International Monetary Relations

International Monetary Relations:
Theory, History, and Policy / Second edition

Leland B. Yeager
UNIVERSITY OF VIRGINIA

Harper & Row PUBLISHERS · NEW YORK, EVANSTON, SAN FRANCISCO, LONDON

Sponsoring Editor: John Greenman
Project Editor: David Nickol
Designer: Gayle Jaeger
Production Supervisor: Francis X. Giordano
Compositor: American Book–Stratford Press, Inc.
Printer and Binder: Halliday Lithograph Corporation
Art Studio: J & R Technical Services Inc.

International Monetary Relations:
Theory, History, and Policy,

Second Edition

Library of Congress Cataloging in Publication Data

Yeager, Leland B
    International monetary relations.

    Includes index.
    1. International finance.   2. Foreign exchange
problem.   3. Balance of payments.   I. Title.
HG3881.Y4   1976   332.4′5   75-1724
ISBN 0-06-047323-1

Contents

part II History and Policy

Preface

This book surveys the monetary side of international economics. It focuses on international balance and imbalance and related policies. It does consider some topics that concern the practical merchant and banker (forward exchange and the like), but only insofar as they bear on the main theme. The great emphasis that writings and policy-making in this field have traditionally given to supposed historical "lessons" has prompted a fairly detailed reconsideration here.

The last several years have been a difficult period in which to revise this book, first printed late in 1965. So much has been happening, both in theorists' ivory towers and in the real world. But waiting for history to sort out the relatively important from relatively unimportant developments, as well as waiting for new figures of kinds that are so annoyingly susceptible to being revised, would keep a new edition from ever seeing print. If I were only now beginning my long-drawn-out work on a new edition, I would do some things differently from the way I have done them. I would be more careful with the assumption, tacitly made in several places, that aggregate demand for goods and services, when "wrong," is unambiguously either deficient and deflationary or excessive and inflationary. Inflationary recession would receive more attention. Its ex-

planation, it seems to me, hinges largely on differential lags. Since changes in rates of growth of a country's money supply affect price levels or trends more slowly than they affect production and employment, it is possible for an economy to be suffering simultaneously from too fast and too slow money-supply growth, the excessive growth having occurred further in the past than the deficient growth. This possibility is one argument for reasonably steady monetary growth and for international monetary arrangements least likely to disrupt such a policy.

In the realm of abstract theory, recognition of the monetary nature of balance-of-payments disequilibrium and adjustment seems to undergo long-term cycles of popularity and neglect. This book's first edition gave the monetary approach more emphasis than was usual at the time. Nowadays, the continuing cycle has restored that approach to popularity.

In the realm of events, theories of international transmission of inflation through exchange-rate pegging and of the inflationary bias of pegged rates have been massively illustrated during the period of last-ditch defense of the Bretton Woods system that stretched out over several years before finally coming to an end in March 1973. Domestic money was created on a massive scale as the central banks and governments of countries with balance-of-payments surpluses bought up foreign exchange in efforts to keep exchange rates fixed. (During the single year 1971, foreign authorities bought more U.S. dollars than they had bought cumulatively through all history until then, and further episodes of great money creation ensued.) With a lag, as usual, price trends responded. Once a country has become hooked on rapid inflation, however innocently (as by importing it rather than generating it at home), its addiction is hard to cure, for the withdrawal pangs (recession and unemployment) would likely be severe. It is tragic, in my opinion, that the world did not abandon the Bretton Woods system several years before 1973. Intellectually, that system never was abandoned; rather, repeated efforts to maintain it finally collapsed.

This is not to blame the recent acceleration of worldwide inflation all on the exchange-rate system. Plenty of inflationary biases (some connected with democratic politics) exist within countries; but when international monetary relations are under discussion, particular attention to international aspects is appropriate.[1]

Worldwide inflation has been spurred not only by domestic policies and not only by the monetary consequences of defending the Bretton Woods system to the bitter end but also by an unfortunate conjunction of particular shortages and cartel actions epitomized in the phrase "wheat, oil, and anchovies." (Not all of these events, however, are entirely independent of monetary inflation. Oil-country spokesmen may well be right when they suggest that depreciation of the dollar against goods and services and other currencies played some part in strengthening the cohesion and aggressiveness of the oil cartel.) These particular events are unfortunate not only in themselves but also because they provide a superficially obvious explanation of inflation, tending to draw attention away from its basically monetary nature. They heighten the danger that we will not salvage anything—not even a lesson—from our recent monetary traumas.

Furthermore, contemporary discussion illustrates again a distressingly familiar phenomenon mentioned in this book's first edition: floating exchange rates get blamed for unsatisfactory conditions that had caused the earlier rate-fixing to collapse and to which the fixed rates may themselves have contributed.

With the exchange-rate flexibility prevailing since March 1973, the world has at least escaped the kind of major currency crises that had become so frequent up to then. The present system functions, after a fashion, amidst extraneous difficulties even more serious than those amidst which the fixed-rate system had proved incapable of continuing to function at all. True, it has not lived up to exaggerated expectations. For example, floating rates have not equilibrated trade balances specifically (note recent German experience). But economic theory never promised that, as distinguished from equilibration of overall balances of payments.

We should be clear, furthermore, about *what* system, or nonsystem, now prevails. It is *not* a system of freely floating rates deliberately adopted, intended to be permanent, and providing a known basis for the evolution of market institutions and practices. On the contrary, inhibiting uncertainty prevails about the nature and future of the system itself. What we now have are the remnants of a pegged-rate system that collapsed after a disastrously prolonged defense. Much rate-pegging remains, as between the German mark and several other European currencies and as in a shrunken but still significant dollar bloc. Adjustments and rumors of adjustment of pegged rates, though less frequent than under the Bretton Woods system, continue to occur. Much official intervention takes place even in the markets of supposedly floating currencies. (It is symptomatic that the International Monetary Fund did more business in 1974 than in any earlier year.) Controls over capital movements and other controls abound, undergoing frequent modification. Discussions of international monetary reform—so called—keep reviving from time to time.

Some observers call for a return to fixed exchange rates. In a conceivable sense, permanently fixed rates among national currencies of stable purchasing power—or, even better, a stable worldwide currency—would be an ideal goal. But merely to advocate fixed exchange rates—implying a situation in which fixed rates could work—boils down to saying that what our monetary problem needs is a solution. That remark is true but empty. It is empty because it jumps over identifying and diagnosing the problem (including its domestic political aspects). Furthermore, to advocate (or reject) fixed (or floating) exchange rates after brooding over the pros and cons of one single system or the other is a misguided approach. One more in tune with economists' way of thinking is to compare the alternatives, recognizing that any system has some disadvantages. Bliss is not an available option.

I should like to echo, if only briefly, the gratitude expressed in the preface of my first edition to Professors James W. Angell and Ragnar Nurkse. (Particularly because I take issue with the late Professor Nurkse on exchange-rate policy, I am anxious to stress how much I admire him and his teaching and seminal writings.) Again I thank my Virginia colleagues for their courtesies, Messrs. Marvin Phaup, Gary Lee, and David Tuerck for assistance with computations and other chores, Professor and Mrs. Paul Homan for encouragement, the Relm Foundation and the University of Virginia Institute for Research in the Social Sciences (and now also the University's program of leaves for chairholders) for support of closely related research, and Harcourt Brace Jovanovich, Inc., and Van Nostrand Reinhold

Co. for permitting the lengthy quotations appearing at the end of Chapter 15.

Among the people to whom I am indebted for discussions stretching out over many years, I should particularly like to mention Professor Alexandre Kafka, Executive Director of the International Monetary Fund, Dr. David Tuerck, Dr. Daniel James Edwards, Professor William R. Allen, and the late Professor James M. Waller. I am also indebted to the former graduate students whose doctoral dissertations are cited in this new edition.

I corrected proof while a Visiting Professor at the University of California, Los Angeles, from January to June 1975. I am indebted to Professors J. C. La Force and William R. Allen and Miss Lorraine Grams for their considerateness at that stage of my work.

My thanks go to Messrs. Charles Robert Coates and Lincoln Anderson, who expertly prepared the indexes to the first and second editions, respectively, of this book. Among the typists who labored so competently over several drafts of the first and second editions, Mrs.

Betty Tillman Ross and Mrs. Marion Haddow deserve special thanks.

LELAND B. YEAGER
Charlottesville, Virginia
July 1975

1. Since writing this preface, I have seen further corroborating argument and evidence concerning exchange rates and inflation in two publications that amply deserve the reader's attention: the "World Inflation" issue of Federal Reserve Bank of San Francisco, *Business Review*, Spring 1975 (containing articles by Edward S. Shaw, Michael W. Keran, Hang-Sheng Cheng and Nicholas P. Sargen, and Joseph Bisignano), and "Flexible Rates—the Monetary Shock Absorber," First National City Bank of New York, *Monthly Economic Letter*, July 1975, pp. 12–15.

Theory

The study of international monetary relations (international finance)
covers prices, wages, incomes, money supplies, monetary standards,
financial policies, international loans, balances of payments, exchange
rates, external reserves, and international liquidity. Monetary magnitudes
serve as indicators of, and guides to, such underlying "realities" as
resource allocation, trade in goods and services, and international transfer
of command over resources by way of loans and investment. The chapters
of Part I investigate the theory of how the several alternative systems
of international monetary relations operate. These chapters include some
abstract analysis of policy measures, leaving until Part II a survey of policy
in the context of past and current history.

CHAPTER ONE

Realities Behind the Veil of Money and Prices

The gain from trade

A quick review of some leading principles of international economics will introduce our study of the role of money and prices. First, let us recall the sources of gain from trade. Admittedly, the idea of gain for a country as a whole is fuzzy. Relaxing or abolishing restrictions on trade, like any other policy, cannot be proved right or wrong on purely scientific grounds. Appraising any policy whatsoever depends not merely on "positive" propositions, but also on value judgments—personal opinions about how desirable or undesirable various results are. Any supposedly beneficial change in national circumstances harms some people. If a mere act of Congress could abolish hurricanes, some persons would suffer a loss of business, including meteorologists, construction workers, and the present generation of undertakers. The same is true of inventions: people in general gain, but some lose. A vast literature deals with the problem of weighing benefits to some persons against damage to others in assessing social gain or loss. These subtleties concern economic theory and policy in general but do not have an especially strong or direct bearing on international finance in particular. Here, "gain from trade" will mean gain of the same admittedly debatable kind as gain from techno-logical progress or from abolishing hurricanes. Like technological progress, trade widens the range of available ways of transforming labor and other resources into desired goods and services. Technological progress and geographic specialization both make this transformation more "efficient" (to use a loose but convenient word). The basis for specialization and trade among countries of the world is the same as for specialization and trade among states of the United States.[1]

Trade is most obviously beneficial when it bring us goods we could hardly produce at home at all. The gain from cheaper foreign supplies of things we could well make ourselves requires more discussion. Under the conditions of an idealized competitive model, price relations indicate opportunity costs, or how much each product costs in sacrificed production of other things.[2] Suppose we can produce widgets in our country for $5.00. This means, under ideal competitive conditions, that producing a widget costs sacrificing the production of other goods that would also have been worth $5.00 to us.

Suppose, now, that we can buy a widget abroad for only $3.00. If imports and exports pay for each other, an imported widget costs us $3.00 worth of our export products. Supplying these exports means our sacrificing their consumption or the production and consumption of other goods that would also have been worth $3.00 to us. Importing a widget at $3.00 involves only three-fifths as much sacrifice as making it ourselves at $5.00. Importing a product at a money price below the cost of making it ourselves represents a real saving in the amounts of other desirable things forgone.

---

1. This is no place to appraise all the various arguments for interference with international trade, such as the argument for protection of defense industries. Valid as these arguments may be, they do not disprove the gain from trade discussed here but merely point out other considerations that must be weighed against it in policy-making.

A convenient way of presenting some pieces of analysis is to apply them to examining and demolishing fallacious arguments. But the use of fallacious arguments in behalf of certain policies does not in itself prove that no valid arguments are available and that the policies themselves must be rejected. On the other hand, analytical *validity* is not the same as *conclusiveness* in policy arguments. Economic analysis is part, but only part, of what is relevant in policy discussions.

2. See "Realities and Money Prices," p. 6.

Our opportunity for gain is genuine regardless of *why* foreigners sell so cheaply. Perhaps the foreign widgets are cheap because the climate is ideal for their production in foreign countries, or because the land or capital used in widget production is especially abundant there, or because a broad home market there gives scope for cheap mass production, or because the foreign producers have skills stemming from a long tradition of widget production. Perhaps general wage levels in the widget-producing countries are lower than ours or perhaps foreign widget-workers in particular are shamefully underpaid even in relation to the generally low wage levels of their own countries. Perhaps the exchange rate translates prices in the foreign currency at an "unfairly" low value, whatever that might mean. Perhaps foreign governments are subsidizing widget exports. Perhaps widgets grow wild on bushes abroad and need only be gathered at slight expense. What difference does any of this make to us? How can it matter *why* the foreign widgets are so cheap?[3] What matters to us is whether prices *in our own country* correctly indicate realities—whether our prices correctly indicate how much each product costs in required sacrifice of others, given the state of technology and the demands on and scarcity of our resources. The opportunity that foreign prices offer to us is genuine from our point of view, regardless of whether any "distortions" in the foreign price system may be causing foreigners to offer us this opportunity. Refusing this opportunity is the same as refusing any other kind of opportunity for making or getting goods more efficiently or cheaply than before.

The principle of comparative advantage

Some people who take part in controversies over tariff legislation fail to understand this. They warn about supposed distortions: trade is harmful unless goods of the kinds imported can be produced with greater *absolute* or *physical* efficiency in the foreign country supplying them than in the home country importing them. A reply to this error need not rest on quibbles about how difficult or impossible it is to give a clear meaning to the notion of absolute efficiency. We can assume an extreme case for the sake of analysis; we can imagine one country so inefficient that, in all lines of production, more man-hours of labor, acre-weeks of land, machine-hours of capital goods, etc., are required per unit of final product than elsewhere. Conversely, we can imagine an extremely efficient country where each unit of product requires fewer real inputs of labor and other resources than anywhere else. Yet trade can be beneficial if the country with all-around inferior efficiency specializes in the lines of production where its inferiority is slightest and the country with all-around superior efficiency specializes in the lines of its greatest superiority. International real-cost comparisons are a red herring; what counts is comparing the opportunities available in domestic production and in foreign trade.

This is the *principle of comparative advantage*. It is an "even-if" proposition: it demonstrates how trade can yield benefits *even* in the almost unimaginable situation in which absolute all-across-the-board inferiority and superiority might seem, at first, to rule trade out. Actually, the principle is unnecessary in a demonstration of the gains from trade; elaborating on the example of the $5.00 and $3.00 widgets could provide a satisfactory demonstration. But to accommodate people who persist in supposing that comparisons of absolute efficiency are somehow relevant, the principle accepts their premises for the sake of argument.

The principle of comparative advantage does *not* agree that the gain from specialization comes from having each item produced in the place where it can be produced with the greatest absolute efficiency, i.e., where the inputs of real resources needed per unit of final product are least. Assuming that "absolute efficiency" were meaningful, this misinterpretation of the principle would have an all-around-efficient country produce everything and an all-around-inefficient country produce nothing—in short, there would be no specialization and trade at all (since trade in only one direction could hardly be acceptable to both sides).

A simple variant of traditional examples will help clarify comparative advantage. Considering only two countries and two commodities will suffice to make the point. (Here and in later chapters we adopt the convenient German terminology of naming the home country "Inland" and another country, or all other countries together, "Outland.") Suppose that with a given assortment of labor and other resources (which might be a different given assortment in each country), production possibilities are as shown in the following table.

TABLE 1.1. *An example of comparative advantage*

Country	Output of wheat (bushels) or cloth (yards)	Opportunity cost[a]
Inland	90 W *or* 30 C	1 C for 3 W; 1 W for ⅓ C
Outland	40 W *or* 20 C	1 C for 2 W; 1 W for ½ C

a. How much more of each product could be produced by reallocating labor and resources and cutting back the production of the other product.

In Inland, 1 additional bushel of wheat can be had by sacrificing production of ⅓ yard of cloth. In the same sense, the cost of a bushel of wheat in Outland is ½ yard of cloth. As for cloth, producing 1 additional yard costs the sacrifice of 3 bushels of wheat in Inland and only 2 bushels in Outland. These opportunity-cost figures reflect how effectively labor and other resources can shift within each country from one line of production to the other, either directly or in an indirect and complex reallocation.

The conclusions of the example do not depend on any measures of absolute efficiency or absolute real cost in terms of physical quantities of inputs required per unit of output. For all it mattered, we could suppose that the assortment or package of labor and resources necessary to yield the outputs shown in the table is of the same size in Outland as in Inland—or even is much bigger; Outland would be unquestionably less efficient in both lines of production. Still, in the *relative* sense just explained, wheat would be cheaper in Inland and cloth in Outland. Inland gains from trade if it can acquire cloth at a cost per yard any lower than 3 bushels of wheat, i.e., if it can get anything more than ⅓ yard of cloth in return for 1 bushel of wheat. Outland gains if it can get anything more than 2 bushels of wheat in return for 1 yard of cloth, i.e., if giving up anything less than ½ yard of cloth will pay for a bushel of wheat. Clearly, terms can be found at which both countries gain[4]—for example, 1 yard of cloth for 2½ bushels of wheat (1

bushel of wheat for ⅖ yard of cloth). By partially or perhaps completely switching out of cloth into wheat production and exporting wheat to pay for imported cloth, Inland can acquire cloth at less sacrifice of wheat than if it produced all its wheat at home. Outland can gain by switching from wheat into cloth production. If consumers so desired, each country could have more of each product for domestic use than in the absence of trade.

There is a further kind of gain that our example does not reveal. *Even* if a country's cloth and wheat production were rigid and unchangeable but if its people could trade on the world market at terms of 1 for 2½, they could gain as long as they were not indifferent between having 1 yard of cloth and having 2½ bushels of wheat. (This other kind of gain, not necessarily connected with production, was well illustrated in prisoner-of-war camps, where the prisoners swapped their rations and the contents of their Red Cross packages to get additional satisfactions from fixed total quantities of goods in view of their own differing tastes.) In short, trade permits greater efficiency both in using resources to produce goods and in using goods to "produce" satisfactions.

How much each country gains depends on the terms of trade. These must fall somewhere between the Inland opportunity cost of one cloth for three wheat and the Outland cost of one cloth for two wheat; at terms of trade outside these limits, people in one country would

3. One possible answer concerns not how genuine but how dependable an opportunity the cheap foreign widgets give us; this is the problem considered in a properly sophisticated version of the "dumping" argument for tariffs. Certain arguments concerning special cases of "external diseconomies" involved in accepting imports or supplying exports could also provide possible answers to the question in the text.

4. This depends on opportunity costs being different in the two countries; otherwise, the international exchange of wheat for cloth would be pointless. If Inland's absolute efficiency exceeded or fell short of Outland's by the same degree in every line of production and if tastes were the same in both countries—unrealistic and almost meaningless conditions—then trade could provide no gain.

be especially eager for trade but people in the other would refuse. Just where the terms fall depends on supply and demand conditions. Incidentally, the nearer the terms of trade fall to the limit of 1 to 3, the greater is the share of the gain going to Outland; and the nearer to 1 to 2, the greater Inland's share. This is understandable: trade offers gain by providing opportunities different from those already available in domestic production; the farther the terms of trade fall from the domestic opportunity cost, the more significant are the new opportunities offered by trade. The more a country's export products are worth in terms of its import products, the greater is its share of gain.

Gain by a country as a whole is a fuzzy concept, as already admitted. Some producers in each country must cut back their output and switch, if possible, into a relatively more efficient line of production. How do we weigh sectional gains and losses in assessing the national outcome? If the benefited cloth consumers and wheat producers in Inland were considered to be undeserving people whose welfare should count for very little and if the harmed cloth producers and wheat consumers were considered to be especially deserving people whose welfare should count heavily, one might conclude that Inland as a whole lost from trade. On a less special set of judgments about what people deserved, however, we still might say that the country did gain. Trade would *allow* the country to have more of each product than otherwise. The gainers from trade could more than afford, if necessary, to buy the consent of everyone who would otherwise lose. Actually, of course, the gainers wouldn't bother. Here, however, we may gloss over such problems of welfare economics, since our purpose is only to prepare for describing how wage levels and exchange rates play a part in guiding trade along lines of comparative advantage.

The wheat-and-cloth example is not meant to show how large the volume of trade would be. As long as opportunity costs remain different in the two countries and neither country is yet fully specialized on one product to the exclusion of the other, further specialization and trade would yield further gain. Actually, changes in opportunity cost as specialization went on might prevent complete specialization. As resources shifted out of cloth into wheat production in Inland, still further shifts might become less and less rewarding. Eventually each additional bushel of wheat might cost the sacrifice of perhaps $2/5$ rather than only $1/3$ yard of cloth. In Outland, cutbacks in wheat and expansion of cloth production might result in each additional yard of cloth costing $2\frac{1}{2}$ rather than only 2 bushels of wheat. But until the two countries' opportunity costs had thus come together, further specialization and trade would be beneficial. (Transportation costs and tariffs—ignored here as irrelevant to showing the nature of the gain—would in reality narrow the scope for beneficial trade.)

Realities and money prices

One vital point still remains to be cleared up. Practical businessmen don't know or care anything about comparative advantage and don't need to: they want to buy where *money prices* are lowest and sell where *money prices* are highest. If all lines of production really were less efficient in Outland than in Inland, how could Outland businessmen price any of their goods low enough to capture foreign markets? How could Outland sell anything abroad and earn money to buy abroad? The answer hinges on a generally low level of wages and other incomes in Outland (low, that is, as translated at prevailing rates of exchange and compared with wage and income levels in Inland). Low wage levels—the famous "cheap labor"—are an inevitable result of Outland's inefficient production, but they are also what lets Outland export the products in which it has the smallest disadvantage and so pay for imports that could be produced at home only at still greater disadvantage. Low wages permit Outland to share the benefits of international trade and so be less poor than otherwise.

Inland also gains, even when trading with an inefficient, "cheap-labor" country. Shrinkage of particular Inland industries as a result of trade does not in itself prove otherwise. Shifting labor and resources out of lines of least superior production into lines of most superior production is a key part of the process of reaping the benefits of trade. It would be just as questionable for the Inland government to restrict trade merely on the grounds that Outlanders employed "cheap labor" or had an "unfairly depreciated currency." The difference between Inland and Outland wage levels—wages being translated through the exchange rate into one currency—is necessary to reflect overall differences in efficiency or productivity and so to allow the product price relations that lead profit-seeking businessmen to carry out trade of the sort described by the principle of comparative advantage.

In a competitive economic system no one has to measure directly how much each product costs in terms of the forgone physical output of others. No one has to take these opportunity costs consciously into account. As long as the system works fairly well along the lines of the textbook competitive model, money prices measure them, and people have ordinary profit-and-loss incentives to take them into account. Under competition, if the selling price of a particular commodity happened to exceed or fall short of the change in total cost involved in producing one more or one less unit of it, firms would have a profit incentive to expand or cut back production. Under competition, therefore, the price of a commodity tends to equal the sum of the prices times quantities of the additional ingredients necessary to produce one more unit of it. (These ingredients—resources, factors of production, or factor services—include not only labor and materials but also business enterprise, or whatever the factor receiving profit may be called. So-called normal profit thus counts among the payments for ingredients used in making the commodity.)

Under competition, the prices of these ingredients are determined by the bidding for them among various uses. Each firm has a profit incentive to employ each ingredient in such an amount that the effect on the total value of output of employing one more or one less unit of it is equal to its price.

Here we return to the main argument. The price of a product tends to equal the sum of the prices times quantities of the additional ingredients needed to make an additional unit of it. Each ingredient tends to have a price equaling the value of what one unit of it could contribute to production in the various lines employing it. Hence, under competition each product tends to be priced at the additional cost of making an additional unit of it, which in turn tends to equal how much of other products—valued in terms of what consumers were prepared to pay for them—could have been made instead with the necessary ingredients. Prices of $20.00 for a radio and $10.00 for a hat indicate that an additional radio costs

twice as much as an additional hat in terms of other-products-in-general forgone. The opportunity cost is two hats for one radio.

No doubt reality and the competitive model diverge from one another. But to the extent that the price system does work, the tendencies just outlined, hampered though they may be, do operate.

Prices and exchange rates

The argument so far has prepared for showing how a pattern of prices and exchange rates emerges at which businessmen and consumers will have the incentives, under competition, to conduct the trade that yields the gain described by the principle of comparative advantage. Suppose that cloth has a price of $6.00 per yard and wheat a price of $2.00 per bushel in Inland. In Outland, the prices are 36 pesos for cloth and 18 pesos for wheat. (These figures merely illustrate prices reflecting the opportunity costs previously assumed.) To know where they can buy each commodity most cheaply or sell it most dearly, businessmen must consider the dollar-peso exchange rate. At any more than 9 pesos per dollar, both products would be cheaper in Outland than in Inland. Outland would tend to export both and import neither—a situation that could not last if cloth and wheat were the only tradeable products. At the opposite extreme, a rate of fewer than 6 pesos per dollar would make both products cheaper in Inland. A workable exchange rate must fall somewhere between P9 = $1.00 and P6 = $1.00, the exact rate being the one at which each country's exports and imports are equal in total money value.

A more elaborate example will now be instructive. It shows that different patterns of *relative* prices within countries, reflecting different patterns of opportunity costs, set the stage for determining absolute prices at which each country imports some things and exports others. In Inland, according to Table 1.2, a pair of shoes costs 7½ times as much as a bushel of wheat and 15 times as much as a hammer; while in Outland, a pair of shoes costs only 5 times as much as a bushel of wheat and only 7 times as much as a hammer. In Outland a bushel of wheat costs more than a gallon of wine; in Inland it costs less. In Inland a gallon of wine has an opportunity cost of 4 hammers; in Outland a gallon of wine costs only 1⅕ hammers.

These different patterns of relative prices and opportunity cost are translated by the exchange rate into differences in absolute prices (both countries' prices being translated into one currency or the other). At a rate of 1 peso per dollar, *everything* would be cheaper in Inland. (We assume, for simplicity, that the four goods listed are the only ones tradeable.) People would want to buy everything in Inland and nothing in Outland. Attempts to buy dollars to pay for Inland goods would create lopsided pressure on the foreign-exchange market to exchange pesos for dollars. Unless officially fixed, the exchange rate would move in the direction of more than 1 peso per dollar. At the opposite extreme, a rate of 6 pesos per dollar would make everything cheaper in Outland. As Inlanders eager to buy Outland goods flooded the market with dollars, the rate would move in the direction of fewer pesos per dollar. This shows one of the reasons why the law of demand holds true for foreign exchange as well as for ordinary commodities in ordinary markets. The cheaper one country's currency is in terms of foreign currencies, other things being the same, the wider will be the range of products underselling similar foreign products and the greater will be the quantity of the currency demanded by foreigners to buy that country's relatively inexpensive goods.

Table 1.2 shows that a workable exchange rate must lie somewhere between 1½ and 5 pesos per dollar. At 3 pesos per dollar, for example, Outland would undersell in shoes and wine and Inland in wheat and hammers. The example is not detailed enough to determine the exact exchange rate or export list of each country. These results depend on how strong the preferences for the various goods are and on how local prices, reflecting opportunity costs, would change as output changed. In any case, Inland will export hammers and Outland wine, and the exchange rate will be one at which the flows of trade in the two directions pay for each other. (Complications such as international lending are not yet taken into account.) The exchange rate and the international terms of trade are determined together in the interplay of supply and demand.

Trade does not leave local commodity prices unchanged. The Outland demand for hammers, added to the Inland demand, bids the Inland price above $1.00; in Outland, the supply of hammers coming from Inland lowers the price below 5 pesos. Wine shipments from Outland to Inland tend to raise the peso price in Outland and lower the dollar price in Inland. Were it not for transportation costs and other obstacles to trade, prices would move toward being everywhere the same (as translated at the exchange rate emerging from the same process).[5] This equalization of commodity prices would reflect changes in resource allocation and production patterns within countries that made opportunity costs equal among those commodities still produced in at least some amounts in the trading countries. Trade would expand and specialization in production would develop until no further expansion and specialization was worthwhile. But price and cost equalization would not destroy trade. It would destroy incentives for further *expansion* of trade (unless underlying conditions changed, such as population, tastes, technology, etc.). Trade might conceivably wipe out price differences among countries. In a sense, though, the trade would still be motivated or guided by *virtual* price differences— differences that *would have* existed in the absence of trade and that would appear if trade were cut off or restricted.

TABLE 1.2. *Translation of relative into absolute price differences*

Commodity	Dollar price in Inland	Peso price in Outland	OUTLAND PRICE CONVERTED INTO DOLLARS AT RATE OF					
			P1 = $1	P1½ = $1	P2 = $1	P3 = $1	P5 = $1	P6 = $1
Shoes (pair)	$15.00	P35	$35.00	$23.33	$17.50	$11.67	$7.00	$5.83
Wheat (bushel)	2.00	7	7.00	4.67	3.50	2.33	1.40	1.17
Wine (gallon)	4.00	6	6.00	4.00	3.00	2.00	1.20	1.00
Hammers (each)	1.00	5	5.00	3.33	2.50	1.67	1.00	.83

The general-equilibrium theory

The principle of comparative advantage is a proposition in welfare economics; it demonstrates the gain from trade when patterns of opportunity cost differ from country to country. It takes for granted these different patterns and does not try to explain them. A notable attempt at explanation is Bertil Ohlin's general-equilibrium theory of international trade.[6] Ohlin's theory does not necessarily clash with the theory of comparative advantage. Each emphasizes aspects of trade that the other takes for granted. Ohlin's theory, for its part, largely takes the gains from trade for granted and instead tries realistically to describe how and why trade takes place.

We have already seen how differences between countries in opportunity costs and *relative* prices give rise to *absolute* price differences. But what underlies and explains the different patterns of relative prices? What determines a price? The stock answer is "supply and demand." These, however, are categories of influences that in turn need explaining. *Demand* is the relation between various prices and desired purchases of a commodity and depends on: (1) the needs and preferences of consumers, (2) consumers' incomes, which depend on ownership of and the prices of factors of production, and (3) prices of other commodities. *Supply* is the relation between various prices of the commodity and the quantities offered and reflects the cost of producing and marketing various amounts of the commodity and so depends on: (1) physical conditions of production—climate, the state of technology, and other conditions determining the relation between inputs and ouput—and (2) the supplies of factors of production actually or potentially used in making the commodity, as well as the bidding for these factors from other uses. Under competition a long-run tendency prevails for the quantity supplied and quantity demanded of each commodity to be equal at a price just covering cost (counting the "normal" profit of enterprise among the costs). A complete theory must therefore probe into costs and into the prices of factors of production. The price of each factor itself depends on "supply and demand." Demand derives from the technological capacity of the factor to contribute to the production of various goods and from the consumer demands for these goods. Supply, for some factors of production, is a fixed or almost fixed quantity provided by

nature (for example, land area). For most factors, supply is a price-quantity relation, with the quantity offered depending on the factor's own price and on other prices. The quantity of electrical engineers, for instance, presumably depends not only on the salaries of electrical engineers but also the salaries of civil engineers, the fees of doctors, etc. Commodity prices and supplies and demands, factor prices and supplies and demands, incomes—all interact intimately and in complex ways. The various prices and quantities determine one another; no single one is a dominating cause.

All this helps us approach the question: When will internal patterns of relative prices differ from country to country and so set the stage for beneficial trade? In each country some factors of production will be more abundant and cheaper in comparison with other factors than in the outside world; other factors will be relatively scarce and expensive. In the absence of trade, goods produced with relatively large amounts of a country's abundant factors will tend to be relatively cheap; goods requiring large amounts of scarce factors will be expensive. Let us suppose that land is abundant and labor scarce in Inland and that labor is abundant and land scarce in Outland. In Inland high-land-content food is cheap relative to high-labor-content clothing. In Outland the opposite price pattern prevails. As a result, an

5. The translation of comparative advantage into price-and-profit incentives for trade is simplest to explain when exchange rates are flexible. If the monetary systems of various regions and countries are unified, variations in *price and income levels* replace the flexibility of exchange rates. An explanation of this more complicated process appears in Chapter 5.

In the process discussed here exchange rates are not entirely *determined* by the patterns of local-currency prices prevailing in various countries in the absence of trade. On the contrary, exchange rates also *affect* local prices; everything depends on everything else. This is not to say that the influence of exchange rates on *general* price levels is anywhere near as strong as the opposite influence.

6. Bertil Ohlin, *Interregional and International Trade*, Cambridge, Mass.: Harvard University Press, 1933.

exchange rate (or a relation between general price levels) can emerge at which Inland will undersell in food and export it and Outland will undersell in clothing and export it.

Just conceivably, different consumer preferences in the two countries might so match the different endowments of factors of production as to keep the internal relative price patterns from diverging. Inlanders might have especially strong preferences for food and Outlanders for clothing. On the other hand, even if the different factors of production were available in the same proportion in both countries, tastes might differ in such a way as to create differences in relative prices. Though both countries had land and labor in the same proportions, Inlanders might so prefer clothing and Outlanders so prefer food that prices would emerge which would promote the exchange of Inland food for Outland clothing.

We shall have to make some qualifications soon. Loosely speaking, meanwhile, it is differences in factor endowments—differences, rather, in the relations of factor supplies to the demands for factors derived from consumer demands for goods and services—that create the patterns of comparative advantage giving rise to international trade. An exchange rate translates differences in relative prices into international differences in absolute prices (differences that trade itself tends to wipe out). Incidentally, the exchange rate permits comparing absolute factor prices, making it possible to say that a particular kind of labor is cheaper in one country than in another. The exchange rate at which a country's imports and exports pay for each other depends largely on reciprocal demand and supply. The more intense the Outland demand for Inland goods and the offer of Outland goods in payment and the weaker the Inland demand for Outland goods and the offer of Inland goods in payment, the stronger will Inland's currency be on the foreign-exchange market and the more favorable Inland's terms of trade.

The general-equilibrium theory suggests the following probable consequences of trade:

1. The price of each commodity traded tends to become the same everywhere except for transportation costs, tariffs, and the like.

2. The same is true for the price of each factor of production. A country tends to export products embodying relatively large amounts of its abundant factors, and the export-derived demand for them lessens their relative abundance and cheapness. Similarly, importing products whose production at home would require relatively large amounts of scarce factors tends to relieve the relative scarcity and expensiveness of these factors. Trade in goods and services spells trade in the factors of production they embody. The tendency toward factor-price equalization would be complete, however, only under highly restrictive and unrealistic assumptions concerning pure competition, costless transport, internationally identical constant-returns-to-scale production functions, incomplete specialization, identity in kind of the factors in the different countries, substitutability among factors, fewness of factors relative to products, etc. The equalization tendency has almost no chance at all of prevailing in reality. But even if it did, it would in no way imply equalization among countries of relative factor quantities, of real incomes per person, or of standards of living. Equalization of wage rates, in particular, does not mean equalization of average output per person or of average income per person from all factors. Trade would continue to provide a gain even for countries favored with an especially great abundance of natural resources, capital, and entrepreneurial ability in relation to population. Incidentally, if the necessary but almost impossible conditions did hold true and factor prices were equalized among countries, would this not destroy international differences in commodity cost patterns and so destroy the basis for trade? The answer is practically the same as to the earlier question about commodity price equalization. Complete factor-price equalization would destroy the basis not for trade but for its further *expansion*. Assuming costless transport and so forth, a volume of trade any smaller than what would equalize both commodity and factor prices in different countries would leave profit incentives in existence for further expansion of trade. The volume of trade per time period that just accomplishes equalization is motivated by the price differences that *would* exist at any smaller volume; it would be motivated, that is, by *intramarginal* differences.

3. Another consequence of trade and a corollary of the factor-price-equalization tendency is modification of domestic income distributions. Trade tends to reduce the shares going to previously scarce factors of production and to increase the shares of previously abundant factors.

4. A fourth consequence is an *increase* in the international disparity of factor quantities,

so far as these respond to price. Opportunities to import fruit may result in maintaining fewer orchards than otherwise. If a country exports chemicals, more chemists may be trained; if it exports automobiles, more capital may be accumulated in factories and heavy machinery. Supplies of natural resources *economically* available may respond to trade through the influence of prices on the rate of discovery or of development for exploitation. Recognizing how trade may increase the factor-supply disparities that cause it does not contradict what has already been said about modification of the scarcity or abundance of factors: a particular factor can become more abundant in absolute amount while less abundant relative to demand or become scarcer absolutely while less scarce relative to demand.

5. Trade affects patterns of demand in several ways: by increasing consumers' real incomes, by modifying domestic income distributions, and by acquainting people with a broader variety of goods and services and thus modifying tastes.

6. The general-equilibrium theory suggest a catchall category of effects of trade, including broader gains than those from specialization and resource reallocation as described by the principle of comparative advantage. By expanding the markets open to individual producers and entire industries, trade improves opportunities for efficient mass production. Trade and specialization could thus provide an improvement over national self-sufficiency even if countries had otherwise identical conditions. Just as occupational specialization permits individuals to *acquire* comparative advantages, so trade may do the same for countries (as may restrictions on trade). Trade presumably weakens local monopolies. In short, trade does more than merely promote efficient allocation of existing productive resources; it affects industrial structures, tastes, labor supplies, and the types of natural resources and capital equipment in actual use. At best it helps transmit techniques and ideas as well as goods, promoting modern development. (None of this amounts to claiming that free trade provides the best of all conceivable worlds. Judicious restrictions could conceivably increase a country's gains from trade or promote escape from stultifying overspecialization.)

Recognizing the foregoing effects of international trade undermines the relative-factor-endowment explanation of it. No longer can we simply stress international differences in the

relative abundance of various factors. Factor quantities are a result as well as a cause of trade. In reply it might be argued that things such as chemical engineers, factories, hydroelectric sites, and fields prepared for particular crops are not what the theory means by factors of production; instead, these are only intermediate embodiments of the more fundamental factors, whose relative abundance is indeed somehow objectively given apart from the flow of trade. Perhaps so, but then it becomes a problem in metaphysics to specify what the underlying factors of production are and how abundant each is. Consider capital, for example. Its supply is no doubt related to the propensity of the population to save and invest, which is in turn related to attitudes and traditions. But how can these be described as objectively *given* and be quantitively specified? The kinds and quantities of labor available might also be traced back to propensities of the population to absorb training and experience and even to propagate, but this, too, would be a meaningless dodge. A similar problem concerns such things as meteorological, intellectual, social, and political "climates." These profoundly influence possibilities for advantageous international specialization; yet only extreme straining at the accepted meanings of words can assimilate them to "factors of production."

The proposition that a country exports abundant-factor-intensive goods and imports scarce-factor-intensive goods now also appears too simple. Sheer technological necessity does not always make some products inherently labor-intensive, for instance, and others inherently land-intensive. The proportions in which various factors are used depend, among other things, on their prices. Of two products, A might be the more labor-intensive and B the more land-intensive at one ratio of labor and land prices; yet B might be the more labor-intensive and A the more land intensive at another factor-price ratio.[7] Yet factor prices

7. Supposed evidence for such possibilities appears in Bagicha S. Minhas, "The Homohypalligic Production Function, Factor-Intensity Reversals, and the Heckscher-Ohlin Theorem," *Journal of Political Economy*, April 1962, pp. 138–156.

largely result from trade and are not independently given. Apart from the consequences of the very flow of trade to be explained, one cannot always unambiguously say which commodities embody relatively large proportions of which factors of production.

Still another difficulty with the factor-proportions theory is that the absolute scarcity or abundance of factors in a country does not itself determine the flow of trade. What counts is scarcity or abundance relative to the demands for these factors deriving from demands for goods and services embodying them. Yet these demands or tastes, whose role parallels that of factor endowments, themselves largely result from trade. Even if taste patterns were identical from country to country and were left unaffected by changed possibilities of gratification, international trade would raise real incomes and so effect the *marginal* pattern of demand. Even given fixed patterns of consumer preference, consumers' appraisal of the relative importance of various goods at the margin presumably varies with the level of consumers' incomes.

The attempt of the general-equilibrium theory to explain trade in terms of factor endowment thus breaks down when pursued literally.[8] The theory is still useful in discussing some of the most important types of conditions that give rise to comparative advantages and in suggesting the unfathomable complexity of the conditions interacting through the price system in guiding the patterns of geographic specialization and trade. In the last analysis, however, there is no single explanation of what *causes* comparative advantage and of *why* trade takes place. We can only illustrate various types of influence. Ultimately we must take different patterns of opportunity cost for granted. We must lamely admit that comparative advantage stems from unfathomably complex differences among countries in climates, resources, populations, tastes, ideologies, and so forth, most of which are consequences as well as causes of trade. But this conclusion need not be disconcerting. The main thing is to recognize that, whatever the reason may be, countries do have comparative advantage in different lines of production and that specialization and trade provide gains like those from technological progress. ". . . the production of one good to exchange for another is an *alternative method of producing* the second commodity. Under competitive conditions, productive resources will not be used in this indirect process of production unless the yield is greater than that obtained by the use of the direct method."[9] Profit incentives lead businessmen to engage in trade yielding the gains the theory describes. Our main interest is in the role of exchange rates, money supplies, and price and wage levels in this working of the international price system. We must now take a closer look at exchange-rate determination.

---

8. The criticisms reviewed above are stressed by Romney Robinson, "Factor Proportions and Comparative Advantage," Parts I and II, *Quarterly Journal of Economics*, **LXX**, May 1956, pp. 169–192, and August 1956, pp. 346–363. Robinson recognizes that Ohlin takes account of such things as the influence of trade on factor supplies and tastes; but he thinks that Ohlin is pursuing two separate and rather incompatible theories, one less fully worked out than the other.

9. Frank H. Knight, *The Ethics of Competition*, New York: Kelley, 1951, p. 234.

CHAPTER TWO

Foreign Exchange: Rates, Instruments, and Markets

International remittances

Foreign exchange includes actual foreign coins and banknotes. Mostly it consists of claims on foreign currency, such as bank accounts and negotiable short-term paper. If a merchant in Inland needs foreign funds to pay for goods imported from Outland, he may buy a check drawn by his own bank on its Outland-peso account kept with some Outland bank. (If the merchant's bank does not itself keep funds on deposit abroad, it will presumably have a correspondent relationship with some other Inland bank that does.) The merchant then mails the peso check to the seller in Outland, who deposits or cashes it as he would any other check written in his home currency. Other ways of making payments in foreign currencies will be considered later; meanwhile, it serves our purpose to think of checks drawn by home banks against their accounts kept with foreign banks.

The Inland bank in the example has drawn down its peso balance in Outland. (It has also increased its holdings of Inland dollars, or has reduced its dollars liabilities by deducting the price of the peso check from its customer's balance.) How does the Inland bank now replenish its Outland bank account? (Actually, a bank doesn't have to maintain foreign-currency balances large enough to meet its customers' future demands; it can buy foreign currencies on the market as needed. But we still have to consider how the market is supplied with foreign currencies.) The bank may buy peso checks on Outland banks earned by Inland exporters who have taken payment from their customers in this form. It may also buy peso checks from Outlanders who need dollars to spend in Inland. If Outlanders paying for purchases in Inland buy dollar checks on their own banks' balances with Inland banks, the Outland banks have to replenish their dollar balances and may do so by buying dollar checks earned by Outland exporters or offered by Inlanders needing pesos to spend in Outland. Foreign-exchange transactions thus basically appear to be exchanges, through the intermediary of banks as dealers, of bank balances in different currencies.

These examples should not be taken to imply bilateral balancing of payments. Each country need not pay to each other country exactly as much as it receives from it. The contrary is more typical. Inland banks replenish their Outland balances by burying pesos not only from Inland exporters to Outland but also from third-country exporters to Outland or from third-country banks holding larger peso balances and smaller dollar balances than they consider convenient.

A country's import trade typically involves exchanging home for foreign bank balances; it involves a demand for foreign exchange to be bought with home money or, in other words, a supply of home money to be sold for foreign exchange. This is true regardless of whether the import goods are priced and payment is required in home or foreign money. If an Inland importer must pay in Outland money, he takes the initiative in exchanging dollars for pesos. If the importer pays in dollars, then the Outland seller must take the initiative in exchanging these dollars for the pesos he wants. Either way, home money demands (is supplied for) foreign money. The currency in which Inland exports are priced is similarly unimportant; it only determines whether the buyer or the seller must take the initiative on the foreign-exchange market. Nor does it much matter if goods are priced and payment is called for in the currency of some third country. The transaction involves an exchange of the importer's home money for foreign money and an exchange of foreign money for the exporter's home money.

Arbitrage

If governments impose no restrictions (as we usually assume until Chapter 7), we hardly need concern ourselves about the nationality of the person taking the initiative in a particular transaction or about the country where particular parts of the transaction take place. Arbitrage links transactors in different countries together into what is in effect a single uniform market. Arbitrage consists of seeking profit from discrepancies between prices prevailing at the same time in different submarkets. Suppose that the pound sterling was quoted at $2.45 in London and $2.35 in New York. In the London part of the market, arbitrageurs would sell pound balances in English banks for dollar balances in American banks, receiving $2.45 for each pound. In New York the arbitrageurs would buy pound balances in English banks with dollar balances in American banks, paying only $2.35 for each pound. The arbitrageurs' eagerness to sell pounds dear in London and buy them cheap in New York bids the exchange rate toward a common level, perhaps $2.40, in both places. Arbitrage quickly destroys the price discrepancies that motivate it.

Arbitrage in unrestricted markets also works to maintain orderly *cross rates* of exchange, that is, to keep exchange rates among numerous currencies consistent or compatible. Exchange rates would be inconsistent or disorderly—cross rates would be "broken"—if at one time, for example, quotations prevailed of 60 Belgian francs per dollar, 3 Belgian francs per Mexican peso, and 10 Mexican pesos per dollar. An arbitrageur could profit by buying 60 Belgian francs with $1.00, buying 20 Mexican pesos with the 60 Belgian francs, and, finally, buying $2.00 with the 20 Mexican pesos. Large-scale attempts to do this would strengthen the franc against the dollar (perhaps toward a rate of 50 francs per dollar), strengthen the peso against the franc (perhaps toward 4 francs per peso), and strengthen the dollar against the peso (perhaps toward 12½ pesos per dollar). This or some such consistent pattern of rates would emerge at which no further arbitrage was profitable.

Large banks conduct most of the arbitrage.

TABLE 2.1. *Correspondence between two viewpoints in the foreign-exchange market*

PESOS DEMANDED WITH AND SUPPLIED FOR DOLLARS

DOLLARS DEMANDED WITH AND SUPPLIED FOR PESOS

(1) Price of peso in dollars	(2) Millions of pesos per time period Demanded	(3) Supplied	(4) Price of dollar in pesos	(5) Millions of dollars per time period Demanded	(6) Supplied
$.40	P37.500	P600.000	P2.50	$240.000	$15.000
.35	48.980	459.375	2.857	160.781	17.143
.333	54.000	416.667	3.00	138.889	18.000
.30	66.667	337.500	3.333	101.250	20.000
.25	96.600	234.375	4.00	58.594	24.000
.20	150.000	150.000	5.00	30.000	30.000
.167	216.000	104.167	6.00	17.361	36.000
.15	266.667	84.375	6.667	12.656	40.000
.125	384.000	58.594	8.00	7.324	48.000
.10	600.000	37.500	10.00	3.750	60.000

NOTE: This table was drawn up by assuming two demand functions to start with:

1. The demand for pesos as a function of the price of the peso in dollars (the function represented by Columns 1 and 2). The equation is $q = \dfrac{6}{p^2}$, where $q =$ the number of millions of pesos demanded and $p =$ the price of the peso in dollars. This demand function has a constant elasticity of 2.

2. The demand for dollars as a function of the price of the dollar in pesos (the function represented by Columns 4 and 5). The equation is $Q = \dfrac{3750}{p^3}$, where $Q =$ the number of millions of dollars demanded and $P =$ the price of the dollar in pesos. This demand function has a constant elasticity of 3.

Their foreign-exchange traders keep constantly in touch with colleagues at home and abroad by telephone, teletype, and cable and keep constantly alert to the latest quotations. Even small discrepancies of the sort exaggerated in our examples will motivate arbitrage prompt and voluminous enough practically to wipe out the discrepancies literally within minutes. The checks mentioned earlier are written instructions for changing the ownership of deposit claims against banks; instructions of the same kind are commonly transmitted by cable.

The prompt effectiveness of arbitrage justifies assuming that, in the absence of restrictions, traders and institutions scattered all over the world form one single foreign-exchange market. It also justifies assuming that, from the standpoint of an individual country at a given time, foreign exchange is a single uniform commodity. In the absence of restrictions, one foreign currency can be converted into any other foreign currency almost instantly and at a competitively determined rate. Furthermore, changes that affect the foreign-exchange value of the home currency but not the values of foreign currencies among themselves will cause the home currency to appreciate or depreciate by a uniform percentage in relation to all foreign currencies.[1] In a preliminary analysis we may properly express the strength of the home currency by its rate on one foreign currency chosen to represent foreign exchange in general. We may regard the demand for foreign exchange as arising from imports and other transactions typically involving payments to foreigners and the supply of foreign exchange as arising from exports and other transactions typically involving receipt of payments from foreigners. It hardly matters—as already explained—whether goods are priced in home or in foreign currency.

Supply and demand

Inland's imports and other transactions involving payments to Outlanders give rise to a demand for Outland pesos to be bought with Inland dollars or, in other words, to a supply of dollars to be sold for pesos. Inland's exports and other transactions involving receipt of payment from Outlanders give rise to a supply of pesos to be sold for dollars or, in other words, to a demand for dollars to be bought with pesos. We can view the determination of the rate of exchange that clears the market either in terms of supply and demand for pesos and the price of the peso in dollars or, alternatively, in terms of supply and demand for dollars and the price of the dollar in pesos. Table 2.1 illustrates the translation from one viewpoint to the other. The three columns on the left show the demand for and supply of foreign exchange in terms of home money. Columns 1 and 2 reflect the fact that the lower the price of the Outland peso in Inland dollars and the cheaper Outland goods and services appear to Inlanders, the more of them Inlanders want to buy and the more pesos they demand to pay for them. Columns 1 and 3 show that the higher the price of pesos, the more of them are supplied. The reason is that a "high" dollar price of pesos means a "low" peso price of dollars; Inland goods appear cheap to Outlanders and attract a larger volume of peso expenditure on them than would occur if the buying power of the peso over Inland goods were not so high. (A conceivable exception is considered on the next pages.) The three right-hand columns show the same price-quantity relations from the alternative point of view. The cheaper the dollar in pesos, the more dollars are demanded to pay for Outlanders' purchases of the correspondingly cheap Inland goods. The more valuable the dollar in pesos, the more dollars are supplied as Inlanders spend them to buy the correspondingly cheap Outland goods. For any row the prices in Columns 1 and 4 are reciprocals ($.40 per peso is the same as 2.50 pesos per dollar). Columns 2 and 6 correspond: if 37.5 million pesos are being demanded at $.40 each, then 37.5 million × .40 = $15 million are being spent for pesos or, in other words, are being supplied on the foreign-exchange market. If 96 million pesos are being demanded at $.25 each, then 96 million × .25 = $24 million are being supplied in exchange for pesos. Similarly, columns 3 and 5 correspond: 600 million pesos being supplied at $.40 each amounts to 600 million

1. This simplification is appropriate here, although, realistically, changes in world-market conditions may require a new pattern of rates of each currency against many others.

× .40 = $240 million being demanded; and 37.5 million pesos being supplied at $.10 amounts to $3.75 million being demanded. In Fig. 2.1, part A represents the left side and part B the right side of Table 2.1; the two sides of the table and the two graphs represent the same conditions. The same equilibrium exchange rate ($.20 per peso, 5 pesos to the dollar) emerges regardless of which point of view is adopted. At a rate "overvaluing" the peso ("undervaluing" the dollar), some suppliers of pesos (demanders of dollars) would be frustrated; at a disequilibrium rate in the opposite direction, the opposite kind of frustration would prevail; and in an unhampered market, competition among frustrated transactors would bid the rate toward the equilibrium level.

A situation that will call for detailed attention later invites mention here. Conceivably, the demand for and supply of foreign exchange might be so inelastic—the quantities demanded and supplied might respond so slightly to price—that the market would be unstable. In a loose and preliminary way this amounts to saying that the demand curve slopes downward so steeply and the supply curve slopes backward so markedly as to intersect as shown in

Fig. 2.2. At an above-equilibrium price of foreign exchange, the quantity *demanded* would exceed the quantity *supplied*, and competition among frustrated demanders would bid the rate further upward from equilibrium; at a below-equilibrium rate, competition among frustrated suppliers would bid the rate further downward. The same instability would appear in a view of the market as a supply of and demand for home currency in terms of foreign exchange.

An inelastic demand for one currency implies a backward-bending supply curve of the other currency. Table 2.2 and the corresponding two parts of Fig. 2.3 illustrate the translation of the demand for dollars in terms of pesos into the supply of pesos in terms of dollars. Columns 1 and 3 show equivalent ways of expressing the exchange rate, and columns 2 and 4 also correspond (for example, $25 million demanded at 10 pesos each corresponds to 250 million pesos supplied at $.10 each). At prices above 17.5 pesos per dollar, the demand for dollars is elastic: a specified small percentage change in price results in a larger percentage change in the opposite direction in the number of dollars demanded, or, in other

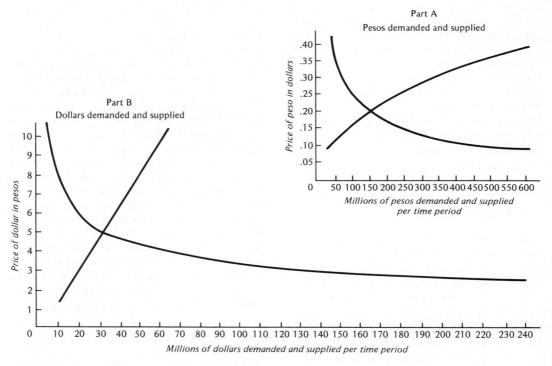

FIGURE 2.1

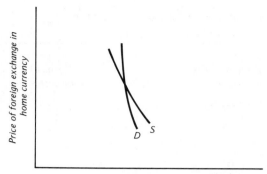

Quantities of foreign exchange supplied
and demanded per time period

*Price of foreign exchange in
home currency* (vertical axis label)

D   S

FIGURE 2.2

words, a change in price results in a change in the opposite direction in the total number of pesos that would be spent to buy dollars. This range of elastic demand for dollars corresponds to dollar prices of the peso below $.05714; the lower the price of the peso, the fewer pesos would be supplied, as is true of a normally sloping supply curve. The demand for dollars is *inelastic* at prices below 17.5 pesos each: a change in price results in a change in the same direction in the total number of pesos that would be spent to buy dollars. This range corresponds to dollar prices of pesos higher than $.05714. Within it, the higher their price, the fewer pesos would be supplied.[2] Even a backward-bending peso supply curve of this sort might be cut in the normal way by a sufficiently elastic demand curve, yielding a stable equilibrium. For two reasons, though, the unlikely possibility of an unstable market is worth understanding: first, as Chapter 8 will explain, it enters into discussions of the workability of free markets; and second, applying principles to strange cases as well as ordinary cases is a useful exercise in understanding the principles themselves.

Some warnings are necessary to keep our numerical examples, with their definite schedules and curves, from being misleading. Reality is not that simple. Events that would shift any supply or demand curve would to some extent shift the other curve also. This is notably true of foreign exchange. An export boom that brought more foreign exchange onto the market than before at each exchange rate would presumably raise incomes at home and so raise import demands and the quantity of foreign exchange demanded at that rate. Or a shift in tastes toward imports would not only increase

the demand for foreign exchange but also shunt some resources away from producing the commodities now in weakened demand into export production instead, stimulating exports by lowering their prices and so increasing—or if the foreign demand were inelastic, decreasing—the quantity of foreign exchange supplied at a given exchange rate. Even an adjustment from disequilibrium to equilibrium in a particular market shifts the curves that describe the market. If official controls that had been artificially supporting the foreign-exchange value of the home currency were dropped and if international trade expanded as a result, the whole economic system would in principle be affected, including the positions and shapes of the foreign-exchange supply and demand curves themselves.[3] Such interdependence of supplies and demands is true of foreign exchange and ordinary commodities alike, with perhaps a difference only in degree. Inventions that cheapen some commodity will affect the incomes of its producers, as well as incomes in competing and complementary industries, and so will affect consumer demands for the commodity. Removal of an official price ceiling on some commodity will increase its production and consumption, bidding factors away from other lines of production and affecting factor prices and the production costs and supply schedule of the commodity in question. (This

2. Pondering the relation between columns 1 and 3 of the table will dispel any momentary puzzlement over the fact that while the inelastic range of the demand-for-dollars curve takes up only half the length of the entire curve, the backward-sloping range of the supply-of-pesos curve takes up much more than half the length. The two price scales are different. High pesos-per-dollar rates correspond to low dollars-per-peso rates, and conversely; the equivalents of rates above 17.5 pesos per dollar are squeezed into the range below $.05714 in the dollars-per-peso scale.

3. Svend Laursen hints at some such considerations in his strictures against applying ordinary partial-equilibrium supply-and-demand analysis to foreign exchange as well as to ordinary commodities. See his "The Market for Foreign Exchange," *Economia Internazionale,* **VIII**, November 1955, esp. pp. 762–766.

TABLE 2.2. *Correspondence between demand for one currency and supply of the other*

DOLLARS DEMANDED WITH PESOS		PESOS SUPPLIED FOR DOLLARS	
(1) Price of dollar in pesos	(2) Millions of dollars demanded	(3) Price of peso in dollars	(4) Millions of pesos supplied
P 0	$35	$Infinite	P 0
2	33	.50	66
3	32	.33333	96
5	30	.20	150
10	25	.10	250
15	20	.06667	300
17.5	17.5	.05714	306.25
20	15	.05	300
25	10	.04	250
30	5	.03333	150
32	3	.03125	96
33	2	.03030	66
35	0	.02857	0

is just one reason why the total amounts of a commodity that *would be* supplied per time period at various prices depend on what amount is in fact *being* supplied.) In principle, a partial view of the market for foreign ex-

change or of anything else is incomplete; and it should be supplemented with general-equilibrium considerations whenever they are particularly relevant. But negativistic carping at partial-equilibrium analysis is pointless.

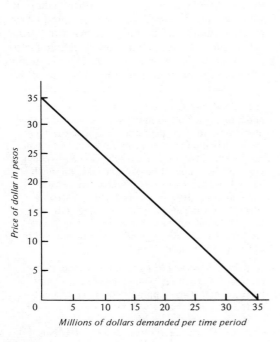

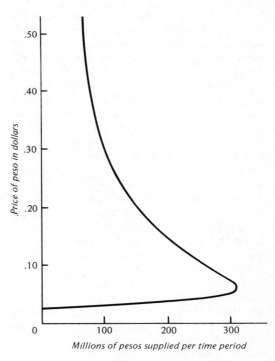

FIGURE 2.3

There are still other reasons why a supply curve or a demand curve does not portray a definite price-quantity relation. The amount of something that would be supplied or demanded per time period depends not only on the price supposed to prevail but also on the previous price, on how long this previous price had prevailed, on how long a time actual and potential producers and buyers are considered to have to adjust to the new price, and other such things. The quantity of something supplied or demanded depends not only on tastes, incomes, the prices of other things, and the price of the thing itself but on the whole historical constellation of circumstances, including the thing's price history.

For all the foregoing reasons, and others, a supply or demand curve is not, and does not even *represent*, some definite entity in or property of the real world—something perhaps difficult to measure but none the less objectively "there." Instead, supply and demand curves are pedagogical devices for illustrating the direct and inverse price-quantity relations asserted by the law of supply and the law of demand and for aiding explanations of the competitive price-determining and market-clearing tendencies asserted by the law of supply and demand. Sometimes it is useful to discuss how sensitively or insensitively quantities supplied or demanded respond to price, to consider what conditions make for relatively high or low responsiveness, to consider how different conditions of these kinds affect the consequences of particular economic changes, and even to assume definite "elasticities" in numerical or graphical examples. Doing so need not mean really believing in definite supply-and-demand entities having definite numerical elasticities. Supply-and-demand analysis should not suffer discredit because of the error of taking too literally the simplified

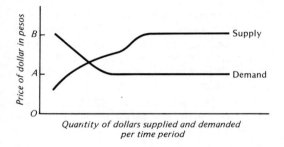

FIGURE 2.4

pedagogical devices sometimes used in expounding it.

Pegged rates and the gold standard

So far we have assumed an exchange rate freely determined by private supply and demand. Usually, however, rates are officially pegged. Figure 2.4 reflects a policy in one or both countries of preventing the exchange rate from going outside the range of OA and OB pesos per dollar. If the authorities are willing to supply practically unlimited amounts of dollars out of officially held reserves at the price OB and are willing to absorb practically unlimited amounts into official reserves at the price OA, the supply and demand curves become horizontal at these levels. No matter how the curves shift, their intersection cannot be outside the range of official pegging. By narrowing the spread between the official selling and buying prices of foreign exchange, the authorities could keep the range of possible fluctuation as small as they pleased.

The international gold standard pegs exchange rates indirectly. Under the gold standard a country's monetary authority keeps the national monetary unit and a certain quantity of gold equal in value on free markets by maintaining two-way convertibility. It stands ready both to buy unlimited amounts of gold at a definite price (or to coin all gold brought to the mint by private owners) and also to sell unlimited amounts of gold at the same or very nearly the same price—perhaps by redeeming its paper money in gold coins. (How the authority can remain able to honor these commitments, and the consequences of its doing so, are topics for later chapters.) An *international* gold standard exists among all countries that tie their moneys to gold and allow the unrestricted import and export of gold. If the Inland dollar "contains" 1 gram of gold and the Outland peso $\frac{1}{5}$ gram, the so-called mint par between them is 5 pesos per dollar. This par has no more claim to the title of the equilibrium exchange rate, however, than any other rate within a certain narrow range on either side of it. Suppose, for example, that the rate became 5.01 pesos per dollar. Wouldn't arbitrageurs do the following on a huge scale: redeem 5 pesos in 1 gram of gold in Outland, ship the gold to Inland, sell it to the authorities there for $1.00, and sell the dollar on the market at the assumed 5.01 rate for a profit of 0.01 peso? No. This margin would probably be more than eaten up by the expenses of office work, of telephone calls and cables, of perhaps actually melting down one country's coins and refining them into pure gold before delivering it to the monetary authority of the other country, of crating and shipping and insuring the gold, and even of losing interest on capital tied up in gold in transit. If these expenses total 0.05 peso per gram of gold, it would become profitable to ship gold from Outland to Inland only if the peso depreciated to more than 5.05 per dollar. Arbitrage would then tend to check further depreciation.

To clarify the principles of gold arbitrage, let us suppose, at the other extreme, that the peso had strengthened on the market to a rate of only 4.94 per dollar. Arbitrageurs would then redeem $1.00 in 1 gram of gold, ship it to Outland, and receive 4.95 pesos net for it, even after covering the expenses of 0.05 peso. Buying back $1.00 at the assumed 4.94 rate, they would still have 0.01 peso left as profit. Arbitrage of this sort on a large scale would add to the ordinary supply of pesos and demand for dollars and so move the rate toward 4.95, making more arbitrage no longer profitable.

These examples explain why the rates of 5.05 and 4.95 pesos per dollar are known, respectively, as the gold import and export points for Inland and the gold export and import points for Outland. It is also clear why the exchange rate will not go or remain much outside these limits. But the gold points are not absolutely definite and unchanging figures. Since the distance of each gold point from mint par depends on shipping and insurance costs, interest costs, administrative costs, and even the implicit and uncertain costs of diverting the arbitrageurs' time and effort from other activities, the gold points are bound to be somewhat different for different arbitrageurs and to move with changes in interest rates and other conditions. Even the prices at which national monetary authorities buy and sell gold may be subject to some slight fudging. (For historical examples, see p. 306.) But the principle remains that exchange rates among gold-standard currencies, while not absolutely

rigid, do move within narrow if imprecise limits and that temporary breakouts from these limits set up corrective tendencies.[4]

Gold arbitrage explains how imbalances between ordinary commercial and financial payments into and out of a country or between the amounts of the country's currency being demanded and supplied on the exchange market are "settled" under the international gold standard. No authorities need somehow estimate and deliberately fill any such gap. Given fixed interconvertibility between gold and national moneys and freedom of gold shipments, private parties will undertake the appropriate shipments without any official planning. Weakness or strength pressing the exchange value of a country's currency to one gold point or the other will cause gold movements that tend to shrink or expand the country's money supply. How strongly the money supply responds, and with what further consequences, is something to be examined later.

Even without standing ready to buy and sell practically unlimited amounts of foreign exchange or gold at specified rates, the authorities could conceivably stabilize a country's exchange rate just by rigorously suppressing transactions at rates outside specified narrow limits. The demand curve for foreign exchange would be horizontal at its upper left because no one would be allowed to exercise any effective demand at a higher rate, and the supply curve would be horizontal at its lower left because no one would be allowed to supply foreign exchange at a lower rate. Such control would of course have wide repercussions.

Methods of international remittance

Before Chapter 3 introduces the concept of the balance of international payments, it will be helpful to know some factual or "mechanical" details about foreign-exchange and related transactions. A quick survey—too quick to benefit practical merchants and bankers—will furnish a background for the theory and policy discussions still to follow. Institutional facts will prove relevant to such topics as the complexity of international banking and of administering and complying with official controls over it; the comparative complexity and expense of systems of pegged and of free exchange rates; the possibilities of speculation on short-run wobbles and on major adjustments in pegged and in free rates, and the possibilities of speculation by banks, merchants, professional operators, and others; and the influence of official stabilization funds on rates and on the expectations and actions of private operators.

The foreign supplier of an Inland importer may either require payment in advance or require cash on delivery.[5] At the opposite extreme, he may sell on open-book account and wait some weeks or even months for payment. Sooner or later, the importer will have to transfer funds. The simplest method, if not forbidden by the government, is probably to mail an ordinary check written on his regular Inland bank account. The foreign supplier will be able to sell this check to his own bank for Outland currency, since Outland banks can use such checks to replenish their working balances with Inland banks.

But perhaps the Outland supplier will insist on payment in his own currency. If so, the Inland importer may buy a bank draft from his own bank.[6] This is a check drawn by his bank on a bank balance in Outland. Alternatively, the importer may buy a mail transfer or a telegraphic or cable transfer. There is little difference. Instead of obtaining a draft from his bank and mailing it himself to his foreign supplier, he simply has his bank instruct its foreign branch or correspondent to make the payment to the foreign payee. (What the remitting importer receives from his own bank is not a document to mail abroad but simply a receipt for the Inland money paid for the transfer.) Since the instructions constituting a mail or telegraphic transfer go directly by airmail, telegraph, or cable, they ordinarily arrive sooner than a draft bought and sent by the importer. The deduction from the Inland bank's deposit abroad thus occurs sooner; and to take account of the interest for this difference in time, the price charged for an airmail transfer and especially for a telegraphic transfer may be slightly higher than for a bank draft.

Banks also buy cable transfers from their customers. An American exporter who has received payment in British pounds may sell them for dollars to an American bank, which will have the pounds transferred to its own account by cabling the London bank in which they had been deposited. The telegraphic or cable transfer is the major instrument for effecting payments in the leading exchange markets throughout the world.[7]

FOREIGN EXCHANGE: RATES, INSTRUMENTS, AND MARKETS

For purposes of analysis we have perhaps said enough already about the origin and use of the instruments that actually convey ownership of or claims on foreign currencies and bank accounts. These include various types of checks, drafts, and mailed or cabled instructions, and also, to a small extent, actual foreign

---

4. Under the gold standard before 1931 and especially before 1914, the dollar rate on the pound sterling almost always kept within a very few cents of the mint par of $4.86656.

In view of the inherent vagueness of the gold points, it is puzzling to see the gleeful iconoclasm with which one student of the gold-standard era reported that exchange rates often did push beyond the gold points, and for long, continuous intervals. See Oskar Morgenstern, *International Financial Transactions and Business Cycles*, Princeton, N.J.: Princeton University Press, for the National Bureau of Economic Research, 1959, *passim*; e.g., p. 567. Morgenstern's remarks are particularly puzzling because he does not say how he knew precisely what the gold points were at each time and does not indicate how big any breakouts of actual exchange rates from the gold points would have to be discredit standard theory. Morgenstern expresses similar vague doubts about arbitrage tending to maintain orderly cross rates of exchange.

5. When the terms are C.O.D., the seller will arrange for release of the bill of lading or other documents necessary to obtain the goods from the transportation company only when the buyer makes payment in the agreed way. The seller will send the bill of lading and other shipping documents to an agent of his in the buyer's country (perhaps a foreign branch or correspondent of his own bank), and the agent will release the documents to the buyer at the proper time.

6. Here, *bank draft* means a check drawn by one bank on another. The term is also used as a synonym for *banker's bill*, that is, a bill of exchange (draft) drawn by a commercial firm on a bank under a letter of credit (as explained in the appendix). The two types of bank draft are alike in both being drawn *on* a bank. Whether the drawer is another bank or a commercial firm is usually clear from the context.

7. Alan R. Holmes, *The New York Foreign Exchange Market*, New York: Federal Reserve Bank of New York, 1959, p. 18.

coins and banknotes. The appendix gives some further detail and some information about types of document not yet mentioned.

Foreign-exchange trading

Trading on the foreign-exchange market in the United States takes place: (1) between banks and their customers, who are the ultimate suppliers and demanders of foreign exchange, (2) between different American banks, and (3) between American and foreign banks.[8] Dozens of American banks, mostly in New York City, maintain working balances of foreign exchange abroad, though fewer than half of them do most of the business. The New York market also includes some branches and agencies and representative offices of foreign banks and dealers specializing in foreign paper money and coins.

A firm wanting to buy or sell foreign exchange will deal with its bank, ordinarily by telephone. A large firm doing business with several banks will probably shop around for the best rate. If the firm is not located in a major city or for some other reason does not deal with a bank active in the exchange market, its regular bank will act as an intermediary in arranging the transaction with one of its large correspondents. Customers of small outlying banks are more likely to be buying foreign exchange in small amounts than selling it, since they would rarely be drawing drafts or receiving payment in foreign currencies. The city banks list the rates at which the small banks, as agents, may sell exchange. These "retail" rates are high enough to allow some margin of safety and are valid only up to a specified daily total amount and only for a few days, unless altered sooner.

During a day, a large bank will be buying a particular currency from some customers and selling it to others. To some extent these transactions will match, but the chances are that the bank will still be making net purchases or net sales and will want to offset them on the interbank "wholesale" market, where banks with a surplus of a particular currency trade with banks short of it. This is an "over-the-counter" market, with no specific location or formal organization in New York. Trading takes place by mail, telegraph, and cable, and above all by telephone. In Germany, however, several foreign-exchange bourses have been organized. Although they are open less than an hour a day and account for only a small fraction of total foreign-exchange turnover in Germany, the rates established on them influence over-the-counter transactions, especially transactions between banks and their business customers. Paris also has a foreign-exchange bourse, which accounts for a larger fraction of total turnover than the German bourses. In London and Zurich, as in New York, all transactions are over-the-counter.[9]

The local banks in New York and in several foreign centers, instead of shopping around among themselves directly, ordinarily deal through brokers. In this way the banks keep their facilities and personnel freer for dealing with their customers. The brokers are in an ideal position to keep themselves and their clients informed about actual exchange rates and about bids and offers. In addition, using these middlemen lets banks remain anonymous as long as possible. Anonymity can be important for large banks whose transactions might be taken as indicating or even determining rate trends; they would risk pushing the rate against themselves when trying to deal directly. Smaller banks known by the kinds of customers they serve to be mainly either buyers or sellers at wholesale might also risk not getting the best possible rates if they dealt directly.

A bank wanting to buy or sell a particular currency phones an inquiry to one of the brokers. The broker phones other banks to seek a counterparty to the transaction. He receives his commission by quoting foreign exchange at a slightly lower price to the selling bank than to the buying bank. Since competition keeps the commission down to a very small fraction of 1 percent, his profit depends on a large and rapid turnover.[10] As of 1965, eight foreign-exchange brokers were operating in New York (in the 1930s, when the market was more active, there were about 45). Some of the brokers specialize in particular currencies, but all handle the most active ones. Sterling is far in the lead in volume of transactions on the New York market, followed by the Canadian dollar and trailed by Continental European and South American currencies.

The preference of American exporters for quoting prices and receiving payment in dollars limits the commercial supply of foreign exchange on the New York market. And anyway, American banks do not try to offset all imbalances among themselves before dealing with foreign banks; all types of transactions go on at the same time. When an American bank can get a better rate directly from a foreign bank than through a broker from another American bank, it will do so. The foreign banks, for their part, are always alert to chances of advantageously buying or selling dollars in New York.

A bank's market activity centers in its trading room.[11] Each of several traders works with a set of direct telephone connections to the foreign-exchange brokers, the cable companies, and perhaps one or more correspondent banks outside New York. He uses regular telephones for customer contacts and foreign calls. The typical trading room also has a direct teletype link with correspondent banks at home and abroad. At the start of each business day, the traders face the overnight accumulation of mail orders. They learn the latest exchange-rate trends by telephone from London and the Continent, where the markets have been open for several hours. Throughout the day, assistants keep a running record of the bank's short or long position in each currency so that the traders can always judge how eager they should be to buy or sell each currency when quoting rates and when responding to the quotations of others. Profit depends on speed and large volume, since the typical spread between a bank's buying and selling rates for large blocks of a currency is in the range of one-tenth of 1 percent, or even less.[12] The traders also watch for opportunities for arbitrage profit provided by small fleeting discrepancies between rates quoted in New York and elsewhere or between the cross rates of exchange involving two or more foreign currencies. A foreign-exchange trader needs a keen memory, a facility for fast and accurate mental arithmetic, and nerves that can stand the strain of continual decisions involving many thousands of dollars in a few seconds.

In addition, an expert trader needs a "feel" for market trends, an ability to interpret clues about short-run shifts in supply and demand. Although a bank's traders are not deliberate speculators and although they *do* strive for an even balance between their sales and purchases of each currency, they do not immediately offset each individual transaction with a commercial customer by an opposite transaction in the interbank market. Except when the latest transaction has created an uncomfortably large imbalance, they may wait a while to see what offsetting occurs in the course of ordinary busi-

8. The following description draws on Holmes, *op. cit.* (and also the second edition, co-authored by Francis H. Schott, 1965), as well as on Helmut Lipfert, *Devisenhandel*, Frankfurt/Main: Fritz Knapp Verlag, 1958.

9. Lipfert, *op. cit.*, pp. 53–57, 147–149.

10. Since World War II, the Canadian Bankers Association has hired brokers at fixed salaries, also paying their office rent and other expenses. This arrangement, replacing the earlier system of private brokers charging percentage commissions, has increased the volume of transaction in the Canadian market and has attracted some business from New York banks dealing through Canadian banks. (Donald B. Marsh in Robert Z. Aliber, ed., *The International Market for Foreign Exchange*, New York: Praeger, 1969, pp. 145–146.)

11. Cf. Holmes, *op. cit.*, chap. VI, and Lipfert, *op. cit.*, chap. B.

12. Paul V. Horn and Henry Gomez, *International Trade Principles and Practices*, 4th ed., Englewood Cliffs, N.J.: Prentice-Hall, Inc., 1959, p. 314; Charles N. Henning, *International Finance*, New York: Harper & Row, 1958, p. 252.

According to Harry Eastman, Canadian banks quote their largest business customers, as well as foreign banks, a spread of $\frac{1}{32}$ of 1 cent per U.S. dollar between buying and selling prices. U.S. and European banks quote still smaller spreads. (Eastman in *Canadian–United States Financial Relationships*, Boston: Federal Reserve Bank of Boston, 1972, pp. 149–151.) Norman Fieleke has assembled figures on monthly average asked-bid spreads for several currencies in the New York interbank market in 1970 and 1971. (Most of his figures refer to *forward* exchange rates, explained later in this chapter.) Until the beginning of monetary upheavals in May 1971, the great bulk of such spreads amounted to well under $\frac{1}{10}$ of 1 percent of the rate. Except for a rise to $\frac{1}{10}$ of 1 percent in the turbulent month of August 1971, the spread on the Canadian dollar, which had been floating since June 1970, hardly reflected those upheavals. (Fieleke in *Canadian–United States Financial Relationships*, especially table on p. 181, and "Exchange-Rate Flexibility and the Cost of Using the Foreign-Exchange Market," *New England Economic Review*, July/August 1972, especially charts on pp. 21, 22, and 24.)

Even if the foreign department of a bank is not profitable in itself, it may be indirectly profitable by helping to attract and retain the deposits and loan business of internationally active corporations.

ness. How willing a trader is to wait depends in part on which way he expects the exchange rate to move over the next few minutes or hours. In fact, his job includes trying to profit from such short-run predictions without running too much risk. How much is "too much" is a matter of opinion. A trader might win compliments if events bore out his judgment and draw criticism for speculating if they did not. Banks have occasionally profited from being short of currencies at the time of large devaluations, as in 1931 and 1949, but some banks have lost heavily on their working balances of foreign exchange.[13]

Foreign-exchange traders must worry not only about their bank's overall long or short position in each currency but also about its time pattern. They must take account of the precise form of the exchange bought and sold—cable transfers, mail transfers, sight drafts, time drafts, actual currency—since this affects the time when funds sold must be made available and when funds bought become available. Even differences of a day or two matter. Furthermore, banks not only buy and sell currencies "spot" (for delivery at once or in the next few days) but also make contracts with their customers for purchases and sales some weeks or months later. During a day, a bank may have made net sales of spot sterling matched by net purchases for future delivery. Yet the prospect of a surplus of sterling in the future is no full offset to a deficiency in the present. The bank may therefore want to arrange a "swap" in the interbank market—in this particular example, a sale of "forward" (future) sterling accompanied by a simultaneous spot purchase. Since no two banks are likely to have exactly offsetting patterns of imbalance, some banks have to be satisfied with swaps that meet their needs only roughly; but a clever broker can go a long way toward meeting the exact needs of his clients by working out a set of transactions involving perhaps three or even four or five parties. The participant banks will receive or pay the differences between the spot and forward rates on the currencies involved; these rates are not in general identical. Despite its concern for its net position in each foreign currency in the present and for various future dates, a bank is not determined to keep the time pattern of its position exactly in balance from moment to moment or even from hour to hour. That would be too difficult. If the bank has developed a £100,000 short position in forward

sterling and it does not seem about to be offset by further forward or spot transactions with commercial customers, the bank's trader may approximately correct the unbalanced forward position by promptly buying £100,000 spot. The bank now risks a much smaller loss from an unfavorable change in the spread between the forward and spot quotations than it would otherwise have risked from an unfavorable move in the dollar quotation on sterling generally (with the forward and spot rates moving approximately together). A closer adjustment of the time pattern of the bank's position can be left for correction by swap transactions later and in less haste. Incidentally, swap transactions (like arbitrage transactions) can be carried out not only by banks but also by commercial firms if they are familiar enough with the market and have the funds available.

Actual trading is similar for both spot and forward exchange. Suppose that a bank wants to cover a £100,000 short position in sterling by a purchase in the interbank market. One of the bank's traders will phone one of the foreign-exchange brokers and inquire, "What's sterling?" He does not reveal at first whether he wants to buy or sell.[14] The answer will be a pair of fractions, perhaps "¼–⁵⁄₁₆" (traders know the prevailing range of the exchange rate so well that only the fractions of a cent need be mentioned). The inquiring bank can sell at the lower rate and buy at the higher rate unless, as a bit more conversation will make clear, these rates are merely the broker's judgment of the market instead of actual bids and offers made by some of his other clients. The bank's trader may decide to accept an actual offer at once. Alternatively, and especially if the broker has quoted mere estimates, the trader may state his bid; and the broker will inquire around among his other clients. In quoting the rate to a potential seller he will deduct a small fraction to allow for his commission. After arranging a deal, the broker identifies each party to the other so that the actual exchange of sterling for dollars may be carried out.

If the quantity of sterling offered in the interbank market comes to exceed or fall short of the quantity demanded at the then prevailing rate, the brokers will propose some new rate to match desired transactions on the two sides of the market. The rates established in the interbank market influence the rates that banks quote to their commercial customers. At the same time, the interbank rates reflect the banks' transactions with their commercial customers. For example, when sterling would be in excess supply at the previous exchange rate in transactions among banks, the reason probably is that, on balance, commercial customers have been making net sales of sterling to the banks. The exchange rates that emerge in banks' transactions among themselves and with their customers are "administered"; they are proposed and agreed to by definite persons. Yet to all intents and purposes, these rates emerge in sensitive response to competitive pressures and almost as impersonally as the prices on an organized commodity or stock exchange.

It is true that the range within which an exchange rate is freely determined will be narrow if central banks or other authorities are actively making bids and offers in the interbank market to keep the rate within set limits on either side of an official parity. Under an international gold standard, the interconvertibility of gold and national currencies and the operations of gold arbitrageurs had essentially the same effect. In the United States, until some official transactions were begun in 1961, neither the Treasury nor the Federal Reserve Bank of New York intervened directly on the exchange market to influence rates; but they accomplished the same result by keeping dollars and gold interconvertible for foreign monetary authorities at $35.00 per ounce, plus or minus one-quarter of 1 percent. Furthermore, the Federal Reserve Bank of New York, whose foreign-exchange trading room is linked by direct wire to the trading rooms of several of the largest banks, will place orders in the New York market on behalf of foreign authorities. Even when these authorities carry out their rate-pegging operations at home, arbitrage of course makes the results felt in New York also.

Whether exchange rates fluctuate freely without any limit or only within narrow limits maintained by official pegging, banks and their large customers must remain alert even to brief and minor fluctuations. Continual interbank trading occurs, and the whole apparatus of foreign-exchange traders and brokers (or alternative arrangements for the same purpose) remains necessary. The persons most directly active in the exchange market devote most of their energies to considering and acting upon hour-by-hour and minute-by-minute fluctuations of small fractions of 1 percent. Their work is necessary, no matter whether the range within which fluctuations *could* occur is limitless or is narrowly limited. Neither the international gold standard nor the typical sort of official exchange-rate pegging simplifies and cheapens the operation of the market decisively as compared with a system of freely fluctuating rates. This advantage would exist only if continuous official transactions at substantially identical buying and selling rates kept the rates rigid. Banks would then hardly be foreign-exchange dealers in their own right. In practice if not in name, they would be mere intermediaries between their customers and the exchange-pegging authorities. (If the authorities wished to maintain buying and selling rates rigid but with a spread between them, private transactions at other than the two limiting rates would have to be forbidden; and the banks would even more fully have to be mere agents of the authorities.) Nothing short of such official monopoly over the foreign-exchange

13. Henning, *op. cit.*, pp. 252, 252n., 281. On the respectability of not always promptly covering unbalanced positions, see Paul Einzig, "Some Recent Changes in Forward Exchange Practices," *Economic Journal*, **LXX**, September 1960, p. 492; Einzig, *A Dynamic Theory of Forward Exchange*, London: Macmillan, 1961, pp. 74, 101; Eastman, *op. cit.*, pp. 152–153; Helmut Lipfert in Aliber, *op. cit.*, pp. 125–127; and Samuel I. Katz, *Exchange-Risk Under Fixed and Flexible Exchange Rates*, New York University, *The Bulletin*, June 1972, pp. 29–33. Katz maintains that the banks' willingness to hold unbalanced positions, even though of limited size and duration, contributes materially to the smooth functioning of the market.

14. In international dealings directly between banks, custom entitles the party initiating and paying for a telephone or teletype conversation to expect the party called to state first his buying and selling rates in the currency inquired about. If the party called quoted "too big" a spread, failed to allow his caller a reasonable time to react (perhaps 10 or 20 seconds at the phone and a minute or two at the teleprinter), or failed to back up his rate quotations on a major currency by trading at least a customary sizable minimum amount, his reputation would suffer. A poor reputation would discourage inquiries and so erode the bank's opportunity to maintain continual contact with the market. Lipfert, *Devisenhandel*, pp. 66–68, and Lipfert in Aliber, *op. cit.*, pp. 129–130.

business would keep rates rigid enough to cut much from the cost of exchange-trading facilities and personnel employed by banks and business firms. But if pegging could hold rates within limits narrow, *permanent*, and *dependable* enough to eliminate substantially all risk of changes, then merchants would no longer need the risk protection that forward-exchange facilities nowadays afford. Elimination of forward exchange would permit some economies in exchange-trading equipment and personnel. Whether or not rates could be pegged permanently and dependably enough to eliminate the risk of changes, and if so at the cost of what disadvantages, are matters considered in later chapters.

Forward exchange[15]

Forward-exchange contracts, as already mentioned, specify the purchase and sale of foreign exchange to be delivered some weeks or months later and to be paid for then at an exchange rate agreed on in advance. Forward exchange is akin to futures in commodities. If there were no such facilities, an importer or exporter of goods due to be paid for in foreign currency some time in the future would run the risk of an unfavorable change in the exchange rate in the meanwhile. Since dealing only in terms of one's own currency merely shifts the risk to the foreigner and does not eliminate it, insistence on this privilege might rule out some advantageous transactions. Forward exchange is a better answer. By telephoning his bank, an importer or exporter can determine the local-currency equivalent of foreign exchange to be paid or received in the future. A merchant trading in staple commodities at a very small profit margin can obtain a firm forward-rate quotation to guide his final decision about whether or not to agree to a contemplated transaction at a particular price in foreign currency. He can telephone his bank in advance and arrange for it to keep its rate quotation available for perhaps 30 minutes or an hour.[16]

Forward exchange is also a convenient vehicle for speculation, or would be if banks did not generally shy from forward contracts with persons known to be outright speculators. Buying a foreign currency spot to bet on its rise is a rather amateurish approach. Instead, the speculator can buy it forward, take delivery at the agreed time, and then sell at the new spot rate to realize his gain (or loss). Forward sales, conversely, are a convenient method of bear speculation. Finally, forward contracts are used not only for reducing risk in commercial transactions and for speculation but also in interest arbitrage, as explained presently.

In the New York foreign-exchange market, pounds sterling and Canadian dollars are the two currencies in which forward contracts are most commonly written. The U.S. dollar is so widely used in international trade that the active markets for forward contracts involving it and minor foreign currencies are located abroad rather than in New York, but American banks can often arrange through their correspondents abroad for forward contracts in these other currencies. Forward rates are commonly quoted for contracts of 30, 60, and 90 days' maturity, but banks will tailor the length of contracts to meet the needs of their customers. Rather long maturities are often obtainable. (See pp. 266–267.)

Banks can write forward contracts with little risk. Unlike insurance companies, which take essentially unavoidable risks onto themselves and receive insurance premiums for doing so, banks play a part in arranging for opposite risks to cancel each other out.[17] Their customers' forward purchases and sales of a particular currency ordinarily will match to a considerable extent. Banks deal among themselves in the forward market to even out their individual positions. Even if the overall commercial demand for forward sterling exceeded the overall supply, banks could cover the risk of their excess sales of forward sterling by buying spot sterling and investing it at short term in London until the time for delivery under forward contracts. The willingness of banks to cover unbalanced forward positions by spot transactions, and accordingly the forward rates that the banks are willing to quote, depend on interest rates at home and abroad.

The Chicago Mercantile Exchange inaugurated futures trading in foreign currencies on its International Monetary Market on May 16, 1972.[18] The new market displays the characteristic features of futures trading (as distinct from forward trading, to split terminological hairs): trading takes place on an organized exchange rather than over the counter, contracts are standardized rather than tailored to the exact requirement of the individual parties, an explicit brokerage fee replaces a spread between buying and selling rates, and most contracts are settled by payment of gain or loss rather than by actual delivery of the currency traded. Outright speculative activity is welcome, whereas banks generally shun forward contracts with recognizable speculators.

Interest parities

The principle of *interest parities* explains interrelations among spot, forward, and interest rates. It gives insight into possibilities of inexpensively covering future needs for or receipts of foreign exchange by making forward contracts. To an importer, the cost of eliminating risk is how much more he must pay for exchange bought forward than he would have to pay for a spot purchase. To an exporter, the cost is how much less he receives for foreign exchange sold forward than he would have received in a spot sale. Since the forward rate may be either higher or lower than the relevant spot rate,[19] the cost of avoiding risk may just as conceivably be negative as positive.

Ordinarily, the forward and spot rates quoted at the same time will diverge only slightly, the divergence corresponding to the difference between short-term interest rates in the two countries concerned. If short-term interest rates were higher in London than in New York by 4 percentage points a year, or by 1 point per three months, then the three-months forward rate for pounds in terms of dollars would stand at about a 1 percent discount from the spot rate. *Interest arbitrage* tends to maintain this relation.[20] To see how, we may suppose that the interest rates are as just mentioned but that the spot and forward exchange rates on the pound were equal. Arbitrageurs would have an incentive to buy pounds spot and at the same time sell them three-months forward at the same rate. During the three months, the funds could be lent in London for more interest than was obtainable in New York, and the risk-free reconversion into dollars would already have been provided for. Arbitrageurs not holding dollars at the start could borrow in New York, convert to spot pounds for relending at higher interest in London, and, under a forward contract made at the start, reconvert capital and interest at the end of the three months into enough dollars to repay capital with interest in New York with profit to spare. The eagerness of arbitrageurs to buy pounds spot and sell them forward would tend to bid up spot pounds and bid down forward pounds, establishing a for-

ward discount in correspondence with the excess of London over New York interest rates. The eagerness to borrow in New York and lend in London would also tend, perhaps only slightly, to narrow the interest-rate differential between the two centers.

Some simple algebra will specify more precisely the conditions in which no one would have incentives either to expand or to shrink the volume of covered interest arbitrage.[21] (Covered interest arbitrage means interest-motivated short-term international transfers of funds protected against exchange risk by forward contracts.) Let

S = spot exchange rate in dollars per pound
F = three-month forward exchange rate in dollars per pound
$p = \dfrac{F - S}{S}$ = premium on the forward

---

15. The standard reference is Paul Einzig, *The Theory of Forward Exchange*, London: Macmillan, 1937. The 1961 edition is *A Dynamic Theory of Forward Exchange*. Also see Holmes, *op. cit.*, pp. 26–27, 34, 36–54, and Paul Einzig, *Economic Journal*, September 1960, pp. 485–495.

16. Lipfert, *Devisenhandel*, pp. 153–154.

17. Chapter 13 comments further on the false analogy between forward exchange and insurance.

18. For statistics as well as institutional description, see *International Monetary Market Year Book 1972–1973* and *1973–1974*, Chicago: IMM, 1973, 1974.

19. This phrasing is deliberately vague about just what spot rate belongs in the comparison. Chapter 13 faces this question.

20. The major arbitrageurs are banks, as well as such operators in short-term funds as international oil companies. Katz, *op. cit.*, p. 40.

21. The following basically derives from S. C. Tsiang, "The Theory of Forward Exchange and Effects of Government Intervention on the Forward Exchange Market," IMF *Staff Papers*, **VII**, April 1959, pp. 79–80; and John Spraos, "Speculation, Arbitrage and Sterling," *Economic Journal*, **LXIX**, March 1959, p. 2n.

Readers familiar with the condition for portfolio equilibrium that the marginal expected returns be equal on all assets held will recognize interest parity as a particular example of this condition.

pound (a negative p means a discount on the forward pound)

N = short-term interest rate in New York per three months

L = short-term interest rate in London per three months

(p, N and L are understood to be expressed as decimals.)

There is no incentive to expand or shrink the volume of covered interest arbitrage when one dollar plus New York interest for three months just equals one dollar's worth of spot sterling plus London interest for three months reconverted into dollars at the forward rate. In symbols,

$$1 + N = \frac{1}{S} (1 + L) F$$

It follows from the definition of p that $F/S = 1 + p$. Thus the equilibrium condition becomes:

$$1 + N = (1 + p)(1 + L)$$
$$1 + N = 1 + p + L + pL$$
$$p = N - L - pL$$

This equation might be solved for p ($= \frac{N - L}{1 + L}$) to give the precise interest-parity condition. It is a useful simplification, however, to note that p and L are ordinarily both small decimals, so that their product, pL, is negligibly small. To a close approximation, then, the interest-parity condition becomes

$$p = N - L$$

We arrive at the same result if we consider arbitrageurs who want their profit in sterling instead of dollars. There is no incentive to expand or shrink the volume of arbitrage when one pound plus London interest for three months just equals one pound's worth of spot dollars plus New York interest for three months reconverted into pounds at the forward rate. In symbols,

$$1 + L = S (1 + N) \frac{1}{F}$$

By seeing that $S/F = \dfrac{1}{1 + p}$ and recalling that pL is negligibly small, we reach the same result as before.

This approximate equilibrium condition $p = N - L$, which underlay the earlier example,

corresponds to the usual verbal statement of the interest-parity condition: the forward premium on the pound expressed as a fraction of the spot dollar rate on the pound corresponds to the excess of New York over London interest rates (or the forward discount corresponds to the excess of London over New York interest rates).

Consider what would happen if this condition were not satisfied. An unrealistically large discrepancy will help make our new example clear: the three-month interest rate is 3 percent in London and 1 percent in New York, while the three-month forward discount on the pound is 4 percent instead of the theoretical 2 percent. Arbitrageurs can profit by borrowing pounds in London, converting them into dollars at the spot rate and at the same time contracting for their later reconversion into pounds at the forward rate, and meanwhile lending them in New York. Although the interest paid in London exceeds the interest earned in New York, this difference is more than outweighed by the opportunity to sell pounds spot and buy them back forward at an abnormally large discount. In their eagerness to do so, arbitrageurs weaken the spot pound and strengthen the forward pound and thus narrow the forward discount into line with the interest rates. (In principle, all these variables are interdependent; and the interest rates themselves would be somewhat affected.)

Departures from interest parities

The simplification of regarding pL in the equilibrium formula as negligibly small is only a minor reason why this interest-parity condition does not describe reality exactly.[22] A more important complication is that the short-term interest rates of the formula cannot be specified unambiguously. Different rates prevail for different instruments (even ones with the same name), for different maturities, and for different borrowers. Securities issued and bank balances held in different countries differ in the political risks involved, including the risk of imposition of exchange controls. The interest rate at which arbitrageurs can borrow in given country probably exceeds the rate at which they can lend, and borrowers' rates may well rise with the amount borrowed. (Banks holding balances in various countries, however, may perhaps be considered able to borrow at their own lending rates in the sense that they may use funds for arbitrage that they might otherwise have lent.) Statistical workers may choose some particular interest rate in each country—perhaps the treasury bill rate—as an indicator of short-term interest rates in general, but the chosen rate is hardly "the" rate of the formula. Costs associated with arbitrage also help explain departures from interest parity. Arbitrageurs must pay commissions on their transactions (in the form of a slight spread between the bid and asked prices of foreign exchange), as well as telephone and teletype charges and other costs of being in business and of conducting their transactions.

For these and other reasons, the discrepancy between the actual and the theoretical forward premium or discount on a currency may have to exceed some *minimum sensibile* before arbitrageurs find their transactions worthwhile.[23] Small deviations from interest parity may go uncorrected. Official restrictions on short-term capital movements, or even the possibility of their imposition, can also impede interest arbitrage. Or not enough funds might be available to arbitrageurs to finance operations on a large enough scale to wipe out deviations from interest parity. In reality, of course, there is no precise limit to the volume of arbitrage funds available. In principle, arbitrageurs might always borrow additional money by offering high enough rates of interest to bid funds away from other potential borrowers; in principle, interest rates in various countries belong just as fully to a system of mutually determining variables as do the spot and forward rates of exchange. In practice, however, credit rationing and the like may pose at least a vague and elastic limit to the arbitrage funds available at any particular time and place. For example, banks must not divert so much funds into interest arbitrage that they lose their reputation for taking care of the credit needs of their regular customers. Still another qualification is that short-term investments or cash balances in various currencies yield their holders some intangible benefits of convenience or liquidity in addition to explicit interest. Banks and other potential arbitrageurs presumably tend to distribute their short-term holdings in various forms and in various financial centers so as to equate the marginal yields of interest plus intangible advantages. The interest-parity formula might in principle be adapted for each arbitrageur so as to take into account not only the objectively quoted interest rates and spot and forward exchange rates but also the sub-

jectively appraised convenience yields of short-term assets denominated in various currencies.[24] The parity level of a forward premium or discount would thus become fuzzy, but specified changes in interest rates would still have qualitatively the same effects on arbitrage operations and on forward premiums or discounts as those predicted by the usual simple formula.

The entire preceding discussion assumes that spot exchange rates are flexible or are at least subject to uncertainty. This is a reasonable assumption, for the chief purpose of forward exchange is to enable businessmen to overcome the attendant risk. If perfect confidence prevailed that a spot exchange rate would not move outside definite limits, however, then these limits would pose a further constraint, in addition to the principle of interest parities, on the movements of the forward rate. (A corollary useful in interpreting historical episodes is that a forward rate outside the support limits of a pegged spot rate proves lack of confidence

---

22. Cf. Tsiang, *op. cit.*, pp. 80ff.

. 23. The traditional supposition was that arbitrage would not take place unless motivated by a prospective gross profit margin of at least ½ percent a year. This margin was required to cover transactions costs, allow for inaccurate parity calculations, and provide some net remuneration. More recently, however, 1/16 percent or 1/32 percent has been said to be often enough. (This is consistent with a decline in transactions costs as arbitrage facilities become more fully developed.) In fact, banks may sometimes conduct arbitrage at no direct profit at all, just to enjoy the prestige of operating on a large scale and so to attract other business. See Einzig, *Economic Journal*, September 1960, pp. 485–488, and *A Dynamic Theory of Forward Exchange*, pp. 50, 167, 169, 170, 201–202. William H. Branson econometrically estimated that the minimum covered differential necessary to generate a flow of U.S.-U.K. and U.S.-Canada arbitrage in Treasury bills in the early 1960s was 0.18 percent a year. "The Minimum Covered Interest Differential Needed for International Arbitrage Activity," *Journal of Political Economy*, Vol. 77, November/December 1969, pp. 1028–1035.

24. See Tsiang, *op. cit.*, pp. 81–86.

in maintenance of the peg.) Let us assume perfect confidence that spot sterling will stay within official support limits of $2.38–$2.42. Forward sterling would never rise above $2.42 even if interest rates were very much higher in New York than in London. The interest-rate spread would indeed motivate heavy temporary transfers of funds to New York, but the arbitrageurs would not pay more than $2.42 to get pounds again under forward contracts if they were certain of getting pounds spot for $2.42 or less. They could safely leave their interest-arbitrage funds uncovered. Similarly, the forward pound would never fall below $2.38, no matter how much higher interest rates were in London than in New York. No one would accept less than $2.38 in a forward contract when planning to transfer funds back to New York after temporary investment in London, for at least as favorable a spot rate would certainly be available. (Interest rates and interest arbitrage would still affect just where within the assured spot limits the actual spot and forward rates fell. A very great excess of London over New York interest rates, for example, would tend to put the spot rate at $2.42 and the forward rate at $2.38.)

It follows that if the spot rate were pegged not merely within a range but at one precise figure, and if confidence were absolute that this rigid pegging would continue, then the forward rate would coincide with the spot rate. Or, rather, no forward rate and no forward market would exist. All commercial transactions and all interest-motivated transfers of funds would be uncovered, since, by assumption, no exchange risk would exist to be eliminated.[25]

Paradoxically, strong distrust in a prevailing spot rate of exchange, as well as perfect confidence in it, could cause the forward premium or discount to deviate from the theoretical interest parity. If a currency were definitely and generally expected to depreciate, merchants would be especially sure to sell scheduled future receipts of it forward but would be inclined to let scheduled future payments in it go uncovered. If they expected an appreciation, merchants would be especially sure to cover scheduled future payments in the currency by forward purchases but would be inclined not to sell future receipts forward. Failure to cover the exchange risk in an ordinary commercial transaction means deliberately bearing the risk in hope of profiting by the expected movement in the rate. In short, this is speculation. (Or, rather, it is speculation unless the exchange risk serves as a hedge against some other risk in the

opposite direction, as, for example, of change in the domestic price of an inventory of imported goods.) Apart from such passive commercial speculation, furthermore, outright speculators would operate in the forward market or in the forward and spot markets both.

Yet not even the passive and outright speculation mentioned in the preceding paragraphs would necessarily distort the forward-spot relation far from interest parity. If a trusted rigid peg left people with no reason for forward transactions, no forward-spot discrepancy could exist. If the spot pegging were the only departure from free-market conditions, *uncovered* temporary transfers of funds would tend to shrink any interest-rate differential between two countries. Uncovered interest arbitrage would work similarly, though more loosely, when the spot rate was pegged not rigidly but within a firmly trusted narrow band. With possible exchange loss correspondingly limited, such arbitrage would tend to keep any interest differential from remaining large in relation to the width of the band. If confident expectations limited the deviation of the forward rate from the spot rate, those same expectations would limit the interest differential also.

Suppose, at the other extreme, that adjustment of a pegged spot rate is overwhelmingly expected (and is foreshadowed in the forward rate). Arbitrageurs borrow heavily in the weak-currency country and lend heavily in the strong-currency country, temporarily transferring funds with little prospect of loss and much prospect of gain on the exchange rate. These transfers combine spot speculation with uncovered interest arbitrage, which tends to raise interest rates in the weak-currency country and depress rates in the strong-currency country. The result is qualitatively, if not with quantitative precision, what the interest-parity theory envisages—relatively high interest rates in the country with a forward discount on its currency and relatively low rates in the country with a forward premium. Even if *covered* arbitrage were inadequate by itself to hold the discrepancy between forward and spot exchange rates in line with a relatively normal interest differential, as is likely in the speculative situation envisaged, the just-mentioned uncovered arbitrage would supplement it and tend to widen the interest differential into line with the abnormal forward-spot spread. Speculative distortions of forward exchange rates and interest rates thus need not destroy all tendencies toward the interest-parity *relation*.

Suppose, now, that there is no pegging. If the spot rate really were free of official intervention, it would already, at any moment, reflect a balance of bullish and bearish opinion. Expectations would *not* run one-sidedly toward further appreciation or depreciation, except as they were also reflected in the international interest-rate differential.[26] Speculation might dominate both spot and forward rates; but the two would tend to move in parallel.

Speculation *in itself* thus does not create forward premiums or discounts far out of line with interest parity. Such misalignment would more plausibly be due to market imperfections, lags in responses, and the like, to official interference with interest-arbitrage movements of capital, or to one-sided expectations of change in an officially pegged spot rate. As long as a spot rate remains pegged, it cannot do its share in alignment to the interest-parity relation. As shown in Chapter 13 and in Part II, history does offer examples of abnormally large forward discounts on currencies pegged in the spot market but beset by fears of impending devaluation.

In summary, the principle of interest parities describes the forward-spot relation most accurately for a regime of freely fluctuating rates and least accurately for a regime of fixed rates that either are firmly trusted or are strongly and one-sidedly distrusted. Under ideal free-market conditions, a deviation from interest parity—in other words, an "intrinsic" forward premium or discount, also called a covered interest margin—would not serve as a reliable indicator of speculative sentiment. The less fully such conditions prevailed, however, the more accurate or plausible would such an indicator be.[27] In general—and even when rates are pegged but are neither implicitly trusted nor strongly distrusted—forward premiums and discounts do in fact correspond rather closely to the relations between short-term interest rates in the various financial centers. Chapter 13, which compares exchange risks and the possibilities of protection against them under different exchange-rate regimes, will draw some implications from this fact.

The "modern theory" of forward exchange

We may gain further insight into the influence of expectations by reviewing a theory suggested

by some writers as more sophisticated and accurate than the interest-parity theory.[28] The so-called modern theory envisages the equilibrium forward rate between two currencies as a weighted average of the forward rate corresponding to interest parity and the possibly distinct forward rate that would equilibrate speculative supply and demand in the forward market; the latter is generally interpreted as the expected future spot rate.[29] Among other supposed advantages, the modern theory is said to justify the use of the intrinsic forward premium or discount (covered interest margin) as an indicator of speculative sentiment even under freely fluctuating exchange rates.

25. The analysis of the two preceding paragraphs derives from Bent Hansen, "Interest Policy, Foreign Exchange Policy and Foreign Exchange Control," *Skandinaviska Banken Quarterly Review*, **XL**, January 1959, p. 17.

26. As explained further in the next section, expectations of more severe price inflation in Outland than in Inland could depress both the expected future spot rate and the forward rate on the Outland peso below its current spot rate; but if these expectations also expressed themselves in the two countries' interest rates, market operators would *not* immediately dump spot pesos and so depress the current spot rate to its expected future level. A high enough nominal interest rate in Outland would motivate retention of balances there despite the expected price inflation and exchange depreciation. Compare Chapter 12, particularly p. 235.

27. This proposition gains theoretical and empirical support in John Van Belle's University of Virginia dissertation (May 1974), "An Analysis of Objective Indicators of Speculative Activity under a System of Flexible Exchange Rates."

28. Cf., e.g., Jonathan Kesselman, "The Role of Speculation in Forward-Rate Determination: The Canadian Flexible Dollar 1953–1960," *Canadian Journal of Economics*, **IV**, August 1971, pp. 279–298; and Hans R. Stoll, "An Empirical Study of the Forward Exchange Market Under Fixed and Flexible Exchange Rate Systems," *Canadian Journal of Economics*, **I**, February 1968, p. 59–78.

29. Forward rates and the relevant expected future spot rates differ with the contemplated forward-contract maturity, of course; but the language used in the text is convenient and unlikely to cause misunderstanding.

Within its own spirit, however, the modern theory has the defect of overlooking another possibly distinct forward rate, the one that would equilibrate supply and demand from international traders covering themselves against risk.[30] If a country's trade balance or current account[31] were in deficit over the relevant time period, one would expect the traders' forward purchases of foreign exchange to exceed forward sales; and for these covering purchases and sales just to match each other, the forward quotation on the home currency would probably have to be weaker than the one corresponding to interest parity.

Extended to take account of commercial covering, then, the modern theory views the equilibrium forward rate as a weighted average of the forward rates that would correspond to interest parity, that would balance speculative supply and demand, and that would balance commercial hedgers' supply and demand. The weights, totaling unity, would be estimated by regressions fitted to recent historical data. Since the future spot rate expected by speculators and the forward rate that would balance hedgers' supply and demand cannot be observed directly, estimates of them would have to be used in the regressions; the trade balance or current-account balance of one or both countries involved would no doubt figure in estimating the latter rate.

Estimates of an overall equilibrium forward rate made along these lines might be useful in some situations and for some purposes. There seems little reason to expect the econometrically estimated weights to stay the same, however, in different historical circumstances; experience with extreme forward discounts or premiums at times of preponderant speculation against pegged spot rates rather suggests the contrary. It is a misconception, furthermore, to view the modern theory as a superior rival of the interest-parity theory. It is irrelevant to parade instances in which regressions containing additional variables achieve higher coefficients of multiple correlation than regressions containing only the variables considered in the interest-parity theory.[32] A theory of a parity is not supposed to take account, within itself, of everything that might obscure or distort the relations it describes. Instead, it is meant to describe tendencies at work when the variables it considers are free to adjust to each other. The interest-parity theory shows how arbitrage would work under free-market conditions if the

equilibrium relations it describes did not initially hold. It is not discredited by such interferences with equilibrating tendencies as transactions costs, incompleteness and costliness of knowledge, other market "imperfections" (such as differences between the money-market instruments available in different countries and differences between borrowing and lending rates of interest), and official spot-rate pegging either reinforced or threatened by expectations of the future. Like any good theory, its function is to highlight key influences and relations by abstracting from innumerable peripheral complications.[33] The modern theory, by contrast, is eclectic in the worst sense when appraised as a theory rather than as a possibly useful tool for empirical estimation.

Any supposition that the modern theory rivals and displaces the interest-parity theory deserves a further answer: recognizing how spot-rate expectations may influence and even dominate the forward rate does not necessarily clash with the interest-parity theory. The latter, while describing equilibrium *relations* among spot and forward exchange rates and the two countries' interest rates, leaves room for additional factors, including expectations, to enter into explanations of the absolute *levels* of these rates.

An example will be helpful. Suppose that the purchasing power of the Inland dollar is expected to remain stable, while inflation in Outland is expected to depress the dollar rate on the Outland peso by 10 percent in the coming 12 months.[34] The 12-month forward rate on the peso, equaling the expected future spot rate, therefore stands at a 10 percent discount from the current spot rate. This discount is in line with interest parity; for the Outland interest rate, like the forward exchange rate, would reflect the expected Outland inflation and so exceed the Inland interest rate by 10 percent. If we assume definite expectations of the future, consistency requires allowing them to show themselves in interest rates as well as in forward exchange rates.

The 10 percent differential in nominal interest rates implies that real interest rates become equal in Inland and Outland. (A real interest rate is the nominal rate minus any allowance-for-inflation component.) Arbitrage is the explanation. If the Outland interest rate happened to exceed the Inland rate by more than the 10 percent inflation allowance, temporary transfers of loanable funds would occur, tending to raise the Inland rate and lower the Outland rate. If the Outland interest rate exceeded the Inland rate by less than 10 percent, the transfers would run in the opposite direction, lowering the Inland rate and reinforcing the upward push of the inflationary expectations on the Outland rate. Such interest arbitrage could take place without forward cover against exchange risk; yet it would hardly be speculative from the arbitrageurs' point of view, given the hypothesized definiteness of expectations about the future spot exchange rate. At the same time, arbitrageurs less sure of their own foresight might be carrying out covered temporary transfers to profit from any forward discount on the Outland peso not yet fully matched by the interest-rate differential. In principle, the current spot rate is one of the magnitudes adjusting to each other. Assuming that the peso's spot depreciation is restrained by its not-yet-eroded purchasing-power parity, however, the current spot rate is unlikely to perform a larger share of the adjustment than the Inland interest rate. It would be far-fetched to assume expectations definite enough to become embodied in both forward and current spot exchange rates but not definite enough to become embodied in the Outland interest rate. An adjustment is more plausible whereby the current and expected future spot exchange rates roughly correspond to current and expected future purchasing-power parities, the current forward rate both equals the expected future spot rate and stands in the interest-parity relation with the current spot rate, and nominal interest rates reflect any inflation that may be expected.

It is admittedly extreme and unrealistic to assume definite expectations about the future. But remember the context: we have made these assumptions in order to consider, on its own grounds, a so-called modern theory that seems at first sight to challenge the interest-parity theory. The latter remains tenable after all, reconciling nicely with an expectations

does tend to support the interest-parity theory, particularly by serving as evidence of interest arbitrage at work. Examples of such calculations appear in Victor Argy and Zoran Hodjera, "Financial Integration and Interest Rate Linkages in the Industrial Countries," IMF *Staff Papers*, **XX**, March 1973, pp. 1–77.

33. Compare similar remarks in Chapter 11 about the purchasing-power-parity theory.

34. For definiteness, the example assumes, as John Pippenger does, that expectations of the future spot rate rest on expectations of the future ratio of the purchasing powers of the two currencies. (On the purchasing-power-parity doctrine, see Chapter 11.) Pippenger shows that the expectations and interest-parity theories of the forward rate, the purchasing-power-parity theory of current and expected future spot exchange rates, and Irving Fisher's theory of the allowance-for-inflation component of interest rates all interlock and support one another in the assumed context of no transactions costs, accurate expectations, and so forth. See his "Spot Rates, Forward Rates, and Interest-Rate Differentials," *Journal of Money, Credit, and Banking*, **IV**, May 1972, pp. 375–383. For a lucid exposition, also see Mark Fitzsimmons, "The Forward Premium: Three Theories or One?", *Virginia Essays in Economics*, **V**, Spring 1974, pp. 9–17.

Does it beg any questions to attribute expected exchange-rate changes to expected changes in purchasing powers? What if the expectations center around prospective collapse of a spot peg that is already out of line with the relative purchasing powers of the currencies? As suggested in the preceding section, speculatively uncovered interest arbitrage would then make interest rates bear the brunt of the adjustment. With exchange rates floating freely, the most plausible reason for changes in them to be definitely expected is different rates of price inflation (or deflation) in the different countries.

Even if we blur the reason for expectations about the future, tendencies toward interest parity would still be plausible. As Wilfred Ethier remarks, "the argument is that if monetary policies should cause domestic and foreign interest rates to differ, then, under a system of floating rates, arbitrage would cause the exchange rate to steadily appreciate at a rate to compensate for the difference, thus causing the expected future spot rate, the interest parity level, and the actual forward rate to coincide." "International Trade and the Forward Exchange Market," *American Economic Review*, **LXIII**, June 1973, p. 497n.

30. John Van Belle, "A Neglected Aspect of the Modern Theory of Forward Exchange," *Southern Economic Journal*, Vol. 40, July 1973, pp. 117–119. Van Belle shows how unbalanced hedgers' supply and demand could invalidate the supposed speculative indicator.

31. Chapter 3 explains these concepts.

32. However, a highly significant coefficient for the interest-rate differential in multiple regressions

theory of the forward rate. The interest-parity theory basically applies to free-market conditions and does not pretend to be the complete and exact story when pegging and other interventions are at work.

Conclusion

This chapter almost defies summarizing because its purpose has not been so much to reach conclusions as to introduce concepts needed later on. It explains the supply-and-demand analysis of exchange-rate determination and considers the influences of currency arbitrage and of rate pegging by direct official intervention or by gold arbitrage under a gold standard. To provide a background for later inquiry into such matters as exchange controls, exchange risk, speculation, and the administrative feasibility of alternative exchange-rate systems, it surveys some institutional aspects of international remittances and the foreign-exchange market. It describes forward exchange, presents the interest-parity explanation of forward premiums or discounts, and shows how that explanation reconciles with an expectational theory that superficially appears to challenge it.

Appendix to Chapter 2:

Documents

of International Finance

International finance involves many documents besides those that directly transfer ownership of existing bank balances. These include other types of bill of exchange or draft. A bill or draft is a negotiable instrument in which one party orders a second to pay a definite sum of money to the order of a third (though the three parties need not all be distinct).[1] The most familiar type is an ordinary check. Other types may originate in various ways. An Inland exporter may arrange to collect payment by drawing a bill on his Outland customer. This document is known as a *commercial* bill or draft, since the drawee is an ordinary business firm rather than a bank. If payable upon presentation, it is known as a *sight draft*. If the seller wishes to grant his customer credit and accordingly draws a bill not payable until some weeks or months in the future, the instrument is known as a *time draft*. If the seller uses a time draft, he may wish to have an agent of his in the buyer's country present it to the buyer for acceptance. By signing the time draft on its face to confirm his obligation to pay it when due, the drawee converts it into an *acceptance*, akin to a promissory note.

If the draft or acceptance is expressed in Outland currency, it is a foreign-exchange instrument from the Inland point of view, and the Inland drawer may wish to sell it on the foreign-exchange market, that is, to his bank. The sale ordinarily is "with recourse": if the drawee fails to pay, the drawer must reimburse the holder. Credit risk may make it difficult to sell the instrument at an advantageously low rate of discount, however, especially if the drawee is not well known and does not enjoy an outstanding reputation. For this reason, it is quite usual to arrange to draw the drafts on the foreign importer's bank rather than on the importer himself.

This introduces the topic of *bankers' bills* (also called *bank drafts*), *bankers' acceptances*, and *letters of credit*. If the exporter wishes to draw his bill of exchange on a bank rather than on his customer directly, he will ask the customer to make the necessary arrangements. The importer's bank agrees to honor a draft or drafts drawn in accordance with specified provisions. The importer agrees to furnish the bank the necessary funds shortly before the draft is to be paid; if all goes as expected, the bank ties up no funds of its own. Instead, it in effect merely sells the use of its good name and credit standing for a moderate commission. If the importer fails to meet his obligation to the bank, the bank must pay the draft anyway and stand the loss itself. The exporter is protected. The bank, for its part, will take precautions to protect itself against default by its customer, the importer. For example, it may insist on receiving the bill of lading or other documents necessary to obtain the goods from the transportation company. Then the bank can withhold these documents from the importer until he pays the money or provides suitable guarantees.

The bill drawn on the bank may be a sight or a time draft. A time draft allows credit to the importer, who will not have to provide the money until shortly before his bank must pay the draft. A time draft will ordinarily be converted into a *banker's acceptance*. An agent of the exporter in the importer's country (typically a foreign branch or correspondent of the exporter's bank) will present the newly drawn bill to the importer's bank. If it is in good order, if the bill of lading and other specified

---

1. The first and third parties are the same, for example, when the drawer of the bill names himself as payee. The second party, or drawee, has no legal obligation to honor a draft drawn on him unless it was drawn under an arrangement to which he had already agreed or unless he subsequently accepts an obligation to pay.

documents accompany it, and if the other stipulated conditions have been met, then the bank will sign, confirming its obligation to pay the draft when due. The resulting banker's acceptance, as the short-term obligation of a well-known bank, is a prime credit instrument. If the exporter wants cash before the acceptance comes due, he can probably sell it at only the small discount from face value characteristic of high-grade short-term obligations.

The conditions under which the exporter may draw on the importer's bank are specified in a *letter of credit*. This is not in itself a credit instrument or a type of foreign exchange; it is a formal letter from the bank authorizing the exporter to draw a draft or drafts on it up to a specified total amount and promising to honor the drafts provided that all stipulated conditions have been met. Letters of credit typically specify in close detail the time period within which the drafts must be drawn, the amounts of money available, the identifying notations to appear on the drafts, and the documents that must accompany them to evidence shipment of specified goods within a specified time period and by specified means of transport.

The letter of credit is useful to the exporter not only as a set of instructions but also as evidence that a bank has authorized him to draw drafts and has promised to honor them. This evidence greatly improves the salability of a draft. The exporter and anyone who might buy the draft from him can rely on the bank and need not worry about the solvency and trustworthiness of the foreign importer. Even when these are not in doubt, the letter may provide worthwhile assurance: it minimizes the risk that government controls in the importing country may prevent or delay payment, since the importer's bank has presumably taken account of any such problems before issuing the letter and since the government would usually hesitate to force banks to dishonor promises that were permissible when made.[2] Use of a letter of credit benefits the importer as well. The low degree of credit risk helps persuade the exporter to offer his lowest prices and best discounts. Furthermore, the exporter is prodded to ship goods of the qualities and in the amounts specified in the letter of credit and to ship them on time.

Letters of credit are of many kinds. They may be *revocable* or *irrevocable*. Irrevocable letters are the more usual and are what we have had in mind so far. Such a letter conveys a firm promise that may not be withdrawn or modified without the consent of all parties concerned. Revocable letters, by contrast, convey no firm promise and amount to hardly more than instructions about the preparation and presentation of drafts and documents. Letters of credit may also be classified as *circular* (also called *negotiation*) or *straight* (domiciled). In a circular letter, the opening (issuing) bank mentions no other particular bank through which the drafts are to be negotiated; the exporter may send his drafts directly to the opening bank for payment or may route them through his own bank or any other bank willing to handle them. A straight letter is more usual. It is sent to the beneficiary (the exporter) by way of some other bank, typically a bank in his own city, which is instructed to pay drafts drawn under it on behalf of the opening bank. The latter still has responsibility for providing the necessary funds.

If the exporter wants the second bank's promise to honor his drafts even if the opening bank should fail to do so, the document used is known as a *confirmed* letter of credit. A Brazilian importer might arrange for his local bank to issue a letter of credit in favor of an American exporter. Instead of notifying the American beneficiary directly, the Brazilian bank might ask its New York correspondent to prepare and deliver the letter. Although the Brazilian bank is opening the credit, the letter would provide for the drafts to be drawn on the New York bank, which promises to pay them. The Brazilian bank is supposed to collect from its own customer and pay the New York bank (probably by authorizing a deduction from its balance with the latter); but regardless of what may go wrong, the New York bank binds itself to pay the exporter's drafts if properly drawn and accompanied by the proper documents. The letter issued by the New York bank is known, from the American point of view, as a confirmed irrevocable export letter of credit. Under an alternative arrangement, the New York bank might issue its own letter of credit in favor of the American exporter on behalf of the Brazilian importer, with the Brazilian bank acting as a mere intermediary. Only the New York bank would then be obligated, not both banks. Arrangements in one way or another involving an American bank in the issue of an export letter of credit are quite common in U.S. export trade.

A *traveler's letter of credit* is a document carried by the beneficiary on his foreign travels.

It authorizes him to write drafts on the opening bank within a specified time period and up to a specified total amount. (He agrees to reimburse the bank. The amounts drawn may be deducted from his regular account with the bank, or he may deposit collateral.) In the letter, the opening bank requests its correspondents throughout the world to cash drafts drawn by the properly identified traveler and to note on the letter itself the amounts drawn so that banks visited later can tell whether the entire amount of the credit has yet been used up. The traveler cashes his drafts on his home bank in the local currency of the country visited at the prevailing exchange rate for bankers' sight drafts. The issuing bank gives the traveler a list of its correspondents. (*Traveler's checks* are in some ways more convenient. They are orders by the issuing company to its paying agencies to pay the indicated sum to the order of the traveler.)

These and still other types and modifications of letters of credit need no detailed discussion

here. Neither do the other documents called for in letters of credit or otherwise involved in international business—bills of lading, insurance policies, consular invoices, certificates of inspection, and many more.

2. American export business has shown a trend toward less use of letters of credit and more selling on open account and related practices common in domestic business. Reasons for the change include increased competition in foreign trade, better knowledge of foreign buyers and their creditworthiness, and reductions in risk because of export-credit-guarantee programs and also, presumably, because of dismantling and simplification of foreign government controls over trade and payments. See American Bankers Association, *A Banker's Guide to Financing Exports*, New York: 1963, p. 9.

CHAPTER THREE

The Balance of International Payments

Balance-of-payments concepts

Transactions that typically involve payments by foreigners to Americans and thus involve supplying foreign money for sale against dollars are classified as "credit" or "plus" transactions. Transactions that typically involve payments by Americans to foreigners and thus involve demanding foreign money with dollars are classified as· "debit" or "minus" transactions. Transactions are grouped on the two sides of a statistical record known as the *balance of international payments* of the United States. It summarizes all transactions—buying and selling, borrowing and lending, transfer of investment earnings, and gifts—that have taken place between residents of the United States (including businesses and other institutions) and foreigners during a year or some other definite period. Actually, the term *balance of international payments* is misleading and has nothing to recommend it except long-standing usage; a better term would be *balance of international transactions*.[1] Transactions are not classified according to actual receipts or payments of money that may or may not occur. Instead, they are classified according to the direction of payment that they would *typically* entail sooner or later, whether or not money is paid in each transaction. Commodity imports,

for example, appear on the debit or "pay-ments"-to-foreigners side of a country's balance of international payments not because the act of bringing goods into a country in itself is an outpayment—of course it is *not*—but because commodity imports *typically* have to be paid for. A particular import is still classified this way even if it is not paid for (it may come as a gift or as part of a barter deal, or the importer may default on his obligation to make payment). This is just one among many examples of how confusion can arise from the all-too-common practice of referring to transactions as *receipts* or *inpayments* on the one side and *payments* or *outpayments* on the other. These words *seem* so familiar that people are apt to forget the special sense in which they are used. The colorless language of *credits* or *pluses* and *debits* or *minuses* is safer precisely because it lacks any deceptive familiarity and so reminds everyone that the matter under discussion is a technical one. It is worth repeating that "credit" items are not in themselves receipts, but simply transactions that ordinarily, but not necessarily, call for payment sooner or later by foreigners to residents of the home country. They way that the words *debit* and *credit* are used here could be reconciled with ordinary accounting language, but the trouble is hardly worthwhile. We may as well simply accept the fact, without worrying why, that balance-of-payments statisticians use these words as they do.

Table 3.1 is meant to list all categories of items in the balance of payments. There is no single correct list; how many categories appear depends on how broadly or narrowly each is defined. The listing in the table is a convenient one for discussing some balance-of-payments principles, though not necessarily for arranging actual statistics.

Consider items 1, 2, and 3 in the credits list. Americans are shipping goods, selling transportation, meals, hotel accommodations, and sightseeing tours, and selling shipping services, engineering consultation, legal advice, banking and brokerage services, insurance protection, and other intangible goods to foreigners. Commodity exports (item 1) are sometimes called *visible exports*, since they consist of tangible goods visibly leaving the country. Item 2 and 3 are sometimes called *invisible exports*, since, while representing sales to foreigners, they do not consist of tangible goods visibly leaving the country. The distinction is a matter of physical detail rather than

TABLE 3.1. *Categories of the balance of payments*

Credits = Plus Items = Transactions of Kinds Ordinarily Involving Foreign Payments to Americans = Transactions of Kinds Ordinarily Involving a Supply of Foreign Exchange to be Sold for Dollars (A Demand for Dollars to be Bought with Foreign Exchange)

1. Commodity exports from the U.S.
2. Foreign travel in the U.S.
3. Foreign purchases of American services.
4. Receipt by Americans of current earnings on their loans and investments abroad.
5. Gifts, reparations, and other "unilateral transfers" from foreigners to Americans.
6. Capital imports through new loans and investments made in the U.S. by foreigners, including increases in foreign-owned deposits in American banks.
7. Capital imports through recovery by Americans of their loans and investments and bank accounts previously placed abroad.
8. Exports of monetary gold from the U.S.

Debits = Minus Items = Transactions of Kinds Ordinarily Involving American Payments to Foreigners = Transactions of Kinds Ordinarily Involving a Demand for Foreign Exchange to be Bought with Dollars (A Supply of Dollars to be Sold for Foreign Exchange)

1. Commodity imports into the U.S.
2. American travel abroad.
3. American purchases of foreign services.
4. Payment to foreigners of current earnings on their loans and investments in the U.S.
5. Gifts, reparations, and other "unilateral transfers" from Americans to foreigners.
6. Capital exports through new American loans and investments abroad, including increases in American deposits in foreign banks.
7. Capital exports through repayment to foreigners of their earlier loans and investments and bank accounts in the U.S.
8. Imports of monetary gold into the U.S.

of economic importance. Visible and invisible exports alike typically (but not always) involve foreigners' having to make payments to Americans and so involve an exchange of foreign money for dollars. (Of course, exchanges of

currencies are not themselves the transactions classified under these headings.)

Item 4 might also be described as an invisible export. Americans are making available —are "exporting"—to foreigners the continuing services of American capital that was placed abroad some time in the past through investments in government and private bonds, corporation stocks, American-controlled business enterprises, etc. Item 4 does not refer to new transfers of capital. It comprises interest, dividends, and profits received by Americans on their foreign investments and may be regarded as measuring the value of the services continuing to be currently rendered by capital lent or invested some time ago. This sale of capital services to foreigners appears on the same side of the balance of payments as the sale of the services of American insurance companies, engineers, and lawyers.

Items 1 through 4, taken together, make up the credit side of the so-called *good-and-services account*. This account comprises all or most—depending on the definitions adopted—of the *current account*. All four types of transaction on the credit side are of the sort whereby Americans, by *currently* furnishing goods and services to foreigners (including the continuing services of existing investments), are typically becoming entitled to receive payments from abroad.

The opposite current-account transactions appear as items 1 through 4 in the debits list. Here Americans are engaging in the types of transactions that ordinarily require their making payment to foreigners: they are importing goods, consuming goods and services as travelers in foreign countries, buying freight carriage and legal advice and other services from foreigners, and continuing to have the use of foreign capital already invested in American securities and in businesses in the United States.

The credits and debits of item 5 might be regarded as forming a *unilateral-transfers account* of their own or, alternatively, might be counted as part of the current account. The

1. Cf. Charles N. Henning, *International Finance*, New York: Harper & Row, 1958, p. 17.

choice between these two classifications is a matter of plausibility and convenience, not of right or wrong. The case for including unilateral transfers in the current account is strongest if they are of a routine and recurring nature, like pensions.

On the credits side, item 5 is the value of foreign gifts and war reparations and other unilateral or currently unrequited transfers being made to Americans. For example, an Englishman might be contributing to the support of a poor relative living in Chicago, or—less plausibly—the United States might be squeezing reparations out of a defeated enemy. Note that the item does *not* refer to the actual transfer of currency or bank deposits from foreign to American ownership. For one thing, the gift or reparations may be made in securities or commodities and not involve money at all. More fundamentally, acceptance of commodities or securities or money has to do with the *form* in which Americans take the gift or reparations transfer, that is, the *use* to which they put its value; and this is something distinct from the *fact* that foreigners are somehow making unilateral transfers of a certain value to the United States. The latter is what item 5 refers to.

More familiar is its counterpart in the debits list: the value of current American donations to foreigners. If someone living in the United States gives money to relatives abroad, the gift involves making a payment to foreigners and so involves a demand for foreign money with dollars (a supply of dollars for foreign money). There is no mystery about why this gift appears on the debit side of the American balance of payments. But the gift itself should be kept in mind, as distinct from the foreigners' acquisition of currency or bank balances or other assets. The very making of the gift is what *typically* involves payment to foreigners and so counts as an American debit; the particular form in which the foreigners receive the gift or the use to which they put its value is something else again. There is still no mystery about the classification even if the donor is the United States government rather than a private person. But a commodity gift instead of a money gift may be confusing. An individual American might send a CARE package or the government might send surplus farm products abroad as a gift. In principle, either of two treatments would conform to the logic of a balance of payments: we could either ignore the commodity gift completely on the grounds that it gives rise to no international payments or else we could count the actual export of the commodity as an ordinary example of credit item 1 and at the same time count the money value of the gift as a unilateral transfer under debit item 5. The latter is the more usual treatment (except for military goods). In a way, it amounts to pretending that we Americans sell the commodity to foreigners, at the same time giving them the funds with which they immediately pay for it. The commodity-export aspect of the whole operation appears as a credit in the American balance of payments, the gift aspect as a debit.

To clinch the point that credits are not actual receipts and debits not actual payments, let us suppose that Americans give foreigners some ten-dollar bills, which the foreigners simply hoard. The debit in the American balance of payments is *not* the actual transfer of American currency to foreigners. On the contrary, by acquiring American money to hold, the foreigners are investing in short-term claims against the United States (for that is what American money is). As a new foreign loan or investment in the United States—as an example of item 6 in the upper half of the table—this aspect of the transaction is a *credit* in the American balance of payments. The debit aspect consists of the gift abstractly considered, apart from its particular form: Americans are *giving* the foreigners the wherewithal to invest in hoards of American money or to buy American goods or to do anything else with the gift. The particular use to which the foreigners put the gift, such as acquiring a hoard of American currency, does not affect the classification of the gift aspect of the transaction as a *debit* in the American balance of payments.

Under item 6 in the list of credits, foreigners are making new investments or increasing their investments in American government bonds, American corporation stocks and bonds and other claims against Americans, and in branch offices and factories and other properties in the United States. Accomplishing such transactions typically involves exchanging foreign for American money. These so-called capital imports into the United States belong on the same side of the balance of payments as commodity exports. It is helpful to remember that capital imports are typically evidenced by *exports* of stocks, bonds, and title deeds. A type of capital import worth special attention was already mentioned in the last paragraph: increases in foreign holdings of American paper money or coins or deposits in American banks. Foreigners, in acquiring American currency, are investing in or lending to the United States just as if they were acquiring American bonds. The same is true of increased foreign deposits in American banks: since a bank deposit is a debt of the bank to the depositor, increases in foreign-owned bank balances represent foreign lending to American banks.

Item 6 in the debits list consists of American capital exports through purchase ("import") of deeds to properties abroad and of foreign securities and other claims against foreigners. A noteworthy example is acquisition of claims against foreigners in the form of foreign currency or of deposits in foreign banks.

Item 7 in the credits list represents American capital imports through reversal of earlier American capital exports. Americans are engaging in transactions entitling them to receive payment from foreigners: they are re-exporting foreign securities and title deeds previously bought. Similarly, by spending or otherwise drawing down their hoards of foreign currency and by drawing down their balances in foreign banks, Americans are recovering their previous investments in these obligations of foreigners. Under item 7 in the debits list, Americans are exporting capital by discharging some of their previously existing debts to foreigners. In other words, foreigners are selling back their holdings of American securities and properties; Americans are reimporting claims previously sold. In particular, foreigners may be spending their previous holdings of American bank accounts and currency and to that extent ceasing to be creditors of American commercial and Federal Reserve banks and the U.S. Treasury.

For understanding whether particular transactions are classified as debits or credits, it does not matter whether capital movements (headings 6 and 7) are "long-term" or "short-term." The distinction between long- and short-term capital movements is important in analyzing equilibrium and disequilibrium in the balance of payments, but that is another story, to be taken up later.

Under credit item 8, the United States is selling gold to foreigners; such sales would ordinarily call for foreign payments to Americans. In the debit list, the United States is buying foreign gold. Gold exports and imports belong on the same side of the balance of payments, respectively, as commodity exports and imports. In principle, gold transactions could be lumped together with commodity transactions. They are usually shown separately, however, because gold plays a role in intergovernmental settlements and national monetary reserves that makes it something especially interesting to government officials and economists.

The equality of credits and debits

The balance of payments must balance. If full and accurate figures were available, total credits and total debits would have to be equal. Lack of full and accurate figures is a mere practical detail that does not impair this principle. The two sides must have the same total because of the way a balance of payments and the items in it are defined and the way these definitions interlock. A balance of payments must balance for the same general reasons as why a company's balance sheet must balance.

There are two ways of further convincing ourselves that balance is logically necessary. First, we can see the double-entry nature of a balance of payments: each transaction has a debit aspect and a credit aspect of equal size. For example, a commodity export is a credit entry, but it must somehow be paid for or matched. Perhaps the American exporter has engaged in a barter deal, so that a commodity import directly matches the commodity export. Perhaps the American exporter accepts payment in the form of foreign currency or of a deposit in a foreign bank, thus making a loan to foreign monetary authorities or banks, which is a debit in the U.S. balance of payments. Perhaps the foreigner pays for the American goods by drawing on his holding of American currency or on his deposit in an American bank, in which case Americans are discharging debt previously owed to foreigners —again a debit. Perhaps the American exporter sells the goods on credit or gives them to foreigners as a gift; in this case, the loan or gift aspect of the transaction is a balance-of-payments debit, matching the credit aspect consisting of the actual commodity export. Suppose the American exporter expects to get paid but the foreign buyer defaults: it turns out that the American has made an involuntary unilateral transfer, which is an example of debit item 5.

As another example, consider an American gift to foreigners. The gift aspect of the transaction is in itself a debit; the way in which the foreigners take the gift is a credit from the American viewpoint. The gift may actually take the form of a commodity; or the foreigners may immediately use a money gift to buy American commodities. Either way, an export appears in the American balance of payments. The foreigners may use the gift to pay off old debts owed in the United States or else to increase their holdings of American securities, currency, or bank accounts; any of these transactions would represent a capital inflow into the United States and count as a credit.

A second way to see why total debits and credits must be equal is to realize that a country, like an individual or other economic unit, cannot buy goods and services worth more than what it sells unless it draws down its cash reserves (as of gold, foreign money, and bank accounts abroad), sells off some of its investments, receives repayment of debt owed to it, borrows (perhaps by buying on credit), or receives gifts or indemnities or the like. Conversely, a country cannot sell more than it buys in goods-and-services transactions unless it engages in matching debit transactions by accumulating cash reserves, investing, lending,

TABLE 3.2. *U.S. balance of international payments for the calendar year 1973*

	Credits or plus items	Debits or minus items
	(Millions of dollars)	
Merchandise trade, excluding military transactions	70,277	69,806
Military transactions, net		2,201
Income on private and government investments, net	5,291	
Travel and transportation, net		2,710
Other services, net	3,540	
TOTALS SO FAR	79,108	74,717
DIFFERENCE BETWEEN THESE TOTALS = BALANCE ON GOODS AND SERVICES	4,391	
Remittances, pensions, and other transfers, net		1,943
U.S. government nonmilitary grants		1,933
Private long-term capital movements, excluding changes in bank liabilities to foreign official agencies, net	127	
U.S. Government capital flows, excluding transfers and changes in special liabilities, net		1,538
TOTALS SO FAR	79,235	80,131
DIFFERENCE BETWEEN THESE TOTALS = BALANCE ON CURRENT PLUS LONG-TERM-CAPITAL ACCOUNTS		896
Additional "above-the-line" items		
Private nonliquid short-term capital flows, net		4,276
SDR allocation	0	
Errors and omissions		2,624
TOTALS SO FAR	79,235	87,031
DIFFERENCE BETWEEN THESE TOTALS = NET LIQUIDITY BALANCE		7,796
"BELOW-THE-LINE" SETTLEMENT OF THIS NET LIQUIDITY BALANCE (details in next table)	7,796	

NOTE: Because of the netting done in some of the items, the "totals so far" have no special significance.

SOURCE: See Table 3.3.

paying off debt, or giving gifts or paying indemnities.

To clinch an understanding of the balance-of-payments concept, it is worthwhile to draw the analogy between a country and a single family. Examples of credits in the family's balance of payments might be: (1) sales of goods, such as crops grown or cakes and carvings produced by members of the family, (2) provision of lodgings to tourists, (3) work done by wage-earning members of the family, (4) earning of interest and dividends on bank accounts and bonds and stocks, and earning of profit from a family-owned business, (5) receipt of gifts, perhaps from relatives or from public-relief authorities, (6) new borrowing, including the obtaining of credit from sellers of goods bought on the installment plan, (7) undoing loans and investments previously made, including, for example, selling stocks, cashing savings bonds, spending wads of currency kept in the mattress, and drawing down bank accounts, and (8) sale of gold coins from a collection. Debits might include: (1) purchase of groceries and other goods, (2) traveling, staying in hotels, and eating in restaurants, (3) buying medical and legal and repair services, (4) incurring interest on money previously borrowed, (5) making gifts, (6) repayment of borrowing, including payment of installments on credit purchases, (7) purchases of stocks and bonds and increases in bank accounts and hoards of currency, and (8) purchase of gold coins. The family clearly cannot be spending more than it earns on current account (items 1 through 4) without at the same time receiving gifts, borrowing, drawing down bank accounts and hoards of cash, otherwise recovering old loans or selling off investments, or selling gold. Conversely, a family cannot be earning more than it spends on current account without lending, investing, making gifts, accumulating cash and bank accounts, or the like.

The necessary balance of debits and credits is a matter of sheer definitions and arithmetic and gives no guarantee of "equilibrium" in any reassuring sense of the word. Total debits would equal total credits even for a family or a country in terrible economic straits.

This necessary equality has a corollary: the *principle of compensating balances.* If the balance-of-payments items are classified into various categories or "accounts," an excess of debits (or credits) in one or more of them must be matched by an equal excess of credits (or debits) in the remaining ones.

An example of a balance of payments

Tables 3.2 and 3.3 illustrate these principles with actual figures for the United States. They also provide a factual background for a more abstract discussion, later in this chapter, of concepts of imbalance or disequilibrium in international payments.

On goods-and-services account, Americans in 1973 were exporting merchandise ·worth slightly more than what they were importing, buying travel and transportation services from foreigners worth more than what they were selling, and earning more on their investments abroad than foreigners were earning on their investments in the United States. The United States was spending heavily to maintain its military establishment abroad. Earnings exceeded expenditures on miscellaneous services. All in all, the country ran a surplus of $4.4 billion in goods and services. Private and governmental gifts and other unilateral transfers by Americans to foreigners exceeded gifts and so forth in the opposite direction. This is true even though government grants for military purposes are not counted. (The goods in which the military grants were transferred are likewise left out of the figure for commodity exports. Without disturbing the necessary equality of total debits and total credits, the dollar amount involved could, alternatively, have been included as both a unilateral-transfer debit and a merchandise credit.) Various distinctions between "above-the-line" and "below-the-line" transactions are explained later in this chapter. In any case, most capital movements may be regarded as "independently motivated," in a sense explained later, and so appear above the line. The net credit figure of $127 million reflects an overall inward balance on account of transfers of U.S. private capital abroad for "direct" investment (meaning, for the most part, investment in business properties abroad

TABLE 3.3. *Three alternative concepts of imbalance in the U.S. balance of payments, 1973* (*millions of dollars*)

Above-the-line items	Net liquidity Plus	Net liquidity Minus	Gross liquidity Plus	Gross liquidity Minus	Official reserve transactions (official settlements) Plus	Official reserve transactions (official settlements) Minus
Net balance of items counted above the line by all three concepts		7,796		7,796		7,796
Changes in U.S. nonliquid but readily marketable liabilities (including long-term liabilities of U.S. banks) to foreign official agencies			1,118			
Changes in U.S. bank and nonbank liquid claims on foreigners				1,944		1,944
Changes in U.S. government nonliquid liabilities to foreign official reserve agencies				475		
Changes in U.S. liquid liabilities to foreign commercial banks, international and regional organizations, and other foreigners					4,436	
COLUMN TOTALS		7,796	1,118	10,215	4,436	9,740
DIFFERENCE BETWEEN COLUMN TOTALS = BALANCE		7,796		9,097		5,304

Below-the-line items	Net liquidity Plus	Net liquidity Minus	Gross liquidity Plus	Gross liquidity Minus	Official reserve transactions Plus	Official reserve transactions Minus
Changes in U.S. reserve assets (gold, convertible foreign currencies, reserve position in I.M.F., and SDR's)	209		209		209	
Changes in U.S. liquid liabilities to foreign official agencies	4,452		4,452		4,452	
Changes in U.S. nonliquid but readily marketable liabilities (including long-term liabilities of U.S. banks) to foreign official agencies	1,118				1,118	
Changes in U.S. bank and nonbank liquid claims on foreigners		1,944				
Changes in U.S. government nonliquid liabilities to foreign official reserve agencies		475				475
Changes in U.S. liquid liabilities to foreign commercial banks, international and regional organizations, and other foreigners	4,436		4,436			
BELOW-THE-LINE COLUMN TOTALS	10,215	2,419	9,097		5,779	475
DIFFERENCE BETWEEN COLUMN TOTALS = SETTLEMENT OF IMBALANCE	9,097		7,796		5,304	

SOURCE: Department of Commerce figures, rearranged from *Federal Reserve Bulletin*, October 1974, p. A60.

controlled by U.S. companies) and for investment in securities and other long-term portfolio assets, reversals in 1973 of such capital movements made earlier, and similar transfers and repatriations of foreign-owned capital. As reflected in the net debit figures of $1538 million and $4276 million, above-the-line movements of U.S. government capital and private nonliquid short-term capital were outward on balance. Issue to the United States of Special Drawing Rights represents a kind of gift to the United States by the International Monetary Fund, as explained in Chapter 20. No such issue occurred in 1973, but the o in the credit column indicates where the transaction would appear (as it did appear in the U.S. balances of payments of 1970, 1971, and 1972).

By any of three ways of distinguishing between above-the-line and below-the-line transactions, two categories of transaction appear below, in the settlement account. The first is reflected in the net credit figure for transactions in reserve assets: U.S. sale of gold, convertible foreign currencies, and Special Drawing Rights, together with any rundown of the U.S. reserve position in the International Monetary Fund, exceeded U.S. acquisition of such assets by $209 million. (The reader should make sure he sees *why* gold exports would count as a credit, just as ordinary commodity exports do. Any idea that credit items are necessarily "good" and debit items "bad" causes serious confusion, especially here.) Second, U.S. government and private institutions ran up liquid liabilities to foreign official agencies—U.S. liabilities of kinds that those foreign agencies count as part of their own official reserves—by $4452 million. These two categories, along with one other, comprise the entire settlement account in the gross-liquidity arrangement of balance-of-payments figures. Different groupings of transactions appear below rather than above the line in the net-liquidity and official-reserve-transactions arrangements.

"Errors and omissions," finally, is a "cheating item." Its existence and size serves as a warning to regard most figures in all balances of payments as no better than rough approximations. (The way that revisions and reclassifications keep changing published figures underlines this warning, which should be understood even if not actually repeated whenever a balance-of-payments figure is quoted.) Because of inaccuracies and gaps in estimates of other items, total *recorded* debits fell $2624 million short of total *recorded* credits, and to make the statement balance, an equivalent debit was entered under "errors and omissions." This item in no way casts doubt on the principle that if all items are fully and accurately stated, their totals *must* balance. It is necessary solely because of practical difficulties in gathering absolutely full and accurate statistics. Tourist spending abroad, for example, must be estimated from information supplied from memory by a sampling of returning travelers. The fact that some people change their residence to or from the United States during the course of a year causes complications. Some smuggled goods go unrecorded. The international lending implied in the shipment of goods that have not been paid for by the end of the year is hard to keep close track of. In some years when errors and omissions is a plus item in the U.S. balance of payments, it may include a considerable hidden transfer of capital into the United States in violation of exchange controls imposed by foreign governments; when it is negative, as in recent years, it presumably includes unrecorded capital outflows.

The balance of payments and the national accounts

The distinction between the goods-and-services account and other parts of the balance of payments conveniently leads to seeing the relation between a country's foreign transactions and its national income and production. In a "closed" economy (without foreign trade),

National Expenditure = National Income or
Product

during a given time period. That is to say, total spending to buy all final goods and services produced (including consumption goods and services and investment goods, both private and governmental) equals the total market value of the things produced and so equals the income that this production generates or amounts to.[2] The term *absorption* conveniently covers all private and governmental consumption and real investment (as distinguished from mere financial investment in securities and other claims) toward which expenditure is directed. For a closed economy, absorption necessarily equals national income and product: there is no source of consumption goods and services and investment goods except domestic production,[3] and, on the other hand, there is no outlet for what is produced except to consume or invest it at home.

Foreign trade makes the truism slightly more complicated:

National Expenditure − Imports + Exports
= National Income or Product

The imports and exports are of currently produced goods and services. Imports have to be subtracted on the left side of the equation to cancel out the imports that are already included in national expenditure (which means expenditure *by* the economic units making up the home economy, not necessarily expenditure *on* home production only). This canceling is necessary because imports are part of foreign, not home production; and expenditure on them, though "out of" home income, gives rise to foreign income, so far as its direct impact is concerned. Exports must be added to the left side for the opposite reason: they are part of national production, and expenditure on them gives rise to national income, yet the expenditure on them is foreign, not domestic.

By rearrangement,

Exports
− Imports = National Income or Product
− National Expenditure

or

Imports
− Exports = National Expenditure − National Income or Product

Since national expenditure "absorbs" consumption and investment goods and services, it follows that

An export surplus = an excess of production over "absorption"

and

An import surplus = an excess of "absorption" over production

An open economy, unlike a closed one, need not always have production and absorption equal. On the one hand, it may be producing goods and services worth more than those it itself consumes or devotes to real capital formation, so that it is building up claims on or paying off debts to foreigners. The claims built up may include foreign securities, business properties and other investments in foreign countries, and foreign currencies and bank deposits and gold. The only other possibility is for the country simply to give the value of its export surplus to foreigners. On the other hand, an open economy may be absorbing into consumption and real investment goods and services worth more than those it itself is producing; it could finance the difference by disposing of its previously acquired foreign investments and gold and foreign exchange or by borrowing from or receiving new investment funds or gifts from foreigners.

What all this means for the behavior of actual persons and business firms and government units is something still to be investigated. We must avoid personifying countries too much and must make it clear who it is that makes decisions and takes actions. In any case, an imbalance between imports and exports of goods and services is the same thing as an imbalance between national production and absorption. Nothing said so far implies that this imbalance is necessarily a bad thing.

Equilibrium and disequilibrium in the balance of payments

Discussions about "surpluses," "deficits," "gaps," and "disequilibriums" in balances of payments and about "active" and "passive" and "favorable" and "unfavorable" balances, as well as governmental measures to deal with these troubles, are all too familiar. What can such terms mean, considering that total debits and credits must be equal? Precisely because it must hold true by definition of the terms involved, this *ex post* equality is hardly reassuring. It no more demonstrates equilibrium than does the fact that actual purchases and sales of any commodity are always equal, even though a shortage caused by a price ceiling may be leaving many would-be buyers unsatisfied. What matters is equality or inequality between the debt and credit totals of certain intentional transactions, or transactions that were considered desirable for their own sakes, as distinguished from other transactions undertaken automatically or passively or without being especially desired and undertaken only as arithmetically necessary counterparts of an imbalance between desired transactions.

We are already familiar with the ideas of a surplus or deficit on account of goods and services.[4] We also know how excess imports can be financed—by drawing down foreign assets, borrowing, or receiving gifts. Unless some such transactions on the credit side were available to the country, it could not be running the deficit in the first place. A country simply cannot be importing more goods and services than it can pay for in some way or other (at least by getting them on credit).

There may be grounds for worry, however, if such a deficit is being financed in a merely stopgap way, as by drawing down bank accounts abroad, selling off gold or investment assets, receiving stopgap loans from abroad, or receiving gifts granted by foreigners precisely in order to tide the country over the crisis. The worry is that such stopgaps cannot go on forever: eventually, foreign bank accounts and gold and other salable assets will be exhausted, and foreigners will become tired of making bad loans and unrequited gifts. The deficit country may suddenly be caught up by the unpleasant need to live within its income. A persistent current-account deficit may indicate the impending need for sudden unpleasant readjustments.

Financing a goods-and-services deficit or a current-account deficit in stopgap ways is fundamentally different from financing it by a long-term capital inflow. Long-term international capital movements typically reflect investors' own judgments about where they can lend their money at highest rates of interest or invest it for highest dividends or profits (and borrowers consider where they can borrow most advantageously). The individual investors take account as they themselves see fit of such factors as different degrees of risk on various investments and of marketability of the securities involved. These profit considerations pre-

sumably correlate with the prospective productivity of the capital. Long-term capital entering

2. "Final" goods and services are distinguished from "intermediate" goods that go through further stages of processing and marketing. Counting all values *added* at each stage would be the same thing as counting only final goods and services.

Income and product are measured gross or net according as investment is counted gross or net of depreciation (i.e., without or with subtraction of that part of total investment that simply offsets wear and tear on and damage to capital goods).

Goods and services are valued at market prices, including whatever taxes may go into them. Our purposes permit slurring over this matter of "indirect business taxes."

"Expenditure" is not meant absolutely literally. If a company constructs new capital equipment itself instead of buying it from some other firm, it is still considered to have "spent" money on the equipment (or on everything that went into it). Inventory investment also counts as expenditure. If a commercial farmer diverts some of his crop to his own consumption, he "spends" on these consumer goods.

3. Consumption plus *new* investment can exceed total production if disinvestment is going on at the same time. But if consumption and investment are added together with the proper negative sign for disinvestment, the statement in the text remains true.

4. The difference in value between exports and imports of *commodities* alone is traditionally called the *balance of trade*. (Some writers, however, use this expression to mean the difference between exports and imports of goods *and services*. See for example, J. E. Meade, *The Balance of Payments*, The Theory of International Economic Policy, Vol. One, London: Oxford University Press, 1951, pp. 7–8; and W. M. Scammel, *International Monetary Policy*, London: Macmillan, 1957, pp. 18–20). An excess of commodity exports over imports is called an "active" or "surplus" or, rather misleadingly, "favorable" balance of trade; the opposite, a "passive" or "deficit" or "unfavorable" balance. Economically, the concept of the balance of commodity trade alone is unimportant, as is the distinction between "visible" trade in commodities and 'invisible' trade in services.

a country presumably tends to increase the country's capital formation, its productive capacity, and its attainable level of consumption, as well as its ability to provide for transfer of interest and profits on the capital and eventual repayment of the capital sums themselves.

A net inflow of long-term capital of this sort is almost inevitably accompanied by a deficit in the country's current account (reserve gains or short-term capital outflows providing conceivable exceptions). This current-account deficit, far from being grounds for alarm, is the way in which capital in "real" terms comes into the country as the counterpart of the financial transfer. The rise in the country's goods-and-services imports relative to its exports is how additional amounts of real resources become available to the borrowing government units and businesses and even consumers. Machinery and other capital goods may be imported, or increased imports and reduced exports of consumer goods may free domestic resources for real capital formation. To welcome an inflow of long-term investment capital while deploring a current-account deficit is to fight sheer arithmetic.

A current-account deficit met by *short-term* capital imports, such as stopgap borrowing or use of gold and foreign-exchange reserves, is something quite different. It is but a temporary expedient that may not long be available. Besides, short-term borrowing soon may have to be repaid.

The distinction often drawn between "long-term" and "short-term" capital movements might perhaps better be drawn between *independently motivated* and stopgap or *compensatory* transactions instead.[5] Independently motivated capital movements are typified by long-term international investments made in hope of gain, but short-term private transfers of capital also may sometimes be motivated by different interest rates in different countries and be equally uninfluenced by a desire to finance imbalances in other parts of the balance of payments. Ordinary private trade in goods and services is almost all independently motivated in the present sense. Stopgap or compensatory financing, on the other hand, is officially provided or arranged for, with perhaps some minor exceptions, precisely to cover (and thus permit) an imbalance between other debits and credits.

The distinction between independently motivated and compensatory transactions serves to define a deficit in a country's balance of payments: it is an excess of independently motivated debit over independently motivated credit transactions. In other words, it is an imbalance requiring or permitted by net resort to compensatory credit transactions. Quite conceivably, an independently motivated capital outflow might more than counterbalance a current-account surplus and so produce an overall deficit, as was true of the United States in the 1960s. More typically, though, a country in overall deficit will be running a current-account deficit not fully financed or matched by an independently motivated capital inflow. In other words, it will be financing an import balance of goods and services at least in part by stopgap methods.

A balance-of-payments surplus, conversely, is an excess of credits over debits in independently motivated transactions, which typically means net exports of goods and services not fully matched by an independently motivated capital outflow and so matched at least in part by passive official accumulations of gold and foreign exchange or by the granting of stopgap loans and gifts to foreigners. A disequilibrium in this direction poses a less pressing problem for a country's authorities than a deficit. A deficit cannot go on without any limit to its stopgap financing; a painful retrenchment may become necessary; but a country with a surplus faces no equally definite limit to the reserves it can accumulate and the help it can give to foreigners. It may be a waste but it is not a critical problem to continue exporting goods and services worth more than those imported and receiving nothing better for the excess than claims on foreigners that would not have been an attractive investment in their own right.

Balance-of-payments *equilibrium* means the absence of any surplus or deficit as just defined: debits and credits on account of goods-and-services trade, together with other independently motivated transactions, add up to equal amounts. To avoid tediously long phrases in theoretical discussions, however, it is often convenient to blur the distinction between trade and other independently motivated transactions, such as long-term capital movements, and speak simply of whether or not the country's "trade" is in balance or whether or not the country is "living within its income."

A country may be in equilibrium as far as is shown by the actual statistics, appropriately classified, and yet be in "latent" or "potential" or "suppressed" disequilibrium. The only thing warding off an actual deficit might be import controls or a domestic financial policy resulting in heavy unemployment. The "equilibrium" shown by the statistics might then be described as "artificial," "forced," "precarious," or "unsatisfactory." But though some such adjective may be attached, it does seem simplest to call even this situation an "equilibrium." We might as well define the term without connotations of approval: by *how desirable a method* equilibrium is maintained is a separate matter from *whether* equilibrium prevails. Sometimes it is convenient to refer to actual and to latent or suppressed disequilibrium alike as balance-of-payments "trouble."

Multilateralism and bilateralism

Related to equilibrium and disequilibrium is the concept of *multilateralism*. By its derivation, the word means "many-sidedness"—here, a many-sided balancing of transactions. Ordinarily, a country's transactions will not balance separately with every other country with which it trades; yet the excess of purchases over sales in transactions with particular countries in no way implies disequilibrium. Balance in total transactions with the rest of the world as a whole is what counts—at least, when currencies can be exchanged for one another without restriction. (When restrictions prevent currency earned by excess sales to one country from being freely exchanged to pay for excess purchases from another country, the story is different.)

Multilateralism is normal; it characterizes the balance of payments of every family. The opposite would be *bilateralism*—avoiding, as far as possible, purchases in excess of sales in dealing with each particular person or firm. The plumber would try to avoid buying groceries worth more than the plumbing work he sold to the grocer and avoid buying medical care worth more than the plumbing work he sold to the doctor. Such bilateralism interferes with achieving efficiency through specialization. The same misgivings apply to national regulation of imports and exports out of concern for a supposed proper balance in transactions with separate foreign countries. (When foreign countries kept their currencies from being freely exchangeable for one another, however, bilateral policies might conceivably be a necessary evil for a country that would otherwise deplore them.)

Alternative concepts of equilibrium and disequilibrium

It might seem that one country's deficit or surplus must necessarily be matched by a surplus or deficit of all other countries taken together: Inland and Outland must have equal but opposite balance-of-payments positions. In theoretical discussions this is a convenient assumption, but it does not necessarily hold true of real-world statistics. Certain transactions might be considered independently motivated by the statisticians of one country and compensatory by the statisticians of another. Gold exports might be independently motivated for a gold-producing country, but adding this gold to the official reserves of another country might be compensatory. The authorities of one country might commandeer foreign securities owned by its citizens and sell them abroad to provide compensatory finance, yet people in other countries might buy these securities for ordinary private motives.[6]

---

5. J. E. Meade's terms *autonomous* and *accommodating* transactions are often used for essentially the same distinction meant here. Unfortunately, the term *autonomous* has a confusing variety of meanings in economics. In the theory of balance-of-payments adjustment, autonomous changes in imports and exports are those motivated otherwise than by changes in income, yet commodity transactions that Meade would label "autonomous" in the present context might very well be motivated by income changes, though independently of anyone's concern about the overall state of the country's balance of payments.

6. Meade, *op. cit.*, chap. II.

As these examples suggest, the distinction between independently motivated and compensatory transactions is not precise. This vagueness cannot be helped; it corresponds to reality. The size and very meaning of a disequilibrium in a country's international transactions depends on just how the line is drawn between their two types. For this reason, incidentally, the distinction is often described—with reference also to the physical arrangement of balances of payments—as a distinction between "above-the-line" and "below-the-line" transactions. A disequilibrium is measured by the difference between the totals of "above-the-line" credits and debits and is "settled" or "financed" by the equal but opposite difference between the two "below-the-line" totals. This neutral language has the advantage of emphasizing the arbitrary element in the distinction between independently motivated and compensatory transactions and therefore in reported figures of surpluses and deficits.

Some further examples may be worthwhile. If an official agency sells foreign exchange out of its reserves to keep an imbalance between other supply and demand from upsetting the officially desired exchange rate, the balance-of-payments credit that this use of reserves represents is pretty clearly a stopgap or compensatory item. This is true even though the authority does not plan the amount of reserves used and just passively supplies whatever amount may be necessary to keep the exchange rate fixed. If a foreign country simply gives or lends gold or money to a country with alarmingly low reserves precisely in order to tide it over this trouble, the transaction is also clearly compensatory, even though the amount of stopgap financing in this case was planned deliberately instead of determined passively. But suppose a deficit country deliberately raises domestic interest rates to attract funds from abroad. If the policy works, investors will transfer funds for their own advantage and probably with no thought of plugging up any gap. From the private point of view, these transfers are motivated just as independently by private economic advantage as transactions in commodities. Yet the policy that attracted the funds was an emergency measure adopted with the balance-of-payments trouble in mind. How, then, should the capital movement be classified? Or, for another example, suppose that importers build up their indebtedness to foreign suppliers because the government, anxious

about its dwindling foreign-exchange reserves, is putting obstacles in the way of its citizens' prompt payment of their external debts. If the foreign exporters acquiesce in the delay because they do not want to lose future business by insisting too obnoxiously on prompt payment and because they are confident of being paid in the end, their extension of the loans may be called voluntary and in accordance with estimates of private advantage. Is the growth of the indebtedness of the deficit country then compensatory or independently motivated? Another example would not even involve any change in government policy. If imports and exports are both habitually bought and sold largely on short-term credit, development of an import surplus (perhaps independently caused by some such development as domestic inflation or foreign depression) would almost automatically be accompanied by a net capital import, since importers are now receiving more total credit than exporters are granting. Are these loans to be classified above or below the line? There are no unequivocal answers to these questions; it is not easy to present statistics of transactions classified by anything so indefinite as motive. But despite all this fuzziness, the distinction between independently motivated and accommodating transactions, and so between equilibrium and disequilibrium, is meaningful.

The definition of disequilibrium introduced in these pages is essentially the same as the third of the "three concepts of the balance of payments" distinguished by Fritz Machlup.[7] This, the *accounting balance*, is the difference between the totals of certain categories of debit and credit items selected from the necessarily balancing complete list of items. (The particular selection made depends on one's view of the motives underlying various transactions.) The accounting balance is an *ex post* concept: it uses figures for a period of time that is over and done with and not figures planned or intended for the current period or for the near future. The idea of planned or intended transactions does come into the concept, but only to distinguish independently motivated transactions (which presumably *had been* planned or intended without regard to the country's overall international accounts) from compensatory transactions not undertaken just for those ordinary motives. The accounting balance has an affinity with Machlup's first concept, the *market balance*, which is the difference between the amounts of foreign exchange effectively demanded and supplied over a period of time by buyers and sellers not motivated by a desire to influence the exchange rate. (This distinction between transactions that are and those that are not officially undertaken to influence the exchange rate is probably the most clear-cut example of the distinction between independently motivated and compensatory transactions.) The state of the accounting balance for immediate past time periods may furnish clues to the probable state of the market balance in the immediate future and to the volume of official transactions that would be necessary to keep the exchange rate unchanged. This knowledge can be helpful to the authorities in deciding what if any change in the rate may be advisable, after all, or what other policies they should adopt to head off a prospective market imbalance. The information provided by the accounting balance has only a loose and uncertain relevance, however; too much depends, among other things, on what exchange rates, financial policies, trade and exchange controls, and other economic conditions and policies were affecting the various items in it. The amount and kind of compensatory financing provided also presumably had been affecting the size of some of the supposedly independent items.

Machlup's remaining concept is the *program balance*, the difference between the amount of foreign exchange that some authority considers it necessary or desirable to have available over some future period and the amount that it expects to become available from regular sources. A certain amount of foreign exchange is obviously "necessary" or "desirable" only with reference to some sort of economic plan or program, however vague, and with reference to desired levels of national consumption and investment. An example is the plan drawn up by the West European countries in 1947 to show the excess of foreign-exchange expenditures over foreign-exchange earnings that their postwar reconstruction would "require" in the following few years. More recent examples are the foreign-exchange deficits involved in economic development plans of underdeveloped countries. Serious confusion (though, one suspects, confusion not always unwelcome to authorities with programs to promote) results from not distinguishing sharply between a "program" balance on the one hand and an "accounting" or a "market" imbalance on the

other hand. The latter two refer to what has happened or is happening under certain conditions. But the program balance refers to what is supposedly necessary *to meet certain desires.* If the desired foreign aid is not forthcoming to cover a program deficit, then a deficit of that size cannot materialize in reality; it remains an unsatisfied wish. (To point out confused thought is not necessarily, of course, to condemn the programs whose adoption the confusion might possibly serve.)

Measurement of disequilibrium in the U.S. balance of payments

The purpose of presenting some actual U.S figures in Tables 3.2 and 3.3 was to emphasize and illustrate the concept of a balance of payments and the necessary equality of debit and credit totals. The later historical chapters discuss actual disequilibria of particular countries. Here, though, it is worth noting the measures of disequilibrium suggested by publications of the U.S. Department of Commerce and usually adopted in the financial press.

Until around 1971, probably the most usual concept was the "liquidity balance," now out of favor and now, as in Table 3.3, renamed the *"gross* liquidity balance." This old concept is still worth attention not only because official figures for other concepts of disequilibrium are

7. "Three Concepts of the Balance of Payments and the So-called Dollar Shortage," *Economic Journal*, **LX**, March 1950, pp. 46ff.

The text that follows modifies some details of Machlup's definitions. In particular, his definition of the "market balance" specifies that the amount of foreign exchange demanded is what would-be purchasers would want to buy if "not restricted by specially adopted or discretionary government control measures." This may or may not be the most useful definition. There is something to be said against defining away the very possibility of achieving equilibrium by controls. It may be more useful to recognize this possibility and to discuss separately whether or not controls are preferable to other measures.

not published for years before 1960 but also because it helps emphasize the arbitrary element unavoidable in *any* measure of disequilibrium. The gross-liquidity concept viewed the U.S. deficit as settled or financed by net losses of gold and other official reserves plus the growth of foreigners' liquid claims on the United States. The latter included not only bank accounts, short-term securities, and similar quickly cashable claims, but also, because of their ready marketability, ordinary U.S. government securities of *all* maturities, as well as certain special medium-term convertible securities sold by the government to foreign monetary authorities precisely to help palliate the U.S. balance-of-payments problem. Changes in claims held by private foreigners counted just the same as changes in claims held by foreign official agencies. Furthermore, the gross-liquidity concept treated flows of short-term private capital in an asymmetrical way.[8] Changes in U.S. liquid liabilities to private foreigners went below the line, while changes in private U.S. claims on foreigners went above. Suppose that a U.S. commercial bank acquired a £1000 balance in an English bank and gave it a $2400 (=£1000) balance in return. The first part of the transaction counted above the line as an independently motivated outflow of U.S. capital, worsening the U.S. deficit, while the inflow of English capital counted below the line as a settlement item. On the gross-liquidity concept, this swapping of bank accounts swelled the U.S. deficit by $2400! The excuse for this asymmetry was that U.S. liquid liabilities even to private foreigners were a potential claim on the U.S. gold stock: they might readily be transferred to foreign central banks or governments, to whom the United States would sell gold for dollars on demand. Yet private U.S. capital outflows counted above the line, since private claims on foreigners, even short-term claims, are not readily available to the authorities as reserves for supporting the dollar on the foreign-exchange market. Far from being arbitrary, the asymmetry supposedly reflected the real world, including the special role of the dollar in international finance and the importance of the ratio of U.S. official reserves to *all* U.S. liquid liabilities, those owed by and to private parties as well as those owed by and to official agencies.

This defense of the old concept is open to various replies. In any case, the Commerce Department replaced it in 1971 with the concept of "*net* liquidity balance."[9] The new concept removes the above-mentioned asymmetry by putting changes in U.S. liquid claims on and liabilities to foreigners both below the line, among the settlement items. It also changes the handling of certain special financial transactions, as reflected in Table 3.3.

A few years earlier, after a government-appointed committee of experts (the Bernstein Committee) issued its report in 1965,[10] the Commerce Department began publishing figures arranged according to the "official-reserve-transactions" (ORT) concept of overall imbalance of payments. Also called the "official-settlements" concept, it, like both liquidity concepts, measures the settlement of an overall deficit or surplus by what has happened to U.S. holdings of gold and other reserve assets and to certain types of claims against the United States. The difference comes in the classification of foreign claims on the United States. The gross- and net-liquidity concepts differ in their handling of changes in U.S. claims on foreigners, but both put changes in foreign claims on the United States above or below the line according to whether they are nonliquid or liquid claims. The ORT concept draws the line according to whether the foreign claims belong to private foreigners or to foreign authorities. The ORT balance equals the net-liquidity balance plus the flow of U.S. and foreign *private* liquid capital.[11]

The ORT concept treats any increase in foreign private claims on the United States, whether liquid or illiquid, as an ordinary capital inflow, just as it treats an increase in private American claims on foreigners as an ordinary capital outflow. It recognizes that satisfying the normally growing desire of private foreigners for dollar holdings should not count as measuring and settling a United States deficit. It recognizes that movements of short-term as well as long-term capital owned by private foreigners generally reflect personal and business motives and so differ in character from the transactions of U.S. and foreign monetary authorities. The ORT concept focuses attention on U.S. gold and other reserves and on the dollar claims that foreign monetary authorities acquire or dispose of, usually in trying to stabilize exchange rates.

The ORT concept recognizes the artificiality of distinguishing, as the gross-liquidity concept did, between liquid and certain nonliquid U.S. liabilities to foreign authorities. It puts changes in both below the line. The decision on which nonliquid liabilities are to be handled that way is admittedly somewhat arbitrary. The ones in question consist chiefly of nonmarketable, nonconvertible U.S. government securities issued to foreign authorities.

According to the Bernstein Committee, the rationale of the ORT presentation of the figures is that a summary indicator of the balance of payments is wanted because central banks and treasuries are responsible for maintaining stable exchange rates. To carry out this responsibility, these authorities settle the net deficits and surpluses arising from all other international transactions by gaining or losing reserve assets and by increasing or decreasing their liabilities to foreign authorities. The size of a country's official transactions both in its own reserves and in its liabilities held as reserves by foreign authorities supposedly measures the scale of market intervention necessary to maintain exchange stability. (However, a "deficit" in the ORT balance of the United States does not necessarily spell a disequilibrium in the sense of a bad and unsustainable condition if foreign authorities have been purposefully building up their dollar reserves instead of passively finding dollars thrust upon them by weakness of the dollar in the market. With exchange rates generally fluctuating since early 1973, furthermore, the very meaning of the ORT measure of imbalance, as of the other measures, has become even fuzzier than before.)

The distinction that the ORT concept makes between private and official dollar claims can itself be rather artificial. Suppose that a foreign central bank transfers a dollar deposit that it holds in a U.S. commercial bank to a commercial bank at home, acquiring a dollar claim on the latter. On the ORT basis, the U.S. balance of payments improves! The increase in the liability of the U.S. bank to the foreign commercial bank counts above the line, as an ordinary capital inflow, while the decrease in the liability to the foreign central bank counts below the line, among the settlement items. Furthermore, central banks in many foreign countries manipulate the dollar holdings of commercial banks. The liquidity measures of the U.S. deficit, on the other hand, are not affected by policy-induced shifts of dollar claims between central and commercial banks, since changes in both private and official foreign liquid claims go below the line anyway. No clear line separates foreign dollar holdings that do from those that do not stand

as offsets to the gold and foreign-exchange reserves of the United States.

Government publications now report both the net-liquidity and official-settlements measures of the overall U.S. payments position, as well as the "balance on current account and long-term capital." The latter concept, often called the "basic balance," seems to fluctuate in popularity over the years. Above the line it puts trade in goods and services, private and government unilateral transfers, flows of U.S. and foreign private long-term capital, and flows of U.S. and foreign government capital other than changes in U.S. official reserve holdings and foreign official reserve holdings in the United States. Below the line, along with the traditional settlment items, it puts short-term capital movements and errors and omissions. Transactions in these categories are supposedly more volatile and less accurate as a reflection of fundamental trends than are the "basic" transactions.

Still further measures of deficit and surplus could be mentioned. The multiplicity of measures explains how official American and international publications of the early 1950s could describe the U.S. balance of payments for 1951 as in *surplus* by various amounts ranging up to $5 billion, although later publications came to describe the imbalance in the same year as a *deficit* ranging nearly to $1 billion.[12] As early theories of "dollar short-

8. Walter R. Gardner, "An Exchange-Market Analysis of the U.S. Balance of Payments," IMF *Staff Papers,* **VIII,** May 1961, pp. 195–211.

9. See David T. Devlin, "The U.S. Balance of Payments: Revised Presentation," *Survey of Current Business,* June 1971, pp. 24–64. Devlin also explains the concepts of official-reserve-transactions balance and balance on current account and long-term capital (basic balance), discussed below.

10. Review Committee for Balance of Payments Statistics, *The Balance of Payments Statistics of the United States,* Washington: Government Printing Office, 1965.

11. Devlin, *op. cit.,* p. 24.

12. See Fritz Machlup, "The Mysterious Number Game of Balance-of-Payments Statistics," chap. VII in his *International Payments, Debts, and Gold,* New York: Scribner's, 1964.

age"[13] and of chronic deficit tendencies in European payments positions underwent revision, transactions relating to U.S. foreign aid, military spending, and capital outflows were reclassified from "below the line" to "above the line."

All this illustrates what we have been insisting on all along: there is no single unambiguously correct measure of a country's international payments position. When one financial writer told the Bernstein Committee, "All I want is one number, with no if's, but's, or maybe's," he was asking the impossible. Deficits and surpluses are not definite things objectively existing in the real world and waiting to be described with precision. What they are depends on *theories* and on definitions that economists and statisticians are free to choose as they think best for various purposes. In work with actual statistical raw material, hairsplitting and arbitrariness are necessary because the figures do not automatically fall into neat categories according to the motives underlying the transactions. In abstract analysis, however, it is ordinarily legitimate to assume a clear distinction between independently motivated transactions and settlement transactions, thus sidestepping any worry over the exact meanings of deficit and surplus.

Personal and national balances of payments

The analogy between a country and a family can serve again in analyzing equilibrium and disequilibrium. A family enjoys equilibrium in its balance of payments if its spending on goods and services plus its repayment of old loans and its independently motivated lending and investing are just equal to its sales of goods and services plus its independently motivated disinvestment, recovery of loans previously made, and nonstopgap borrowing. As for borrowing, the key distinction is between borrowing judged worthwhile in its own right (as to buy a house or to finance an education) and borrowing as an emergency expedient to keep abreast of current bills. If the family is covering expenditure beyond its income only by the temporary expedient of cashing its savings bonds, drawing down its bank account, or otherwise using up its liquid assets, or by emergency borrowing, it has a deficit The

opposite imbalance, matched by passive accumulation of cash, bank accounts, and the like, is a surplus. For a family as for a country, the key conceptual distinctions are a bit fuzzy. (One defect in the analogy will prove important in explaining the possibility of national balance-of-payments crises. For a family, decisions to spend beyond current income and to finance this overspending interlock closely. A country is much less a single decision-making unit. For a country, an official agency may find itself passively supplying foreign exchange to finance an import surplus that it had no direct part in deciding upon. Related to this contrast is the fact that a country, unlike a family, has an exchange rate to peg, alter, or leave free.)

A country's surplus or deficit is an aggregate of the separate imbalances of the various individuals, families, business firms, banks, foreign-exchange offices, treasuries, and other private and government institutions making up the country's economic system. All of these are represented in Table 3.4 by just three men.

TABLE 3.4. *Individual balances of payments*

Buyers / Sellers	Jones	Brown	Smith	Outside world	Total sales
Jones		20	25	0	45
Brown	50		30	10	90
Smith	20	40		5	65
Outside world	15	20	10	—	45
Total purchases	85	80	65	15	245
Surplus (+) or deficit (−)	−40	+10	0	+30	

The numbers show their transactions among themselves and with outsiders in goods and services and in claims and investments bought and sold for nonstopgap motives. For example, during the period covered, Smith buys $25.00 worth of such things from Jones; Smith sells $5.00 worth to the outside world; Brown's sales exceed his purchases by $10.00. Table 3.5 washes out the three men's transactions with each other and shows only the group's transactions with the outside world. The group's balance (−30) equals the total of the balances of

TABLE 3.5. *Consolidation of individual balances of payments*

Buyers Sellers	Jones + Brown + Smith	Outside world	Total Sales
Jones + Brown + Smith		15	15
Outside world	45		45
Total purchases	45	15	60
Surplus (+) or deficit (−)	−30	+30	

each member with all other transactors, fellow-countrymen and outsiders alike (−40, + 10, and 0).

The point illustrated is obvious but important. If a country is making purchases and independently motivated loans, investments, repayments, and gifts abroad in excess of its independently motivated transactions in the opposite direction—if it is resorting to compensatory or stopgap finance—then some of the economic units composing it must be doing the same. If all of its units were "operating within their means" (in the sense just implied by contrast), or if the surpluses of some just balanced the deficits of others, the country as a whole could not have an external deficit.

There should now be no mystery about what tends to prevent persistent disequilibrium in a country's balance of payments: individual economic units strive to keep their own affairs in order. In a country with a deficit, some economic units must be having financial troubles. Troubled individuals and firms will try to expand their sales or cut their purchases, and some transactions with the outside world will be affected. Not even careless spendthrifts can go ever deeper into debt, if only because their creditors will get tired of making bad loans to them.

Any mystery, then, is not about equilibrating tendencies but about how they could fail as often as they apparently do. Sometimes the trouble might seem to be the aftermath of war. Ruritania's industries have been ruined by the fighting; her import "needs" are great, her balance-of-payments deficit is unavoidable. But this argument falls into the "fallacy of misplaced concreteness." Ruritania, an abstraction, cannot be impoverished; it is the *Ruri-*

tanians who are impoverished. If they had used up their external reserves and could not get help abroad, they could not possibly keep on running a deficit. They might starve, but they would starve with their balance of payments in equilibrium.[14] Foreign aid permits and in a sense *is* their deficit. It is illogical to argue that they should receive aid *because* they have a deficit. Rather, they should be permitted a deficit because they are impoverished and deserve help in gratitude for their wartime sacrifices.

The inhabitants of Geneva, as Professor Röpke explains,[15] found themselves comparatively poor at the end of World War II. The League of Nations had been liquidated. Trade with the French hinterland had been impeded. Income from tourists had declined. The inhabitants had suffered losses on their foreign investments. Yet nobody worried about Geneva's balance of payments. Not the city, but rather its inhabitants, had been impoverished. People had to refrain from buying more goods and services than they could afford, and this behavior took care of the city's balance of payments.

This apparent denial of the very possibility of balance-of-payments trouble can be reconciled with experience. A country with a deficit must contain individuals or institutions that are living beyond their means, dissipating their resources in a stopgap way, to a greater extent than others are doing the reverse. Even if the national government were creating money to cover a yawning budget deficit, however, the country as a whole would not necessarily have a balance-of-payments deficit

13. See the appendix to Chapter 27.

14. "International adjustment always takes place in some fashion, but this statement offers little more comfort than the observation that an airplane always gets back to the ground somehow. For adjustment can be a wretchedly painful affair." Randall Hinshaw in Hinshaw, ed., *The Economics of International Adjustment*, Baltimore: Johns Hopkins Press, 1971, p. 4.

15. Wilhelm Röpke, *Internationale Ordnung*, Erlenbach-Zürich: Rentsch, 1945, pp. 227–230.

(though it could have if foreigners were acquiring some of the inflated currency, thereby in effect making loans or perhaps ultimately gifts to the inflating government). By inflation, amounting to a tax on money and government securities, the government might be wresting real wealth from the public and forcing it to absorb less than its current production. We must look further for the institution whose deteriorating finances would explain a country's balance-of-payments deficit. This would be the central bank or other official agency selling foreign exchange to peg the rate. If this agency is being called upon to sell more foreign exchange than is being offered to it—in other words, if it could not replenish its foreign-exchange reserves in a free market at the same price at which it is selling them—this very fact shows that it is dealing in foreign exchange at a below-equilibrium price in home currency. In so doing, it is dissipating its assets—"operating beyond its means"—since only nominally, but not at free-market values, is the home currency it takes in fully worth the foreign exchange it pays out.

Foreign loans or gifts, if obtained, could explain a country's continuing deficit. The argument still stands: a country as a whole can have an external deficit only if individuals and institutions are, on balance, using up assets or going into debt or cadging gifts as a stopgap—behaving without ordinary financial prudence. If the country has mere balance-of-payments "trouble" because various *ad hoc* import and exchange controls are suppressing a latent deficit, an exchange-pegging agency is in corresponding trouble. It would be dissipating its assets (or incurring debt to foreigners), were not the controls choking off the demand for the foreign exchange being sold unduly cheap.

As a matter of analysis, though not necessarily as a policy recommendation, it is worth remembering that a country could avoid balance-of-payments trouble (though not all economic trouble) simply by not having any agency dealing in foreign exchange in ways that ran counter to its own financial self-interest. Either of two extremes would satisfy this condition: complete international monetary unification or complete national monetary independence. These extremes and intermediate arrangements will be considered next.

CHAPTER FOUR

Monetary Systems and International Adjustment

The 100 percent gold standard

When different countries shared a common monetary system to the fullest conceivable extent, no agency could be dealing in foreign exchange to influence rates because none would exist. All members of the system would use the same single kind of money. No national authority could have the slightest independence in creating money and determining the local money supply. Even fractional-reserve banking would be ruled out: no one could issue demand deposits or any other means of payment unless they were backed unit-for-unit by the sole standard money. Monetary unification would thus be even more complete than it is at present between Switzerland and Liechtenstein or among the states of the United States. The sole money might conceivably be fiat money issued by a single international authority, but it is even simpler to suppose that nothing but actual gold serves as a medium of exchange. The system would not really be different, though, if some or all of the money in circulation consisted not of actual gold coins but of more convenient fully backed gold certificates in the form of subsidiary token coins, paper currency, or demand deposits. The total quantity of money would still coincide with the total quantity of monetary gold. In redeeming other kinds of money in gold, a bank or other issuing agency would not be *pegging* them to gold but simply honoring them as claim checks on gold actually held in storage. For the same reason, no issuing agency could ever be in danger of running out of gold reserves.

As a practical matter, such complete monetary unity is impossible. It is worth analyzing because of the way it highlights, by contrast, some crucial features of more realistic systems. Under complete unity, each country's money supply—its share of the total quantity of monetary gold in all countries—would be determined solely by the concern of individual persons and institutions not to let their cash balances shrink or expand to sizes that they themselves considered inappropriate to their own circumstances.

Suppose that the Outland demand for Inland goods declines or that some Inland demand switches from domestic to foreign products. Inlanders in the affected export or import-competing industries, with their sales reduced and their cash dwindling, have clear incentives to push their own sales at home and abroad (perhaps by cutting prices) and to retrench on their purchases. They will retrench on buying Outland goods and on buying from fellow Inlanders. These others, also seeing their incomes and cash dwindle, will in turn push their sales and limit their purchases, again partly affecting exports and imports. Individual families and firms have adequate incentives to try to keep solvent and hold enough cash; beyond this, there is no distinct problem for the country as a whole. Of course, the underlying shift of demand away from their products does worsen the Inlanders' terms of trade, but this in an inexorable "real" development, not avoidable by mere financial devices. One of the things Inlanders may economize on in view of their changed circumstances is the holding of cash balances. They will draw down their cash while figuring out how to rearrange their purchases and sales; this is one of their reasons for holding cash in the first place—to have it as a buffer to draw on while making orderly adjustments to changed circumstances. Meanwhile, their own (and the country's) balances of payments are temporarily in deficit. But private incentives effectively limit the size and duration of their deficit. This is one key feature of the 100 percent gold standard.

The same incentives work in the opposite direction to prevent opposite initial changes from causing a troublesome balance-of-pay-

58

ments surplus. Individuals will not accumulate cash without limit.

Other portfolio assets

In reality, other portfolio assets besides money play a part in the adjustment process just described. Let us return to our assumption that demand has shifted either in Inland or in Outland away from Inland onto Outland goods. As long as any trade deficit persists, despite the corrective tendencies already described, some Inlanders are spending more money on goods and services than they are currently earning. Besides running down their money balances to pay for this overspending, they may be selling securities or other assets from their investment portfolios. (Any borrowing by them also counts as the sale of securities.) Individual Inlanders do not much care whether they sell securities to fellow countrymen or to foreigners. The decline in the prices of the securities sold—the rise in their interest or dividend yields—attracts some purchases from Outland investors. The securities moving to Outland in heaviest volume are ones that enjoy a ready international market. (Others, such as stocks and bonds of enterprises known only locally, do not enjoy such a broad market, and some kinds of Inland assets, such as land, enjoy little international market at all.)

As a result of these transactions, Inlanders' financial positions come to show larger ratios than before of debt to income and to assets and smaller ratios of money and securities to income. Internationally traded securities make up smaller proportions than before of investment portfolios held in Inland. Now, people and business firms have some ideas about suitable ratios of money balances, investment portfolios, and debt to income. They have ideas about suitable proportions of money, readily marketable securities, and other assets, including physical assets, in their portfolios. These desired ratios and proportions depend to some extent on interest rates, dividend yields, and expectations of capital gain and loss. These rates, yields, and expectations are unlikely to change so sharply, however, and the desired ratios and proportions are unlikely to respond so sensitively as to mean that people are effectively indifferent to the changes that have been going on.[1] On the contrary, people do care about what has been happening to their ratios of debt and money and other assets

to income and to the compositions of their portfolios. As such changes went on, people would become increasingly uncomfortable about them (as well as about their shrunken incomes) and increasing anxious to check or reverse this deterioration of their portfolios. Accordingly, they would strive to cut their purchases of goods and services, including their purchases from Outland, and to increase their sales, including their sales in Outland. The result of such efforts, from the national point of view, is further shrinkage of Inland's trade deficit.

Of course, people do not go on blithely overspending on goods and services until they belatedly wake up and see what has been happening to their asset and debt positions. Decisions about buying and selling goods and services interlock with decisions about debt and asset portfolios. Concern about portfolios restrains overspending—which is Inland's trade deficit—in the first place. In fact, this is the point of the present discussion.

Prices play a part in shrinking or preventing the trade deficit. People's efforts to restrain their purchases and increase their sales of goods and services tend to depress prices of goods and factors of production in Inland. (In other words, their eagerness to acquire or hang on to money means that people value it more highly than before in their market transactions.) The resulting price-and-cost decline affects mainly goods and services (like labor, haircuts, and houses) in which interregional and international trade is relatively inactive. Actively traded goods are affected less because their prices are determined by international supply and demand. Thus, local goods fall in price relative to goods of kinds actively imported and exported; import-and-export-type goods rise in price *relatively*. Inland consumers have an incentive to switch their buying away from imports, while producers have an incentive to switch their production or sales efforts onto export goods. In Outland, purchasers have price incentives to switch from Outland to Inland sources of supply and sellers to switch from Inland to Outland markets.[2]

The special emphasis on money

This chapter pays more attention to the role of money in particular than of asset and debt portfolios in general. Several considerations justify this emphasis. First, and in summary, "balance-of-payments deficits and difficulties are essentially monetary phenomena. . . ."[3] Second, international transactions in securities and other investment assets conventionally go "above the line" in balance-of-payments accounting. Because money balances serve as a buffer, rising or falling in almost passive initial response to surges of income relative to expenditure or of expenditure relative to income, a rundown of money balances is the very prototype of the "below-the-line" financing of an overall payments deficit. Third, this "domestic financing" of the deficit, as it might be called, is matched by "external financing" when an official agency pegs the exchange rate by running down its reserves of foreign exchange.[4] Such pegging is, after all, the pegging together of domestic and foreign *money* in particular and not of domestic and foreign financial assets in general. A fourth reason for focusing on money is that assets more broadly conceived, as well as debts, have a different role in the payments-adjustment process. Their role relates more to the financing and adjustment of a deficit or surplus in goods-and-services trade than to adjustment of the overall balance of payments as conventionally defined. When we are concerned with overall imbalance, with unbalanced private desires to exchange domestic for foreign money, with the consequent rundown of official foreign-exchange reserves, and with the short-run danger of a currency crisis, the narrowly monetary view is more relevant. Fifth, desired money balances are to some extent geared to total portfolios as well as to income. Conversely, quantities of near-moneys, and even the nominal values of physical assets, are geared to the quantity of money through the influence of money on nominal incomes and price levels.[5] Because of this gearing together, building up or running down money balances is the prototype of, or is symbolic of, building up or running down portfolios conceived more broadly. A sixth and final reason concerns a characteristic of money that other assets do not share. As the medium of exchange, money has a routine flow. Efforts to conserve dwindling balances of money—the one thing routinely spent—constitute practically in themselves a reduction in the flow of spending. Efforts to conserve on holdings of

tion with Outland restrains this rise, or until domestic business recession reverses it. A rise in Inland interest rates causes Inlanders to desire smaller money balances than before in relation to income and to other portfolio assets. On the other hand, the interest-rate rise tends to work against Inland's trade deficit by restraining consumption and real investment; it discourages indebtedness and promotes the holding of interest-bearing securities.

2. In the imaginary extreme case of a standardized good traded without transport costs throughout a purely competitive world market, the price differentials necessary to switch purchases from one source of supply to another and to switch sales from one market to another would be infinitesimally small. We could still think of price differentials at work causing such shifts, but the responses would be so sensitive that the differentials would be imperceptible. Thus we need not contradict the Law of One Price for a homogeneous good in a unified competitive market.

Other sections of this book, especially pp. 93–95, pay closer attention to the role of prices in the international adjustment process. Here, we are mainly concerned with the role of asset portfolios and debts in affecting propensities to spend income on goods and services.

3. Harry G. Johnson, *International Trade and Economic Growth*, Cambridge, Mass.: Harvard University Press, 1958, p. 157. Compare Robert A. Mundell, *Monetary Theory*, Pacific Palisades, Cal.: Goodyear, p. 93: "The balance of payments, of course, is a monetary phenomenon, and its correction requires monetary policies." Arnold Collery notes that the very concept of balance-of-payments disequilibrium would be practically meaningless in a world of barter. *International Adjustment, Open Economies, and the Quantity Theory of Money*, Princeton Studies in International Finance, No. 28, Princeton, N.J.: Princeton University, 1971, p. 1.

4. On the terms "domestic financing" and "external financing," see Fritz Machlup, "Adjustment, Compensatory Correction, and Financing of Imbalances in International Payments," in Robert E. Baldwin *et al., Trade, Growth, and the Balance of Payments*, Chicago: Rand McNally, 1965, esp. p. 203. By "domestic financing," however, Machlup means re-creation by the monetary authority of the money being cancelled by the external deficit.

5. See my "Essential Properties of the Medium of Exchange," *Kyklos*, **XXI**, No. 1, 1968, pp. 45–68.

1. The conditions that caused Inlanders to overspend in the first place, together with their efforts to finance their overspending, tend to raise Inland interest rates—unless close financial integra-

other assets do not constitute so *direct* a cutback in spending.

In short, assets besides money, as well as liabilities, play a part in the international adjustment process. However, concern about money balances is the very prototype of concern about portfolio positions. Money is distinctive as the thing routinely received and spent and as the thing routinely pegged to foreign money. Balance-of-payments accounting conventions also direct special attention to money.

Fractional reserves and the reinforcement of drains

The automaticity of adjustment under a 100 percent monetary system is easier to understand if we contrast it with a fractional-reserve system. An official agency has issued fiduciary money amounting to several times as much as its gold reserve. Ordinarily it has no trouble honoring the relatively few demands for redemption that actually are made. But now an initial shift in home or foreign demand causes Inlanders to buy more than they sell. They may be willing to pay for excess purchases for a while by drawing down their cash balances. But since Outlanders are not willing to accept final settlement in Inland currency, it must be redeemed in gold. The resulting drain is a bigger fraction of the agency's gold reserves than of the cash balances of individuals. If the gold reserves had amounted to only 10 percent of the total money supply, a drain equaling only 5 percent of this total would amount to fully *half* of the reserves. The drain can pose a serious problem for the agency pegging its monetary liabilities to gold—a serious problem for "the country," as is commonly said. Yet the drain can be so small in relation to cash balances of ordinary Inland money that people are willing to draw their balances down that far and even farther. Since cash balances are swollen with fiduciary money (and since the price level is correspondingly high), a drain of an absolute size (that is, size measured in dollars rather than as a percentage) that might have been ample to make people pull their expenditures and receipts back into balance under a 100 percent gold standard might not be big enough under the fractional system. An other-wise large enough drain would be too small in relation to all the money pyramided onto a fractional gold base and in relation to the corresponding price level. Partial-reserve money *dilutes* the otherwise adequately corrective cash-balance effect.[6]

The problem is not that the deficit might continue forever. Dwindling cash balances would strengthen people's incentives to retrench on their purchases or push their sales. Unfortunately, adjustment might not be complete before the agency ran out of reserves and had to stop pegging the exchange rate. How can it undo the dilution of the cash-balance effect and make individuals behave so that, as under the 100 percent standard, what is financially sound for themselves is financially sound for itself also? It must make the cash balances of individuals vary not merely by the same absolute amount as its own gold reserve, but by roughly the same *percentage*. Then, since individuals simply will not draw down their cash balances to anywhere near zero, the gold reserve cannot run out either. Complete safety requires complete proportionality. A $1-billion gold drain must make the money supply shrink by $2 billion under a 50 percent reserve system, by $10 billion under a 10 percent reserve system, and so forth. This "reinforcement" of the money-supply effects of a gold drain conforms to the so-called rules of the game of the fractional-reserve gold standard. (For discussion in a historical context, see Chapter 15.) Reinforcement corrects for the above-mentioned "dilution" inherent in a fractional-reserve system. The country's central bank can contract the money supply by reducing its loans and investments and thus its monetary liabilities; the government can get money out of circulation by collecting taxes in excess of its expenditures.

This centralized reinforcement is not automatic. To those who are denied loans or loan renewals or government services that they had been counting on or who must pay higher taxes, the deflationary policies must seem arbitrary. Under the 100 percent standard, people see their cash balances shrinking in obvious relation to their increased purchases or reduced sales and independently of any deliberate policy. Under the fractional standard, the shrinkage of cash balances is not in such close and obvious relation to people's own overspending. It comes, instead, from identifiable acts of the monetary or fiscal authorities. Even people not directly affected by the deflationary policies as borrowers or taxpayers are affected indirectly by reduced sales to the first group. In a sense soon to be examined more fully, the reinforcement necessary to safeguard a fractional-reserve standard makes correction of a balance-of-payments deficit objectionably harsh and rapid.

Could the necessary reinforcement work more satisfactorily if the only money issued on a fractional-reserve basis were the demand deposits of private banks? The only reserve requirements might be those that banks themselves individually adopted to compromise prudently between safety and immediate earnings. If depositors demanded gold to pay foreigners for an excess of imports over exports, the banks would have to protect their reserve ratios by shrinking their loans and investments and their deposit liabilities by probably several times as much as their loss of gold reserves. This magnified shrinkage in individuals' cash balances would stop them from overspending before the gold reserves were gone. To persons denied new bank loans and pressed for repayment of old ones, the deflation would seem almost as arbitrary as if it had been imposed by a central authority. The process is more automatic only in minor respects. First, the decisions to deflate are made decentrally, by dozens or hundreds or thousands of individual bankers rather than by a single authority. Second, bankers are less likely than an authority to avoid or delay reinforcing the gold drain in hope that the underlying balance-of-payments disturbance will soon reverse itself of its own accord and without corrective action. The individual banker may not even be aware of the rather indirect connection between the country's balance-of-payments deficit and the drain on his own reserves. In any case, he cannot wait to see how things work out. He must avoid insolvency. If he lags behind other banks in deflating, a disproportionate fraction of the national gold drain will impinge on his reserves. He has no recourse to the controls over trade, the legal suspension of gold payments, and the excuses ultimately available to a governmental authority. The contrast holds for a gold gain, too; while a non-profit-seeking official agency might refrain from expanding its money issues in full proportion, growing excess reserves of unprofitable gold would soon prod a laggard banker into step with a general expansion. But the similarities between systems of officially issued and privately issued fractional-reserve money are normally more basic than the contrasts.

The contrast is greater between 100 percent money on the one hand and fractional-reserve money, by whomever issued, on the other. With 100 percent money, to repeat, the concern of individuals to maintain cash balances that they consider adequate but not excessive in the light of their real incomes and wealth is all that is necessary to avoid national balance-of-payments trouble. Furthermore, cash-balance changes fully sufficient to correct over- or underspending are inseparably linked with that over- or underspending. It is unnecessary to draft innocent parties into the adjustment process, contracting or expanding their cash balances in an apparently arbitrary way by measures of banking or fiscal policy. Adjustment need proceed no faster or more harshly than individuals see fit in the light of their own unmanipulated circumstances.

Offsetting the impact of reserve changes

The 100 percent standard seems appealing because the internal adjustments to an external disturbance of any given size can proceed more impersonally and slowly than under fractional reserves. But even setting aside quibbles about whether "slower" adjustment has a precise and unambiguous meaning, one might ask whether a slower adjustment is necessarily preferable, after all. If slowing down is always desirable, even apart from detailed knowledge about the particular circumstances, then why aren't 200 percent reserves better than 100 percent, and

6. To speak of a cash-balance effect is not to assert that an excess demand for or excess supply of money necessarily has its main impact *directly* in the markets for goods and services. Direct impacts may occur mainly in the markets for securities and other investment assets, with the markets for currently produced goods and services being affected through a chain of repercussions.

so on indefinitely?[7] A 200 percent standard would mean a monetary gold stock twice as large as the ordinary money supply. Inflows and outflows of gold would expand and contract the money supply by only half as much. When an export surplus draws in gold, the country's authorities adopt restrictive banking and fiscal policies in order to acquire half of the gold for themselves and cut down the growth of the money supply in the hands of the public. When an import surplus draws gold out, expansionary policies cut down the shrinkage of the money in the hands of the public. The cash-balance incentives for individuals to bring their sales and purchases back into equality are weakened.

In analyzing such policies, it is convenient to recall the term *absorption*, introduced in Chapter 3. It means the total of private and public consumption and capital accumulation in the country. An export surplus of goods and services is the same thing as an excess of the value of current production over the value of current absorption; an import surplus is this difference in reverse. Now, policies that partially offset any addition of gold to the money supply amount to taxing absorption. Open-market sales of securities or other contractionary central-bank operations make credit more expensive and less readily available, while "overcharging" for public services through a government budget surplus is an even more obvious tax on absorption. Credit-cheapening operations and a government budget deficit, conversely, subsidize absorption and put gold into circulation in partial replacement of the outward drain. By operating a 200 percent gold standard, the authorities are apparently not just slowing down the correction of external surpluses and deficits but are eliminating part of the correction. Actually, this distinction is empty. Over the fullness of time and apart from gifts and loans and so forth, a country's imports and exports, like its absorption and production, must be equal. (Admittedly, authorities may occasionally suffer the embarrassment of running out of *fractional* reserves.) The policies of alternately taxing and subsidizing absorption under a 200 percent standard keep absorption and production from matching each other as closely in each individual month or year as they otherwise would. The time pattern of absorption is partially smoothed out in the face of fluctuations in production. (These can be fluctuations in the real value of production, corresponding to changes in the terms of trade and caused by changes in supplies and demands, rather than fluctuations in the physical level of output. For that matter, absorption is smoothed out in the face of fluctuations not only in output but also in the *propensity* to absorb.) The authorities accumulate gold reserves when restraining absorption and decumulate gold reserves when subsidizing it. Even under a mere 100 percent standard, some smoothing takes place, but only in accordance with the decisions of private individuals and firms, who use temporary spurts in their real incomes partly to build up cash balances and who draw down their cash balances to maintain absorption when their real incomes slump temporarily. The most obvious conceivable justification for official policies to accomplish still more smoothing—in effect, for building up and drawing down additional reserves *on behalf of* the private economy—is that the authorities either know better how much smoothing is proper or know better what the future holds in store and how likely various developments are to prove temporary.

Perhaps a more realistic reason for *offsetting* the monetary effects and adjustment incentives that gold gains and losses would produce is to save the home economy from disruptive *reinforcement* occurring through the profit-and-safety-motivated decentralized responses of a private banking system. But this danger means that the monetary system was not based on at least 100 percent gold reserves after all. Marginally, however—that is, in the face of gold movements that are small in relation to the total gold reserve—the authorities can operate *as if* they were on a 100-percent-or-more standard: they can keep gold gains and losses from swelling or shrinking the ordinary money supply several times as much or just as much or even at all. The authorities can absorb or disgorge gold, allowing their reserve ratio, even if it is only a fractional ratio, to go up or down. They have comparatively little difficulty absorbing a gold *inflow* by restrictive central-bank and fiscal operations and may have ample motive. Unless it were thus kept out of the reserves of the commercial banks, the new gold would serve as the basis of a multiple bank-credit and bank-deposit expansion. A resulting inflation of prices and money incomes might be unwanted both because of its immediate consequences and because of the difficulties that a gold drain would later involve in view of well-known resistances to downward adjustments in incomes and prices. Contraction imposed by a drain of gold from the reserves of the commercial banks, even when not set against a background of recent inflation, can have unpleasant domestic consequences, and the authorities may well want to offset it by expansionary central-bank and budget operations.[8] They may consider the risk of an excessive drain on their reserves well worth taking in view of the deflationary difficulties thereby avoided, especially if they believe that the underlying balance-of-payments disturbance responsible for the country's gold loss is temporary and likely to reverse itself soon even without any corrective process or action.

The dilemma of a fractional-reserve system

This last proviso is important, for the policy just outlined does fully or partially destroy equilibrating incentives. The authorities are in a dilemma under a fractional-reserve system. Suppose they aim at balance-of-payments equilibrium and so reinforce the monetary impact of gold inflows and outflows, either by themselves creating and destroying fiduciary money or by permitting or causing the banking system to do so. This means using fiscal and banking policies to manipulate the cash balances even of persons who had not been "absorbing" more or less than their incomes. Suppose, on the other hand, that the authorities "offset" domestic monetary responses, impeding external adjustment. A continuing surplus implies taxing away domestic income or wealth to build up gold reserves that hardly represent an attractive national investment in their own right. A continuing deficit endangers the gold reserves and threatens to force departure from the gold standard.

Whatever the authorities do under a fractional-reserve standard, their behavior is incompatible with a fully automatic gold standard. They cannot even pursue a meaningful "passive" policy, for if they neither promote nor prevent certain responses, they at least *permit* responses different from those that would have occurred under a 100 percent standard. "There is . . . a fundamental conflict between the principles of central banking and the principles of the gold standard." "A so-called managed gold standard is . . . not a gold standard at all. . . ."[9]

Further comparison of 100 percent and fractional standards

The distinctiveness of the 100 percent gold standard does stand up well, after all, despite questions of whether its supposed superiority over fractional reserves does not imply the still greater superiority of more than 100 percent reserves. It safely allows private parties alone to decide how far to finance temporary imbalances by building up or drawing down their cash reserves. Local money supplies go up or down in each time period only by the absolute amount of a voluntarily accepted temporary

7. J. E. Meade, *The Balance of Payments*, London: Oxford University Press, 1951, p. 185, presents the slower-adjustment argument for 100-percent reserves. Milton Friedman, *Essays in Positive Economics*, Chicago: University of Chicago Press, 1953, p. 186, questions the necessary superiority of slower adjustment and mentions the idea of 200 percent reserves.

8. An "offsetting" policy is not always and necessarily domestically stabilizing; it depends on what the initial disturbance to the balance of payments was. If it was an inflation originating at home, the resulting balance-of-payments deficit would exert deflationary influences as a partial counterweight. Offsetting these deflationary influences would actually mean perpetuating the original inflation.

9. The two quotations (though not the details of this analysis) are from John H. Williams, *Postwar Monetary Plans and Other Essays*, New York: Knopf, 1944, pp. 183–184; and Frank D. Graham, *Fundamentals of International Monetary Policy*, Essays in International Finance, No. 2, Princeton, N.J.: Princeton University, 1943, p. 12. Williams seems to mean only that passivity or "offsetting" is incompatible with gold-standard principles. Triffin shows that "reinforcement" in accordance with the traditional "rules of the game" is also a great departure from the mechanism of the pure gold standard; see his "National Central Banking and the International Economy" in Lloyd A. Metzler, Robert Triffin, and Gottfried Haberler, *International Monetary Policies*, Postwar Economic Studies, No. 7, Washington: Board of Governors of the Federal Reserve System, 1947, pp. 48–54.

surplus or deficit.[10] And since the world money supply remains constant, with transfers of money between residents of different countries having no basically different impact than transfers between residents of a single country, overall levels of demand do not change, so far as they depend on the quantity of money. The pattern of demand changes as tastes and technology change, of course, and so do relative prices. But even changes in *national* price levels and terms of trade are hardly more than statistical fabrications, less significant than changes in the relative prices paid and received by the particular groups affected by the underlying real changes. The relevant groupings are not mainly by nationality. Even the concept of each country's local money supply is unimportant. The absence of national fractional-reserve system avoids most of the difficulties blamed on the gold standard of historical experience, under which currencies were largely fiduciary and only imperfectly international.

But not even a 100 percent gold standard guarantees completely smooth adjustment to all economic changes. Because of various price inflexibilities and frictional resistances to sudden rearrangements of spending patterns, a sudden shift in demand is likely to impose transitional losses radiating beyond the persons first affected by the underlying changes in tastes or technology.[11] Even within countries, the existence of "depressed areas" illustrates the difficulties of reallocating resources promptly when patterns of demand alter. Perhaps little can be done about these frictions within countries. Internationally, however, any arrangements that could improve effective price flexibility and also preserve balance-of-payments equilibrium without shrinkage in national money supplies should score a point in comparison with even a 100 percent gold standard.

What scores decisively is practical considerations. The 100 percent standard can be nothing more than a theoretical extreme useful for understanding, by comparison, the characteristics of other systems. One difficulty is that its full logic would require all countries to adhere to it. If some countries were on 100 percent and others on fractional reserves, payments disequilibria and gold movements would affect the total world volume of money (gold plus fiduciary money pegged to it). No longer would adjustments take place against the background of an approximately stable average

world purchasing power of gold; instead, price levels must change. The burden of making these changes falls unevenly among countries, depending largely on their different gold reserve ratios. Furthermore, the need for larger and more pervasive price changes under mixed standards than under a universal pure gold standard gives more scope for wage and price inflexibilities to make adjustments inefficient and burdensome. In practice, not even a single country can maintain the 100 percent standard, let alone all countries together. Not only central banking but also commercial banking as we know it would have to be suppressed. All the obstacles familiar from discussions of the 100 percent reserve-banking proposal would have to be overcome. The authorities would have to be vigilant against strong private profit incentives to invent money substitutes and devices for "economizing" on money in ingenious new forms as soon as older forms had been suppressed. (Nevertheless, a few economists do argue that the benefits of a 100 percent standard would be worth the efforts necessary to attain and maintain it. Their arguments are summarized in Chapter 31.)

Types of gold and foreign-exchange standard

The gold standard of historical experience was a fractional-reserve standard. Various types are distinguishable. Under a *gold-coin standard*, all other kinds of money are convertible on demand into gold coin. The actual circulation of gold coins, together with at least short-run stability in the public's preferred ratio of gold coins to other types of money held, is supposed to provide a fairly stable and not too highly geared connection between a country's monetary gold stock and its total money supply. One advantage claimed for this system is that the threat of drains on their gold reserves will restrain the government and the central and commercial banks from following inflationary policies. They must take care not to alarm the man in the street, who, by demanding or not demanding redemption of his money in gold coin, can exercise control over financial policies.

Under a *gold-bullion standard*, the authorities stand ready to buy and sell uncoined gold at a fixed price, but only in large minimum amounts.[12] The absence of gold coins from circulation and the obstacle this poses to redemption and gold hoarding by the ordinary citizen permit "economies" in the use of gold, that is, a smaller and probably more flexible gold reserve ratio.

A *gold-exchange standard* permits still further "economies." The monetary authority of a country ties its currency to gold not directly but by dealing on the foreign-exchange market to maintain a substantially fixed exchange rate with some foreign currency that *is* on a gold-coin or gold-bullion standard. The authority holds its reserves as bank deposits and other liquid claims in the foreign currency. The opportunity to earn interest is one reason for holding reserves in this form rather than in actual gold. The gold reserves of the country on the actual gold standard—the so-called center country—do double duty: they "back up" its own currency directly and the currencies of one or more members of the system at one remove. The total money supplies of the member countries are pyramided onto a smaller and presumably more variable percentage of actual gold than would prevail if each held its own gold reserve. Still, the authorities of each country must pay attention to the relative sizes of their monetary liabilities and their foreign-exchange reserve so they can keep domestic money redeemable *de facto* in foreign exchange.

A *foreign-exchange standard* need not be a *gold*-exchange standard: the foreign money held as reserves and to which the home currency is pegged need not be a gold-standard currency, after all. One notable example was the system maintained by members of the Sterling Area during the 1930s, when the British pound was not linked to gold. As long as a country is anxious to keep its exchange rate fixed, maintain an adequate reserve of foreign exchange in relation to its domestic money supply, and allow gains and losses of foreign exchange to expand and contract the latter, it limits its monetary independence in the same general way as it would under an actual gold standard.

Intermediate positions are conceivable between being on a gold standard and being on an exchange standard. The national monetary authority might hold its reserves partly in gold and partly in foreign currencies tied to gold and deal on the foreign-exchange market to keep the exchange rate so close to par that private gold arbitrageurs would seldom if ever

find it worthwhile to operate. Even if the authority stood ready to buy and sell actual gold at a fixed price, it might seldom be called on to do so.

Except for major restrictions on the right of domestic private parties to demand interconvertibility at a fixed rate between the local currency and either gold or foreign exchange, many countries were on some such intermediate standard until around 1971. Practically all members of the International Monetary Fund defined their currency units in gold. To maintain its exchange parity, each country had to take care not to get too far out of step with monetary conditions and price levels in other countries; yet balance-of-payments surpluses and deficits were not allowed to have any tight automatic effect on domestic money supplies. That compromise system was often called a gold-exchange standard, though the little-used term *gold-par standard* seems more descriptive.[13]

There is no clear-cut line between being on

---

10. This paragraph, as well as almost the entire discussion of 100 percent versus partial-reserve gold standards, abstracts from new gold production, withdrawal of gold into nonmonetary uses, and secular economic growth.

11. For hypothetical examples, see Philip H. Wicksteed, *The Common Sense of Political Economy*, London: Macmillan, 1910, p. 643; or Wilhelm Röpke, *Die Lehre von der Wirtschaft*, 4th ed., Erlenbach-Zürich: Rentsch, 1946, pp. 94–96.

12. From 1934 until it was changed by the events of 1968–1971, the monetary system of the United States was sometimes called a "limited gold bullion standard." The Treasury would buy gold from anyone at $34.9125 per fine troy ounce and would sell it at 35.0875, but only to licensed industrial users and foreign monetary authorities. Private ownership and export of gold were severely restricted. The total money supply was not geared automatically to the gold stock. The system thus lacked the essential characteristics of a gold standard as it was understood earlier, except for the stability of exchange rates with other currencies—and even this stability commanded only limited confidence.

13. Cf. Henrik Akerlund, *Guldparistandarden*, Stockholm: Grafiska Konstanstalten Trykeri, 1959.

and being off a gold or exchange standard. International monetary linkage is a matter of degree, to be judged by how large or small and how variable the ratio is between a country's gold or foreign-exchange reserves and its domestic money supply and by how closely the money supply responds to the balance of payments. The linkage is largely window-dressing if fixed exchange rates are maintained by controls over imports and other expenditures abroad and if the money supply is insulated from balance-of-payments developments.

At the opposite extreme from the 100 percent gold standard stands complete national monetary independence. Each country's money then has its total supply determined solely by domestic considerations, is not pegged to or backed by or redeemable in gold or anything else, and has its rates of exchange against foreign currencies determined by the free play of private supply and demand. As later chapters will try to show, either extreme system may have a logic and coherence not found in any compromise arrangement.

Palliatives of disequilibrium

Before considering further how balance-of-payments disequilibriums are corrected under different monetary arrangements, we may mention some temporary *palliatives* of disequilibrium. Most of what is said about a deficit will apply in reverse to a surplus. Most obviously, the authorities can draw upon their external reserves to peg the exchange rate, but perhaps this is less a palliative of a deficit than a means of financing and therefore perpetuating it.

A more genuine palliative operates under an international gold standard of unquestioned permanence. As the foreign-exchange value of the home currency falls near the gold export point, people will realize that depreciation cannot go much further and that if the exchange rate moves at all it must bounce back from the limit. A practically risk-free opportunity prompts speculators to sell foreign exchange and buy the home currency. This "equilibrating" inflow of short-term capital covers the deficit and checks the drain on the gold reserves that would otherwise occur. Speculation is similarly equilibrating even under a nongold foreign-exchange standard when full confidence prevails that the authorities will maintain the pegged exchange rates within narrow predetermined limits.

Speculators respond quite differently when they suspect that the gold parity or the official support limits may collapse. If they see that only the drawing down of limited gold or foreign-exchange reserves is staving off the depreciation of the currency, they will want to get rid of it while it is still enjoying artificial support. An outflow of short-term private capital then compounds instead of palliates the deficit from ordinary transactions.

Palliative, or "equilibrating," speculation is not necessarily confined to a fully trusted gold or exchange standard; it may even occur under freely fluctuating exchange rates. A depreciation that is expected to prove only temporary will attract purchases of the currency—in other words, an inflow of short-term funds that helps cover a temporary deficit. Whether this or destabilizing speculation is more likely is an important question for later chapters.

A second genuine palliative involves short-term capital movements motivated by differences in interest rates at home and abroad. A deficit in the goods-and-services account itself suggests that people and institutions of a country are in the aggregate spending beyond their incomes; voluntary domestic saving has fallen short of intended investment. Unless the external deficit is associated with a continuing domestic cheap-money policy, interest rates are likely to rise as a result of an excess demand for loanable funds that would otherwise prevail. Higher interest rates not only keep some short-term funds invested in the country that would otherwise have moved abroad but perhaps even attract some funds from abroad. The authorities of the deficit country may strengthen this automatic palliation by actively promoting a rise in domestic interest rates. Short-term funds are presumably more likely to respond to interest rates in this helpful manner when exchange rates are fixed and trusted than when they are subject to change.

These palliatives can at best provide time for adjustments affecting trade and long-term capital movements; they can hardly stave off the need for adjustments indefinitely. Reserves cannot hold out forever. Speculators will not go on acquiring a weak currency if the causes of its weakness prove more than temporary. Short-term investors will not continue pouring funds into a deficit country in response to a mere interest-rate advantage if a persistent disequilibrium in other transactions threatens the value of its currency.

Balance-of-payments correctives

There are three ways in which a balance-of-payments disequilibrium can be cured "automatically," that is, without direct orders from some authority but rather through appropriate incentives to private economic units, concerned as they are with their own incomes and cash balances and expenditures.[14] To correct a deficit (and conversely for a surplus), each of these three involves a fall in the ratio of total home money income to total foreign money income. This ratio is not, of course, an indicator by which persons and firms govern their decisions and actions. Mentioning it is simply a device for organizing a comparison of the three mechanisms: (1) The ratio could conceivably fall without any decline in the physical volume of domestic production and employment; home money income could fall simply through cuts in the prices and wages at which goods and services were valued; (2) Home income and its ratio to foreign income could fall through a shrinkage in the physical volume of goods and services produced, with prices and wages unchanged; and (3) The ratio could fall through a change in the exchange rate used in making home and foreign money incomes comparable. Or the ratio could fall through changes partly in prices, partly in real income, and partly in exchange rates.

Which mechanism or combination of these three mechanisms operates depends on the monetary relations among the various countries. Under a gold standard or a foreign-exchange standard requiring governments to conduct their domestic monetary and fiscal policies so as to keep fixed exchange rates workable without direct controls over international trade and payments, the first and second mechanisms operate together. Their relative importance depends on how frictionlessly price and wage levels adjust up and down. If the countries have independent fiat moneys free to fluctuate against one another, the third mechanism operates. If exchange rates are not free to fluctuate and yet national monetary and fiscal policies do not operate enough in parallel to keep fixed rates workable without controls, the combination of mechanisms at work depends on the exact nature of monetary and fiscal and exchange-rate policies. If these policies prevent any of the three "automatic" mechanisms from operating, direct controls over international trade and payments appear necessary.

14. These three possibilities should perhaps be counted *in addition to* the cash-balance effect, which plays a role in all of them but may deserve mention as a separate corrective mechanism in its own right. The cash-balance effect is discussed in the early pages of this chapter and again in the next chapter.

CHAPTER FIVE

International Adjustment Under Fixed Exchange Rates

This chapter describes balance-of-payments adjustment when national monetary systems are closely linked, though linked less completely than under a 100 percent gold standard. (Adjustment under that standard is too simple to need further explanation.) Several sections of the chapter give attention to aspects of the adjustment process that dominate standard treatments of the topic.

The price-level mechanism

Though adjustments involving price levels and production-and-employment levels actually operate together, considering each separately at first will contribute to clarity. In explaining adjustment under the gold standard, economists until the 1930s traditionally emphasized a theory based on the price-specie-flow mechanism of Richard Cantillon and David Hume. Developments making for a deficit in Inland's balance of payments push its exchange rate to the gold export point. Outward gold shipments by arbitrageurs shrink the reserve base and in turn shrink the home money supply. Inland's general price and wage levels fall accordingly. Opposite developments take place in Outland, where a balance-of-payments surplus corresponds to Inland's deficit: gold flows in, the money supply expands, and prices and wages rise.

Since Outland is the entire rest of the world, these effects of trade with Inland will probably be diluted almost to imperceptibility over its entire vast economy. The important thing, however, is that Inland's price level falls and Outland's rises, each *relatively* to the other's. Now consider some Inlanders who have been hesitating between buying certain goods from their fellow Inlanders and importing similar goods from Outland. The relative cheapening of Inland goods will tip their decisions in favor of *not* importing. Similarly, Outlanders will have reason to buy the relatively cheapened Inland goods.

How sensitively these responses to price occur depends on how closely substitutable for each other Inland and Outland goods are in the minds of consumers in both countries and how readily factors of production in each country can shift from one line of production into another. These conditions of substitutability in consumption and production underlie the elasticities of import and export supply and demand. To understand why proper operation of the gold-flow and price-level mechanism depends on high enough elasticities, let us consider the most unfavorable case conceivable. Both demand elasticities are zero: Inlanders will buy a certain physical quantity of imports and Outlanders will buy a certain physical quantity of Inland's exports, no more and no less, regardless of price. Now, when the gold drain lowers the prices of Inland goods (and their prices go down in terms of both Inland and Outland money, since both moneys are tied to gold), Inlanders will receive a smaller total amount of money than before for their physically unchanged exports. Furthermore, Inland's total expenditure on its imports of Outland goods rises slightly, since the physical volume of trade remains unchanged and the expansion of Outland's money supply raises Outland prices slightly. The worsened balance-of-payments deficit results in bigger gold flows, greater price deflation in Inland and inflation in Outland, more of the perverse response that brings a still bigger disequilibrium, and so on in a vicious circle. And this perverse result could still occur even if export and import quantities did respond to price in the normal way to *some* extent, provided this response was very slight. This perversity could not last indefinitely, however: the limited sizes of their incomes and their concern not to let their cash balances fall dangerously low would ultimately *make* Inlanders behave with enough price-sensitivity to assure a normal corrective effect. The bothersome question under a fractional-reserve standard (but not under a 100 percent standard) is whether the monetary authority might not run out of gold reserves before Inlanders had finished drawing down their cash balances to the extent they individually saw fit.

Sufficient price-elasticity of demand makes the adjustment successful rather than perverse. Even though the price per unit of Inland's imports rises slightly because gold gains have increased Outland's money supply and prices, imports might fall enough in quantity to reduce their total money value. And even though the price per unit of Inland's exports falls, exports might rise enough in quantity to increase their total money value. One or both of these adjustments must occur. Just how much demand elasticity is "enough" is a complicated matter and will be considered in Chapter 8 in connection with the effectiveness of exchange-rate variation. There we shall see that the requirements for normal balance-of-payments adjustment are not very stringent and are almost certain to be satisfied in reality. The theory of unduly low elasticities is mentioned here only as a basis for emphasizing later on how similar the gold standard and variable exchange rates are in this respect: it is not the exchange-rate mechanism alone whose proper working depends on high enough demand elasticities.

The role of cash-balance management

Our example of what happens to countries' general price levels, while illuminating in a preliminary way, is crude. The relative shift in national price levels is not the only influence to motivate the appropriate shift in flows of trade: a more direct influence is the monetary developments to which the shift in price levels is itself a response. In the gold-losing deficit country, the cash balances of individuals and business firms shrink. They become and remain smaller than before not only in nominal money amount but also in terms of real purchasing power, at least until (and probably even after[1]) prices and wages have fully responded to the monetary deflation. Out of concern not to let their cash balances shrink too far, people in the deficit country become less eager than before to buy capital assets and consumption goods

alike. Decisions about buying and selling and managing cash balances interlock.[2] It is strange that this adjustment effect should have been so widely overlooked even in the traditional analysis relying on the quantity theory of money; for anything better than a purely mechanical version of the quantity theory must emphasize how the money supply interacts with demands for cash balances so as to affect people's market behavior and *thereby*—rather than in some direct magical way—affect prices. This "absorption"-depressing cash-balance effect is part of the answer to the skeptical question sometimes asked: How can mere changes in price levels correct a country's tendency, evidenced by its external deficit, to consume and invest in overall excess of its current production?

This effect need not be entirely lost even if a palliative inflow of short-term capital postpones a gold outflow. For Inland cash balances may go into the possession of speculators motivated by confidence that Inland's currency will rebound from the gold export point. Ordinary persons and businesses in Inland still see their own cash dwindling as they spend in excess of their incomes, and this gives them incentives to retrench on consumption and investment. The resulting decline in spending accompanies a decline in the money supply available to ordinary Inland residents or—which is the same

1. In the new position, with the price level reduced and balance-of-payments equilibrium restored in the former deficit country, individuals and businesses, from their own points of view, find their real incomes smaller than they were while the deficit was furnishing a net inflow of desired goods and services. The drawing down of the country's gold reserves in paying for this net inflow had represented a kind of subsidy to the incomes or absorption of individual economic units. Its discontinuance now represents a fall in real incomes from private points of view, tending to deter people from as much consumption and investment—and as much holding of real cash balances—as before. Later pages and chapters give further explanation.

2. For reasons why the analysis puts more emphasis on cash balances than on other portfolio assets, recall pp. 58–60 in the preceding chapter.

thing here—a decline in the average velocity of the entire Inland money supply held by all holders (since the balances acquired by speculators presumably have an unusually low velocity). This cash-balance effect probably imposes less correction of Inland's balance of payments than a gold outflow would, however, since the palliative inflow of short-term capital postpones or avoids the multiple contraction of currency and deposits that a drain of gold reserves would otherwise have imposed on a fractional-reserve monetary and banking system.

Adjustments in relative prices and in subsidization

Besides the cash-balance effect and movements of general price levels, shifts in *relative* prices also tend to restrain absorption in the deficit country. Our preliminary assumption that export prices fall and rise along with general price levels in the deficit and surplus countries is an oversimplification. The prices of each country's imports and exports—the very prices supposed to be decisive in adjusting flows of trade—tend to move by smaller percentages than countries' general price levels because they are determined by supplies and demands on the world market rather than by money supplies of individual countries. The monetary contraction in a gold-losing deficit country does not lower all prices in the same proportion. The relevant distinction is between international goods and services, which are imported and exported, and domestic goods and services, like houses and haircuts and labor, which do not typically move in international trade. Of course, the dividing line is fuzzy and shiftable: even local services can be "exported" by sale to visiting foreigners, and large enough spreads between foreign and domestic prices could motivate trade in goods ordinarily too bulky in relation to value. Still, the distinction is meaningful. As for the goods belonging most fully to the "international" category, their prices are determined largely by worldwide supply and demand and are not much affected by monetary contraction in the gold-losing deficit country. Monetary contraction there has its main impact, instead, on prices of domestic goods and factors of production.

Because domestic goods become relatively cheaper, Inlanders have reason to shift their buying away from imports and exportable goods onto domestic goods and to concentrate their production and sales efforts on the more favorable foreign market. Corresponding but opposite price shifts and incentives in Outland may slightly reinforce the balance-of-payments adjustment. These substitution effects are important and deserve attention far out of proportion to the space needed to state them.

Among the most "domestic" of a country's noninternational goods and services are labor, land, and other factors of production. Wage rates, land rents, and other factor prices fall as gold losses deflate the money supply of a deficit country,[3] while prices of international goods fall little if at all. This implies a fall in the real purchasing power of productive factors and in the real incomes of their owners. Their worsened situation joins with and perhaps even overshadows the cash-balance effect already mentioned in restraining overabsorption. Neither this change nor the response of individuals in reducing their consumption and investment necessarily means that overall production and employment drop. Nor is the change identical to a worsening of the terms of trade in the ordinary sense of the ratio of export to import prices.

The fall in the real value of individuals' incomes in the adjustment process may be traced to discontinuance of what had amounted to a subsidy. This subsidy is best explained with examples of the sort of disturbance that might have originally caused a deficit in Inland's balance of payments. Consider first a "real" (as distinguished from a monetary) disturbance: the world demand for Inland's exports declines because of changes in tastes or technology or in competition from other suppliers. (A depression in Outland would also count as a real disturbance from Inland's point of view; the unemployment and the drop in production make Outland a less effectively eager trading partner. This is true even though the depression in Outland stemmed from monetary causes there.) The consequent worsening of the terms of trade is much the same for Inland as a deterioration in technology: the process of converting Inland factors into Inland exports and then into imports from Outland now gives a reduced "yield." Inevitably, Inland's real national income has fallen. Yet this fact escapes being fully brought to bear on the decisions of individuals and businesses as long as corrective tendencies are somehow kept from working (in particular, as long as domestic factor prices do not fall relative to international-goods prices in the way just described) and as long as outward shipments of gold continue to pay for imports in excess of the value of exports. In effect, sale of gold from the reserves at a fixed price too low to equate private supply and demand subsidizes the incomes of and absorption by individuals and businesses. The fall in factor prices relative to international-goods prices, when it finally occurs as the domestic money supply shrinks, represents an offset to or a discontinuation of this subsidy. The country's worsened real economic position comes to bear on the decisions of individual economic units. The unchanged price of gold again becomes an equilibrium price. The overabsorption that constituted the external deficit is restrained and the gold shipments that had been associated with the income subsidy shrink or cease.

One related development also offsets the subsidy represented by gold outflows in the face of not-yet-adjusted price relations. This offset is the very process of reinforcing the monetary contraction imposed by gold losses under a fractional-reserve standard. In the process of getting more money out of circulation, credit becomes more expensive and less readily available, or a government budget surplus overcharges the public for government services. These policies impede absorption. They need not continue or be pushed further after they have ended the subsidy to absorption by raising the equilibrium value of the currency up to its pegged level.

Next consider a monetary (rather than real) disturbance to balance-of-payments equilibrium—monetary inflation in Inland. If the money supply expands through a government budget deficit, undercharging the public for government services subsidizes absorption. So does putting new money into circulation by making credit artificially cheap and abundant. The rise in the money supply also directly stimulates absorption. Since under fixed exchange rates the domestic monetary inflation has a lesser upward impact on the prices of goods and services supplied and demanded in world markets than on the prices of domestic goods and services, the real incomes of workers and other owners of factors of production rise. Although the real economic position of the country as a whole has not improved (except perhaps to a minor extent through improved terms of trade), the positions of individual economic units have improved because their incomes and absorption are being subsidized by

sale at a bargain price of gold from the official reserves.

Any correction of the resulting overabsorption and balance-of-payments deficit involves bringing to the attention of the decision-making economic units the fact that the country's real economic position has *not* improved. The disinflation imposed by gold losses reverses the subsidization of incomes and absorption just described. In particular, the lowering of the temporarily increased prices of domestic factors of production, relative to the prices of internationally traded goods, brings the real incomes of owners of productive factors back into correspondence with the real economic position of the country. (Insofar as factor prices are on a ratchet and will not fall again once they have risen, unemployment develops; and a fall in employment and in real income produced comes to the aid of balance-of-payments adjustment in the unpleasant manner still to be described.)

Real and monetary disturbances to the balance of payments require comparison. A failure of cash balances and the ratio of domestic factor prices to international-goods prices to go down in response to a real disturbance, together with the drain on gold reserves, subsidizes the *maintenance* of previous levels of absorption despite real economic deterioration from the national point of view.[4] When

---

3. If frictions keep factor prices from responding to monetary deflation, unemployment develops and real-income aspects of balance-of-payments adjustment come into play.

4. A long-term independently motivated capital outflow is an example of a real disturbance. It is true that this response to attractive investment opportunities abroad does not spell a worsening of the country's real economic position, but the quantity of of resources available for *current* absorption at home is reduced. This fact must be brought to bear on the decisions of individual economic units, and absorption must not be subsidized, if the country is to escape an overall balance-of-payments deficit. Independently motivated capital movements are the most typical examples in the literature of balance-of-payments disturbances; but here, adjustment to them is considered separately in the appendix to this chapter.

domestic monetary inflation expands cash balances and raises the ratio of domestic factor prices to international-goods prices, a failure of these changes to reverse themselves, together with gold outflows, subsidizes an increase in absorption, even though the country's real economic position has not improved. The actual mechanism of balance-of-payments adjustment —money-supply shrinkage and a fall of domestic factor prices relative to international-goods prices—remedies either of these failures.

The income mechanism

In the 1920s Professor Frank Taussig and some of his graduate students at Harvard studied examples of balance-of-payments adjustment under the gold standard before World War I. The process seemed to have worked surprisingly well—too well and too promptly for traditional theory to explain everything. Traditional theory, as usually presented, had emphasized gold flows and price-level shifts in the light of too mechanical a version of the quantity theory; it had not adequately shown the role of cash-balance or purchasing-power effects on consumption and investment. In reality, Taussig and his students sometimes found disturbances met without appreciable gold flows and price shifts.[5] Of course, to the very extent that trade did respond sensitively and promptly to even slight changes in cash balances and prices, no sizable disequilibrium would develop in the first place and no conspicuous gold flows and price shifts would be necessary. But this did not seem to be the full explanation. Some unknown equilibrating mechanism also must have been at work. But what? The application of modern income theory to international trade, following publication of Keynes's *General Theory of Employment, Interest and Money* in 1936, helped solve Taussig's puzzle.[6] Ironically, this neo-Keynesian theory of international adjustment is more relevant to the pre-1914 era of close international monetary linkage than to the era of independent national full-employment policies that has followed its own development. Still, the theory affords valuable if only partial insights, holds an important place in present-day literature, and is worth considering at length.

For a preliminary view of the income-adjustment mechanism, consider a disturbance to the trade of New England, whose monetary system is tied to that of the rest of the United States.

Whether competition from other sources has weakened the outside demand for New England goods or New Englanders themselves have switched some purchases from local to outside goods does not much affect the example: in either case, a slump in the demand for local goods causes a deficit in the region's balance of payments. Businessmen and workers who had been making these goods now find their profits and wages smaller than before. Production and employment decline. Those who first suffer drops in income now must cut back their spending on goods and services, causing a second "round" of New Englanders to lose sales and jobs, wages, and profits. As poverty spreads, New Englanders cut their purchases not only of each other's goods and services but also of imports from outside the region. This cut in imports in response to a fall in income reduces the deficit by partially matching or offsetting the initial export slump or import spurt.

An initial disturbance in the opposite direction causes an external surplus and touches off a chain reaction of rising production, employment, profits, and wages. (For real income to rise in this way, some labor and resources must have previously been idle, available to meet demands for increased output.) Prosperity spreads as New Englanders buy more than before of each other's goods and services. They also tend to buy more from outside the region, thus partially correcting the balance-of-payments surplus.

A *quick review of income theory for a closed economy*

To prepare for a closer look at how home income and foreign trade interact, we shall review in a simplified way the Keynesian theory of income determination in a closed economy. Persons earn income by selling labor and other productive factors. The demand for these factors depends on a flow of spending to buy the goods and services made from them. Incomes thus arise from spending and at the same time are the main source of people's spending. The two big categories of private spending are *consumption* and *investment*. (*Investment* means purchases not of stocks and bonds but of newly produced capital goods and inventories.) *Saving* is defined as the difference between income and consumption. Considering how much of their incomes people save is an indirect but convenient way to consider how much they consume. We can focus attention on the relation between saving and investment (rather than on the total of consumption plus investment). Saving is a "leakage" from the stream of spending and income; it may or may not be matched by an "injection" of investment spending.

Private saving and investment are not the only types of leakage and injection. We can conveniently regard government tax collections in excess of government spending as a leakage from the spending stream and thus as a kind of saving; government spending in excess of tax collections is an injection into the spending stream and in that sense is a kind of investment. (Government spending covered by taxes is neither leakage nor injection but a part of the main spending stream, a kind of government consumption on behalf of the taxpayers.) This simplifying dodge yields the following definitions, which will be understood in what follows:

Saving = amount of private after-tax income
   not spent on consumption
  + the government budget surplus
   (if any);

Investment = expenditure to build private
    capital goods, inventories, etc.,
   + the government budget deficit
    (if any)

Expenditure generates money income, but income may be less or more than fully respent. Saving is a gap between income and consumption that needs to be closed, as by investment in newly produced capital goods. Intended investment (also called *voluntary* or *planned* or *scheduled* investment) may either less or more than fully fill the gap of intended (voluntary, planned, or scheduled) saving, since different groups of people generally make investment and saving decisions. An excess of intended saving over intended investment depresses production and employment. An excess of investment over saving expands production and employment if idle resources provide scope for this expansion (and also inflates prices, especially if "full employment" has already been reached). When intended saving and intended investment are equal, money income is in equilibrium.

Given the existing level of prices and wages,

5. See F. W. Taussig, *International Trade*, New York: Macmillan, 1927, pp. 239–244, 260–262; and Harry D. White, *The French International Accounts 1880–1913*, Cambridge, Mass.: Harvard University Press, 1933, esp. chap. 1, which reviews several earlier studies. While not rejecting the classical mechanism of gold flows and sectional price adjustments, White was more inclined to stress that international transfers of purchasing power and consequent shifts in demand schedules could take place without large net shipments of gold. His purchasing-power-transfer and demand-shift effect seems loosely related to the cash-balance effect of the present chapter.

6. A recent commentator on the "smoothness of the transfer process under the gold standard that puzzled Taussig and his students" argues that variations in employment and real income of the sort envisaged in Keynesian theory could not have played an important role; these variations were not large, and their effects could have operated only with too much delay. Nor could price effects have accomplished the necessary variations in real absorption relative to real income at substantially full employment. The smooth adjustments historically experienced must have been due to the influence on total absorption of interest-rate changes (upward in deficit and downward in surplus countries). Saving and investment must be (or, in the days of the gold standard, must have been) sufficiently responsive to interest rates in the ways supposed by classical theory. (As for actual gold movements, they were supposedly kept small by equilibrating speculation based on confidence in the existing gold parities.) See Egon Sohmen, *Flexible Exchange Rates: Theory and Controversy*, Chicago: University of Chicago Press, 1961, pp. 35–38, 60–64.

Especially in the light of how casual the evidence offered is, Sohmen's emphasis on interest rates as the key element in the adjustment process seems strained indeed. The present text puts the emphasis, instead, on interrelations between cash balances and propensities to save or spend and on the role of prices and exchange rates in conveying to individual economic units right or wrong information about the sizes of real incomes out of which absorption may be undertaken. In this view, any effective adjustment process or policy works by correcting prices that initially convey incorrect information. The exposition in the text can hardly help reflecting the misunderstandings and lack of consensus that still prevail among economists.

some level of money income is just high enough but not too high to support full employment and full-capacity production. There is no automatic tendency, however, for saving and investment to be equal at just this right level of money income. Adjustments in interest rates, for instance, do not automatically keep saving and investment equal at the ideal level of income. (Even if interest rates did keep the amounts of loans supplied and demanded equal, this would not be the same as keeping saving and investment equal. Saving is not necessarily a supply of loans: for instance, savers may hoard some of their savings. Investment is not necessarily a demand to borrow savings; it may be financed, for instance, out of accumulated holdings of money or with newly created money.)

Although there is no automatic tendency for saving and investment to be kept equal at the level of national money income that is just right for full employment at the existing level of prices and wages,[7] there is *some* tendency for saving and investment to become equal. They are made equal not so much by changes in the level of interest rates as by changes in the level of income itself. The explanation hinges on Keynes's "fundamental psychological law": the marginal propensity to consume is less than 1. In plain English, consumption does not ordinarily change by the full amount of a change in income, i.e., people save more dollars out of a large income than out of a small income. If saving is greater than investment, income falls. In accordance with Keynes's "law," people reduce their saving. Eventually it no longer exceeds investment. Now suppose the reverse: Investment exceeds saving. Income rises. Eventually the rise of income to its equilibrium level raises saving to equality with investment.[8] The equilibrium level is not necessarily ideal. It may be too low to employ all willing workers and buy all potential output at prevailing wages and prices. On the other hand, it may be so high that reaching it involves price inflation.

In the elementary Keynesian theory reviewed here, investment, unlike consumption and saving, does not depend on income in any fairly definite way. Technological innovations, businessmen's expectations and moods, interest rates, and other influences affect it. Government deficit spending counts as what Sir Dennis Robertson called "honorary" investment. Suppose investment rises by $40 billion a year above its previous level, while the consumption-income relation is such that consumption changes by $\frac{2}{3}$ and saving by $\frac{1}{3}$ of any change in income. Saving will rise by $40 billion and thus match the increased investment only if income rises by 3 times as much, or by $120 billion.[9] Until income has risen to its new equilibrium level, an excess of investment over saving will keep driving it up. The change in investment thus has a multiple effect on income. Soon we shall extend this principle of the *multiplier* to cover the effects of changes in imports and exports.

Meanwhile, a more intuitive grasp of what the multiplier means will be helpful. Suppose that investment rises to a sustained level of $1000 per time period more than before; perhaps the government is deficit-spending on new defense programs. Suppose, also, that people in general save $\frac{1}{10}$ and consume $\frac{9}{10}$ of any increase in their incomes. Now, a first round of people—construction workers, owners of companies supplying construction materials or ordnance, etc.—have $1000 of extra income in all. These first-round people spend an extra $900 on consumption, providing extra income for a second round of people—grocers, tailors, etc. These second-round people spend an extra $810 on consumption, providing extra income for a third round of people, and so on. Each figure in the series of extra incomes is $\frac{9}{10}$ of the figure before it. Ultimately the total of extra incomes would be $10,000. (Carrying this arithmetic into a great many rounds will bring the total as close as one pleases to $10,000, without ever exceeding it.) Since an initial addition of $1000 to the rate of spending per time period ultimately gives rise to $10,000 of additional income, the multiplier is said to be 10.[10]

These examples show that the greater the respending on consumption and the smaller the leakage into saving at each round of income, the greater the ultimate effect of an initial increase in spending will be. The multiplier works in the downward direction, too. Suppose there is an initial drop in investment. To arrive at a new equilibrium, saving will have to fall by the same amount; and since changes in saving are only a fraction of any changes in income, income must fall by several times as much as the fall in saving and investment.

Our examples have supposed that investment (including government deficit spending) is what initially changes to touch off the multiplier process. Keynesian theory does often suppose that investment is the type of spending most subject to independent change, while consumption depends passively on income. However, if independent changes in consumption did occur—if the consumption-income relation changed in such a way that consumption would be $10 billion more or less than before, for instance, at any given level of income—then these changes would have multiplier effects of the sort already described.[11]

While it is true that an initial rise or fall in a particular type of spending will typically raise or lower income by more than its own amount,

---

7. This proviso is crucial to getting the analysis straight (as distinguished from deriving policy recommendations). It is now generally recognized that Keynesian underemployment equilibrium depends on downward rigidities in prices and wages. Without them, not even the famous "liquidity trap" could cause underemployment equilibrium.

8. The reader to whom this is not thoroughly familiar may benefit by constructing a numerical example. Prepare a table with columns headed Income, Consumption, Saving, Investment, and Consumption + Investment. (Leave space at the right for adding two more columns later.) In the Income column, write figures of 20, 50, 80, 110, and so on, standing for billions of dollars a year. To represent the Keynesian assumption that consumption depends on income in a fairly definite way and changes by less than the full amount of any change in income, write 50 for consumption out of income of 50 and make consumption larger or smaller by 20 for every increase or decrease of income by 30. Saving, being income minus consumption and thus changing by one-third as much as any change in income, is —10 at income of 20, 40 at income of 170, and so on. Assume that investment is given at 30 and write this figure in each position down the investment column. Finally, fill in the Consumption + Investment column. Observe that saving equals investment and consumption plus investment equals income only at the income level of 140. Discrepancies at any other level tend to drive income toward this equilibrium level.

9. To complete the example of the last footnote, add an Increased Investment column with figures of 70 all the way down. In a Consumption + Increased Investment column, add this 70 to whatever consumption still would be at each level of income. Note that saving equals increased investment and consumption + increased investment equals income only at income of 260. At any other level, discrepancies drive income toward this new equilibrium. The rise of income by 120 (from its old level of 140) is 3 times as large as the increase of investment by 40 (from its old level of 30).

10. This example assumes that the initial increase in spending is an increase in the *flow*: spending is a certain amount higher than before in *each* of the time periods to which the figures relate. As a result, the total increase in the flow of income equals the initial increase in the flow of spending multiplied by the Multiplier. On the other hand, if the initial increase in spending is a one-shot dose, not repeated in later time periods, income at first spurts up by the amount of this dose and then gradually drops back to the original level. In the meanwhile, income is larger than it otherwise would have been; and over time these dwindling increments to what income would otherwise have been add up to the initial shot of extra spending multiplied by the Multiplier. This standard Keynesian conclusion depends, incidentally, on slurring over what is happening to the quantity and circulation of money.

11. Recall that for the sake of simplicity we have been regarding tax-financed government spending as a kind of consumption, a government budget surplus as a kind of saving, and a government budget deficit as a kind of investment. From this one might think that an increase in government spending cannot raise income if it is financed entirely by increased tax collections and therefore produces no government deficit to count as a kind of Investment. But this conclusion would be wrong. The part of private incomes that the government taxes away and spends itself is *entirely* spent on what has been defined as a type of consumption, whereas the part of private incomes not taxed away is partly saved and only partly spent on consumption. Therefore, an increase in tax-financed government spending means an increase in the part of incomes that is *entirely* rather than only partly spent on consumption and so means an upward shift in the relation of total consumption to total income. The result is a rise in the equilibrium level of income. This effect could be illustrated by systematically raising the consumption figures and lowering the saving figures in the table referred to in footnotes 8 and 9. Conversely, a drop in government spending exactly matched by a drop in tax collections can lead to a lower equilibrium level of income, even though no government budget surplus appears. An extensive literature on the "balanced-budget multiplier" explores these effects in detail. The reasons why this principle does not necessarily provide an argument for ever larger government budgets (or against cutting the budget if the Russian menace ever somehow vanished) should be too obvious to dwell on.

the apparent precision of the multiplier analysis is deceptive. Gardner Ackley offers an analogy concerning the number of students in his national-income course. If the "marginal propensity of men to enroll" is ⅗—if, from one year to the next, the increase in men's enrollment is ⅗ of the increase in total enrollment—then the increase in total enrollment is 2½ times the increase in women's enrollment. The "sex multiplier" is 2½.[12] A less pretentious way of considering what multiplier analysis deals with is to recognize that an initial increase in spending either brings new money into circulation or speeds up the circulation of existing money and will ultimately raise total money income by perhaps several times its own amount. Money is continually spent and re-spent. Conversely, an initial decline in spending either takes money out of circulation or slows velocity down and will ultimately reduce total money income by perhaps several times its own amount, since the money would otherwise have kept getting spent and respent.

Income effects and international trade

Imports and exports now enter the picture. Spending on imports, like saving, is something "done with" income that does not, by itself, maintain the continued flow of spending and income at home. Spending on imports does provide a demand for goods and services and in turn for labor and other factors of production—but for *foreign*, not domestic, factors (at least not directly). Imports are indeed a leakage from the domestic income stream. Exports, like investment, are an injection: they represent spending on domestic goods and services and so are a source of income for domestic factors of production that does not proceed from domestic income. In what follows, then, leakages include imports as well as saving (including any government budget surplus), and injections include exports as well as investment (including any government budget deficit).

Suppose that Inland's income is in equilibrium: total injections equal total leakages. The balance of payments is also in equilibrium. Now an autonomous increase in exports disturbs this twofold equilibrium; that is, exports rise because of some change occurring independently of income-and-expenditure or other relationships built into the theoretical model. Perhaps Outlanders' tastes shift in favor of Inland goods; perhaps the Outland government cuts tariffs. Even a business boom in Outland would be an autonomous stimulus to exports from Inland's point of view. Anyway, the injections into Inland's home income stream now exceed the leakages from it. Income rises. Producers of exports do more spending out of their increased incomes, including more spending on domestic goods and

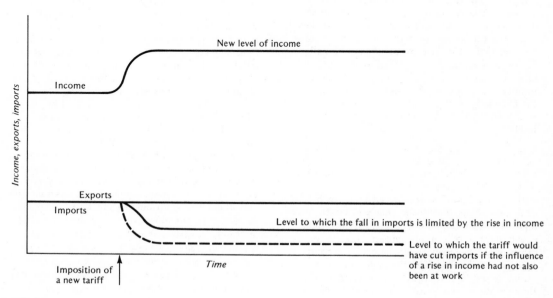

FIGURE 5.1

services, which provides more income for additional "rounds" of Inlanders. The export boom multiplies Inland income.

Inlanders can afford not only to spend more than before on domestic goods and services but also to do more importing and saving. These leakages rise until they reach the increased level of injections. Inland income rises by more than the amount of the new export injections because people spend much or most of all additional income on domestic goods and services; only part of any additional income goes for additional imports and saving. Suppose that an autonomous increase in exports provides $100 per time period of additional injections, which must be matched by additional leakage to restore income equilibrium; and suppose that people will use one-third of any additional income for additional saving plus importing. The necessary $100 of additional leakage is one-third of $300, which is therefore the amount by which income must increase to arrive at its new equilibrium level. An additional $100 of exports brings about 3 times as large a rise in income.

What happens if injections initially come to exceed leakages not because of an increase in exports but because of an autonomous cut in imports (perhaps due to Inland's imposition of a tariff)? Some spending that used to leak out of the home income stream to buy imports now goes toward home goods and services instead. Inlanders producing replacements for imports enjoy increased incomes; and they can afford to spend more for consumption, providing additional income for still further "rounds" of Inlanders. The initial excess of injections over leakages thus makes income rise. Since total leakages must rise until they again equal total injections and since probably only a fraction of additional income goes into leakages, the rise in income may be several times as large as the initial excess of injections over leakages. Again a foreign-trade multiplier is at work.[13]

The last example has a bothersome complication: the initial *cut* in imports generates a rise in income, which in turn generates a rise in leakages, including imports. Which really occurs—a cut or a rise in imports? The answer is that the autonomous cut in imports is partly offset by an income-induced *tendency* for imports to rise. The rise in income makes imports rise *relative to what they would have been* if the new tariff had been the only influence at work. Figure 5.1 shows a continuing surplus of the unchanged exports over the reduced imports, the effect of increased income on imports goes only part-way toward maintaining balance-of-payments equilibrium. This outcome is based on plausible assumptions. In particular, imports are not the only leakage: saving also rises with income. At the new equilibrium level of income, the injection represented by an excess of exports over imports is matched by a leakage in the form of an excess of domestic saving over domestic investment. Because changes in total leakage are made up only partly of changes in imports (changes in saving being another part), income effects considered alone (separate, for instance, from changes in cash balances and prices) are unlikely to do the full job of maintaining balance-of-payments equilibrium. This incompleteness of adjustment will have to be considered more fully later on.

The foreign trade multiplier can lower as well as raise domestic income. An autonomous fall in exports or rise in imports makes injections fall short of leakages. Income falls until it has dragged leakages down to the level of injections. Since only a fraction of income leaks into saving and imports, income will have to fall by more than the amount of the necessary fall in leakages.

Figure 5.2 illustrates all this. It shows Inland's investment, exports, saving, and imports (measured vertically) in relation to the level of home income (measured horizontally). The horizontal lines for investment and exports show the preliminary assumption that these two quantities are determined by influences outside the model and not by the level of home

12. Gardner Ackley, *Macroeconomic Theory*, New York: Macmillan, 1961, pp. 309–312.

13. The fact that a new tariff or other import controls may lead to a rise in home income is hardly an argument for these controls or hardly a refutation of the traditional analysis of protective tariffs. A rise in *money* income may represent mere price inflation rather than a rise in real production. But even if unemployment and underproduction had been prevailing, the question remains whether import restrictions are the best remedy. There are several reasons for doubt—in particular, the availability of more direct ways of providing enough effective demand for full employment.

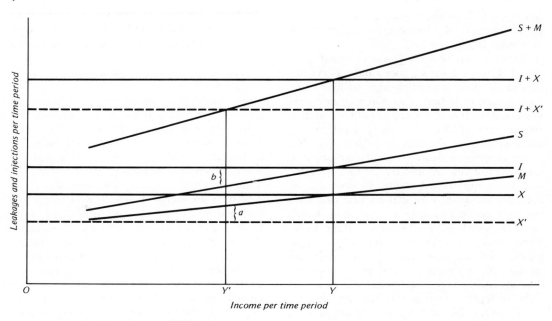

FIGURE 5.2. *An autonomous fall in exports*

income. The height of the $I + X$ line, representing total injections, is the combined height of the I and X lines. The lines for saving and imports slope upward from left to right in such a way as to show that of any increase in income, part—but only part—goes for additional saving and additional imports (and the rest, presumably the bulk, goes for additional consumption of domestic goods and services); similarly, when income drops, part but only part of the necessary cutbacks are in saving and imports (and the rest of the economizing is done on domestic consumption). The $S + M$ line is the vertical summation of the saving and import lines.

Originally, income is in equilibrium at the level OY, where the intersection of the $I + X$ and $S + M$ lines shows injections and leakages equal. The balance of payments is also in equilibrium, as shown by the intersection of the X and M lines. Now exports fall autonomously to the level shown by the dotted line X'. Correspondingly, there is a new and lower total-injection line $I + X'$. As long as the level of income has not yet fallen, total injections are now less than total leakages. This excess of leakages makes income fall to the level OY', where, as shown by movement down and leftward along the $S + M$ line, leakages are finally cut down to the reduced level of injections. The drop in income, YY', is larger than the autonomous drop in exports, illustrating the

multiplier. Imports do not fall fully as much as exports because only part of the reduction in leakage takes the form of a reduction in imports; the rest is a reduction in saving. The bracketed distance a shows the continuing though reduced excess of imports over exports. This excess of expenditure leakages from income over injections into income through international trade is matched by an excess of investment over saving at home, shown by the bracketed distance b. The country's trade deficit a equals its overabsorption b, this overabsorption being (as explained in Chapter 3) the excess of private and governmental consumption and investment over national income produced. Under the assumptions underlying the diagram, the fall in income and in turn of imports only partially corrects the initial disturbance to balance-of-payments equilibrium.[14]

The foreign repercussion

The developments just surveyed from Inland's point of view have counterparts in or repercussions on Outland, the rest of the world. May not these help bring trade completely back into balance, after all? The initial autonomous fall in Inland's exports may have been due to a change in tastes and may be an autonomous fall in imports from Outland's point of view. This fall in the schedule of leakage out of Outland income causes Outland income to rise, with the result that Outland's imports do not fall as much, after all, as the initial change would otherwise have dictated. From Inland's point of view, the decline in its exports is restrained (the export lines does not shift downward as much, after all, as Fig. 5.2 shows). This restraint on the decline in exports contributes, along with the already considered income-induced fall in Inland imports, to a more nearly complete balancing of trade.

A foreign repercussion may also be at work when the initial autonomous disturbance is internal to one country. Suppose that Inland develops an investment and income boom, causing a rise in imports and an external deficit. This implies a rise in Outland's exports and income and, in turn, in Outland's purchases from Inland. The repercussion tends to hold down the size of Inland's external deficit.

In neither of these examples, however, is the repercussion likely to be strong enough to restore complete balance. The reason is a positive marginal propensity to save in each country: in neither country will upsetting the initial equality between leakages and injections bring about such a change in income that the import leakage undergoes the entire change necessary to restore equality; the domestic saving leakage will make part of the response to the change in income. This may be understood by supposing the contrary for the sake of argument: in Outland, the domestic saving leakage is either zero or does not *change* at all with income; imports are the only leakage that responds. If, then, leakages fall below injections because of a downward shift in the relation of imports to income in Outland, as in the first example considered, equality can only be restored by a large enough rise in Outland income to *induce* a full recovery of the import leakage in accordance with the import-income relation. If injections exceed leakages because of a rise in exports to domestically booming Inland, as in the second example, then equality can only be restored by a large enough rise in Outland income to induce a matching rise in imports. A response in the saving leakage has been ruled out by hypothesis. But when we realistically allow saving to respond and to play a part in restoring equality between leakages and injections, we see that a rise in Outland income will not induce a change in imports fully large enough, by itself, to undo the autonomous fall in imports in the first example or to match the rise in exports in the second example. And since

balanced trade is not restored for Outland, it is not restored for Inland either.

One practical consideration (if it is not out

---

14. Since an external deficit is an excess of absorption over real income, it may seem odd at first thought that a *fall* in real income should contribute even partially toward shrinking the deficit. Why should absorption fall more than income? The reverse seems more plausible: faced with a drop in income, people typically retrench only in part on consumption (or on consumption plus real investment, if the latter is also recognized as variable) and make the rest of their adjustment, at least in the short run, by retrenching on their saving also (or even by dissaving).

A partial answer to the paradox is that the initial autonomous fall in exports imposes a drop in income to which absorption has not yet adjusted. People temporarily find themselves absorbing more in relation to income than they intend. Even if income fell no further, they would retrench. But this retrenchment imposes a still further fall in income, and so on and on as Multiplier theory describes. Since each successive drop in income has itself already been imposed by retrenchment in absorption, it does not exceed the latter; and there remains the deficit-shrinking effect of people's original efforts to pull absorption down into line with what they consider appropriate to their reduced income. The merely partial removal of the trade deficit reflects the fact that the marginal propensity to absorb is less than unity—that retrenchment impinges only partly on absorption and for the rest impinges on saving.

This whole point may be put briefly if less exactly: if absorption is in excess of income and if the two are geared together in a fairly definite way, then simultaneous declines in both can reduce the *absolute* excess of absorption. Income, absorption, and the difference between them all shrink to a smaller scale.

A further answer to the paradox, though not part of the income-effect theory being reviewed, is nevertheless realistic. As a continuing trade deficit shrinks the country's money supply, people try to conserve their dwindling cash balances and so absorb less goods and services than they otherwise would at each level of income.

While the paradox raised by the absorption approach can thus be answered, the income-adjustment mechanism does prove inefficient in requiring *both* absorption and real income to fall to shrink an excess of the one over the other.

of place amidst these abstractions) also argues against a complete balancing of trade through the foreign repercussion: foreign governments need not just sit back and allow the influence of trade with Inland to multiply home incomes up or down; domestic policy measures are available.

Induced investment

Induced investment, that is, the response of domestic investment to changes in income, provides a conceivable if not very realistic exception to the conclusion about incomplete balancing of trade. Let us consider both a model that does not and a model that does allow for induced investment. Both models start with trade and income in equilibrium, with total injections equalling total leakages:

$$I + X = S + M$$

Now exports increase autonomously. (Circled algebraic signs attached to the letters indicate autonomous changes; uncircled signs indicate income-induced changes.) Injections thus exceed leakages, and income accordingly rises:

$$I + X\oplus > S + M$$
$$Y\uparrow$$

At a new higher level of income, total injections are again matched by total leakages. But exports and imports may or may not be back in balance, depending on whether or not a rise in investment interacts with a rise in income.

Without induced investment

$I + X\oplus = S^+ + M^+$
Since $S^+ > I$,
$\quad X\oplus > M^+$

Thus there is a continuing (though reduced) export surplus.

With induced investment

$I^+ + X\oplus = S^+ + M^+$
Since I^+ *may* $\geqslant S^+$,
$\quad M^+$ *may* $\geqslant X\oplus$

Thus full correction or even overcorrection of the export surplus is possible. The actual outcome depends on how strongly investment responds to the export-initiated rise in income.

In an example of overcorrection, a country in deep depression somehow enjoys an autonomous increase in exports. The increased income and employment in export industries touch off an upward spiral of business recovery. With activity and confidence improved, businessmen step up their investment in buildings, machinery, inventories, and other capital goods. The return of prosperity leads people to buy not only more domestic goods and services but also more imports, and the rise in imports may conceivably outstrip the autonomous increase in exports that started the whole process off.

The key element in full adjustment or overadjustment is that investment responds to a change in income at least as strongly as saving. In our earlier examples, even those recognizing the foreign repercussion, what prevented complete external adjustment was a response of the domestic saving leakage in the same direction as income, investment being unaffected. But in our present example, the investment injection can respond as fully as the saving leakage, or more so; the marginal propensity to *save-net-of-investment,* so to speak, can be zero or negative. An economy with a negative *net* marginal propensity to save would be unstable in isolation from foreign trade: a random disturbance to income equilibrium would make total spending rise or fall cumulatively. It is farfetched to suppose given "propensities" to consume, invest, and save out of real income that could cause such behavior; instead, cumulative income changes presuppose propensities changing along with the quantity of money.

Money in the income-adjustment theory

Even less farfetched examples of the income-adjustment mechanism tacitly assume that the flow of money income and expenditure in a country can go up and down in passive response to influences arising from foreign trade. This implies a variable domestic money supply. In abstract logic, variations in velocity could conceivably accommodate wide variations in money income and expenditure, even with a constant money supply. To some slight extent, this accommodation is even plausible. When Inland is running an external deficit, foreigners may be willing to accept some of the net payments due them by acquiring balances in Inland currency and simply holding them for a while; or speculators may acquire balances in the belief that the weakness of the Inland currency (within the gold points) is only temporary. These foreign-held or speculator-held balances presumably have a lower velocity than balances held by typical Inlanders, and the average velocity of the Inland money supply falls somewhat.[15] When Inland develops a balance-of-payments surplus, conversely, the average velocity of money may rise as cash balances return from foreigners' or speculators' ownership into ordinary domestic use. Expectations may also influence velocity in the same direction. When developments in foreign trade are tending to depress income, Inlanders may become more cautious than before and desire larger cash balances relative to income and expenditure, just as the reverse may happen when trade developments are tending to raise income.

Yet these accommodations in demands for cash balances relative to income and spending are but fringe possibilities. Realistically, the multiplier theory must presuppose a variable money supply.[16] Under a gold standard or a system of pegged exchange rates, it is obvious, furthermore, how developments in foreign trade do change a country's domestic money supply in the same direction as income.

Once we recognize all this, we see what limited applicability the theorem about incomplete balance-of-payments adjustment has. As long as an initial export surplus persists, even though shrunken, acquisitions of gold or foreign exchange still are expanding the local money supply. (This is true unless the monetary and banking authorities pursue an "offsetting" policy. Ad hoc suppositions about policy or other autonomous developments can of course play havoc with the conclusions of any strand of theory.) Increased cash balances will promote more spending, on imports as well as on other things. As long as foreign transactions are out of equilibrium, home income cannot be in equilibrium either. Theories of incomplete external adjustment that assume fixed "propensities" to import, to consume domestic goods, and to save miss the point that such propensities simply cannot remain fixed indefinitely in the face of persistent change in the money supply. The cash-balance effect may be weak, but its existence and not its strength is the crucial point. (As a practical matter, of course, waiting for this effect to cure a deficit might be disastrous for the money and banking authorities, whose gold reserves might run out in the meanwhile.)

Income or multiplier theory was in a dilemma. Because changes in velocity could not fully account for the income changes it described, it had to recognize the money supply as variable. And once this was recognized, the notion of an external imbalance persisting even after income reached a new equilibrium level would have implied that velocity undergoes passive changes *opposite* to those dismissed as inadequate to support the theorized movement in income. For example, if a persistent export surplus were to keep adding to the money supply, yet income were to level off, velocity would have to keep falling; people would have to be demanding ever larger cash balances in relation to their incomes and expenditures. This is implausible.

The cash-balance effect not only rules out income equilibrium without balance-of-payments equilibrium but also suggests how adjustment to an export spurt may conceivably overshoot the mark and cause an import sur-

15. If the foreign creditors or the speculators acquire short-term securities in Inland instead of actual cash balances, they tend to make interest rates lower than they otherwise would have been. With the opportunity cost of holding cash balances correspondingly lower for foreigners and speculators and members of the domestic economy alike, desired cash balances relative to income and expenditure are likely to be larger—velocity is likely to be lower—than otherwise. (On the other hand, the overabsorption that the deficit represents would have tended to raise interest rates in the first place.)

The present discussion does not maintain that these effects are important. Rather, it illustrates what sort of theoretical straws one would have to grasp at to explain how income might vary as described by the foreign-trade-multiplier theory solely through accommodations in velocity rather than in the quantity of money.

16. For emphasis on the importance of explicit attention to the quantity and velocity of money in income theory, see J. J. Polak, "Monetary Analysis of Income Formation and Payments Problems," IMF *Staff Papers*, VI, November 1957, pp. 1–50; J. J. Polak and Lorette Boissonneault, "Monetary Analysis of Income and Imports and Its Statistical Application," IMF *Staff Papers*, VII, April 1960, pp. 349–415, and J. Marcus Fleming, "Money Supply and Imports," IMF *Staff Papers*, VIII, May 1961, pp. 227–240.

plus. This is most easily conceivable if the money and banking system practices "reinforcement," engaging in multiple expansion on the basis of increased gold or exchange reserves, if income responds fully to monetary expansion and imports respond fully to income growth only with substantial lags, and if the development making for the original export spurt was temporary in the first place. In this way, a favorable development could conceivably lead to a balance-of-payments crisis later on.

Export responses and combined adjustment effects

In reviewing foreign-trade-multiplier theory, we have so far considered only how imports respond to changes in home income, how exports respond to changes in *foreign* income, and how exports and imports *affect* home income. We have said nothing about how exports respond to home income. Yet at an increased level of income, the home population is likely to bid more vigorously not only for imports but also for exportable goods and for domestic goods producible by diverting labor and resources away from export production. This response contributes to increasing any import surplus due to a domestic boom or to reducing any export surplus originating in the foreign-trade sector.

These export responses have received relatively little attention in the abstract application of income theory to international trade. The reason is apparently related to neglecting or assuming away price and wage changes, so that changes in money income correspond entirely to real changes in production and employment. Nowhere in the range of variation considered does real income come close enough to the maximum level set by limitations of resources and technology for additional spending to push up wages and prices; nowhere in the range considered does real income fall from close enough to this full-employment limit to worsen unemployment so significantly in comparison with what it already was that the additional downward pressure on wages and prices at last breaks their rigidity. All changes in income and employment must be tacitly supposed to leave *changes* in the pool of idle resources small in relation to the great unemployment existing even at both extremes of the range of variation considered. If this is so, a rise in home income

and expenditure does not withhold any exportable goods from the foreign market or any resources from export production because plenty of idle resources still remain available to meet both domestic and foreign demands. A fall in income and expenditure does not divert any home-consumed exportables to the foreign market or any resources into export production because only the state of foreign demand, not resource limitations, had been keeping exports no greater than they were. The possibility of a price decline that might stimulate foreign purchases is ignored or assumed away. At a certain level of theoretical abstraction, such simplifications may be defensible.

In actuality, changes in money income consist partly of changes in real production and employment and partly of changes in prices and wages. Export responses then do play a role both in intensifying an external disequilibrium due to domestic disturbances and in correcting an external disequilibrium due . to external disturbances. A boom of domestic origin tends not only to raise imports but also to shrink exports. (Conceivably, of course, exports could rise in money value while shrinking in quantity; foreign demand might be inelastic. In the real world of less-than-perfect competition, though, changes in the tightness of nonprice terms of sale as well as in price can affect the quantities and values of goods sold.) A domestic slump, conversely, tends on the export and import sides alike to cause a balance-of-payments surplus. (These remarks refer, of course, to cyclical variations in the degree of utilization of a given total of resources. Secular growth in resources and total output may well tend to expand exports.)

If a rise in foreign demand for Inland exports raises home income, Inland demand strengthens not only for imports but also for exportable goods and for domestic goods using factors otherwise available for export production. Higher prices or reduced availability, or both, tend to keep exports from increasing in full and unhampered response to the initial rise in foreign demand. (This restraint on export growth accompanies the promotion of imports resulting from a rise in Inland's domestic prices relative to import prices as well as from the rise in income.) Foreign demand may also be discouraged and restrained by a lengthening of export delivery dates.

For another example, suppose that Inland demand shifts autonomously from home to imported goods. The resulting fall in income tends not only to restrain the initial rise in import demand but also to cut down home purchase of exportable goods and of domestic goods made with factors capable of shifting into export production. Foreigners take additional exports in response to Inland's more eager sales efforts (which may include faster deliveries).

The combined operation of cash-balance, real-income, price, delivery-time, and sales-effort effects, fully effective though it may be in maintaining or restoring balance-of-payments equilibrium if policy does not thwart or counteract some of its aspects, still gives only slight grounds for satisfaction. The variation of real income as one corrective for external disturbances represents a *departure* from a theoretically ideal system frictionlessly maintaining equilibrium on all goods and factor markets through prompt price and wage adjustments.[17] Regrettable though the fact may be, real-income variations do play an important part in adjustment under conditions of international monetary linkage.

So far we have considered only the relations between income and trade in goods and services. Taking capital movements into account, routine originality can spin out a variety of plausible and weird cases concerning the overall balance of payments. Capital may move not only in response to interest rates but also in response to anticipated business profits and stock-market trends. Conceivably, a domestic business boom might cause an overall balance-of-payments surplus by attracting a capital inflow larger than the deficit in goods-and-services trade. Conversely, a domestic deflation engineered to cure a trade deficit might so worsen profit prospects that capital outflows would widen the overall payments deficit.

Interregional adjustments

Real-income, cash-balance, and price effects work together to keep transactions in balance among regions of a single country. Regional balance-of-payments crises rarely develop, regional balances of payments are seldom even mentioned, and marked differences in price-level and income-level changes from region to region are seldom conspicuous in the short run; all this testifies to how smoothly palliatives and adjustments can occur under monetary unification. The lesser degree of protectionist interference with interregional than with international

tional trade, as well as the smaller burden of transportation costs, leaves interregional trade especially responsive to price differentials. Equilibrating shifts in relative price and income levels are ordinarily hardly noticeable. Moreover, when the money and capital markets are active and nationally integrated and when liquid and nationally marketable securities are widely held, compensatory flows of short-term capital are likely to cushion the impact of temporary balance-of-payments disturbances and make multiple contractions and expansions of regional money supplies unnecessary. (Compensatory capital flows come especially close to being automatic where all banking is conducted by a few large banks with branch offices throughout the country; close correspondent relationships among unit banks can provide an approximation to this financial integration.) Suppose, for example, that newly recognized opportunities cause an investment boom in one state. Local incomes rise and so do purchases from other states. Balance-of-payments difficulties are avoided, however, when the local banks sell some of their U.S. government securities and other short-term assets in the national money market in order both to finance the local investment spending and to meet the drain on their reserves and avoid a multiple contraction of their credit and deposits. Furthermore, the original improvement in local investment opportunities may well attract long-term capital from other parts of the country. Or suppose that the outside demand drops for the products of a particular state. Money and bank reserves tend to leave the state in payment for its excess imports, but again, banks will cushion the impact by selling some of their security holdings on the national market. Borrowing externally through the

---

17. This is not quite the same thing as denying that external disturbances would affect real income at all in a theoretically perfect system. Changes in supplies and demands in international trade and thus in the terms of trade would still affect the quantity of goods obtainable for domestic use from a full-employment level of production. What *would* ideally be absent is waste through unemployment, as well as changes in its extent.

intermediary of the district Federal Reserve Bank or in the Federal funds market is another possibility, as is a deliberate transfer of U.S. Treasury deposits into the deficit region to lessen the strain on banks there. The Federal tax and expenditure system may operate helpfully, and even spontaneously through its elements of "built-in flexibility," by transferring funds into deficit regions.

In the face of persistent disequilibrium in interregional trade, such palliation of deficits could not continue indefinitely: sooner or later the banks would run out of salable assets; and sooner or later the adjustment mechanism working through money supplies, incomes, and prices would have to be allowed its full effect. But the palliation may suffice to keep the adjustment from being sharp and conspicuous.

Some effects connected with export of securities from a deficit region go beyond palliating disequilibrium and contribute to restoring equilibrium by tending to restrain absorption. Selling securities at any cut in their prices represents a rise in interest rates. Closely connected with this is the tendency of interest rates to be bid up in the deficit region because of the excess of investment over saving that the deficit amounts to. If increased interest rates do anything to promote saving or restrict investment, the effect is in the direction of reequilibrating the balance of payments. Furthermore, selling securities represents running down the total of financial assets held in the deficit region. Just as people are unwilling to run down their cash balances without limit, so are they unwilling to run down their other financial assets without limit; the decline in security holdings, like a decline in cash balances, helps restrain absorption. (Even financial assets not actually sold have their total money value reduced to some extent by any decline in their prices.) Furthermore, flexibility of security prices contrasts with the official pegging of the gold or foreign-exchange value of a country's money under a fractional-reserve system. Securities contrast with money, then, in that no official price-propping constitutes a subsidy making real wealth or income seem larger from the viewpoint of individual economic units than it actually is from the community's point of view. The larger security holdings are relative to money supply and income, the smaller is the relative scope for pegging the external value of money to falsify price signals and partially shelter individual economic units from full awareness of aggregate economic circumstances.

Within a country, no regional currencies exist to be pegged together. Regional monetary authorities, which conceivably would try to neutralize regional money-supply changes and thus interfere with the trade-balancing cash-balance effect, do not exist. No scope exists for regional policy-makers to give different weights to the goals of full employment and price-level stability. Interregional competition, interregional mobility of goods, labor, capital, and enterprise, and perhaps also the activities of nationwide unions prevent large price and cost disparities among regions from developing in the first place.

The just-mentioned factor mobility provides a final reason why payments disequilibria and their correction are generally inconspicuous within the United States. Differences in legal systems, traditions, and language impede interregional mobility much less than international mobility. When demand shifts away from the traditional products of a region, conspicuous deflation need not occur there. Some of the inhabitants will move to work elsewhere, while others will find jobs in industries attracted by idle facilities and manpower or perhaps aided by favoritism in the award of Federal government contracts.

But interregional adjustments do not always work inconspicuously and smoothly. Several decades ago, before the establishment of the Federal Reserve System and especially before banks held large quantities of government securities readily salable throughout the country, interregional payments problems *were* noticeable in the United States. Bank credit creation in frontier regions caused local money incomes, prices, and imports from the rest of the country all to rise. Readjustment sometimes occurred harshly through serious strains on bank reserves for which no ready palliative was available.[18] Even today difficulties in adjustment (in which minimum-wage laws may perhaps play a part) are sometimes evident in localized depressions in regions that have suffered a drop in the national demand for their products. (This matter of "depressed areas" will come up again in a comparison of the exchange-rate adjustment mechanism with the combined price-and-income mechanism.) Even the more typical interregional synchronization of business conditions raises some questions about the convenience of the price-

and-income mechanism, as well as providing evidence of the mechanism at work.

International transmission of business fluctuations

Examples already considered have illustrated a double relation between domestic business conditions and foreign trade. Domestic prosperity or depression and external surplus or deficit do not go together in any simple way; the relation depends on how the causation runs. On the one hand, the *adjustment* process operates: autonomous developments causing an export (or import) surplus tend to raise (or lower) home income and so to affect imports in such a way as to reduce the imbalance in trade. On the other hand, a *transmission* process operates; impulses of depression or inflation originating within a country cause an external surplus or deficit and communicate themselves abroad. (Exceptional responses—such as might occur if a country's imports were on the whole "inferior goods"—are hardly worth detailed attention.) This transmission process now deserves a bit more attention. First, contagion

occurs as described by multiplier theory. Depression cuts a country's imports, which are other countries' exports. Their export slump depresses business in the other countries. Conversely, a country undergoing inflation stimulates expenditure in other countries by increasing its imports from them. Countries thus confronted with an export slump or export boom also find their gold or exchange reserves and their money supplies shrinking or expanding in consequence; money-supply changes accommodate the income changes described by the multiplier theory. Deliberate domestic policy may conceivably offset these contractionary or expansionary tendencies transmitted through international trade, though, under fixed exchange rates, at the cost of perpetuating external disequilibrium and, for a deficit country, of risking a crisis. But the *spontaneous* process is clearly one of international contagion.

A study by Oskar Morgenstern documents the international connection of business conditions under the gold standard. His findings, summarized in Table 5.1, indicate that the four countries considered were all undergoing general business expansions or contractions together more often than not. (Yet if months of expansion and months of contraction had been equally likely and if there had been nothing more than a chance association between business conditions in different countries, then one would have expected four countries all to share the same trend of business only one-eighth of the time.) The table shows, furthermore, that the international conformity of business trends was greater before World War I, when the

TABLE 5.1. *Percentages of months in which the indicated countries were undergoing general business expansions or contractions together*

	Prewar (Sept. 1879– Aug. 1914: 419 months)	Postwar (June 1919– July 1932: 157 months)
Great Britain and France	86.2%	68.8%
Great Britain and Germany	90.2%	60.5%
France and Germany	89.7%	61.1%
All three European countries	83.1%	45.2%
All three European countries and the United States	53.5%	35.6%

SOURCE: Reprinted from Oskar Morgenstern, *International Financial Transactions and Business Cycles*, Princeton, N.J.: Princeton University Press, 1959, pp. 45, 49. By permission of Princeton University Press. Copyright 1959.

18. On this historical point as well as on the cushioning by interregional transactions in securities and flows of short-term capital, see James C. Ingram, "State and Regional Payments Mechanisms," *Quarterly Journal of Economics*, LXXIII, November 1959, esp. pp. 626–629. In this article, in his *Regional Payments Mechanisms: The Case of Puerto Rico*, Chapel Hill: University of North Carolina Press, 1962, and in his proposals for international monetary reform (reviewed in a later chapter), Ingram has made important contributions to adjustment theory; the foregoing discussion has drawn heavily on them.

international gold standard was flourishing, than after the war, when the gold standard was restored only in a modified form and for only part of the period considered. As Morgenstern himself says with particular reference to Great Britain, France, and Germany before World War I, the parallelism maintained during both shorter and longer business cycles supports the thesis of not merely a covariation of independent factors but of a "transmission and an interlocking of the cycles."[19]

Economic interdependence under the gold standard is illustrated not only in general business activity but also in interest rates. During the period 1880–1913, and especially the last 20 years of this period, the heyday of the international gold standard, the central-bank discount rates of virtually all of twelve major countries tended to rise and fall together, at least in their larger movements.[20] This parallelism seems mainly due to the inverse correlation of discount rates and central-bank reserve ratios and, in turn, to both the inverse correlation of these ratios with levels of economic activity and to the international parallelism of business fluctuations. In addition, the parallelism of discount rates may have been partly due to "defensive" changes: when one or more important central banks raised their rates, others may have done the same to guard against outflows of short-term funds and gold; and when some lowered their rates, others may have felt safe in following suit. (A more detailed discussion of the international effects of discount rates appears in a historical context in Chapter 15.)

Conclusion

A brief closing comment can only mention, not meaningfully summarize, the main theme of this chapter. When the monetary systems of different countries are closely linked together through fixed exchange rates, balance-of-payments disturbances tend to be met by movements in money supplies, price levels, the relative prices of domestic and international-trade goods, incomes, and interest rates. The more completely rigidities keep changes in money incomes from taking the form of changes merely in money prices and wages, the larger must changes in real incomes and employment be. The same factors that operate in the balance-of-payments adjustment process under fixed exchange rates also operate in the international transmission of business fluctuations.

19. Oskar Morgenstern, *International Financial Transactions and Business Cycles*, Princeton, N. J.: Princeton University Press for the National Bureau of Economic Research, 1959, p. 52.

It seems plausible, incidentally, that Morgenstern's method of counting the months in which different countries shared the same business trend is more likely to understate than overstate the international conformity of business fluctuations. Lags in this conformity presumably characterize a genuine causal process; yet these lags would introduce a rather spurious element of nonconformity into the counting of months. For brief remarks on differences in phase of business cycles in the late nineteenth century and on what Clark Warburton called a seesaw movement between the United States and Great Britain, see Milton Friedman and Anna Jacobson Schwartz, *A Monetary History of the United States, 1867–1960*, Princeton, N.J.: Princeton University Press for the NBER, 1963, p. 98.

20. The discount rates are charted and their parallelism noted in Arthur I. Bloomfield, *Monetary Policy Under the International Gold Standard: 1880–1914*, New York: Federal Reserve Bank of New York, 1959, pp. 35–38.

Appendix to Chapter 5:
The Adjustment of Trade to Capital Movements

Independently motivated capital movements

An independently motivated capital movement has been the traditional theoretical example of balance-of-payments disturbance. For some reason not directly connected with trade in goods and services, Inlanders want to invest funds in Outland: higher interest rates or better profit prospects there, changes in taxation or other government policies in one country or the other, or a rise in saving, of which part seeks placement abroad. Perhaps Outlanders take the initiative, seizing favorable opportunities to float new securities on the Inland market. Or perhaps Inland has lost a war and must pay cash reparations.

Starting with international transactions in balance, the capital movement now means overall disequilibrium in independently motivated transactions. Restoring equilibrium involves cutting the capital-exporting country's goods-and-services imports or expanding its exports, or both, and conversely for the capital-importing country. How can trade so adjust? The answer is trivial if the capital movement occurs by way of a loan "tied" to use of the proceeds in the lending country or by way of credit granted by commodity exporters. The question arises most clearly if the Outland borrowers want to spend the proceeds mostly in their own country rather than especially on Inland goods. All parties, by assumption, are interested only in the transfer of *money* capital and do not know or care about the necessary adjustments in trade. Yet if the loan is to make more resources available in the borrowing country and fewer in the lending country, a "real" counterpart to the merely financial operation must somehow occur.

It makes no important difference whether the bonds are denominated in the currency of the lending or of the borrowing country and whether it is the Outland borrowers or the Inland lenders who must take the initiative in exchanging one currency for the other on the foreign-exchange market. Either way, holdings of domestic money by the ordinary public (the public excluding banks and other dealers or speculators in foreign exchange) initially go down in Inland and up in Outland. The banks or other foreign-exchange dealers, for their part, initially increase their assets (or reduce their liabilities) in lending-country currency and reduce their assets (or increase their liabilities) in borrowing-country currency. If the banks and other dealers are willing simply to accept these changes for a while, without trying to reverse them in the wholesale foreign-exchange market, they are making possible a transfer of cash balances and purchasing power from the lenders to the borrowers. This transfer is still possible even though the banks and dealers do reverse the initial changes in their positions, provided that speculators, in their stead, are willing to increase their balances of Inland currency and reduce their balances of Outland currency.[1] If speculators did so (or, for that matter, if the banks and dealers speculatively refrained from reversing the initial changes in their currency positions), their motive would be confidence that the market weakness of Inland and strength of Outland

---

1. Whether done by banks and other dealers or by speculators, this amounts to a transfer of short-term capital from the long-term borrowing country to the long-term lending country. In this way a temporary offsetting of the main capital flow helps accomplish the transfer of cash balances and purchasing power between the ordinary publics of the two countries that in turn helps translate the main financial operation into a net flow of real goods and services from the lending to the borrowing country.

currency would prove only temporary and that the exchange rate would bounce back from Inland's gold export point. (Even under flexible exchange rates, in fact, accommodating speculation is conceivable.)

Perhaps, however, neither banks and other lenders nor outright speculators will accept these accommodating changes in their currency positions. Gold will then flow, or the foreign reserves of Inland's exchange-pegging authority will be drawn down. Repercussions on money supplies and price and income levels will then promote the adjustment of trade.

Incomplete adjustment by purchasing-power transfer

Before returning to these other aspects of adjustment, we should look more closely at the transfer of purchasing power. It is true that if the Outland borrowers had not borrowed abroad, they might have borrowed at home, but then other Outlanders would have had less purchasing power at their disposal than in the absence of the international loan. Slightly lower interest rates and easier credit rationing than in its absence may help to bring the more abundant purchasing power to the attention of Outlanders generally. If this goes to buy Inland goods and services, the international real transfer occurs without further ado. To the extent that the borrowers spend the proceeds of the loan at home instead, they are passing on the additional purchasing power to their fellow Outlanders, some of whom may increase their imports. Inland lenders, to be able to grant the foreign loan, may cut down their buying of both home and Outland goods. More probably, they reduce or eliminate loans that they would otherwise have made at home; would-be borrowers, and their fellow Inlanders from whom they would have bought goods and services, now have less purchasing power than otherwise at their disposal and so buy less of both home and Outland goods.

For several reasons, however, a complete international transfer is unlikely to take place in this way alone. First, Inlanders and Outlanders will probably not reduce and increase their respective total spending—at least not "on the first round"—by the full amount of the loan; changes in domestic leakage will account for the difference. Second, changes in total spending will probably impinge only fractionally on purchases abroad rather than at home. For example, if total expenditure in each country goes down or up by only 80 percent of the purchasing power transferred or received and if expenditures on foreign goods and services change by only 30 percent of the change in total expenditure, then external expenditure goes down by only $.80 \times .30 = 24$ percent of the loan in the lending country and goes up by only the same percentage in the borrowing country. The balance of trade in goods and services moves "in favor" of the lending country by only $24 + 24 = 48$ percent of the amount of the loan.[2]

But this "first round" is not the whole story. The cut in domestic spending on output in the lending country has not been fully matched by a rise in export sales, and the rise in domestic spending on output in the borrowing country has not been fully offset by a fall in export sales. Total sales and hence total incomes fall in Inland and rise in Outland. Changes in income affect further "rounds" of spending, and contraction and expansion may proceed in the respective countries as multiplier theory describes. Will not incomes continue to change until Inland has reduced its imports and Outland has increased its imports enough fully to accomplish the real transfer of the loan? If behavior of the money supply and the velocity of circulation permit and if policy does not interfere—and these are important provisos— further rounds of adjustment may indeed result in a more nearly complete real transfer than the first round alone suggests (depending on just how people allocate their incomes or purchasing power among imports, domestic spending, and saving).

Even so, a complete tranfer is unlikely. Total leakages out of the stream of spending on each country's products will have responded enough to the change in income to stop any further change in income before trade has fully adjusted to the loan. A fall in saving will help check the fall in Inland income and a rise in saving will help check the rise in Outland income before incomes have changed enough fully to adjust the two countries' imports. This result is comparable to the already explained incomplete adjustment to other balance-of-payments disturbances by way of income effects alone, strictly conceived.[3]

Other elements of the adjustment process

An analysis of narrow purchasing-power-transfer and income effects is incomplete and oversimplified, especially if it assumes definite parameters regarding saving and domestic and import spending. Actually, for example, the lenders or their fellow countrymen might not reduce their own spending; if the foreign loan opportunity had not been available, they might simply have hoarded the money, perhaps because a depression was discouraging home consumption and investment. What happens to the velocity as well as quantity of money is an important question. Another is whether the monetary-fiscal authorities of the two countries resist any cumulative inflationary or deflationary processes for the sake of domestic stability or promote them for the sake of fixed exchange rates or gold parities.

Under a fractional-reserve gold or foreign-exchange standard, magnified money-supply and price-level developments go beyond the purchasing-power-transfer effects mentioned so far and make a distinct contribution to the otherwise incomplete adjustment of trade to the loan, much the same as in our earlier examples of autonomous disturbances in goods-and-services trade. The shrinkage of cash balances and the decline in the prices of domestic factors of production relative to the prices of internationally traded goods make people in the lending country see that fewer real resources are currently available than would have been available in the absence of the loan. They see that they must cut their absorption of goods and services accordingly. Opposite developments promote absorption in the borrowing country. Corresponding supplements to adjustment by purchasing-power transfer under flexible exchange rates are a matter still to be considered.

Intergovernmental transfers

Unrequited intergovernmental transfers, such as postwar reparations, introduce no new principle. Yet they deserve special notice because of the famous Keynes-Ohlin controversy of the late 1920s[4] and because of the distinction it introduced between the budgetary and transfer problems. In meeting the Allies' demand for

reparations payments, the German government faced the budgetary problem of levying taxes or otherwise raising the necessary amounts of home money. The transfer problem concerned possible difficulties in achieving the German export surplus necessary to provide the required foreign exchange. Keynes did mention how the purchasing-power transfer itself tended to promote German exports, but he assigned it a minor role and focused attention on the price changes disadvantageous to Germany that would be needed to produce a large enough export surplus. The *real* disposable incomes of Germans would thus be lowered not merely by the taxes levied to pay reparations (the budgetary burden) but also by the price changes (the transfer burden). Furthermore, Keynes thought, even this change in relative prices might not achieve the necessary German export surplus. Perhaps physical limitations would prevent any great expansion of German exports. Or perhaps foreign demand for them might prove inelastic, so that price cuts would

2. But a full (or more than full) "real" transfer is conceivable. If the marginal fractions of purchasing power spent and of expenditure devoted to imports were $9/10$ and $5/9$ respectively in each country, the balance of trade in goods and services would move in favor of the lending country "on the first round" by $9/10 \times 5/9 + 9/10 \times 5/9 = 100$ percent of the loan. Realistically, though, countries do not devote large enough fractions of their total expenditure to buying each other's goods rather than domestic goods. Furthermore, the repercussions occurring (unless prevented by policy) on subsequent "rounds" of income and expenditure may partially neutralize rather than reinforce the "first-round" international adjustment.

3. Numerical examples to clarify this point have had to be sacrificed for the sake of brevity. For the general approach, however, see J. E. Meade, *The Balance of Payments*, London: Oxford University Press, 1951, pp. 125–148.

4. See their articles, reprinted from the *Economic Journal*, March and June 1929, in American Economic Association, *Readings in the Theory of International Trade*, Philadelphia: Blakiston, 1949, pp. 161–178, as well as the article immediately following: Lloyd A. Metzler, "The Transfer Problem Reconsidered," reprinted from the *Journal of Political Economy*, June 1942.

lower their total gold value.[5] Keynes concluded: "Only those who believe that the foreign demand for German exports is very elastic, so that a trifling reduction in German prices will do what is required, are justified in holding that the Transfer Problem is of no great significance apart from the Budgetary Problem."[6]

Ohlin, on the other hand, apparently envisaged no great depreciation of the German currency or deflation of the German price and wage level. The Germans, having surrendered purchasing power to pay reparations, would be less able to afford imports, while the foreign recipients would have more purchasing power with which to buy German exports. Of course, only fractions of the cutbacks in spending made by German taxpayers and of the additional spending done by the foreign beneficiaries would impinge directly on internationally traded goods. But the changes in spending on domestic goods also—decreases in Germany and increases abroad—would tend to produce secondary contraction and expansion, giving further reason for labor and capital to concentrate on export production in Germany and to shift from it into home-market production abroad. Important aspects of the adjustment mechanism would operate even if German prices did not decline at all relative to prices in the countries receiving reparations.

To illustrate his optimistic view, Ohlin pointed out that during the few preceding years Germany had borrowed sums abroad considerably outweighing its reparations payments; if any transfer problem existed, it had been one of accomplishing a "real" transfer *into* Germany. Yet no such transfer problem had become conspicuous enough to arouse discussion.

The role of government budgeting deserves more emphasis than Keynes and Ohlin gave it. If the governments of two countries wanted to do all they could to accomplish a "real" transfer between them, the paying government should raise the necessary sum (or more) by increasing taxes (thereby reducing the disposable income of its citizens) or by cutting its own domestic expenditures; and the other government should use the payments received (or more) to cut taxes or to expand its own domestic expenditures. The purchasing-power-transfer effect would be completely absent if, in contrast, the paying government neither increased taxes nor cut its spending but simply inflated the necessary funds into existence and if the receiving government neither cut taxes nor increased its spending but simply held the funds received idle. The paying government might conceivably withdraw some gold coins from circulation, replacing them with newly printed paper money, and then deliver the gold to the receiving government, which might simply hold it against some future contingency without letting it influence the budget or the country's money supply. Such a situation would be uninteresting, for no genuine transfer problem would exist if gold were the ultimate means of settlement and no room remained for further repercussions.

Though unfavorable shifts in the relative prices of import and export goods and home factors of production may indeed lay a transfer burden on a paying country in addition to the budgetary burden, this does not necessarily prevent an adjustment of trade to the payment. Consider postwar reparations imposed in a world of barter. The victors might say in effect to the vanquished: "You must expand your deliveries of goods to us, or reduce your acquisitions of goods from us, or both, so much that your total deliveries of goods to us, valued in terms of our own goods, exceed our total deliveries to you by the amount we specify." The task of complying is greater than it would be if barter exchange ratios did not move against the defeated country, but this is simply an aspect of the kind of reparations demand made. The defeated country will be unable to discharge this obligation only if its people cannot accomplish the necessary production and bear up under the necessary deprivation—only if they are too poor. In other words, the transfer problem is included in the budgetary problem and can be solved if the latter can be solved. Admittedly, though, the defeated country might already be importing so little that little room remained for creating an export surplus by further import cuts, and the victors' demand for its exports might be so inelastic that increased physical amounts would be worth only reduced value amounts on their markets (even though the increased real disposable income of the victors was shifting their demand curves rightward). Two types of unfavorable foreign demands—the insistence on reparations measured in a particular way and the inelastic market demand—would be imposing poverty on the defeated country. This and the transfer problem would be intermingled.

Direct investment abroad

Direct investment abroad means, for the most part, investment in business properties located abroad but controlled by the investors. Immediately, directly, transfers of funds for that purpose have a negative impact on the balance of payments of the tranferring country. On the other hand, various plus items in its balance of payments may increase. The investing country may export more equipment and components and parts and more goods and services of types complementary to those produced in the foreign facilities. Its residents may earn technical fees and royalties and, eventually, profits. The foreign facilities may make imports available to the investing country more cheaply, either reducing or increasing their total value. Not all feedbacks will strengthen its balance of payments; perhaps production abroad will displace some goods formerly exported from the investing country itself.[7]

Multilateral aspects of capital movements

Complications appear when we go beyond the usual two-country model and recognize that many countries exist. How can trade adjust to capital movements if borrowers or their fellow countrymen increase their purchases not in the lending country but elsewhere and if lenders or their fellow countrymen reduce their purchases not in the borrowing country but elsewhere? The purchasing-power transfer and other gold-standard processes then tend to give the lending country an export surplus in trade with third countries. The adjustment process can best be understood by considering it while still incomplete. Perhaps the consolidated balances of payments of the third countries are in overall equilibrium, but their trade deficits with the lending country and their surpluses with the borrowing country still do not fully match the flow of capital to be transferred. There would then still be "too much" lending-country currency and "too little" borrowing-country currency being offered on the foreign-exchange market, promoting further gold flow and further monetary contraction and expansion in the respective countries. They would accordingly tend further to expand their respective net sales to and net purchases from the third countries, if not from each other directly. Another conceivable transitional stage of incom-

plete adjustment would have the third countries in overall balance-of-payments surplus, with excess exports to the borrowing country outweighing excess imports from the lending country. With their currencies in overall excess demand (not merely bilateral excess demand, thanks to arbitrage), the third countries would then gain gold; but the rises in their money supplies, incomes, and prices relative to those of the contractionary lending country would be in some sense more extreme than the relative declines in their money supplies, incomes, and prices in relation to those of the expansionary borrowing country. As an appropriate result, the discouragement of exports and encouragement of imports in third countries' trade with the lending country would be stronger than the continuing encouragement of exports and discouragement of imports in their trade with the borrowing country.

It would be tedious to explore all conceivable halfway stages in the multilateral accommodation of trade; the possibility of real capital transfer *through* third countries as well as directly is clear in principle. Whether the tendencies just described work swiftly enough to avoid difficulties under a gold standard is a serious question. They are more *understandable*, at least, under flexible exchange rates (or will be, after a study of the next chapter). If the third countries had trade surpluses with the borrowing country outweighing their deficits with the lending country at one stage of the

---

5. Supposed physical limits to amounts of existing German exports were something of a red herring. New goods might have come onto the list of exports. Price changes as well as heavy taxation could have motivated cutbacks in German home consumption and so have increased the quantities of goods available for export even if total production of export-type goods had been physically limited. And even if the foreign demand for German exports had been inelastic, price changes might have played a further role in contributing to an export surplus by cutting *imports*.

6. The cited *Readings*, p. 167.

7. Various possibilities are reviewed in Ingo Walter, *International Economics*, New York: Ronald Press, 1968, pp. 286–290, 292.

incomplete adjustment, then supply and demand on the foreign-exchange market would tend to strengthen third-country currencies in relation to the borrowing-country currency (or restrain the original tendency toward relative weakening) to a greater extent[8] than this pattern tended to weaken third-country currencies in relation to the lending-country currency (or restrain the original tendency toward relative strengthening). As a result, third countries would find their surplus in trade with the borrowing country either tending to shrink or else tending to expand less than their trade deficit with the lending country was tending to expand. The balances of payments of third countries would tend back into multilateral equilibrium.

The discussion of international capital movements is not meant to appraise their effects on welfare but merely to consider further the adjustment to balance-of-payments disturbances. Still, we should notice a parallel between the multilateral possibilities of the "real" transfer process and the fact that the transfer need by no means take the form of whatever capital goods the borrowers may wish to buy with the proceeds of the loan. Instead of exporting the particular goods that the borrowers may want, the lending country may export goods in whose production it has a comparative advantage, even though these may be demanded by persons in the borrowing country other than the actual borrowers or even only by persons in third countries. Similarly, the borrowers need not obtain the particular goods they desire from the lending country or, for that matter, from any foreign country. If they can obtain these goods more advantageously from some third country or even at home, a net transfer of real goods and services into their country still means that they are obtaining more real resources for their own projects without, on the whole, taking resources away from their fellow countrymen. International real transfers can take place "automatically" on a multilateral basis. The direct financial arrangements for an international loan or transfer may take place between persons in two countries only, but this financial bilateralism need not deprive trade of its multilateral character or distort it out of conformity with comparative advantage.

---

8. This extent would be measured not necessarily in percentage movement of rate quotations but rather in the influence of the exchange-rate movements on the flow of trade (which involves various demand and supply elasticities).

CHAPTER SIX

Exchange-Rate Adjustment and Other Mechanisms: A Preliminary Comparison

The exchange-rate mechanism

How exchange-rate variation can equilibrate the balance of payments should be easy to understand now that other mechanisms have been explained. Some disturbance causes a deficit in Inland's balance of payments. At the old exchange rate, Inland's dollar is in excess supply and Outland's peso in excess demand. Depreciation of the dollar under free-market pressures, or its devaluation if the rate had been officially pegged,[1] raises the price of foreign goods in dollars, restraining imports, and lowers the price of Inland goods in pesos, promoting exports. Adjustment of trade in this way, as through the price-level-adjustment mechanism of the gold standard, might conceivably go awry if demands were extremely inelastic. With the total Outland-peso value of Inland's exports reduced more than that of Inland's imports, the worsened imbalance on the exchange market would make the dollar depreciate further, making Inland's deficit still greater.

Setting aside this theoretical curiosity until Chapter 8, we shall take a closer look at the "normal" adjustment process. In reality, export prices in home currency do not remain constant, and shifts occur in the relative prices of domestic and internationally traded goods. As the dollar depreciates under pressure of a balance-of-payments deficit, the dollar prices of Inland's imports rise. Dollar prices rise even though what appears from the Outland point of view as a drop in Inland demand may somewhat reduce the *peso* prices of the Outland goods sold to Inland. For trade moving in the opposite direction, the new exchange rate cheapens Inland exports in Outland pesos and so stimulates Outland purchases. From the Inland point of view this appears[2] as an increase in the demand for exports, bidding up their dollar prices. At the new exchange rate, in short, Inland's imports and exportable goods alike tend to rise in price relative to domestic goods. Domestic or nontraded goods include such things as houses and haircuts and, in particular, labor and other factors of production. The price rise of internationally traded goods relative to domestic goods and factors of production leads Inlanders to cut down on importing and on domestic consumption of goods they could export and to concentrate more than before on production for export. The fuzzy dividing line between international and domestic goods shifts so as to make more goods than before profitably exportable. In the theoretical extreme case of infinite price elasticity in all relevant supplies and demands, no *actual* shift in the relative price levels of international and domestic goods would be observed: an infinitesimal exchange depreciation would slash Inland's imports and would spur her offer of exports in response to what, from her point of view, appeared as an increase in the Outland demand for them. The sectional-price-level shift would then be virtual; loosely speaking, Inland's imports and exports would respond to the relative price rise of international goods that would otherwise have occurred. The more sensitively quantities demanded and supplied

---

1. *Depreciation* is the broader term. When a distinction is intended, *devaluation* implies official action to fix the foreign-exchange value of a currency at a lower level than before.

2. The increase in Outland demand is *apparent* only, since the demand schedule relating Outland's desired purchases of Inland goods to alternative prices *in pesos* is pretty much the same as before. Outlanders will buy more than before at any given dollar price, not because their demand has become more intense but because that price now represents fewer pesos. Inlanders, however, perceive that the schedule of desired Outland purchases in relation to *dollar* prices has shifted to the right.

respond to price changes, the smaller need observed price changes actually be.

A sectional-price-level shift occurs in reverse in Outland, the surplus country. Exchange appreciation of the peso lowers the peso prices of imports from Inland and also causes an apparent decline in Inland demand for Outland exports, lowering their prices as well. Outland domestic goods and factors of production rise in price, relatively. Outlanders shift toward buying international goods and away from producing them. The more sensitively Outlanders respond to prices, the less marked does the actual shift in prices have to be in order to correct the initial surplus in Outland's balance of payments.

The ideal similarity of exchange-rate and price-level mechanisms

Ideally, the ultimate real changes that preserve or restore equilibrium in a disturbed balance of payments are essentially the same under the exchange-rate mechanism as under the price-level mechanism of international monetary linkage. The qualification *ideally* means that the adjustments considered are those that would take place if each mechanism operated in a theoretically perfect way. We abstract from frictions and suppose that both mechanisms operate with equal promptness, smoothness, and ease, and with equal absence of unwanted side effects. (Differences in these respects will be explored later.) We also abstract from such complications as debts fixed in the money of one country or another and speculation on exchange-rate or price-level changes. *Ultimate* changes refer to the new equilibrium that either mechanism would attain, considered apart from the processes and timing of getting there and apart from the influence that the path followed would, in reality, have on the final position. *Real* changes refer to physical quantities produced and traded, real incomes, and relative prices (price *ratios*)—all distinguished from mere money magnitudes and absolute levels of prices in money.[3]

To see the similarity of adjustment, consider some change in tastes that shifts demand partly away from Inland onto Outland goods. Preventing or curing a deficit in Inland's balance of payments requires bringing to bear on the decisions of Inland's families and firms the fact that the country's real economic position has worsened and that absorption must be restrained. The buying power of Inland's domestic factor incomes over internationally traded goods must be reduced. But keeping the gold parity or exchange rate of the Inland currency fixed without allowing the loss of gold or foreign-exchange reserves to deflate Inland's money supply and prices would mean blocking the change in economic signals needed fully to apprise individual decision-makers of the country's worsened real circumstances. Blocking these signals means subsidizing continued absorption by drawing on the gold or foreign-exchange reserves. Allowing either the gold-standard or the exchange-rate adjustment mechanism to operate, in contrast, does change the signals appropriately and does discontinue the subsidy to overabsorption. Under the gold standard, real cash balances fall as gold losses shrink the nominal money supply. Under the exchange-rate mechanism, depreciation or devaluation of the Inland currency lowers the purchasing power of the existing nominal money supply over import and export goods. Under either system, domestic goods and services fall in price relative to internationally traded goods; and the real buying power of the incomes of Inland factors of production falls. Under the gold standard, the general levels of domestic prices and money incomes fall while the gold prices of internationally traded goods remain more nearly unchanged; with exchange-rate adjustment, the Inland-currency prices of internationally traded goods rise while domestic prices and money income remain nearly unchanged. But *relative* movements are ideally the same. Under either method of allowing the economic signals to change and of avoiding continued subsidy to overabsorption, real incomes fall in Inland (and rise in Outland) because of the hypothesized initial shift in demand from Inland to Outland goods, just as one would expect if all trade were by barter and no money existed.[4]

A comparison of adjustment processes turns out similarly if the initial disturbance is an independently motivated capital flow from Inland to Outland. Insofar as the international transfer of purchasing power and the associated tightening of credit in Inland and loosening of credit in Outland do not by themselves restrain absorption in the one country and promote it in the other strongly enough to accommodate trade fully to the capital movement, further signals are needed. Inlanders must realize that fewer real resources are *currently* available for their absorption than before the loan was made. Either monetary contraction in response to gold flows or exchange depreciation of the Inland currency has the effects already described on real cash balances and on the relation between prices and factor incomes in Inland (and conversely in Outland).

These similarities, it must be repeated, refer to real outcomes in the absence of frictions. General price levels tend to move in opposite directions under the two mechanisms, and so do production and employment levels, in the absence of wage and price flexibility. Under fixed exchange rates, an independently motivated capital outflow tends to *deflate* the domestic money supply, prices, and production and employment. These changes are not the *result* of a goods-and-services export surplus but rather a part of the means of bringing the surplus about. Under fluctuating exchange rates, the capital outflow causes exchange depreciation and an export surplus directly. With the money supply remaining under domestic control, this net withdrawal of goods and services tends to *raise* prices in home currency, as well as production and employment.[5]

For a final comparison, consider a monetary rather than a real disturbance causing a deficit: inflation in Inland at a time of already full employment. The way that new money is put into circulation (government expenditures in excess of tax collections or an easing of credit), the rise in cash balances, the rise in money incomes relative to the less fully inflated prices of internationally traded goods, the drawing down of gold and foreign-exchange reserves—all cause apparent improvements in the economic positions of individuals, even though the country's real economic position has by hypothesis not improved; and all subsidize overabsorption while they last. Ideally, the gold-standard process reverses these monetary and price changes (or prevents them in the first place). Alternatively, depreciation of the Inland currency undoes these distortions by allowing the Inland-currency prices of internationally traded goods to keep pace with domestic cash balances and prices and incomes; it stops the overabsorption promoted by false price signals and financed by drafts on the country's external reserves. Of course, an exchange rate that equilibrates the balance of

EXCHANGE-RATE ADJUSTMENT AND OTHER MECHANISMS: A PRELIMINARY COMPARISON

payments cannot by itself offset *all* consequences of inflation, including the transfer of wealth from creditors to debtors. A gold or foreign-exchange standard, in contrast, does tend to check the domestic inflation.[6]

This is one of the practical differences be-

3. Even on this level of extreme abstraction, at least one dissimilarity between the two mechanism must be noted. Under a gold standard, some real resources go into providing monetary expansion over the long run, diverting them from other uses; the absolute level of prices affects the profitability and volume of gold mining and so, because of general economic interdependence, in principle affects all prices and quantities in the economic system to some extent. Some other dissimilarities on this same level of detail might be mentioned.

4. An original disturbance in the reverse direction would leave Inland's currency *under*valued at the old exchange rate if the resulting balance-of-payments surplus were kept from expanding the local money supply and so from bidding up the prices of domestic goods and factors of production relative to import and export prices. In maintaining an undervalued currency by accumulating foreign exchange at a higher local-currency price than it would be worth on a purely private market and thus in keeping import and export prices artificially high in local currency, the authorities would in effect be subsidizing what might be called either "underabsorption" or the net "production" of foreign exchange through an export surplus. Either appreciating the Inland currency or allowing the local money supply to expand would rectify the signals given by relative prices and bring the country's improved economic circumstances to bear on the decisions of private families and firms.

5. Cf. Gottfried von Haberler, *Prosperity and Depression*, new ed., London: Allen & Unwin, 1958, pp. 446–450; Egon Sohmen, *Fluctuating Exchange Rates: Theory and Controversy*, Chicago: University of Chicago Press, 1961, pp. 25–26; and Rudolf R. Rhomberg, "A Model of the Canadian Economy Under Fixed and Fluctuating Exchange Rates," *Journal of Political Economy*, LXXII, February 1964, p. 21.

6. This does not mean that a gold or foreign-exchange standard is inherently less inflationary than rival systems, but simply that it tends to keep each country in step with monetary conditions in other countries—stability, inflation, or deflation alike.

tween the two ideally similar adjustment mechanisms. Another concerns how long drafts on external reserves continue to subsidize over-absorption while adjustment of the price signals is still incomplete. In making prices signal a changed real situation and in avoiding drains on any external reserves, the flexible exchange rate operates more quickly. A closely related difference concerns the frictions that bedevil the ideally similar operation of the two mechanisms. Ideally, fluctuations in employment and in overall real economic activity are neither an integral part of the gold-standard or exchange-rate mechanisms nor a distinct adjustment mechanism in their own right. They represent frictions in the response of prices and wages to changes in expenditure patterns and money supplies. Ideally, overall production and employment never undergo deflation; only prices and wages do.

Ideally, in short, the adjustment mechanisms operating under monetary linkage and under flexible exchange rates are similar; in practice, they depart from the ideal in different ways and degrees. A realistic comparison must emphasize the frictions that may impede and the production-and-employment variations that may accompany one or both of them. As part of this fuller comparison, we must next examine the problem of maintaining both internal and external balance.

Expenditure and price policy for internal and external balance

External balance simply means balance-of-payments equilibrium. *Internal balance* means aggregate equality between quantities of goods and services and productive factors supplied and demanded on the markets of the home economy. More normatively, it might be defined instead as full employment *plus* price-level stability, except that even purely domestic obstacles may keep these two domestic goals from being entirely compatible.[7] More realistically, then, internal balance must refer to a high level of employment and production with no more movement of the general price level than is necessary to this primary goal. Yet still another difficulty remains. If monetary inflation somehow occurs and if the price system is not to be thrown out of commission by the general shortages characteristic of suppressed inflation, policy must allow the price level to rise. In short, internal balance represents whatever compromise is considered best on domestic grounds between the goals of full employment, a smoothly working market mechanism, and price-level stability.

Two general types of policy are available for pursuing internal and external balance. The first is expenditure (or expenditure-adjusting) policy. It affects a country's flow of aggregate demand. The second, sometimes called expenditure-switching policy, may also be called price policy, since price changes are the prototype of expenditure-switching developments. "Prices" include not only the prices of ordinary goods and services but also wage rates, prices of other factors of production, and exchange rates. Our abstract comparison of the gold-standard and exchange-rate mechanisms gave equal status to the price adjustments working through domestic price levels and those working through exchange rates. With both mecha-

TABLE 6.1. *Inland responses to domestic and foreign disturbances* (*expenditure policy alone*)

	Initial domestic disturbance		Initial foreign disturbance	
Type of disturbance	Home inflation		Foreign depression, or cheapening of foreign goods, or shift of demand from Inland to Outland goods	
Internal tendency in Inland	Inflation		Deflation	
Tendency in Inland's trade	Deficit		Deficit	
Expenditure policy for internal balance in Inland	Contractionary	Required policies coincide	Expansionary	Required policies clash
Expenditure policy for Inland's external balance	Contractionary		Contractionary	

nisms working frictionlessly, flows of *real* expenditure were all that mattered, and these were ideally unaffected by the money expenditures that corresponded to them. But now, realistically allowing for frictions that cause variations in real demand and hence in production and employment, we must recognize price-level and exchange-rate adjustments as *sub*categories of price policy, which contrasts with policy governing flows of money expenditure.

Actually, it is a bit narrow to speak of price and expenditure *policy*. Changes may occur in spontaneous response to market forces, without any deliberate official action. "Policy" to cure a balance-of-payments deficit might simply consist of passively permitting either the deflation of the money supply, spending, and prices or the exchange depreciation that the deficit would itself touch off. Even internally, adjustments may occur of their own accord: the price-and-wage cuts appropriate for curing depression and unemployment in the absence of positive expenditure policy would tend to come about, though slowly and painfully, under the pressure of gluts of labor and commodities. For this reason, "policy" will usually mean either passively *permitting* the appropriate adjustments or, if necessary, actively *promoting* them. The word will not always refer to deliberate official action.

Expenditure policy alone

The policies required for internal and external balance will sometimes coincide and sometimes clash. Let us first consider expenditure policy alone, putting aside any possibility of corrective adjustment through prices, wages, and exchange rates. Table 6.1 considers two alternative types of disturbance tending to inflict an external deficit on Inland: (1) an inflationary impulse originating at home, and (2) any of several kinds of disturbance originating wholly or partly abroad, such as a foreign depression, a cheapening of foreign goods, or some change in tastes or technology or tariffs causing demand to shift from Inland onto Outland goods. Previous discussion should make the items in the table self-explanatory; for example, an export slump would inflict both a trade deficit and income deflation on Inland, requiring expenditure contraction to remedy the former and expenditure expansion to remedy the latter. Not only trade in goods and services but also capital movements may respond to expenditure policy. This is true if expenditure

policy works through, or involves, changes in interest rates. The reduction in interest rates (reduction, at least, until the policy had succeeded in restoring domestic prosperity) would tend to worsen a balance-of-payments deficit (or reduce a surplus) not only by affecting trade but also by promoting an outflow (or reducing an inflow) of capital.

If the initial disturbance were the opposite of those shown in the top line of Table 6.1, each of the entries below would also be the opposite of the one shown.

The table suggests that when a disturbance originates at home, the expenditure policies required for internal and external balance coincide. When the disturbance originates abroad, or in the foreign-trade sector, the internal and external requirements clash. In general, when a deflationary or inflationary disturbance originates within one country, the ideal expenditure policy, from its own and foreign viewpoints alike, is correction of the disturbance at the source.

Some disturbances can be at least partially external to *all* countries concerned, as when a change in tastes or technology or tariffs shifts demand from Inland onto Outland goods. Inland develops internal deflation and an external deficit; Outland, internal inflation and an external surplus. If both adopt expenditure policies for internal balance—expansionary in Inland and contractionary in Outland—the imbalance in trade grows all the worse. If both adopt expenditure policies for external balance —contractionary in Inland and expansionary in Outland—the domestic imbalances grow all the worse.

Is there any way to avoid policy clashes by somehow having one country pursue internal balance and the other external balance? Outland, toward whose goods demand has shifted, might concentrate on getting rid of its external surplus by an expansionary expenditure policy, while Inland would concentrate on sustaining

---

7. Obstacles include those stressed in theories of "wage-push inflation." These and other aspects of the problem of internal and external balance are examined in J. E. Meade, *The Balance of Payments*, London: Oxford University Press, 1951, esp. chaps. VIII–X.

domestic income by a similar expansionary policy. If both expand expenditure with appropriate vigor, both could achieve external balance and Inland could achieve internal balance. But Outland's inflation then becomes all the worse; the entire conflict is concentrated into a worsened internal imbalance in Outland. The reverse pairing of objectives—contractionary policies in both countries as Inland sought external and Outland internal balance—produces no better result: again, balanced trade is conceivably attainable, but at the cost of shifting the entire conflict into Inland in the form of intensified deflation.

Even when internal and external policy requirements coincide in *direction*, they may clash in *degree*. More precisely, they may coincide in direction until policy has changed conditions to the extent that the requirements then clash even in direction. Consider a country sharing a worldwide depression[8] and running an export surplus. Both internal and external objectives call for an expansionary policy. But it would be extreme coincidence if the same degree of expansion were needed for both. On the one hand, if the export surplus were relatively slight, it might vanish while internal depression was still only partially remedied. Further expansion to finish curing the depression would shift the balance of payments into deficit. On the other hand, if the internal depression were relatively slight, it might be completely cured while an export surplus still persisted. Further expansion to cure this surplus would cause domestic inflation.

Conflicts of direction and degree arise be-cause only one policy weapon, expenditure policy, has as yet been considered for pursuing two policy goals.[9] The problem is to hit two targets with a single shot. If the two targets just happen to be perfectly in line with each other, the feat is possible, but policy-makers cannot always count on this happy coincidence.

Price policy alone

The previous section set price policy aside to consider expenditure policy alone; this section does the reverse. Downward price policy lowers a country's wages and prices relative to those of other countries either by actual cuts in terms of local currency (if it is rigidly linked to foreign currencies) or else by exchange devaluation or depreciation. Upward price policy works either through price-and-wage increases in terms of local currency or through a rise in the currency's foreign-exchange value. Again we must emphasize that *policy*, in this context, does not necessarily mean positive action by the authorities. It may simply mean passively *allowing* market pressures to work their normal effects on domestic prices or the exchange rate. Table 6.2 lists some disturbances and the appropriate remedies.

This table requires somewhat more explanation than Table 6.1. Even some of the terminology is different. The inflationary domestic disturbance is here called "boom" rather than "inflation" because the price increases that would tend to occur are considered a policy response, even though passive, and a

---

TABLE 6.2. *Inland responses to domestic and foreign disturbances (price policy alone)*

	Initial domestic disturbance	Initial foreign disturbance
Type of disturbance	Boom at home	Foreign depression, or cheapening of foreign goods, or shift of demand from Inland to Outland goods
Internal tendency in Inland	Boom	Depression
Tendency in Inland's trade	Deficit	Deficit
Price policy for internal balance in Inland	Upward ⎫ Required policies clash	Downward ⎫ Required policies coincide
Price policy for Inland's external balance	Downward ⎭	Downward ⎭

different word is needed for the condition that would prevail in their absence. Barring price increases, the inflation would be a "suppressed" one, involving general shortages of labor and goods and sabotage of the price mechanism. A cure for inflation in this sense would be inflation in the quite distinct sense of upward price adjustments; an excessive flow of purchasing power can be cut down by a cut in the purchasing power of each unit of money spent.

Even when working through exchange appreciation rather than through price and wage increases in home currency, upward price policy would tend (though more feebly) to restore internal balance: the new price relations would divert some purchases, by both Inlanders and Outlanders, onto Outland and away from Inland goods. This diversion, though appropriate to Inland's domestic situation, would tend to cause inflation in other countries previously enjoying internal balance. A related difficulty is that Inland's upward price policy would worsen the external deficit already associated with her domestic boom.

The table suggests downward price policy, perhaps rather misleadingly, to remedy the balance-of-payments deficit. Forcing down the Inland price level would make the "suppressed" character of the suppressed inflation all the worse, and though it might make Outlanders more *eager* to buy Inland goods, it might not make more such goods actually available to them. After all, however, an extreme enough devaluation of Inland currency might make import and export goods so expensive in Inland currency that Inlanders, despite their generally excessive purchasing power, would cut down their purchases of such goods enough to get rid of the country's deficit.

Let us now consider an initial domestic disturbance opposite to the one shown in the table: a depression that originates at home, causing an export surplus. An active policy to promote money expenditure is ruled out by our consideration of price policy alone. Downward price policy is the next best answer. Wage and price cuts in terms of home currency tend to restore real production and employment because each nominal money unit of cash balances and of expenditure represents more real purchasing power than before and goes further in buying goods and hiring labor. Expenditure in real terms thus goes up, even though changes in the nominal money supply and in money expenditure are ruled out. Wage and

EXCHANGE-RATE ADJUSTMENT AND OTHER MECHANISMS: A PRELIMINARY COMPARISON

price cuts would also have an expansionary domestic impact through their influence on Inland's foreign trade. They would divert some Inland and Outland purchases alike from Outland to Inland goods, stimulating Inland economic activity (at the cost, though, of tending to "export" unemployment to Outland).

This price-induced shift of purchases from foreign to domestic goods, not any increase in the real purchasing power of the existing expenditure flow and money supply, provides the expansionary impetus to domestic economic activity when downward price policy works through exchange depreciation rather than

8. A clear-cut example requires an at least partially external disturbance. For if the country were suffering from a purely domestic depression that had not yet spread to other countries, policy might conceivably just remedy this depression and therefore also just remedy the export surplus it would cause.

9. Expenditure policy employs various sub-weapons—open-market operations, debt management, and adjustments in taxes, government spending, bank reserve requirements, and central-bank discount rates. Whether this fact can make control of the flow of money expenditure count as more than a single policy weapon is considered in the appendix to this chapter. The argument there reaches a generally negative answer. Meanwhile, we continue to regard the choice among various budgetary or central-bank operations for affecting expenditure as an essentially administrative detail. It is unable to split expenditure policy into aspects as distinct from each other as any of them is from price policy (including exchange-rate policy).

A noteworthy discussion of the required relation between the number of policy goals and the number of policy weapons is presented by Jan Tinbergen in *The Theory of Economic Policy*, Amsterdam: North-Holland Publishing Company, 1952, chaps. IV and V and esp. pp. 39–40; and in *Economic Policy: Principles and Design*, Amsterdam: North-Holland Publishing Company, 1956, esp. p. 55 and chap. 4. Tinbergen counts exchange-rate variation as a possible policy weapon, but there is little difference between regarding the adoption of rate flexibility as the addition of a policy weapon and regarding it as abandonment of the policy goal of a particular rate. Either way, any excess of the number of policy goals over the number of policy weapons is reduced by one.

through wage and price cuts. Since it lacks the internal real-purchasing-power effects of such cuts, downward price policy is a feebler stimulus to domestic activity when it works through exchange depreciation alone. It is true that devaluation to a sufficiently low pegged rate can also help promote internal balance by creating or expanding an external surplus that brings reserve gains, money-supply growth, and positive operation of the foreign-trade multiplier, as well as an opportunity for expenditure policy to become actively expansionary without causing balance-of-payments difficulties. But this means using price policy and at least passive expenditure policy *in combination,* something we are not yet ready to consider.

In ideal theory, price policy alone is adequate to achieve internal balance eventually. But to show this is not to endorse it for this purpose. Working through the exchange rate, it has only relatively indirect and feeble effects at home. Working in the downward direction through wage and price cuts, it is unattractive and impractical for familiar reasons involving wage and price stickiness, expectations, and the like. But the ultimate effects are as described. Even if price policy did work in ideal frictionless fashion, conflicts between internal and external objectives would sometimes bedevil reliance on it alone, and it is important to understand when and how.

Luckily, this conflict is absent—at least in direction, if not in degree—when the initial disturbance is of external origin. As Table 6.2 shows, downward price policy is appropriate for coping with both the external deficit and the domestic depression caused by an export slump of external origin.

There is a notable contrast between the clashes of internal and external objectives that may occur when expenditure policy is used alone and when price policy is used alone. The required *expenditure* policies clash when an initial disturbance is external to a country and coincide when the disturbance is internal. But the required *price* policies clash when the disturbance is internal and coincide when it is external.

Dilemma and nondilemma cases— a graphical view

Figure 6.1 illustrates cases of compatibility and of clash between the policy requirements of internal and external balance.[10] The horizontal axis measures what expenditure policy seeks to control, the total real demand by Inlanders for both home and foreign goods and services. The vertical axis measures what price policy controls (or allows), namely, the ratio of foreign to home prices. A rise in this ratio, through either a reduction of home prices at a fixed exchange rate or a devaluation of the home currency on the exchanges, would spell what we have called a downward price policy. A fall in the ratio through either of the opposite moves would be an upward price policy. The labeled arrows serve as reminders of this interpretation. For definiteness in what follows, let us think of downward or upward price policy as working through exchange-rate changes.

One line on the diagram represents the combinations of exchange rate and Inland demand that would yield balance in foreign trade; the other represents combinations yielding internal balance. To understand why the trade-balance line slopes upward from left to right, consider a position *on* that line, representing a zero trade balance. It is convenient to start from the point of intersection with the other line. Now an arbitrary increase in Inland demand takes place and spills over onto imports and export-type goods. A rightward move to point 1 represents this occurrence. What would remedy the trade deficit? Devaluation of Inland's currency would affect relative prices so as to switch some purchases both at home and abroad away from Outland and onto Inland goods. This development is represented by a vertical move from point 1 back to the trade-balance line at a new

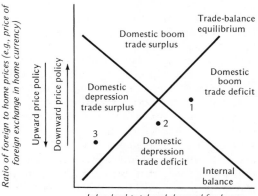

FIGURE 6.1

point on it.[11] Alternatively, consider that we start from the original balanced position and arbitrarily revalue the Inland currency upward, as represented by a downward move to point 2. The resulting trade deficit might then be cured by a demand-contracting policy, represented by a leftward move to the trade-balance line at a new point on it.

To explain the downward slope of the internal-balance line, we start from the same internally and externally balanced position as before and consider an expansionary demand policy, represented by the rightward move to point 1. This would cause an inflationary boom at home unless something switched away the excessive Inland spending onto additional imports and onto goods that would otherwise have been exported. This switch, worsening the trade deficit, could be accomplished by upward revaluation of the Inland currency, represented by a move downward from point 1 to the internal-balance line at a new point on it. If currency revaluation instead of demand expansion were the initial disturbance, we would have a situation represented by point 2. Overcoming the depression at home at the new exchange rate would require an expansionary expenditure policy; its results would be represented by a rightward move back to the internal-balance line at a new point on it.

We now see why positions to the southeast of the trade-balance line represent trade deficits and positions to the northwest represent surpluses. Positions northeast of the internal-balance line represent internal boom and positions to the southwest represent depression. The surplus-and-boom sector at the top of the diagram and the deficit-and-depression sector at the bottom represent the classic "dilemma" cases: expenditure policy alone, represented by leftward or rightward moves, cannot cure both the internal and external imbalances. On the contrary, a cure for one imbalance makes the other all the worse. A move left or right from a dilemma point brings us closer to one line but further away from the other.

In the two *nondilemma* sectors, a horizontal move, representing expenditure policy, brings us closer to both lines. However, expenditure policy alone, unaccompanied by any change in prices or the exchange rate, could achieve both internal and external balance only if we started from a special case of disequilibrium represented by some point, such as point 1, exactly level with the intersection. A point like 3 represents the more general case in which the pol-

EXCHANGE-RATE ADJUSTMENT AND OTHER MECHANISMS: A PRELIMINARY COMPARISON

icies required for internal and external balance "clash in degree though not in direction." A policy just expansionary enough to cure the trade surplus leaves the home economy still in depression; a policy expansionary enough to cure the depression reverses the trade balance into deficit. Again we see that, in general, it is impossible to cure both imbalances with expenditure policy alone—to hit two targets with a single shot, to achieve all policy goals with a smaller number of policy weapons.

Dilemmas for price policy receive less attention than dilemmas for expenditure policy, since the exchange rate is less commonly regarded as the sole policy weapon than is expenditure. Anyway, points in the east and west sectors represent dilemmas for price policy alone, and north and south points represent nondilemma cases. In a situation such as point 3 represents, a revaluation of the home currency sufficient to cure the trade surplus would make the depression all the worse; a devaluation sufficient to cure the depression would make the trade surplus all the larger. (Currency devaluation tends to cure a depression, remember, through price incentives that switch purchases in both Inland and Outland away from Outland onto Inland goods.) In the nondilemma cases, the required price policies would clash neither in direction nor even in degree only in the special cases represented by points exactly above or below the intersection.

The same Fig. 6.1 helps us consider the relations set forth in Tables 6.1 and 6.2. An expansionary domestic disturbance appears on the diagram as a rightward move from the intersection. To correct the resulting boom and deficit both, the same expenditure policy is re-

10. The diagram is an adaptation of one devised by Trevor W. Swan for a paper of 1955, reprinted in American Economic Association, *Readings in International Economics*, Homewood, Ill.: Irwin, 1968, pp. 455–464.

11. This line, as well as the internal-balance line, is drawn on the assumption that import and export demand elasticities are high enough for the trade balance to respond normally rather than perversely to the exchange rate. Chapter 8 will explain and justify this assumption.

quired, namely, one represented by reversal of the rightward move. If price policy were to be used instead, it would have to go in one direction to correct the internal boom and in the opposite direction to correct the trade deficit.

One different kind of domestic disturbance would be an increase in population or productivity that raises the real productive capacity of the economy. The internal-balance line shifts northeastward. (To maintain full employment at an unchanged exchange rate, an expansion of Inland expenditure would be necessary; at an unchanged total of Inland expenditure, a higher price of foreign exchange would be necessary to switch some expenditure from Outland onto Inland goods.) The trade-balance line presumably shifts southeastward, if at all, indicating that the increased Inland productive capacity tends to promote a trade surplus through greater exports or lesser imports.[12] The original point of intersection, representing Inland's original expenditure level and exchange rate, now lies in the depression-and-surplus sector formed by the new lines (which the reader should draw for himself.) Reaching the new internal and external equilibriums requires a rightward movement; the expenditure-policy requirements coincide for the two goals. (They coincide in direction, though probably not in degree.) With a change in expenditure ruled out, the price policies required for the two goals clash.

One of the foreign disturbances mentioned in Tables 6.1 and 6.2, such as a foreign depression, throws Inland into both depression and deficit. The internal-balance line shifts northeastward, representing the need either for an increase in Inland's total expenditure or for an exchange-rate change to switch demand from Outland onto Inland goods. The trade-balance line shifts northwestward, representing the need either for a cut in Inland's total expenditure or for a devaluation. The old intersection lies in the depression-and-deficit sector formed by the new lines. The price policies required for both internal and external balance are the same in direction if not in degree—devaluation of the Inland currency—but the expenditure policies required for the two goals clash.

The diagram thus leads to the same conclusions as the reasoning summarized in Tables 6.1 and 6.2. These conclusions are the basis for a presumption, to be discussed presently, about the proper pairing of expenditure and price policies with the internal and external goals.[13]

Our use of the diagram has regarded equilibrium in trade in goods and services as the prototype of overall balance-of-payments equilibrium; tacitly, we have ruled capital movements out of the picture. Formally, it is not hard to take account of them. For overall equilibrium, an independently motivated capital outflow or inflow requires a trade surplus or deficit of the same size. To match a trade surplus to a capital outflow, the price of foreign exchange would have to be higher or total Inland expenditure lower than otherwise. Diagrammatically, the conditions for overall external equilibrium would be represented by a balance-of-payments line drawn northwestward of the trade-balance line for the no-capital-movement case. Otherwise, the analysis and its qualitative conclusions would be the same as before.[14]

Alternative policy combinations

The pattern of coinciding and clashing policy requirements that we have reviewed yields a presumption about the proper pairing of expenditure and price policies with internal and external goals. So does the consideration that price policies for internal balance are feeble when working through the exchange rate and impractical and unattractive when working through domestic wage and price levels. The presumption favors using expenditure policy mainly for internal balance and price policy mainly for external balance. Strictly speaking, it is not legitimate to pair particular weapons with particular goals: all weapons and goals intertwine in a single integrated system, and a change in any one aspect of this system in principle affects all the others. Still, pairing weapons and goals according to their *main* interconnections has a certain plausibility.

Expenditure policy for internal and price policy for external balance, while intuitively attractive, is not the only conceivable pairing. The alternative is price policy primarily for internal and expenditure policy primarily for external balance.[15] This comes close to the idealized theory (if perhaps not the actuality) of the traditional gold standard. A country with an externally caused balance-of-payments deficit incurs a deflation of expenditure and money supply through operation of the foreign-trade multiplier and loss of gold, which checks the tendency to overimport. This deflation would also cause unemployment and a slump in production, however, unless wage and price cuts so raised the purchasing power of the money unit that the flow of expenditure, though shrunken in money terms, nevertheless remained adequate in real purchasing power to provide enough demand for a full-employment level of production. Ideally, the necessary wage and price cuts would occur automatically, under the pressure of the oversupplies of labor and goods that would otherwise glut the market.

Further consideration of this expenditure-and-price mechanism demonstrates why it is not possible to identify one aspect of it strictly with external and the other with internal goals. Some cross-association is bound to occur. The drop in wages and prices tends, for example, to sustain domestic economic activity not only in the way previously described but also by shifting purchases from foreign to domestic goods and by permitting, without danger to the balance-of-payments position, an active or passive policy of moderating the monetary contraction otherwise being imposed by the external deficit. The more promptly wages and prices adjust downward and the more sensitively trade responds to the changed relation between domestic and foreign prices, the less severe the expenditure deflation must be for the sake of the balance of payments.

Now consider this same "gold-standard" policy combination in a country with depression and an external *surplus*. (The cause might have been some spontaneous increase in the thriftiness or liquidity preferences of the public.) The consequences of the external surplus tend to sustain income and expenditure at home, but since this tendency is probably not strong enough by itself, wages and prices fall under the pressure of gluts on the market. These price adjustments help restore full employment both by diverting some additional purchases from foreign to domestic goods and by making each money unit "go further" in providing real demand. The recovery of domestic economic activity and purchasing power encourages imports and restrains exports and so overcomes the external surplus that the price adjustments would otherwise perpetuate. The more readily the domestic economy recovers, the smaller do these downward price adjustments have to be.

The intuitively preferable first pairing of

EXCHANGE-RATE ADJUSTMENT AND OTHER MECHANISMS: A PRELIMINARY COMPARISON

weapons and goals—expenditure policy for internal and price policy for external balance—would accomplish price adjustments most easily through the exchange rate. Expenditure policies to resist internal disturbances would ordinarily also be appropriate to correct the impact of these internal disturbances on the balance of payments; but so far as the expenditure policy required for internal balance does not exactly coincide in degree with the require-

12. Furthermore, if the increased demand for real money balances associated with the growth in the real size of the Inland economy is met neither by domestic monetary expansion nor by a price-level decline and currency appreciation, then it tends to be met through a balance-of-payments surplus. See p. 186.

13. The analysis is not particularly helpful for illustrating the use of trade controls as a policy weapon. This omission here is not intended to prejudge the case for or against controls; a judgment must await Chapter 7.

14. This statement assumes that expenditure policy and the exchange rate affect the trade balance but not the capital account, or that if they do affect the capital account, they do not do so in such a way as to make the overall balance of payments change in the opposite direction from the change in the trade balance. In reality, of course, all sorts of effects on the capital account, including interest-rate and expectational effects, may enter the picture. An expansionary monetary policy might tend, on the one hand, to promote capital outflow through a (temporary) reduction in Inland interest rates but, on the other hand, to promote capital inflow through improved business activity and profit prospects in Inland. (On the latter possibility, the so-called income-mobility of capital, see Harry G. Johnson, "Some Aspects of the Theory of Economic Policy in a World of Capital Mobility," *Rivista Internazionale di Scienze Economiche e Commerciali*, XII, June 1965, pp. 545–561, reprinted in Tullio Bagiotti, ed., *Essays in Honour of Marco Fanno*, Padua: Cedam, 1966, pp. 345–359.) Going into these complications would take us far afield from the relations between policies and goals that concern us here.

15. These two pairings are what Meade calls "principle 1" and "principle 2." See Meade, *op. cit.*, pp. 157–162.

ment for external balance, the exchange rate can help take care of the latter. As for external disturbances to the balance of payments, the exchange rate can provide the required adjustment. It is true that removing or preventing a deficit through exchange depreciation, for example, tends to expand or at least resist contraction of domestic expenditure, with results that run counter to the primary effect of the new exchange rate on trade. But this means not that depreciation must be ineffective but simply that it must go further than would have been necessary if domestic expenditure had been allowed to shrink. Again we see the need for two types of policy for the successful pursuit of two goals. Chapter 8 will argue an important corollary: if each country were to pursue a policy of stabilizing domestic expenditure (or its growth trend, in line with "real" economic growth), the income and expenditure responses that might weaken the external effectiveness of exchange-rate variation would be avoided.

Further practical differences between the two policy combinations

Both pairings of policies with goals are abstractly logical. The difference is in how practical each is. Price policy for internal balance, or even for external balance when exchange-rate variation is ruled out, sometimes requires adjusting the whole level of wages and prices in local money, which is especially awkward when the adjustment has to be downward. In correcting external imbalance, the relative behavior of sectional price levels is ideally the same under both mechanisms: relative to the prices of internationally traded goods, the prices of domestic goods and factors of production must go down in a deficit country and up in a surplus country. But with flexible exchange rates, this shift takes place mainly by changes in the local-currency prices of international goods, with the prices of domestic goods and factors of production being less directly and sharply affected.[16] Under the gold standard or a similar system, the shift takes place mainly by changes in the prices of domestic goods and factors of production; and if rigidities limit or retard price and wage cuts necessary to correct a balance-of-payments deficit and to maintain full employment in the face of shrunken expenditure, the outcome is unpleasant. Adjust-

ments to a balance-of-payments deficit must permeate the whole domestic economy, reducing prices and wages and incomes in various degrees. The gold standard requires a crude, "shotgun" process of adjustment; and since it will not work frictionlessly, deflation to remedy the external deficit cuts production, employment, and real incomes as well as prices, wages, and money incomes. "But what a paradox! The country has been buying abroad more than it can afford. Surely the remedy should be to produce *more* rather than *less*."[17]

The gold-standard mechanism changes a wrong exchange rate into a right one not by changing the rate itself but by adjusting everything else. This approach reminds Professor Röpke of a circus clown who, seeing that the chair was too far from the piano, tried, with sweat streaming down his face, to push the piano towards the chair.[18] Exchange-rate adjustment pushes the chair instead; it is a more delicate and selective method, operating directly where changes are really required—in the markets for internationally traded goods and services. Professor Friedman has made a similar comparison. General price and income adjustments resemble arranging for more daylight hours after work on summer evenings by having everyone adjust his daily schedule so that he does everything one hour earlier. Instead of making these myriad detailed changes in our habits, we simply adopt daylight saving time. Changing one price, the exchange rate, rather than a multitude of internal prices, offers similar simplicity.[19]

Exchange rates and quasi flexibility of wages and prices

The greater ease of changing one price than many suggests how fluctuating exchange rates can in effect put flexibility into sticky wages and prices. The importance of flexibility is best grasped by imagining its absence. As wants, resources, or technology change, resources would have to shift not in response to increases in the prices and costs of some products and resources and declines in the prices and costs of others but in response to the more wasteful and unpleasant spurs of shortages of some products and resources and gluts or unemployment of others. Flexible exchange rates could make the prices of each country's labor and products flexible, after all, as translated into the currencies of other countries. This we shall call "quasi flexibility." If demand for a country's products falls off, exchange depreciation could partly absorb the impact by lowering their foreign-currency prices and so helping to sustain foreign purchases. It would also benefit the country's import-competing industries and ease some transfer of resources out of the damaged export industries.

Consider the United States during a nationwide slump in the demand for automobiles. In order either to keep up sales and output or to guide resources into other lines of production under the spur of something less stark than actual unemployment, automobile prices would have to fall in terms of the single nationwide currency that in fact exists, and at least an interruption in wage increases for automobile workers would also be necessary. Now suppose, instead, that each state has its own independent fluctuating currency. (What follows is a piece of analysis only and is not meant as even a hint at a policy proposal.) The slump in demand for Michigan's automobiles depresses the exchange value of Michigan's "edsel." This depreciation cuts automobile prices outside Michigan, helping maintain sales and production despite the reduced demand. It also benefits Michigan's other export industries and import-competing industries, providing some job opportunities there for displaced automobile workers. Depreciation of the edsel raises prices in Michigan of imported and exportable goods (other, presumably, than automobiles); in fact, this is how a necessary cut in real wages is accomplished despite obstacles to a cut in money wages.[20] If the industries burdened with increased costs of imported materials are export industries, higher selling prices in edsels will partly compensate. The burden is heavier for industries importing materials but selling their products at home, but discouragement of these industries is appropriate to the unavoidable real worsening in Michigan's external trade opportunities. So is the price incentive to substitute local for imported materials.

We must not paint too cheerful a picture. Since depreciation of the edsel does nothing by itself to expand the Michigan money supply and thus is not generally inflationary,[21] the rise in import and export prices implies deflationary pressure on other prices and wages inside Michigan. If these are rigid downward, the deflation of demand causes cutbacks in production and employment. Depreciation of the edsel may shift the problem of unemploy-

EXCHANGE-RATE ADJUSTMENT AND OTHER MECHANISMS: A PRELIMINARY COMPARISON

ment partly from the automobile industry to other industries. But under the alternative of fixed exchanges, actual shrinkage of the money supply in Michigan and contractionary operation of the external-trade multiplier would have made the spread of unemployment worse.

Still another consideration suggests that flexible exchanges do provide some net protection against unemployment. An initial drop in the outside demand for Michigan products and so in the derived demand for Michigan factors of production could conceivably exert its effect in either of two extreme forms: unemployment,

16. Some adjustment in domestic prices must still occur, as the principle of general economic interdependence teaches. Domestic-goods prices would generally move opposite to international-goods prices under a policy of keeping the home currency stable in overall purchasing power. However, the necessary domestic adjustments are less extreme under flexible exchange rates than under the gold standard. The exchange-rate mechanism operates *primarily* on the prices of international goods, whereas the gold-standard mechanism operates primarily on domestic prices and income.

17. R. G. Hawtrey, *Bretton Woods for Better or Worse*, London: Longmans, Green, 1946, p. 10.

18. Wilhelm Röpke, "Le rideau de fer monétaire," *Revue Economique et Sociale*, **VIII**, January 1950, p. 32. This quip is especially interesting, coming as it does from an economist who favors return to a gold standard.

19. Milton Friedman, "The Case for Flexible Exchange Rates," *Essays in Positive Economics*, Chicago: University of Chicago Press, 1953, p. 173.

20. This does not mean that a Michigan cost-of-living index constructed by any reasonable method would vary in full proportion to exchange rates. Even in a single state the cost of living is not wholly made up of imported and readily exportable items: consider shelter, services, and the local-labor component of goods at retail. But collective bargains gearing wage rates to a cost-of-living index, together with an acquiescent monetary policy, would seriously impair quasi flexibility; see p. 224.

21. The original real worsening in trade opportunities does tend to raise prices somewhat, on the average, since real income would unavoidably fall even if the flow of money income were kept unchanged.

with Michigan factor prices rigid, or factor-price cuts sufficient to maintain purchases and avoid unemployment. A flexible exchange rate makes prices of Michigan factors flexible in terms of outside currencies and goods and thus enables the effect of the drop in demand to approach the second extreme form more closely than otherwise. In short, a fluctuating edsel permits Michigan factors to absorb the effects of reduced demand more fully in the form of worsened terms of trade and less in the form of unemployment. If the former coal miners of West Virginia could have accepted their economic misfortunes of some years ago in reduced real wage rates rather than in unemployment, they might have been better off than they actually were. West Virginia coal would have been able to hold its market better in the face of competition, or other local industries might have expanded or new industries have been attracted into the area. The existence of depressed areas in the United States even in prosperous times testifies to the importance of wage-price flexibility or some substitute for it.

Quasi flexibility through exchange rates would have the further though minor advantage of promoting price competition.[22] The producer of each particular product would find that the prices quoted by outside competitors, as translated at fluctuating rates, were undergoing continual (though usually slight) changes relative to his own price. It would be difficult to maintain a rigid price not only in terms of all currencies but perhaps even in terms of the local currency. The more nearly standardized a product, the less feasible would quasi-oligopolistic price inflexibility be. Continual slight fluctuations in the prices of rival producers, as translated at flexible rates, would pose some slight obstacle to collusion or a live-and-let-live policy of rigid prices. Even "pattern" wage bargaining could be impeded somewhat.

But this overstates the case. Exchange-rate flexibility is, after all, only a crude and unselective substitute for flexibility in each individual wage and price. The more individually flexible wages and prices were, the less a free exchange rate would have to move when world-market conditions for some particular product changed. This is no reason for rejecting quasi flexibility, however, when detailed flexibility is inadequate. The two types of flexibility are by no means rivals: fixed exchange rates do not necessarily promote, and flexible rates do not necessarily impair, detailed flexibility.

Substitute flexibility would be most satisfactory if currency areas coincided with economically homogeneous territories. If we could start with a blank slate in designing an ideal world, we would not carve out currency areas according to today's national boundaries. The smaller the area in which each currency circulated and the less varied the economic activities carried on there, the more nearly would exchange-rate flexibility approximate industry-by-industry or even firm-by-firm wage and price flexibility. Obviously, though, there is such a thing as moving too far in this direction.

Particularly when monetary unification already exists among regions of a country, undoing it is not an attractive idea. But when countries have not unified their fiscal and monetary systems and when currency exchanges already are necessary for international payments, the question of "optimum currency areas" becomes relevant. Appendix 2 to this chapter reviews the arguments for and against large currency areas.

The sharing of adjustment burdens

One supposedly important point of comparison between rival mechanisms concerns how deficit and surplus countries share the burden of adjustment.[23] The supposed burden has several aspects. Correction of a deficit, and specifically of a deficit in goods-and-services trade, means that the country ceases to enjoy the pleasure of living beyond its means; its people no longer have their consumption and investment subsidized from its international reserves or from official borrowing abroad. (For a surplus country, conversely, restoration of equilibrium means *shedding* the earlier burden of holding its consumption and investment below its total production.) Apart from defaulting on its debts or otherwise getting foreigners to transfer wealth to it, a country cannot go on running a deficit indefinitely. If a country cannot avoid living within its means in the long run, the question of the burden of doing so is rather idle. It would hardly be more pointless to theorize about the burden of having to breathe to live. We may make one concession, though, to the present concept of burden: if the people of a country have become accustomed to living beyond their means, as they can do in the short run, a rapid return to reality brings unpleasant disappointment of expectations and revisions of habits. By not getting accustomed in the first place to the cheap foreign goods and cheap foreign travel temporarily permitted by an overvalued currency, the people of a country could avoid this sort of burden.

As already mentioned, restoration of equilibrium *relieves* a surplus country of one kind of burden. The deficit country as well as the surplus country sheds a burden of a different kind, namely, a misallocation of resources due to the wrong price relations that also account for the international disequilibrium. Export and import-competing industries had been too small in the deficit country and too large in the surplus country relative to domestic-goods industries; patterns of production and resource allocation had been relatively inefficient. Terms such as "misallocation" and "inefficiency" are admittedly loose, but the topic at issue is not important enough for the long discussion necessary to explain or avoid them. What they mean is relatively obvious when special tariffs and controls are imposed to palliate the payments disequilibrium. The inefficiency involved is similar to that described in the standard case against tariff protection (and the qualifications applying to that case apply here also). A smoothly working market mechanism of payments adjustment avoids that inefficiency and the associated restriction of opportunities for international trade.

One of the burdens of adjustment, assuming that change is itself unpleasant for people, is the unpleasantness of shifting labor and other resources between the international-trade-goods and domestic-goods industries. These shifts are part and parcel of the adjustment, however, and it is probably splitting hairs to distinguish between this burden and the adjustment itself. *Working ideally*, the exchange-rate and general-price-level adjustment mechanisms accomplish identical shifts of resources (apart from minor qualifications about gold-mining and the like). These shifts are what they are in each country, and it is meaningless to ask how deficit and surplus countries share the burden of undergoing them.

This question becomes meaningful only when we recognize frictions. Because people need time to acquire, digest, and act on information about changes in market conditions, because of long-term contracts, because of the costs of revising prices, and so forth, prices are "sticky," especially in the downward direction. Prices cannot keep all markets always cleared. When, therefore, a payments-adjustment mechanism shifts demands from some sectors of

EXCHANGE-RATE ADJUSTMENT AND OTHER MECHANISMS: A PRELIMINARY COMPARISON

an economy to others, some unemployment and idle capacity appear in the sectors from which demand has shifted. It does matter *how* the required adjustments in trade, production, and resource allocation are made—how fast they occur, how nearly automatically, in response to what kinds of signals and incentives, and in response to whose, if anyone's, deliberate policy actions.[24] Some methods of balance-of-payments adjustment are more likely than others to entail unpleasant side effects such as transitional unemployment. The exchange-rate mechanism shifts the chair to the piano—to recall the analogy introduced on page 104—while the price-level mechanism of the gold standard tries to shift the piano to the chair. If countries rely on the latter mechanism, then, to the extent that surplus countries resist inflating, deficit countries must undergo all the more money and price deflation, risking the side effects of unemployment and loss of output. The more inflation the surplus countries accept, the less the deficit country shares in burdensome side effects.

All this is a reason for considering degrees of marginal pyramiding of domestic money onto international reserves and to compare the positions of a center country and peripheral countries under a foreign-exchange standard. Under a gold or foreign-exchange standard, flows of

22. Wolfgang Kasper argues that flexible exchange rates, by facilitating changes in international prices, would tend to promote competition across borders and impede international collusion among sellers. See George N. Halm, ed., *Approaches to Greater Flexibility of Exchange Rates*, Princeton, N.J.: Princeton University Press, 1970, p. 386n.

23. William P. Culbertson critically reviews the literature in his 1972 University of Texas doctoral dissertation, *The Burden of Balance-of-Payments Adjustment*. He emphasizes how nearly meaningless much of the supposed issue is. I am indebted to Professor Culbertson for use of his dissertation and for discussions with him, but he is not to blame for all of my formulations.

24. Closely related is the question of how to avoid unnecessary and inappropriate adjustments. That question is relevant when disturbances of balance-of-payments equilibrium have been essentially monetary rather than "real"; see p. 114.

international reserves affect money supplies and spending more strongly in the countries with the greater marginal pyramiding, other things being equal. Equal absolute changes are, of course, different percentage changes for countries of different size, but for an external imbalance of a given size *relative* to a country's economy, the country presumably shares the adjustment burden in inverse relation to its reserve ratio. Differences in monetary velocities and in the marginal propensities to import and save that determine foreign-trade multipliers blur this presumption. Price changes may not correspond closely with expenditure changes because of countries' different initial degrees of unemployment and slack in production and different degrees of price-and-wage flexibility. But we certainly would not say that a deficit country escapes its share of the adjustment burden to the extent that monetary deflation affects real activity instead of prices and wages; quite the contrary.

Even apart from all this hedging, the question of how burdens are shared is particularly complex when some countries are on a gold-exchange or foreign-exchange standard instead of a gold coin or bullion standard.[25] Consider a drain of reserves between two ordinary members of such a system, each of which holds its monetary reserves in the currency of some center country. The impact on each will be much the same as if each had been on an actual gold standard, and the size of its reserve ratio is relevant. A drain between an ordinary member and the center country will work asymmetrically. The ordinary member will be affected much as if gold had flowed under a gold standard, but in the center country the domestically held money supply (understood to include not only actual money but also near-moneys that other countries might hold as reserves) will change only by the absolute amount of the international reserve flow. When the center country runs an external surplus or deficit, its ordinary bank balances (and near-moneys) move into or out of the possession of its own residents and out of or into the possession of foreigners. It experiences no multiple expansion or contraction of money.[26] There is no such multiplication, anyway, unless its authorities deliberately engineer it out of concern for the *difference* between the country's gold reserves and the amount of its money and near-moneys held as reserves by foreigners. If its authorities fail to

do so, the center country leaves the bulk of the adjustment to the member country. The center country largely avoids the "discipline of the gold flows" that it would experience under a full-fledged international gold standard. This avoidance is particularly significant when the center country is running a deficit, for the member countries with the corresponding surpluses may not cure the imbalance by allowing their reserve gains to have their full impact on their own money supplies, incomes, and price levels. Their authorities may want moderate surpluses to continue as a way of building up their reserves of center-country currency in step with their general growth of income and international trade. The imbalance may then continue indefinitely, with the center country's external liabilities growing ever larger in relation to its gold reserves. The danger heightens that a scramble for actual gold may some day pull down the whole increasingly precarious structure. In some degree, at least until around 1968–1971, the United States was a center country of the kind described. The growth of American external liabilities in settlement (or perhaps one should say *non*settlement) of chronic deficits since 1950 convinced many observers that the dangers mentioned were indeed realistic. Chapter 27 will have more to say about this problem.

The center country is affected even by imbalances between two other countries if one of them belongs to the exchange-standard system and uses its currency as reserves but the other does not. A member country gaining actual gold from a nonmember will presumably exchange it for balances of center-country currency, following whatever motives led its authorities to choose an exchange standard rather than a gold standard in the first place. The center country gains gold reserves, then, even without running a balance-of-payments surplus itself. If the imbalance between the other countries is in the reverse direction, then the authorities of the nonmember country, unwilling to hold their new reserves in the form of foreign exchange, will convert them into gold drawn from the center country.

This possibility may lead the authorities of the center country to subtract member-country holdings of its currency from its total gold reserves to estimate its net or effective gold reserves. So defined, the net gold reserves of the center country will be unaffected by transfers among other countries, regardless of which are or are not members of the exchange-standard system. For example, if a nonmember gains reserves from a member and converts them into gold, the drain on the gross gold reserves of the center country is matched by an equal fall in its foreign liabilities. Even imbalances between the center and a member country will have effects much as under a regular gold standard if it is the *net* gold reserves that govern monetary responses in the center country. A rise or fall in liabilities to a member spells a fall or rise in the center's net gold reserves, to which its domestic money supply is now supposed to be more or less definitely geared.

But if this is how the center country responds to external imbalance, then the gold-exchange standard does not "economize" on gold after all; the multiple pyramiding of domestic money supplies in both center and member countries onto the central gold base is avoided. Either net reserves govern money supplies and the exchange standard does not economize on gold (though in historical fact this was its main purpose) or else the system is a precarious one. (Economizing on gold is precarious both because the center country has to shoulder part of the burden of readjusting to imbalances between member and nonmember countries and also because, for an indefinite period, the center country escapes "the discipline of the gold flows" that imbalances with member countries would otherwise impose on it.) Actual practice under the exchange standard has usually come closer to landing on the second horn of this dilemma.

Still another asymmetry may occur in the sharing of adjustment burdens under a fractional-reserve gold or exchange standard. It is implied in the question whether or not ratios between gold reserves and domestic money supplies remain fairly stable when gold flows in or out. The marginal gold-reserve ratio may well be larger, and the response of the domestic money supply smaller, for inflows than outflows. An imbalance leading to an inflow of reserves is seldom if ever a serious difficulty requiring prompt correction; the authorities may simply allow the reserves to pile up without promoting all the multiple domestic monetary expansion required to maintain a constant reserve *ratio*.[27] Of course, complete "sterilization" of inflowing reserves is neither easy nor likely; their purchase by the authorities as required to keep exchange rates fixed tends to expand domestic bank reserves and the money

EXCHANGE-RATE ADJUSTMENT AND OTHER MECHANISMS: A PRELIMINARY COMPARISON

supply much as would a central-bank open-market purchase of securities, and actual counterexpansionary action would depend on deliberate policy. But even partial sterilization by surplus countries throws an all the larger share of the adjustment burden onto the deficit countries. Furthermore, deficits call more urgently for action, since reserves losses are a more critical problem than gains. Even if a country had previously built up a comfortable margin of reserves beyond the legal or the supposedly prudent ratio, the limit to what it can stand to lose is much more definite than the almost nonexistent limit to the reserves that a surplus country can absorb. Much more than is true of a surplus country, a deficit country must act to restore balance and protect its reserves; and if it is to abide by the gold-standard rules against exchange depreciation and *ad hoc* controls over trade and payments, this action can only be to deflate. Because adjustment burdens fall more urgently on deficit than on surplus countries and because adjustment to a deficit means deflation, the gold standard has a deflation bias *if actually adhered to*. (This is not to say that the gold standard cannot be inflationary; it has been, as from about 1896 to 1914. The foregoing refers to whatever bias may be inherent in the relative intensities of pressures to adjust on deficit and surplus countries.)

25. The following relies in part on Meade, *op. cit.*, pp. 183–189.

26. However, if the foreign banks or monetary authorities insist on holding their external reserves as deposits with the central bank of the center country rather than as ordinary commercial-bank deposits or near-moneys, their losses and gains of such reserves can spell gains or losses of domestic monetary reserves for the commercial banks of the center country. These may then engage in multiple expansion or contraction of credit and deposits.

27. France and the United States were accused of such a "sterilization" of gold gains during the 1920s. A more recent and conspicuous example is West Germany's understandable reluctance to let the massive growth of her gold and dollar reserves since 1950 have its full domestic inflationary impact.

The adjustable peg: asymmetries and imported inflation

The foregoing discussion is much more relevant to systems of firmly fixed exchange rates than of flexible rates. Under flexible rates, deficit and surplus countries undergo more nearly symmetrical changes. This symmetry is less nearly complete when flexible rates are managed rather than free. The "adjustable peg"—the system of making deliberate changes in officially fixed rates—is an attempted halfway house between the two extremes of full international monetary linkage and full national monetary independence. Insofar as countries are reluctant to adjust their exchange parities and instead make both maintaining them and avoiding controls a leading policy goal, the system approximates the gold or gold-exchange standard and distributes adjustment burdens as already described. But since World War II, at least, countries have been understandably reluctant to deflate for the sake of external balance; "full employment" is the watchword of policy. A country will simply try to "ride out" an external deficit; its authorities will hope that the imbalance will somehow or other vanish of its own accord before too long. Meanwhile, they will continue to peg the exchange rate by drawing on reserves or international loans. But it is still true that deficits and reserve losses pose a more pressing problem than surpluses. A country with a persistent deficit will ultimately impose controls as a palliative or, in accordance with the logic of the adjustable-peg system, will devalue. But it will not actively deflate.

Just as under the gold standard, the need to act falls more urgently on deficit than on surplus countries. But the preference for devaluation over deflation makes the adjustable-peg system contrast sharply with a gold standard that is meant to be permanent and whose rules are obeyed. An inflationary bias emerges in several ways. In the sometimes lengthy intervals between exchange-rate adjustments, when some countries are hopefully "riding out" deficits and losing reserves, others are running surpluses and gaining reserves. Without wanting to, a surplus country tends to "import" inflation in four overlapping ways. (1) Local-currency prices of imports, import-competing goods, and exportable goods are linked, through the fixed exchange rate, with rising prices in the inflationary outside world.[28] (2)

An export surplus spells withdrawal of real goods and services from the home economy; less than the full value of its current production is available for satisfying demands on the home market. (3) The foreign-trade multiplier operates in the expansionary direction. (4) The authorities create new domestic money as they buy the local residents' surplus earnings of foreign exchange to keep exchange rates pegged. Capital inflows, if they occur, have a similar monetary effect.

Under a fractional-reserve banking system, official purchases of foreign exchange or gold, as of securities or anything else, expand the volume of bank reserves and set the stage for a multiple expansion of ordinary deposit money. Deliberate monetary or fiscal measures can conceivably counteract or neutralize these spontaneous inflationary pressures, but successful neutralization tends to frustrate balance-of-payments adjustment, perpetuating the troublesome surplus and the need for domestic measures to resist its inflationary impact. For the sake of being able, without inflation, to make the involuntary loans to foreigners that the foreign-exchange accumulations represent, a country must impose higher taxes or tighter credit on the economy than would otherwise be necessary. The dilemma is compounded if anti-inflation policy involves interest rates high enough to attract funds from abroad, increasing the amount of foreign exchange that the central bank must buy to maintain exchange-rate stability. These purchases further tend to expand the domestic money supply, and borrowers of the inflowing foreign funds presumably pay higher interest rates on them than the authorities earn on their involuntary foreign-exchange accumulations. Domestic policies for monetary stability cannot be as consistent, vigorous, and relatively painless as they could if some mechanism were continuously correcting balance-of-payments disequilibria. Despite everything, though, it is possible that surplus countries might succeed at least for a while in "sterilizing" their reserve gains, sometimes completely and often partially. But if they sterilize less completely and less typically than deficit countries avoid deflation—which is probable—the adjustable peg has an inflationary bias.

Sterilization by surplus countries has already been noted as an at least minor problem for deficit countries under the gold standard. From the standpoint of surplus countries, the prospects for successful sterilization are probably dimmer under the adjustable-peg system than under the gold standard. Imbalances are likely to be larger and longer-lasting because authorities in deficit countries, knowing that they can always devalue or impose controls as a last resort, are less willing to deflate as a corrective. Furthermore, a general desire to keep exchange rates fixed except for infrequent adjustments breeds international arrangements to help deficit countries "ride out" their supposedly temporary troubles. The more these devices enable deficit countries to avoid or postpone or mitigate the controls or devaluations otherwise necessary, the slighter is their immediate need to restrain imports and push exports and the stronger, therefore, are price-raising demands relative to supplies in the world markets for their imports and exports. And better-financed deficits for some countries mean larger and more persistent surpluses for other countries, together with problems of imported inflation. The hope that deficits and surpluses will alternate is hardly reassuring, for the alternation will take place at generally higher levels of spending than if special finance for deficits had not been provided.

A surplus, with its inflationary impact, may indeed reverse itself in time. But the deflationary impact of a subsequent deficit is hardly a full and satisfactory offset to what may have happened earlier. Trying belatedly to undo an accomplished inflation courts unemployment and recession. A country will resist deflationary pressures from abroad even when they come against a background of inflation imported earlier. A "ratchet" is at work.

A related aspect of this "ratchet" shows up in a radically simplified example concerning either several industries within a single country or several countries in a world of pegged currencies. Suppose that something, such as changed consumer preferences, shifts demand away from the products of industry or country A onto the products of industry or country B. Prices and wages are bid up in B but exhibit downward rigidities in A. Demand next shifts from B to industry or country C, again raising some prices and wages without correspondingly reducing others. Now demand may shift back toward A, perhaps still in a depression from the first shift. Wages and prices may or may not go up there; in any case, they have gone up and stayed up in B and C. Mere shifts—perhaps only temporary shifts—in the pattern of demand may thus raise the *average* level of wages and prices.[29] Under the unlikely policy of

EXCHANGE-RATE ADJUSTMENT AND OTHER MECHANISMS: A PRELIMINARY COMPARISON

stabilizing money supplies or total spending, these wage-and-price increases would entail unemployment, but acquiescent monetary expansion would consolidate them. Within a country, this dilemma stems from inadequate two-way flexibility of wages and prices; internationally, it stems from lack of continuous balance-of-payments adjustment through either domestic price-and-wage flexibility or continuous exchange-rate flexibility.

Perhaps it is not yet clear what serves as the growing reserve basis for the expansion of national money supplies. Without monetary expansion the inflationary tendencies already described could not go very far. One answer may be the creation of "international liquidity" under various schemes to shore up the adjustable-peg system. Even apart from this, the devaluation bias of the system provides an answer.

Because deficits and reserve losses are more critical problems than surpluses and reserve gains, countries are more likely to devalue in response to deficits than to revalue their currencies upward to escape inflationary pressures from abroad. History seemed to bear out this generalization, anyway, until around the end of the 1960s.[30] (Many of the revaluations that did occur in 1971–1973 can be seen as incidents in the relative devaluation of the U.S.

28. This aspect of the process is stressed in Gerhard Fels, *Der internationale Preiszusammenhang*, Köln: Heymanns, 1969. Fels's arguments and other aspects of imported inflation are considered further in the chapter in Part II on the German experience. See also Samuel I. Katz, *"Imported Inflation" and the Balance of Payments*, The Bulletin, Nos. 91–92, New York University, October 1973.

29. Charles L. Schultze reports detecting some such ratchet mechanism at work domestically. *Recent Inflation in the United States*, Joint Economic Committee Study Paper No. 1, Washington: U.S. Government Printing Office, 1959.

30. For earlier historical documentation of the devaluation bias of fixed exchanges, see Henrik Akerlund, *Guldparistandarden*, Stockholm: Grafiska Konstanstalten Tryckeri, 1959, pp. 85–88. Upward revaluations, when such rarities occurred, were likely to err on the small side.

dollar, which, because of the dollar's special role in the crumbling gold-exchange-standard system, was a process that stretched out piecemeal over time.)

One important check to upward revaluation is the prospect of domestic political opposition from the interests whom it would harm. (The greater influence of special producer interests than of the general consumer interest is a familiar fact of practical politics, amply illustrated in tariff legislation.) People attached to the export and import-competing industries are likely to complain that revaluing means accepting an unfair penalty for the country's economic success. The government of a surplus country escapes this political onus if, instead, deficit countries devalue. Furthermore, since no one knows how to calculate a new equilibrium exchange rate, there is always the danger that a revaluation might prove excessive. Or the conditions that had seemed to justify it might blow over of their own accord. A related problem with deliberate revaluation is the risk that other countries will not follow suit appropriately. Suppose, for example, that Germany and Japan are both running heavy surpluses while the United States is heavily in deficit. If either Germany or Japan revalues first, it runs the risk that the other will not follow and that it will lose competitiveness in a wrong pattern of exchange rates. Each prefers that the other act first, or that the United States devalue. In contrast with what is true under freely floating exchange rates, the question of distribution of an adjustment burden of a particular kind thus does arise when a new multilateral pattern of exchange rates has to be reached by deliberate adjustment of pegs. The temptation is to sit tight and wait.

Similar temptations tend to delay action when conditions call for devaluation. The move would harm people interested in cheap imports and would otherwise affect the distribution of income. The secrecy necessary in preparing a devaluation inhibits full consultation among all affected departments even within a single government. Supposed national prestige may be at stake. Political opponents may cite the devaluation as evidence of earlier financial bungling or may encourage public uproar about "letting the speculators get away with it." Still, conditions can eventually force devaluation in a fuller sense than they can force revaluation. If devaluation must finally come, it is more likely to err on the large side

than on the small side. Since the authorities in any case incur the odium of changing the rate, they might as well avoid a change so small as to raise the question whether it really was necessary. They might as well play safe and avoid risking the need for a confidence-shaking second devaluation soon afterward. Also, a switch from overvaluation to undervaluation of the currency may give the authorities a chance to rebuild their depleted reserves. Excessive devaluation sets the stage for inflationary influences working through the balance of payments.

Although national governments feel inhibitions against "taking the *initiative* in making parity changes, it is difficult to prevent a chain reaction once a major parity change is announced. Other countries feel they must make an overnight decision, and may well be tempted to decide that they have a golden opportunity to put the blame for unpopular action on forces outside their control."[31] Over the long run, the devaluation bias of the system means that even a fixed world stock of gold (or whatever else serves as basic international reserves) would grow in value expressed in national currencies; and given the modern insistence on a large measure of national freedom to pursue full-employment policies, an abundance of international liquidity is more likely to promote than a scarcity is to restrain the inflation of national currencies.

Even the gold standard, like the adjustable-peg system, suffers from this inflationary devaluation bias. Despite the firmest of intentions, gold parities cannot be kept fixed forever; forced devaluations and depreciations are a familiar historical fact. Over the long run, the gold standard *is* an adjustable-peg system, but with the adjustments infrequent. The *deflationary* bias previously attributed to the gold standard operates in the relatively short run, the inflationary bias secularly. There is no incompatibility between these two biases. Both operate because adjustment burdens fall more urgently on deficit than on surplus countries. This means deflation as long as deficit countries can manage to stick to the gold-standard rules, devaluation when the game is up. In practice, forced devaluations are seldom reversed. Sporadic long-run currency erosion is no less real just because short-run deflations interrupt the process. Short-run and long-run troubles do not just compensate for each other. When a streamroller is rolling over you from south to north, it is no consolation to know that later on it will probably roll over you again from north to south.

In favor of the gold standard, on the other hand, its supporters claim that it poses a healthy "discipline'" against the inflationary propensities of governments.

Fluctuating exchanges

The system of independent national currencies with freely fluctuating rates stands at the opposite extreme from the gold standard. Whether it has asymmetries and biases of different kinds than those discussed here, whether it suffers from and promotes various kinds of instability, whether it impedes trade and investment and generally disrupts international economic integration, and whether it has still other disadvantages—all these questions will be explored in later chapters. Meanwhile, it is worth noting that it largely escapes several of the specific asymmetries and biases of the gold standard and the adjustable-peg system.

Most fundamentally, free rates avoid imposing the more urgent need for action and the bulk of the adjustment burden on deficit rather than surplus countries. This two-sidedness is a distinctive feature which deserves emphasis. No authority need decide about allowing or promoting deflation or inflation; the short-run deflation bias of the gold standard is absent. No authority need decide about adjusting a pegged rate downward or upward. No authority operates with the understandable human tendency to err on the large side when deciding on devaluations and on the small side when deciding on upward revaluations. The rate adjusts itself under impersonal market pressures. It moves upward for a country that would otherwise have had an external surplus just as readily as it moves downward for a country otherwise in external deficit (both movements considered relative to the currencies of countries in approximate external balance). The asymmetry and the inflationary devaluation bias of the adjustable peg are absent.

Since imbalances do not go uncorrected for long periods, countries otherwise in surplus can avoid the inflations—inflations irreversible in practice, because of downward wage and price stickiness—that they might otherwise sometimes import or that they could neutralize only with difficulty. Continuous balance-of-pay-

EXCHANGE-RATE ADJUSTMENT AND OTHER MECHANISMS: A PRELIMINARY COMPARISON

ments adjustment, together with the effective two-way flexibility that fluctuating rates give to each country's wages and prices in terms of foreign currencies, counters the international aspects of the inflationary "ratchet" associated even with nothing worse than mere temporary shifts in patterns of demand. (See pp. 111–112.)

More broadly, free rates permit compartmentalizing inflationary tendencies. Consider an inflation originating in certain countries under a fixed-rate system. Whether it is due to monetary expansion pure and simple or to acquiescent monetary policy in the face of a "wage push" is immaterial. Trade becomes unbalanced. Other countries experience the familiar monetary and "multiplier" effects of balance-of-payments surpluses. Increased costs of importing from the originally inflationary countries hasten these effects by directly pushing costs and prices upward. (All these effects may be imperceptibly slight if the first countries make up only a small fraction of the world economy and develop only mild inflations; the nature rather than strength of international contagion is what is at issue here.) Under free rates, by contrast, other countries escape not only external surpluses and their consequences but also the apparent "cost push" of increased import prices. Wages and prices in the inflationary countries, though increased in local currency, are translated at promptly depreciated exchange rates. This keeps the export prices of inflationary countries and their demands for the exports of other countries from increasing from the viewpoint of the latter. The *pattern* of prices and demands seen by other countries does change somewhat, since wages, prices, and demands in terms of local currency in inflationary countries do not all rise in equal proportion. As translated at the new exchange rates, some individual prices and demands rise and others fall. But the new ex-

31. Stephen Marris, *The Bürgenstock Communiqué: A Critical Examination of the Case for Limited Flexibility of Exchange Rates*, Princeton Essays in International Finance, No. 80, Princeton, N.J.: Princeton University, May 1970, p. 17.

change rates do prevent any unequivocal increases, from the viewpoint of other countries, in the general level of prices charged by and demand emanating from the first.

Depression as well as inflation can be compartmentalized under free rates. Exchange depreciation under free-market pressures can save countries not originally involved in foreign depressions from balance-of-payments deficits and their deflationary consequences. "The free-exchange system eliminates . . . the most important carrier of the boom and depression bacillus—namely, the flow of money across frontiers."[32]

A flexible exchange rate not only accomplishes necessary adjustments of resource allocation in a relatively efficient way but also helps avoid unnecessary adjustments. To understand how, we must distinguish between adjustments to "real" and to monetary disturbances. A monetary inflation abroad, raising all foreign prices uniformly, would be the prototype of a purely monetary disturbance. The resulting appreciation of the home currency on the exchanges would make it possible to *avoid* changes in prices and resource allocation at home. A monetary disturbance is unlikely to be *purely* monetary, however, especially in the approximately opposite case of foreign *deflation*. In practice, foreign countries cannot experience deflation without also suffering a depression of production and employment and real income and so becoming less effectively eager trading partners for the home economy than before. Thus, some "real" adjustment—some repatterning of resource allocation and of production and consumption—is necessary. But the adjustment is easier than if the home country had to adjust to foreign depression under fixed exchange rates. The adjustment even to a purely "real" disturbance is also easier under flexible than under fixed rates. If foreign demand shifts away from the home country's export products, the otherwise necessary fall in export prices or production is cushioned by currency depreciation. Depreciation avoids the *general* deflation of the home money supply and price level that would be necessary under the fixed-exchange-rate mechanism.

None of the foregoing means that free exchange rates, in and by themselves, can ward off all troubles, ranging from hangnails to unemployment. Nothing short of total prohibition of foreign trade could insulate a country completely from foreign economic developments. Independently motivated capital movements, for example, would still have an impact, though probably opposite in direction from and weaker in intensity than their impact under fixed exchange rates. (An inflow would tend to strengthen the home currency on the exchanges, thereby cause imports of goods and services to exceed exports, and in turn have an adverse multiplier effect on domestic economic activity.) Free exchange rates are no substitute for appropriate domestic policy, but they do at least free domestic policy from balance-of-payments constraints. They free it to resist the economy-wide inflation or deflation that foreign disturbances might otherwise impose.

According to one line of reasoning, the free flexibility of exchange rates actually increases the effectiveness of monetary policy for domestic stability. Expanding the money supply and reducing interest rates to counter a recession—or even just letting interest rates fall spontaneously, as they typically do in a recession—tends to cause a capital outflow. The balance of payments would be in overall deficit—*except* that the home currency depreciates on the exchanges to whatever extent necessary to cause an export surplus of goods and services large enough to match the capital outflow. This export surplus represents a timely addition to the demand for domestic output and domestic factors of production. An anti-inflationary monetary policy, conversely, influences capital movements so as to make the home currency appreciate, bringing a net inflow of goods and services into the country and imposing restraint on the pricing policies of domestic producers. This reinforcement of domestic policy, says Egon Sohmen, no doubt exaggerating, "is perhaps the most persuasive reason for the advocacy of flexible exchanges. . . ."[33]

Even if the free-rate system avoids some asymmetries and biases of rival systems, doesn't it have other and perhaps worse ones of its own? No systematically unequal imposition of adjustment burdens is apparent, particularly if rates are allowed to respond just as freely to potential surpluses as to potential deficits. Nor is any deflation bias apparent.

The absence of deflation bias raises suspicion of an inflation bias; a perfectly neutral system is implausible. Under free rates, concern for its balance of payments never forces a country to deflate nor restrains it from inflating. The problem of downward inflexibility of wages and prices is not necessarily any worse than under other exchange-rate systems; but anyway, accidental inflationary impulses that might otherwise prove temporary and remediable threaten to become consolidated in wage and price structures. A "ratchet" operates. The exchange depreciation that avoids a balance-of-payments deficit allows import and export prices to rise in local currency and, together with the monetary expansion that may have been the initial disturbance, allows a general rise in prices. Exchange-rate pegging, by contrast, lets the country enjoy the anti-inflationary assistance of an actual deficit: the real goods and services in effect borrowed from abroad help hold down prices, while the sale of foreign exchange drawn from official reserves or borrowed abroad mops up liquidity at home. In broader terms, the gearing of the home economy into a not-yet-inflated world environment provides time

---

32. Gottfried von Haberler, *op. cit.*, p. 446. No country ever seems to have made a thoroughgoing experiment with free exchanges as a buffer against foreign business fluctuations, but some accidental examples illustrate the possibilities revealed by theory. As price and income levels sank in gold-standard countries after 1929, the Spanish government reluctantly alowed the peseta to depreciate severely against gold currencies. The Spanish price level sagged only moderately, and the depression was less severe in Spain than in other countries. Walter H. Delaplane, "The Spanish Peseta since 1913" (unpublished dissertation), Durham: Duke University, 1934, pp. 128–129, 135, 138, 158, 207; Anon., "Eine 'systematisch unstabile Währung'. Die spanische Peseta," *Währung und Wirtschaft*, IV, August 1935, p. 130. Spanish national income held up well in the early 1930s; Colin Clark reproduces the figures in *The Conditions of Economic Progress*, 2nd ed., London: Macmillan, 1951, p. 156.

Exchange depreciation of her silver-standard currency spared China internal deflation and the contagion of the world depression for the first two years after its outbreak in 1929. See p. 355.

Considerable other evidence suggests that countries with depreciated currencies weathered the 1929 depression better than countries that clung longer to their old gold parities. See James W. Angell, "Exchange Depreciation, Foreign Trade and National Welfare," *Proceedings of the Academy of Political Science*, XV, June 1933, p. 291; and Richard A. Lester, *Monetary Experiments*, Princeton, N. J.: Princeton University Press, 1939, p. 275.

Besides being much weaker under flexible than under fixed exchange rates, the international contagion of business fluctuations even tends to work in the opposite way. At least, so goes one plausible

EXCHANGE-RATE ADJUSTMENT AND OTHER MECHANISMS: A PRELIMINARY COMPARISON

line of reasoning. (See Svend Laursen and Lloyd A. Metzler, "Flexible Exchange Rates and the Theory of Employment," *Review of Economics and Statistics*, **XXXII**, November 1950, pp. 281–299. Egon Sohmen gives a lucid and on the whole concurring discussion of this argument in *Flexible Exchange Rates*, revised ed., pp. 138–140.) Suppose that a depression in Outland lowers the demand for Inland's exports, causing its currency to depreciate on the exchanges. Import prices rise in Inland currency, while the primary effect of the drop in Outland demand keeps the depreciation from raising export prices to the same extent (if at all). Since import prices rise relative to export prices while imports and exports remain equal in value (though at a new level—one key assumption, incidentally, is the absence of any capital movements accommodating a temporary imbalance), import *quantity* falls relative to export *quantity*. Real demand is shunted toward Inland's domestic output and domestic factors of production. Employment tends to rise, unless already existing full employment puts the entire demand pressure on prices. (Nothing in the process just outlined would tend spontaneously, apart from policy, to cause an offsetting shrinkage in the Inland money supply.)

A more intuitive way of seeing all this is to note that depressed Outland has become an effectively less eager trading partner, which causes Inland's terms of trade to worsen and real income (at the previously existing level of employment) to fall. The worsening of Inland's opportunities for international trade has the same kind of employment-creating or price-raising impact, loosely speaking, as would a bad harvest or an earthquake.

33. *Op. cit.*, 1961 ed., p. 84. See also pp. 83, 85, 123–124, as well as Sohmen, *International Monetary Problems and the Foreign Exchanges*, Special Papers in International Economics, No. 4, Princeton, N.J.: Princeton University, International Finance Section, 1963, pp. 6, 51–54, 65, 70; and J. Marcus Fleming, "Domestic Financial Policies Under Fixed and Under Floating Exchange Rates," IMF *Staff Papers*, **IX**, November 1962, pp. 369–379.

The contrast with fixed exchange rates is striking. An anti-inflationary policy of tight money and relatively high interest rates tends to attract capital, expand foreign exchange reserves and domestic bank reserves, and so promote unwanted monetary expansion. The German experience with this problem in the 1950s, reviewed in Chapter 24, is instructive.

to correct the inflationary impulse before it is irreversibly consolidated in wages and prices.[34]

What this really means is that the country not so much prevents all inflation as makes inflation of domestic origin inconspicuous by diluting it into the outside world. It shoves its problem onto other countries in many small inconspicuous bits. It may use this opportunity to gain time while correcting inflationary pressures. Or it may not. Inflation, especially "wage-push" inflation, has aptly been characterized as an attempt by different groups to divide up among themselves more than the total national output. Under fixed exchange rates these excessive claims against national output can partly be met—for a while—by dipping into reserves or borrowing abroad. It is not unprecedented for a regime currently in power to subsidize the temporary delights of living beyond the country's means by dissipating its external reserves, passively hoping that the longer-run necessary adjustment will somehow take care of itself and leaving it to some successor regime to impose "austerity." Monetary insulation under fluctuating exchanges, on the other hand, leaves each country more immediately and fully exposed to the wanted or unwanted consequences of its own policies. This is a disadvantage for the less prudent countries and an advantage for the more prudent ones.

Free rates allow a country to drift carelessly into inflation; at the other extreme, they allow it to pursue monetary stability even in an inflationary world. Monetary independence means freedom for recklessness and prudence alike. This is a relevant comment on the further point that under fixed exchange rates, the "discipline of the balance of payments"—the need to worry about deficits—restrains inflationary domestic policy. Sometimes, by coincidence, the "discipline" will work in a welcome direction; at other times, not. And as for "discipline," a free exchange rate may itself be a useful alarm signal, indicating domestic inflationary tendencies more conspicuously than an external deficit would and rallying public protest more promptly. Conceivably, of course, the opposite is true: dwindling reserves may be a greater impulse to timely action than a falling exchange rate; the impression that the exchange rate alone will take care of the balance of payments may make the public apathetic about fighting inflation.[35] But these indecisive considerations relate to the psychology of central bankers, politicians, and voters and not to biases inherent in instituional arrangements.

Conclusion

The expenditure policies required for both internal and external balance coincide when a disturbance is domestic and clash when it is external; the required price policies clash for a domestic and coincide for an external disturbance. This fact, together with difficulties in using price policy for internal balance, tells in favor of expenditure policy as the main weapon for internal and price policy for external balance. Adjustment works more simply in practice through exchange rates than through general levels of domestic prices, even though the two mechanisms are *ideally* the same. Exchange-rate flexibility contributes to effective flexibility of wages and prices in accordance with the logic of a price system.

The burden of correcting external imbalances fall unevenly on different countries under the gold standard. The incidence depends in part on their different sizes, reserve ratios, marginal propensities to import, and initial degrees of prosperity. How the burden falls is even more complicated under a gold-exchange or foreign-exchange standard, depending in addition on whether each country involved is a center country, an ordinary member of the system, or a nonmember.

In assessing possible inflation or deflation biases of different exchange-rate systems, two considerations stand out. First, deficit countries feel more urgent pressures to correct disequilibriums than do surplus countries, except under freely fluctuating exchange rates. Second, countries have stronger incentives to resist deflation than to resist inflation. The first consideration tends to make for a deflation bias under permanently fixed exchange rates but for a devaluation and inflation bias under fixed-but-adjustable exchange rates. Under the latter (adjustable-peg) system, surplus countries have a tendency to import inflation irreversibly, and devaluations are more likely than upward revaluations. The second consideration used to be weakened by acceptance of the gold-standard mystique and the associated willingness to deflate to cure balance-of-payments deficits. Since the best of intentions cannot maintain gold parities forever, however, even the gold standard is a system of (infrequently) adjustable pegs and so has a long-run inflation bias in addition to its shorter-run deflation bias. The system of free exchange rates, whatever its other defects may be, apparently has no deflation bias and has an inflation bias only in the sense of not yoking the financially less prudent countries together with the financially more prudent ones.

duce exchange depreciation that spreads irreversibly into the whole wage and price structure. It is noteworthy, however, that he explicitly assumes a passively expanding money supply. With the money supply so completely out of control, flexible prices of *anything*, and not just of foreign exchange, would seem to be unsafe.

Emil Küng, *Zahlungsbilanzpolitik*, Zurich: Polygraphischer Verlag, 1959, p. 582, reviews the opinions of several other writers on which is more effective as an alarm signal for mobilizing opinion against inflationary policies—reserve drains or exchange depreciation.

34. See Robert Triffin, *Gold and the Dollar Crisis*, New Haven, Conn.: Yale University Press, 1960, pp. 82–86.

35. Lionel Robbins, *The Economist in the Twentieth Century*, London: Mamcillan, 1954, pp. 98–101 and esp. p. 100. Robbins worries that some otherwise minor disturbance, perhaps an unfavorable "real" change on the world market, will pro-

Appendix 1 to Chapter 6: Separate Weapons of Financial Policy

Separation of fiscal and monetary policy

Chapter 6 considered cases in which expenditure or financial policy alone, without price policy, could not achieve both internal and external balance; the trouble lay in having more goals than weapons. One conceivable solution might be to split expenditure policy into two separate weapons, monetary policy (interpreted as interest-rate policy) and fiscal policy.[1] For controlling the overall balance of payments, including the private (or independently motivated) capital account, interest-rate policy has a comparative advantage, so to speak. Fiscal policy has a comparative advantage in controlling aggregate demand. While the interest rate and the government budget both affect aggregate demand and, through it, affect the current account of the balance of payments, the interest rate has an additional effect on capital movements.

Let us consider the two "dilemma" combinations of internal and external disequilibrium. The authorities might raise the interest rate to deal with an external deficit. An existing domestic slump would then tend to grow worse, but a cut of a certain size in the government budget surplus (or increase in the budget deficit) could just offset this deflationary ten-dency, leaving some external improvement through the response of capital movements to the raised interest rate. The current account would not fully wipe out this improvement even if some further fiscal ease now actually expanded aggregate demand. Part of this expansion could now survive a further rise in the interest rate for balance-of-payments purposes. Policies might conceivably combine so that the high interest rate outweighed the fiscal ease fully enough in affecting the balance of payments to cure the external deficit, while the fiscal ease outweighed the same high interest rate fully enough in affecting demand to cure the domestic slump.

In the opposite case of conflicting disequilibriums, the suggested remedy includes cutting the interest rate to reduce an external surplus. The unwanted inflationary tendency could just be offset by a definite degree of fiscal tightening, leaving the response of international capital movements as desired. The current account would not fully undo this move toward overall external balance even if some further fiscal tightening now actually shrank demand. This desired shrinkage could now partially survive a further cut in the interest rate. Conceivably, a low interest rate could outweigh fiscal tightness fully enough in affecting the balance of payments to cure its surplus, while the fiscal tightness could outweigh the low interest rate fully enough in affecting demand to cure the domestic inflation.

In the sense suggested by these last two examples, interest-rate policy corrects the balance of payments while fiscal policy corrects the level of aggregate demand. In accordance with Mundell's Principle of Effective Market Classification,[2] each policy aims at the objective on which it has the relatively greater influence. Since the two policies pull in opposite directions, each one has to be more extreme than would be necessary if the objective it is paired with were the only objective in view; but since each policy has a comparative advantage in reaching one of the two objectives, an overall reconciliation may be found.

Starting in late 1960 or early 1961, the United States attempted something like this solution (with the further refinement of trying to split interest-rate policy itself into two parts —see p. 569). Besides this unsatisfactory experience, several general considerations cast doubt on the idea. Except perhaps for mild and temporary clashes between internal and external requirements, it counts more as a piece of academic ingenuity than as serious policy advice. For one thing, the idea assumes away concern about the makeup of the balance of payments and tacitly regards a current-account deficit matched by an artificially stimulated capital inflow as just as satisfactory as a closer approach to balance in the two external accounts separately. Maintenance of capital inflow could become increasingly difficult as a larger and larger fraction of the total stock of internationally mobile funds had *already* moved. Payment of interest on a growing debt to foreigners could itself eventually become an important minus item in the balance of payments. This burden would be particularly regrettable if capital had been artificially lured in the first place from countries where its marginal productivity was relatively high to a country where its marginal productivity was relatively low. Furthermore, the government budget, the government debt, the money supply, the compositions of investors' portfolios, interest rates, the behavior of the price level, and rates of capital formation and economic growth are all interrelated. How strongly a budget deficit spurs total demand, for example, surely depends on how it is financed, which also affects interest rates. The performance of the home economy could suffer unless something distinct from monetary-fiscal policy helped serve external balance.

Most fundamentally, the whole analysis reviewed here rests on the question-begging assumption that there does exist some combination of interest rate and budget position capable of achieving both goals at the same time. Yet what assures each policy enough potency to achieve its goal even while the other policy pulls in the opposite direction? Suppose that the United States arbitrarily marked the dollar up to twice its present foreign-exchange value. Could *any* attainable combination of interest rate and budget position cure the resulting external deficit without internal deflation or direct controls?

Forward-rate policy to cope with interest-rate differentials

Another suggestion for reconciling internal and external balance without altering the exchange parity has a longer history of academic discussion. Official intervention in the forward-exchange market could selectively manipulate

the interest rates relevant to international capital movements. In effect, these rates could be kept high enough for external balance without requiring a domestic interest-rate and money-supply policy any tighter than necessary for the health of the home economy.

To understand the idea, we must first expand on our earlier explanation of how capital movements respond to interest rates and spot and forward exchange rates. Funds are presumably the more mobile, the more narrowly spot exchange rates are allowed to fluctuate and the more confidence these limits command. With the range zero and confidence absolute, a country with relatively low interest rates would either have to align its rates with those abroad or else risk seeing its foreign-exchange reserves shrink, perhaps to the point where speculation joined higher earnings, after all, in drawing capital out. The possibility of even moderate exchange-rate fluctuations, however, should restrain enthusiasm for uncovered interest arbitrage. A mere one-quarter of 1 percent adverse movement while funds were on loan abroad for three months would cancel the gain from an interest differential of 1 percentage point a year. Arbitrageurs would therefore seek forward-exchange cover for their return into their home currency. In obtaining this protection they would bid up its cost. The rise would be sharp if other persons showed only a limited and price-inelastic willingness to deal on the other side of the forward market as counterparties to the interest arbitrageurs. The scope for profitable interest arbitrage and the national danger from interest-motivated capital outflow would be limited. Anyway, this was a reassuring view commonly held and apparently supported by experience while postwar exchange restrictions

1. Robert A. Mundell, "The Appropriate Use of Monetary and Fiscal Policy for Internal and External Stability," IMF *Staff Papers*, **IX**, March 1962, pp. 70–76.

An alternative suggestion for increasing the number of policy weapons has hardly been developed in the literature: price policy might conceivably be split into price-level and exchange-rate policy.

2. *Ibid.*

and exchange-rate uncertainty continued until the late 1950s.

To make the idea clear, let us consider an interest-motivated temporary transfer of funds abroad. To avoid risk on moving back into home money (crowns), the interest arbitrageurs would sell foreign money (gold) forward at the very time of buying it spot. Spot gold would tend to strengthen against the crown. A weakening of forward gold would probably be more pronounced, since the arbitrageurs would probably be undertaking a larger fraction of total forward than of total spot transactions (especially with the central bank dealing to limit spot rate fluctuations). The arbitrage would thus, as usual, tend to use up the opportunities motivating it. This limit to profitable arbitrage would be especially narrow if, as the reassuring view supposed, forward gold would have to fall sharply to induce even a limited volume of additional commitments on the *other side* of the arbitrageurs' forward contracts.

William H. White has pointed out why, after all, the volume of funds available for commitment on the other side of arbitrageurs' forward contracts is *not* likely to be so small and so insensitive to price.[3] His crucial assumption is firm confidence that the spot exchange rate will hold within set limits. Exporters and importers will not then *routinely* make forward contracts to cover future receipts and payments of foreign money; their decisions will depend on the forward rate. Suppose the spot rate is fluctuating within firmly trusted limits of 1.98 and 2.02 crowns per gram of gold. Merchants do not know just where within these limits the rate will be in three months (or whatever the relevant period is); they can only guess in comparing spot rates then and now. An importer due to pay gold in three months can, however, compare the current forward rate with the two spot limits. The closer the forward rate on gold is to the trusted upper spot limit of Cr2.02, the less he risks losing and the more he stands to gain by simply waiting to buy gold spot in three months instead of arranging for it now at such a high forward rate. With the current forward rate exactly *at* Cr2.02, the importer has every reason to shun a forward contract. But when a current forward rate at the opposite spot limit of Cr1.98 presented no chance at all of getting gold more cheaply spot and great risk of its costing more, he would have every reason to make a forward purchase.

The same argument, properly modified, applies to an exporter due to receive gold in three months. A comparison of possible gains and losses counts the more strongly for making a forward sale, the closer the current forward rate lies to Cr2.02; it counts the more strongly for simply awaiting a better spot rate, the closer the forward rate lies to Cr1.98.[4]

Considering the responses of importers and exporters together, we see that the closer the current forward rate is to Cr2.02, the larger the net quantity of forward gold supplied; the closer to Cr1.98, the larger the net quantity demanded. This responsiveness of traders' supply and demand puts flexibility into the volume of commitments available to match the desires of arbitrageurs. When arbitrageurs are heavily supplying forward gold to cover the return of funds temporarily moved abroad, their supply need not run up against so limited and nearly rigid a demand as to require a sharp fall in the forward rate to clear the market. On the contrary, a sag in the forward rate would tend to cushion itself—and so preserve the scope for profitable interest arbitrage—by inducing ordinary traders to demand a larger net quantity of forward gold.

A key assumption warrants emphasis again: the forward-rate-sensitive behavior of traders that accommodates interest-arbitrage transactions depends on confidence in the spot-rate limits. Without it, traders would seek forward cover against their exchange risks more completely as a matter of routine and with less regard to the level of the forward rate. Their transactions accommodating those desired by interest-arbitrageurs would be less flexible in volume, the forward-rate movement caused by any given change in the volume of interest arbitrage would be larger, and the self-limiting character of this arbitrage would be all the more pronounced.

This reasoning raises doubt whether observations about the interest-sensitivity of capital movements in times of low confidence in spot rates are relevant to times of high confidence. Experience in one situation may have little bearing on another and quite different one. The reasoning also suggests that widening the spot-rate limits might impede troublesome interest-motivated capital movements The forward rate would then have to rise or fall over a wider range to create a given state of opinion among traders about the chances of the future spot rate's being higher or lower; a given change in the forward rate would elicit a smaller change in traders' net use of forward contracts. There would be less cushioning of the forward-rate movements whereby interest arbitrage destroys its own profitability. A given international interest-rate differential would motivate a smaller transfer of funds. The closer the system came to complete lack of any spot rate limits, the slighter the problem such transfers would pose.

Recognizing all this does not mean condemning all aspects of interest arbitrage and forward exchange. On the contrary, the theory of interest arbitrage provides the main reason for expecting reasonably priced protection against traders' exchange risks. Is it inconsistent to welcome this aspect, yet regret that rate-sensitive, nonroutine forward covering by traders accommodates interest arbitrage? Is it contradictory to suppose that interest arbitrage *will* accommodate commercial covering but that, under flexible spot rates, variations in commercial covering will *not* greatly accommodate interest arbitrage? Mere consistency does not prove an argument correct, of course, but it is a necessary condition.

To consider these questions, we should distinguish between two types of sources of opportunity for profit from interest arbitrage. If the source is an actual interest differential between countries, the authorities would presumably like to see only a small capital outflow suffice to establish the spread between spot and forward rates that would make any larger volume of outward arbitrage unprofitable; they would regret an arbitrage-accommodating response by ordinary traders. Admittedly, a large forward-spot spread would burden commercial covering. Actually, though, the thing to regret would be the interest differential occasioning that spread; and either of the alternatives—a heavy capital outflow or alignment of domestic with foreign interest rates—might be still more regrettable. A prompt, uncushioned adjustment of the forward rate to the interest differential might really be the best attainable outcome.

A contrasting source of opportunity for arbitrage would be an initially *wider* forward-spot spread than any interest differential called for. Besides motivating capital flows, this discrepancy would spell an abnormally high cost of risk protection for some traders. (Others, covering opposite positions, would enjoy a negative cost; but their gain would hardly console the first group.) The authorities would then be glad if only a small flow of arbitrage funds sufficed to shrink the forward-spot spread and hold it at interest parity. Again, they would like to see variations in commercial covering cushion the self-destroying tendency of interest arbitrage as little as possible.

In the first example, arbitrage *expanded* an initially inadequate forward-spot spread into line with a supposedly troublesome interest differential; in the second, arbitrage *shrank* an initially excessive spread into line with the interest differential (which

could be zero). In both cases, the authorities would like to see the interest-parity forward premium or discount reached with a minimum actual flow of arbitrage funds; they would regret variations in commercial covering that accommodated interest arbitrage and kept a large volume of it profitable. Such unwanted accommodation would be slight when traders always routinely sought forward coverage against exchange risk. Variations in commercial covering would also be absent, of course, when rigidly fixed exchange rates commanded complete confidence; but then, unfortunately, interest-arbitrageurs would no more need forward cover than traders would.

When spot exchange rates dependably kept within narrow limits do accommodate interest arbitrage, some palliative for the problem of capital flows may seem all the more necessary. Now we are ready to consider official operations in forward exchange, as suggested by Keynes in the early 1920s and often by others since then.[5] Suppose the Ruritanian author-

3. "Interest Rate Differences, Forward Exchange Mechanism, and Scope for Short-Term Capital Movements," IMF *Staff Papers*, **X**, November 1963, pp. 485–501.

4. The convenience of supposing that the imports and exports of Ruritania (the home country) are all priced in gold does not affect the conclusions. If some are priced in crowns, it is the foreign merchant rather than the Ruritanian who must decide whether or not to make a forward contract; but the influence of the forward rate on these decisions remains as described in the text.

5. See Paul Einzig, A *Dynamic Theory of Forward Exchange*, chap. 32. As Einzig notes in chap. 34, the idea had been anticipated in practice by the Austro-Hungarian bank.
The following paragraphs have benefited from John H. Auten's examination of the idea in "Monetary Policy and the Forward Exchange Market," *Journal of Finance*, **XVI**, December 1961, pp. 546–558. (Auten, pp. 556–557, interprets Keynes as advocating the separation of external and internal interest rates by means of forward-rate policy to make possible attracting an actual capital inflow to match a current-account balance-of-payments deficit. Auten himself would use forward-rate policy merely to avoid an unwanted capital outflow. He thus does not reject forward intervention but merely cautions against too ambitious a use of it.)

ities want to check an outflow or even promote an inflow of private funds, but without letting interest rates rise at home. They could support the forward crown by selling forward gold as cheaply, relative to the spot price, as would correspond to interest parity, or even more cheaply. The artificially high price of a covered return into crowns would check an interest-motivated outflow of funds in the first place. A foreigner wanting to return eventually into his own gold currency could move into crowns at the spot rate (say Cr2.01 per gram) and at the same time arrange to buy gold back later at the supported forward rate on the crown (say Cr1.99 per gram). By thus selling gold and contracting for its cheaper repurchase, he would in effect collect a subsidy on the interest received on a loan of the crowns in the meanwhile. Foreigners with funds already on loan in Ruritania would have a similar inducement not to take them home.

Might the Ruritanian authorities risk not having the gold to honor their forward contracts with? Apparently not; there would be no danger beyond any possible problem of having scanty reserves anyway. In part, the authorities merely commit gold forward that they would otherwise have lost sooner because of capital outflows through the spot market. Any actual capital inflows currently bring in the gold that the authorities sell forward (or else reduce the country's existing external liabilities). The authorities pay the *de facto* interest subsidy in home, not foreign, currency. The only additional problem directly involved is that foreigners might want to convert into gold the crowns they receive as interest and the crowns they save in buying back their original gold at its officially cheapened forward price. But continued official forward operations might keep reattracting or retaining these and other foreign-owned funds.

Can Ruritanians as well as foreigners collect the interest subsidy? Apparently not: the way it is offered makes it available only to persons who start and *finish* in gold, with protection against exchange risk in the meanwhile. (Strictly speaking, of course, citizenship does not matter; what does matter is the currency begun and ended with.) However, the range of fluctuation permitted in spot exchange rates does bear on the question. Suppose the authorities peg the forward crown at 520 milligrams of gold (only Cr1.92 per gram), considerably stronger than its upper spot limit of 505 milligrams (Cr1.98 per gram). Now even a Ruri-

tanian can profit at his own government's expense. He buys a gram of gold forward at Cr1.92 and counts on selling it spot at maturity of his contract for not less than Cr1.98. In effect the government sells for Cr1.92 the gold it will buy back if necessary to keep its price no lower than Cr1.98. People would seize this opportunity on a vast scale. The cost to the government would be in home rather than foreign money, true enough, but it could be a heavy cost.

The opportunity for profit at government expense is no longer limited to persons starting with and wanting to end with gold because everyone is (by assumption) confident that the crown will *not strengthen* above its existing upper spot limit. This disbelief in any upward revaluation would be especially firm and prevalent when the occasion for the official forward support was some fundamental *weakness* in the crown's general position. To keep some distinctions clear, let us repeat: general weakness further constrains forward-rate policy when the spot rate limits are so narrow that, whatever the exact current spot rate may be, a wide enough forward premium on the crown to make short-term investments in Ruritania attractive to foreigners would require a forward rate above the crown's upper spot limit, for then Ruritanians could profit at their own government's expense by means of *uncovered* arbitrage. On the other hand, *strength* of the crown in the sense of a currently high spot rate would complicate the authorities' dilemma in a slightly different way by narrowing the scope for pushing the forward rate on the crown to an adequate premium while still keeping it within the upper spot limit. (If a high current spot rate does happen to be a symptom of a strong general position, however, official support operations of any kind are less likely than otherwise to be needed. Ironically, the constraints just described are likely to matter least when forward policy is least needed.)

Adequate scope for differentiating interest rates from the home and foreign points of view therefore requires not too narrow a range of spot-rate fluctuation (as Keynes and other advocates of the policy have realized). The crown's spot rate needs room to be low currently so that its current forward rate can be high in comparison without being above the upper spot limit. Ruritanians would then shy away from what would otherwise seem bargains in forward gold for fear that when they took delivery at the maturity of their contracts, they could resell the gold spot only for still fewer crowns. Once again, the more exchange flexibility is allowed, the more freedom domestic policy can have from problems of international interest differentials. Barring that flexibility, authorities might understandably and desperately wish that interest differentials did not have much influence on capital movements, after all, and so did not pose much of a problem to be somehow palliated (but then the alternative idea of using actual interest-rate policy for external balance while fiscal policy served internal balance would not have much relevance, either).

Even if the interest subsidy offered by official forward pegging could be confined to foreigners, a questionable feature would remain. Effectively paying foreigners higher interest

APPENDIX 1
TO CHAPTER 6

rates than correspond to the marginal productivity of capital at home spells a waste of national resources. True, the waste would doubtless be less than that of unemployment due to too tight a domestic financial policy pursued for the sake of the balance of payments. This means only that successful forward intervention would at best reduce the cost of facing the conflict between internal and external policy considerations under fixed exchange rates; it does not banish that conflict.

Appendix 2 to Chapter 6:
Arguments for and Against Large Currency Areas

A currency area is the domain of a single currency or of two or more currencies linked closely enough together to be equivalent to a single currency. The links involve fixed exchange rates, unrestricted convertibility, and unified or tightly coordinated monetary management. This definition of currency area is unavoidably a bit fuzzy, since policy coordination may be more or less complete and, like exchange-rate fixity, may sooner or later break down. The term "currency union" or "monetary union," incidentally, implies the merger of formerly separate currency areas into a larger area of which they become mere "regions." "Territory" is a neutral term here and implies nothing about monetary arrangements.

The literature of "optimum currency areas"[1] weighs the arguments for having only a few large currency areas—at the extreme, a single currency for the entire world—against the arguments for a great many independent currencies each circulating in a small area. The weights to be given to arguments pulling toward opposite conclusions depend on the economic characteristics of the currency areas supposed to exist initially, of the currency unions that might be formed, and of the smaller areas into which existing areas might conceivably be split. The relevant characteristics—defined later on—include degree of wage and price flexibil-

ity, size, openness or closedness, homogeneity or diversity, factor mobility, and political circumstances.

The general economic principle of diminishing marginal returns and increasing marginal costs yields an enlightening presumption: the further we have already moved toward either extreme of monetary unification or monetary fragmentation, the slighter are the incremental advantages and the greater the incremental disadvantages of moving still further in the same direction. The optimum lies between the two extremes. Just *where* to draw currency boundaries depends, furthermore, on the characteristics of the territories contemplated.

Largely for noneconomic reasons, a wholesale redrawing of boundaries is neither likely nor desirable. Theorizing about it might seem irrelevant to real issues. Yet the discussion provides a way of organizing some widely applicable theoretical points, including points concerning the functions of money and prices. It is relevant to the choice of currency policy within common markets, to a country's choice of a fixed or floating exchange rate, and to international monetary reform.

We shall first review the arguments for extreme monetary unification and for extreme fragmentation and then the rebuttals to each case. Next we shall examine the territorial characteristics governing how much weight each of the arguments and counterarguments deserves. We shall also try to clear up some apparent inconsistencies in the discussion.

Arguments and replies

Arguments for extreme unification. As a medium of exchange, money saves the costs of barter transactions. The larger the area in which a single currency circulates, the more fully it performs this function; for example, it saves the costs of otherwise necessary foreign-exchange transactions. A single currency also economizes on the expense of printing and coining many separate currencies and administering many central banks. At the opposite extreme, with each person having his own currency, money loses its very meaning as purchasing power routinely acceptable by most of the other economic units to which the holder might wish to make payments.

As a unit of account, money economizes on acquiring and using knowledge. It simplifies keeping aware of the exchange ratios among various goods and services. It simplifies accounting. It facilitates quantifying and comparing the costs and benefits of contemplated activities, such as producing incremental amounts of particular goods and services; it facilitates economic calculation. Quoting prices in money facilitates comparing the terms offered by rival sellers and rival buyers and so presumably enhances competition. Having to keep track of a great multiplicity of currencies, of prices quoted in them, and of changing exchange rates would undermine money's performance of its unit-of-account function.

A medium of exchange must to some extent be a store of value. Holding money or claims fixed in money can serve as a hedge against fluctuations in the relative values of other goods and services. As explained on page 126, money would perform this function poorly in a very small currency area whose external exchange rate dominated local wages and prices. But once a currency's domain is of a certain size, a still larger domain would improve its store-of-value function relatively little. Furthermore, linkage to political units more likely than one's own to pursue inflationary policies would undermine the store-of-value function.

A multiplicity of currencies would complicate money's function as a standard of deferred payments. Perhaps more important than the stability or instability of the exchange rate between a debtor's and a creditor's currency, however, is the stability or instability of the purchasing power of whichever currency the loan is denominated in.[2]

In the ways mentioned, money, as compared with barter, facilitates the functioning of markets and the balancing of supply and demand. Increased monetary unification improves the unity of markets and the integration of the economic system and so facilitates reaping the gains from trade and specialization, *except* as it impairs the effective flexibility of wages and prices, a point considered presently. The *additional* net benefits of these kinds presumably become smaller as complete monetary unification is more and more closely approached.

Arguments for many small currency areas.
Exchange-rate flexibility, as explained above in the example of Michigan's edsel (p. 105), can provide quasi flexibility of prices and wages. For well-known reasons (not all of which hinge on money illusion), wages and prices would probably not be flexible enough everywhere within a huge currency area to avoid the prob-

lems of depressed regions and of interregional balance-of-payments adjustment in the unpleasant way described by the theory of the income mechanism. (An areawide monetary policy expansionary enough to inflate away all localized unemployment would entail price inflation and probably could not accomplish its purpose over the long run anyway.)

Quasi flexibility through exchange rates would help prices and wages perform their functions of conveying information and incentives, facilitating decentralized decision-making, balancing supply and demand on individual markets, balancing the aggregates of transactions that appear in a country's or a region's balance of payments, linking individual markets together, coordinating different sectors of the economy, and facilitating economic calculation. In short, flexibility improves the functioning of the price system. Money itself could thus perform its functions better by *not* being everywhere the same. If prices and wages are sticky, while too wide a currency area rules out quasi flexibility, prices and money fail to perform their functions well. A price that, because of changed conditions, no longer clears

1. Notable contributions include Robert A. Mundell, "A Theory of Optimum Currency Areas," *American Economic Review,* LI, September 1961, pp. 657–665; Bela Balassa, *The Theory of Economic Integration,* Homewood, Ill.: Irwin, 1961, pp. 263–268; Ronald I. McKinnon, "Optimum Currency Areas," *American Economic Review,* LIII, September 1963, pp. 717–725; McKinnon, "Optimum World Monetary Arrangements and the Dual Currency System," Banca Nazionale del Lavoro *Quarterly Review,* XVI, December 1963, pp. 366–396; Delbert A. Snider, *Optimum Adjustment Processes and Currency Areas,* Princeton Essays in International Finance, No. 62, Princeton, N.J.: Princeton University, October 1967; Peter B. Kenen, "The Theory of Optimum Currency Areas: An Eclectic View," in Robert Mundell and Alexander Swoboda, eds., *Monetary Problems of the International Economy,* Chicago: University of Chicago Press, 1969, pp. 41–60; and Thomas D. Willett and Edward Tower, "Currency Areas and Exchange-Rate Flexibility," *Weltwirtschaftliches Archiv,* Vol. 105, No. 1, 1970, pp. 48–65.

2. See pages 273–274.

its market is conveying *mis*information and wrong incentives and causing wider disruptions.[3] It is a mistake to suppose that monetary unification necessarily promotes economic integration in the ways that count for human welfare.[4]

Separate currencies tend to compartmentalize macroeconomic disturbances and policy blunders, lessening the contagion of inflation and depression. For an analogy, consider the advantage of having several watertight compartments in the hold of a ship. Separate currencies make it easier for a country's authorities to pursue domestic stability (or the best compromise between unemployment and inflation, if such a tradeoff really exists) despite instability in the outside world. On the other hand, one could argue that monetary linkage to the outside world at a fixed exchange rate tends to dilute an individual country's disturbances and blunders, giving time for their correction before they have irreversible consequences, in particular, price and wage inflation.[5]

Reply to the arguments for unification. The benefits of unification cost sacrificing the advantages of quasi flexibility and of compartmentalization. Little can be saved from the expense and nuisance of foreign-exchange transactions, anyway, if countries retain their own currencies, even though exchange rates among them are fixed. Currencies tightly tied together are not fully equivalent to a single currency. The necessary coordination among the operations of national central banks or monetary authorities also has costs and may involve difficult negotiations. As for the political unification necessary for genuine financial and monetary unification, an extreme degree of it would probably not be desirable for reasons of political philosophy, even if it were realistically attainable.

Reply to the arguments for fragmentation. The quasi flexibility offered by fragmentation is only a crude substitute for flexibility in each individual price and wage. (On the other hand, a crude substitute may be better than nothing when the genuine article is unavailable.)

Beyond some admittedly indefinable point, multiplying independent currencies and shrinking the domain of each would begin to negate the very concept of money. Already-mentioned expenses and nuisances count against fragmentation. Having a great many independent currencies would leave each one with a thin market on the foreign exchanges, lacking "breadth, depth, and resiliency." Individual transactions might be large enough relative to total supply or demand to cause sharp, random exchange-rate fluctuations. Speculation would be inadequately stabilizing, and groups of speculators might even be able to dominate the market for individual currencies and manipulate rates to their own advantage.

Territorial characteristics and the weights of the arguments

What weights the foregoing arguments and replies deserve depends on the characteristics of the territories considered.

The more *flexible wages and prices* are in local currency, the less the advantage of quasi flexibility through exchange rates. The degree of flexibility depends on how prevalent monopolies, cartels, labor unions, and long-term contracts are, on the characteristics of products and production processes, on how markets are organized, on the nature of taxation and government regulation, and on innumerable other technological and institutional factors. Flexibility does not mean that prices and wages oscillate wildly. It means, rather, that they are free from impediments to the changes necessary to keep markets cleared. Though flexible, prices would be stable when their fundamental determinants remained unchanged. Flexible prices and wages would keep balances of payments equilibrated in the face of underlying disturbances, even under fixed exchange rates, without large fluctuations in output and employment.[6] Extreme flexibility, by the way, is not unequivocally desirable. Inertia or friction has some merit in economic as well as mechanical affairs. Excessively frequent price changes, including small and reversible ones, would raise the costs of acquiring and using knowledge. Would-be sellers and buyers who experience frustration in finding trading partners can rationally keep the prices they are asking and offering unchanged for a time while canvassing the market to see whether changed market conditions really do call for price changes. It may even be beneficial if exchange-rate fluctuations reduce the need for fluctuations in individual prices and wages, particularly in view of the greater simplicity, described by the chair-and-piano analogy, of changing one price rather than a great many.

Still, a high degree of price and wage flexibility in the territories considered does add weight to the arguments for monetary unification and lessens the weight due the opposing arguments.

The economic *size* of a territory means the volume of its resources, population, and economic activity. If one needed a single indicator, total real GNP would be a plausible candidate. The smaller a currency area, the less fully money performs its standard functions (except as independent currencies are needed for quasi flexibility). Smallness makes for a thin foreign-exchange market. These considerations lend weight to the reasons why small territories should form a monetary union. Others may of course pull the other way. A small territory is by that token likely to be a "drop in the bucket" on world markets and therefore to face highly elastic demands for its exports and supplies of its imports. High elasticities contribute to the exchange-market stability and therefore to the viability of an independently fluctuating currency.[7]

A territory's *openness* is its degree of involvement in transactions with the rest of the world relative to internal transactions. Indicators would be such figures as the share of total output of goods and services exported, share of imports in total domestic absorption of goods and services, and ratio of imports plus exports to gross national product. Other considerations being equal, great openness lends weight to the major arguments against monetary independence and for monetary union among regions highly open to each other. The more open a territory is, the more significant (though perhaps not very significant) are the nuisance and expense of the correspondingly many foreign-exchange transactions. The greater is the danger, furthermore, that exchange-rate fluctuations might dominate the internal price and wage level, impairing the quasi flexibility of prices and wages otherwise

---

3. The contagion of market imbalances is a leading theme of the disequilibrium economics inspired by the work of Clower and Leijonhufvud. See, for example, Robert W. Clower, "The Keynesian Counterrevolution: A Theoretical Appraisal," in F. H. Hahn and F. P. R. Brechling, eds., *The Theory of Interest Rates*, London: Macmillan, 1965, pp. 103–125; and Axel Leijonhufvud, *On Keynesian Economics and the Economics of Keynes*, New York: Oxford University Press, 1968.

4. As Wolfgang Kasper says, the view of "professional Europeans" that economic integration requires monetary unification "is too much centered around an institutional, organizational, and legalistic, not to say bureaucratic, notion of what in-

ternational integration means. Rather, international integration should first of all aim at the welding together of national markets, so that potential buyers have an undiscriminated choice between homemade and imported goods—with the organizational and legal superstructure to come later.

"If functional integration (in the sense of larger markets with equal competitive opportunities throughout) is the prime concern, the fixity of exchange rates may, rather, be seen, in the light of past experience, as a disintegrating factor." See Kasper in George N. Halm, ed., *Approaches to Greater Flexibility of Exchange Rates*, Princeton, N.J.: Princeton University Press, 1970 (hereafter cited as Bürgenstock Papers), p. 385.

It is instructive to compare the views of the "monetarists" and the "economists" on the sequence of steps to be taken in the economic unification of Europe. (In this context, the term "monetarist" means something entirely different from the sense in which it labels a position contrasting with that of the "fiscalists" on matters of monetary theory and macroeconomic policy.) The monetarists would fix exchange rates early, even using controls over capital movements if necessary, to prod policy-makers into other aspects of unification. The economists call for economic unification first, including freedom of capital movements, with exchange rates helping take care of balance-of-payments problems until finally the rates could be permanently fixed. Cf. John R. Presley and P. Coffey, "On Exchange Rate Unification—A Comment in Relation to the European Economic Community," *Economic Journal*, Vol. 82, December 1972, pp. 1380–1382. W. M. Corden warns that a "pseudo-exchange-rate union" may create balance-of-payments stresses leading to imposition or tightening of controls over current- or capital-account transactions; "the movement toward one aspect of monetary integration (the exchange-rate union) may well set back the movement to the other (capital-market integration)." Corden, *Monetary Integration*, Princeton Essays in International Finance, No. 93, Princeton, N.J.: Princeton University, April 1972, pp. 29–30.

5. On this and the related "discipline" argument for fixed exchange rates, see pp. 132, 639–643.

6. See pp. 94–96.

7. To understand this point about elasticities, as well as the superficially contradictory point made in the following paragraphs on "openness," the reader will have to understand Chapter 8 first. Also see Willett and Tower, *op. cit.*, pp. 54–55.

to be expected from an independent currency. Practically by the definition of an extremely open territory, the cost of living in it is composed largely of the prices of imported and readily exportable goods; other things (such as local services and the local-labor component of shelter and of goods sold at retail) account for only a small part of the cost of living. People would be highly aware of the exchange rate and alert to adjust local-currency prices in line with it. Labor contracts gearing wages to the cost of living would in effect gear wages to the exchange rate. If the Michigan of our example were an extremely open economy, exchange depreciation of the edsel would not be effective in reducing the real wages of automobile workers. (More generally, economic policy faces a dilemma when powerful interests resist adjustment of their selling prices to adverse supply-and-demand changes.) In a highly open economy, people would be inclined effectively to use outside currency not only as a unit of account, as just suggested, but also as a liquid reserve of purchasing power, undermining the viability of the local currency. All these difficulties are compounded if the open economy is also small, as it is empirically likely to be.

The foregoing argument tacitly takes it for granted, however, that the flexible exchange rate of an open currency area would be highly unstable; for otherwise, it is unlikely that people would be pathologically alert to fluctuations. But why should the exchange rate be so unstable, given stability of the local money supply and reasonable stability in the outside world? The argument tacitly envisages disturbances of a *micro* nature—changes in "wants, resources, or technology." Suppose, however, that the disturbances are *macro*—general price-and-income inflation or deflation. Suppose, further, that these macro disturbances originate abroad. Appropriate exchange-rate changes would then tend to insulate the home economy from foreign instability, preserve the liquidity value of the home currency, and reduce risk in foreign trade. Openness, furthermore, tends to increase the proportion of disturbances to internal and external balance that originate abroad (or in the territory's foreign-trade sector) rather than at home. (A completely closed economy would feel *no* disturbances from outside.) As we have seen, price policy, which includes exchange-rate variation, is more appropriate than expenditure policy for coping with outside disturbances.[8] While a flexible exchange rate would be useful for warding off the external disturbances characteristic of an open economy, the smallness likely to be associated with openness does pose difficulties for the working of a flexible rate. The clash between these considerations is a feature of hard reality, not a sign of logical flaw in the analysis.

Another suggested reason why a highly open territory should shun monetary independence is that expenditure policy can serve the requirements of balance-of-payments equilibrium rather well. (Basically, it would be a policy of keeping in step with other regions of the monetary union.) Since a large part of total expenditure goes for imports and exportable goods, expenditure restraint corrects a payments deficit with relatively little deflation of internal output and employment. A substantially closed economy, by contrast, would have to endure widespread domestic deflation to obtain the desired deflation of expenditure on imports and exportables; the foreign-trade tail would be wagging the domestic dog. Such an economy needs the monetary independence allowed by a flexible exchange rate.

A rather abstract and unimportant reason for monetary union in order to avoid openness concerns elasticities. In a very open economy, competing domestic production and consumption are slight relative to imports and exports respectively. These circumstances hold down the degree to which the elasticity of demand for imports in particular exceeds the elasticity of total demand for import-type goods and the degree to which the elasticity of supply of exports in particular exceeds the elasticity of total supply of export-type goods. In holding down the import-demand and export-supply elasticities, openness tends to detract from the exchange-market stability of an independent currency. Smallness, on the other hand, as we have seen, tends to raise the other two of the four key elasticities. Since a small economy tends to be open and a large economy to be relatively closed, we might seem to have run into a contradiction regarding whether smallness-and-openness contributes to or detracts from the elasticity conditions conducive to a stable foreign-exchange market. The contradiction is not genuine, however; for smallness and openness are logically distinct though empirically associated concepts. Smallness contributes to the elasticity conditions for a stable foreign-exchange market, and what pulls the other way is not smallness as such but the openness likely to be associated with it.

This distinction between logical and empirical association is easier to understand in connection with the possibility of an awkwardly thin foreign-exchange market: smallness pulls that way, while openness pulls for "breadth, depth, and resiliency." For a monetary area of a given degree of openness, smallness makes for a thin market; but for a monetary area of a given size, openness makes for breadth.

Financial openness may be distinguished from openness to trade in goods and services. Indicators of its degree might be ratios of debts to and claims on outsiders to debts to and claims on fellow residents and ratios of flows of loan and investment transactions with outsiders to such transactions with fellow residents.

On might distinguish between the actual openness of a territory and the potential openness that a monetary union would bring into effect. One might also conjecture that the distinction is more relevant for financial than for commercial openness, on the grounds that monetary fragmentation impedes financial transactions more seriously than it impedes trade. In either case, if the impediment is serious, that fact strengthens the case for monetary unification. On the other hand, if underlying characteristics are such that there both actually is and still would be relatively little financial intercourse among the regions (as well as little goods-and-services trade), the convenience and freedom from exchange risk provided by monetary unification would be correspondingly unimportant.

The last point bears on the question of what monetary arrangements are desirable in view of the degree of financial openness or integration promoted by conditions more basic than policy. A different question concerns whether a high or low degree of financial openness or integration would be more conducive to the smooth working of a specified monetary arrangement. The conjecture seems plausible that great financial openness is more conducive to the smooth working of either extreme monetary independence or extreme monetary unification than to some intermediate monetary arrangement. At the one extreme, a large volume of actual and potential capital movements, free of controls, would link the foreign-exchange market and the money and capital markets in different territories together, lending "breadth, depth, and resiliency" to each, lessening the likelihood that random imbalances of supply and demand arising from commercial transactions would cause sharp exchange-rate fluctuations, and facilitating stabilizing speculation. At the other extreme of monetary unification, highly interest-sensitive

capital movements would readily finance interregional balance-of-payments imbalances while the corrective processes characteristic of unification were at work. These corrective processes would themselves be enhanced by ready marketability of important categories of financial assets throughout all regions of the currency union. Changes in the ratios of assets to income and of interregionally marketable to local assets in portfolios would motivate persons and firms to make readjustments tending to restore interregional equilibrium on current account.[9] This asset-transfer adjustment process would work better if investors were wealthy enough to hold large portfolios relative to income and if wealth, tastes, economic organization, and the like were similar throughout the monetary union. Under such circumstances, tight monetary unification would itself lessen the danger that unification would break down.[10] That danger is relatively great, however, under the intermediate arrangement of distinct currencies pegged together at "irrevocably" fixed exchange rates. Capital movements become highly sensitive to interest and profit incentives. But as long as the member regions of the union have separate currency reserves with which to carry out the exchange-rate pegging and have the potential for balance-of-payments problems, one currency will occasionally come to be regarded as stronger or weaker than the others, and one-way-option speculation may become massive as "everybody begins to expect the irrevocable to be revoked."[11]

---

8. Cf. pp. 102–104; Corden, *op. cit.*, pp. 18–19; and Herbert Giersch in Bürgenstock Papers, p. 149.

9. Recall p. 58.

10. See pp. 634–635.

11. Marshall Hall and Dhiru Tanna, "On Exchange Rate Unification: A Comment," *Economic Journal*, Vol. 82, December 1972, p. 1378. Corden also urges that "an attempt to maintain fixed rates without absolute assurance that they can be maintained . . . is an invitation to increased destabilizing capital movements." See Corden, *op. cit.*, p. 29. On one-way-option speculation, see pp. 248–250 below.

Homogeneity and diversity are opposites. A territory is homogeneous if its component parts are similar in their resource endowments and economic activities. (In some contexts it might be useful to distinguish between potential and actual diversity. Two territories possessing similar patterns of economic activity might become diverse if an economic union between them fostered regional specialization that their separate economic policies had previously inhibited. It seems empirically likely, however, that the dismantling of trade barriers would contribute more toward specialization and diversity than would the abolition of regional monetary independence.)

All other considerations being equal, a currency area should be homogeneous in its resources and economic activities so that quasi flexibility of wages and prices through the exchange rate is effective rather than crude. Other considerations being equal, a diverse area should be split into internally homogeneous monetary areas. An independent currency would be helpful for a "depressed area" suffering from demand or production conditions not typical of the country as a whole. (On the other hand, a central government sophisticated in using a wide range of policy tools would lessen the importance of regional monetary independence.) The fact that a given area is homogeneous is no argument against its joining with other areas economically the same as itself, so that their union would still be homogeneous.

Empirically, of course, large size and diversity (and closedness), small size and homogeneity (and openness) tend to go together. This fact poses perhaps the most prominent tradeoff discussed in the optimum-currency-area literature: large size is desirable for the functions-of-money, transactions-economy, and broad-exchange-market reasons already explained; small size is desirable, not for its own sake, but for the greater homogeneity likely to prevail in a small area.

Peter Kenen (cited in footnote 1) has argued that diversity is desirable in a currency area. More precisely, he seems to have meant that diversity is desirable for a region somehow inexorably fated to belong to a larger currency union. With an independent currency ruled out of consideration, the homogeneity that would argue for independence loses most of its attractiveness. Diversity, on the other hand, provides insurance against big terms-of-trade or balance-of-payments changes. Because of the law of large numbers, the independent microeconomic disturbances influencing each sector of a diversified economy will tend to have mutually canceling effects on the territory's aggregate trade balance at a fixed exchange rate and on its terms of trade. Diversity increases the probability that an adverse shift of demand or a poor harvest affecting one industry or locality is offset in another, thus avoiding the balance-of-payments imbalance that would have occurred if the industries and localities had belonged to different countries. Extreme benefits of diversification of this kind accrue to the world as a whole, which can never have any balance-of-payments deficits.[12] A single-product economy, by contrast, has all of its eggs in one basket, so that its trade balance would be subject to wide variations at a fixed exchange rate and so that a flexible exchange rate, as well as the terms of trade, would be subject to wide fluctuations.[13]

Kenen further argues that when a diversified economy does face a drop in demand for its exports, unemployment will rise less than in a specialized economy. Variations in investment at home will be slighter and will magnify the employment impact of export variations to a lesser degree. Diversification presumably spells opportunities to replace lost foreign trade with expanded domestic trade. It not only diminishes the likelihood of major external shocks but also mitigates the damage such shocks do and eases the burden to be borne by internal policies.

It should be noted that the foregoing arguments refer to external shocks (or to internal production shocks, such as bad weather might cause) of a *microeconomic* nature; the shocks considered are essentially independent of each other rather than pervasive along a broad front. Kenen does not intend his arguments to give reassurance about the workability of a fixed exchange rate in the face of serious business-cycle fluctuations or irresponsible monetary policies in the outside world.

In stressing the advantages of diversity, Kenen seems to be contradicting Mundell (also cited in footnote 1), who described the advantages of internally homogeneous monetary areas. The contradiction is apparent only; for the two writers are asking different questions. Mundell is taking the characteristics of territories as given and is asking how to draw boundaries. He is not ruling out the possibility of achieving internally homogeneous monetary areas. Kenen, by contrast, is doing one or both of the following: (1) contemplating a territory yoked with others in a monetary union and asking whether homogeneity or diversity within the region would be better for the working of this assumedly irrevocable arrangement; (2) contemplating a diverse territory, assumed unsplittable, and asking whether its diversity recommends its joining a still wider currency union. His answer to (1), as we have seen, finds diversity desirable. His answer to (2) is in effect as follows: since both the prospective member and the contemplated wider union would in any case each be diverse within itself and since forming the union could therefore not cost the loss of a nonexistent homogeneity, the standard arguments for a currency area's being both large and closed would argue for the union. These arguments are buttressed by the reasons already noted why internal diversity is beneficial for a region within a union. Mundell says that the first step toward yoking mutually diverse territories together is very disadvantageous, other considerations being the same. Kenen, in answering question (2), assumes that this first step has already been irrevocably taken and notes that the incremental disadvantages of further unification are relatively slight, perhaps slight enough to be outweighed by the advantages of greater size and closedness.[14]

Mobility of factors concerns how readily labor, capital, and business enterprise can shift among localities and occupations. Obstacles to mobility might be termed either "sociological" or "occupational." Examples of the former would be people's slavishness to tradition and lack of adaptability, strong family and other local ties, language barriers, nonportability of pensions and social-insurance benefits, labor-union restrictions, and the like. Occupational barriers would be differences between lines of production in the mixes and qualifications of the factors they employ such that factors displaced from one economic sector have little usefulness in another.

Poor factor mobility enhances the importance of wage and price flexibility so that adjustment to adverse changes in "wants, resources, and technology" can occur through wage and price decreases rather than through unemployment. Poor mobility of factors between areas argues against sacrificing quasi flexibility by yoking those areas together in a monetary union. Conversely, the more readily factors can move between occupations and between localities specialized in particular occupations, the more easily can an area adjust to changed conditions, including changes in outside supplies and demands, by changes in its pattern of production and resource allocation.[15] Its authorities are less embarrassed than they would be in the case of immobility by the question of whether to try to inflate away pockets of unemployment at the cost of areawide price inflation.

In this respect, mobility and homogeneity are substitutes; either condition reduces the weight of arguments for carving an area up into monetarily independent parts. Unfortunately, the two conditions and their opposites tend to be associated. In particular, great similarity among a territory's economic activities and in the characteristics required of the factors they employ promotes mobility. Actual homogeneity of occupations would promote mobility but also make it pointless, since factors displaced from some jobs would find their other potential employers facing the same drop in demand for their output. (If the automobile industry falls into depression, what good does it do if labor is highly mobile among automobile firms?) Mobility due to homogeneity would be empty and would not reduce the need for price and wage flexibility or quasi flexibility. The kind of mobility that would reduce this need is perhaps empirically rather

12. Herbert G. Grubel, *The International Monetary System*, Baltimore: Penguin Books, 1970, pp. 54–55.

13. Empirically, however, it is a disputed question whether countries undiversified in exporting tend to have especially unstable foreign trade.

14. This paragraph is not guaranteed as a faithful *account* of what Mundell and Kenen actually said. Instead, it suggests an *interpretation* that reconciles their positions.

15. Even so, high labor mobility is a poor substitute for wage-and-price flexibility or for quasi flexibility through the exchange rate, especially when mobility takes the form of outward migration of unemployed labor. The costs of adjustment are concentrated on the unfortunate emigrants rather than being spread more thinly and evenly through reduction of real wage rates. Cf. Corden, *op. cit.*, pp. 15–16.

unlikely: mobility compatible with diversity of occupations.

A country's degree of *policy prudence*—its likelihood of avoiding deflationary or inflationary blunders—is a consideration in deciding whether or not to join prospective partners in a monetary union. If it were less prudent, it would find some advantage in the "discipline" of being yoked to more prudent partners. This "discipline" argument seems most relevant for countries that have an intermediate propensity to inflate. The most inflationary governments are hardly restrained by fixed exchange rates; in fact, they cannot keep their rates fixed for long. Their currencies are pegged at disequilibrium rates most of the time; they are undervalued for a while after each devaluation but become increasingly overvalued again as inflation proceeds and makes another devaluation necessary. Wrongly pegged rates simply disrupt business without exerting effective discipline. At the other extreme stand the most prudent countries. Their resistance to inflation gains nothing from monetary linkage to foreigners. On the contrary, impulses of imported inflation may sometimes inconvenience them.[16] In between stand the countries whose inflations are not fast enough to require frequent devaluations. Their pegged exchange rates do not become quickly and seriously wrong again after each (infrequent) adjustment. Such countries can benefit from external restraint on inflation. Unfortunately, their benefit is accompanied by the weakening of restraint that their partners experience from being linked to them.

Prospects for political unification form one of the most decisive and obvious considerations in weighing the arguments for monetary fragmentation and monetary unification against each other. Monetary union or the firm fixing of exchange rates requires a high degree of coordination of money-supply policies, which would hardly be possible unless member countries sacrificed their fiscal and budgetary independence to a considerable degree. Fiscal and monetary policies best go hand in hand and, for an "optimum policy mix," should have the same domains. It would be awkward for the domain of fiscal policy to span the domains of several independent currencies. ". . . a major difference between the currency composition of government receipts and the currency composition of government spending would force the treasury into the exchange market where, will-fully or otherwise, it might well become the single speculator capable of altering regional exchange rates."[17] The opposite noncoincidence of monetary and fiscal domains would be a more serious difficulty: what a regional government could do with fiscal policy for macroeconomic purposes would be constrained by its inability to pursue a monetary policy of its own.[18] Not only monetary, fiscal, and budgetary policies but also policies toward trade-union aggressiveness and toward the choice of tradeoff between unemployment and inflation would have to be coordinated. And such extensive policy coordination would require a corresponding degree of political unification. Possibilities of it depend on geographical contiguity (a minor matter in these days of rapid communication and transportation), ethnic factors, national traditions, and the like. If political unification is not feasible or desirable, the prospective partners might as well forget about tight monetary unification also.

Reasons of political philosophy tell against a centralized world government (with powers extending beyond those necessary to prevent armed aggression) and against a world of a few Leviathans only. It is probably realistic, moreover, to take existing nation-states and the general degree of independence that each desires as given. The live issue is not how to carve the world from scratch into currency areas, but whether or not each country should have an independent currency and flexible exchange rate or join with other countries in some sort of monetary union.

Resolving apparent contradictions

Before summarizing, let us remind ourselves of three sources of apparent contradiction between different strands of the currency-area literature. One is the blurring of distinctions between particular economic characteristics of a territory because of our empirical knowledge that certain of them tend to go together while others tend not to. For example, it is desirable that a currency area be both large and homogeneous, yet it is empirically unlikely that an area would in fact be both. Closedness and homogeneity would argue for an area's having an independent currency with a fluctuating exchange rate against the rest of the world; yet homogeneity is likely to go with an area's being open to trade, not closed. And closedness, while arguing against the fixed-exchange-rate payments-adjustment mechanism, also argues (for an area of a given size) against a fluctuating rate because of the corresponding thinness of the exchange market.

A second and closely related source of apparent contradiction is that a particular economic characteristic, or it together with some other one empirically associated with it, may favor monetary unification in some respects and fragmentation in other respects. Diversity, as we have seen, provides an example. Smallness tends to favor the smooth working of a territory's foreign-exchange market by promoting high elasticities of demand for its exports and supply of its imports in the outside world; on the other hand, smallness makes for a thin market; and the openness associated with smallness detracts for the elasticities of the territory's demand for imports and supply of exports. Both of these observations remind us of the banal point that not all considerations bearing on a policy choice always pull in the same direction; decisions in the real world can be tough.

A third source of apparent contradiction—as between Mundell and Kenen in regard to diversity—is ambiguity about just what question a stated conclusion comes as an answer to. Consider the following questions: (1) What economic characteristics of its own territory make a country a good or a poor candidate for joining with others in a monetary union? (2) What characteristics of countries in relation to each other make them good or poor prospects for forming a union? In other words, what characteristics that a union would possess if formed would argue for or against its being formed? (3) Given that a territory is monetarily unified within itself and has a fluctuating exchange rate against outside currencies, what characteristics of the territory and its component regions would most facilitate the smooth functioning of these arrangements? (4) If currency boundaries were to be redrawn from scratch, how should they be drawn? (This question presupposes that territories have given characteristics and investigates reasons for grouping some into a currency union and for keeping others separate from each other. It leaves open the possibility, as some other questions do not, of splitting a country and perhaps of allotting the split parts to different currency unions.)

Summary and conclusion

What characteristics would lend weight to the arguments for monetary union? It is impossible to answer both briefly and precisely, since some characteristics, as we have seen, cut one way in some respects and the other way in others. On the whole, though, we can say that the following characteristics of the individual country would count in favor of its joining a union: flexible prices and wages, smallness, openness, diversity, factor mobility, policy imprudence, and willingness to sacrifice political sovereignty. The opposite characteristics would argue for monetary independence. The following characteristics of the proposed union would argue for its formation: flexible prices, large size, openness of its members to each other but closedness to the outside world, homogeneity, factor mobility, policy prudence, and acceptability of a union-wide government.

Realistically, there is much to be said for treating at least the sovereign industrial states as separate currency areas.[19] The live question for each of them is whether to retain monetary independence or to join with others in fixing exchange rates or adopting a common currency.

Monetary independence and floating exchange rates afford scope for diverse experi-

16. Samuel Brittan has suggested that it would make little sense to treat a country like France, with a record of inflation and devaluation, and one like Germany, with a record of more nearly stable prices and of revaluations, as an optimum currency area. *The Price of Economic Freedom*, New York: St. Martin's Press, 1970, p. 173.

17. Kenen, *op. cit.*, pp. 45–46; quotation from p. 46 n.

18. Among the minor reasons why a currency area coinciding with a fiscal area is relatively feasible is that the fiscal system helps accomplish palliative transfers of income or wealth from regions with surpluses to those with deficits in their balances of payments. Also relevant are other reasons why balance-of-payments adjustment is particularly easy among regions of a well-unified country.

19. Brittan, *op. cit.*, p. 73.

ments in trying to reconcile full employment with money of stable purchasing power. Countries blessed with better tradeoffs between unemployment and inflation or with more favorable political, sociological, or ideological conditions have a better chance to succeed independently than they would have if fixed exchange rates transmitted to them the inflations of less prudent or less fortunate countries. (The Bretton Woods system was indeed a powerful international transmitter, and even a generator, of inflation.) With monetary independence, the relatively successful countries could provide healthy examples and lessons for the others. This argument for diversity of monetary authorities bears an obvious analogy to the political arguments for federalism as opposed to highly centralized national governments.

CHAPTER SEVEN

Balance-of-Payments Adjustment by Direct Controls

Barring adjustment through prices, incomes, or exchange rates, direct controls are necessary to force an equilibrium in the balance of payments. But putting the matter this way is not quite exact. A deficit can persist only so long as it can be financed. If no more resources are available for exchange-rate pegging, yet both exchange depreciation and formal controls over expenditures abroad are ruled out, the rate can be maintained only in some such manner as by strictly enforced prohibition of transactions in foreign exchange at other than the official rate. Unofficial rationing would then develop and would favor persons most friendly with exporters earning foreign exchange or persons who (figuratively) stood in line earliest at the offices of the exchange dealers. Or, more probably, persons earning foreign exchange would not sell it for home currency at all but would spend it abroad on goods to be imported and sold at prices reflecting a *de facto* devaluation of the home currency. If the authorities were still unwilling to tolerate market methods of adjustment, they would probably introduce official controls, after all, to force equilibrium in a tidier manner.

Types of control available include quantitative restrictions (quotas) and *ad hoc* duties on imports, as well as exchange control (including systems of multiple exchange rates). Special measures to increase earnings of foreign exchange, such as export subsidies, are akin to these controls in being *ad hoc* remedies for a deficit. (Reverse types of control, incidentally, might be used to banish a balance-of-payments surplus, but since a surplus is a less pressing problem, the discussion that follows will assume a deficit.)

Quotas and import licensing

Restricting imports by quantity seems like a straightforward remedy. The authorities allow only so many automobiles, cameras, tons of wheat, or gallons of wine into the country each month or year. But setting a quota is a complicated job, even for one single product. A *global quota* simply limits the total amount of the product allowed into the country during each year or other time period but does not specify where the product may come from or who is entitled to import it. The difficulties are obvious: home importers and foreign exporters will stampede to get their shipments into the country before the limit has been reached. Stockpiles build up at the beginning of the quota period, leaving no more imports allowable until the beginning of the next period. Merchants whose goods arrive too late to win entry suffer extra expense, and all bear some risk. Wasteful haste pays better than judicious market research and shopping for the best terms. The profits of trade in the quotaed commodities go largely by luck to the particular importers and foreign suppliers able to get their goods into the country first, though the expenses of abnormal haste eat into these profits. Furthermore, the global quota tends to discriminate against the most distant foreign suppliers because of the expenses of shipping back goods denied entry.

For all these reasons, governments in practice reject global quotas in favor of licensing administered to keep imports within some intended limit. But then an allocation problem arises. How, for example, are the scarce privileges of marketing the commodity to be parceled out among the various exporting countries without unfair discrimination? It is no answer to say that each foreign country may supply the same percentage of the total allowable imports, for some countries are naturally more and others less important as suppliers; equal allocations would in fact discriminate.

One answer is to allocate trading rights among foreign suppliers in proportion to the amounts supplied in some "previous representative period." But this tends to freeze the pattern of trade according to historical accident and the more or less arbitrary choice of a base period. It discriminates against countries whose comparative advantages as a supplier of the commodity in question have increased since then and in favor of those whose competitive position would have weakened in a free market. It hampers importers of the home country in shopping around for the best bargains.

When controls wielded by other governments keep surplus earnings in transactions with one foreign country from being freely usable to cover excess expenditures in transactions with another, the home authorities are likely to feel compelled to discriminate among foreign sources. But when this problem is absent, the simplest approach is to allocate import licenses only among home importers, leaving each free to buy from whatever foreign source seems best to him. But how should this allocation take place? To grant or refuse licenses simply on the merits of each individual application is open to obvious abuses. Permitting each importer an equal volume of imports would be nonsensical because of the different sizes and fields of specialization of the various firms and because of the difficulties of deciding who qualifies as an importer of each commodity. Granting licenses in proportion to the shares of importing done in some "previous representative period" tends to assure relatively inefficient firms their historic shares of the market, while restraining firms that could have expanded by virtue of greater efficiency or smaller profit margins. Any base period that might be chosen is likely to have involved some untypical circumstances that result in unfair treatment of particular importers, and no provision for adjustment in such "hardship cases" can be fully satisfactory. The question of admitting new firms to the trade is particularly thorny. The restriction of total imports to a smaller quantity than what the home population would want to buy at a price just covering the foreign supply price plus transportation and marketing expenses and normal profit gives the imports a special scarcity value, and the chance to cut themselves in on the corresponding abnormal profit spurs newcomers to seek admission to the field. Reserving part of the total import quota to newcomers tends to encourage this socially functionless entry into a field probably already overfilled with facilities and personnel, yet barring entry tends to suppress new and protect stagnant methods of service.[1]

Artificially restricting imports gives the licenses a scarcity value. Who receives the quota profit depends on just how the licenses are allocated. The importers favored by history and the choice of a base period may receive the profit if the licenses are allocated in this way. If some system of domestic price control tries to keep the importers from charging higher prices than would have prevailed if imports had been unrestricted, then the benefit may go to the fortunate consumers who happen to get the scarce but price-controlled imports. Foreign suppliers may cut themselves in on the quota profit, raising their prices to correspond to the imposed scarcity of their wares in the importing country, if the restricted trading privileges are allocated to them rather than to the importers.[2] The foreigners may also gain if the licenses, though issued to domestic importers, carry restrictions about the amounts to be bought in designated countries. This arrangement reserves a definite share of the market to each foreign source, provided that the overall degree of import restriction and the resulting scarcity value of the commodity in question are great enough to make it worth the importers' while to import the full amounts permitted to them despite the need to pay more for imports from some countries than from others.

A system that leaves some of the quota profit to the foreigners spells higher prices for the restricted imports and worsened terms of trade. Carelessness with controls might even worsen instead of improve the restricting country's balance of payments. Suppose, for example, that the country had been importing ten automobiles per week at a price of $2,000 each. Now a quota of five cars per week is imposed. Demand for imported cars is so inelastic that no price below $5,000 will cut the number demanded down to five. Also assuming circumstances enabling the foreigners to collect the entire scarcity premium, the country's total expenditure on imported cars is $25,000, as against the $20,000 previously spent, the balance of payments deteriorates by $5,000.[3] Anomalies of this sort could be avoided by more careful licensing or by limiting imports not in physical quantity but in total value. This would be on the borderline between quotas and exchange control. Even then, the scarcity premium might fall to persons considered undeserving.

Ad hoc import duties

Perhaps the simplest solution is for the restricting government to collect the quota profit itself by charging fees for import licenses. It might decide the total amount of each particular commodity to be admitted into the country per month or year and then auction off the corresponding licenses.[4] This arrangement amounts to levying import duties designed to restrict imports of each commodity to the desired quantity. The only real difference is an administrative one: under the licensing system, the government fixes the total import quantity and lets the license fee set itself at auction at whatever level makes the quantity demanded conform; under the tariff system, the government can only in principle but not in practice know the precise rate of duty necessary for the desired restriction.

Charging duties or license fees has several advantages over limiting quantity alone. Reserving the scarcity premium to the government is not only probably fairer than arbitrarily giving it to private traders but also avoids promoting overcapacity in the importing business. By operating through the price system instead of trying to override it, duties or the equivalent are less likely to require bolstering by additional interventions (such as domestic price control or rationing of the restricted imports). By raising revenue, duties or fees have some effect against any domestic inflation that may be playing a part in the balance-of-payments difficulties. Levying or increasing a duty makes the domestic but not the foreign price of the imported commodity higher than it would be in the absence of restrictions and therefore, unless demand is completely inelastic, reduces the quantity demanded in terms of physical volume and foreign-currency value both.

Not only import duties but also export duties and subsidies might be used to help correct a balance-of-payments deficit. An export tax might be levied on commodities known to be in inelastic foreign demand, so that the foreigners would spend a larger total amount of their own money on reduced physical quantities. The terms of trade of the taxing country would also improve. For products known to have a highly elastic foreign demand, an export subsidy could be granted to cheapen them and increase their total foreign-currency proceeds. The balance of payments would then improve at the expense of worsened terms of trade.

As a balance-of-payments corrective, import duties and export duties and subsidies are less suitable than exchange-rate adjustments in affecting invisible transactions. (If it were possible to collect a uniform rate of duty on foreign exchange bought for all purposes and to pay a subsidy at the same uniform rate on sales of foreign exchange acquired in all ways, this would be equivalent to exchange depreciation of the home currency.)

Advance deposit requirements

Just as tariffs discourage imports by raising their cost, so do advance deposit requirements for imports.[5] Under this system, when an

1. On this and several points developed later, cf. Emil Küng, *Zahlungsbilanzpolitik*, Zürich: Polygraphischer Verlag AG., 1959, Part 5, esp. pp. 640–643.

2. Some such arrangement is not unknown: the United States and other countries have occasionally pressured Japanese and Hong Kong industries into "voluntarily" limiting their exports of particular products.

3. Cf. J. E. Meade, *The Balance of Payments*, London: Oxford University Press, 1951, pp. 276–280.

4. How such an auction might operate is described in *ibid.*, p. 286n. A similar system for auctioning off foreign exchange to be made available for other than "essential" purposes had already been proposed by Robert Triffin in "National Central Banking and the International Economy," in Lloyd A. Metzler *et al.*, *International Monetary Policies*, Washington: Board of Governors of the Federal Reserve System, 1947, pp. 69–70; and such systems have been used in Brazil and some other Latin American countries.

5. See Eugene A. Birnbaum and Moeen A. Qureshi, "Advance Deposit Requirements for Imports," IMF *Staff Papers*, VIII, November 1960, pp. 115–125.

importer applies for permission to import particular goods or to buy the necessary foreign exchange, he must deposit funds amounting to some specified percentage of the value of the goods. In some countries and for goods judged particularly nonessential, this figure may range up to several hundred or even a few thousand percent. The funds, deposited in a commercial bank, must usually be transferred to a special account at the central bank. The authorities will not return the deposit to the importer until a period has elapsed that ranges, under the systems of different countries, from a few days to many months. The importer bears the cost of tying up his own funds during this period, suffering a possibly sizable loss in their purchasing power in countries with rapid inflation, or else he must borrow funds at a corresponding interest rate. In extreme cases, the unavailability of a loan frustrates the import transaction, though such loans are usually rather easy to get (one reason being that the required deposit serves as a guarantee of the loan).

Import duties can have an anti-inflationary effect through the government budget; advance deposits can serve as a tool of anti-inflationary monetary policy by temporarily reducing the liquidity of claims on the banking system and by sequestering commercial bank reserves at the central bank. These effects go into reverse when the deposits are released, and the timing may prove awkward.

Advance deposit systems are most common in Latin America but have also been tried elsewhere—even in the United Kingdom in 1968. Several reasons have prompted resort to this bizarre type of control. It may be comparatively easy to adopt, especially if international agreements hamper manipulation of tariffs or other controls. It may be convenient for domestic monetary policy in countries where using other weapons requires legislative approval obtainable only with delay, or where a more obvious tightening of credit would meet public resistance. It may, in effect, compel importers to lend funds wanted to cover a government budget deficit. The system is usually regarded as temporary, but the larger an accumulation of required deposits has been allowed to grow, the more awkward dismantling it becomes. Another disadvantage is that it tends to harm competition by discriminating against new and small importing firms and in favor of those with stronger finances and better connections.

Exchange control

The desire to regulate capital transfers and invisible as well as commodity trade leads to exchange control. This may be defined as a system of regulations designed to assure both that foreign exchange coming into the possession of residents of the controlling country is sold in official channels and that this exchange is used only for approved payments abroad. The regulations usually try to plug up the evasion of conducting international business in ways that keep foreign exchange out of the possession of citizens of the controlling country in the first place. Exporters may be required to insist on payment in prescribed foreign currencies; or if the foreign buyers are allowed to make payment in the currency of the exporting country, they must have acquired this currency only in approved ways. Exchange control is almost always associated with fixed exchange rates, since there would otherwise be little need to requisition and ration foreign exchange. Conceivably, though, the rate could be left unpegged, with the controls modifying private supply and demand to make the home currency stronger than it otherwise would be.

Thorough control requires an extensive apparatus to block many ways of obtaining foreign exchange outside official channels. Residents of the controlling country who want to buy some unauthorized import or spend money abroad for some other unauthorized purpose might, for instance, simply mail domestic paper money abroad. This smuggled currency would sell in the foreign market at a discount from the official rate, since foreigners buying it to pay for imports from the controlling country would have to use it illegally. To fully prevent the *de facto* depreciation of the domestic currency involved in such transactions, the exchange-control authorities would have to search both mail and persons leaving and entering the country.

Another way to acquire unauthorized foreign exchange, or, rather, to accomplish the result for which it was wanted, would be private compensation. Merchants in Inland and Outland might agree that each would buy specified goods in his own country for shipment to the other. Since it is the Inlander, we suppose, whom government controls are making especially eager to carry out the deal, he would have to offer goods worth more than the Outland goods received for them as valued at the domestic prices prevailing on the two markets and at the official exchange rate. The deal would thus imply a *de facto* devaluation of the Inland currency. Furthermore, the Inland authorities would lose the foreign exchange that they might have acquired for disposal through official channels if their country's exports had been sold in the normal way instead. To stamp out private barter, the authorities would need, at least in principle, to supervise all import and export transactions.

Tourists might make similar compensation arrangements. Suppose that some Inlanders want to spend more than their foreign-exchange allotment while traveling in Outland. They might have friends or relatives pay their expenses there in return for a promise to reciprocate when the Outlanders later visited Inland. The matching of expenses to be paid by the Outlanders and by the Inlanders would presumably imply a rate of exchange discounting the Inland currency below its official parity. This example suggests how difficult it would be to plug all loopholes. The Inland authorities could hardly investigate each occasion when an Inlander bought a restaurant meal or paid a hotel bill for a visiting foreigner on suspicion that this hospitality might be part of a private compensation arrangement.

Another complication is the need to check whether each foreign-exchange allotment really is used for the specified purpose—to see, for instance, that exchange allotted for imports of "essential" food or raw materials is not in fact diverted to some unauthorized "luxury." It would even be necessary to supervise import prices. Otherwise, an Inland importer who wanted foreign exchange for unauthorized purposes might arrange for his Outland supplier of some authorized import to bill him at too high a price but pay him a secret rebate. Supervision of export pricing would also be necessary. Otherwise an Inland exporter might underbill his foreign customer and deliver only the corresponding amount of foreign exchange to the control authorities, while receiving a prearranged secret extra payment from the foreign customer. These last examples illustrate the difficulty of confining controls to capital movements alone (even though such limited control was envisaged, for instance, in the Articles of Agreement of the International Monetary Fund). Capital transfers could be accomplished by way of ordinary and apparently legitimate import and export transactions unless detailed supervision were undertaken to uncover irregularities.

Similarly, so-called leads and lags in commercial payments could be a vehicle for capital transfers. Suppose people want to get funds out of Inland, perhaps fearing devaluation. Inlanders exporting goods priced in foreign currency will be anxious to delay receiving payment in order to hold claims in foreign currency as long as possible. The foreign purchasers will probably cooperate in this delay, especially if they receive credit from their Inland suppliers on advantageous terms. Inlanders importing goods to be paid for in foreign currency have an incentive to hasten their payments for fear of a rise in the local-currency price of foreign exchange, and the resulting reduction in the debt owed to foreigners amounts to a capital export. It is a complicated matter to control business in such detail as to specify how fast Inlanders must collect their claims on foreigners and how slowly they must pay their foreign debts. The complexities are similar if goods are priced and are to be paid for in Inland currency. The foreign buyers of Inland exports will have an incentive to delay their payments in hopes of devaluation, and the resulting growth of Inland claims on foreigners amounts to a capital export. Foreigners who have sold goods to Inland will press for especially prompt payment of the amounts due them in Inland currency, thus reducing Inland's outstanding foreign debt. Changes in timing may affect not only payments but also the placement of orders: Inland's imports will tend to be hastened and exports delayed. It is probably true that the capital movements and similar effects on Inland's balance of payments accomplished by changes in timing are inherently both temporary and limited in potential amount: a return to more normal payments practices implies a reversal of the capital outflow. But the original capital outflow can be very unwelcome to the Inland authorities while it goes on, and they may be hard put to control it. It may even help force a devaluation.

Another method of capital export akin to leads and lags involves credit obtained by companies doing business both in Inland and abroad. Such a company might reduce its borrowing from Outland banks and increase its borrowing from Inland banks, accomplishing what would amount to an outward transfer of capital. So many devices are available for evading control confined to capital movements alone that really tight control would involve supervising all foreign transactions, all imports and exports of goods and services, all commercial credit granted in international trade, and all borrowing and lending by companies doing business at home and abroad. If motives for international capital transfers were very strong, controls would have to be correspondingly strict. In historical reality, they have sometimes gone as far as "the surveillance of correspondence and telephone conversations, for clandestine foreign-exchange operations can be carried out in these ways."[6]

Quite apart from outright evasion, the fungibility of money and capital can impede the intended working of capital controls, especially as time permits the adaptation of market institutions and practices. For example, if U.S. controls over capital exports prod U.S. corporations to raise more of the funds for their European projects in Europe, then the resulting changes in capital-market conditions may induce Europeans to reduce or reverse their own placements of funds in the United States.[7]

An exchange-control system requires precautions to minimize interference with legitimate international banking. If Inland is a country of leading importance in international trade, its currency is widely used in normal times for quoting prices and stipulating payments. Traders in many countries ordinarily hold working balances of its currency, and banks and other firms providing financial services to foreigners might account for a good part of Inland's international earnings. Exchange control might make foreigners reluctant to hold bank accounts in Inland unnecessarily or to invest funds in its market. A trend might develop away from pricing commodities and stipulating payments in Inland currency. Foreigners would dislike having the convertibility of their funds into other currencies subject to the whim of the Inland controllers. To assuage foreign fears on this score, the Inland authorities could establish a system of nonresident accounts. Bank accounts owned by nonresidents could remain freely convertible into foreign exchange at the official rate of exchange at any time and for any purpose. Except for possible fears of devaluation or of changes in the regulations, then, Inland currency might be just about as suitable for holding by foreigners

as it had ever been.[8] Under this system, payments by residents into nonresident accounts would have to be just as strictly controlled as residents' purchases of foreign exchange, for funds once transferred to a nonresident become freely convertible into foreign exchange.

Multiple exchange rates

In exchange-control systems of the type considered so far, foreign exchange is allocated for various types of import or payment abroad according to *ad hoc* decisions or rules of thumb. Instead, exchange might be allocated by selling it at different prices to importers of different products or to persons making payments abroad for different purposes. It might be sold relatively cheap, for example, to pay for imports officially considered "essential" or for goods being imported by agencies of the government itself. For transactions considered less worthy of encouragement—"luxury" imports perhaps, or travel, donations, or investment abroad—exchange might be sold at a relatively high price. Charging an especially high price for foreign exchange to pay for imports of certain goods resembles levying import duties on such goods under a unitary exchange-rate system, except that the duties can be levied not only on commodities but also on invisible transactions. Sale of foreign exchange cheap for other purposes amounts to an import subsidy.

On the export side, the authorities may pay a comparatively high local-currency price for the foreign-exchange proceeds of certain exports so as in effect to subsidize them, perhaps on the supposition that the foreign demand for them is highly elastic. A relatively low price might be paid for the foreign-exchange proceeds of other exports, including staple exports for which foreign demand was thought to be inelastic. The system of multiple exchange rates can operate as a selective system of import and export duties and subsidies, with the rate calculated for each particular type of transaction according to supposed essentiality, demand elasticity, or other attributes.

Multiple rates also resemble duties in providing revenue. By buying foreign exchange more cheaply on the average than it sells, the government can profit from its monopoly of exchange transactions. Such a system would tend to mop funds off of the domestic market and so have a deflationary or anti-inflationary effect. If the domestic-currency prices of foreign exchange were higher on the average for import transactions than for export transactions, the country might conceivably even have an export surplus with trade valued in foreign currency but an import surplus with trade valued in domestic currency. Even though trade in goods and services produced larger earnings than expenditures of foreign exchange, an import balance as measured in domestic currency might be exerting an anti-inflationary influence on the domestic economy.[9]

Many variations on the multiple-rate system are possible. One would combine fixed official rates and fluctuating rates. Importers of favored commodities could buy foreign exchange at the fixed rate, while importers of less-favored commodities would be shunted to the "free" market, where foreign exchange would command a higher price. Purchases of foreign exchange for travel, capital transfer, and other invisible transactions might also be confined to the free market. A gamut of different effective rates of exchange might be established by defining several categories of transactions, for each of which the buyers of foreign exchange would be allowed a specified percentage at the favorable official rate and required to buy the remainder in the less favorable free market. A multiplicity of exchange rates would appear on the export side of the market, also, if the regulations permitted different percentages of the foreign-exchange proceeds of various commodities to be sold at the advantageous free-market rate according to the degree of encouragement officially intended for each category of exports.

Multiple exchange rates have been employed in many countries and have been quite common in Latin America, though considerable simplification has taken place over the years. The Brazilian system in effect at the end of 1960 is an example.[10] (It represented a radical simplification of systems previously in effect and gave way to still further simplification in 1961.) The official and parity rates of 18.36, 18.50, and 18.92 cruzeiros per dollar had very limited applicability. The Bank of Brazil requisitioned the foreign-exchange proceeds of "first-category" exports (cocoa beans and green and roasted coffee) at a rate of 90 cruzeiros per dollar and the proceeds of "second-category" exports (cocoa derivatives, castor beans, and crude mineral oil and derivatives) at 100 cruzeiros per dollar. Proceeds of all other exports, of most invisible transactions, and of capital

BALANCE-OF-PAYMENTS ADJUSTMENT BY DIRECT CONTROLS

imports had to be surrendered at a so-called free-market rate. This rate was fluctuating in the vicinity of 190 cruzeiros per dollar at the end of 1960, but immediate cash payment of only 130 cruzeiros was made, with the balance paid in six-month notes of the Bank of Brazil. On the import side, foreign exchange to pay for newsprint bought by printers whose publications weighed 80 grams or less was available at 67.57 cruzeiros per dollar. Exchange was available at 100 cruzeiros per dollar for imports of newsprint by printers whose publications weighed more than 80 grams, as well as for government payments, specified government imports, wheat, petroleum and petroleum derivatives, imports for the petroleum and printing industries, and certain other preferential imports, and also for amortization and interest on registered loans, credits, and financing. A "free-market" rate fluctuating in the vicinity of 195 cruzeiros per dollar applied to most invisible imports and all capital transactions not carried out at preferential rates. Exchange for imports of most commodities had to be

6. Robert Mossé, *Les Problèmes Monétaires Internationaux*, Paris: Payot, 1967, p. 205.
For a survey of measures to regulate capital movements imposed by the major industrial countries since the late 1950s, including various kinds of instructions to the commercial banks, see Rodney H. Mills, Jr., *The Regulation of Short-Term Capital Movements in Major Industrial Countries*, Washington: Board of Governors of the Federal Reserve System, 1972.

7. See Mordechai E. Kreinin, *International Economics: A Policy Approach*, New York: Harcourt Brace Jovanovich, 1971, pp. 139–140.

8. This paragraph implicitly refers to the system of nonresident accounts since December 1958 and of American accounts before then in the exchange controls of the United Kingdom.

9. On this last point, see Shu-Chin Yang, *A Multiple Exchange Rate System, An Appraisal of Thailand's Experience, 1946–1955*, Madison: The University of Wisconsin Press, 1957, pp. 77–78.

10. International Monetary Fund, *Twelfth Annual Report on Exchange Restrictions*, Washington: 1961, pp. 52–59, *International Financial Statistics*, August 1961, pp. 60–63.

bought in auctions held separately for two categories of goods. For "general-category" imports (raw materials, equipment, and other production goods, as well as consumer goods deemed to be in short domestic supply), the auction rate was about 229 cruzeiros per dollar at the end of 1960. For "special-category" imports (other goods, comprising only about 5 percent of all auction imports), the rate was about 640 cruzeiros per dollar. The auctioned foreign exchange was generally not made available until after the lapse of 150 days, though successful bidders had to pay for it within a very few days. Special exchange auctions were held from time to time for separately listed goods used in agriculture and for fruits from Uruguay. Special regulations were in effect for trade with countries with which Brazil had bilateral payments agreements. In addition to being subject to the various foreign-exchange regulations just described (and described in an oversimplified way, at that), exports and some imports were subject to licensing.

Multiple-rate systems permit selective adjustments to equilibrate a country's balance of payments. In effect, the home currency can be devalued only for those types of import and export transactions in which the response to price is thought to be most sensitive. The only important advantage over duties and subsidies is that the multiple-exchange-rate system can more easily cover a broader range of transactions, invisible as well as visible.[11] Extensive supervision of exchange transactions is necessary, however, to prevent unauthorized arbitrage—for example, to keep people from buying foreign exchange relatively cheap, supposedly for one of the favored purposes, and then reselling it to other persons who want foreign exchange for less favored purposes and who would otherwise have to buy it at a less favorable rate.[12]

A relatively simple multiple-rate system, that of the split or dual market, was given additional importance in Belgium-Luxembourg in 1971, where it had long prevailed. France adopted the system in 1971 and Italy in early 1973, both abolishing it in 1974. In principle, capital transactions, especially short-term capital transactions, were confined to a "financial market," where supply and demand might establish a different rate than prevailed on the "commercial market." The rate differential was supposed to discourage officially undesired capital inflows or outflows while allowing trade transactions to take place at a rate acceptable to or

even pegged by the authorities. Arbitrage was a problem: transactors ingeniously sought ways to get the benefit of whichever rate was more advantageous for themselves.[13]

An appraisal of possible advantages

Complexities in enforcing particular types of control do not necessarily condemn the whole approach. A judicious combination of controls might be the answer. An appraisal involves value judgments as well as facts and analysis. It also implies a *comparison* with the more nearly "automatic" mechanisms of adjustment; and since some of their possible defects still remain to be examined, the present appraisal can be tentative only.[14]

In the next few pages, some comments immediately follow each statement of an advantage claimed for controls. This arrangement merely serves convenience and is not meant to dismiss each advantage as completely illusory.

1. Controls can keep balances of payments in order when other methods of adjustment would work painfully, if at all. Controls make less deflation of expenditure necessary to improve the balance of payments by any given amount (or they increase the scope for an expansionary policy to combat depression at home). Deflation of aggregate expenditure is an inefficient way of improving the balance of payments, especially if consumption of imports and exportable goods responds downward only slightly, if resources have little mobility from home-market into export production, and if foreign demand for additional exports is absent. Furthermore, expenditure deflation impinges more heavily in the aggregate on home-market goods than on imports and so causes unemployment (unless goods and factor prices are more completely flexible than is likely). Controls, on the contrary, tend to create employment by switching demand away from imports onto home-market goods. They offset some of the damage to employment done by expenditure deflation and make a given balance-of-payments improvement possible with less unemployment than if deflation had been the only weapon used.[15] This gain presumably outweighs any unemployment that carelessly designed and administered controls might inflict on factors of production employed together with imported materials. As for sparing a country from deflation for the sake of the balance of payments, however, controls are

not the only method of adjustment capable of doing that. The case for controls depends on defects in other mechanisms.

A related argument is that direct controls could work more rapidly and effectively than any alternative in coping with sudden severe disturbances such as war, foreign depression, or domestic harvest failure. Market mechanisms might not be absolutely unworkable—the home currency might be allowed to depreciate sharply to a level that, barring speculation or extremely low demand elasticities, would be bound to equilibrate the balance of payments—; but adopting direct controls as an emergency measure might prove less burdensome than severe, even if temporary, exchange-rate movements.[16] (Why and how may be seen from arguments still to follow.) On the other hand, the tightening and loosening of controls in response to changes in supply and demand, or even the knowledge that the authorities stood ready to wield controls when they saw fit, could also hamper trade. Adjustable controls could require wasteful temporary

certainly must be appropriate. A loose analogy with the general economic principle of marginalism suggests that neither complete reliance on nor complete rejection of controls is sensible; the best position must be somewhere in between. Not to control the balance of payments directly in any way or to any extent seems like a highly exceptional policy. Rejection of controls can be imputed to some sort of superstitious trust in the magic of the price system, to a callously comfortable belief that things will work themselves out for the best if left alone, to a doctrinaire insistence on laissez-faire. Advocacy of controls—if not of one particular kind, then of some other kind—can, by contrast, be represented as a more pragmatic, practical, realistic position. The clash of opinions can be represented as a dispute between ivory-tower dogma and practical awareness. In my judgment, this way of thinking provides the most deep-seated basis for advocating direct controls. The anticontrols position, as well, admittedly has a basis in psychology and political philosophy. But whatever the psychological underpinnings of the different points of view may be, it should be possible to discuss rationally how well rival policies harmonize with the value judgments that anyone would avow openly.

11. For an appraisal of the possibilities of using multiple exchange rates to manipulate trade in the interest of economic development programs, see Eugene R. Schlesinger, *Multiple Exchange Rates and Economic Development*, Princeton, N.J.: Princeton University Press, 1952.

12. For further arguments against multiple exchange rates, see IMF, 1967 *Annual Report*, pp. 45–46.

13. See German Bundesbank, *Geschäftsbericht für das Jahr 1971*, pp. 35–36; German Council of Economic Experts, *Toward a New Basis for International Monetary Policy* (translated from the Experts' Annual Report of November 1971), Princeton Studies in International Finance, Princeton, N.J.: Princeton University, No. 31, October 1972, pp. 18–19; and remarks by Armin Gutowski and Wolfgang Kasper in American Enterprise Institute for Public Policy Research, *International Monetary Problems*, Washington: AEI, 1972, pp. 69–72 and 88–93.

14. There is always the danger, in appraising some line of policy, of setting up and blowing down straw men or of reporting arguments in weak versions only. The best an admitted skeptic can do is keep this danger in mind and *try* to present the case for controls fairly. With one exception, the discussion that follows covers what seem to be the real arguments. The exception concerns a psychological basis for shifting the burden of proof onto the opponents of controls. So many kinds are available that if some are demonstrably inappropriate, others almost

15. See M. F. W. Hemming and W. M. Corden, "Import Restriction as an Instrument of Balance-of-Payments Policy," *Economic Journal* LXVIII, September 1958, pp. 483–510. The authors devote only incidental attention to exchange-rate adjustment but do recognize it as an alternative to controls and even mention (esp. pp. 509–510) that whereas import restriction tends to increase employment only by diverting expenditure from imports onto home-produced goods, the shift in relative prices resulting from devaluation does so both by discouraging imports and by increasing the efficiency with which expenditure deflation tends to shift goods and resources into meeting a stimulated export demand.

16. Not all considerations, however, count in favor of the supposed relative sureness of controls. With quotas controlling imports and with conditions changing over time, it becomes increasingly difficult to guess what the pattern of trade would be if quotas were removed. Importers cease to apply for import licenses when they expect refusal, and the number of applications ceases to indicate the strength of demand. As an example, I. F. Pearce cites Australia's experience in 1960, when imports soared far more than predicted upon the lifting of controls. *International Trade*, New York: Norton, 1970, p. 251.

shifts of factors of production into and out of import-competing industries in the controlling country and into and out of foreign export industries.[17] Incidentally, the argument for controls in exceptional emergencies implies reliance on other adjustment mechanisms in normal times.

2. Just as controls over trade might be warranted in emergencies, so exchange control might be useful to check speculative "hot money" movements or other unwanted capital transfers. As already emphasized, though, close supervision of all international transactions would be needed to block many ways of transferring capital indirectly. (Extensive supervision might not be necessary if the authorities were content to restrain only certain major long-term capital outflows—those accomplished by floating foreign security issues in the home market, for example. But such capital outflows presumably pose a less sudden and critical problem than the others that are so difficult to control.) Furthermore, control confined to capital movements, with current-account transactions supervised but permitted if judged bona fide, would be no complete adjustment mechanism and no substitute for one affecting current-account as well as capital transactions.

3. When something happens that would otherwise cause a balance-of-payments deficit, resort to controls may perhaps prevent or lessen the rise in the home price level and the worsening of the terms of trade that would have accompanied exchange depreciation instead. Later chapters examine these two worries about depreciation in greater detail; here we mention only the main points of comparison. In tending to make imported goods more expensive, import controls are similar to depreciation, not different from it. (Strictly speaking, it is neither depreciation nor controls that tend to raise prices, but the unfavorable occurrences requiring some response or other.) Controls also tend to raise prices in the way a reversal of technical progress would, since they interfere with the gains from international specialization. As for the terms of trade, the use of import restrictions or duties can avoid cheapening exports in favor of foreigners the way devaluation would.[18] Foreign suppliers of imports may shave their prices somewhat to help hold their market. In principle, if not very accurately in practice, the authorities could judiciously apply different rates of duty or degrees of restriction to different goods so as to achieve the best possible combination of effects on the terms and balance of trade in the light of different supply and demand elasticities. A vast literature relevant to appraising this possibility covers such matters as the sacrifice in trade volume to obtain better terms, the attendant concept of an "optimum" degree of trade restriction, questions of the amount and permanence of improvement obtainable in the light of long-run demand and supply elasticities, practical difficulties of actually estimating the relevant elasticities for the purpose of adopting suitable restrictions and continually modifying them, attempts by other countries to counter-manipulate the terms of trade, alternatives to terms-of-trade manipulation as a vehicle for agreed international redistribution of wealth or income, and fundamental ambiguities in the very concept of terms of trade.

Furthermore, if controls really can ward off the bad effects of some occurrence tending to worsen both the balance of payments and the terms of trade, then, it would seem, controls to improve the terms of trade would already have been advisable in the first place. The terms-of-trade argument for controls or duties does not make a case against relying at the same time on one of the "automatic" mechanisms as the primary method of balance-of-payments adjustment. The key presumption to be examined is that some new development tending to cause a deficit and otherwise to require deflation or exchange depreciation increases at the same time the stringency of control that is optimal on terms-of-trade grounds.[19]

4. The question of how countries share the gains from trade brings to mind a broad range of issues that will also turn out to involve the distribution of income or wealth, but now the *domestic* distribution. Though often only dimly seen, these considerations probably have great importance in actual policy-making.

Direct controls can restrict imports more selectively than "the blind forces of the market" would. Controls can keep foreign exchange from being wasted on "nonessential" or "luxury" imports and can conserve it for "essentials." At least, selective import duties or multiple exchange rates can penalize its nonessential use. In this way, the relatively poor consumers of imported essentials can escape and can shift to the relatively rich consumers of imported luxuries some of the burden of abstinence that a market method of adjustment would otherwise indiscriminately impose. If wealthy playboys were allowed to take lengthy pleasure trips abroad, they would bid up the price of foreign exchange and so raise the prices of imported food consumed by the poor and the prices of imported capital goods needed for industrial reconstruction or development. It was no doubt considerations of this sort that led European countries at the end of World War II to fix their currencies at overvalued levels in relation to the dollar, to cope with the attendant balance-of-payments difficulties by direct controls, and, in general, to impose "austerity" in a deliberate and overt manner.

These arguments, like those for consumer rationing in wartime, do have considerable force. But they need some qualification. For one thing, it is hard to distinguish clearly and consistently between luxuries and essentials. Suppose, for example, that the British authorities tightly ration foreign exchange for Mediterranean cruises but classify oil as an essential import. Some of the oil may go for heating at English vacation resorts that operate on a larger scale than they would have done if the cruises had not been restricted. The restrictions may in effect divert English labor and other factors of production from other activities into providing recreation services that other countries could provide at lower cost. In view of the English climate, it may well be that the marginal units of foreign exchange spent on imported oil and so forth go to satisfy wants no more urgent—while satisfying them less effectively—than the wants otherwise satisfied by marginal units of exchange spent on foreign travel.

Such examples suggest at least two lessons. First, restricting imports of supposed nonessentials is likely to promote imports of their substitutes and also divert domestic and imported resources or materials into home production of substitutes. The diversion may hamper exports as well.[20] Second, it is idle to try to decide on some abstract, philosophical basis which wants and commodities are frivolous and which essential. The controllers cannot know except in a very rough-and-ready way how relatively important various imports and foreign expenditures are. They must rely in part on expert advice from persons engaged in the affected lines of business. The allocation of foreign exchange is influenced by a "competition in lamentation"; there is a tendency to consider

(*op. cit.*, esp. p. 510), the only clear-cut advantage over devaluation they claim for controls concerns the terms of trade. (They also barely mention speed of operation, political and administrative considerations that might cut either way, and the opportunity to discriminate according to how restricting imports from various sources might affect the supply of credit and export sales as well as the terms of trade.) Hemming and Corden conceive of an optimum policy combination determined by balancing three effects at the margin: of controls in distorting resource allocation (but improving the terms of trade), of expenditure deflation in causing unemployment, and of devaluation in worsening the terms of trade. Ideally, they say, marginal damages should be equal for a marginal degree of balance-of-payments improvement in each of the three ways.

19. Sidney S. Alexander, "Devaluation versus Import Restriction as an Instrument for Improving Foreign Trade Balance," IMF *Staff Papers*, I, April 1951, pp. 379–396, esp. pp. 388–389, seems to assert such a presumption. The appropriate tightening of import restriction accompanies devaluation automatically if the restriction is imposed in the form of an *ad valorem* tariff.

More precisely, Alexander appears to envisage a devaluation undertaken, independently of any change in supplies and demands in foreign trade, in order to shrink a previously existing trade deficit. The real issue, however, is the presumption that a tightening of previously optimal import restrictions is the best response to a *change* in supplies and demands that would otherwise *cause* a trade deficit. Egon Sohmen, *Fluctuating Exchange Rates: Theory and Controversy*, Chicago: University of Chicago Press, 1961, pp. 14–15, further questions whether Alexander's argument tells in favor of tighter controls when nobody knows whether or not those already existing are or are not above the "optimum" level.

20. Licenses to import materials might be made contingent on using the materials in export production, but enforcement would be difficult. What could the authorities do, for example, if producers claimed that they *had* produced their goods for export but had not been able to sell them abroad because of the overvalued exchange rate and so had had to sell them on the home market after all? And anyway, earmarking imported materials for export production would tend to release similar domestic materials for home-market production. On some of these and other awkward repercussions, see Küng, *op. cit.*, pp. 644–645, 654–655, 666, and *passim*.

17. Cf. Küng, *op. cit.*, pp. 586–587.

18. When Hemming and Corden finally face the issue squarely in their article on import restriction

needs the greatest in the sectors that howl the loudest.[21] The controllers may even consider how foreign governments might react to their decisions. A more fundamental part of the problem hinges on one of the major teachings of economics: things are not useful because of their physical characteristics alone. Usefulness is a relation between things and human wants; and the marginal usefulness or utility is the smaller the more abundant the particular thing considered. Ideally, decisions about restricting the supply of various things ought to consider their essentiality or usefulness *at the margin*. It is easy to imagine circumstances in which an additional dollar's worth or an additional ounce of penicillin or polio vaccine would contribute less to human satisfaction than an additional dollar's worth or an additional ounce of orchids.

Official attempts to lay down distinctions between luxuries and necessities sometimes become ridiculous. At one time the Norwegian government restricted purchases of bathtubs to persons whose doctors had certified their need for one. Sir Stafford Cripps, during his tenure at the British Exchequer, was once questioned in the House of Commons about the possibility of allowing imports of French cheese; he replied that only "serious cheese" could be permitted.[22]

It is particularly dubious to try to distinguish between essential and frivolous imports according to whether they contribute to production or merely to "unnecessary" consumption. All production supposedly aims at satisfying human wants, immediately or ultimately. Producing machinery or constructing factories is not inherently more worthy than producing restaurant meals or nightclub entertainment, for the machinery or factories are pointless unless they can sooner or later give rise to goods or services (including, perhaps, national defense) that do satisfy human wants. Similarly, it would be odd to administer import controls so as to discriminate against some goods and in favor of others merely because these others were raw materials to be embodied in exports. For the export trade is not carried on as an end in its own right; exports are in effect the price paid for the imports whose ultimate services consumers desire. To favor production-oriented or export-oriented imports over consumption-oriented imports is to prefer a roundabout achievement of ultimate consumer satisfactions to a more direct achievement merely because of

its greater roundaboutness; it is to confuse ends and means.

One possible answer to this point is that certain distortions in the economic system cause businessmen and consumers to choose the immediate satisfaction of wants, even though indirect methods of satisfaction have a yield sufficiently greater to more than justify postponing the ultimate satisfactions. In comparison with some sort of social point of view, private decision-makers might be taking too much thought for the present and not enough for the future. Controls could then conceivably compensate or correct for existing distortions. But if so, a convincing case would have to specify what these other distortions were and why direct controls over international transactions were the best way of dealing with them; slogans are not enough. Incidentally, if controls over trade really were desirable to offset other distortions in the economy, the case for them would seem to be a general one, not especially related to balance-of-payments difficulties.

Barring specific known distortions for which controls might be a corrective, the idea naturally arises of letting ultimate consumers appraise "essentiality." Give up trying to make sweeping philosophical comparisons; instead, let people act on their own comparisons of the satisfactions expected from another dollar's worth of this and another dollar's worth of that. Let consumers and businessmen judge and act on the intensities of the wants that various domestic and imported goods can satisfy, either directly or by contributing to further processes of production. Let them bid for the imports they want and for the foreign exchange with which to pay for them.

This advice can be challenged. In effect, it calls for "rationing by the purse." How meaningful is it to judge the essentialities or utilities of various goods by what people are prepared to pay for them? The wealthy man's $5000 vacation abroad may have less social importance than the imported food or machinery that the same amount of foreign exchange would have bought. The price system cannot take account of facts like this.

This argument, if sound, applies at home as well as in foreign trade. So applied, the argument is familiar: the unhampered price system perversely provides cream for the dowager's pampered cat while the poor widow's baby lacks milk. The choice of policies lies between direct remedies for the problems of poverty, including direct taxes and transfer payments, and redistribution attempted through rationing and excise taxes and subsidies to keep real incomes from corresponding to money incomes. While the latter approach cannot be condemned completely, it does have familiar disadvantages, especially those connected with its making things have different price ratios and different marginal rates of substitution for different persons.

If applying direct controls and selective excise taxes and subsidies to domestic transactions is a clumsy and indirect way of redistributing real income, how much more so it is to try pinching and squeezing international transactions in particular for the same purpose. If luxury imports are restricted to maintain a favorable exchange rate for imports of essential goods used by relatively poor persons, the redistributory purpose of the import controls calls for corresponding controls over domestic production and trade as well. Otherwise, resources would be diverted into the relatively inefficient local production of substitutes for the restricted luxury imports. It would be ironic if the controls permitted imports of machinery for domestic luxury industries. Anomalous results might occur in all sorts of indirect ways; for example, even though the local luxury industries fostered by the import controls used locally built machinery, the resulting total demand for machinery might be great enough to stimulate imports by other industries that might otherwise have bought their machinery at home. Restricting the use of foreign exchange for frivolous purposes might intensify the use of foreign exchange for apparently serious purposes, all without blocking the satisfaction of supposedly frivolous desires but simply causing them to be satisfied in a less efficient way. Restrictions on imports of flowers, for example, might stimulate growing flowers locally in greenhouses heated by coal, and a consequent reduction in coal exports might mean that the foreign exchange saved in one direction was lost in another.

Curing a trade deficit involves cutting the country's total of private and public consumption and investment. Income-distribution considerations may perhaps argue for cutting back on luxury consumption in particular. Even so, as long as some goods in each category will still be consumed in the new situation, it is not clear why the cut in luxury consumption should be especially concentrated on imports.

BALANCE-OF-PAYMENTS ADJUSTMENT BY DIRECT CONTROLS

Perhaps the pattern of opportunity costs even calls for cutting imports mainly of essential rather than luxury goods; an import-replacing expansion of domestic production of essentials could be aided by cutbacks on the domestic production of luxuries.[23]

If, despite everything, possibilities of influencing the domestic distribution of real income are thought to justify selective controls over trade, the question arises why their use should hinge on balance-of-payments difficulties. Should redistributionary controls be relaxed whenever the balance-of-payments situation happens to turn favorable? If redistribution is the purpose, why shouldn't the controls be administered accordingly, with balance-of-payments equilibrium being taken care of in some further way? One more possible argument for controlling luxury imports may be mentioned for the sake of completeness, even though saying much about it would arouse suspicion of blowing down straw men. It involves the international demonstration effect.[24] If people in a poor country become acquainted with the high standards of living prevalent abroad and with the attractive goods available there, their propensity to consume may be higher and their propensity to accumulate capital lower than if they had remained more nearly in ignorance of foreign consumption

21. *Ibid.*, p. 690.

22. Wilhelm Röpke, *Internationale Ordnung—heute*, Erlenbach-Zürich: Rentsch, 1954, p. 286.

23. If the foreign supply is elastic for the imported luxuries and inelastic for the imported necessities, and if domestic industry could rather easily convert from luxury to essential production, terms-of-trade considerations would call for concentrating import restrictions on the essentials rather than on the luxuries. On all this, see Meade, *op. cit.*, p. 318n. Incidentally, this point is not meant to recognize a clear distinction between "luxuries" and "essentials"; it merely mentions some problems to consider *even if* the distinction could meaningfully be made.

24. Cf. Ragnar Nurkse, *Problems of Capital Formation in Underdeveloped Countries*, Oxford: Basil Blackwell, 1953, esp. pp. 58–75.

standards. Restrictions on luxury imports may be a way of protecting this salutory ignorance.

One further argument for controls is considered in the appendix to this chapter.

Further problems with controls

Some general remarks about controls still need to be pulled together.

1. Controls are open to the same sorts of objections on "efficiency" grounds as are developed in the traditional analysis of protective tariffs versus free trade, and whatever qualifications apply to that analysis apply here also.[25] Even though intended solely for balance-of-payments purposes, furthermore, controls give at least incidental protection against foreign competition to domestic producers of items in which the country had a comparative disadvantage. Vested interests develop and press for continuance of the controls even after the original need for them has passed. Vested interests also develop in the "quota profits" created by certain types of restriction. And speaking of vested interests, one might mention trade experts and controllers who like to think that their services are too important for their country to dispense with.[26]

Sometimes the inefficiency caused by controls is obvious even to noneconomists. When the Mexican government was trying to stave off the devaluation of 1948, it banned imports of trucks but not of spare parts. Mexicans found it worthwhile to import parts and assemble trucks locally at a greater cost, even in foreign exchange, than the cost of ready-built trucks. Under a system adopted in Brazil in 1953, petroleum could be imported at a preferred exchange rate of 33.82 cruzeiros per dollar, while repair parts for trucks and buses had to be imported at a rate fluctuating up towards 150 cruzeiros per dollar. This made maintaining and repairing trucks and buses artificially expensive relative to the cost of gasoline. It did not pay truck operators to spend 1 dollar for repairs that would improve engine efficiency enough to save 3 dollars' worth of gasoline, since the differential exchange rates meant that 3 dollars for gasoline cost fewer cruzeiros than 1 dollar for repair parts. This was one reason why the average truck consumed 4.3 tons of gasoline a year in Brazil compared with 2.7 tons in the United States. Other inefficiencies of this type were also apparent, such as the use of limestone to make cement instead of fertil-izer while fertilizer was being imported at preferred exchange rates. Because newsprint was imported at a preferential rate of 18.82 cruzeiros per dollar, Brazilian producers could not compete and began switching their output into other kinds of paper. More and more foreign exchange was used to import newsprint, leaving less available for the import of machinery and parts.[27]

2. One fundamental difficulty with relying on controls for equilibrium is that a deficit on current account corresponds to attempts by the country's residents to "absorb" goods and services in excess of aggregate production. At full employment, no room remains for a remedy through greater production; in fact, the inefficiencies caused by controls would, if anything, interfere. People's attempted overspending accompanies an excess of liquid purchasing power in ther hands: given the prevailing level of prices (including the prices of internationally traded goods and services at prevailing exchange rates), the purchasing power of the total money supply is larger than the aggregate of real cash balances that persons and institutions desire to hold. Barring a disinflationary policy, the market method of adjustment is for the real money supply to be cut down to what people are willing to hold by a rise in prices, notably including the home-currency prices of internationally traded goods as translated at increased quotations on foreign currencies. In addition to this, the cheapening of domestic goods and factors of production *relative* to internationally traded goods brings substitution and real-income effects into play.[28] If these market adjustments are prevented, merely introducing import controls will not remedy the generally overblown demand. If people are restricted from spending their money on certain imports, they are likely to spend part of it on other imports. If controls apply broadly and tightly enough to cut *total* spending on imports, people will divert their expenditure to goods produced at home, including exportable goods and home-market goods employing resources diverted from export production. Damming up purchasing power in one place lets it seep through in another. Import restrictions cannot eliminate a trade deficit unless they can somehow restrict total—including domestic—consumption and investment and make people more acquiescent than before in saving and holding cash balances. Temporarily, controls may do this: when people are blocked in spending their money in some ways, they may

need some time to decide how else to spend it. Some disinvestment, including disinvestment in inventories of imported materials, may occur. But continued success would require not merely maintaining but repeatedly tightening the controls.[29]

Professors Röpke and Brozen each have described the problem picturesquely. When the government forbids people to import gourmet cheese or bathtubs or automobiles or to take other than strictly limited vacations abroad, it leaves money "burning holes in their pockets" and possibly itching to be spent on other imports or on exportable goods or on goods and services using resources that might otherwise have gone into import-competing or exportable goods. To keep a wealthy Brazilian from spending his money on an imported automobile or on foreign travel may accomplish little saving of foreign exchange. Instead, he may use it for a luxurious home or for other domestically produced luxuries. If import restrictions keep an Englishman from giving his wife a Swiss watch for Christmas, "it is scarcely to be assumed that he will give her a savings-account passbook instead; rather, he will try to hunt up some other luxury good."[30]

Some writers have concluded that import restrictions at full employment can in themselves do substantially nothing at all to shrink absorption and so shrink a trade deficit.[31] But this conclusion goes too far. The undoubted possibility of curing a deficit by completely prohibiting *all* imports suggests that less sweeping restrictions should be able to reduce imports directly by somewhat more than they reduce exports indirectly. The case against controls is not that they are totally ineffective but that they are inefficient. While they leave in operation the subsidy that an artificially low price of foreign exchange gives to absorption, they do narrow the range and restrict the quantities of goods on which people can in fact collect this subsidy. Controls shrink the effective real purchasing power of the existing money supply not by allowing the prices of foreign exchange and internationally traded goods to rise in free markets but by creating shortages that make prices rise anyway and also by directly keeping people from spending their money as they wish. Prices alone do not measure the entire loss in the purchasing power of money and of money incomes.

The absorption approach suggests one further problem when an external deficit is associated with a policy of suppressed inflation and extreme "austerity." Having a country live within its means may involve not only restraining consumption but also stimulating production, yet enforced austerity tends to hamper it. The state may try to limit luxury spending, but there is one luxury that, without going totalitarian, it can hardly deprive people of—leisure. Although people may still care about earning money to spend later, after austerity will have been relaxed, their incentives to work harder or longer for more mere money become relatively weak if their present incomes already cover their ration of artificially cheap "necessities" permitted by the controls, if social services take care of other necessities such as medical care, and especially if purchases of additional "luxuries" are restricted or forbidden. Perhaps the best example is Germany before the reforms of mid-1948. The contrasting policy of allowing the price mechanism to operate offers people the incentive of using any additional money earnings for whatever goods and services they themselves desire.

25. For a discussion with particular relevance to developing countries, see Derek T. Healey, "Development Policy: New Thinking About an Interpretation," *Journal of Economic Literature*, **X**, September 1972, pp. 757–797, esp. pp. 779–783.

26. Cf. Küng, *op. cit.*, pp. 671–672.

27. Yale Brozen, "Solutions for the Brazilian Dollar Shortage," *Current Economic Comment*, May 1955, pp. 22–23.

28. None of this means, of course, that a deficit can result only from actual monetary inflation. A deterioration of trade opportunities can reduce a country's real income, leaving the previously appropriate money supply and money income level excessive, until prices adjust.

29. Cf. J. J. Polak, "Monetary Analysis of Income Formation and Payments Problems," IMF *Staff Papers*, **VI**, November 1957, p. 30.

30. Brozen, *op. cit.*, p. 23; Röpke, *op. cit.*, pp. 287–288. The translated quotation is from Röpke. His pages 282ff., which have largely inspired the present treatment, examine "austerity" in foreign-trade policy as an aspect of suppressed inflation in general.

31. For example, Hemming and Corden, *op. cit.*, esp. pp. 495 and 509.

3. For the reasons already reviewed, and others, direct controls tend to be self-necessitating: the existence of certain controls not conforming to the logic of a price system tends to create conditions that appear to call for more such controls. One illustration concerns exchange control in particular. If foreign countries keep their currencies from being freely convertible into others, the residents of a country still lacking such controls would find that their surplus earnings in transactions with some countries could not be freely sold to meet excess expenditures in other countries. Their authorities would now worry not merely about a multilateral balance of transactions with the rest of the world as a whole but also about balance with other countries separately. Unless they were to allow a free exchange market in which the controlled foreign currencies would very probably be quoted at broken cross-rates of exchange, the authorities would find themselves driven to institute controls of their own to increase the degree of bilateral balance. Of course, countries might collaborate to lessen the necessities for bilateralism by establishing some arrangement such as the European Payments Union to improve the external convertibility of their currencies. The possibility that cooperative relaxation of some controls can facilitate relaxation of others illustrates in reverse their self-necessitating nature.

Capital controls as well as trade controls tend to be contagious. By the early 1970s, capital inflows and their possible inflationary impact were causing concern in Europe. It became "a familiar practice for some countries to try to avert an inflow or to instigate an outflow of volatile funds. While such measures [might] bring relief to one country for a while, this procedure unfortunately [led] to these funds moving toward other countries which, faced with the same discomfort, soon resort[ed] to similar measures in their turn. The outcome [was] a game of 'pass the buck,' played with foreign exchange controls. . . ."[32]

A more sweeping way in which controls breed controls is in tending to reduce the price-responsiveness of flows of trade, creating the very inelasticities of demand that seem to make reliance on automatic market adjustments risky. When the very purpose of direct controls is to override price incentives in international trade, it is hardly surprising when they do just that and, consequently, discredit reliance on the price mechanism. This pessimistic proposition has an optimistic corollary: removal of direct controls over world trade should be a cumulative process, each stage helping to restore the price-responsiveness of trade and so facilitating still further decontrol.

4. The consequences of using direct controls are at least potentially unfair. For one thing, controls almost inevitably discriminate not only among the purposes for which foreign exchange may be used but also among persons and firms and perhaps among foreign countries. *Discrimination* is admittedly a pejorative term here, and controls might instead be called wholesomely *selective*. But whatever word is used, controls do involve numerous arbitrary decisions by the authorities. It is difficult to be precise, for example, about what might constitute administering import quotas and exchange controls so as not to give especially unfavorable or favorable treatment to the exports of particular countries. And reliance on direct controls may create opportunities for playing favorites among local importers or other users of foreign exchange, opportunities that in some countries may put a strain on the moral standards of the officials.[33]

Exchange control, bluntly characterized, deprives some persons of their property at less than its market value for the actual or supposed benefit of others. A man who sells goods or delivers lectures or writes for publication abroad and thus earns foreign exchange in an honest and proper way may not use it as he wishes but must surrender it for home currency at a price that is almost certain to be artificially low (since there is little reason for exchange control except in connection with a policy of officially setting or influencing exchange rates). George Winder mentions the allocation of hundreds of thousands of dollars to a well-known British retailer for opening a shop in New York. At the rate of $4.03 per pound sterling prevailing at the time, a rate at which "every importer in England was begging for dollars," this allocation virtually gave away many thousands of pounds to the fortunate retailer. And who in effect paid for this gift? Other British businessmen from whom honestly earned dollars were compulsorily requisitioned. The government was taking dollars from one and giving them to another at a price below what the parties would have freely agreed upon.[34]

To worries over requisitioning some person's property for the benefit of other persons, the reply may be made: "So what? Taxes do that, too, but only anarchists condemn all taxation.

Furthermore, all property rights are creations of the law, and none are absolute." In turn one may ask how well the kind of requisitioning associated with exchange control accords with acceptable canons of taxation and with conceptions of property rights worthy of being fostered by law. Can the particular redistributions of income and wealth that result from exchange control be defended in their own right, or are they haphazard and capricious?

The courts, the legislature, public opinion, the press, and the academic community all are handicapped in resisting unfairness in the administration of controls. The issues are too technical. The courts, for example, must depend largely on the determinations of the experts—that is, the controllers themselves—as to matters of fact; and independent scholars can concern themselves with basic principles but hardly with details of administration.[35]

5. A list of arguments pro and con must mention some still broader and less "economic" consequences of having controls extensive and strict enough to suppress extreme disequilibrium. Many kinds of opportunities for evading controls or for avoiding their intended results need to be suppressed. In allocating foreign exchange, the difficulty of distinguishing between business trips and pleasure trips abroad suggests just one of many respects in which controls do the opposite of putting the burden on the big operator for the sake of the little man. On the contrary, a system of controls puts a premium on having "contacts" and on engaging in far-flung and diversified activities.[36]

Exchange control is a kind of regulation that has built-in incentives for violation. The more generally the regulations are obeyed, the more profitable does violation become for a law-breaking minority. For by staying out of the black market and shunning questionable deals, the law-abiding citizens are refraining from bidding up the black-market or *de facto* price of foreign exchange. This makes its illegal acquisition more attractive for the law-breakers than it would be if they had more competition. The law-breakers reap something in the nature of a scarcity rent from the scarcity of their willingness to break the law. Law-abiding citizens may feel with some justification that they are being dupes and that their own very obedience is providing illegal profit for less conscientious persons. This point becomes clearer when one contrasts a law against capital export with a law against murder. By refraining from

BALANCE-OF-PAYMENTS ADJUSTMENT BY DIRECT CONTROLS

murder, law-abiding persons do nothing to make murder significantly easier or more profitable for others.

The gift of a scarcity rent to violators is only one reason why direct controls are sometimes said to breed cynicism and disrespect for law. Enforcement requires declaring illegal many things that are not in themselves morally wrong and so tends to blur the distinction between right and wrong. Furtheremore, if the prohibitions are to be strictly enforced—if borders are to be closely patrolled, if travelers are to be thoroughly searched, if suspects are to be shadowed—many policemen and much of the time of the courts must be diverted from dealing with crimes that are morally wrong as well as illegal.

All this raises questions about the effect of controls on freedom. Some persons are inclined to classify restrictions on spending as interferences with mere "economic freedom," supposed to be less worthy than other types. But they may be less complacent about controls

---

32. Wolfgang Schmitz, Governor for Austria, in International Monetary Fund, *Summary Proceedings of the Twenty-Seventh Annual Meeting of the Board of Governors*, Washington: September 1972, p. 132.

33. Applicants for import licenses may find it worthwhile to invest money "to help the official to decide to whom he shall hand out the valuable permit." Meade, *op. cit.*, p. 277.

34. George Winder, *The Free Convertibility of Sterling*, London: The Batchworth Press, 1955, pp. 58–59.

35. Cf. Küng, *op. cit.*, pp. 674–675.

36. The British restriction on foreign travel expenditures, as Samuel Brittan explains, was "quite spurious in its egalitarianism. It did not affect those who wanted and could afford to travel to Sterling Area pleasure resorts in the West Indies. Nor did it affect those who could travel on private or official business, or who knew the ropes in other ways. In addition, those who could afford to maintain personal establishments overseas were inevitably hit less badly than those who could only afford to stay at hotels." Samuel Brittan, *The Price of Economic Freedom*, New York: St. Martin's Press, 1970, p. 23.

extending to purchases of foreign books and periodicals, contributions to causes or organizations headquartered abroad, and foreign travel for scholarly or other serious nonbusiness purposes. Restrictions on the transfer of capital by a person wishing to emigrate from his home country perhaps belong in the same category, as does requisitioning foreign exchange earned on lecture tours abroad or from books sold abroad. Intentionally or not, such controls interfere not merely with material pursuits but even with the expression and propagation of knowledge and opinion. Different aspects of life do not fall neatly into separate compartments.

To point this out is not to erect freedom into an absolute and condemn all interferences with it. Different aspects or segments of freedom—freedom for particular actions and of particular persons—necessarily clash. The liberal ideal is to devise social institutions that minimize such conflicts. According to this ideal, the key economic fact of scarcity should be brought to bear on consumption and investment decisions in a more impersonal and less arbitrary way than by government control. Each person would decide for himself how to restrict his activities to correspond with his limited resources and his own circumstances and preferences. If he wishes to stint himself on material goods in order to spend money on intellectual or ideological activities, he is free to do so.

Conclusion

The presumption in favor of market processes depends on whether they can work satisfactorily, and our investigation of this question is far from completed. We cannot condemn all alternatives regardless of circumstances and purposes. Perhaps a respectable if not conclusive case can be made for direct controls—or more probably for tariffs instead—to improve the terms of trade of certain countries; and the familiar arguments are not downright fallacious for using import controls to foster infant and defense industries, to promote economic development, and to promote the diversification of economies judged to be precariously specialized in and dependent on the export of one or a few primary commodities. To restate and appraise all of these possibilities would take us into the traditional discussion of free trade versus protection and would range too far afield from an examination of alternative methods of balance-of-payments adjustment.

Appendix to Chapter 7:
A Case for Discriminatory Direct Controls

Discrimination to minimize the destruction of trade

Ragnar Frisch has developed a case for making direct controls *discriminatory*, if they are to be used at all, when the balance-of-payments deficits of a number of countries correspond to the surplus of one particular country or of only a few countries.[1] The argument is that if each deficit country nondiscriminatorily restricted its imports from all sources, from surplus countries and fellow deficit countries alike, the total cut in world trade would be greater than under discrimination.

A numerical example will prove helpful. Table 7A.1 supposes a world of two deficit countries and one surplus country. The figures shown for exports and imports per time period are supposed to include all credit and debit items on current account and independently motivated capital account, so that the deficits and surpluses refer to the needed accommodating movements of international reserves and short-term capital.

The figures outside the parentheses describe the initial situation. Ruritania's and Graustark's deficits of 15 and 4, respectively, match the US surplus of 19. Ruritania's exports equal only one half of her imports, and Graustark's export/import ratio is 9/10. Now the author-

ities in each deficit country try to correct their imbalance by restricting imports to the level of existing exports. Thus, Ruritania and Graustark cut back imports to 50 and 90 percent, respectively, of their earlier levels. Each country's restriction is nondiscriminatory: its same percentage cutback applies to imports from all sources.[2]

The new situation is shown by the figures in parentheses in each cell and by such of the original figures as remain unchanged. (US imports do not change; perhaps the US has a full-employment policy that neutralizes any deflationary influence stemming from the decline in its exports.) Although each country has restricted its imports by a percentage calculated to cut them down into line with its previous exports, the deficits have not been eliminated; more than one-third of the original total imbalance remains, and Graustark's deficit has actually increased. The reason is that the nondiscriminatory import restrictions of each deficit country have also shrunk the export market of the other. To this extent, the restrictions have merely shuffled the burden of the deficits around between the deficit countries instead of concentrating the restrictions on the exports of the surplus country. Even the merely partial removal of the imbalances has cut total world trade (total exports = total imports) from 101 to 82. If nondiscriminatory restrictions are to eliminate the imbalance completely, they will have to be tighter and the shrinkage in world trade even greater.

The advantage of discriminatory controls can be shown by going back to the original unbalanced position and supposing that each

---

1. Ragnar Frisch, "On the Need for Forecasting a Multilateral Balance of Payments," *American Economic Review*, **XXXVII**, September 1947, pp. 535–551.

2. This way of interpreting "nondiscrimination" is open to some question. If the same cuts were to be accomplished by *ad valorem* import duties rather than by direct controls, the pattern of supply and demand elasticities might well require each deficit country to apply different rates of duty to imports from different sources. Nondiscrimination in the sense of uniform import cuts does not, in general, coincide with nondiscrimination in the sense of restrictions equivalent to uniform *ad valorem* duties. Defining nondiscrimination in the former sense simplifies the discussion, however, without affecting the principle being illustrated. See Meade, *op. cit.*, p. 406n. in particular, as well as his chapters XXVIII through XXXI in general.

TABLE 7A.1. *An example of imbalance and its removal*

Exporting country	Importing country			Total exports	Deficit (−) or Surplus (+)
	Ruritania	Graustark	US		
Ruritania		7 (6.3)	8	15 (14.3)	−15 (−0.7)
Graustark	13 (6.5)		23	36 (29.5)	− 4 (−6.5)
U.S.	17 (8.5)	33 (29.7)		50 (38.2)	+19 (+7.2)
Total imports	30 (15.0)	40 (36.0)	31	101 (82.0)	

deficit country leaves imports from the other unaffected while discriminatorily cutting imports from the US by the amount of its own previous overall deficit. The new situation is as in Table 7A.1, except that Ruritania's imports are 2 from the US and 15 in total, Graustark's imports are 29 from the US and 36 in total, total US exports are 31, all deficits and surpluses are 0, and world exports (= world imports) are 82. This shrinkage of total world trade is the same as had been necessary for only *partial* elimination of imbalances and smaller than would be necessary for *complete* elimination of imbalances by tighter nondiscriminatory controls. Total world trade has had to shrink by only the amount of the previous total deficits (= total surpluses). In fact, the discriminatory method would probably shrink total trade even less than this, since the restrictions on imports from the US might induce residents of Ruritania and Graustark to import more from each other. In part, that is, the restrictions could cause a mere diversion rather than destruction of trade.

This happy outcome could fail if the US retaliated. While perhaps politically understandable, retaliation would have little economic rationale. The US might consider it "unfair" that only her exports should be cut. But even if the deficit countries restricted their imports from all sources in equal proportion, the US would suffer the same total reduction in its export trade. Balancing trade without any change in US imports means cutting US exports by a definite amount—down to the level of these imports—no matter *how* this cut is made. The only advantage the US could gain by insisting on nondiscrimination would be the *Schadenfreude* of seeing other countries suffering cuts in their exports also.

The US of our examples is a hypothetical country, but it may not be amiss here to introduce a well-phrased comment on policy of the real US. The former editor of the London *Economist* noted that official American opinion had recovered from its immediate postwar resentment of anything smacking of discrimination against American exports.

After all, Europeans cannot be expected to spend more dollars than they have and, having exhausted their dollars, it is really not reasonable to object to their using the pounds and francs and lire they do have. Why should I be prevented from spending my vacation at Monte Carlo simply because I do not have the dollars to go to Miami?[3]

The example of imbalance considered so far was easy to remedy (on paper) because each deficit country's overall deficit was smaller than its imports from the surplus country. A more challenging pattern of imbalance would have one country's overall deficit larger than its imports from the surplus country. Restricting imports from the surplus country alone would not suffice; one deficit country would have to restrict imports from the other deficit country as well.

In an example of many countries and with still more complicated imbalances, direct restrictions might cut a deficit country's imports from another country, either in deficit or in balance, which would in turn cut its imports from still another deficit or balanced country, which would finally in turn cut its imports from a surplus country. The indirect nature of the adjustments would require total world trade to shrink by more, perhaps much more, than the amount of imbalances being eliminated. Where the cuts are made is crucial. No one country should concentrate its import cuts on a second country if some third country has still greater need, in some sense, to concentrate its own cuts on that second country. The general objective is "the quickest ultimate concentration of the cuts upon the surplus countries."[4] A carefully planned program would damage trade less than a spiral of indiscriminate import restrictions, with countries successively intensifying their own restrictions to match the drop in exports caused by earlier rounds in the process of restriction by other countries.

These considerations reveal an inadequacy of the "scarce-currency clause" of the Articles of Agreement of the International Monetary Fund. (See Chapter 20). This clause authorizes discriminatory exchange restrictions in special circumstances against transactions with a country whose overall payments surplus is so large that its currency becomes generally "scarce." The inadequacy is that the best program of direct controls may go beyond requiring discriminatory restrictions on expenditures by deficit countries in the scarce-currency country: it may also require discrimination against other surplus countries and even against balanced or deficit countries.

The merits of an internationally coordinated program are perhaps easier to appreciate if we think of it as an inititally nondiscriminatory control system modified by the partial *removal* of controls, namely, of certain controls on trade *among* the countries that would be in deficit or in balance in the absence of any remedial measures. Yet despite the superiority of planned discriminatory controls over haphazard nondiscriminatory controls, the method, even at its best, does have shortcomings.[5] First, trade restrictions do little toward reaching adjustment by stimulating the exports as well as restraining the imports of deficit countries. (In this one respect, discriminatory controls may compare unfavorably with nondiscriminatory controls; for the latter, by hampering trade even among deficit countries, may prod their exporters into greater sales efforts in the surplus countries.) Second, establishing an optimum pattern of controls runs into practical difficulties: in obtaining relevant, accurate, and timely data about trade patterns, about substitutabilities in production and consumption, and about elasticities of supply and demand; in factually comprehending the immensely complex interrelations involved; in

obtaining loyal cooperation among countries in adopting and enforcing precisely the controls and only the controls recommended by the international experts in charge of the program; and in making prompt modifications as circumstances change. Third, difficult though it is to contrive restrictions that shrink total world trade by the least possible amount, even this is not the real goal. The mere volume of trade is only a crude indicator of welfare obtained by international specialization. Nothing ensures that the particular flows of trade designated for elimination or shrinkage would be the relatively most dispensable ones. (In ideal competitive equilibrium, all flows of trade are in some sense of equal importance at the margin; but this does not mean that *intra-marginal* chunks of equal money value also represent equal chunks of welfare.) An internationally planned program of controls would ideally try to take account of how essential trade in particular commodities from particular sources to particular destinations was, but international agreement on this would be elusive. Finally and most generally, discriminatory trade controls merely palliate the balance-of-payments symptoms of underlying maladjustments in prices, costs, incomes, and production patterns at existing exchange rates. They do not fully allow trade to develop in accordance with comparative advantage.

Though open to these strictures, the case for discriminatory controls is instructive. It serves as a reminder of how complex the adjustments are that a changing world continually calls for.

3. Geoffrey Crowther, *Balances and Imbalances of Payments*, Boston: Harvard University, Graduate School of Business Administration, 1957, pp. 60–61.

4. Meade, *op. cit.*, p. 414.

5. A number of criticisms of Frisch's approach are summarized in Charles P. Kindleberger, *The Dollar Shortage*, New York: The Technology Press of MIT and John Wiley & Sons, Inc., 1950, pp. 228–229; William R. Allen and Clark Lee Allen, eds., *Foreign Trade and Finance*, New York: Macmillan, 1959, pp. 491–495; and Meade, *op. cit.*, pp. 414–417.

It shows the advantage of selectivity over indiscriminate restriction. Finally, it prompts the question whether some alternative might not be a more practical means of selectivity.

Selectivity without discrimination

To approach this question, we may note the parallelism between the idea of imposing discriminatory controls or duties on imports from surplus countries and the idea of discriminatorily subsidizing (or taxing, if demand is inelastic) exports to the surplus countries. If a deficit country has import restrictions effectively equivalent to a 10 percent *ad valorem* duty on imports from a surplus country and also has a 10 percent *ad valorem* subsidy on exports to that country, this combination corresponds, ignoring nontrade transactions, to a 9.1 percent depreciation of its own currency in terms of the surplus country's currency.[6] The selectivity desired in a system of controls and subsidies to balance trade might as well be achieved by a multilateral pattern of exchange-rate adjustments.

Appreciation of surplus-country currencies and depreciation of deficit-country currencies (relative to the currencies of countries roughly in balance) would selectively influence trade patterns in several ways. Exports from deficit to surplus countries would be spurred by: (1) the cheapening in surplus countries of imports from deficit countries relative both to home-produced goods and to imports from other surplus countries and from balanced countries; and (2) the increased profitability, for producers in deficit countries, of export sales to surplus countries relative both to sales at home and to sales in other deficit countries and in balanced countries. Imports of deficit from surplus countries would decline because of: (3) the increased prices in deficit countries of imports from surplus countries relative both to home-produced goods and to imports from other deficit countries and from balanced countries; and (4) the decreased profitability, for producers in surplus countries, of export sales to deficit countries relative both to sales at home and to sales in other surplus countries and in balanced countries.

This repatterning of trade would share a selective feature with a scheme of discriminatory controls: deficit countries would reduce their imports from surplus countries while reducing trade among themselves little if at all. Trade among deficit countries might even increase in substitution for their reduced imports from surplus countries; but, on the other hand, the increased exports of deficit to surplus countries might displace some trade among deficit countries. This adjustment by way of exchange rates would presumably shrink total world trade either not at all or less than even judiciously discriminatory restrictions would.

Flexible exchange rates could correct complicated imbalances (or, rather, avoid them in the first place). Suppose that Ruritania has no room to correct her overall deficit solely by cutting her imports from the US, the surplus country, and so (if relying on import restrictions alone) must also cut her imports from another deficit country, Graustark, with the latter in turn cutting her imports from the US by more than the amount of her original overall deficit. Exchange-rate flexibility might work by expanding exports to the surplus country, but we rule out this possibility for the sake of closer comparability with reliance on import controls alone. Suppose the Ruritanian crown and Graustark florin initially depreciate by equal percentages against the US dollar. Since the original trade pattern left little scope for cuts in Ruritanian imports from the US, since export expansion has been ruled out by assumption, and since no change in the crown-florin rate has yet affected trade between the two deficit countries, Ruritania's overall deficit is not yet fully corrected. Since Graustark had ample room for cutting imports from the US, however, depreciation of the florin against the dollar brings Graustark all or part of the way toward balance while Ruritania remains in overall deficit. The crown now depreciates further against the dollar and at last also against the florin. (Actually, of course, these changes would occur concurrently.) The new pattern of rates restrains Ruritanian imports from Graustark. Despite her appreciation relative to Ruritania, Graustark can have depreciated enough relative to the US so that the cut in her imports from the US exceeds her original overall deficit by enough also to match the drop in her exports to Ruritania. In final effect, then, Ruritania makes up for limited room to cut imports from the US directly by cutting them indirectly through the intermediary of Graustark.

This example gives an unrealistically *un*-favorable account of the market process of multilateral adjustment, since we have ruled out export stimulation for the sake of comparability with the controls scheme.

Market adjustments take place without the need for any centralized gathering of data and formulation of plans and without anyone's crudely regarding all flows of trade between particular countries and in particular products as comparable for welfare purposes in terms of money value alone. They also avoid the alternative of crude official judgments about the relative dispensabilities of the various flows of trade. Such judgments can be made marginally rather than globally and can be made in a

decentralized way by the persons most closely concerned and possessing the relevant detailed knowledge.

6. On the similarities among selective trade controls, duties and subsidies, and exchange-rate adjustments, see Meade, *op. cit.*, pp. 418–419.

CHAPTER EIGHT

The Stability Conditions

Stable and unstable markets

So far, other methods of balance-of-payments adjustment seem less attractive than exchange-rate variation. But this conclusion cannot stand without further attention to possible defects of that method.

The present chapter returns to the danger that the exchange-rate mechanism, like the price-level mechanism of the gold standard, might work perversely because demand was not price-sensitive enough. The chapter seeks to formulate more precisely the so-called stability conditions for normal operation. The analysis refers to exchange rates but could readily be modified to refer to the price-level mechanism also.

Consider the supplies and demands for foreign exchange diagrammed in the three parts of Fig. 8.1. (Why only the parts of the curves in the immediate vicinity of the intersection have been drawn will become apparent later.) In parts (a) and (b) of the diagram, random deviations from the unpegged equilibrium exchange rate are self-correcting. The directions of the arrows show this. At "too high" a price of foreign exchange in home currency, an excess quantity of exchange supplied would drive the rate down. At "too low" a rate, an excess quantity demanded would bid it up. In part

(c), however, deviations from equilibrium are self-aggravating. At too high a rate, excess demand bids the rate still higher; and a rate too low would sink still lower. The trouble stems from a backward-sloping supply curve of foreign exchange, although, as (b) shows, even this cannot cause instability if the normally sloping demand curve is elastic enough. A backward-sloping supply curve would reflect an inelastic foreign demand for home exports (as explained in Chapter 2).

None of the diagrams (a), (b), and (c) has an upward-sloping demand curve for foreign exchange, for that would show an exception to the ordinary law of demand, and such a theoretical curiosity is out of the question here. A rise in the price of foreign exchange and thus in the home-currency prices of foreign goods would hardly make home buyers want to buy increased quantities of foreign goods and of the foreign exchange with which to pay for them. Thus the question of stability boils down to whether the supply curve of foreign exchange is backward-sloping and, if so, whether this peculiarity is offset by sufficient elasticity of the downward-sloping demand curve.

The stability formula

The elasticities of supply and demand for foreign exchange trace back to the elasticities of supply and demand for import and export goods and services with respect to their prices in the currencies of the sellers and buyers. (For simplicity, the following analysis supposes that imports and exports of goods and services make up the only items in the balance of payments. Suitable interpretation, however, could take other items into account; see the section on "Money and Elasticities" in Chapter 9.) A lively dispute has raged over these elasticities. They supposedly express the responsiveness of quantities to price. But what things besides price are tacitly allowed to vary, and what other things really are considered constant? How meaningful, legitimate and useful are these elasticity concepts? The whole issue will be clearer if, before facing it, we first ponder the formulas in which the elasticities appear.

In the formulas that follow, the e's stand for supply elasticities and the η's for demand elasticities; the subscripts m and x refer to the imports and exports of Inland, the home country. Thus:

e_m = elasticity with respect to price in Outland currency of Outland's supply of Inland's imports.

e_x = elasticity with respect to price in Inland currency of Inland's supply of exports to Outland.

η_m = elasticity with respect to price in Inland currency of Inland's demand for imports from Outland.

η_x = elasticity with respect to price in Outland currency of Outland's demand for Inland's exports.

The elasticities of supply are positive for normal upward-sloping supply curves. The elasticities of demand are positive, too, on the definition whereby normal downward-sloping demand curves are said to have positive elasticity.

In terms of these elasticities, the criterion of normal rather than perverse influence of exchange-rate changes on the balance of payments is

$$\frac{e_x\,(\eta_x - 1)}{e_x + \eta_x} + \frac{\eta_m\,(e_m + 1)}{e_m + \eta_m}$$

If this expression is positive, the market is stable; if negative, unstable. The derivation of this expression is left to the appendix of this chapter; the chapter itself tries only to draw the implications of the expression and make them seem intuitively reasonable. The criterion applies precisely, with the elasticities in it interpreted as nearly ordinary price elasticities, only if domestic income levels remain stable—only if domestic money supplies and incomes do not somehow get out of control as a direct or indirect consequence of exchange-rate variation. The derivation of the formula assumes, furthermore, that cross-elasticities beween exports and imports are zero—that export prices do not influence the demand for imports and vice versa. This assumption is justifiable only if the exchange-rate change in question is a small one and if attention focuses—as it does in this chapter—on the question of the stability of the foreign-exchange market.[1] Such preliminary simplifications seem necessary to a manageable analysis; we can consider complications later.

The text expression can be negative, indicating a perverse exchange-rate mechanism, only if η_x, the elasticity of Outland's demand for Inland's exports, is less than 1, making $\eta_x - 1$ negative.[2] Even if η_x were actually as small as

zero, however, the entire test expression could be kept positive by the other elasticities in it. Earlier chapters have made it clear, without algebra, that high demand elasticities are favorable to normal responsiveness of the balance of payments. The role of the supply elasticities may be investigated by rewriting the algebraic criterion as

$$\frac{\eta_x - 1}{1 + \dfrac{\eta_x}{e_x}} + \frac{\eta_m + \dfrac{\eta_m}{e_m}}{1 + \dfrac{\eta_m}{e_m}}$$

When $\eta_x > 1$ and the left-hand term is positive, it is "desirable" (for the sake of stability) that this term be large, thus that the denominator $1 + \eta_x/e_x$ be small, and thus in turn that e_x be large. When $\eta_x < 1$ and the left-hand term is negative, however, it is "desirable" that the absolute value of this negative term be small and thus that e_x be small.

In the right-hand term, when $\eta_m > 1$, a given absolute decrease in η_m/e_m represents a larger percentage decrease in the denominator $1 + \eta_m/e_m$ than in the numerator $\eta_m + \eta_m/e_m$ and thus increases the value of the ratio. It follows that when $\eta_m > 1$, a low value of η_m/e_m, and so a high value of e_m, is favorable to stability. On the other hand, when $\eta_m < 1$, a given absolute increase in η_m/e_m represents a larger percentage increase in the numerator $\eta_m + \eta_m/e_m$ than in the denominator $1 + \eta_m/e_m$ and thus increases the value of the ratio. It follows that when $\eta_m < 1$, a high value of

1. For a sizable change in the exchange rate, the interaction terms cannot properly be neglected; yet including them would make the formula hopelessly complicated. See Richard N. Cooper, "Devaluation and Aggregate Demand in Aid-Receiving Countries," in Jagdish N. Bhagwati *et al.*, eds., *Trade, Balance of Payments and Growth*, New York: American Elsevier, 1971, pp. 361n., 374.

2. The two supply elasticities (like the demand elasticities) must almost certainly be positive (or at worst zero); the conditions necessary for a backward-sloping supply curve are especially unrealistic when applied to the exports in general of a whole country.

160

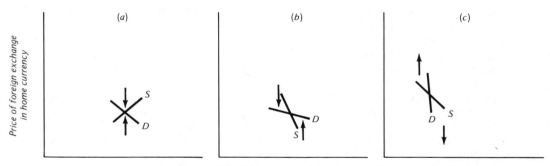

FIGURE 8.1. *Stable and unstable exchange markets*

η_m/e_m, and so a low value of e_m, is favorable to exchange stability.

Each of these conclusions about supply elasticities will now be restated, together with a verbal attempt to make it seem intuitively reasonable:

When the Outland demand for Inland exports is elastic, it is "desirable" (for the sake of stability) that Inland's supply of exports be elastic also. Reason: if depreciation of Inland's currency and the consequent cut in Outland-currency price of Inland's exports is effective enough in stimulating Outland's purchases to increase their total Outland-currency value, then it is "desirable" that there be as little interference as possible with this price cut. In particular, the depreciation should raise the Inland-currency price of exports as little as possible: slight price increases should suffice to call forth the necessary increases in the quantity of exports supplied.

When the Outland demand for Inland exports is inelastic, it is "desirable" that Inland's supply of exports be inelastic also. Reason: if depreciation and the consequent cut in the Outland-currency price of Inland's exports is so ineffective in stimulating Outland's purchases that their total Outland-currency value falls, then it is desirable that there be as much interference with this price cut as possible. In particular, the depreciation should greatly raise the Inland-currency price of exports: large price increases should be required to call forth increases in the quantity of exports supplied.

When Inland's demand for imports is elastic, it is "desirable" that the Outland supply be elastic also. Reason: if depreciation and the consequent rise in the Inland-currency price of imports is very effective in restraining imports, it is desirable that there be as little interference as possible with this price rise. In particular, the Outland-currency price should fall as little as possible: slight price drops should suffice to curtail the quantity of imports supplied from Outland to Inland.

When Inland's demand for imports is inelastic, it is "desirable" that the Outland supply be inelastic also. Reason: if depreciation and the consequent rise in the Inland-currency price of imports is rather ineffective in restraining imports, interference with this price rise does little damage. On the contrary, a better chance of reducing the total Outland-currency value of Inland imports hinges on a drop in their Outland price. Thus Outlanders should be relatively dependent on the Inland market: sharp price reductions should be necessary to curtail the quantities supplied even slightly.

Returning to the original algebraic criterion

$$\frac{e_x\,(\eta_x - 1)}{e_x + \eta_x} + \frac{\eta_m\,(e_m + 1)}{e_m + \eta_m}$$

we readily see that, regardless of demand elasticities, if both supply elasticities are zero, a normally-working exchange market is assured, for the expression reduces to $\frac{\eta_m}{\eta_m}$, or 1, which is positive.

The zero import supply elasticity means that when depreciation of Inland's currency causes what from Outland's point of view appears as a drop in Inland's demand, Outlanders are so dependent on the Inland market that they act to keep their sales unchanged by absorbing the entire effect of the depreciation through price cuts in terms of their own currency. Inland's zero export supply elasticity means that despite depreciation, the quantity of Inland's exports and hence their Outland-currency price and total Outland-currency value all remain unchanged. The net result for Inland is a reduction in the Outland-currency value of its imports, no change in the Outland-currency value of its exports, and thus an improvement in its balance of payments.

In fact, if either one alone of the supply elasticities is zero, stability is still assured. As just shown, a zero export supply elasticity keeps the total Outland-currency value of exports unchanged when Inland's currency depreciates, thus ruling out the shrinkage of export proceeds that would have to characterize a perversely working mechanism. When the import supply elasticity is zero, the stability criterion reduces to

$$\frac{e_x\,(\eta_x-1)}{e_x+\eta_x}+\frac{\eta_m}{\eta_m} \quad \text{or} \quad \frac{\eta_x-1}{1+\dfrac{\eta_x}{e_x}}+1$$

Now, no matter how near zero η_x is, the left-hand term cannot be larger negatively than 1, so that the entire expression cannot be negative. At worst, with $\eta_x=0$, the expression reduces to $-1+1$, or 0, indicating the borderline between normal and perverse response of the balance of payments to the exchange rate.

The well-known case of both supplies being infinitely elastic can best be approached by rewriting the test expression as

$$\frac{\eta_x-1}{1+\dfrac{\eta_x}{e_x}}+\frac{\eta_m\!\left(1+\dfrac{1}{e_m}\right)}{1+\dfrac{\eta_m}{e_m}}$$

Making all the e's infinite reduces to zero all the little fractions of which they are denominators, so that the test expression becomes simply $\eta_x+\eta_m-1$. Thus the stability condition is satisfied if either demand elasticity, or even if merely the sum of the two of them, exceeds 1. This simple condition for the case of infinitely elastic supplies has long been familiar[3] and is sometimes mistaken for the *general* stability condition. Actually, even lower demand elasticities will suffice when the supply elasticities are less than infinite.

In the extreme case of a country so small that it faces a perfectly elastic foreign supply of its imports and foreign demand for its exports, the test expression reduces to $e_x+\eta_m$. Thus, any price sensitivity at all either in export supply or import demand (or both) assures a normal response of trade to the exchange rate.

When each of the supply and demand elasticities is *between* zero and infinity, as in reality, the stability condition can usefully be rewritten[4]

$$\frac{e_m\,e_x\,(\eta_m+\eta_x-1)+\eta_m\,\eta_x\,(e_m+e_x+1)}{(e_m+\eta_m)\,(e_x+\eta_x)}$$

Now, since each of the individual elasticities is positive, the denominator of this expression is assuredly positive and may be ignored. In the numerator, the only negative element is the -1 in the first parentheses. Again we see that stability is assured if the two demand elasticities add up to 1 or more and is still easily possible even if their total is less than 1. Substituting numbers into $e_m e_x(\eta_m+\eta_x-1)+\eta_m\eta_x(e_m+e_x+1)$ shows that when each supply elasticity is 10, it suffices for stability that each demand elasticity be only a shade over $^{10}\!/_{21}$ (or one can be lower with the other enough higher). When each supply elasticity is 5, demand elasticities of just over $^5\!/_{11}$ each suffice; when each supply elasticity is 2, demand elasticities of just over $^2\!/_5$ each suffice; when each supply elasticity is 1, demand elasticities of just over $^1\!/_3$ each suffice; when each supply elasticity is $\frac{1}{2}$, demand elasticities of just over $\frac{1}{4}$ each suffice, and so on.

Empirical clues about elasticities

All this makes the elasticity requirements for a normally working exchange-rate mechanism hardly appear very exacting. Familiar facts suggest that they are likely to be satisfied in the real world. First, the world demand for a single country's exports is likely to be elastic because of competition with similar exports from other countries; buyers in the world market may have plenty of opportunity to shift toward or away from a particular country's exports according to price comparisons. The principle is the same as that which explains why the demand for

---

3. Abba P. Lerner, *The Economics of Control*, New York: Macmillan, 1947, p. 378.

4. By straightforward though tedious manipulation. Incidentally, this is the form in which the stability condition seems most commonly to appear in print. It is essentially the same, for instance, as appears in Lloyd A. Metzler, "The Theory of International Trade," in Howard S. Ellis, ed., *A Survey of Contemporary Economics*, Philadelphia: Blakiston, 1948, p. 226.

wheat grown on a particular farm is extremely elastic even though the overall demand for wheat may be extremely inelastic. (The chief exception would be for a country the great bulk of whose exports consisted of one or more products in highly inelastic overall demand and facing no great competition on the world market.) The principle can be expressed by the formula

$$\eta_x = \frac{1}{a}\,\eta_w + \frac{b}{a}\,e_c$$

in which η_x = the elasticity of world-market demand for a particular export commodity supplied specifically by Inland, η_w = the elasticity of world-market demand for that commodity from all exporting countries in general, e_c = the elasticity of export supply from countries completing with Inland, a = Inland's share of the world export market, and b = the competitors' share of the market.[5] If Inland has half the world market for exports of the commodity and all its competitors together have the other half, if the elasticity of world-market demand is ½, and if the elasticity of competitors' supply is actually as unfavorable as zero, the elasticity of demand for Inland's export is still

$$\frac{1}{\frac{1}{2}} \cdot \frac{1}{2} + \frac{\frac{1}{2}}{\frac{1}{2}} \cdot \text{o, or 1.}$$ If Inland has ⅓ and its

competitors ⅔ of the world market and if the elasticities of world demand and competitors' supply are each only ½, Inland faces an export demand elasticity of 2½.

A second consideration is that the existence of some domestic production of an import-type commodity makes the elasticity of demand specifically for the import higher than the elasticity of demand for the commodity in general. This is expressed by a formula whose derivation parallels the one given in the last footnote:

$$\eta_m = \frac{1}{f}\,\eta_D + \frac{h}{f}\,e_s$$

where η_m = the elasticity of import demand, η_D = the elasticity of demand for the commodity in general, e_s = the elasticity of supply from domestic production, f = the share of foreign goods in the total home market for the commodity, and h = the share of home goods in the market. For example, if the elasticity of general demand and the elasticity of supply from home production were each only ½ and if imports and the home-produced com-

modity were sharing the market half-and-half, the elasticity of import demand would be 1½. Even if supply from home production were completely inelastic, the elasticity of import demand would still be greater than the elasticity of general demand. This may be seen by substituting o for e_s in the above formula, which then becomes $\eta_m = \frac{1}{f}\,\eta_D$. Now, since f is a fraction smaller than 1 and $\frac{1}{f}$ a number greater than 1, $\eta_m > \eta_D$. Furthermore, even if general demand for the commodity had zero elasticity, the existence of some domestic supply with some elasticity would give some elasticity to the import demand. Substituting o for η_D makes the formula become $\eta_m = \frac{h}{f}\,e_s$.

If the general demand had zero elasticity, if home supply had an elasticity of 1, and if imports were furnishing half of total consumption, the import demand would have an elasticity of 1. Algebraic precision vanishes when domestically produced commodities are not substantially identical to the competing import goods. Still, the broad conclusion holds that domestic production of import-competing goods contributes to elasticity in the specific demand for imports and that this contribution is the greater, the greater is the substitutability between domestic and imported goods and the greater the volume of domestic production relative to imports.

By close analogy with the formula for import demand elasticity, a formula can readily be derived for export supply elasticity (the task is left to the reader as an exercise). This shows that the existence of some domestic consumption of export goods makes the export supply elasticity greater than the total supply elasticity. This is true even if the domestic consumption demand is completely inelastic. Furthermore, even if the country's total production of the export commodity were completely unresponsive to price, the supply for export would still have some price elasticity as long as there were some domestic demand having some elasticity. These principles of export supply elasticity are relevant because when import and export demand elasticities are greater than 1, large values of the corresponding supply elasticities strengthen the normal operation of the exchange-rate mechanism.

A third general consideration about elasticities is that price changes can affect not only the quantities imported and exported of goods already traded but also affect the composition of the list. Depreciation of Inland's currency not only will increase sales of goods already being exported but also may make possible the export of some new goods. At the level of the exchange rate at which the export of some new Inland good just becomes possible, the elasticity of export demand for it is infinite. Similarly, depreciation not only will restrict Inland's imports of particular goods but also may cause some goods to drop off the import list entirely. For this reason, among others, a statistical study of demand elasticities for the particular goods already entering into a country's trade will tend to understate the overall elasticities of demand for the broad range of actual and potential imports and exports; yet these are the elasticities relevant to the question of exchange stability.

Elasticity measurements

For several years after World War II, attempts to measure import and export demand elasticities kept being reported for many individual countries. Almost invariably the elasticities were surprisingly low, occasionally low enough to suggest taking the perverse-elasticities case seriously. Soon, however, critics explained a number of statistical pitfalls causing such a bias toward zero in the measured elasticities as to make them practically meaningless. (Furthermore, some of the apparent inelasticity of demand in international trade had been due to quotas, tariffs, and other government controls precisely intended to keep trade from responding sensitively to price. That the price mechanism shows signs of being affected by deliberate interferences with its responsiveness is no evidence against is workability under more favorable policies.) A start was also made on developing refined methods yielding elasticities more nearly like those to be expected on general grounds. For several reasons it now seems sufficient simply to give citations to this literature rather than review it here.[6] First, the

5. Except for some change in symbols and in the sign convention for demand elasticities (here the definition is used whereby demand elasticity is positive), this formula is taken from Fred C. Shorter, "Jute Production Policies of India and Pakistan," *Indian Economic Journal*, **III**, July 1955, p. 44 and footnote.

Derivation: Let W = world-market quantity demanded, C = quantity supplied from competing countries, $W - C$ = quantity demanded of Inland's export, and P = price. By the definition of elasticity,

$$\eta_x = \frac{-P}{W-C} \cdot \frac{d(W-C)}{dP}$$

$$= \frac{\dfrac{-P}{W}\dfrac{dW}{dP}W}{W-C} + \frac{\dfrac{P}{C}\dfrac{dC}{dP}C}{W-C}$$

$$= \frac{W}{W-C}\,\eta_w + \frac{C}{W-C}\,e_c$$

Now $a = \dfrac{W-C}{W}$, $b = \dfrac{C}{W}$, and $\dfrac{b}{a} = \dfrac{C}{W-C}$.

6. J. Hans Alder, "United States Import Demand during the Interwar Period," *American Economic Review*, **XXXV**, June 1945, pp. 418–430; Tse Chun Chang, "The British Balance of Payments, 1924–1938," *Economic Journal*, **LVII**, December 1947, pp. 475–503; Chang, "The British Demand for Imports in the Inter-War Period," *Economic Journal*, **LVI**, June 1946, pp. 188–207; Chang, "International Comparison of Demand for Imports," *Review of Economic Studies*, **XIII**, (2), 1945–1946, pp. 53–67; Chang, "A Statistical Note on World Demand for Exports," *Review of Economics and Statistics*, **XXX**, May 1948, pp. 106–116; J. Tinbergen, "Some Measurements of Elasticities of Substitution," *Review of Economic Statistics*, **XXVIII**, August 1946, pp. 109–116; Randall Hinshaw, "American Prosperity and the British Balance-of-Payments Problem," *Review of Economic Statistics*, **XXVII**, February 1945, pp. 1–9; A. J. Brown, "The Rate of Exchange," pp. 75–106 in T. Wilson and P. W. S. Andrews, eds., *Oxford Studies in the Price Mechanism*, Oxford: Clarendon Press, 1951; Fritz Machlup, "Elasticity Pessimism in International Trade," *Economia Internazionale*, **III**, February 1950, pp. 118–137; Guy H. Orcutt, "Measurement of Price Elasticities in International Trade," *Review of Economics and Statistics*, **XXXII**, May 1950, pp. 117–132; Arnold C. Harberger, "Some Evidence on the International Price Mechanism," *Journal of Political Economy*, **LXV**, December 1957, pp. 506–521. Hang Sheng Cheng has surveyed these and other published studies in "Statistical Estimates of Elasticities and Propensities in International Trade, IMF *Staff Papers*, **VII**, April 1959, pp. 107–158. He provides greater detail in a lengthy mimeographed supplement to his paper.

apparent outcome of this discussion itself suggests that the danger of critically low elasticities has received attention entirely out of proportion to its importance for the real world. Second, the purchasing-power-parity doctrine (explained in Chapter 11) permits side-stepping some statistical difficulties and empirically judging whether demand elasticities in the real world are above or below the value critical to exchange stability. Third, an analysis to be reviewed below shows that stable equilibrium levels of exchange rates must necessarily exist. Even if demand elasticities were perversely low at prices corresponding to some levels of exchange rates, other rates would necessarily exist at which these elasticities simply could not remain perversely low.

Secondary effects: income changes

Before showing this, we should mention two or three effects that could modify the stability criterion already developed. First are various "income effects." For example, a country may have been maintaining the exchange value of its currency only by tolerating persistent depression at home. If the government now decides to resolve this conflict between the goals of external balance and domestic prosperity by devaluing the currency, it may be able to pursue an expansionary monetary and fiscal policy. As business improves, spending on imports increases along with spending on domestic goods and services. This income effect could conceivably swamp the influence of changed relative prices resulting from devaluation. Two distinct influences are at work. (Though devaluation and an expansionary financial policy would no doubt be linked in the minds of the policy-makers, they are two distinct changes in the situation: devaluation does not automatically and inevitably impose the change in domestic policy.) For the sake of manageable analysis, the effects of separate causes must be considered separately; different strands of analysis may be combined later. No one strand is disproved by showing that other influences join in determining the complex outcome in the real world.

A more relevant challenge to the price-elasticity analysis might show that interfering income effects result spontaneously from the change in the exchange rate. Suppose that currency depreciation or devaluation shrinks the country's import surplus or expands its export surplus. The associated multiplier effect tends to raise national income (assuming unemployment before). With increased incomes people import more than otherwise. Currency depreciation improves the country's balance of payments less than if its effect had not been diluted by the income effect.

Can we go further and conclude that the income effect could turn an otherwise stable foreign-exchange market into an unstable one? Probably not. If the income effect did make the exchange-rate mechanism work perversely, then currency depreciation would cause the balance of payments to *deteriorate*. But then, contradictorily, the foreign-trade multiplier would reduce rather than increase national income; and imports in turn would be restrained rather than stimulated. At worst the income effect would deprive exchange depreciation of all effect on the balance of payments, but it would not turn an otherwise stable mechanism into a perverse one. As long as an import-stimulating rise in home income depends on a depreciation-induced improvement in the balance of payments, the income effect merely weakens but does not reverse the net response to the balance of payments to a change in the exchange rate.

Another thought bolsters this tentative conclusion. Suppose that the country starts with a deficit in its balance of payments. As shown in the second footnote to the Appendix to this chapter, the deficit makes the elasticity requirements for a normal mechanism less exacting than they would be with initial equilibrium. If, despite this, the elasticities are only barely favorable enough for normality, then depreciation will reduce the deficit as measured in *foreign* money but will increase it as measured in *home* money. (A decreased amount of foreign money can equal an increased amount of home money if the home-money price of foreign money has risen.) As to whether the foreign-exchange market works normally and whether the country has balance-of-payments trouble or not, the deficit measured in foreign money is the one that counts. But the deficit measured in home money is the one relevant to the multiplier effect on home income.[7] If the deficit measured in home money increases (though the foreign-exchange deficit decreases), then the foreign-trade multiplier tends to reduce home income. This, in turn, tends to restrain imports. In short, the secondary income effect due to currency depreciation tends, in the borderline case, to reinforce the normal primary effect of depreciation. Now let us consider a case in which the country originally enjoys balance-of-payments equilibrium, or perhaps even a surplus. Assuming for the sake of argument, contrary to the conclusion so far, that income effects made the otherwise stable exchange market work perversely, then currency depreciation would create a balance-of-payments deficit. Now, since by hypothesis the import and export supply and demand elasticities would have been favorable enough for a normally working exchange market had it not been for the income effects and since the existence of a balance-of-payments deficit relaxes the elasticity requirements for normality, it seems that the new deficit could cause the market to work normally (at least if the import and export supply and demand elasticities are no less favorable at the new than at the old points on the respective curves). Even if the market is only barely normal in the new situation, further depreciation would, as already explained, reduce the foreign-exchange deficit while increasing the deficit measured in home currency. If so, the secondary income effects would reinforce the new-found stability of the exchange market.

The income effects so far canvassed, other than the one resulting from policy, have all involved changes in income stemming from the initial change in the balance of payments. But if currency depreciation somehow affects the level of home income directly, rather than only through the balance of payments, the conclusions reached so far become less definite. For example, since depreciation changes the pattern of relative prices, some residents of the home country are better off and some worse off than before, and if the persons benefited have a higher propensity to consume than the persons harmed, the country's overall propensity to consume may rise. Thus both home income and imports tend to rise. Another possibility for a rise in the propensity to consume and thus in income and imports lies in the fact that depreciation tends to lower the prices of home factors of production *relative* to the prices of internationally traded goods, thus lowering the real income corresponding to any given level of money income from the viewpoints of income-receivers. If the fraction of real income saved falls as real income falls, as is conceivable in some situations, this means that the schedule of consumption expenditure in relation to money income rises, with the consequences already mentioned.[8] Still another conceivable "direct" income effect hinges on the inducement provided by the depreciation for people to switch some demand toward the relatively cheapened products of the depreciating country and away from the relatively more expensive products of the rest of the world. This increased demand would tend to have a multiplier effect on home income, stimulating imports in turn.[9] The rise in income and imports occurring by way of any of these three effects could mean a perverse net response of the balance of payments to depreciation even when the price elasticities of import and export supply and demand, considered by themselves, indicated a neutral or weakly normal response. The stability condition would then be more stringent than our formulas indicate.

7. Albert O. Hirschman, "Devaluation and the Trade Balance: A Note," *Review of Economics and Statistics*, **XXXI**, February 1949, p. 53.

8. Cf Lloyd A. Metzler, "Exchange-rate Stability Considered," *Econometrica* Supplement, **XVII**, July 1949, pp. 109–110; and Svend Laursen and Lloyd A. Metzler, "Flexible Exchange Rates and the Theory of Employment," *Review of Economics and Statistics*, **XXXII**, November 1950, esp. pp. 286–291, 297. A further discussion in the same *Review* clarifies this argument: William H. White, "The Employment-Insulating Advantages of Flexible Exchanges: A Comment on Professors Laursen and Metzler," **XXXVI**, May 1954, pp. 225–228, and Laursen and Metzler, "Reply," pp. 228–229 in the same issue. For further skeptical comment on the Laursen-Metzler effect, see Richard N. Cooper in Bhagwati, *op. cit.*, pp. 358 and 358–359n. Also see footnote 32 in Chapter 6 above.

9. The increased demand operates directly and not just through the balance of payments. Even though the relation between the total money values of imports and exports remained unchanged or even worsened (because of a decline in the total foreign-currency value—though not quantity—of exports), depreciation would still tend to stimulate home-currency expenditure on home-produced goods. Cf. Arnold C. Harberger, "Currency Depreciation, Income, and the Balance of Trade," *Journal of Political Economy*, **LVIII**, February 1950, p. 51.

The analysis becomes hopelessly untidy when one tries to allow for all the income effects already described and others readily invented. Effects are even conceivable that tend to make depreciation more effective; the change in relative prices might redistribute incomes, for example, in such a way as to lower the national propensity to consume. It does seem that such roundabout effects of depreciation directly on income and, in turn, of income on imports are likely to be weak in comparison with the primary influence of depreciation on imports and exports, so that the stability condition already derived in terms of price elasticities does not need to be modified much—but this statement admittedly defies quantification. It must be emphasized that these income effects presuppose instability in national incomes. For changes in *real* rather than money income, in particular, to interfere seriously with the normal results of currency depreciation, unemployment and subcapacity production must have previously prevailed. The effects are incompatible, then, with a successful policy of maintaining stable and prosperous domestic business conditions. Yet part of the rationale of exchange-rate flexibility is that it would permit independent national stabilization policies. Successful domestic stabilization would help preserve the effectiveness of exchange-rate variations in equilibrating the balance of payments. Though the stability condition expressed in terms of price elasticities might have to be modified for analyzing the effectiveness of deliberate adjustments in pegged exchange rates in a world of passively unstable national incomes, the condition seems roughly correct for appraising the workability of freely fluctuating rates for a country pursuing a successful domestic policy.

Secondary effects: price levels

Besides income changes, price-level changes might also be thought to threaten making an otherwise normal exchange-rate mechanism work perversely. Could this happen if currency depreciation somehow pushed up the internal prices of goods and services in full or partial sympathy with the price of foreign exchange? Probably not. Currency depreciation corrects a balance-of-payments deficit by making internationally traded goods more expensive in relation to domestic goods and factors of production in the depreciating country and cheaper in relation to domestic goods and factors elsewhere.[10] In the worst realistically conceivable situation—which would presuppose expansion of the home money supply—all prices would rise in the depreciating country in proportion to the price of foreign exchange. Foreign-currency prices of exports would remain the same as before, and so, presumably, would the quantities and total foreign-currency proceeds of exports. Quantities and total foreign-currency values of imports would also remain unchanged, since imports would not have become more expensive in relation to labor and other domestic goods. The balance of payments in terms of foreign currency would be unchanged.

Depreciation could hardly make prices of domestic goods rise *faster* than prices of internationally traded goods, so encouraging imports and discouraging exports; on the contrary, it is precisely the internationally traded goods whose prices are most directly pulled upward along with the price of foreign exchange. Thus, while responses of the internal price level to the exchange rate might possibly lessen the sensitivity of the balance-of-payments to exchange-rate changes, they would not make an otherwise normal mechanism perverse. At worst, sympathetic movement of the internal price level would render exchange-rate variations ineffective in equilibrating the balance of payments. This issue of induced instability in the domestic price level provides a familiar objection to flexible exchange rates (and is explored in Chapter 11), but it is distinct from the question of elasticity requirements for a normal adjustment mechanism.

Secondary effects: imported materials

Another complication has to do with imported raw materials embodied in exports.[11] Even if depreciation did increase the foreign-exchange proceeds of exports, part of these would have to go to pay for the necessary additional imports of raw materials. Furthermore, the use of imported raw materials lessens the degree to which depreciation enables a country's exporters to attract customers by quoting lower prices in foreign currency, since depreciation raises cost in home currency.

In doing so, depreciation raises the schedule of home-money prices necessary to call forth various quantities of exports. In effect, using imported materials make a country's export supply less elastic than otherwise. How export supply elasticity enters into the stability conditions has already been shown: when foreign demand is elastic, a low supply elasticity lessens the effectiveness of exchange-rate variations, but when foreign demand is inelastic, a low supply elasticity contributes to a normal effect. It seems to follow that a high import content in exports lessens the sensitivity of the balance of payments to exchange-rate variations when foreign demand is elastic but might contribute to a normal reaction when foreign demand is inelastic.

Imports of materials need not necessarily increase in proportion to any increase in exports. The volume of materials imported depends not on exports alone but on the country's overall production. At any given level of production, an increase in exports might simply divert imported materials from making goods for domestic consumption into making the additional export goods. Furthermore, to assume that the proportion of imported materials in export products stays constant whatever the exchange rate is illegitimately to assume away any substitution between home and foreign materials, as well as any shift from high-import-content toward low-import-content exports.

All this further suggests that while the use of imported materials in exports may conceivably make the balance of payments less sensitive to exchange-rate variations than otherwise, it does not make the elasticity requirements for normality any more stringent. In any case, the imported-materials effect· is hardly decisive. Even for countries with very "open" economies, like those of Western Europe, imported raw materials account for only a small fraction of the value of the exports embodying them. The fraction is still smaller for a country like the United States.[12]

Secondary effects: summary

Canvassing secondary income, price-level, and imported-materials effects yields no conclusive indication that the stability requirements already derived are either too stringent or not stringent enough. (The likeliest exception has to do with income changes produced directly by an exchange-rate variation.) There is some reason, however, for thinking that secondary

effects may lessen the sensitivity of the balance of payments to exchange-rate variations, damping normal and perverse reactions alike. But the dividing line between normality and perversity remains at least approximately specified by the algebraic sign of the previously-stated expression

$$e_m \, e_x \, (\eta_m + \eta_x - 1) + \eta_m \, \eta_x \, (e_m + e_x + 1)$$

The discussion of secondary effects has been tedious and unrealistic but was necessary in order to not simply ignore matters considered important by competent students. In the real world it is unlikely—as later pages try to show —that an exchange market would be in that dubious borderline where secondary effects might be decisive.

Short-run instability

One might suppose that since a country's demand for imports and the foreign demand for its exports are both very inelastic in the very short run, the foreign-exchange market might work perversely in the short run. And since time is just a succession of short runs, a free exchange market might be unstable in the long run also. The quantity of something demanded at a newly established price depends, among other things, on how long a time buyers have had to react to the new price (as well as on

10. There is no conflict between the stability-condition and sectional-price-level analyses. The stability condition concerns *how strongly* import and export quantities must respond to price changes for depreciation to succeed. The sectional-price-level analysis investigates *why* and *how* imports and exports respond to exchange-rate variations.

11. Cf. Metzler, *Econometrica* Supplement, **XVII**, July 1949, p. 109; Metzler, "The Theory of International Trade," in Ellis, *op. cit.*, p. 230n.; A. J. Brown, *op. cit.*, p. 78; and G. Stuvel, *The Exchange Stability Problem*, Leiden: Stenfert Kroese, 1950, pp. 172–174.

12. J. J. Polak and T. C. Chang, "Effect of Exchange Depreciation on a Country's Export Price Level, IMF *Staff Papers*, **I**, February 1950, p. 51.

what the previous price was). The shorter this time, the less responsive buyers are. Strictly speaking, one ought not to speak of *the* demand curve: there is a whole sheaf of demand curves, one for each of the infinitely many conceivable lengths of adjustment period. Similar comments apply to supply curves also.

If demands for internationally traded goods are inelastic in the short run, so too—and presumably even more so—are supplies, and their inelasticity is then a stabilizing element. It would be odd indeed if short-run demands were too inelastic yet short-run supplies too elastic for normality.[13] But if this peculiar short-run situation did prevail, shrewd speculators might well realize that perverse movements in a free exchange rate were only temporary. They would not think in the economists' jargon of stability conditions, but that would not matter. If they succeeded in profiting from short-run rate fluctuations, they would be tending to iron them out and would be providing unofficial financing for "riding out" temporary disequilibriums.

Granted that the supply of and demand for foreign exchange arising from actual exports and imports are inelastic in the very short run, so are the production-supply of and consumption-demand for any ordinary commodity. Though the analogy is not perfect, since a short-run commodity supply curve could hardly slope negatively, it is still instructive. Why don't the continual shifts in the short-run inelastic supply and demand curves for any competitively marketed commodity make price fluctuate violently? Because absorption and release of the commodity into and from stocks— in a sense, speculative stocks—prevent this. Similar absorption and release of foreign exchange into and from stocks held by private dealers and others would tend to keep short-run supply and demand inelasticities from causing extreme fluctuations in a free market. (A full appraisal of how likely this is must await a separate chapter on speculation.)

One might fear perverse exchange markets in a war-devastated world where urgent relief and reconstruction needs made import demands inelastic. Apart from the possibility that inelastic demands might be accompanied by the stabilizing inelasticity of the corresponding supplies, there is the fundamental point that urgency of need is not the same thing as inelasticity of demand. The only demand that counts on a market is demand backed up by willingness and ability to pay. Despite urgent needs, impoverishment itself may force people to behave on the market with great price-sensitivity. (Arguments for helping war-impoverished people, if persuasive, need not be adorned with references to inelastic demands and perverse markets.)

Instability due to fixed obligations

The existence of fixed obligations to foreign countries, such as interest and amortization payments or indemnities, might conceivably keep the exchange-stability conditions from being satisfied, provided the foreign demand for exports were very inelastic at the same time. If the obligations to foreigners were fixed in domestic currency, they would affect the foreign-exchange market like imports of demand elasticity equal to 1 and so could not cause perversity. Obligations fixed in foreign currency, however, would have the same effect on the exchange market as imports in absolutely inelastic demand.

Recognizing this does not contradict what is said a few pages later on about the elasticity conditions for exchange stability necessarily being satisfied at *some* level of the exchange rate. Some price of foreign exchange is so high in terms of home currency that the debtors obliged to make the fixed payments to foreigners would have to default. Despite the rigidity of the obligations fixed in foreign currency, the effective demand for foreign exchange with which to actually meet these obligations would come to have some elasticity.

Perverse elasticities under free and under fixed exchanges

In the unlikely case of perversely low demand elasticities, not only free exchange rates but any other system allowing unrestrained private international dealings in currencies and commodities would be unworkable. Government controls would have to maintain an artificial equilibrium. Currency depreciation and deflation of the home price level, currency appreciation and inflation of the home price level, are alternative methods of correcting a balance-of-payments deficit or surplus. If the relevant elasticities were too low for normal operation of the exchange rate, then (as mentioned in Chapter 5) the price-level mechanism of the gold standard would also work perversely.[14] Correcting a deficit would then call for either currency appreciation or price-level inflation. Inflation would raise export (as well as domestic) prices, but foreigners, having an inelastic demand, would spend a greater total amount on the inflating country's exports. Since the country's import demand is also inelastic, the cheapening of imports relative to inflated domestic prices would expand imports only slightly.

The parallelism between the price-level and exchange-rate processes provides a further chance to test the theory of perverse elasticities against experience. Why do we not observe balance-of-payments troubles among the regions of a single country? Their absence from interregional trade, free from government controls, is perhaps not quite conclusive evidence, however. Deflation of real income and employment and cash balances as well as of prices and money income in the region that would otherwise have a deficit might account for balance-of-payments equilibrium even in the perverse-elasticities case. On the other hand, the explanation might be that the reduction in real income restores equilibrium not in spite of perverse elasticities but rather by making the people of the deficit country unable to afford an inelastic effective demand for imports. Whatever the explanation, it is worth pondering how, if the perverse-elasticities case is anything more than a theoretical toy, trade *within* countries stays in balance nowadays and how international trade stayed in balance under the historical gold standard.

A paradox and the solution

By now the reader surely has sensed a paradox. Chapter 3 suggested that balance-of-payments problems (as distinguished from problems of sheer poverty) are impossible if the government does not concern itself with trade, exchange rates, reserves of gold or foreign exchange, and so forth. After the people of a deficit country have used up their holdings of foreign exchange and exhausted their credit with foreigners, the country's current international accounts are bound to come into balance, regardless of "essential needs" for imports "or any other of the obfuscating phenomena with which the matter has been, and continues to be, surrounded."[15] Yet the theory of perverse elasticities still implies otherwise.

How can common sense be reconciled with this theory? Are the stability conditions wrong, or is common sense superficial? Neither. Demand elasticities must necessarily become high enough to satisfy the conditions. If all else fails to assure a normal adjustment process, then the country's demand for imports must turn elastic. The reason becomes clear when we think what the contrary would mean. The people of the deficit country would spend larger and larger total amounts per time period of their own money on imports as import prices, tied to the price of foreign exchange, rose higher and higher. But they could not keep doing this on and on because they do not have infinitely large incomes and accumula-

13. Without causing nonsatisfaction of the stability condition, short-run inelasticities of demand and supply may cause trade balances to respond to exchange rates more feebly in the short run than in the long run. Helen B. Junz and Rudolf R. Rhomberg calculated the average price elasticities of market shares and of exports at a given size of export markets for thirteen industrial countries exporting to fourteen markets over the years 1958–1969. When calculated with market shares lagged three to five years behind prices, the estimated elasticities were more significant than unlagged elasticities. The authors rationalized their findings in terms of lags of recognition, decision, delivery, replacement, and production. Junz and Rhomberg, "Price Competitiveness in Export Trade Among Industrial Countries," *American Economic Review*, **LXIII**, May 1973, pp. 412–418.

14. Joan Robinson, "The Pure Theory of International Trade," *Review of Economic Studies*, **XIV** (2), 1946–1947, No. 36, pp. 102–103, carries on her analysis in terms of varying money wage rates with rigid exchanges, although, as she emphasizes, her argument could readily be transposed into terms of variable exchange rates. Similarly, Abba P. Lerner, *op. cit.*, pp. 377–378, discusses the elasticity requirements for balance-of-payments stability in terms of gold flows and variable price levels rather than exchange rates.

15. Frank D. Graham, *The Theory of International Values*, Princeton, N.J.: Princeton University Press, 1948, p. 275. Cf. Graham, *Exchange, Prices, and Production in Hyper-inflation: Germany, 1920–1923*, Princeton, N.J.: Princeton University Press, 1930, pp. 26–27.

tions of assets from which to spend. Eventually, as import prices rise, total home-currency expenditure on imports could no longer rise. Some price of foreign exchange must be so high that the country's import demand would become elastic, itself satisfying the condition for a normally reacting balance of payments. At worst, the borderline case would be reached.

Admittedly, though, it is just abstractly conceivable that even this conclusion might fail: no matter how high-priced imports might become in local currency, total spending on them might always rise just a bit further, asymptotically approaching but never quite reaching the complete exhaustion of income. But this picture of people devoting 99 percent and 99.99 percent and ever closer to a full 100 percent of their entire incomes to imports, no matter how high their prices and thus no matter how low the import-purchasing-power of the country's exports, presupposes downright negligible possibilities of switching consumption away from imports toward home-market or export-type goods and of switching production away from exportables into home-market goods or import substitutes. No elaborate statistical investigation is necessary to rule out this truly weird picture; even empirical knowledge of the kind pervasive enough to force itself on the most resolutely abstract of theorists is enough.

It is still conceivable that people might have no faith in the future value of the home currency and refuse to hold cash balances larger than they considered absolutely necessary for transactions purposes. In trying to get rid of money almost as soon as received, they would be bidding up the prices of foreign exchange and other things. Surely, one might say, there can then be no stable equilibrium in the exchange market. A more defensible interpretation, however, is that the equilibrium exchange rate keeps rising because of continuous shifts in supply and demand in an inflationary environment. As long as the money supply keeps rising or the demand for real cash balances keeps falling, domestic prices and money incomes would be rising, and with them the demand for and the price of foreign exchange. If this monetary inflation did not keep on swelling domestic money incomes, people could not keep on spending more and more money on imports. Genuinely perverse elasticities would not be the correct interpretation. Incidentally, if the perverse-elasticities case really did prevail, then domestic price inflation would reduce the defi-

cit or increase the surplus in the balance of payments of the inflating country. The very fact that inflation did *not* have this result would disprove the perverse-elasticities hypothesis.

Multiple equilibriums

Beyond some degree of exchange depreciation of Inland currency, import demand would be elastic and the reaction of the balance of payments normal. A symmetrical argument demonstrates a degree of appreciation of Inland currency beyond which the foreign demand for Inland exports would be elastic and the reaction of the balance of payments again normal: if the Outland-currency price of Inland currency rose still higher, Outlanders could no longer afford to go on spending ever larger amounts per time period of their own money to buy Inland goods. Any unstable equilibrium exchange rate and its range of balance-of-payments perversity would thus be flanked above and below by ranges of normal reaction.[16] These considerations do not provide absolutely airtight theoretical proof, however, that an unstable equilibrium would be flanked by upper and lower equilibrium rates. For reasons already mentioned (but dismissed on inescapable empirical grounds), it is abstractly conceivable that the relevant elasticity might approach but never reach or exceed unity as the exchange rate moved extremely high or low. Or it is just barely conceivable that even though the two ranges of normal reaction did exist, the respective rise or fall of the exchange rate within them would promote balance-of-payments equilibrium so feebly as never quite to achieve it. (For one thing, as the exchange rate raises the price of imports in one country toward infinity, it lowers the price toward zero in the other, and while the budget restraint implies that the import demand elasticity must at the very least become almost unitary in the country with rising import prices, the corresponding elasticity may approach zero in the other country as imports become almost free.) Nevertheless, it is overwhelmingly likely that the two stable equilibriums *would* exist on either side of the unstable one. Inland's demand curve for foreign exchange touches the price axis at some very high price—if at none lower, then when the smallest unit of foreign goods worth having costs Inland's entire national income. This demand curve would have a normal intersection with the supply curve, which could not be more backward-sloping than a rectangular hyperbola: At the other extreme, there must almost surely be some price of foreign exchange so low that the supply curve, after intersecting the demand curve normally, touches the price axis; some Outland price of Inland currency must be so high that Outlanders would buy no Inland goods whatever. This same conclusion about the supply curve also follows from looking at the matter from the standpoint of the suppliers of foreign exchange, that is, Inland's export producers. These exporters might be so dependent on the Outland market that, to hold it, they fully or partially offset the effect of the Inland-currency appreciation on the Outland-currency price of their goods by marking down their Inland-currency price. But there must be some degree of appreciation so extreme and therefore some Inland-currency price of exports so low that exporters would be unwilling to go further in trying doggedly to hang on to any remnant of their Outland market. This might happen because the opportunities either to sell all former export goods on the home market instead or to switch from export goods into other lines of production had finally become less unattractive than such unrewarding export business.

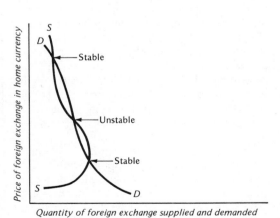

Quantity of foreign exchange supplied and demanded per time period

FIGURE 8.2

Figure 8.2 illustrates multiple intersection of the foreign-exchange supply and demand curves. (The reader now knows why the graph of unstable equilibrium at the beginning of the chapter showed only the parts of the curves in the immediate vicinity of the intersection.) A freely fluctuating exchange rate would tend to shoot away from the unstable equilibrium toward one or the other of the stable levels, which one being pretty much a matter of chance. The lower of the stable equilibrium levels provides the more favorable terms of trade for Inland. Furthermore, the Inland authorities could nudge the exchange rate towards this level, around which it would then gravitate under the influence of private market forces. Official sales of foreign exchange (borrowed if necessary) would do the trick. After the rate had moved toward the self-maintaining favorable equilibrium, the authorities could profitably buy back the foreign exchange at a

16. Cf. Alfred Marshall, *Money Credit & Commerce*, London: Macmillan, 1923, p. 352; Heinrich Freiherr von Stackelberg, "Die Theorie des Wechselkurses bei vollständiger Konkurrenz," *Jahrbücher für Nationalökonomie und Statistik*, **CLXI**, September 1949, pp. 40–41, and the graph on p. 60; Milton Friedman, *Essays in Positive Economics*, Chicago: University of Chicago Press, 1953, p. 160n.; Egon Sohmen, "Demand Elasticities and the Foreign-Exchange Màrket," *Journal of Political Economy*, **LXV**, October 1957, pp. 431–436. The present discussion tries to take account, as well, of an attack on Sohmen's reasoning by Jagdish Bhagwati and Harry G. Johnson in "Notes on Some Controversies in the Theory of International Trade," *Economic Journal*, **LXX**, March 1960, esp. p. 93n.; and also of Sohmen's "Comment" and the two authors' "Rejoinder" in *Economic Journal*, **LXXI**, June 1961, pp. 423–430.

Experimentation with Marshallian offer curves of the kind that Bhagwati and Johnson present in their 1960 article, p. 91, suggests that what they call "terminability" of each country's import demand suffices for Sohmen's conclusion. As the two authors state in their 1961 rejoinder, "the proposition that an unstable equilibrium is always bounded by stable rates . . . does not hold in strict theory but requires an empirical assumption of insatiability *or* terminability to support it. . . ." (p. 427; emphasis on *or* supplied). Now "terminability" simply means that there is *some* limit beyond which people would rather discontinue trade than accept still more unfavorable terms of trade. Everyday observation amply justifies an inference that in no country would people give their entire annual national output for one single milligram per year of imported goods.

lower home-currency price than that at which they had sold it.[17]

Perverse elasticities: summary

The perverse-elasticities case would not be un-favorable for a deficit country and would not make a free exchange market unworkable. It would depend upon peculiar local bulges or dents in the relevant supply and demand curves, so to speak, and could easily be escaped from into a position of improved terms of trade and a normally working exchange-rate mecha-nism. In the real world, though, each exchange rate very probably has only one equilibrium, a normal one. The stability condition is not at all exacting and ought to be easily met. Many internationally traded products are supplied competitively by producers in several countries, and many imports and exports constitute only a fraction of the consumption and production of similar goods in the importing and exporting countries. These facts imply that demands in international trade are amply elastic. So does the purchasing-power-parity doctrine (ex-plained in Chapter 11), which shows why currencies tend to exchange, on free markets, at rates that approximately translate their re-spective purchasing powers. If this doctrine is true, the picture of rates perversely shooting away from these equilibrium levels is quite implausible.

Referring to the theory that equilibrium in international trade might be unstable, Alfred Marshall said, ". . . it is not inconceivable, but it is absolutely impossible.". Frank Graham called it "solemn nonsense." Wilhelm Röpke mocked "hypothetical-curiosity" theories ex-hibiting that "characteristic combination of a maximum of ingenuity more geometrico and a minimum of 'judgment.' . . ." Gottfried Haberler found it "difficult to understand why anyone should find it necessary to fall back on such implausible and farfetched hypotheses as the sudden appearance in the fourth decade of the 20th century of stubborn real inelasticities of international demand (of whole continents and a great variety of countries). . . ."[18]

Challenges to the elasticities analysis: the absorption approach

The elasticities approach to the analysis of exchange-rate variation has drawn much criti-cism, notably from S. S. Alexander.[19] Accord-ing to him, to say that the response of the balance of payments depends on certain elastic-ities is mere implicit theorizing unless the elas-ticities are independently specified. The stabil-ity formula derives purely from the manipula-tion of definitions and has no operational con-tent unless the nature is specified of the functions whose elasticities are involved. The functions might be specified so that the elas-ticities are "partial" elasticities, indicating how sensitively import and export quantities re-spond to their own prices when other prices and national incomes all remain unchanged. In fact, however, exchange-rate adjustment cannot leave those other things unchanged. Import and export prices are interdependent, for example, and imports and exports respond to the other prices as well as to their own. Such repercussions may well work against the primary effects. The stability formula thus has no application if the elasticities in it are interpreted as "partial". On an alternative interpretation, the elasticities are "total," measuring the price-responsiveness of import and export quantities when not only their own prices but also incomes and other prices change as they will change in direct or indirect response to the exchange-rate adjust-ment. The usual stability formula is then tautologically correct—and empty. If the elas-ticities are defined as referring to price-quantity relations when all things change as in fact they would in response to an exchange-rate adjust-ment, then no one could know how large these elasticities were without *already* having a complete analysis of the whole response of domestic and foreign economies to the rate adjustment. To say that the effect on the balance of payments depends on the (total) elasticities boils down to saying that it all depends on how the economic system be-haves.[20]

Finding this not very helpful, Alexander suggests his "absorption" approach instead. As earlier chapters have recognized, an import surplus is identical to an excess of absorption (consumption plus investment) over national output or income, and an export surplus is identical to underabsorption. If exchange de-preciation is to improve a country's balance of payments, it must somehow increase national income or output relative to absorption or—the same thing—decrease absorption relative to income or output.

Next Alexander lists and discusses various "effects," or ways in which devaluation might either increase output or restrict absorption. First is the "idle-resources effect": somehow or other, unemployed resources, if there were any, might be put back into productive use. No reason suggests itself why devaluation would have a powerful effect of this sort. Furthermore, for any such effect to improve the balance of payments, the "marginal propensity to absorb" would have to be less than 1: additional consumption and investment would have to absorb less than the full amount of any increase in income or output, and this is uncertain. Second is the "terms-of-trade effect": devaluation presumably makes foreign goods and services more expensive relative to home goods and services and factors of production, thereby reducing the real buying power of and real absorption by the home population. This effect tends to be outweighed, says Alexander, by an adverse primary impact on the foreign balance, since the worsening of the terms of trade tends to cheapen the money value of exports relative to that of imports. Third is a set of possible "absolute-price-level effects." Among these might be the effect of devaluation in reducing the total real value of cash balances; and in their efforts to rebuild their real cash balances into an appropriate relation with levels of real income and transactions, individuals and businesses might reduce their consumption and investment relative to income. Or aggregate absorption might be reduced by a shift in the distribution of income, perhaps toward taxes and profits at the expense of wages (i.e., toward low-absorption from high-absorption economic units). A particularly dubious possibility hinges on what Alexander calls "money illusion": an increased price level might (or might not) dissuade people from some purchases, even though their money incomes had risen in proportion. Finally, there may be various miscellaneous minor price-level effects. Some of these may even influence the balance of payments unfavorably; for example, a rise in prices resulting from devaluation may unleash inflationary expectations that actually increase absorption.

None of these "effects" appears powerful and dependable. Some are likely to prove fleeting. For example, the domestic money supply may respond to the needs of trade at the increased price level, thereby both undoing the shrinkage in real cash balances that would otherwise tend to restrict absorption and also supporting a general price inflation that impedes any equilibrating shifts in relative prices.

17. By abstracting from shifts in the curves—that is, from dynamic developments such as inflation, deflation, speculation, and changes in tastes—the discussion here remains in the context of the perverse-elasticities controversy, which is concerned with possible absence of a stable static equilibrium. It continues to follow Sohmen's 1957 article.

18. Marshall, *op. cit.*, p. 354; Graham, *The Theory of International Values*, p. 297; Röpke, "Devisenzwangswirtschaft: das Kardinalproblem der internationalen Wirtschaft," *Aussenwirtschaft*, **V**, March 1950, p. 29n.; Haberler, "Monetary and Real Factors Affecting Economic Stability," *Banca Nazionale del Lavoro Quarterly Review*, **IX**, September 1956, p. 97.

19. See "Effects of a Devaluation on a Trade Balance," IMF *Staff Papers*, **II**, April 1952, pp. 263–278; and "Effects of a Devaluation: A Simplified Synthesis of Elasticities and Absorption Approaches," *American Economic Review*, **XLIX**, March 1959, pp. 22–42.

20. In a vein similar to Alexander's, I. F. Pearce (*International Trade*, New York: Norton, 1970, *passim*) disparages the use of total elasticities because the ultimate of this approach is to say—quite emptily—that what happens depends on the elasticity of the balance of payments with respect to the exchange rate. Pearce prefers to work with consumption-demand and production-supply elasticities. But the futility of an approach, carried to its ultimate, does not imply futility if carried only part way. The ultimate of Pearce's approach would be to work with the parameters of individual persons' demand functions for individual commodities and supply functions of factors of production and the parameters of all relevant production functions, which would be unmanageable. We must strike some compromise between meaningfulness but unmanageability at one extreme and apparent simplicity but meaninglessness at the other extreme. Such a compromise may well involve "total" elasticities of import and export supply and demand. Somewhat fuzzy concepts like these can serve as elements in a filing system (like the terms in the equation of exchange $MV = PT$). They help us organize a discussion of what conditions would contribute and what conditions would detract from "normal" response of the balance of payments to the exchange rate. Furthermore, the total-elasticities approach does not claim exclusive attention. It illuminates some aspects of the response, while the absorption and monetary approaches (described below) illuminate other, though overlapping, aspects.

(Alexander finds such a passive response of the money supply quite realistic.) The impression emerges that devaluation can do little to correct a deficit.

This analysis is illuminating but calls for some comment. For one thing, the use of a parameter labeled "propensity to absorb" plays down the question whether price changes accompanying devaluation might not helpfully alter this propensity.[21] The opinion that devaluation may worsen the terms of trade so as to increase import value relative to export value despite a slight favorable change in physical quantities invites two comments. First, devaluation does not *necessarily* worsen the ratio of export to import prices (see Chapter 10). More important, the question whether adverse price movements will outweigh favorable quantity movements touches the essence of the "elasticities" approach, and the answer is far from immediately obvious. The absorption approach does not actually deny that the changes in relative prices brought about by devaluation are effective in encouraging substitution, both at home and abroad, between domestic and internationally traded goods, but it buries these response to price rather obscurely among the apparently feeble "effects" that it does consider. The opinion that effects working through changes in the total real value of cash balances would probably be washed out by a passive monetary expansion in the devaluing country concerns responses that are, after all, a matter of policy and deserve forthright emphasis as such. Lax management of the money supply abetting a spiral of domestic inflation and repeated devaluation would prevent reaching any equilibrium. The persistence of balance-of-payments trouble would then imply nothing about how effective devaluation would be under different domestic policies.

A reconciliation of the absorption and elasticity approaches

J. Black has restated the absorption approach and its pessimistic implications with a clarity that points the way toward reconciliation with the elasticities approach.[22] An excess of absorption (consumption plus investment) over income produced becomes, in Black's equivalent terminology, an excess of domestic investment over domestic saving. Devaluation or any other measure to correct a balance-of-payments deficit must somehow reduce investment or increase saving or do both. Black thinks a cut in investment unlikely and proceeds to search for possible additions to saving. Devaluation might raise saving by raising real income, but only in an economy with unemployment and slack productive capacity. At full employment, the repercussions of devaluation might conceivably redistribute real income toward high-saving classes. The opposite is equally conceivable. The effect is either weak or perverse. By itself, devaluation at full employment can do little to remedy a deficit.

Paradoxically, a different view makes the deficit itself, rather than its cure, seem implausible and in need of explanation. (Recall Chapter 3.) Since a country's balance of payments is an aggregate of the balances of the individuals and institutions composing the country, it as a whole could not have a deficit unless some individuals or institutions in it were living beyond their incomes or dissipating their resources. The central bank or other official exchange-rate-pegging agency may be doing so by drawing down its reserve of gold and foreign exchange and receiving in return domestic currency whose lesser equilibrium value would be evidenced by the very fact that the agency was being called upon to sell more foreign exchange than was being offered to it at its pegged price. Only in terms of the price imposed by its own unbalanced transactions does the agency appear to be maintaining rather than dissipating the value of its assets.

For an instructive parable, suppose that Ruritania's balance of payments has been in equilibrium at a freely fluctuating exchange rate hovering around 1 Ruritanian crown per U.S. dollar. Now an eccentric wealthy Ruritanian with ample bank deposits in New York, acting on some strange whim, offers dollars for sale at only ½ crown each. This rate prevails for all transactions; no one will pay more for dollars earned by Ruritanian exporters. The exchange appreciation of the crown cheapens import-and-export-type goods relative to domestic goods, including Ruritanian labor and other factors of production. Laborers and other factor-owners gain buying power over international-trade goods and scarcely lose buying power over others. The wealthy eccentric is in effect subsidizing his fellow countrymen's purchases. Because of the effective increase in their real incomes, Ruritanians buy more goods and services, especially the cheapened imports and export-type goods. Ruritania develops a balance-of-payments deficit. In the outside world, the depreciation of currencies relative to the Ruritanian crown lowers factor incomes in terms of goods imported from and exported to Ruritania. (By enabling his fellow countrymen to spend the balances that he had previously been holding idle in the outside world, the Ruritanian eccentric is reducing the real resources currently available to the foreigners.) Because of the great size of the outside world in comparison with Ruritania, however, this income effect would discourage purchases from and encourage sale to Ruritania only rather feebly in comparison with the pattern of relative prices caused by exchange-rate pegging.

If some worried official were now to ask what might remedy the deficit in Ruritania's balance of payments, an "elasticities" economist might suggest depreciation of the crown, that is, an end to exchange-rate pegging by the wealthy eccentric. An "absorption" economist would be doubtful, pointing out that removal of a deficit implies an increase in saving or an even less likely reduction in investment and that exchange depreciation can do little to promote either.

Ruritania's deficit admittedly does imply "overabsorption" or "undersaving" on the part of the country as a whole, *including* the eccentric. *Other* Ruritanians as a group may nevertheless be living within their real incomes as they see them. The country's deficit stems from a dissipation of the eccentric's resources and a related distortion of the prices that give meaning to money incomes and that guide consumption and investment decisions. An end to exchange pegging would remove the price distortions that had been making real income seem larger from the viewpoint of ordinary persons than it was from the national viewpoint.

Black's skeptical question is a crucial one: "How . . . does devaluation tend to bring about an increase in savings?"[23] How, in other words, does it raise the propensity to save (or reduce the propensity to absorb) out of a given income? An answer must emphasize the fundamental ambiguities in the very concepts of total production, total income, and total absorption and especially in the concepts of the difference between absorption and production or income, of saving, and of an import or export surplus. These concepts are particularly tricky when the magnitudes are supposedly measured in real terms. In an open economy, for instance, real income and real output are not necessarily identical: some home production is sold abroad, and some foreign goods are imported for use at home, and the real income corresponding to a given pattern of physical production depends on prices.[24] Any sum or difference of heterogeneous goods and services requires measurement in money terms; prices are necessarily involved. A change in prices will change the relation between income and absorption (between saving and investment) both as a matter of sheer arithmetic and also by confronting buyers and sellers with new price incentives. A rectification of distorted price signals is what, from one point of view, reduces the propensity to absorb or increases the propensity to save, even out of a given real income, in a devaluing country.[25] From the point of view of individuals themselves, however, the change in absorption reflects not so much a reduced *propensity* to absorb as a cut in the real size of the incomes out of which their absorption must take place. A further but possibly minor aspect of adjustment through devaluation is the "real-balance effect" already mentioned. Domestic currency loses some of its purchasing power over international-trade goods, impoverishing individuals and businesses to some slight extent, disrupting the desired composition of asset-holdings, and tending to promote frugality in buying goods and services.

---

21. Fritz Machlup, "Relative Prices and Aggregate Spending in the Analysis of Devaluation," *American Economic Review*, XLV, June 1955, pp. 255–278, esp. p. 275. This article has suggested some of the comments that follow.

22. J. Black, "A Savings and Investment Approach to Devaluation," *Economic Journal*, LXIX, June 1959, pp. 267–274.

23. *Ibid.*, p. 269.

24. Machlup, *American Economic Review*, June 1955, pp. 268–270. Machlup especially criticizes Alexander's concept of a " 'real' trade balance."

25. *Ibid.*, pp. 265–266, suggests that the liberalization of trade made possible by abandoning an unrealistic exchange rate may improve the allocation of resources and so raise real income. This is a further, though probably minor, way in which an excess of real absorption over real income might be reduced.

This last effect presupposes that domestic goods and services do not fall in price enough to compensate for the rise in international-trade goods and so maintain the overall purchasing power of cash balances. To justify this presupposition, let us *try* to conceive of such exactly compensating price movements. No fall in real cash balances would then be at work to restrain total absorption, while the reinforced shift in relative prices would switch expenditure away from international-trade goods and toward domestic goods. Domestic prices would again be bid up, some rise in the general price level would occur after all, and the shrinkage of real balances would come into play. In fact, any expenditure-switching policy (such as devaluation or the tightening of import restrictions) tends to raise the price level unless accompanied by a separate expenditure-reducing policy (such as monetary or fiscal measures).[26] For an expenditure-switching policy to produce a helpful real-balance effect, it need not necessarily be accompanied by an *active* expenditure-reducing policy, though the monetary expansion that would neutralize the effect must be avoided.

Even when the money supply is not actually expanding, "balance-of-payments deficits and difficulties are essentially monetary phenomena";[27] and it is a merit of the absorption approach to illuminate this fact. For an excess of expenditure over income implies that individuals and businesses are running down their cash balances. Domestic money disappears from circulation when it is paid into the official exchange-rate-pegging agency to buy foreign exchange. People's willingness to content themselves with reduced cash balances in real terms and relative to income and expenditure spells a rise in velocity. A continuing balance-of-payments deficit depends on a continuing rise in velocity of this sort. This is true, that is, unless the monetary authority continually creates new domestic money to replace what it absorbs from circulation through its sales of foreign exchange. Whichever corresponds to the balance-of-payments deficit—the implausible continuing rise in velocity or a continuing re-creation of domestic money—deserves emphasis as a monetary phenomenon.[28]

Absorption economists are uneasy about the switch from a saving-and-investment analysis to the elasticities analysis of how "imports and exports are determined as the result of the interplay of supply and demand in particular markets, with no reference at all to savings and investment."[29] But we have good reason to focus attention on particular markets and especially on the foreign-exchange market. It is natural to inquire how effectively an increase in the home-currency price of foreign exchange would reduce the quantity of it demanded from an official agency offering it at a pegged price. Furthermore, it is natural to focus attention on the size and consequences of the subsidy that currency overvaluation gives to absorption. The higher the relevant elasticities, the more scope and meaning this subsidy has. The higher the income-elasticity of demand for import-and-export-type goods and the closer their substitutability with domestic goods, the more the home population as a whole currently gains from the artificial cheapening of the former goods. The greater, accordingly, is the exaggeration of real national income from private points of view relative to the national point of view.

Finally, we are particularly concerned with the foreign-exchange market in order to appraise the workability of free price determination in it. The elasticities approach is useful in organizing this appraisal. It helps bring commonplace empirical facts to bear on the question, such as that competition occurs between imported and domestic goods at home and between the exports of various countries on the world market, that not all resources are irrevocably specialized in the production of particular goods, and that incomes are of finite size.

In summary, each of the two approaches to devaluation analysis deals only implicitly with the aspects of adjustment that hold the center of the stage in the other. As usually presented, the absorption approach is preoccupied with propensities to consume, save, and invest and seems to have little room for the incentives created by changes in relative prices. The elasticities approach is preoccupied with relative prices and seems to ignore the question of total absorption out of total income. The two approaches can be reconciled by recognizing how exchange rates and prices affect the sizes of real incomes and real cash balances from the point of view of the persons who make decisions about absorption and how the conditions underlying the elasticities affect the scope and size of the subsidy that overvaluation affords and the size of the discrepancy between private and national views of real income. Reconciliation dispels the "devaluation pessimism" spawned by the pure absorption approach.

Another criticism
of the elasticities approach

Like Alexander, E. Victor Morgan calls the whole elasticities approach into question, but in a different spirit and on different grounds.[30] The concept of demand or supply elasticity strictly applies only to a physically homogeneous commodity and only when all relevant variables other than its own price (including incomes and the prices of all other goods) stay unchanged. Yet imports and exports are far from homogeneous, and the response to a change in exchange rates involves changes not merely in import and export quantities but also in the "mix" of goods traded. The fundamental impact effect of a depreciation is to cheapen home factors of production relative to foreign factors. The depreciating country's goods, in turn, become relatively cheaper, but the response is by no means simple. It may become profitable to export some goods not previously exported and to discontinue some imports entirely. Changes will occur in the relative importance of various goods in both the import and export lists. Export- and import-competing industries will exert strengthened demands for factors of production. Home-currency prices will rise sharply for some factors and only slightly for others, depending for each on whether its supply elasticity is low or high and on how intensely other industries bid to retain it. Industries using large proportions of factors still remaining relatively cheap will tend to expand; industries using large proportions of factors becoming relatively expensive will expand little or will shrink. Similar but opposite changes occur in nondepreciating countries.

The language of supply and demand elasticities for imports and exports as a whole masks this thoroughgoing reallocation of resources and repatterning of production. Any such elasticity must involve the relation between price and quantity indexes of some sort; yet no index number can take account of the changes in import and export mixes that are the very essence of adjustment. "When we use the words elasticity of demand (or supply) for imports (or exports) we quite literally do not know what we are talking about."[31]

But is it necessary to throw out elasticities entirely? Perhaps they need only be reinterpreted a bit, in a way that the elasticity approach has presumably taken for granted all

along. What matters for the stability of the foreign-exchange market is how *total money values* of imports and exports respond to price changes. If a 1 percent reduction (through exchange depreciation) in the foreign price of a country's exports would cause foreigners to spend a 1 percent smaller total amount of their own money on the export goods, the elasticity of foreign demand may be said to be zero. If a 1 percent price reduction causes a 3 percent rise in total foreign expenditure, the demand elasticity is 4. Price elasticity of demand is approximately 1 + the elasticity of total expenditure with respect to price (the sign convention is understood whereby demand elastic-

26. Cf. Harry G. Johnson, *International Trade and Economic Growth*, Cambridge, Mass.: Harvard University Press, 1958, pp. 153–168 and esp. pp. 165–167. Johnson's terms "expenditure-switching" and "expenditure-reducing" refer to *real* expenditure rather than its nominal money value.

The rise in the price level upon which the real-balance effect depends (unless, of course, devaluation is accompanied by measures to shrink even the nominal money supply) does not mean that devaluation is inflationary *tout court*. First, without continuing monetary expansion, the rise in prices is a one-time adjustment and not a continuing process. Second, whether avoiding a devaluation prevents even this rise in prices depends on what the alternative is. Import restrictions are equally an expenditure-switching policy (cf. Johnson, p. 167) and are likely to affect the price level much as devaluation would. For further explanation, see Chapter 11.

The role of the real-balance effect in balance-of-payments adjustment is recognized in Michael Michaely, "Relative-Prices and Income-Absorption Approaches to Devaluation: A Partial Reconciliation," *American Economic Review*, L, March 1960, pp. 144–147.

27. Johnson, *op. cit.*, p. 157.

28. For further reconciliation of the monetary, absorption, and elasticity approaches to balance-of-payments analysis, see the following chapter.

29. Black, *op. cit.*, p. 268.

30. "The Theory of Flexible Exchange Rates," *American Economic Review*, XLV, June 1955, pp. 279–295.

31. *Ibid.*, pp. 282–284.

ity is normally positive). Supply elasticity may be similarly interpreted. If a 1 percent rise in the home-currency price of a country's exports would cause only a 1 percent rise in the total home-currency value of exports supplied, the supply elasticity may be said to be zero. If a 1 percent price rise would cause a 3 percent rise in value supplied, the elasticity of supply is 2. The elasticity of supply is less by 1 than the elasticity of total value supplied with respect to price. Since this way is available for translating the usual elasticities approach into terms of meaningful elasticities of total expenditure or value, it is no serious defect of the usual approach that it analyzes total money values of imports and exports into prices multiplied by rather fictitious homogeneous physical quantities. This fiction allows the convenience of the familiar terminology used in discussing ordinary commodity markets. The criticism best applies not so much to the standard elasticity criterion of exchange-market normality itself as to econometric attempts to estimate elasticities by observing how price and quantity indexes vary together over time. These attempts presumably underestimate the effectiveness of the exchange-rate mechanism by failing to allow for the *changing* nonhomogeneity of imports and exports.

Morgan also criticizes the usual elasticity approach as unable to take adequate account of the changes in income necessarily associated with changes in exchange rates. In particular, he criticizes the use of marginal propensities to import as parameters. Goods entering into or disappearing from trade or increasing or diminishing in relative importance do not all have the same income elasticity of demand, and the supposed parameters will themselves change with devaluation. Supply and demand curves are likely, furthermore, to shift independently of devaluation-linked changes in income. All

this is true. Yet however complex the process of response of import and export values to exchange-rate changes may be, it is meaningful to discuss its sensitivity. Far from impugning the conclusions of the traditional elasticity approach, an emphasis on changing import and export mixes and on other kinds of response to changed relative prices only reinforces them.[32]

---

32. In fact, reinforcing these conclusions is Morgan's purpose. Besides criticizing the elasticity approach, he makes a positive contribution. If devaluation and the consequent cheapening of Inland relative to Outland factors of production is to *worsen* Inland's balance of payments, a necessary (but not sufficient) condition is that Outlanders spend a smaller amount of their own money on Inland goods than before. This implies an increase in Outlanders' expenditure on their own goods, provided that the total flow of their expenditure does not change. (Given a successful stabilization policy, the total flow of Outland money expenditure would not fall. In the face of a cheapening of Inland goods in terms of Outland factors of production, analogous to an improvement in productivity, a policy of price-level stabilization would even call for some slight monetary expansion in Outland.) This increase in Outland expenditure on Outland goods would be diffused over numerous goods, with complicated substitutions perhaps taking place. Still, there would have to be at least one good for which the increase in Outland demand was greater than the reduction in Inland demand. For this one good, at least, an increase in relative price would have to tend to increase the excess quantity demanded. Only if the market for at least one good were unstable, therefore, could Inland's depreciation have a perverse effect on the balance of payments. This would be an odd situation indeed. (*Op. cit.*, p. 281; cf. pp. 285–286, 289–293.)

For somewhat similar remarks about exchange instability implying instability in the market for at least one individual commodity, see Harry Johnson, *op. cit.*, p. 164.

Appendix to Chapter 8: Derivation of the Exchange-Stability Conditions[1]

Symbols

e_f = elasticity of supply of foreign exchange with respect to its price in home currency. (If e_f is 2, for example, this means that a 1 percent rise in the home-currency price of foreign exchange so stimulates exports that their total foreign-currency value becomes 2 percent more than before.)

η_f = elasticity of demand for foreign exchange with respect to its home-currency price. (An η_f of 3 means that a 1 percent rise in the home-currency price of foreign exchange would lead to a 3 percent reduction in imports valued in foreign currency. An algebraic sign is built into this definition of demand elasticity so that a normally sloping demand curve is said to have a positive elasticity.)

e_m, e_x, η_m, and η_x are as defined on p. 159. In these symbols, the e's stand for supply elasticities and the η's for demand elasticities; the subscripts m and x refer to the imports and exports of the home country. The elasticities of supply are algebraically positive for normal upward-sloping curves. Demand elasticities are positive, too; for we adopt the sign convention whereby normal downward-sloping demand curves are said to have positive elasticity.

A 1 percent devaluation of the home currency—a 1 percent cut in its foreign-currency value—is approximately the same as a 1 percent rise in the home-currency price of foreign exchange. Of course, it is not strictly and precisely the same; but the smaller the devaluation is, the more nearly are the two percentages identical. Throughout the present derivation, it is convenient to take 1 percent as representing an extremely small change in the rate, though the resulting formula is strictly true only for an infinitesimally small change. The same infinitesimality assumption made explicit here is implicit in the derivation of the formula by calculus.

Assuming initial balance-of-payments equilibrium, with the quantities of foreign exchange supplied and demanded equal, an autonomous devaluation by 1 percent will raise the quantity of foreign exchange supplied by e_f percent and decrease the quantity demanded by η_f percent and so make the quantity supplied exceed the quantity demanded by $(e_f + \eta_f)$ percent of the quantity initially supplied-and-demanded.[2] This expression is positive except in the perverse-elasticities case.

---

1. This method of derivation, though tedious, uses only the simplest algebra. It follows up some hints given in A. C. L. Day, *Outline of Monetary Economics*, Oxford: Clarendon Press, 1957, chaps. 30 and 31.

2. If the country originally had a balance-of-payments deficit, with the quantity of foreign exchange demanded for imports exceeding the quantity supplied by exports, an η_f percent reduction in the quantity of foreign exchange demanded would amount to *more than* η_f percent when expressed as a percentage of the quantity of foreign exchange *supplied*. Consequently, a 1 percent devaluation would reduce the *excess* quantity of foreign exchange demanded by somewhat more than $(e_f + \eta_f)$ percent of the original quantity of foreign exchange supplied. Even if $e_f + \eta_f$ totalled only zero, the excess quantity of foreign exchange demanded would still be reduced somewhat. The point of this is that when we consider a country with an already-existing balance-of-payments deficit, the elasticity requirements for devaluation to improve the balance of payments as measured in foreign currency (which is the relevant measurement) are somewhat less exacting—somewhat *easier* to satisfy—than the requirements stated in a formula derived on the assumption of initial equilibrium in the balance of payments. The worse the balance-of-payments deficit, the more likely it is that depreciation would be effective in reducing it. Albert O. Hirschman makes this point in *op. cit.*, pp. 50–53.

The expression for e_f

To translate this criterion into terms of the import and export supply and demand elasticities used in the text of this chapter, we must first develop expressions for e_f and η_f separately. A 1 percent exchange depreciation of the home currency leads to the following percentage increase in the quantity of foreign exchange supplied:

1. The percentage increase in the total home-currency value of exports − 1.
[The subtraction of 1 takes account of the fact that the depreciation has reduced by 1 percent the foreign-currency equivalent of amounts expressed in home currency.]

2. This = the percentage increase in the home-currency price of exports + the percentage increase in the quantity of exports − 1.

3. = the percentage increase in the home-currency price of exports + η_x (1 − the percentage increase in the home-currency price of exports) − 1.
[The expression in parentheses is the percentage reduction in the foreign-currency price of exports, which is the 1 percent depreciation less the—almost certainly smaller—percentage increase in the home-currency price of exports. This expression multiplied by the elasticity of foreign demand for the exports yields the percentage increase in the quantity of exports.]
This, by straightforward rearrangement, becomes

4. The percentage increase in the home-currency price of exports $\times$ (1 − η_x) + η_x − 1.

5. Now, the percentage increase in the home-currency price of exports = the percentage increase in the quantity of exports $\div e_x$
[Recall that e_x is defined as the percentage increase in the quantity of exports supplied $\div$ the percentage increase in the home-currency price of exports.]
Recalling steps 2 and 3 above, we see that

6. The percentage increase in the home-currency price of exports = η_x (1 − the percentage increase in the home-currency price of exports) $\div e_x$
Straightforward solution of this equation yields

7. The percentage increase in the home-currency price of exports = $\dfrac{\eta_x}{e_x + \eta_x}$

Substituting this into step 4 shows that the initially assumed 1-percent depreciation makes the quantity of foreign exchange supplied increase by the following percentage:

8. $\dfrac{\eta_x}{e_x + \eta_x} (1 - \eta_x) + \eta_x - 1$, which can be rearranged into

9. $\dfrac{\eta_x - \eta_x{}^2 + e_x\eta_x + \eta_x{}^2 - e_x - \eta_x}{e_x + \eta_x}$ and into

10. $\dfrac{e_x (\eta_x - 1)}{e_x + \eta_x}$

This is e_f.

The expression for η_f

The assumed 1 percent depreciation of the home currency brings about a percentage decline in the total foreign-currency value of imports and of foreign exchange demanded equalling:

11. The percentage decrease in the quantity of imports + whatever percentage decrease there may be in the foreign-currency price of imports.
The home-currency price of imports rises by 1 percent because of the devaluation, mitigated by whatever percentage decrease there may be in the foreign-currency price of imports. This net percentage multiplied by the elasticity of home demand for imports yields the percentage decrease in the quantity of imports. Thus the expression in step 11 becomes:

12. η_m (1 − the percentage decrease in the foreign-currency price of imports) + the percentage decrease in the foreign-currency price of imports.

13. = η_m + (1 − η_m) the percentage decrease in the foreign-currency price of imports.
We now recall that the elasticity of foreign supply of imports is defined as percentage decrease in quantity of imports supplied $\div$ percentage decrease in foreign-currency price of imports.
Thus:

14. The percentage decrease in the foreign-currency price of imports = the percentage decrease in the quantity of imports $\div e_m$
By the reasoning used in going from step 11 to step 12, we now have:

15. The percentage decrease in the foreign-currency price of imports $= \eta_m(1 -$ the percentage decrease in the foreign-currency price of imports$) \div e_m$

Straightforward solution of this equation yields

16. The percentage decrease in the foreign-currency price of imports $= \dfrac{\eta_m}{e_m + \eta_m}$

Substituting this into 13 makes the expression for the percentage decrease in the quantity of foreign exchange demanded become:

17. $\eta_m + (1 - \eta_m) \cdot \dfrac{\eta_m}{e_m + \eta_m}$ which simplifies via

18. $\dfrac{\eta_m e_m + \eta_m{}^2 + \eta_m - \eta_m{}^2}{e_m + \eta_m}$ into

19. $\dfrac{\eta_m (e_m + 1)}{e_m + \eta_m}$

This is η_f.

Combination of the two preliminary expressions

With expressions now derived for e_f and η_f, their sum, whose algebraic sign provides the desired stability criterion, becomes

$$\frac{e_x (\eta_x - 1)}{e_x + \eta_x} + \frac{\eta_m (e_m + 1)}{e_m + \eta_m}$$

This is the expression already introduced in the text of this chapter. Straightforward manipulation reduces it to the form more commonly found in the literature:

$$\frac{e_m e_x (\eta_m + \eta_x - 1) + \eta_m \eta_x (e_m + e_x + 1)}{(e_x + \eta_x)(e_m + \eta_m)}$$

CHAPTER NINE

Money in Analysis and Policy: Reconciliations with Other Approaches

ANALYSES OF DISEQUILIBRIUM: A PREVIEW

The monetary approach to balance-of-payments analysis links a deficit to an excess supply of money.[1] The absorption approach views a deficit (on current account, specifically) as an excess of the country's total absorption of goods and services (real expenditure on them) over its total production. The elasticities approach attributes a deficit to wrong prices, including exchange rates, and centers attention on how sensitively imports and exports respond to price changes. On the domestic scene, the monetary approach attributes a depression to an excess demand for money and an inflationary boom to an excess supply.

Though superficially different, the three approaches to the balance of payments reconcile rather straightforwardly.[2] Contradiction is most apparent between the monetary views of external and internal imbalance; in some cases, the diagnoses are "excess supply of money" for one imbalance and at the same time "excess demand for money" for the other. These contradictions are examined toward the end of this discussion; the reconciliation will hinge on clarifying concepts and making distinctions.

In a discussion of this kind, understanding anything depends on understanding everything else first. The following pages will therefore sketch out the problems and solutions in a preliminary way before returning to them in detail.

Let us consider a payments deficit; the analysis of a surplus is approximately the converse. The *monetary approach* notes that private and governmental units (other than the monetary system) are, in the aggregate, running down their money balances, or are failing to retain in their balances the full amount of any domestically created new money. With their unwanted home money, they are buying foreign currency from the reserves of the exchange-rate-pegging monetary authority and using it to pay for imports of goods, services, and securities in excess of exports. Because the unwanted home money is canceled in the process, it is a convenient metaphor to speak of its "leaking" abroad in payment for net imports of other things. (This terminology would be literally correct if exactly the same kind of money circulated abroad as at home, so that no agency exchanging one kind for another entered the picture.)

The *absorption approach* makes contact with the monetary approach through the fact that market transactions are two-sided. While the monetary approach focuses on disposal of unwanted domestic money, the absorption approach focuses on the excess imports being bought with this money. While the monetary approach considers the country's overall payments position, including the capital account, the absorption approach, narrowly conceived, focuses attention on the current account. It views net imports of goods and services as corresponding to an excess of private plus governmental consumption plus investment over total domestic production of goods and services. Broadened into an interpretation of the overall payments deficit, the absorption approach notes that net exports of securities (i.e., net capital imports) are not fully financing the overabsorption of goods and services, so that people must be drawing down their money balances (or must be failing to retain in their cash balances the full amount of any new money obtained by selling securities to the monetary system). (Conceivably, of course, the rundown of cash balances could correspond to net imports of securities in excess of net exports of goods and services.)

The *elasticities approach* makes contact with the monetary approach by noting that when members of the home economy are in the aggregate exchanging home money for foreign money to spend on excess imports, the desired volume of such transactions depends not only on real incomes, propensities to consume and invest, and the stock and rate of creation of home money but also on the *price* at which the pegging agency stands ready to sell foreign money for home money. This price affects the prices paid and received for imports and exports and the purchasing powers of home money incomes and money balances. The elasticities approach focuses attention on how desired transactions respond to the level of this price, or to changes in it, or to deviations of it from the level at which the foreign-exchange market would clear without official intervention. Here is where the "four elasticities" of import and export demand and supply enter the picture.[3] The elasticities approach makes contact with the absorption approach by noting that the pegging agency's net sales of foreign exchange from its reserves normally indicate that the agency is asking a lower price in home money than would clear the market without its intervention. In this way the agency is in effect subsidizing absorption of goods and services, and of imports and exportable goods in particular. In an analysis of the extent to which domestic economic units respond to this absorption subsidy, the "four elasticities" again enter the picture.

The three balance-of-payments approaches reconcile in their descriptions not only of deficits and surpluses but also of corrective processes. The monetary and absorption approaches intersect in describing why the home money supply, shrinking through a deficit at a fixed exchange rate (if not continually replenished by fresh creation), would eventually no longer be excessive. No longer would people be disposing of excess money to finance overabsorption. From the standpoint of the elasticities approach, the reduction in people's eagerness to exchange domestic for foreign money makes the wrong fixed exchange rate right after all. That approach pays particular attention to rectification of that unchanged rate through declines in domestic prices—rise in the purchasing power of the home money unit—and through responses of exports and imports to changed price relations. After these responses, the fixed exchange rate would no longer constitute a subsidy to overabsorption.

Exhaustion of official foreign-exchange reserves might prevent keeping the exchange rate

MONEY IN ANALYSIS AND POLICY: RECONCILIATIONS WITH OTHER APPROACHES

fixed until the "automatic" process just mentioned had fully corrected the deficit. Or devaluation might be welcomed as less painful than the consequences of money-supply deflation.

1. Recall the quotations from Harry G. Johnson and Robert Mundell in Chapter 4, section on "The Special Emphasis on Money." Arnold Collery asks: "In a world of barter, what possible meaning can be given to a balance-of-payments deficit?" *International Adjustment, Open Economies, and the Quantity Theory of Money*, Princeton Studies in International Finance, No. 28, Princeton, N.J.: Princeton University, 1971, p. 1. Collery rephrases an old proposition of Ricardo's to the effect that "Balance-of-payments deficits exist . . . only when money is redundant." "Excess Supplies of Money and Balance-of-Payments Deficits," *Kyklos*, Vol. 24, No. 4, 1971, p. 777.

2. The present discussion builds on partial reconciliations already in print. See Sidney Alexander, "Effects of a Devaluation on a Trade Balance," IMF *Staff Papers*, **II**, April 1952, pp. 263–278; Alexander, "Effects of a Devaluation: A Simplified Synthesis of Elasticities and Absorption Approaches," *American Economic Review*, **XLIX**, March 1959, pp. 22–42; J. Black, "A Savings and Investment Approach to Devaluation," *Economic Journal*, **LXIX**, June 1959, pp. 267–274; Randall Hinshaw, "Further Comment," *Quarterly Journal of Economics*, **LXXII**, November 1958, pp. 616–625; Fritz Machlup, "Relative Prices and Aggregate Spending in the Analysis of Devaluation," *American Economic Review*, **XLV**, June 1955, pp. 255–278; Michael Michaely, "Relative-Prices and Income-Absorption Approaches to Devaluation: A Partial Reconciliation," *American Economic Review*, **L**, March 1960, pp. 144–147; Ivor F. Pearce, "The Problem of the Balance of Payments," *International Economic Review*, **II**, January 1961, pp. 1–28; S. C. Tsiang, "The Role of Money in Trade-Balance Stability: Synthesis of the Elasticity and Absorption Approaches," *American Economic Review*, **LI**, December 1961, pp. 912–936; and Leland B. Yeager, "Absorption and Elasticity: A Fuller Reconciliation," *Economica*, n.s., Vol. 37, February 1970, pp. 68–77.

3. This description of the elasticities approach could be rephrased to apply to a gold-standard or single-currency world in which no exchange-rate pegging was taking place. The outflows or inflows of money desired by residents of a particular country would be shown to depend on various prices and elasticities.

The monetary approach views devaluation as discontinuing the excessively favorable terms on which domestic money was exchangeable for foreign money. With their purchasing power reduced (particularly over imports and exportable goods), domestic money balances cease being considered excessive. In terms of the absorption approach, devaluation removes the previous subsidy to overabsorption. The elasticities approach pays particular attention to changed price relations brought about by devaluation.

Definitions

Listing the symbols used in covering all this ground more thoroughly provides an opportunity to make the related concepts more precise and to specify the economic units or sectors to which they refer. This, rather than any need for ambitious manipulations, is the chief purpose of introducing the symbols.

$Y =$ national income or product. This and other flow magnitudes are measured in home money value per time period. Unless otherwise mentioned, prices are assumed to be constant and money and real magnitudes therefore to move in parallel.

$A =$ absorption of, or real expenditure on, domestic and foreign goods and services by the nonmonetary sector of the home economy. This sector consists of all persons and private and governmental organizations *other than* the monetary and exchange-rate-pegging system. (This "monetary system," as we call it for short, is assumed to deal only in financial claims and liabilities and not to engage in any "real" production or absorption.) A is therefore private and governmental consumption plus real investment.

$B =$ Balance of payments on current accounts $=$ exports minus imports of goods and services. (We abstract from unilateral transfers or banish them to the capital account, although transfers are often included in the current account in real-world statistics.)

$Y = A +$ exports $-$ imports $= A + B$. (This formulation expresses the usual macroeconomic demand-determination theory of national income or product. Aggregate demand for domestic output consists of total absorption of goods and services by home economic units, *less* imports, which represent demand for foreign rather than domestic output, *plus* exports, which represent foreign demand for domestic output. An export surplus thus represents an injection into and an import surplus a subtraction from the total real spending stream that determines national income and product.)

$B = Y - A$. This follows immediately from the foregoing and expresses the key idea of the absorption approach: a current-account surplus means absorption falling short of real income or product, while a current-account deficit means overabsorption.

$K =$ net international capital flow, positive for net inflow (net exports of securities) and negative for net outflow (net imports of securities). The capital transactions covered are those of all domestic economic units other than the monetary system; exchange-rate-pegging transactions are therefore *not* included. (Some such demarcation is necessary to make the concept of overall balance-of-payments deficit or surplus meaningful.) The term "securities" is to be understood very broadly, including "thank-you letters" for unilateral transfers and even including foreign money acquired and disposed of by domestic economic units other than the monetary system.

$B + K =$ the country's overall balance-of-payments position, positive for a surplus and negative for a deficit. It is the net balance of international transactions of all domestic economic units except the monetary system. (This whole discussion applies more straightforwardly to a country whose currency is not used by others as international reserves than to a reserve-currency country. For a reserve-currency country, the location of the "line" between above-the-line and below-the-line transactions is fuzzy or arbitrary, and so, therefore, is the very concept of overall payments surplus or deficit. Suitable conventions can make the analysis applicable, however, even to a reserve-currency country.)

F = net foreign assets of the monetary system, the system's foreign-exchange holdings and similar claims on foreigners minus debts to foreigners.

$\triangle F = B + K$, since a rise or fall in F represents gain or loss of external reserves associated with exchange-rate pegging, which is the below-the-line settlement of an overall payments surplus or deficit.

D = net domestic assets (loans and investments less nonmonetary liabilities) of the monetary system. (If the system has been providing deficit finance to the nonmonetary sector of government, then D includes the corresponding claims on the government, which may admittedly have a rather fictitious character.)

M = monetary liabilities of the monetary system to domestic holders = domestically held money supply[4] = $D + F$. The domestic monetary liabilities comprising one side of the system's balance sheet are matched by its net domestic plus net foreign assets on the other. (We either assume away any nonmonetary or quasi-monetary liabilities of the system or else handle them as deductions from assets. Exactly how to draw the distinction between money and near-money is not crucial here.) The present formulation in effect assumes that the central bank alone constitutes the entire monetary system; it makes no distinction between the central bank and commercial banks and thus no distinction between the primary and the total monetary expansion or contraction touched off by the central bank's net purchases or sales of domestic and foreign assets. For the purposes at hand, this simplification is acceptable.

$\triangle M = \triangle D + \triangle F$. This follows from the foregoing. The symbol $\triangle M$ does not distinguish between an actual and a

desired change in total domestic money holdings, but the distinction can be introduced as needed in interpreting the formulas. $\triangle D$ and $\triangle F$ may conveniently be identified with domestic and foreign "sources" of change in the domestically held money supply.

Money and absorption

The fundamental expressions for the country's overall payments position, positive for a surplus and negative for a deficit, are

For the monetary approach:

$$\triangle F = B + K = \triangle M - \triangle D$$

and

For the absorption approach:

$$\triangle F = Y - A + K = \triangle M - \triangle D$$

In words, the overall balance, equaling the balances on current plus capital account, or underabsorption plus the capital-account balance, equals the change in net foreign assets of the monetary system, which in turn equals the change in the domestically held money stock in excess of the change attributable to the system's expansion of credit by acquisition of domestic assets.

To focus attention on an overall payments *deficit*, expressed as a positive number, we reverse the signs:

$$-\triangle F = -B - K = A - Y - K = \triangle D - \triangle M$$

---

4. This formulation allows for the possibility that a payments deficit need not shrink and surplus need not expand the *total* outstanding stock of domestic money. A deficit may be financed by transfer of some domestic money to foreigners, who hold it during the period considered; and a surplus may be financed by reacquisition of domestic money formerly held by foreigners. When the home nonmonetary sector finances a deficit by transferring home money to foreigners, M goes down, matched in the monetary system's balance sheet by a decline in F, since a rise in the system's monetary liabilities to foreigners spells a decline in its *net* foreign assets.

The overall deficit equals the nonmonetary sector's overabsorption of goods and services plus its excess of purchases over sales of securities $(-K)$ in transactions other than with the domestic monetary system, i.e., in transactions with foreigners. In other words, the deficit equals overabsorption of goods and services in excess of net sales of securities abroad $(+K)$. This, in turn, equals the monetary system's domestic asset acquisition, which is the nonmonetary sector's borrowing from it, in excess of the nonmonetary sector's additions to its money balances.

The position of the ΔM term in the foregoing expressions might seem to suggest—contrary to intuition—that monetary expansion contributes to a surplus and monetary contraction to a deficit in the balance of payments. What resolves the paradox? The actual change in the money stock is assumed to equal the desired change; the ΔM term must be interpreted as both actual and desired change. The equations therefore say that if members of the nonmonetary sector are succeeding in adjusting or maintaining their money balances as they desire, their overall balance-of-payments surplus or deficit must equal the amount by which the desired money-supply change exceeds or falls short of that part of the change being furnished by the domestic credit operations of the monetary system. If domestic money-and-credit expansion, measured by ΔD, just equals desired increments to money balances, then the overall balance of payments is in equilibrium. If ΔD falls short of desired additions to money balances, the remainder of the money is obtained through a balance-of-payments surplus. If, on the contrary, domestic credit expansion is *tending* to create more new money than is wanted for additions to money balances, then the unwanted new money is being canceled by a negative ΔF.

This view accords well with intuition. It does not deny that the "unwanted" new money is wanted in some sense: people are glad to get it by borrowing from the domestic monetary system; but if they want it for spending rather than for additions to cash balances, they dispose of it through what shows up for the country as a whole as an overall payments deficit. This is true when the nonmonetary sector is engaging in overabsorption of goods and services in excess of what it is financing by net capital imports (net securities exports). The overabsorption is then being financed domesti-cally by sales of securities to the monetary system, externally by drain on the country's foreign-exchange reserves. A slightly different case would involve overabsorption financed neither by securities exports nor by borrowing of newly created money from the domestic monetary system. In that case, the nonmonetary sector would necessarily be running down money balances previously held, metaphorically letting them "leak abroad." In still another instructive case, the nonmonetary sector would be in current-account balance, engaging in no overabsorption, but engaging in net imports of securities $(-K)$. It would then necessarily be either borrowing from the monetary system (a positive ΔD for the system) or running down its money balances.

In these various cases, the monetary nature of either a desired change in money balances (ΔM) or domestic money-and-credit expansion or contraction (ΔD) is obvious.

Suppose that population growth, increases in productivity, or other real factors are tending to raise real income and in turn the total real volume of money demanded. If the monetary system is not satisfying this demand by its domestic operations, the country's balance of payments tends into surplus. People's desires to build up their money holdings are reflected in their actions to become net sellers of goods plus services plus securities; and since they cannot be net sellers in the aggregate in transactions among themselves alone, they must become net sellers in transactions with the outside world. Thus, contrary to what naive Keynesianism would suggest, real factors making for economic growth tend, in themselves, to produce a balance-of-payments surplus. The reason is that people desire to devote increments to real income partly to increasing their portfolios of financial assets rather than entirely to additional absorption of goods and services. In fact, real growth factors might tend to produce a larger surplus on current account than in the overall balance; for, on the plausible assumption that real economic growth raises desired net holdings of securities as well as of money, net capital exports occur.[5]

The most obvious link between the absorption and monetary approaches, to summarize, is the *quid-pro-quo* nature of market transactions. The two approaches are mirror images of each other, *except* that the absorption approach focuses on goods and services, while the monetary approach focuses on the *quid pro quo*, money, that changes hands in transactions in goods and services and also in securities, broadly conceived.

Money and elasticities

Like the absorption approach, the elasticities approach has traditionally focused attention on the current account in particular. Like the monetary approach, however, it can focus attention on how an overall imbalance is financed through transactions in domestic money and in foreign exchange added to or drawn from the official reserves. When running an overall deficit, the nonmonetary sector is exerting an excess demand for foreign exchange that is being met from the official reserves and whose size depends in part on the pegged exchange rate. The nonmonetary sector's incentive to run down domestic cash balances (or to fail to retain in its cash balances the full amount of any new money obtained by borrowing from the monetary system) depends on how great a bargain other things are in domestic money. The "other things" include the foreign exchange being sold by the pegging agency and the internationally traded goods and services and securities whose prices are affected by the exchange rate. The bargain prices of these other things spell an artificially high purchasing power of the domestic money unit, which explains, from an explicitly monetary standpoint, the desire of the nonmonetary sector to reduce its cash balances (or to shun additions to them). An overall payments surplus, conversely, can be viewed as the nonmonetary sector's accumulation of domestic money, and of more of it than is being created by domestic credit expansion. Its incentive is that exchange-rate pegging is keeping the purchasing power of the home money unit artificially low; home money is a bargain in terms of other things and, in particular, in terms of foreign exchange and foreign-trade goods.

If we may ignore the capital account, an excess demand to exchange home for foreign money or foreign for home money that is being accommodated by the exchange-rate-pegging agency is the difference between the quantities of foreign exchange being demanded and earned in international transactions in goods and services. These quantities depend on how sensitively imports and exports respond to the exchange rate or, more generally, to price. The

formula introduced in Chapter 8 for the conditions of "normal" response is relevant here. What we need is not new manipulations but further interpretations. On one interpretation, the four elasticities in the formula are not straightforward *ceteris paribus* price elasticities. Rather, they are "total" elasticities, expressing how sensitively imports and exports respond when not only their own prices change but also incomes and other prices change as they do in direct or indirect response to an exchange-rate adjustment. The formula is tautologically correct—and allegedly empty. To say that the response of the balance of payments to a change in the exchange rate depends on these total elasticities boils down to saying that all depends on how the economic system behaves. Sidney Alexander finds this not very helpful.[6] Yet the four elasticities, though total elasticities, do serve to organize an assessment of such circumstances as degrees of competition and of substitutability between domestic and foreign goods, circumstances that do affect how trade responds to the exchange rate. Although the import demand elasticity—to mention just one of the four—is not strictly a price elasticity, it is related to a price elasticity in the sense that it would be affected in the same direction by circumstances tending to make a price elasticity high or low.

Although the elasticity approach is concerned with the price-responsiveness of "imports" and "exports," these terms might be interpreted broadly enough to include securities (i.e., the counterpart of capital movements) as well as goods and services. If this dodge seems too strained, we could confine the elasticity approach to the current account and handle the capital account separately. Analyses of the current account and of the overall bal-

5. See Robert A. Mundell, *International Economics*, New York: Macmillan, 1968, chap. 9. On the point about a larger current-account than overall surplus, see Ryutaro Komiya, "Economic Growth and the Balance of Payments: A Monetary Approach," *Journal of Political Economy*, Vol. 77, January/February 1969, pp. 35–48.

6. Articles of 1952 and 1959, cited in footnote 2.

ance of payments should not conflict fundamentally. In the theoretical literature dealing with exchange-stability conditions, "one usually abstracts from capital movements on the legitimate assumption that the level of the exchange rate does not, when it is expected to prevail (the usual presumption in comparative-static analysis), directly influence capital flows." This is not the same as assuming that the capital-account balance is zero in the real world.[7]

Elasticities and absorption

The relation of the elasticities approach to the absorption approach requires a more complicated description than its relation to the monetary approach. The reason is that the transactions in goods and services and securities through which people adjust their money balances are more varied and subject to more complex influences than their acquisition and disposal of money. An immediate qualification is necessary: transactions in money and in other things are, of course, two sides of the same operations; but we can focus attention more simply, or superficially, on the money side than on the other side.

We now turn to the more complicated side. When the pegging agency is running down its foreign-exchange reserves, this normally indicates that it is asking a lower price in home currency for foreign exchange than would clear the market without its intervention. The bargain price of foreign exchange is making imports and export-type goods artificially cheap in home money, exaggerating the purchasing powers of home money incomes and money balances and thereby subsidizing total absorption of goods and services. From their own points of view, members of the nonmonetary sector are not engaging in consumption and investment out of line with what their incomes and financial resources appear to warrant.

A suitable devaluation corrects the price distortions that had been exaggerating the purchasing powers of money incomes and financial resources. This correction is what appears to reduce the national propensity to absorb goods and services even despite a substantially unchanged real national income. Individuals and business firms and nonmonetary units of government cut their consumption and investment not so much because their propensities have changed as because their real incomes and real money holdings, as they see them, have fallen.

To understand in greater detail the link between price elasticities and the subsidization of overabsorption, let us consider, in particular, the demand for imports. If people demanded imports in almost rigid quantity, regardless of price, their scope for taking advantage of the subsidy afforded by artificially cheap foreign exchange would be relatively small. If, on the contrary, purchases of imports were highly price-sensitive, the scope and significance of the subsidy would be correspondingly great. (For a family that had been spending equal fractions of its income on beef and gasoline and whose demand for beef was the more elastic, a subsidy on beef would raise real income more than a subsidy of the same percentage on gasoline.) High price elasticity of demand means that the subsidy itself greatly expands the base on which it is paid. This consideration immediately brings into contact with the absorption approach all the familiar discussions of the importance for the balance of payments of the elasticity of import demand and, in turn, of the overall price elasticity of demand for import-type goods, the elasticity of domestic supply of competing goods, the smallness of import volume in relation to competing production, and the degree of substitutability between imports and domestic goods.

While artificially cheap foreign exchange subsidizes buyers of imports, it in effect taxes suppliers of exports. Export suppliers, perceiving real income as smaller from their points of view than it is from the national point of view, tend to restrain their consumption and investment. Normally, however, overvaluation of the home currency makes imports exceed exports, so that imports provide a larger base for absorption-promoting subsidization than exports provide for absorption-deterring taxation. (The word "normally" serves as a reminder that these concepts of exaggeration and understatement of real income can handle the theoretical-curiosity case of "perverse elasticities," in which the balance of payments reacts perversely to the exchange rate.)

Another element in reconciling the elasticity and absorption approaches is a terms-of-trade effect. To an extent described by the four elasticities, the level of the exchange rate affects the prices in foreign currency that foreigners receive for home-country imports and pay for home-country exports. By thus affecting the size of the home-country's gains from trade, the exchange rate affects the size of real national income. Both the subsidy-tax effect and the terms-of-trade effect of a disequilibrium exchange rate cause divergence between individual perceptions of real income and the national reality of how much real income there is to be absorbed "out of." Within the framework of the absorption approach, a behavioral interpretation of the elasticities formula of Chapter 8 can derive its conclusions concerning how the effectiveness of exchange-rate adjustment relates to both supply elasticities and demand elasticities.

The required interpretation is tedious and is omitted here.[8] Its key idea is that a disequilibrium exchange rate causes various economic units to have wrong perceptions of the real income available to cover absorption. Devaluation of an overvalued currency removes these wrong perceptions; it discontinues a net subsidy that had been causing overabsorption. Devaluation thus has not only a demand-switching but also a demand-shrinking effect.

Internal and external monetary disequilibrium

Although the three approaches to balance-of-payments analysis reconcile nicely, an apparent conflict can still arise between the monetary views of internal and external imbalance. The monetary approach attributes a depression at home to an excess demand for money: the money supply is too small to support a flow of spending on domestically produced goods and services adequate for full employment. (A definite money supply may be said to "support"

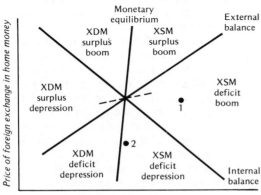

FIGURE 9.1

that level of aggregate spending at which the quantity of money demanded would be equal to the money supply. Aggregate spending serves as a scale variable in the demand-for-money function.) The same approach attributes an inflationary boom to an excess supply of money: the real quantity of money is larger than people desire to continue holding, and shortages of goods and resources generally prevail because their prices have not yet adjusted upward fully enough to keep their markets cleared.[9]

No problem arises with the *non*dilemma cases for expenditure policy (described on pages 96–102). It is easy to understand why an excess demand for money resulting from a domestically caused shrinkage of the money supply or an intensification of demand for money balances should show itself in both depression and a balance-of-payments surplus. It is understandable why an excess supply of money originating at home should show itself in both inflationary boom and payments deficit. The problem arises in the cases of depression with deficit and boom with surplus.

An adaptation of Fig. 6.1 can illuminate the problem. In Fig. 9.1, as before, the vertical axis measures the Outland/Inland price ratio; but it is a convenient simplification to regard both price levels as constant in local currency and take the exchange rate as indicating their vari-

7. Gert Haller, book review in *Journal of Money, Credit, and Banking*, **IV**, November 1972, p. 1020.

8. See Yeager, *op. cit.*

9. The monetary approach describes a central aspect of depression and boom but does not purport to tell the *whole* story. Its rationale is too familiar and is not squarely enough in the realm of international finance to call for full repetition here. See, for example, my "A Cash-Balance Interpretation of Depression," *Southern Economic Journal*, **XXII**, April 1956, pp. 438–447; and "Essential Properties of the Medium of Exchange," *Kyklos*, **XXI**, No. 1, 1968, pp. 45–69.

On internal balance and imbalance, recall pages 96–99. Inflationary boom is a state or process of incomplete adjustment to an inflationary monetary disturbance, as distinguished from an equilibrium situation in which, purely as a matter of history, the price level is higher than it once was.

able ratio.[10] To pay explicit attention to money, we measure its quantity on the horizontal axis, rather than expenditure, as before (but expenditure is positively correlated with the quantity of money). The internal- and external-balance lines have essentially the same meaning and rationale as in Fig. 6.1 (except that the latter line refers here to equilibrium in the overall balance of payments rather than specifically in trade). The chief novelty requiring explanation is the slope and position of the monetary-equilibrium line, which divides situations of excess demand for and excess supply of money (XDM and XSM). Starting from the all-around-equilibrium situation represented by the intersection, an arbitrary increase in the quantity of money is represented by a move to point 1. Money is now in excess supply. People could be led to desire their increased money holdings if the purchasing power of the Inland dollar became sufficiently low. The only change of this general sort representable on the diagram is a rise in the price of foreign exchange. That rise spells a fall in the purchasing power of the dollar over foreign-trade goods and thus over goods on the average. The exchange-rate change that restores equilibrium between the demand for and supply of money is represented by an upward move from point 1 to the monetary-equilibrium line at a new point on it. As an alternative disturbance, consider an arbitrary exchange appreciation of the Inland dollar, represented by a move from the intersection to point 2. Because the purchasing power of the dollar over foreign-trade goods has increased, people would be holding larger real money balances than they desired unless the money supply shrank to a quantity represented by a point on the monetary-equilibrium line to the left of point 2.

Next we must see why the money line is placed as drawn rather than in the position of the dashed line. The dashed position would imply that a relatively small increase in the price of foreign exchange would raise the quantity of money demanded enough to match an arbitrary increase in the money supply. This seems implausible; for against the background of a stable Inland price level, the rise in the price of foreign exchange would have to be relatively great to spell such a reduction in the overall purchasing power of the dollar that people would want to hold all of the increased money supply. The dashed position implies the implausible circumstance, furthermore, that a

smaller increase in the price of foreign exchange would be required to restore monetary equilibrium than to remove the balance-of-payments deficit, even though the initial disturbance was a domestic increase in the money supply and though the exchange rate relates more directly to the balance of payments than to the demand for money holdings.

A less loose and intuitive reason for ruling out the dashed line is that in cutting through the east and west sectors formed by the other two lines, it would imply the conceivable coexistence of deficit, boom, and excess demand for money and of surplus, depression, and excess supply of money. In certain subsectors, that is, the dashed line would imply a counterintuitive kind of association of monetary disequilibrium with internal and external imbalance both. Drawn in the solid position, the money line avoids this double-barreled contradiction. Although it avoids the paradoxical kind of association of monetary disequilibrium with both internal and external disequilibrium at the same time, it does permit one paradox or the other. This is the difficulty that we have to clear up.

One disturbance bringing a balance-of-payments deficit accompanied by depression at home would be an arbitrary upward revaluation of the Inland dollar. Point 2 suggests the result. Alternatively, Outland demand for Inland exports has dropped off, perhaps because of a change in tastes, a new tariff, or a depression in Outland. If so, the lines for external, internal, and monetary balance were formerly located so as to intersect somewhere in one of the two bottom sectors formed by the new lines—perhaps at some such point as point 2. From its undrawn old position to its new position as drawn, the external-balance line has shifted northwestward, indicating that either exchange depreciation of the home currency or domestic monetary deflation is necessary to cure the payments deficit. The internal-balance line has shifted northeastward, indicating the need either for currency deprecation to remove the payments deficit and its siphoning of demand away from the home economy or else for domestic monetary expansion sufficient to offset the demand leakage due to the payments deficit. Just how, if at all, the money line shifts is less clear, partly because of an ambiguity, to be explained, about the very meaning of monetary equilibrium and disequilibrium. Meanwhile, we may note a presumption of a northwestward shift, small in comparison with the shifts of the other two lines. The hypothesized drop in Outland demand for Inland goods entails worsened terms of trade, reduced real income, and thus a reduction in real money balances demanded. With the home price level assumed fixed, a matching reduction in the real money supply could be accomplished either by shrinkage of the nominal money supply or by a rise in the price of foreign exchange; and this is what a northwestward shift of the money line indicates.

Let us assume, then, that point 2 was the intersection of the undrawn old lines. With respect to the new equilibrium lines, it now represents a situation of deficit, depression, and excess supply of money. The nature of the excess supply of money associated with the payments deficit should be clear from earlier sections of this chapter. With sales to Outland reduced, some Inlanders suffer a fall in their incomes. They do not immediately cut their purchases of goods and services by the full amount of the fall in their incomes; instead, they take some time to adjust, financing their overspending in the meanwhile by drawing down their cash balances (as well as, probably, by disposing of other investment assets or running up debt). One of the functions of cash balances is to serve as a buffer against just such shocks. With their incomes cut, furthermore, Inlanders cannot "afford" cash balances as large as before. While running down their cash balances, Inlanders are expressing an excess supply of money of a sort that corresponds to the country's payments deficit.

The puzzle, instead, is one of depression apparently associated with an excess supply of money rather than excess demand for it. The domestic trouble is not merely a money supply inadequate for a full-exmployment level of aggregate demand. It is also a misdirection of aggregate demand, too much of it going onto Outland goods and not enough onto Inland goods for internal balance. (Recall what the initial disturbance was—a switch of demand away from Inland goods, or an inappropriate exchange-rate change causing such a switch.) But misapportionment of demand is not the whole story, either. Money's being in excess supply in relation to the balance of payments does not preclude its being in excess demand, in another sense, on the domestic scene. With reference not merely to money but to goods and services in general, the theoretical litera-

ture has become pervaded in recent years with distinctions among notional demand, effective demand, successful demand, frustrated demand, and so forth, and similar distinctions for supply. For money in particular, by its very nature and by the way that people acquire and dispose of it, the concept of "demand" bristles with ambiguities and the need for careful distinctions.[11]

We must also distinguish between the *kinds* of equilibriums represented and disequilibriums demarcated by the internal-balance and external-balance lines of our diagram. Internal balance means either full employment without excess demand and price inflation or the attainable compromise between these desirable conditions deemed best on domestic grounds. External balance, by contrast, has less normative content; it means balance-of-payments equilibrium, however obtained. Because internal and external balances and imbalances are different in kind, so too are the associated monetary equilibriums or disequilibriums. Where the diagram shows an excess supply of money paradoxically associated with depression, the explanation is that the XSM is of the kind straightforwardly associated with a payments deficit; and where the diagram shows an

10. For our purposes, it is legitimate to overlook the realistic complication that an exchange-rate change could hardly leave prices or price levels unchanged in local currency. We can regard each country's unchanged price level as that of goods other than those whose prices are most closely linked to the exchange rate.

11. See Robert Clower, "The Keynesian Counter-revolution: A Theoretical Appraisal," in F. H. Hahn and F. P. R. Brechling, eds., *The Theory of Interest Rates*, London: Macmillan, 1965, pp. 103–125; Axel Leijonhufvud, *On Keynesian Economics and the Economics of Keynes*, New York: Oxford University Press, 1968, esp. pp. 81–89; and many writings inspired by these contributions. Ambiguity about the very concept of demand for money is a leading theme of Donald P. Tucker, "Macroeconomic Models and the Demand for Money under Market Disequilibrium," *Journal of Money, Credit, and Banking*, III, February 1971, pp. 57–83.

excess demand for money associated with a payments deficit, the XDM is of the kind straightforwardly associated with a depression.

The kind of monetary disequilibrium characteristic of depression may be called a full-employment excess demand: the real money supply is smaller than the real quantity of money *that would be demanded* at a flow of real spending adequate for full employment, given the apportionment of the spending flow between Inland and Outland goods and services. Given the nominal money supply, the purchasing power of the money unit is too low. As the medium of exchange routinely traded on all markets, money differs from all other goods in having no market specifically its own. It has no price of its own that adjusts flexibly to maintain equilibrium between its supply and demand. Neither does any agency stand ready at home to accommodate an excess demand for or supply of money at a fixed price in any such definite way as occurs on the foreign-exchange market. In contrast with the satisfaction of excess demand or supply by the exchange-rate-pegging agency, a domestic full-employment excess demand for money remains frustrated. This frustration has more pervasive repercussions than it would have if the excess demand focused on a specific market; it takes the form of dispersed, generalized frustration in selling things and earning incomes. Efforts to conserve cash balances make the flow of spending and income shrink because money is the routinely circulating medium of exchange. Depression deepens—barring the attractive but usually unavailable alternative of a rapid and sufficient fall in the price level—until the scale of economic activity has fallen sufficiently to choke off the quantity of money actually demanded to the quantity in existence. But a suppressed or virtual excess demand for money remains. This, essentially, is the monetary interpretation of depression.

Our hypothesized initial diversion of demand away from Inland goods causes a full-employment excess demand for money in the following sense. Given the changed apportionment of total demand, the total Inland demand for goods and services necessary for full employment becomes larger than before and requires support by a larger money supply. Not only does the quantity of money necessary for full employment increase, but the actual quantity decreases as money disappears through the balance-of-payments deficit. Because it is the

routine medium of exchange, money flows *through* cash balances, out as well as in. Some outflows would always be taking place, even when people were wanting to maintain or increase their balances. In spending money, people spend it in the ways they consider most advantageous; and if a wrongly pegged exchange rate makes it advantageous to spend money on excess imports of goods and services, that is what people will do, even though no one desires the resulting shrinkage of Inland's money supply and its macroeconomic consequences. There is no contradiction between an excess supply of money being accommodated by the pegging agency on the foreign-exchange market and an excess demand for money being frustrated at home and being worsenened by money's disappearance through the balance of payments. The two monetary disequilibria are not so much different in direction as different in kind.

The fall of income in the depression-and-deficit dilemma case itself helps account for the overabsorption of goods and services in relation to income that constitutes the deficit in foreign trade. The fall in income also causes a decline in the actual demand for money, as distinguished from the full-employment demand. Hence people willingly resort to running down their actual money balances, and in the ways made most advantageous by the pegged exchange rate.

The opposite dilemma case of domestic inflationary boom associated with balance-of-payments surplus is empirically familiar.[12] It can be similarly explained. The domestic monetary disequilibrium that results when an external disturbance changes the apportionment of aggregate demand in favor of Inland goods may be described as a full-employment excess supply of money: more money exists than people desire to hold at a flow of aggregate demand compatible with a full-employment level of real income and with the existing price level; if a high enough level of real income is unattainable, then a higher price level is necessary to make people content to hold the entire money supply. With regard to the balance of payments, underabsorption of goods and services may be attributed to the hypothesized shift of demand onto Inland goods, which causes a rise in real income (if not through restoration of previously absent full employment, then at least through improved terms of trade). The additional income is not immediately matched by a rise in absorption. Inlanders willingly devote part of their increased income to a buffer-like accumulation of domestic money balances, especially when exchange-rate pegging is making domestic money available artificially cheap in terms of foreign money and ultimately in terms of internationally traded goods and services. In short, the excess demand for money associated with the balance-of-payments surplus is being gratified on a particular market at a particular price (the exchange rate) and is different in kind from the excess supply of money associated with the domestic inflationary boom.

The monetary interpretations of dilemma cases in an open economy with a fixed exchange rate are admittedly more complicated or strained than the monetary interpretations of depression or inflationary boom in a closed economy. Domestic monetary analysis of an open economy is simpler if a floating exchange rate is avoiding dilemma cases by keeping the balance of payments in equilibrium. In a closed economy, it is highly implausible that a deficiency of demand for currently produced goods and services could persist accompanied not by a (full-employment) excess demand for money but by an excess demand for securities or "Old Masters" instead. The argument, not fully reproduced here,[13] hinges on the fact that securities and Old Masters, unlike money, are traded on markets and at prices of their own. Their prices tend to adjust to clear their individual markets; and if price rigidity did interfere, frustrated demand for the assets in question would spill over harmlessly into other markets rather than cause the pervasive disruptions caused by an excess demand for money. It is at least as difficult in an open economy with a floating exchange rate as in a closed economy to conceive of depression associated not with excess demand for money but with excess demand for securities or Old Masters instead. What might otherwise be excess demand for such things would tend to be met by imports, causing depreciation of the home currency on the foreign-exchange market. The resulting export surplus of currently produced goods and services would stimulate rather than impair domestic production and employment. In an open economy with a floating exchange rate, perhaps even more so than in a closed economy, depression is straightforwardly attributable to a full-employment excess demand for money.[14]

The internal-external reconciliation summarized

Reconciling the monetary views of external and internal imbalance in the dilemma cases hinges on distinctions between various concepts of excess demand for and excess supply of money. The deficit-and-depression case exhibits, on the one hand, an excess supply of money which is actual or effective, which centers on a particular market and relates to a particular price (the exchange rate), and which is being gratified by transactions with a particular agency. On the other hand, frustration is pervasive as a virtual excess demand for money prevails in the sense that the actual money stock is smaller than the stock that would be demanded at full employment. This domestic disequilibrium is related to money's role as a medium of exchange and to its not having a market and price distinctively its own, so that suppression of the disequilibrum must occur in a roundabout and painful way.

In one respect, the reconciliation runs into embarrassment. In a dilemma case such as a switch of demand away from Inland goods might cause, domestic depression corresponds not to inadequacy of total spending and of the money supply but rather to a changed apportionment of spending between Outland and Inland goods. Or so one might object. The reply contends that given the changed apportionment, the total Inland spending and money supply required for full employment are indeed bigger than before, so that money is in full-employment excess demand even at its initial quantity, and all the more so as its quantity shrinks through the balance-of-payments deficit. If this answer seems strained, the reason lies with the real-world situation envisaged rather than with any error in the analysis. Dilemmas really are awkward.

12. See in particular Chapter 24.

13. See the articles in footnote 9.

14. This straightforward applicability of the monetary interpretation of domestic imbalance may be a psychological reason, in addition to the several objective reasons, why many economists favor floating exchange rates.

MONETARY AND FISCAL POLICIES UNDER FREE AND FIXED EXCHANGE RATES

A large literature, teeming with detailed assumptions, has developed on the proper pairing of free or fixed exchange rates with monetary or fiscal policies intended to influence domestic aggregate demand and income.[15] Appraisals of Canadian policy in the late 1950s illustrate the importance of the topic; the Canadian authorities seem to have pursued an inappropriate combination of policies.[16] The following pages try to convey the main points of consensus that emerge from the discussion while avoiding strands whose conclusions depend sensitively on special features of specific models.[17] One fairly robust conclusion, not hopelessly dependent on special detailed assumptions, is that a floating rather than fixed exchange rate enhances the effectiveness of both fiscal and monetary policy by freeing policy from balance-of-payments constraints. (Exceptions are conceivable; we will particularly note an exception for fiscal policy when capital is extremely mobile.) Furthermore, a floating exchange rate enhances the effectiveness of monetary policy relatively more, so that fiscal policy may be said to have a *comparative* advantage under fixed exchange rates, while monetary policy has a comparative advantage under floating rates.

For definiteness, we shall consider domestic financial policy operating in the expansionary direction. Monetary policy means expansion of the home money supply through central-bank open-market operations without any government budget deficit. We measure the scale of monetary policy by the change it would make in the money supply in a closed economy (i.e., by the central bank's acquisition of domestic assets) and not by the *net* change occurring in an open economy. The effects of exchange-rate pegging on the money supply[18] are important to much of the analysis that follows, but those effects are attributed to that pegging and do not count as modifying the scale of monetary policy. If money should "leak abroad" through a balance-of-payments deficit at fixed exchange rates, this leakage counts as interfering with the policy's effectiveness rather than as holding its scale down in the first place. Similarly, money-supply growth through a balance-of-payments surplus does not indicate an expansionary monetary policy. Fiscal policy is defined as operating through government deficit spending financed by the issue of bonds, not money. (Deficit spending financed with newly issued money could be handled as a combination of a bond-financed government deficit and an open-market operation of buying back the bonds with newly issued money.) To focus attention on how external developments reinforce or impair the effectiveness of domestic financial policy, we shall assume away the realistic complication of endogenous changes in the government budget. That is to say, although a rise in income tends to cause a budget surplus or shrink a deficit, causing government bonds (or money) to be retired or their rate of issue to be reduced, we shall assume that such a change is prevented by tax adjustments or by the fixing of tax collections as well as of government expenditures as lump sums in the first place.

We shall assume normal rather than perverse elasticities (in the sense of Chapter 8): exchange-rate movements affect the balance of payments, and specifically the balance of trade in goods and services, in the normal way. We assume that speculation neither accentuates nor damps the movements of free exchange rates. We do not consider the price movements under fixed exchange rates that would be equivalent in their real consequences to movements of free exchange rates. In this respect, our discussion rests on Keynesian assumptions. With complete price and wage flexibility, there would be no need for expansionary policy for the sake of employment.

Regarding capital mobility, our two polar cases are zero and perfect interest-sensitivity. At one extreme, no capital movements occur. At the other, Inland is so small in relation to the world financial market and other necessary conditions are so fully satisfied that Inlanders can import and export unlimited amounts of securities at an unchanged interest rate; securities arbitrage keeps the Inland interest rate constant at the world level. We suppose that capital movements are responsive only to interest-rate differentials (or, strictly speaking, to the differentials that *would* emerge if arbitrage were not sensitive enough to keep them from emerging in the first place). We rule out the response of capital movements to such things as rates of profit on equity capital[19] and to exchange-rate expectations. Various special assumptions could multiply cases and apparently paradoxical results almost endlessly.

In the expectation that they will also provide insights about intermediate cases found in the real world, we shall examine the eight possible combinations (shown in Table 9.1), of pure fiscal or pure monetary policy, free or fixed exchange rates, and zero or perfect capital mobility. We need not *separately* consider the benchmark cases of fiscal and monetary policy in a closed economy, since, for the purpose at hand, the case of a free exchange rate with zero international capital mobility is formally equivalent to a closed economy.[20] With the exchange rate balancing the overall balance of payments and with the capital account nonexistent, the current account must always be in balance. No net leakage from or injection into the domestic spending stream can then occur through the current account, just as no leakage from or addition to the country's money supply can occur through the overall balance of payments. Policy actions and any resulting movements of the exchange rate may indeed cause changes in the composition of a country's imports and exports and in the level at which they balance, as well as in the patterns of the country's production and absorption. But the balance of payments cannot cause unambiguous changes in the levels of production or absorption, any more than in domestic spending and in the money supply. In that sense the case is equivalent to the closed-economy case.

Table 9.1 summarizes some conclusions, to be justified in what follows. In the abbreviated labeling, "free" and "fixed" refer to exchange rates and "zero" and "perfect" to interest-sensitivity of capital movements. The numbers in the cells refer to the rankings of policy effectiveness, from 1 for most to 4 for least effective in influencing income.

The table ranks fiscal-policy and monetary-policy cases separately. Only in cases where one policy is and the other is not totally ineffective can we compare monetary and fiscal policy with each other and say that one is unambiguously more effective than the other. The diffi-

15. Numerous citations appear in Akira Takayama, "The Effects of Fiscal and Monetary Policies under Flexible and Fixed Exchange Rates," *Canadian Journal of Economics*, Vol. 2, May 1969, pp. 190–191n. Noteworthy contributions not cited there include Egon Sohmen, *Flexible Exchange Rates*, rev. ed., Chicago: University of Chicago Press, 1969, chap. V; Ronald I. McKinnon and Wallace E. Oates, *The Implications of International Economic Integration for Monetary, Fiscal, and Exchange-Rate Policy*, Princeton Studies in International Finance, No. 16, Princeton, N.J.: Princeton University, 1969; Ronald I. McKinnon, "Portfolio Balance and Inter-

MONEY IN ANALYSIS AND POLICY: RECONCILIATIONS WITH OTHER APPROACHES

national Payments Adjustment," in Robert A. Mundell and Alexander K. Swoboda, eds., *Monetary Problems of the International Economy*, Chicago: University of Chicago Press, 1969, pp. 199–234; Komiya, *op. cit.*; Robert W. Baguley, Appendix A to Richard E. Caves and Grant L. Reuber, *Capital Transfers and Economic Policy: Canada, 1951–1962*, Cambridge, Mass.: Harvard University Press, 1971; and Victor Argy and Michael G. Porter, "The Forward Exchange Market and the Effects of Domestic and External Disturbances Under Alternative Exchange Rate Systems," IMF *Staff Papers*, **XIX**, November 1972, pp. 503–532.

16. See pages 556–559.

17. A model, should the reader care to work it out, is useful as a guide to and check on verbal reasoning. In it, $Y = A + B$ (the symbols are as defined on pp. 184–185). A is a function of Y, the interest rate i, and a fiscal-policy parameter. B is a function of A and the exchange rate. The stock of money demanded is a function of Y and i. For continuing monetary equilibrium, the change in the quantity of money demanded equals the change in the money supply, which equals the sum of the external current- and capital-account balances and the change in the domestic assets of the monetary system (as on page 185). The procedure is to take total differentials and solve for dY. For the perfect-capital-mobility cases, it is instructive to consider the implications of $di = 0$ in the monetary-equilibrium equation.

Like the models used in most of the literature, this one does not explicitly allow for a direct real-balance effect on absorption nor take explicit account of bonds. (In so simple a model, what tends to raise the interest rate in the case of expansionary fiscal policy is not the issue of government bonds but the tendency of rising income to increase the demand for cash balances in the face of a money supply unchanged by domestic action.) Yet the model is adequate to highlight some key relations.

18. Recall earlier sections of this chapter.

19. In particular, we rule out capital inflow or outflow incited by a rise or fall in income. See Harry G. Johnson, "Some Aspects of the Theory of Economic Policy in a World of Capital Mobility," *Rivista Internazionale di Scienze Economiche e Commerciali*, **XII**, June 1965, pp. 545–561, also in Tullio Bagiotti, ed., *Essays in Honour of Marco Fanno*, Padua: Cedam, 1966, pp. 345–359.

20. Cf. Baguley, *op. cit.*, p. 378; and McKinnon in *Monetary Problems*, p. 224.

TABLE 9.1. *Degrees of policy effectiveness*

	Fiscal policy		Monetary policy	
Closed economy or free-zero	2		2	
Free-perfect	4	Totally ineffective	1	Highly effective
Fixed-zero	3		3	
Fixed-perfect	1	Highly effective	4	Totally ineffective

culty is that there exists no common unit of policy intensity enabling us to compare monetary and fiscal policies of equal scale. (A common unit could be devised, but it would have to be conventional rather than compellingly natural.) A related problem of measurement concerns the distinction between one-shot and continuing policy actions. Quantity-theory reasoning suggests that a one-shot addition to the money supply, if not reversed, makes money income larger thereafter than it otherwise would have been, whereas discontinuance of government deficit spending allows income to drop back toward its initial level. An expansionary fiscal action, unlike an expansionary monetary action, has to be maintained or repeated indefinitely to keep income above its original level. The monetary and fiscal actions that would make and keep income $1 billion a year higher than it otherwise would have been are different not only qualitatively but also in duration.

Let us consider the cases of Table 9.1 in order, from left to right and top to bottom.

Fiscal-free-zero (*equivalent to a closed economy*). According to standard macroeconomic theory, government deficit spending, being equivalent to a rise in the national propensity to spend, raises income. In monetary terms, loosely speaking, the government borrows money out of relatively idle balances and restores it to the spending stream; an increased interest rate raises the velocity of the unchanged money supply. A rise in the interest rate is necessary to make people accept increasing ratios of bonds to money in their portfolios (except in the limiting case of infinite substitutability between money and bonds) and to accept lower ratios of money to income (except

in the limiting case where a rise in income does not cause people to desire larger money balances). In this and the other fiscal-policy cases, the tendency of the interest rate to rise is attributable not only to the government's borrowing but also to the tendency for income to rise and for people accordingly to demand larger money balances at an unchanged interest rate. (These tendencies are thwarted in some of the other cases.)

One restraint on the effectiveness of fiscal policy unsupported by monetary policy in a closed economy or equivalent is the partial "crowding out" of private expenditure.[21] In financing its deficit by selling bonds, the government competes with other borrowers. The more sensitively private consumption and investment decline in response to a rise in the interest rate (and, correspondingly, the more interest-sensitive private demands for and issues of bonds are), the more significant this crowding out tends to be. A high interest-sensitivity of demand for money balances is favorable, on the other hand, to the effectiveness of fiscal policy; for it facilitates the government's borrowing money out of idle balances.

The wealth effect of increased private bondholdings might tend to raise the propensity to spend out of income. On the other hand, people might desire additional money in their portfolios to match their growing holdings of bonds. If bondholdings grew relative to income, so also might desired money-holdings, spelling a decline in income velocity.[22] This difficulty could be significant if demands and supplies of bonds and goods and services were highly interest-sensitive and if demands for money balances had only slight interest-sensitivity and were strongly influenced by notions of appropriate portfolio composition. Generalization about such matters of personal taste is difficult. It seems clear, though, that nothing settles to equilibrium as long as government deficits continue adding bonds but not money to private portfolios. The increasing difficulty of bond financing, epitomized in a rising interest rate, might eventually lead the government to abandon its deficit spending or to reinforce it with an expansionary monetary policy.

In short, the standard macroeconomic theory of the effectiveness of pure fiscal policy in a closed economy is subject to several qualifications. Such considerations bolster an intuition that achieving a definite increase in income would require a more massive fiscal policy than monetary policy—an intuition that fiscal policy is less effective. Such a comparison must remain intuitive only, however, because there is no clear-cut way to specify what might be meant by fiscal and monetary policies of equal intensity.

The analysis of fiscal policy in a "free-zero" open economy is similar to the analysis for a closed economy, except that currency depreciation rather than absence of foreign economic relations is what keeps spending and money from leaking abroad.

Monetary-free-zero (*equivalent to a closed ecomony*). As contrasted with fiscal policy, monetary policy directly increases the money supply and raises money income as described by the quantity theory. The expansionary open-market operation withdraws bonds from private portfolios and injects money into them. The fall in the interest rate necessary to make people accept this change in the composition of their portfolios is likely to raise desired money-to-income ratios (i.e., to reduce velocity), so that income rises less than in proportion to the money supply. Standard theory points, however, to an at least partial reversal of this interest-and-velocity restraint on the effectiveness of money-supply expansion. As income does rise, private borrowing and lending also expand, lodging more bonds in private portfolios. With regard to portfolio balance, private indebtedness and holdings of private bonds are not simply the opposites of each other; and as income and private borrowing and lending do expand, the withdrawal of government bonds by the initial open-market operation becomes relatively less and less significant for portfolio balance.

Fiscal-free-perfect. What difference does perfect capital mobility make in comparison with the two zero-mobility cases just considered? The issue of bonds to finance government deficit spending, along with any tendency for income to rise, *tends* to raise the Inland interest rate. Bond exports (capital imports) respond so sensitively to this tendency, however, that the Inland interest rate does not in fact rise above the world level. If the interest rate does not change, yet the supply of and demand for money balances are to remain equal, then at least one of the following conditions must hold: (1) the demand for money is perfectly interest-elastic; (2) the demand for money has zero income-elasticity; (3) the change in demand for money due to a change in income is accommodated by a change in the money supply; (4) income does not change.

Conditions (1) and (2) are highly unrealistic extreme cases, and condition (3) is ruled out by the hypothesis of pure fiscal policy and a free exchange rate; so condition (4) holds: income does not rise. In brief, neither the money supply nor velocity rises.

Inland's surplus on capital account strengthens the currency on the foreign exchanges, which causes a current-account deficit of equal size, since the free exchange rate maintains balance in the overall balance of payments. In effect, the government's overabsorption of goods and services corresponds to the country's overabsorption as measured by its trade deficit, and the government finances this overabsorption by selling bonds to foreigners. In effect, the government is engaging in overabsorption covered in real terms by net imports of goods and services and in financial terms by capital imports.[23] Any stimulus to domestic

---

21. Roger W. Spencer and William P. Yohe, "The 'Crowding Out' of Private Expenditures by Fiscal Policy Actions," Federal Reserve Bank of St. Louis, *Review*, Vol. 52, October 1970, pp. 12–24.

22. For a thought-provoking hint about how a government budget deficit financed by bond issues could have an eventually deflationary influence, see Allan Meltzer and Karl Brunner, "The Place of Financial Intermediaries in the Transmission of Monetary Policy," *American Economic Review*, LIII, May 1963, p. 381.

23. Two points of terminology may require clarification. "The government's overabsorption" means government purchases of goods and services in excess of those withheld from private consumption and investment by the collection of taxes. The phrase "in effect" means this: actually, the Inland government may be acquiring its deficit-financed goods and services from Inlanders and may be selling its bonds to Inlanders. Private Inlanders, however, will be acquiring a corresponding net amount of goods and services in unbalanced trade with foreigners. Similarly, Inlanders buying bonds from their government will either resell those same bonds to foreigners or sell foreigners other bonds that, by the assumption of perfect capital mobility, are effectively identical. *In effect*, then, Inlanders are mere intermediaries in transactions whereby their government acquires goods and services from foreigners in exchange for newly issued bonds.

spending from the government budget deficit is offset by the country's deficit on current account. Because the government is in effect implementing its fiscal policy by transactions with foreigners alone, the policy has no domestic macroeconomic impact.

The degree of currency appreciation involved in the outcome just described depends on what fraction of additional Inland expenditure would go for additional net imports at a fixed exchange rate. In the extreme case of a small and open Inland economy whose domestically produced and consumed goods and services were perfectly substitutable with import and export goods, the fraction just mentioned would be unity. The additional expenditures resulting from the government budget deficit go entirely for net imports without the flexibility of the exchange rate coming into play. In this extreme case, fiscal policy could not raise Inland income even if the exchange rate were fixed.

Except in this extreme case, some appreciation of the Inland currency would be involved in the impotence of fiscal policy, which is why, given perfect capital mobility, a free exchange rate impairs the effectiveness of fiscal policy. The less interest-sensitive capital movements are and the greater the propensity to devote expenditure to net imports, however, the greater the tendency for Inland's currency to depreciate rather than appreciate, as in the "fiscal-free-zero" case.

Monetary-free-perfect. In contrast with frustrated fiscal policy, monetary policy comes into its own when the exchange rate is free and when perfect capital mobility stabilizes the interest rate against a decline caused by the open-market operation. No interest-induced decline in velocity offsets the effect of an expanded money supply. In contrast with what happens under a fixed exchange rate, the additional domestic money remains in circulation. Any attempt to dispose of it and to replenish bond portfolios depleted by the initial open-market operation causes the currency to depreciate and the current account to move into surplus. Inlanders pay for imports of bonds with net exports of goods and services. The capital-account deficit and current-account surplus continue until people are content with their bond and money portfolios again, but at a risen level of income. Holding more money and having larger incomes than before, people will probably want more bonds than before, so

that the replenishment of bond holdings will be more than complete.

In Keynesian terms, the current-account surplus represents an injection into the Inland spending stream and is a further reason why capital mobility and a free exchange rate interact to enhance the effectiveness of monetary policy. This interaction, which might be called the Sohmen effect,[24] is transitional only, occurring only during the period of adjustment to the open-market operation. Its effect in speeding both the restoration of portfolio balance and the full response of income to the open-market operation is a further reason, however, why monetary policy is more powerful in this case than in any of the others considered.

Fiscal-fixed-zero. This case is equivalent to that of a closed economy or of a free exchange rate without capital mobility except that a fixed exchange rate allows expenditure and money to leak abroad through a current-account deficit. Only in the extreme case where no part of any additional expenditure was devoted to additional net imports—a case of the economy's being closed "at the margin," so to speak—would these leakages not occur. These leakages resist the tendency of bond-financed deficit spending to raise incomes; in particular, the shrinkage of money balances restrains private absorption. The interest rate must keep rising to keep people content with rising ratios of bonds to money in their portfolios. The increased interest rate tends not only to restrain private consumption and investment in favor of bond-holding but also to restrain the holding of money relative to income, which explains why income need not fall in the face of money-supply shrinkage. (An actual fall in income and expenditure would restrain itself through reversal of the current-account deficit and leakage of money). As in the closed economy, an equilibrium outcome is hardly conceivable as long as the government deficit keeps adding to holdings of bonds which, by the hypothesis of capital immobility, cannot be sold abroad.

Fiscal policy counts as less totally ineffective in this case than in the free-perfect case because its frustration depends on leakage of money abroad through a current-account deficit caused by a temporary rise in income and expenditure. In the other case, exchange-rate appreciation *promptly* opposes the expenditure leakage of a current-account deficit to the expenditure injection of the government deficit.

Monetary-fixed-zero. With monetary policy as with fiscal policy, openness to trade in goods and services at a fixed exchange rate allows a current-account deficit to develop and drain expenditure and money out of the economy, provided that any part of additional expenditure goes for net imports. In contrast with the cases of a closed economy or free exchange rates, income need not rise and remain risen to make people desire, after all, to hold the entire money supply as expanded by the open-market operation. Instead, unwanted money can leak abroad. This leakage continues until, as a result of its restraint on absorption of goods and services, income and expenditure are no higher than originally and the current account no longer is in deficit. Monetary policy counts as less totally ineffective in this case than in the fixed-perfect case because the leakage can occur only through a current-account deficit rather than through deficits on both current and capital account.

Fiscal-fixed-perfect. Perfect capital mobility under a fixed exchange rate gives fiscal policy its greatest effectiveness and monetary policy its least effectiveness of all the cases considered. Bond-financed government deficit spending promotes an export of bonds and an inflow of money at a steady interest rate. This inflow is analogous to a feature of the closed-economy case in which fiscal policy is highly effective because of a highly interest-sensitive activation of money out of idle cash balances. In both these cases, furthermore, a stable interest rate keeps the government deficit spending from "crowding out" private spending.

In the present case, fiscal policy is effective in raising income not despite an unchanged money supply but because the money supply *does* increase. Since this increase occurs endogenously, through the balance of payments, instead of being directly imposed by policy, the policy counts as fiscal rather than monetary.

The government deficit spending and resulting rise in Inland income do tend to cause a current-account deficit and a corresponding outward drain of money. Only when income stabilizes at a new higher level, however, do this deficit and drain fully offset the inflow of money corresponding to the surplus on capital account. Meanwhile, a cumulative addition to the money supply has flowed into the country to sustain an increase in income.

One exception is conceivable—the extreme case (already noted on p. 198) in which the entire amount of any additional expenditure goes for net imports. In that case, a current-account deficit would already fully match the government deficit spending and the bond exports at an unchanged level of income. Right from the start—as distinguished from ultimately, at an increased level of income—the Inland government would in effect be doing its deficit spending entirely on foreign goods and paying with bonds. That is the extreme case in which the exchange rate would not change even if free from official pegging.

In general, when less than the full amount of additional Inland expenditure goes for net imports, there is a difference between free and fixed exchange rates. A free exchange rate appreciates to keep the overall balance of payments in equilibrium, matching a current-account deficit to a capital-account surplus and preventing any inflow of money. When the exchange rate is kept fixed, the level of income has to rise before a current-account deficit fully matches the capital-account surplus and prevents continuation of the money inflow that does occur in the meanwhile. This contrast explains why fiscal policy enjoys its maximum effectiveness in the present case.

This polar case, however instructive, could hardly correspond to reality. It supposes that until the new equilibrium of income and the overall balance of payments is reached, Inland and Outland are willing and able to finance exchange-rate pegging by transfers of international reserves. Inland expands its domestic money supply only passively, as a by-product of exchange-rate pegging, and not by domestic action. In the new equilibrium, Outland is willing to go on indefinitely financing Inland's overabsorption of goods and services by buying more and more Inland bonds. This assumption

---

24. See Egon Sohmen, *Flexible Exchange Rates*, rev. ed., pp. 112–115, 119–123, 212–216. Sohmen's sophisticated argument distinguishes between spot and forward exchange rates. See also Robert A. Mundell, "Capital Mobility and Stabilization Policy Under Fixed and Flexible Exchange Rates," *Canadian Journal of Economics and Political Science*, Vol. 29, November 1963, esp. p. 148.

of persistently perfect capital mobility is unrealistic, particularly in view of the stock rather than flow character of internationally mobile capital.[25]

Monetary-fixed-perfect. As compared with the "fixed-zero" case, capital mobility further impairs the effectiveness of monetary policy because new money leaks abroad not only on current account but also on capital account, and regardless of whether any temporary rise in income occurs. The thwarting of policy is quicker or more decisive in the present case because it is double-barreled. In either case, a fixed exchange rate allows what a free exchange rate would prevent—leakage of new money abroad through an overall payments deficit. Right from the start, in the present case, the open-market operation leaves Inlanders holding fewer bonds and more money in their portfolios than they wish to continue holding at an unchanged level of income. (They were willing to sell bonds to the monetary authority in the first place, of course, because the authority offered them a slightly higher price than the unchanged one at which they could replace their bonds with effectively identical ones from abroad.) At the fixed exchange rate, Inlanders dispose of their excess money in exchange for the bonds bought abroad. But in doing so, they become in effect mere intermediaries through which their government trades away its foreign-exchange reserves for bonds bought from foreigners, leaving no impact on domestic expenditure or the money supply. In contrast to the free-exchange-rate case, in which income adjusts upward until people do desire to hold the entire increased money supply, new money is canceled through the balance of payments—specifically, through the capital account—leaving income unaffected. If the authorities attempt to offset this leakage by still bigger open-market purchases, the outflows of capital and money will become all the larger; and the policy will remain frustrated.

Conclusion about policies. The polar cases considered suggest a couple of generalizations that are also relevant to intermediate situations in the real world. They afford insight into the problems of reconciling national monetary policies with fixed exchange rates in a world of capital mobility and help to explain, if not to justify, the frequent resort to controls to interfere with capital mobility. First, monetary policy is always more domestically effective under free than under fixed exchange rates, regardless of how interest-sensitive capital movements are; but the combination of monetary policy with free exchange rates is especially appropriate when capital movements are highly interest-sensitive. Second, fiscal policy may be more effective either under fixed or under free rates, depending on how sensitively the capital account responds to interest rates and the trade balance to the level of income. (In Table 9.1, fiscal policy contrasts with monetary policy in that the two fixed-rate cases rank neither both behind nor both ahead of the two free-rate cases.) An expansionary fiscal policy exerts two opposing influences on the balance of payments at a fixed exchange rate: by raising the home interest rate, it tends to strengthen the capital account; but by raising income, it tends to weaken the current account. If the latter effect prevails (because of relatively low capital mobility and a relatively high propensity to import), then money drains out of the economy through an overall balance-of-payments deficit, thwarting the tendency for income to rise. In that case, preventing the drain by freeing the exchange rate and allowing the currency to depreciate would preserve the effectiveness of fiscal policy. In the opposite case of a relatively strong tendency toward a capital-account surplus and a relatively weak tendency toward a current-account deficit, the appreciation of the currency at a free exchange rate would thwart the inflow of money that would occur under a fixed rate. In that case, fiscal policy and exchange-rate pegging would go appropriately together, since that combination of policies would enlist money-supply expansion through the balance of payments in support of a rise in income.

---

25. Some such considerations as these may perhaps account for Paul Wonnacott's cryptic remark "that, in a country such as Canada, with a close connection to international capital market, exchange rate flexibility probably dulls [i.e., a fixed exchange rate probably enhances the] effectiveness of fiscal policy *in the short run*" (emphasis supplied). *The Floating Canadian Dollar*, Washington: American Enterprise Institute, 1972, p. 21. Short-run conditions in which a fixed exchange rate aids fiscal policy may not endure in the long run.

CHAPTER TEN

The Terms of Trade

This chapter tries to organize and extend the scattered remarks already made about the relation between a country's exchange rate and terms of trade. This relation is of theoretical interest and also bears on policy issues, since a familiar worry about either devaluing or freeing the rate to cure a balance-of-payments deficit is that the terms of trade would worsen.

Some necessary distinctions

In considering how a change in the exchange rate affects the terms of trade, we have to distinguish among: (1) an "autonomous" change in the rate, considered apart from changes in supplies and demands in international trade and apart from changes in controls, (2) the underlying supply-and-demand changes themselves, which would make a free rate change or would put trade out of balance and eventually lead the authorities to after a pegged rate, and (3) the changes in controls that the authorities may make in response to supply-and-demand changes or in association with an exchange-rate adjustment.

We shall first inquire how an autonomous rate change, with other things equal, affects the terms of trade. In fact, of course, the authorities presumably do not make an autonomous rate change out of sheer whim but in response to conditions produced by some earlier underlying change. Here, though, we are interested in how the terms of trade move from their level of just before the exchange-rate adjustment, and the earlier change in underlying conditions is ancient history.

If a devaluation shrinks or removes a balance-of-payments deficit that was actually somehow being financed (rather than being suppressed by controls), it necessarily worsens the country's so-called gross barter terms of trade.[1] This decline in the ratio of the country's total import quantity to total export quantity is trivially obvious: the country retrenches toward living within its means.

Another familiar consequence of devaluation is that it reduces the real purchasing power of domestic factor incomes over internationally traded goods; it does so by discontinuing or reducing the subsidy that was, in effect, being paid out of the country's dwindling external reserves. This is not a change in any generally recognized terms-of-trade concept, but it is akin to a kind of terms-of-trade change and deserves mention again because it may be what people vaguely have in mind if they suppose that devaluation necessarily worsens the terms of trade.

The most usual concept is the so-called net barter or commodity terms of trade—the quantity of imports obtainable for a given quantity of exports, i.e., the ratio of an export price index to an import price index. A loose impression sometimes prevails that devaluation must necessarily worsen the terms of trade even in this sense, since it can succeed in improving the balance of payments only by making exports cheaper and imports more expensive. Devaluation lowers export prices in *foreign* currency but raises import prices in *domestic* currency. The relevant comparison, however, is between export and import prices expressed in the same currency. Which one does not matter; the relative price change is the same either way. Considering prices in the home currency is perhaps a bit more convenient.

---

1. For definitions of this and other terms-of-trade concepts, see Jacob Viner, *Studies in the Theory of International Trade*, New York: Harper & Row, 1937, pp. 319, 558ff.

Devaluation and the net barter terms

As the analysis of balance-of-payments adjustment showed, devaluation raises the home-currency prices of exports and imports alike. There is no conclusive presumption which prices rise by a larger percentage. If the Outland demand for Inland exports is highly elastic, the demand increase apparent from the Inland viewpoint is substantial; and if the Inland supply is inelastic, the upward impact is more strongly on price than quantity. On the import side, if Inland demand is highly elastic and Outland supply highly inelastic (that is, if Inlanders would cut their imports severely rather than pay substantially increased prices and if Outlanders are dependent on the Inland market and would absorb substantial price cuts in their own currency rather than suffer substantial loss of sales), then the Inland prices of imports rise only slightly. Inland's terms of trade, the ratio of export to import prices, thus improve. In the opposite circumstances, with export prices rising but little because of inelastic foreign demand and elastic home supply and import prices rising much because of inelastic home demand and elastic foreign supply, devaluation worsens Inland's terms of trade.

The effect of devaluation on these "commodity" or "net barter" terms can be described more precisely with the elasticity symbols already defined in Chapter 8. Devaluation will *improve* (and appreciation worsen) a country's terms of trade if the demand elasticities are high relative to the supply elasticities, that is, if

$$\eta_m \eta_x > e_m e_x$$

or $$\frac{\eta_x}{e_x} > \frac{e_m}{\eta_m}$$

or $$\frac{\eta_x}{e_m} > \frac{e_x}{\eta_m}$$

With these inequalities reversed, devaluation worsens the terms of trade.[2] For a country too small to influence the world-market prices of its exports and its imports, the terms remain unchanged.

Joan Robinson finds it reasonable to suppose that η_x/e_m, the ratio of export demand elasticity to import supply elasticity, is typically less than 1. In general, each country is more specialized in production than in consumption and thus tends to be a more important factor in the world market for its exports than in the world market for its imports. For this reason, the world demand for a country's exports is likely to be less elastic than the supply to it of its imports. The ratio e_x/η_m, on the other hand, is likely to exceed 1, particularly since dependence on imports for products not produced at home tends to make for a low import demand elasticity. But these observations are very casual, and the inference Mrs. Robinson draws from them that an autonomous devaluation is likely to worsen the terms of trade is no more than a weak presumption. The reverse is readily conceivable.

The relation between the effects of devaluation on the balance of payments and on the net barter terms of trade can be summarized as follows:

	Improves balance of payments	Worsens balance of payments
Improves terms of trade	Possible	Impossible
Worsens terms of trade	Possible	Possible

When the balance-of-payments reacts normally, devaluation can either improve or worsen the terms of trade; in the perverse-elasticities case, devaluation can only worsen the terms of trade. This relation may occasionally be of use in factual studies. If (but not only if) devaluation improves a country's terms of trade, the relevant demand elasticities are shown to be high enough for the balance of payments to respond normally—assuming, of course, that it is the devaluation which has changed the terms of trade and not other changes in the total situation. After the French and Finnish devaluations in the late summer of 1957, for example, each country's commodity terms of trade appeared to *improve* slightly. (See the export and import price indexes published in monthly issues of *International Financial Statistics*.)

The relation just stated is intuitively reasonable. For depreciation to affect the balance of payments normally, supply elasticities may be either high or low absolutely or in comparison with demand elasticities, except that when demand elasticities are extremely low, the corresponding supply elasticities must also be low.

(The words *high* and *low* are to be understood in the light of the formulas already presented.) In general, then, demand elasticities may be either high or low in relation to supply elasticities, and this relation is, loosely expressed, the test of how devaluation affects the terms of trade. For devaluation to affect the balance of payments perversely, demand elasticities must be low both absolutely and in relation to supply elasticities. This relation between elasticities indicates that devaluation then worsens the terms of trade.[3]

The effect of underlying real changes

Next we shall consider the second type of change listed on the first page of this chapter—not devaluation itself, but an underlying supply-and-demand change that would create a balance-of-payments deficit and sooner or later lead the authorities to devalue or that would cause a free exchange rate to depreciate spontaneously. The changes to be considered are real ones—the kind represented by shifts in Marshallian reciprocal-demand curves—rather than purely monetary changes such as Inland inflation, which currency depreciation could ideally just take account of so as to leave the real situation unchanged. One standard example of a real development unfavorable to Inland and her terms of trade is a decline in the Outland demand for her exports.[4] The price of these exports would fall in both currencies, but with nothing directly happening to import prices, so long as the exchange rate remained unchanged. If Inland tastes spontaneously shifted toward imports from Outland, import prices would rise in both currencies with nothing directly happening to export prices, given an unchanged rate. Again the original change, by itself and even apart from the appropriate exchange-rate adjustment, worsens the terms of trade. The same is true of the original change *accompanied* by the rate adjustment necessary to maintain balance-of-payments equilibrium (as can be understood by imagining the terms-of-trade changes necessary to maintain continuous supply-and-demand balance in a world of barter).

Do we have a paradox? We have seen that an unfavorable demand shift, whether or not accompanied by devaluation to avoid an external deficit, worsens the terms of trade. Yet the devaluation considered by itself, apart from

whatever made it necessary, may either improve or worsen the terms. It follows that the unfavorable demand shift, by itself, may worsen the terms of trade either more or less than is appropriate for full adjustment with a new exchange rate. This is understandable. With Inland's export supply inelastic, exchange rate unchanged, and import prices not

2. These expressions coincide with the criteria stated by Joan Robinson, "Beggar-My-Neighbor Remedies for Unemployment," *Readings in the Theory of International Trade*, Philadephia: Blakiston, 1949, pp. 399–400. For a derivation, see the appendix to this chapter.

3. Mere numerical examples of elasticities suffice to show that the terms of trade may move either way when the balance of payments reacts normally to devaluation. A proof that perverse response of the balance of payments to devaluation necessarily entails worsened terms of trade is slightly more complicated. In symbols, the proposition is that if

$$e_m e_x (\eta_m + \eta_x - 1) + \eta_m \eta_x (e_m + e_x + 1) < 0,$$

then

$$\frac{\eta_m \eta_x}{e_m e_x} < 1$$

The first expression may be rearranged into

$$\frac{\eta_m \eta_x}{e_m e_x} < \frac{1 - \eta_m - \eta_x}{e_m + e_x + 1}$$

Now, the fraction on the right side must be smaller than 1 (though not negative, since the sum of the two demand elasticities is less than 1 in the perverse case under consideration). The required conclusion follows:

$$\frac{\eta_m \eta_x}{e_m e_x}$$

is smaller than an expression itself smaller than 1.

An intuitive explanation can be brief: if devaluation reduces the ratio of total export value to total import value while raising the ratio of export quantity to import quantity, as it in any case will, then the ratio of export prices to import prices must fall.

4. Not much will be said about real developments tending to worsen the terms of trade yet *favorable* to Inland, though examples readily come to mind, such as technological progress in Inland's export industries. Of course, this progress could be an unfavorable development if Inland's exporters were competing among each other in the face of an inelastic world demand.

directly or immediately affected, a drop in Outland demand causes Inland's export prices and terms of trade to fall substantially. Devaluation, when it finally comes, raises export prices in Inland currency part way back to their initial level, especially if Outland demand is elastic; and while Inland's import prices now tend to rise, their rise is proportionately less than that of export prices if Inland's import demand were highly elastic and the Outland supply inelastic. All in all, devaluation partly— but only partly—reverses the worsening of the terms of trade caused by the initial demand shift. But if the elasticities are such that devaluation by itself worsens the terms of trade, then the initial demand shift, by itself, brings only part of the ultimate worsening. It should not be necessary explicitly to write out all conceivable cases in order to justify the conclusion that an unfavorable real change accompanied by an appropriate or free-market exchange-rate change necessarily worsens the terms of trade, that the rate change by itself may move the terms either way, and that, accordingly, the unfavorable real change by itself may either underworsen or overworsen the terms as compared with full adjustment to a new balance-of-payments equilibrium.

The reader may think he sees an exception, after all, to the proposition that the unfavorable real change, together with the appropriate or free-market exchange-rate adjustment, necessarily worsens the terms. With demand elasticities perversely low, *upward* revaluation of the Inland currency would seem to be appropriate to remedy the balance-of-payments deficit otherwise emerging; and (since devaluation in the perverse-elasticities case necessarily worsens the terms of trade) upward revaluation would improve the terms. However, the Inland currency would not appreciate under free-market pressures, so the proposition remains unimpaired for a *free-market* movement of the rate. As for an upward revaluation, it would have to be an officially contrived rather than a free-market adjustment; and, as such, it need not have awaited any unfavorable demand shift in trade. As long as the perverse-elasticities case prevails in a country's balance of payments, its authorities are not fully taking advantage of its monopoly-monopsony position in international trade (just as a monopolist in an ordinary market is not taking full advantage of his position if he is charging a price for his product so low as to leave the demand still

inelastic). With adequate information and nationalistic motivation, the authorities would have avoided the perverse-elasticities case and had the country's balance of payments in stable equilibrium in the first place, so that the appropriate contrived exchange-rate adjustment would be in the same direction as the free-market adjustment. Thus the foregoing statement is correct: the commodity or net barter terms of trade move in the same direction as an appropriate exchange-rate adjustment accompanying some initial real disturbance.

None of the conclusions reached so far establishes a case for or against flexible exchange rates as compared with the alternative price-level mechanism of equilibrating the balance of payments, since, apart from sticky prices, outstanding debts and other long-term contracts, and other frictions, both accomplish the same real adjustments—in the terms of trade as well as in other relative prices and in quantities. As far as the terms of trade are concerned, the issue is between either of these "market" mechanisms, on the one hand, and the use of controls (including *ad hoc* duties) on the other. For two reasons, exchange-rate pegging cannot maintain favorable terms of trade by itself in the face of an unfavorable event causing a balance-of-payments deficit: first, even by itself, the event worsens the terms; second, a deficit cannot be financed indefinitely.

Artificial improvement of the terms of trade

Even tariffs and other controls cannot keep the terms of trade unchanged, though they may keep them more favorable than otherwise. How they can is a familiar story. They and the currency overvaluation they support are ways for the country to exploit the less-than-perfect price elasticity of the foreign demand for its exports and of the foreign supply of its imports. In effect, they establish a selling cartel in the sale of home currency and goods and a buying cartel in the purchase of foreign currency and goods. Controls and overvaluation restrain competition among the country's individual importers and individual exporters, enable the country to act more nearly as a unit on the world market, and make it appear from the foreign point of view less eager to trade than it would be under free-market conditions. This reduced eagerness enables it to exact a better deal from foreigners.

Also familiar are the reminders that improvement in the terms of trade comes at the expense of the volume of trade, that there is therefore such a thing as going too far in improving the terms of trade and reducing the country's gains from trade, defined in any plausible way, that high long-run supply-and-demand elasticities in international trade limit opportunities for much lasting success in manipulating the terms,[5] that optimum manipulation of the terms of trade would require overcoming administrative and other practical difficulties and exercising detailed and adaptable control over individual import and export goods in the light of detailed and constantly revised knowledge of the changing and interdependent supply and demand elasticities for each, that one country's gain in this way would be other countries' loss, and that rounds of manipulation and counter-manipulation might very well result in a net loss for all concerned.

Ideally devised and administered tariffs or other controls could indeed change a country's supplies and demands in international trade so that the equilibrium exchange value of its currency would be higher than otherwise. The rate would then not even have to be pegged; it would fluctuate around the higher level under the influence of supplies and demands modified by the controls.

It is not enough to consider the terms of trade of a country as a whole. We must ask who "the country" is and what actual persons gain from their manipulation. The strengthened exchange value of the home currency as a result of controls keeps down both the quantity and home-currency prices of exports, so that export producers do not gain. Because an import surplus cannot be financed indefinitely, controls or duties (or, in their absence, haphazard rationing of scarce foreign exchange) must eventually keep imports down to what export earnings can pay for. The population thus does not enjoy its "improved" terms of trade in the form of larger quantities of imports than would otherwise be available (except in the unlikely case that the foreign demand for the country's exports is actually inelastic at free-market prices). The restricted imports must be rationed somehow, if not by

price. It is little consolation to deprived consumers to know that foreign suppliers may be receiving a lower price than they otherwise would.

If consumers in general do not enjoy more imported goods than would otherwise be available, who *does* benefit from the improved terms of trade? The answer depends on just how imports are restricted to what can be paid for. Chapter 7 considered how import quotas or licensing or foreign-exchange rationing can give a special scarcity profit to favored importers (or even, conceivably, to foreign suppliers)—unless the expense of scrambling for the scarce import privileges dissipates this profit. The government might try to suppress this abnormal profit and divert the benefit to consumers by putting price ceilings on imported goods, but this still would not make any more goods available. The consumers who benefited would be, for instance, those who were lucky enough to arrive at the stores when some cheap but scarce imports happened to be on sale. Other consumers would lose—those who would have bought the imports under free-market conditions but cannot find what they want under the regime of controls. Coupon-book rationing might be used to avoid this haphazard result, as well as to deprive importers of abnormal profits and keep down prices. The consumers who then benefit are those whose ration permits them to buy more imports than they would have bought at prices corresponding to unmanipulated terms of trade; others lose. So far as controls really do succeed in restricting imports yet keeping down their cost to consumers, money that cannot be spent on them tends to be diverted onto other goods and to raise their prices. The most plausible bright spot in the picture so far is that manipulation of the terms of trade keeps available at home some goods that would otherwise have been exported.

The government itself is the beneficiary if it

5. This is one of the main themes of Frank D. Graham, *The Theory of International Values*, Princeton, N.J.: Princeton University Press, 1948, esp. pp. 343–344.

maintains improved terms of trade by collecting high enough import duties or import-license fees. The government could use these revenues to reduce domestic taxes or to increase government services. Ideally, the terms-of-trade improvement would accrue in this way to the general population. This is presumably preferable to letting the improvement fall to not-particularly-deserving private traders in restricted imports or to particular consumers who happen to be favored by official rationing or by price control and haphazard rationing.

Actually, favorable terms of trade resulting from unconstrained supply and demand and favorable terms maintained by hampering free choice in the purchase of imports are two different things. The people of a country may gain little from knowing that their imports have been kept artifically cheap in relation to their exports or in relation to their labor and other productive factors, if they are not free to buy all they want on these "improved" terms. It is as if price controls had made shirts attractively cheap but almost unobtainable. There is so vast a difference between the price at which one *can* buy and the price at which one *cannot* buy that the two concepts ought not to bear the same label *price*. And the same could be said about the concept *terms of trade*.

Terms of trade and real income

When official devaluation or free-market depreciation replaces controls as a means of suppressing a balance-of-payments deficit, worsened terms of trade need not bring a cut in real income. To show this, Fritz Machlup suggests the analogy of a free-lance writer who has been selling fewer magazine articles than he has time to write. Now he cuts the high price that he had previously been asking; he worsens his terms of trade. Quite conceivably the reduced price so effectively promotes the sale of his articles that the writer earns more income than before and cures an actual or threatening deficit in his personal balance of payments. To change the analogy a bit, the writer may have been fully occupied even before cutting his price but spending only part of his working time writing and the rest of the time doing his own housework. Cutting the price enables him to sell more articles, take in more money, and hire a housekeeper who will free his time for writing the additional articles. He avoids a personal financial crisis and enjoys a higher standard of living than before. This happy result depends, of course, on an adequate degree of price-sensitivity in the demand for his articles. What was true for the writer may be true for a country: abandoning currency overvaluation and the controls that had been supporting overvaluation may raise real national income in any plausible sense of the term. The freer flow of trade may employ previously idle resources, and a higher degree of international specialization may permit reallocation of resources into relatively more productive lines. Accepting "worse" terms of trade may be necessary to obtain the beneficial reemployment-of-idle-resources and resource-reallocation effects.[6] Of course, none of these possibilities discredits the theoretically sound (if actually impractical) concept of controls that provide the optimal compromise between trade shrinkage and terms-of-trade improvement. But experience suggests that controls are likely to err on the tighter-than-optimal side (especially in view of high long-run supply-and-demand elasticities), and it is worth realizing why devaluation that brings worsened terms of trade is by no means necessarily harmful on balance.

The foreign debt burden

Just as controls and currency overvaluation may improve a country's terms of trade, so they may conceivably lighten its burden of foreign debt. If businessmen or the government must pay interest and repay capital sums fixed in foreign currency, keeping up the exchange value of the home currency will keep down the home-currency cost of these payments. But this will not necessarily make it easier for the country as a whole to pay its foreign obligations; overvaluation hampers exports and, unless foreign demand is actually inelastic, makes foreign-exchange earnings smaller than otherwise. The real debt burden depends more on the purchasing power of the money in which the debt is fixed than on anything that might be accomplished by manipulating the exchange rate with controls. Actually, the debt burden for a country as a whole is a vague concept. Private or governmental organizations with foreign debts to pay may indeed benefit from being able to buy foreign exchange cheap; but they benefit at the expense of others, such as exporters and some consumers of imports, who are harmed by currency overvaluation or the controls necessary to maintain it. Overvaluation does not so much lighten the debt burden as shift some of it onto other persons.

Conclusion

This chapter does not dismiss the terms of trade or foreign debt burdens as unimportant. If the foreign demand for a counry's exports falls off, if foreign supply prices of imports rise, if intensified buying competition from other countries raises the cost of imports, or if the currencies in which external debts are expressed rise in purchasing power, the country suffers. But it is not so much the changes in exchange rates in response to shifts in international supplies and demands as these shifts themselves that are responsible for changes in the terms of trade. Exchange-rate policy can neither avert the unpleasantness of unfavorable real developments nor create the benefits of

favorable developments that have not actually occurred. Insofar as terms-of-trade considerations warrant exchange-rate pegging, what they more basically warrant is the duties or other controls that make the rate-pegging feasible. This argument is well known, and subject to well-known limitations. Ideally, it calls for selective duties or controls on individual items entering into trade according to their individual supply and demand elasticities; overall control to keep up the exchange value of the home currency is only a crude substitute.

6. Fritz Machlup, "The Terms-of-Trade Effects of Devaluation upon Real Income and the Balance of Trade," *Kyklos*, **IX**, 1956, pp. 417–449, esp. 429–436.

ample, if a certain exchange-rate change makes export prices rise by 3 percent and import prices rise by 2 percent, then the terms of trade improve by $3 - 2 = 1$ percent. This formulation is approximately correct and approaches being exactly correct when the changes involved are extremely small.]

Note again that all of the above symbols refer to proportionate changes rather than to absolute magnitudes.

The elasticity symbols are the same as previously defined.

Appendix to Chapter 10: Derivation of the Formula for the Effect of Exchange-Rate Variation on the "Commodity" or "Net Barter" Terms of Trade

Symbols

m = proportionate change in quantity of imports $\left(\dfrac{\Delta M}{M}\right)$

x = proportionate change in quantity of exports $\left(\dfrac{\Delta X}{X}\right)$

p_m = proportionate change in the home-currency price of imports $\left(\dfrac{\Delta P_m}{P_m}\right)$

p_x = proportionate change in the home-currency price of exports $\left(\dfrac{\Delta P_x}{P_x}\right)$

c = proportionate change in the foreign-exchange value of the home currency $\left(\dfrac{\text{new value} - \text{old value}}{\text{old value}}\right)$. For depreciation of the home currency, c is negative; for appreciation, positive.)

$p_m + c$ = proportionate change in foreign-currency price of home imports.

$p_x + c$ = proportionate change in foreign-currency price of home exports.

$t = p_x - p_m$ = proportionate improvement $(+)$ or worsening $(-)$ in the home country's terms of trade (in the ratio of export prices to import prices). [For ex-

The expression for p_x

1. $p_x = \dfrac{x}{e_x}$ [Because $e_x = \dfrac{x}{p_x}$]

2. $x = -\eta_x (p_x + c)$ [Because $\eta_x = -\dfrac{x}{p_x + c}$]

3. $p_x = -\dfrac{\eta_x (p_x + c)}{e_x}$

[Note the tacit assumption that quantity of exports supplied equals quantity demanded and the corresponding assumption, below, for imports.]

4. $p_x = -\dfrac{\eta_x c}{e_x + \eta_x}$

The expression for p_m

5. $p_m = -\dfrac{m}{\eta_m}$ [Because $\eta_m = -\dfrac{m}{p_m}$]

6. $m = e_m (p_m + c)$ [Because $e_m = \dfrac{m}{p_m + c}$]

7. $p_m = -\dfrac{e_m (p_m + c)}{\eta_m}$

8. $p_m = -\dfrac{e_m c}{e_m + \eta_m}$

The expression for t

9. $t = p_x - p_m = -\dfrac{\eta_x c}{e_x + \eta_x} + \dfrac{e_m c}{e_m + \eta_m}$

$= c\left(\dfrac{e_m}{e_m + \eta_m} - \dfrac{\eta_x}{e_x + \eta_x}\right)$

This means that the terms of trade move in the same direction as the foreign-exchange value of the home currency when the expression in parentheses is positive. The two move in opposite direction—depreciation of the home currency would *improve* the terms of trade—when the expression in parentheses is negative.

The expression in parentheses may be rewritten:

$$10. \quad \frac{e_m\, e_x + e_m\, \eta_x - e_m\, \eta_x - \eta_m\, \eta_x}{(e_m + \eta_m)\,(e_x + \eta_x)}$$

$$= \frac{e_m e_x - \eta_m \eta_x}{(e_m + \eta_m)\,(e_x + \eta_x)}$$

Since the denominator is bound to be positive, it may be neglected. Depreciation improves or worsens the terms of trade according to whether the numerator is negative or positive.

In other words, depreciation *improves* the terms of trade if

$$\eta_m\, \eta_x > e_m e_x$$

that is, if

$$\frac{\eta_x}{e_x} > \frac{e_m}{\eta_m}$$

or if

$$\frac{\eta_x}{e_m} > \frac{e_x}{\eta_m}$$

If the inequalities are the other way around, depreciation worsens the terms of trade.

CHAPTER ELEVEN

Exchange Rates and Price Levels

Exchange rates interact not only with balances of payments and terms of trade but also with national price levels. How do price levels govern exchange rates? Is an opposite influence—from exchange rates to prices—of any real importance? Might this influence even sabotage balance-of-payments adjustment? Can the relation between exchange rates and price levels offer any evidence on demand elasticities in international trade and thus on prospects for exchange-market stability?

Purchasing-power parity

The purchasing-power-parity doctrine bears on these questions. It observes that people value currencies for what they will buy.[1] If one Inland dollar buys as much goods and services as three Outland pesos, a free exchange rate would hover in the range of 3 pesos per dollar. An actual rate that unmistakably undervalued the peso ($.25, say, instead of the equilibrium $.33) would make Outland goods and services seem like bargains to Inlanders, whose eagerness to snap them up would flood the market with dollars seeking to buy pesos. From the Outland point of view, the high Inland prices as translated into pesos at the disequilibrium rate would discourage buying. Imbalance on the foreign-exchange market would bid the rate back toward the purchasing-power-parity level. Corrective pressures would operate not merely through changes in the volume of trade in a given list of goods and services but also through changes in the composition of that list. Currency undervaluation makes the general level of prices of a country's productive factors low relative to foreign levels, enabling the country's businessmen to compete in world markets with an expanded variety of products, while restricting imports in variety as well as in volume.[2] Responses of trade that might be small in relation to a country's total imports and exports could still be large in relation to any deficit or surplus in its balance of payments.

The purchasing-power-parity doctrine in no way denies that supply and demand determine a free-market exchange rate. Rather, it points out certain properties of supply and demand and of the level toward which they tend to push the rate.

If the doctrine is correct, the theory of elasticities so low as to permit cumulative and disequilibrating fluctuations does not apply to reality. Strong pressures tend to keep the actual rate in the vicinity of a determinate equilibrium level at any given time, even though this level does change over time if the price levels of the two countries concerned move out of step with each other. The purchasing-power-parity doctrine is not merely or even chiefly a formula for actually calculating precise equilibrium rates. More basically, the doctrine describes stabilizing pressures that keep an exchange rate from oscillating chaotically and instead keep pushing it toward a definite equilibrium level, hard though it may be to specify a precise figure.

Rival doctrines

Before reviewing standard criticisms of the doctrine, we should note what other theories it was intended to answer. Chief among these was the balance-of-payments theory, which attributed market strength or weakness of a currency to strength or weakness of the country's balance of payments. During the Napoleonic Wars, explanations of the depreciation of the paper pound (or rather, as some insisted, of the appreciation of gold) commonly stressed Britain's heavy flow of outward payments. Early difficulties in pegging the Austrian crown at its newly established gold value in the 1890s were likewise blamed on a passive balance of payments. The rapid fall of the German mark after World War I was widely ascribed to heavy reparations obligations.[3] Now, no one denies that external influences working through the balance of payments can affect a country's internal monetary conditions. But it is misleading to insist on the balance-of-payments explanation of a currency's weakness on the exchange market to the *neglect* of how the domestic money supply and price level are behaving. Balance or imbalance in a country's external transactions, far from one-sidedly determining the exchange rate, is largely a *consequence* of the relation between the exchange rate and relative price levels. When Professor Cassel, after World War I, directed attention to the different degrees of inflation in different countries and to the relative purchasing powers of their currencies, he was certainly making an advance over the man-in-the-street economics of the balance-of-payments theory.

That theory was in some respects resurrected in a more sophisticated notion of the equilibrium rate of exchange. At a currency's equilibrium foreign-exchange value, a country's reserves of gold and foreign exchange might fluctuate quite a bit from month to month or even from year to year but would remain approximately stable (or approximately on a long-run growth trend) on the average over a period of at least several years. According to the doctrine, this medium-run equilibrium-on-the-average in the balance of payments must not depend on *ad hoc* trade and exchange controls or on toleration of domestic depression or inflation.[4] The International Monetary Fund seems to have been initially predicated on some such notion—that there is some pattern of fixed exchange rates which, unsupported by direct controls and by unwanted depressions and inflations, would keep a country's balance of payments in equilibrium on the average over a period of several years at least. Whenever an unmistakable disequilibrium appeared, the adherents of this doctrine could agree that the equilibrium rate pattern did not in fact prevail but would presumably argue that some other fixed rate pattern, though hard to specify, *would* satisfy their criteria. It is difficult to see what kind of observational evidence could bear on such a contention. To try to establish the concept of a durable equilibrium rate by sheer definition is to beg crucial questions. The doctrine vaguely defines the equilibrium rate of exchange

as one which, if fixed for at least several years, would make things work out just fine. But it does not tell how to calculate the rate even approximately, nor even set forth the general principles determining it. The purchasing-power-parity doctrine, incomplete though it may be, comes closer than any of its rivals to having a specific content. One need not believe any naively rigid version of the doctrine in order to recognize this merit.

Numerical calculations: a subsidiary aspect

Two versions of the parity doctrine—the absolute or positive version and the comparative version—have been put forth. Actually, these are not so much two different versions of the doctrine itself as two approaches to implement-

1. Rudiments of the purchasing-power-parity doctrine date back at least to British discussions of the depreciation of the paper pound during the Napoleonic Wars. Cf. Jacob Viner, *Studies in the Theory of International Trade*, New York: Harper & Row, 1937, pp. 124–126, 379–380; Gottfried Haberler, *A Survey of International Trade Theory*, rev. ed., Princeton, N.J.: Princeton University, International Finance Section, 1961, pp. 45–47. Gustav Cassel reformulated and vigorously urged the doctrine during and after World War I.

2. E. Victor Morgan has emphasized these and related points, though without relating them to purchasing-power parity. See "The Theory of Flexible Exchange Rates," *American Economic Review*, XLV, June 1955, esp. pp. 282–284; cf. Gustav Cassel, "International Trade, Capital Movements, and Exchanges," *Foreign Investments*, Chicago: University of Chicago Press, 1928, pp. 15–16.

3. See Viner, *op. cit.*, pp. 138–148; Howard S. Ellis, *German Monetary Theory, 1905–1933*, Cambridge, Mass.: Harvard University Press, 1937, esp. chaps. 12 and 14; and Theodor Hertzka, *Wechselcurs und Agio*, Vienna: Manz, 1894, pp. 94, 156.

4. Cf. Ragnar Nurkse, "Conditions of International Monetary Equilibrium," *Readings in the Theory of International Trade*, Philadelphia: Blakiston, 1949; and W. M. Scammell, *International Monetary Policy*, London: Macmillan, 1957, pp. 49–54.

ing its rate-calculation aspect, which, in turn, is less fundamental than the stabilizing-pressures aspect already mentioned. The absolute or positive approach tries to compare the purchasing powers of two money units at a given time. An Outland price level three times as high in pesos as the Inland price level in dollars suggests an exchange rate of roughly 3 pesos per dollar. But price levels could be compared in so straightforward and simple a way only if some one assortment of goods and services could be priced in both countries and if that assortment accurately represented the types and relative quantities of various goods and services produced and consumed in each country. In fact, no one assortment can typify economic life in both of two countries at the same time; national patterns of production and consumption differ too much.

Attempts at calculations according to the absolute or positive version of the doctrine are not unknown,[5] but their difficulty usually forces resort to the comparative version. This makeshift relates the current parity exchange rate to changes in the purchasing powers of the two currencies since some past base period when the actual exchange rate was supposedly in equilibrium. If the Inland price level has tripled over a certain period of time while the Outland price level has been multiplied by six—if Outland has suffered twice as much price inflation as Inland—then the Inland dollar should command about twice as many Outland pesos as before.

These ideas may be expressed in formulas. In them, *then* refers to the base period and *now* to the period for which the theoretical parity exchange rate is being computed. The formula for this rate in units of home currency per unit of foreign currency is:

Theoretical price of foreign currency now
= actual price of foreign currency then ×

$$\left\{ \dfrac{\dfrac{\text{home price level now}}{\text{home price level then}}}{\dfrac{\text{foreign price level now}}{\text{foreign price level then}}} \right.$$

Thus, the larger the increase in the home relative to the foreign price level, the more home cents it takes to equal one foreign peso. (Incidentally, the year for which the price index stands at 100 may be different for the two countries; all that matters is how much each country's own price index has changed between *then* and *now*.)

In calculating a time series of purchasing-power parities between two currencies, always using the same base period, the following arrangement simplifies the arithmetic:

Theoretical price of foreign currency now
= actual price of foreign currency then ×

$$\dfrac{\text{foreign price level then}}{\text{home price level then}} \times \dfrac{\text{home price level now}}{\text{foreign price level now}}$$

All of this expression except the last ratio on the right can be worked out once and for all and used repeatedly in calculating the theoretical rate for each successive month or year.

To calculate purchasing-power parities for a number of foreign currencies, all for the same current period and all based on the same past period, the most convenient arrangement is:

Theoretical price of foreign currency now
= actual price of foreign currency then ×

$$\dfrac{\text{foreign price level then}}{\text{foreign price level now}} \times \dfrac{\text{home price level now}}{\text{home price level then}}$$

The last ratio can be calculated once and used in all the calculations. Suppose price levels and base-period exchange rates are as shown in Table 11.1.

TABLE 11.1. *Price indexes and base exchange rates for illustrative purchasing-power-parity calculations*

Country	1937 price index	1975 price index	1937 Actual exchange rate in Inland cents per foreign unit
Inland	65	130	
Ruritania	40	160	75¢
Graustark	90	170	50¢
Laputa	30	570	20¢

The ratio of the 1975 price level to the 1937 price level for Inland is 130/65, or 2. Multiply-

ing this figure by the 1937 exchange rate ×
$\dfrac{1937 \text{ price-level}}{1975 \text{ price-level}}$ for each of the foreign countries yields purchasing-power parities for 1975
of 37.5¢ for Ruritania, 52.9¢ for Graustark,
and 2.1¢ for Laputa.

For exchange rates expressed not in cents
per foreign unit but in foreign units per Inland
dollar, the parity formula becomes:

Theoretical number of foreign units per dollar
now = actual number of foreign units per dollar
then ×

$$\begin{cases} \dfrac{\text{foreign price level now}}{\text{foreign price level then}} \\[2ex] \dfrac{\text{home price level now}}{\text{home price level then}} \end{cases}$$

As before, rearrangements will simplify the
arithmetic of calculating a time series of theoretical exchange rates between two currencies
and the theoretical rates of a number of foreign currencies on the home currency at the
same time for all. It is instructive to recalculate
the previous example in terms of foreign units
per dollar, noting the equivalance.

Comparative vs. absolute versions

The great convenience of the comparative approach is that it sidesteps direct comparison of
the purchasing powers of different currencies at
a given time. No standard assortment of goods
and services, representative of economic activity at home and abroad, need be devised and
priced in both places. Instead, each country's
own price index, constructed in its own way
and representative of local economic life, can
be used. All that need be compared internationally are the degrees of change in the separate
national indexes. Whatever general price indexes are available may be used—wholesale
price indexes, cost-of-living indexes, etc.—
though the same type of index should presumably be used for both countries whenever possible. If wholesale and cost-of-living indexes are
both available for both countries, two purchasing-power parities can be calculated; fairly good
agreement between the two would strengthen
confidence in them.

The convenience of the comparative version
is also the source of its weaknesses. It is only an

expedient made necessary because the theoretically more relevant absolute version is so awkward to apply statistically. The purchasing-
power-parity doctrine is primarily concerned
with the forces at work determining an exchange rate at a given time; what may have
happened in the past is, in principle, ancient
history. Yet the comparative version deals with
price-level changes over a span of time. Any
inaccuracies in the price indexes of the two
countries concerned affect the calculated parity
exchange rate. Long time spans rob price indexes of both accuracy and even clear meaning.
The assortment of goods and services whose
prices constitute each country's price level has
changed. The degree of similarity or dissimilarity between the two national economies may
also have changed, thus further vitiating any
international comparison. Moreover, the base-
period actual exchange rate necessary to comparative-version calculations may not have been
an equilibrium rate at the time, perhaps because of government pegging or other controls,
because of anticipations stemming from rapid
price changes, because of other temporary or
special influences, or because of mere accidental or random deviations from equilibrium.
A disequilibrium base-period exchange rate impairs all purchasing-power-parity calculations.
Still another complication is that transporta-

5. For example, the German Statistical Office
publishes "consumer-currency parties" (*Verbraucher-
geldparitäten*) between the mark and some 25
foreign currencies. Most of the calculations are done
twice, with the German and the foreign consumption patterns as weights; and as one might expect
(see the section on "Bias Due to Income Differentials," below), the mark appears relatively
stronger with the German weighting and the foreign
currency relatively stronger with the foreign weighting. It is noteworthy that direct price comparisons
were made in each case for one definite time only;
calculations were extended to subsequent months
and years by use of German and foreign cost-of-
living indexes. The Statistical Office also publishes
"travel-currency parities" (*Reisegeldparitäten*) between the mark and some ten foreign currencies. See
Statistisches Bundesamt, *Statistisches Jahrbuch für
die Bundesrepublik Deutschland* 1973, Stuttgart:
Kohlhammer, 1973, green pages 104–105.

tion costs and the severity of tariffs and other trade barriers may have changed since the base period. All these difficulties relate to a makeshift way of calculating parities; they do not impugn the logic of the parity doctrine itself. In particular, they do not discredit its more fundamental stabilizing-pressures aspect—the analysis of automatic correctives of overvaluation or undervaluation.

Some objections apply to the comparative and positive versions of the doctrine alike. Either involves the notion of purchasing powers of currencies over things *in general*. How does this square with the analysis of Chapter 6, which shows how exchange-rate changes affect trade by causing shifts *within* general price levels, shifts in the relative prices of internationally traded and domestic goods? If relative price changes are crucial, what becomes of the notion of general price levels and general purchasing powers? One answer is that actual shifts in sectional price levels will not be large when supply and demand elasticities in international trade are high and when small shifts suffice to modify production and consumption patterns. Consider the extreme case of infinite elasticity in Inland's demand for imports and supply of exports. Then, if Inland's currency were somehow to tend to depreciate on the foreign exchange market, the Inland price level of internationally traded goods would not rise at all. The resulting decline in consumption and increase in production by Inlanders of internationally traded goods would be "caused" by the virtual sectional-price-level shift that would *otherwise* have actually occurred. Now, to the extent that the purchasing-power-parity doctrine holds true, the supply and demand elasticities are indeed high; the tendency of exchange rates to hover around their purchasing-power-parities is incompatible with low elasticities requiring large divergent shifts in the prices of domestic and international goods.[6] The fuzziness and shiftability of the line between domestic and international goods is another reason why the concept of sectional-price-level shifts does little damage to the logic of the purchasing-power-parity doctrine. In some circumstances, moreover, the free adjustment of an exchange rate tends not so much to cause a sectional-price-level shift as to avoid one that would otherwise occur (consider, for example, the case of depression or inflation abroad). Finally, it is a matter of common observation and elementary monetary theory that sizable changes in the monetary determinants of a currency's purchasing power cause a general correspondence in the broad movements of domestic- and international-goods and prices—correspondence far overshadowing any divergence associated with exchange-rate changes. And the parity doctrine is basically a theory of monetary influences on exchange rates.[7]

Standard objections to the parity doctrine

Obscurities in the concepts of general price levels and general purchasing powers of currencies provide one set of objections to the parity doctrine in either its positive or its comparative version. Another is that transportation costs, tariffs, quotas, exchange controls, and other obstacles to trade may allow an existing exchange rate to overvalue or undervalue a currency in relation to a calculated purchasing-power parity without corrective tendencies operating through alterations in the flow of trade. For an extreme example, consider a country whose very restrictive tariffs and import quotas limit imports (and indirectly exports) to an insignificant percentage of total domestic production and consumption. At prevailing exchange rates, foreign goods might seem great bargains to the citizens of this country, yet these people might be unable to bring these bargain goods in over the wall of trade barriers, and so they could not undo the overvaluation of their home currency by eagerly demanding foreign exchange.

As for transportation costs, these merely keep the actual exchange rate from adhering closely to purchasing-power-parity but do not discredit the concept of parity itself. Similarly, because of costs related to shipping gold, an exchange rate under the international gold standard need not stay exactly at mint par—it can fluctuate within the gold points—without discrediting the concept of mint par. In permitting deviations from exact parity, transportation costs under the international gold standard and under independent paper currencies have differences in degree but not in kind. How great this difference is is a factual question about which more must be said later.

Tariffs, quotas, exchange controls, and other man-made trade barriers, if restrictive enough, could admittedly ruin the responsiveness of trade to prices and so make the parity doctrine irrelevant.[8] The doctrine is meant to deal with relatively free markets and, in fact, to help appraise their workability. Rigorous controls may make the doctrine, like many other propositions of economic theory, incomplete descriptions of reality.

A further line of objection, which critics generally (but mistakenly) regard as decisive against the purchasing-power-parity doctrine, stresses how many transactions besides those in goods and services can give rise to supply and demand on the foreign-exchange market. Loans, loan repayments, unilateral transfers of gifts, royalties, and indemnities—all can affect exchange rates without necessarily involving relative price levels. Quite true. Yet there are limits to how far out of line with relative price levels such nontrade transactions can push exchange rates. These limits (imprecise though they may be) are essentially what the parity doctrine is all about. A marked rise of a currency above purchasing-power parity, perhaps as a result of borrowing abroad, would create price incentives tending to spur imports and check exports. This, together with a direct reduction of current spending power in the lending country and an increase in the borrowing country, is how the financial aspects of a capital movement are translated into a real net inflow of goods and services into the borrowing country (or a reduction in a previous net outflow). Such responses in the flow of trade may add to the quantity of foreign exchange demanded for imports and subtract from the quantity supplied by exports so as largely to match the increased quantity supplied by the loan without calling for any great change in the exchange rate. If this translation of financial into real capital movement met temporary obstacles or delays, speculators might well realize the situation and buy and thus support the temporarily depressed currency of the lending country.

Nontrade transactions could similarly be cited, and not much less properly, as an objection to the theory of mint par under the gold standard. Many types of transactions besides gold transactions give rise to supply of and demand for gold-standard currencies without discrediting an emphasis on their relative gold contents. Gold arbitrage limits deviations of gold-standard exchange rates from their mint pars. Under free exchanges, analogously, shifts in goods-and-services trade can limit deviations from purchasing-power parity. Both mint par and purchasing-power parity are theories of

par. Neither theory insists that exchange rates stay precisely at their par values; neither stands or falls according to whether or not they do.

The analysis of nontrade transactions applies also to the further argument that not only prices but also income levels influence trade and exchange rates. This is true; yet price-induced trade readjustments can restrain large deviations from purchasing-power parity. Besides, cyclical developments affecting incomes are likely to affect prices in the same direction, so that there need be no conflict between price and income influences on exchange rates. As for long-run growth or decay of real economic activity, an economy's import demands and export supplies are likely to be affected in the same direction.

The purchasing-power-parity doctrine does not deny that "structural" changes—changes in technology and tastes apart from monetary changes—can affect both exchange rates and the terms of trade (particularly of persons

6. This is not a circular argument. It does not pretend to furnish independent support for the parity doctrine but only seeks to clear up an apparent logical inconsistency between the sectional-price-level and purchasing-power-parity analyses.

7. Per Meinich has generalized the quantity theory of Don Patinkin's *Money, Interest, and Prices* (New York: Harper & Row, 1956, 1965) to an open economy. Making *ceteris paribus* assumptions similar to Patinkin's and working on a similar level of abstraction, Meinich shows, for example, that doubling the supply of domestic money would result in a doubled price level and a doubled home-currency price of foreign exchange. See his *A Monetary General Equilibrium Theory for an International Economy,* Oslo: Universitetsforlaget, 1968.

8. Interferences severely distorting an exchange rate away from the purchasing-power-ratio of the two currencies might, however, still leave the rate powerfully related to the relative purchasing powers. Suppose, as an extreme example, that uniform *ad valorem* import duties and export subsidies create such a spread between the home and foreign prices of a country's imports and exports that the foreign-exchange value of its currency is double what it would otherwise be. Even so, a change in relative price levels could still bring about a roughly proportionate change in the distorted exchange rate, and random rate fluctuations could still be self-correcting.

heavily specialized in producing or consuming the individual commodities most directly involved).[9] However, the doctrine does describe price-induced adjustments in trade flows that will limit nonmonetary exchange-rate movements.

Bias due to income differentials

Like "structural" differences between countries, differences in per capita real incomes may keep the equilibrium exchange rate between two currencies from being the simple ratio of their purchasing powers. In a comparison of the purchasing powers of the Inland dollar and Outland peso, which country's consumption or production pattern should determine the makeup of the "basket" of goods and services to be priced in both currencies? At the pattern of exchange rates that would balance each country's overall payments, the cost of.Inland-style living is likely to be lower in Inland than in Outland. The reason is that certain goods and services figure more heavily in the Inland than in the Outland consumption pattern precisely because they *are* cheaper in relation to other goods in Inland than in Outland. At the same time and at the same equilibrium rate, and for a similar reason, the cost of an Outland assortment of goods is likely to be higher in Inland. The purchasing power of each currency seems greater when its own country's basket of goods, rather than the other's, is used in the comparison. An extreme example will make this clear: if the Inland basket contains some good or service completely unobtainable in Outland, its price in pesos in Outland is infinitely high, while its price in Inland in dollars is some definite figure only.

How is all this relevant? The commodity-arbitrage strand of purchasing-power-parity reasoning—explained in the following section —applies only to goods that do or could enter into international trade. But if the price-level comparison is made with a basket including some goods that are especially high-priced in Inland but absent from or unimportant in international trade, the comparison will make the dollar's purchasing-power parity seem weaker than its trade-balancing equilibrium rate on the peso. A country's relatively high per capita income level may cause an underestimate of its equilibrium value in this way. The reason is that in a rich country, nontradable goods—services, typically—tend to be relatively high-priced and to make the country's *general* price level too high in relation to the narrower price level of tradable goods.

But *why* are nontradable services more expensive relative to tradable goods in rich than in poor countries? A country is likely to be rich precisely because its labor and other factors of production are used more productively than those of a poor country. But its advantage in productivity is not uniform all across the board. It is greater in tradable goods, smaller in services. The reason is that technological advances in production are more likely to affect tradable goods of farm and factory than nontradable services. High-labor-content goods like custom-made articles and buildings also tend to lag behind in technological advance. Since labor of similar qualifications tends to receive the same wage in all equally attractive occupations, high-labor-content services and non-traded goods tend to be high-priced relative to traded goods in high-productivity rich countries and low-priced relative to traded goods in low-productivity poor countries. Residents of rich countries traveling abroad commonly notice this: as translated at payments-balancing exchange rates (in determining which the prices of traded goods are particularly relevant), prices in poor countries seem quite low for domestic help, haircuts, and other services.

Within each country, the prices of tradable and domestic goods and services are linked together, although not rigidly. The links operate through costs of production and values in use—through use of some goods as ingredients in making others, through the competition among different lines of production for the same labor and other productive factors, and through substitutabilities among different goods and services in consumption as well as in production. These links justify going beyond truistically comparing the price levels of traded goods only and comparing countries' general price levels instead. The links operate in different patterns of relative prices, however, within rich and poor countries. The purchasing powers of rich countries' currencies are relatively higher in buying traded goods than in buying goods and services in general, including nontraded ones. Yet the narrower purchasing powers over traded goods are the ones directly relevant to equilibrium exchange rates. Thus, purchasing-power parities calculated with general price levels seem to call for weaker exchange rates for the currencies of rich countries than the rates that would in fact equilibrate their balances of payments.

Bela Balassa tested this proposition by studying how the ratios of purchasing-power parity to actual exchange rates were associated with real per capita gross national products for a number of countries.[10] Accepting actual exchange rates as approximations to equilibrium rates, he found that the higher a country's per capita gross national product, the weaker, by and large, was its calculated parity exchange rate relative to its actual rate. This relation between a country's productivity and per capita income, on the one hand, and the ratio of the *general*-price-level calculation of its parity exchange rate to the rate that would balance its international payments, on the other hand, may, if it proves fairly dependable, serve as a way of correcting the crude parity calculation in estimating whether an existing exchange rate undervalues or overvalues a particular currency. More important, we have another example of a key point. International income differentials, like various "structural" conditions, may indeed distort a free-market exchange rate away from some calculated purchasing-power parity. Yet the rate can still be stable in the sense that price incentives will limit or reverse, rather than intensify, random fluctuations.

In case the bias in question is still not quite clear, a look at it from another angle may be helpful. Translating the money incomes of different countries at the exchange rates that balance their international payments tends to exaggerate the differences between their real incomes. The relative cheapness of nontraded goods in poor countries does not directly affect the actual or equilibrium exchange rates used in comparing money incomes, but it does affect the domestic purchasing powers of those incomes. The purchasing powers of money incomes in poor countries are larger than translation at equilibrium exchange rates suggests. The exchange rates yielding payments equilibrium are weaker for poor countries' currencies and stronger for rich countries' currencies than the rates appropriate for international income comparisons.

In describing the bias toward underestimating both the domestically relevant purchasing power of a poor country's currency and the internationally relevant purchasing power of a rich country's currency, we have been assuming the absolute or positive method of estimating

parities. Does the same bias affect what we have called the "makeshift" comparison of *changes* in the purchasing powers of currencies since some base period? Will the relative purchasing power of a rich country's currency appear to have risen too little or sunk too much, so that the comparison of price indexes, like the direct price-level comparison, would misrepresent the equilibrium exchange rate as an overvaluation of the rich country's currency? Yes, the bias would operate if, over time, the extent had widened to which the rich country enjoyed a greater productivity advantage in traded goods than in nontraded services. This may well be a realistic case because of the tendency of technical progress to continue occurring especially on the farms and in the factories of advanced countries. If this sectoral unevenness of productivity advantage had not increased, however, a comparison of purchasing-power *changes* would sidestep the bias in question.

Commodity points and commodity arbitrage

At about the time that Gustav Cassel began resurrecting purchasing-power parity, his fellow countryman, Eli Heckscher, introduced a concept that should have tempered the enthusiasm of attacks on the doctrine. Just as gold-standard exchanges fluctuate within the gold points, so paper exchanges fluctuate within "commodity points." Just as the spread of upper and lower gold points from mint par depends on the costs of shipping gold, so the spread of upper and lower commodity points from "price

---

9. A change in the terms of trade does not necessarily even require a change in purchasing-power parity. A country's export and import prices might change in opposite directions, leaving a general price level unchanged in some average sense. Cf. Haberler, *op. cit.*, p. 50.

10. "The Purchasing-Power Parity Doctrine: A Reappraisal," *Journal of Political Economy*, LXXII, December 1964, pp. 584–596.

parity" (as Heckscher called it) depends on the costs of and other obstacles to shipping commodities.[11] There are, of course, differences: tariffs and other trade barriers contribute to making the spread between commodity points larger than the spread between gold points; and commodities are not, like gold under an international gold standard, supplied and demanded at government-guaranteed prices. Commodity points are more nebulous than gold points (though even gold points are not absolutely precise), and, as considered later, price parities are partly resultants rather than purely determinants of exchange rates.

Heckscher's analysis can be improved by explicitly noting that an exchange rate has not just a single pair of upper and lower commodity points but many—one pair for each good or service that actually or potentially enters into international trade.[12] Strictly speaking, an exchange rate also has a great many purchasing-power pars: for each commodity or service marketed in both of two countries, there is some potential level of the exchange rate that equates the two local-currency prices. The purchasing-power parity may be conceived of as some sort of central tendency among these individual parities.

Commodity points and price parity suggest the concept of commodity arbitrage (in analogy to the gold arbitrage under an international standard). If, under freely fluctuating exchange rates, the price of foreign exchange sinks below the import point for a particular commodity, traders will import the commodity at a profit. Their arbitrage demand for foreign exchange will tend to buoy up the rate. If the price of foreign exchange rises above a commodity export point, traders will profitably export the commodity and help to hold down the exchange rate. If an actual exchange rate were to depart further and further from its average purchasing-power parity, it would pass the import or export points of more and more individual commodities; and arbitrage in those commodities would provide "defense in depth" against further movement of the rate.[13]

Though such arbitrage is hardly distinguishable from ordinary international trade, the arbitrage concept is useful: it fits in well with the worldwide character of supply and demand for the staples of commerce when intermeshing of national markets is not deliberately restricted. L. B. Zapoleon, writing around 1930 of factors tending to narrow international differences among prices as translated at going exchange rates, stressed such things as organized commodity exchanges; the alertness of traders and speculators in raw materials and of manufacturing consumers of raw materials; improvements in transportation; methods of preserving "perishable" foods; transmission of price quotations and conclusion of arbitrage operations by cable, telegraph, and radio; establishment of commercial information services, definite commodity standards, facilities for settling commercial disputes, and modern banking and credit systems; the "interindustry competition" arising in part from development of synthetic materials and working to tie together the prices of seemingly unrelated commodities; and the reduction in differences in consumer demand arising from local custom as education and international contacts develop. While government policies have sometimes made the worldwide interconnection of markets less tight than when Zapoleon wrote, other factors he stressed—in particular, those related to technological progress—have continued to gain in relevance. For all these reasons, neither the actual volume of international trade nor the presence or absence of trade in particular commodities indicates the full interconnection among prices on domestic and world markets. Even mere potential shipments help maintain international price alignment.[14]

Some evidence on purchasing-power parity

These considerations are qualitative only. In trying to give more definite meaning to such terms as *narrow* spread between commodity points and *close* price interconnections, we must consider whatever purchasing-power-parity calculations can be made, imperfect though they are. Of course, not even a close correspondence between actual and calculated rates would mean much if the actual rates determined the prices entering into the parity calculations much more strongly than the prices determined the rates. This question of which way the causation mainly runs will require a section to itself later on. In view of the reassurance to be offered there, the considerable correspondence found between actual and calculated rates testifies in favor of the more basic stabilizing-pressures aspect of the parity doctrine. Correspondences are all the more impressive in view of the statistical and logical difficulties, already discussed, of specifying parities precisely. Actual exchange rates of, say, half or twice parities calculated in any plausible manner are highly unusual, yet if there were nothing at all to the parity doctrine, actual exchange rates of only a few percent or of several hundred percent of calculated rates would not uncommonly appear by chance. Haberler remarks on the "great theoretical interest" attaching to the "considerable degree of correlation" observed in the movements in different countries even of retail prices, as made comparable at prevailing exchange rates. When trade is not drastically controlled and when no wars or other great structural upheavals separate the periods compared, "it would hardly be possible to find . . . a case where an equilibrium rate is, say, 15–20 percent off purchasing power par."[15] Some examples will bring to mind the kind of evidence readily available.

During the American Civil War, when the West Coast continued using the gold dollar as the unit of account while the rest of the Union used the paper greenback, the commodity price level in the East rose by roughly the same percentage as the greenback price of gold. The price level in the East roughly doubled from 1860 to 1864, while prices stayed about the same on the West Coast. A Federal employee earning 100 greenback dollars a month could buy roughly the same amount of goods, whether he spent his greenbacks in the East or exchanged them for 50 gold dollars and spent them in the West.[16] Over the whole period 1861–1879, the ratio of the actual to the purchasing-power-parity exchange rate of gold in greenbacks (these rates being practically equivalent to greenback rates on the pound sterling) fluctuated between a maximum of about 121 percent and a minimum of about 88 percent on an annual basis. The first major discrepancy, the wartime rise of the price of gold to at most about 20 percent above its calculated parity, seems remarkably small in view of its important cause, namely, the interruption of cotton exports as a source of foreign exchange. The second major (but smaller) discrepancy, the low price of gold in relation to purchasing-power parity from the end of the war through 1871, seems due to heavy foreign

al., *Sweden, Norway, Denmark, and Iceland in the World War*, New Haven, Conn.: Yale University Press, 1930; Heckscher is here more concerned with the fallacy of the purchasing-power-parity doctrine interpreted as a precise formula than with its broad truth, but his intentions do not impair the usefulness of his concepts. Cf. L. B. Zapoleon, "International and Domestic Commodities and the Theory of Prices," *Quarterly Journal of Economics*, **XLV**, May 1931, pp. 422–423.

12. Writing in apparent unawareness of Heckscher's and Cassel's work, Kurt Schmaltz makes this improvement in *Das Valutarisiko im deutschen Wirtschaftsleben und seine Bekämpfung*, Stuttgart: Poeschel, 1921, especially chaps. III, IV, and V. He explicitly draws analogies between commodity and gold parities, points, and arbitrage. He says (p. 114) that "the general purchasing power parity [is] the average parity of all commodity parities. . . ."

For later but less explicit treatments, see Gottfried von Haberler, *The Theory of International Trade*, 3d impression, London: Hodge, 1950, pp. 32, 34; and J. B. Condliffe, *The Commerce of Nations*, New York: W. W. Norton & Co., 1950, p. 307.

13. Without using the term "defense in depth," Schmaltz, *op. cit.*, does in effect expound that theory of why an actual exchange rate will not deviate far from the neighborhood of its average parity. He notes how an exchange-rate movement will lengthen or shorten, as the case may be, the lists of profitably importable and exportable commodities. He comes very close to arguing (pp. 53–55, 59–60, 63–64) that trade tends to promote a clustering together of the individual commodity parities and import and export points and the actual exchange rate, all of which tends to narrow the range of random rate fluctuations. His argument, if correct, implies that the "depth" of the "defense" is a thick clustering of many defenders, so to speak, rather than their deployment over a wide range.

14. Zapoleon, *op. cit.*, pp. 409–459. See also Condliffe, *op. cit.*, pp. 301–311, for a description of how closely world markets were integrated in the late nineteenth century, when the general extent of governmental trade restrictions was relatively slight.

15. Haberler, *The Theory of International Trade*, p. 39, and *A Survey of International Trade Theory* (1961 edition), p. 51.

16. Richard A. Lester, *Monetary Experiments*, Princeton, N.J.: Princeton University Press, 1939, pp. 169–170.

11. Eli F. Heckscher, "Växelkursens grundval vid pappersmynfot," *Ekonomisk Tidskrift*, **XVIII**, 1916, pp. 309–312; see also Heckscher, "Price Levels and Rates of Exchange: The Theory," in Heckscher *et*

purchases of U.S. government bonds and railroad securities.[17]

The currency upheavals after World War I furnish some more recent experience. In his study of the fluctuating pound-dollar rate from 1919 to 1925, W. F. Stolper found that speculation apparently played little part in determining the actual rate. Although cost-of-living indexes are generally supposed to reflect prices of internationally traded goods less strongly than do wholesale indexes, Stolper found that purchasing-power parities corresponded with actual exchange rates even better when calculated with cost-of-living indexes than when calculated with wholesale or raw-materials price indexes.[18]

Frank D. Graham calculated comparative-version purchasing-power parities in United States cents (based on wholesale price indexes and 1913 mint pars) for twelve fluctuating European currencies during the period 1919–1923. He then expressed each parity as a percentage of the actual exchange rate for that month. Discrepancies were large only for Germany, whose exchange rate during the hyper-inflation doubtless reflected anticipation of a continued fall of the mark. For the eleven other countries (Sweden, Switzerland, Spain, Norway, Netherlands, Czechoslovakia, Great Britain, Denmark, Belgium, France, and Italy), Graham gives 492 monthly "observations" in all (not a full 660 because data are missing for some countries in some months). His results may be summarized by saying that purchasing-power parity fell above or below the actual exchange rate by not more than 35 percent in 97.2 percent of the country-months; by not more than 25 percent in 91.5 percent of the country-months; by not more than 15 percent in 72.2 percent of the country-months; and by not more than 5 percent in 27.2 percent of the country-months. In conclusion, Graham pointed out "in most cases a rather close correspondence between actual exchange rates and the theoretical pars based on relative prices. . . . If we exclude Germany, the clustering around the 100% figure is marked and aberrations were apparently self corrective."[19]

J. M. Keynes made similar calculations of the purchasing-power-parity dollar rates of the pound, franc, and lira from August 1919 to June 1923. Comparing the calculated and actual rates, he reached conclusions similar to Graham's: ". . . the influences, which detract from the precision of the purchasing power parity theory have been in these cases small, on the whole, as compared with those which function in accord with it. . . . The Purchasing Power Parity Theory, even in its crude form, has worked passably well."[20]

Since the Spanish peseta fluctuated all through the 1920s (and for several decades before), it provides particularly interesting evidence. A frequency distribution of actual monthly-average dollar rates on the peseta expressed as percentages of the corresponding purchasing-power parities for 1920 through 1929 shows that in only two months of this period did this percentage fall as low as the 77.5 to 82.5 range; in only three months did it rise as high as the 117.5 to 122.5 range. The actual rate kept within the range of 12.5 percent below to 12.5 percent above purchasing-power parity in 82.5 percent of the months.[21]

The period since World War II provides additional evidence. In the 81 months from October 1950, the actual monthly average of the fluctuating rate between the U.S. and Canadian dollars kept close to a calculated purchasing-power parity. With wholesale price indexes used in the calculations, the actual rate was within 3.5 percent of parity in 96 percent of the months; with cost-of-living indexes used, the actual rate stayed this close to the calculated parity in 83 percent of the months. Even *changes* from one quarter-year to the next in actual and in parity rates were generally correlated, feebly for calculations using cost-of-living indexes but to a statistically significant degree for calculations using wholesale price indexes.[22] Any such detectable short-run correspondence at all between exchange-rate and price movements is noteworthy, especially considering the narrow range of fluctuation of the relevant variables in the Canadian experience. Consider a correlation of short-term changes in body weight and in food intake for a person whose weight and eating habits were both quite stable; given the narrowness of fluctuations actually experienced, statistical methods could hardly be expected to detect the obvious association.

Peru, Mexico, and Thailand all experienced longer or shorter periods of exchange-rate variation beginning in the late 1940s; and they too exhibit an unmistakable correspondence between price levels and exchange rates, a correspondence that seemed to improve upon adjustment or abandonment of exchange-rate pegging or upon simplification of systems of fluctuating rates.

The Peruvian and Mexican experiences cover

17. Milton Friedman and Anna Jacobson Schwartz, A *Monetary History of the United States 1867–1960*, Princeton, N.J.: Princeton University Press for the National Bureau of Economic Research, 1963, pp. 61–80, 85–86. The figures of 121 and 88 percent were read off charts on pp. 65 and 74.

Gerald Thompson ran regressions for the greenback price of gold, using, as the independent variable, annual purchasing-power parities calculated with U.S. and English, German, or French price indexes. (An English price index for half-years, as well as a monthly U.S. index, made some calculations with half-yearly figures possible also.) In general, purchasing-power parity accounted for the great bulk of change in the actual greenback-gold rate; adding estimates of capital flows as an additional independent variable improved the explanatory power only slightly. Recognizing that the wholesale price indexes he used were heavily weighted with internationally traded goods, Thompson also used figures enabling him to calculate a U.S.-English purchasing-power parity based on domestic prices only. Reassuringly, that parity differed only slightly from ones calculated for all commodities. See Gerald Richard Thompson, "Expectations and the Greenback Rate, 1862–1878," University of Virginia dissertation, 1972, especially chap. III.

18. W. F. Stolper, "Purchasing Power Parity and the Pound Sterling from 1919–1925," *Kyklos*, II, 1948, esp. pp. 244, 247–249, 251. Calculating comparative-version parities on the basis of the pre-war exchange rate and changes from prewar price levels in Britain and the United States, Stolper presents a chart of actual and theoretical exchange rates, but not the actual numbers. My calculations yield actual dollars-per-pound exchange rates for July as the following percentages of the corresponding purchasing-power-parity rates derived from United States and British cost-of-living indexes based on 1914: 113.8 in 1919, 98.8 in 1920, 101.7 in 1921, 106.0 in 1922, 99.4 in 1923, 94.8 in 1924, and 102.2 in 1925 (after the return to the gold standard). The underlying data are from League of Nations, *International Statistical Year-Book*, 1929, Geneva, 1930, pp. 241, 243, and from Board of Governors of the Federal Reserve System, *Banking and Monetary Statistics*, Washington, 1943, p. 681. For reference to a study of the dollar-sterling rate using wholesale price indexes and other explanatory variables, see pp. 320–321.

19. The term "100% figure" refers to the purchasing power parity as a percentage of the corresponding actual exchange rate. Frank D. Graham, *Exchange, Prices, and Production in Hyperinflation: Germany, 1920–1923*, Princeton, N.J.: Princeton University Press, 1930, quotations from pp. 117, 121, underlying figures from

pp. 118–120. Lester (*op. cit.*, pp. 200, 212) carried purchasing-power-parity calculations for the Danish and Norwegian kroner forward by quarter-years to 1927 and 1928 and found deviations of actual from calculated rates to be almost always within a few percent. In his study of trade and exchange rates after World War I, Jean Weiller encountered, among other difficulties, the fact that deviations from purchasing-power parity were seldom large enough to show clearly the effects of over- or undervaluation of a currency. *L'influence du change sur le commerce extérieur*, Paris: Rivière, 1929, pp. 132–133, 192).

20. J. M. Keynes, A *Tract on Monetary Reform*, London: Macmillan, 1923, pp. 99, 105.

Lloyd B. Thomas has run regressions, using monthly data for 1920 to mid-1924, to "explain" the exchange rates between the dollar and the currencies of some ten European countries, as well as Canada and Japan. His explanatory variables included the "fundamental" determinants of price-level ratio, interest-rate ratio, and ratio of indicators of income or production, as well as quarterly dummy variables and a time-trend indicator. The results generally showed close correspondence between actual exchange rates and rates predicted by the fundamental determinants, with the regression coefficients of the price-ratio terms having especially high statistical significance. Except for the French exchange rate, furthermore, the coefficient of the price-ratio term was such as to suggest that changes in that ratio tended to be associated with *less* than fully proportionate changes in the exchange rate. This fact, considered in conjunction with the purchasing-power-parity doctrine, counts as evidence against the hypothesis that speculation was tending to exaggerate exchange-rate fluctuations. See Thomas, "Behavior of Flexible Exchange Rates: Additional Tests from the Post-World War I Episode," *Southern Economic Journal*, **XL**, October 1973, pp. 167–182.

21. Derived from the actual and purchasing-power-parity rates in United States cents (computed with wholesale price indexes on a 1913 base) given in Walter H. Delaplane, "The Spanish Peseta since 1913" (unpublished dissertation), Durham, N.C.: Duke University, 1934, pp. 251–55.

22. For details on this and other postwar evidence mentioned on the following pages, see my "A Rehabilitation of Purchasing-Power Parity," *Journal of Political Economy*, Chicago: The University of Chicago Press, **LXVI**, December 1958, pp. 524–528. Copyright 1958 by The University of Chicago.

periods when exchange rates were sometimes pegged rather than continuously free to fluctuate, and pegging has been all but universal for other countries since the war. Comparison of fixed rates with purchasing-power parities, though a rather unfairly hard test of the doctrine, is not entirely irrelevant. Respectable correspondence would suggest either that relative price levels influenced what exchange rates could successfully be fixed or else that the domestic money supply in each country had to be regulated actively or passively so as to keep the home price level in line with foreign prices at prevailing exchange rates. Cassel himself noted that the rate of exchange between two gold-standard currencies must correspond to the ratio of their purchasing powers. "The purchasing power of each currency has to be regulated so as to correspond to that of gold"; only then will it be possible to keep exchange rates near their mint pars.[23]

Such considerations suggested working out purchasing-power parities for all countries whose relevant figures appeared in *International Financial Statistics*. Their actual exchange rates against the dollar in July 1957 were expressed as percentages of the calculated rates. (For countries with multiple exchange rates clustering fairly close together, the average rate was used; countries with widely divergent multiple rates had to be omitted.) For countries publishing two or more wholesale indexes, the one *least* inclusive of internationally traded goods was chosen; for countries publishing both wholesale and cost-of-living indexes, an average of the two purchasing-power parities was compared with the actual exchange rate. A prewar base period was used (1937 for most countries), making the results reflect price and exchange-rate changes over an eventful span of about 20 years. For no one of the 30 countries that could be considered was the actual exchange rate in U.S. cents as low as 80 percent or as high as 200 percent of purchasing-power parity (the Philippine figure of 197 percent appeared quite exceptional). The actual-to-parity ratio fell inside the range of 75 to 125 percent for three-fourths of the countries; two-thirds of the countries had ratios between 80 and 120 percent.[24]

Implications for exchange stability

Room hardly remains to doubt a broad correspondence between actual and purchasing-power-parity exchange rates, especially in comparison with the huge discrepancies to be expected if the doctrine were quite wrong. But "how close is close"? How rough can this correspondence be and still discredit the worry about exchange-market instability due to low demand elasticities? An instance of poor correspondence between an actual and a calculated rate might be due to one or both of two conditions—low and perhaps perversely low elasticities, or the familiar statistical inaccuracies and ambiguities and "ancient-history" element in comparative-version parity calculations.

In considering the first of these possibilities, we must remember that if an unstable-equilibrium exchange rate did exist, stable equilibriums would necessarily flank it above and below. Now suppose that an actual and a purchasing-power-parity exchange rate diverge widely: each is half or double the other. The new actual rate would be half or double the base-period rate as adjusted into a parity in accordance with any change in price levels over the span of time involved in the calculations. If the new exchange rate and the price-adjusted old exchange rate would both be workable and if we exclude the second (statistical-difficulties and "ancient-history") explanation of the discrepancy between them, then each must approximate one of three multiple-equilibrium levels explained in Chapter 8. Over the vast range of values in which the three multiple equilibriums (one unstable and two stable) might lie, they are in fact so close together that each is no less than half or no more than twice the other. Within this narrow range positions exist in which demands in international trade are inelastic enough to cause perverse operaton of the exchange market. Yet the price level of imports would only have to rise from these positions by under 100 percent in order to press buyers so sharply against their budget restraints as to convert seriously inelastic import demands into elastic demands. It seems implausible that imports (from both the home and the foreign viewpoints) would be in such extremely inelastic demand as to cause exchange-market instability and yet would bulk so large in budgets that a less than doubling of their prices would bring the budget restraint into play enough to render the demand elastic. In view of these implications, even such large discrepancies as actual exchange rates of half or double the corresponding purchasing-power parities would hardly demonstrate the existence of multiple equilibriums and perverse elasticities. In fact, discrepancies so large are not at all common. If the perverse-elasticities case is advanced to explain such discrepancies as have actually been found, the multiple equilibriums implied by the argument would have to be implausibly close together.

It follows that observed discrepancies must be explained largely in terms of the second group of difficulties: inappropriate base periods; disequilibrium exchange rates (including base-period rates), often imposed by official pegging; tariffs, quotas, and other interferences with trade, payments, and exchange rates, and changes in the stringency of these interferences; the attenuated meaningfulness of price-level comparisons over long spans of time; the crudity of some price indexes; distortion by price controls and rationing of some prices entering into indexes; distortions of relative prices by not yet digested inflations; and changes in the structure of national economies.

Most fundamentally, the comparative version of the purchasing-power-parity doctrine, used in all the calculations mentioned, is not the doctrine itself—and, in particular, is not its basic stabilizing-pressures aspect—but is, rather, a mere makeshift method of statistical application. The reasons for bothering with makeshift calculations of this sort are, first, that alternative approaches seem even worse and, second, that even the observed approximate validity of the rate-calculation aspect of the parity doctrine, despite all the statistical difficulties that might interfere, speaks well for its stabilizing-pressures aspect. Even crude calculations can indirectly provide some further "bits and pieces of evidence" on whether demand elasticities are high enough for proper operation of the international price mechanism.

The influence of exchange rates on prices

As already noted, the statistical evidence in apparent support of purchasing-power parity loses force if exchange rates *determine* rather than reflect the price levels used in the calculations. But meaningless statistics would be among the least of the troubles from causality running in this direction. Exchange-rate variations might be ineffective or even self-aggravating. Either spontaneous depreciation of a free-market exchange rate or deliberate devaluation

of a pegged rate might push up the country's general price level.[25] Any such inflationary impetus would be objectionable both in its own right and also for tending to frustrate improvement in the balance of payments. Depreciation or devaluation does not become ineffective, however, merely because the home-currency prices of internationally traded goods go up; the sectional-price-levels analysis reveals this to be a key part of the adjustment mechanism. The worry is that not only internationally traded goods but goods in general might rise in price, frustrating the necessary change in price relations.

How might this happen? As the price of foreign exchange in home currency rose, so would

23. Gustav Cassel, *Post-War Monetary Stabilization*, New York: Columbia University Press, 1928, p. 31.

24. Henry J. Gailliot compared changes in price levels and exchange rates over an even longer time span. He used the 1900–1904 and 1963–1967 averages of exchange rates and wholesale price indexes of the United States and seven other industrial countries. Despite imperfections in the data and despite changes in economic structures and policies, depressions, and two world wars that occurred in the interval of more than six decades, the calculations conformed remarkably well to the purchasing-power-parity doctrine. Gailliot also made decade-by-decade calculations. Sizable discrepancies, in the few instances when they did occur, generally tended to shrink in the subsequent period. "Purchasing Power Parity as an Explanation of Long-Term Changes in Exchange Rates," *Journal of Money, Credit and Banking*, **II**, August 1970, pp. 348–357.

25. See Lionel Robbins, *Economic Planning and International Order*, London: Macmillan, 1937, pp. 288–289; Robbins, *The Economist in the Twentieth Century*, London: Macmillan, 1954, pp. 98–101; Paul A. Samuelson, "Disparity in Postwar Exchange Rates," in Seymour E. Harris, ed., *Foreign Economic Policy for the United States*, Cambridge, Mass.: Harvard University Press, 1948, p. 404; Hubert Henderson, "The Function of Exchange Rates," *Oxford Economic Paper*, n.s., **I**, January 1949, esp. pp. 6–9; Sidney S. Alexander, "Effects of a Devaluation on a Trade Balance," IMF *Staff Papers*, **II**, April 1952; pp. 270–272, 274; and Scammell, *op. cit.*, pp. 91–92.

the prices of imports and exports. These price increases might communicate themselves to domestic goods for which internationally traded goods were direct or indirect substitutes or into which they entered as raw materials. The cost of living would rise, unleashing pressures for higher wages, which in turn would push up costs of production and further feed the price spiral. The problem would be especially serious if contracts linked wages and other payments to price indexes. This is the general line of argument, anyway, and it is not to be dismissed summarily. Later pages of this chapter will mention historical episodes in which exchange depreciation did seem to spur inflationary spirals.

Much depends on whether domestic monetary conditions permit such a spiral. Given "monetary stability"—whose meaning will become more definite as the discussion proceeds —not even the prices of import and export goods and services would rise fully in proportion to the price of foreign exchange. (They would not do so anyway, unless home import demand and export supply were totally inelastic, which monetary stability itself seems to preclude, and unless the corresponding foreign supply and demand were infinitely elastic.) In fact, some domestic prices would tend to go down. This can be shown in a preliminary way by adapting Fisher's equation of exchange so as to split up PT into prices of and transactions in domestic and internationally traded goods and services. Thus,

$$MV = P_dT_d + P_iT_i$$

Suppose that MV, the total flow of expenditure of domestic money, does not rise. Then any rise in P_i the price index of internationally traded goods, must be accompanied by a fall in one or more among T_i, T_d, and P_d. There is no strong reason to expect a fall in T_i, the total physical volume of transactions in internationally traded goods occurring on the home market and settled in home currency. Devaluation presumably increases exports and thus the total of home-market transactions in goods destined for export. On the other hand, devaluation *tends* to reduce imports. There is no need, however, for transactions in imports to fall by more than transactions in exports rise, particularly if expanded export earnings permit import purchases that had formerly been choked off by foreign-exchange rationing or import controls. T_d, the total physical volume of transactions in

home-market goods, would hardly fall, either, unless as one result of a deflation of effective demand that would also tend to lower the prices of these goods. Hence increased prices of internationally traded goods will make P_d, the price index of domestic goods, tend to fall. Incidentally, "goods" is understood to include "services"; and the domestic price level whose fall is likely is a very inclusive one, taking into account, among other things, the prices of domestic factors of production.

Our reassuring conclusion rests so far on little more than an algebraic tautology. We may have to make some qualifications that hinge on what causes and what accompanies the exchange depreciation of the home currency, a question faced in the next section of this chapter. Meanwhile, it may be helpful to recast our reasoning with closer attention to the quantity of money and to velocity or the demand for cash balances. Suppose that depreciation does raise the home-currency prices of internationally traded goods. With no compensating declines in other prices, people would begin to find their cash balances too small in relation to their transactions, incomes, and wealth at the new higher average price level. They would therefore try to enlarge their cash balances by becoming less ready to buy goods and securities and more ready to sell. As a result, prices would eventually fall until people again were satisfied with their cash balances (which add up to the existing money supply, assumed to be kept unchanged in nominal size). Though these downward price adjustments might encounter frictions and delays, causing recession and unemployment, the conclusion stands that any initial price rise provoked by exchange depreciation would be accompanied, on balance, not by further inflation but by some compensatory deflation.[26] If the initial price rises are not reversed, then prices of other goods must fall—still assuming, of course, no inflation of the money supply. Conversely, if exchange appreciation depressed some prices, others would rise in compensation.

Even with a stable money supply, however, it is abstractly conceivable that depreciation could increase total spending and the general price level. It and the accompanying rise in the prices of international goods might undermine confidence in the future purchasing power of money and so lead people to economize more than before in demanding cash balances.[27] During rapid monetary inflation, velocity does indeed rise in this way. But with a stable money supply, any effect of depreciation on velocity should prove temporary. A continuing inflation of expenditure and prices would presuppose a continuing rise in velocity and not merely a shift to a higher level (not merely, that is, a once-and-for-all shift to greater economizing on real cash balances). Yet a single upward shift in velocity is the normal response to expectations of steadily continuing price inflation: a continuing rise in velocity would presuppose expectations of continually *accelerating* inflation, which, to be well justified, would in turn presuppose a continuous acceleration of velocity. Theoretical-curiosity models of inflation proceeding by its own bootstraps must rely on utterly unrealistic and implausible assumptions about the speed and frequency with which people form and keep revising their expectations about the pace of further price inflation. Actually, when people saw that the money supply was remaining stable and that the dreaded inflation was not accelerating, they would seek to replenish their temporarily and inconveniently small holdings of real cash balances. This drop-back in velocity would stop or reverse any initial rise in the general price level. (No one argues that velocity always returns to one definite level. Innumerable factors influence it. The present argument merely denies that movements in velocity are *self*-perpetuating.) Inflationary anticipations would be especially unlikely if domestic policy were known to be aiming resolutely at domestic monetary stability.

The most plausible worry is that the domestic money supply might passively *respond* to changes in exchange rates and prices. The monetary and banking system might adjust the money supply to the "needs of trade" in the sense of the real-bills doctrine; increased money values of goods might, for instance, be thought to justify bigger bank loans to finance their production and marketing. If escalator clauses or labor-union pressure geared domestic prices or wages to import and export prices, the authorities might permit accommodating increases in the money supply to avoid unemployment. A government budget deficit might enter the picture. *Excessive devaluation* could bring a balance-of-payments surplus and the importing of money-supply and price inflation; here again, it is important to distinguish between an adjustably *pegged* exchange rate and a *free-market* rate. Whenever money-supply

variations do permit a causal chain running from exchange rates to general price levels, the situation is due not to inexorable linkages but to policy, including policy about institutional arrangements.

Aside from the matter of which way causation ran, such situations, if observed, would support rather than refute the purchasing-power-parity relation between price levels and exchange rates. They would further suggest that if the money supply had been autonomously controlled, the exchange rate would not have dominated the price level.

Skepticism about observed correlations between exchange rates and ratios of price levels might perhaps be saved by contending that the price indexes used in purchasing-power-parity calculations are made up chiefly of those prices that are governed by exchange rates, with the prices that undergo compensating opposite changes largely left out. Indeed, we should be willing to calculate purchasing-power parities with very inclusive price indexes, when available, and not solely with price indexes for internationally traded staples or even solely with wholesale price indexes. In addition, we should consider whether the structure of a country's relative prices is so subject to the alleged distortion as to rob purchasing-power-parity calculations of significance. Actually, as explained on p. 216, various links operate between the prices of domestic and international goods and

26. Richard N. Cooper has developed a similar argument. By raising the prices of imports and import-competing goods, devaluation exerts a deflationary effect similar to that of an excise tax and so withdraws purchasing power from expenditure on domestic goods. "Devaluation and Aggregate Demand in Aid-Receiving Countries," in Jagdish N. Bhagwati *et al.*, eds., *Trade, Balance of Payments and Growth*, New York: American Elsevier, 1971, pp. 355–376, especially Cooper's summary statement on p. 373.

27. Completeness requires mentioning one additional but probably minor reason: the lessened buying power of the earnings of home factors of production over internationally traded goods may make people feel too poor to afford holding as much purchasing power as before in the form of cash.

services.[28] Furthermore, the monetary factors which primarily determine a country's general price level cause a parallelism in major price movements of domestic and international goods that overshadows any divergence associated with exchange-rate changes. If some random or speculative force were to move a free exchange rate counter to the fundamentals of monetary conditions at home and abroad, a "defense in depth" through commodity arbitrage would resist that movement. The rate could hardly dominate all the many individual commodity price parities and pairs of commodity points.

A crude analogy illustrates the stronger influence of prices on free exchange rates than of rates on prices. Suppose we put a large magnet and a needle close together on a slippery table. Each will attract the other, but the final position of the two depends more on the magnet's than on the needle's initial position. Similarly, in free markets prices dominate exchanges rather than the reverse. An uncontrolled exchange rate is a sensitive and mobile price. Many goods and services have "sticky" prices. Price levels will sooner or later respond to the pressure of changed monetary conditions, but, barring monetary instability and barring an accompanying widespread use of escalator clauses, it is farfetched to suppose that flexible exchange rates will dominate even the relatively sticky prices of a great many goods and services. With an exchange rate officially and persistently pegged at a disequilibrium level, however, the story is different. Money and prices adjust to the rate.

Devaluation, controls, and prices

How devaluation or free-market depreciation of a currency affects a country's price level depends very much on the previous state of the balance of payments. If a realistic new exchange rate *replaces* trade-throttling import and exchange controls that had been maintaining an artificial equilibrium in the face of currency overvaluation, the result may be the opposite of inflationary. If controls had previously been concentrating inflationary pressures entirely on the home economy, a devaluation that permits exports and so also imports to expand need have no net inflationary effect. Devaluation may help undo previous distortions in the relations between prices and incomes at home and abroad. "Indeed, devaluation may be an essential part of the process of

change from inflation to stability."[29] Trade flows more freely. A more efficient pattern of specialization results and tends to raise what is loosely but traditionally called the total real income of the devaluing country. If the flow of expenditure and *money* income remains unchanged, the rise in *real* income implies a fall in the general price level.

The argument in this simple version assumes not only constant money expenditure[30] but also competitive conditions and full employment both before and after the devaluation. (If noncompetitive distortions and underutilization of resources had previously prevailed, it would be trivial to show that remedies involving devaluation might not necessarily raise the general price level.) The argument further assumes price and wage flexibility, so that shifts of demand away from particular goods and services will cause price reductions rather than just reduced purchases and output. (Even if prices and wages are "sticky," however, their downward *tendencies* mean that devaluation is not unequivocally inflationary.)

Perhaps the chief qualification has to do with the possibility that the trade controls associated with the earlier currency overvaluation might have been improving the country's terms of trade; sacrifice of this improvement may cost the country more in welfare or real income than it gains from an improved allocation of resources. In other words, the country's trade restrictions and currency overvaluation might have been approximately "optimal" (in the sense of the terms-of-trade argument) before devaluation and might become definitely suboptimal afterwards. It is unnecessary to repeat here the questions of Chapter 10 about how individuals benefit from "the country's" artificially favorable terms of trade, about how relevant to actual policy the concept of optimum terms is when conditions are always changing and detailed knowledge is unavailable, and about whether retaliation might not obstruct a country's efforts to benefit at the expense of its neighbors. Conceivably, anyway, devaluation and trade liberalization might reduce real national income, implying a rise in the general price level.[31]

In brief, any price-*lowering* tendency of devaluation presupposes the conditions in which trade liberalization would be beneficial in the traditional sense. But the full benefits depend on a time-consuming adjustment toward a new pattern of production more nearly in accordance with comparative advantage. In the short run, however, there is no conclusive presumption that devaluation will lower rather than raise the general price level. Whatever happens to other prices, the home-currency prices of exports will rise.[32] The possibility of a short-run upward average price movement despite the downward long-run tendency points to the moral "that there is all the more reason to take those measures early whose fruits are known to take some time to mature."[33]

Further doubt concerns just what type of price level it is that sooner or later tends downward. Declines in the prices of domestic goods and services, including labor and other factors of production, may indeed offset rises in the prices of international goods in a very comprehensive price index. But this gives no assurance that a more ordinary wholesale or retail price index will go down or even hold steady. Neither the equation-of-exchange nor the cash-balance analysis ensures that devaluation will not raise the money cost of living to consumers. A partial answer is that devaluation will necessarily tend to raise import prices only if imports had previously been free of restrictions. But if restrictions had existed to force balance-of-payments equilibrium despite an overvalued currency and are now simply replaced by an equilibrium exchange rate, imports need not become any scarcer and more expensive within the devaluing country than before. Expanded export earnings may even permit more abundant and therefore cheaper imports.

The argument, to summarize, is that removal of exchange-rate disequilibrium tends to make the use of resources more efficient and the price level lower, given stable monetary conditions. A technical characteristic of index numbers tends to obscure this result, however, in historical examples of actual devaluations. For practical reasons, most available price indexes are of the Laspeyres type, in which prices are weighted by the quantities of goods and services bought in some base period. Such an index has the bias of not being able to do justice to the "qualitative" improvements in real income, including an increase in the variety of foreign goods and services possibly made available by relaxation of trade controls. For goods and services that become available only with devaluation and trade liberalization, the predevaluation prices are in effect infinite; yet their cheapening cannot show up in the usual price index. For other goods the bias still exists, though to a slighter extent. In the as-

sortment of goods bought after devaluation, those whose prices have fallen will have gained ground relative to those whose prices have risen; yet this shift in buying patterns is not reflected in price indexes of the usual kind.[34]

The worry that depreciation tends to be inflationary implies that overvaluation of a cur-

---

28. The close price interdependence among supposedly "domestic" and supposedly "international" commodities is the main theme of Zapoleon's article, already cited; see also Condliffe, *op. cit.*, pp. 306–310.

29. Edward M. Bernstein, "Strategic Factors in Balance of Payments Adjustment," IMF *Staff Papers*, **V**, August 1956, pp. 166–168. Egon Sohmen formalizes this general line of argument in "The Effect of Devaluation on the Price Level," *Quarterly Journal of Economics*, **LXXII**, May 1958, pp. 273–283.

30. Bernstein even sees one case in which devaluation would cut expenditure relative to available output. In a country with full employment and a trade deficit financed by foreign aid or a capital inflow, devaluation means that importers pay more than before for foreign exchange and exporters receive more for their foreign-exchange earnings. Real income is transferred from importers to exporters. Also, the government receives more from importers for whatever foreign exchange is provided by foreign aid. This may help cut expenditure and bring it into balance with output plus aid. *Op. cit.*, pp. 166–167.

31. Sohmen (*loc. cit.*) explicitly recognized this possibility but judged that trade is typically restricted to far more than the optimal extent in the world of today, so that devaluation and relaxation of controls would mean moving toward rather than away from the optimum.

32. Randall Hinshaw, "Further Comment," *Quarterly Journal of Economics*, **LXXII**, November 1958, pp. 624–625.

33. Egon Sohmen, "Reply," *Quarterly Journal of Economics*, **LXXII**, November 1958, p. 629. Referring to a country suffering inflation of domestic origin, Fritz Machlup argues similarly: "If a postponement of devaluation slows down the price inflation temporarily, it may aggravate it in the longer run." *The Alignment of Foreign Exchange Rates*, New York: Praeger, 1972, p. 66.

34. Cf. Sohmen, "Reply," pp. 628–629.

rency on the exchanges can be anti-inflationary. This idea must rest on some implicit contrast between overvaluation accompanied by a current-account deficit and a devaluation which restores balance-of-payments equilibrium. Actually, the emphasis belongs on whether or not a current-account deficit exists rather than merely on the exchange rate. An excess of imports over exports can indeed have an anti-inflationary influence while it lasts. Excess imports are a net addition to the goods and services available on home markets and do tend to hold down prices. Furthermore, the sale from official reserves or from the proceeds of foreign loans or gifts of foreign exchange to pay for the excess imports can act like an open-market sale of securities, enabling the authorities to mop up some of the domestic supply of bank reserves and money. When a current-account deficit actually exists in the balance of payments, the price level is being kept down by a subsidy in effect being granted to domestic purchasers either by their own government, which is selling its accumulated external reserves at an artificially low price, or else by foreigners who may be making loans or grants. These anti-inflationary effects can last only so long as finance is available for an actual deficit.

When a country devalues to remove an actual deficit—rather than to get rid of controls that had previously been forcing an equilibrium—the resulting price increases, particularly of international-trade goods, are appropriate. They tend to discourage consumption in general by lowering the real purchasing power of the current incomes of domestic factors of production.[35] This reduction in current real incomes from the point of view of individual recipients is not necessarily a matter for regret, since continued subsidization of current consumption by drafts on foreign reserves or loans or grants would mean risking a sudden forced return to reality in some future crisis. An end to this subsidization out of the reserves does, however, mean an end to the temporary net inflow of goods and services that had corresponded to the deficit. In this respect, the impact is inflationary.

The anti-inflationary possibilities of currency overvaluation as long as an actual balance-of-payments deficit can be financed are symmetrical with the already familiar ways in which undervaluation and a surplus can be inflationary. The latter is a more realistically important possibility because the limits to a surplus in size and duration are looser than the limits to a deficit. Recognizing the inflationary impact of undervaluation does not discredit the purchasing-power-parity doctrine. On the contrary, it accords with the doctrine to say that if the exchange rate is kept from adjusting to purchasing-power parity, then purchasing-power parity must adjust to the exchange rate. That process involves expansion of the domestic money supply and could not go far without it. Furthermore, the doctrine is particularly relevant to a system of free exchange rates; yet undervaluation of a currency, together with inflationary official purchases of more and more foreign exchange, is characteristic of pegged rates.

Historical examples of exchange depreciation and domestic inflation

Historical experience, by itself, cannot settle the question whether devaluation is inflationary. Devaluation or free-market depreciation has often registered inflation due to other causes. Yet striking instances are well known, as in Europe after World War I, in which exchange depreciation appeared to push up internal prices. In Austria after late 1920, and especially in the second half of 1921 and in the summer of 1922, the price of foreign exchange appeared to lead the rise of the price level and of the bank-note circulation. Rising prices of imported materials boosted domestic production costs. Producers began estimating costs in foreign currency, adding a profit margin, and translating the result into Austrian crowns at the latest exchange rate. Retailers adopted similar practices. Escalator clauses in labor contracts reinforced the influence of exchange rates. The spiral of exchange rates dramatized the folly of holding savings in the form of rapidly melting crowns. The printing presses rolled to cover government budget deficits, which, from 1919 through 1922, amounted to half or two-thirds of government expenditures. The more the crown sank, the harder financial reform looked. Government spending, including costly food subsidies until their belated abolition in 1922, rose roughly in step with the price level. Specific taxes and the prices of goods sold by the state (such as tobacco and rail transportation) lagged, and much of the real value of income taxes vanished in the lag between assessment and collection. Superficially, at least, exchange depreciation *caused* the price increases, the deficits, and the swelling issues of paper money. This interpretation gains apparent support from the fact that exchange-rate stabilization in August 1922 preceded price-level stabilization in September. Exchange stabilization was started artificially: when supply and demand were not equal at the desired rate, an official agency made up the difference. Foreign loans and government pledges of financial probity helped restore confidence and make stabilization possible. With confidence returning, the demand to hold purchasing power in the form of crown balances revived; and to prevent this slump in velocity from causing a disastrous deflation, the Austrian National Bank issued much additional money, paying out crowns to acquire foreign exchange.[36]

The German hyperinflation that climaxed in 1923 is an even more striking example of the apparent sequence of exchange depreciation, price increases, swollen government deficits, and fresh issues of paper money. It is hardly surprising that depreciation of the mark on the foreign exchanges often ran ahead of price increases inside Germany, since the government's chief method of getting foreign exchange for reparations payments to the Allies was to have the Reichsbank print new mark notes and sell them on the exchange market.[37] Frenchmen, in the mid-1920s, could not be sure that their franc would not suffer the same virtual annihilation as the crown and mark. From 1922 (and especially from 1924) through the middle of 1926, fears of mounting inflation centered on the government's financial difficulties and showed themselves most promptly on the foreign-exchange market.

In Austria, Germany, and France alike, the stage of inflation in which exchange-rate movements loomed as a causal element came only after several years of wartime and postwar government deficits financed by the printing press. Even in the advanced stage of the German inflation, according to Bresciani-Turroni, continuing exchange depreciation and price increases were dependent on continuing currency issues. Whenever monetary expansion slackened, German merchants and industrialists had to dishoard some of their foreign exchange onto the market, and the exchange rate improved. If the government and the Reichsbank could have held the line against fresh issues of money, confidence in the mark would have returned, the abnormally low demand for real cash balances would have proved

temporary, and the mark would have strengthened. This is suggested by developments in November 1923, when the government finally mustered the energy for monetary and budget reforms.[38]

A lag of monetary expansion behind price spurts and exchange depreciation in the process of rapid inflation proves little or nothing about true causation. The sequence typically reflects anticipations. When a government has pumped out new money month after month, people may reasonably expect the money to keep on deteriorating. A lag of prices behind exchange rates proves similarly little. A currency does not lose value at one stroke or at a uniform pace with respect to all goods and services. Some prices are "stickier" than others. An unpegged exchange rate is among the least sticky of prices. It is especially prompt to reflect actual and anticipated changes in price levels and monetary conditions.[39] But this is not at all the same thing as *determining* price levels and monetary conditions.

China after 1870 provides a plausible example of the exchange rate appearing to determine the prices not only of internationally traded goods but also of services and immovable goods. China was on a silver standard.

35. For a parable illustrating why this is appropriate for correcting a deficit, see Hinshaw, *op. cit.*, esp. pp. 620–623.

36. J. van Walré de Bordes, *The Austrian Crown*, London: P. S. King & Son, Ltd., 1924, *passim*.

37. Benjamin M. Anderson, *Economics and the Public Welfare*, New York: Van Nostrand, 1949, p. 94; Graham, *op. cit.*, pp. 135–136.

38. Costanino Bresciani-Turroni, *The Economics of Inflation*, London: Allen & Unwin, 1937, pp. 398–402.

39. For supporting examples from the history of the greenbacks during the American Civil War, see two works by Wesley C. Mitchell: *A History of the Greenbacks*, Chicago: University of Chicago Press, 1903, esp. pp. 187–238, 209–210, 276–279; and *Gold, Prices, and Wages under the Greenback Standard*, Berkeley: University of California Press, 1908, esp. pp. 40–41, 251, 282.

After about 1870, when the major trading countries began to demonetize silver, the gold price of silver dropped year by year. After an intermediate rise during World War I, the price of silver resumed its downward trend in 1920. As China's silver currency depreciated in relation to gold currencies, wholesale commodity prices rose in port cities. The prices increases spread inland, affecting retail markets, the cost of living, and wage rates. Even rents, leases, and land values were gradually reappraised.[40] Yet this experience does *not* show that exchange depreciation, in itself, can push up the general domestic price level. Not only did China's currency depreciate on the exchanges; the money supply also rose. The decline in the world commodity value of silver made silver flow into China, where, if the inflow had not occurred, silver would have retained a higher purchasing power than elsewhere. Growth of the money supply is the true explanation of rising prices. Instead of showing anything about how exchange fluctuations would affect internal prices under a system of independently managed national paper currencies, the Chinese experience illustrates the repercussions on trade, money, and prices of exchange undervaluation of a currency on a commodity standard.

Summary

The purchasing-power-parity doctrine is more concretely meaningful than rival theories of exchange-rate determination. The usual *a priori* objections to the doctrine, though casting doubt on its usefulness for calculating equilibrium levels for pegged exchange rates, do not discredit its relevance to appraising the probable stability of free exchange markets. Comparisons of actual exchange rates with calculated purchasing-power parities generally show a correspondence which is particularly impressive in view of all the statistical difficulties (as distinguished from errors of principle) that might blur it.

The possibility of causation running from exchange rates to prices hardly discredits the parity doctrine. Regarding whether devaluation or depreciation is generally inflationary, certain distinctions are crucial. First, a devaluation that cures a previous actual balance-of-payments deficit and thus ends the temporary pleasures of living beyond current national resources does tend to raise prices. Devaluation to replace controls that had previously been forcing an equilibrium is quite another matter. Second is the question whether devaluation carries the foreign-exchange value of the home currency toward an equilibrium level or away from and below it. Equilibrium exchange rates and the avoidance of trade-balancing controls tend to promote resource allocation in accordance with comparative advantage and thus tend to be anti-inflationary, at least in the long run. It is pegged undervaluation of a currency, together with the resulting export surplus and money-supply expansion, that tends, in contrast, to be inflationary. Third is whether or not the domestic money supply is being kept stable (that is, either fixed or growing only in line with real economic growth). Only if monetary inflation is occurring at home or is being precariously suppressed in a psychologically inflationary atmosphere is exchange depreciation likely to feed an inflationary spiral. A policy of internal balance would leave little reason to fear domestic inflation resulting either from devaluation to an equilibrium level or from free exchange-rate fluctuations in lieu of controls to maintain balance-of-payments equilibrium. But if a country cannot or will not maintain internal balance independently and if it needs the anti-inflationary discipline of potential balance-of-payments crises at a fixed exchange rate, then, by assumption, exchange flexibility is inflationary in a permissive sense.

---

40. Condliffe, *op. cit.*, pp. 307–309, 396–397.

CHAPTER TWELVE

Speculation

This chapter reviews the grounds for perhaps the most common worry about free exchange rates—that disruptive speculation might dominate the market. The chapter tries to clarify distinctions between self-aggravating and stabilizing speculation and show what conditions are conducive to one kind or the other. In reviewing theories of speculative behavior, it considers equilibrium positions from the viewpoints of speculators themselves, the supposed natural selection of speculators, and analogies between speculation in currencies and in commodities and securities. It compares and contrasts speculation under free and under pegged exchange rates.

When a currency shows signs of depreciating or appreciating, speculators may hasten to sell or buy it and so intensify the movement. Even commodity trade might react perversely: the rise of import and export prices expressed in a currency depreciating under speculative pressure, instead of checking the country's imports and spurring its exports in the normal way, might breed expectations of further price movements and so hasten imports and retard exports. With exchange speculation and perverse responses of trade reinforcing each other, even the country's internal economic conditions might be disrupted. At least, so goes a familiar line of argument.[1]

Speculators' equilibrium

How generally applicable is that argument? To begin an appraisal, let us consider the decision-making of an individual speculator. For expository convenience, we assume that he operates in the spot rather than forward market.[2] Equi-

1. See Ragnar Nurkse, *International Currency Experience*, League of Nations, 1944, esp. pp. 210–211.

One must be careful in worrying about speculation on capital account and current account both. As Milton Friedman has pointed out (*Essays in Positive Economics*, Chicago: University of Chicago Press, 1953, p. 176n.), Nurkse seems to be asserting an arithmetical impossibility—that destabilizing transactions may occur on both accounts simultaneously in a context in which the two exhaust the balance of payments.

For lurid textbook visions of speculation under fluctuating exchange rates, see Leland J. Pritchard, *Money and Banking*, Boston: Houghton Mifflin, 1958, pp. 541–544; and Theodore Morgan, *Introduction to Economics*, 2d ed., Englewood Cliffs, N.J.: Prentice-Hall, 1956, pp. 667–668.

As Joseph A. Schumpeter remarks, currency disorders have caused weakness and fluctuations of exchange rates ever since international trade became significant enough. "And the first 'theory' that people had about them was that the exchange rate was the work of evil speculators, enemies of the country, whose activities must be put down." *Das Wesen des Geldes* (edited from manuscript by Fritz Karl Mann), Göttingen: Vandenhoeck & Ruprecht, 1970, p. 59.

2. Though choosing to frame their own discussions in terms of forward speculation, S. C. Tsiang and Egon Sohmen do note a close relation between spot and forward speculation. See Tsiang, "The Theory of Foward Exchange and Effects of Government Intervention on the Forward Exchange Market," IMF *Staff Papers*, **VII**, April 1959, p. 92; Sohmen, *Flexible Exchange Rates*, rev. ed., Chicago: University of Chicago Press, 1969, p. 92. For example, a speculative forward purchase of foreign exchange can be regarded as a speculative spot purchase coupled with a nonspeculative interest-arbitrage transaction consisting of a simultaneous spot sale and forward purchase. The present analysis of spot speculation maintains contact with much of the literature. Some important kinds of speculation do occur in the spot market, notably through *uncovered* interest arbitrage and through decisions on the timing of otherwise nonspeculative transactions. (On the latter, see "Speculation under Pegged Exchange Rates," later in this chapter.) Furthermore, the spot-market view facilitates considering the influence of home and foreign interest rates on speculators' decisions and considering the gains and losses

librium in his holdings of foreign exchange may be described by the equation

$$e = (I - i) + (r - c),$$

where

$e =$ the expected percentage rise in the home-currency price of foreign exchange (e is negative if foreign exchange is expected to decline on the market; the following discussion refers to speculative purchases of foreign exchange, but it could be modified to deal with transactions in the opposite direction.)

$I =$ the interest rate in the home country

$i =$ the interest rate abroad

$r =$ the subjective allowance for risk involved in holding foreign exchange and, in particular, for uncertainy about the expected movement in the exchange rate

$c =$ the marginal yield of intangible convenience provided by foreign-exchange assets. (For many speculators, c may be substantially zero, or, if the marginal convenience yield of domestic assets is also taken into account and c interpreted as the excess of the marginal convenience yield of foreign assets over that of domestic assets, it may even be negative.)

These symbols all refer to percentages over time spans of the same length, perhaps one month.

The equation describes the situation in which a speculator would wish neither to increase nor decrease his holdings of foreign exchange: the marginal revenue he expects on them equals the marginal cost, adjusted to allow for uncertainty. At the margin, his expected gain on foreign exchange equals the net interest cost of borrowing (or not lending) funds at home and placing them abroad (a negative cost if the interest rate were higher abroad than at home) plus risk allowance net of convenience-yield.

As a speculator's holdings of foreign exchange grow, other things being equal, the total of the terms on the right side of the equation rises. His subjective risk allowance rises as he puts more and more of his eggs into one basket. Any partially offsetting convenience-yield on foreign assets declines in accordance with the principle of diminishing returns or diminishing marginal utility. The interest rate the speculator must pay on domestic money borrowed to finance his operations may rise as lenders grow wary of his increasing debt at home and his increasing long position in foreign exchange. More realistically, we may regard I as indicating not only a rising domestic interest rate in the strict sense of the term but also a tighter rationing of credit to the speculator as his debt grows.

For speculators as a class, the risk premium, convenience-yield, and home and foreign interest rates must be taken as averages, in some sense, of the ones pertaining to individual speculators. Still, as speculative holdings of foreign exchange grow, $r - c$ moves in the same direction as for an individual speculator, and so do interest rates. Increased borrowing at home and lending abroad would tend to raise interest rates or tighten credit rationing at home and depress interest rates abroad.[3]

The behavior of e, the expected increase in the price of foreign exchange, is more uncertain. Although purchases by a single atomistic speculator would hardly influence present and expected future exchange rates, the aggregate purchases of all speculators might well do so. At the worst, speculative purchases might cause or intensify an uptrend in the rate, raising e and perhaps even raising it faster than the terms on the right side of the equation. Expectations might become self-justifying. This argument cuts two ways: if the fundamental determinants of exchange rates are stable and if speculators happen to operate in accordance with them, the idea of a normal range of rates arises and, barring sharp changes in fundamentals, becomes self-reinforcing. Random break-outs from the normal range would seem like fleeting opportunities for profit, and seizing them would tend to reverse them.[4]

Even if speculators kept adding to their *stocks* of foreign exchange for some time, this would not necessarily imply continued growth in their demand for a *flow* into these stocks per day, week, or month. Even while still adding to their stocks, they might no longer be contributing to bidding up the exchange rate (as distinguished from keeping it up). While the total on the right side of the equation continued to rise, the basis for self-justifying upward revisions in e would disappear. Unless nonspeculative fundamentals were tending to push the rate up, the flow of speculative demand would hold steady, slow down, stop, or reverse itself.

Speculative trends lacking an objective basis meet still other built-in checks. At any hour and at any price prevailing in a free, unpegged market, effective bullish and bearish sentiments are pretty evenly matched. Otherwise, the free-market price would already be different from what it in fact is.[5] The mere fact that it has been rising for some time does not mean that people quite generally expect it to be still higher an hour or a month later. A speculator can switch sides. While some new bulls may appear as a price climbs, some bulls turn into bears, and conversely as a price falls. In one respect, the rate movements caused by speculation themselves tend to weaken the incentives for more such trading. Suppose speculators expect the peso to weaken to 60 to the dollar from the current rate of 50. Their initial sales depress the peso to, say, 52 per dollar, and the knowledge that profit-taking will later add to the demand for pesos tends to support the expected future rate at, say, 58. The expected profit margin shrinks from 10 pesos per dollar to 6; some speculation tends to reduce the expected profit from further speculation.[6] Even when operating on the basis of wrong forecasts, speculators tend to move the current and expected future rates against themselves, thus limiting their expected profit and the volume of their operations.

This mention of selling pesos in hopes of buying them back cheaper reminds us obliquely that speculators may operate in forward exchange. Do our insights based on the equation $e = (I - i) + (r - c)$ still remain valid? Consider speculators buying some foreign currency forward. The dealers making contracts with them will buy spot exchange to keep their positions covered, temporarily withdrawing funds from the domestic loan market and supplying them to the foreign market. If these dealers for some reason failed to cover by buying spot exchange, the bid-up forward rate and the not yet affected spot rate would give others an opportunity for profitable arbitrage in buying spot and selling forward exchange, temporarily transferring loanable funds abroad. Interest rates would tend, though perhaps only weakly, to rise at home and fall abroad. In accordance with the principle of interest parities, this would mean a larger premium (or smaller discount) on forward exchange in relation to spot than in the absence of the specula-

from speculation. The concluding paragraphs of the present section, however, do take note of speculation in the forward market.

The analysis centered around the equation that follows in the text leans primarily on an earlier article by Tsiang, "A Theory of Foreign-Exchange Speculation under a Floating Exchange System," *Journal of Political Economy*, **LXVI**, October 1958, pp. 399–418. There, where he develops ideas of J. M. Keynes and Nicholas Kaldor, Tsiang tacitly deals with speculation in the spot market. Several modifications here require absolving him from possible errors while crediting him with the general approach.

3. The home interest rate rises under two influences: (1) the primary effect of the increased demand for loans (or reduced supply of loans) by the foreign-exchange speculators, and (2) the secondary effect of the reduced supply of loans (or increased demand for loans) by people in general, who may desire to hold increased transactions cash balances because of the increased flow of income and expenditure (perhaps at a slightly increased price level) that may have been caused by the country's export surplus corresponding to the net speculative purchases of foreign exchange.

The more flexibly the interest rate responds to these two pressures, the less induced change will occur in money income and in the price level. In the extreme case where the money supply is kept constant and where the level of the interest rate has no effect whatever on desired cash holdings, the rise of the interest rate in response to the pressure of the speculators' demands for funds will suffice to choke off an equal amount of demand for funds for investment and consumption, so that the inflationary effect on total expenditure will be absent. The overall "cost-push" effect of the rise in the prices of foreign exchange and of imports and exports would then presumably be negligible, since it would be unsupported by an increase in the total flow of spending. See Tsiang's 1958 article, pp. 406–407.

4. See Guillermo Subercaseaux, *Le Papier-Monnaie*, (trans. from Spanish), Paris: M. Giard and E. Brière, 1920, pp. 201–204. According to Subercaseaux, the idea of normality had a stabilizing influence in the markets for the Russian and Austrian paper currencies in the nineteenth century.

5. This statement abstracts from expectations of continuing price inflation or deflation at home or abroad. The next section of this chapter considers such a situation.

6. Cf. J. E. Meade, *The Balance of Payments*, London: Oxford University Press, 1951, pp. 219–220.

tion and the resulting arbitrage. The relation between spot and forward rates would move in a way unfavorable to further speculation. (In oversimplified terms, the speculators would bid the forward rate against themselves.) These movements correspond, loosely, to the rise in $I - i$ in the earlier analysis. As for c, the marginal convenience-yield, it does not accrue to the speculators themselves when they are not holding spot exchange; but it does accrue either to the dealers who acquire spot exchange to cover their positions as counterparties in forward contracts with speculators or to others who acquire it in arbitrage. Their c presumably does go down as their holdings go up, affecting their willingness to make contracts and thus affecting the spread between forward and spot exchange rates much as a rise in home and fall in foreign interest rates do. The risk premium r rises on the more-eggs-in-one-basket principle as speculators go longer in foreign exchange, regardless of whether they do so by forward or spot transactions.

On the left side of the equation, the expected rise in the price of foreign exchange likewise presumably behaves in pretty much the same way, regardless of whether speculators operate spot or forward. Current rate movements still affect and respond to expectations. The currently prevailing spot and forward rates move closely together, any spread conforming to the interest-parities relation, in turn affected by changes equally taken into account in the analysis of pure spot speculation (changes, that is, in I, i, and c).

The self-limiting aspect of speculators' bidding rates against themselves also still holds good when speculators operate by buying forward and later, after taking delivery of foreign exchange under their maturing contracts, selling spot. (Typically, the speculators will not take actual delivery and then resell the exchange in a separate transaction; they will simply receive or pay the net amount of their gain or loss. The effect, though, is the same.) Whether we suppose speculation to take place only in the spot market or in the forward market also thus leaves the analysis the same in its essentials.

Self-aggravating speculation

Having justified glossing over the distinction between spot and forward speculation, we return to search for further ways in which ex-

change speculation might conceivably be self-aggravating rather than self-limiting. Bear speculation on the home currency (bull speculation on foreign exchange) could conceivably contribute to continuing inflation of domestic prices and money incomes. Far from restraining itself as it ran counter to the fundamental conditions governing the relative values of currencies, speculation might determine these fundamentals. Conceivably the rise in the price of foreign exchange might discourage any *actual* capital outflow in the aggregate; speculators on the two sides of the market might just be dealing with each other. Any actual net purchases of foreign exchange by speculators as a group must be matched by sales by nonspeculators; any actual net outflow of capital must be matched by an export surplus in goods and services; sheer arithmetic demands this. Under free exchange rates, as Chapter 6 has shown, the combination of capital outflow, exchange depreciation, and current-account surplus has an expansionary tendency in the home economy.

The process has two interrelated aspects. First, the rise in the price of foreign exchange may exert an upward "cost push" on domestic prices and wages by way of increased home-currency prices of import and export goods (perhaps including both raw materials and cost-of-living items). The export surplus means that real goods and services in the aggregate have become scarcer than before at home. Second, the rise in exports or fall in imports may have an expansionary "multiplier" effect on home incomes. The velocity of money rises. The persons who reduce their demands for domestic cash balances relative to income and expenditure are the speculators themselves or the persons induced to cut down their cash balances by a rise in interest rates or by expectations of inflation. So far as the factors considered here are concerned, the process will not level off until speculators become content with their holdings of domestic and foreign money. The inflationary process is essentially the same as one due to a widespread desire to shift from cash into real goods. In fact, we might well think of speculators as shifting into the real goods corresponding to the country's export surplus and then selling these goods to the foreigners for foreign money. This fiction illuminates the principles involved.

Merely describing these effects raises doubts about their strength. Desired shifts from domestic cash balances into foreign exchange must ordinarily be small in relation to the total domestic money supply and the flow of domestic income and expenditure. Except in a time of rapid inflation, the foreign-exchange speculators would be only a minority of the population. Even the speculators cannot reduce their domestic cash balances below zero, and there is also a fuzzy limit, at least, to how much they might borrow from the cash balances of others. Not only their ability but also their desire to keep on exchanging domestic for foreign money weakens as their speculative positions grow, as our earlier analysis suggests. Conceivably, self-justifying bear speculation on the home currency might hinge on expectations that kept an inflationary rise in velocity. going—it is often easy to obscure economic principles by an *ad hoc* appeal to expectations —but whether the expectations can persist in the absence of any basis more objective than their own consequences is open to the doubts mentioned in Chapter 11.

The only really plausible ways that speculation might remain cumulatively self-reinforcing all involve monetary expansion. The central bank might create fresh domestic monetary reserves to rescue commercial banks beset by unexpectedly large adverse clearing balances in the unstable economic climate or beset by a run of depositors anxious to have actual currency immediately available for buying foreign exchange or other assets. The initial upward push on the price level and spending stream might cause monetary expansion through a government budget deficit or a banking policy compliant with the supposed "needs of trade." An economy whose money supply thus responded passively, continually "ratifying" or "supporting" otherwise limited upward pushes on prices, would be unstable even without international contacts. Foreign exchange is just one more asset persons may fly into when they fear for the value of the home currency; it is just one among many potential triggers of disturbance. The lack of positive control over the money supply, rather than speculation in particular, is what calls for a remedy.

Even in this most unfavorable case of continuing monetary inflation, speculation need not drive exchange rates cumulatively out of contact with the purchasing-power ratio of home and foreign money. In a severe and continuing inflation, interest rates include a "price premium": lenders insist on and borrowers will pay enough to cover the expected rise in the price level. The high money cost of borrowing to finance speculative purchases of foreign exchange and the alternative opportunity to preserve the real value of one's capital by making loans at interest rates high enough to compensate for the expected rise in prices tend to restrain the speculative demand for foreign exchange. (This is another implication of the equation $e = I - i + r - c$.) If people should come to expect an accelerated rise in the prices of domestic goods and foreign exchange alike, then the domestic interest rate is likely to incorporate a still larger price premium, and what would otherwise be a stimulus to intensified demands for foreign exchange again is counterbalanced.[7]

Speculation and welfare

More will be said later about speculation that is less violent but still destabilizing. Meanwhile, the foregoing discussion should not suggest that speculation is characteristically harmful and that the only apology for it concerns possible limits to its extent. On the contrary, speculation at its best can contribute to welfare, understood in any common-sense way. Suppose that the market rate on the Ruritanian crown, free from official intervention, keeps Ruritania's external transactions on current account always in balance in the absence of private borrowing, lending, and speculation. Now the foreign demand for Ruritanian products slumps. The crown weakens from an old rate of 5 to a new rate of 6 per dollar, restricting imports and supporting exports. At home, imports become scarcer and more expensive in relation to wages and other factor earnings. Assuming omniscience, we further suppose that the slump in foreign demand, the worsened trading opportunities, the crown's depreciation, and the corresponding scarcity of foreign-trade goods inside Ruritania all are temporary: the situation is fated to right itself again in six months. If so, it would be a particular hardship for the Ruritanians to concentrate their neces-

7. Tsiang considers this point quite important. *Journal of Political Economy*, October 1958, p. 412.

sary frugality with foreign-trade goods solely during these six months. They would benefit if they could somehow transfer some foreign-trade goods from the future, when they will be relatively abundant again and of correspondingly low marginal utility, to the present time of scarcity and high marginal utility. Speculators might in effect give Ruritania a loan of foreign exchange to cover a temporary excess of imports over exports by seizing the opportunity to buy crowns during their temporary depreciation and holding them for resale after their recovery. The crown would weaken less than otherwise. (The subsequent recovery would also be slightly weaker, for if speculation were to restrain the dip and leave everything else unaffected, it would amount to a never-withdrawn capital inflow into Ruritania. The deterioration of Ruritania's fundamental trading opportunities, even though temporary, requires the exchange value of the crown, averaged over the fullness of time, to be very slightly below what it otherwise would have been.)

To vary the example, consider a permanent deterioration of Ruritania's international trading opportunities. In time, the Ruritanians might be able to readjust without undue pain by directly and indirectly shifting factors of production out of the hardest-hit export industries into other export industries and into import-competing industries. In the short run, however, factors are less mobile and supplies and demands less elastic, and continuous balance in Ruritania's international current account might require massive price changes. Without a cushion of speculation, the crown might sink to 8 per dollar from the initial rate of 5. Later, as time eased readjustments in production and consumption, the rate might recover to 6. Though trading opportunities have worsened permanently, there is, as in the first example, an interval of particular scarcity of foreign-trade goods, corresponding to the temporary depreciation of the crown even below its new long-run-equilibrium value. As before, speculators who profitably bought crowns during their deepest dip and sold them after their recovery would be not only smoothing out rate fluctuations but also, in effect, granting Ruritania a short-term loan to cover a temporary import surplus. They would be transferring foreign-trade goods from the future to the immediate period of relative scarcity and high marginal utility.

In stabilizing the crown against the later-to-be-reversed part of its depreciation, the specu-

lators are helping to cushion adjustment to the underlying deterioration of opportunities. Two extremes are conceivable. One is no cushioning at all: Ruritania's exports must pay for its imports at all times; and at first, a painful curtailment of imports and drive to export is necessary under the prod of a particularly severe depreciation of the crown. The opposite extreme is complete cushioning: the prolonged financing of a Ruritanian import surplus either by (mistakenly excessive) speculation or, until its international reserves ran out, by an official agency. Eventually, a crisis and sharp depreciation would probably occur after all. The best degree of cushioning and best pace of adjustment is somewhere in between. Difficult to define though this optimum admittedly is, it is a standard in comparison with which official exchange-rate management tends to make adjustment sometimes too slow and sometimes too fast: sometimes the bulk of the reserves goes to prop up an uneconomic rate; at other times, a sharp devaluation occurs.[8]

In a third example, emerging conditions will eventually cut the foreign demand for Ruritanian exports or worsen Ruritania's export-supply capacity. Because these trends are gradual and because of long-term contracts and other elements of inertia, however, the pattern of international trade would not change much for a while. If there were no speculation and if current-account transactions alone held sway on the foreign-exchange market, the rate would remain at about its old level. Only later, as the changing fundamental conditions took effect, would the crown depreciate. But if speculators foresaw these developments, they would sell crowns at once (perhaps by forward contracts), hoping to buy them back later more cheaply. The hastened depreciation would begin stimulating exports and retarding imports at once, and a commodity export surplus would match the speculative capital outflow. Later, as speculators moved capital back to collect their profits, the country could have an import surplus. In effect, the speculators would lead Ruritanians to postpone some consumption from a time when foreign-trade goods were still relatively abundant and of low marginal utility to the later period of relative scarcity and high marginal utility. Price incentives for reallocating resources would also come earlier. Speculation would smooth the adjustment to worsened trading opportunities by causing it to begin sooner. The process is roughly similar to what happens when speculators foresee a poor grain harvest and, by bidding up the price in the present, induce consumers to stint their present consumption of relatively low-marginal-utility grain so that it will be available as high-marginal-utility grain in the future. As this comparison shows, speculation need not always *resist* price or exchange-rate movements in order to be appropriate (in the light of plausible value judgments); sometimes it is appropriate for future developments to cast their shadows before them as hastened price signals.

A fourth example supposes a domestic price inflation not significantly related to international transactions or foreign-exchange speculation and not generally expected to keep getting worse. Without speculation, elements of inertia in the supply of and demand for foreign exchange (such as existing contracts for import and export transactions) might delay a full depreciation of the crown in line with its diminished purchasing power. Meanwhile, there would be a resulting distortion, unrelated to real changes in supplies and demands, in the relative prices of import and export goods, on the one hand, and domestic goods and factors of production on the other hand. Speculators would be helping prevent this tempoary distortion if they foresaw the ultimate effects of the inflation on the exchange rate and sold crowns.[9]

Speculation has benefited Ruritania in all four examples. From the viewpoint of the rest of the world, the first two examples involve temporary cheapness of Ruritanian goods. Speculative stabilization of the exchange rate would stretch out over time not only the Ruritanians' necessary economies in the consumption of foreign-trade goods but also the foreigners' enjoyment of their temporarily improved terms of trade with Ruritania. In the third example, from the foreign viewpoint, also, speculation both advances the adjustment in time and stretches it out. Even when the adjustment is to improved conditions, this stretching-out might be an advantage: a benefit presumably means more if it can be accepted at an orderly pace than if it must be accepted suddenly. In the fourth example, speculation would overcome temporary distortions of relative prices from both the Ruritanian and foreign points of view. In all four examples, then, the gains do not go to Ruritanians only at the expense of foreigners.

These examples suggest an analogy between speculation and arbitrage. Arbitrage moves something from a submarket or place where it

is less valuable to a submarket or place where it is more valuable. Speculation based on a correct diagnosis of fundamental supplies and demands is arbitrage in time. Speculators "move" foreign exchange (and, ultimately, the foreign-trade goods corresponding to it) from a point in time of lesser value to a point in time of greater value. The source of speculators' profits is akin to that of arbitrageurs' profits, or, for that matter, of truck drivers' wages: speculators, arbitrageurs, and truck drivers alike share in the values that they almost literally create by transforming lower-valued into higher-valued goods through a relocation .in time or space.[10] The difference between arbitrage and speculation is the uncertainty connected with dealing at different points in time. The arbitrageur *knows* the prices ruling in the markets both where he buys and where he sells; the speculator must guess the future. Furthermore, the time sequence of the speculator's markets gives rise to notions of trends, which may sometimes help and sometimes hinder forming sound judgments about future prices. This difference relates to how generally speculators succeed in buying cheap and selling dear but does not detract from the similarity between the values created by arbitrage and by speculation when speculators *do* succeed.

Mistaken and excessive speculation

Since speculators sometimes fail, we should modify our earlier examples to consider speculation in the wrong direction. In the first two, speculators were supporting the Ruritanian

8. On the question of the optimum pace of adjustment and optimum cushioning, see Milton Friedman, *op. cit.*, pp. 184–186.

9. Cf. Tsiang, *Journal of Political Economy*, October 1958, p. 414.

10. This statement refers to the aggregate of all speculative profits and losses. Qualifications will be made later about profits that some speculators make at the expense of less competent speculators. Incidentally, nothing said here implies a judgment about how ethically entitled to their incomes speculators, arbitrageurs, or truck drivers may be.

crown during what would otherwise have been temporary or temporarily excessive weakness. Mistaken speculation, by contrast, would mean interpreting the early depreciation as a sign of still more to come and selling the crown and depressing it further. Later, when the speculators finally realized their mistake and bought back crowns (sold foreign exchange) to cut their losses, they would make the crown recover, temporarily, still further than it would otherwise have done. By moving some of the foreign exchange available to nonspeculative traders from the earlier period of its greater to the later period of its lesser value, the speculators would in effect have been moving the foreign-trade goods available to the Ruritanian economy from a time of relative scarcity to a time of relative abundance. Such speculation, based on a wrong forecast even of the *direction* in which nonspeculative supply and demand would move the rate, has aptly been named "perverse."[11] Transforming high-marginal-utility goods into low-marginal-utility goods impairs total welfare, on any plausible interpretation of welfare.

Even so, it is not certain that nonspeculators in general are harmed. If speculators have no monopsonistic or monopolistic influence over the prices at which they buy and sell, the losses of mistaken speculators may well exceed the aggregate loss. If the speculators bear their own losses and do not impose them on other persons by bankruptcy or default, a net gain may conceivably remain for nonspeculators as a group.[12] When the speculators buy, they raise the price against themselves, benefiting the nonspeculative sellers, and when they sell, they lower the price against themselves, benefiting the nonspeculative buyers. It is true that nonspeculative buyers are harmed the first time and nonspeculative sellers the second. On the whole, however, nonspeculators' gains presumably exceed nonspeculators' losses each time. When the speculators buy and raise the price, the nonspeculative sellers enjoy their gain on a correspondingly increased volume of sales, while the nonspeculative buyers suffer their loss on a reduced volume of purchases; when the speculators sell and lower the price, the nonspeculative buyers enjoy their gain on an increased volume of purchases, while the nonspeculative sellers suffer their losses on a reduced volume of sales. In other words, when speculators are buying, the losses imposed on nonspeculative buyers are matched by the gains of the nonspeculators who sell to them, and

there remains the net gain on the nonspeculators' sales to the speculators. When speculators are selling, the losses imposed on nonspeculative sellers are matched by the gains of the nonspeculators who buy from them, and there remains the net gain on the nonspeculators' purchases from the speculators.

It hardly seems worthwhile to press this point by a fuller analysis, complete with diagrams. The argument would still suffer from interpersonal comparisons and the other familiar defects of the crudest (but most usable) version of the concepts of consumers' and suppliers' surplus. The argument does not distinguish between Ruritanians and foreigners, and there is no obvious ground for ruling out the possibility that all or more than all of the aggregate gain of nonspeculators might go to the foreigners. Furthermore, any manageably simple version of the argument assumes that the nonspeculative supply and demand schedules are definitely given at any particular time. In fact, however, any price change shifts at least one of the schedules. Even for any ordinary competitively traded commodity, the supply and demand schedules and the price all are interdependent; this is notably true of foreign exchange. Finally, the worsened instability of exchange rates caused by perverse speculation may cause damage offsetting any benefit of the kind just described. Thus we do not have an actual proof that even perverse speculation benefits nonspeculators. But we do have reason to question any contrary idea that perverse speculation necessarily harms nonspeculators on the whole. A net benefit is easily conceivable on the basis of an interpersonal comparison of gains and losses that, while crude, at least has no special bias contrived to yield this result.

Besides correct speculation and perverse speculation, "grossly excessive" speculation should be mentioned. Instead of perversely intensifying a merely temporary depreciation and instead of appropriately hastening a depreciation called for by changing fundamentals, speculation might, for a while, stabilize exchange rates too much. The price incentives for necessary readjustments of production and consumption would be delayed. Eventually speculators would see their error and rush to undo their positions, temporarily driving the rate to the other side of its new equilibrium level. Too much stability in the short run would have been bought at the cost of too much instability later on. In effect, speculators would have transported foreign-trade goods in time, keeping them unduly abundant in the present at the cost of undue scarcity for a while later on. (Even so, the foregoing considerations still apply: the speculators might conceivably bear all of or more than all of the aggregate loss themselves.)

Speculative exchange-rate stabilization might be considered excessive for still another reason. Exchange-rate flexibility is a form of price flexibility, which has a role to play in continually adjusting production and consumption to changing circumstances. Even seasonal fluctuations may have their value. For a clear-cut example, suppose that all of Ruritania's imports and exports consist of nonstorable services—tourism, perhaps. The factors of production used in producing tourist services are typified by resort hotels, specially trained personnel having little opportunity for slack-season employment at acceptable wages, and the like. When tourist services are not bought, the factors specialized in producing them go to waste. From December to March, demand is weak for tourism in wintry Ruritania but strong for tourism in summery Graustark, in the opposite hemisphere. Nevertheless, for institutional reasons (cartel or government regulations, the awkwardness of frequent changes, or the like), the local-currency prices of tourist services are not flexible enough to equate supply and demand at all times. From December to March, tourist facilities are largely idle in Ruritania, while in Graustark they are in excess demand and are crudely rationed by the necessity of making reservations far in advance. A flexible exchange rate between the Ruritanian crown and the Graustark florin would partially overcome this difficulty. A depreciation of the crown between December and March would, in effect, cut the prices charged Graustarkians for tourism in Ruritania and raise the prices charged Ruritanians for tourism in Graustark, and so give residents of both countries alike a price incentive to substitute tourism in Ruritania for tourism in Graustark in these months. The seasonal underutilization of Ruritanian facilities and the excess demand for Graustark facilities would both find a partial remedy. Of course, exchange-rate flexibility is a crude and unselective substitute for the flexibility of individual prices and wages, and industries other than those in a position comparable to that of tourism might be adversely affected. Still, the example is pertinent in showing that ironing out fluctuations is not always and necessarily an unqualified good even when the fluctuations are fated to reverse themselves. When exchange-rate flexibility is supplementing inadequate flexibility of individual prices and wages and, in particular, when *nonstorable* goods and services are involved and a temporary slump in buying them would mean a waste of factors of production, then speculative stabilization of exchange rates might plausibly be judged inappropriate.[13] This point is probably not very important in reality. It is worth making, however, as a counter to any idea that stabilization is necessarily a good thing and that speculation is to be praised or condemned according to how much or how little stability it produces. If exchange-rate fluctuations were quite clearly temporary or seasonal, private speculation would probably iron them out; but even if it did not, this failure would not necessarily be a matter for regret.

The analogy between foreign exchange and commodities

For ordinary commodities, the role of flexible prices in balancing supply and demand is generally recognized, even though official price-pegging might supposedly eliminate harmful speculation and relieve producers, traders, and users of some risk. Continually changing con-

---

11. On "perverse" speculation and "grossly excessive" speculation, see Meade, *op. cit.*, pp. 220–224.

12. See A. P. Lerner, *The Economics of Control*, New York: Macmillan, 1944, pp. 88–95; and J. E. Meade, "Degrees of Competitive Speculation," *Review of Economic Studies*, **XVII** (3), no. 44, 1949–1950, esp. pp. 160–161.

13. The earlier analysis of how the loss from incorrect speculation might be more than fully borne by the speculators themselves, leaving a gain for nonspeculators, does not seem applicable here. That analysis presupposed flexible prices always equilibrating speculative plus nonspeculative supplies and demands. Here, by contrast, the difficulty stems from excessively rigid prices and exchange rates and the consequent imbalances between quantities demanded and supplied.

ditions call for continual adjustments in resource allocation; keeping prices from fulfilling their rationing and production-motivating functions might be more disruptive than price fluctuations and the speculation that may feed on them. Why, then, do not these same considerations tell against pegging exchange rates?[14] Well, some writers reject the analogy between exchange rates and ordinary prices. It allegedly ignores the fundamental fact about money—that it is important primarily as a unit of account and that everything priced in one money is affected by its value in terms of other moneys.[15] Such arguments do not distinguish sharply enough between the foreign-exchange value and the purchasing power of a currency. To Americans, the price of French francs *is* like the price of any ordinary commodity; it is the price of an "ingredient" used in "producing" imports from France, just as the price of cotton cloth is the price of an ingredient used in producing shirts. To Frenchmen, likewise, the price of dollars is similar to an ordinary commodity price. As for the interdependence between exchange rates and other prices, there is no evident difference of principle between this and the general interdependence of commodity prices in a closed economy. Any argument about an especially disruptive interdependence involving exchange rates must be explicitly developed to be meaningful; interdependence in itself does not destroy the commodity analogy. Emphasis on the distinctive functions of money—its use as a unit of account and debt-paying medium—would seem a better argument for stabilizing the domestic purchasing power of money than for stabilizing exchange rates.

Jacob Viner develops a more sophisticated objection to the commodity analogy. As in the market for short-term loans and the short-term interest rate and in the price of gold under a gold standard, he finds something peculiarly crucial in the foreign-exchange market and exchange rates. Its zero storage cost and low financial carrying cost make foreign exchange especially subject to speculation. He distrusts routine application of standard speculation theory to "a commodity whose supply and whose demand have no upward or downward limitations arising out of cost limitations on output or out of want limitations on 'marketability.' "[16] By this, Viner means that the price of one country's fiat money in terms of another's has no ceiling or floor derived from real costs affecting supply or from direct or indirect utility either as a consumer good or as an ingredient in production. Fiat money can be produced in unlimited amounts at negligible cost. Similarly, sellers of commodities or of other currencies will accept it in unlimited amounts, though at a correspondingly low value. The implication is that the limits within which speculation can push exchange rates around are much less close and definite than those ruling in commodity markets. Commodity prices are dominated by supply and demand factors reflecting costs of production and utilities, but the domestic or international value of a currency can be practically anything, since cost and utility play practically no role.

To individual persons and firms, however, a foreign currency does indeed have a cost of production and a utility, quite as an ordinary commodity does. To the businessmen who "produce" foreign exchange for the home economy, it has a real cost of "production" in the export goods that are "transformed" into it on the international market and, more basically, in the domestic factors of production used in making these exports. Similarly, the businessmen who demand foreign exchange as an "ingredient" in "producing" import goods find that it does have a utility or productivity, much as any other ingredient or intermediate good. The exchange rate between two currencies does have an objective basis, after all, in their respective purchasing powers over goods and services. Even if only loosely controlling, this basis contradicts any notion that no cost or utility factors limit the play of speculation.

Money is essentially costless to the authorities or institutions that create it, though not to ordinary persons and firms. Exchange depreciation of a currency may put pressure on the issuing authorities "to increase its output, to speed up the printing presses, or to make larger entries in the books which in the monetary field represent, in relation to the stock of money, what farms and factories represent in relation to stocks of other commodities."[17] Our whole earlier analysis of mutual influences among exchange rates, price levels, and money supplies bears on this worry. The trouble would be with policies and institutional arrangements and not with speculation as such. Viner himself recognizes that his distinction between speculation in commodities and in foreign exchange would not be valid if countries were successfully stabilizing their price levels.[18]

Firm control over the domestic money supply provides little reassurance about speculation feeding on the domestic instability of *foreign* currencies. Still, the damage that domestically stable countries would suffer, with rate fluctuations intensified by speculation, might well be less than the damage from linkage to the unstable foreign currencies at fixed rates.

In comparison with most staple commodities traded on organized markets, foreign exchange presumably has a high elasticity of demand and supply and a correspondingly low susceptibility to price fluctuations caused by random shifts in supply and demand. Foreign exchange is like a commodity with many uses; it is an "ingredient" of a wide variety of goods and services imported from many places, whereas wheat, tin, or any other single commodity has a narrower range of uses. Similarly, foreign exchange has many sources of supply, being obtainable by producing a wide variety of goods for a wide range of foreign customers. Ordinarily, then, there is reason to doubt whether foreign exchange is a commodity subject to the wide price fluctuations and the kind of speculation often characteristic, for instance, of wool, sugar, rubber, tin, cocoa, and other staples.[19]

The natural selection of speculators

One line of reasoning emphasizes a *natural selection* of successful speculators, whose activities generally tend to be stabilizing. Other speculators, it is true, may be unable to assess the fundamental supply and demand conditions governing prices; they may be unduly inclined to expect short-run price fluctuations to continue in the same direction; they may buy and sell according to whim or emotion or mass mood. Precisely because they are so often wrong, however—so goes the argument—they will lose money and be forced to curtail or cease their operations. More competent and better-informed speculators will make profits and be able to expand their operations. Their very profits suggest that their operations are tending to stabilize prices, for speculators can make profits only if they succeed, on the average, in buying at lower prices than they sell at. When buying, they make low prices less low than they would otherwise be; and when selling, they make high prices less high. The natural selection of profit and loss rewards and promotes stabilizing speculation and penalizes and eliminates destabilizing speculation.[20]

Two closely related objections challenge this reasoning. First, it is not certain that profitability necessarily implies a stabilizing effect. Second, the shrewder speculators may make profits not so much by assessing fundamental supplies and demands as by predicting price swings caused by the moods of amateur speculators; speculation as a whole still may be destabiliz-

14. See Charles R. Whittlesey, *International Monetary Issues*, New York: McGraw-Hill, 1937, p. 32.

15. Michael Lindsay Hoffman, "The Economics of Fluctuating Exchanges" (unpublished dissertation), Chicago: University of Chicago, 1942, p. 352. Hoffman is elaborating on F. A. von Hayek, *Monetary Nationalism and International Stability*, London: Longmans, Green, 1937, pp. 5–6.

16. Jacob Viner, "Some International Aspects of Economic Stabilization," in Leonard D. White, ed., *The State of the Social Sciences*, Chicago: University of Chicago Press, 1956, p. 291.

17. *Ibid.*, p. 292.

18. *Ibid.*, p. 294.

19. Further objections could be raised to regarding foreign exchange as the output of the home country's export firms and the chief input of its import firms: for example, movements in its price tend to drag prices of certain other goods along with it; its supply curve could conceivably bend backwards; and price changes (even merely speculative price changes) tend to affect the *schedule* of its cost of "production." But such things are equally conceivable for commodities in the literal sense of the word. The commodity analogy remains suggestive.

20. More than a century ago and in remarkable detail, John Stuart Mill argued that neither an individual speculator nor speculators in the aggregate can profit from price movements caused solely by their own transactions and that profitable speculation is generally both stabilizing and beneficial to the public. See his *Principles of Political Economy*, Book IV, chap. II, sec. 5 (pp. 67–71 in the edition edited by Donald Winch, Baltimore: Penguin Books, 1970).

"People who argue that speculation is generally destabilizing seldom realize that this is largely equivalent to saying that speculators lose money. . . ." (Friedman, *op. cit.*, p. 175). While recognizing the possibility, Friedman argues against any presumption that a changing body of money-losing amateur speculators would in fact dominate the market.

242

ing. Let us examine these two doubts in turn.

Speculators clearly both make profits and exert a stabilizing influence if they buy at the troughs and sell at the peaks of swings in prices. But they seldom can time their actions so accurately. They may not recognize a price trough or peak until it has passed and given way to an uptrend or downtrend. Instead of trying to call the turns in prices exactly, they

may choose a better chance of a smaller profit by waiting to see which way the wind is blowing before taking action. Speculative purchases at low but rising prices and sales at high but falling prices will sharpen the price movements and, in this narrow sense, may be considered destabilizing.[21]

In another and probably more meaningful sense, even tardy speculative purchases and

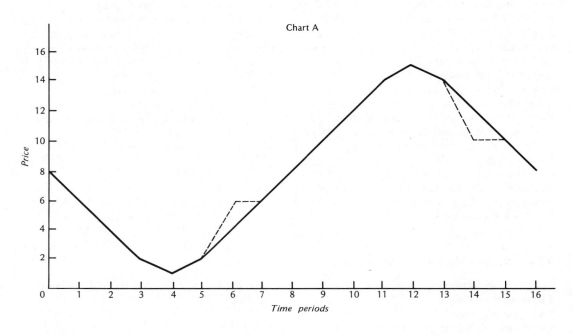

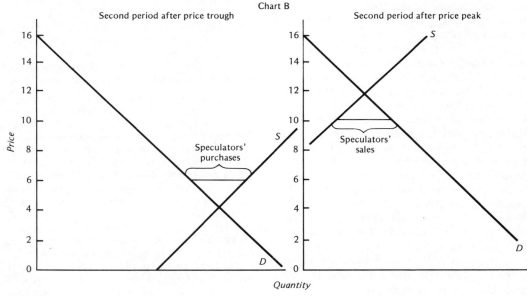

FIGURE 12.1

sales can still be stabilizing. Since the sole purpose of the next page or two is to show a possibility rather than prove a necessity, it is legitimate and convenient to postulate nonspeculative supply and demand functions and nonspeculative shifts in supply and movements in price of very simple kinds. For further simplicity, the speculators are assumed to buy in only one period and sell in only one period of each price cycle. In Fig. 12.1, the solid line of Chart A shows how the price of some commodity would move through time in the absence of speculation. The dashed line, where it deviates from the solid one, shows how speculative buying in the second period after the price trough and speculative selling in the second period after the price peak modify the time series of prices. The two parts of Chart B relate to the two periods in which speculators operate. They show the nonspeculative supply and demand and the price they would determine in each period in the absence of speculation, the quantity brought by speculators in the one period and sold in the other, and the prices as modified by speculation. These prices correspond to the dashed line on Chart A. As is clear from Chart B, nonspeculative demand and supply are assumed to depend only on current price and not at all on past price. Furthermore, the nonspeculative demand schedule is assumed to be always the same; the price fluctuations are due to shifts in the supply schedule (perhaps because of seasonal weather changes). Speculative demand or supply presumably depends on future price as predicted in the light of past and present prices, but it is unnecessary here to explore just how the speculators make their decisions; it is enough that they buy and sell in the amounts and at the times shown.

The new series of prices, shown by the dashed lines, is less regular or tidy than the nonspeculative one. Nevertheless, it represents greater stability in the sense that the average deviation (ignoring sign) of the price in each period from the average price over the entire cycle is smaller: the total of these deviations is 58 for the speculation-distorted price pattern and 62 for the nonspeculative pattern. (This result is obvious at once: the nonspeculative and speculative prices are always the same except in periods 6 and 14, when the nonspeculative price deviates by $4.00 and the speculative price by only $2.00 from the $8.00 average price over the cycle.) Speculators make profits because they buy at a price of $6.00 and sell at

$10.00. Furthermore, the speculation is appropriate in the sense that it transfers some of the commodity from a period when its nonspeculative value would have been only $4.00 to a period when its nonspeculative value would have been $12.00. It is true that the speculators would have been acting even more appropriately if they had concentrated their buying and selling at and around the troughs and peaks of prices, instead of waiting to see uptrends and downtrends already under way. But the example shows that imperfect speculation can, though need not, be better than none at all; it can be "stabilizing" and "appropriate," in reasonable senses of these words, even when intensifying parts of upswings and downswings in prices.

By delaying the bulk of their purchases and sales until later than they do in our example, out of anxiety to see price trends still more firmly established before acting, speculators might perversely be buying at above-average and selling at below-average prices. They would be intensifying the instability of prices and transferring the commodity or the foreign exchange they dealt in from times of greater to times of lesser value. But then the speculators would be losing money. The presumption that profitable speculation is stabilizing speculation still seems intact. The easiest way to challenge this presumption is to postulate that speculation affects price trends and price expectations in such a way as to modify nonspeculative supplies and demands. But when nonspeculators take account of price trends and act according to the resulting expectations, they are no

21. See William J. Baumol, "Speculation, Profitability, and Stability," *Review of Economics and Statistics,* **XXXIX,** August 1957, pp. 263–271.

The text above appears to make the unrealistic suggestion that prices move in regular cycles. For the sake of mere convenience in providing periods of relatively high and relatively low prices for consideration, such a model is legitimate. However, arguments (such as Baumol's) that depend in an essential way on unchanging (though complicated) supply and demand functions with fixed parameters are considerably more suspect. This point deserves more repetition and emphasis than, for fear of boring the reader, it receives in the following pages.

longer "pure" nonspeculators. The problem of drawing a clear distinction between speculators and nonspeculators will require further examination.

By including a speculative element even in the decisions of nonspeculators, it is possible to construct examples in which even profitable speculation by the professionals both sharpens and widens price fluctuations. W. J. Baumol[22] has constructed a model of this sort to serve as a counterexample to and refutation of the reassuring notion that profitable (nonmonopolistic) speculation is necessarily stabilizing. Baumol has prices fluctuating in a sine wave in the absence of speculation. The nonspeculative supply and demand functions generating this pattern are assumed to include recent as well as current prices: high prices tend to create excess supply but *rising* prices tend to create excess demand. The functions describing the behavior of speculators involve their buying shortly after upturns and selling shortly after downturns in prices. Baumol's functions further imply, as a critic has pointed out,[23] that speculators raise their predicted price when the actual price trend is concave upward even though falling and lower their predicted price when the actual price trend is concave downward even though rising. With suitably chosen parameters in the model, speculation can increase the amplitude of price fluctuations. The professional or pure or conscious speculators can destabilize the market while profiting at the expense of others.

We must remember that the supposed nonspeculators are not free from speculative behavior; their transactions are assumed to depend on price trends as well as on prices.[24] Everyone in the model behaves partly in accordance with overt or tacit predictions of future prices and thus is to some extent a speculator. But it is an old story that some speculators might profit and others lose more, with speculation being destabilizing on the whole. While this deserves to be taken seriously (and will later be considered at length), it does not mean that speculators can make profits *in the aggregate* and yet destabilize the market. This is the point at issue.

Anticipating these objections, Baumol constructed another counterexample. In it, nonspeculative purchases depend solely on the current price and not at all on past prices. Nonspeculative sine-wave fluctuations in price stem from shifts in supply, which in turn might be due to seasonal changes in weather. Grafting speculative demand and supply onto this "real cycle" could change the constant-amplitude pattern of price fluctuation into an unstable explosive movement: the price increases produced by speculative purchases would incite still further speculative purchases, and so on, indefinitely. Though destabilizing, this speculation could be profitable in the sense that the speculators' holdings became more and more valuable. But it is premature to describe the speculators' operations as profitable while they are still in mid-stream, before the paper profits have been cashed. Actually, if the speculators tried to sell and cash their profits, prices would collapse. Baumol concedes, in fact, that his is not actually "an example of destabilizing *profitable* speculation."[25] An autonomous desire to unload speculative holdings is not the only thing that might break the speculative spiral. The rising interest cost of financing speculative holdings might dampen the enthusiasm for further purchases, stop the price rise, and prick the bubble.[26] Interest rates would in fact be likely to rise as progressively more funds were demanded (or withheld from supply) on the loan market to finance the growing speculative positions.

The models just reviewed sought to undermine the proposition that profitability for the aggregate of all speculators (including incidental and partial speculators) implies a stabilizing influence. In fact, the *ad hoc* peculiarities of those counterexamples tend to support the proposition as a useful generalization if not an airtight theorem.[27] To further rehabilitate it, Lester Telser constructed a model of great generality in which nonspeculative excess demand is inversely related to current price and is unaffected by past prices, while speculative excess demand or supply is proportional to the expected rise or fall in price. The better the speculators predict future prices, the larger are their profits. Mathematics grinds out the conclusion that positive speculators' profits do indeed imply a price-stabilizing influence, on the plausible definition that the variance of actual prices from the mean price measures the degree of instability.[28] In fact, as Telser remarks, speculators may conceivably stabilize prices to some extent even when suffering losses. A radically simple example (not given by him) illustrates this possibility. Suppose that the speculators buy when the price would otherwise be $.75 below average and in so doing bid up the price by $1.00 to $.25 above average; they sell when the price would otherwise be $.75 above average and thus bid the price down to $.25

below average. The speculators lose money, since they buy more dearly than they sell, but they make prices deviate less from the average than they otherwise would have.

The issue is still not completely decided. Perhaps Telser's proof that profitable speculation is stabilizing is not a general one but rather is just one more example of the undisputed fact that it *can* be stabilizing. Baumol still insisted that the relation between profitability and stability is in part an empirical question, not to be settled by *a priori* arguments.[29] Yet the question whether aggregate profitability necessarily implies a stabilizing effect is *not* an "empirical" question; it is a question of logical implication. It is the job of logical analysis to explore under what conditions the suggested proposition would not hold. No number of historical examples in which profitable speculation has been stabilizing can prove that it logically *must* be. And no number of historical examples in which speculation seems to have been destabilizing yet profitable will settle the issue unless the profit-and-loss figures refer to fully cashed rather than mere paper profits and unless they refer to all speculators—amateur as well as professional, inadvertent as well as conscious.

The practical issue apparently resolves into whether *professional* speculation is generally stabilizing. When even predominantly nonspeculative trading is partly based on attempts to predict future prices, when no satisfactory distinction can be drawn between speculative and nonspeculative trading, or when amateur speculators are active, then profitable professional speculation is not necessarily stabilizing. This is a second objection to the natural-selection argument; it must be emphasized and closely examined.

The natural-selection argument expects incompetent speculators to be weeded out, leaving profit-making speculators dominant with their stabilizing influence. The argument is persuasive only when speculative supply and demand are small in relation to total trading. Otherwise, though a speculator still needs superior foresight to succeed, his superiority may lie in sensing the opinions and moods of other speculators rather than in predicting fundamentals. Especially if speculative transac-

22. *Ibid.*

23. Lester G. Telser, "A Theory of Speculation Relating Profitability and Stability," *Review of Economics and Statistics*, XLI, August 1959, p. 300.

24. Baumol himself has recognized and Telser has emphasized this point.

25. W. J. Baumol, "Reply," *Review of Economics and Statistics*, XLI, August 1959, p. 301.

26. Telser, *op. cit.*, p. 301. This point is, of course, part of Tsiang's analysis of speculators' equilibrium.

27. A more recent example of destabilizing profitable speculation involves multiple equilibriums of the exchange rate in the absence of speculation! Murray C. Kemp, *The Pure Theory of International Trade*, Englewood Cliffs, N.J.: Prentice-Hall, 1964, pp. 259–260.

28. Telser, *op. cit.*, pp. 298–299.

29. Baumol, *Review of Economics and Statistics*, August 1959, p. 302.
Writings published since the first edition of the present book have apparently failed to yield simple and secure generalizations about the profitability-and-stability issue. The conclusions reached depend on what is meant by the degree of price stability (possible criteria include variance around the mean or around a trend over the time period considered and average absolute percentage change between successive daily, weekly, or monthly quotations), on whether or not the supposedly nonspeculative demand and supply functions take account of price expectations as influenced by price experience, on the exact characteristics of those functions (linearity or whatnot), on transactions costs, and so forth. See M. J. Farrell, "Profitable Speculation," *Economica*, n.s., XXXIII, May 1966, pp. 183–193; Fred R. Glahe, "Professional and Nonprofessional Speculation, Profitability, and Stability," *Southern Economic Journal*, XXXIII, July 1966, pp. 43–48; N. P. Obst, "A Connection between Speculation and Stability in the Foreign Exchange Market," *Southern Economic Journal*, XXXIV, July 1967, pp. 146–149; Sohmen, *op. cit.*, rev. ed., chap. III; and Jörg Schimmler, "Speculation, Profitability, and Price Stability—A Formal Approach," *Review of Economics and Statistics*, LV, February 1973, pp. 110–114.
We are left with the nonrigorous and defeasible presumption that profitability implies a stabilizing tendency. Perhaps we should try (as Baumol did) to devise precise models in which speculation, though profitable for the aggregate of all persons who behave at all speculatively, even though not all of them are pure speculators, is nevertheless destabilizing. We should then compare the characteristics of such models with the real world.

tions are a large part of the total, this may be the profitable way to operate. Speculators as a group may suffer losses, but with a successful minority winning from the losses of an unsuccessful and changing mass. Keynes likened professional speculation to a contest to pick out the six prettiest faces from a hundred pictures, the prize going to the contestant whose selection most nearly corresponds to the average selection of all contestants. Each has to pick the faces not that he finds prettiest, but that the other contestants, who are looking at the problem in the same way, seem likeliest to pick.[30] Why, then, bother with fundamentals? Why not join in and profit from any ignorant speculative stampede while it lasts?

The distinction between professional and amateur speculation suggests a related distinction between calm and excited times. Unusual excitement grows from prospects of winning large gains (as on the stock market during a boom) or of avoiding large losses of purchasing power (as on the foreign-exchange market during rapid inflation at home). A population seized with speculative mania is looking for big profits in a hurry. Exchange rates between domestically stable currencies, however, would hardly vary sharply or rapidly enough to have strong get-rich-quick appeal to amateur speculators. Fluctuations about a gradually changing equilibrium are the sort of thing that only professionals might hope to profit from.

While ironing out clear deviations from equilibrium, even professional speculators could not be sure of the precise rate called for by commercial supply and demand. Small short-run oscillations, more so than large movements, may be unrelated to nonspeculative fundamentals. If speculation is oriented around the fundamentals, there is thus more reason to expect it to resist oscillations outside of a certain range than within that range. The size of this range differs among markets according to the influence of some idea of a "normal price."[31] As shown a few pages later, this stabilizing idea of a normal price is likely to be more powerful in foreign-exchange markets than in security markets. Another reassuring consideration about speculation on small short-run wobbles in exchange rates is that it is undertaken by banks—though perhaps not deliberately—insofar as they may sometimes be willing to let unbalanced positions developed in transactions with their commercial customers ride for a few minutes or hours. For this reason, very-short-run imbalances between commercial supplies of and demands for particular currencies need not cause correspondingly frequent and violent rate movements. Nevertheless, the question of how wide the range is within which speculation is likely to dominate exchange rates is an empirical one, to be illuminated by historical experience.

The stock-market analogy

Worry over the activities of inexpert speculators feeds on a supposed analogy between speculation in currencies and in stocks. Experience with speculation in freely fluctuating exchanges is less common than acquaintance with the lore of the stock market. It is easy to become impressed by similarities between the two markets,[32] but the differences are at least as noteworthy.

One of the most important differences is the greater strength of the idea of normal price in foreign exchange than in stocks. There is hardly such a thing as a normal price for a share of stock. Presumably it would equal the stream of expected future dividends discounted by the going rate of interest on loans of comparable risk. Except for the very near future, no one knows what future dividends will be. The proper discount factor is also unknown. The price of a stock is a kind of crude average judgment sometimes liable to sharp change, which intrigues amateur speculators. The normal rate of exchange between two currencies is definite by contrast. One can ordinarily be confident that a purchasing-power-parity calculation approximates the equilibrium exchange rate within, say, 20 or 30 percent. If there is a marked discrepancy between the rates of inflation or deflation in the two countries, one can also judge in which direction purchasing-power parity is tending to change. Judging the nonspeculative value of one currency in terms of another requires less expert knowledge than judging the nonspeculative value of a stock.

Under free international trade, commodity arbitrage would keep exchange rates from deviating far from purchasing-power parity. But there could be no comparable arbitrage in stocks, even if each stock did have a normal value. Even if one could know that speculation was undervaluing a stock, an individual arbitrageur would have no way to buy the stock and then sell the physical plant, inventories, goodwill, and other underlying assets. And if a stock were known to be overvalued, there would be even less chance of buying assets for conversion into the stock.

Speculative supplies of and demands for foreign exchange are merely added onto supplies and demands arising out of international trade. But in the stock market, speculative supplies and demands more nearly dominate. Except perhaps for the flotation of new issues, it is hard to imagine what stock-market transactions correspond to nonspeculative sales and purchases of foreign exchange. It is doubtful whether many people buy stocks as a long-run investment, paying sole attention to income prospects and no attention at all to possibilities of capital gain. Where speculators can gauge nonspeculative supplies and demands, as in the foreign exchange market, prices are less subject to emotional influences than where speculators must rely on sensing the moods of other speculators, as in the stock market.

The large volume of commercial transactions tends in another way to make functionless price fluctuations less violent in foreign-exchange markets than in stock markets (particularly than in the stock markets of some decades ago). Large commercial supplies of and demands for a currency, together with arbitrage that keeps various exchange rates mutually consistent, make it difficult for a pool of speculators to dominate the market in some currency and engineer profitable price fluctuations. Monopolistic manipulation of exchange rates would require greater boldness and larger resources than any pool of private speculators is ordinarily likely to have.

Another reassuring fact is the greater two-sidedness of the exchange market than the stock market. Bullish and bearish sentiments have more nearly equal opportunities to express themselves. Suppose, for example, that speculators think the dollar price of sterling is higher than fundamental conditions warrant. Bearishness on pounds can easily express itself as bullishness on dollars: Englishmen and other owners of pounds can buy the undervalued dollars. It is more difficult for bearishness on the dollar price of some stock to find full expression, for no country uses that stock as money. Furthermore, well-organized forward markets furnish good vehicles for bearishness on currencies but not on stocks. Admittedly, bears can sell a stock short after first borrowing it, but this method is rather inadequate. (Members of the uninitiated public are plausibly alleged to feel uncomfortable in the un-

familiar position of being in debt for shares of stock. Active bearishness on stocks is discriminated against by rules such as that short sales can be made only after upward price movements and that profits from short positions, no matter how long outstanding, cannot have the benefit of the lower tax rate on capital gains.) Even if stocks were actively bought and sold for forward delivery, as on some European markets, there still would not exist the same systematic relation between spot and forward prices as in the exchange market. A decline in the forward rate on a currency affects the spot rate through interest arbitrage, but if the forward price of a stock were to sink, arbitrage communicating the effect to the spot price would have to depend on the inadequate expedient of borrowing stock. Inadequate outlets for bear sentiment probably enter into an explanation of the exaggerated and precarious Wall Street bull market of 1927–1929. With bears acting mainly by withdrawing from or staying out of the market rather than by taking positive action, bull sentiment seemed even more dominant than it actually was. This impression encouraged still further bull speculation. Finally, when the rise in prices could no longer be maintained, the crash had to be sharp. It would have been less sharp if many speculators had had short positions to cover. Things would be different on free foreign-exchange markets. Bear speculation on a currency would be just as easy as bull speculation. Short selling would tend to check any unbalanced speculative rise in a currency, and covering of short positions would cushion any subsequent decline.

The reasons why impressions of the stock market cannot be carried over into considering speculation in currencies apply even more strongly to impressions about speculation in

30. J. M. Keynes, *The General Theory of Employment, Interest and Money*, New York: Harcourt, Brace, 1936, esp. p. 156. Keynes was referring to the stock market in particular.

31. Nicholas Kaldor, "Speculation and Economic Stability," *Review of Economic Studies*, **VII**, October 1939, p. 10.

32. See Hoffman, *op. cit.*, pp. 220–221, 223n.

land, tulip bulbs, or Old Masters. Something like the boom and collapse of Florida land values in the 1920s, for example, is quite unlikely in the foreign-exchange market. One vitally relevant difference is the practical impossibility of active bear speculation in land. (How can one actively speculate on a fall in land values except by selling whatever holdings one already has, thereby withdrawing from speculation?) Of all speculative markets, the market in foreign exchange seems least vulnerable to booms and crashes resulting from inadequate means of continuous expression for bearish and bullish sentiments alike.

Speculation under pegged exchange rates

The reassurances of the last section apply only to markets in which exchange rates fluctuate freely. Things are different when rates are fixed. They are different, also, when a fixed-rate system is in the process of crumbling and when episodes of "dirty floating" characterize this process.[33] It is true that speculation is unlikely to cause trouble under a *full-fledged* international gold standard, for exchange rates are then understood to be fixed permanently, and defense of the gold parity of its currency is the overriding aim of each country's financial policies. Speculation then works in support of gold parities and helps provide accommodating finance for temporary balance-of-payments disequilibriums. A gold standard commanding this degree of confidence existed, however, for at most a few decades in the world's history. Nowadays, exchange-rate adjustments are acceptable, at least as last resorts, in dealing with "fundamental disequilibrium." Even when rate adjustments are not in fact made, their very possibility can unleash troublesome speculation.[34] If exchange-rate adjustments were to be discussed at international conferences, the result would be general uncertainty between conferences and chaos during them. If exchange-rate adjustments were to be made according to some formula (even a supposedly secret one), speculators still would have a great advantage. In practice, exchange rates are adjusted at the discretion of individual governments. Rumors keep springing up about possible impending adjustments, and these rumors flag speculation on. The historical chapters to follow offer many examples.

Those who speculate on adjustments in pegged exchange rates have practically a *sure thing*, a so-called one-way option. When a currency is under suspicion, everyone knows whether it is overvalued or undervalued. There may be some doubt about whether the government will make a rate adjustment, and to what extent, but there is practically no doubt about the direction of any change. If rumors have the government contemplating devaluation of a clearly overvalued currency, its holders have an incentive to sell it quickly before the devaluation takes place. They can profitably buy their balances back afterwards. People committed to make future payments in the suspected currency can speculate against it simply by failing to buy it forward. Considering its obvious overvaluation, there is almost no chance that the suspected currency will be revalued upward rather than devalued. The possibilities are simply devaluation or no change. Devaluation gives the bear speculators an easy profit; no change lets them break even. (The only possible losses are from a small rise in the currency within its narrowly pegged band of fluctuation, the commissions and other minor expenses of selling a currency and later buying it back, and a small interest loss if short-term interest rates are lower in the country where the speculative funds are temporarily transferred than in the country whose currency is suspected.)

This assurance that any loss will be slight ordinarily applies fully only to speculation in the spot market, whether by outright currency transactions or by the "leads and lags" to be mentioned presently. If devaluation is strongly and generally expected, the forward quotation on the currency will tend to be below the pegged spot rate. If the expected devaluation does not occur after all, bearish speculators who have operated by selling the distrusted currency forward at its depressed forward rate will have to fulfill their forward contracts and close out their positions by buying the currency at its successfully defended higher spot rate. It should be emphasized *why* speculation in forward exchange is not a sure thing: there is some risk because forward rates are allowed to fluctuate and get out of alignment with spot rates. Even so, the extreme unlikelihood of appreciation of the spot rate enables speculators to calculate their maximum possible losses, and the interest-parity linkage of forward and spot rates, though weakened in a time of extreme distrust and bearish speculation, still has an influence. For this reason, even speculation by way of the unpegged forward market is less risky and approximates a "one-way option" more closely than it would if the spot rate were unpegged also. Speculators enjoy a one-way option just as much when an upward revaluation is expected as when a devaluation is expected. By buying the currency in question, they seize an opportunity for easy profit with practically no danger of loss.

The one-way option is not the only incitement that a system of fixed-but-adjustable exchange rates offers to speculators. Another is the fact that speculators do not, as under a system of fluctuating rates, bid the rate up against themselves as they bullishly buy a currency or bid the rate down against themselves as they bearishly sell. Nor do they again bid the rate against themselves as they later undertake the reverse transactions, closing out their positions (and collecting their profits, if the expected rate adjustment has been made). Under a system of pegged rates, the authorities in effect subsidize speculation by keeping the rate steady except at the very moment of the expected adjustment. Furthermore, the profit from speculation on an official rate adjustment promises to be large.[35] Adjustments in fixed exchange rates are momentous and well-publicized events. They must be substantial to justify the publicity and sometimes odium involved. A devaluing government is likely to make the step large not only to convince the public that it really was necessary but also to leave a margin of safety; devaluing too far seems better than devaluing too little and perhaps soon being forced to devalue again. Besides, the official reserves of gold and foreign exchange may have sunk very low during the period of currency overvaluation; the government may even be in debt for borrowed foreign exchange. Consequently, devaluation, when it comes, may go further than just enough to restore equilibrium in the country's balance of payments; it may aim at a surplus so that the government can rebuild its reserves and repay its borrowings.

Another advantage of fixed-but-adjustable rates over free rates—from the speculators' point of view—is that bear speculation against a weak currency may actually force the hoped-for devaluation. The bears win if they can exhaust the official reserves or the willingness of the authorities to use the reserves in continued pegging. The costs and risks of speculation are small in relation to the possible profit. The lower the reserves fall, the more imminent the collapse of the pegged rate becomes, and the stronger the motives for continued bear specu-

lation. Even if the original rumors were quite untrue, they might force devaluation and so make themselves true.[36] This could happen even if the speculation were not justified by underlying long-run commercial supplies and demands in the exchange market, so that the exchange rate could otherwise be maintained. When the government is about to run out of exchange reserves, mere lectures about the silliness of speculation against underlying supply and demand conditions will not discourage speculators who see a good opportunity. It is less rewarding under pegged than under free exchange rates to operate according to one's assessment of the "fundamentals." Although the herd as a herd may be behaving irrationally in some sense, it can still be rational for each individual member to run with the herd.[37]

33. On "dirty floating," that is, official manipulation of floating exchange rates, see the concluding section of Chapter 14, as well as certain sections of the historical chapters.

34. Contrasts in the character of speculation under different exchange-rate systems are emphasized in John Burr Williams, *International Trade under Flexible Exchange Rates*, Amsterdam: North-Holland Publishing Company, 1954, pp. 243–244.

35. Successful speculation against a pegged exchange rate is the case that Jerome L. Stein describes in his "Destabilizing Speculative Activity Can Be Profitable," *Review of Economics and Statistics*, XLIII, August 1961, pp. 301–302. This case is irrelevant, of course, to the profitability-and-stability discussion surveyed earlier in this chapter. In effect, the rate-pegging authorities turn out to be unsuccessful speculators.

36. Cf. J. Kymmell, *De Ontwikkeling van het Internationale Betalingsverkeer*, Leiden: Stenfert Kroese, 1950, p. 109.

37. Around the beginning of March 1973, the U.S. dollar, recently devalued for the second time in fourteen months, again came under heavy bear attack. Although many qualified observers believed that the dollar had *already* been devalued excessively, it was rational for corporation treasurers and oil-country central bankers to join in the bear movement. Even if already undervalued, the dollar was obviously not going to be revalued upward any time soon; and any further movement in the short run would be further downward. See the details in Chapter 28.

Speculation on adjustably pegged rates offers few if any compensating advantages. Perhaps its only useful function is to dramatize the unsoundness of existing conditions and force the hand of a government that has procrastinated too long. Speculation is rewarded at the expense of the authorities, meaning at the expense of the taxpayers. In defending an untenably overvalued currency, the authorities sell foreign exchange to speculators cheap, only to buy it back at a higher price after the defense collapses. This loss seems particularly regrettable if some of the foreign exchange sold in the futile pegging of the home currency was borrowed abroad; it later must be bought at an increased home-currency price to repay the foreign lenders. The authorities (and general public) also lose, to the benefit of speculators, in the rarer operation of trying to maintain an untenable exchange undervaluation of the home currency. At first the authorities are buying foreign exchange from speculators at an unduly high price in terms of home currency; later, after resistance to appreciation of the home currency has collapsed, the authorities sell foreign exchange to speculators at a lower price. In either type of futile pegging, the losses of the authorities are, from the speculators' point of view, a subsidy and an incitement to their operations. It is no coincidence that pegging breeds an apparent need for controls over capital movements. Unfortunately, the controls may be circumvented unless the authorities extend comprehensive supervision even to ostensibly nonspeculative current-account transactions.

The Bretton Woods system of pegged exchange rates presupposed a low degree of capital mobility, whether because of controls, habit, or other obstacles. Yet the 1960s, in particular, brought a tremendous growth in international capital movements. Multinational corporations play a large role in this development. Though they may not like to think of themselves as engaging in speculation, their self-protective management of their holdings and debts in various currencies does have similar consequences. The many ways available to multinational corporations for moving funds around are an embarrassment to the pegged-rate system.[38]

Speculation by way of so-called leads and lags in commercial payments is almost impossible to stamp out. If the Ruritanian crown comes under suspicion, foreigners with crown debts may delay payment as long as possible, awaiting devaluation. Ruritanians owing debts in foreign exchange will hasten to settle them before the foreign-exchange value of their money is reduced. Foreign purchasers of Ruritanian goods and services who would ordinarily cover their future needs for crowns in the forward market will now refrain from doing so, thereby speculating, and Ruritanians who would ordinarily cover future receipts of foreign exchange by selling them forward will now wait, hoping to sell the exchange at an increased crown price. Speculation may even take the form of postponing foreign purchases of Ruritanian goods and hastening Ruritanian purchases of foreign goods. Even when operating in these passive or indirect ways, speculators enjoy an only slightly impaired one-way option. Like overt speculation, this indirect speculation eats into the reserves of the exchange-pegging authorities.[39]

There are some grounds for believing that a currency like the U.S. dollar, widely used in pricing and payments for much trade even between countries other than the United States and widely used as a vehicle in converting funds from one nondollar currency to another, may become especially vulnerable when exchange rates are fixed but shaky. When the dollar comes under suspicion, exporters will hasten to collect and sell the dollars due them, or will hasten to sell forward the dollars they expect to receive, while importers will delay their payments and delay spot purchases or avoid forward purchases of the dollars they will need. Hence a widely used currency can come under the bearish pressure of leads and lags and of covering or noncovering in the forward market even in connection with trade among countries other than its own.[40]

Some students see the dangers of speculation less as an argument against pegging spot rates than as one in favor of supporting forward exchange rates as well. The prospects of finding a solution along these lines will be one of the two main topics covered in Chapter 14.

Summary

Theoretical considerations suggest that the standard worries about speculation in foreign exchange are most fully justified in cases of internal financial disorder. (Later chapters consider historical experience.) Yet even in the most unfavorable case of rapid and continuous inflation of the domestic money supply and prices, speculation would not make exchange rates cumulatively lose contact with the purchasing-power ratios of currencies as long as domestic interest rates were allowed to rise apace with inflationary expectations. Several considerations about calmer times are rather reassuring, such as purchasing-power parities as guides to "normal" exchange rates, the closer resemblance of foreign exchange to a commodity than to stock, and the natural selection of speculators by profit and loss. Fixed-but-adjustable rates are more likely than free rates to incite speculation on one-way options through leads and lags. Proposals for palliating this problem are examined later.

38. See Richard N. Cooper in Randall Hinshaw, ed., *The Economics of International Adjustment*, Baltimore: The Johns Hopkins Press, 1971, p. 78.

39. Paul Einzig has written a whole book on this topic: *Leads and Lags: The Main Cause of Devaluation*, London: Macmillan, 1968. Also see Einzig's *Foreign Exchange Crises*, London: Macmillan, 1968, chap. 10.

40. See Paul Einzig, *The Destiny of the Dollar*, London: Macmillan, 1972, esp. pp. 54–57.

CHAPTER THIRTEEN

Exchange Risk as an Obstacle to International Trade and Investment

The risk and nuisance of fluctuations

Even if not intensified by speculation, exchange-rate fluctuations might still be harmful. In selling or buying goods on credit at a price specified in foreign currency, a businessman runs the risk that the exchange rate may have moved to his disadvantage by the time he receives or makes payment. A less obvious risk confronts a businessman who imports goods for resale at home, either after or without further fabrication. A subsequent decline in the price of foreign exchange will reduce the home-currency value of his inventories by cheapening new imports of such goods. Exchange fluctuations may also cause the nuisance of requiring frequent changes in markets and sources of supply or even in inputs and products. They may complicate accounting and price-setting. (These are unpleasant aspects of competitively flexible prices in general, however; and it is not certain that the price rigidities of imperfect competition are on balance preferable.) The various risks and nuisances of exchange fluctuations might make businessmen refrain from some otherwise profitable international transactions. Businessmen would try to compensate themselves by adding larger mark-ups to their selling prices than under stable exchanges. The

volume of international trade would be smaller; some potential benefit from the international division of labor would be lost. Or so goes the argument. (Increased prices to compensate for exchange risk would not affect the volume of trade much, however, unless demands had considerable price elasticity; it is inconsistent to worry about fluctuating exchanges on the grounds of possibly perverse elasticities and serious shrinkage from exchange risk both.)

For obvious reasons it seems practically certain that exchange risk tends to hamper trade to some extent. But there are some partial offsets. The risk of loss also involves the chance of gain. Sometimes, furthermore, the risk is more nominal than real. It might then be less risky for a trader to deal in terms of a foreign currency of stable purchasing power than to deal in terms of his own, if it is subject to rapid inflation. Elimination of the nominal exchange risk would mean assumption of a greater risk of loss of purchasing power.

Importers of competitively traded staple commodities may find some compensation for uncovered exchange risk. An importer who must pay later in a foreign currency suffers by any rise in its rate in the meanwhile, but his loss may be partially offset by the corresponding rise in the home-currency price of his imported inventories.

Historical clues about exchange instability and trade volume

Such minor compensations, however, hardly alter the fact that exchange-rate instability must, in itself, deter trade. It is of interest, therefore, to see whether this effect is strong enough to show up in actual experience. One possible approach is to compute a correlation between the volume of a country's international trade during individual years and a measure of how widely the country's exchange rate fluctuated during the same years. A clear inverse association would presumably appear if exchange risk had been an important influence. The failure of this test would not, however, actually disprove the thesis of trade deterrence.[1] The burden on trade consists not so much in the fact or the size of fluctuations during particular years as in *uncertainty* about possible changes. In accepting this point, however, one must also recognize that a system of temporarily fixed exchanges subject to official adjustment at any time does not fully remove this risk.

Though correlating measures of rate instability and trade volume may be irrelevant, the same is not true of comparing trade in a period of dependable exchange stability with trade in a period of fluctuating exchanges. The United States slid onto an irredeemable greenback currency during the Civil War and did not restore stable exchanges with gold-standard countries until January 1879. The Civil War greatly interfered with American trade, of course, and prolonged postwar deflation in preparation for resumption of gold payments also presumably restrained economic activity. Nevertheless, there seems to be no upward break after 1878 in the trend of postwar trade growth to suggest that exchange instability had in itself previously been an important deterrent. Such evidence fails to appear whether imports plus exports are measured in current dollars or in dollars deflated by a wholesale price index.[2] Evidence of damage done by exchange-rate fluctuations before 1879 still is absent when one compares trade with gross national product, as in Table 13.1, remembering that the entire decade 1869–1878 and the first half of the overlapping decade 1874–1883 were a period of unstable exchanges.

A number of European countries experienced fluctuating exchange rates after World

EXCHANGE RISK AS AN OBSTACLE TO INTERNATIONAL TRADE AND INVESTMENT

War I before struggling back onto the gold standard during the 1920s. The years of fluctuating and then of fixed rates until the Great Depression were so few, however, that computed trends of growth in their international trade in each period would be practically meaningless. Even the yearly figures mean little, for reasons that will be mentioned, but they are presented here because they inevitably come to mind as *possible* sources of meaningful evidence. A clear and unmistakable jump in the trend of each country's trade volume at the time of its exchange-rate stabilization, or the clear and unmistakable absence of such a jump, might have suggested whether or not rate fluctuations had seriously been hampering trade until then. In considering the figures of Table 13.2, the reader should bear in mind the period of immediate postwar reconstruction, the depression after 1929, and the dates of each country's currency stabilization. The United Kingdom returned to the gold standard in April 1925. France stabilized the franc-dollar rate *de facto* in December 1926 and returned to gold *de jure* at about one-fifth of the prewar parity in June 1928. Denmark reestablished the gold standard in January 1927. Italy stabilized the lira *de jure* in December 1927, after approximate *de facto* stabilization several months earlier. The Norwegian krone fluctuated at values only slightly below its prewar dollar parity throughout 1927 and became redeemable in gold again in May 1928. The trade figures for each country's year of stabilization are circled in the table.

No reason is apparent why the figures in

TABLE 13.1. *Total of American imports and exports as a percentage of gross national product, overlapping decades, 1869–1908*

Decade	Percentage
1869–1878	14.4
1874–1883	14.1
1879–1888	13.2
1884–1893	12.9
1889–1898	13.2
1894–1903	12.5
1899–1908	11.9

SOURCE: Import and export values and Kuznets's estimates of gross national product from *Historical Statistics of the U.S.*, pp. 15 and 244–245. (Relating trade to gross national product is simply a rough way of taking account of secular economic growth and price changes and does not imply that total trade is a component of gross national product.)

1. Michael L. Hoffman, who disapproves of fluctuating exchanges, has insisted on this point. "The Economics of Fluctuating Exchanges" (unpublished dissertation), University of Chicago, 1942, pp. 305–306. The test did fail, incidentally, in the two lengthy nineteenth-century experiences to which I was able to apply it, those of Chile and Austria-Hungary.

2. For trade values and the price index, see U.S. Bureau of the Census, *Historical Statistics of the United States, 1789–1945*, Washington: Government Printing Office, 1949, pp. 233–234, 244–245.

TABLE 13.2. *Quantum of exports plus imports of five European countries, 1919–1931*[a]

	United King-dom	France	Den-mark	Italy	Norway
1919	100		100	100	100
1920	109	100	127	106	99
1921	87	79	138	102	65
1922	106	83	164	93	82
1923	114	81	199	105	86
1924	123	91	203	125	88
1925	(126)	92	195	144	90
1926	123	(101)	201	137	92
1927	131	104	(232)	(138)	98
1928	129	108	242	152	(103)
1929	134	115	242	158	114
1930		114	272	148	118
1931		106	278	138	102

[a] Indexes: 1919 = 100, except 1920 = 100 for France. The circled figures are those of the year in which each country's stabilization occurred; see text.

SOURCES: Total quantum indexes of merchandise exports plus merchandise imports (not including invisible trade) were pieced together from separate quantum indexes and from figures of trade at constant prices found in three League of Nations publications: *Memorandum on Balance of Payments and Foreign Trade Balances, 1911–1925*, vol. I, Geneva: 1926; *Memorandum on International Trade and Balances of Payments, 1927–1929*, Vol. I, Geneva: 1930; and *Review of World Trade, 1931 and 1932 (First Half)*, Geneva: 1932. The figures for the United Kingdom were adjusted to preserve comparability despite separation of the Irish Free State in April 1923. The Italian figure for 1921 had to be estimated on the basis of the first six months only.

Table 13.2 might be systematically biased either toward exaggerating or toward concealing any damage inflicted on trade by exchange-rate fluctuations in the periods before stabilization. Nevertheless, skepticism is in order. One reason hinges on the conceptual problems of index numbers generally and, in particular, on the frankly makeshift nature of the trade-quantum indexes shown in the table. Other reasons concern the shortness of the time periods covered, particularly after stabilization, and the unrepresentativeness of the periods, particularly before stabilization. Toleration of fluctuating rates as an expedient, despite the weight of opinion condemning them, is itself

evidence of this. Fluctuating rates were not accepted as a permanent system; little incentives existed for full development of appropriate institutions, such as forward-exchange facilities. Instead, countries were consciously struggling back toward exchange stability, at prewar parities if possible, meanwhile undergoing postwar readjustments, the depression of 1920–1922, and price-level instability. Furthermore, the dating of periods "before" and "after" stabilization is difficult. Even when it can be pinned down, the date of a particular country's stabilization against the dollar is not necessarily the date when its trade came to be conducted essentially at fixed rates, since some of its trading partners may have stabilized later. Finally, should the figures showing stagnation of trade after 1929 or 1930 be ignored? Obvious considerations suggest excluding depression periods, but if the artificial fixity of exchange rates actually had anything to do with the origin or severity of the depression (as can plausibly be argued), then it would be these methodological considerations rather than pure empiricism that saved the fixed-rate system from showing poor performance.

Since World War II, Thailand, Peru, and Canada have experienced several years of fluctuating exchange rates. Comparisons of their trade with total world trade, as well as comparisons between periods of fixed and fluctuating rates, seem worth trying. Of course, innumerable reasons justify skepticism about the apparent results. In considering the tables that follow, one should remember certain dates. The bulk of Thailand's trade since the war had been conducted at fluctuating exchange rates, and the reform of September 1955 marked neither the abandonment nor the introduction of an effectively fixed rate but rather the unification of a multiple-rate system in which fluctuating rates had long predominated. Thailand finally adopted a fixed par value in October 1963, after holding the exchange rate rigid for about a year and a half. Late in 1948, Peru introduced a fluctuating rate and broadened its use for specified purposes. In November 1949 the fixed rate was abolished completely in favor of two fluctuating rates that diverged only narrowly from each other. From about October 1950 to August 1951 and again from about October 1954 on, however, the central bank intervened so actively on the exchange market (sometimes holding the rate rigid for more than a year at a time) that the system defies definite classification. This ambiguity weakens whatever lessons the Peruvian experience might seem to provide. Canada unpegged its exchange rate at the beginning of October 1950 and abandoned all remnants of its exchange controls in December 1951. It began manipulating the exchange rate in June 1961 and returned to a fixed rate in May 1962. (Chapter 26 discusses the Canadian experience more fully, which explains the dearth of Canadian statistics here.)

For a first comparison, the dollar value of the exports plus imports of each of the three countries has been expressed as a percentage of the dollar value of the exports plus imports of the entire world (excluding Mainland China, the Soviet Union, and Soviet satellites). Table 13.3 shows that the three countries gen-

TABLE 13.3. *Dollar values of exports plus imports of Thailand, Peru, and Canada expressed as percentages of the total dollar values of world exports plus imports*

Year	Thailand's percentage	Peru's percentage	Canada's percentage
1928	0.29	0.30	4.26
1938	0.30	0.31	3.72
1947	0.24	0.31	5.66
1948	0.37	0.28	5.36
1949	0.44	0.28	5.22
1950	0.44	0.31	5.38
1951	0.40	0.32	5.17
1952	0.41	0.34	5.96
1953	0.43	0.34	6.19
1954	0.38	0.31	5.68
1955	0.38	0.33	5.70
1956	0.36	0.35	5.99
1957	0.37	0.34	5.64
1958	0.36	0.34	5.62
1959	0.38	0.30	5.74
1960	0.37	0.35	5.16
1961	0.40	0.40	5.07
1962	0.39	0.42	4.91
1963	0.38	0.39	4.80

SOURCE: Calculated from December 1964 and earlier issues of *International Financial Statistics*. The "world" excludes Mainland China, the Soviet Union, and some Eastern European countries. Canada includes Newfoundland from 1949 on (i.e., Newfoundland's foreign trade becomes included in the Canadian figure, but trade between Newfoundland and the rest of Canada becomes domestic rather than international trade); this complication is of small importance.

EXCHANGE RISK AS AN OBSTACLE TO INTERNATIONAL TRADE AND INVESTMENT

erally had at least as large a share of world trade after World War II as before. This fact by itself proves nothing, of course, though really serious interference from fluctuating rates might have been expected to reveal itself.

Another comparison employs postwar rates of growth of rough indexes of the physical volume of trade of the world and of the three countries. Growth rates in the subperiods of first fixed and then fluctuating rates are also shown for Canada and Peru (though the qualification about informal pegging of the Peruvian sol at times since 1950 must be remembered). It should be clear, incidentally, that a growth rate for the whole postwar period is in no sense an average of the rates for subperiods. The figure for Thailand is included for completeness, but, for reasons explained in the note to Table 13.4, the apparent faster growth of Thailand's trade than of world trade deserves little attention. Peruvian trade apparently grew somewhat faster than world trade, especially since the reform of the exchange system in November 1949. Canadian trade apparently grew somewhat more slowly than world trade, surprisingly enough, though the disparity became less marked after Canada adopted the fluctuating rate in October 1950. The slightly slower growth of Canadian than of world trade seems to clash with the earlier finding that Canada's *share* of world trade did, if anything, grow slightly after 1950. The apparent discrepancy must be attributed to a difference in concepts: one approach deals with growth of quantum indexes, the other with percentages of a total expressed in current U.S. dollars.

For Peru,[3] it may be of interest to see how well trade kept pace with national income before and after abandonment of the fixed rate in 1948–1949 and return to a *de facto* pegged rate around 1960. This is shown in Table 13.5.

Unfortunately for providing evidence, Mexico had a fluctuating exchange rate for less than a year, from July 22, 1948 until June 17, 1949. (Official intervention kept the rate from

---

3. Thailand made no clear transition from fixed to fluctuating rates in the period considered, and the figures for Canada appear in Chapter 26.

fluctuating *freely*; but since the peso was not firmly repegged until it had lost 44 percent of its earlier value, any exchange risk was presumably at least as great as it would have been under a system of completely free rates.) One slight compensation, however, was that the brief period of fluctuating rates was flanked on

TABLE 13.4. *Rates of growth of the physical volume of trade: the World, Thailand, Peru, and Canada, 1946–1958*

Inclusive period	YEARLY AVERAGE PERCENTAGES			
	World	Thailand	Peru	Canada
1946–1958	6.8	14.6	7.8	4.5
1946–1949	8.2		0.6	
1946–1950	8.9			1.0
1950–1958	5.7		7.6	
1951–1958	5.5			4.3

SOURCES AND METHODS: Each of the yearly average percentages of growth was obtained by fitting an exponential trend to the annual trade-quantum figures for the period indicated (i.e., by fitting a linear trend to the logarithms of the trade figures). A quantum index of world exports was spliced together from various issues of the United Nations *Yearbook of International Trade Statistics* and the United Nations *Monthly Bulletin of Statistics*, January 1960. For Thailand, separate export and import quantum indexes through 1949 are given in the UN *Yearbook of International Trade Statistics*, vol. I, 1956, p. 557. Various issues of *International Financial Statistics* give current baht values of exports and imports, as well as a wholesale price index with which to deflate these current values roughly, making it possible to piece together a crude total quantum index for the entire period. (It is thus clear that the quantum index for Thailand is especially a makeshift. An additional reason for this is that Thai trade statistics were complicated by the multiple-exchange-rate system in effect until September 1955. Furthermore, the very sharp growth of Thai trade in the earliest postwar years, as shown in the footnote, takes much of the meaning away from the growth trend for the entire postwar period, which includes these years.) For Peru and Canada, all underlying data come from *International Financial Statistics*. Peruvian export and import values in current soles were deflated by separate export and import price indexes and then added together. Canadian export and import quantum indexes were averaged into a total trade index by use of base-year Canadian-dollar values as weights.

The quantum indexes thus derived and to which the trends were fitted are shown in the following table. They have been shifted to a common base year for easier comparison.

Quantum Indexes of Exports Plus Imports, 1953 = 100

Year	World	Thailand	Peru	Canada
1946	58	13	64	72
1947	69	34	58	80
1948	70	57	47	77
1949	75	59	70	75
1950	85	96	70	78
1951	95	112	78	86
1952	94	93	87	96
1953	100	100	100	100
1954	105	109	98	95
1955	114	115	104	106
1956	124	118	118	120
1957	131	129	127	118
1958	129	114	123	113

either side by a period of fixed rates. A 15 percent *ad valorem* tax was imposed on most exports when the fixed rate was abandoned, and the American recession beginning in the fall of 1948 might also have been expected to hamper Mexican trade. Nevertheless, the total of imports and exports for the year from mid-1948 to mid-1949, 6446 million Mexican pesos, does not compare badly with the totals of 5344, 5718, 7192, and 9313 million pesos

TABLE 13.5 *Ratio of Peruvian exports plus imports to national income*

Year	Percentage
1946	41.0
1947	37.6
1948	29.6
1949	50.5
1950	45.9
1951	53.1
1952	50.1
1953	50.4
1954	51.7
1955	52.2
1956	58.0
1957	57.9
1958	52.7
1959	50.2
1960	52.9
1961	56.8
1962	58.2
1963	53.7

SOURCE: *International Financial Statistics*, March 1955, January 1960, and December 1964.

for the calendar years 1947 through 1950. Furthermore, the postwar uptrend in the ratio of exports plus imports to national income continued during the period of fluctuating rates. This ratio averaged 19.3 percent in 1946 through 1948, 21.3 percent from mid-1948 to mid-1949, and 25.6 percent from 1949 through 1958. It is interesting to note that Mexican trade increased in relation to national income not only during and after the prolonged depreciation of July 1948 to June 1949 but also after the devaluation of April 1954. The ratio rose to 26.8 percent in 1951, fell to 24.0 percent in 1953, rose after the 1954 devaluation to a peak of 29.0 percent in 1956, and by 1958 had fallen to 22.9 percent.[4] One plausible interpretation is that trade had become hampered as the fixed exchange rate became progressively more unrealistic and then spurted up again for a while after each devaluation approximately readjusted the rate to the degree of inflation thus far experienced in Mexico.

The preceding pages offer apparent examples both of trade damaged by fluctuating exchange rates and of trade flourishing under fluctuating exchange rates. The exchange-rate system is only one of numerous changing conditions that may affect the level of trade at different times. In general, the evidence is inconclusive. Still, exchange-rate instability has not hampered trade severely enough to make the effect unmistakably clear.

Some scraps of evidence gathered by other writers point to this same negative conclusion. The United States Tariff Commission investigated American trade during the period from October 1931 to about March 1932 to see whether the depression had harmed trade with countries that had left the gold standard more or less severely than trade with countries still clinging to gold. The Commission found no clear difference between changes in American trade with the two groups of countries.[5] James W. Angell classified a number of countries according to the stability or instability of their currencies in 1932 and compared the value and weight of the imports and exports of each group in 1932 with the corresponding averages of the figures for 1929 and 1931. He found that the trade of the unstable-currency group had declined distinctly less than the trade of the stable-currency group.[6] Seymour Harris also collected statistics suggesting that in the early 1930s, the trade of paper-currency countries generally declined less than the trade of gold-standard and exchange-control countries.[7]

EXCHANGE RISK AS AN OBSTACLE TO INTERNATIONAL TRADE AND INVESTMENT

Some broader and more impressionistic observations are also available. According to Bertil Ohlin, the volume of world trade grew about as fast during the period 1850–1870, before the full international gold standard came into existence, as in the early twentieth century, and faster than during the period of falling prices from the mid-1870s to the mid-1890s. Besides, trade between gold-standard and silver-standard countries grew even when the gold quotations of silver currencies were changing considerably.[8] According to Whittlesey, the years from 1846 to 1880 were not only a period of very active foreign lending but also probably the era of greatest freedom in world trade; an incipient decline of economic internationalism accompanied the emergence of the

4. All figures are derived from *International Financial Statistics*. The national income figure used for mid-1948 to mid-1949 is the average of the incomes for the two calendar years; the trade figure is the sum of the monthly figures.

5. United States Tariff Commission, *Depreciated Exchange* (Report No. 44, second series), Washington: U.S. Government Printing Office, 1932–1933, esp. Part I, pp. 2, 4, 5, and Part III, pp. 352, 357, 366, 370, 376. Also see the Commission's *Sixteenth Annual Report*, 1932, Washington: U.S. Government Printing Office, 1933, pp. 59–61.

6. James W. Angell, "Exchange Depreciation, Foreign Trade and National Welfare," *Proceedings of the Academy of Political Science*, XV, June 1933, pp. 290–291. In considering this result and the one mentioned in the next sentence of the text, it should be remembered that gold-standard countries did not conduct all their trade at stable exchange rates, since they were trading with some unstable-currency countries. Nevertheless, gold-standard countries must have done a smaller fraction of their trade at fluctuating exchange rates than unstable-currency countries, so that comparison of the two groups is not meaningless.

7. Seymour Harris, *Exchange Depreciation*, Cambridge, Mass.: Harvard University Press, 1936, pp. xxiii, 98–107, and *passim*.

8. Bertil Ohlin, "International Economic Reconstruction," in Joint Committee, Carnegie Endowment—International Chamber of Commerce, *International Economic Reconstruction*, Paris: International Chamber of Commerce, 1936, p. 36.

international gold standard toward the end of this period.[9] Frank Graham goes so far as to maintain that between the two world wars, the "volume, variety, and general beneficence" of international trade tended to be greater when exchange rates were flexible than when they were fixed.[10]

Since the end of the 1960s, as described in the historical chapters to follow, episodes of floating rates have multiplied. In time they may provide evidence on the trade-volume issue; the early evidence seemed rather encouraging. It is probably relevant to remember, though, that the floats have generally been "dirtied" by official intervention.

Exchange rates and trade barriers

Innumerable assertions that fluctuating exchanges cut down the volume of international trade have been published without the support of clear historical evidence. The fragmentary evidence reviewed in this chapter leaves such assertions still unsupported. Yet, as seems obvious, the risk of exchange fluctuations must almost certainly eliminate some trade that would otherwise occur. Perhaps it is unreasonable to expect historical or statistical support for this proposition since, as Michael Lindsay Hoffman points out, there is no way of measuring the trade "that would exist under otherwise similar circumstances."[11]

This is a key phrase. Granted that, *ceteris paribus*, exchange instability hampers trade, governments cannot stabilize exchange rates while keeping circumstances "otherwise similar." The very policies necessary to maintain fixed exchange rates, and their fixity at disequilibrium levels, may impede trade more severely than the mere risk of fluctuations.[12] Consideration of these matters, as well as of the ways merchants can guard against exchange risks, may help explain the inconclusiveness of the relevant statistics.

If policy keeps both the exchange-rate and price-and-income mechanisms of balance-of-payments adjustment from operating, tariffs or other controls may arise as a substitute. Alternatively, accepting deflation in the interest of external balance hampers trade. According to several interpreters, the rebirth of protectionism even before the collapse of the historical gold standard is not attributable solely to the self-seeking of producer interests. The unpleasantness of the domestic monetary adjustments required by the gold standard led to evasion of its "rules" by devices not generally recognized as evasions. Especially in the depression of the early 1930s, events dramatized the strongest motives for tariffs, quotas, export subsidies, and exchange controls—to conserve gold and defend the national currency.[13] Even when imposed for these reasons, however, import restrictions tend, for political reasons, to outlast the balance-of-payments crisis that may have occasioned them.

Fixed exchanges have a political tendency to promote import barriers by hiding their adverse effects. The benefit to protected home industries is evident; the burden on other industries is not. Under fixed exchanges, adjustments to balance-of-payments disturbances must take place through a pervasive process of wage-and-price-level changes understood only by special students. Under free exchanges, by contrast, one needs little special knowledge to see that a tariff increase would lower the price of foreign exchange and that while the new tariff would benefit the industries given tighter protection, its repercussions would injure other producers of import-competing goods, as well as exporters. These interests could voice definite objections to proposed tariff increases.[14]

Under fixed exchanges, a country may use commercial policy as a tool for creating or enlarging a balance-of-payments surplus to promote home employment. Examples are found in the 1930s. Under free exchanges (as distinguished from variable but manipulated exchanges) such a "beggar-my-neighbor" policy works less well. If one country does reduce the exports of another by tariffs against its goods, the other country's currency depreciates, tending to counteract the aggressive country's tariff and restore trade equilibrium. Under free exchanges, with trade enabled to jump tariff walls, governments might see the futility of tariffs as "beggar-my-neighbor" weapons.

Trade barriers and exchange depreciation are different in regard to retaliation. Retaliatory trade barriers can cancel out whatever benefit a single country might have got from its commercial policy, harming all countries involved by interference with the international division of labor. But retaliatory exchange depreciation does not leave any comparable interference with trade: two countries cannot impose and maintain a depreciation of their own currencies in terms of each other's. And *free* exchanges, by definition, leave no opportunity for beggar-my-neighbor or retaliatory depreciation.

Some economists have worried that trade barriers are more likely to result from fluctuating than from fixed exchanges. The reason seems to be that if some countries allow their currencies to depreciate, other countries, finding themselves in balance-of-payments trouble, will adopt protectionist measures in self-defense. These measures may in turn make the fluctuating currencies depreciate further, calling forth additional protectionism by the other countries, and so forth. Besides, exchange instability may make governments cautious in drawing up commercial treaties. When the danger of sudden and substantial exchange-rate changes exists, governments may hesitate to commit themselves to cuts in trade barriers. They may keep the machinery of emergency import control in readiness. Commercial treaties may be subject to denunciation on short notice or may include reservations regarding exchange-rate changes.[15]

This reasoning tacitly recognizes that protectionism is more likely to flourish in countries trying to maintain fixed exchange rates than in free-exchange countries. The erection of trade barriers against alleged exchange dumping is an effect not so much of fluctuating exchanges in particular as of general horror at all opportunities to obtain foreign goods on particularly favorable terms. While fluctuating foreign currencies may give protectionists a superficially plausible argument for stricter import barriers, the same necessary connection does not exist between fluctuating currencies and trade barriers as exists between overvalued currencies and trade barriers.

Furthermore, when free currencies depreciate on the exchange market, they must do so in response to conditions that would otherwise have caused balance-of-payments trouble for the countries concerned. If these countries did not allow their currencies to depreciate, they might have had to meet the situation with extra import barriers or export subsidies or internal deflation or disinflation. These measures, like depreciation, would cut down on imports from other countries. A country with an overvalued currency cannot avoid trade barriers simply by not depreciating unless it has such ample reserves of foreign exchange that the authorities can use them freely without fear of their possible exhaustion.

The argument about how depreciation may impel *other* countries to erect trade barriers usually seems to contemplate a sudden overcorrection of a previous overvaluation, so that the

EXCHANGE RISK AS AN OBSTACLE TO INTERNATIONAL TRADE AND INVESTMENT

depreciating country's new undervaluation puts other countries under strain. But this is less a characteristic of *freely* fluctuating exchanges than of flexibly pegged or managed exchanges. When a free currency depreciates, it does not necessarily put pressure on foreign countries. Suppose that as a country reflates at home in order to promote recovery from a depression, its currency depreciates passively on the exchanges. This does not steal markets from foreign countries, for the income effect of the reflation tends to offset the price effect of the

9. Charles R. Whittlesey, *International Monetary Issues*, New York: McGraw-Hill, 1937, pp. 89–91, 237.

10. Frank Graham, *The Cause and Cure of "Dollar Shortage,"* Essays in International Finance, No. 10, Princeton, N.J., Princeton University, 1949, p. 12.

11. Hoffman, *op. cit.*, p. 306.

12. In his *"Ceteris Paribus: Some Notes on Methodology," Southern Economic Journal*, XXIV, January 1958, pp. 259–270; James M. Buchanan has incisively dissected the errors in a number of economic theories purporting to keep constant some magnitudes that simply *cannot* remain constant in the face of changes in the magnitudes considered. A similar criticism should apply to analyses that purport to study the effects of certain policy changes while keeping constant other circumstances that *cannot* remain constant.

13. See Arthur D. Gayer, *Monetary Policy and Economic Stabilisation*, 2nd ed., New York: Macmillan, 1937, pp. 44–47; and Jørgen Pedersen, *Pengeteori og Pengepolitik*, Copenhagen: Busck, 1944, p. 195.

14. Henry C. Simons, "Currency Systems and Commercial Policy," in Commission of Inquiry into National Policy in International Economic Relations, *International Economic Relations*, Minneapolis: University of Minnesota Press, 1934, pp. 346–347.

15. T. E. Gregory, "The Reports of the Experts to the Joint Committee: A Personal Survey," *International Economic Reconstruction*, Paris: International Chamber of Commerce, 1936, pp. 171, 189–190. See also "Report of the Expert Committee" in *ibid.*, p. 222; and Margaret Gordon, *Barriers to World Trade*, New York: Macmillan, 1941, pp. 12–13.

depreciation. Adjustment of exchange rates to equilibrium levels promotes trade; depreciation puts pressure on the outside world only if it carries the exchange value of a currency below equilibrium.

As for the danger that fluctuating exchanges would obstruct international commercial agreements, this much seems true: fluctuating exchanges do complicate appraisals of the worth of proposed "concessions" in commercial policy and do complicate intergovernmental planning as to precisely what degree of protectionism each contracting government shall retain. But free exchanges facilitate rather than obstruct *voluntary* steps toward freer trade, as contrasted to unenthusiastic participation in a game which, to judge from reference to tariff cuts as "concessions" or sacrifices, is seen as a game of "You cut your throat and I'll cut mine."

Since the late 1960s, resort to controls, especially controls over capital movements, and episodes of ("dirtily") floating exchange rates have become commonplace. This association does not mean that the floats necessitated the controls. Both expedients appeared, rather, as the earlier pegged-rate system crumbled. Doctrinal influences were also at work: policymakers rejected free rates as a permanent system.

Disequilibrium exchange rates

It is superficial to blame interference with trade on trade barriers when clinging to wrong exchange rates is what makes these barriers seem necessary. In the 1930s, for example, exchange controls and quotas were probably less responsible for the contraction in trade than the maintenance of overvalued parities. Professor Nurkse has put the point well:

That the mere rate at which one currency is exchanged for other currencies can [affect the volume of trade] is not an easy or familiar notion to the general public, whereas the instruments used to support an overvalued currency—exchange control and quotas, among others—are immediately evident and so are apt to be regarded as the real cause of the fall in trade. But it should be clear that a country with an overvalued currency necessarily suffers a decline in its competitive capacity to export and that consequently its imports, in so far as they must be paid for by exports, have to be cut down accordingly; the means by which the cut is effected are of secondary interest; they may be exchange restrictions,

import licenses, quotas, prohibitions or even tariffs. In the conceivable extreme case where a currency's external value is so high that exports decline to zero, the result would be complete national autarky.[16]

If a government decrees and rigidly enforces too high an exchange value for its currency, it makes exports unprofitable and foreign exchange for imports correspondingly scarce. In the absence of official import controls or exchange rationing, unofficial and haphazard equivalents would inevitably develop. Undervaluation of the currency, on the other hand, will discourage imports by making them unduly expensive. Exports seem very profitable, but unless private parties or the authorities are willing to go on and on accumulating foreign exchange without using it (thus making interest-free or low-interest loans or ultimately even gifts to foreigners), or unless foreigners have inexhaustible reserves of the undervalued currency, export as well as import trade will decline. (Imports and, in turn, exports would revive, however, if a decline in the purchasing power of the domestic currency were to end the underevaluation. This might occur if the authorities created additional domestic money to finance their accumulations of foreign exchange at the fixed rate.)

This reasoning suggests that the volume of trade is larger at equilibrum than at disequilibrium exchange rates, just as the amount of a commodity changing hands per time period in any ordinary competitive market is greater at the price that equates supply and demand than at some different floor or ceiling price. This conclusion may not apply, however, when the overvalued-currency countries have enough reserves to satisfy all demands for foreign exchange at the official rates. The increase in their imports over what the volume would be at equilibrium rates might then be as large as or larger than the reduction in their exports. But this exception depends on truly ample foreign-exchange reserves. Maintaining exchange stability by import barriers is not at all the same thing as maintaining it by the lavish use of inexhaustible reserves.

Since underlying supplies and demands are continually changing, a fixed exchange rate is usually a disequilibrium rate, just as an officially fixed commodity price would usually be a disequilibrium price. If an exchange rate or a price is fixed by the government—and can be counted on to stay fixed—trade is no longer hampered by the risk of fluctuation. But does removing this risk tend to promote trade more than the disequilibrium price tends to hamper it? Merchants may indeed *worry* less about risk under fixed exchanges than under free exchanges, but part of the reason may simply be that fixed disequilibrium rates rule some potential trade so completely out of consideration that there is no point in worrying about risk connected with it.

Something can even be said in favor of clearly temporary or seasonal exchange-rate fluctuations. If shifting supplies and demands cause the equilibrium rate to change seasonally, stabilization at some average level would cause a discrepancy between actual and equilibrium rates throughout most of the year and so might hamper trade. (Think of the regrettable consequences that would flow from officially stabilizing Florida hotel rates at some average level throughout the year.) Generally speaking, seasonal fluctuations seem particularly useful in the prices of nonstorable goods and services. Now, many services enter into international trade—shipping services, harbor and dock use, the labor of stevedores and of employees of trading firms, and so forth. Also, not all internationally traded commodities are storable. Seasonal rate fluctuations may be useful in tending to even out the quantities of these nonstorable goods and services demanded throughout the year.

The case for pegging still would not be conclusive even if fluctuations were clearly a *net* deterrent to trade. This might not be too high a price to pay for greater freedom in domestic monetary and fiscal policy. Furthermore, any trade that exchange risk might destroy would probably be trade in articles whose international cost differences would be the smallest— trade in articles in which the exporting countries had the smallest comparative advantages over the importing countries.[17] More precisely, the *segments* of trade destroyed would be those for which the *marginal* comparative advantages would rise most slowly as trade shrank. Even though welfare cannot actually be measured, a presumption emerges that exchange risk shrinks welfare less than in proportion to the total volume of trade. The same cannot be said of controls adopted to support disequilibrium exchange rates, since they are often imposed in notorious disregard of comparative advantage.

Finally, exchange risk is not peculiar to a system of freely fluctuating rates. It also characterizes any other system under which rate changes are possible. When countries pursue

independent and uncoordinated monetary and fiscal policies, the choice cannot lie between fluctuating exchange rates and permanently fixed rates. It lies, rather, between more or less even fluctuation and temporary stability interrupted by occasional sharp changes.[18] Changes need not actually occur frequently in order to cause apprehension.

Protection against exchange risk

A full comparison of rival systems on this score must consider the possibilities of shedding risk. In one respect, as the following discussion will show, the possibilities are sometimes less satisfactory under pegged-but-adjustable rates than under free rates.

A merchant can largely avoid the risk of an unfavorable change in the fluctuating price of foreign exchange by creating an offsetting liability or asset in the foreign currency as soon as he becomes committed to receive or pay it in the future. An American exporter due to receive payment in sterling in 90 days might immediately borrow the sterling in London and sell it for dollars. The cost of this precaution would be any excess of interest paid to the British lender over interest obtainable on the dollars. A foreign electric system ordering heavy machinery in England might borrow *all* the necessary money at home at once, buy pounds at once, and place the money on loan in England until the sterling payments to the English engineering firms fell due. Difficulties, delays, and expenses in borrowing are, of course, obstacles to this approach.

A merchant might find it convenient to have a bank account in foreign money, either abroad or with his bank at home. When he incurred an obligation to pay foreign currency in the

---

16. Ragnar Nurkse, *International Currency Experience*, League of Nations, 1944, p. 184. Also see p. 169.

17. L. L. B. Angas, *The Problems of the Foreign Exchanges*, London: Macmillan, 1935, pp. 176, 180.

18. Frank D. Graham, "Achilles' Heels in Monetary Standards," *American Economic Review*, **XXX**, March 1940, p. 28.

future, he could immediately buy it and add it to his account, from which he could make payment at the proper time. When he became entitled to receive foreign currency in the future, he could immediately sell the corresponding amount from his account, replenishing it upon receipt of the expected payment. Unfortunately, this requires the merchant to tie up capital; any interest received on foreign-currency accounts might not be an adequate compensation. Furthermore, a merchant doing business with several countries would have to hold several foreign-currency accounts. Such arrangements would be satisfactory only for companies regularly both receiving and making payments in foreign countries. An English insurance company, for example, might guard rather well against fluctuations in the pound-dollar rate by leaving a large part of its premiums collected in the United States invested or on deposit there as a fund from which to make indemnity payments to American customers.

Forward exchange and some minor inadequacies

The foregoing methods are probably less important than forward exchange. An American importer or exporter due to pay or receive sterling in 90 days can protect himself against appreciation or depreciation of the pound in the meanwhile by buying or selling sterling forward. That is, he makes a contract with his bank to buy or sell a given number of pounds in 90 days at a price agreed on in advance. An importer does not have to lay out dollars to buy pounds until he needs them, yet he can be sure of the price at which he will get them. An exporter can grant credit to his foreign customer without running the risk of exchange loss.

All this was explained in Chapter 2, and details need not be repeated here except in considering some inadequacies of forward exchange. One is that forward-exchange contracts do not actually eliminate risk; rather, they offset one risk by another in the opposite direction. For example, an American exporter who is to receive future payment in British pounds stands to lose by depreciation of sterling in terms of dollars and stands to gain by an appreciation. By selling the same number of pounds forward, the exporter takes a position

in which he stands to gain by depreciation of sterling and to lose by appreciation. Now, if the export transaction that is the reason for the forward contract somehow falls through or if the foreign customer is delinquent in paying his debt, the exporter has an uncoveed position in foreign exchange and stands to lose if he has to buy sterling at an appreciated price to deliver it to the bank under his forward contract. This is hardly a serious problem, however. At least those firms that import or export in large volume can learn from experience how to make allowance, in buying or selling forward exchange, for the fraction of their commercial transactions that will not be completed as originally planned.

Forward exchange cannot simultaneously protect the importer of a competitively traded staple commodity against both of the risks mentioned earlier—the exchange risk and the price risk. If the importer buys foreign currency forward to guard against its appreciation between the time he orders the goods and the time he is to pay, he still stands a risk of the second kind: if the currency of the supplying country depreciates against the home currency before the importer has disposed of the goods, the value of his inventory falls, since his competitors can now import more of the same goods at a lower home-money price than he paid. By neglecting to make any forward-exchange contract at all, the importer would let the two kinds of exchange risk partially offset each other. If the foreign currency appreciated, he would lose in buying foreign exchange to pay his supplier but would gain on the home-money value of his inventory. If the foreign currency depreciated, he would gain in buying foreign exchange to pay his supplier but would lose on the home-money value of his inventory. Unfortunately, the two risks do not exactly offset each other, and the importer must estimate how and to what extent, on balance, he stands to gain or lose by a change in the exchange rate. Having made this estimate, the importer can judge, though not very accurately, how much foreign exchange to buy.

An importer's dilemma may be particularly troublesome if he is importing some staple commodity from a country that accounts for a major fraction of the total world supply and whose currency is threatened with devaluation. (Essentially the same dilemma exists if upward revaluation of the home currency is a strong possibility, except that it is not necessary for a large fraction of total imports to be bought in some particular foreign country.) If he does cover his foreign-exchange needs by a forward purchase, he risks the inventory loss just explained. If he hedges against this risk by *not* buying exchange forward and if the expected foreign devaluation is somehow avoided, he may find that his competitors have obtained a price advantage by grasping the opportunity to buy the foreign currency forward at the heavy forward discount reflecting the general distrust of its spot rate. It should be noted, however, that the large forward discount causing the special problem in this example is unlikely to occur except when spot exchange rates are (adjustably) pegged; in the absence of pegging, spot and forward rates would fluctuate fairly closely together, in accordance with the principle of interest parities.

The foregoing examples no doubt exaggerate an importer's problems. Inventory risk is ordinarily likely to be small relative to exchange risk, and an importer would ordinarily do well to obtain forward cover for the bulk of his foreign-exchange needs. (The terms *covering* and *hedging* are often used loosely as complete synonyms. When a distinction is intended, *covering* means arranging for protection against the exchange risk involved in a definitely scheduled commercial or financial transaction. *Hedging* then means arranging for protection against an indefinite and indirect risk linked with a possible rate change, such as the risk of a fall in the home-currency value of business properties located abroad.)[19]

The cost of forward-exchange cover

Even if forward contracts do offer protection against exchange risk, the possible objection remains that its cost would deter trade under free exchanges.[20] Just what is this cost, and how large is it likely to be? To an importer billed in foreign currency, it is how much more he pays for foreign exchange bought forward rather than spot; to an exporter billing in foreign currency, it is how much less he receives for foreign exchange sold forward rather than spot. This cost is negative for a trader who finds the forward rate more advantageous to himself than the spot rate. Whether positive or negative, this cost need not fall entirely on only one of the two parties to an international transaction; it may well be split between the seller and the buyer through its effect on the pricing of the goods traded.

Strictly speaking, the cost of or the gain from forward cover per unit of foreign currency is the difference between the currently quoted forward rate and the spot rate that will prevail at the relevant future date.[21] Because no one can know the future spot rate at the time of making a forward contract, this cost of forward cover cannot be known then, either. Uncertainty about the future is, after all, why traders make forward contracts, thereby eliminating both their risk of loss and chance of gain on a change in the spot rate. With forward protection, traders need feel no cost in the sense of risking such losses or gains. They can take the forward rate into account when calculating their prospective profits from contemplated international transactions. They no more suffer a cost than they would if for some reason they were dealing currently in the spot market at the known spot rate. "What matters in connection with foreign trade is the exchange rate at which exporters and importers transact their business." A change in the forward rate "is simply a change in the exchange rate that many traders use as the basis of calculation."[22]

19. See Paul Einzig, A *Dynamic Theory of Forward Exchange*; London: Macmillan, 1961, esp. pp. 3–4, 34, 82–85, 89–92, 234–236.

20. Cf. Nurkse, *op. cit.*, p. 210.

21. The "miscellaneous costs of forward cover" mentioned a few pages later may make this formulation only approximately correct.

John Van Belle (in an unpublished manuscript) has calculated the cost of cover as the percent per year discrepancy between forward rate and spot rate at time of maturity of forward contract for transactions between the United States and Canada, the United Kingdom, and Germany in 1955–1960 and 1970–1973. Such discrepancies, ignoring sign, turned out much larger than ordinary forward premiums and discounts. This finding stands to reason: covered interest arbitrage links forward and spot rates quoted at a given time, whereas current forward and maturity-of-contract spot rates are separated by time, which only speculation and not arbitrage could bridge.

22. Fritz Machlup in George N. Halm, ed., *Approaches to Greater Flexibility of Exchange Rates*, Princeton, N.J.: Princeton University Press, 1970, p. 309; see p. 300 also.

Since the future spot rate can be compared with the current forward rate only later, with hindsight, and not at the time of a decision about making a forward contract, an alternative comparison suggests itself—one between the current forward rate and the *current* spot rate. The spread between them, the forward premium or discount in the ordinary sense, is widely regarded as some sort of indicator of the cost of forward cover. Instead of making a forward contract, a trader could conceivably complete his foreign-exchange transaction promptly at the current spot rate, borrowing and lending funds at home and abroad as appropriate until the time of final settlement with his foreign trading partner. Taking the forward premium or discount as the desired indicator can admittedly be justified only intuitively, not rigorously, which serves to underline the vagueness of the very concept of the cost of forward cover.[23]

Anyway, the cost of risk avoidance, as thus approximated, is ordinarily not large either negatively or positively in fully free markets, since forward and spot rates are closely related. One reason is that commercial demands and supplies of forward exchange partly match each other. While importers want to buy exchange forward, exporters want to sell. Banks and brokers make a business of enabling traders to satisfy each other's requirements, and competition tends to keep margins small enough just to compensate the middlemen for their work. Under normal conditions, furthermore, the spread between the spot and forward rates is aligned with the international difference in short-term interest rates. The explanation, already given in Chapter 2, involves interest arbitrage and the principle of interest parities. Even if home and foreign interest rates differed by four percentage points a year, for example, the premium or discount from spot on 90-day forward exchange would be only about 1 percent.

Whether estimated by the currently unknowable spread between the current forward rate and the future spot rate or by the currently known forward premium or discount, the cost of forward cover can just as well turn out negative as positive; and if positive for either importers billed or exporters billing in foreign currency, it is negative for the other group. This fact underlines the fallacy of regarding forward-exchange transactions as *insurance* against exchange-rate risk, since insurance premiums are never negative.[24] In making

forward contracts with their customers and in evening-out their positions in the interbank market, banks are not acting as insurance companies. Instead, they are agreeing to sell foreign exchange in the future to some customers while agreeing to buy it from others. Instead of spreading the losses from essentially unavoidable risks around in sure but small pieces known as insurance premiums, as insurance does, forward-exchange transactions *destroy* risk by canceling opposite risks out against each other. Traders using forward contracts are *not* paying insurance premiums to pool or share risks; they are not dealing at forward-exchange rates systematically less favorable to themselves than the relevant spot rates would have been. They are not paying any risk premiums supposedly shifted partly onto producers and partly onto consumers in the prices of internationally traded goods.

Forward rates under pegged spot rates

Large discrepancies sometimes observed between forward and spot rates are often cited as evidence of the high cost or impossibility of avoiding risk under free exchanges. This is ironic, for such discrepancies occur during episodes of speculation against *pegged* rates (or officially manipulated flexible rates).[25] The historical chapters of this book describe episodes since World War II. Some prewar examples are also noteworthy. During 1935 the discounts on three-month forward French francs, Dutch guilders, and Swiss francs reached 27, 22, and 29 percent per annum respectively.[26] The forward French franc was even weaker in 1936. At times before the devaluation in September, the discount on three-month francs went to 37 or 38 percent per annum.[27] Under these conditions, protection against exchange risk was expensive indeed. If an American owner had hedged an asset valued in a fixed number of French francs by a three-month forward sale on January 2, 1935 and by six successive renewals, the cost would have amounted to more than half of the loss that the owner would otherwise have suffered from the devaluation in September 1936. The high cost of hedging induced many businessmen to leave their long positions in francs unprotected.[28]

These large forward discounts betrayed general distrust of the currencies of the European "gold bloc." Demand and supply of forward exchange were very one-sided. At forward rates in line with spot rates, few traders with future obligations in francs would have wanted to buy francs forward to guard against such an unlikely event as appreciation. But those with claims to future francs, or Frenchmen with future obligations in foreign currencies, were eager to sell francs forward, at least if the discount did not seem too large. Outright bear speculation also took place in the forward market.

Why didn't interest arbitrage compensate for the one-sidedness of other supply and demand? It was indeed profitable for holders of francs to sell them spot and repurchase them forward. As these operations involved the sale of spot francs, they increased the gold outflows from France and also tended to reduce the supply of loanable funds, increasing French interest rates.[29] Though arbitrage *was* tending to equate the forward franc discount to the difference between French and foreign interest rates in two ways—by supporting the forward franc and by raising French interest rates—it could not do the job completely. For one thing, arbitrage could not pull the spot franc appreciably down toward the forward franc as long as France still clung to the gold parity. Furthermore, some Frenchmen, once having got their money out of France, were presumably reluctant to bring it back again by buying forward francs. Perhaps even more important was the fact that the French government tried to discourage interest arbitrage. Also, Great Britain and other countries tried to help the gold-bloc governments in their fight against what they considered speculation.[30]

Since commercial demand for and supply of forward exchange are seldom equally strong and are especially unlikely to be so when the spot rate is inappropriate, "legitimate" traders can be sure of finding cover at moderate discounts or premiums only in an active market broadened by speculation and interest arbitrage. Exchange restrictions, even if confined to capital transfers, interfere with interest arbitrage. To the extent that "legitimate" traders can find cover only with their fellows dealing in the opposite direction, forward rates may have to deviate far from spot rates in order to equate "legitimate" supplies and demands.

One side or the other of the forward market is especially likely to languish when a pegged spot rate is generally distrusted. When a cur-

EXCHANGE RISK AS AN OBSTACLE TO INTERNATIONAL TRADE AND INVESTMENT

rency is expected to fall, holders of claims to future payment in it will be able to cover them only at unattractive forward rates. Even if outright speculators are prevented from selling the distrusted currency forward, selling pressure on the forward rate still exceeds buying pressure, for people committed to make future payments in the currency have ample reason not to buy it forward.

Because of large and unstable discrepancies

23. Since a forward contract and an immediate spot transaction are alternative methods of avoiding exchange risk, the ordinary forward premium or discount is an aspect of the *difference* between the costs of those methods rather than the cost of cover itself. Other aspects of this cost difference include the differences between home and foreign interest rates and between the transactions costs of the two methods. Mention of transactions costs suggests still another possible indicator of the cost of cover: the excess of the bid-asked spread on forward exchange over the bid-asked spread on spot exchange at the time of maturity of the forward contract. It is empirically unusual but quite possible for this excess to be negative.

24. On the fallacy of the insurance conception of forward exchange, see Egon Sohmen, *The Theory of Forward Exchange*, Princeton, N.J.: Princeton University, International Finance Section, 1966.

25. Egon Sohmen, *Flexible Exchange Rates*, rev. ed., Chicago: University of Chicago Press, 1969, pp. 109–110.

26. A. A. van Sandick, "Memorandum on the Technique of the Forward Exchange Market and the Elimination of Uncertainty," *The Improvement of Commercial Relations between Nations and the Problems of Monetary Stabilization*, Paris: International Chamber of Commerce, 1936, p. 306.

27. Paul Einzig, *The Theory of Forward Exchange*, London: Macmillan, 1937, pp. 480–481; Martin Wolfe, *The French Franc Between the Wars*, New York: Columbia University Press, 1951, p. 164. The figures refer to pound-franc rates.

28. Charles P. Kindleberger, "Speculation and Forward Exchange," *Journal of Political Economy*, XLVII, April 1939, p. 176.

29. Einzig, *The Theory of Forward Exchange*, pp. 192–193.

30. *Ibid.*, pp. 377–378; Kindleberger, *op. cit.*, p. 172.

between spot and forward rates, exchange risk can at times be a bigger deterrent to international trade under pegged-but-adjustable exchanges than under fluctuating exchanges. How often precariously pegged rates actually do change is not decisive. The point is that traders bear in mind the risk of changes and that protection against this risk becomes expensive under pegged exchanges precisely when traders most feel the need for it. Under free rates, by contrast, there is no general opinion that the spot rate will move only in one particular direction, since the current spot rate *already* reflects the balance of opinion. Consequently, neither buying nor selling pressure predominates in the forward market. Under free rates, furthermore, use of the forward market probably becomes more general and routine than under pegged rates, leaving less scope for one-sided stampedes to obtain the forward cover usually neglected.[31] If capital movements are unrestricted, interest arbitrage tends to keep forward rates near their interest parities in relation to spot rates. Realizing this, speculators contribute to keeping discrepancies between forward and spot rates small and transitory.

Miscellaneous costs of forward cover

This optimistic conclusion perhaps needs to be slightly qualified. Pledging collateral, if required, is an additional cost of risk protection. When a bank finds itself with a net long or short position in some currency as a result of forward contracts with its customers, it offsets this position by selling or buying the currency. If one of its customers defaults on his forward contract, the bank has an uncovered position in the currency and may suffer an exchange loss. To protect itself, the bank may require a customer to put up some collateral or margin to guarantee performance of his forward contract. The collateral required would be worth only a fraction of the amount of the contract, since default by a customer costs the bank not the whole amount, but only the possible loss on that amount because of an unfavorable exchange-rate movement. Still, putting up even a relatively small capital in collateral or margin might increase the true cost of protection. In practice, however, banks seldom ask traders to guarantee their forward contracts with collateral. The reason is that a bank ordinarily makes forward contracts only with its regular customers, whom it has learned to trust and who probably have deposits in the bank anyway.

In appraising the total cost of forward-exchange protection, one should remember several facts. First, while provision of forward-exchange facilities does use up some labor and resources, so does the operation of spot markets. Even if forward exchange vanished, much of the cost would probably still have to be incurred in maintaining ordinary exchange facilities. Second the many kinds of governmental and intergovernmental activities involved in trying to keep exchange rates pegged have costs of their own. Actually, these various costs come in addition to rather than instead of the costs of forward-exchange facilities, since when exchange rates are pegged but insecure, traders still feel the need of forward-exchange cover. Furthermore, cost-cutting competition among banks prevails in supplying forward-exchange facilities, whereas there can be no similar competition in the supply of governmental and intergovernmental measures. One final point rests on a value judgment that costs should ordinarily be borne by the people in whose interest they are incurred: the cost, such as it is, of protection against free-market exchange fluctuations falls on the producers and consumers of internationally traded goods, whereas the expense of governmental measures is widely diffused.

Long-term exchange risk

Forward exchange does not provide perfect protection against long-term exchange risk. If a construction company is doing work in a foreign country and is to receive payment in the foreign currency only after the lapse of well over a year, how can it protect itself against exchange risk? Special arrangements can sometimes be made, and long-term forward contracts might become regularly available if sufficient demand arose and exchange restrictions did not interfere; the trend of forward-exchange practice is encouraging in this respect.[32] But the construction company in our example has no really good answer to its problem if banks do not make forward contracts of maturities as long as it requires. Still, it can eliminate most of its exchange risk by selling the currency it expects to receive by a three-month forward contract and then renewing the contract every three months.

For the sake of as simple an explanation as possible, let us consider what an American exporter might do to avoid exchange loss on £1 to be received six months in the future, even though three-month contracts were the longest obtainable. First, he sells £1 to his bank three months forward at a price of about $3.00. (We assume that the spot rate at the time is exactly $3.00; *about* means plus the forward premium or minus the forward discount.) If the spot rate is unchanged when the forward contract comes due, our exporter buys £1 in the spot market for $3.00, delivers it to the bank to fulfill the contract, and receives the agreed price of "about $3.00." Then he again sells £1 three months forward at a price of about $3.00 (but probably not precisely the same forward price as before). (Actual practice, of course, telescopes these separate steps together.) By the time this second contract comes due, the exporter has received from his English customer the £1 that is the occasion for these procedures. He delivers it to the bank and receives the agreed price of about $3.00, no matter what may have happened to the exchange rate during the second three months.

Now let us suppose the same situation, except that by the end of the first three months the spot pound has depreciated to $2.00. To fulfill his forward contract, the exporter buys £1 in the spot market for $2.00 and delivers it to the bank for the agreed price of about $3.00. Then, to guard against further depreciation, he again sells £1 forward for three months, this time at a forward rate of about $2.00. This he receives when he finally delivers £1 at the end of the second three months. This price, together with the profit of about $1.00 taken in closing out the first contract, amounts to approximately the rate of "about $3.00" that the exporter had originally counted on. If the pound, instead of depreciating, had appreciated to $4.00 during the first three months, the exporter would have lost about $1.00 in closing out his first contract, but this loss would be approximately offset by his receipt of about $4.00 under the second forward contract.

If an American importer is committed to pay £1 six months in the furure, he can protect himself by buying £1 three months forward and then renewing. The original forward rate is approximately equal to the $3.00 spot rate. At the end of three months, the importer takes delivery, paying the agreed price of about $3.00. If by then the spot pound had appreci-

ated to $4.00, the importer would collect a profit of about $1.00. Because of this, he would in effect pay only the approximate net price for the pound that he had originally counted on, even though he took delivery at the end of the second forward contract at the new rate of about $4.00 specified in it.

These examples show that a series of short-term forward contracts can remove most of a long-term exchange risk. Most, but not all. For one thing, a merchant risks not being able to get a new forward contract when an old one expires. Barring the outbreak of war or the imposition of crippling exchange controls, however, the forward market will not suddenly vanish. More substantial is the risk of being able to renew a forward contract only on unfavorable terms. The forward seller risks the emergence of a large forward discount from the spot rate, and the forward buyer risks the

31. In nonspeculative periods under pegged rates, business firms show relatively little interest in forward cover, but their eagerness for it rises one-sidedly when a rate comes under suspicion. See Helmut Lipfert in Robert Z. Aliber, ed., *The International Market for Foreign Exchange*, New York: Praeger, 1969, p. 236; and Edwin A. Reichers and Harold Van B. Cleveland (officials of the First National City Bank of New York) in Halm, *op. cit.*, p. 325. Samuel I. Katz reviews some of the admittedly fragmentary and inconsistent information available on business use of forward facilities in *Exchange-Risk Under Fixed and Flexible Exchange Rates*, New York University, *The Bulletin*, Nos. 83–84, June 1972, pp. 56–57.

32. Availabilities of forward contracts for a year or more in New York, in Sweden, in Britain, and on the Continent are mentioned in, respectively, Alan R. Holmes, *The New York Foreign Exchange Market*, Federal Reserve Bank of New York, 1959, p. 38; Bent Hansen, "Interest Policy, Foreign Exchange Policy and Foreign Exchange Control," *Skandinaviska Banken Quarterly Review*, **XL**, January 1959, p. 16; Einzig, *Economic Journal*, September 1960, pp. 486, 493; and Einzig, *A Dynamic Theory of Forward Exchange*, pp. 58, 548. "Today," according to a book published in 1971, "yearly contracts are routine in the major world currencies and arrangements are made for up to 7 years." Bernard A. Lietaer, *Financial Management of Foreign Exchange*, Cambridge, Mass.: The MIT Press, p. 71.

emergence of a large premium. The risk consists not in the possibility of large fluctuations in spot or forward rates, which in themselves are relatively harmless, but in the possibility of *divergent* spot and forward rate movements. Interest arbitrage ordinarily prevents large divergences.

Here we see another difference between exchange risk under freely fluctuating and under pegged-but-adjustable rates. The forward rate can deviate considerably from a *pegged* spot rate because of one-sided selling or buying pressure in the forward market when the spot rate is generally considered untenably high or low. Also, precisely because the spot rate is pegged, it cannot move to help close the gap between itself and the forward rate. Finally, controls sometimes used in maintaining a fixed spot rate may interfere with the interest arbitrage that would otherwise keep the gap between spot and forward rates narrow.[33] Under pegged rates, changing rumors about the imminence and size of an exchange-rate adjustment are sometimes likely to make the forward premium or discount not only large but also highly unstable.

A businessman may feel almost as much risk in a long-term position in a foreign currency under pegged exchanges as under free exchanges. No one can be certain that a pegged rate will not be altered within the next few months or years. Yet because the forward premium or discount may vary widely, a trader cannot count on hedging his risk economically by successive renewals of short-term contracts. Under free exchanges, possible variations in the forward premium or discount are a less serious threat to advantageous renewal of forward contracts. Therefore, irremovable long-term exchange risk may even be a less serious problem under free exchanges than under pegged exchanges. This point deserves thoughtful consideration. And in reality, the makeshift of renewals is unnecessary when long-term contracts are available.

We must now recognize a kind of exchange risk that forward contracts cannot remove. It is the long-run, enduring uncertainty of being in a line of business—foreign trade, or production for export, or domestic use of imported materials—whose revenues or costs are subject to unpredictable fluctuation not only for all the ordinary reasons but also through change in exchange rates. This uncertainty remains even though the forward market enables businessmen to deal at exchange rates known firmly at the time of final decision on individual transactions. Individual transactions may enjoy forward cover, but not the entire stream of transactions that affect a firm's long-run profitability. Businessmen will allow for exchange-rate-related uncertainty in the prices that they charge and pay, and these allowances will tend to hamper trade. The relevant exchange rates, even though forward rates, are likely to be more changeable under flexible than under securely fixed spot rates, since forward rates tend to stay in close relation to spot rates.[34]

This point is valid but must be viewed in perspective. For one thing, businessmen cannot be certain that fixed rates will remain fixed. (Contrary expectations, as we have seen, can sometimes move forward rates to sizable premiums or discounts.) A large devaluation or revaluation that suddenly alters the profitability of being in a particular line of business may well be more seriously disruptive than gradual changes in profitability associated with gradual changes in free exchange rates. A hybrid system straddling monetary nationalism and monetary internationalism may well pose a worse problem of exchange risk than either extreme.

A system of *permanently* fixed exchange rates would avoid the uncertainty of both sudden and gradual changes. Under a full-fledged and enduring international gold standard, for example, each country would sacrifice full employment and price-level stability, if need be, to the supreme goal of preserving the parity of its currency. But the necessary financial policies would entail uncertainties of their own. The changes in underlying conditions that would cause either exchange-rate movements or active or passive adjustments in financial policies, depending on the exchange-rate system in effect, occur under any system. The associated burden of uncertainty would fall on different groups of persons under different systems. Keeping exchange rates fixed represents an attempt to "socialize" some of this burden, shifting it away from firms engaged in international transactions and onto other groups. Such a shift is not obviously efficient and equitable. Floating exchange rates, by contrast, leave the burden of coping with risk more nearly squarely on the shoulders of those who directly profit from international transactions.[35]

Worries about exchange risk often tacitly assume that exchange rates move for no fundamental reason. Actually, rate flexibility may just as well provide shelter against disturbances as pose an independent disturbance; exchange-rate changes may sometimes benefit rather than harm firms engaged in international trade. Consider an export firm selling on a competitive world market and squeezed by costs rising in line with inflation at home. Discontinuance of exchange-rate pegging would relieve such a firm of a burden, not saddle it with a fresh one.[36]

Types of forward-exchange contract

After considering whether forward exchange contracts provide a hedge against long-term risk, we should ask whether or not forward contracts are available only in standard maturities—30, 60, and 90 days. What recourse is open to a trader who wants to buy or sell a currency in 45 or 75 days or who does not know the exact date when he will need to buy or sell it? For one thing, a combination of spot and forward transactions should be able to meet the problem at no great expense. Odd-length contracts are also possible. Banks will tailor the lengths of contracts to suit their customers. Banks also offer contracts permitting the customer to make or take deliver whenever he chooses during a specified week or half-month or month.

Similarly, banks will tailor the denominations of contracts as customers wish; it is possible to sell, say, £716 forward. Large importing and exporting firms might be content, however, to make contracts in round numbers.

If fluctuating exchange rates were to become an enduring system, option trading in foreign exchange, analogous to puts and calls in securities, might well develop. Such facilities have existed in the past, as in Berlin in the late nineteenth century. Suppose, for example, that a German coal company quoted a price in rubles and allowed its prospective Russian customer several weeks to decide on the offer. With the ruble fluctuating and the customer's decision not yet made, the coal company would expose itself to exchange risk whether it made a firm forward sale of rubles or did nothing. The solution was to make a contingent forward sale, which was in effect the purchase of an option to sell rubles at a specified exchange rate.[37]

EXCHANGE RISK AS AN OBSTACLE TO INTERNATIONAL TRADE AND INVESTMENT

Availability of forward-exchange facilities

A common worry about forward exchange as protection against exchange risk is that its facilities are available only to the traders of a few leading countries. However, even if a small trader in some remote country were ignorant of forward exchange, his trading partner in an

33. Ironically, arguments against free exchange rates often stress the observed thinness of markets in long-term forward exchange, even though that thinness stems partly from actual or feared restrictions on interest arbitrage amidst the balance-of-payments troubles characteristic of the pegged-rate system. Arbitrage, not speculation, is what matters. It is a mistake to argue that long-term forward markets are unlikely to flourish because speculators will not assume the long-term risk supposedly involved. Sohmen, *Flexible Exchange Rates*, rev. ed., pp. 111–112.

34. Related points are a theme of Wilfred Ethier, "International Trade and the Forward Exchange Market," *American Economic Review*, Vol. 63, June 1973, pp. 494–503; Peter B. Clark, "Uncertainty, Exchange Risk, and the Level of International Trade," *Western Economic Journal*, XI, September 1973, pp. 302–313; and Samuel I. Katz, *op. cit.*, esp. pp. 39, 69.

35. Cf. Machlup in Halm, *op. cit.*, p. 300; and Anthony Lanyi, *The Case for Floating Exchange Rates Reconsidered*, Princeton Essays in International Finance, No. 72, Princeton, N.J.: Princeton University, February 1969, especially p. 16.

36. A somewhat similar example appears in Samuel Brittan, *The Price of Economic Freedom*, New York: St. Martin's Press, 1970, p. 50. For further remarks about how dependable or how uncertain profits are under fixed and under fluctuating exchange rates, see p. 638.

37. This example appears in Germany, Börsen-Enquete-Kommission, *Bericht*, Berlin: Reichsdruckerei, 1893, p. 94. Other examples of the advantageous use of puts and calls in German-Russian trade appear in Gerhart v. Schulze-Gävernitz, *Volkswirtschaftliche Studien aus Russland*, Leipzig: Duncker & Humblot, 1899, p. 510, citing Max Weber in *Zeitschrift für Handelsrecht*, XLV, p. 58.

important foreign market might be willing to quote prices in the small trader's own currency in order to get his business. According to Einzig, German exporters, who had access to forward exchange facilities, made striking headway before World War I in such outlying districts as the interiors of Brazil and China.[38]

A similar worry is that exchange markets could not be expected to quote minor currencies in terms of one another. A Finnish importer of goods from Honduras could hardly hope to buy forward lempiras in terms of markkas. However, if there were a forward market between the markka and sterling and a forward market between the lempira and sterling, then the markka and lempira would be linked indirectly by forward-exchange facilities. If it were to their advantage, importers and exporters in little countries could, as they largely do now, agree on prices in terms of sterling or some other important currency and then avoid exchange risk by forward dealings in the local currency and sterling. Little countries would need to have a forward market in only the one or two most important foreign currencies. Alternatively, the custom might arise of pricing exports and imports of small countries in grams of gold, so that a market in gold futures in each country would suffice to protect local exporters and importers against exchange risk.

History gives encouragement about the likelihood that adequate forward markets would develop under free exchanges, if given a chance. Throughout the 1880s the Vienna bourse dealt actively in German mark notes for forward delivery, and forward dealings had probably begun several decades earlier. There were also occasional forward dealings in Vienna and Trieste in sterling and French francs against fluctuating Austrian guldens. Berlin had an irregular market in forward rubles after the Russian paper money became inconvertible during the Crimean War. This market gained importance in the late 1870s, when a large and steady export of grain from Russia developed and when the Russian government printed paper money to finance its war with Turkey. St. Petersburg had a less important forward market. The United States had active forward-exchange markets several decades before World War I; these markets probably originated during the period of the Civil War greenbacks. At that time New York definitely had a well-organized market in gold futures, which was practically equivalent to a

market in forward sterling. Long before World War I, fluctuations in the exchange rate between silver and gold gave rise to a forward sterling market in Shanghai. Japan had forward exchange facilities in sterling, dollars, and francs. Argentina, Brazil, Chile, Egypt, Spain, Portugal, and most other civilized countries, according to Einzig, had active forward markets before World War I. Forward exchange markets were especially active in the period of exchange fluctuations after World War I. During the 1930s, merchants could buy and sell forward sterling, dollars, French and Swiss francs, guilders, belgas, escudos, Canadian dollars, Scandinavian currencies, and the major Latin American and Oriental currencies. Before interference from exchange restrictions or internal troubles, good forward markets had also existed in other currencies, such as reichsmarks, lire, and pesetas.[39]

An account of the forward-exchange market in as small a country as Chile before World War I is relevant to judging whether adequate hedging facilities might arise under free exchanges. The Chilean peso was so unstable that all purchases and sales of foreign exchange were forward transactions, unless otherwise specifically agreed. Spot transactions were for small amounts only. Since mailboats sailed from Valparaiso for Liverpool every other Tuesday morning, most forward-exchange contracts were arranged to fall due on the Monday before each departure. Forward contracts were made for the nearest mail-day and for each of the 25 following, so that traders could cover foreign-exchange commitments for as long as a year in the future. Most contracts were for multiples of £500. Traders dealt in forward exchange, free from government control, on a bourse, in the banks, and even on the streets. There was also a well-developed renewal market, giving speculators the opportunity to continue their forward-exchange positions.[40]

Exchange risk and international lending

A twin to the worry that exchange fluctuations would hamper international trade is the worry that they would discourage international borrowing and lending. If a lender makes a loan in the currency of a foreign borrower, whether for 30 days or for 30 years, he runs the risk that the foreign currency will be worth less in his own currency at the time of repayment than when he made the loan. If the loan is in the lender's currency, the borrower risks having to repay at a time when that currency has appreciated against his own. Of course, the chance of gain from a favorable rate movement stands against the chance of loss from an unfavorable one. This obvious point should be remembered throughout the present discussion.

If forward-exchange facilities can overcome the exchange risks associated with trade, why can't they do the same for the risks associated with international lending? In fact, individuals *can* protect themselves from exchange risk on short-term international loans. Interest arbitrage is a prime example: an arbitrageur who is temporarily transferring funds abroad sells the foreign currency forward at the same time he buys it spot. However, borrowers and lenders can all get rid of their exchange risks only when the flows of capital into and out of a country match each other. Forward exchange cannot get rid of the exchange risk on a *net* outflow or inflow. Lenders placing funds abroad will not only buy the foreign currency spot to pay for the securities bought but will also want to sell the currency forward to cover bringing their funds home again. If the capital movement is supposed to be a *net* outflow from the lending country, the safety-minded lenders will predominate as sellers of the foreign currency in the *forward* market. Now, who are the corresponding buyers of forward foreign exchange, i.e., forward sellers of the currency of the *lending* country? They must largely be arbitrageurs who, in order to be able to sell the lending country's currency forward without risk, have bought it spot. (These arbitrageurs may, of course, be nationals of the lending country who are buying their own currency spot with funds borrowed abroad.) In buying and holding the currency of the lending country, the arbitrageurs are transferring capital *into* that country. The ordinary capital export in the form of foreign security purchases is matched by a capital import through arbitrage in the spot and forward markets. Thus, if capital exporters insist on covering all of their exchange risk, they will fail to accomplish any net capital export at all.[41]

The same is true of an international loan expressed in the lenders' currency. The borrowers will want to cover their repayment by buying that currency forward. But the arbitrageurs who sell it forward will cover themselves by buying it spot. As before, this amounts to an offsetting flow of capital into the country that superficially appears to be exporting capital.

This analysis requires some qualification. Not all those who serve as counterparties in forward contracts with risk-avoiding lenders or borrowers need be risk-avoiding arbitrageurs; some may be speculators who deliberately assume exchange risk by leaving their forward sales of the lending country's currency uncovered by spot purchases. A net international capital movement can then take place with nonspeculative borrowers and lenders protected against exchange risk.

Still, it remains true under unstable exchanges that international lending inevitably involves exchange risk to be borne by *somebody*. There are no obvious grounds for assuming that speculators would operate in the right direction and shoulder enough of the risk to leave international lending just as active under unstable exchanges as, other things being equal, it would be under stable exchanges. Exchange instability apparently is a genuine deterrent to international capital movements.[42]

This disadvantage is not peculiar to *freely fluctuating* exchange rates, however; rather, it characterizes all systems of changeable exchange rates, including pegged-but-adjustable

---

38. Einzig, *The Theory of Forward Exchange*, pp. 50–51.

39. *Ibid.*, pp. 37–39, 42–46, 379–380; Van Sandick, *op. cit.*, p. 297; Schulze-Gävernitz, *op. cit.*, *passim* between pp. 499–536.

40. Rudolf Dunker, "Kursspekulation und Kurssicherung in südamerikanische Valuten, speziell in chilenischer Währung," *Bank-Archiv*, 15 Oct. and 1 Nov. 1909, esp. pp. 40–41.

41. This reasoning expands on Harold Barger, "Speculation and the Risk-Preference," *Journal of Political Economy*, **XLVI**, June 1938, p. 402. Also see *Bretton Woods for Better or Worse*, London: Longmans, Green, 1946, pp. 100–104, where R. G. Hawtrey reaches the same conclusion: if no one were willing to bear the risk of exchange-rate instability, net lending would cease to be international.

42. For historical examples, see Guillermo Subercaseaux, *Le Papier-Monnaie*, Paris: Giard & Brière, 1920, pp. 228–234.

rates. If the exchange rate changes in the harmful direction during the life of an international loan, it makes no difference to the losers whether the change occurred through free-market fluctuations or through one or more adjustments in official pegging. It is not enough that governments try to avoid frequent rate adjustments. To eliminate exchange risk over the life of medium- and long-term international loans, countries must sacrifice enough of their national monetary and fiscal independence to make exchange-rate adjustments unnecessary. For encouragement of international lending, artificial stabilization of exchange rates cannot take the place of a thoroughly international monetary system. Exchange control might interfere with the initial transfer of whatever international loans people were willing to make. Existing or possible future exchange controls would make lenders worry about difficulties in getting their capital and interest earnings, as well as dividends or profits on equity investments, out of the borrowing country when the time came. Such potential difficulties discourage international lending just as exchange risk does—and without really eliminating the risk. It is an oversimplification to argue that freely fluctuating exchange rates discourage and fixed exchange rates encourage international investment. Rather, the distinction is between fluctuating or pegged rates under independent national monetary systems, on the one hand, and permanently fixed rates under an international monetary system such as the full-fledged gold standard, on the other.

In at least one respect other than through one-way-option speculation, exchange-rate pegging can have a positively perverse effect on international capital movements. Consider a country experiencing price-level inflation while other countries maintain price stability. Expectations of continuing inflation tend to show up in an excess of the actual rate of interest over the "real" rate. Then, although the real rate of interest and the real marginal productivity of investment were the same in the inflationary country as elsewhere (or even a bit lower), that country could have a higher actual rate of interest and so attract funds from abroad. That flow of capital in response to a distorted interest-rate differential would presumably represent an international misallocation of resources. Under free exchange rates, a sustained depreciation of the inflationary currency would tend to discourage the capital flow as much as the interest differential encouraged it. Under fixed rates that still commanded confidence, however, that offset could not occur. The very inflow of capital in question (not to mention controls and other *ad hoc* measures) could help sustain the pegged exchange value of the inflationary currency for some time. In short, pegged exchange rates can promote counterproductive capital movements.[43]

A bit of business arithmetic helps us avoid an exaggerated impression of how seriously the risk of an adverse movement of a free exchange rate would weigh against the interest-rate incentive for an international loan. Suppose that Inlanders are considering the issue of bonds denominated in Outland pesos. By how much would the dollar have to depreciate against the peso just to offset the advantage of borrowing at the lower Outland interest rate? Table 13.6 shows the answers for a few interest rates and bond maturities. The calculations underlying the table rest on the most *un*favorable assumption that the dollar depreciates to the critical level immediately after the loan is contracted and stays there until the maturity of the loan.

TABLE 13.6. *Exchange risk versus interest advantage on an international loan*

Inland interest rate, percent	Outland interest rate, percent	Percentage of depreciation of dollar against peso that would just wipe out the interest-rate advantage of borrowing for the indicated number of years		
		2 Years	10 Years	20 Years
5	3	3.72	15.44	24.92
7	5	3.62	14.06	21.19

SOURCE: Richard E. Caves and Grant L. Reuber, *Capital Transfers and Economic Policy: Canada 1951–1962*, Cambridge: Harvard University Press, 1971, pp. 38–40.

A gradual depreciation could be ultimately larger than the table shows without wiping out the interest-rate advantage, for the delay in the depreciation reduces the number of annual interest payments having to be made in a correspondingly increased number of dollars. It should be remembered, furthermore, that Inland borrowers face the chance of gain as well as of loss on exchange-rate movements.

Exchange rates and purchasing powers

The purchasing-power-parity doctrine suggests that large real exchange losses or profits on an international loan under flexible exchange rates are improbable unless financial and price-level conditions in the two countries have diverged substantially during the life of the loan. When the relative purchasing powers of the two currencies have changed, the exchange profit or loss may come as an approximate offset to what would otherwise be a loss or gain in real purchasing power. To illustrate, let us suppose that an international loan is denominated in the lending country's currency, that the lending country avoids deflation and inflation, and that the exchange rate is free to fluctuate. If inflation has occurred in the borrowing country by the time that the loan must be repaid, the borrower must pay more of his local money for the necessary amount of lending-country currency than he originally expected. Because of the inflation in his country, however, the average borrower may find it no more difficult to earn the increased amount of local money than it would have been to earn the amount originally expected if the local money had not depreciated in purchasing power and exchange value. If everything is as just described except that deflation rather than inflation occurs in the borrowing country, the borrower enjoys an exchange profit: repayment of the loan in the currency of the lending country requires less of his appreciated local currency than he originally expected to need. However, the average borrower suffers an offset to this exchange profit in the fact that deflation increases the difficulty of earning local money.

The outcome differs according to whether the loan is expressed in the currency of the lending or the borrowing country. The various possibilities involving price-level stability in one country and inflation or deflation in the other are summarized in Table 13.7. In the table, B and L stand for *borrower* and *lender*, respec-

tively. *Exch gain* and *exch loss* mean, respectively, that the rate at which one buys or sells foreign exchange in connection with debt repayment is more favorable or more unfavorable than originally expected. *PP gain* means that the borrower repays in (or buys the needed foreign exchange with) domestic money units of lower purchasing power than originally expected, or that the lender receives repayment in (or sells the foreign exchange received for) domestic money units of higher purchasing power than originally expected. *PP loss* means that the borrower repays in (or buys the needed foreign exchange with) domestic money units of higher purchasing power than originally expected, or that the lender receives repayment in (or sells the foreign exchange received for) domestic money units of lower purchasing power than originally expected. *Neutral* means that debt repayment is made or received in domestic currency which has remained stable in purchasing power.

The table shows a capricious redistribution of wealth between lender and borrower when the loan is expressed in a currency of unstable purchasing power. When it is expressed in a currency of stable purchasing power, one of the parties experiences a "neutral" affect, while the other experiences exchange-rate and purchasing-power effects that run in opposite directions (if they occur) and tend roughly to compensate for each other. The advantage of expressing loans in a currency of stable rather than unstable purchasing power holds true of domestic and international loans alike. For countries where domestic borrowing and lending are greater than international borrowing and lending, purchasing-power stability seems correspondingly more important than exchange-rate stability, if a choice between the two policies must and can be made. A domestically stable currency would also provide a good standard of deferred international payments.

43. Friedrich A. Lutz, "Money Rates of Interest, Real Rates of Interest, and Capital Movements," in William Fellner *et al.*, *Maintaining and Restoring Balance in International Payments*, Princeton, N.J.: Princeton University Press, 1966, pp. 161–166.

TABLE 13.7. *Gains and losses on international loans*

	Loan in lender's currency	Loan in borrower's currency
Stability in lending country		
Inflation in borrowing country	B: Exch loss offset by PP gain L: Neutral	B: PP gain, not offset L: Exch loss, not offset
Deflation in borrowing country	B: Exch gain offset by PP loss L: Neutral	B: PP loss, not offset L: Exch gain, not offset provided B does not default
Stability in borrowing country		
Inflation in lending country	B: Exch gain, not offset L: PP loss, not offset	B: Neutral L: Exch gain offset by PP loss
Deflation in lending country	B: Exch loss, not offset L: PP gain, not offset provided B does not default	B: Neutral L: Exch loss offset by PP gain

Exchange loss on capital transfers

Professor Nurkse has noted another characteristic of fluctuating exchanges that tends to impede capital movements. Suppose that Americans borrow £10 million in England, the debt being expressed in pounds. Selling these borrowed pounds for dollars drives down the pound from an initial rate of $5.00 to, say, $4.00. After the capital transfer is completed, the exchange rate reverts to the normal $5.00 per pound. When the time comes to pay back the loan, the American debtors must buy £10 million. The extra demand for pounds drives the pound rate to, say, $6.00, and the Americans have to spend $60 million to repay the sterling for which they had earlier realized only $40 million. If the loan had been expressed in dollars rather than in pounds, the English lenders rather than the American borrowers would have suffered the exchange loss. The loan agreement might arrange some shifting or sharing of the loss, but it could not contrive to avoid it entirely.[44]

The initial depreciation of the pound is part of the process that translates the financial capital movement into a real net flow of goods and services into the United States by way of increased imports or reduced exports or both, and the later appreciation of the pound is part of the process that translates the financial repayment into a real repayment. We must consider whether a comparable effect does not occur under fixed exchanges. Real transfer of a large international loan by means of the price-specie-flow mechanism of the gold standard theoretically causes price-level movements analogous to the exchange-rate movements just described. As a result of an international flow of gold, American borrowers find the purchaing power of the loan lower in America than they had expected, while Englishmen find that they have lent money of higher purchasing power than they had expected. Repayment of the loan involves another flow of gold, lowering prices in America and raising them in England. Thus the borrowers repay the loan in money whose purchasing power in America is higher than at the time of borrowing, and the lenders receive repayment in money whose purchasing power in England is lower. It is not obvious which are more harmful: these purchasing-power losses or the corresponding losses under fluctuating exchange rates.[45] Neither type of loss is apparent under a system in which countries pursue monetary and fiscal independence and yet try to keep exchange rates fixed. Under this hybrid system, "automatic" price effects play no fundamental part in transferring capital internationally or in equilibrating balances of payments, which is one reason why such a system is fragile.

Under fluctuating exchanges, the loss described by Nurkse falls largely on the borrowers or lenders in the unmistakable form of a money loss. Under an international money standard, the corresponding purchasing-power loss is less evident and is more fully diffused onto third parties. There is something to be said for keeping any such loss clearly apparent to the persons responsible for it, especially when the capital movements involved would be of the hot-money rather than the investment variety.

Nurkse's example admittedly exaggerates the loss for the sake of clarity in exposition. In normal times, net capital movements are small enough in relation to the value of trade in goods and services that changes in them produce only moderate changes in the total demands for or supplies of currencies, and the resulting exchange-rate movements should not be disruptive. Furthermore, the purchasing-power-transfer mechanism—that is, decreased spending by lenders (or by fellow citizens to whom they would otherwise have lent) and increased spending by borrowers (or by fellow citizens from whom they would otherwise have drawn funds)—supplements the exchange rate mechanism in translating the financial transfer into a net international flow of goods and services. When the borrowers spend the entire loan on goods of the lending country, transfer of the loan has no direct effect on the exchange rate, and the same is true, *mutatis mutandis*, of the eventual repayment.

Still, it does seem probable that the purchasing-power-transfer mechanism would ordinarily work less well under free exchanges than under the gold standard. Under an international standard, gold movements or the equivalent can facilitate the appropriate contraction of spending in the lending country and expansion of spending in the borrowing country. But under independent national standards, no money flows between countries. Instead, the exchange rate moves, tending to shift purchases of internationally traded goods toward the lending country, causing expansion there, and away from the borrowing country, causing contraction there. The respective upward and downward price-level tendencies are intensified by the fact that the real transfer of the loan, so far as it begins to succeed, makes fewer goods available to be bought within the lending country and more available in the borrowing country. These tendencies, which run counter to the primary and appropriate cut in spending by the lenders and rise in spending by the borrowers, might conceivably be resisted by continued adherence to policies of internal monetary stabilization.[46]

To say that the purchasing-power-transfer mechanism may work with difficulty under free exchanges is not to say that it will not work at all. The long-term American borrowers of Nurkse's example can spend their borrowed English funds in America only by selling them for dollars. Potential purchasers include not only importers of English goods but also holders of idle dollars who might be induced to switch temporarily into sterling assets. Speculators, in particular, might do so in the justifiable belief that any impact effect of the original loan in depressing sterling exchange would be only temporary. Speculative purchases of sterling amount to a short-term loan to England. Thus, a short-term loan *to* the long-term lending country by persons dishoarding funds held in the long-term borrowing country facilitates the tranfer of purchasing power appropriate to the primary loan.[47] This lessens the exchange-rate change necessary to effect a real transfer of capital.

Fixed exchanges as window-dressing

Encouragement of international lending is not much of a point in favor of fixed exchanges if the fixity is only temporary. Anyone lending to a foreign borrower should realize that he is taking a risk not only on the individual borrower himself and on the exchange rate (if the loan is expressed in the foreign currency) but

44. Ragnar Nurkse, *Internationale Kapitalbewegungen*, Vienna: Springer, 1935, pp. 70–73.

45. Cf. Whittlesey, *op. cit.*, pp. 171–175. The foregoing discussion of loan losses under the gold standard considers only price effects and abstracts from purchasing-power-transfer and income effects; it is on the same level of abstraction as Nurkse's discussion of the loss under free exchanges.

46. Cf. P. B. Whale, "The Theory of International Trade in the Absence of an International Standard," *Economica*, n.s., **III**, February 1936, pp. 29–32; and Gottfried von Haberler, *Prosperity and Depression*, 4th ed., London: Allen & Unwin, 1958, pp. 446–447.

47. Cf. Carl Iversen, *Aspects of the Theory of International Capital Movements*, Copenhagen: Levin & Munksgaard, 1935, pp. 312–324, esp. pp. 316–317.

also on the ability of the foreign country as a whole to achieve an export surplus (or an inflow of new capital) by which interest payments and capital repayment can eventually be made. Far from eliminating such risk, precarious exchange stability increases it if currency overvaluation impairs the debtor country's ability to export. If exchange stability *is* assured by keeping internal monetary and business conditions in step with external developments, the deflation and recession (and to a lesser extent, the inflation) that may accordingly have to be imported from time to time may hamper the debtor enterprises or governmental units in earning enough money or collecting enough taxes to service their external debts. Exchange stability imitated by such expedients as exchange control and moratoria on foreign debt payments clearly does not benefit foreign creditors. Under freely fluctuating exchanges, some countries, no longer able to conceal unfavorable conditions or policies behind a façade of exchange stability, might indeed have more trouble than otherwise in obtaining foreign loans.[48]

Equity investment

Fluctuating exchanges might discourage some international borrowing and lending but would not rule it all out. (Canada's reassuring experience under fluctuating exchange rates is discussed in Chapter 26.) Exchange risk certainly would not rule out all international investment, though it presumably would induce some investors to buy shares of stock rather than bonds of foreign enterprises. There is little reason to suppose that fluctuating exchanges would thwart international direct investment. Equity investment provides some protection against depreciation of the currency of the capital-importing country, for if inflation occurs, the money profits of enterprises should rise accordingly.[49] Exchange risk poses a particularly small obstacle to international investment when a parent enterprise intends to bring home income from its foreign properties in kind rather than in money, as in the form of oil or iron ore. Besides providing investors with some hedge against depreciation of the foreign currency, equity investments should ease the problem of tranferring earnings out of the host country. Unlike bonds, shares of stock do not entail a fixed amount of service charges that are supposed to be transferred abroad every

year despite the condition of the balance of payments. A country can transfer large volumes of dividends to foreign investors when it is prosperous, making only small transfers during difficult times. A further advantage of foreign equity investment, and particularly of direct rather than portfolio investment, is that when the exchange value of the host country's currency is unusually weak, foreign investors have an incentive to plough current earnings back into their properties, waiting until the balance-of-payments situation is more favorable to repatriation of profits.[50] Capital inflow by way of direct rather than portfolio investment also tends to be accompanied by entrepreneurial and technical ability, which underdeveloped countries typically need as much as foreign capital.

A wrongly pegged exchange rate is likely, in several ways, to make a prospective host country less attractive to foreign investors than a floating rate would. Overvaluation of its currency poses price disincentives against investment there to produce goods for import replacement or for export to third countries. Overvaluation is likely to breed inhibiting controls and to pose the threat of sudden sharp devaluation, which could come as an embarrassment to the particular executives responsible for a corporation's decision to invest in that country. Currency *under*valuation, in ways of its own, distorts international capital movements.[51] A floating exchange rate and any resultant relative concentration on equity investment would help avoid the distortion of capital movements when inflation affects interest rates, bringing "a closer correspondence of the actual flow of foreign investment to that justified by international differences in capital productivity."[52]

Risk, trade, and investment: summary

On *a priori* grounds it seems practically certain that, other things being equal, the risk of exchange fluctuations tends to reduce the volume of international trade. However, the resulting loss of welfare would, if measurable, probably turn out to be less than proportionate to the loss of trade volume. Besides, fixing exchange rates itself violates the condition of other things being equal. Any shrinkage in trade because of risk may well be outweighed by the trade-promoting effect of rates allowed to adjust toward changing equilibrium levels. Even rate-pegging, incidentally, does not remove risk as long as danger remains that pegged rates will have to be changed. Free exchange rates are conducive to trade so far as they enable countries to dispense with controls for balance-of-payments purposes and provide the opportunity for independent domestic stabilization policies. Finally, both theory and history suggest that forward-exchange facilities would offer merchants adequate and inexpensive protection against the risk of rate changes in free and unrestricted markets. This protection might even be more satisfactory under freely fluctuating than under pegged-but-adjustable exchanges, since forward premiums or discounts are apt to become comparatively large and unstable when pegged spot rates come under suspicion.

Exchange risk probably would deter international borrowing and lending to some extent. However, the fault is not peculiar to free exchanges. A system of fixed-but-adjustable exchanges, or even an insecure gold standard, presents similar, though less constantly conspicuous, risk. The relevant distinction is not so much between free rates and pegged rates as between either fluctuating or pegged rates under independent national monetary systems on the one hand and permanently fixed rates under an international monetary system on the other. The purchasing-power-parity doctrine teaches that borrowers and lenders would be unlikely to experience large gains or losses of real wealth from changes in free exchange rates except when the currency in which the loan was expressed suffered a change in purchasing power. The monetary problem involved in credit operations, domestic as well as foreign, is not just the narrow one of exchange-rate instability but rather the broader one of purchasing-power instability.[53] To try to peg exchange rates when this problem remains unsolved is to palliate symptoms. Finally, risk under fluctuating exchanges does not strangle all international investment; in particular, it is probably

not an important deterrent to direct and other equity investments, types of investment that have much to recommend them relatively.

48. John E. Floyd calls it a "sophisticated error" to regard future exchange-rate changes as a more significant source of risk affecting international investment than the alternative changes necessary under fixed exchange rates to maintain balance-of-payments equilibrium. See a book review by Floyd in *American Economic Review*, **LVIII**, September 1968, pp. 1018–1020.

49. "The fundamental hedging in long-term capital movements between countries, as within a country, comes from the fact that the investment is made in real terms not nominal terms. . . . And you do not need any further forward market for long-term hedging." Milton Friedman in Federal Reserve Bank of Boston, *The International Adjustment Mechanism* (conference of October 1969), Boston: 1970, p. 116.

50. Whittlesey, *op. cit.*, pp. 167–170.

51. David L. Grove (chief economist of IBM), "The Wider Band and Foreign Direct Investment," in Halm, *op. cit.*, pp. 151–166. Grove (p. 159) notes the irony "that critics of proposed floating-exchange-rate systems almost always assume that the underlying demand and supply forces would be inherently and strongly unstable, and then proceed to present illustrations that show how hopeless it would be for businessmen and bankers to operate under such a system; yet, they then proceed to describe the benefits of the present fixed-exchange-rate system within a framework of stability of underlying demand and supply forces."

52. Lanyi, *op. cit.*, p. 10. Compare p. 272 above.

53. To split hairs, the problem is not one of instability but of unpredictability; for if the purchasing power of a currency were going to change in a way fully known in advance, free-market interest rates would allow for the change and avoid unwanted redistributions between debtors and creditors.

CHAPTER FOURTEEN

Stabilizing
Official Intervention

The first two sections of this chapter, together with the summary following them, review proposals for solving a problem described toward the end of Chapter 12—the problem of one-way-option speculation under the system of pegged exchange rates. The proposed policy weapon is official intervention in the forward-exchange market. The remaining sections of the chapter review the compromise idea of giving up on fixed exchange rates but still retaining official market intervention to smooth out the movements of floating rates.

Speculation and arbitrage

Some students see the dangers of self-justifying speculation against a pegged currency less as an argument against pegging spot rates than as one in favor of supporting forward rates also.[1] They interpret the immediate cause of a drain on the official reserves as arbitrage rather than as speculation as such. Suppose that bearishness on the Ruritanian crown (expressed in speculative demands for forward foreign exchange, more universal forward covering of commercial commitments to pay foreign currency, and lesser prevalence of forward covering of commercial commitments to receive foreign currency) drives the crown's forward rate

to an abnormally large discount from spot. Arbitrageurs can now profit by selling crowns spot and buying them back forward. In defending the spot rate against the arbitrageurs' spot sales, the authorities lose reserves. Covered interest arbitrage, not speculation, is the immediate cause of the drain; it transmits to the spot market the speculative pressure in the forward market. The covering part of the arbitrage operations, considered by itself, amounts to taking a position opposite to that taken by speculators; it tends to hold down the speculative forward premium on foreign exchange (i.e., forward discount on the crown). The more powerfully even a small volume of arbitrage can shrink this premium to the point of making any larger volume of arbitrage unprofitable, the slighter the danger to the official spot reserves. On the other hand, the less powerfully arbitrage tends to destroy its own profitability, the stronger seems the case for official intervention to destroy it.[2]

Another example of arbitrage seen as the immediate cause of pressure in the spot market concerns a foreign buyer of Ruritanian goods. He can speculate against the crown by getting his trade financed in Ruritania, contriving to owe crowns. Alternatively, he may finance his trade at home, at the same time taking a bear position in crowns on the side by selling them forward. If he chooses the former course (which tends to delay an inflow of foreign exchange into the Ruritanian reserves), it must be because the relations among spot and forward exchange rates and different countries' interest rates make this a cheaper form of speculation than the latter course; and these are arbitrage considerations. A foreign company with funds on deposit in Ruritania, fearful of devaluation, could either sell its crowns spot, thus tending to drain the Ruritanian reserves, or else keep holding its crowns while covering them with a forward sale. If the company expected not only a devaluation of the crown but also an upward revaluation of the Graustark florin, it could buy florins with crowns either spot or forward. In each example, the choice could be described as an arbitrage decision. The same may even be said of speculation by way of leads and lags. Suppose that a foreign buyer of Ruritanian goods priced in crowns lags his remittance or even his purchases, awaiting a devaluation. Why should he do this unless he can speculate against the crown more cheaply this way than by leaving his schedule of payments and purchases undisturbed and selling crowns forward? Suppose that a Ruritanian importer, afraid of being caught with a foreign-exchange obligation if the crown is devalued, hastens his remittance or his purchases. What, if not a cost advantage, could be a sound reason for doing this instead of buying foreign exchange forward? The leads and lags that harm the Ruritanian reserves are due not to speculation as such but to the particular form of speculation that arbitrage considerations recommend. More generally, whenever people shun forward transactions in favor of transactions that immediately strain official reserves, their decision must involve the very interest-rate and spot-and-forward-rate relations that govern ordinary interest arbitrage. In this sense, even outright speculation in the spot rather than forward market could be described as arbitrage.

Counterspeculative support of forward exchange

This interpretation seems like a sterile attempt to lay down substantive propositions by changing the accepted meanings of words. Its advocates say, however, that their terminology has the advantage of emphasizing the remediable aspects of speculative situations. It suggests how official manipulation of arbitrage incentives could make all bear speculation against the crown take the form of forward sales, "thereby rendering it harmless to the . . . reserves."[3]

If the authorities bought crowns (sold foreign exchange) forward on a large enough scale to keep the forward crown from sinking to any abnormal discount, they could deprive arbitrageurs of any chance to profit from selling crowns spot and repurchasing them forward. The intervention would likewise eliminate speculators' incentive to go bearish on crowns by reserve-depleting spot rather than forward sales. Importers and exporters who would otherwise speculate by leads and lags would find that they could take equivalent short positions more advantageously in the forward market.[4] Not even "one-way option" speculation could eat into the reserves as long as official intervention lured it all into the forward market.

Several objections to the proposal have been

1. A. E. Jasay, "Bank Rate or Forward Exchange Policy," *Banca Nazionale del Lavoro Quarterly*

Review, No. 44, March 1958, pp. 56–73; A. E. Jasay, "Forward Exchange: The Case for Intervention," *Lloyds Bank Review*, October 1958, pp. 35–45; John Spraos, "Speculation, Arbitrage and Sterling," *Economic Journal*, LXIX, March 1959, pp. 1–21. Bent Hansen discusses the proposal sympathetically but without complete agreement in "Interest Policy and Foreign Exchange Policy" and "Interest Policy, Foreign Exchange Policy and Foreign Exchange Control," *Skandinaviska Banken Quarterly Review*, Vol. 39, October 1958, pp. 114–121, and Vol. 40, January 1959, pp. 15–27. Further discussion appears in J. H. Auten, "Counter-speculation and the Forward Exchange Market," *Journal of Political Economy*, LXIX, February 1961, pp. 49–55; R. Z. Aliber, "Counterspeculation in the Forward Exchange Market: A Comment," *Journal of Political Economy*, LXX, December 1962, pp. 609–613; Henry Goldstein, "Counter-speculation in the Forward Exchange Market: Some Further Comments," *Journal of Political Economy*, LXXI, October 1963, pp. 494–500; R. Z. Aliber, "More About Counter-speculation in the Forward Exchange Market," *Journal of Political Economy*, LXXI, December, 1963, pp. 589–590; and Paul Einzig, *A Dynamic Theory of Forward Exchange*, London: Macmillan; New York: St. Martin's Press, 1961, chaps. 44–48, esp. 44 and 45.

2. Unfortunately, variations in commercial covering might accommodate the arbitrage: shrinkage of the forward premium on foreign exchange might be resisted by increased buying of forward foreign exchange by importers (whose speculative motive for being especially sure to cover is reinforced by improvement of the price at which they can do so) and by reduced sales of forward foreign exchange by exporters (whose speculative motive for not covering and instead waiting to sell foreign exchange spot later on is reinforced by the less attractive forward rate). As explained in Appendix 1 to Chapter 6, however, commercial covering is more likely to vary in response to the forward rate when the support limits of spot exchange rates are trusted than when they are distrusted or nonexistent.

3. Spraos, *op. cit.*, p. 8.

4. However, traders might not behave so "rationally." They might consider outright forward-market speculation unpatriotic or otherwise undesirable, yet consider shrewd timing of their trade and payments only a matter of sound business judgment. Even worse, some might continue leading and lagging while speculatively selling crowns forward besides. Cf. Goldstein, *op. cit.*, p. 497 and footnote.

made, and answers have been offered. First, keeping the forward discount on a suspected currency small not only affects the form of bear speculation but also tends to increase its total amount by in effect subsidizing it. This effect may only be slight if speculators do not operate on fine margins and if their general distrust of the pegged currency swamps alertness to the forward-spot spread, seen as the cost of taking a bear position.[5] On the other hand, the forward rate itself is not the only influence: the accompanying publicity designed to persuade speculators of the "rationality" of operating forward instead of spot might well induce some speculation that would not otherwise have occurred at all. A more cheerful thought is that avoiding a conspicuous forward discount might promote confidence in the crown and so deter speculation against it—but such arguments appealing to psychological influences are notoriously unsure.[6] Besides possibly affecting the total volume of speculation, forward support may also attract additional *net* forward sales of crowns to the authorities by parties other than outright speculators. Importers committed to future payments in foreign exchange will be especially sure to cover their commitments by buying these currencies forward if their forward quotations are held down. Exporters committed to future receipts of foreign exchange will be especially reluctant to sell it forward and especially content to maintain an uncovered long position if its forward price is held down. (On the other hand, the whole speculative atmosphere may so dominate traders' decisions that the level of the forward rate is only a comparatively slight influence on covering practices.) Net forward sales of crowns to the authorities might also increase in connection with an increase in imports relative to exports, as explained a few pages later on.

Advocates of the forward-support policy would not be alarmed by even a vast growth of the authorities' forward contracts to buy crowns and deliver foreign exchange, provided that these contracts matched pure speculation only. There is no limit to official support of a currency in the forward market comparable to the limit to spot support posed by exhaustible reserves. The authorities need only keep their nerve (whereas nervously discontinuing intervention as pressure mounted would probably intensify the speculation). Speculative short-sellers of crowns will have to buy them spot with foreign exchange when the time comes to deliver crowns under their forward contracts;

foreign exchange will thus flow into the official reserves at the same time that the authorities have to deliver it under their maturing contracts. Meanwhile, speculation cannot force a devaluation and saddle the authorities with the costs of carrying out their contracts, for its successful diversion into the forward market means that it depletes no reserves, and, as just mentioned, the official forward operations could be as large as necessary for this diversion. As for forward sellers of crowns who need buy none to make delivery because they had been holding crowns (or assets readily salable for crowns) all along, they could have sold the crowns spot in the first place anyway; hence the proposed policy does no harm and even has the merit of delaying such drains as the reserves could in any case have suffered.

This view is too optimistic. Surely the authorities cannot be indifferent to how much of their forward activity matches pure speculation by short-sellers who will have to buy crowns spot to make delivery and how much matches forward sales by persons already holding crowns—perhaps foreign companies operating in Ruritania and hedging to protect the value of their crown assets. Some holders who would simply have stood pat and taken their chances in the absence of an attractive opportunity to hedge might move out of crowns by delivering them when their forward contracts matured in the event of devaluation in the meanwhile. If devaluation had not then yet occurred, hedgers might make delivery of crowns they already held but could spare only temporarily (or, for example, might obtain crowns to deliver by temporarily running down inventories held in Ruritania), hoping to buy their crown assets back again profitably after the still momentarily expected devaluation. Since the authorities cannot know who will eventually take delivery of the foreign exchange they are selling forward and what the unknown ultimate recipients will do with it, they remain in the dark about the nature and extent of the pressure against the crown. By not intervening forward and by suffering spot reserve losses instead, the authorities would at least know where they stood and would be less inclined wishfully to postpone fundamental corrective measures.[7]

Honoring a massive volume of contracts made under the forward support policy would prove costly to the authorities if they did lose their nerve and finally devalue. In effect, then, they lose their freedom to devalue; but, on an optimistic view, this nearly ironclad guarantee against devaluation itself further deters speculation.[8] A worry harder to dispel concerns the possible upward revaluation of one or more of the foreign currencies in which the Ruritanian authorities had been operating; that decision would be out of their hands. And anyway, even the best of intentions and strongest of nerves might not be able to prevent devaluation of the crown. Just as going deeper and deeper actually into debt to foreigners to obtain foreign exchange for ordinary spot support of a currency would leave the currency's existing parity increasingly suspect, so suspicion would grow as official forward commitments grew bigger and bigger in relation to actual reserves. The size of these commitments might not be published, but it would be the subject of rumor—rumor perhaps even more disturbing than actual figures. Speculators might begin to wonder where in the world, even with the most honorable of intentions, the authorities were going to get the foreign exchange to meet their mounting commitments in case their heroism somehow failed. (Sales of foreign exchange by short-sellers buying crowns for delivery at the maturity of their contracts would then not provide the full answer, since each crown would be worth less foreign exchange, after devaluation, than at the rate specified in the maturing contracts.) Speculators and others might reasonably fear the imposition of controls to their disadvantage. Official publicity about the cost advantages of confining speculation to the forward market would seem less relevant and convincing. Transfers through the spot market could grow. Knowing that a forced devaluation *could* be the outcome, speculators might expect the authorities to give up before they had taken on disastrously heavy forward commitments.

Mention of heavy forward commitments brings to mind an oversight in the reassuring argument that these commitments can hardly become much heavier than spot reserve losses would have been anyway in the absence of forward support. Perhaps the argument is right that forward support only changes the form of speculation and does little to increase its total volume. But this is true, if at all, only of the volume per time period. The longer a speculative situation lasts before coming to a climax—the more time that distrust of the crown has to grow and to motivate new speculators and embolden old ones—the greater the cumulative volume of speculation can be. The time that

can elapse until speculation in the spot market comes to its climax is limited by the size of the reserves; the duration of speculation diverted to the forward market is not so limited. A denial that this consideration is relevant would have to rest, again, on the assumption that devaluation simply *will not* occur.

On a highly abstract level, there is much to the argument that pure speculation, completely unjustified by any adverse fundamentals in trade and normal capital movements, could not defeat a bold, resolute, and if necessary unlimited forward support policy. But the distinction between pure speculation and speculation related to fundamentals can be made confidently only with hindsight.[9] Fundamental disequilib-

5. R. Z. Aliber, "Counterspeculation in the Foreign Exchange Market: A Comment," pp. 609, 612.

6. Paul Einzig quotes a European central banker to the effect that forward support of a currency at an obviously artificial rate "attracts an amazing volume of selling from the most unexpected quarters." Einzig also notes that the British authorities stopped supporting forward sterling during the 1957 crisis when they found that the artificial forward rate, far from relieving the pressure, stimulated speculative and quasi-speculative pressure. "Some Recent Developments in Official Forward Exchange Operations," *Economic Journal*, **LXXIII**, June 1963, pp. 241, 252.

7. This point, particularly concerning the dangers of unavoidable ignorance about the counterpart of official forward transactions, has been much stressed by Paul Einzig, A *Dynamic Theory of Forward Exchange*, p. 510, and *Economic Journal*, June 1963, pp. 248–249.

8. Auten, *op. cit.*, p. 55n., attributes this argument to A. E. Jasay's evidence before the Radcliffe Committee.

9. Cf. Paul Einzig, A *Dynamic Theory of Forward Exchange*, p. 506: ". . . I came to realise in the light of experience the difficulty of drawing the line between speculative pressure unwarranted by deep-lying disequilibrium, and speculative pressure that is but a manifestation of such disequilibrium." J. Marcus Fleming and Robert A. Mundell explain why the forward-support technique is appropriate only for meeting a deficit whose cause is not merely temporary but inherently self-reversing. Something like a harvest failure would not be an appro-

rium, absent at first, might develop later, forcing a devaluation that would be costly in proportion to the counterspeculation meanwhile undertaken. One reason why forward support is only a short-term palliative is that it affects only transactions that can have forward cover, and these do not ordinarily include long-term capital transfers. A domestic interest-rate level too low in view of foreign levels and of the exchange rate is likely to promote an outflow of long-term capital, despite forward intervention to manipulate short-term flows.[10] Even the current account of the balance of payments could worsen because of forward support of the currency. The prevailing forward rate affects the profitability of an import or export transaction involving a future payment or receipt to be covered against exchange risk. Imports are more attractive to Ruritanians and Ruritanian exports less attractive to foreigners if the forward crown is kept strong than if it is allowed to weaken.[11] Overvaluation of a currency in both the spot and forward markets is more of an overvaluation than overvaluation in the spot market alone. (Strictly speaking, the distinction is between forward overvaluation due to direct support and lesser forward overvaluation loosely paralleling the spot overvaluation.) In the face of continuing unmistakable overvaluation, an import surplus will eventually drain the reserves and put an end to spot support. This will happen, anyway, unless forward operations can go beyond merely deterring capital outflow and can promote an actual continuing capital inflow matching the current-account deficit. This would imply keeping the forward quotation on the home currency stronger than its interest parity. It would imply that the home government kept subsidizing the build-up of a heavier and heavier debt to foreigners. Outward interest payments would grow. If declining credit-worthiness would limit straightforward borrowing to finance ordinary support of the spot rate, it is not clear how equivalent indirect efforts could succeed without limit.

Summary

The foregoing survey does not necessarily condemn all sorts of official forward operations under all circumstances; the case against die-hard rigid pegging is not in itself a case against all intervention.[12] It does cast doubt, though,

on whether forward intervention can effectively banish trouble from speculative capital movements under pegged spot rates. Paradoxically, troublesome capital movements are likely to arise both from speculation when fixed parities are distrusted and, as already shown in Appendix 1 to Chapter 6, from interest differentials when the parities are trusted.

The dual purpose of exchange equalization accounts

Policy-makers disillusioned with fixed exchange rates yet worried about speculative disorders and burdensome risk under freely fluctuating exchanges might seek an answer in operating an exchange equalization account, also called an exchange stabilization fund. The idea represents a compromise between fixed and free rates, but a different compromise than the adjustable-peg system. The exchange-rate mechanism would be allowed to keep balances of payments in equilibrium over the long run, but routine official trading in the market would iron out speculative, accidental, and otherwise purely temporary fluctuations.

A stabilization fund might strive, as its second purpose, to cushion the domestic monetary and credit impact of disturbances arising from international trade or capital movements. Strictly speaking, the fund would neutralize not so much the foreign disturbances themselves as what would otherwise be the consequences of moderating their influence on exchange rates. Buying or selling foreign exchange to resist appreciation or depreciation of the home currency has an expansionary or contractionary domestic monetary impact much the same as that of central-bank open-market operations in domestic securities. The fund could try to neutralize this impact by selling or buying securities whenever it bought or sold foreign exchange.

Problems of domestic monetary insulation

The best known of the funds operating in this way has been the British Exchange Equalisation account, managed by the Bank of England as agent for the Treasury. At its beginning in 1932, it held only British Treasury bills and so could operate in only one direction, buying gold or foreign exchange with sterling. In its early years, the Account did, in fact, operate most (but not all) of the time to resist tendencies toward an appreciation of the pound. Its foreign assets kept growing, and the government repeatedly had to give it fresh sterling assets. Despite the original idea that the Account should merely smooth out erratic exchange-rate fluctuations due to "hot-money" transfers or other temporary influences, it came increasingly to resist trends and actually to determine the rate. Even when the Account was given the explicit task of not merely smoothing the rate but of fixing it within definite narrow limits, its function of insulating domestic monetary and credit conditions remained pretty much the same as before.[13]

The Account holds sterling almost entirely in "tap" Treasury bills.[14] It finances purchases of gold or foreign exchange by cashing some of its tap bills, obliging the Treasury to sell that many more tender bills to private investing institutions. When it sells gold or foreign exchange, the Account puts the sterling received into tap bills; and the Treasury reduces by that much its issue of tender bills to the private money market. The Account and the Treasury, taken together, in effect pay for foreign exchange bought and dispose of the sterling proceeds of foreign-exchange sold by increasing and reducing their borrowing from the public; the open-market operations in foreign exchange and in Treasury bills run in offsetting directions.[15]

Numerous complications prevent perfect insulation of the home economy. As an example, let us consider a flight by foreigners from their own money into British bank deposits.[16] The Exchange Equalisation Account absorbs the inflowing foreign exchange or gold to resist an unwanted appreciation of the pound; but since it acquires the necessary sterling by selling Treasury bills from its own portfolio (through the intermediary of the Treasury), it avoids the net creation of additional domestic bank reserves. If the commercial banks buy these bills, they have more of them as assets, more foreign-owned deposits as liabilities, and unchanged reserves. But on the one hand, the rise in deposits reduces their reserve ratios, while on the other hand, their increased bill holdings raise their ratios of total liquid assets (cash, bills, and call loans) to deposits. Since British

priate occasion, since no reversal would necessarily occur to allow the authorities to undo their forward-exchange position. A more appropriate occasion would be a nervous flight of funds, based on some misunderstanding, from a basically sound currency. "Official Intervention on the Forward Exchange Market: A Simplified Analysis," IMF *Staff Papers*, **XI**, March 1964, pp. 15–17.

10. Hansen, *Skandinaviska Banken Quarterly Review*, Vol. 39, October 1958, p. 121.

11. *Ibid.*, p. 120; Paul Einzig, *The Theory of Forward Exchange*, London: Macmillan, 1937, chap. 23; Einzig, *A Dynamic Theory of Forward Exchange*, pp. 212–213, 272; and S. C. Tsiang, "The Theory of Forward Exchange and Effects of Government Intervention on the Forward Exchange Market," IMF *Staff Papers*, **VII**, April 1959, pp. 104–105. Subject only to the obvious qualification that the balance of payments must be normally rather than perversely responsive to the spot rate as well, Tsiang's reasoning is recognized as valid amidst otherwise critical comments by Auten, *op. cit.*, pp. 53–54. Also see Fleming and Mundell, *op. cit.*, pp. 11–12, 15.

12. Resisting a speculative and quasi-speculative *inflow* of funds by pegging down the forward premium on the home currency can have awkward consequences but, unlike resistance to an outflow, cannot lead to calamity. How long in foreign exchange the authorities can afford to go has no limit comparable to that on going short.

Note, incidentally, that the bulk of the academic discussion about the pros and cons of various forward support strategies takes for granted a pegged spot rate that may require some sort of defense or other.

13. Cf. R. S. Sayers, *Modern Banking*, 4th ed., Oxford: Clarendon Press, 1958, p. 159.

14. "Tap" bills are short-term securities issued and redeemed by the Treasury at any time for the convenience of government departments and certain overseas monetary authorities having funds for temporary investment. They are distinguished from "tender bills," which the Treasury auctions off to the general investing public every week in predetermined amounts.

15. Committee on the Working of the Monetary System, *Report* ("The Radcliffe Report"), *Cmnd.* 827, London: Her Majesty's Stationery Office, August 1959, pp. 34, 268.

16. See W. Manning Dacey, *The British Banking Mechanism*, 2nd rev. ed., London: Hutchinson & Co., 1958, pp. 104–107.

banks traditionally strive for both cash reserves and total liquidity amounting to rather definite percentages of deposits, the operation just described presupposes that the banks had previously had some excess cash reserves and probably, as a reason for buying the Treasury bills, some deficiency of noncash liquid assets. If the Exchange Equalisation Account had had to absorb the speculative inflow of foreign funds when the banks had had no slack in their cash ratios, it could have avoided actual deflationary pressure only by selling some of the Treasury bills to the Bank of England for sterling it needed, instead of selling all the bills to the commercial banks. One may wonder why the Account and the Treasury could not have mopped up the bank reserves that purchase of the inflowing foreign funds would otherwise have produced by selling bills to the British public generally instead of to the banks. One complication in either approach is uncertainty about who would be the ultimate new holders of the bills. Even if the authorities could somehow sell bills to the public alone, simply releasing bank deposits from domestic to foreign ownership with no change in their total or in bank reserves, the effect of the total operation might still be slightly deflationary, since deposits would presumably be less active under foreign than domstic ownership (as in fact is implied by the foreigners' assumed motive in acquiring the deposits). To offset the domestic monetary effects of speculative capital movements completely, then, the authorities cannot aim at anything so relatively simple as stabilizing total bank reserves, or the total of domestically owned deposits, or the total of deposits under domestic and foreign ownership alike; they would have to know and take account of the different velocities of deposits under different ownership. Incidentally, if the foreigners fleeing from their home currency wished to hold their new sterling assets entirely in the form of Treasury bills, and if the British authorities knew this, then their task would be simpler. At the other extreme, complete insulation would not be even theoretically possible if the foreigners wished to acquire assets whose total supply the authorities could not manipulate (shares of corporation stock, for example).

It makes some difference to the task of the authorities whether the disturbance to be offset is a "hot-money" tranfer or is something more nearly "normal," such as a supposedly temporary imbalance on goods-and-services account. When a speculative capital inflow occurs, it may be appropriate to allow almost as large an increase in the total volume of bank-account money if the foreigners are going to treat their new accounts pretty much as idle hoards. But when the authorities acquire foreign exchange corresponding to a balance-of-payments surplus on current account, allowing an equivalent increase in bank-account money would be inflationary, since it would be held by residents and would presumably be about as active as the bank accounts already in existence. If official purchases of foreign exchange were financed by selling bills to the commercial banks, the banks' reserves, at least, could be kept unchanged. As in the preceding example of the capital inflow, however, this operation would presuppose that the banks had had above-normal cash reserves (and probably below-normal total liquidity) in the first place; otherwise, the Bank of England would have to create some additional reserve cash for the banks by buying some of the Treasury bills sold by the Account—which implies allowing the country's international current surplus to retain some net expansionary domestic effect. The task of approaching complete neutralization would be easiest for the authorities if they could persuade the British nonbank public to hold fully as much in additional Treasury bills as the country's surplus earnings of foreign exchange; in the final position, ignoring intermediate stages, the public would then be holding additional bills equivalent to the net excess exports of goods and services, the Exchange Equalisation Account would be holding fewer bills and more foreign exchange, and the commercial banks would find their reserves, deposits, and ratios unchanged. (Yet even this outcome would not spell complete neutralization. The public's additional holdings of highly liquid Treasury bills, together with the increased interest rate necessary to attract into the bills funds fully equal to the external surplus, would presumably promote a slight increase in the velocity of circulation of actual demand deposits and currency.)

Given a British current-account deficit, the Exchange Equalisation Account must release gold and foreign exchange to support sterling. Its task is simplest if the British public wishes to pay for its net surplus purchases of foreign goods and services with Treasury bills previously held. If the public wishes to draw down its bank accounts instead, the banks will lose reserves and have to sell Treasury bills or other assets to replenish them. If the banks were the sole sellers of the bills bought by the Exchange Equalisation Account, their reserves would remain unchanged, their cash reserve *ratio* would rise (because of the fall in deposits), and their liquidity ratio would fall (because bill holdings and deposits fell by equal absolute amounts). If the banks could not respond this way because they had not held superabundant total liquidity in the first place, and if, as assumed, the public did not sell all the bills sought by the Account, then the Bank of England would have to sell some bills to the Account and absorb some cash from it, partially tolerating the original deflationary tendency. The alternative would be to cut the yields on government securities enough to make the public, as a whole, part only with securities and not with demand deposits in paying for the foreign exchange needed for the surplus imports. Again, the question remains whether an unchanged volume of bank reserves and bank deposits spells complete neutralization if a change in interest rates is necessary in the process.[17]

In summary, exact neutralization of the effect of external transactions on a country's domestic monetary and credit situation is usually impossible, not only in practice but even in theory. Any pronounced expansionary or contractionary influence, however, can at least in principle be restrained.[18] The techniques of an exchange equalization account are not the only weapons available; there is also the whole armory of monetary and fiscal policy. Detailed attention to the domestic operations of an exchange account is thus rather uninteresting. The separation between exchange account, central bank, and treasury is chiefly legalistic. If their actions are coordinated—and in practice, no one of them can overlook the consequences of the others' actions—the three can be considered together under the collective name of the "monetary authorities." Not the exchange account but rather these "authorities" decide whether, when, and how to try to insulate the domestic structure of money and credit from the effects of external disturbances or exchange-stabilization operations.[19]

Official exchange-market operations

Official measures to insulate the domestic economy interfere with balance-of-payments equilibration through price-and-income effects. The question arises of how far domestic stabili-

zation is compatible with official operations in foreign exchange.

The answer implied by the distinctive purpose of exchange-stabilization funds is—indefinitely. For the idea of stabilization, as distinguished from rigid pegging, is that rate variations should indeed serve as the chief method of achieving external balance. A fund should do no more than smooth out functionless erratic wobbles (perhaps due to random mismatching-in-time of commercial supply and demand or due to speculation). Avoiding merely fluky exchange-rate movements would avoid the temporary and wasteful reallocations of productive resources that those movements might otherwise cause.[20] Functional exchange-rate movements—those in response to the changing fundamentals of tastes, technology, weather, harvests, price levels, monetary and fiscal policies, and reasonable expectations about all of these—would have full scope to maintain balance-of-payments equilibrium at

17. The foregoing examples concern transactions between Britain and countries outside the Sterling Area. Given the practices actually followed during the heyday of the Area, a British surplus or deficit in trade with the rest of the Area produced effects on bank deposits and reserves in Britain not much different from those that would occur in a region of a monetarily unified country. On this and on the consequences of imbalances in trade between the outer Sterling Area and the outside world, see Sayers, *op. cit.*, esp. pp. 163–164.

18. Recall from Chapter 9, however, the extreme difficulty of pursuing an independent monetary policy under fixed exchange rates when international capital movements are highly interest-sensitive.

19. Cf. W. A. Brown, Jr. in chap. VI of Ragnar Nurkse, *International Currency Experience*, League of Nations, 1944, p. 154.

20. Fritz Machlup replies, however, that traders and producers are no less aware that price signals may sometimes be false "than are the warners who, in fear of false signals, advocate arrangements which eliminate all signals." He questions the tacit assumption that the managers of official intervention would consistently act with information, intelligence, and judgment superior to those possessed by private specialists. *The Alignment of Foreign Exchange Rates*, New York: Praeger, 1972, pp. 81–82.

all times except perhaps in the very short run. The fund would not resist fundamental rate trends. Its intervention would not involve exchange control in the specific sense of requisitioning and rationing foreign exchange. Since the fund would buy and sell gold and foreign exchange in the open market rather than directly control private transactions, its activity would be fully as compatible with a free-market economy as are open-market operations for domestic monetary policy.

This prospectus is attractive. The chief question about implementing it concerns how the managers of the fund are to distinguish promptly between fundamental and temporary rate movements. Hindsight is not enough. If the managers were as able to foretell the future or to diagnose the present as they ideally should be, they could speculate as private parties, iron out temporary fluctuations without risking public money, and earn handsome profits. But then, according to one point of view, no *official* fund would be necessary. If the authorities possessed information not generally available to private speculators, they might best simply make this information public (unless it had to be kept secret for security reasons).

Spokesmen for this point of view have indeed argued that for private competitive speculators and official stabilization funds alike, profit and loss indicate whether or not their operations have had a stabilizing effect.[21] The profit-and-loss test is meant to apply to a market in which oscillations occur around an unchanging average rate; an uptrend or downtrend over the period considered would raise the problem of revaluing the fund's foreign assets and would blur the profitability criterion. Ideally, the profitability criterion also presupposes that the fund, like each individual speculator, carries out only a very small fraction of the total transactions in the market. For if the fund's own purchases and sales had an appreciable effect by themselves on the prices paid and received, then the most profitable volume of operations would fall short of the most stabilizing volume. Extreme examples show why. If the fund were to stabilize the rate completely, it would always buy and sell at the same stabilized price and would make zero profits. At the other extreme, a very small volume of operations would narrow the range of fluctuation hardly at all; properly timed purchases and sales could yield a maximum profit per unit, but on such a small volume of transactions that the total profit would be negligible. The most profitable volume of operations is somewhere in between. The fact that profitable operations are stabilizing does not

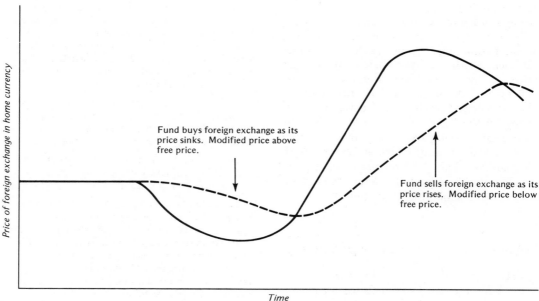

Fund buys foreign exchange as its price sinks. Modified price above free price.

Fund sells foreign exchange as its price rises. Modified price below free price.

Price of foreign exchange in home currency

Time

FIGURE 14.1. *Exchange fund operations*

imply that stabilizing operations are necessarily profitable; least of all does it imply a simple correspondence between degree of profitability and degree of stabilizing effect.

This consideration seems to discredit the profitability test in appraising the success or failure of an official fund. It is hard to imagine a fund that acted as a perfect competitor: its very purpose implies operations large enough to influence the rate.[22] But if a fund did operate on so small a scale as not to affect the rate appreciably, it would be idle to use the profitability criterion (or any other criterion) to judge whether its influence had been stabilizing or not; by hypothesis, the influence would be negligible.[23] Continued insistence on the profitability criterion of success reflects a policy opinion that a fund *ought* to keep its operations small; profit or loss might then indicate whether its intentionally slight influence had been slightly stabilizing or slightly destabilizing.[24] (Whether the fund "ought to" exercise such self-restraint is a topic for discussion a few pages later on.)

Resistance to all rate movements would presumably have a stabilizing influence if the fluctuations were around a steady average rather than around an uptrend or downtrend.[25] Figure 14.1 will help show this. The "free rate" is the exchange rate that would have prevailed in the absence of official intervention; the solid line shows its time path. The "modified" or "observed" rate is the one actually prevailing under the influence of the fund's transactions; the dashed line shows its path. Under the assumed policy of resisting all observed movements, the fund begins buying foreign exchange as its price sinks. The observed or modified rate continues to sink, since the fund does not aim at complete stabilization. Nevertheless, its purchases of foreign exchange keep the falling observed rate above the free rate. When the downtrend of the observed rate finally gives way to an uptrend, the fund's policy of resistance calls for a switch from buying to selling. But from then on, with the fund selling foreign exchange, the observed or modified rate lies below the free rate. To the left of its own trough, the observed rate is above the free rate; to the right of its trough, the observed rate is below the free rate.[26] The trough of the observed rate must, therefore, lie on the path of the free rate. Furthermore, this point must lie to the right of and above the free-rate trough. (A coincidence of the observed and free troughs is a barely conceivable limit-

ing case. As a little experimenting with the diagram will show, it is impossible for the observed trough to lie on the free-rate path to the left of the latter's trough and yet for the observed rate to the left of its own trough to be above the free rate and to the right of its own trough to be below.) The same reasoning, *mutatis mutandis*, shows that the peak of the observed rate lies on the path of the free rate to the right of and below the latter's peak. In short, the extremes of the observed rate occur after the corresponding extremes of the free rate and deviate less from the longer-run average rate. Operations that counter all fluctuations

21. Milton Friedman, *Essays in Positive Economics*, Chicago: University of Chicago Press, 1953, p. 188; Harry C. Eastman and Stefan Stykolt, "Exchange Stabilization in Canada, 1950–4," *Canadian Journal of Economics and Political Science*, **XXII**, May 1956, pp. 221–233.

22. Charles P. Kindleberger, "Exchange Stabilization Further Considered: A Comment," *Canadian Journal of Economics and Political Science*, **XXIII**, August 1957, p. 408.

23. Paul Wonnacott, "Exchange Stabilization in Canada, 1950–4: A Comment," *Canadian Journal of Economics and Political Science*, **XXIV**, May 1958, pp. 262–265.

24. Harry C. Eastman and Stefan Stykolt, "Exchange Stabilization Once Again," *Canadian Journal of Economics and Political Science*, **XXIV**, May 1958, pp. 266–272.

25. The conclusion about a stabilizing influence would still hold true even if the rate fluctuated up and down around a longer-run trend; but such behavior is of little interest because it would imply that the fund, in resisting all movements, was developing a cumulatively and untenably unbalanced position over the longer run.
The analysis that follows was introduced by Wonnacott and extended by Eastman and Stykolt in the articles cited in the two preceding footnotes.

26. The conclusion that the observed rate is falling and above the free rate whenever the fund is buying and is rising and below the free rate whenever the fund is selling apparently depends on a tacit assumption that the free rate at each point of time is affected neither by the fund's earlier interventions nor by expectations about its later interventions.

around a trendless average rate are indeed stabilizing. It is not obvious that such operations must be profitable, but if they are, there must be some most profitable volume of them, in between a negligibly small volume and a volume large enough to produce absolute rate stability and zero profits.

Tactics and problems of intervention

Even though the profit criterion turns out to have a very limited applicability and even though something may be said, under certain hypothetical circumstances, for a policy of countering all rate movements, the practical case for official intervention gains little from this discussion. For one thing, even if it could be known that particular rate movements will prove purely temporary, it is far from clear that they are functionless. (See p. 239.) More important, no fund *can* be sure that the rate movements it observes are mere oscillations around a steady longer-run average. In practice, any fund faces the formidable problem of distinguishing promptly between rate movements that do and those that do not represent the beginnings of fundamental shifts in trend. Even speculation-induced movements in exchange rates cannot be presumed independent of the main trend, since informed speculators may be taking account of basic supply and demand conditions in international trade and of expected changes in them. Even if a stabilization fund attempts only to offset supposed speculative influences, buying when speculators are thought to be selling and selling when speculators are thought to be buying, it may find itself working against anticipations of the basic trend. Instructing the account to offset speculative movements presupposes that it can know what the nonspeculative equilibrium exchange rate is going to be. A policy supposedly confined to ironing out unwarranted fluctuations can drift into a policy of pegging exchange rates at levels that ultimately prove inappropriate. This danger was illustrated by various funds during the 1930s, including the British.[27] Several Latin American experiences with supposedly fluctuating exchanges in the 1950s and early 1960s also illustrate the drift from smoothing into pegging.

If a fund holds a currency close to a definite level for months at a stretch, changing to a new level only occasionally, it is likely to affect speculation much as would a policy of fixed-but-adjustable rates. When speculators come to realize that the account is temporarily maintaining an undervaluation or overvaluation of the currency, they can be fairly confident of which way the exchange rate will move if it does. Like explicit pegging, exchange-fund operations can actually encourage functionless capital movements by giving speculators time to get into the market at attractive prices. An overvalued currency is probably more of an invitation to bear speculation than an undervalued one is to bull speculation: if the bears can exhaust the fund's exchange reserves or its willingness to continue selling foreign exchange cheaply, they force the depreciation they had been betting on.

Even if a fund manages to steer clear of actual rate pegging, it still may worsen the very speculation that it is supposed to neutralize. To avoid giving speculators tips on a sure thing, it must keep at least some of its activities and intentions secret. But then speculators will guess. Intervention increases the range of things on which expectations can focus and about which expectations can change. The decisions and activities of a relatively small number of officials, and expectations about them, are probably more subject to sudden jumps and reversals than are the fundamentals of price levels and of supplies and demands in international trade. An appearance of hesitation and uncertainty on the part of an exchange fund can make the impact of an intervention be the opposite of what it intended.[28] The idea of a "normal" exchange rate is less likely to prevail and to exert its stabilizing influence when speculators must guess at the whims of an agency not limited to profit-seeking than when they need consider the fundamentals only. Destabilizing speculation feeds on mysteries, gossip, and rumor.

These generalizations about exchange-fund operations and speculation have a striking parallel in the officially stated reasons why the Federal Reserve System, from 1953 until late 1960, usually avoided intervention in the market for long-term government securities and confined its domestic open-market operations to "bills only." Because of their short maturity and the relatively great activity of their market, Treasury bills fluctuate much less in price than do long-term bonds when the Federal Reserve undertakes a given volume of purchases or sales. Yet operations in bills and in bonds have substantially the same power to affect the quantity of bank reserves and bank deposits, which is the main channel through which open-market policy works. The Federal Reserve could therefore regard the following disadvantage of operating in the thinner and more price-volatile bond market as ordinarily decisive: Professional dealers, realizing that the Federal Reserve was in a position to dominate the market, would necessarily attach great importance to clues about its current intentions. They would be anxious to avoid bucking any price trend that they suspected the Federal Reserve of setting; on the contrary, they would try to increase or reduce their bond inventories according to whether they thought the Federal Reserve had embarked on a program of buying or of selling. With the Federal Reserve potentially dominating the market, dealers would almost unavoidably try to divine the deeper or longer-run significance of each bit of trading that it was known or thought to be undertaking; they would try to get on its side. Unfortunately, the traders might sometimes read undue significance into minor shifts in Federal Reserve operations; they might sometimes jump onto a bandwagon that in fact was going nowhere. They might bid bond prices up or down to a level that proved untenable, and the original sharp fluctuations would give way to another in the reverse direction. Price instability of this sort would result, to repeat, from speculation based on anticipations about the operations and intentions of a powerful official trader.[29] Freely fluctuating foreign-exchange rates are presumably supposed to resemble long-term bond prices in their potential unsteadiness (otherwise there would be little grounds for official stabilization in the first place), but if the supposition is true, the difficulties of official intervention in the one market seem relevant to the other market as well.

Sometimes the suggestion is made that an exchange fund could do more to combat disruptive speculation than to incite it. In particular, the fund could manipulate the exchange rate aggressively to punish unwarranted bear speculation against the home currency.[30] The fund would first suck the bears into a trap, letting the home currency show signs of weakness to attract plenty of short selling. Then, after the speculators had acquired a large short position, the fund would pursue a strong counteroffensive, driving the exchange value of the currency above where it stood when the bear attacks began. Forced to cover their short sales at high prices, the speculators would suffer big losses, to the profit of the fund. They

would soon learn their lesson, and the problem of speculation would be alleviated—or so the proposal goes.

There *are* a few historical examples of official manipulation of this sort. Throughout the

27. Cf. Brown's chapter in Nurkse, *op. cit.*, p. 143; Leonard Waight, *The History and Mechanism of the Exchange Equalisation Account*, Cambridge: Cambridge University Press, 1939, pp. 138–140; Walter A. Morton, *British Finance, 1930–1940*, Madison: The University of Wisconsin Press, 1943, pp. 126, 128.

During his experience as financial advisor to the Chinese government, Arthur N. Young also noted a tendency for efforts to "check undue fluctuations" to drift into pegging, overvaluation, and controls. A government may come to feel that its prestige is at stake. Under managed flexibility, the managers may be tempted to seek personal profit or to practice favoritism with their interventions, or may at least be accused of doing so. Young concludes, however, in favor of fixed rather than freely fluctuating rates. See his comments in Randall Hinshaw, ed., *The Economics of International Adjustment*, Baltimore: The John Hopkins Press, 1971, pp. 96–97.

28. Helmut Lipfert makes some of these observations in Robert Z. Aliber, ed., *The International Market for Foreign Exchange*, New York: Praeger, 1969, pp. 134–136.

29. An official rationale of the bills-only policy, largely along this line, appears in Winfield W. Reifler, "Open Market Operations in Long-Term Securities," *Federal Reserve Bulletin*, XLIV, November 1958, pp. 1260–1274. The answers of government securities dealers to a questionnaire distributed by the Joint Economic Committee, Eighty-Sixth Congress, generally endorsed the official theory; see Part 6C, especially pp. 1861–1874, of the Committee's *Hearings on the Government's Management of its Monetary, Fiscal, and Debt Operations*, Washington: U.S. Government Printing Office, 1959.

30. Cf. Lowell M. Pumphrey, "The Exchange Equalization Account of Great Britain, 1932–1939: Exchange Operations," *American Economic Review*, XXXII, December 1942, p. 815; Frank D. Graham, "Achilles' Heels in Monetary Standards," *American Economic Review*, XXX, March 1940, p. 23; Charles R. Whittlesey, *International Monetary Issues*, New York: McGraw-Hill, 1937, pp. 121–122.

1880s the Russian press had been campaigning against speculation in rubles on the Berlin market; and after making improvements in government finances, the Russian Finance Minister, Sergei Witte, finally moved to squelch it. In 1892 he forbade Russian subjects to deal in forward exchange. In 1893 he imposed a tax, mostly for statistical purposes, of 0.01 percent on exports of ruble notes. When considerable speculative short selling of rubles developed in 1894, agents of the Russian government in Berlin bought large amounts of ruble notes for forward delivery. Then Witte suddenly forbade the export of ruble notes from Russia. Since the forward contracts called for delivery in actual notes and since the Russian government's agents insisted on actual delivery and refused mere payment of an exchange difference, the short sellers were at Witte's mercy. He finally authorized export of the necessary ruble notes at a penalty price. Because of the discouragement that these losses gave to further speculation and also because of official exchange stabilization during the process of putting the ruble onto the gold standard, dealings in forward rubles were on a very moderate scale thereafter.[31]

A better-known example is the punishment of bear speculators against the French franc in March 1924. Armed with a loan of dollars from the House of Morgan and supported by an abatement of inflationary anticipations following a tax increase, the French government was temporarily able to drive up the exchange value of the franc to a level that meant heavy losses for the bears.

A government agency may create a bear squeeze by exercising the monopoly power that individual private speculators do not have in an active market. Armed with official power and prestige, a fund's managers may feel little moral restraint against playful or vindicative treatment of speculators. Even so, it is hard to see how the bear-squeeze technique could discourage supposedly undesirable speculation without also risking discouragement of the useful sorts of speculation. Sometimes underlying supply and demand conditions do warrant a decline in a currency, and bear speculation may be useful in hastening a smooth transition. But if speculators knew that an exchange fund was watching them and that it had a sadistic propensity to play cat and mouse with them, they might decide to quit the market. Or speculation might tend to become one-sided, with speculators willing to take long positions but unwilling to take short positions in currencies managed by exchange funds. This one-sidedness might tend to permit exaggerated bullishness in the managed currencies, making the reactions all the more sharp when they finally came. Such one-sidedness would not necessarily and always develop, however. Speculators against a clearly overvalued currency might count on outlasting the fund's ability to prolong a bear squeeze.

Historical examples illustrate how official intervention may sometimes be more disruptive than equilibrating. Agents of the Russian government tried to support the ruble in 1861, 1862–1863, and 1875–1876. After the stock of foreign exchange had run out and the government had suffered losses, the ruble depreciated —probably more sharply than it would otherwise have done. Made wiser by these experiences, the Russian government usually refrained until the 1890s from further attempts to control the exchange rate.[32] In 1906 the Spanish Treasury, apparently seeing a chance to restore the long-depreciated peseta to par, began selling French francs on the exchange market to intensify an appreciation of the peseta that was already under way. At first, this intervention incited short sales of francs and panicky selling by holders of foreign exchange. Later, realizing that the peseta's support was at the cost of Spain's foreign-exchange reserves, Spaniards took advantage of the temporary bargain price of francs in terms of pesetas. A contemporary Spanish economist judged that speculators' efforts to infer the intentions of the Finance Ministry from each development on the market were aggravating the instability of the rate and that a market free from official intervention would have been more stable.[33] In June 1928 the Spanish government created the Exchange Intervention Committee, which fought exchange fluctuations with funds borrowed abroad. The Committee apparently did narrow the range between weekly highs and lows of the peseta but could delay the downward trend only for short periods. Support of the peseta exhausted the Committee's foreign funds and caused it to suspend operations between February and June 1929. After a few months of resumed activity, the Committee again ceased functioning in October, when foreign banks refused fresh credits. Again, the peseta sank. With commodity prices in Spain holding steady in the face of an incipient worldwide deflation, the government was unable to peg the exchanges. Its efforts, though, left the government in debt to London and New York banks. Raising an internal gold loan to repay the external debt increased the demand for foreign exchange and drove the peseta to still lower levels from December 1929 to January 1930. In April 1930 the Exchange Intervention Committee was finally abolished. Later in 1930 and in 1931 the government imposed strict exchange controls, yet the peseta kept sinking still lower as depresson deepened in the outside world.[34]

A few months after its establishment, the British Exchange Equalisation Account saw sterling weakening in the second half of 1932. The pressure stemmed in part from tension about the war debt payment to the United States coming due in December. Though for a time the Account tried to defend the pound, it declined in the step-wise manner characteristic of a currency with a weak underlying trend but with artificial support. Finally, not having had time to acquire enough gold and foreign exchange, the Account had to stop supporting the pound and let it sink to a low of $3.17 in November. Early in 1933 the situation was reversed. The Exchange Equalisation Account kept the pound from rising above $3.45, although many observers thought that it would have gone to $3.80 or more in a free market. The Account was supplying cheap pounds for speculative buyers and thus enabling them to win profits later. After the depreciation and devaluation of the American dollar in 1933–1934, the British Account helped keep the exchange rate close to $5.00 until mid-1938. Then, at last, Britain's increasingly adverse trade balance drew tardy recognition that the pound was overvalued. The Account met growing demands for gold and dollars, letting the pound depreciate only in small steps. The delay in letting the pound find its free-market level naturally incited purchases of gold and dollars while they were still being kept relatively cheap. In August, the developing crisis over Czechoslovakia intensified this speculation. By February 1939 the Account had retreated to a rate of $4.68 per pound. There the Account held until just before the outbreak of World War II, although that rate—generally recognized as indefensible in the long run—was a standing invitation to bear speculation.[35]

"Dirty floats," as episodes of managed fluctuation came to be known, became almost worldwide during the second half of 1971 and especially after March 1973. Early experience seemed to bear out the distinction between

such a system, or nonsystem, and freely floating rates. Difficulties attributable to official intervention and rumors about it were apparent. However, not all the evidence is in yet.

In contrast to all the foregoing, there is at least one prominent example of an official exchange fund that seems neither to have engaged in unduly persistent pegging nor to have disrupted the market by breeding speculation about its own intentions. This is the Canadian fund, operating from October 1950 until June 1961 under circumstances described in Chapter 26. The fact that the Canadian fund operated with rare and notable self-restraint tends,

---

31. Einzig, *The Theory of Forward Exchange*, pp. 40–41; G. W. M. Huysmans, *Termijnhandel in Valuta*, Roermond: J. J. Romen & Zonen, 1926, p. 81; Gerhart v. Schulze-Gävernitz *Volkswirtschaftliche Studien aus Russland*, Leipzig: Duncker & Humblot, 1899, pp. 524–526; various issues of *Aktionär* (Frankfurt, Germany), September–November 1894.

32. Schulze-Gävernitz, *op. cit.*, pp. 528–530. It should be added, however, that there does seem to have been official intervention at times during Ivan Vyshnegradsky's tenure as Finance Minister, 1887–1892. Then, incidentally, the ruble rate displayed unusually wide fluctuations. According to Arthur Raffalovich, futile support of the ruble around 1863 left the Treasury burdened with a new debt of 15 million pounds and cost it a loss of 70 million rubles. "Histoire du Rouble-crédit," *Journal de la Société de Statistique de Paris*, **XXXVII**, October 1896, p. 365.

33. Francisco Gil y Pablos, *Estudios sobre la Moneda y los Cambios*, Madrid: Hijos de Reus, Editores, 1906, Appendix, esp. pp. 334, 347–351.

34. Walter H. Delaplane, "The Spanish Peseta since 1913" (unpublished dissertation), Duke University, 1934, pp. 118–123, 150—156, 213–214.

35. Waight, *op. cit.*, pp. 21, 111–114, 119–120; Morton, *op. cit.*, pp. 128–129; William Adams Brown, Jr., *The International Gold Standard Reinterpreted*, New York: National Bureau of Economic Research, 1940, **II**, 1137–1138, 1146–1147; Pumphrey, *op. cit.*, p. 811. The floating French franc of 1937–1938 provides still another example of speculation against an exchange stabilization fund; see pp. 364–366 below.

"if anything, to support, by contrast, the lessons apparently taught by experience with more ambitious funds.

Concluding comments

When official accounts are at work, exchange-rate determination becomes at least potentially, a political matter. Though the managers of a fund may sincerely intend only to iron out undue fluctuations, they necessarily must use their own judgment about what fluctuations are "undue." Rates thus become a matter of official decision. Though exchange funds may be used as instruments of international cooperation, they may also be used at cross purposes, or even as instruments of currency warfare. At least, their very existence makes accusations of competitive exchange depreciation (or appreciation) plausible. The same is true if the national authorities are known to be operating in the exchange markets even without establishing separate funds for this specific purpose;

unequivocal renunciation of all official intervention would presumably be necessary to allay suspicion. The internationally owned and operated exchange stabilization fund proposed by Lerner and Meade[36] as a substitute for national funds would presumably avoid nationalistic manipulation of exchange rates; but even if the various diplomatic and administrative difficulties could be overcome, it would still face some of the problems characteristic of national funds: a drift from rate smoothing to actual rate pegging and incitement of destabilizing speculation based on interpretations and anticipations of its own activities and intentions. It is an open question whether a fund operating modestly enough to avoid these dangers would really be missed if abolished.

---

36. Abba P. Lerner, *The Economics of Employment*, New York: McGraw-Hill, 1951, pp. 360–362; J. E. Meade, *The Balance of Payments*, London: Oxford University Press, 1951, pp. 225–226; Meade in American Enterprise Institute, *International Payments Problems*, Washington: AEI, 1966, pp. 76–77.

part II

History and Policy

A series of historical chapters begins here. They survey the policies pursued as circumstances unfolded, and they close by surveying present-day proposals for the reform of international monetary policies. Attention to history is worthwhile because historical references abound in the traditional lore of international monetary economics and because the supposed "lessons" of historical experience have played a great role in the formation of policy. For the interwar period, whose "lessons" have been so influential, and for the period since World War II, a rather detailed chronicle of events seems appropriate. For the period before World War I, a broader survey will suffice.

CHAPTER FIFTEEN

The Gold Standard Before World War I

Rise of the international gold standard

An international gold standard exists when most major countries maintain two-way convertibility between gold and their national monetary units at substantially fixed ratios and leave inward and outward shipments of gold substantially free from interference. This system is a normal state of grace, hallowed by centuries of practice, from which the world has fallen away only in recent decades—or so goes a widely believed myth. In fact, a full-fledged international gold standard held wide sway for at most about 40 years just before World War I. True enough, the use of gold (and silver) coin dates back to antiquity, but a fixed and supposedly permanent value relation among various types of money is a development of the past two centuries. Before then, even within single countries, various kinds of money had circulated in chaos. Fixing the value of all moneys in relation to standard gold coin became common only in the nineteenth century.

The full-fledged gold standard arose in Great Britain. The background of its evolution from a loose bimetallism goes back to the seventeenth and eighteenth centuries. Sir Isaac Newton, as Master of the Mint, played a part

by calculating the value of the gold guinea in terms of silver shillings. We may conveniently take up the story at the time of the Napoleonic wars. England was then experiencing wartime inflation and an irredeemable paper currency. The Bank Restriction Act, in force from 1797 to 1821, forbade the Bank of England (at its own wish, of course) to redeem its notes in gold. An act of 1798 foreshadowed further development away from bimetallism and toward the full gold standard by suspending the free coinage of silver and reaffirming a £25 limit on the legal-tender power of silver coin. The Coinage Act of 1816 authorized the gold sovereign, a 20s. or £1 gold piece first coined the following year. Its gold content confirmed the mint price of a standard ounce of gold (11/12 pure) that had been recognized since the middle of the eighteenth century: £3.17s. 10½d. Silver money was subordinated to gold and further limited in its legal tender power only to payments up to £2. The continued irredeemability of the paper pound and the market quotation of gold at a premium above its theoretical value deprived the 1816 coinage law of its full significance for a while. Finally, a law of 1819 required the Bank of England to make its notes redeemable in gold bars at the coinage price of gold by May 1821 and in coin by May 1823. Actually, full redeemability in coin was achieved in 1821, but at the cost of rapid credit contraction, further price deflation, industrial distress, and widespread unemployment. The law of 1819 had already repealed restrictions on the melting of coin and the export of coin and bullion. The paper pound was equivalent to the gold sovereign, and England was on a full gold standard.[1]

The United States at this time was legally on a bimetallic standard: the Coinage Act of 1792 had defined a gold dollar and a silver dollar 15 times as heavy. (Gold dollars were not actually minted until 1849, but the gold content of the dollar was implied by the weight of gold coins of larger denominations.) The American mint ratio of 15 to 1 clashed with a ratio of about 15½ to 1 prevailing on world markets. Since the U.S. Mint was accepting

1. R. G. Hawtrey, *The Gold Standard in Theory and Practice*, 5th ed., London: Longmans, Green, 1947, chap. III; Albert Feavearyear, *The Pound Sterling*, 2nd ed., rev. by E. Victor Morgan, Oxford: Clarendon Press, 1963, esp. pp. 152–155, 172, 188, 212–213, 221, 223.

gold at less than its market value, little gold came to it for coinage, and the United States was in effect on a silver standard.

The Coinage Acts of 1834 and 1837 reversed this disparity by slightly cutting the gold content of the dollar and setting a new mint ratio of very nearly 16 to 1. Since the United States was now valuing silver less highly relative to gold than was the world market, little silver was offered for coinage, and the United States was in effect on a gold standard. Considering this development, should we say that the international gold standard arose in the 1830s? Probably not. For one thing, the United States was on gold only accidentally; bimetallism was still the legally prescribed standard. Second, the United States was still too small a country for its practice to carry much weight in an assessment of world monetary arrangements. Third, the United States was not permanently on gold; the Civil War was to interrupt its metallic standard. The international gold standard as a system consciously adhered to by the major trading countries still had not arisen.

The ratio of 15½ to 1 ruled on world gold and silver markets because of the dominance of France's bimetallic system, dating from the period of the French Revolution and embodying this ratio. Being in effect on both the gold and silver standards at the same time, France was standing ready to deal in the two metals in unlimited quantities and at fixed prices. France was prepared to hold a large enough stock of each in relation to world demand and supply to govern the price ratio.

French bimetallism incidentally tended to stabilize exchange rates between gold-standard and silver-standard currencies. The British pound and French franc, for instance, were linked by their relative gold contents, while the French franc and Indian rupee were linked by their relative silver contents. The exchange rates between gold and silver currencies, such as the pound and the rupee, could fluctuate more widely than within the range of gold points of two gold currencies, of course, since silver was more expensive to ship than a quantity of gold of the same value and since a kind of combination of gold points and silver points was operative, with the spread reflecting the costs of shipping, melting and recoining both metals.

Around 1850, gold from newly discovered fields in California and Australia began pouring onto world markets and revolutionizing the relative values of gold and silver. Yearly world gold production had averaged under £2 million in the period 1821–1830 and about £7½ million in 1841–1850 but reached about £31 million in 1853.[2] With increased supplies thus tending to depress the value of gold, the French bimetallic ratio of 15½ to 1 came to overvalue gold, making the franc in effect a gold currency. The same was all the more true of the dollar at the U.S. mint ratio of 16 to 1.

In hopes of promoting an international standardization of currencies on a bimetallic basis, the Latin Monetary Union was formed in 1865 by countries whose standard monetary units were equal to the French franc: France, Belgium, Switzerland, and Italy. Greece joined in 1868. Each member was to issue standard coins in denominations of 100, 50, 20, 10 and 5 francs in gold and 5 francs in silver,[3] and these coins were to circulate freely throughout the union. In addition, each member country could mint subsidiary coins in amounts up to 6 francs per inhabitant, and public offices of all member countries were to accept these coins in payments of up to 100 francs.

The situation around 1870 was, in short, still far from an international gold standard. England was fully on gold. Several legally bimetallic countries were in effect on gold. Germany, Holland, Scandinavia, and the Orient still had silver standards. Various wars and revolutions in the period 1848–1871 had inflated several important countries, including Russia, Austria-Hungary, Italy, and the United States, onto irredeemable paper. Even the French franc suffered a slight and brief depreciation as a result of the Franco-Prussian War.

Then, in the early 1870s, movement toward an international gold standard gained momentum. The German Empire, newly established and due to receive a sizable war indemnity from France, led the way. Germany's earlier silver standard had been credited with some advantages, such as stability of exchange rates in trade with Russia and Austria, but this advantage had been lost for some time because of inflation off silver onto inconvertible paper in the latter two countries. The German government now adopted the gold mark as its new monetary unit, discontinued the free coinage and unlimited legal tender of silver, and began selling silver on a large scale in order to buy gold. The glut of silver on world markets was swollen by new discoveries in Nevada and elsewhere, by the eventual effects of the discontinuance of the free coinage of silver in the United States in 1873, and by the subsequent demonetization of silver in various other countries. The overabundant silver at first began flowing into the monetary systems of countries whose silver or bimetallic standards still guaranteed a market for it. These countries faced the threat of monetary inflation and a corresponding drop in the buying power of their money units. Suspending the free coinage of silver seemed to offer the only protection. France and her associates in the Latin Monetary Union limited the coinage of standard silver pieces in 1874 and entirely discontinued it in 1878, thus transforming their bimetallism into a "limping gold standard." Holland and the Scandinavian countries acted similarly. Gold replaced silver as the standard money in all European countries except the few still on irredeemable paper. The collapse in the monetary demand for it of course made silver depreciate all the more sharply in relation to gold.

The United States was also gradually moving toward the international gold standard. In 1873, when Congress omitted the silver dollar from the list of coins to be minted, the country was still using the inconvertible greenbacks, dating from the Civil War inflation. For this reason and also because the worldwide depreciation of silver had not yet become pronounced, this end to the government's unlimited market for silver brought forth no strong protest at the time. Only later did mining interests label it the "Crime of '73." The act of 1873 did, however, mark the end of bimetallism as the legal standard from which the inconvertible paper was regarded as a temporary departure. (In a sense, though, the limited legal tender of the silver "trade dollar" between 1873 and 1876 was still providing a latent bimetallism at the ratio of $16\frac{1}{3}$ to 1.) A return to convertibility would now mean gold monometallism. By 1879 the economy had "grown up" enough to the money supply and price deflation had gone far enough to permit resuming convertibility at the prewar gold content of the dollar.

Only after the early 1870s did the dollar-sterling exchange rate exhibit the degree of stability commonly associated with the pre-1914 gold standard. (For the greenback period, this remark applies to the sterling rate not only of the paper dollar but even of the *gold* dollar.) Before the early seventies, with financial institutions and transatlantic transportation and communications relatively undeveloped,

THE GOLD STANDARD BEFORE WORLD WAR I

exchange rates varied widely. Only as improvements occurred in banking, the foreign-exchange market, and communications, as transportation (including gold shipments) became quicker and cheaper, and as arbitrage became routine were fluctuations confined to a narrow range between gold points.[4] (Not until 1865, for example, was the transatlantic cable successfully laid.)

The role of silver under bimetallism died harder in the United States than in Europe. Silver-mine interests wanting price support for their product formed a political alliance with farmers burdened by debt and hopeful of relief through inflation. (Actually, the long-term trend in prices had been downward since the end of the Civil War, and some extra expansion of the money supply would have been appropriate.) The miner-farmer alliance found its most conspicuous expression in the Populist movement of the 1890s, which campaigned, among other things, for the free and unlimited coinage of silver at the ratio of 16 to 1. Though the alliance never succeeded in reestablishing full bimetallism, it did secure passage of the Bland-Allison Act of 1878 and the Sherman Silver Purchase Act of 1890. These compromises required the Treasury to buy specified amounts of silver each month and issue corresponding amounts of silver dollars or silver certificates. With the money so issued contributing to a threatened exhaustion of the country's gold reserve and a forced abandonment of the gold standard, President Cleveland persuaded a special session of Congress in 1893 to repeal the Silver Purchase Act. McKinley's defeat of Bryan, who campaigned in 1896 for the free coinage of silver, helped seal the fate of bimetallism. The Gold Standard Act of 1900 consolidated the monetary

2. Hawtrey, *op. cit.*, pp. 47, 81.

3. Troubles with irredeemable paper money kept Italy and Greece from fully joining this system.

4. See L. E. Davis and J. R. T. Hughes, "A Dollar-Sterling Exchange, 1803–1895," *Economic History Review*, **XIII**, August 1960, pp. 52–78, plus a fold-out chart. This article is largely based on detailed records of purchases of sterling bills by a Philadelphia importing firm.

standard that had existed in the United States since 1879.

The events preceding adoption of the gold standard in Austria-Hungary and in Russia are of particular theoretical interest. After a long record of paper-money inflation interrupted by periods of stabilization on silver, both countries were again driven off their traditional silver standards around the middle of the nineteenth century by issues of paper money to meet the expenses of revolutions and wars. Then, as silver depreciated on world markets in the 1870s and afterwards, the value of the silver "contained" in the standard gulden and ruble threatened to sink down to the purchasing power of the paper units. Once the value of silver began sinking still lower, owners of silver bullion would have taken advantage of the guaranteed market provided by the free coinage of silver into guldens and rubles. Silver would have poured into Austria-Hungary and Russia, inflating their money supplies and pulling down the purchasing powers and foreign exchange values of their currency units in step with its sinking value. To forestall this unwelcome development, both countries suspended the free coinage of silver, Austria-Hungary in 1879 and Russia in 1893. Thus Austria-Hungary began 13 years and Russia 4 years during which the national currency unit was "hanging in mid-air," with a value exceeding that of its traditional metallic content. This phenomenon, a puzzle to some economists of the time, illustrates the quantity theory of money; suspension of free coinage helped maintain the scarcities and so the purchasing powers of the two moneys. In 1892 Austria-Hungary began adopting a gold-exchange standard, replacing the paper gulden with a gold crown worth half as much. Russia, after building up a gold reserve, moved onto a gold standard in 1897. The story of the Spanish peseta, another former silver currency inflated into inconvertibility, partially parallels that of the gulden and ruble. Spain also aimed at a gold standard, but unsuccessfully.

India traditionally had a silver standard, and during the years when French bimetallism at 15½ to 1 was dominant, the exchange rate between the rupee and the British pound was fairly stable. But with the decline of silver in the 1870s and afterward, the rupee-pound rate underwent widening fluctuations. In 1893 the Indian government suspended the free coinage of silver to check further depreciation, but the rupee continued sinking for a while in partial sympathy with silver until it briefly reached a low point of barely more than half its earlier gold value. Until 1898 the rupee resembled the gulden and ruble in having a scarcity value greater than the bullion value of its silver content. Then it was pegged against the pound sterling at two-thirds of its earlier value by adoption of the gold-exchange standard, that is, by official buying and selling on the foreign-exchange market to maintain the chosen rate.

Similar measures put other Far Eastern currencies onto gold. The Philippine peso, for example, was tied to the dollar under a gold exchange standard after the United States took over the Philippines. Japan adopted a gold standard in 1897. By World War I China was almost alone among major countries still clinging to a silver standard. In Latin America, it is true, several countries still had inconvertible paper money. But the gold standard was the target and the prevailing idea of normal; going back to silver was no longer a live issue.

Beginning in the 1890s, growing supplies of gold eased the worldwide transition to the gold standard. Gold was found in the Klondike-Yukon area and in South Africa. The cyanide process of refining gold was introduced. The more abundant supply of gold helped countries such as Austria-Hungary and Russia to acquire reserves for their new gold currencies. Along with growing use of checking-account money, it also helped to stop and reverse the downtrend in prices that had been going on for two or three decades. Pro-silver agitation in the United States slackened. From 1896 to 1910, wholesale prices in the United States rose on the average by some 50 percent—all while the dollar was firmly tied to gold.

It may seem paradoxical that increased output of gold after 1849 and 1896 and the resulting depreciation of gold and increased output of silver in the 1870s and the resulting depreciation of silver both contributed to the spread of the gold standard. Yet there is no real contradiction. The two depreciations of gold were comparatively mild: the earlier one tended to ease legally bimetallic countries onto a *de facto* gold standard, and the later one worked to avoid deflationary pressure as countries newly adopting the international standard built up their gold reserves. The later depreciation also helped quiet the fears of bimetallists that two monetary metals were necessary to avoid a deflationary scarcity of reserves. By contrast, the depreciation of silver that began in the 1870s was sharp, supposedly threatening price inflation in countries clinging to silver or bimetallism (which would in effect have become a silver standard). This threat brought action to downgrade silver.

The international gold standard was a comparatively brief episode in world history. We cannot specify a precise date when it began. It did not exist in 1870 and did exist in 1900. World War I marked its end, for the postwar attempts at restoration can hardly be considered successful. The international gold standard was in full sway only from perhaps 1897 to 1914, less than 20 years.[5]

London as the center

Before World War I the pound sterling was by far the currency most commonly used in pricing goods and services and making international payments. Ordinary British merchants dealt only in pounds, shillings, and pence, letting the foreigners struggle with the mystery of the foreign exchanges.[6] Even much trade that never touched British shores was priced in sterling and financed with sterling drafts and acceptances. For example, an American importer of Japanese silk might arrange for his own bank to honor sterling drafts drawn by his supplier. The Japanese exporter would sell these drafts to his bank for yen. The American importer would pay dollars to his own bank, which would either deal through a correspondent bank in New York to buy the necessary sterling or else would use balances of its own already held in London. The Japanese bank would collect the sterling due on the draft at its maturity and so in effect take over a sterling balance previously owned by an American bank.[7]

What had made sterling such an international currency and London such a dominant financial center? Britain's leading position as importer, exporter, and source of long- and short-term capital made it convenient for foreign suppliers, customers, and debtors to hold working balances in sterling: funds temporarily to spare could be lent at interest in London with great safety. The unrivaled facilities of the London money market assured that any bill endorsed by one of the British acceptance houses could be discounted at the world's most favorable rates. Britain's commercial and financial leadership stemmed in turn from a combination of historical factors, including: the policy of free trade, which was firmly estab-

lished by the middle of the nineteenth century, a head start in industrialization, generating wealth and savings available for loan and investment abroad, and early reestablishment of a firm gold standard in 1821. Actually, it hardly occurred to people in those days to speak of sterling as convertible: there was nothing better to convert it into. The identity of gold and sterling seemed almost a law of nature. Even more than the link with gold, sterling's general acceptability and unrestricted transferability promoted confidence. The Bank of England operated before World War I with a gold reserve often below and only very rarely above the range of £30 to 40 million, in contrast with reserves in the neighborhood of £50, £100, and £120 million held by central banks with lesser responsibilities, those of Austria-Hungary, Russia, and France. (Since World War II, in further contrast, British reserves have been regarded as dangerously low even when over £600 million.) At the end of 1913, the central banks and governments of seven countries held larger gold reserves than the British authorities; the United States held almost eight times as much, and even Argentina held more than half again as much. (With almost 12 percent of the world total of gold reserves plus gold coins in circulation in 1913, however, Britain ranked third by that criterion, behind the United States and France.) ". . .

5. J. B. Condliffe, *The Commerce of Nations*, New York: Norton, 1950, p. 362, singles out 1897 as the starting date. Perhaps he had it in mind as the year when Russia and Japan went on gold, when Austria-Hungary enjoyed its first full year of uninterrupted success in operating a gold-exchange standard, when McKinley became President of the United States after campaigning in defense of the gold standard, and when price indexes registered a rise after decades of deflation.

Arthur I. Bloomfield dates the international gold standard as indicated in the title of his monograph, *Monetary Policy Under the International Gold Standard: 1880–1914*, Federal Reserve Bank of New York, 1959.

6. William Adams Brown, Jr., *The International Gold Standard Reinterpreted*, New York: National Bureau of Economic Research, 1940, **I**, 638.

7. Condliffe, *op. cit.*, pp. 383–384.

contemporaries were torn between criticism . . . and admiration" of how "such vast transactions, both domestic and external, [were] handled with so small a reserve."[8]

Rough equality between payments to and from Britain kept the world well supplied with sterling: no "sterling shortage" developed at all comparable to the "dollar shortage" experienced in the early years after World War II. Britain generally ran a surplus on current account in the balance of payments, with earnings from exports and on foreign investments exceeding expenditures on imports. Rather than accumulate it in barren gold, Britons constructively made this surplus available for additional overseas loans and investments. Furthermore, there was some tendency for the British balances of trade and of long-term lending to move in offsetting directions over the business cycle, which contributed to overall external equilibrium of the rest of the world as well as of Britain itself. London investment banking houses were highly specialized according to types of securities, types of enterprises, and overseas geographical areas, just as stockmarket operators and commodity experts were similarly specialized. By World War I an estimated one-third of all accumulated British wealth had taken the form of private foreign investment. Adjusted to the size of the American economy in 1955, this could mean something like $300 or $400 billion, as against an actual figure of about $25 billion. In the four decades preceding World War I, about 40 percent of British savings was invested overseas. Corresponding figures for America in the 1950s would have amounted to a capital outflow upwards of $20 billion a year, as contrasted with an actual net private outflow of some $1 to $3 billion. In the few years just before World War I, one-tenth of British national income consisted of returns on overseas investment; the comparable American figure in the 1950s was well under 1 percent. British foreign investments shortly before World War I amounted to roughly twice the French, more than three times the German, and many times as large as the foreign investments of any other country. Probably something over half of the British foreign investment was outside the British Empire, largely in the United States and Latin America.[9] Figures such as these highlight the contrast between Britain's financial leadership in the days of the international gold standard and America's less dominant

position nowadays; they show the special nature of the historical circumstances in which the international gold standard worked as well as it apparently did.

Britain's role in international economic affairs before World War I took the form of *private* trade and investment, not of government grants and loans. Much of the British foreign investment and lending, though privately supplied, went to foreign government units or to government-guaranteed enterprises. The bulk of British capital export in the period 1870–1913 took the form of purchases of fixed-interest securities. Overseas government bonds and railway securities together accounted for about two-thirds of the total international investment in this period, and further British investment went into other public-utility undertakings. No major proportion of investment went for "colonial"-type ventures—that is, mines, plantations, and similar undertakings producing for the investing countries.[10]

The British money market played an even more direct role than the long-term-capital market in the working of the international gold standard. When England returned to gold after the Napoleonic Wars, banking was carried on almost entirely by private partnerships. Several hundred operated outside London, free from any significant special regulation, keeping reserves in whatever form and amount they themselves saw fit, and making loans and issuing paper money. Deposits and checks were still little used in the provinces. Inside London, about 60 banks were operating, including the country's largest and soundest. Except for the Bank of England, they did not issue their own banknotes. Instead, they granted loans by crediting the borrower with a deposit or by paying out Bank of England notes. London businessmen were already well accustomed to checking accounts.[11]

As the British money market evolved further, businessmen increasingly made payments to each other by tranferring claims on London banks. The use of checks spread from London throughout the country and was well established by the 1880s. Joint stock banks, better able to amass large capitals, grew at the expense of banking partnerships. Through mergers and otherwise, the number of banks fell from around 600 in 1824 and 250 in 1865 to 55 in 1914 and even fewer after that. Most of the banking business eventually came into the hands of the "big five"—the Midland,

Westminster, Lloyd's, Barclay's, and National Provincial. (This is true of England and Wales; Scotland and Northern Ireland have banking systems of their own, and commercial banks there even today have limited banknote-issue privileges.) England, like Canada but in contrast with the United States, developed a branch banking system, with a few giant banks operating many offices throughout the country.

Certain functions now performed by banks in the United States gravitated in England into the hands of special *acceptance houses*, which evolved from leading London mercantile firms. They profited by knowing the credit-worthiness of a great many merchants and manufacturers in Britain and throughout the world. The typical client of an acceptance house was a merchant buying goods or otherwise becoming obligated to make a payment in the near future. Foreign trade gave rise to the bulk of the acceptance business. The client would arrange to pay the house, and his supplier or creditor would be authorized to draw a draft ("bill") on the house instead of on the merchant himself. The house would "accept" the draft when properly drawn and presented, thus guaranteeing payment when due. Bills accepted by one of the specialized houses had a much higher credit standing than bills drawn directly on their clients would have had. As high-quality obligations, they could be sold on the London money market at the most favorable rates of discount available. For a commission, little-known but reliable firms could thus take advantage of the credit standing of acceptance houses, which were in effect guaranteeing the soundness of paper rather than actually providing loans. The lending was done by discount houses and others who bought paper and held it until maturity.

The *discount houses* were a small number of firms that profited by judicious investment in short-term paper. They operated with their own capital and with funds borrowed from the banks and deposited by the public. They had evolved from bill brokers (middlemen between short-term investors and merchants wishing to discount bills) and from bill dealers, who combined the brokerage function with the holding of bill portfolios of their own.

The institutions of the late-nineteenth-century London money market illustrate remarkable specialization. According to Walter Bagehot, "a very great many of the strongest heads in England spend their minds on little else than on thinking whether other people will

pay their debts." The typical bill-broker or banker

. . . is a kind of "solvency-meter," and lives by estimating rightly the "responsibility of parties," as he would call it. . . . The moment any set of traders want capital, the best of them, those whose promises are well known to be good, get it in a minute, because it is lying ready in the hands of those who know, and who live by knowing, that they are fit to have it.[12]

8. Paul Bareau, "The Position of Sterling in International Trade," *Banking and Foreign Trade*, London: Europa Publications Limited for the Institute of Bankers, 1952, pp. 152–53; Brian Tew, *International Monetary Cooperation*, London: Hutchinson's University Library, 1952, pp. 121–122; F. Robert Vanes, *De Internationale Gouden Standaard: Een onderzoek naar de oorzaken van zijn verval in de tussenoorlogse periode*, Antwerp/Amsterdam: Standaard-Boekhandel, 1951, pp. 99, 416; Feavearyear, *op. cit.*, p. 314 (from where the quotation is taken).

The continuing stability and convertibility of sterling and other leading gold currencies were never seriously questioned, and major or sustained 'runs' on them virtually never occurred. Confidence held firm despite continuing public concern in England and some other countries regarding the adequacy of the gold reserves. Bloomfield, *op. cit.*, p. 21.

9. Most of these estimates are from the statement of John H. Adler, citing A. K. Cairncross, in *Foreign Economic Policy*, Hearings before the Subcommittee on Foreign Economic Policy of the Joint Committee on the Economic Report, Washington: U.S. Government Printing Office, 1955, pp. 453, 463, and from Condliffe, *op. cit.*, pp. 325–327.

10. Ragnar Nurkse, *Problems of Capital Formation in Underdeveloped Countries*, Oxford: Blackwell, 1953, pp. 28–29.

11. This and the next few paragraphs draw in part on P. T. Ellsworth, *The International Economy*, New York: Macmillan, 1950, pp. 243–257; Condliffe, *op. cit.*, chap. XI, and Committee on Finance & Industry, *Report* (The "Macmillan Report"), London: His Majesty's Stationery Office, 1931, pp. 25–45.

12. Walter Bagehot, *Economic Studies*, London: Longmans, Green, 1880, pp. 45–46.

Bank rate and the gold standard

Responsibility for administering the country's gold reserve gradually fell upon the Bank of England. The Bank had originally been established in 1694, largely to make loans to the government, act as its banker, and issue paper money. Private stockholders owned it until 1946. Gradually the ordinary commercial banks in London and many in the rest of the country grew accustomed to keeping reserves against their own demand liabilities partly in the form of Bank of England notes and partly in deposits at the Bank. The ordinary banks held shrinking fractions of their reserves in gold coin. Even before the gold standard had become internationally established, the Bank of England had come to hold Britain's only important gold reserve. It had acquired special responsibilities, in fact, though the directors of the Bank shrank from admitting them explicitly and preferred to insist that theirs was just one, though the largest, among profit-seeking banks. Only tacitly did the Bank admit special responsibility by keeping a reserve larger in proportion to liabilities than ordinary banks did. Even so, the Bank's gold reserve was precariously small in relation to the total volume of claims directly and indirectly pyramided upon it; in the late nineteenth century it amounted to only 2 or 3 percent of the country's total money supply.[13]

Furthermore, the Bank came to function as a "lender of last resort" in time of stringency. Occasionally, when exceptionally large demands for credit or drains of currency into circulation or of gold abroad menaced the liquidity of ordinary financial institutions, the Bank would come to the rescue, providing funds by heavy rediscounts of bills and advances. The Bank could hardly have shouldered this responsibility unless the British government had been willing in emergencies to waive the requirements of the Bank Act of 1844. This act had split the Bank of England into a banking department and a note-issuing department and had required pound-for-pound gold backing (or, to a limited extent, silver backing) for all bank notes beyond a specified fiduciary issue (originally £14 million, later increased from time to time as the note-issue privileges of other banks lapsed). Parliament had intended to give Britain an "automatic" or unmanaged money supply in accordance with the classical theory of the gold standard: the country's currency stock would supposedly vary by the absolute amount of inward and outward flows of gold. The emergency waivers of this Bank Act took the form of so-called "Chancellor's letters" or "crisis letters." The Chancellor of the Exchequer issued them in 1847, 1857, 1866, and at the start of the war in 1914. Such a letter was a message urging the Bank to rediscount abundantly to make available the funds necessary for relieving the panic on the money market. The Bank was not to worry if such action led it to issue banknotes in excess of the provisions of the Bank Act; the Chancellor promised that, in such an event, the government would have Parliament pass a special law making the action legal retroactively.

This willingness to waive the principles of the 1844 law spelled abandonment of the ideal of a self-regulating, unmanaged monetary system. Another development relieving the British money supply of a rigid tie to the gold stock was the increasing growth of checking-account money relative to currency and coin. Actually, it is questionable whether a money supply rigidly geared to the gold stock would have proved acceptable even in the unlikely event that such a system could have been maintained. The remarkable growth of the British economy in the nineteenth century probably required an adaptable money supply. According to Barrett Whale, "the Act of 1844 has worked satisfactorily because it did not work in the way designed."[14]

Ever since publication of Walter Bagehot's highly influential *Lombard Street* in 1873, the Bank of England's special duty was generally recognized. "Bagehot's rule" called for the Bank to lend copiously in times of critical credit stringency, but at a high rate of interest. By custom, commercial banks needing funds did not go directly to the Bank of England. Instead, they would press the discount houses to repay loans and would let their own holdings of bills mature without replacement. In this way the pressure was transmitted to the discount houses, which were "forced into the bank"—forced, that is, to rediscount some of their paper at the Bank of England.

The rate charged on such rediscounts, known as "Bank rate," was analogous to the discount rate of the Federal Reserve banks in the United States nowadays, but far more important. The dominance of the Bank of England among British financial institutions and a conventional linkage of commercial-bank deposit and loan rates to Bank rate meant that the whole structure of rates in the money market, and to some extent even long-term interest rates, moved in sympathy with Bank rate. Its manipulation was a vital weapon for the custodian of remarkably slender gold reserves. Drains of currency into circulation or of gold abroad, perhaps in response to temporary deficits in the British balance of payments, fell on the reserves of the Bank. To counter such losses Bank rate would go up. Conversely, the Bank would lower its rate when gold reserves were unusually plentiful. Changes were frequent: Bank rate was changed 195 times between 1880 and 1913, every two months on the average.[15] The Bank had learned to heed Bagehot's advice: keep a margin of safety in the reserves, and adjust Bank rate before the reserves fall too close to a safe minimum.

Just how did Bank rate influence inflows and outflows of gold? A rise in the rate, together with the sympathetic rise in other money-market rates, would make London a relatively more attractive place to lend and a relatively less attractive place to borrow. The resulting shift in international capital movements would support or strengthen sterling on the foreign exchanges, changing the incentives for gold arbitrage so as to discourage an outflow of gold or even promote an inflow. A cut in Bank rate tended to work in the opposite way. London's undisputed position as world financial center avoided any problem of two or more centers of the same rank acting at cross-purposes. London was dominant both as international borrower and as international lender: it borrowed heavily in the form of foreigners' holdings of bank deposits and money-market paper and lent heavily through the long-term securities market and by discounting the bills that financed trade throughout the world. New loans in each direction were always being made afresh and old loans always coming due and subject to renewal or repayment. Even if there were no increase in British borrowing abroad, a restraint on lending would make gold flow in as foreigners paid off maturing old debts. Bank rate could control flows of capital and gold effectively because it had so much material to work on.

According to the traditional interpretation, which may or may not suit historical reality, Bank rate worked through a second channel also in correcting the balance of payments. Besides palliating temporary disequilibriums by guiding flows of capital, it provided a more fundamental cure. An increase in the rate tended to tighten credit generally, thereby retarding investment in inventories and fixed capital goods, slowing the general pace of business, and depressing prices and perhaps employment also. These price and income effects would tend to check imports and promote exports. A cut in Bank rate would unleash opposite tendencies. This traditional interpretation is well summarized in the report of the Cunliffe Committee, which was set up in Britain towards the end of World War I to make recommendations about postwar monetary policy:

4. When the exchanges were favourable, gold flowed freely into this country and an increase of legal tender money accompanied the development of trade. When the balance of trade was unfavourable and the exchanges were adverse, it became profitable to export gold. . . . [If the gold drain reduced the Bank of England's ratio of reserves to liabilities] in a degree considered dangerous, the Bank raised its rate of discount. The raising of the discount rate had the immediate effect of retaining money here which would otherwise have been remitted abroad and of attracting remittances from abroad to take advantage of the higher rate, thus checking the outflow of gold and even reversing the stream.

5. If the adverse condition of the exchanges was due not merely to seasonal fluctuations, but to circumstances tending to create a permanently adverse trade balance, it is obvious that the procedure above described would not have been sufficient. It would have resulted in the creation of a volume of short-dated indebtedness to foreign countries which would have been in the end disastrous to our credit and the position of London as the financial centre of the world. But the raising of the Bank's discount rate and the steps taken to make it effective in the market necessarily led to a general rise of interest rates and a restriction of

13. Jacob Viner, *International Economics: Studies*, New York: Free Press, 1951, p. 124.

14. P. Barrett Whale, "A Retrospective View of the Bank Charter Act of 1844," in T. S. Ashton and R. S. Sayers, eds., *Papers in English Monetary History*, Oxford: Clarendon Press, 1953, p. 130.

15. Richard N. Cooper in Richard E. Caves and associates, *Britain's Economic Prospects*, Washington, D.C.: Brookings Institution, 1968, p. 150n.

credit. New enterprises were therefore postponed and the demand for constructional materials and other capital goods was lessened. The consequent slackening of employment also diminished the demand for consumable goods, while holders of stocks of commodities carried largely with borrowed money, being confronted with an increase of interest changes, if not with actual difficulty in renewing loans, and with the prospect of falling prices, tended to press their goods on a weak market. The result was a decline in general prices in the home market which, by checking imports and stimulating exports, corrected the adverse trade balance which was the primary cause of the difficulty.

6. When, apart from a foreign drain of gold, credit at home threatened to become unduly expanded, the gold currency system tended to restrain the expansion and to prevent the consequent rise in domestic prices which ultimately causes such a drain. The expansion of credit, by forcing up prices, involves an increased demand for legal tender currency both from the banks in order to maintain their normal proportion of cash to liabilities and from the general public for the payment of wages and for retail transactions. In this case also the demand for such currency fell upon the reserve of the Bank of England, and the Bank was thereupon obliged to raise its rate of discount in order to prevent the fall in the proportion of that reserve to its liabilities. The same chain of consequences as we have just described followed and speculative trade activity was similarly restrained. There was therefore an automatic machinery by which the volume of purchasing power in this country was continuously adjusted to world prices of commodities in general. Domestic prices were automatically regulated so as to prevent excessive imports; and the creation of banking credit was so controlled that banking could be safely permitted a freedom from State interference which would not have been possible under a less rigid currency system.[16]

One striking thing about this quotation is how complacently the Committee, entranced with supposedly automatic correctives, viewed adjustments working through deflation of money, prices, production, consumption, and employment.

Various parts of the traditional view have been challenged. Robert Triffin, for one, believes that the adjustment mechanism operated in Britain itself in the opposite way, in important respects. Increases in London interest rates readjusted the balance of payments not so much through their effects on the British economy as through their effects elsewhere, especially in primary-producing countries.[17] Triffin's argument is that a rise in Bank rate attracted capital and gold from abroad so effectively that it tended to relieve rather than accentuate deflationary pressures in Britain; deflation would be more likely to fall upon the countries from which the capital was drawn. A cut in Bank rate, conversely, would promote an outflow of capital, tending to reduce expansionary impacts upon the British economy. International capital movements thus thwarted or delayed the fundamental price readjustments that changes in the rate were designed to stimulate.[18]

British experience did not conform to the classical picture, which really portrayed price relations among a large number of equally important countries. Because of Britain's dominance in the world economy before 1914, however, expansionary and contradictionary tendencies in Britain tended to engulf most other nations at the same time. Since the bulk of foreign exports was financed through London and since foreign bills far outweighed inland bills in the London discount market, a tightening or loosening of credit in Britain could be expected to affect the prices of foreign goods more drastically and directly than domestic prices. These movements might be further magnified by induced contraction or expansion in the foreign banking systems, especially as tightened credit there would not, as in London, attract compensatory capital movements from abroad. Another point in Triffin's skepticism about the classical view of relative price movements is that Britain's imports, consisting mainly of foodstuffs and raw materials, presumably responded more sensitively in price to changes in credit and business conditions than did Britain's largely industrial exports. If Britain's Bank-rate policy failed to accomplish the price-level readjustments of classical theory, as Triffin argues, the main reason is the thoroughly *international* character of the London money market. The system approximated the automatic gold standard of the classical model less than it did a centralized sterling exchange standard managed by the Bank of England.[19] ". . . the automatic operation of the gold standard . . . was more or less limited to the sphere of the Bank of England and was satisfactory in its results only because London was then by far the most powerful financial centre in the world . . . and could thus by the operation of her bank rate almost immediately adjust her reserve position. Other countries had, therefore, in the main to adjust their conditions to her."[20]

The Bank had charge of the reserves not only of the London money market but of the worldwide trade and investment cleared through London. Yet the myth of an automatic, self-regulating system was so strong that even when the directors of the Bank took positive action in raising or lowering Bank rate in response to depletion or growth of the gold reserve, they thought of themselves not as active managers but as middlemen giving effect to impersonal market forces.[21] Actually, there was some scope for discretionary management, even though in England, as in other gold-standard countries, maintaining the gold parity of the currency was the overriding objective of policy and the reserve ratio its major guide.

---

16. Committee on Currency and Foreign Exchanges after the War, *First Interim Report* (Cd. 9182), London: His Majesty's Stationery Office, 1918, pp. 3–4.

17. Robert Triffin, "National Central Banking and the International Economy," in Lloyd A. Metzler, Robert Triffin, and Gottfried Haberler, *International Monetary Policies*, Washington: Board of Governors of the Federal Reserve System, 1947, p. 59. Compare P. Barrett Whale, "The Working of the Pre-war Gold Standard," in Ashton and Sayers, *op. cit.*, pp. 151–164.

18. Triffin, *op. cit.*, p. 60. This argument tacitly presupposes a mechanical adjustment of market interest rates in step with Bank rate—"mechanical" in the sense that interest rates rise or fall apart from any domestic restriction or expansion of the money supply. This presumption may or may not be historically justified—quite possibly things did work that way in the short run—but the argument would hardly apply if the rise or fall of interest rates was associated with domestic restriction or expansion of the money supply. Restrictions on growth of the money supply of which higher interest rates were simply one aspect, or acceleration of monetary growth of which lower interest rates were simply one aspect, should affect the balance of payments in the classical way.

19. *Ibid.*, pp. 58–63. Triffin's interpretation has by no means gone unchallenged. William P. Culbertson concludes that the conditions postulated by Triffin are dubious and are unnecessary for explaining observed movements in Britain's terms of trade under the gold standard. *The Burden of Balance-of-Payments Adjustment*, University of Texas dissertation, 1972, chap. IV. D. E. Moggridge concludes that "The short-run adjustment mechanism seems to have hinged almost entirely on capital movements rather than real factors." *British Monetary Policy 1924–1931*, Cambridge: Cambridge University Press, 1972, p. 13.

20. Committee on Finance & Industry, *op. cit.*, p. 125.

The view of the pre-1914 system as a managed sterling standard has been challenged. There is no evidence to show that the Bank of England regarded itself as money manager for the world or as acting otherwise then to protect its reserves. It did not accumulate excess reserves in good times and release them in times of strain in order to counteract inflationary and deflationary tendencies. Its reserves were inadequate for the global task of stabilization, and it sometimes had to impose otherwise unwanted deflationary pressure on the British economy in order to protect both its slender reserves and the gold convertibility of sterling. For this interpretation, see John M. Letiche, *Balance of Payments and Economic Growth*, New York: Harper & Row, 1959, p. 23; and Lloyd Mints, *Monetary Policy for a Competitive Society*, New York: McGraw-Hill, 1950, p. 107.

If "management" means a "conscious attempt to influence the trend of commodity prices, there was certainly no management; at that time the Bank of England never sought to prevent the variations in the output of gold from producing their normal effect on the currency and credit structure and consequently on prices. Neither can it be said that the Bank of England or other central banks regarded it as their task to control the business cycle, except that, in accordance with their customary practice, they would react against speculative excesses by increasing interest rates and, conversely, lower their rates when, in times of depression, the demand for credit became less acute." Bank for International Settlements, 13th *Annual Report* (1942–1943), p. 126.

The fact that the Bank of England raised and lowered Bank rate almost solely out of concern for its own reserves hardly settles the issue of management, however. The Bank *did* manage the nineteenth-century gold standard in the sense of dominating it—which is not to say that the Bank's actions were in accordance with modern ideas of contracyclical policy and not to deny that they appeared to be dictated by circumstances instead of being freely chosen.

21. Condliffe, *op. cit.*, p. 359. In a more general context, Albert O. Hirschman writes: ". . . in the minds of many economists, the central banker became a sort of honorary member of the market forces." *The Strategy of Economic Development* (paperbound ed.), New Haven: Yale University Press, 1961, p. 64n.

Central bankers did not operate by rigid, mechanical rules. They constantly exercised judgment on such matters as whether or not to act in a given situation, on how and how vigorously and when to act, and on the policy instruments to be used (for the discount rate was not their sole weapon).[22]

Critics of the traditional view may be right in maintaining that English Bank-rate policy operated less to keep domestic money, credit and price conditions passively in step with world conditions than actively to dominate and determine those conditions. They may be right in questioning the price-income-and-employment channel through which Bank rate supposedly operated. They do seem right in questioning the supposed automaticity of the pre-1914 gold standard. But, in any event, there seems little doubt that countries outside Great Britain had to keep fairly well in step, forgoing any major degree of monetary independence, if they meant to keep their currencies on the gold or sterling standard. And there seems little reason to doubt the effectiveness of Bank rate in influencing international flows of capital, whatever may be said about the further consequences of the rate and of these flows. Belief in its effectiveness was epitomized in the old City saying that 7 percent would bring gold from the North Pole.[23] Funds would not have moved so sensitively from country to country, of course, if the confines of the gold points had not kept exchange-rate fluctuations so small that potential losses on this score were overshadowed by the profits offered by the international differentials in interest rates.

Supplements to bank rate

Bank rate was not the only means of influencing international gold flows. In addition, there were the so-called gold devices—expedients enabling the Bank of England to vary somewhat the prices at which it bought gold and at which it redeemed banknotes in gold.[24] The Bank was legally required to redeem its notes on demand in gold sovereigns. The gold content of a full-weight sovereign implied an official selling price for coined gold of £3.17s. 10½d. per standard ounce (11/12 pure). The Bank was also required to issue banknotes in exchange for bar gold at the price of £3. 17s. 9d. per standard ounce. But nothing prevented the Bank from paying more than the specified buy-

ing price for gold when anxious to attract additional gold into its reserves. Of course, the Bank could not offer so much more that arbitrageurs would find it profitable to redeem banknotes in sovereigns, melt the sovereigns into bars, sell the bars to the Bank at the especially favorable price, redeem the banknotes so obtained, and so on. Another way of in effect slightly raising the buying price for gold was to accept foreign coins instead of standard bars, sparing gold importers the expense of melting and refining. Occasionally the Bank offered gold importers interest-free loans equal to the value of gold in transit. Conversely, when unnecessarily abundant reserves made the Bank willing to facilitate gold exports, it might redeem its notes in bars or in foreign coin for exporters who found gold in this form more suitable than sovereigns. As the Bank became less willing to see gold go abroad, it might offer bars and foreign coins to exporters on increasingly less favorable terms. It might even insist on its legal right to redeem banknotes in sovereigns alone, thereby saddling gold exporters with the possible expenses of melting and reminting into coins of the country of destination. The ultimate in protecting the Bank's gold reserve this way was to redeem notes in worn sovereigns of barely the minimum legal weight. Such expedients were not unusual, at least after 1890, and may occasionally have made it possible to keep Bank rate lower than otherwise would have been necessary.

Various "gold devices" were also often used by American and continental authorities. All central banks, according to Oskar Morgenstern,[25] sometimes tried to attract or hold gold by means other than the discount rate, no matter how often they denied it. In Germany, interest-free loans were given to importers of specie, and exports of specie were impeded. Similar devices were employed in France, where, for example, the central bank sometimes insisted on its legal right to redeem its notes in silver 5-franc pieces rather than in gold. These devices put some slight variability into the gold values of monetary units and slightly increased the range of possible exchange-rate fluctuations. So doing, they nibbled at the fringes of the very idea of an international gold standard. In addition, several central banks, notably the Austro-Hungarian Bank, influenced exchange rates by direct transactions on the market.

Fostering noncurrency methods of payment

and the issue of small-denomination notes in efforts to economize further on the use of gold[26] amounted to further nibbling; for measures that deliberately modify and loosen the linkage between the quantity of gold and the quantity of money run counter to the idea of an impersonally regulated money supply. These measures foreshadowed the massive attempts to economize on gold under the gold-bullion and gold-exchange standards of the late 1920s.

Still other features of later systems, including some aspects of present-day arrangements, also were occasionally, though not typically, evident before World War I: destabilizing speculation and hot-money movements, bear attacks that threatened to force departure from the gold standard and that required resort to extraordinary remedies, concern about the volume of short-term foreign indebtedness, concern about inadequacy of the reserves of individual countries and of international liquidity in the aggregate, and warnings about the need for institutionalized cooperation among the authorities of different countries.[27]

The myth of the gold standard

Understandably, these less attractive and less typical facts tend to be forgotten more readily than the sound features of the international monetary system destroyed by World War I. That system even today exerts a peculiar fascination. Gold itself, and hence a currency tied to it, is material for fond legends. Christopher Columbus said, "Gold constitutes treasure, and he who possesses it has all he needs in this world, as also the means of rescuing souls from Purgatory and restoring them to the enjoyment of Paradise."[28] The administrator of the gold system, the Bank of England, was also a symbol: "The old lady of Threadneedle Street, very much like the contemporaneous old lady on the throne, had become a symbol of the

halt secular economic expansion than to impose an absolute deflation of incomes and prices.

23. Mention of 7 percent does not mean that so high a rate was typical. On the contrary, from January 1876 to July 1914, Bank rate moved rather narrowly around an average somewhat above 3 percent. Never in that period did it stand at or above 5 percent for longer than 26 consecutive weeks. Long-term interest rates were also remarkably stable. Only twice in the 50 years before 1914 did the rate on Consols move by one-quarter of 1 percent or more within a single year. Such figures tend to bear out the impressions of contemporary British observers that the balance of payments seldom severely troubled monetary policy.

24. See R. S. Sayers, "The Bank in the Gold Market, 1890–1914," in Ashton and Sayers, *op. cit.*, pp. 132–150; and Feavearyear, *op. cit.*, p. 330.

25. *International Financial Transactions and Business Cycles*, Princeton, N.J.: Princeton University Press for National Bureau of Economic Research, 1959, p. 441. Also see Bloomfield, *op. cit.*, pp. 52–55; and Kurt Schmaltz, *Das Valutarisiko im deutschen Wirtschaftsleben und seine Bekämpfung*, Stuttgart: Poeschel, 1921, pp. 95–97.

For a contemporary Continental description of gold devices and a defense of them as giving the central bank some freedom to manage monetary and credit conditions as seemed appropriate for domestic business, see Julius Landesberger, *Ueber die Goldprämien-Politik der Zettelbanken*, Vienna: Manz'sche k.u.k. Hof-Verlags-und Universitäts-Buchhandlung, 1892.

26. Bloomfield, *op. cit.*, p. 22.
On the eve of World War I, gold accounted for scarcely more than one-tenth of the world's estimated total monetary circulation and silver for perhaps only one-half or one-third as much as gold. Paper currency and bank deposits already accounted for nearly nine-tenths of the total. Robert Triffin, *The Evolution of the International Monetary System: Historical Reappraisal and Future Perspectives*, Princeton Studies in International Finance, No. 12, Princeton, N.J.: Princeton University, 1964, p. 15.

27. Arthur I. Bloomfield, *Short-Term Capital Movements under the Pre-1914 Gold Standard*, Princeton, N.J.: Princeton University, 1963, pp. 2, 28–29, 44–45, 83–92.

28. Quoted in R. H. Tawney, *Religion and the Rise of Capitalism*, New York: Harcourt, Brace, 1926, p. 89.

22. Bloomfield, *op. cit.*, esp. pp. 23, 25–26.
Bloomfield (pp. 43–44, 61) also expresses skepticism about the importance of the "second channel," involving prices, incomes, and employment, through which discount-rate policy was supposed to affect the balance of payments. Clinging to the gold standard sometimes was a hardship for individual countries, especially the less developed ones; but there is not much evidence that discount-rate increases were harshly deflationary and caused severe unemployment. Restrictive credit policies apparently served more to slow down or temporarily

solidity, the glory, the far-flung interests, and the incorruptible and beneficent omnipotence of the British Empire."[29] It is natural, though perhaps not logical, to associate the international gold standard with the serene economic progress that prevailed at the same time throughout the world, or at least in Europe and in countries settled by peoples of European descent.

Conditions almost unique in history smoothed the operation of the system. Currency parities, instead of being arbitrarily chosen over short time spans, expressed an equilibrium that had evolved gradually between themselves and national price levels. Rising world prices after 1896 happened to facilitate *relative* adjustments of prices and wages, while the uptrend had not lasted long enough to cancel its possible benefits by becoming embodied in expectations. Even money prices and wages were probably more flexible, downward as well as upward, than they later became. Relative calm in social and political affairs and the absence of excessively ambitious programs of government spending and taxation all favored confidence in monetary stability.[30] The age of the gold standard was an age of relative peace: though limited wars were numerous enough between 1815 and 1914, conflagrations involving many countries were unknown.

By and large, people were freer from government regulation—freer to transact any honorable business as they saw fit, to make investments, to transfer funds, to travel without formality—than in any age of history before or since. There is a certain charm in the reminiscences of an old German banker of how, during his student days at Heidelberg, he and some friends, one of whom had just inherited some money, left on the impulse of the moment for a tour of Italy, where the Italian banker in the first town they stopped in considered it an honor to cash in gold coin the large check written by the young stranger. There is a similar charm in Jules Verne's story of Phineas Fogg, who left on short notice for his 80-day tour of the world, paying his expenses from a carpetbag full of Bank of England notes, accepted everywhere. The civility and internationality prevalent during the age of the gold standard have such charm for us nowadays that it seems almost sacrilege to ask whether these benefits resulted from the gold standard or, instead, coexisted with it by mere coincidence.

The gold standard, in short, evokes the "good old days." This association is well illustrated by two quotations, the first from Benjamin M. Anderson, a lifelong champion of the gold standard, and the second from John Maynard Keynes, his generation's leading critic of the gold standard:

Those who have an adult's recollection and an adult's understanding of the world which preceded the first World War look back upon it with a great nostalgia. There was a sense of security then which has never since existed. Progress was generally taken for granted. . . . We had had a prolonged period in which decade after decade had seen increasing political freedom, the progressive spread of democratic institutions, the steady lifting of the standard of life for the masses of men. . . .

In financial matters the good faith of governments and central banks was taken for granted. . . . No country took pride in debasing its currency as a clever financial expedient.

London was the financial center, but there were independent gold standard centers in New York, Berlin, Vienna, Paris, Amsterdam, Switzerland, Japan, and the Scandinavian countries. There were many other countries on the gold standard, with some tendency for the weaker countries to substitute holdings of sterling or other means of getting increased earnings. For their purpose the sterling bill was quite as good as gold. . . . But, in general, the great countries held their own gold. They relied upon themselves to meet their international obligations in gold. At times of great crisis a country under very heavy pressure would seek international cooperation and international assistance, and would get it—at a steep rate of interest.[31]

What an extraordinary episode in the economic progress of man that age was which came to an end in August, 1914! The greater part of the population, it is true, worked hard and lived at a low standard of comfort, yet were, to all appearances, reasonably contented with this lot. But escape was possible, for any man of capacity or character at all exceeding the average, into the middle and upper classes, for whom life offered, at a low cost and with the least trouble, conveniences, comforts and amenities beyond the compass of the richest and most powerful monarchs of other ages. The inhabitant of London could order by telephone, sipping his morning tea in bed, the various products of the whole earth, in such quantity as he might see fit, and reasonably expect their early delivery upon his doorstep; he could at the same moment and by the same means adventure his wealth in the natural resources and new enterprises of any quarter of the world, and share, without exertion or even trouble, in their prospective fruits and advantages; or he could decide to couple the security of his fortunes with the good faith of the townspeople of any substantial municipality in any continent that fancy or information might recommend. He could secure forthwith, if he wished it, cheap and comfortable means of transit to any country or climate without passport or other formality, could despatch his servant to the neighboring office of a bank for such supply of the precious metals as might seem convenient, and could then proceed abroad to foreign quarters, without knowledge of their religion, language, or customs, bearing coined wealth upon his person, and would consider himself greatly aggrieved and much surprised at the least interference. But, most important of all, he regarded this state of affairs as normal, certain, and permanent, except in the direction of further improvement, and any deviation from it as aberrant, scandalous, and avoidable. The projects and politics of militarism and imperialism, of racial and cultural rivalries, of monopolies, restrictions, and exclusion, which were to play the serpent to this paradise, were little more than the amusements of

his daily newspaper, and appeared to exercise almost no influence at all on the ordinary course of social and economic life, the internationalization of which was nearly complete in practice.[32]

29. Viner, *op. cit.*, p. 129.

30. See Vanes, *op. cit.*, pp. 100–102.

31. B. M. Anderson, *Economics and the Public Welfare*, New York: Van Nostrand, 1949, excerpts from pp. 3–4, 6.

32. John Maynard Keynes, *The Economic Consequences of the Peace*, New York: Harcourt, Brace & World, Inc., 1920, pp. 10–12.

CHAPTER SIXTEEN

Suspension and Attempted Restoration of the International Gold Standard

The end of an era[1]

War ended the brief reign of the full international gold standard late in July 1914. A foreign-exchange deadlock resulted at first. As usual, the whole world had debts coming due in London. British financial houses, anxious to play safe by bringing their short-term funds home from abroad, swelled the demand for sterling. London banks sought to bolster their reserves against possible panic by shrinking their loans to the discount houses. On July 27, when London acceptance houses stopped granting new acceptance credits, foreigners lost their most important single current source of sterling. They could still get it by selling their British securities in London. Dumping of securities caused the stock exchange to close on July 31 and stay closed several months. Other European security exchanges closed under similar pressure.

In New York, nervous foreigners hastened to sell their American securities and take home the proceeds. Preparations to export gold strained bank reserves, restricted credit for carrying securities, and worsened the threat of a market collapse. The New York Stock Exchange closed the same day as the London exchange. The United States had already been losing gold because of a passive trade balance

and German, French, and Russian accumulations of gold in readiness for war. Further gold shipments would ordinarily have filled the gap between the intensified demand for sterling and the shrunken supply. But hostile cruisers were on the seas, and insurance against wartime risks was unavailable for a few days. Despite a mint par of $4.86656, the pound sterling rose to $6.35 in New York in the last week of July and to $7.00 at the beginning of August for a few transactions in a very thin market. On August 12 the Bank of England agreed to accept gold in Ottawa, and sterling dropped to a more normal rate. Large gold shipments proved unnecessary.

The unusual rise of sterling would have been only temporary, anyway, for wartime demands for American goods soon mounted. By December 1914 the dollar rate on sterling sank to and below par. The franc, the mark, and other belligerent currencies were also weakening.

The international gold standard did not break down completely or all at once. Most countries clung to its legal fictions for some time. "The date when England 'returned to gold' after the war is a landmark in world history, but it is very difficult to determine the date when England left the gold standard to which she returned in 1925."[2] The gold content of the sovereign remained unchanged. Until 1925, private persons still had the legal right to bring gold to the mint for coinage. The Bank's obligation to buy all gold offered at the official price remained in force until 1939. Throughout World War I, private persons still had the legal right to import gold. In fact, though, the Bank of England arranged to buy all incoming gold, leaving none for private parties. Private gold exports also remained legal, though only theoretically so. Redemption of banknotes in gold, still legally possible, was all but prevented by appeals to patriotism, inquisition into motives, regulations against the melting of gold coin, a ban on buying or selling gold at a premium, and pegging of the exchange value of sterling (from January 1916 on) at only about 2 percent below mint par. The most important departure from the gold standard was quite unofficial: bullion dealers, like the general public, felt that gold exports would be unpatriotic and simply did not undertake any.

The gold standard evaporated piecemeal on the Continent also. Germany, Austria-Hungary, Russia, and France suspended redemption in coin and embargoed gold exports. Yet official obligations to buy gold at fixed prices still stood, and gold imports remained legal. The neutral Dutch government at first embargoed gold exports and authorized the Netherlands Bank to suspend specie payments. More typically, however, neutrals interfered with gold imports. Holland did so in 1915, when commodity imports began to lag behind exports and capital and gold flowed heavily inward; and under its "gold repulsion policy," the Netherlands Bank sometimes refused to buy gold. In February 1916, Sweden suspended both the free coinage of gold and the Riksbank's obligation to buy gold at fixed prices, thus restricting the entry of gold imports into the monetary system. Denmark and Norway agreed to adopt similar measures when necessary. Spain also became reluctant to accept gold. Such measures sought—not very successfully, as events turned out—to limit the contagion of the belligerents' inflation through balances of payments.

The United States kept most of the legal forms of the gold standard. After American entry into the war, however, persons trying to redeem their paper money in gold ran into unofficial difficulties; and in September 1917, gold exports became subject to official license. The two chief requirements of the gold standard, interconvertibility between paper money and gold and the free international movement of gold, lapsed in one way or another.

Paradoxically, violating the substance of the gold standard enabled many governments to preserve its reassuring symbols—comfortable reserves and familiar exchange rates. Governments badgered their citizens in various ways and degrees to get gold coins out of circulation into official hands. Several countries supplemented these "gold-concentration" campaigns with steps to mobilize foreign exchange. In 1915 the British government began encouraging and in January 1917 began requiring private holders to sell it their foreign securities, which it could then sell for foreign exchange. The French government persuaded but did not compel its citizens to sell it their foreign securities. Germany, too, used persuasion and did not resort to compulsion until March 1917; and even then, the German government promised to replace the commandeered securities three years after making peace with England.

Belligerents used resources so obtained in efforts to support the prewar pattern of exchange rates. Late in 1915 some neutral currencies were tending to rise against sterling and

SUSPENSION AND ATTEMPTED RESTORATION OF THE INTERNATIONAL GOLD STANDARD

dollars, while the currencies of Italy, Austria, Germany, and Russia were tending to fall. Even the sterling-franc-dollar relation was growing shaky. Control of the sterling-dollar rate began in August 1915, and in January 1916 the rate was definitely pegged at $4.76⅞₆, about 2.1 percent below mint par. In April 1916 the British and French governments arranged to stabilize franc exchange. The resources available for allied exchange-rate pegging began running out by the fall of 1916 but were replenished by advances from the U.S. Treasury after the United States joined the war the following spring. Lacking such support, the German and Austrian exchanges continued to sink, and efforts to restrain the fall of the mark definitely failed early in 1918.

Towards the end of the war speculation centered on belief that exchange rates would soon return to "normal." At the time of the armistice, the rates of the Netherlands, Spain, the United States, Great Britain and the Empire, Japan, France, Sweden, Argentina, Brazil, and Italy diverged remarkably little from the prewar pattern, considering the circumstances.[3]

Postwar financial conditions

Faith in a prompt return to "normal" overlooked the profound changes that war had brought. Physical changes included casualties, property destruction and deterioration, and subtler types of erosion of productive capacity. Political changes included the dismemberment of Austria-Hungary, the communization of Russia, and widespread acceptance of extensive government intervention in economic life. Financial changes included the consequences of government borrowing in ways that inflated

1. General references for this section include W. A. Brown, Jr., *The International Gold Standard Reinterpreted*, New York: National Bureau of Economic Research, 1940, **I**, Book One; and Benjamin M. Anderson, *Economics and the Public Welfare*, New York: Van Nostrand, 1949, Part I.

2. Brown, *op. cit.*, p. 28n.

3. *Ibid.*, p. 70.

money supplies. Even the United States government covered roughly 72 percent of its wartime expenditures by borrowing instead of taxation. The French Finance Minister expressed a typical attitude. When questioned in Parliament about the financing of military expenditures, he referred to future indemnities: "The Boche will pay."

War financing more than tripled the French public debt between the end of 1914 and the end of 1918, and between March 1914 and March 1919 the public debt was multiplied more than thirty-fold in Germany and almost nine-fold in the United Kingdom.[4] Table 16.1 shows what happened to currency supplies and price levels in Europe. Inflation was less severe in the United States. Currency outside banks multiplied by about $2\frac{1}{3}$ from mid-1914 to mid-1919, and total deposits and currency multiplied by about 1.8. Wholesale prices in 1919 averaged about twice and in 1920 about $2\frac{1}{4}$ times the level of 1914. (This was a slightly greater degree of price inflation, incidentally, than had been experienced under the Civil War "greenbacks.") Price-level figures for the immediate postwar years must be taken with great reservations because of such distortions as price control and rationing.

Price inflation reached a peak in most countries in 1920 and then gave way to a couple of years of business depression. The United States, with its comparatively mild inflation, was able to discontinue controls over gold exports and so return to a full gold standard in June 1919. Particularly in Germany, France, and central and eastern Europe, however, inflation went on for several years. The old money units of Austria, Hungary, Poland, Germany, and Russia were practically wiped out. By the end of their respective inflations, prewar price levels had been multiplied by roughly 14,000 in Austria, 23,000 in Hungary, $2\frac{1}{2}$ million in Poland, and 4 billion in Russia.

The German inflation

The German experience was worse.[5] As one of the classic hyperinflations of history, this episode deserves special notice. The prewar mint par had been 4.2 marks per dollar. In 1918 the quotation averaged 6 marks per dollar. It was 14 in June 1919, 39 in June 1920, 69 in June 1921, 317 in June 1922, nearly 18,000 in January 1923, and around 100,000 in June 1923. From then on the mark sank faster and faster

TABLE 16.1. *Currency supplies and price levels in Europe after World War I as percentages of their prewar figures (end-of-year data)*

	1918	1919	1920
United Kingdom			
Currency circulation	248	274	294
Wholesale prices	246	297	264
Cost of living	230	236	278
France			
Currency circulation	433[a]	533[a]	541[a]
Wholesale prices	355	432	444
Cost of living	248	285	424
Germany			
Currency circulation	503	760	1230
Wholesale prices	260[b]	803[b]	1440[b]
Cost of living			1158
Italy			
Currency circulation	486	649	769
Wholesale prices	296	416	596
Cost of living	260[c]	323[c]	455[c]
Switzerland			
Currency circulation	248	263	268
Cost of living	211	245	243
Spain			
Currency circulation	173	200	224
Wholesale prices	213	204	214
Sweden			
Currency circulation	348	323	330
Wholesale prices	335	317	267
Cost of living	238	263	271
Norway			
Currency circulation	348	323	386
Wholesale prices	345	322	377
Cost of living	264	291	335

NOTE: The base for the wholesale indexes is the average for 1913; the cost-of-living figures are mostly based on July 1914.

[a] The base figure for 1913 excludes gold coins, most of which were not in active circulation.

[b] End-of-year price indexes for 1918, 1919, and 1920 were 289, 1508, and 2023 for imported goods and 250, 633, and 1323 for domestic products alone.

[c] Average of two indexes for retail prices in Rome and Milan.

SOURCE: League of Nations, Secretariat, Economic, Financial, and Transit Department, *The Course and Control of Inflation*, League of Nations, 1946, p. 88.

until the climax in November 1923. Wholesale prices averaged about 35 times their prewar level by December 1921. A year later, prices were 1475 times the prewar level. Already, even before the final phase of astronomical figures, inflation was dislocating economic activity.

One source of dislocation was the fact that people were reluctant to hold melting marks and snapped at the chance to buy commodities. Bidding inventories and goods-in-process away from their normal uses tended to impair the smooth flow of production and distribution. Relative prices became distorted as some prices responded more promptly than others. It was often cheaper to travel from one town to another by railroad than from one block to another by streetcar. Wages moved slowly at first and later were tied to prices. Salaries and pensions lagged.

At times the exchange depreciation of the mark ran ahead of the rise in internal prices. The iconoclastic view that this timing shows cause and effect finds some support in the association of a particularly sharp fall in mark exchange in September 1921 with a heavy reparations payment from Germany to the Allies.[6] This payment increased the demand for foreign exchange to be bought with marks. Prices of German imports and exports rose in sympathy with foreign-exchange rates; domestic prices followed. Government expenditures rose with prices. Revenues lagged because specific taxes and nontax revenues (such as railroad fares) were adjusted slowly to the inflation and because income taxes collected in a given year were based on incomes of the year before, when nominal prices and incomes had been much lower. Since the government met its growing deficit by borrowing freshly printed money from the Reichsbank, one might contend that the mark's depreciation was more directly a cause than a consequence of money-supply inflation. Private as well as government demands for credit rose with prices.[7]

This process, at least in its early stages, drew remarkably little effective protest. Inflation creates its own vested interests. For the government, inflationary financing meant following the (temporarily) easiest course. Budgetary laxness possibly fed on the thought that financial chaos could serve as an argument or excuse for scaling down reparations to the Allies. Industrialists and merchants learned to live with inflation and to profit—at least apparently, in terms of nominal marks—from price increases between the time of buying materials, labor, or inventories and the time of selling the product. Exaggerated profitability stimulated capital formation and the capital-goods industries. Labor enjoyed full employment, and arrangements were made for more frequent paydays and for wages scaled to keep pace with prices. Of course, not all persons were able to protect themselves. Creditors lost real wealth to debtors. Great hardship fell on pensioners, holders of insurance, endowed institutions, and small savers inexperienced in putting their liquid wealth into satisfactorily hedged forms.

In January 1923 French and Belgian troops occupied the industrial Ruhr valley to prod the defaulting Germans into fuller and more prompt reparations payments. The Germans responded with "passive resistance," including deliberate absenteeism from industrial jobs. Support of the resisting workers further burdened the German government budget. By the end of October 1923 the government's ordinary receipts were covering only about 0.8 percent of expenditures; the government was raising money almost exclusively by borrowing at the Reichsbank, which in turn simply rolled the printing presses. New money also poured out on loan to private businessmen, who eagerly borrowed with the prospect of repaying some weeks or months later in marks that would have depreciated much further in the meanwhile.

4. Paul Alpert, *Twentieth Century Economic History of Europe*, New York: Henry Schuman, 1951, pp. 34–35.

5. See W. Arthur Lewis, *Economic Survey 1919–1939*, London: Allen & Unwin, 1949, pp. 23–29; Frank D. Graham, *Exchange, Prices, and Production in Hyperinflation: Germany, 1920–1923*, Princeton, N.J.: Princeton University Press, 1930; and Costantino Bresciani-Turroni, *The Economics of Inflation*, London: Allen & Unwin, 1937.

6. See John H. Williams, "German Foreign Trade and the Reparations Payments," *Quarterly Journal of Economics*, XXXVI, May 1922, pp. 502–503.

7. For an analysis of similar experiences during the Austrian inflation that reached its climax in 1922, see J. van Walré de Bordes, *The Austrian Crown*, London · King, 1924.

Businessmen took to figuring costs and quoting prices in gold or foreign currency (and some bonds were denominated in dollars, wheat, rye, or other things of relatively stable value). Prices were translated into marks at the moment of sale at the latest exchange-rate quotations. This practice hastened depreciation by increasing the demand for foreign exchange: a merchant, having assumed the obligation to pay a sum in paper marks depending on the exchange rate on the day of payment, might hedge by buying foreign exchange in advance.

This practice is only one reason why the mark should have lost foreign-exchange value more rapidly than internal purchasing power. Another is that persons flying from marks found foreign exchange a convenient asset, stable yet liquid. A more general reason is that a sensitive and competitive market where prices are the very opposite of "administered" is bound to be one of the promptest of all markets in responding to both objective and psychological influences. Moreover, the German government raised foreign exchange for reparations payments by dumping newly printed marks on the exchange market. With fresh banknotes having their first impact there, it is no wonder that exchange depreciation outpaced the mark's loss of internal purchasing power. This phenomenon would probably have been even more striking, had not gullible foreigners, until the last stages of inflation, continued buying up mark notes in the belief that the mark must have reached bottom and was due to recover.

In view of all these facts, the role of exchange depreciation in the German inflationary process provides no valid evidence against the quantity theory of money.[8] The inflation first began with monetary expansion to pay for the war and could not have gone on without continued expansion. As for reparations in particular, the depreciation of the mark must be blamed not so much on these payments themselves as on how the government raised money for them. If the government had bought foreign exchange only with marks raised by taxation or by genuine noninflationary loans, so that the wealth transferred to the Allies had been wrested from the German population in these orthodox ways, the depreciation would have been limited. Whether such a Spartan budget policy would have been practical politics is another question, but a *policy* question

of this sort upsets no propositions in economic *analysis.*

Ideological influences were at work. A League of Nations report has made pertinent comments:

. . . the "ideological" soil of German economic thought was favourable to inflation. The quantity theory of money had never gained much ground in Germany. The majority even among the trained economists refused to believe in a chain of causation running from the issue of money to the rise in prices. Most economists attributed the rise in prices to the unfavourable balance of payments and to the consequent fall in the external value of the mark. Helfferich, Minister of Finance in 1923, was a leading proponent of the balance-of-payments theory. Havenstein, President of the Reichsbank, in so far as he had any theoretical notions at all, adhered to a form of the "banking principle" which told him that the rise in prices created a need for money on the part of business men as well as the government, a need which it was the Reichsbank's duty to meet, and which it could meet without any harmful effects. . . . German economic thought failed to apprehend that the expansion in the money supply was at least an essential *condition* without which the general rise in prices could not have gone far. And this intellectual failure accounts in great part for the weakness of the defences which the spring tide of inflation encountered in Germany.

The management of the Reichsbank . . . followed the old Banking Principle and refused to believe that printing money in favour of business men against genuine commercial bills could have any inflationary effect. The Reichsbank had kept its discount rate unchanged at 5% up to the summer of 1922. Thereafter, it raised the rate by several stages to 90% in September 1923. But even at that rate it was practically giving money away. The fall in the value of the currency was more closely reflected in the market rate on short-term loans, which rose as high as 20% *per diem* or approximately 7300% *per annum*. At the rates maintained by the Reichsbank, the rediscounting of bills made it possible for the commercial banks to extend credits on very favourable terms to business men. For business men, indeed, it became one of the rules of good management to contract as many debts as possible, debts which were later repaid in depreciated money.[9]

Undervaluation of the mark on the exchanges in relation to its purchasing power made it abnormally cheap for foreigners to live or buy goods and services in Germany. This much-deplored *Ausverkauf,* or clearance-sale, of the German economy ended when business-men started adjusting their prices in step with exchange rates and finally, toward the end of the inflation in 1923, in step not just with current but with expected *future* exchange rates. Internal prices again, as in the early mild stages, rose faster than foreign exchange rates.

By this time prices were not simply rising at a faster rate than the money supply—a phenomenon easy to understand. They came to rise faster even than money supply times velocity. In terms of Fisher's equation of exchange $MV = PT$, T, the physical volume of transactions carried out with money, fell: inflation had caused such disruption that real business activity and employment actually slumped in the last few weeks of inflation in 1923.

Prices had risen so much faster than the money supply that complaints became common of an acute *shortage* of money, despite eventual issue of denominations as high as 100 trillion marks. At one point, Havenstein, the President of the Reichsbank, seriously expressed hope that new high-speed currency printing presses soon to be installed would help overcome the shortage.[10] Of course, the terrific shrinkage of the German money supply in terms of real purchasing power or gold merely reflects how fully people had come to understand the fantastic real cost of holding money.

The currency "shortage" just mentioned explains how Dr. Hjalmar Schacht could succeed in launching a new "Rentenmark" currency (which, as a kind of public-relations device, was supposedly backed by land). The public had been so inconvenienced by lack of stable currency that it was eager to believe in the reform. The demand for Rentenmarks to rebuild depleted real cash balances gave the government a breathing space in which to cover its expenditures with new issues of money while taking steps to balance its budget through spending cuts and tax increases. A drop in velocity offset further monetary expansion. Timely receipt of an international loan under the Dawes Plan of 1924 also helped.

As the inflation of the old Reichsmark reached its climax late in November 1923, a newspaper cost 200 billion marks. Wholesale prices averaged about 1.4 trillion times as high as before the war. The currency reform set one new mark equal to 1,000,000,000,000 old ones. Germany had experienced the most severe inflation in history up to that time. (The Hun-

garian inflation of 1946 produced statistics even more astronomical.)

Reparations and war debts[11]

The financial problems of Germany intertwined with a problem that conditioned international monetary relations throughout the 1920s and early 1930s. In the Versailles Treaty of 1919, Germany acknowledged war guilt and undertook to compensate her victims. Pending final determination of compensable damage, Germany was to begin an interim payment of roughly $5 billion, largely in commodities, mainly coal. Meanwhile, the Reparation Commission produced successive tentative estimates of the total amount due, which was scaled down in 1921, partly in view of Germany's supposed capacity to pay, to 132 billion gold marks (about $31½ billion). Bonds were to be delivered for this amount and payments on them

---

8. In a study of a number of hyperinflations, including the German, Phillip Cagan has shown that velocity depended on expectations about the future rate of increase in prices, as inferred from the observed rate of increase in prices in the recent past, which in turn was related to the rate of expansion of the money supply. See "The Monetary Dynamics of Hyperinflation," in Milton Friedman, ed., *Studies in the Quantity Theory of Money*, Chicago: University of Chicago Press, 1956, pp. 25–117.

9. Pp. 16–17 and 31 respectively (in the section written by Ragnar Nurkse) of League of Nations, *The Course and Control of Inflation* (1946).

10. Frank D. Graham later observed that Havenstein's death at the time of currency reform and introduction of the new mark was "a demise which cannot be thought of as other than opportune." *Op. cit.*, p. 12.

11. This section draws in part on Alpert, *op. cit.*, pp. 53–61; William Ashworth, *A Short History of the International Economy, 1850–1950*, London: Longmans, Green, 1952, pp. 189 ff.; and James W. Angell, "Reparations," in the *Encyclopedia of the Social Sciences*, New York: Macmillan, 1930, vol. 13, pp. 300–308.

to be made in yearly installments of 2 billion gold marks plus the proceeds of a 26 percent tax on German exports. More than half of the money was to go to France. An Allied ultimatum prodded Germany into accepting these terms.

Not only Germany's ability but also her willingness to pay was a key question. Another was whether other countries would forego excessive tariffs and let Germany achieve the export surplus necessary for transferring large sums of money. Great Britain generally favored reasonableness and compromise. The French government, engaged in deficit spending to finance reconstruction work, wanted large reparations. In 1922, with reparations transfers contributing to the downward slide of the mark, Germany asked for a further delay in payments, but France refused. In 1923, after more than half a year of passive resistance in the Ruhr—absenteeism, sabotage, neglect of French·orders—the Germans gave in and began cooperating with the technicians of the occupation forces.

The final collapse of the mark in 1923 brought a new study of the issue. A special committee of the Reparation Commission, headed by an American banker, produced the Dawes Plan in 1924. It sought to improve Germany's paying capacity by rehabilitating her economy and finances. To support transition from the temporary Rentenmark currency to a gold standard, Germany received an international loan of almost $200 million, about half subscribed in the United States. This amount equalled four-fifths of the reparations installment payable during the first year of the Dawes Plan. The annual installments were to rise gradually over five years to a standard amount of 2½ billion gold marks (about $600 million). They were to vary thereafter according to changes in the value of gold and were to rise with an index of German prosperity. An Allied agent in Berlin was to supervise German finances related to obligations under the plan. A transfer committee was to see that the transfer of reparations payments abroad took place in such amounts and at such times as not to endanger the new mark.

The Dawes Plan worked well for 5 years, but it had been conceived as a merely temporary solution and had not set a total reparations figure. In 1929 another international committee drew up the Young Plan. For agreeing to supposedly definite and firm obligations, Germany got a further scaling-down of payments, an end to international control of her finances,

and withdrawal of remaining Allied troops. Annual payments under the plan would run for 59 years, until 1988, when 121 billion marks (about $29 billion) would have been paid. The discounted present value of this stream of payments was estimated at 37 billion marks, or under $9 billion. This burden was far below the 132 billion marks set by the Reparation Commission in 1921 (since that was a principal sum, with interest to be extra) and even somewhat below the Germans' own proposal of 1921. Annual Young Plan payments were set on a slowly rising scale beginning at only two-thirds of the standard annual payment under the Dawes Plan and averaging only four-fifths of that amount. Payments could be postponed under various circumstances. If the United States should reduce its war-debt claims on its allies, part of the benefit would pass on to Germany in a still further scaling-down of her payments. Part of the German obligation could be commercialized by the issue of interest-bearing bonds, which claimant countries might sell at once for cash. Conditions on the international capital market were so unfavorable at the time, however, that only about $200 million worth of the bonds were actually floated.

The Bank for International Settlements was established in Basel, Switzerland, in May 1930 and given the task of assisting with German reparations transfers. Until 1966, when a settlement with Germany took effect, the Bank still carried some of the Young Plan bonds on its balance sheet, together with a reservation by the public accountants as to their actual value.

Linked with the problem of reparations was that of interallied war debts. Wartime and early postwar loans left the United States government a net creditor for over $10 billion. Great Britain had both borrowed and lent and emerged a net creditor for about $4½ billion. France owed over $3½ billion net. These amounts do not include interest. Other countries owed smaller sums. France, a net debtor, argued that the wartime loans should be regarded as contributions made among allies in a common cause. Britain, though a net creditor, took a realistic view of its chances of collecting on its claims and pressed at the peace conference of 1919 for cancellation of all war debts. In August 1922 Britain announced that it would expect no more from its debtors than it itself had to pay to the United States. The United States denied any legal connection between the interallied debts and reparations from Germany, though France in particular insisted on the economic connection. The United States—"Uncle Shylock" in some circles—saw its loans as binding business transactions, though interest rates might properly be scaled down. With its high-tariff policy during the 1920s clashing with insistence on debt repayment, the United States was able to collect some money from its debtors chiefly because private American loans to Germany and other European borrowers made possible some reparations payments and in turn some interallied debt repayments.

With minor exceptions, war-debt payments came to an end, together with German reparations, less than two years after the Young Plan took effect. (Some details are given in the next chapter.) The United States finally recovered about $2.7 billion, or a little over one-fourth of its claims. How much the Allies received from Germany is not clear, partly because so much was transferred in goods. According to some guesses, Germany paid about 25 billion gold marks from Versailles until the Dawes Plan and about 11 billion under the Dawes and Young Plans, totaling roughly $8½ billion.[12] Payments in 1928–1929 amounted to 12.4 percent of the total cost of government in Germany and to 3.4 percent of the estimated national income. All in all, Germany paid a little under $5 billion, according to estimates of the Reparation Commission, and more than three times that much, according to padded German claims. In comparison, Germany received some $8 or $9 billion from abroad during this period, mostly as loans after 1924 but nearly one-fourth of it earlier by way of losses by foreigners on their holdings of depreciating marks.[13] After 1924, German borrowings abroad ran roughly double German reparations payments; thus the problem of achieving a current-account surplus in the German balance of payments large enough to effect the reparations tranfers—and foreign reluctance to accept German goods might have contributed to this problem—was actually sidestepped.

History seldom teaches clear lessons; so much depends on the selection and interpretation of the facts. There seems to be a consensus, however, that the futile effort to collect sizable reparations kept Europe in a turmoil for a dozen years or more. Given the financial policies then prevailing in Germany, reparations transfers contributed to the hyperinflation; and international wrangling fed German grievances. With regard to intergovernmental debts as well as reparations, the prospect of large

international payments unrelated to current production and trade presumably hampered a return to economic and financial tranquility. Lumpy transactions connected with reparations and debt payments, together with the way that related events and negotiations affected expectations, presumably contributed to strains on the foreign-exchange markets.[14] The outcome probably would have been better if Germany's victims had contented themselves with a definite indemnity collectable within a few years[15] and if the United States had taken a less legalistic attitude toward war debts.

Britain off gold

A background has now been set for reviewing two experiences during the 1920s that are widely thought to teach lastingly relevant lessons. These are the contrasting experiences of Britain and France.

World War I destroyed Britain's unchallenged financial dominance.[16] Her already noticeable lag behind newly industrialized countries in production and export growth grew worse. Wartime trade interruptions spurred industrialization in several of Britain's traditional markets. Britain lost ground in shipping and, partly because of wartime sales of assets,

---

12. Some other estimates are much lower—for example, less than 10 billion gold marks until the Dawes Plan and about 20 billion in all. André Piettre, *Monnaie et Économie Internationale*, Paris: Cujas, 1967, p. 173.

13. Cf. Alpert, *op. cit.*, p. 60; Angell, *op. cit.*, p. 307; and Étienne Mantoux, *The Carthaginian Peace*, New York: Scribner's, 1952, pp. 152–155.

14. F. Robert Vanes, *De Internationale Gouden Standaard; Een onderzoek naar de oorzaken van zijn verval in de tussenoorlogse periode*, Antwerp/Amsterdam: Standaard-Boekhandel, 1951, pp. 260–262.

15. Nothing is implied here about any supposed *economic* impossibility of Germany's paying and transferring reparations in the amounts originally demanded.

16. Facts in the following paragraphs come from a number of sources, including, in particular, parts of chapters 7–12 of Brown, *op. cit.*

as a foreign investor. Reduced current-account surpluses and new demands for capital to re-equip industries at home shrank Britain's capital exports and weakened her position as international banker. Even her traditional free-trade policy was dented by import duties imposed during the war to raise revenue and conserve foreign exchange and shipping space and by duties imposed in 1921 to protect stategic industries. These duties applied only to selected goods and were not far-reaching enough to warrant dating the real end of British free trade before 1931, but they were straws in the wind.

The American dollar destroyed the preeminence of sterling without itself taking over sterling's old role. The United States became an international financier during the war, lending abroad to finance an export surplus during its neutrality and later to aid its Allies. Sterling acceptances lost ground to telegraphic transfers because of specific wartime developments, trends in the British banking structure, and gradual changes in trade-financing methods. American cotton exporters, for instance, instead of receiving payment by drawing sterling bills, began using revolving credits granted by American banks while awaiting telegraphic transfers from their British customers. A market for dollar acceptances had already been developing in New York under the encouragement of the Federal Reserve Act, passed in 1913. Foreign-owned bank balances began building up in New York early in the war as belligerent governments prepared for war purchases and as capital took refuge from Europe. After April 1915, when an emergency system

of security price floors was abolished, New York had the world's only stock exchange not restricting trading in foreign securities. Belligerents, neutral borrowers whose usual accommodations had been cut off, and even some private British borrowers floated securities in New York.

Meanwhile, the London market saw further changes: (1) the rise of the Treasury bill, (2) reduced power to "compel" and more need to "attract" foreign deposits, and (3) rise of the tied-loan principle.[17] To conserve the resources of the money market for its own Treasury bills, the British government restricted the use of trade bills. The acceptance and discount houses saw their distinctive functions gradually undermined. Second, the strength of sterling on the exchanges depended on London's holding the foreign deposits abnormally built up during the war. Yet with the erosion of prewar practices, international traders no longer felt "compelled" to hold London balances. They would require attractive yields from now on. Third, criticism was growing of loans to foreign countries whose industries were encroaching on former British markets. Departing from the traditional British indifference to where the proceeds of loan flotations were spent, the feeling grew that borrowers ought to spend the loans in the lending country.

The report of the government-appointed Cunliffe Committee, issued in August 1918,[18] recognized that sterling had suffered a still-concealed depreciation against gold in some moderate degree then impossible to measure. It worried about the danger of gold losses, once

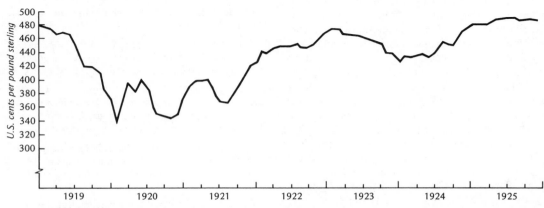

FIGURE 16.1. *Sterling-dollar exchange rate, monthly averages, 1919–1925.* (SOURCE: *Banking and Monetary Statistics, Board of Governors of the Federal Reserve System, 1943 p. 681.*)

obstacles to gold shipments were removed. The report recommended an early end to government borrowing, a start on repayment of government securities held by the banks, resumption of traditional credit control through Bank rate, and shrinkage of the currency circulation. Without even analyzing whether prewar exchange rates were still appropriate, the report took a return to prewar gold parity for granted. According to some tacit ethical code, apparently, the British paper pound was a binding promise to pay a certain quantity of gold. Continuing inflation abroad could be hoped for to ease domestic deflation and the return to normalcy.

Wartime artificialities had to be cleared away first, including extensive price control and government domination of food marketing. The most notable decontrol step came early: the wartime peg of the pound-dollar rate lapsed on March 20, 1919. A temporarily fluctuating rate would measure progress in deflating British prices enough more than American prices to make prewar parity workable again. Less than two weeks after the unpegging, paradoxically, gold exports were legally forbidden for the first time (until then, they had been restricted by wartime shipping risks, by appeals to the patriotism of the bullion dealers, and by exchange-rate pegging that made them unprofitable). The exchange rate was freed from the influence of import and capital-export controls only by degrees, and its freedom was not complete until late 1919 or early 1920. Administrative arrangements made in September 1919 and a law passed in 1920 permitted the reexport from Britain of newly mined South African gold. Its price in London paralleled the sterling-dollar exchange rate. From 1920 through 1924, the rate fluctuated almost completely free from official intervention.[19]

From the start, the rate fluctuated in an unstable environment. British government spending was running far ahead of revenue, with the deficit for 1918–1919 amounting to almost two-thirds of expenditure. Almost one-third of the national debt had a maturity of under five years, and almost one-fifth of under three months. Revenue increases and drastic expenditure cuts, however, reversed the budget into surplus in 1920–1921. Deflationary policies, as well as the world depression, depressed prices and employment. By December 1922 the wholesale and cost-of-living indexes had fallen to 48 and 64 percent of their respective peak levels of 1920, and unemployment among

union members averaged 15.2 percent in 1922.[20]

The pound reached a monthly average low of $3.38 in February 1920. The lowest single quotation was $3.18, or 35 percent below prewar par. A year and a half of indecisive swings followed. The monthly average rate next rose almost without interruption from a low of $3.63 in July 1921 to a high of almost $4.70 in March 1923. After that it gradually sank to a low of $4.26 for January 1924 and then, with minor interruptions, rose again to near parity in April 1925.[21]

The movement of the exchange rate in relation to purchasing-power parity provides some clues about speculation.[22] Three notable fluctuations occurred in 1919–1921, the immediate postwar years of abnormal scarcity and inflation followed by sharp recession. Since the

---

17. *Ibid.*, pp. 154ff.

18. Committee on Currency and Foreign Exchanges after the War, *First Interim Report* (Cd. 9182), London: His Majesty's Stationery Office, 1918.

19. It is true, however, that the Bank of England might have influenced the rate through the timing of its purchases, as agent for the Treasury, of dollars to service the U.S. and Canadian debts. The Bank's gold reserve was practically unchanged from the end of 1920 until April 1925, and its great increase during 1920 was due to transfers from the commercial banks rather than to official intervention on the market. S. C. Tsiang, "Fluctuating Exchange Rates in Countries with Relatively Stable Economies: Some European Experiences After World War I," IMF *Staff Papers*, VII, October 1959, p. 245.

20. D. E. Moggridge, *British Monetary Policy 1924–1931*, Cambridge: Cambridge University Press, 1972, pp. 24–25.

21. Most of the monthly average exchange rates in this chapter are taken from Board of Governors of the Federal Reserve System, *Banking and Monetary Statistics*, Washington, 1943, p. 681 for the United Kingdom and p. 670 for France.

22. Tsiang, *op. cit.*, pp. 249–256. Tsiang calculated purchasing-power parities on a 1913 base, using the Federal Reserve Board's indexes of wholesale prices in the United Kingdom and the United States.

major depreciation of the pound that started in June 1920 was apparently in step with the greater fall of American than of British prices, only two of the episodes remain as possible examples of destabilizing speculation. The first began late in 1919. The initial depreciation of the pound against the dollar, which had thus far corresponded to the movement in relative purchasing powers, now speeded up and carried further. The similar behavior of other European currencies at the same time suggests that destabilizing speculation was not the only influence at work. A tightening of monetary policy in the United States suddenly choked off a flow of export credits to Europe. The European exchange depreciations were apparently due less to a self-aggravating flight of capital than to a policy-induced cessation of a previous stabilizing flow. Furthermore, the depreciation reversed itself as early as February 1920. March brought a sharp uptrend in the sterling rate. As judged by almost all plausible criteria, the rate was more volatile in March 1920 than in any other month of the floating-pound period. Economic fundamentals were running strongly in favor of sterling. Britain's trade deficit with the United States was shrinking, and the climate of expectations was becoming ever more favorable to sterling.[23] By April the pound was stronger than it had been in December 1919.

A second possible example of destabilizing speculation was the pound's rapid climb, after an intervening dip, from December 1920 to May 1921. The rate outran purchasing-power parity. Steps to establish U.S. government export credits for farm products and negotiations for refunding the British debt to the United States had supposedly stimulated bullishness on the pound. An 8 percent reversal in June and July shrank the pound's premium over purchasing-power parity. Abatement of the earlier overoptimism might have been partly due to strikes in Britain's two chief export industries, coal and textiles, in the spring of 1921. In addition, the dollar was strengthened by heavy German buying in late May and early June in order to pay reparations. In August 1921, when the exchange rate had come more into line with purchasing-power parity, the pound began to appreciate gradually as it gained in purchasing power relative to the dollar.

From this time on, the exchange rate moved broadly in line with purchasing-power parity. From March to October 1922, however, the exchange rate was sticky despite a rise in the relative purchasing power of the pound. Failure of the pound to appreciate may have been connected with British labor disputes and a deadlock over German reparations. From September to November 1922 the threat of war in the Dardanelles area also seems to have had some influence. From then until the return to gold, movements in both the exchange rate and purchasing-power parity were generally mild and closely associated. A so-called "flight from the pound" does seem to have influenced the rate, however, from October 1923 until early 1924. The impression was growing that heavy unemployment might weaken the British government's commitment to deflation aimed at restoring the pound to prewar parity. Defeat of the Conservatives in the December elections and formation of a Labour government in January contributed to the uncertainty. Confidence gradually returned after the new government, in February, officially went on record in support of the orthodox doctrines of the Cunliffe Report.[24]

The conclusion suggested by narrative history finds support in a statistical study by John S. Hodgson. Hodgson ran regressions for the monthly-average pound-dollar rate from March 1919 to April 1925. The actual rate conformed closely to the rate calculated on the basis of such "fundamentals" as the interest-rate differential, national money supplies, and—especially—price indexes; it also conformed to the rate calculated on the basis not only of these fundamentals but also of dummy variables for seasonal influences and certain newsworthy events. Regression coefficients of low significance for dummy variables representing political and economic disruptions on the Continent suggest that these events, contrary to contemporary impressions, were not important in determining the exchange rate. (The calculations suggest, however, that the 1923–1924 episode of "flight from the pound" did have some influence.) The dominance of the fundamental influences, together with regression coefficients on the price-level variables suggesting that the exchange rate tended to change in less than full proportion, casts doubt on any idea that speculation generally intensified exchange-rate fluctuations. This inference refers to monthly-average rates, however, and does not rule out the possibility of destabilizing speculation within months. Since evidence of other kinds suggests that speculative buying or selling seldom persisted in one direction for more than a week or two, it does seem doubtful that speculation was cumulatively destabilizing.[25]

In summary, the fluctuations of sterling exchange after the immediate postwar years of inflation and recession were in accordance with purchasing-power parity and, on the whole, were not even as wide as those of either purchasing-power parity or the United Kingdom price level. This relative stickiness suggests that exchange speculation was mainly in a stabilizing direction.[26]

Britain on the gold-bullion standard

British motives for finally returning to par strengthened in 1924 when the new German mark was stabilized on gold and when sterling improved following the success of Germany's Dawes Plan loan. The Gold and Silver (Export Control) Act of 1920, which had been protecting the gold reserves of the Bank of England, was due to lapse at the end of 1925. The government would soon—probably in the Budget Speech of April 1925—have to declare whether or not it would extend the act, giving reasons.

Discussions of what to do were largely qualitative; the statistical work was superficial. Bank of England and Treasury officials relied heavily on their "feel" for the situation. Many thought that postponement of the return to par would reverse market expectations and so require costly efforts to check a sharp relapse of the sterling rate. Considerations of international prestige also told against postponement. The view prevailed that Britain was somehow morally committed to the old parity. Sentiment yearned for the pound once more to "look the dollar in the face." American inflation, people hoped, would help make this possible.[27]

A Committee on the Currency and Bank of England Note Issues had been appointed in June 1924. In a report of February 1925 (not made public until April 28), the Committee found Britain financially strong enough for reestablishment of a free gold market, provided that the internal purchasing power of the pound were raised somewhat further and provided that foreign investments were restricted to the country's normal current-account surplus. The return to the gold standard should be announced soon, said the report, and control over gold and silver exports allowed to

lapse. Foreign credits, though not necessary, would help promote confidence in the restored parity. The circulation of gold coins was considered a nonessential and undesirable luxury.[28]

During this period the Bank of England continued holding total bank reserves, deposits, and earning assets stable. In November 1924, informal restrictions were tightened on the placement of new foreign loans in London; and during the year this embargo was in effect, British loans to foreign borrowers were negligible. Early in 1925 American standby credits were obtained to help defend sterling after the return to gold. In March 1925 Bank rate was raised to 5 percent to keep British interest rates above the rising rates in New York.

The stage was now set for the Budget Speech of April 28. The Chancellor of the Exchequer, Winston Churchill, announced

23. John S. Hodgson, "Fluctuations of the Pound Sterling, 1919–1925," University of Virginia dissertation, 1971, pp. 198–205.

24. Tsiang, *op. cit.*, and Hodgson, *op. cit.*, pp. 125–128, 260–266.

25. Hodgson, *op. cit.*, and Hodgson, "An Analysis of Floating Exchange Rates: The Dollar-Sterling Rate, 1919–1925," *Southern Economic Journal*, **XXXIX**, October 1972, pp. 249–257. The close conformity between actual and calculated rates appears in time-series charts, high coefficients of determination, and significant regression coefficients for the "fundamental" variables. Regression of the exchange rate on the ratio of U.S. to British price indexes alone yields an R^2 of 0.81. The price-index ratio was also significant, and was the only significant quantifiable variable, in a regression of month-to-month percentage changes in the exchange rate on changes in the explanatory variables. These findings, says Hodgson, lend strong support to the purchasing-power-parity theory. (Dissertation, p. 268.)

26. Tsiang, *op. cit.*, esp. p. 256. E. Victor Morgan, *Studies in British Financial Policy, 1914–1925*, London: Macmillan, 1952, pp. 364–366, also found "a very close correlation between movements of the exchange and relative prices," apart from the short-lived drop of the pound in mid-1921.

27. Moggridge, *op. cit.*, esp. chaps. 3 and 10.

28. Brown, *op. cit.*, pp. 375–377.

that the restrictions on gold and silver exports would lapse at once and that the Bank of England would redeem legal tender in gold for export. The Gold Standard Act of 1925, passed on May 13, required the Bank to sell gold in ingots of not less than 400 fine ounces for legal tender at the traditional price of £3.17s. 10½d. per ounce 11/12 fine. Sterling could thus be redeemed in gold in amounts worth no less than almost $8300. Redemption in coin was not required. Only the Bank was to have the right to bring gold bullion to the mint for coinage. The Bank remained obliged, as it had been without interruption ever since 1844, to buy all gold offered to it at £3. 17s. 9d. per ounce 11/12 fine.

Omitting gold coins from actual circulation aroused little comment; attitudes had changed. During the war the fiction prevailed that money was still redeemable in gold coin, even though gold for export was not actually available. Now the gold standard was proclaimed in effect again because gold exports were again permissible, even though the redemption of money in gold was restricted to this purpose.[29] Other European countries apparently shared this new view. For example, when the Netherlands followed England back onto the gold standard, the Netherlands Bank would sell gold only if exchange rates justified its export.[30] While Americans saw domestic redeemability as the essence of the gold standard, Europeans apparently welcomed the bullion standard as a way to economize on gold and yet have the benefits of the full gold standard.[31]

Britain did not regain parity without trouble. Considerations of legislative timing and of international prestige had forced action before the British and American price levels had been fully aligned at exchange parity. Although nothing better than a very rough measurement is possible, the figure of 10 percent has become the traditional informed guess of how far the restored parity was above the pound's equilibrium value. It is true that the discount on the fluctuating pound had shrunk below 10 percent in July 1924 and below 2 percent early in 1925, but by then exchange-rate quotations were supposedly reflecting speculation on the imminent official restoration of parity.[32]

Most prominent among British economists warning against overvaluation was John Maynard Keynes. Keynes was already famous as the author of *The Economic Consequences of the Peace*, which dissected the economic provisions of the Versailles Treaty. He testified against returning to gold in the Currency Committee hearings in the summer of 1924. Along with Reginald McKenna, chairman of the Midland Bank, he recommended aiming at stability of the price level instead.[33] In 1925 he published a pamphlet entitled *The Economic Consequences of Mr. Churchill*,[34] warning that the old parity would hamper exports and necessitate further painful deflation in Britain. Similar warnings had been made about returning to parity after the Napoleonic Wars, and on both occasions the warnings seem to have been borne out by experience. The deflation in the United States from 1865 to 1879 in preparation for restoring the greenbacks to the parity in effect before the Civil War is another example.

The further downward adjustment of British prices and wages required to make parity an equilibrium rate might not have been too difficult for a flexible economy (which is not to say that this would have been the best policy even then), but the British economy was not flexible enough. B. M. Anderson cites as typical the example of four companies that had agreed on fixed prices and sales quotas. Three of them could profitably have cut prices to attract new business, but the fourth was burdened by a poor location and outmoded equipment and could have been ruined by price competition. Precisely because the cartel agreement was not legally enforceable (though not itself illegal), the three strong companies felt all the more honor-bound to abide by it.[35] Furthermore, a widespread tendency among British businesses to cling to old production methods and obsolete plant and equipment made cost-and-price cutting all the more difficult. Britain seemed to be in the middle of the theoretical gold-standard adjustment process, stuck there, with unemployment having no marked tendency to depress wages and prices. Union wage scales, unemployment insurance, and unemployment relief tended to hold wages up. Recurrent labor disputes, including a general strike and a lengthy coal strike in 1926, dramatized how hard it was to reduce costs and prices. In time the hope became clearly futile that domestic deflation would restore equilibrium. Foreign countries, either by internal deflation to restore their own parities with the dollar or by stabilizing their currencies at undervalued levels, killed Britain's alternative hope that price inflation abroad would make adjustment easy.

Industrial production generally stagnated.

British industry had traditionally specialized in meeting basic rather than readily expansible wants. Depression in the old basic industries (including iron and steel, coal, and cotton textiles, now faced with competition from rayon) was not fully offset by prosperity in newer ones, such as electrical apparatus and appliances, chemicals, and automobiles. Coal production never regained the prewar level during the entire interwar period. Reasons included increased efficiency in using coal to produce electricity, increased competition from foreign mines and from other fuels, and the inefficiency and high labor costs of the British coal industry. The decline in exports of coal compounded the troubles of British shipping. The total volume of world trade regained the 1913 level only in 1929, then promptly fell off again. Shipbuilding, like shipping, was hard hit: over half of British shipyard workers were unemployed during the 1920s. Even while most other countries were enjoying prosperity, well over 10 percent of the total British labor force was usually unemployed. The "dole," given to families proving their need for relief after exhaustion of unemployment benefits, supported an actual majority of the population in some particularly depressed areas. The deflation, depression, and chronic unemployment of the 1920s, and their worsening after 1929, created durable memories and presumably contributed to the growth of anticapitalist sentiment in Britain, to the increasing strength of the Labor Party and its election victory in 1945, and to the lasting importance of "full employment" as a political slogan.[36]

Signs of trouble appeared in the balance of payments and the foreign-exchange market. Small current-account surpluses, seldom reaching one-third or one-half of the prewar real size (after adjustment for the higher prices), did not cover the long-term foreign security issues floated in the highly developed London capital market, and the necessary funds came as short-term inflows from abroad. By 1928 the London market had run up short-term external liabilities of about £500 million gross and £200 million net, in contrast with its net short-term creditor position before the war. Sterling was generally weak from 1925 on. The market

29. The Currency and Bank Notes Act of July 1928 provided, among other things, that any person in the United Kingdom owning more than £10,000 worth of gold coin or bullion could be made to sell it to the Bank of England at the legal price, unless

the gold were being held for immediate export or for industrial use. Thus, if necessary, the Bank could keep private gold hoarding from seriously interfering with its own policies. *Ibid.*, pp. 682–683.

30. Besides the Netherlands and the Netherlands East Indies, Australia and South Africa also, by agreement, returned to gold at the same time as Britain, while New Zealand returned to its old parity on a kind of sterling-exchange standard. (Moggridge, *op. cit.*, p. 84 and footnote.) Sweden had grown tired of waiting and had returned to gold alone in March 1924. (Stephen V. O. Clarke, *Central Bank Cooperation: 1924–31*, New York: Federal Reserve Bank of New York, 1967, p. 80.)

31. Brown, *op. cit.*, p. 382.

32. According to W. M. Scammell, "It is generally agreed that . . . the pound was approximately 10 percent over-valued" between 1925 and 1931. *International Monetary Policy*, London: Macmillan, 1957, p. 52n.

After reviewing the academic discussion and some relevant figures, Moggridge (*op. cit.*, p. 105) concludes: "An exchange rate at least 10 percent lower than $4.86 would probably have been somewhat more appropriate for sterling." For an unconvincing challenge to the judgment that sterling was overvalued, see John T. Walter, *Foreign Exchange Equilibrium*, Pittsburgh: University of Pittsburgh Press, 1951, pp. 14–16. A better-based challenge appears in John Hodgson's dissertation, already cited, pp. 273–274. The restored parity was not substantially higher than the equilibrium rate calculated by Hodgson on the basis of "fundamental" factors; mere speculation on the return to gold does not appear to have produced a substantial overvaluation. Hodgson recognizes, however, that the British deflation policy may have contrived a higher "fundamental" exchange rate, and with it higher levels of unemployment, than could be maintained indefinitely. The "structural" worsening of Britain's international competitiveness, mentioned in the text of this chapter, should also be taken into account. For mention of evidence supporting the standard view about bullish speculation on sterling, see Moggridge, *op. cit.*, p. 93.

33. Moggridge, *op. cit.*, pp. 42–44.

34. London: L. and V. Woolf, 1925. The American edition, published by Harcourt, Brace, was entitled *The Economic Consequences of Sterling Parity.*

35. Anderson, *op. cit.*, 164–165.

36. Alpert, *op. cit.*, chap. 6.

price of gold in London persistently tended to stay at or near the selling price of the Bank of England, which was almost continually resisting a tendency to lose gold. Exchange rates in the late twenties contrasted with those of 1888–1914, when the annual average rate on sterling in New York had been below mint par only four times and above par 23. But from 1925 through 1931 the annual rate reached the mint par of $4.8666 only once—in 1928, when, supported by substantial losses of foreign-exchange reserves in the second half of the year, it averaged just that figure.[37]

Did the pains of the 1925 revaluation yield no comparable benefits? Well, no sober weighing of prospective benefits and costs had led to that policy. Superficially, it might seem a benefit that the "City" of London, while never regaining its unchallenged prewar supremacy, did regain the prestige of a gold-standard center and did attract short-term foreign funds in heavier volume than before the war. In particular, London attracted deposits from the central banks of countries that had adopted the gold-exchange standard. In linking their currencies to the dollar or pound and holding their monetary reserves largely in dollar or sterling bank balances or short-term securities, these countries could earn at least some interest on their otherwise barren reserve funds. This arrangement seemed satisfactory to London bankers also, for it cheaply provided them with funds for profitable relending. Another source of foreign balances in London was the flight of funds to safety during the French monetary difficulties of 1924–1926; these French funds were not immediately repatriated after the franc was stabilized. The French banks, into whose hands these funds gradually drifted, were inclined to retain them to earn the relatively high interest rates offered in Britain's defense of the gold standard. In fact, an abnormally large volume of international short-term money existed in the late 1920s, ready to flit from one financial center to another as risks and earnings opportunities changed. Before the crisis of 1931, London harbored much of these funds.[38]

The advantage of having foreign balances in London was shaky. If they should be quickly withdrawn, as finally did happen, a house of cards would come tumbling down. Though exchange rates on the pound were still stable within the gold points, the situation bristled with latent instability.

In short, British monetary experience in the 1920s consisted of: several years of deflationary struggle back to prewar parity; temporary success in this questionable effort; and then continued business stagnation and chronic unemployment, the need for relatively high interest rates, and a precarious accumulation of mobile short-term foreign funds—all under the influence of an inappropriate exchange rate.[39]

France before stabilization

French monetary inflation continued until mid-1926 and went far enough to prevent a return to prewar parity. A new parity was finally adopted that somewhat undervalued the franc and caused a balance-of-payments surplus and gold accumulation during the late 1920s.

The franc, like the pound, had been pegged near par during the war. A decline after the unpegging in March 1919 seemed temporary and hardly disastrous; Frenchmen apparently expected an early return to normal. But inflationary government finance continued. The franc fell in relation to the dollar more rapidly than did the pound, and by April 1920 it stood at slightly under one-third of the prewar rate. Then new taxes and the flotation of loans provided a respite from inflationary finance. Moreover, the French government obligated itself by a convention with the Bank of France and by a law of December 1920 to repay earlier advances at a rate of 2 billion francs a year. Though these repayments were later made either only partially or by means of subterfuges (such as borrowing from other sources, including private banks to which the Bank of France was compelled to lend the necessary funds),[40] the announced policy did at first promote confidence in the currency. The franc moved on the exchange market in general harmony with sterling. From April 1920 to April 1922 it rose from 6.25 to 9.23 U.S. cents. That was to prove the highest monthly level ever reached since December 1919.

The franc was subject to worse strains than sterling. Expenditures on postwar reconstruction from 1919 to 1926 resulted in government budgets that were as large as or larger than wartime budgets (larger in nominal francs, though smaller in real purchasing power). These expenditures, together with war-related pension and interest costs, produced a "consecrated deficit" in a confusing morass of special government budgets. The national debt rose from 173 billion francs in 1918 to 428 billion in 1924. "Le Boche paiera" was the cry. The franc was vulnerable when the wrangle over reparations came to a head in mid-1922. The adamant Raymond Poincaré had already replaced Aristide Briand as premier, interrupting Briand's relatively conciliatory policy towards Germany. Already in May the franc had begun to fall against the dollar and sterling. Later in the year foreign bear speculation became active, undermining the confidence of the French in their own currency. The franc fell to an average rate of 6.86 cents in November 1922. The Ruhr occupation episode began in January 1923.

Until early 1922 speculation and capital flight clearly had not dominated the exchange market; in fact, capital tended to enter France each time the franc slumped considerably. But then a kind of speculation developed that was later to be authoritatively described as illustrating the general "dangers of . . . cumulative and self-aggravating movements under a regime of freely fluctuating exchanges. . . ."[41]

For this reason the entire experience deserves detailed reexamination. The decline of the franc in 1922 cannot plausibly be explained by trouble with the balance of payments, which actually improved. Neither does the still moderate expansion of the money supply provide the full explanation. Some French economists (notably Albert Aftalion) later propounded a so-called "psychological theory" to explain the exchange rates of the franc in the period then beginning. The public's willingness to hold francs and, in turn, the supplies and demands on the foreign-exchange market reacted to growing uneasiness about the government budget. Yet the French government persisted in unrealistically counting on reparations to cover its outlays for reconstruction and pensions. The deficit was being reduced year by year, but not eliminated, and the national debt kept rising. Furthermore, when the government had trouble selling its securities to the public, it borrowed directly or indirectly from the Bank of France, which in effect ran a printing press on its behalf. Psychological influences on the foreign-exchange market thus centered on real factors.

In 1923 the government was again unable to comply with the law of December 1920 regarding repayments to the Bank of France. January 1924 saw the failure of a loan floated by the Crédit National, an association of the principal French banks that had been set up in October 1919 to sell its own government-guaranteed

SUSPENSION AND ATTEMPTED RESTORATION OF THE INTERNATIONAL GOLD STANDARD

bonds to the public and use the proceeds for term loans to industry and for advances to war-damage victims on the security of their claims for indemnity. The failure of this loan was ominous because the government was dependent on the willingness of the public to buy its obligations if it was to escape outright inflationary finance.

Under the continued pressure of bear speculation that had resumed the previous November, the franc kept falling. The rate hit 3.49 cents on March 8, 1924. Increases in the discount rate of the Bank of France in January had proved unable to stop the decline. On March 22, in an atmosphere of crisis, Parliament authorized several fiscal reforms, including a 20 percent increase in most direct and indirect taxes. This law symbolized Parliament's first official recognition that the "Germany-will-pay" program had been wishful thinking.[42] Largely thanks to this show of fiscal realism, Raymond Poincaré's new coali-

---

37. Bank for International Settlements, *The Sterling Area*, Basel: 1953, p. 22; Brown, *op. cit.*, pp. 603, 709. The Federal Reserve's *Banking and Monetary Statistics* quotes an average rate of $4.8662 for 1928. On the Bank of England's intervention, see Moggridge, *op. cit.*, pp. 136–137, 176–198.

38. Lionel Robbins, *The Great Depression*, New York: Macmillan, 1936, pp. 89–91.

39. This interpretation is not fully shared, however, even by all economists who understood what was at issue. As sensitive an observer as Gustav Cassel felt that promoting international confidence and international trade through restoration of sterling to its old position as the principal world currency was worth the small sacrifices of the moderate price deflation still necessary. (Cassel estimated that a 6 percent further reduction of the British price level was necessary at the beginning of 1925.) *The Downfall of the Gold Standard*, Oxford: Clarendon Press, 1936, pp. 37, 40.

40. Tsiang, *op. cit.*, p. 265.

41. Ragnar Nurkse, *International Currency Experience*, League of Nations, 1944, p. 118.

42. Robert Murray Haig, *The Finances of Post-War France*, New York: Columbia University Press, 1929, pp. 97–98.

tion government was able to borrow $100 million through J. P. Morgan and Company in New York and £4 million through Lazard Frères in London. These foreign funds were promptly used to support the franc on the exchanges, raising it to 6.71 cents on April 22. This "bear squeeze" succeeded in inflicting heavy losses on speculators who had sold francs short. These operations, together with the new tax law and the Dawes Plan, which was due to go into effect in the autumn and which would improve the basis for estimating future receipts from Germany, reversed speculative sentiment. The swing carried so far that the government was able to buy back all the dollars and pounds previously sold to support the franc.

The violent and rather artificial rise gave way to a reaction late in April. On June 1 the franc was down to just under 5 cents. Nervousness stemming from the recent fluctuations persisted. The large size and short average maturity of the floating government debt remained a threat. At the end of 1924 the floating debt was about 60 billion francs, including about 54½ billion francs of *bons de la défense nationale*, of which about 7 or 8 billions were coming due monthly. In addition, about 27½ billion francs worth of longer-term bonds were to mature from July 1925 to May 1926. If the public for any reason became unwilling to renew the maturing debt, the government would have to resort to inflationary borrowing at the Bank of France. Distrust in government economic policies was in fact heightened by the victory in the May 1924 elections of a union of Socialists and Radical-Socialists and replacement of Poincaré in June by the fiscally less conservative Edouard Herriot. (Public dismay at the tax increases enacted in March had probably contributed to the election result.) Toward the end of 1924 and early in 1925 public holdings of *bons de la défense nationale* fell by several billion francs. Current government deficits had now become a less crucial inflationary element than past deficits in the form of a large volume of short-maturity government debt. The government was borrowing from Peter to pay Paul with increasing difficulty.

In April 1925, just when England, by contrast, was returning to the gold standard, the Herriot government had to confess a subterfuge whereby State borrowing at the Bank of France had exceeded the legal limit, with the excess concealed in the Bank's balance sheet

under the heading *portfolio*. Herriot's defense was that earlier cabinets had been guilty of similar irregularities. Another disclosure was that the Bank's end-of-1924 balance sheet (and possibly others) had been falsified by concealment of note issues beyond the legal limit under the heading "miscellaneous liabilities." Worry over the fate of the franc was so general that not only merchants and financiers but also working people understood and scrutinized the figures for "advances to the State" on the asset side and "note issue" on the liability side of the weekly balance sheets of the Bank of France. Repeated increases in the legal limits to these two amounts were taken as ominous signs. Hence the disclosure of actual subterfuges was a particular blow to confidence.

These disclosures, together with the unpopularity of proposals for a 10 percent capital levy or a forced loan, forced the Herriot ministry to resign in April 1925. Caillaux, Finance Minister in the successor cabinet, then tried to meet the financial difficulties by an internal loan to consolidate the floating debt and by further borrowings in America. The internal loan was poorly received and the American loan negotiations fell through in October. Caillaux resigned.

Wholesale prices and the cost of living had continued rising moderately throughout 1925. The franc was sinking gradually under the pressure of a persistent outward transfer of capital, often through purchases of foreign securities payable in gold. Official support helped keep the New York rate on the franc at about 5.18 cents during March, April, and May and at about 4.70 cents during July, August, and September. Though further restrictions were placed on capital export in October, the temporary pegging of the franc gave way to a rapid decline. The monthly average rate sank to 3.74 cents in December. Emergency taxes calculated to raise about 3 billion francs in a hurry failed to restore confidence. "By the end of 1925 the seemingly uncontrollable wave of exchange depreciation had brought a hysterical note" into financial discussions. The ordinary citizen became panicky, and a general flight from the franc and from monetary securities into commodities and foreign assets got under way, presaging the virtual hysteria of mid-1926.[43]

Here is a good point to summarize the stages of crisis up to the final climax. Though actual government budget deficits and increases in the national debt remained moderate, they were large enough and had persisted long enough to sap confidence. This in turn hampered the sale of new government securities as fast as old ones came due. With the government having to borrow at the Bank of France, increases became necessary in the legal limits of the Bank's advances to the state and its note issue—either forthright increases or devious subterfuges. These inflationary omens still further discouraged public subscriptions to government securities. By July 1926 the Bank's advances to the state had increased 77 percent, notes in circulation had increased 38 percent, and notes in circulation plus demand deposits with four leading commercial banks had increased 43 percent over the levels of only 18 months before.[44]

Business as well as government borrowing fed the inflation. The French banking system was dangerously responsive to the "needs of trade"; as rising prices swelled the monetary volume of business, bank credit expanded correspondingly. Banks could get funds to meet their customers' demand for loans by drawing on their deposits previously made with the Treasury, by cashing government securities as they matured without buying new ones, or by discounting at the Bank of France. Their doing so caused the government all the more financial embarrassment.

Finance minister replaced finance minister in a "waltz of the portfolios." From October 1925 to July 1926 a new minister took office every 37 days, on the average. The climax came in July 1926 when Caillaux, again Finance Minister, spurred by the urgent tone of a report just released by a nonpolitical committee of financial experts, demanded—and was refused—decree-making powers. The Briand-Caillaux government was overthrown and replaced—for two days only—by another Left coalition under Herriot.

The old Finance Ministry had previously asked the Bank of France to buy from the Treasury the $31 million still left from the Morgan loan of 1924. On July 19 the Bank agreed on condition of a corresponding increase in its legal note issue. The Treasury was facing a serious drain from redemption of the short-term *bons de la défense nationale*, yet the new ministry was unwilling either to force their holders to take longer-term securities in exchange (which would have amounted to partial default) or to take the openly inflationary step of increasing the Bank's legal note issue. The

SUSPENSION AND ATTEMPTED RESTORATION OF THE INTERNATIONAL GOLD STANDARD

Bank remained firm in refusing to buy the Morgan dollars without a legal increase in its note circulation. On July 21, 1926, in order to forestall illegal subterfuges, the governor of the Bank sent a letter to Herriot's finance minister warning, in effect, that the Treasury's small remaining balance at the Bank of France would probably run out by the end of that very day. The balance sheet to be made up that night and published the next day would probably show advances by the Bank to the State in excess of the legal limit, obliging the Bank to cease making payments for the account of the Treasury. Only one means was available, concluded the letter, to prevent this disaster: immediate parliamentary approval of the proposed transaction on the Bank's terms.

The Treasury's balance at the Bank did not, in fact, quite run out on July 21. That evening the government was overthrown after submitting a bill to sell the Morgan dollars to the Bank *without* raising the note-circulation limit. Immediately after the overthrow, a special session of both chambers of Parliament enacted a bill embodying the Bank's terms.

On this same eventful day, the franc fell on the foreign-exchange market to 2.05 U.S. cents. People had the fate of the German mark in 1923 freshly in mind. The cost of living was rising day by day. The Paris mob was protesting against inflation by rioting and by threatening the deputies. On the morning of July 22, Raymond Poincaré agreed to form a cabinet; and the next day Parliament installed the conservative old lawyer, a former premier and a wartime President of the Republic, as premier and finance minister with special powers. Poincaré promised to save the franc by cutting expenditures, cutting pensions, dismissing unnecessary government employees, and raising taxes. His reputation for fiscal conservatism was so great that the mere news of his nomination for office pulled the franc up from its low point of 2.03 cents. Its average quotation rose

43. Martin Wolfe, *The French Franc between the Wars, 1919–1939*, New York: Columbia University Press, 1951, pp. 38–39.

44. Calculated from a table in Tsiang, *op. cit.*, p. 269.

to 3.42 cents in November and 3.95 cents in December.

Poincaré's task was not unduly difficult. Speculation had brought the franc lower than fundamentals justified. Unlike Germany during its inflation, France relied primarily on indirect taxation and on the revenue of fiscal monopolies instead of on taxes on incomes of the year before, and government revenues thus rose with the price level. Government expenditures rose more slowly: approximately 53 percent of them in 1926 went for service on the internal debt and for pensions and so were fixed in terms of francs. Poincaré balanced the budget and even achieved a surplus. To clinch his success, he had some of his basic fiscal reforms enacted into constitutional law.

Toward the end of 1926, after recovering from its panic level to about one-fifth of pre-war parity, the franc was stabilized *de facto* by official dealings on the foreign-exchange market. To restrain its further recovery, the Bank of France bought foreign exchange heavily.[45] Before the end of December its net purchases had totaled £5.3 million. They were over £20 million by February 1927 and reached £100 million by May 1927. Most of the purchases were of sterling, giving the Bank of France great power to influence the London money market.

By now it was apparent that the exchange value of the franc was hardly likely to fall in the near future, and rumors persisted that the official pegging which was keeping it down might be relaxed. A speculative flight *to* the franc got under way. The Bank of France did not want to let the franc appreciate, fearing damage to the competitive position of French industry. Neither did it relish the inflationary creation of more francs with which to keep on buying foreign exchange. The Bank believed that the troublesome speculative purchases of francs were being financed by borrowings in foreign money markets at interest rates lower than those prevailing in France. Accordingly, it urged tighter credit abroad, especially in London and Berlin. It began drawing gold from London in May 1927 and threatening further withdrawals unless the Bank of England raised its discount rate. The Bank of England was unwilling to yield, since tighter credit would have been burdensome to the British economy at the time and since it doubted that the problem of one-way-option bullish speculation on the franc could be so easily solved.[46] It is ironic that the problem of speculation on a pegged franc should so soon have replaced the problem of speculation on a fluctuating franc.

Now that a historical survey has prepared the ground, it is appropriate to ponder and appraise the lessons of the French prestabilization experience. The interpretation presented in the League of Nations publication *International Currency Experience* is often cited as the "basis" or "proof" that speculation is destabilizing under freely fluctuating exchange rates.[47] "The post-war history of the French franc up to the end of 1926 affords an instructive example of completely free and uncontrolled exchange variations. . . ." "The dangers of . . . cumulative and self-aggravating movements under a regime of freely fluctuating exchanges are clearly demonstrated by the French experience of 1922–26." "Self-aggravating movements [of exchange rates and trade], instead of promoting adjustment in the balance of payments, are apt to intensify any initial disequilibrium and to produce what may be termed 'explosive' conditions of instability. . . . we may recall in particular the example of the French franc during the years 1924–26."[48]

Actually, the historical details already reviewed undermine these conclusions. Up to early 1922, there was no question of speculation and capital flight dominating the market. For about eight years after the start of inflationary wartime and postwar government finance and about three years after the breakdown of fixed exchange rates, no foreign exchange crisis developed. Actual panic did not ensue until 1926, after about 12 years of inflation and seven years of fluctuating exchanges. The panic came only after protracted budgetary and debt difficulties, price inflation, exchange depreciation, and the recurrent political crises stemming from these troubles, and only after the spread of fear that the franc was about to suffer the fate of the German mark. In view of these circumstances, the French episode hardly supports any general proposition about exchange speculation. If anything, it demonstrates the consequences of irresolution and ineptitude in debt management and in dealing with inflation, especially when the officials in charge suffer from "simple ignorance of monetary economics."[49] With the supply of money and credit as extremely expansible as it in fact was, pegged exchange rates would have worked at least as badly as the fluctuating rates.[50] In fact, although firm exchange fixing had broken down in 1919, there were some official interventions and some unsuccessful attempts at supporting franc exchange during the period 1924–1926. It is ironic that after an end to the internal financial crisis again made exchange pegging feasible, fixed exchange rates came on the scene to take credit for the improved situation.

As for exchange speculation during the French episode, one can plausibly argue that it was equilibrating rather than disequilibrating, apparently being based on a correct diagnosis of underlying financial trends. And it was stabilizing rather than destabilizing in that by dramatizing a bad financial situation with which politicians had temporized too long, it turned attention toward the political improvements necessary to reverse the trends and save the franc.[51]

The undervalued franc

The inflation, serious and potentially disastrous though it had been, paradoxically left some elements of strength in the French situation. First, the outward transfer of capital during the years of distrust had built up an accumulation of foreign assets. Depreciation of the franc had stimulated exports and so translated the financial outflow into real terms. Repatriation of funds as profitable investment opportunities appeared at home would tend to strengthen the franc on the exchanges. Second, the chronic monetary crisis had forced necessary tax increases in 1920, 1924, and 1925, and in 1926 had forced fiscal probity under Poincaré's leadership. Finally, the franc had fallen far enough to frustrate attempts to "return to normal" and to spare France England's costly deflationary struggle. Since the franc had already fallen further in foreign-exchange value than in domestic purchasing power, its stabilization was possible without the preliminary step of a confidence-shaking further depreciation.

The de facto exchange stabilization achieved in 1926 was eventually ratified de jure. After the parliamentary elections of May 1928, the Bank of France again had to buy large amounts of foreign money to hold down the franc on the exchange market. Hopes revived that temporary pegging would give way to upward revaluation. Even Premier Poincaré continued to harbor the quixotic feeling that national honor called for a return to prewar par, the same feeling that had been so decisive

in Britain. Governor Moreau of the Bank of France threatened to resign, however, unless de jure stabilization were enacted at once. Advocates of revalorization were championing a hopeless cause; undoing an 80 percent depreciation was out of the question. The French public had become accustomed to the 3.9-cent franc. A law of June 25, 1928 redefined the gold content of the franc in line with that exchange rate and required the Bank of France to buy and sell gold bars under a gold bullion standard at the corresponding fixed price of 15,383 francs per kilogram. The law obscured the Bank's authority to buy foreign exchange, and it decided to convert further gains of foreign exchange into gold. It was even reluctant to keep holding all the foreign exchange it already had. Governor Norman of the Bank of England thought it only reasonable for France to cooperate by continuing to hold rather than converting its London balances; but Governor Moreau, who wanted a "real" gold standard, thought he was being generous in holding any London balances at all. He thought London

45. The Bank had been authorized to buy gold and foreign exchange at premium prices and issue banknotes against them that would not count against the legal maximum. Vanes, op. cit., pp. 184–185.

46. Lester V. Chandler, Benjamin Strong, Central Banker, Washington: Brookings Institution, 1958, pp. 371–374.

47. On the great influence that this book has had, see Milton Friedman, Essays in Positive Economics, Chicago: University of Chicago Press, 1953, p. 176n.; and Tsiang, op. cit., p. 244.

48. Nurkse, International Currency Experience, pp. 117, 118, 211.

49. Wolfe, op. cit., p. 70.

50. The extreme elasticity of the money supply, the close statistical correlation between the money supply and the exchange rate, and the difficulties that would have beset a fixed rate system under the circumstances all are emphasized by Tsiang, op. cit., pp. 245, 261, 264, 267–273.

51. Cf. Friedman, Essays in Positive Economics, p. 176n.; and Harry C. Eastman, "French and Canadian Exchange Rate Policy," The Journal of Economic History, XV, December 1955, p. 408.

was trying to have the advantages of an international banking center without the obligations.[52]

The new parity slightly undervalued the franc; and, to the particular discomfort of Britain, a balance-of-payments surplus continued bringing gold into France through the rest of the 1920s and in fact through 1932. (The effect of current-account deficits on gold movements in 1931 and 1932 was more than counterbalanced by continued inflows of capital.)[53]

Stabilization of other countries

Little needs to be added about American postwar monetary experience. The dollar returned with ease to the full gold standard as early as 1919 and thereafter was the guidepost for realignment of other currencies. Rebuilding the gold standard was a gradual worldwide process. Some countries sooner or later regained their prewar gold parities; besides Great Britain, these included the Dominions, Switzerland, the Netherlands and her colonies, Argentina, the three Scandinavian countries, and Japan (which did not drop her wartime gold export embargo until January 1930). The revaluation of some currencies was hastened by bullish anticipation of it. In 1925 and 1926, for example, speculation restored the Danish crown to an overvalued level at which the internal economy suffered deflationary pains.[54] Other countries stabilized after devaluation; besides France, these included Belgium, Italy, Finland, Chile, Czechoslovakia, Yugoslavia, Greece, Bulgaria, Rumania, Estonia, Latvia, and Portugal (which, after three years of approximate stability and two years of *de facto* stabilization, did not return to gold *de jure* until June of the fateful year 1931). Austria, Hungary, Poland, Germany, and Russia adopted new currency units (some with the old names) after hyperinflation had destroyed their old currencies. By the end of 1925 some 35 currencies in addition to the U.S. dollar had either been stabilized on gold or had displayed exchange-rate stability for a full year. Three years later the apparent reconstruction of the international gold standard was substantially complete.[55]

The most prominent currency left unstabilized was the Spanish peseta, which had been fluctuating for several decades even before World War I. In 1920 its wartime premium above its theoretical parity disappeared. During the next five years wars in Morocco damaged Spanish finances, and the peseta sank to about three-fourths of its theoretical parity. In 1926 victory in Morocco and establishment of a firm if dictatorial government seemed to promise financial improvement, but the repegging of other European currencies and uncertain expectations of official Spanish pegging at par influenced speculation on the peseta. Official efforts to support the peseta in 1928–1931 kept breaking down, at considerable cost in foreign resources spent and foreign debt incurred. Elaborate exchange controls introduced after the overthrow of the monarchy in the spring of 1931 did not succeed in preventing further depreciation.[56]

The successive stabilizations of the 1920s were separate acts of national sovereignty. Each country mistakenly thought it was tying its currency to gold. Actually, countries were tying their currencies to each other in a piecemeal, uncoordinated fashion. Some parities were chosen under the influence of abnormal short-term capital movements, some for considerations of prestige. The new pattern of rates did not adequately reflect the different degrees of inflation in different countries. Countries generally thought to have adopted overvalued parities include the United Kingdom, Denmark, Norway, and Italy, while the currencies of Germany, France, and Belgium were undervalued.[57] "The piecemeal and haphazard manner of international monetary reconstruction sowed the seeds of subsequent disintegration," according to one widely accepted interpretation; it would have been better to set up the network of exchange rates "by simultaneous and coordinated international action. . . ."[58] It was partly in hopes of profiting from this lesson that the International Monetary Fund was established after World War II.

Troubles with the new system

Before examining this lesson later in its historical sequence, we should note other difficulties plaguing the restored exchange stability of the 1920s. Before World War I, international payments had typically been made in a relatively simple way, by transfer of ownership of bank balances in London. The postwar system had more than this one focus. New York, and to a lesser extent Paris, competed with London.

Dollar deposits and drafts rivaled sterling in international clearings and payments. Having more than one major financial center made international clearing more complex and less efficient. The various centers now had to arrange for offsetting claims among themselves and to hold balances with one another for this purpose. Cash and liquid assets had come under foreign ownership in much greater volume than before the war. Funds were liable to move erratically from one financial center to another in response to changing interest rates, changes in confidence or distrust in currencies, and other developments besides deep-seated disequilibriums. This "hot-money" danger had been far less serious before 1914, when no center rivaled London as a place where short-term funds might move and profitably be held.

Not only ordinary traders and banks but also many central banks had grown into the habit, since the war, of holding balances in the financial centers. Their shift to holding their legal monetary reserves largely as bank accounts or liquid securities in the gold-standard countries was a key aspect of the widespread adoption of the gold-exchange standard.[59] This had been recommended by the Financial Committee of the Genoa Conference in 1922. (Another Genoa recommendation had been stabilization of the purchasing powers of currencies and gold through domestic anti-inflation policies and cooperation among central banks.) The objective of the Genoa system was to make the world's supposedly inadequate gold supply do double duty, "backing" full-gold-standard currencies directly and gold-exchange-standard currencies at one remove. Critics would regard this as a paradoxical attempt both to have and to escape from the link between gold stocks and money supplies that forms the essence of a real gold standard.

Another difficulty was that the arrangement could not be relied on as permanent. The actions of Germany, France, and Italy were examples. After stabilization of the mark in 1924, the Reichsbank held more foreign exchange than any other European central bank, but it drew down its holdings rapidly in 1925 and again in 1927. In December 1924 foreign exchange made up 63.2 percent of its total of foreign exchange plus monetary gold; in December 1928 this figure was down to 17.5 percent. In 1926 and 1927 the Bank of France acquired the largest stock of foreign exchange of any central bank in the world. Its motive was to prevent an unwanted appreciation of

SUSPENSION AND ATTEMPTED RESTORATION OF THE INTERNATIONAL GOLD STANDARD

the franc rather than to adopt the gold exchange standard, yet it dominated the whole new system.[60] Late in 1928 and early in 1929 the Bank of France did convert about 4½ billion francs' worth of its foreign exchange into gold. According to its Annual Report for 1932, the Bank had wished to liquidate its foreign exchange ever since 1928; one presumed reason for its delaying was its concern for international repercussions. Other signs of impermanence in the gold-exchange standard were the activities of the "undisclosed buyer"[61] in the

---

52. Chandler, *op. cit.*, pp. 378–379.

53. Wolfe, *op. cit.*, pp. 128–129.

54. Bertil Ohlin, *La Politique du Commerce Extérieur*, Paris: Dunod, 1955, pp. 90–91, cites the Danish episode as an example of disequilibrating speculation under fluctuating exchange rates. This is a less apt example of that system itself than of eagerness to find fault with it, since the speculation was anticipating an official *policy* of raising the crown and then *stopping* its fluctuations.

55. Brown, *op. cit.*, pp. 394, 402; and League of Nations, *The Course and Control of Inflation*, pp. 92–93.

56. Brown, *op. cit.*, **II**, pp. 1031–1034.

57. Vanes, *op. cit.*, pp. 171–188, 191.

58. Nurkse, *International Currency Experience*, p. 117.

59. *Ibid.*, p. 30, lists the following countries as allowing their central banks, during all or part of the period 1922–1931, to hold their legally required reserves wholly or partly in the form of foreign exchange: Albania, Austria, Belgium, Bolivia, Bulgaria, Chile, Colombia, Czechoslovakia, Denmark, Ecuador, Egypt, Estonia, Finland, Germany, Greece, Hungary, Italy, Latvia, Peru, Poland, Portugal, Rumania, Spain, Uruguay, the USSR, and Yugoslavia. India, New Zealand, Argentina, and Venezuela lacked central banks but were on an exchange standard.

60. Brown, *op. cit.*, **II**, 742, 747, 765, 767, 770.

61. The "undisclosed" or "unknown" buyer was the collective name on the London bullion market for the central banks of Belgium, Switzerland, Poland, and Italy. Their activities from 1925 to 1928 formed part of a so-called "scramble for gold." *Ibid.*, pp. 633–634.

London gold market and Italian legislation permitting the central bank to convert its foreign-exchange holdings into gold. Attempts to liquidate foreign-exchange holdings played a key part in the collapse of 1931. Even two or three years before then, the gold-exchange standard was apparently on the decline.[62]

"Offsetting" versus an adjustment mechanism

The postwar system differed in operation as well as in structure from the gold standard as traditionally conceived. In a dimly held and perhaps historically inaccurate conception of the supposed "rules of the game," a central bank had more than the passive duty of interconverting domestic and international currency. With an eye on its reserve *ratio*, it was supposed to make the domestic money supply rise or fall not merely by the same *amount* but roughly by the same *percentage* as the country's gain or loss of gold or other international liquidity. It was supposed to *reinforce* the monetary impact by adjusting its discount rate or its use of other policy weapons to make its domestic assets move in the same direction as its international assets. Gold-gaining and gold-losing countries were supposed to meet each other half way in adjusting domestic money supplies, incomes, and prices to the requirements of international equilibrium. But things did not work this way in the middle and late 1920s. The evidence appears in Ragnar Nurkse's tabulation of changes in the international and domestic assets of the central banks of 26 countries.[63] During the period 1925 through 1929, the international and domestic assets of central banks changed from year to year in the same direction only 26 out of 106 times; they changed in opposite directions 73 times, and changes in one type of asset or the other were negligible 7 times. Over the longer period 1922 through 1938, changes were in the same direction in 32 percent of the instances and in opposite directions in 60 percent. Thus the traditional reinforcement of gold flows was the exception rather than the rule; by and large, central banks appeared to be "offsetting" or "neutralizing" the internal monetary effects of gold inflows and outflows. Surprisingly enough, a similar conclusion appears to hold true for the pre-1914 gold standard as well: year-to-year changes in the international and domestic assets of central banks were in opposite directions more often than in the same direction.[64]

Neither for the period before nor the period after World War I, however, is this conclusion certain. Conceivably the traditional reinforcement of gold flows did generally occur, but with such a lag as to be concealed in the figures of year-to-year changes. Furthermore, and especially before World War I, the apparent neutralization may often have been "automatic" rather than the result of deliberate policy, with international and domestic assets of central banks tending to move in opposite directions under the influence of the business cycle. Also, an inflow of gold, by increasing the liquidity of the money market, may sometimes have caused repayments of debts to the central bank; conversely, an outflow of gold may have tightened the market and increased borrowing from the central bank. Mere passive response to credit demands, even quite apart from any active neutralization, could have made a central bank's domestic and international assets move in opposite directions. (One might argue in reply that keeping the central-bank discount rate unchanged or changing it insufficiently in the face of changes in the supply of or demand for credit is in itself a policy and that the money supply is more appropriate than the discount rate as an indicator of policy.) Another type of automatic neutralization sometimes working during the years 1925–1928 rested on mobility of private short-term credit in response to interest-rate differentials between various money markets. The traditional interest-rate increase in reaction to a balance-of-payments deficit might attract funds from abroad, and foreign assets would replace part of the central bank's domestic assets. Such "equilibrating" capital flows tend to cushion, or delay the need for, the domestic monetary responses of traditional gold-standard theory.

Allowing for possible lags and for mere passivity in central-bank policy still hardly upsets the conclusion that traditional correctives did *not* occur promptly and actively under the restored gold standard of the 1920s. At times neutralization was clearly deliberate and so was a departure not only from traditional ideas but also from prewar historical reality. From 1920 to 1924 the United States, then the only major country back on the gold standard, received heavy gold shipments in payment for her large postwar surplus of exports, especially to Europe. Rather than let this inflowing gold feed inflation, the Federal Reserve authorities offset its effects, sometimes reducing their holdings of bills and securities on their own initiative and keeping some of the gold outside the credit base by circulating it as gold certificates.[65] In the five years after 1924 the U.S. gold stock changed little on balance, but its year-to-year changes were offset by changes in the domestic assets of the Federal Reserve banks. The Federal Reserve's ratio of gold to demand liabilities remained at nearly twice the legal requirement, further suggesting that the United States did "sterilize" gold during the 1920s. When reproached for this interference with the traditional adjustment mechanism, the Federal Reserve authorities were inclined to give the obvious answer that they were in effect holding much of the gold merely in trust for gold-exchange-standard countries, who might withdraw it whenever they saw fit.[66] The policy followed was no doubt justified from the domestic point of view, but it did interfere with international equilibration. That this interference did not put an immediate and unbearable strain on world payments is probably due in part to heavy American capital exports at the time. During the four years 1925–1928 the net total amount of foreign long-term securities floated in the United States was twice the amount floated in London. In addition, American businesses were making heavy direct investments abroad.[67]

Not until the second half of 1927 did the Federal Reserve reverse its gold sterilization. This reversal seems to have been the chief outcome of discussions among British, German, French, and American central bankers from July 1 to 6. (An attempt was made to preserve the secrecy of their discussions, held on a Long Island estate.) Besides international considerations, a slight recession in the United States prompted the Federal Reserve to cut its discount rates and buy securities vigorously. The balance of payments shifted in favor of Europe, gold flowed out of the United States, and the major European currencies strengthened on the exchanges. Sterling benefited notably.[68] Unfortunately, according to a widely accepted interpretation, this brief episode of cheap money fed a stock-market boom that grew highly speculative in 1928 and 1929. The profitability of bull speculation in Wall Street and the high yields obtainable on call loans to speculators shrank American capital exports and attracted funds from overseas. The efforts of the Federal Reserve to check the stock-

62. End-of-year figures for 24 European central banks show their total foreign-exchange holdings reaching an absolute peak in 1928. The share of foreign exchange in their end-of-year totals of gold and foreign exchange had peaked at 42.5 percent in 1927, dropped to 41.9 percent in 1928, and dropped more sharply thereafter. Vanes, *op. cit.*, pp. 333–334.

63. The years of 1922 through 1938 were covered so far as figures were available. On all this, see Nurkse, *International Currency Experience*, chap. IV and especially pp. 69, 237–240; and Committee on Finance & Industry, *Report*, pp. 83–84.

64. Arthur I. Bloomfield applied Nurkse's test to 11 central banks for the period 1880–1913, or such parts of that period as seemed relevant and for which statistics were available. International assets (gold, foreign exchange, and silver) and domestic income-earning assets (discounts, advances, and securities) moved in opposite directions 60 percent of the time and in the same direction 34 percent of the time (and in the remaining instances, one or the other of the two asset categories underwent virtually no change). *Monetary Policy Under the International Gold Standard: 1880–1914*, Federal Reserve Bank of New York, 1959, pp. 48–50.

Insofar, however, as variation in a central bank's domestic portfolio offset *only a fraction* of any opposite variation in its international assets, the latter might still have a multiple impact on the domestic money supply. Robert Triffin, *The Evolution of the International Monetary System: Historical Reappraisal and Future Perspectives*, Princeton, N.J.: Princeton University, 1964, p. 5.

65. The Federal Reserve decided to contract credit in the spring of 1923 despite an unprecedentedly large gold reserve. According to R. F. Harrod, this was the first great peacetime step away from the idea that monetary management should be primarily related to the international situation. *The Pound Sterling*, Essays in International Finance, No. 13, Princeton, N.J.: Princeton University, 1952, p. 4.

66. Nurkse, *International Currency Experience*, pp. 73–75; John T. Madden and Marcus Nadler, *The International Money Markets*, Englewood Cliffs, N.J.: Prentice-Hall, 1936, pp. 11–13.

67. Committee on Finance & Industry, *op. cit.*, p. 70.

68. Clarke, *op. cit.*, pp. 123–130.

market boom by renewed tight money, together with the efforts of European countries to check the loss of gold to the United States, led to tight money in many countries almost at the moment when, as hindsight reveals, business activity was turning downward.

The Bank of England apparently followed a policy of neutralization during the six years after the return to gold in 1925, trying to hold the total volume of credit available to the British economy stable within broad limits and match gains or losses of gold with reductions or increases in domestic earning assets.[69] This hardly meant managing credit with primary regard to the domestic economy; for the credit expansion appropriate to remedy unemployment would have made the gold position even more precarious. In France, the increase in gold and foreign-exchange assets of the central bank following stabilization of the franc at an undervalued level in 1926 was not allowed to have the full "rules-of-the-game" influence on domestic money and credit; the country was in no mood for a renewal of inflation.[70] In 1929 France had a larger gold stock per inhabitant than any other country except Argentina, and its gold stock was to double in the following three years.[71]

The general conclusion suggested so far had already appeared in the Macmillan Report, issued in England in June 1931. The report blamed "the instability of post-war international finance" partly on the fact that "Movements of gold have ceased of late to have what used to be considered their 'normal' effect on the domestic credit policy of certain countries, notably France and the United States. In recent years it has been impossible to rely on action being taken by both the country losing gold and the country gaining gold to preserve international equilibrium, the one meeting the other half way. . . ."[72]

The façade of a restored gold standard

In summary, the gold standard of the late 1920s was hardly more than a façade. It involved extreme measures to economize on gold through withdrawing gold coins and adopting gold-bullion or gold-exchange arrangements. It involved the neutralization or offsetting of international influences on domestic money supplies, incomes, and prices. Gold-standard methods of balance-of-payments equilibration were largely destroyed and were not replaced by any alternative. The new system has aptly been described as "a temporary exchange pegging device"; it consisted of "pegging operations on a vast scale."[73] Some of the pegs were at clearly wrong levels. With both the price-and-income and the exchange-rate mechanisms of balance-of-payments adjustment out of operation, disequilibriums were accumulated or merely palliated, not continuously corrected. Too much depended on *ad hoc* policies and switches in policy. Mistakes in diagnosis and lags in the effectiveness of policies threatened perverse results.

---

69. Nurkse, *International Currency Experience*, pp. 75–76.

70. *Ibid.*, p. 77.

71. Vanes, *op. cit.*, pp. 224–225. This book, pp. 197ff. and *passim*, reviews the facts and a considerable literature concerning gold sterilization in the twenties.

72. Committee on Finance & Industry, *op. cit.*, pp. 68–69.

73. Brown, *op. cit.*, **II**, 805. The epithet "façade" is also Brown's.

CHAPTER SEVENTEEN

The Great Depression and the End of the Gold Standard

The background of depression

Continuing our historical survey will help show in what degree and in what ways the international monetary system was precarious. The conditions menacing international arrangements and general business activity were thoroughly intermingled. Precarious positions were being shored up and adjustments delayed in individual lines of production, in currency parities, and in international payments. Agriculture is a notable example of the first kind. The quick postwar recovery in European agriculture brought no corresponding cutbacks in North America and other areas of great wartime expansion in farm output. The prices of the staple foodstuffs and fibers of international commerce came under severe downward pressure in the middle and late 1920s. Governments or government-encouraged cartels were trying to support the prices of wheat, sugar, coffee, rubber, tin, copper, nitrates, and other primary products by such devices as holding supplies off the market. These interferences with the price signals that would otherwise have promoted gradual cutbacks in excessive production threatened, together with growing stockpiles, to make a crash in prices all the more severe when it finally came and all the more damaging to the balance-of-payments

positions and the currency parities of the primary-producing export-oriented countries. The farm depression in the United States accounted for most of the bank suspensions, numbering an average of 700 a year in the last four years of the 1920s.

International imbalances, such as reflected in the American current-account surplus, were to a large extent being temporarily palliated by international lending. In this way, the strong suction of gold into the United States from 1921 through 1924 was on the whole stopped and even very slightly reversed from 1925 to the beginning of 1929. American loans in the immediate postwar years had been mainly for relief and rehabilitation in Europe. In the early and middle 1920s a number of loans were arranged through intergovernmental cooperation to help such countries as Austria, Hungary, Germany, Belgium, Poland, and Italy put their finances in order and stabilize their currencies. Then German borrowing offset and more than offset German reparations payments. American private lending to Central Europe, especially Germany, expanded vastly in the late 1920s. Many of the loans went for commercially unprofitable projects that contributed little to the ability of the debtors to pay interest and repay the principal when due. National and municipal governments floated bonds in the American capital market to pay for public works. In some areas, such as Latin America, much of the international investment did contribute to production, but of coffee and other commodities already in oversupply. Toward the end of the decade an increasing proportion of international lending, British as well as American, was at short term, and many short-term loans were being used to finance long-term capital projects.

The gold-exchange standard, with many central banks holding substantial parts of their legal reserves in the form of the bank deposits or securities of London and a few other financial centers rather than in actual gold, spelled a precarious direct and indirect pyramiding of claims on a narrow ultimate gold base. Any serious strain on a full-gold-standard center would cause difficulties for its satellites, and conversely, heavy withdrawals by the satellites would cause difficulties for the center.

The system of the 1920s was not merely precarious; it contained seeds of monetary deflation in particular. Whether or not there was an overall shortage of gold—a question much discussed at the time—the existing supply was unevenly distributed. The United States in the early 1920s and France in the late 1920s acquired and kept exceptionally large shares of the world's gold. Other countries, including England, were in much the same position as if there had been an overall shortage. Their external positions required restrictive policies at home, while countries with relative surpluses of gold were reluctant, for fear of inflation, to pursue the expansionary policies that would have eased the strain on the others. For the world economy as a whole, monetary policies were thus bedeviled by a clash, manifesting itself differently in different countries, between domestic and balance-of-payments considerations. Policy could not aim at a single consistent set of objectives.[1]

The worldwide downward drift in commodity prices even several years before the depression struck may well be evidence that the international monetary system had a deflationary bias. Between 1923 (after recovery from the postwar depression) and 1929, sensitive commodity price indexes compiled on the same basis for different countries showed declines ranging from 10 percent in the United States to 20 percent in Great Britain. Between 1925 and 1929 the average prices of commodities moving in international trade fell by over 10 percent.[2] In the United States, the annual average index of wholesale prices had recovered by 1925 to only 7 percent above its 1922 depression trough. From 1925 to 1929 the index fell 8 percent. By 1928, in fact, it was already down to its previous trough on an annual average basis. The U.S. consumer price index recovered by 6 percent between 1922 and 1926 and then fell to 3 percent below the 1926 level in both 1928 and 1929.

Growth of the U.S. money supply during the 1920s was slow in comparison with the annual growth of 4 percent or so that seems appropriate in the light of long-run experience. Defined as total deposits adjusted and currency outside banks, the money supply in mid-1929 was 38.4 percent above the level of mid-1920, 14.2 percent above mid-1925, and 0.9 percent above mid-1928. Defined as demand deposits adjusted and outside currency, the mid-1929 money supply was only 10.4 percent above mid-1920, 4.9 percent above mid-1925, and 1.2 percent above mid-1928. (At a 4 percent annual rate of growth, the mid-1929 money supply would have been 42.3 percent above the 1920 level and 17.0 percent above the 1925 level.)

These figures perhaps suggest incipient tendencies but certainly do not warrant any sweeping conclusions about unmistakable deflation in the late 1920s. One familiar contrary line of interpretation of the subsequent crash emphasizes credit expansion and an unusual inflation without general price inflation. The most conspicuous signs of inflation were localized, notably in Wall Street. By September 1929, Standard and Poor's monthly average index of common stock prices had shot up to twice the level of less than two and a half years before. The Federal Reserve had begun its most notable episode of cheap money in the second half of 1927 with the partial purpose of easing the strain on the gold reserves of the Bank of England. This is an example of the lack of steady, consistent policies during the 1920s and of the use of *ad hoc* expedients based in variable degrees on internal and balance-of-payments considerations. The policy of 1927 appears to have unintentionally fed the Wall Street boom, so attracting speculative money to the United States and frustrating its own international objectives. The later reversion to tight money, as well as the high interest rates on call money used in financing stock-market speculation, also attracted funds from all over the world, under the system of fixed exchange rates, and gave rise to domestically inappropriate tight-money policies in countries tending to lose gold.[3] On Wall Street, stock market activity had evolved into the stage where the typical speculator kept buying not because he thought earnings and dividends justified the prevailing prices but because experience had taught him to expect that he could sell out later at a profit to other speculators still more daring than himself. By this time, a mere leveling off of stock prices would cause speculators to lose interest and would bring on the crash. Widespread holding of stocks on narrow margins made the crash feed on itself, once it began. But neither the stock market crash nor any other specific shock can properly be blamed for the severity of the depression that followed. The main emphasis apparently belongs on a passive monetary policy that permitted the total U.S. money supply to shrink by more than one-fourth in less than three years.

The foregoing paragraphs sketch in an admittedly oversimplified and incomplete background of a complicated process of economic deterioration. The emphasis on matters related to international monetary arrangements should not give the impression that the entire explanation lies in this sphere.

Signs of depression had already appeared at various times between late 1927 and mid-1929 in Australia, the Dutch East Indies, Germany, Finland, Brazil, Poland, Canada, and Argentina; but serious depression did not spread widely until after the industrial downturn in the United States in mid-1929 and the stock crash in October. The first impact was a reversal of the surge of speculative foreign money that had been coming to New York to share in the stock-market boom; sterling strengthened briefly to an average of 1½ cents above par in December, and London gained gold.

The first half of 1930 brought hopeful signs that the worldwide slump might remain mild. Monetary policies, as gauged by interest rates, generally eased. International lending revived, with new foreign issues being floated in the United States and Britain. By midyear, however, deterioration resumed. By and large, the monetary authorities in major countries did little further to ease credit policies. American lending abroad virtually ceased and gave way to repatriation of funds.[4] The protectionist

---

1. Three of the six conditions listed by Edward M. Bernstein as causing "centers of deflation in the world economy in the 1920's" are the overvaluation of sterling, the undervaluation of the French franc, and "a lack of sufficient gold and foreign exchange reserves to avoid the spread and intensification of depression and deflation." (Bernstein's other three causes are reparations and other German economic problems, agricultural depression in the United States, and highly protective American tariffs.) *International Effects of U.S. Economic Policy*, study paper no. 16 for the Joint Economic Committee; Washington: U.S. Government Printing Office, 1960, p. 8n.

Per Jacobsson, late Managing Director of the International Monetary Fund, suggested that the decline in agricultural prices in the latter half of the decade and the general deflation from 1929 on were partly connected with excessive gold contents of currencies. ". . . if the parities had been fixed at a lower level the individual countries would not have had to worry too much about whether they possessed sufficient cover, particularly in gold, in relation to their notes and sight liabilities." As early as 1917 Jacobsson had insisted that efforts to maintain prewar reserve ratios would threaten a deflationary bias, and in 1931 the Gold Delegation of the League of Nations recommended a reduction in reserve ratios. *Some Monetary Problems International and National*, London: Oxford University Press, 1958, pp. 18–19.

THE GREAT DEPRESSION AND THE END OF THE GOLD STANDARD

In the judgment of J. R. Hicks, the world "was trying to manage with a gold supply, which was . . . extremely inadequate" in relation to the price and wage inflation that had occurred during and after World War I. Inadequate adjustment of exchange rates contributed to the weakness of the Bank of England and the German Reichsbank, interfering with their responsibilities as lenders of last resort. *A Contribution to the Theory of the Trade Cycle*, Oxford: Clarendon Press, 1950, p. 163n.

According to the Macmillan Report, issued in England in 1931, debtor countries were usually unable "to adjust their balance of payments so rapidly and completely as to permit a complete cessation of borrowing; yet, in so far as they export gold, their credit as borrowers suffers. Thus, having lost their gold and not being able to borrow, they are forced off the gold standard. And creditor countries, on the other hand, when they have accumulated more than their fair share of gold, far beyond their legal requirements, fearing to provoke an inflation by letting the new gold produce a rise in prices, try, in effect, to make themselves insensitive to further imports. Thus, when equilibrium is profoundly upset between creditor and debtor nations, the whole world suffers. The adjustments to be made are greater than can be accomplished by a movement of short-money funds or by a small alteration in prices. The debtor countries suffer a serious deflationary crisis and some of them, probably failing to meet their problems by drastic measures, may be forced off the gold standard; the creditor countries will be affected both by the depression in the debtor countries and by the influx of large quantities of gold. Here is, perhaps, the major part of the immediate explanation of the collapse of international prices. . . ." Committee on Finance & Industry, *Report*, London: His Majesty's Stationery Office, 1931, pp. 83–84.

2. H. V. Hodson, *Slump and Recovery*, London: Oxford University Press, 1938, p. 34.

3. Cf. Paul Einzig, *A Dynamic Theory of Forward Exchange*, London: Macmillan, 1961, pp. 316–317, 528–529. On the adverse impacts abroad of reduced capital outflows from and increased capital inflows into the United States in 1928 and 1929, see also Stephen V. O. Clarke, *Central Bank Cooperation: 1924–31*, New York: Federal Reserve Bank of New York, 1967, pp. 147–150; and F. Robert Vanes, *De Internationale Gouden Standaard*, Antwerp/Amsterdam: Standaard-Boekhandel, 1951, p. 292.

4. Clarke, *op. cit.*, pp. 168–173.

Smoot-Hawley Tariff of 1930 reinforced the effects of depression in contracting American imports. All in all, total American spending and lending abroad shrank by two-thirds between 1927–1929 and 1932–1933.

By mid-1932 world industrial production and the real volume of world trade had both fallen to slightly below 70 percent of their 1929 average levels. Industrial production regained its earlier peak toward the end of 1935. World trade recovered more slowly, almost reaching its earlier peak in 1937, only to fall off again.[5] Table 17.1 gives some indications of the depth and duration of the depression in several major countries. Two countries in particular call for comment. The comparatively good record of the United Kingdom is rather deceptive, reflecting the depressed level of economic activity from which the slide into further depression began; but in part it is genuine, showing the relief provided by the depreciation of sterling in 1931 and the stimulus of a vigorous easy-money policy begun in 1932. Japan's record seems partly due to policies of abundant credit and government deficit spend-

ing (largely for military purposes). Furthermore, the yen was allowed to depreciate to whatever level necessary to equilibrate the balance of payments without drastic controls. The yen lost almost two-thirds of its earlier gold value, as compared to a loss of about 40 percent by the pound sterling and the dollar. Yet price inflation was moderate; even in 1937, after the jump associated with the invasion of China, the price index had hardly regained its 1929 level.[6]

As the depression deepened after 1929, countries particularly hard pressed by shrinking exports and payments deficits reacted in either of two ways: by leaving the gold standard and letting the currency depreciate or by imposing exchange and import controls. In 1929 and 1930 currency depreciation was the course taken by countries such as Argentina, Brazil, Paraguay, Uruguay, Australia, New Zealand, Venezuela, Spain, and China (whose currency, still on the silver standard, depreciated against gold). Thus far, none of the dominant countries in international trade allowed their currencies to depreciate. Only a few countries,

TABLE 17.1. *Indicators of the great depression in six countries*

	United Kingdom	France	Germany	Canada	United States	Japan
Industrial production						
Lowest year & production then as percentage of the 1929 level	1931: 86	1932: 74[a]	1932: 58	1932: 68	1932: 55	1931: 92
Year when the 1929 level was regained or passed	1934	1950	1936	1936	1937	1933
Real national income						
Lowest year and income then as percentage of the 1929 level	1932: 93	1934: 83	1932: 80	1933: 76	1933: 68	[b]
Year when the 1929 level was regained or passed	1934	Postwar?	1934	1938	1937	[b]

[a] After a partial recovery, French industrial production relapsed in 1935 to 78 percent of the 1929 level.

[b] Japanese real income did not decline below the 1929 level, though the 1929 figure was about 1 percent below that of 1928.

SOURCES: For industrial production, Organization for European Economic Cooperation, *Industrial Statistics, 1900–1957*, Paris 1958, p. 9. For Germany and Japan, however, the figures are League of Nations data reproduced in Harold G. Moulton, *Controlling Factors in Economic Development*, Washington: Brookings Institution, 1949, p. 374. For real national income, Colin Clark, *The Conditions of Economic Progress*, 2nd ed., London: Macmillan, 1951, pp. 46, 54, 63, 80, facing 101, 136.

including Spain, Iran, and Turkey, imposed new exchange controls at that time. Until the late spring of 1931, the depression in many respects followed the course of ordinary business slumps of the past. The gold standard was still intact in Western Europe and the United States. Steadiness or slight increases in seasonally adjusted figures of industrial production in Germany and the United States even offered some hope during the first few months of the year. In Great Britain and most other countries, however, economic activity kept on sinking.

The 1931 crisis on the continent

Against this background a worldwide financial and economic relapse occurred. A chain reaction involved one currency after another. Telling the story of one crisis such as this seems worth while because it reveals the shakiness of the gold-standard façade, because it illustrates some general characteristics of speculation against pegged exchange rates, and because it offers sheer morbid fascination. The story may begin with the Austrian Credit-Anstalt.[7] This firm, founded by the Rothschilds in 1855 and associated with that family ever since, had assets and liabilities amounting to 70 percent of the total for all Austrian banks. The disintegration of the Austro-Hungarian Empire at the end of World War I had left this bank, like Vienna itself, overextended for the territory remaining to it. Furthermore, the Credit-Anstalt had absorbed another financially weak institution in October 1929. Like other Viennese banks, the Credit-Anstalt had acquired funds at short term in London, New York, Amsterdam, Brussels, and elsewhere and had made short-term and even long-term loans to industry not only in Austria but also in Hungary, Poland, Rumania, and Yugoslavia. The stock-exchange and business slump ate into the value of the bank's portfolio. By the beginning of 1931, its losses had reached an amount estimated at nearly 85 percent of total capital and reserves shown on its balance sheet. In the second week of May, when the difficulties of the Credit-Anstalt were announced to the public, a blind *sauve qui peut* gripped its foreign creditors. The run affected all Austrian banks.[8] The Rothschilds, the Austrian National Bank, and the Austrian government stepped in with financial support,

relieving the situation for a while. Confidence had been shaken, however, and withdrawals from the Credit-Anstalt persisted throughout May.

Political developments were worsening the situation. With tariffs and other trade barriers mounting throughout the world and trenching on her trade, especially with Hungary, Czechoslovakia, and the Balkans, Austria had sought relief in a customs union with Germany. An agreement had been announced on March 21, before the Credit-Anstalt difficulties became acute. France, however, chose to regard the proposed economic arrangement, sponsored by the peace-minded Brüning government of Germany, as an *Anschluss*, or political connection between Germany and Austria, in violation of the postwar treaties. The French Chamber of Deputies debated the question in May. The idea of reconciliation with Germany came under attack, and its chief advocate, Briand, failed to win the French presidency. France's great financial power at the time—the large gold and foreign-exchange holdings of her banks—made her government's attitude ominous. Rumors circulated that French bankers were pulling funds out of Austria.[9]

Meanwhile, the finances of the Credit-Anstalt and of the Austrian government were becoming more and more intermingled

5. Chart in Bank for International Settlements, 10th *Annual Report* (1939–1940), p. 41.

6. On Japan, see W. Arthur Lewis, *Economic Survey 1919–1939*, London: Allen & Unwin, 1949, pp. 118–120, and for the price index, Colin Clark, *Conditions of Economic Progress*, 2nd ed., London: Macmillan, 1951, p. 137.

7. Full name: Oesterreichische Credit-Anstalt für Handel und Gewerbe. *See, inter alia*, Hodson, *op. cit.*, chap. III.

8. Vanes, *op. cit.*, p. 319.

9. According to Gottfried Haberler, the collapse of the Credit-Anstalt was "triggered by the withdrawal of French credits in reprisal for the proposed Austro-German customs union. . . ." *International Payments Problems*, Washington: American Enterprise Institute, 1966, p. 4.

through the state of public confidence. By late May, when the Austrian Parliament passed a law authorizing a government guarantee of new liabilities of the Credit-Anstalt, the shakiness of the government's own credit robbed the gesture of real significance. The run on Austrian banks and the public's demand for foreign exchange was temporarily stemmed by a foreign-currency loan made available to the Credit-Anstalt on May 31 by the Bank for International Settlements and eleven central banks. The total amount of $14 million, however, was inadequate under the circumstances. Negotiations for further foreign credits fell through, largely because the French were making their cooperation conditional on abandonment of the proposed customs union.[10] Unwilling to accept these conditions and also facing domestic opposition on the question of guaranteeing the foreign liabilities of the Credit-Anstalt, the Austrian government resigned on June 16. Hours afterwards, the Bank of England advanced to the Austrian National Bank the amount of the abortive international loan, thereby arousing some resentment in France.

Armed with the British loan, the new Austrian government guaranteed the Credit-Anstalt's existing liabilities to foreign creditors. The chief creditors, for their part, accepted a standstill agreement not to press their claims for two years. The government also guaranteed deposits at the bank, superseded its management, and retrenched on its expenses. Representatives of the foreign creditors took part in this reorganization.

The standstill arrangements were fairly well observed for a time, but they did not entirely stop the run on Austria. In the following months the Austrian National Bank lost most of its large stock of foreign exchange. Exchange controls were imposed in October to restrain capital flight by Austrian nationals, collect foreign-exchange receipts, and conserve foreign exchange for meeting the country's foreign obligations; the international system of unrestricted multilateral payments was beginning to crumble. Furthermore, the standstill of foreign claims on Austria created doubts about the soundness of banks holding such claims and about the continued convertibility of creditor-country currencies at existing exchange rates.[11]

Austria's plight had its parallels in Hungary, Rumania, and elsewhere. As early as May and June it was raising doubts about the financial condition of Germany. German short-term foreign liabilities were almost double German short-term claims on foreigners. The danger was evident. The Reichsbank lost nearly one-third of its gold and foreign-exchange reserves in the first 12 days of June alone,[12] and an increase in its discount rate from 5 percent to 7 percent on the 13th failed to stop the run. On June 20, President Hoover proposed a one-year moratorium on all governmental war debts and reparations.[13] The French delayed agreement until July 6, depriving the gesture of much of its psychological effect. June 25 brought the announcement that the Bank for International Settlements, the Bank of England, the Bank of France, and the Federal Reserve Bank of New York had put together $100 million worth of credit for the Reichsbank. This credit was originally intended as a temporary measure to meet end-of-month strain on the Reichsbank and was due to expire in mid-July. In fact it proved inadequate, and repayment was not even started until the following year. Dr. Luther, the president of the Reichsbank, hastened to London, Paris, and the Bank for International Settlements in Basel in search of a new loan. His zeal perturbed foreign financiers and Germans alike. Partly because the French insisted upon unacceptable political strings, he had to return from his journey with only vague promises. The proposed customs union with Austria was finally abandoned, anyway, on September 3.

On July 13, the very day when Dr. Luther and other central bankers were meeting unsuccessfully in Basel, the Darmstädter und National Bank closed. It fell victim to a run touched off by failure of the largest German textile company, to which it had large loans outstanding. The textile failure at the beginning of July had helped convert a run mainly of Germany's foreign creditors into a flight from the mark into foreign exchange by Germans as well. The Danat Bank, as it was called for short, was reopened later in the month under restrictions, including a moratorium on its debts until July 31 and a government guarantee of its deposits thereafter.

Upon the Danat failure, the German government decreed a two-day bank and stock-exchange holiday and a partial bank moratorium lasting until August 5. Rudimentary exchange controls were introduced. When the financial markets reopened on July 16, the

Reichsbank raised its discount rate to 10 percent. Briefly in early August the rate rose to 15 percent. Further international conferences in July and August produced little more than a limited standstill agreement affecting German indebtedness to foreign banks. By this time, however, Germany was learning to rely more on proliferating exchange controls than on additional foreign loans.[14]

The 1931 crisis in Great Britain

Runs on the currencies of Austria, Germany, Great Britain, and other countries overlapped in time. The standstill agreement and earlier events froze about £70 million of British short-term assets in Germany. Against the background of almost chronic weakness in the British balance of payments, the Danat Bank failure and bank holiday in Germany had already shaken the London stock market and the foreign-exchange value of the pound, making gold export profitable for arbitrageurs. "In the two weeks ended July 29 the Bank of England lost $200 million in gold and dollars, one quarter of its international reserves."[15] In response, the Bank raised its discount rate from 2½ to 3½ percent on July 23 and to 4½ percent on July 30—still a "very modest figure," according to pro-gold-standard historians.

On the very day of the Danat failure and of the fruitless Basel meeting, July 13, the Committee on Finance and Industry issued its report, the so-called Macmillan Report. The report unintentionally emphasized the vulnerability of sterling by revealing that while London's known short-term sterling claims on foreigners at the end of March had amounted to only about £153 million, much of which was now being immobilized on the Continent, foreigners' deposits and sterling bill holdings in London amounted to about £407 million.[16] Furthermore, it was generally known that foreign holdings of the 5 percent War Loan alone amounted to hundreds of millions of pounds. Of course, London was a world banking center, and there is nothing unusual about a banker's having short-term liabilities far in excess of immediately liquid assets. (In fact, the Macmillan Committee even considered its figures more reassuring than alarming.) In time of crisis, though, the fact is inconvenient. Furthermore, the Macmillan Report recommended a cheap-money policy to central banks as an antidepression measure. This recommendation intensified foreign worries about whether England would defend the gold standard to the utmost.[17]

On August 1 the Bank of England announced that the Bank of France and the Federal Reserve Banks had agreed to lend it a total of $250 million. An increase of £15 million in the permissible fiduciary banknote issue also expanded the available gold reserve. One conservative observer interpreted the foreign loan as a sign that the British authorities were indisposed to let the outflow of gold tighten the internal money market and so call the classical corrective forces into play.[18] The deflationary effects of the gold losses were largely offset; about two-thirds of the contraction of the credit base that would otherwise have accompanied the loss of gold was replaced by central-bank credit.[19] For better or worse, the "rules of the game" of the gold standard were still being violated.

The financial markets apparently took the foreign credits as a sign of weakness and the

10. Clarke, *op. cit.*, pp. 186–188.

11. Clarke, *op. cit.*, pp. 186, 189.

12. Calculated from figures in Vanes, *op. cit.*, p. 320.

13. As things worked out, reparations never were resumed after the Hoover Moratorium year. Except for a few token payments, the Allies ceased paying installments on their war debts to the United States. Only Finland continued paying in full.

14. Vanes, *op. cit.*, p. 320; Clarke, *op. cit.*, pp. 190–193, 199–201, 227.

15. Clarke, *op. cit.*, p. 296.

16. The Bank of England's gold reserves at the end of March amounted to 35 percent of the latter figure. Calculated from Vanes, *op. cit.*, p. 322.

17. On this last point, see Vanes, *op. cit.*, p. 325.

18. B. M. Anderson, *Economics and the Public Welfare*, New York: Van Nostrand, 1949, p. 245.

19. W. A. Brown, Jr., *The International Gold Standard Reinterpreted*, New York: National Bureau of Economic Research, 1940, **II**, p. 1022.

increase in the fiduciary issue, together with the report of the Committee on National Expenditure (the May Committee), as an omen of inflation. With firm official support delayed, the sterling exchange rate broke badly on Wednesday the 5th. Rumors of French uncooperativeness flooded the markets.[20]

The May Report, published on July 31, worried about growth of the government budget deficit and recommended cuts in unemployment relief, government salaries, and other expenditures, as well as tax increases. Given the pre-Keynesian notions then prevalent in all three political parties about the evil of a government deficit even in time of depression, the revelations of the May Report were alarming. Prime Minister MacDonald and his government resigned on August 24 because of resentment among fellow members of the Labor Party, both inside and outside his cabinet, over some of the proposed economies. At the urging of the King and of Conservative and Liberal leaders,[21] MacDonald then promptly organized a National government, whose Labor members were repudiated by their own party. The new coalition cabinet was expected to save the gold standard. In a radio speech on the evening of August 25, MacDonald warned of hyperinflation, no less, that would follow a fall of the pound.[22]

Reassured by the new government's economy program, a group of French and American commercial banks agreed to lend the British authorities a total of about $400 million. Announcement of his aid on August 28, together with presentation on September 10 of a revised and balanced government budget, gave only a brief respite. Financial aid in two separate arrangements, with the second coming only after virtual exhaustion of the first batch of credit had become common knowledge, formed a strategy far inferior to what a single impressive package would have been. Resentment was spreading in the Labor Party and in union circles about the budget economies, feared wage cuts, and the supposed pressure of foreign bankers. With the Bank of England supporting sterling in the spot and forward markets, the proceeds of the foreign loans were soon used up. Counting forward as well as spot sales, the Bank's losses of gold and foreign exchange from mid-July through September 19 totaled over £200 million. (The equivalent amount in dollars of 1972 purchasing power would be over $3 billion.) At the close of business on Saturday the 19th, the Bank of England's remaining gold and foreign exchange exceeded by only £5 million the total of its obligations under forward-exchange contracts and the debts to the central banks and the New York and Paris commercial banks.[23]

The flight of funds and the reserve losses had accelerated in mid-September. On September 15 the Admiralty announced that pay cuts had caused "unrest" among sailors at Invergordon. Some foreign newspapers exaggerated this incident into a "mutiny." On September 18 the Treasury's request for further credits in New York and Paris met with friendly and sympathetic, but negative, replies. By the close of the short market session in New York on Saturday the 19th, the sterling rate plunged to $4.17.[24]

That evening the Bank of England, after consulting with the British government all along, finally stated that its gold reserve had fallen to the point where it could no longer maintain the gold standard. The Cabinet ratified the inevitable decision the following day, Sunday, and released an official statement announcing that it would introduce the appropriate bill in Parliament, that it had already authorized the Bank of England to suspend gold payments, and that the Stock Exchange would remain closed Monday. Appealing to patriotism, the announcement warned British citizens against further straining the exchanges by buying foreign securities. The banks had agreed to cooperate by restricting British purchases of foreign exchange to those required for the actual needs of trade or for meeting existing contracts. The government would take further measures if they seemed advisable. The announcement concluded:

His Majesty's Government are securing a balanced Budget, and the internal position of the country is sound. This position must be maintained. It is one thing to go off the Gold standard with an unbalanced Budget and uncontrolled inflation; it is quite another thing to take this measure, not because of internal financial difficulties, but because of excessive withdrawals of borrowed capital. The ultimate resources of this country are enormous, and there is no doubt that the present exchange difficulties will prove only temporary.[25]

All on the next day, Monday the 21st, the Commons and Lords passed and the King signed the Gold Standard (Amendment) Act, confirming the cabinet's action and thus

"amending" the gold standard out of existence.[26] One section of the new act authorized
such exchange controls as the Treasury might
see fit. On Tuesday the Treasury issued the
following order, which was not rescinded until
March 2, 1932:

. . . until further notice purchases of foreign exchange or transfers of funds with the object of
acquiring such exchange directly or indirectly by
British subjects or persons resident in the United
Kingdom shall be prohibited except for the purpose
of financing: (1) Normal trading requirements;
(2) contracts existing before September 21, 1931;
(3) reasonable travelling or other personal purposes.[27]

Britain left the gold standard with Bank rate
still at 4½ percent, a rate which, according to
some pro-gold-standard observers, was too low
and indicated failure to employ classical
weapons in a real battle to defend the pound.
On the other hand, a very high Bank rate during the crisis might have been taken as a sign
of desperation and so have even intensified the
panicky run on the gold reserves. In any event,
the Bank of England raised its rate to 6 percent on the very first day off gold, presumably
as a gesture of determination to resist inflation
and to rally confidence in the unattached
pound.

During the first week, the pound fluctuated
between about $4.30 and $3.40 (in comparison with the previous mint par of $4.86656).
Foreign holders of sterling suffered a corresponding loss. The depreciation cost the Bank
of France, for instance, an amount equal to
seven times its capital. The loss of the Netherlands Bank, though only approximately equal
to its capital, was the more shocking because it
directly resulted from trust in the word of the
Bank of England. Dr. Vissering, head of the
Netherlands Bank, had telephoned the Bank of
England on Friday, September 18, asking
whether the gold value of his sterling balance
was safe. Though the truth was almost certainly already known to be just the opposite,[28]
Dr. Vissering received reassurances. The
Netherlands Bank thereupon decided to support the Bank of England by refraining from
converting its sterling into gold, as it still could
have done. For the resulting loss, the Netherlands Bank was severely blamed by its government; and its next annual report was bitter on
the matter. The episode cost Dr. Vissering his
job.[29]

Depreciation of sterling had wider repercussions. Most European stock exchanges closed
immediately for various periods of time. The
markets in New York, Tokyo, and elsewhere
declined. Credit tightened and central-bank
discount rates went up in many countries, most
strikingly in Scandinavia. Within a few days
the Swedish Riksbank lost about 100 million
kroner of gold and foreign exchange reserves.
Despite closing of the stock exchange, increase
in the bank rate, official assurances that the
country would stay on gold, and attempts to
borrow in New York and Paris, Sweden was
driven off the gold standard one week after
England. Norway left gold the same day, September 27, and on the 28th, Denmark confirmed the departure from gold already represented by its gold export embargo of the 22nd.

20. Clarke, *op. cit.*, p. 207.

21. See the authorities quoted in Reginald
Bassett, *Nineteen Thirty-One Political Crisis*, London: Macmillan, 1958, pp. 149–150, 155–157, 160,
343, 358–375.

22. Quoted in *ibid.*, pp. 178–179n.

23. Clarke, *op. cit.*, pp. 204, 209–216; D. E.
Moggridge, *British Monetary Policy*, 1924–1931,
Cambridge: Cambridge University Press, 1972, p.
193 and footnote.

24. Chart in Clarke, *op. cit.*, p. 208.

25. Bassett, *op. cit.*, pp. 238–239.

26. J. M. Keynes, exaggerating, said that sterling
had not left gold, but that gold had left sterling.
(Brown, *op. cit.*, II, p. 1052.) Keynes's witticism
presumably meant that gold had been appreciating
in purchasing power and that in September 1931
sterling finally ceased appreciating in step with gold.

27. *The Economist*, 26 September 1931, p. 555.

28. Cf. Brown, *op. cit.*, II, pp. 1092–1093.

29. Anderson, *op. cit.*, pp. 246–247, 252–253;
Walter A. Morton, *British Finance*, 1930–1940,
Madison: University of Wisconsin Press, 1943, p.
46n. Montagu Norman, Governor of the Bank of
England, was out of the country at the time for a
rest. He had collapsed of physical exhaustion on
July 29 and was almost entirely out of action until
the crisis was over. Bassett, *op. cit.*, pp. 62–63n.;
Clarke, *op. cit.*, pp. 204, 210.

At least 35 countries left the gold standard from April 1929 to April 1933, as shown in the following list,[30] though some of the dates are uncertain because of the piecemeal and unofficial manner in which some countries acted at first.

1929
    April   –Uruguay
    November –Argentina
    December –Brazil

1930
    March   –Australia
    April   –New Zealand
    September–Venezuela

1931
    August   –Mexico
    September–United Kingdom, Canada, India, Sweden, Denmark, Norway, Egypt, Irish Free State, British Malaya, Palestine
    October   –Austria, Portugal, Finland, Bolivia, Salvador
    December –Japan

1932
    January   –Colombia, Nicaragua, Costa Rica
    April   –Greece, Chile
    May   –Peru
    June   –Ecuador, Siam
    July   –Yugoslavia

1933
    January   –Union of South-Africa
    April   –Honduras, United States

As the gold standard disintegrated, many countries decided to keep their currencies at least approximately stable in terms of sterling and fluctuating with it against the currencies still on gold. Typically they had close trading and financial ties with Britain. As Britain introduced restrictions on overseas lending after the 1931 crisis and again in 1934 and 1936, preferential access to the British capital market became an additional reason for maintaining the link with sterling. Thus the Sterling Area was born as an informal group of countries pegging their currencies to sterling and holding their official external reserves largely in the form of sterling balances. Its early members—the British dominions and colonies (except Canada, Newfoundland, and Hong Kong), Ireland, Portugal, Egypt, and Iraq—

were joined within a few years by Thailand, the Scandinavian countries, Estonia, Latvia, and Iran. Several other countries, including Japan and Argentina, kept their exchange rates stable on sterling for several years without generally being regarded as members of the Area. (On the other hand, the Free City of Danzig, whose gulden had been on a sterling-exchange standard since 1923, switched to a gold peg in September 1931.) As the exchange controls of World War II gave the Sterling Area a more formal status, its non-British members began dropping away.[31]

Free sterling in 1931–1932

The first week of wild fluctuations in sterling exchange in September 1931 was followed by a few weeks of relative dullness, with quotations in the neighborhood of $3.90, about 20 percent below the old par. A sharp decline then carried the rate to a low of $3.23 on December 1, 34 percent below par. Thereafter the pound oscillated upward toward a brief peak of about $3.80 at the beginning of April 1932. Apparent influences early in the new year included weakening of confidence in the dollar by the Glass-Steagall Act and a budget deficit in the United States, British announcement that debts to the United States and France would be paid on time, and the start of a considerable return flow of capital to London. On April 19 Chancellor of the Exchequer Neville Chamberlain announced that makeshift methods of intervention in the foreign-exchange market would be replaced by an Exchange Equalisation Account. The Account (which did not actually begin operations until June or July) would be managed by the Bank of England under Treasury control. Its dealings in the market, whose details were to be kept secret, were supposed to smooth out excessive short-run rate fluctuations.[32] Bullishness on sterling abated, and the rate fell back to just under $3.70, where it held during May and early June. In subsequent months sterling drifted gently downward against the dollar. Table 17.2 shows the monthly average quotations through the end of 1932. The lowest of the immediate postdepreciation months was December 1931 and the lowest of the entire 1930s was November 1932.

Surveying sterling's first year off gold, the

TABLE 17.2. *Sterling exchange in 1931–1932*

	Monthly average rate in U.S. cents	Percentage of old parity
1931		
August	485.7725	99.83
September	453.1260	93.11
October	388.9291	79.92
November	371.9934	76.44
December	337.3707	69.33
1932		
January	343.1210	70.51
February	345.6316	71.02
March	363.9304	74.78
April	374.9994	77.06
May	367.5140	75.52
June	364.6648	74.93
July	354.9564	72.94
August	347.5721	71.42
September	347.1062	71.33
October	339.6163	69.79
November	327.5267	67.30
December	327.8679	67.37

SOURCE: Federal Reserve, *Banking and Monetary Statistics*, p. 681.

London *Economist* felt that "on the whole sterling has thrived better than might have been expected—certainly much better than might have been inferred from the lugubrious prophecies heard immediately before the suspension of the gold standard."[33]

This judgment is contradicted by the League of Nations' authoritative survey of *International Currency Experience*. It cites the period between abandonment of gold in September 1931 and establishment of the Exchange Equalisation Account the following spring as an example of the unsatisfactory operation generally to be expected of freely fluctuating exchanges. It argues that disequilibrating capital movements were at work in the first few months off gold. The outflow of foreign funds largely determined the depreciation of sterling, while prospects of further depreciation largely determined the outflow itself. After a return of confidence early in 1932, the movement became cumulative in the reverse direction. "It was the realization of the exchange market's

inability to maintain a stable equilibrium, at any rate in the short run, that led to the establishment of the Exchange Equalization Fund and thus to the abandonment of the principle of freely fluctuating exchanges."[34]

The pound fluctuated in 1931–1932 under circumstances very different from those likely to characterize freely fluctuating exchanges adopted as a permanent system. England had been pushed off the gold standard by a flight from the pound that had been gathering momentum for some time. Whatever bearish speculation the free pound inherited from the gold pound might more justly be blamed on the earlier maintenance of currency overvaluation and on its incitement to one-way-option speculation than on the workings of the free market itself. Furthermore, the continued outflow of funds from England for several weeks after September 20 was not due entirely and perhaps not even mainly to private speculation: general abandonment of the gold-exchange standard meant that several foreign central banks were hurriedly selling their previously accumulated sterling reserves. In fact, a number of central banks *had* to withdraw their balances from England because their statutes required them to hold their exchange reserves exclusively in gold or gold-standard currencies.[35] As will be emphasized later, this scramble for gold put pressure on the gold-standard dollar as

30. Brown, *op. cit.*, **II**, p. 1075, citing Bank of Nova Scotia, *Monthly Review*, September 1933.

31. Ragnar Nurkse, *International Currency Experience*, League of Nations, 1944, chap. III; Benjamin J. Cohen, *The Future of Sterling as an International Currency*, New York: St. Martin's Press, 1971, pp. 68, 80–81.

32. See, *inter alia*, Frederic Benham, *Great Britain Under Protection*, New York: Macmillan, 1941, pp. 157–160; and Maxwell White Hudgins, Jr., *Currency Exchange Rate Fluctuations Under a System of Stabilization Funds: The Case of the Pound-Dollar Rate, 1931–38*, University of Virginia dissertation, 1973, pp. 11–12 and chap. III.

33. *The Economist*, 24 September 1932, p. 537.

34. Nurkse, *op. cit.*, p. 118.

35. *Ibid.*, pp. 39–40.

well as on the fluctuating pound, leading to increases in the Federal Reserve rediscount rate in order to protect the U.S. gold stock. Another difficulty was that confidence in sterling was partially linked to possibilities of extending the credits obtained in France and the United States during the unsuccessful defense of the gold standard. Even before establishment of the Exchange Equalisation Account, the Bank of England was trading on the exchange market, on balance buying more foreign exchange than it was selling in order to repay the French and American loans. Incidentally, complete freedom for private transactions did not prevail during the period of supposedly free fluctuations; the previously quoted regulations about capital movements must have interfered with private arbitrage and speculation. Furthermore, uncertainties over political, legislative, and economic developments at home and abroad influenced the fluctuations of sterling. Several of these developments in turn came partly as responses to the unsatisfactory operation of the earlier system of exchange-rate pegging that was now cracking up. The British Parliament was dissolved on October 7, for example, and the election on October 27 gave an overwhelming victory to MacDonald's coalition, in which Conservatives inclined toward protectionism were heavily represented. The severe decline of sterling in November was due, among other things, not only to seasonally heavy imports but also to a rush to get imports into the country before enactment of a stopgap tariff on November 19. The subsequent rise of sterling was partly due to the drop in imports after the stopgap tariff went into effect. (A more permanent general tariff replaced it on March 1.) Similarly abnormal influences on the sterling-dollar rate included preoccupation with news about the British and American government budgets, uncertainties about whether or not war debts would be reduced or cancelled, fears late in November about an increase in the fiduciary note issue of the Bank of England, uncertainties about the expansionary consequences of the Reconstruction Finance Corporation and the Glass-Steagall Act in the United States, and exports of gold from India as India moved from a gold to a sterling standard. Speculation was by no means centered on the fate of the pound alone.

Some broader observations are relevant to an appraisal of the fluctuating pound of 1931–1932. Instability is to be expected in a currency that has just come unpegged. With the old value inappropriate, no recent history of equilibrium exchange rates exists to guide buyers and sellers in making their bids and offers on the market. Since the currency could hardly rise in value above the level that had just proved untenable, the immediate speculative pressure is overwhelmingly bearish. Quite understandably, this pressure may temporarily carry the rate below the level corresponding to fundamental supply and demand conditions, setting the stage for an upward reaction. After the initial shock of coming loose from an inappropriate peg had worn off and after the reaction from that shock had run its course, the British pound might well have settled down to narrow fluctuations about a gradually changing equilibrium rate. But the pound never had this chance; the Exchange Equalisation Account came onto the scene and took credit, rightly or wrongly, for whatever degree of stability was observed thereafter. In any case, it is wrong to cite the fluctuating pound of 1931–1932 as a horrible example of what is to be expected from free rates generally. To do so is to criticize fluctuating rates in a situation in which fixed exchange rates could not—and did not—work at all.

American gold and banking crises, 1931–1933

After England left gold in September 1931, the international panic centered briefly on the United States. A foreign run on U.S. gold caused a 15 percent drop in the gold stock from mid-September to the end of October. (The gold drain temporarily ceased in November and December but resumed at the end of the year and continued with some interruption until June 1932.) Within the United States, confidence in the gold standard still endured, and there was little new gold hoarding. Hindsight shows that the country was in little danger at the time of exhausting its reserves and being forced off gold.

Nevertheless, the episode interrupted the half-hearted easy money policy that should have been maintained and intensified if overcoming the depression at home had been the dominant consideration. Allegedly because of legal technicalities tying up gold as collateral for its notes, the Federal Reserve considered that during the fall of 1931 it had practically exhausted its power to buy government securities on the open market to relieve the domestic credit stringency. The rediscount rate of the Federal Reserve Bank of New York jumped from 1½ to 2½ percent on October 9 and to 3½ percent on October 16. The owned (non-borrowed) reserves of banks belonging to the Federal Reserve System fell from $2.1 to $1.3 billion between early September and the end of the year. Given the low reserve requirements then governing banks and the smallness of their excess reserves, the further reserve losses provoked a powerful multiple contraction of bank credit. The country suffered "one of the most violent deflations in our banking history."[36] Between September 1931 and February 1932, demand deposits declined by $2.7 billion, or almost 14 percent. Toward the end of 1931, hundreds of banks were closing each month, tying up hundreds of millions of dollars of deposits. In the last three months of 1931 and the first six months of 1932, the volume of commercial bank loans was shrinking by more than half a billion dollars a month.[37] From August 1931 to January 1932 the money stock fell at the unprecedented annual rate of 31 percent.[38] In the words of one sound-money economist not given to undue worry about deflation, the country had "real money pressure." Although the situation was not so bad in New York, "There were important parts of the country where good merchants had their loans reduced or even cut off because the banks themselves were short of money." Many banks that could have made loans hesitated out of fear of sudden runs by their depositors.[39] According to A. G. Hart, the whole deflationary episode reflects "panic" on the part of America's financial leaders, including the Federal Reserve. The 1931 Annual Report of the Federal Reserve Board lamely explained that "after the middle of September, in view of the outflow of gold from the country and of currency into hoarding, the Federal Reserve Banks increased their rates on discounts and acceptances."[40]

The drain on U.S. gold reserves had a deflationary influence on fiscal as well as monetary policy. Former Vice President Garner, who was speaker of the House of Representatives at the time, recalled leaving the Speaker's chair to beg for passage of a tax bill to stop the gold outflow and guard the dollar. "At the end of my speech, I said: Now every man in this House that believes in levying a tax bill sufficient to

sustain the American dollar, I want him to rise. Every one of the members rose. We did pass a tax bill and it saved the situation."[41]

The technicalities which had supposedly tied up an unusually large part of the country's gold stock as collateral against Federal Reserve notes were overcome by passage of the Glass-Steagall Act in February 1932. The Federal Reserve authorities delayed about ten weeks, however, in buying enough securities on the open market to take advantage of the act's provisions. Partly because of the opportunities provided by the Glass-Steagall Act, the United States was able to weather the renewed foreign drain on its gold stock during the first half of 1932 (especially in May and June) without further credit-tightening; in fact, the New York rediscount rate was cut to 3 percent in February and to 2½ percent in June (though all other Federal Reserve Banks except Chicago kept their rates at 3½ percent). The Reconstruction Finance Corporation, created by act of Congress in January 1932 and equipped with funds for lending to banks, railroads, and other pivotal institutions in temporary trouble, also was useful in checking the contagion of financial distress.

In the middle of 1932, signs of business revival appeared: mining, manufacturing, payrolls, department-store sales, commodity prices, and stock prices rose. These good omens were soon to evaporate. Events of that summer were

36. H. H. Villard, "The Federal Reserve System's Monetary Policy in 1931 and 1932," *Journal of Political Economy*, **XLV**, December 1937, p. 725.

37. Albert Gailord Hart, *Money, Debt and Economic Activity*, 2nd ed., Englewood Cliffs, N.J.: Prentice-Hall, 1953, p. 321.

38. Milton Friedman and Anna J. Schwartz, A *Monetary History of the United States, 1867–1960*, Princeton, N.J.: Princeton University Press, 1963, pp. 317–318.

39. Anderson, *op. cit.*, pp. 264, 266.

40. Quoted in Hart, *op. cit.*, pp. 321–322.

41. "John Garner at 90 Tells an Inside Story," *U.S. News & World Report*, vol. **XLV**, No. 21, November 21, 1958, pp. 98–105, quotation from p. 100. The tax bill was passed in 1932.

already preparing another tight-money crisis. The Central Republic Bank & Trust Company of Chicago appeared vulnerable to runs. General Charles G. Dawes, who had headed this bank before becoming Vice President of the United States and afterwards Ambassador to Great Britain, was now the head of the Reconstruction Finance Corporation. When danger threatened his old associates and depositors, Dawes resigned from the RFC and went to Chicago to attempt a rescue. In his efforts, Dawes found it necessary to ask the RFC for help. Its loan, supplemented by others from some New York and Chicago banks, made possible a reorganization of the Central Republic Bank that protected the depositors, including a large number of country correspondent banks, and perhaps even staved off a chain of bank failures. The assistance of the RFC seemed in accord with both the letter and the spirit of the law creating the agency. Nevertheless, an outcry arose that Dawes as a government official was rescuing himself as a private person.[42] Though apparently unjustified, suspicion grew that the RFC was making loans on a political basis, and its lending policy became more timid thereafter. With Democrats in control of the House of Representatives, the RFC was required first, in August, to report new loans to the Clerk of the House, and later, in January 1933, to report loans previously made. These reports were speedily given to the press, subverting the RFC practice of keeping loans confidential for fear that knowledge of a bank's borrowing would arouse worry among its depositors. Some institutions hesitated to borrow from the RFC for fear of bad publicity. Disclosures in congressional hearings were already shaking trust in banks generally.

Meanwhile, President Hoover was defeated for reelection. This blow to confidence among conservatives may have had something to do with a fresh wave of currency hoarding and bank failures that set in in December. During the interregnum until Franklin D. Roosevelt took office the following March 4, neither man was in a position to frame long-range policy; and efforts to arrange cooperation between them broke down. Rumors circulated that the new president might take the country off the gold standard despite the Democratic platform. Foreigners began to withdraw gold again early in 1933, and domestic depositors withdrew currency from banks for hoarding or conversion into gold. The difficulties of the Union Guardian Trust Company of Detroit grew worse in January when its indebtedness to the RFC became known. Depositors hastened to transfer their funds elsewhere. The bank's difficulties became critical in February, yet its strategic importance argued against allowing it to fail. On February 14 the governor of Michigan decreed an eight-day statewide bank holiday. (Limited bank restrictions had already been adopted in Nevada, Iowa, and Louisiana.)

With their Michigan funds now blocked, businessmen had ample reason to draw on any bank accounts they happened to have in other states. Bank holidays quickly followed in Indiana, Maryland, Arkansas, and Ohio. Some states enacted legislation permitting bank commissioners to restrict withdrawals, and an act of Congress of February 25 authorized the Comptroller of the Currency to give national banks emergency privileges similar to those protecting state-chartered banks. The wave of bank holidays continued into the first few days of March. The governor of Kentucky, lacking any other constitutional means to suspend banking business, declared successive "Days of Thanksgiving."

As member banks sought funds by rediscounting, the reserves of the Federal Reserve banks themselves slid down toward what they considered the bare minimum level. The Federal Reserve Bank of New York came to the end of its own lending power and was being carried by the other Reserve banks. Since the New York Bank was chiefly responsible for meeting the general run on the Federal Reserve System, its position impeded any further large extensions of credit.[43] The New York and Chicago banks responded on March 3 and 4 by raising their discount rates from 2½ percent to the 3½ percent level already in effect at the other ten Reserve banks. The *New York Times* described this increase as "a perfectly normal and customary expedient in a time of large gold withdrawals"—which is a revealing commentary on the state of economic thinking at the time. The whole episode deserves emphasis. For the second time during the depths of severe depression, the Federal Reserve authorities tolerated and even abetted a deflationary tightening of credit. Of course, it is unfair to blame particular men, given the rules under which they were working and the economic ideas then prevalent.

Significantly, both this episode of early 1933 and the previous one in the fall of 1931 had involved preoccupation with gold reserves and with precautions actually or supposedly necessary to maintain the gold standard in the face of foreign drains. Recovery from the depression required a vigorous easy-money policy (and perhaps other measures as well). Yet concern about the gold standard required, in the judgment of the Federal Reserve authorities, keeping the monetary policy only half-heartedly easy, and required punctuating even this, in the fall of 1931 and the early months of 1933, with bouts of outright monetary tightness. One can of course argue that if only the gold reserve requirements had been lower or had been administered more flexibly, the country could have had the necessary monetary expansion at home while meeting the gold demands of foreigners. But this is an admission that a rigid gold standard is unacceptable. Furthermore, there is surely a limit, even though not a precise one, to how far expansionary policy can go without upsetting the balance of payments or exchange rates.

New Deal currency policies

On March 3, inauguration eve, it seemed that the Federal Reserve banks themselves could not long carry on business as usual. Warned of imminent collapse of the whole banking system, President Hoover agreed to proclaim a nationwide bank holiday only if the incoming President would share responsibility. Roosevelt refused. On Saturday, March 4, the Federal Reserve banks and all the leading exchanges closed; and, as the Federal Reserve Board later reported, "business in general was practically at a standstill."[44] New York, Illinois, and 23 other states proclaimed bank holidays. Before the end of the day, banks almost everywhere in the country were either closed or under restrictions. The banking crisis was at its very climax as President Roosevelt took office early that afternoon.

One remark in Roosevelt's inaugural address had special significance for international monetary policy: "Our international trade relations, though vastly important, are, in point of time and necessity, secondary to the establishment of sound national economy. I favor as a practical policy the putting of first things first."

President Roosevelt immediately summoned Congress to a special session. At one o'clock Monday morning, the 6th, claiming authority under the Trading with the Enemy Act of 1917, he proclaimed a four-day nationwide

bank holiday, a cooling-off period. Except with the permission of the Secretary of the Treasury, no bank was to "pay out, export, earmark, or permit the withdrawal or transfer in any manner or by any device whatsoever, of any gold or silver coin or bullion or currency or take any other action which might facilitate the hoarding thereof. . . ."[45] A further proclamation of March 9 continued the bank holiday, but the ban on banking business was progressively relaxed. The ban on obtaining gold was generally regarded as a temporary technicality of little significance. Secretary of the Treasury Woodin said, "We are definitely on the gold standard. Gold merely cannot be obtained for several days."[46] Doubt whether the mere private holding of gold had been made illegal was not dispelled until an order of April 5 expressly prohibited "the hoarding of gold coin, gold bullion and gold certificates within the continental United States."

When Congress met on March 9, Roosevelt asked for immediate legislation authorizing him to exercise control over banks to protect depositors, to reopen banks found in sound condition, and to reorganize unsound banks and reopen them later. He also asked authority for additional currency issues in case of heavy demands. The Emergency Banking Act, overwhelmingly passed on that very day, reaffirmed the President's authority under the Trading with the Enemy Act to regulate or prohibit transactions in foreign exchange and the export, hoarding, melting, or earmarking of gold and silver coin, bullion, or currency. It also authorized the Secretary of the Treasury, at his discretion, to require delivery to the Treasury

---

42. Anderson, *op. cit.*, pp. 274–275. Hodson, *op. cit.*, chap. VII, contains a useful survey of the American crisis.

43. Brown, *op. cit.*, II, p. 1240.

44. *Ibid.*, p. 1249.

45. The proclamation is reprinted in James Daniel Paris, *Monetary Policies of the United States, 1932–1938*, New York: Columbia University Press, 1938, pp. 164–165.

46. Ray B. Westerfield, *Money, Credit and Banking*, New York: Ronald, 1939, p. 788.

of any or all gold coin, gold bullion, or gold certificates.

By Wednesday, March 15, most of the country's banks were back in business. The wave of panicky distrust had passed. Hoarded currency poured back into the banks. When the New York Stock Exchange reopened on March 15, prices were buoyant. When dealings in the dollar were resumed in London on March 13, it was slightly higher in relation to sterling than before the banking crisis. The banks' foreign-exchange transactions were still restricted, however, and paying out gold or gold certificates was still forbidden. The United States government allowed exports of gold under earmark for foreign governments or central banks or for the Bank for International Settlements, and a very few other gold-export licenses were issued in mid-April. The exchange value of the dollar against the French franc (still on gold) remained within the gold points.

On April 18, 19, and 20, while British Prime Minister MacDonald was en route to Washington for conferences, the United States unequivocally left the gold standard. The government announced that it would issue no further gold export licenses, except perhaps under very special conditions. The Secretary of the Treasury was also given power to investigate, regulate, or prohibit all foreign-exchange transactions. These surprise announcements made the dollar fall sharply; the pound rose from $3.44⅝ on April 15 to $3.81½ on April 20, that is, by 10.7 percent.

A Congressional Joint Resolution of June 5 abrogated the gold clause in public and private contracts and made all outstanding obligations to pay in gold coin payable dollar for dollar in any legal tender. The gold clause—almost routinely included in bonds—called for repayment in dollars of the original "weight and fineness" or the equivalent in total gold content. Many bondholders brought suit to recover the larger number of depreciated dollars "containing" the original total amount of gold. The Supreme Court decided in February 1935 that the constitutional right of Congress to regulate the value of money included the right to annul the gold clause in contracts of private parties and state and local governments. As for the gold clause in the U.S. government's own bonds, Congress could not rightly repudiate it. Nevertheless, said the Court, the bondholder had not shown that he had been damaged by the Congressional action. To forestall efforts to show such damage and collect more than the face value of outstanding government bonds, Congress then took away the jurisdiction of the Federal courts to hear such suits. The United States government quite specifically repudiated its own promises.

Unlike Great Britain, the United States had not been driven off the gold standard. Though both imports and exports had fallen, the American balance of payments still showed a surplus on current account. By the beginning of 1933, American short-term debts to foreigners had been so largely paid off that the remainder outstanding fell short of American short-term claims on foreigners. The flight of American capital had not assumed menacing proportions after the end of the banking panic in March, and such flight as there was stemmed from expectations of deliberate departure from the gold standard. Nor was the United States forced off gold by a price level already too high relative to foreign price levels (though vigorous reflation might have created balance-of-payments trouble later on). The departure from gold was deliberate.

The early Roosevelt administration adopted a hodge-podge of deflationary and inflationary measures. The delay in reopening all but unquestionably sound banks was deflationary. So was the economy budget submitted shortly after the banking crisis. The agricultural programs sought to adjust production to a shrunken volume of monetary demand, rather than the other way around. The law establishing the National Recovery Administration called on each industry to draw up a "code of fair competition" to prescribe maximum hours, minimum wages, and other working conditions, to foster collective bargaining, and to limit price competition. Rising prices as a typical *symptom* of recovery from depression were confused with rising prices as a *cause* of recovery. Rising prices as a frequent *consequence* of monetary expansion were apparently confused with the necessary monetary expansion itself.

On the side of potential inflation was Roosevelt's acceptance on April 18 of the Thomas Amendment to the pending farm bill, which was passed in May. The amendment gave the President discretionary power to cut the gold content of the dollar by as much as 50 percent, to open the mints to unlimited coinage of silver and fix the ratio between silver and gold, to accept silver up to specified amounts in settlement of war debts, to sell up to $3 billion worth of government securities to the Federal Reserve banks, and to put up to $3 billion of new paper money into circulation by redeeming Federal debt. Roosevelt did not use this authority for forthright monetary expansion.

General economic conditions improved remarkably from March to around July. The spurt in prices, production, employment, and payrolls apparently rested on expectations of recovery and on spending to beat the rise in costs that NRA was likely to impose. With its basis so weak, the spurt gave way to relapse in the summer of 1933.

The London economic conference

Meanwhile, the United States took the lead in getting countries to forswear additional trade barriers at least until after the forthcoming World Economic Conference. The conference duly opened in London on June 12, with 64 countries represented. France and other gold countries wanted to restore an international monetary standard before lowering trade barriers. Britain and other paper-currency countries feared that an international standard would break down unless excessive tariffs, internal deflation, and other unfavorable conditions were dealt with first. The cleavage of opinions was fundamental. "But the London Conference was held under the auspices of that sort of statesmanship which strives to escape awkward problems by elaborating formulas so vague and so noncommittal that everybody may be able to subscribe to them."[47] Domestic antidepression measures also came up for discussion. If we are dismayed that Daladier of France and Dollfuss of Austria should have called for cutting production down into line with consumption, we can console ourselves with the thought that economic understanding has gained some ground since then.

The American position on exchange stabilization was unclear and remained so after dispatch of Professor Raymond Moley, Assistant Secretary of State, to brief the American delegation. Heightened uncertainty following a statement by the American delegation on June 22 seemed to threaten the few remaining gold currencies and touched off a bear movement against the Dutch guilder, pushing the gold countries toward cooperation in a formal gold bloc. Yet President Roosevelt's apparent attitude left room for hope that some sort of

reassuring compromise declaration could be worked out to accommodate the gold countries.

Instead, Roosevelt sent a message made public on July 3 warning against "a catastrophe amounting to world tragedy" if economic recovery measures should be sidetracked "by the proposal of a purely artificial and temporary experiment affecting the monetary exchange of a few nations only." A nation's internal economic soundness, he argued, is more important to its well-being than the price of its currency in terms of other currencies. The American objective of stabilizing the purchasing power of the dollar "means more to the good of other nations than a fixed ratio for a month or two in terms of the pound or franc." Gold or gold and silver can be important as currency reserves, but discussion of a better distribution of them can properly await "concerted policies in the majority of nations to produce balanced budgets and living within their means. . . ." Restoration of world trade is important, but "temporary exchange fixing is not the true answer." The conference must not be diverted from its purpose of seeking cures to fundamental economic ills.[48]

Roosevelt's message is commonly said to have "torpedoed" the conference. Much of its economic substance would probably command wide agreement nowadays (though one may question its preoccupation with gold and silver reserves and with balanced government budgets even during depression). Perhaps the main fault of the message was the bad diplomacy behind it. Roosevelt was thoughtless in not deciding sooner just what his policy was, in blowing hot and cold about American cooperation in what most delegations regarded as the main objectives of the conference, in giving the initial false impression that he would agree to some sort of exchange stabilization, and finally in making a unilateral decision bound to hurt morale and create bad will. As Moley, Roosevelt's special emissary, reminisced many years

47. Gustav Cassel, *The Downfall of the Gold Standard*, Oxford: Clarendon Press, 1936, p. 141.

48. Roosevelt's message is reprinted in Paris, *op. cit.*, pp. 166–167.

later, the "delegates wandered around in a fog" after the conference began, "trying to learn by remote control what Mr. Roosevelt was currently thinking. The whole conference fell to pieces."[49] Yet the delegates lingered around a few weeks more, agreeing on minor matters and finally, as a gesture of unwillingness to confess failure, merely "adjourning" the conference but not closing it.

The New Deal gold program

By mid-July, the dollar had dopped more than 30 percent against, gold-bloc currencies. (Nevertheless, the government continued selling gold bars to the arts and industries at the old price of $20.67 an ounce until late in August.) Yet the spring spurt in production soon gave way to relapse. Farm prices were sagging. On October 22, 1933, Roosevelt made a radio speech stressing the need first to raise prices and then to stabilize the purchasing power of the dollar. His way was to "control the gold value of our own dollar at home," out of range of "the accidents of international trade, . . . the internal policies of other nations and . . . political disturbance in other continents." As part of his plan for manipulating the dollar, the Reconstruction Finance Corporation was authorized to buy gold from American mines and, when necessary, on world markets. The price was to be set from time to time in consultation with the Secretary of the Treasury and the President.[50]

Roosevelt apparently adopted his gold-buying program under the influence of the well-known Warren-Pearson theory concerning a supposed line of causation running from the dollar price of gold to the general price level. Untroubled by the dubiousness of the theory, the RFC went ahead buying gold, first domestic and later foreign also. Short-term funds speculatively leaving the United States drove the dollar down on the foreign-exchange market at a more rapid pace than the actual rise in the price of gold. On November 6, 1933, the pound sterling appreciated against the dollar beyond its former parity of $4.8666. On November 15, the dollar fell to $5.50 to the pound before a reaction set in.

In January 1934, the President asked Congress to give the government title to all monetary gold held by the Federal Reserve banks (which had acquired the gold previously surrendered by the public). Taking the gold over at the former parity would let the Treasury reap any revaluation profit. The President also asked for an upper limit on the new gold content of the dollar at 60 percent of the old one (the Thomas Amendment already authorized devaluing the dollar to a lower limit of 50 percent). These and related proposals became the Gold Reserve Act of 1934, signed on January 30. Next day Roosevelt fixed the gold content of the dollar at $15\frac{5}{21}$ grains of gold, 9/10 fine, corresponding to 59.06 percent of the pre-1933 gold content and to a price of $35 an ounce for pure gold. The book profit on revaluation of the Treasury's gold reserves was $2.8 billion.

From this amount, $2 billion was set aside to establish an Exchange Stabilization Fund. The Secretary of the Treasury was given wide discretion, with the approval of the President, to deal in foreign currencies or make other expenditures or investments from the Fund. As might be expected with the dollar again linked to gold, the American fund behaved more passively in the foreign-exchange market than did the British Exchange Equalisation Account; the latter seems to have had the greater influence on the pound-dollar rate. Still, the American fund might help see to it that the price of gold in private markets stayed near the official price.[51]

The government announced that it would buy all gold offered to it at $35 per ounce, less charges for handling and the equivalent of minting. Gold would also be sold for export to central banks. Thus the United States was back on a kind of gold standard. It was a "limited gold-bullion standard," with redemption in gold "limited" to dollars held by foreign central banks and governments (and licensed users of gold for the industries and arts).

Heavy gold shipments from Europe and elsewhere began what Graham and Whittlesey called the "golden avalanche."[52] By January 1935 the dollar value of the American gold stock was more than double, and by the end of 1936 almost triple, what it had been in January 1934. The inflow kept on until checked by foreign restrictions during World War II, and it resumed in the early postwar years. One short-run reason for the golden avalanche was the return of American capital that had fled abroad during the protracted depreciation of the dollar in 1933–1934. Other reasons included the attractiveness of the high gold price to foreign producers and the balance-of-payments consequences of a dollar that was undervalued in terms of gold and foreign exchange; the failure of American prices as a whole to rise as fast a the dollar depreciated confronted foreign countries with the competition on world markets of what appeared to be predatory excessive depreciation. In the later 1930s, the gold inflow was largely the counterpart of the inflow of foreign capital taking refuge from political and economic uncertainties abroad.

The fluctuating dollar, 1933–1934

The exchange rate of the dollar against gold currencies was fixed again after January 1934. Exchange rates with Sterling Area currencies were also in practice kept fairly stable. But for a time, from April 1933 to January 1934, the dollar had been fluctuating on the foreign-exchange market. This episode provided the author of *International Currency Experience* with yet another supposed example of disequilibrating speculation under freely fluctuating exchange rates. The dollar depreciated, mainly in response to an outflow of short-term funds, but the American export surplus fell rather than rose. Foreign buyers postponed purchases in the hope that the dollar would become still cheaper. Americans imported heavily in anticipation of a continued rise in foreign-exchange rates.[53]

Speculation in the fluctuating dollar was based not so much on assessment of free-market forces as on guesses about the government's exchange-rate policy and internal fiscal and monetary policy.[54] The definite embargo on gold exports in April 1933 made known official intentions of staying off the gold standard. The President was anxious to have the dollar depreciate and apparently wanted to make sure that all speculation against the dollar would be fully effective and that gold exports would not ease the pressure of demands for foreign currencies. The very announcement of this policy was bound to intensify the speculative capital movements that had already made some dent in American gold stocks. Fear of inflation helped to depress the dollar. This fear grew stronger when, at the time of the embargo on gold exports, the committee considering the farm bill adopted the Thomas ("Inflation") Amendment, which became law on May 12.[55]

People knew that the government intended to raise commodity prices by such devices as reduction in the gold content of the dollar, silver policy, open market operations, credit expansion, public-works spending, NRA, and AAA. Still other influences on exchange speculation were the ban on gold hoarding, the congressional gold-clause resolution, and rumors about what the World Economic Conference in London would decide on. For example, rumors that the British, French, and American authorities had agreed or shortly would agree on temporary exchange stabilization caused the dollar to advance sharply in the exchange markets on June 15.[56] On July 3,

49. Quoted in Anderson, *op. cit.*, p. 331, from the Los Angeles *Times*, 7 April 1945. Reading Roosevelt's mind was important because, for one thing, the Thomas Amendment had given him vast discretionary powers to alter the American monetary system.

50. The relevant part of the speech is reprinted in Paris, *op. cit.*, pp. 168–169.

51. Hudgins, *op. cit.*, pp. 51ff. and *passim*.

52. F. D. Graham and C. R. Whittlesey, *Golden Avalanche*, Princeton, N.J.: Princeton University Press, 1939.

53. Pp. 118, 120, citing U.S. Department of Commerce, *The Balance of Payments of the United States in 1933*, p. 9.

54. "For several months, exchange rates were left to be determined . . . by the consensus of speculative opinion as to what the government might do later." Hart, *op. cit.*, p. 378.

55. Cf. Seymour E. Harris, *Exchange Depreciation*, Cambridge: Harvard University Press, 1936, pp. 249–250; Anderson, *op. cit.*, p. 317; Milton Gilbert, *Currency Depreciation and Monetary Policy*, Philadelphia: University of Pennsylvania Press, 1939, pp. 108–109. Not only exchange speculators but also reputable economists worried in 1933 about the possibility of inflation in the United States. Eleanor Lansing Dulles wrote *The Dollar, the Franc and Inflation*, New York: Macmillan, 1933, to warn against inflation by drawing parallels between apparent American trends and French experiences during the 1920s. Also see James W. Angell, "Exchange Depreciation, Foreign Trade and National Welfare," *Proceedings of the Academy of Political Science*, XV, June 1933, pp. 295–296.

56. Anderson, *op. cit.*, p. 330.

however, President Roosevelt practically broke up the conference by rejecting exchange stabilization.

Renewed rumors of inflation spurred further flight from the dollar in August and September, intensifying depreciation. The dollar showed strength, however, by recovering from a discount of 35.3 percent in terms of the French franc on September 23 to a discount of only 28.8 percent on October 21. The next day Roosevelt made his speech announcing a deliberate depreciaton of the dollar in order to restore commodity prices to predepression levels. He practically told speculators to be more bearish against the dollar.[57] As Nurkse says, "the principal effect of the [gold-buying] policy was to encourage private speculation against the dollar."[58]

In November 1933, rumors of impending stabilization reversed speculative attitudes, and the dollar started to rise. Early in 1934 a large return flow of capital actually embarrassed the government in its attempts to depreciate the dollar. The volume of gold imports necessary to depress the dollar at that time suggests a high elasticity of demand for dollars.[59] Finally, at the end of January, the dollar was tied back onto gold at a fixed price.

This review of history shows that the exchange value of the dollar was *not* free from official influence throughout the months of fluctuation in 1933 and 1934. Speculators and traders had to keep guessing what President Roosevelt and his advisors had in mind. At times the Administration actually incited bearish speculation. Clearly, then, the American experience supports no generalizations about speculation in free markets.

U.S. *silver policy and its repercussions*[60]

The story of American silver policy from 1933 to around 1936 is worth reviewing because it further documents the experimental nature of New Deal monetary policies, provides insights about behavior in a market dominated by official transactions, and illustrates how a country (China) may suffer deflation imposed from abroad. The open-market price of silver reached an all-time low of 24¼ cents per fine ounce ($\frac{1}{85}$ of the price of gold) late in December 1932 and then turned upward early the following year under the influence of rumors about policies to be adopted by the new Administration.

The congressional silver bloc made its influence felt. In December 1933, under authority of the Thomas Amendment, enacted in May, President Roosevelt proclaimed what amounted to a buying price of 64.64 cents per fine ounce for all newly mined domestic silver. A Silver Purchase Act was enacted in June 1934. One strange argument used in its favor had been that it would benefit China by raising the value of her monetary standard, increase her national purchasing power, and stimulate Chinese-American trade. Leaving him considerable discretion as to where and when and at what prices to buy, the Act directed the Secretary of the Treasury to buy silver at home or abroad until either the price had risen to $1.29 an ounce or silver had come to make up one-fourth by value of the government's total gold and silver stock. A 50 percent tax was levied on profits from speculative transactions in silver. Silver exports were made subject to license. In August, privately owned silver bullion in the United States, with certain exceptions in favor of the industries and arts, was "nationalized" at 50.01 cents an ounce.

During 1935, further policy developments and expectations about them caused a series of speculative upheavals on the world silver market. The world price, the U.S. Treasury's buying price, and expectations about that price all interacted upwards. Late in April a slide began after it became apparent that the Treasury would not continue raising its price. When a market crisis developed in July, apparently because of bearish speculation, the Treasury responded with heavier purchases. A slight reduction in the Treasury's buying price in mid-August caused speculative panic and again prodded the Treasury into large remedial purchases. Later the Treasury slackened its buying.

The world price was down to about 45 cents by early 1936 and to about 35 cents in 1939, before recovering during the war. Meanwhile, the high domestic support price had caused the physical volume of American silver production to triple between the ends of 1933 and 1936. The domestic price was cut in December 1937 and then raised again by a law of July 1939. (The Silver Purchase Act of July 1946 raised the price to 90.5 cents an ounce for domestic and foreign silver alike. The open-market price hovered close to this figure until late in 1961.

By then, the Treasury had been selling silver for some time to hold the price *down*. Discontinuance of Treasury sales at this fixed price allowed a rise until a silver dollar was worth a full dollar as bullion. Steps begun in 1963 and 1964 very much reduced the monetary role of silver, and silver dollars practically disappeared from circulation into hoards.)

The vicissitudes of American silver policy had particularly sharp repercussions on China. The price of silver had sagged in world markets after 1929, accentuating a decline already under way before. The foreign-exchange value of the Chinese silver yuan had moved in sympathy, depreciating from yearly averages of 56.9 cents in 1925 and 50.0 cents in 1926 to 41.9 cents in 1929 and 21.7 cents in the trough year of 1932. As late as the time of the London Economic Conference in 1933, Chinese representatives considered this severe depreciation upsetting to their country's trade and were eager for measures to prevent its resumption, though they were not looking for the sharp appreciation soon to be engineered by the United States. Actually, the inflow of increasingly cheap silver to the Chinese cities from the provinces and from abroad had been swelling bank reserves and contributing to a mildly inflationary boom from about 1926 on. This boom continued for some two years after the start of the world depression in 1929; the abundance of its depreciating silver-standard currency insulated China from the contagion of worldwide deflation. In the words of the special economic adviser to the Nanking government, "China benefited substantially in 1930 and 1931 from the fact that the depreciation of silver in terms of gold was saving her from currency deflation. . . ."[61] Business activity held up rather well.

China's two years of prosperity in the face of world depression and the reversal that took place in the second half of 1931 both illustrate the essentially monetary nature of boom and depression. Beginning toward the end of 1931, as England, India, Japan, and other countries left the gold standard, including the United States in 1933, China's silver currency appreciated against the currencies of the countries with which she traded. The yuan's monthly average quotation more than doubled from a low of 19.5 U.S. cents in December 1932 to a high of 41.1 cents in May 1935. As the price of silver rose abroad, arbitrageurs demanded redemption of Chinese paper currency to obtain silver for export. Withdrawals depleted Chi-

nese bank reserves. Money became scarce, credit tightened, prices fell, banks and other businesses failed, and trade stagnated.

The American silver purchase program did not originate these trends, but it prolonged and intensified them. Several times during 1934 the Chinese government reminded the United States about the consequences of the program. In September the Chinese Finance Ministry prohibited until further notice "purchases and sales of foreign exchange . . . except for the purpose of financing (1) legitimate and normal business requirements, (2) contracts entered into on or before September 8, 1934, and (3) reasonable traveling or other personal requirements."[62] This order failed to stop the outflow of silver. In October, after the reply to their latest protest had made the Chinese see the uselessness of trying to sway the United States, the government imposed a 10 percent export tax on silver, together with an equalization charge varying with the world price of silver and intended to be prohibitive. The yuan then fell briefly by some 13 or 14 percent in relation to sterling. In effect China had been forced off the silver standard as far as the foreign-exchange value of her currency was concerned. Internally, however, the deflation continued, since the link with the world silver market had not been cut completely. Hoarding went on in expectation that the currency would be devalued or the silver export restrictions re-

57. Gilbert, *op. cit.*, p. 110.

58. Nurkse, *op. cit.*, p. 123n.

59. Harris, *op. cit.*, pp. 13–14.

60. This section draws facts from L. Y. Shen, *China's Currency Reform: A Historical Survey*, Shanghai: Mercury, 1941; Hodson, *op. cit.*, pp. 257–266; Paris, *op. cit.*, chap. III; and John Parke Young, *The International Economy*, New York: Ronald, 1942, chap. 24. Monthly and annual average exchange rates are from Federal Reserve, *Banking and Monetary Statistics*, p. 667.

61. Sir Arthur Salter's report to the government, February 1934, quoted in Hodson, *op. cit.*, p. 259. Also see Salter, "China and Silver," *Economic Forum*, **II**, Spring 1934, Section II (Supplement), esp. pp. 3–8, 48, 108.

62. Shen, *op. cit.*, p. 83.

laxed. The continuing rise in the world silver price was still making itself felt. In Shen's picturesque words, "crafty methods of smuggling silver out of China were incessantly employed by unprincipled miscreants."[63] Between November 1934 and May 1935 the monthly average quotation of the yuan in U.S. cents rose by 23 percent. China was beset with "extreme contraction of currency and credit, rising interest rates and falling commodity prices, declining value of real estate and securities, and widespread business failure and unemployment." In short, the situation became "most critical" in 1935.[64]

The decline in the world price of silver and the exchange value of the yuan after April 1935 gave the Chinese economy some but not enough relief. During the autumn rumors recurred that China would still more completely leave the silver standard. Finally, on November 3, the government announced an irredeemable paper currency. The government banks were to deal on the market to stabilize the foreign-exchange value of the Chinese yuan at the existing level, slightly over 40 percent of its 1929 gold value. Monetary deflation was stopped and reversed; business activity improved. Hong Kong followed the Chinese reform in November and December 1935 by embargoing exports of silver coins and bullion and setting up an exchange fund to regulate the external value of the currency.

Besides China, other countries in several continents were inconvenienced when, by early 1935, the bullion values of their silver coins had either risen above their face values or seemed likely soon to do so. Mexico, Costa Rica, Peru, Colombia, Danzig, Persia, and the Straits Settlements, among others, made preparations to replace their silver coins and save them from the melting pot. Ironically enough from the standpoint of silver producers, these measures, and therefore the American policy that had led to them, tended to reduce the world's monetary use of silver.

In summary, a clumsy U.S. silver policy seriously inconvenienced a number of countries. China particularly suffered—and at a time, incidentally, when the friendly Nanking government was still insecure and was having difficulty with the Japanese and with Communists at home. The nature of the turmoil on the world silver market showed once again how important it is to be clear whether notable episodes of speculative instability reflect the play of decentralized private supply and demand or instead reflect the destabilizing dominance of official transactions and of changing rumors about them.

---

63. *Ibid.*, p. 89.

64. *Ibid.*, p. 91.

Further Currency Experience in the 1930s

Early struggles of the gold bloc

After the widespread depreciations of 1931 and especially after the American devaluation of 1933–1934, the currencies of France, Switzerland, Belgium, the Netherlands, Luxembourg, Italy, Poland, and the Free City of Danzig were still on gold but clearly overvalued. Some of these countries, notably France and Belgium, had returned to the gold standard in the later 1920s at new parities that undervalued their currencies. Protected by the resulting lowness of her prices relative to world prices, France in particular enjoyed a "golden glow" of remarkable immunity to the world depression for its first year or two. French industrial production stayed practically as high in 1930 as in 1929 and in 1931 was down by only 13 or 14 percent.[1] (U.S. industrial production, by contrast, dropped 31 percent from 1929 to 1931.) Though the current-account surplus gave way to a deficit in 1931 and afterwards, the inflow of gold continued to mount for a while, reaching levels of 18.5 billion francs (over $700 million) in each of the years 1931 and 1932. French banks were continuing to repatriate their balances held abroad, and flight capital was flowing in from abroad.[2] After foreign devaluations had raised the relative value of the franc (to 6.6 U.S. cents, for example,

from 3.9 cents), deflationary pressures began operating through the balance of payments.

The "gold bloc" was formalized during the London Economic Conference of July 1933, when France, Belgium, the Netherlands, Switzerland, Italy, and Poland issued a joint statement of intention to stay on gold at existing parities. At the time, the first four countries mentioned held larger gold stocks than ever before in history. Only a few years before, all the signatory countries except the Netherlands and Switzerland had experienced extreme price inflation and exchange depreciation. Leaving gold would have seemed risky. Considerations of national prestige were also at work.[3] At a conference in Geneva in September 1934, the gold countries declared themselves more determined than ever to defend their parities. To do so, they had to endure depression well after recovery had begun elsewhere. Internal economic difficulties that in themselves stemmed largely from prolonged deflation—stagnant trade, strikes, budget deficits, weak credit reputations—contributed to the menace of speculative flights from their currencies.

The struggles of France will serve as representative for those of the whole group. In response to the falling prices and increasing imports that confronted French industries, quantitative import limitations were imposed in 1931 as emergency measures. At first the quotas were mainly on farm products, but as the franc became more and more overvalued, quota protection was extended. By 1934 over half the items in the French tariff list were subject to quotas; imports of many items were restricted to less than half the predepression quantities. Internal price deflation also seemed necessary. Wholesale prices in mid-1935 aver-

1. It is perhaps significant that the French money supply increased from year to year through 1931. F. Robert Vanes, *De Internationale Gouden Standaard*, Antwerp/Amsterdam: Standaard-Boekhandel, 1951, p. 229.

2. William H. Wynne, "The French Franc, June, 1928–February, 1937," *Journal of Political Economy*, **XLV**, August 1937, esp. pp. 489–493. In 1932 and 1933, however, losses of foreign exchange by the Bank of France outweighed its gains of gold. Vanes, *op. cit.*, p. 230 and footnote.

3. Maxwell W. Hudgins, Jr., *Currency Exchange Rate Fluctuations under a System of Stabilization Funds: The Case of the Pound-Dollar Rate, 1931–38*, University of Virginia dissertation, 1973, p. 14.

aged barely more than half of their 1929 level. Farmers especially suffered from the low level of prices. Wages fell and unemployment rose moderately.

Reduced incomes and tax yields created a deficit in the French government budget, which was regretted as a sign that deflationary public finance had to press still further if earlier efforts to save the franc were not to prove in vain. None of the French governments or parties dared question the goal of a balanced budget. "What we now call 'deficit financing' was then known as 'national bankruptcy.' "[4] The Budget Bill of March 1934 authorized the government of the venerable Gaston Doumergue, who had come out of political retirement to form a "Cabinet of National Union," to impose economies by decree. Government jobs and salaries and even veterans' pensions were cut. Yet a continued drop in revenue outstripped the saving in expenditure; new issues of government securities brought in barely enough funds to keep abreast of old issues falling due.

Discontent with the deflation policy and wrangles over a proposed constitutional reform overthrew the Doumergue government in November 1934. The finance minister of the old government remained in the new one, trying as vigorously as ever to defend the existing gold parity. However, the new premier, Pierre Flandin, apparently had some notion that deflation of prices of final goods had gone far enough and that production might now be made profitable by reduction of costs. His government began gradually relaxing state support of wheat prices and at the same time undertook to restrict planting and adopt other expedients to deal with wheat surpluses. In January 1935 an industrial-cartellization bill was enacted reminiscent of the American NRA: self-regulation in industry was to be reinforced by law. One of the objects of the new law was to spread employment by shortening the work week, cutting out overtime, and raising the age for leaving school. Steps taken toward the end of 1934 and early in 1935 to lower interest rates formed another recovery measure. The government tried to switch from long-term to short-term borrowing to lessen its competition with private business in bidding for long-term capital. A forced change in its governors made the Bank of France somewhat less reluctant than before to absorb Treasury bills. In the Chamber of Deputies, Paul Reynaud, who had previously urged devalua-

tion, again insisted on a choice between devaluation and deflation and warned that Flandin's interest-rate policy would tend to raise prices and worsen the overvaluation of the franc. Not much came from Flandin's mild attempt at reflation on the gold standard. Even the lowering of long-term interest rates proved only temporary.[5]

First cracks in the gold bloc

What menaced the French gold standard was not so much actual balance-of-payments deficits as the threat of potental capital flight, a threat intensified by the Belgian devaluation of March 1935. The current-account deficit was shrinking steadily from 1932 to 1935,[6] and in 1934 the Bank of France had actually gained gold and foreign exchange reserves. None of this, however, means that the franc was not overvalued after all, since the balance-of-payments and reserve positions were being maintained by internal deflation and import controls.

The smaller gold countries were less fortunate: Switzerland, the Netherlands, and Belgium were losing gold. Though her remaining gold reserves were still well above the minimum legal requirement, Belgium was generally considered the financially weakest member of the group. She was suffering from unemployment and from a collapse of the international trade on which her economy had so heavily depended; between 1929 and 1934 imports had fallen from 35.6 to 14 billion francs and exports from 31.9 to 13.7 billion francs.[7] Public confidence in the banking system was shaky. The belga (a unit worth 5 Belgian francs, introduced in 1926 for exchange-market purposes to emphasize the independence of the Belgian currency from the then unstable French franc) was subject to bear speculation. Rumors of devaluation and the consequent capital outflow became particularly intense in November 1934, but loans from American, Dutch, and Swiss banks saved the situation for the time being. A slump in the exchange value of the British pound late in February and early March 1935 thrust a fresh crisis upon the gold countries. Further rumors touched off a new bear attack, and on March 17 the government centralized control over all foreign-exchange operations and bullion dealings and forbade noncommercial sales of belgas. Next the cabinet resigned, saying it did not have the overwhelming parliamentary support necessary for successful defense of the currency. The belga weakened on the exchanges while a new coalition was being put together. The impact of increased British tariffs on iron and steel products largely imported from Belgium, the perilous state of the banks, and the impracticality of further deflation and wage cuts combined to force a decision. The new premier, Paul van Zeeland, had been in office only a few days at the end of March 1935 before announcing a devaluation, whose extent was soon afterwards specified as 28 percent. The government reaffirmed belief in gold-standard principles and called (in vain) for an international conference to consider general restabilization of currencies. Belgian economic conditions improved over the next two years, but it is difficult to measure the role of the devaluation in this recovery. A royal decree of March 31, 1936 reestablished the gold standard at the new devalued parity.

The fall of the belga renewed bearishness on the currencies of the Netherlands, Switzerland, Italy, and France. Danzig devalued by 42 percent on May 2, 1935. To meet a gold drain, the Dutch authorities introduced legislation to cut state expenditure and raised the discount rate of the Netherlands Bank. The leading commercial banks were asked to prevent speculation against the guilder, to assure customers that the currency was in no danger, and to keep from expressing doubts about Holland's ability to stay on gold. At the expense of continued internal economic stagnation, the guilder weathered attacks against it in April and May and again in July 1935. Even the Swiss franc, which had a metallic backing of over 100 percent at the end of 1934, came under bear attack after the Belgian devaluation. In May 1935 the forward quotation on the Swiss franc in terms of sterling fell to a discount of 28 percent a year. Swiss authorities raised the discount rate, asked commercial banks to withhold credit from hoarders of goods, gold or foreign exchange, and called for penalties on persons contributing toward depreciation of the currency. By June 1935, the run on the Swiss franc subsided.

In France, Premier Flandin denied any tie between the French and Belgian currencies. Early in April his government announced that it would mint gold coins to insure confidence in the franc (though a delay of perhaps a few years was likely before enough coins would be ready for circulation and though the coinage was bound to trench upon official gold reserves). His compromise policy of trying to combine cheaper credit with budgetary deflation to defend the franc was failing. The Bank of France raised its discount rate three times in close succession toward the end of May 1935. Budget deficits were continuing to undermine confidence. Despite a technically strong banking position and a gold reserve that would ordinarily have been ample, a run on the franc was in full swing in May and June. On one day in May the discount on three months forward francs in London touched 40 percent a year.[8] The "speculators" who were blamed for these troubles were by no means professionals only, but included ordinary French and foreign businessmen trying to get rid of francs out of ordinary prudence. After being refused power to decree further government economies, Flandin resigned on May 31. His successor survived in office less than four days.

Renewed attempts at price deflation in France

On June 8, 1935, Pierre Laval's new government obtained from Parliament the very emergency powers denied to its predecessors. Trying to balance the budget, Laval raised some taxes and decreed a 10 percent reduction in practically all payments made by the government, including subsidies, salaries (not only in government employment but even in some subsidized private enterprises), pensions, and inter-

4. Martin Wolfe, *The French Franc between the Wars, 1919–1939*, New York: Columbia University Press, 1951, p. 105.

5. H. V. Hodson, *Slump and Recovery*, London: Oxford University Press, 1938, pp. 364–368.

6. See table in Wolfe, *op. cit.*, p. 218.

7. Walter A. Morton, *British Finance, 1930–1940*, Madison: University of Wisconsin Press, 1943, p. 157.

8. Bank for International Settlements, 6th *Annual Report, 1935–1936*, p. 12. Hodson, *op. cit.*, pp. 369–377, provides many of the other facts above.

est on domestically held government securities, which spelled partial repudiation of a government contract. (Some exceptions were made for hardship cases, such as those involving the pensions of totally disabled veterans and the salaries of the lowest-paid government employees.) Thousands of government employees and unemployed workers rioted in Paris against these cutbacks. Other decrees attempted to deflate prices in the private economy. All rents were cut by 10 percent. Landlords were allowed a 10 percent cut in interest payable on mortgages. Prices of gas, electricity, bread, and fertilizer were reduced. By the time his special powers expired in October, Laval had issued no less than 549 decree-laws, some of them interfering with private contracts to a degree unprecedented outside totalitarian countries. Whatever the reasons may be, the country did enjoy a brief calm; the Bank of France regained some of its lost reserves, and signs of slow economic recovery were noted. Some economic logic actually can be claimed for Laval's program. If defending the exchange rate rules out monetary expansion to promote recovery from depression—if domestic purchasing power must not be expanded by increasing the number of francs in circulation—then the next best approach is to expand total real purchasing power by raising the purchasing power of each existing franc. Given the number of money units in circulation, it is price-and-wage cuts rather than price-and-wage increases that will tend to promote recovery. Laval's program was roughly the opposite of NRA in the United States, and it made better theoretical sense. The mistake was insistence on doing things the hard way.

Actually, France under Laval was inconsistently deflating and reflating both at the same time. While cutting ordinary budget expenditure, his government was incurring heavy extrabudgetary charges for armaments and public works and was borrowing not only from the public but also from the Bank of France. By the end of 1935 the public debt was 338 billion francs, up 64 billions since 1931. Forty percent of all budget expenditure went to service the national debt, and another 20 percent went for military expenses and pensions.[9] By January 1936 Laval was unwilling to push economy any further and was under fire for the Hoare-Laval proposals to appease Italy in Ethiopia. His resignation created another run on the franc. His successor tried to carry on until the election of a new Chamber of Deputies. During this interlude, on March 7, Hitler reoccupied the Rhineland. The expenses that mobilization would have entailed figured among the reasons for French vacillation at this time.

Italy and Poland off gold

Italy's currency policy during the mid-1930s contrasted with that of other members of the gold bloc. Step by step Italy left any semblance of a real gold standard. Although decrees had cut prices and wages, deflation by credit restriction had not been used before 1934. Public-works spending was contributing to a budget deficit. A fall almost to the legal minimum in the gold reserve ratio of the central bank promoted capital flight and prompted action to defend the balance of payments. The Bank of Italy already had a practical monopoly of exchange transactions. In April 1934 imports of copper, coffee, and wool were subjected to licensing, which would be administered to affect trade with particular countries. A rise in the Bank of Italy's discount rate in November was taken as a sign of threatening devaluation and accelerated the gold loss. In December 1934 Italians were required to declare their foreign securities and balances abroad in case the government should later want to requisition them. Export prices were supervised to prevent undervaluation as a device for secretly accumulating funds abroad. Quotas were used to promote bilateral balancing of imports and exports. These devices for maintaining the lira at an artificial parity meant that Italy had in practice left the gold bloc and was to be classified with exchange-control countries such as Germany. Government control over the Italian internal economy and over the foreign exchanges (with requisitioning of privately held foreign securities) was further extended in 1935, especially after the invasion of Ethiopia and the voting of sanctions by the League of Nations that fall.

Poland never had been considered a full-fledged member of the gold bloc. In April 1936 she unmistakably left it by abolishing free dealings in gold and instituting exchange control. The old parity of the zloty was kept, but it had become artificial.

France in 1936

In 1936 the spotlight was back on France.[10] A rather detailed survey is necessary as background for appraisal of the supposed lessons of the ensuing currency experiences. Price deflation had run its course by mid-1935 but still had not cured the overvaluation of the franc. Overvaluation was even worsening: in the six months between September 1935 and March 1936, the wholesale price level rose by nearly 10 percent. Political developments pushed toward a climax. Elections in May gave the Popular Front a majority in the Chamber of Deputies, and at the beginning of June the Socialist Leon Blum formed a Communist-supported ministry. A wave of sitdown strikes by triumphant workers ended with the government-sponsored "Matignon agreement" of June 8, in which employers accepted collective bargaining and granted wage increases, shorter hours, and fringe benefits—all pushing up production costs. Premier Blum's legislative proposals dealt with public works, farm price supports, nationalization of the armaments industry, reorganization of the Bank of France in the direction of ultimate nationalization, a rise in the age for leaving school, vacations with pay, promotion of collective bargaining, a 40-hour work week with no cut in weekly wages, and modification of Laval's salary and pension cuts. (Blum argued that higher wages would mean increased purchasing power and so benefit the whole nation.) Later he intended to enact a scheme of old-age pensions, further measures to deal with unemployment, and tax reform at the expense of inherited wealth.

Given the increased spending and higher costs and prices that this program involved, it was natural to expect an accompanying devaluation of the franc. Paul Reynaud once again warned that delay would make matters all the more difficult. Even some persons who until then had wanted to stay on gold by means of deflation, such as the statesmen Caillaux and Germain Martin and the economist Charles Rist, now called for devaluation in one guise or another. Blum's finance minister, Vincent Auriol, a former advocate of devaluation, had changed his mind in the opposite direction, however, and now argued against the step lest it lead other countries to devalue in retaliation and tend to raise internal prices without guaranteeing an improvement in foreign trade. He attacked persons who called devaluation "inevitable" and castigated "traitors" secretly holding funds abroad.

Premier Blum hoped for some kind of reflation on the gold standard. Despite economic realities emphasized by his critics, he found reasons for still giving assurances against de-

FURTHER CURRENCY EXPERIENCE IN THE 1930S

valuation. His Communist supporters suspected that devaluation would raise the cost of living and rob workers of their recent gains. Besides, they were not particularly concerned about the health of a capitalist economy. Second, his Popular Front had made campaign promises against devaluation. Finally, Blum feared that devaluation would be fruitless and dangerous unless in accord with some sort of international agreement.

Assurances and exhortations apparently had some brief success. During the summer the franc rallied on the exchanges, the capital outflow abated, and in July the Bank of France even regained some gold. More fundamental conditions determined that this improvement in confidence could be only temporary. Measures were either in effect or in preparation to raise wages and grant fringe benefits, to expand public works, to support wheat prices, and to bring the Bank of France (which was not merely the central bank but also a commercial bank with hundreds of offices) more nearly under government control. Under a new governor, the Bank repeatedly cut its discount and loan rates in the first few weeks after the Blum government took office. Unaccompanied by devaluation, however, the government's attempts to promote business recovery failed in almost every sector of the economy. By August the industrial production index had sagged as low as in the worst months of 1932 and 1935. Unemployment grew. Yet, paradoxically for a time of stagnant production, wholesale prices rose spectacularly from June to October 1936; "reflation" was being absorbed in higher prices rather than in general business revival. International developments in 1936 contributed to nervousness: Germany remilitarized the Rhineland in March; Italy completed its conquest of Ethiopia in May, marking the end of the League of Nations as an instrument for collective security; and the Spanish Civil War started in July.

In the midst of these disturbances, during

9. Wynne, *op. cit.*, p. 504; Wolfe, *op. cit.*, p. 116.

10. Cf. Wolfe, *op. cit.*, pp. 138–145, 156–158; Hodson, *op. cit.*, pp. 403–414; Wynne, *op. cit.*, pp. 504–510.

the summer of 1936, the government was having familiar difficulties in paying its bills. It sought a credit at the Bank of France, intending not to draw on it if an issue of one-year and six-month "baby bonds" sold well. The issue was floated in July, bearing interest rates of 3.5 and 4 percent, which would have been attractive to British and American investors but for the risk of loss on depreciation of the franc. Subscriptions were disappointing.

By late summer, the respite was over. The government vainly tried to check the outward seepage of capital. A law of August 13 supplemented earlier measures for registering the export of securities and declaring capital held abroad. Buying foreign banknotes was restricted, sale of gold coin was virtually forbidden, and travelers had to declare any precious metals being taken out of the country. It is noteworthy, however, that the Blum government never did impose full-fledged exchange control. Punishment was provided for spreading rumors to shake confidence in the currency and for inciting withdrawal of deposits or sales of government securities, though advocacy of devaluation in good faith was not forbidden.

Further blows to confidence came in September: strikes in the textile industry brought wage increases, and a League of Nations report cited the disparity between internal and external currency values as the greatest obstacle in the way of worldwide recovery and hinted in favor of devaluation of the gold-bloc currencies. The spot exchange value of the franc was still pegged (by gold outflows amounting to $320 million worth between August 7 and September 25), but the forward quotation gave a truer picture: the discount on forward three-month francs at times reached 37 or 38 percent a year. A rise from 3 to 5 percent in Bank rate on September 24, reversing Blum's cheap-credit policy, was taken as indicating not strength but desperation in the face of gold losses. On the next day, rumors drove the discount on forward francs to a level said to represent an approximately even bet on devaluation by 25 percent within three months.

French devaluation and its repercussions

During the night of September 25–26, in almost identical statements released in Paris, London, and Washington, the three governments announced a devaluation of the franc. (The three statements are reprinted at the end of the 7th *Annual Report* (1936–1937) of the Bank for International Settlements.) Though intergovernmental negotiations had been going on for several months, the secret had been well kept. The devaluation apparently surprised the many Frenchmen who had come to trust Premier Blum's guarantees against it. Some earlier statements of the Premier and the Finance Minister had, it is true, listed possible international complications among the reasons for not devaluing, and the French government could now claim that intergovernmental agreement to avoid these complications had changed the situation. In fact, this public-relations aspect, rather than any substantive provisions, was probably the chief purpose of the so-called Tripartite Monetary Agreement. In the joint announcement, the British and U.S. governments "welcomed" the "readjustment" of the franc, promised to avoid disturbing responses to it, barred competitive exchange depreciation, called for relaxation of trade and exchange restrictions, and invited other nations to join in similar pledges.

A supplement to the original declaration, the so-called Gold Agreement, was announced on October 12–13. Each day the monetary authority of each participating country would cable the other two the price in its own currency at which it would buy and sell gold. Since these quotations would be valid for 24 hours, each monetary authority would know the exchange rates at which it could deal in the other two currencies during the next 24 hours without risk of exchange loss. This assurance would facilitate cooperation among the three countries' exchange-stabilization funds in managing exchange rates. By late November 1936 Belgium, Holland, and Switzerland also adhered to the agreement. A modified gold bloc was thus created.[11]

The French Parliament ratified the devaluation of the franc on October 1. The Bank of France no longer had to redeem its notes in gold bullion, though the franc was still defined as a gold currency. The cabinet was to fix its new gold content at somewhere between 25.2 and 34.4 percent below the old. When the exchange markets reopened, the franc settled at not quite 4.7 U.S. cents, representing a devaluation of about 30 percent. The Exchange Stabilization Fund set up by the new law supported the franc at this level until late in March 1937. Under the law, private holders of gold were not to profit from the devaluation: they could either sell their gold to the Bank of France at the old rate or hold it and pay the government the amount of increase in its franc value. Undeclared gold could be confiscated. In fact, this provision was neither obeyed nor enforced.[12]

The story so far shows how much economic misery and political turmoil over several years stemmed from the inappropriateness of a single pegged price—that of the French franc. This sacred price, so long and painfully defended, finally had to be adjusted anyway. The final step was brought on not by a massive actual deficit in the balance of payments nor by exhaustion of gold reserves but by a flight from the franc. Perhaps the flight might have been weathered for some time, or even temporarily checked again, but the necessary measures no longer seemed worthwhile. The flight was likely to recur from time to time as long as French political and economic disorder undermined confidence and, in particular, as long as the opinion prevailed that the franc was overvalued.

The French franc pulled other currencies down with it. The Swiss Federal Council met in emergency session on Saturday morning, September 26, and announced that the Swiss franc would *not* be devalued; the Councilors apparently felt that Switzerland faced no such special necessity for devaluation as France had faced. But heavy gold losses prompted a reversal that same afternoon, and the following day the Federal Council instructed the National Bank to cut the gold content of the Swiss franc by between 25.9 and 34.6 percent. The final devaluation, like the French, amounted to about 30 percent. The Swiss decision caused the Dutch government to reverse its initial decision the same day, the 26th; for Holland, with the only important currency still on its predepression gold basis, would have faced unbearable pressure. The government embargoed gold exports, saying ironically that it did so "to prevent being forced to abandon the gold standard."[13] No definite margin of devaluation was set, but a newly established equalization fund kept the exchange rate against the dollar in the vicinity of 20 percent below the old parity. The currency of the Dutch East Indies followed that of the mother country. The Italian lira was already so much subject to exchange control as not to be genuinely on the gold standard. Nevertheless, it was devalued on October 5 to 59.06 percent of its former gold content—a degree of devaluation identical, significantly, to that of the United States dollar in 1934. This step must have been embarrassing to Mussolini, who, in a speech at Pesaro in 1926, had sworn to defend the lira to the last drop of blood and had ordered his words graven in stone. The Czechoslovak crown, which had already been devalued by 16⅔ percent in February 1934, was cut again by from 13 to 19 percent, or to between 28 and 32 percent below its pre-1934 gold content. Latvia devalued by about 40 percent, reestablishing its pre-1931 parity with sterling. Some currencies previously linked to the French franc, such as those of Greece and Turkey, now linked themselves to sterling. Despite rumors of devaluation of the Reichsmark, the German authorities decided against passively following in a move on which they had not been consulted. Anyway, Germany already had multiple exchange rates and comprehensive exchange controls. The only country remaining on gold at the predepression parity and without exchange controls was now Albania. From the start, the currency adjustments of 1936 involved much more official intervention in exchange markets and much more management of the rates than had been undertaken in the early months of wide fluctuations after the wave of depreciation in 1931.

Further weakness and the floating franc

The new pattern of exchange rates soon came under renewed strain. Not enough refugee capital returned to France to save the franc from occasional weakness, especially in the forward quotations. A moderate and spotty increase in production in France after the devaluation faded in the spring of 1937. A drop in unemployment was due less to the devaluation than to the work-spreading 40-hour

11. Hudgins, *op. cit.*, pp. 22–23, 171, 179–180.

12. Wolfe, *op. cit.*, pp. 146–147.

13. Hodson, *op. cit.*, p. 418.

law. Retail and wholesale prices continued rising. All through January and February 1937 Finance Minister Auriol repeated assurances against further devaluation and waged a campaign against rumors. The discount rate of the Bank of France, which had been lowered after the devaluation, was raised again on January 28, but without checking speculative pressure. On the 29th the Stabilization Fund revealed that it had kept the franc pegged only by using its entire allotment of gold, and now it had to borrow more gold from the Bank of France. In February, for the sake of businessmen's confidence, Blum announced a "pause" in further social and economic reform. Some fiscal retrenchment was undertaken. Free trade in gold was reestablished, and the earlier law against undeclared gold holdings was reversed. Blum was determined to maintain a free foreign-exchange market.

Around the beginning of April, the Exchange Stabilization Fund, now managed by a commitee of monetary experts, relaxed the peg. The franc soon sank to the minimum support level specified in the law of October 1, or to some 6 percent below the preceding support level and about 34 percent below the old gold parity.

Renewed difficulties for the Exchange Stabilization Fund provoked further capital flight in May 1937. By this time, government promises of no further devaluation only made the speculators more suspicious. The balance of payments on current account was also taking a turn for the worse. The export stimulus of the devaluation was being offset by higher labor costs and general distrust. Earnings from tourism, though improved, were still well below the levels of 1925–1931, and other invisible exports also responded poorly. On the import side, quota and tariff restrictions had been liberalized soon after the first devaluation. The current-account deficit, measured in billions of francs of the gold content of the 1928 law, rose from 0.8 in 1935 to 2.9 in 1936 and to 4.0 in 1937.[14]

By mid-June 1937, the discount on forward francs exceeded 35 percent a year. During June the Stabilization Fund and the Bank of France lost about $350 million worth of gold in resisting speculative attacks. The government, in familiar domestic financial difficulties, had to arrange for loans directly from the Bank of France. Blum resigned on June 21 after being refused emergency decree-making powers to deal with the financial panic.

A second Popular Front government was formed on June 24, with the more moderate Radical-Socialists under Camille Chautemps replacing the Socialists in predominance. Chautemps obtained, until the end of August, the decree-making powers denied to Blum. A decree-law of June 30, 1937 cut the franc from any specific support limits, leaving the Exchange Stabilization Fund now committed only to what Finance Minister Bonnet called a "mobile defense of the franc." The Americans and British had approved what they regarded as a forced rather than a competitive depreciation.

Bear attacks on the floating franc grew intense in September 1937. The Stabilization Fund, retreating from a support level that it had held for about six weeks, allowed the franc to slip almost down to half of its pre-1936 gold value. A reassuring official declaration of rather conservative tone, together with an influx of funds into France following the New York Stock Market crash in the fall of 1937, then came to the rescue. The Stabilization Fund was able to keep the franc steady in November and December, and the discount on the forward franc narrowed. But France entered 1938 in renewed political and economic turmoil. The continuing rise in French prices and the worldwide business recession hampered exports. Disagreement over how to handle a wave of sit-down strikes led in January to organization of a third Popular Front government, with Chautemps still premier and with Blum and other Socialists completely out of the cabinet. Government finances and the exchange value of the franc continued deteriorating. Parliament refused Chautemps new decree-making powers. Hitler annexed Austria. The fourth and last Popular Front government, formed by Blum on March 13, 1938, lasted only one month.

Edouard Daladier put together a new government drawn from the moderate Radical-Socialists and parties on the Right. At the time, the franc had been floating at around 170 to the pound sterling. Armed with decree-making powers, Daladier announced on May 4 that the franc would be fixed at about 179 to the pound and further depreciation stopped.[15] This retreat to a level which, as Daladier hoped, could be "defended victoriously" amounted to a devaluation against the dollar of some 36 to 38 percent below the level prevailing just before the franc was unpegged on June 30, 1937. In terms of gold, the franc was now

worth only 42 percent of its value of before
September 1936 and only 8½ percent of its
value before World War I.[16] Thus eroded, the
franc was successfully stabilized in relation to
sterling until the outbreak of World War II.
During the winter of 1938–1939, for the first
time in several years, France experienced a sustained homecoming (chiefly from England) of
funds that had previously taken flight. Sterling
itself declined against the dollar during the war
scares of 1938, however, and the franc went
along, sinking from an average of 2.81 U.S.
cents in May 1938 to 2.63 cents in November.
It held near that level until the war.

The vicissitudes of the French exchange rate
occurred against a background of domestic
failure on the part of the Blum government
and its successors. Even when the brief business recovery of the spring of 1937 had carried
practically to full employment, industrial production was well below predepression levels.
This anomaly stemmed from near-stagnation
in population growth, a back-to-the-farm
movement during the depression, and the
legally imposed 40-hour work week; between
1929 and 1937, total hours worked in industry
had fallen by one-third. On the eve of World
War II, France was less of a manufacturing
nation and more of a rural nation than it had
been during the 1920s. With qualifications
about the problems of comparison over a long
time span, it even seems that the level of
French industrial production just before
World War II was not much greater than just
before World War I. Other aspects of the
Popular Front program also proved disappointing, including the quasi nationalization of the
Bank of France and the nationalization of the
railroads and some heavy industry. Lack of
confidence hampered business investment.

A closer look at the floating franc

It is during this period, specifically, between
the unpegging of the franc on June 30, 1937
and the repegging on May 4, 1938, that the
author of the influential *International Currency Experience* finds his fourth historical
example of the speculative disorders supposed
generally to characterize fluctuating exchange
rates.[17] But the origin and special features of
the situation should be remembered. The unpegging of June 1937 had been preceded by
heavy bear speculation on the pegged franc
during 1936 and earlier and then, in violation
of repeated promises, by the devaluation in

September. After this, despite inducements to
repatriate capital and more assurances against
another devaluation, the expected large-scale
reversal of capital flight did not occur. The
growing danger of war, alarm at Popular Front
policies, the continual rise in wages and prices,
the sluggishness of industrial recovery, the deteriorating balance of payments, and fears of
another devaluation all sapped confidence. The
Exchange Stabilization Fund had to keep selling gold and foreign exchange to support the
franc, and even after its forced retreat to a
lower support level in March 1937, the fund
kept on losing gold. Finally, on June 30, the
franc was completely cut from gold, and discretionary intervention replaced support within
specified limits.

This unpegging of the franc came, significantly, as a last resort, after efforts to hold it
steady had collapsed the previous September
and had collapsed again in March. Even during the period of the floating franc, exchange
rates were not left to private supply and demand alone. The French Fund, sometimes
helped by the British Exchange Equalisation
Account, intervened in the market from time
to time, losing gold in costly efforts to sustain
the franc.[18] During the fall of 1937, clues to
the fund's gains and losses of gold appeared in
the weekly balance sheets of the Bank of
France. Gold losses, thus publicized, tended to
intensify capital flight by showing that the
franc would have been still weaker if it had not
been for the official support. Bear speculators
profitably knew that any change in the support
level would very probably be downward rather

14. Wolfe, *op. cit.*, pp. 154–155, 218.

15. André Piettre, *Monnaie et Économie Internationale*, Paris: Éditions Cujas, 1967, p. 188.

16. Wolfe, *op. cit.*, p. 181.

17. Nurkse, *op. cit.*, pp. 118, 120, 123.

18. On official intervention during this period,
see Robert Solomon, "The French Exchange Stabilization Fund," *Federal Reserve Bulletin*, January 1950, pp. 36–37; Leonard Waight, *The
History and Mechanism of the Exchange Equalisation Account*, Cambridge: Cambridge University
Press, 1939, pp. 109, 111; and Wolfe, *op. cit.*,
pp. 178–179.

than upward. Yet complete secrecy about the fund's operations might not have helped much; as long as some kind of official intervention was known to be taking place from time to time, guesses about the intentions of the authorities would have furnished material for rumors and speculation.

In short, the experiences of France in 1937–1938 have little to do with *freely* fluctuating exchange rates. They are probably less relevant as evidence against that system than as evidence against the adjustable peg.

A review of four historical examples

Now that we have met with this last, in historical order, of Nurkse's horrible examples of speculation (the others were France in 1922–1926, Britain in 1931–1932, and the United States in 1933–1934), it is appropriate to make some summarizing comments on all four of them. The examples suggest, at most, that fluctuating rates do not work well when exchange-rate pegging does not work at all and has in fact broken down. The examples are instructive in showing some of the conditions that do give rise to actually or apparently disruptive speculation: domestic inflation and disordered government finances; the shock of suddenly unpegging a previously overvalued currency under attack by bear speculation, and the reaction from that shock; prospects for unorthodox fiscal and monetary measures, such as deliberate manipulation of the gold value of a currency as a means of influencing prices and business conditions; domestic policies regarded as hostile to business; and clumsy official intervention in the exchange market, particularly when it repeatedly presents speculators with "one-way options."

Professor Edward C. Simmons has made some pertinent comments on why historical episodes provide poor laboratory data in economics. Floating currencies have always appeared after the supposedly temporary collapse of metallic parities. History cannot tell us what would happen if countries abandoned fixed parities once and for all, stopped intervening in foreign-exchange markets, and managed money at home according to an announced rule. Eagerness to seize on history for supposed evidence of disruptive foreign-exchange speculation makes one wonder if anything can be learned from history. A "misreading of economic history . . . underlies the mistaken foreign exchange policies of the present day."

It is disheartening "to think that men are so firmly set in their minds about the necessity of fixed exchange rates that they are willing to believe all sorts of distortions of past events."[19]

German economic nationalism[20]

The chief currencies to escape the wave of exchange depreciation in the 1930s were those of some countries in Central and Eastern Europe. Exchange control maintained predepression parities, and such currency depreciation as occurred did so in concealed forms. Germany provides the classic example of this policy. For the first two years after the start of the depression in 1929, drastic internal deflation kept the mark from becoming seriously overvalued at its fixed gold content. Monetary deflation was supplemented, under the Brüning government, by attempts to lower wages, prices, rents, and interest by administrative decree. Germany developed a "favorable" balance of trade, which grew from 36 million marks in 1929 to 1.6 billion in 1930 and 2.9 billion in 1931; in the latter year, exports, though down from predepression levels, were 43 percent in excess of the even more sharply reduced imports. This commodity export surplus reflects the capital outflow that had replaced the heavy predepression inflow.

During the international liquidity crisis of 1931, a panicky flight of capital led the German government to impose exchange control. The controls that the Nazis were later to perfect into tools for the conscious economic exploitation of foreigners thus originated earlier, as emergency expedients. In September, two months after the unilateral German action, a "Standstill Agreement" was reached with creditors in the United States, the United Kingdom, and West European countries except Spain. This agreement, which initially applied to slightly more than one-fourth of Germany's total external debt, was continued with modifications every year until 1939. It provided for only gradual withdrawal of mark balances owned by foreigners and for extension of foreign trade credits granted to Germans. Controls and standstill arrangements thus gave rise to blocked marks, balances available only for restricted purposes. These blocked marks, bought and sold at a discount abroad, were the first of the many special types of mark later to characterize the complex German currency system.

As foreign currencies were devalued, the

German mark became increasingly out of line. With a theoretically unchanged gold content, it went from a predepression parity of 23.8 U.S. cents to a new parity of just over 40 cents. Reflation and public works begun under Hitler in 1933 to remedy unemployment raised German incomes and prices and contributed to overvaluation. This was a serious handicap to a country as dependent on international trade as Germany (even in the depression year of 1931, Germany had exported over one-third of her industrial production and had depended on foreign sources for some 40 or 45 percent of her raw materials). A sizable cut in the gold value of the mark would have been necessary simply to keep pace with foreign devaluations, but considerations of prestige apparently told against this. At least in the panic conditions of mid-1931, furthermore, devaluation might have seemed a sign of weakness and have intensified attempts at capital flight. Still remembering the hyperinflation of 1923, the public tended to associate exchange depreciation with impending collapse of the currency, and businessmen feared demands that wage rates be linked to exchange rates.

The Nazi regime tightened the partial moratorium already in effect on payments of interest and principal on external debts. Effective in mid-1933, interest and dividends on foreign-held German securities could be paid only to the Conversion Office for German Foreign Debts. Up to half the amounts so paid were made available to the foreign creditors in free currency, with scrip issued for the blocked remainder. The Golddiskontbank then offered to buy the blocked marks with free currency at a discount from the mark's official value. In effect, foreigners could collect only about three-fourths of the payments due them. In 1934, when a worsening in the German balance of trade endangered the Reichsbank's gold reserves, official conversion of interest and dividend payments into free currency was suspended completely, effective on July 1. Instead, foreign creditors were offered ten-year bonds in exchange for their blocked marks. Also discontinued at this time was the arrangement whereby German sellers of so-called "additional exports" (exports considered unsalable without subsidy at official exchange rates) had been allowed to use their foreign-currency earnings to buy German securities, trading on foreign markets at severe discounts from their prices as translated at official exchange rates, in order to bring the securities home and resell them at a profit in marks. This arrangement

FURTHER CURRENCY EXPERIENCE IN THE 1930S

had in effect enabled the favored German exporters to collect subsidies from foreign investors, whose German claims had been depreciated by the inconvertibility of the mark. Now, after mid-1934, "additional exports" were to be subsidized in other ways.

Blocked marks continued to be traded abroad, but only at growing discounts. Various types of blocked mark retained what value they did because the German authorities allowed their use for some purposes, primarily tourist travel in Germany, investment in German securities, and gifts to Germans, as well as for purchase of German exports when bilateral agreements with foreign countries so stipulated. The German tourist industry benefited from the cheap marks available to its foreign customers.

Not only capital movements but also trade in goods and services came under tightening control. Even before the Nazis took power, exporters had been required to sell their foreign-exchange earnings to control authorities, who supervised export transactions and export prices to prevent hidden capital transfers. Foreign exchange was rationed among importers, the allotments initially being specified percentages (successively reduced) of the amounts of foreign exchange bought by each importer in a 1930–1931 base period.

In 1932 and 1933, particularly, "private compensation" served as a means of trading under conditions of currency overvaluation and exchange control. Barter deals were at first undertaken chiefly by firms regularly engaged in both import and export business or by German firms trading with foreign subsidiaries.

19. "Edward C. Simmons, "Discussion," *Journal of Economic History,* **XV,** December 1955, pp. 413–414.

20. The sections on Germany draw mainly on Ragnar Nurkse, *op. cit.,* pp. 167–183; Frank A. Southard, Jr., *Foreign Exchange Practice and Policy,* New York: McGraw-Hill, 1940, pp. 192–197; P. T. Ellsworth, *The International Economy,* New York: Macmillan, 1950, pp. 621–625, 631–641; Ralph H. Blodgett, *Comparative Economic Systems,* rev. ed., New York: Macmillan, 1949, pp. 526–532; and Frank C. Child, *The Theory and Practice of Exchange Control in Germany,* The Hague: Martinus Nijhoff, 1958.

German exporters soon began accepting payment in foreign commodities, which they would then sell to import firms. In 1932, dozens of private and semi-official information agencies sprang up to bring firms together and arrange these transactions. Private compensation trade required government permission, since exports bartered away would not yield foreign exchange for compulsory sale to the authorities. Permission was generally granted only if the exports were considered unsalable in the regular way at official exchange rates and if the imports to be received were considered advantageous to the German economy. The government itself presumably took part in some of the larger deals, such as the barter of coal for Brazilian coffee and of fertilizer for cotton owned by the Egyptian government. In 1934, when importers' rations of free foreign exchange were drastically cut and when demand, strengthened by the return of prosperity at home, was also raising the scarcity value of German imports, private compensation changed in character. Importers rather than exporters now took the initiative. They offered exporters premium prices in marks for foreign goods against which German goods had in effect been bartered. In this way the importer paid more marks for his purchase than corresponded to its foreign-currency value translated at the official rate of exchange, and the exporter received more marks for his merchandise than corresponded to its translated foreign value. Transactions of this sort amounted to a selective devaluation of the mark. Official permission was of course required.

In mid-1934 rationing of foreign exchange according to official judgments about the national importance of various imports replaced rationing according to the base-period purchases of individual importers. The so-called New Plan took formal shape in September with the establishment of numerous commodity control boards, each responsible for detailed licensing and regulation of trade in a particular group of products. German manufacturers requiring a variety of foreign raw materials had to deal with several separate bureaucracies. Detailed control extended to trade both with free-currency countries and with Germany's partners in bilateral clearing agreements. Before long, the controls were supplemented by a program of direct but secret export subsidies financed by a gross receipts tax levied on German businesses. The subsidy scheme discriminated very flexibly among products, firms, and markets. Selective offsets to the overvaluation of the mark spurred the export of commodities considered relatively dispensable in order to pay for imports considered relatively essential. By maintaining the overvaluation of the mark for certain commodities and markets and neutralizing it for others, the German planners were acting like a discriminating monopolist on the international market. The general purposes of the New Plan were to exploit national bargaining power (and foreign weaknesses) in order to exchange exports for imports on the most favorable terms possible, to achieve a degree of national self-sufficiency, and to cultivate import sources most likely to remain dependable in wartime. Increased bilateralism in trade was one method of pursuing these aims. The German authorities openly abandoned any efforts to restore free exchange markets; they preferred to bolster and exploit their bargaining power by discriminatory controls.

Clearing and payments agreements

Bilateral clearing supplemented exchange control in pursuit of the objectives of the New Plan. Some bilateral agreements had been in effect before then. Germany's first, the agreement with Hungary, had been signed even before the Nazi era, in April 1932. (This agreement had a forerunner in the agreement of November 1931 between Austria and Switzerland.) It provided that German importers would pay the Reichsbank in marks for imports from Hungary, while the Hungarian National Bank would pay Hungarian exporters in pengos. The marks received from German importers were to be used, in part, to pay German exporters to Hungary, while Hungarian importers of German goods would provide the pengos paid to exporters. The agreement evidently envisaged a German import surplus in trade with Hungary, since about 10 percent of the marks paid by German importers were to be released to the Hungarian National Bank in convertible funds, and three-fourths and one-fourth of the remainder were to be used, respectively, to pay for current exports to Hungary and to pay Germans holding old blocked commercial claims on Hungary. In general, exchange clearing was a device for bypassing the foreign-exchange market and diminishing the trade-hampering effects of two countries' exchange controls and artificial exchange rates.

Each country maintained an agency to which importers of goods from the other made payment in home currency and from which exporters of goods to the other received payment in home currency. Clearing agreements could cover trade in services as well as in commodities and, as in the German-Hungarian agreement, could even provide for the liquidation of old debts. An important part of a·clearing arrangement was the rate of exchange to be used in translating into one currency or the other the value of the trade in each direction and thus in calculating the debt that might currently develop between the two national agencies. Except as imbalance in bilateral trade was deliberately provided for, such arrangements tended to promote a downward-biased[21] bilateral balancing of imports and exports: if one of the two countries was underimporting, its importers would not be paying enough money into the home clearing agency to satisfy the claims of exporters; and exporters, meeting delays in being paid, would have an incentive to curtail their shipments.

By the mid-1930s, Germany had bilateral trade agreements of this or variant types with almost all European countries and a few Latin-American countries. In the Balkans, particularly, the Nazis used clearing agreements and barter deals for economic domination. With the overvaluation of their own currencies and depression and trade barriers in other countries hampering exports through normal commercial channels, many producers in Southeastern Europe welcomed any chance of greater trade with Germany. Exporters thus unintentionally became something of an "economic fifth column" for Germany, prodding their governments to accept German proposals and to make the concessions necessary from time to time to prevent interruption of bilateral trade. The Germans, for their part, were clever in increasing and exploiting the economic dependence of their small trading partners. Often, for example, Germany imported more from its partners than it exported to them; the Balkan countries developed clearing-balance claims which, as long as they went unspent, represented forced loans to Germany from countries poorer than itself. This situation has been called "double exploitation"—exploitation in addition to that achieved by manipulating the terms of trade.[22] The Nazis seem to have realized that a country gains by what it imports rather than by what it exports and that exports are simply the necessary payment for imports.

The governments of Germany's economic satellites, rather than let their claims acquired by export surpluses go unused, had an incentive to control trade so as to divert purchases toward Germany, even though the desired goods might be priced lower elsewhere. Despite all this, it has been argued that the countries of southeast Europe did reap a net gain from their economic relations with Germany. Something is better than nothing in overcoming the trade-throttling effects of wrong exchange rates. Furthermore, given the depression and the "orthodox" attitudes that blocked vigorous monetary-fiscal remedies, trade with Germany on otherwise unfavorable terms may have been beneficial, after all, in providing employment and expansionary multiplier effects on national income.[23] Inadequately requited exports to Germany may have served the countries of Southeastern Europe as make-work projects; "leaf-raking" in the export sector served as an antidepression measure in the absence of better policies.

Germany's bilateral agreements with West European countries differed from its agreements with its small economic satellites. The West European countries generally took the initiative in seeking agreements. Normally having import surpluses in trade with Germany and so being net sources of free exchange, they saw a bargaining advantage and an opportunity to prod the Germans into making payments on existing blocked debts. By the end of 1933, the Germans had made so-called Sondermark agreements with practically every West European country except the United Kingdom. Apparently these agreements were intended to

21. Downward-biased in comparison with trade under equilibrium exchange rates. Actually, bilateral agreements served to promote trade by partially overcoming the impediments of disequilibrium rates.

22. Child, *op. cit.*, esp. pp. 83, 139, 207. The Greek government, for example, once yielded to the political pressure of export interests and floated a bond issue to get the drachmas needed to meet the claims of exporters, since Greek importers of German goods were not providing enough of them.

23. *Ibid.*, pp. 165–168, 229.

govern only a small portion of the trade between the partners. Germany agreed to allow importers who had used up their ordinary foreign-exchange allotments to make purchases in the partner country, anyway, provided its clearing agency would accept payment in mark balances of restricted usability. The typical agreement also mentioned the intention of the two countries to keep the import-export ratio in their mutual trade the same as it had been in 1931. Since Germany had had an export surplus with most of its West European partners, maintenance of this ratio would keep import concessions from impairing Germany's ability to repay old debts. Part of the payments into the clearing accounts in creditor countries were, in fact, earmarked for debt service. After 1933, however, the creditor countries saw their import surpluses in trade with Germany shrinking. Some of them, like France, restricted exports to Germany rather than tolerate further delays in collecting debt payments.

In July and August 1934 the British finally signed debt-service and Sondermark agreements with Germany, only to find blocked mark balances piling up. In November 1934 these arrangements were replaced by a payments agreement. The Anglo-German agreement was a notable example of a device sometimes worked out between exchange-control and free-exchange countries, principally to promote payments on debts due to residents of the free-exchange creditor country. (A well-known precedent was the payments agreement concluded between Great Britain and Argentina in May 1933.) The Germans agreed to earmark 55 percent of the proceeds of their exports to Britain to pay for imports from Britain, reserving most of the remainder for debt service, though some sterling might remain available to the Reichsbank as free exchange. This arrangement differed from bilateral clearing of the type already described in that the controls over trade and payments necessary to maintain the agreed import-export ratio were to be exercised by the German authorities alone. From the British viewpoint, traders could make and receive payments in sterling bills of exchange and avoid the vexations of a full-fledged clearing system.

Aski marks

For some trade with countries with which she had no clearing or payments agreements (such as the United States and some South American countries and British dominions), Germany adopted another device for selectively overcoming the trade-throttling effects of overvaluation. German exchange-control regulations first mentioned Aski marks in December 1934. *Aski* was an abbreviation for *Ausländer-Sonderkonten für Inlandszahlungen,* meaning "foreigners' special accounts for inland payments." For imports unobtainable at world-market prices translated into marks at the overvalued official rate and yet judged of special importance to the German economy, German firms were allowed to offer foreign suppliers premium prices in marks. Payments were credited to the foreign supplier or to his bank in a special account with a German bank. The foreigner could either use these marks himself to buy specified German goods or else sell them to a fellow countryman; they were not generally transferable. A great variety of Aski marks arose, each identified with the particular commodity for which and particular country to which Germans had made payment, as well as with the kinds of purchases in Germany it might be used for. German imports from the United States gave rise chiefly to "cotton marks" and "copper marks," the former being usable for a somewhat wider range of German goods than the latter. Brazilian exporters earned cotton marks, coffee marks, and so forth, each usable for purchase of different German products.

Trading at different degrees of discount from the parity of the regular mark according to the particular commodities and foreign countries involved, Aski marks in effect provided a selective or discriminatory system of German import duties and export subsidies or a selective or discriminatory system of partial currency depreciation. The United States Treasury recognized the export-subsidy aspect of the system in June 1936 by imposing countervailing import duties on a long list of German goods. To remove this disadvantage, the Germans renounced subsidies on exports to the United States and made the special marks paid to American suppliers completely nontransferable; only the original recipient could use them. The United States Treasury rescinded its countervailing duties in December 1936. In March 1939, the United States Treasury again ruled that the German trading arrangements were export subsidization and again imposed countervailing duties. Even before this time, however, the Nazi authorities themselves were coming to realize that the Aski system was not so much creating "additional" trade as diverting "normal" trade, including export trade that would otherwise have earned free exchange. Changed German restrictions themselves caused Aski trade to decline in 1936, 1937, and 1938.

Nazi trade policy was not, as sometimes supposed, contrived above all to prepare for war. Evolving out of earlier expedients to check panicky flights of capital and palliate difficulties stemming from too high a foreign-exchange value of the mark, the policy aimed at maximizing national gain from trade as German planners conceived it. Though the planners may not have thought of the matter in this way, they were seeking to create and exploit monopoly and monopsony positions in foreign markets in order to achieve an approximation to "optimum" terms of trade.[24]

Sterling and the dollar
in the last five prewar years

While the gold-bloc countries were struggling and ultimately failing to maintain their old parities and while Nazi Germany and other countries were experimenting with exchange controls, the British Exchange Equalisation Account kept the dollar-sterling rate fairly stable, but not rigid.[25] (From 1933 until the agreements of 1936, the Account dealt only in francs, since it was supposed to deal only in currencies convertible into gold; but arbitrage transmitted the influence of this intervention to the dollar rate also.) Over the four-year period from mid-1934 to mid-1938, the rate averaged fractionally above $4.95 per pound. Its monthly average stayed within 5 cents of this figure two-thirds of the time and broke out of the range of 10 cents on either side for only three months (August 1934, when it was higher, and March and April 1935, when it was lower).[26] During the four-year period, the sharpest change from one monthly average to the next occurred at the time of the gold-bloc devaluations of 1936, when the pound lost 2¾ percent against the dollar. A final breakout from the range of mild fluctuation foreshadowed the end of the entire prewar exchange system.

From February to April 1935 the pound rate was depressed by an apparent "gold scare": cases pending in the Supreme Court concerning Congressional abrogation of the gold clause in bonds posed the possibility that the United States would have to lower its price of gold.

Devaluation of the belga in March was another apparent influence. From mid-April to the end of June 1937, the dollar strengthened on new rumors that the United States might cut the dollar price of gold, with other countries perhaps following suit. This second "gold scare" reversed itself into a "dollar scare" late in the same year, after the stock market and business activity had slumped in the United States and some fear had arisen that the dollar might be devalued against gold as an antirecession measure. The speculative outflow of funds from the United States continued through the first half of 1938 and in the ten months up to July amounted to nearly $1 billion. Nevertheless, President Roosevelt's declaration in February that there was no question of devaluing the dollar had helped to restrain the flight from dollars into gold. In the summer of 1938 prices recovered on the New York stock mar-

24. *Ibid.*, esp. pp. 53, 78–79, 226–228.

25. The dummy variable for indications of British official intervention, but not a similar dummy for American intervention, has a statistically significant coefficient in regressions for the monthly average exchange rate. Apparently, then, the British but not the American authorities were significantly affecting the rate. This is not to say that official intervention was powerfully overriding "fundamental" influences. On the contrary, the coefficient of greatest statistical significance in the regressions mentioned was that of the ratio of British to U.S. price indexes. See Hudgins, *op. cit.*, especially chaps. IV and V. A few of the other facts stated in this section of the text also come from Hudgins's work.

26. Advocates of floating exchanges could argue, according to Samuel Brittan, that the British authorities held the rate much too nearly rigid. The Bank of England's gold reserve, including the holdings of the Exchange Equalisation Account, grew from £121 million in 1932 to £840 million in March 1938. Only a small part of this increase represented a rise in the sterling price of gold; the bulk of it represented deliberate resistance to appreciation of sterling. Such a policy could be defended, on the other hand, with the argument that the tendency toward appreciation was due to a potentially reversible inward flow of "refugee capital" from the Continent. Brittan, *The Price of Economic Freedom*, New York: St. Martin's Press, 1970, p. 58.

ket. Apprehension turned toward sterling, especialiy as political tension heightened in Europe. During the acute phase of the international crisis in September, before the Munich conference, a violent outflow of capital from Europe began, and in two months, some $600 million came into the United States. Never before, perhaps, had an international hot-money movement changed direction so abruptly. The flow continued at a slackened rate in November and December and regained intensity early in 1939.[27]

Even before then, as early as the first quarter of 1938, sterling had shown signs of receding from the strength displayed during the period of greatest bearishness on the dollar. Commodity prices fell on the average somewhat further and more rapidly in the United States than in Great Britain during the 1937–1938 recession, and the American balance-of-payments surplus increased while the British current account was in deficit. A number of countries accustomed to holding sizable fractions of their international reserves as sterling balances in London suffered from declines in the prices of their raw-material exports during the recession and began drawing on their London funds to meet deficits with other countries. Withdrawals by India, Australia, New Zealand, Ireland, Norway, Sweden, Finland, and other countries tended to weaken the British position. Authorities in Sweden, Norway, and Ireland, for example, were even converting parts of their sterling reserves into gold and dollars. After the franc apparently was stabilized at last in 1938, French funds shifted home from London, particularly in May and again in the autumn. The international crisis over Czechoslovakia motivated transfers to New York also, more so by foreigners holding funds in London than by the British public itself. The weakness of sterling produced something akin to the speculation through leads and lags familiar since World War II. Foreign exporters, and even some exporters in sterling countries themselves, apparently began quoting prices and writing invoices in sterling less often than before. As a result, merchants were inclined to reduce their working balances of sterling. Alternatively, exporters pricing and granting credit in sterling as usual were inclined to borrow sterling from the banks in order to sell it for dollars or gold at once.[28]

Under these pressures, the British Exchange Equalisation Account let the pound slide gradually down from its level of almost $5.02 in February 1938. By late summer the rate had

definitely broken out below the channel that had so long been maintained of 5 or 10 cents on either side of $4.95. The slide continued evenly (except for a very brief dip to $4.60 at the end of September) down to a low of around $4.67 in December and January. The Equalisation Account had apparently been resisting the decline, but without pegging the rate. But now, and until late August 1939, the Account held the rate practically rigid at fractionally above $4.68.

Various measures to defend sterling were adopted in December 1938 and January 1939. The Bank of England transferred gold worth £350 million to the Exchange Equalisation Account. An embargo was tightened on floating security issues in the United Kingdom if their proceeds were to be transferred abroad. An unofficial embargo on forward dealings in gold and on loans secured by private holdings of gold had been relaxed the previous spring but was now tightened again. The objective was to curb speculation in gold and currencies while not hampering ordinary trade requirements. The London Foreign Exchange Committee advised banks that while no scrutiny of spot operations was necessary, they should be sure, in forward operations, that their customers were covering normal trade requirements only. Forward transactions undertaken merely to protect one's capital were not to be permitted.[29]

The first 7½ months of 1939 saw remarkable, if rather artificial, exchange-rate stability. Never since 1931 had currencies fluctuated so little. Large movements of funds continued, connected particularly with the repatriation of capital to France, the shift of foreign central-bank reserves out of London, and transfer of safety-seeking funds to New York. In addition, the pound remained under the pressure of an adverse balance of payments (due partly to imports for armaments) and of a continued weakness in the demand for raw materials produced in the overseas Sterling Area.

Pressure against sterling made heavy demands on the Exchange Equalisation Account. When international tensions increased after mid-August, the strain became too great. On the 25th, the Account withdrew from the market. The rate fell from $4.68 to $4.40 in one day and to $4.27 by the end of the month. On the 26th, an official ban was imposed on foreign security dealings. England declared war on September 3 and established exchange control the next day to conserve its gold and foreign exchange. The dollar-pound rate was pegged in a range of $4.06–$4.02, later narrowed to $4.03½–$4.02½, or 14 percent below the previous support level.[30]

Wartime exchange controls formalized the Sterling Area. Then, as earlier and later also, Britain was not trying to construct a less-than-worldwide financial region for its own sake. On the contrary, it was trying to limit the decline of sterling's international role. This was the logic of building a fence of controls not around Britain alone but around an entire group of countries willing to enforce similar controls. Within the Area, payments for both current and capital transactions would remain free, with less damage to international trade than if each country controlled its separate payments position with the outside world. At the same time, what became known as the Sterling Area dollar pool took formal shape: member countries would sell surplus foreign-currency earnings for sterling balances to be held as reserves in London.[31]

With these changes, most non-Empire members of the Area dropped out. A number of them, including the Scandinavian countries, did so before their currencies had depreciated against the dollar by more than a small percentage. France kept its 16-month-old link with sterling. (In fact, an Anglo-French monetary and economic agreement of December 1939 hopefully provided for keeping the sterling-franc rate unchanged for the duration of the war and until six months after the signing of peace). Most countries not employing exchange controls before the war now followed Britain and France in adopting them; and by the end of March 1940, only four of the world's major currencies—the dollar, the guilder, and the Swiss and Belgian francs—were still substantially free of controls.[32]

The 1930s in review

Severe depression, recurrent waves of exchange depreciation, and intensified economic nationalism characterized the 1930s. Some countries, including the United States and France, never did fully recover from the depression during peacetime. Eventually the painful deflation of the early 1930s was to bring a general reaction in favor of expansionary financial policies. At first, however, preoccupation with the inflations of the previous decade, as in the gold-bloc countries and Germany, hindered adoption of expansionary policies and

realistic exchange rates. Just as generals are said always to be fighting the last war, policymakers were often treating economic disorders that had already given way to their opposites.

Monetary nationalism, though tempered by rudiments of international cooperation, was bolstered by quotas and increased tariffs, by preferential trade agreements, and, still in a minority of countries, by exchange controls and bilateral clearing. Productive international lending and investment, as distinguished from speculative or panicky transfers of capital, remained far below predepression levels. Under the circumstances, it is hardly surprising that the recovery of international trade lagged badly behind the recovery of production. From 1850 to 1929 the growth of world trade (as well as the decline during World War I and from 1929 to 1932) had proceeded at much the same rate as the growth (or decline) of world industrial production. From the trough in 1932

27. Bank for International Settlements, 8th *Annual Report*, 1937–1938, pp. 19–20, and 9th *Annual Report*, 1938–1939, pp. 23–24, 76.

28. BIS, 9th *Annual Report*, p. 85.

29. *Ibid.*, p. 27.

30. On free markets abroad, however, sterling quotations moved under the influence of private supply and demand. The supply in these markets came from payments in sterling for imports into the U.K. and from existing balances in the U.K. held by nonresidents and transferable to residents or other nonresidents. (Foreigners were thus still able to withdraw funds from London, but not at an officially supported rate.) The demand came from nonresidents having to make sterling payments for which "free" sterling was allowed. Quotations in these free markets fluctuated considerably, briefly touching below $3.20 in May 1940. Free markets and discount sterling never accounted for more than a small percentage of total transactions, however; and they were gradually extinguished after the middle of 1940.

31. Benjamin J. Cohen, *The Future of Sterling as an International Currency*, New York: St. Martin's Press, 1971, pp. 81–83; "Twilight of the Sterling Area," Bank of Nova Scotia *Monthly Review*, December 1972, p. 2.

32. BIS, 10th *Annual Report*, 1939–1940, pp. 18–25.

to the peak in 1937, however, the estimated physical volume of world trade rose hardly more than 50 percent, in contrast to a rise of approximately 85 percent in estimated world industrial production. At the highest point in 1939, when recovery from the recession of 1937–1938 was still incomplete, trade and production were slightly more than 40 and 70 percent, respectively, above their troughs of 1932.[33]

The epidemic of exchange depreciation started in late 1929 and early 1930 as the currencies of several primary-producing countries weakened. It gathered momentum with the crisis of 1931 and the depreciations by Great Britain and the other members-to-be of the emergent Sterling Area. As late as the spring of 1933, a considerable body of opinion regarded the international gold standard as only temporarily suspended, but the American depreciation and final devaluation of 1933–1934 and the failure of the London Economic Conference blasted hopes of an early return to gold. After the painfully delayed collapse of the Continental gold bloc in 1936, almost every currency in the world had been affected. Only one currency avoided both depreciation and exchange control—the Albanian franc—until it too was devalued when pegged to the lira after the Italian occupation of Albania in April 1939.

Paper standards came unwanted into existence when the gold standard had clearly failed. Some conditions predisposing the world economy to the Great Depression can plausibly be blamed on the precarious pegging of currencies to gold in the middle and late 1920s. Exchange depreciations came about under pressure of balance-of-payments deficits due to weak export markets or else were undertaken to permit or aid financial policies for recovery from the depression. Depreciation may occasionally have been a "predatory" measure, adopted more or less intentionally to win a price advantage in export markets, even though this meant "exporting unemployment" to other countries. This "beggar-my-neighbor" policy of "competitive exchange depreciation" was far less widespread, however, than subsequently came to be alleged in sweeping and superficial historical generalizations about the 1930s. The world pattern of exchange rates in that decade was haphazardly determined and was repeatedly subject to haphazard changes. It was the product neither of unhampered free-market forces nor of conscious international planning. Some governments clung to hopelessly high parities for their currencies; others deliberately sought to depress their currencies on the exchanges. Almost everywhere, if not always with consistency, governments sought a freedom for domestic monetary management that was incompatible with earlier traditions of exchange-rate fixity.

Some devaluations in the 1930s were larger than "objective" long-run economic conditions would have called for. Panicky flights of hot money were largely to blame—that is, speculation against currencies whose parities had come under suspicion. Yet paradoxically, by the end of 1936, despite all the upheavals in the meanwhile, exchange rates among the chief currencies still free of exchange control had returned to a pattern not far different from the one prevailing in 1930.[34]

However much the successive depreciations may have reversed each other's effects on exchange rates, they did spell lasting increases in the price of gold in national currencies. This, together with increases in the purchasing powers of the currencies themselves, more than doubled the goods-and-services value of gold. World gold production responded. Including the estimated output of the Soviet Union, it was 1.8 times as great in the four years 1935–1938 as in the corresponding period a decade earlier and was twice as great in 1938 as in 1928. Reported gold reserves of central banks and governments (not counting certain stabilization funds) were half again as large in 1938 as ten years before. These figures refer to physical quantities of gold. Taking account of an average markup of 70 percent or more in terms of national currencies, the money value of world gold production was about three and one-half times as great in 1938 as in 1928, and the money value of central gold reserves was more than two and one-half times as great. Because of general price deflation, the *commodity* value of gold production and gold stocks had increased even more.

Available stocks of international liquidity or international means of payment did not increase in similar degree. The rise of the Sterling Area did not completely take the place of the gold-exchange standard of the 1920s as a means of "economizing" on gold. Furthermore, ownership of gold stocks became increasingly concentrated. In the six years 1934–1939 gold imports added some $10 billion worth to the American hoard. About $6 billion came from new production outside the United States, $1 billion from the hoards of the Orient, and $3 billion largely from central-bank holdings. At least four-fifths of this total gold gain corresponded to a capital inflow of unprecedented nature and size. The rather unwelcome movement of capital into the United States reached its climax in 1939, when some $2 billion was transferred from abroad. (At intervals, however, as during the "dollar scare" of 1937–1938, the capital movement had been in the opposite direction.) In the five-year period 1934–1938 the American share of the world's monetary gold stock rose from 34 to 57 percent. In 1939, the share of the United States and six other leading holders of gold had risen to 88 percent of the world total, as compared to 62 percent ten years before. The functionless excess gold holdings of the United States practically went out of circulation as international means of settlement.[35]

At the start of the 1930s total American investments abroad probably amounted to roughly $15 billion (not counting war-debt claims), offset fractionally by foreign investments in the United States. During the decade the United States repatriated money invested abroad and served as a haven for foreign flight capital to the extent of becoming the world's largest capital *importer*. By the end of the decade the net international creditor position of the United States had shrunk below $2 billion. The shrinkage had been averaging more than $1 billion a year; at this rate, if wartime developments had not intervened, the United States would have become a net international debtor (though still the largest gold-holder) some time in 1940 or 1941.[36]

The flight of funds to the United States, bringing the "Golden Avalanche" with it, was only one example of an abnormal mobility of funds generally prevalent during the 1930s. With liquid deposits earning little or no interest at a time of depressed economic activity, their holders were mainly preoccupied with protecting their capital. When a country's balance-of-payments position seemed to foreshadow either further currency depreciation or the imposition of exchange restrictions, large balances promptly sought refuge elsewhere. Rumors and capital transfers fed on each other. A rise in a central bank discount rate often served less as an inducement for funds to remain in or to enter the country than as a confirmation of financial trouble. Sometimes, after an expected depreciation had taken place or after the crisis had abated without one, the outflow of capital would reverse itself. (As the threat of war increased toward the end of the decade, political considerations replaced purely financial ones as the chief motive of hot-money

transfers.) Capital inflows and outflows produced internal as well as international disturbances by alternately flooding and draining the capital markets, and resistance to internal repercussions was one of the chief tasks of exchange equalization accounts. A country sheltering hot money could not well employ it for productive investment for fear of its sudden withdrawal. Externally, capital transfers were often "disequilibrating," adding to rather than cushioning imbalances between imports and exports. Gold became a vehicle for hot money.[37]

Lessons of the 1930s

There is no denying the historical association between hot-money transfers and exchange-rate variations by uncoordinated national action. They intensified each other. From this and related facts, observers have drawn certain lessons:

. . . the system of flexible exchanges in the 'thirties was associated with disturbances not very different from those associated with freely fluctuating exchanges.

If there is anything that inter-war experience has clearly demonstrated, it is that paper currency exchanges cannot be left free to fluctuate from day to day under the influence of market supply and demand.

33. *Ibid.*, p. 41.

34. The net change in the exchange rate against the U.S. dollar amounted to not more than a very few percent for Argentina, Sweden, India, the United Kingdom, Canada, and Italy; it amounted to larger percentages, ranging hardly above 20 percent, for Brazil, Australia, Czechoslovakia, France, and Belgium. Nurkse, *op. cit.*, p. 129n.

35. Most of these figures are taken or calculated from *ibid.*, pp. 17–19, 26, 90, 132–133, 233, and BIS, 10th *Annual Report*, 1939–1940, p. 83.

36. BIS, 11th *Annual Report*, 1940–1941, p. 98.

37. Capital movements of this type accounted for the great bulk of the changes in French, British, and American official gold reserves in the years 1933–1938. Nurkse, *op. cit.*, p. 16.

. . . any system of exchange rates reached by international consultation will be better than one in which exchanges are determined either by isolated acts of national sovereignty or by markets subject to speculative transfers of funds. To let the exchanges "find their own level" would almost certainly result in chaos.[38]

Now, historical associations, by themselves, never teach lessons. Lessons derive from history as *interpreted* in the light of theories. One theory or assumption apparently underlying the views just quoted is that governmentally managed flexible rates and freely fluctuating rates are essentially the same thing, at least in provoking speculative capital movements. Actually, the supposed lesson of the 1930s requires a more neutral phrasing: flexible management of exchange rates by uncoordinated national action seems to work badly. History does not prove that management by intergovernmental collaboration is the only workable alternative. The 1930s cannot directly provide any lesson about freely fluctuating exchange rates because

freely fluctuating exchanges were far from common in those years. Exchange rates changed indeed; but the changes were usually controlled. For considerable periods at a time, rates were "pegged" or kept within certain limits of variation. . . . [This was a] system of managed though flexible exchanges. . . .

Wide and sudden changes took place in foreign exchange rates. Yet one of the facts that stands out from this experience is that monetary authorities in most countries had little or no desire for freely fluctuating exchanges.

During the 'thirties, exchange rates changed frequently. But *freely* fluctuating exchanges were by no means common. The changes were either controlled or, after brief intervals of uncontrolled fluctuation, were followed by measures of stabilization at a new level.[39]

The emergence of currency blocs, loose and of doubtful durability though they were, is further evidence that exchange rates were not abandoned to market forces. The completely nationalistic management of rates was far from general as a sustained policy. Numerous governments aligned their currencies with sterling or the dollar, or, in the Far East, with the yen. Even the chief fluctuating rate, the dollar-sterling rate, was held within a narrow channel for several years.

As this last example reminds us, exchange stabilization funds were active. The British fund was originally meant to smooth out speculative and seasonal fluctuations, leaving the longer-term course of the rate responsive to private supply and demand. In practice, it had trouble in distinguishing speculative from nonspeculative movements and could hardly avoid influencing even the general trend of the rate. It seemed unwilling to allow much appreciation of sterling against the dollar. The American and French funds also went beyond mere passive smoothing of exchange-rate fluctuations. Yet a system of substantially free exchange rates requires, according to one persuasive interpretation, that *all* countries of major financial importance allow commercial forces to work freely. If the government of one important country tries to dominate the exchange rates with other currencies, the other countries must either accept the leadership of the first or else seek international collaboration in management of the exchanges. Management thus tends to spread and to necessitate international cooperation. "These," according to the alternative interpretation, "are the main lessons of the middle and late thirties."[40] The Tripartite Monetary Agreement of 1936, concerned with cooperation among the British, French, and American exchange funds, may be interpreted as a partial and imperfect recognition of these lessons and even as a forerunner of the International Monetary Fund.

38. *Ibid.*, pp. 123, 137. Cf. W. M. Scammell, *International Monetary Policy*, p. 94; and Thomas C. Schelling, *International Economics*, Boston: Allyn and Bacon, 1958, p. 294. Scammell notes it as a fact "that neither of the pure unmanaged systems," the gold standard and freely fluctuating rates, "has been successful in operation. . . . after nearly a decade of competitive depreciation, we found we had no stomach for free rates. . . ." Schelling refers to "the experience in the 1930's . . . with freely-fluctuating exchange rates" and clearly implies that the experience was unsatisfactory, especially in the violence of rate fluctuations and of speculative capital movements.

39. These passages come, significantly, from the same authoritative source as the "lessons" being considered: Nurkse, *op. cit.*, pp. 8–9, 122, 211.

40. A. C. L. Day, *Outline of Monetary Economics*, Oxford: Clarendon Press, 1957, p. 511. Cf. pp. 503–504.

CHAPTER NINETEEN

Wartime and Early Postwar Financial Developments

Allied financing

In foreign-exchange policy, World War II brought stricter rate pegging, tightened controls, and further displacement of ordinary commercial practices by intergovernmental arrangements. Sterling was rigidly pegged at $4.03. Under exchange control, the Sterling Area became more clearly defined. (Before the war, it had been so loose that it is hard to say whether certain countries belonged or not.) While most of its non-Commonwealth members dropped out, a few foreign countries, such as Egypt, Iraq, and the Free French territories remained or joined.

The British government mobilized privately owned foreign assets to help pay for wartime purchases overseas. By the end of the war, the country had sold nearly £600 million worth of investments in the Sterling Area and about £1.1 billion of foreign investments in all, or nearly one-third of the prewar total. Furthermore, the balances of the sterling countries in London had grown by nearly £3 billion, of which amount the United Kingdom had spent less on supplies for itself than on its defense of India, Burma, and the Middle East. Deferred payment for supplies was also arranged with Canada and some of the neutrals, most importantly Argentina. By the end of the war, the

short-term claims on the United Kingdom of other countries in and out of the Commonwealth—the so-called sterling balances—had been built up to over £3½ billion, including the £½ billion or so of balances already outstanding before the war.[1]

Laws passed in the mid-1930s hampered American aid to the Allies at first: the Johnson Act forbade American citizens to grant loans to foreign governments in default on their obligations to the United States government, i.e., their debts from World War I; and the Neutrality Act embargoed sales of war goods to belligerents. Congress soon repealed the arms embargo, however, and allowed cash-and-carry sales to the Allies. An urgent need for supplies frustrated the desire of the British and French governments to use their gold and foreign exchange sparingly. At first the Allied governments sought to meet their spending by an export drive that trenched on home civilian consumption. After the fall of France, the desperate British had to buy supplies almost without regard to their financial future. By the end of 1940, orders had been placed in the United States that, when paid for, would leave Britain practically without dollars. Despite sales of privately owned dollar investments, the financial situation had become acute. Speaking in November 1941, Prime Minister Churchill said: ". . . this time last year we did not know where to turn for a dollar . . . the end of our financial resources was in sight, nay, had actually been reached."[2]

President Roosevelt outlined the American response to the British plight in December 1940: when your neighbor's house is on fire, you lend him your garden hose to help put the fire out. The Lend-Lease Act became law in March 1941, nine months before Pearl Harbor. Lend-Lease put a great variety of goods at the disposal of the Allies, with settlement to be worked out later. (As it turned out, the goods used up during the war were regarded as an American contribution to the common effort; goods on the way at the end of the war and installations of peacetime value were sold at bargain prices and on credit.) Because of Lend-

1. William Ashworth, *A Short History of the International Economy*, London: Longmans, Green, 1952, p. 225; and Bank for International Settlements, *The Sterling Area*, Basel, 1953, pp. 18–19.

2. Bank for International Settlements, 12th *Annual Report*, 1941–1942, p. 103.

Lease, interallied trade in ordinary commercial channels shrank. The British were able to abandon their export drive and devote the resources saved to war purposes. By 1944, British exports (apart from munitions) were under one-third of their prewar volume.[3]

Thirty-eight countries, including several not involved in the actual fighting, eventually received some Lend-Lease aid. The total amounted to some $48.6 billion through September 1946 (straight Lend-Lease had ended a year earlier, but there were some delayed deliveries and some continued aid to China). Of this total, about 65 percent went to the British Empire, 23 percent to Soviet Russia, 7 percent to France and her overseas possessions, and some to China. The United States received about $8 billion in "reverse Lend-Lease," chiefly as goods, services, and facilities provided to the American armed forces in the British Empire; reverse Lend-Lease from Russia was negligible. The United States also eventually received returns of surplus goods and repayments totaling about $4 billion. The net outflow of Lend-Lease in excess of recoveries of all kinds amounted to about $37 billion, valued at prices averaging perhaps half of present-day levels.[4] Besides giving military and civilian aid, the United States government spent about $15 billion abroad from mid-1940 through September 1945 for supplies and other military purposes, mostly in the British Commonwealth and Latin America.

American policy dominated balance-of-payments trends. During a first phase, mostly coinciding with the period of cash-and-carry sales, the large U.S. merchandise export surplus brought a heavy inflow of gold. From the end of August 1939 to the end of October 1941 (when the movement reversed itself) the gain totaled $5.7 billion. (This followed upon net purchases of foreign gold amounting to $3.5 billion in the 13 months before the start of the war.) Toward the end of 1940 foreigners began supplementing and later replacing gold sales by liquidating their dollar bank deposits and securities. From October 1940 through February 1942 this liquidation amounted to over $700 million, not counting sales of foreign-owned businesses besides. During a second phase of balance-of-payments trends, Lend-Lease largely covered the net exports of the United States and relieved the strain on Allied holdings of gold and dollars. With most war material moving under Lend-Lease and few civilian goods available for export, the heavy overseas wartime expenditures of the United States began rebuilding the gold and short-term dollar reserves of foreign countries. By the end of the war, the total holdings of all foreign countries except Russia had risen above the prewar level by $6.2 billion, or 45 percent. The net losses of the European belligerents were more than matched by the gains of Latin America, South Africa, and the European neutrals in particular. Late in 1945, after the war and most Lend-Lease aid had ended, foreign countries again began running down their reserves.[5]

At the height of the war the chief Allied belligerents were devoting half of their national incomes, more or less, to war spending. By the summer of 1945, the total direct war cost borne by the various national treasuries was estimated at at least four times as much, in real terms, as the cost of World War I.[6]

Divergent production and price changes

The war intensified world economic disparities. Industrial and agricultural production in the first year or so after the war was only three-fourths or one-half or less of prewar levels in Japan, Greece, Austria, Germany, the Netherlands, France, and elsewhere. On the other hand, production gained ground outside the combat zones, notably in Canada, Sweden, and the United States. During the war the United States recovered from the lingering depression of the 1930s and increased its productive plant by nearly 50 percent and its annual physical output of goods and services by more than 50 percent. At the end of the war over half of the world's manufacturing and one-third of total world production of all goods was estimated to be taking place in the United States. Though European countries had lost nearly 40 percent of their merchant shipping tonnage, the world total had risen by 6 or 7 percent; and of this total, the United States owned half, in comparison with 14 percent in 1939. Even two years after the war, the United States was providing one-third of all the world's exports and taking only one-tenth of the imports.[7]

Despite the far greater financial and material costs of World War II than of World War I, the upheaval in prices was smaller. At any rate, controls over prices and exchange rates concealed it better. Episodes of hyperinflation, in particular, were fewer after the second war than after the first; only in Hungary, China, Rumania, and Greece did price levels get quite out of control. Prices were multiplied about 25-fold in Italy, more than 10-fold in Japan and Thailand, and nearly 10-fold in Lebanon. Early postwar prices were about five or six times prewar levels in Finland, France, Iran, and the Philippines and about double, triple, or quadruple prewar levels in Peru, the Netherlands, Portugal, Spain, Mexico, Czechoslovakia, Chile, Paraguay, India, Brazil, Egypt, Belgium, Bolivia, and Turkey (listed in approximate order of least to greatest inflation). Prices rose by about 50 to 100 percent in New Zealand, the United Kingdom, Sweden, Norway, Denmark, Argentina, Switzerland, Ireland, and Costa Rica and only by about 30 to 45 percent in Canada, Australia, the United States, Venezuela, and the Union of South Africa. These figures compare prices in 1946 or at the end of 1945 with levels of 1938 or 1939; inflation in almost all countries continued longer into the postwar period. Furthermore, any international comparison of inflation can be only impressionistic at best; price controls and rationing make figures deceptive.

International transmission of inflation

No country escaped inflation during World War II, not even any neutrals. Several countries, including some in the British Empire, apparently suffered a monetary and price inflation of chiefly external rather than domestic origin. Some of the inactive belligerents provide good examples. Cuban price inflation was unmistakable despite the lack of comprehensive statistics. The index of food prices outside Havana rose by 162 percent between September 1939 and September 1947. Rough estimates suggest that the total cost of living rose some 80 percent from September 1940 to September 1944 and some 125 percent from September 1939 to the end of 1947. The Cuban money supply, consisting of currency and demand deposits in both pesos and U.S. dollars, was multiplied by 4.6 between the ends of 1939 and 1945 and by 6.7 between the ends of 1938 and 1947. Government deficit financing played very little part in this expansion; the inflation of prices and incomes raised tax revenues practically in step with expenditures. Bank credit expansion likewise played only a

small part. Up to 1945, in fact, its influence was technically negative, in the sense that the growth of bank loans and investments amounted to less than the public's acquisition of time and other nonmonetary deposits. During 1946 and 1947 a sharp expansion of bank credit did accommodate the postwar avalanche of imports, but even then, it accounted for only 15 percent or less of the further growth in currency and demand deposits. Throughout the war and early postwar period, the dominant source of inflation was an intensely active balance of international payments. Repatriation of Cuban funds held abroad (and curtailment of new capital exports), partly stimulated by a tax of 0.15 percent a month on Cuban funds held abroad, was an aggravating factor. The main one was a sugar export boom: the peso value of total Cuban exports in 1947 was more than six times the level of 1940. The origins of the money supply can be classified under two headings: (1) domestic credit origin (bank credit and seigniorage on Treasury issues) and (2) international origin (the bullion value of coin, gold bullion and dollars backing silver certificates, dollars in circulation, and dollars in banks and net balances abroad). The international part of the total increase in the money supply amounted to 101 percent between the ends of the years 1939 and 1945, 94 percent between 1938 and 1947, and 85 percent between 1945 and 1947. The Cuban inflation thus occurred under a negative policy of passively tolerating the inflow of money into

3. Ashworth, *op. cit.*, pp. 226–227.

4. BIS, 15th *Annual Report*, 1944–1945, p. 121, 17th *Annual Report*, 1946–1947, p. 98; Thomas C. Schelling, *International Economics*, Boston: Allyn and Bacon, 1958, pp. 420–421. Different sources give slightly different figures covering slightly different time periods, but the general picture is the same.

5. Federal Reserve Bank of New York, *Annual Report* for 1945, New York: 1946, pp. 28–33.

6. BIS, 15th *Annual Report*, 1944–1945, pp. 27, 35.

7. Ashworth, *op. cit.*, pp. 227–228; BIS, 18th *Annual Report*, 1947–1948, p. 15.

domestic circulation that accompanied an export surplus.[8]

The fact that Cuba was technically at war may seem, however irrelevantly, to discredit its experience as an example of imported inflation. For this reason it may be worthwhile to consider a couple of outright neutral countries as well. The Bank of International Settlements reported as follows in 1944:

Portugal is one of the few countries in the world to-day in which the abundance of monetary purchasing power has in no way been derived from internal state financing, the Portuguese budget remaining in good order. The plethora of money has been due to large exports, wolfram and tin being the two most conspicuous commodities for which very high prices have been charged.[9]

Switzerland provides a less clear-cut but better documented example. Despite extensive price controls and rationing, the Swiss wholesale price index in 1945 averaged 107 percent above and the cost-of-living index 52 percent above the level of 1938. Between the ends of these two years, the banknote circulation increased by 119 percent, or by 2084 million Swiss francs. The total net money supply, as defined by the International Monetary Fund, rose by 73 percent, or 3783 million francs. The increase in the gold and foreign-exchange holdings of the Swiss National Bank over the same period amounted to 1770 francs, or 56 percent of the initial holdings.[10] Actually, these figures for the Bank show only part of the official acquisitions of gold and foreign exchange: the Swiss government also shouldered some of this burden and, despite sales of gold bullion to industry and of gold coins on the market, it had acquired 1030.2 million francs' worth of gold at the end of 1945 and 1239.1 million francs' worth at the end of 1946.[11] These facts indicate a creation of Swiss money to finance official purchases of the country's surplus foreign earnings. In peacetime, Swiss commodity exports had almost always fallen far short of commodity imports; the deficiency in value had been 18 percent in 1938 and 31 percent in 1939. But this deficiency shrank throughout the war and finally turned into a surplus of 20 percent in 1945. The quantum indexes of imports and exports in 1945 had fallen to 31 and 57 percent respectively of their 1938 levels.[12]

There is no denying that the Swiss wartime inflation resulted partly from real rather than purely from monetary factors. Some manpower had gone into active military service, and imports became less available and more costly to buy and to transport. The government subsidized domestic production of staple foods, even at the expense of some shrinkage in milk and meat production; and the Swiss-grown portion of food consumption rose from 52 percent in 1934–1936 to 70 percent in 1943–1945. Real national income per person fell by an estimated 10 percent between 1939 and 1945.[13]

The smallness of this decline in available goods and services in comparison with the percentage rise in prices suggests, however, that real economic deterioration by no means entirely explains the inflation. Real causes were abetted by monetary expansion, which, as already suggested, was not mainly of domestic origin. Though tax increases fell far short of increases in defense spending, the resulting large deficit in the federal budget was met by relatively noninflationary borrowing; and the financial positions of the cantonal governments strengthened notably.[14] "Even in the last year of the war, the National Bank had to place financial means at the disposal of the Confederation only temporarily and never in the form of permanent credit." Furthermore, "Because of the considerable liquid resources at the disposal of the banks, the private economy had recourse only in a slight degree to credit from the bank of issue during the second world war." The continued growth of the monetary circulation "could not be attributed to a more important resort by the State or by the private economy to credit from the bank of issue; it stems above all from the acquisition of foreign exchange arising from exports." "Liquidity did not cease to reign on the Swiss money market . . . the continuous acquisition by the bank of issue of export proceeds and of foreign gold furnished it an uninterrupted supply of available funds."[15]

The troublesome afflux of gold and foreign exchange did not originate in ordinary commercial transactions alone. In addition, for instance, the British and U.S. governments needed Swiss francs to meet diplomatic and other payments, including payments to Japan by way of the Red Cross for the care of prisoners of war. They were able to obtain francs up to specified limits for sterling, dollars, or gold at official rates of exchange. During the war the Swiss franc became "the currency most readily accepted in Europe for international settlements, notwithstanding the fact that the

Swiss monetary authorities have deliberately sought to discourage its use for other settlements than those directly connected with the economic life of Switzerland itself."[16]

In trying to discourage these other uses, the National Bank adopted a policy in the latter part of 1940 of requiring information on the origin of foreign exchange offered to it for sale. The Bank wanted to impede the inflow of unstable foreign funds and to keep dollar balances blocked by the American authorities from being liquidated through the Swiss market. It continued, however, to accept all foreign exchange resulting from Swiss exports or from repatriation of Swiss-owned funds.[17] In September 1941 the National Bank worked out a gentlemen's agreement with the commercial banks whereby only the surplus foreign exchange arising from commodity trade and certain other specified transactions would be acquired at the official rates of exchange. Later on during the war the Bank set monthly limits to its purchases of foreign exchange arising from exports of watches and from exports of textiles and certain other products to the Near East. Occasionally dollars arising from non-privileged transactions were quoted at heavy discounts on the Swiss market. The Swiss authorities strove to have importers make use of officially acquired dollars to pay for their imports. But no full remedy was found for the growing glut of gold and foreign exchange. Some efforts were made to sell gold coins and bars to the Swiss public as a kind of anti-inflationary open-market operation; and the Swiss government acquired some of the gold itself, paying with funds borrowed out of circulation rather than simply created. The government thus incurred heavy costs in an effort to restrain monetary expansion.[18]

The wartime experience is nicely summarized in the National Bank's Annual Report for 1946:

After the United States had blocked Swiss assets in June 1941, inflows of dollars to the bank of issue became ever larger, since the exports of certain industries were growing ceaselessly, while opportunities to import goods were diminishing. Gold and foreign exchange arising from various sources thus began flowing to the bank of issue. This state of affairs entailed a continuous creation of means of payment that implied a danger of inflation in spite of price control and rationing. The exigencies of economic policy and of monetary policy obliged Switzerland to use restraint in the creation of francs corresponding to acquisitions of gold and foreign

WARTIME AND EARLY POSTWAR FINANCIAL DEVELOPMENTS

exchange. The measures taken for this purpose consisted in putting quotas on exports consigned to certain countries and in postponing the payment of a part of the equivalent of dollars derived from sales abroad. In general, the transfer of claims on countries using the dollar was ruled out when interest and capital were concerned. This regulation, considered as a makeshift, was to last throughout the whole conflict.[19]

As already shown, these makeshift measures were far from completely successful. As early as 1942 some people were proposing an appreciation of the franc as a more effective kind of

8. Henry C. Wallich, *Monetary Problems of an Export Economy*, Cambridge, Mass.: Harvard University Press, 1950, esp. pp. 151–161. Some of the figures cited above are calculated from Wallich's tables.

9. BIS, 14th *Annual Report*, p. 83.

10. Eidgenössisches Statistisches Amt, *Statistisches Jahrbuch der Schweiz, 1951*, Basel: Verlag Birkhäuser, 1952, pp. 554–555; Swiss National Bank, *44me Rapport*, 1951, Bern: 1952, pp. 56–57; *International Financial Statistics*, December 1948, p. 114.

11. Swiss National Bank, *39me Rapport*, 1946, pp. 13–14, *38me Rapport*, 1945, p. 11, *Geschäftsbericht*, 1944, pp. 10–11, *Schweizerische Nationalbank 1907–1957*, Zürich: 1957, p. 143.

12. *Statistisches Jahrbuch der Schweiz, 1951*, pp. 165, 170.

13. *Schweizerische Nationalbank, 1907–1957*, pp. 36–37.

14. *Ibid.*, p. 67.

15. These quotations are translated from the Bank's *Rapports* for 1945, p. 13, and for 1943, pp. 11, 13.

16. BIS, 14th *Annual Report*, 1943–1944, pp. 36, 38.

17. BIS, 11th *Annual Report*, 1940–1941, p. 38.

18. Swiss National Bank, *Rapports* for 1943, p. 10, for 1945, pp. 10–11, for 1946, pp. 13–14; *Schweizerische Nationalbank 1907–1957*, pp. 140–145; BIS, 14th *Annual Report*, 1943–1944, pp. 36–38.

19. Translated from Swiss National Bank, *Rapport* for 1946, p. 12.

partial insulation from foreign developments. A low enough franc price of foreign currencies would have warded off surplus supplies of foreign exchange clamoring for conversion into newly created Swiss francs. Though imports of goods and services could hardly have been maintained at prewar levels, an appreciated exchange rate could have rectified the trade balance by discouraging unrequited exports. Not even a complete current balancing of trade would have been necessary; for at some raised value of the franc, Swiss businessmen might have regarded foreign exchange as abnormally and temporarily cheap and might have accumulated it for postwar use, relieving the authorities of the burden of absorbing it.

After Sweden and Canada revalued their currencies upward in the summer of 1946, the Swiss authorities were increasingly urged to follow their example. But by this time, doing so would have been belatedly locking the barn door. The Swiss authorities never did consider revaluation a suitable weapon. For one thing, it would have involved writing down the franc value of the National Bank's gold and foreign-exchange reserves. Also, revaluation might have provoked a troublesome capital outflow by causing expectations of some subsequent devaluation.[20] Perhaps just tolerating imported inflation really was the least bad of the courses open.

The examples just considered should not give the impression that monetary expansion connected with a balance-of-payments surplus was *typically* the dominant source of wartime inflation. In most countries, government deficit spending was of course more important. Even in the international transmission of inflation, more than one mechanism was at work. Quite apart from any balance-of-payments surplus, a rise in the real cost of a country's imports because of reduced foreign supplies and increased shipping and insurance rates can begin to percolate through the domestic economy, abetted by practices of pricing goods in accordance with costs and of adjusting wages with the cost of living. A rise in export prices tends to spread similarly. Even apart from any intervening steps, price increases on the world market may lead to a change of market expectations within a country and thus to price markups and to attempts to draw down cash balances. For an inflation transmitted in either of these ways to become general and to carry far within a country, an accommodating expansion of the local money supply is of course necessary; but this is not unusual when money and banking systems are responsive to the "needs of trade."[21]

The Cuban, Portuguese, and Swiss examples of inflation largely transmitted through the balance of payments are admittedly selective. Their merit is in bringing further historical evidence to bear on the analysis of possible conflict between domestic stability and exchange-rate stability. No reference to the war can validly dismiss this evidence as irrelevant unless one can show in what specific respects war overrides the usual economic principles relating to foreign trade, exchange rates, money, and prices. The authorities of the Swiss National Bank grasped part of the lesson to be drawn from their experience:

From the long-run point of view, Swiss economic policy is equally interested in stable exchange rates and in the maintenance of the purchasing power of the franc. As experience teaches, however, these objectives cannot always be simultaneously attained.[22]

Early postwar difficulties

Physical destruction was far greater during World War II than during World War I. The fighting lasted longer and covered a wider area, and the instruments of destruction were more highly developed. Hidden erosion of productive capacity did probably even more total damage than actual shooting and bombing. Wartime urgencies caused postponement and neglect in maintaining and repairing capital equipment: vehicles and railroad cars had been run to ruin, much farm land had gone underfertilized, and many factories and machines were in sorry shape. Inventories of raw materials and goods in process, of consumer durable goods, and of farm livestock had been run down. Populations had been displaced, peacetime productive skills had become rusty, and normal trade and business connections had lapsed or loosened. Years of industrial research and development had been lost, and use of military discoveries for peacetime purposes would take time.

Reconstruction, reconversion, and general economic recovery seemed well under way during the first postwar year in most of the world except for parts of Asia and the East Indies and the devastated industrial regions of Germany and Japan. Before the middle of 1947, however, a number of threats to continued recovery became apparent in Europe. Bilateral trade and payments agreements were having only limited success in moving trade past barriers thrown up to conserve dwindling national reserves of gold and dollars. An unusually cold and snowy winter in Western and Central Europe hampered transportation and production and intensified needs for imported fuel and food. An inclement spring gave way to a dry summer, causing crop failures and curtailing hydroelectric generation, which intensified the coal problem. For the first 2½ years after the end of the war, as in the period just after World War I, probably the most troublesome bottleneck was the shortage of coal, still the primary industrial commodity and needed for power, for heating homes, and as an industrial raw material. In early 1947, British coal production was still some 13 percent below the 1935–1939 level (because of losses in productivity and in the number of miners), and British coal exports had virtually ceased. The coal output of the German Ruhr was 40 percent below the prewar level. Not until the following year, 1948, would the combined effects of abundant rainfall for hydroelectricity, revived coal production, and continued imports from the United States overcome the coal bottleneck. Steel production lagged. Strikes plagued France and Italy. German recovery was foundering on scanty food rations, political unrest, uncertainty about how much industrial activity the occupying powers would permit, and a suppressed inflation that was crippling the operation of the market mechanism. Rising import prices were damaging European terms of trade and balances of payments.

In the 17 countries that later formed the Organisation for European Economic Co-operation, the index of gross national product at constant prices had regained 93 percent of the 1938 level in 1947; population growth kept real per capita gross national product still 13 percent below the prewar level. Consumption and investment expenditures totaled an estimated $148 billion, about $7 billion in excess of the value of aggregate production. This $7 billion of excess "absorption" corresponded to an equal excess of imports of goods and services over exports. The imbalance did not stem from any spurt in imports: controls kept West European imports down to 90 percent of their prewar physical volume, though inflation had approximately doubled their dollar value. Commodity exports had likewise fallen in physical quantity but risen in money value. A large increase in the prewar volume of exports

would have been necessary to make up for the drop in European earnings from foreign investment and from services such as shipping, insurance, and tourism. Europe's trade-balance problem was particularly acute in relation to the United States, since many goods sought for reconstruction were not immediately available elsewhere, since reduced supplies of some goods from customary sources (food from Eastern Europe, for example) increased Europe's dependence on the United States, and since damage had occurred to the multilateral trade in which Europe had formerly earned dollars by net sales to dollar-earning countries of the Far East. To the $7 billion external deficit on current account was added another $2 billion on capital account, including subscriptions to the International Monetary Fund and International Bank, other intergovernmental payments, and private capital transfers. The gross European deficit of about $9 billion was financed mostly by American and Canadian loans and other foreign aid but also by a further loss of some $2½ billion from gold and dollar holdings. At the worst during 1947, exhaustion of the reserves seemed possible within a few months. In August, the British convertibility experiment failed after six weeks, emphasizing how serious the external payments situation was.[23]

20. *Schweizerische Nationalbank 1950–1957*, pp. 128–129.

21. According to A. J. Brown, the worldwide spread of the wartime and postwar inflation was due more to a push from increased import and export prices and to linkages involving expectations than to monetary expansions by way of the balance of payments. See his *The Great Inflation, 1939–1951*, London: Oxford University Press, 1955, especially pp. 70–71, 251–257.

22. *Schweizerische Nationalbank 1907–1957*, p. 103. Switzerland was to suffer essentially the same experience again in the 1960s and early 1970s.

23. On the British convertibility experiment, see Chapter 22.
   The figures in the text are drawn from OEEC, *A Decade of Co-operation*, Paris: 1958, pp. 22–23, 159–160; and Robert Triffin, *Europe and the Money Muddle*, New Haven: Yale University Press, 1957, pp. 31–32, 43–44, 313.

Europe's $7 billion current-account deficit in 1947 represented an excess of total absorption over total production of only about 5 percent and an excess of goods-and-services imports over exports of about 65 percent. The contrast between these two percentages reflects how small external transactions were in comparison with Europe's domestic production and consumption.[24] The 5 percent figure perhaps suggests that the Europeans faced no hopeless task in readjusting to live within their shrunken means; even the estimated 13 percent deficiency of real gross national product per capita below the prewar level does not exactly spell catastrophe. Was the apparently critical disequilibrium of 1947 really due to inexorable physical realities? Or was it partly due to a greater degree of inflation in Europe than in the United States, whether suppressed by controls, as in the United Kingdom, the Netherlands, and Scandinavia, or openly shown in prices, as in Greece, Italy, and France? Exchange rates exaggerated the purchasing power over imports and export-type goods of the money incomes received by individual persons and businesses. Distorted prices did not correctly indicate how much austerity Europe's real economic deterioration required. From their own points of view, individual decision-makers appeared able to afford a level of consumption and investment that nevertheless exceeded the means available from an overall point of view.

Considering how small a further cut in absorption would have brought it into line with production and restored external balance, one wonders whether the simplest way out might not have been to stop distorting the price signals. The objection that too many "nonessentials" and not enough "essentials" would then have been imported makes little sense except as a worry about income distribution: poor persons might have suffered unduly as rich persons outbid them for scarce goods; "rationing by the purse" was unwelcome; controls were needed to distribute effective purchasing power more equally than money incomes. Other relatively respectable worries were that exchange depreciation would worsen the international distribution of incomes by turning the terms of trade against Europe, or that it might worsen European inflation. These standard theoretical arguments need not be reexamined here.

For some countries, the burden of bringing absorption into line with production would have been much heavier than the overall figure

of 5 percent suggests. Germany, Austria, Greece, and Italy, in particular, had already suffered cuts in production and consumption far worse than the average (while Switzerland and the Scandinavian counties had already regained or surpassed prewar levels). Another familiar doubt concerns the feasibility of cutting absorption into line with production in just such a way as to reduce imports and free additional resources for production of exports. Perhaps short-run physical rigidities in the economic structure ruled out a workable realignment: it was common to speak of Europe's incompressible import "needs" and limited export "capacity" in the early postwar period. Conceivably, pricing was almost irrelevant to the problems of the short run. But this seems doubtful. It is practically a denial of economics to speak of "needs" and "capacities" as objective physical magnitudes unrelated to prices.

References to Europe's urgent need for imports and rigidly limited capacity to export might most sensibly have been interpreted as meaning that adjustment through market mechanisms would have been painful and undesirable. The European Allies had made disproportionate sacrifices in the common war effort, had earned the gratitude of the United States, and were entitled to continue living beyond their own resources for the time being. Humanitarian and political considerations called for similar treatment of defeated enemies. A consistent argument for economic aid would not have had to cite balance-of-payments statistics. Ideally, perhaps, countries should have received aid according to some sort of appraisal of their wartime sacrifices, modified by humanitarian and political considerations. It was questionable to earmark aid partly for pegging disequilibrium exchange rates—for that is what linking aid to the balance-of-payments position amounted to.

American aid programs

Assuming continued American aid, it was becoming obvious by mid-1947 that the piecemeal approach was inexpedient. The United States had furnished about $2⅔ billion to liberated countries through the United Nations Relief and Rehabilitation Administration. It had lent $3¾ billion to Great Britain on easy terms. Sizable loans went to liberated Europe and the Far East through the Export-Import Bank and otherwise. Countries under American occupation, chiefly Germany and Japan, got nearly $3½ billion worth of civilian supplies. Congress voted $400 million in May 1947 for aid to Greece and Turkey under the Truman Doctrine. Nearly $600 million was appropriated later that year for interim aid to France, Italy, and Austria. From just before the end of the war until the start of the Marshall Plan in 1948, the worldwide total of piecemeal American aid came to almost $16 billion, about half in grants and half in loans.[25]

In his famous Harvard speech of June 1947, Secretary of State Marshall hinted at American support for a coordinated reconstruction program to be worked out jointly by the European countries. Taking the hint, representatives of 16 countries (not including Soviet satellites) met in Paris the following month, set up a Committee for European Economic Co-operation, and drafted a report for presentation to the United States in September. The report envisaged surpassing prewar levels of industrial and agricultural production and achieving reasonable balance-of-payments equilibrium within four years. Measures to liberate intra-European trade would be a vital part of the program. The report also emphasized that an import surplus would be necessary to achieve the production targets. The necessary balance-of-payments deficit with the Western Hemisphere cumulated over four years was estimated at $22.4 billion, of which about $16.5 billion would be a deficit with the United States.

The Marshall Plan got under way with the Foreign Assistance Act of 1948, passed in April, establishing the Economic Cooperation Administration to operate the aid program, and followed by an appropriations act in June and by subsequent annual appropriations. In April 1948 the 17 European countries (now including West Germany but still not Spain) signed a Convention for European Economic Co-operation, promising to work together for recovery and growth. Among the methods mentioned were a loosening of trade and payments restrictions and maintenance of internal financial stability and "sound rates of exchange." The Convention also promoted the earlier Committee into an Organisation for European Economic Co-operation. One of its purposes was to help in allocating American aid.

The European Recovery Program was originally supposed to last four years, until the middle of 1952. At the beginning, the executive branch of the U.S. government estimated

that the program might call for appropriations of $17 or $18 billion over the entire period. Congress eventually voted a little over $13 billion. The outbreak of the Korean War in 1950 interrupted the original program and shifted the emphasis in American aid from economic recovery to rearmament. The newly created Mutual Security Agency absorbed the functions of the Economic Cooperation Administration in 1951. By the end of that year, aid under the European Recovery Program had amounted to nearly $11½ billion, of which about 10 percent had been in the form of loans and 90 percent in the form of grants.[26]

At its peak, the aid program was providing most recipient countries with additional goods and services worth only about 3 or 4 percent of their own total production. Even after adjustment for the fact that local-currency prices, distorted as they were by rationing and price and exchange-rate controls, probably understated the importance of the aid goods, American aid still seems not to have amounted to more than 5 to 10 percent of Europe's own production.[27] In comparison with imports alone, the aid seems larger. It paid for one-fourth of Europe's total imports of goods and services in the period 1947–1950 and for almost two-thirds of its merchandise imports from the dollar area.[28] For particular commodities of crucial importance, such as cotton, the aid program provided half or more of the imports; but this fact means little, for if aid had not been available, the Europeans would presumably have exercised greater restraint in

24. Triffin, op. cit., pp. 43–44, 313.

25. Schelling, op. cit., pp. 417, 421; Lorna Morley and Felix Morley, The Patchwork History of Foreign Aid, Washington: American Enterprise Association, 1961, pp. 12–16.

26. According to figures compiled for the period from April 3, 1948 to December 31, 1952, American grants (including "conditional aid") amounted to $12.5 billion and loans to an additional $1.3 billion. André Piettre, Monnaie et Économie Internationale, Paris: Éditions Cujas, 1967, p. 413.

27. Schelling, op. cit., pp. 431–433.

28. OEEC, op. cit., p. 33.

buying relatively nonessential goods in order to be able to pay for the relatively essential ones. Only if one believes in urgent and incompressible import "needs" and inexpansible export "capacities" does the fraction of imports financed by the aid program serve as a meaningful indicator of how large and important the aid was. Actually, the great bulk of the recovery effort had to come from the Europeans themselves, as is clear from the smallness of aid compared with local production. According to the OEEC, however, "American aid played the crucial role . . . in financing essential import needs, accelerating investment and reconstruction, and permitting tolerable consumption levels."[29] Partly, perhaps, by providing psychological assurance as well as actual supplies, the program enabled European consumers to tolerate allocation of nearly 20 percent on the average of gross national product into investment. This was about one-third above the average prewar rate.[30]

During the first year of the Marshall Plan, food, animal feed, and fertilizers accounted for over half of the aid shipments. Some aid even went in the form of tobacco (a fact echoing the realities of American politics). Later on, as the emphasis shifted from relief to industrial reconstruction, raw materials, semifinished products, and machinery dominated the shipments. It is not generally possible, however, to judge the purpose or emphasis of an aid program merely by knowing the types of goods provided. If an official program provides certain goods, less of these and more than otherwise of other goods may be bought in ordinary trade channels. Furthermore, when certain goods arrive in foreign-aid shipments, resources are freed for other types of production in the recipient country. It can be quite rational to assist a country's investment in factories, machinery, roads, harbors, and other fixed capital by giving it consumer goods; it depends on the pattern of comparative advantage and the opportunities for gain from specialization and trade.

A reminder is in order, incidentally, that the individual Europeans who received goods under the Marshall Plan—the consumer of American wheat, the farmer who received an American tractor, the manufacturer who received an American machine—were not themselves receiving free gifts. They paid local currency to their own governments for the aid goods, enabling the governments to meet the American stipulation that they set aside local funds equal in value to the grants received.

Five percent of these "counterpart funds" were reserved to the United States for covering the expenses of administering the aid program and for buying materials to be stockpiled in the United States. The remaining 95 percent could be used as agreed upon between the recipient government and the American authorities—for financing public investment projects, for example, or in ways equivalent to cancelling the money as an anti-inflationary measure.

Of the aid provided under the Marshall Plan through 1951, five countries—the United Kingdom, France, Italy, Germany, and the Netherlands—received almost three-fourths. Nearly one-fourth of the total went to the United Kingdom alone, and about one-fifth to France. Decisions on dividing up the American aid apparently took into account such things as the part that each country's own economic recovery could play in the general recovery of Europe, the degree of Communist menace in the various countries, the "requirements" for maintaining "adequate" levels of consumption and investment, and the forecasted balance-of-payments position of each country, especially with the United States. The last criterion is particularly questionable, for reasons already mentioned. Yet when the members of the Organisation for European Economic Co-operation made the first two annual allocations, "The basic criterion for determining the aid allocation to any particular country was the prospective size of its deficit with the dollar area, but if this had been the only criterion it would not have provided incentives to close the dollar gap, for the bigger the gap the bigger the aid would have been."[31] The Organisation tried to lay down some principles to limit the consumption and investment targets used in assessing the probable size of each country's dollar gap. But agreement was difficult, and the OEEC eventually adopted the proportions set in the second annual allocation as the basic guide for the future. This nearly frozen formula gave countries greater incentives to remedy their balance-of-payments deficits than when aid allocations had illogically been subject to adjustment in accordance with balance-of-payments changes.

Accounts of the Marshall Plan customarily try to judge how successful it was in providing relief, promoting industrial and agricultural recovery, restraining inflation, encouraging European unity, aiding political stability, and countering the Communist threat. But no one knows how things would otherwise have worked out, and any judgment must rely heavily on historical intuition. No such attempt is necessary here, since the Marshall Plan has been mentioned at all only to prepare for surveying postwar monetary developments. In considering figures on European economic recovery and growth, it is helpful to recall that 1947 was the last year before the Marshall Plan and that 1951 was the year when the emphasis in U.S. foreign aid shifted away from European recovery.[32]

The special example of German recovery

The remarkable economic recovery and growth of West Germany in particular is worth a closer look. In the immediate postwar years, the German economy labored under heavy physical destruction, political and economic division, displacement of millions of persons, Russian removal of industrial plant and equipment as reparations, and uncertainty due to proposals for permanent de-industrialization to stifle future war potential. A further handicap was a severe wartime expansion of the money supply whose effects on prices were still being suppressed by cumbersome controls. Paradoxically, perhaps, the victorious occupying powers retained the Nazi wartime system of a thoroughly controlled economy, except that, to make matters worse, the national economy of the Hitler period had been split up at the borders of the states into a number of miniature controlled economies. Trade between these was subject to a panoply of controls similar to those over international trade. The internal lines of demarcation became "harder to cross than any ordinary customs barrier."[33] The low level of production burdened not only the Germans but also the occupying powers, which had to stand the costs of the occupation and of relief to their defeated enemies.

For some time after the war, attempts were made to keep wages at least nominally the same as during the war. Wartime wages in turn had been more or less frozen since the wage and price stop of 1936. Apart from some special consideration for workers in key industries such as iron and coal, most wage increases had to take unofficial forms: employers might offer apartments or houses to good workers at low rents and might serve meals in factory canteens. A worker might still be receiving only 150 marks per month, for example, while the cost of the food allowed by the meager

monthly rations might be only 12½ to 25 marks per person. At the same time, a single meal at a black-market restaurant might easily cost as much as his monthly wage. A black-market price of as much as 120 marks for kilogram of butter was not unusual. With the official prices of "essential" items rigidly controlled, relative prices were curiously distorted: a woman's hat might cost as much as several tons of wheat. Since controls held prices and wages far below the equilibrium levels that would have corresponded to the swollen money supply, the typical family had ample cash balances and found ration coupons more meaningful than money as a limit on its purchases. The effect was two-fold: on the one hand, workers lost incentive to stay diligently on the job earning money, since money was not, as in a normal price system, the key to obtaining goods and services; on the other hand, workers had good reason to stay away from work frequently and travel around the countryside in search of food obtainable by bartering with the farmers. Favorite barter articles included cigarettes, nails, small tools such as scissors and screwdrivers, cameras, household effects, and, among miners, coal. Travel on the government-owned railroads was one of the relatively few goods readily available for money at the low official prices. Trains were full of people, even sitting on the roofs and hanging on the sides, traveling to the countryside to engage in barter.[34]

The prevalence of absenteeism and of travel

---

29. *Ibid.* All OEEC countries received American aid except Switzerland. Sweden received a loan but no grants.

30. Morley and Morley, *op. cit.*, p. 23.

31. OEEC, *op. cit.*, p. 33.

32. For a good explanation of the reservations that must accompany the use of industrial-production indexes and of why such indexes may exaggerate increases in economic well-being, see BIS, 22d *Annual Report*, 1951–1952, pp. 38–44.

33. BIS, 17th *Annual Report*, 1946–1947, p. 25.

34. *Ibid.*, pp. 25, 36–37; Jacques Rueff, "Natürliche Erklärung eines Wunders," in A. Hunold, ed., *Wirtschaft ohne Wunder*, Erlenbach-Zürich: Rentsch, 1953, esp. p. 208.

to conduct barter emphasizes how badly the normal channels of internal trade had withered up. Suppressed inflation had undermined co-ordination by prices. Not only normal domestic trade but also production lagged. In 1946, industrial production in the British and American occupation zones stood at only one-third of the 1936 level; in 1947, it was still under 40 percent.[35] At the beginning of 1948, Wilhelm Röpke, an economist who gave decisive advice on the subsequent economic reforms, was still able to say, "Germany is annihilated and transformed into chaos in a degree that no one can imagine who has not seen it with his own eyes." In April 1948, another observer could write, "It appears as if the economic disorganization is continuing and will persist for an unforeseeable period of time."[36]

Then, after June 20, 1948, everything suddenly changed. Previously hoarded or black-marketed goods appeared, overnight, in store windows. Traffic filled the streets. All economic indicators "shot up steeply." Between the second and fourth quarters of 1948, total industrial production rose 45 percent and consumer-goods production 53 percent. The yearly average industrial production index rose 53 percent between 1947 and 1948, 44 percent between 1948 and 1949, and 25 percent between 1949 and 1950. In the period 1950–1957, gross domestic fixed capital formation amounted to one-fifth or more of gross national product; yet despite this heavy emphasis on investment, real private consumption in Germany rose at almost twice the average rate for all OEEC countries.[37]

It would be wrong to credit this dramatic recovery to one single cause. Various things presumably played a part—American economic aid, a zeal for hard work said to be a national characteristic of the Germans, an influx of competent workers, professional men, and business men from the Soviet zone, and moderation in union wage demands. But the most notable event, the one that most definitely invites a "before-and-after" comparison, is the currency reform of June 20, 1948, together with the other reforms directly dependent on it.

Monetary reforms

These reforms ended the suppressed inflation that had been sabotaging the price mechanism.

There are two main ways of doing this. The first is to let the suppressed inflation become an open one: relax or abolish controls and let prices and wages rise into line with the swollen money supply. France and Italy fairly well illustrate this approach. Germany took the second approach: bring the "equilibrium" price level down more or less into line with the existing controlled level by drastically shrinking the quantity of money. The old Reichsmark currency was abolished and a new Deutschemark currency introduced. Initially, at the time of the reform, individuals were entitled to exchange 600 old marks for 60 new marks, and business firms were entitled to a 600-for-60 exchange per employee. The remaining currency and bank-account Reichsmarks were blocked, to be subsequently released and exchanged for the new Deutschemarks. The terms of exchange eventually worked out to be 100 old for 6.5 new. Debts contracted in old marks were written down to one-tenth of their nominal amount in new marks.[38]

For the reform to have the best chance of success, it had to be, and was, accompanied by the almost complete abolition of price controls and rationing. Economics Minister Ludwig Erhard courageously took these steps despite general skepticism and opposition. Severe reduction in the money supply, not controls, was to be relied upon to keep prices from soaring. Money again represented purchasing power. Goods were available to whoever had it. City dwellers no longer had to make barter expeditions into the countryside; they now had the incentive to stay diligently on the job earning money. Businessmen had the incentive to concentrate their energies on producing the items most in demand rather than, as before, producing the items subject only to relatively lax price controls because the authorities considered them nonessential.

Germany's was the most spectacular but by no means the only currency reform in postwar Europe. The reforms fall into three general categories: (1) conversion of old money into lesser amounts of new, without any blocking of funds in the meanwhile, (2) blocking of funds in special bank accounts pending later release (or, in a few reforms, partial cancellation), but without any conversion, and (3) a mixture of conversion and blocking, as adopted by Germany. The mixed reforms occurred only in West and East Germany, Rumania, and Yugoslavia. The pure-conversion reforms were most typical of Eastern Europe, while the blocking reforms occurred in several Western countries, including Austria, Belgium, and the Netherlands. Several countries, including Great Britain, Switzerland, Sweden, France, and Italy, adopted currency reforms of the sort mentioned here either to a negligible extent or not at all.[39]

---

35. Ludwig Erhard, *Prosperity through Competition*, London: Thames and Hudson, 1958, p. 11.

36. Both quoted by Rueff, *op. cit.*, p. 204.

37. *Ibid.*, pp. 204–205; Erhard, *op. cit.*, p. 26; OEEC, *Industrial Statistics, 1900–1957*, Paris, 1958, p. 9; U.S. Congress, Joint Economic Com-

mittee, *Economic Policy in Western Europe* (1959), p. 19. The production indexes cited should probably be regarded with even more than the usual reservations.

38. John G. Gurley, "Excess Liquidity and European Monetary Reforms, 1944–52," *American Economic Review*, **XLIII**, March 1953, p. 87; Dagmar von Erffa, "Währungsreform," in *Wirtschaftslexikon*, Frankfurt: Humboldt-Verlag, 1954, p. 180.

39. See Gurley, *op. cit.*

CHAPTER TWENTY

The International Monetary Fund

Background and purposes

Before continuing with a survey of postwar international monetary experience, we should look at the structure of institutions and ideas within which events unfolded. The core of this "Bretton Woods system" is the International Monetary Fund. Transactions with the Fund will figure prominently in the survey to follow of the experiences of particular countries.

The IMF resulted from lengthy discussions of separate American, British, Canadian, and French proposals drafted during World War II. The British "Keynes Plan" envisaged an international clearing union that would create an international means of payment called "bancor." Each country's central bank would accept payments in bancor without limit from other central banks. Debtor countries could obtain bancor by using automatic overdraft facilities with the clearing union. The limits to these overdrafts would be generous and would grow automatically with each member country's total of imports and exports. Charges of 1 or 2 percent a year would be levied on both creditor and debtor positions in excess of specified limits. This slight discouragement to unbalanced positions did not rule out the possibility of large imbalances covered by automatic

American credits to the rest of the world, perhaps amounting to many billions of dollars. Part of the credits might eventually turn out to be gifts because of the provision for cancelling creditor-country claims not used in international trade within a specified time period. The rival American plan took its name from Harry Dexter White of the U.S. Treasury. White rejected the overdraft principle and the possibility of automatic American credits in vast and only loosely limited amounts. Instead, he proposed a currency pool to which members would make definite contributions only and from which countries might borrow to tide themselves over short-term balance-of-payments deficits. Both plans looked forward to a world substantially free of controls imposed for balance-of-payments purposes. Both sought exchange-rate stability without restoring an international gold standard and without destroying national independence in monetary and fiscal policies. According to the usual interpretation, the British plan put more emphasis on national independence and the American plan on exchange-rate stability reminiscent of the gold standard. The compromise finally reached resembled the American proposal more than the British.

The Articles of Agreement of the International Monetary Fund (and also the articles of its sister institution, the International Bank for Reconstruction and Development) were drafted and signed by representatives of 44 nations at Bretton Woods, New Hampshire, in July 1944. By the end of 1945, enough countries had ratified the agreement to bring the Fund into existence. The Board of Governors first met in March 1946, adopted by-laws, and decided to locate the Fund's headquarters in Washington, D.C. One year later the Fund was ready for actual exchange operations.

According to its Articles of Agreement, the purposes of the International Monetary Fund are to promote international monetary cooperation, facilitate the expansion of international trade for the sake of high levels of employment and real income, promote exchange-rate stability and avoid competitive depreciation, work for a multilateral system of current international payments and for elimination of exchange controls over current transactions, create confidence among member nations and give them the opportunity to correct balance-of-payments maladjustments while avoiding measures destructive of national and international prosperity, and make balance-of-payments disequilibriums shorter and less severe than they would otherwise be.

Recognizing that these goals could not all be achieved promptly, Article XIV of the Agreement provided for a postwar "transitional period" during which the member countries might violate the general ban on exchange controls over current-account transactions. No definite length for the transition period was stated, but countries maintaining exchange controls more than five years after the start of Fund operations (that is, beyond 1952) were expected to consult the Fund about them every year. Actually, consultations about general economic policies have become an annual routine with all members, and not just with members in violation of the standard decontrol obligations. Such consultations, requiring "voluminous documentation," have even become "the main activity of the Fund," the one using up the most man-hours.[1]

The "purposes" just mentioned are vague. More specifically, the Fund provides drawing rights (in effect, loans) to help its members meet temporary deficits without resort to exchange controls, exchange-rate adjustments, or internal deflation. Member countries are supposed to "live with" or "ride out" purely temporary deficits, drawing on the Fund when necessary to supplement their own accumulated reserves of gold and foreign exchange. The Fund is not meant to use up its resources, however, hopelessly palliating "fundamental disequilibrium" (a concept examined later on). A country faced with a "fundamental" deficit in its international transactions may be expected to seek a remedy in devaluing its currency. An opposite situation of "fundamental" balance-of-payments surplus would presumably call for upward revaluation. Such adjustments were expected to be infrequent.

Quotas and par values

The rights of member countries to draw on the Fund, as well as their contributions and voting power, are based on their *quotas*. Each member's quota was negotiated with reference to such factors as national income, international trade, and international reserves. As a general rule, but with an exception in favor of countries with low international reserves, each member contributed 25 percent of its quota to the Fund in gold or U.S. dollars and 75 percent in its own currency (or in non-interest-bearing demand notes payable in its own currency). During 1959 most members agreed to increase their quotas to 50 percent beyond their original sizes.[2] Several countries agreed to larger increases either to reflect their world economic positions more accurately or to have greater access to the Fund's resources. Further general increases of 25 percent and 35.5 percent were agreed on in 1965 and 1970, again with special adjustments for some countries. At the end of September 1974, the quotas totaled 29.2 billion special drawing rights. (The SDR, as explained later, is a unit of account originally equivalent to 0.888671 gram or $\frac{1}{35}$ troy ounce of gold at its rather fictitious official valuation, the same as one pre-1971 U.S. dollar. In 1974 the SDR was redefined in terms of a "basket of currencies.") The largest quotas were those of the United States (23.0 percent of the total), the United Kingdom (9.6 percent), Germany (5.5 percent), France (5.1 percent), Japan (4.1 percent), Canada (3.8 percent), Italy (3.4 percent), and India (3.2 percent). At that time, 126 countries belonged to the Fund. The chief nonmember independent countries were Switzerland, the countries of the Soviet bloc, and Mainland China (but the Republic of China has been a member from the beginning).

Each member of the Fund is supposed to have not only a quota but also a par value of its currency in relation to the gold content of the U.S. dollar in 1944. Few countries failed to declare par values, and most even of these

1. J. Keith Horsefield *et al., The International Monetary Fund 1945–1965,* Washington, D.C.: IMF, 1969, I, p. 320, II, p. 137, and *passim.* This three-volume set is a convenient source of detailed factual information.

2. The increase "was mainly designed to adjust the quotas to compensate for the increase in the level of prices by about 50 percent which had taken place in terms of gold or dollars since the Fund began its operations in 1947." Per Jacobsson, *International Monetary Problems, 1957–1963,* Washington: International Monetary Fund, 1964, p. 271.

maintained *de facto* parities, at least until the periods of floating rates in 1971 and from 1973. The par values chosen in 1946 were the exchange rates then in effect. Many of these initial rates were quite unrealistic, as emphasized by the fact that except for the United States, Mexico, Panama, El Salvador, and Guatemala, all members announced their intentions to maintain exchange controls for the time being under the "transition-period" clause. Between the initial choice of parities and the wave of devaluations in September 1949, however, only two countries, Colombia and Mexico, established new official parities with the Fund. France also devalued during this period but did not declare a new par value.

Transactions between member countries and the Fund are based on the official par values. These values are also supposed to prevail in private transactions: the Articles of Agreement obliged each member to permit spot transactions in member currencies to take place within its territory only at exchange rates not more than 1 percent above or below parity. After the Smithsonian Agreement of December 1971, the Fund authorized its members to widen this range to 2¼ percent above or below the parity or "central rate."[3] A member whose monetary authorities freely bought and sold gold for the settlement of international transactions at prices within margins prescribed by the Fund —as the United States did at least supposedly until August 1971—was deemed to be fulfilling the equivalent of its exchange-pegging obligation.[4] In forward-exchange transactions, the deviations from parity should exceed those for spot transactions by no more than the Fund considered reasonable. In short—and this point deserves emphasis—the International Monetary Fund embodied an international agreement to enforce fixed exchange rates even in private transactions.

A member government may propose a change in the par value of its currency only to correct a "fundamental disequilibrium" in the country's balance of payments. The Fund may not object if the proposed change will not move the exchange rate more than 10 percent away from its initial parity. A country making a larger change without permission may be ruled ineligible to draw on the resources of the Fund and may even be expelled. The Fund may not veto an exchange-rate adjustment necessary to correct a "fundamental disequilibrium," however, even though it may dislike the internal social or political policies of the member country. Changes in parities, when made, call for corresponding changes in the Fund's holdings of the member currencies involved. Incidentally, the Fund may propose (though not impose) uniform percentage changes in the par values of all member currencies. The purpose of such a proposal, which has never been officially made, might be to revalue gold uniformly in terms of all currencies.

Exchange transactions

The Fund's chief financial operations consist of buying currencies from and selling currencies to the treasuries or central banks of member countries. These purchases and sales might better be recognized as loan transactions: when a member "buys" some foreign currency from the Fund, it is borrowing it against the deposit of its own currency; and when the member buys back its own currency with gold or foreign exchange, it is paying off the loan. From the Fund's point of view, its "sale" of a particular currency constitutes a loan, except that when it sells a country its own currency, it is thereby ordinarily receiving repayment of an earlier loan to that country.

Some original limitations on transactions with the Fund have been so modified by the routine granting of waivers as hardly to require description here. As practice has evolved, a member enjoys the "overwhelming benefit of any doubt" in being allowed to buy other currencies at will up to the equivalent of the 25 percent of its quota originally paid in gold (its "gold tranche"). If drawings by other members have reduced the amount of one member's currency held by the Fund to less than the original 75 percent of its quota, its virtually automatic drawing right is enlarged by the difference in question, its so-called super gold tranche. The sum of a member's unused gold tranche and outstanding lendings to the Fund has become known as its "reserve position in the Fund." The Fund encourages its members to count these positions as part of their international liquidity, along with gold and foreign exchange and the new reserve medium (SDRs) to be described presently. Beyond its gold tranche, a member has further drawing rights, known as "credit tranches," whose total amount equals its quota. Since a member draws foreign currencies by buying them with its own, its maximum total drawing rights are conveniently described by saying that the Fund should not hold the member's currency in an amount greater than 200 percent of its quota. At that limit, the Fund would be holding the member's currency in amounts corresponding to the 75 percent of its quota originally subscribed in that form plus the 25 percent gold tranche and the 100 percent of credit tranches. The Fund may waive this limit to drawings, however, and sometimes has. Especially liberal drawing privileges have also been introduced for primary-producing countries troubled by temporary shortfalls in their export earnings, for the financing of "buffer stocks" of commodities, and for the financing of payments deficits stemming from the massive petroleum price increases of 1973–1974. A member can count on very sympathetic consideration of an application to draw on the first of its four equal-sized credit tranches. Drawings on the remaining credit tranches are subject to increasingly close scrutiny of the member's efforts to solve its payments problems but are likely to be permitted when they would, as the Fund says, "support a sound program aimed at establishing or maintaining the enduring stability of the member's currency at a realistic rate of exchange."

These rather flexible limitations on borrowing have, as their implicit counterpart, a limitation on the lending obligations of countries with balance-of-payments surpluses. Each member contributes the amount of its quota, partly in home currency and partly in gold or dollars, and that is all. (A member's obligation to sell foreign currencies for its own currency or for special drawing rights, as described later, hardly counts as an exception to the principle that surplus countries have only limited obligations.) No matter how large its surpluses become or how small the Fund's holdings of its currency, a country cannot be required to furnish any more of its money (except in return for gold). It may be requested but cannot be required to make a loan to the Fund. In 1962, however, the countries later known as the Group of Ten (the United States, the United Kingdom, Germany, France, Italy, Japan, Canada, the Netherlands, Belgium, and Sweden) agreed to the General Arrangements to Borrow, whereby they stood ready to lend the Fund their own currencies up to the total equivalent of $6 billion when needed for relending to fellow participants. (Not all of the $6 billion would be available at once, of course, since a country would not both borrow and lend under the General Arrangements at the

same time.) Switzerland, though a nonmember, agreed to collaborate with the plan.

The rules of the IMF and the availability of its aid are supposed to promote freedom of currencies from restrictions on their usability and the multilateral rather than bilateral balancing of transactions. Under these conditions, an applicant for aid has no special desire to draw the specific currencies of the countries with which it happens to be running bilateral deficits. It is concerned with its overall payments position and with shoring up the general foreign-exchange value of its currency; what it wants is foreign exchange in general in the form of the dollars or other currencies it routinely uses in intervening on the market. The Fund holds the currencies of all its members, however, and not intervention currencies only. Usually, therefore, it supplies aid in a package of several currencies. The ones included are the currencies of countries whose strong payments positions or ample reserves of their own justify their being designated to supply intervention currencies in exchange for

3. After the Agreement, described in later chapters, some countries specified "central rates" rather than par values for their currencies. The new term apparently suggests a particularly informal, tentative, or changeable parity. This book makes no distinction between "par value" and "parity" and usually avoids any distinction between those terms and "central rate."

4. It has been argued that this provision offers a legal loophole for junking the fixed-exchange-rate system, if so desired, without renegotiation of the Articles of Agreement. The Articles say nothing about how narrow the spread between official buying and selling prices of gold must be. The Fund might conceivably prescribe such wide margins that each currency's gold parity became meaningless. Yet by merely standing ready to buy and sell gold at these ridiculously far-apart prices, a member government would be "deemed" to be fulfilling the equivalent of its fixed-exchange-rate obligation. See Robert A. Mundell's remarks in *The United States Balance of Payments*, Part 3, "The International Monetary System: Functioning and Possible Reform," Hearings before the Joint Economic Committee, November 1963, esp. pp. 547–548, 590–591.

their own currencies that the aid-receiving country has jut drawn from the Fund.

The Fund levies interest and service charges on its sales (loans) of foreign exchange. These charges rise according to the size of the Fund's holdings of the borrowing country's currency in excess of its quota and according to the duration of this excess. The twofold progression of these charges emphasizes the expectation that a member country which has drawn on the Fund will reverse the transaction as soon as possible by buying back its own pledged currency. The complicated "repurchase" rules require, in effect, that the member buy back its own currency in the amount of half of any increase in its international reserves or in the amount of half the difference between an increase in the Fund's holdings of its currency and a decrease in its reserves, though it need not do so if its reserves are less than its quota. (Details are given in Section 7 of Article V and in Schedule B of the Articles of Agreement.) According to a policy statement issued in 1952, the Fund expects a borrowing country to buy back its own pledged currency within at most three to five years.

Regardless of the particular foreign currency originally borrowed, the debtor must repurchase its own currency with (repay the loan in) either gold or *convertible* currency. (Loosely speaking, a country is considered to have a convertible currency if it has given up the postwar-transition-period excuse for exchange controls and has accepted the normal obligations of Article VIII of the Articles of Agreement.) Even a convertible currency is not acceptable, furthermore, if the Fund already holds it in excess of 75 percent of the quota of the currency's home country. In 1964, when this restriction barred repayments in dollars, the United States made its own first drawing on the Fund. It drew foreign currencies that were acceptable in repayments and sold them for dollars to countries which would otherwise have redeemed their dollars at the United States Treasury for gold with which to repay the Fund. By drawing on the Fund (and paying the required charges), the United States escaped the drain on its gold stock that would have resulted because of the technicality just mentioned.

The unattractive prospect of having to repay even soft-currency loans in hard currency[5] is one of the chief reasons why fully 85 percent of gross drawings from the Fund from the beginning through February 1961 were in U.S.

dollars, with sterling, marks, guilders, French francs, Argentine pesos, Canadian dollars, Belgian francs, Italian lire, and Danish crowns, in that order, lagging far behind. The major European currencies had become externally convertible *de facto* at the end of 1958, however, and became convertible as defined by the Fund's rules in February 1961. This development, together with the beginning in 1958 of large deficits in the U.S. balance of payments, lessened the overwhelming dominance of the dollar in IMF operations. From the beginning of 1961 through February 1965, only 26.0 percent of all drawings were of U.S. dollars. From the start of the Fund's operations in 1947 through September 1974, 30.3 percent of the SDR value of drawings was in dollars, followed by 17.4 percent in German marks and 6.9 percent in Italian lire; pounds sterling and Japanese yen ranked eighth and ninth, with 4.8 and 4.1 percent. In the five-year period 1968–1972, dollars accounted for 23.3 percent and marks for 18.6 percent; sterling and French francs ranked behind the Dutch, Belgian, Italian, Canadian, and Japanese currencies, and even behind special drawing rights, in which 3.0 percent of drawings were made. In 1972, an exceptional 22.1 percent of drawings were made in special drawing rights. Only SDR10.0 million worth of U.S. dollars were drawn in 1971, none at all in 1972 and 1973, and SDR843.2 million worth (32.1 percent) in 1974 through September.

The Fund's first loan was a sale of $25 million to France in May 1947. After a burst of activity during the first two years, mainly for the benefit of West European borrowers, the Fund's operations shrank to a small scale. In 1950 the Fund made no new loans at all. Disequilibriums in balances of payments throughout the world so overshadowed the Fund's resources that American aid was allowed to carry the burden instead. Really large-scale lending did not resume until late in 1956, when the Fund responded to the balance-of-payments strains stemming from the Suez crisis. In the five months starting in mid-October, the Fund provided a total of over $1.7 billion for immediate withdrawal or as "stand-by credits," chiefly to Britain, France, and India. This figure was about half a billion dollars larger than the total amount of IMF transactions from the beginning through the fiscal year ending in April 1956. The Fund was also especially active in the fall of 1957 during the crisis caused by rumors of impending

European exchange-rate adjustments. Further bursts of activity are reflected in Table 20.1 and are explained in succeeding chapters. The figure include amounts drawn both in the regular way and under standby arrangements, but not unused amounts of standbys.

TABLE 20.1. *Loans by the international monetary fund*

Year	Gross actual drawings	Repayments
	(Millions of Special Drawing Rights)	
1947	468	6
1948	208	11
1949	101	2
1950	0	24
1951	35	74
1952	85	102
1953	230	320
1954	62	210
1955	28	232
1956	693	113
1957	977	64
1958	338	369
1959	180	608
1960	280	681
1961	2,479	770
1962	584	1,490
1963	333	267
1964	1,950	820
1965	2,434	702
1966	1,448	722
1967	835	1,329
1968	3,552	2,157
1969	2,871	1,591
1970	1,839	1,532
1971	1,900	2,866
1972	1,612	1,565
1973	733	614
1974 through September	2,624	1,413
Cumulative total through September 1974	28,876	20,654

NOTE: Repayments include repayments both by the drawer's repurchase of its own currency and by others' drawings of its currency. Until December 1971, dollar amounts are equivalent to amounts in SDRs. The addition is not exact because of rounding.

SOURCE: *International Financial Statistics*, November 1974, April 1965, and earlier issues.

The standby credits just mentioned, like the annual policy consultations mentioned earlier, illustrate a feature that runs through the whole history of the IMF: practices quite unforeseen by the Bretton Woods negotiators have evolved. "The stand-by arrangement is the most original instrument of financial policy that the Fund has created. It is wholly an invention because no suggestion of it can be found in the Articles." ". . . most of the exchange transactions of the Fund now take place under stand-by arrangements and they account for the larger proportion by value as well."[6] Standbys were first arranged for the benefit of Belgium, Finland, Mexico, and Peru in 1952 and 1954, during the Fund's early years of relative inactivity. Together with policy about drawings on successive credit

5. A "hard" currency might be defined as one whose gold or foreign-exchange value is genuine— whose value, that is, does not require bolstering by special restrictions on the currency's salability or usability. "Hardness" thus pretty much coincides with "convertibility," not necessarily in the technical sense of the IMF's rules but in the broad sense of unrestricted salability and usability. A "soft" currency, conversely, is one whose supposed value is somewhat artificial or is impaired by restrictions on use of the currency.

6. Joseph Gold in Horsefield, *op. cit.*, **II**, pp. 532, 535.

The Fund's gold investments furnish another example of bending the Articles of Agreement. During the early years, when scant earnings from drawings left an operating deficit, the idea arose of exchanging some of the Fund's gold for dollars for interest-earning investment in U.S. Treasury bills. At first, the question was much disputed whether such a transaction would not violate the Articles, but a suitable interpretation got around the embarrassing provision. Later, when earnings from heavy drawings had wiped out the Fund's deficit, investment of a larger gold account was interpreted as a permissible way to accumulate a reserve against a future operating deficit. Still later, when a still larger investment of gold in securities of maturities as long as 15 months was obviously being undertaken to help the United States cope with its gold-drain problem, this move—in violation of a straightforward reading of the Articles—was nevertheless somehow interpreted as still permissible.

tranches of quotas, the new invention was a key step in tying strings to the Fund's assistance. A standby virtually guarantees a member the right to draw up to a specified amount of assistance within an agreed period on condition that the member abide by policy intentions declared during the negotiations.

The Fund's arrangement with the United Kingdom at the time of the Suez crisis in 1956 gave strong support to the principle that even major sovereign countries must accept strings attached to large-scale aid. Especially in dealing with underdeveloped countries, the Fund has typically fitted its financial aid into domestic anti-inflation programs whose elaboration "has gradually become one of the main activities of the Fund. These stabilization programs go fairly deeply into internal policies; they include, for example, rather precise undertakings by members with respect to public finance, quantitative limitations on expansion of central bank credit, and minimum reserve requirements for commercial banks."[7] The Fund and its clients have sometimes negotiated limitations on borrowing abroad by both public and private agencies, as well as tax provisions, intended restraints on the growth of government spending, and measures to cut the deficits of government enterprises. The Fund has sometimes joined with other international organizations, U.S. government agencies, and American commercial banks in providing financial support for stabilization programs. These "parallel arrangements" have been made not only for Latin American countries but even for Britain and France as early as 1956 and 1958 respectively.

The Articles of Agreement bar the Fund from approving of fluctuating exchange rates. Yet the Fund has sometimes actually urged (though not approved) a fluctuating rate, especially as part of an anti-inflation program linked with a standby arrangement for an underdeveloped country. It has even gone so far as to insist on "a commitment that the rate would be allowed to move in accordance with the market forces, and that the authorities would intervene in the exchange market only to maintain orderly market conditions." To guard against any more ambitious intervention, the Fund has specified certain "balance of payments tests," framed in terms of the country's reserves. Some stabilization programs have introduced exchange-rate flexibility through periodic adjustments as an alternative to fluctuating rates. Such "programs have pro-

vided that a specified increase in the price index would be followed by an appropriate adjustment of the exchange rate."[8] Such sympathy for exchange-rate flexibility is quite exceptional in relation to the basic Bretton Woods philosophy.

Both in connection with stabilization programs and separately, the Fund has often provided technical as well as financial assistance to underdeveloped countries. Their government officials are reportedly more willing to discuss exchange and trade controls and domestic financial policies with international civil servants than with representatives of private banks or individual governments. The Fund also conducts programs to train officials of member governments in domestic and international fiscal and central-banking operations.

Members that have drawn the largest cumulative amounts of financial aid from the beginning of the Fund's operations through the end of September 1974 were, in order, the United Kingdom (alone accounting for 27.2 percent of the total), the United States (12.3 percent), France, Italy, India, Germany (which made the great bulk of its drawings under exceptional circumstances in 1969), Canada, Argentina, Chile, and Brazil. The members with the largest debt to the Fund (net drawings) still outstanding at the end of September 1974 were Italy (27.6 percent of the total), the United Kingdom (11.5 percent), India, the United States, Chile, and Pakistan.

Special drawing rights

At the Fund's annual meeting in Rio de Janeiro in September 1967, the delegates agreed on general principles for creation of a new kind of international liquidity. The name "special drawing rights" was chosen with deliberate ambiguity to win broad consent for the plan. Some governments, notably the French, were wary of the Fund's creating an actual asset that its holders would own outright; they would have preferred a mere extension of facilities for borrowing from the Fund.[9] The plan took shape in the spring of 1968 in the form of a proposed amendment to the Fund's Articles of Agreement.[10] The amendment achieved the required ratifications in the summer of 1969; and the Fund's Special Drawing Account, distinct from its General Account, came into being on August 6, 1969. Only a few of the Fund's smaller members chose not to participate. Each actual issue of special drawing rights requires the agreement of 85 percent of the voting power. The first issue and allocation of SDRs, totaling 9.3 billion units, was made in three installments on January 1 of 1970, 1971, and 1972. (The unit was originally equivalent to the gold content of one pre-1971 U.S. dollar, 0.888671 gram. After the dollar devaluations of December 1971 and February 1973, one SDR and $1.2063 became theoretically equal in value. On July 1, 1974, the SDR was redefined as the value of a "basket" containing 40 U.S. cents and specified numbers or fractions of 15 other currencies. At the exchange rates prevailing on January 31, 1975, SDR1 was worth US $1.2389.) At the end of August 1974, the SDRs in existence amounted to 5.2 percent of the noncommunist world total of official international reserves (as reported in *International Financial Statistics*, consisting not only of SDRs but also of ordinary IMF reserve positions, foreign exchange, and gold).

The new Account simply created and gave away the SDRs outright: it established balances on its books and allocated them to participants in proportion to their IMF quotas. When a deficit country needs to draw on its international reserves, it can transfer some of its SDR balance to other countries to obtain their currencies or dollars or other currencies for sale on the foreign-exchange market in support of its own currency. (A similar support operation is illustrated by the first use of SDRs. that the United States made in May 1970, when it sold 10 million units to the Netherlands and Belgium in return for dollars they held. Together with a $150 million regular purchase of guilders and Belgian francs from the IMF, the move was designed to mop up dollars that the Netherlands and Belgium might otherwise have presented for redemption in U.S. gold.)

The IMF designates the countries that are to accept transfers of SDRs and supply currencies in exchange. The applicable rules are akin to those governing the choice of currencies to be drawn from the Fund in its ordinary lending operations. Broadly speaking, the designated countries, like the ones whose currencies are paid out in ordinary lending operations, are countries whose strong payments positions or ample reserves of their own enable them conveniently to supply the currencies that the deficit country needs for market intervention in support of its own currency.

Furthermore, countries are supposed to be designated to accept SDRs in such a manner as to promote a balanced distribution of SDR holdings among them. (For example, the fact that a participant has greatly drawn down its original allocations counts toward its being designated to receive SDRs.) No country is required to accept so many SDRs that its total holding of them would exceed three times its cumulative original allocation. Of course, central banks may voluntarily transfer SDRs to each other in settlement of obligations between them. SDRs may also be transferred to the IMF itself in repayment of ordinary borrowings (drawings) from its General Account.

SDRs derive their strength not from a pool of assets held by the IMF but from the obligations of participants to accept transfers of SDRs and provide currencies in exchange. Some mild incentives exist for countries to accept transfers even beyond the amounts that the rules actually require. SDRs carry a gold-value guarantee. A participant earns interest on its holdings of SDRs and pays a charge on its net (i.e., uncancelled) cumulative allocation. Thus, a country that had neither transferred away any of its allocation nor accepted transfers of any additional SDRs would neither pay nor receive interest on balance. A country that had run down its allocation would be a net payer of interest, and a country that had built up its holdings beyond its allocation would be a net receiver. Interest is credited and charges are debited to participants' accounts in SDRs. The rate of interest and the rate of charge are the same; both were initially 1½ percent, with some room for later changes.

A participant's net use of its SDRs must be

7. Margaret G. de Vries in Horsefield, *op. cit.*, **II**, p. 26.

8. Emil G. Spitzer in Horsefield, *op. cit.*, **II**, pp. 506–507.

9. On this happy ambiguity, see Fritz Machlup, *Remaking the International Monetary System: The Rio Agreement and Beyond*, Baltimore: Johns Hopkins Press, 1968.

10. The amendment is reprinted in the IMF 1968 *Annual Report*, pp. 154–170 and is followed, pp. 171–174, by an outline.

such that its average holding over a specified base period (normally, five years) is not less than 30 percent of the average of its net cumulative allocations over the same period. Participants that have transferred away more than 70 percent of their average net cumulative allocations during some part of the base period may, therefore, have to reconstitute their holdings to ensure that their average use over the whole period does not exceed the specified proportion. This partial reconstitution of SDR allocations is not the same thing as repayment of a loan, but it resembles it in a way.

Because of limits to amounts of SDRs that other participants are required to accept and because of the reconstitution rule, each participant finds its SDRs less fully or freely usable than reserves of gold or foreign exchange. This feature of the scheme is another aspect of its compromise between the outright creation of "paper gold," which would be an owned asset of unrestricted usability, and the mere provision of additional borrowing facilities. Nevertheless, SDRs themselves are commonly nicknamed "paper gold."

Article XXIV of the SDR amendment says, in part: "In all its decisions with respect to the allocation and cancellation of special drawing rights the Fund shall seek to meet the long-term global need, as and when it arises, to supplement existing reserve assets in such a manner as will promote the attainment of its purposes and will avoid economic stagnation and deflation as well as excess demand and inflation in the world." Achieving these purposes is quite a large order, in part because regulation of the amount of SDRs will have only a small impact on the total quantity of international liquidity as long as SDRs remain only a small fraction of that total.[11] Instead of rationalizing international liquidity, the SDR amendment compounded the hodge-podge by adding a new—and so far, quantitatively minor—form of liquidity to the forms already in existence. Ironically, as the first SDR allocations were taking place in 1970–1972, the world was being flooded with excess liquidity through the exceptionally large payments deficits of the United States.

While unimportant so far as a means of soundly regulating international liquidity, the SDR has gained stature as a unit of account. The fluctuations of the dollar on foreign-exchange markets, the sharp decline in its purchasing power and that of other currencies, and the sharp rise and oscillations in the open-market price of gold in terms of currencies have undermined the status of the dollar and of gold as measures of value. A few countries have already taken to specifying par values of their currencies in SDRs rather than in gold or dollars, and *International Financial Statistics* publishes par values in SDRs as well as in the two more traditional ways. It is simpler for each country to specify a single parity of its currency in one common denominator than to specify a separate bilateral parity with each of all the other currencies. By devaluing or revaluing its currency against the SDR, a country can achieve an equiproportionate devaluation or revaluation against the currencies of all countries that do not change their SDR parities at the same time. The SDR serves as a common denominator through which currencies are indirectly given parities in terms of each other. Its own original definition in terms of gold has become rather conventional or empty. With the price of gold on the free market diverging as widely as it does from the price of gold for official transactions, there is a radical ambiguity in saying that something is worth a specified quantity of gold. The SDR avoids this ambiguity by being somewhat abstract and by not being traded on any actual open market (but only being transferred among central banks and the IMF in accordance with special rules and at prescribed exchange rates). Actually, the SDR gets its value from its definition (since mid-1974) in terms of a "basket" of 16 currencies, from the parities at which national currencies may be linked to it, and from the rules requiring participants in the scheme to accept SDRs in exchange for currencies. (None of this is to say that the SDR is stable in purchasing power over goods and services, any more than the currencies that define it have such stability.)

Furthermore, the IMF has begun publishing figures on the scale of its own operations and on amounts of international liquidity in terms of SDRs. All this illustrates again the tendency of IMF institutions and practices to evolve in ways quite different from those foreseen in the documents establishing them. As their very name indicates, special drawing rights were supposed to have, in a deliberately ambiguous degree, the character of borrowing privileges; they were not supposed unambiguously to be monetary units. Yet something called *the* SDR has evolved which serves as a measure of value and the common denominator of national currencies.

This evolution of SDRs has not been paralleled, however, by any such growth in importance as a reserve medium and medium of intergovernmental settlements. In those respects, SDRs still remain relatively unimportant.[12]

Other activities

The Fund's chief powers, besides those of administering its General and Special Drawing Accounts, may be summarized as follows. It has authority to limit any member's use of its resources when it considers that they are being improperly used. It may declare members ineligible to draw on the Fund (or even expel them) for unauthorized exchange-rate changes, for use of its resources to finance unauthorized capital transfers (the Fund can permit or even request a country to impose exchange controls against capital outflows),[13] or for failure to remove "transition-period" exchange controls over current transactions when advised to do so. It may veto proposed changes in members' exchange rates beyond 10 percent away from the initial parity if it finds that "fundamental disequilibrium" does not call for such changes. It may invoke the scarce-currency clause to be described below. It may require members to consult with it about any exchange restrictions they may be maintaining. It provides technical assistance to members and prospective members. It may determine the quotas and terms of admission of prospective member countries not represented at the Bretton Woods conference. It may suspend certain provisions of the Articles of Agreement when it considers this necessary.

Besides its activities and powers already mentioned, the IMF has some further functions widely considered of real importance. It provides facilities for semicontinuous consultation among member governments about controls and financial policies and similar matters of mutual concern, presumably fostering compromises and informal understandings. Its annual meetings, in particular, provide forums for momentous declarations, including denials of rumored adjustments in exchange rates. Through its reports and research studies and in other ways, it exerts influence on policies and even on world opinion. Particularly under the leadership of Per Jacobsson, Managing Director from December 1956 until his death in May 1963, it has practiced moral suasion to combat inflation and promote sound or orthodox finance.[14]

The Fund shares with the CONTRACTING PARTIES to the General Agreement on Tariffs and Trade (GATT) the job of supervising and seeking to relax restrictions (including bilateral arrangements) that impede international trade and payments.

The term CONTRACTING PARTIES (in capital letters) refers to the signatories of what is basically an international trade agreement, conceived of not as individual countries but as a loose sort of international organization. The CONTRACTING PARTIES operate(s) through annual meetings, *ad hoc* committees, and a secretariat borrowed from the United Nations; several attempts to establish a more formal organization have failed. GATT today consists of arrangements for international consultation

11. A more profound difficulty, relating to the near-impossibility of achieving appropriate quantities of liquidity on the domestic and international levels both at the same time, is discussed on pp. 624–626.

12. For a discussion of the possible future evolution of SDRs, see Alexandre Kafka, *The IMF: The Second Coming?*, Princeton Essays in International Finance, No. 94, Princeton, N.J.: Princeton University, July 1972; and Fred Hirsch, *An SDR Standard: Impetus, Elements, and Impediments*, Princeton Essays in International Finance, No. 99, Princeton, N.J.: Princeton University, June 1973.

13. Doubt persisted for some years whether the Articles of Agreement permitted the Fund to lend to countries whose balance-of-payments deficits were largely attributable to capital movements. In July 1961 a decision of the Executive Directors confirmed the Fund's practice as it had been evolving: such use of the Fund's resources was permissible. This decision makes sense in view of the "difficulty in separating current and capital payments under a system of convertible currencies." Jacobsson, *op. cit.*, pp. 247, 285.

As for the original idea in the Articles of Agreement concerning control over capital-account but not current-account transactions, the doubts developed in Chapter 7 seem decisive.

14. *Ibid.*, p. 37 and *passim*.

and compromise on trade policies and for negotiation of reciprocal but multilaterally generalized tariff reductions. It is also a body of rules for nondiscriminatory policy (with exceptions in favor of customs unions and historically recognized preferential economic relations), for avoidance of quantitative trade restrictions (with exceptions, particularly concerning balance-of-payments troubles, economic development, and agricultural programs), for moderation in the use of export subsidies, for simplification of customs procedures, for the freedom of transit trade, and, in general, for the liberalization of trade policies and equivalent internal measures.

Ultimately, GATT derives from proposals initiated by the U.S. State Department during World War II for international trade-liberalization agreements and for an organization to administer them. Post-war negotiations for both went forward in parallel. At Geneva, Switzerland, in 1947, pairs of countries negotiated about individual products of which each country was the other's principal supplier. The "concessions" so agreed on were then to be extended to all members of the negotiating group. During the bilateral stage of negotiations, each country was presumably willing to grant its trading partner "concessions" whose benefits would spill over onto third countries because it realized that it would at the same time reap some of the benefits of "concessions" initially negotiated between other pairs of countries. The results of 123 sets of negotiations among 23 countries were incorporated into a single General Agreement on Tariffs and Trade, signed in October 1947. It became provisionally effective the following January 1 among the United States and seven other countries. This agreement contained not only schedules of "concessions" on individual products but also numerous rules of trade policy, broadly the same as those to be administered by a proposed International Trade Organization. The final version of that Organization's charter was drafted at a lengthy conference in Havana and was signed by representatives of 53 nations, including the United States, in March 1948. To obtain such widespread agreement, the ITO charter included so many exceptions, loopholes, and deliberate ambiguities that even its friends could muster little enthusiasm; and only two countries ever ratified it, Australia conditionally and only Liberia unconditionally. The GATT, which was to have been absorbed into the ITO, remained to carry on alone. Since then, officials of the CONTRACTING PARTIES have regularly consulted with member countries maintaining questionable trade restrictions, exercising moral suasion for their removal. The Geneva conference of 1947 was followed by further general conferences at Annecy, France, Torquay, England, and again at Geneva. Additional reductions and simplifications of tariffs have been negotiated on a reciprocal basis. (All along, the President has hinged American participation in GATT, without ratification by the Senate, on authority claimed under the Trade Agreements Act of 1934, as extended and amended every few years, although Congress has explicitly and repeatedly refused either to confirm or repudiate this interpretation of Presidential authority.)

By 1970, GATT membership had grown to 78 countries, with others in provisional or applicant status. Tariff "concessions" in the General Agreement include commitments to reduce, eliminate, or not increase or impose specified duties. At successive annual sessions of the CONTRACTING PARTIES, an increasing range of issues has come under discussion, including not only agricultural protectionism and the export problems of primary-producing countries but also the rise of regional economic arrangements such as the European Economic Community, the European Free Trade Area, and the Latin American Free Trade Association.

The Fund has chief responsibility for campaigning against restrictions on *payments* (i.e., on private transactions in foreign exchange), while GATT concerns itself with *trade* restrictions, such as quantitative import limitations and discriminatory tariffs. This division of responsibility is rather artificial, and is largely due to historical circumstances,[15] since exchange controls and import barriers often serve the same end, differing only in administrative detail. (There need be little difference between strict rationing of foreign exchange made available to *pay* for foreign automobiles and strict allocation of licenses actually to *import* the automobiles.) Member countries are not supposed to use exchange controls to frustrate the intent of the General Agreement or to use trade policy to frustrate the intent of the IMF Articles. GATT members are authorized, however, to employ trade restrictions to reinforce the effectiveness of whatever payments restrictions the IMF, by exception, does permit. GATT members are required to accept the findings of the Fund on their problems of monetary reserves, balances of payments, and foreign-exchange arrangements. They must either belong to the Fund or conclude special agreements with it. The Fund is sometimes asked to decide whether a country's quantitative import restrictions, which GATT will in principle tolerate only as exceptions on specified grounds, are in fact justified by balance-of-payments troubles (i.e., whether they are needed to prevent a serious decline in the country's reserves or to achieve a reasonable rate of increase in very low reserves). If the Fund finds no balance-of-payments justification and the country can find no other approved excuse, it is supposed to remove the restrictions. In October 1959 the Executive Directors of the Fund decided that there was no longer any balance-of-payments justification for discriminatory features in restrictions maintained by member countries whose current receipts were largely in externally convertible currencies. The Fund communicated its decision to GATT, which then issued a similar statement.

The scarce-currency clause

One situation in which the IMF *would* authorize discriminatory controls is worth considering for the further insight it provides into the arrangements contrived at Bretton Woods. The "scarce-currency clause," number VII of the Articles of Agreement, contemplates a situation in which member countries' requests to draw a particular currency exceed the Fund's capacity to supply it. This situation might arise when other countries had exceptionally widespread or severe balance-of-payments deficits with some particular country and were seeking to "ride out" these deficits with the Fund's aid. Unable to meet all of these legitimate calls upon it, the Fund might inaugurate a study of the scarcity and issue a report, seek a loan from the scarce-currency country, or buy the scarce currency with gold. If all else failed, the Fund might formally declare the currency scarce and proceed to ration its available supply among the various applicants. Under the Articles of Agreement, this declaration would authorize member countries to impose discriminatory restrictions on their citizens' expenditures in and payments to the scarce-currency country.

The authors of the scarce-currency clause probably envisaged a situation in which something, probably an American depression, was heavily unbalancing payments between the United States and the rest of the world. Considering all that was said about "dollar shortage" in the early postwar years (see the appendix to Chapter 27), one might expect the scarce-currency clause to have been formally invoked. Yet it was not, and for several reasons. First, members' rights to draw on the Fund were never regarded as fully automatic, so that the Fund in effect rationed its dollars under normal rather than exceptional procedures. Second, American aid programs sup-

plied the rest of the world with dollars and so moderated the demands on the Fund's resources. Third, the kind of discriminatory controls over transactions with the United States that would have been authorized by a formal declaration of scarcity were practiced under the transition-period provisions, anyway, especially during the Fund's early years.

The scarce-currency clause is of interest, then, not for its application but for its recognition that if the balance-of-payments deficits of numerous countries are the counterparts of one particular surplus, the transactions of the deficit countries with the surplus country rather than among themselves are what require adjustment. Deficit countries should not have to hamstring transactions among themselves for the legalistic sake of acting nondiscriminatorily in their efforts to balance their transactions with some third country. (See the appendix to Chapter 7.) Discriminatory controls would then have advantages in comparison with nondiscriminatory controls, but not necessarily in comparison with adjustment by exchange rates.

Balancing of payments under the IMF system

The broader ideas underlying the IMF system as a whole, even more so than those underlying the scarce-currency clause in particular, grew

---

15. For one thing, GATT carried on as a substitute for the stillborn ITO, which was to have operated in tidy parallelism with the IMF. Furthermore, as Brian Tew suggests, voting procedures and degrees of willingness to surrender parts of national sovereignty are involved. In GATT, each member has an ostensibly equal vote; but in the IMF, members have voting power according to (though not strictly proportional to) their quotas. The IMF could hardly have attracted its present near-universal membership if import restrictions for balance-of-payments purposes had been made subject to decisions voted on this basis. Tew, *The International Monetary Fund: Its Present Role and Future Prospects*, Essays in International Finance, No. 36; Princeton University, 1960, pp. 11–12.

out of an interpretation of the monetary experiences of the 1930s. These ideas embody horror of fluctuating exchange rates and competitive exchange depreciation and faith in the virtues of deliberate international monetary cooperation. Insistence on fixed exchange rates is a basic principle. Until the upheavals of 1971–1973, anyway, the Fund's toleration of the few fluctuating-rate systems adopted by its members was "grudging and frigid."[16] (Its attitude toward fluctuating rates of underdeveloped countries pursuing domestic stabilization programs has been an exception.) According to its own staff,

If the Fund finds that the reasons advanced by a member for maintaining a unitary fluctuating exchange rate are persuasive, it may say so, although it cannot concur with the action. The Fund has to emphasize that such a measure must be temporary and that it is essential for the member to remain in close consultation with the Fund.

The system of fixed parities

was written into the Articles of Agreement because it emerged from the experience of the world over a period of many years. No one would deny that the maintenance of a given exchange rate is sometimes made very difficult either by a set of internal policies or by the external economic forces with which countries must deal. . . . Nevertheless, it is a striking fact that the maintenance of stable rates of exchange is virtually the invariable objective of all countries at all times; even those countries that have embarked on a policy of fluctuating rates have in practice generally stabilized their rates within narrow limits over long periods of time.[17]

Another of the key ideas underlying the International Monetary Fund is the distinction, never precisely drawn, between "fundamental" and temporary disequilibriums in balances of payments. Temporary disequilibriums, by implication, stem from accidental or random disturbances and will presently disappear of their own accord; the standard example is a crop failure. Such deficits do not call for controls, devaluation, deflation, or any other corrective action; reserves, and if need be the IMF, can properly be drawn upon until the disturbances reverse themselves. Fundamental disequilibriums, as implicitly defined by contrast, presumably reflect deep-seated and persistent maladjustments, as between one country's income or price and cost levels and those in the outside world. Exchange-rate adjustment

is a proper remedy for such conditions but is presumably expected to be necessary only rarely.

Still, the recognized possibility of adjustment means that the system drafted at Bretton Woods, unlike the pre-1914 gold standard, is not one of exchange-rate stability intended to be permanent. Rather, it is a system of "adjustable pegs." It attempts to reap the advantages of stable and flexible exchanges both. Except during brief periods of deliberate adjustment in pegged rates, international trade and investment will enjoy the benefits of stability. And on the rare occasions when a change has become advisable, it will be made in an orderly manner, after due consultation among experts, and with safeguards against the selfish nationalistic practice of depreciating excessively in order to "export unemployment" or otherwise obtain an unfair advantage for one's own county at the expense of others. (With postwar inflationary conditions being almost the opposite of those that supposedly motivated so many "predatory" depreciations during the 1930s, the Fund in fact has had to restrain unjustifiable devaluations less often than to prod discreetly for adjustments in clearly unrealistic rates.) Actually, the IMF system comes closer to combining the disadvantages than the advantages of truly fixed and truly free exchange rates. It is questionable whether the Fund has even yet established real confidence in currencies. Rate adjustments sometimes occur; and when they do, they are likely to be much sharper—20 or 30 percent over a weekend—than those characteristic of fluctuating rates. Even when no adjustment is in fact made, its mere possibility can at times cause disruptive uncertainties, as several crises since World War II amply illustrate. (See Chapters 21–28.)

The ideas underlying the Articles of Agreement slide over some crucial distinctions, particularly the distinction between truly free exchange-rate fluctuations, on the one hand, and, on the other hand, either governmental manipulation or unsuccessful pegging of rates, as during the interwar period. Paradoxically, though, the Fund is supposed to make some other, extremely delicate, distinctions. How, for instance, can anyone be confident that a given balance-of-payments disequilibrium is temporary rather than fundamental, except with hindsight, *after* the situation has been dealt with or has run its course? And how plausible is still another original key idea, now eroded—the hope of controlling disruptive hot-money movements while leaving current transactions free? The trouble is that capital can be transferred through changes in the timing or other aspects of normal current transactions. The realities of speculation—on a one-way option and by means of leads and lags if not openly—make the idea of deciding on exchange-rate changes only after thorough international consultation seem particularly wishful. As at the time of the devaluations in 1949, the authorities of a country desiring to change its exchange rate typically make up their own minds on the matter and then simply notify the Fund. Though this notification is phrased as a request for permission, the Fund actually faces the choice only between acquiescing or risking loss of face by seeing its authority flouted and the change made anyway. It may be that the administrative structure of the Fund is not conducive to unhurried deliberation among experts—the executive directors tend less to exercise independent judgment than to act as "glorified messenger boys" for the governments appointing them[18]—but the real difficulty inheres in the idea of the adjustable peg.

The IMF system lacks any "automatic" international balancing mechanism. The IMF does lend financial resources for "waiting out" disequilibriums hopefully thought fated to go away of their own accord; it does stand "ready to subsidize this breath-holding policy." Unless by exercising moral suasion over its members' domestic financial policies or by authorizing infrequent deliberate adjustments in levels of exchange-rate pegging, however, it does nothing positive to promote equilibrium. It simply helps improvise *ad hoc* solutions for crises.[19] Trade and exchange controls, which may be sometimes tightened and sometimes loosened and sometimes even hopefully relegated to a standby role, remain as a substitute for a continuously operating adjustment mechanism.[20]

Has the Bretton Woods system been a success?

A full appraisal of the system must await the historical surveys in chapters still to come; the remarks that follow here are preliminary. A favorable verdict requires either a good deal of generosity or else a set of expectations

tempered by the unimpressive performance of the IMF up at least until the time of Suez in 1956. (The trend of general opinion on what goals are practical and realistic may itself be one clue about success or failure, more objectively conceived.) Exchange controls under the transition-period excuse lasted many years beyond the time they were originally expected to lapse. Later years did indeed see important progress, as the next chapter describes. Still, any judgment whether progress has been sufficiently great and rapid implies a comparison of actual developments both with the expectations that prevailed at Bretton Woods and with the probable course of developments under alternative policies. Even today, many countries are still reluctant to dismantle ex-

16. W. M. Scammell, *International Monetary Policy*, London: Macmillan, 1957, p. 182.

17. *The First Ten Years of the International Monetary Fund*, Washington, 1956, p. 14. The second passage is quoted there from the Fund's *Annual Report, 1951.*

18. Robert Triffin, *Europe and the Money Muddle*, New Haven, Conn.: Yale University Press, 1957, p. 137.

19. William R. Allen, "The International Monetary Fund and Balance of Payments Adjustment," *Oxford Economic Papers*, new series XIII, June 1961, pp. 159–164. As for exchange-rate changes, Allen (p. 152) interprets the Fund's view as that they "*conceivably* . . . should be seriously *considered* when rates are so immensely unrealistic that it would be patently *ridiculous*, if not politically and economically *disastrous*, to maintain them." On the other hand, frequent adjustments in pegged rates are hardly the answer, as the Fund itself has noted (1962 *Annual Report*, p. 62).

20. Robert A. Mundell (in the already-cited Joint Economic Committee Hearings of November 1963, especially pp. 546–547, 568) contended that the Bretton Woods system had fallen into desuetude: "the short-run stability of the adjustable-peg mechanism [has] turned into long-run rigidity"; the world has been slipping back to the inflation-stagnation adjustment rules of the gold standard or to "a system of creeping controls." The emerging system is just too costly in terms of the inappropriate discipline it sometimes imposes on national policies.

404

change controls over transfers of funds across national boundaries.

The obvious reason for slowness in dismantling controls is that the IMF system lacks any "automatic" international balancing mechanism. Another possible reason is that the Fund (in contrast with the European Payments Union, described in the next chapter) provided no clearing machinery enabling members to use their surplus earnings in trade with some countries to finance their deficits with others. This omission no doubt reflected an optimistic assumption that convertibility of currencies for nonresidents, at least, would rapidly be achieved, making a centralized clearing machinery superfluous.

By historical standards, world trade has grown rapidly since establishment of the Bretton Woods system. This fact is often cited as evidence that the system has worked and that suitable reforms would merely perfect it rather than change its basic character. Actually, that fact may prove little about the desirability of the par-value system. Several considerations deserve attention. (Although they may not be fully understandable until after a reading of the later chapters, they are assembled here for reference.)

1. The earlier experience with which the postwar period compares favorably covers periods of policy not very conducive to growth of trade. The major countries began shifting away from relatively free trade and back toward tariff protectionism as early as the 1870s. Protectionism and economic nationalism became rampant in the 1930s.

2. Much of what we have been witnessing since World War II has been recovery from the wars and depressions of the first half of the century. Recovery and growth have been particularly strong in Western Europe and Japan. Since their economies are more foreign-trade-oriented than the American economy, their rapid growth has especially boosted world trade.[21]

3. In contrast with the 1930s, full-employment policies have become dominant everywhere. This, certainly more than exchange-rate policy, has stimulated economic activity on the domestic and international scenes alike. It has taken us a long time to reach the stage, which we seem to have been approaching in the last few years, at which people so fully allow for the expected continuation of price inflation that expansionary demand policies grow weak as a stimulus to production and employment. Until recently, however, inflationary policies have succeeded in maintaining approximately full employment and in spurring both production and international trade.

4. An inflationary world environment—to which the Bretton Woods system contributes[22] —makes it easier than it would otherwise be for deficit countries to adjust their balances of payments merely by lagging behind for a while in the inflationary procession, without undergoing actual deflation. Episodes in the experiences of Japan and Italy illustrate this possibility. Even so, quite a few countries occasionally had to resort to exchange-rate adjustment even before the eventful early 1970s, when the system came apart. In this respect, the system worked not because exchange rates were fixed but because their fixity was not defended to the bitter end.

5. Besides occasional lagging in the inflationary procession and occasional exchange-rate adjustments, special historical circumstances were at work to limit or correct payments disequilibria. During the 1950s, the process of adjustment under fixed exchange rates benefited from differential rates of liberalization, especially by European countries, of the trade and capital-movement controls inherited from the immediate postwar years. Surplus countries tended to remove controls more rapidly and more nearly completely than deficit countries. Furthermore, a country could move fast when its payments position was strong but slow down or even temporarily reverse its liberalization when its payments position weakened. Differential liberalization kept the world in better economic balance than it would have experienced if it had entered the postwar period free of controls. This substantial process of adjustment would not be available in the normal state of affairs envisaged by the Bretton Woods philosophy. By around 1960, opportunities for differential liberalization had been pretty much used up.[23]

6. During much of the postwar period, specific historical circumstances made it possible simply to live with payments disequilibria rather than correct them. In the early postwar years, the United States aided countries with deficits. By the criteria used in allocating Marshall Plan funds, a deficit benefited a country by enlarging its share of the aid. To view the situation the other way around, the United States was willing to make gifts to finance surpluses in the rest of its balance of payments. Later, schemes of stopgap international lend-

ing and inter-central-bank cooperation were worked out. After the "dollar shortage" reversed itself into a chronic U.S. deficit, other countries were willing for many years to tolerate the imbalance because of the special role of the dollar as vehicle, intervention, and reserve currency. The United States was supplying other countries with desired increases in their external reserves. It could avoid strong corrective action as long as it could finance its deficits by running up short-term debts to foreigners. As long as the foreigners were willing to acquire these dollar claims as private working balances or as official reserves, the United States did not have to redeem them in gold. Although the foreigners did cash some of their dollar holdings for gold, the United States could pay cheerfully for several years because of the huge size at which its gold stock had peaked in 1949. By the time U.S. gold reserves had fallen far enough to cause alarm, the United States could restrain foreigners from cashing their dollars for gold by exercising various informal pressures.

In short, special circumstances prevailing throughout much of the postwar period enabled sizable imbalances of payments simply to continue without either causing crises or bringing on controls severe enough to impede trade seriously. Up to some time in the 1950s, the United States could run surpluses and other countries deficits; from then until the middle or late 1960s, the United States could run deficits and other countries surpluses—all with relative complacency and without pressure for drastic corrective action. During the 1960s, however, these special circumstances eroded. It became less possible simply to let disequilibriums ride. The change might be dated from the U.S. imposition of "voluntary" capital controls in 1965, or even from the proposal of the Interest Equalization Tax in 1963.

These points, as well as general logical considerations, explain why it is illegitimate to appraise the Bretton Woods system, conceived globally, by reference to historical experience, likewise conceived globally. It is necessary to consider specific features of the system and their relation to specific aspects and episodes of historical experience. This the succeeding chapters will try to do in detail. Throughout the postwar period, and especially from the mid-1960s, the world has been experiencing balance-of-payments crises, otherwise undesirable modifications of domestic policies in response, and controls to palliate the disequilib-

rium. The world has moved to a differential *deliberalization* of controls over trade and especially over capital movements.

Not all of the troubles attributable to the Bretton Woods system fell on the volume of international trade. One might plausibly argue that the system had a global inflationary bias, that it distorted patterns of resource allocation, production, and trade through disequilibrium relative prices associated with wrongly pegged exchange rates, that it led to domestic stop-and-go aggregate-demand policies, that it bred controls impinging on personal freedom, that it caused anxieties over the possibilities of various sudden changes, and that it inflated expenditures on bureaucratic activities.

These troubles and costs may not be very important. They may not much hamper international trade. (Businessmen engaged in international trade, like businessmen in general, seem remarkably capable of learning to cope with difficulties.) Defects of the international monetary system may deserve to rank only 23d or 79th in seriousness on a list of the problems facing mankind. But when the performance of the system is the topic under discussion, one should try to get the analysis straight and not be content with some global appraisal buttressed by a sweeping reference to unanalyzed experience.

Opinions and prospects

Some writers have not shrunk from questioning whether the Fund has achieved the aims set forth in its Articles of Agreement. Perhaps more common, however, was the opinion

---

21. Kenneth N. Waltz, "The Myth of National Interdependence," in Charles P. Kindleberger, *The International Corporation*, Cambridge, Mass.: The MIT Press, 1970, p. 209.

22. Other parts of this book provide theoretical and historical reasons for judging that the system has a definite inflationary bias.

23. Richard N. Cooper in Randall Hinshaw, ed., *The Economics of International Adjustment*, Baltimore: Johns Hopkins Press, 1971, pp. 69–71, 76–77.

406

epitomized in *Business Week* for March 30, 1957 under the heading "IMF Wins Over the Skeptics." According to the article, "a decade of prudent management" had wiped out original suspicions in American banking circles of a supposed "device to allow deficit-financing on an international scale." The sudden spurt of lending to meet temporary payments difficulties at the time of the Suez crisis was in line with the Fund's original objectives. Once maligned but now highly respected, the Fund had played an important role in preaching the merits of anti-inflationary policies.

Yet the "doubts and suspicions" wiped out by "prudent management" were not doubts about the key ideas underlying the Bretton Woods system. Little reassurance flows from almost a decade of prudent near-inactivity followed by heavy lending since then. It is only slightly reassuring to cite particular historical occasions when payments difficulties really did prove temporary and when the Fund's aid did let members wait for a crisis to blow over of its own accord. Some such occasions do of course occur. Skeptics simply maintain that not all disequilibriums are fated to blow over so easily, that the possibility of occasional self-curing disequilibriums hardly justifies dispensing with a continuous adjustment mechanism, that no one can confidently know in advance whether or not each particular disequilibrium is fated to blow over, and that delay in correcting a disequilibrium not so fated may, through speculation and otherwise, make the crisis unnecessarily serious. Some critics would even question the grounds for preferring a payments crisis that does happen to blow over to the alternative of a temporary and perhaps mild depreciation of the currency under pressure. As for episodes of bold, large-scale, and successful IMF activity in times of crisis, these hardly serve as evidence for the success of the system if the system itself tends to breed the opportunities for display of such heroism.

The management and staff of the Fund have no doubt been conservative, prudent, competent, and wise. But perhaps such talent has

been sidetracked into administering questionable principles. Of course, the Fund renders valuable services. It provides "clubrooms," so to speak, for consultations among international civil servants and financial officials of various countries.[24] Its experts give sound advice about domestic as well as international financial policy to some of its economically less advanced member countries, and this advice stands a better chance of being heeded precisely because it comes from a respected international agency rather than from some foreign government. The Fund prepares publications of high quality and great usefulness, such as *International Financial Statistics, Staff Papers, Balance of Payments Yearbook,* and *IMF Survey.* Its *Annual Reports* and *Annual Reports on Exchange Restrictions* are informative documents. Jointly with the International Bank for Reconstruction and Development, it maintains a specialized research library. There is no reason why these services and facilities could not continue even if the ideas underlying the International Monetary Fund were to evolve into something else.

As later chapters describe, the Bretton Woods system of pegged exchange rates fell apart in 1971, was patched together, and fell apart again in 1973. Its early or exact restoration seems unlikely. Changes in the IMF that would apparently be most congenial to its personnel are measures to increase its resources for operations of the kind pursued through most of its history, with perhaps minor modifications. These and other proposals for reform are surveyed in the concluding chapters of this book.

24. This consideration may help justify the Fund's acquisition of land in Maryland, about 20 miles from its headquarters, where it has built "the Bretton Woods Recreation Center, with a golf course, a swimming pool, tennis courts, picnic grounds, and other amenities," as well as the Fund's numerous cocktail parties. See Horsefield, *op. cit.,* I, p. 603; and Robert Mossé, *Les Problèmes Monétaires Internationaux,* Paris: Payot, 1967, p. 259.

CHAPTER TWENTY-ONE

Bilateralism, EPU Convertibility, and Beyond

Early postwar bilateralism[1]

Immediately after the end of World War II, a network of bilateral agreements governed European trade and payments. Each of the two parties to an agreement undertook to regulate its own residents' transactions with the other country to avoid any large bilateral imbalance, promote mutual offsetting of obligations, and so minimize the need for settlements by transfer of gold or hard currencies. The governments in exile of the Netherlands and the Belgium-Luxembourg Economic Union signed the first such agreement in 1943. By the spring of 1947 some 200 bilateral payments agreements were in effect in Europe alone. A few years later, almost 400 agreements (not counting those of Soviet-bloc countries) covered almost the whole nondollar world. Lack of an agreement between two particular nondollar countries usually meant either that trade between them was of little importance or that negotiations had somehow fallen through.

What was the purpose of so apparently restrictive a system? Didn't the very impoverishment caused by the war call for taking fullest advantage of the gains from multilateral trade? Rightly or wrongly, policy-makers thought that desperate conditions called for drastic controls;

free markets seemed a luxury for happier times. At controlled prices and exchange rates, shortages were almost universal. Not the least pressing was the shortage of foreign exchange. Almost every European government felt impelled to control trade tightly to make the best of the shortages and save hard currencies for essential imports not otherwise obtainable. In these circumstances, arrangements between countries to favor imports from each other and avoid use of scarce hard-currency reserves might permit rather than restrict trade. In comparison with the alternative of a nondiscriminatory system of controls, bilateralism had a liberal rather than a restrictive purpose.

Bilateral agreements usually came in pairs: a trade agreement sought to determine or forecast the purchases from the other country that each country would undertake or would permit to its residents, while a payments agreement governed the financing of this trade. Trade conducted by government monopolies could be planned rather simply. To regulate private trade, the two governments agreed to issue import or export licenses for specified quantities or values of goods. The results of this permissive rather than positive regulation were inexact; sometimes, for example, one country's purchases from the other would lag behind the forecasted amounts because of unattractive prices. An agreement therefore typically provided for a joint commission to study possible revisions.

Besides economizing on transfers of hard-currency reserves, countries also sought to safeguard their own exports from import controls exercised at the unilateral whim of other coun-

---

1. Some references for this and the next two sections include Robert Triffin, *Europe and the Money Muddle*, New Haven, Conn.: Yale University Press, 1957, chap. 4; P. T. Ellsworth, *The International Economy*, New York: Macmillan, 1950, pp. 675–681; Raymond F. Mikesell, *The Emerging Pattern of International Payments*, Essays in International Finance, No. 18, Princeton, N.J.: Princeton University, International Finance Section, 1954; Raymond F. Mikesell, *Foreign Exchange in the Postwar World*, New York: Twentieth Century Fund, 1954, chaps. 2 and 5; Merlyn Nelson Trued and Raymond F. Mikesell, *Postwar Bilateral Payments Agreements*, Studies in International Finance, No. 4, Princeton, N.J.: Princeton University, International Finance Section, 1955; and J. Kymmell, *De Ontwikkeling van het Internationale Betalingsverkeer*, Leiden: Stenfert Kroese, 1950, chap. 2.

tries and to obtain essential imports on reasonable terms. Some paradoxes resulted. To win markets for its "nonessential" exports, a country might have to discriminate in favor of certain imports from a bilateral partner and against similar goods obtainable more cheaply elsewhere. Exporting countries were sometimes able to insist on tie-in sales: to get scarce "essentials" such as coal, their partners would have to agree to take "nonessential" imports also. In impoverished immediate-postwar Europe, trade flourished in luxuries such as expensive textiles, cosmetics, perfumes, jewelry, gourmet foods, wines, and vacuum cleaners. Foolish as the resulting pattern of trade may have seemed, each individual country may have been quite rational in bargaining for markets for products in which it had a comparative advantage, even if these were "luxuries."

The payments agreements accompanying postwar bilateral trade agreements differed from the prewar *clearing* agreements typical of Central and Eastern Europe and some Latin American countries in not bypassing the foreign-exchange market by having all payments made in local currency through a clearing office in each country. Instead, the postwar agreements, like the prewar *payments* agreements, allowed use of the normal institutions of the foreign-exchange market. Before the war, one of the two partners in a payments agreement typically had a currency free of exchange control; its currency was used in payments, while the other partner controlled the transactions of its own citizens for the agreed purposes. After the war, both partners, with rare exceptions, had exchange controls and regulated their citizens' transactions.

Degrees of centralization differed widely in the hundreds of postwar payments agreements. Countries with well-developed private-enterprise economies relied on the regular commercial banking systems, which served as agents of the authorities in screening transactions and applying controls. Businessmen dealt with their regular banks to buy foreign exchange for authorized purposes and to sell exchange earned from foreigners. Exports were invoiced and drafts drawn according to normal trade practice. Commercial banks won increasing freedom to hold foreign-exchange balances with correspondent banks abroad, provided they reported fully and promptly. Beginning in 1953, the banks of the main West European countries were even allowed to engage in multi-

lateral arbitrage in spot and forward exchange. (See pp. 415–416.)

Banks running low of foreign exchange demanded by customers for authorized purposes replenished their supply at their country's central bank, where they also sold excess accumulations of foreign exchange. (Reliance on the central bank diminished, of course, as international arbitrage expanded.) Central-bank transactions maintained the exchange rates reaffirmed in the bilateral agreements. Each central bank could supply or absorb the necessary amounts of the other country's money because it maintained an account and enjoyed overdraft privileges with the other's central bank. If necessary, it could draw an overdraft in the other currency and credit the equivalent in its own money to the deposit it owed to its partner. Except for the normal working balances of merchants and commercial banks, each country's foreign-exchange holdings drifted into the hands of its central bank. The central bank ordinarily exchanged any newly acquired deposits in the commercial banks of the partner country for an addition to its account with the partner central bank (or for a reduction in its own deposit liability to the partner central bank).

The net bilateral position developing between partners to an agreement thus tended to show up in the accounts of their central banks with each other. For this reason, discussions of early postwar payments arrangements could personify countries and speak of how much Ruritania owed to Graustark and whether or not Ruritania could use her surplus with Arcadia to cover her deficit with Graustark. Metaphorical language like this requires caution. It can be convenient and harmless only if everyone avoids thinking of countries as monolithic units carrying on trade and finance in great lumps. It is important to understand what actions of individual firms, banks, and government agencies underlie metaphorical references to "countries."

The overdrafts that central banks granted each other made it unnecessary for transactions between two partner countries to balance over short periods of time or to balance exactly. Overdrafts provided a "swing," permitting flexibility in trade and serving much the same purpose as external reserves. Some agreements set no definite limit to the "swing"; agreements with Great Britain, in particular, typically set no limit to the other partner's possible accumulation of sterling. More commonly, though, a limit was set to how much one country might be called on to accumulate of the other's currency. In principle, a balance beyond this limit had to be paid off in gold or in some currency acceptable to the creditor. Alternatively, import and export licensing had to be modified so that altered flows of trade would work off the imbalance. In practice, unforeseen bilateral imbalances became so commonplace that swing limits degenerated from rigid cutoff or gold-payment points to mere "talking points" at which the partners would consult about a remedy. Exporters in a creditor country disliked seeing a debtor partner pressured into balancing its trade by cutting its purchases. Sometimes, instead, traders in the creditor country were allowed to buy goods in the debtor country for resale in third countries. Sometimes the authorities tolerated sales of private balances of debtor currency for creditor currency at depreciated rates. At times, though, reluctance of debtor countries to make settlement in hard currencies and of creditor countries to grant further loans threatened to shrink intra-European trade. This was particularly true during the period of acute "dollar shortage" between the failure of British convertibility in August 1947 and the start of the Marshall Plan the following year. (See pp. 442–444.)

The availability of swing credits with flexible limits shows further how the postwar agreements did not so much force trade into bilateral channels as free it from unilateral and uncoordinated controls. Bilateralism grew looser in several additional ways. Debtor countries sometimes did pay off bilateral imbalances beyond agreed limits in gold or dollars usable as the creditor countries wished. Sometimes bilateral arrangements could be used, officially or unofficially, to finance one country's imports from another for reexport to a third. Bilateral agreements with the United Kingdom, the Belgium-Luxembourg Economic Union, the Netherlands, France, and a few other countries covered their overseas currency areas as well as their home territories and so broadened the scope of multilateral trade. Finally, the transferable-account system set up by the United Kingdom in 1946–1947 and extended and simplified in 1954 enabled foreigners to use pounds earned by exports to the Sterling Area to pay for imports from a wide range of non-dollar countries. (See p. 449.)

The contagion of bilateralism

The early bilateral arrangements had a more dismal side. Like several other types of economic control, they tended to be contagious. Suppose that Arcadia rejected bilateralism and aimed merely at overall equilibrium. Other countries' bilateralism and currency inconvertibility would interfere with Arcadians' using their surplus earnings in transactions with some trading partners to cover their surplus spending elsewhere. Even though they favored multilateralism, the authorities would have to operate their controls with an eye on Arcadia's bilateral positions with its trading partners. They would, that is, unless they tolerated unpegged exchange rates at which the values of any two foreign currencies in Arcadian currency failed (except by coincidence) to correspond to the official parity between them. In comparison with official parities, Arcadian currency would tend to be strong against currencies of countries with which Arcadia would otherwise have had bilateral trade surpluses and weak in relation to currencies of countries with which it would otherwise have had bilateral deficits. The pattern of broken cross rates would promote a certain degree of bilateral balancing in Arcadia's trade after all.

If, alternatively, the authorities encouraged Arcadians to insist on settling all their foreign transactions in U.S. dollars or other hard currencies, other countries' anxiety to conserve dollars would impede Arcadia's export business and, in turn, her ability to buy imports. Furthermore, if Arcadia did not limit the convertibility of its currency, it probably would see its exports discriminated against as individual foreign countries tried to develop trade surpluses with it to obtain dollars. To defend itself against such victimization, Switzerland, for example, made its franc inconvertible for exchange-control countries, even though it remained convertible for residents of Switzerland and other hard-currency countries.[2] With dis-

2. Jacques A. L'Huillier, *Théorie et Pratique de la Coopération Économique Internationale*, Paris: Librairie de Médicis, 1957, p. 206. Canada was another country notably inconvenienced by the bilateralism and currency inconvertibility of others.

criminatory controls and hard bargaining the usual practice, any country failing to join in and use its own bargaining power would suffer from unilateral foreign restrictions. Like Switzerland, some Latin American countries without a dollar problem of their own entered bilateral negotiations largely in self-defense.

The United States was the chief country not drawn into bilateral arrangements. Urgent postwar needs and overvaluation of foreign currencies were spurring its exports. It had no need to bargain in defense of its overseas markets or its foreign-exchange position.

First steps beyond bilateralism

The scope remaining for ordinary foreign-exchange institutions and practices and the flexibility offered by credits among central banks provided a point of departure for further liberalization. The next step was to overcome the incentives countries had to discriminate in favor of imports from partners with which they had bilateral trading surpluses even when goods might have been available on more favorable terms from other sources. Prospects for an early start of the Marshall Plan and the establishment of a Committee of European Economic Co-operation (forerunner of the Organisation for European Economic Co-operation) promoted ideas of a European clearing system. With their convertibility experiment having just failed in August 1947, however, the British were in no mood to risk another failure. (See pp. 442–443.) A compromise took the form of the First Agreement on Multilateral Monetary Compensation, signed in November 1947, and then two successive Agreements for Intra-European Payments and Compensations, signed in October 1948 and September 1949.[3] Under these arrangements, the participating central banks informed the Bank for International Settlements every month of their bilateral debts to and claims on each other in the hope that a worthwhile volume of mutual cancellation or offsetting could be worked out. The process was far from automatic. The only automatic operations were the "first-category compensations," whereby each country settled its indebtedness to a second country by abandoning its claim on a third country but not by increasing its indebtedness to a third country. These automatic

compensations applied in practice only to closed chains in which each country was a creditor of the preceding country and a debtor to the following one. From October 1948 through June 1950, such compensations represented only 2 percent of gross imbalances.[4] "Second-category compensations," in which some countries would exchange debts to or claims on some creditors or debtors for debts to or claims on others, always required the specific authorization of all concerned. In general, these compensations would replace claims on net creditor countries by claims on net debtor countries and replace debts to net debtor countries by debts to net creditor countries. In other words, intermediate countries would find their claims converted into currencies relatively softer than before and their debts converted into currencies relatively harder than before. For this reason, the necessary approval was seldom obtained. In all, compensations of both types cleared only about 4 percent of the positions that would have been cleared under full and automatic multilateral compensation; the remaining imbalance was met by bilateral credits and by U.S.-financed drawing rights.[5]

Under these early schemes, member countries continued to grant each other bilateral drawing rights (lines of credit or overdrafts). American aid under the Marshall Plan was based on advance estimates of each recipient country's deficit in transactions with the Western Hemisphere, but part of this aid was "conditional" on the recipient's grant of equivalent drawing rights to cover other countries' forecasted bilateral deficits with it. Besides depending on inaccurate forecasts, this system gave wrong incentives. Each country had reason to forecast deficits and obtain and use drawing rights. It didn't much matter if the imports financed by the drawing rights were less essential or higher in price than goods obtainable elsewhere, since they were, in effect, gifts; and the sale to importers for home currency of foreign exchange provided under the drawing rights had a welcome anti-inflationary effect. Countries with prospective bilateral trade surpluses, on the other hand, had incentives to grant drawing rights sparingly and obstruct their use, since the "conditional aid" came to be largely unconditional in practice; the drawing rights chiefly affected how a given total of American aid was classified into "conditional" and "direct" segments. By offering or withholding drawing rights, creditor countries could wield bargaining power over deficit countries and so strengthen bilateralism as against competition.[6]

Under this system of drawing rights and American aid, deficits and surpluses between each pair of countries were settled every month, even though they might soon have reversed themselves. Furthermore, countries received aid as compensation for granting drawing rights to their deficit partners even when they were already being compensated by drawing rights with other partners with which they had bilateral deficits. Operating on this monthly and bilateral basis, American conditional aid financed only one-third of the total net intra-European imbalance. Yet, according to Triffin, a smaller amount of aid administered on a cumulative and multilateral basis could have financed the intra-European imbalance completely.[7]

The 1949 agreement on intra-European payments moved slightly further toward multilateralism. One-fourth of the drawing rights could cover deficits with countries other than the grantor itself. Conditional aid went to the countries actually called on to honor them. But since the multilateral fourth was not available until the bilateral three-fourths had been used up, bilateralism remained nearly intact. The expansion of European trade before 1950 was perhaps due less to the monetary transferability provided by the compensation agreements themselves, limited as it was, than to American aid.[8]

The European Payments Union

The early compensation agreements were clearly inadequate. Furthermore, the last of them had hardly been signed in September 1949 when the wave of devaluations ruined its balance-of-payments forecasts. A more adequate multilateral compensation arrangement was worked out in 1950. The agreement for the European Payments Union was signed on September 19 but was made applicable retroactively to transactions that had taken place since July 1. The original agreement was to run two years; subsequent renewals were for a year at a time until the Union disbanded in December 1958. The members of the new system were the countries belonging to the Organisation for European Economic Co-operation,

and indirectly, the Sterling Area and the overseas monetary areas of Belgium, France, Italy, the Netherlands, and Portugal. (Ireland belongs to the Sterling Area and although a member of the European Payments Union, had no separate position with it. Luxembourg's position in the Union was joined with Belgium's.)

The European Payments Union, though only a temporary arrangement, is worth fairly detailed study. Since it operated routinely and continuously, clearing the deficit and surplus positions of its members and receiving and making payments and granting and receiving credit every month, an account of its operations serves as a convenient vehicle for surveying European financial history during its existence. This history underscores some noteworthy lessons about balance-of-payments behavior in the absence of a balancing mechanism. The history of EPU operations provides insight into the complexity of multilateral settlements when balances of payments are matters of direct governmental concern; it helps us appreciate, by contrast, what free exchange markets achieve with little fanfare. Furthermore, the EPU continues to serve as a model for proposed regional clearing arrangements in parts of the world where currency inconvertibility continues to prevail, such as Latin America.

---

3. The texts of the agreements and supplementary protocols appear in the 18th, 19th, and 20th *Annual Reports* of the Bank for International Settlements, pp. 167–170, 232–254, and 262–286. For discussions, see W. M. Scammell, *International Monetary Policy*, London: Macmillan, 1957, pp. 264–278; Mikesell, *Foreign Exchange in the Postwar World*, pp. 100–117; and Triffin, *op. cit.*, pp. 147–160.

4. Triffin, *op. cit.*, pp. 148–149.

5. *Ibid.*, p. 149n.

6. *Ibid.*, pp. 153, 157–158. Cf. L'Huillier, *op. cit.*, p. 218.

7. Triffin, *op. cit.*, p. 155.

8. *Ibid.*, p. 160, and L'Huillier, *op. cit.*, p. 208.

The Union's key features were as follows:[9] Each member's central bank was to continue advancing its own currency to other members as needed for day-to-day stabilization operations in the exchange market. Within months these bilateral credits were practically automatic and unlimited. Every month the Bank for International Settlements, as Agent for the European Payments Union, received reports on each member's bilateral debt to or claim on each other member as a result of the month's transactions. The agent consolidated each member's debts and claims into an overall net debt to or claim on the Union, much as an ordinary clearing house consolidates the items payable and collectable by the various member banks. Each member country's currency was considered equally hard at its official parity against the Union's unit of account (equivalent to one U.S. dollar). Since each member could use its bilateral claims on some partners to cover its bilateral debts to others and had to settle only its net position with the rest of the group as a whole, the clearing system economized on transfers of reserves. Members no longer had reason to reject clearing arrangements that changed the currency in which a debt or claim was expressed; since the Union itself would be the creditor or debtor of each of its members, all members were in effect jointly guaranteeing the credit risks involved. Only central banks, not private parties, enjoyed this automatic transferability of their claims. Still, it removed monetary or balance-of-payments reasons for discrimination in trade among member countries.

Each member's settlement with the Union depended not just on its latest monthly deficit or surplus but rather on its cumulative position since the start of the Union in mid-1950. Each country's cumulative position was covered partly by automatic credit and partly by payment in "gold" (meaning gold or dollars). Beyond each country's *quota*, further settlement would be made entirely in gold or dollars, unless further credit was arranged by exception. With some modifications, each country's initial quota was set at about 15 percent of its turnover of visible and invisible trade within the EPU area in 1949. The quotas totaled $3950 million, the largest originally being those of the United Kingdom (27 percent of the total), France (13 percent), Belgium-Luxembourg (9 percent), the Netherlands (8 percent), and Germany (8 percent).

A country with a cumulative surplus was to grant credit in full up to the first one-fifth of its quota and was to grant credit and receive payment in gold in equal amounts for the remainder of its quota. A cumulative deficit country was to settle increasingly in gold as its deficit approached its quota limit. According to the originally agreed schedules, either a surplus position or a deficit position that had reached the limit of the quota would have been covered 40 percent in gold and 60 percent in credit. The schedules were simplified in mid-1954 so that all positions within quotas would be met 50–50 in gold and credit. In 1955 the shares became 25 percent of the quota in automatic credit and 75 percent in gold. To keep the absolute size of the credit element within quotas the same as before, the 1954 and 1955 amendments also increased the quotas to 1.2 and then to 2.4 times their original sizes.[10] The EPU paid interest to creditors and collected interest from debtors at rates rising with how long a time the debt had existed.

Early experience with heavily unbalanced trade soon undermined any idea that the quotas rigidly limited credit granted or received. The concept of *rallonges* (extensions) was first applied to creditor quotas and later to debtor quotas also: heavy creditors granted credit in excess of their original commitments and heavy debtors received special loans. The main postquota lenders were Belgium-Luxembourg in the early years of the EPU and Germany later on; France was the chief postquota borrower. At the end of the Union in December 1958, 16 percent of the total credit granted by the Union was by way of rallonge, and 55 percent of the total credit granted to the Union was by way of rallonge (all from Germany).[11]

The new system of partial gold settlements weakened earlier perverse incentives to run up deficits and acquire and use drawing rights. Gold losses would call for policies to cure persistent deficits. Similarly, the obligation to grant credit partially to cover surpluses was an incentive not to let surpluses grow. For merely moderate or temporary deficits, on the other hand, their partial coverage by automatic credit could serve as a reassuring shock-absorber, supplementing gold and dollar reserves. "It was hoped that by drawing on these credit lines Member countries would gain sufficient breathing space to take the steps required to restore their balance of payments without having to withdraw trade liberalisation measures."[12]

Under the original gold-and-credit settlement schedules, imbalances of certain sizes within quotas could have called for larger out-payments of gold to creditors than inpayments of gold from debtors. The EPU therefore needed a fund of working capital, so the United States provided $350 million. Because of initial grants-in-aid to so-called "structural" deficit countries, however, the Union's initial capital in fact amounted to only $271.6 million.

In parallel with the EPU, the Organisation for European Economic Co-operation sponsored a program of intra-European trade liberalization. Building on a start made the year before, the member countries agreed in October 1950 to remove quantitative restrictions in a nondiscriminatory way from at least 60 percent of their imports from one another (most of the calculations were based on private imports during 1948). Various devices for evading this liberalization were ruled out. In the following years the OEEC persuaded members to adopt partially standardized lists of quota-free imports and to increase the percentages of trade represented on these lists. These liberalization measures were qualified in several ways. First, countries could be authorized to backslide from trade liberalization in times of balance-of-payments crisis. Second, member countries retained considerable scope for choosing just which products to free from quotas to satisfy the agreed overall liberalization percentages. Third, measures to free intra-European trade from quotas were not fully reinforced for several years by measures to reduce tariffs, to relax restrictions on service transactions, to liberalize imports from nonmember countries, and to limit discriminatory pricing or subsidization of exports. Some progress was made on each of these matters, though.[13] More generally, the OEEC contributed to a trend in trade policy that helped inspire establishment of the European Coal and Steel Community in 1952, the European Common Market in 1958, the European Free Trade Association in 1960, and the European Atomic Energy Community in 1958.

EPU operations in the early years[14]

The Korean War contributed to wide fluctuations in economic conditions and trade. Intra-European deficits and surpluses rose from the previous average of $200 million a month to $260 million in the 1950–51 financial year, to $360 million in 1951–52, and to a peak of $550 million in October 1951. Unexpectedly soon, the EPU faced the problem of abnormally large imbalances.[15]

EPU's first serious difficulty was Germany's import spurt and balance-of-payments crisis of the winter of 1950–1951. During the first half of 1950, expectations of falling prices on world markets had been holding down German imports and the inventories of German firms. When the Korean War broke out, the Germans, sensitized to inflation by two major experiences in a lifetime, were inclined to rush from money into goods. By an unfortunate coincidence, retroactive tax cuts decided upon earlier were swelling the public's spending power. Bank-credit expansion, appropriate earlier, was continuing to feed spending. Germany imported especially heavily from other EPU member countries because their export capacities were continuing to recover, because the 1949 devaluations had made their prices relatively attractive, and because intra-European trade was gradually being liberalized. The current-account deterioration was compounded by capital outflow through changes in ordinary trade credits—another example of leads and lags. By the last quarter of 1950, Germany's foreign-exchange reserves and automatic credit

9. Largely summarized from European Payments Union, *Fifth Annual Report of the Managing Board, Financial Year 1954–55*, Paris: OEEC, 1956, pp. 63ff., and BIS, 21st *Annual Report*, pp. 222ff.

10. Let Q be a country's original quota. Under the original, 1954, and 1955 arrangements, respectively, the credit element within the quota would amount to $.6Q = .5 \times 1.2Q = .25 \times 2.4Q$.

Besides the uniform quota increases just mentioned, the Dutch and German quotas were specially increased in 1951.

11. BIS, 29th *Annual Report*, pp. 206–207.

12. Managing Board of the European Payments Union, *Fifth Annual Report*, p. 63.

13. Cf. L'Huillier, *op. cit.*, pp. 209–217.

14. The following sections draw on the *Annual Reports* of the EPU and of its Agent, the Bank for International Settlements.

15. Triffin, *op. cit.*, p. 180.

with the EPU were threatening to run out soon. The German authorities adopted internal credit-tightening measures and imposed advance deposit requirements for imports. In December, after approving the German program of seeking balance-of-payments equilibrium through tight credit and tax increases, the OEEC Council approved a special EPU loan of $120 million.

After reduced deficits in November and December, a buying wave related to fears touched off by the Chinese Communist intervention in Korea swelled the deficits again in January and February 1951. In March, with foreign-exchange resources at a low level, the German government temporarily suspended import liberalization. The OEEC approved of this step, appointed three independent experts to supervise the distribution of German import licenses, and warned other countries not to retaliate against German exports.

German export trade continued developing favorably, while the monetary and other measures to restrain both imports and speculative capital outflows began showing results. In March and April 1951, Germany ran surpluses with the EPU, and by the end of May the surpluses had grown large enough to permit full repayment of the special EPU credit five months ahead of time. By the end of the year Germany had become a net creditor of the union, had built her dollar reserves up to the highest level in more than 20 years, and had begun progressive removal of the trade and exchange controls restored in March.

The crisis thus ended, but only after drastic changes in financial and import-control policies, after borrowing abroad, and after months of anxiety. According to Triffin, "dynamic and successful handling" of the crisis through national monetary policy and international cooperation gave the young EPU "a prestige and authority far beyond the most optimistic expectations" of its promoters.[16] Speculating on how the situation would have evolved if the exchange value of the German mark had been free to fluctuate all along, Milton Friedman judged that "The whole affair would never have assumed large proportions and would have shown up as a relatively minor ripple in exchange rates."[17] If so, there would have been no crisis and no opportunity for international economic collaboration to get credit for solving one.

France and the United Kingdom provided further early examples of sudden major reversals of position. Both countries experienced initial surpluses so large that the union persuaded them, early in 1951, to step up their liberalization of trade and payments. A reversal began soon afterwards, in the spring of 1951. During the winter and spring of 1951–1952 France suffered a balance-of-payments crisis related to the inflationary impact of the Korean and Indo-Chinese wars, rearmament, and renewed flight from the currency. The EPU helped with a special credit of $100 million; French dollar receipts from American aid, military spending, and offshore contracts continued large; and France temporarily but totally suspended her import liberalization. The sharp resulting decline in imports kept France from exceeding her EPU quota as a debtor until the last quarter of 1952. From then on, except for moderate improvement from the last quarter of 1954 through the third quarter of 1955, the French cumulative deficit kept generally growing. Progress in trade liberalization was slow after being resumed at the end of 1953, and France resorted to export subsidies and "compensatory" import duties to adjust for an uncompetitive level of prices and costs.

The growing cumulative surplus of the United Kingdom (including the Sterling Area) reached a peak in the spring of 1951 as the largest creditor position in the EPU of any member up to that time. Then it began falling rapidly. By September a series of monthly deficits had shifted the position to the debtor side. By the end of May 1952 the debt had gone beyond the quota and had reached the stage of 100 percent gold settlement. The British response to the problem had already begun late in 1951. It, like the French response, spelled partial reversal of European trade liberalization and temporary frustration of one of EPU's chief objectives.[18] The British cumulative net deficit in EPU stopped growing in the summer of 1952, and by the late spring of 1955 a series of monthly surpluses had reduced the cumulative deficit to only about one-fourth of its earlier maximum. Thereafter it grew irregularly again, though keeping well within the quota as increased in mid-1955.

Some EPU members exceeded their quotas as creditors for the first time in 1951—Belgium-Luxembourg in August, Portugal in September, and Italy in November. After long and difficult negotiations, each country agreed to grant credit for part of its beyond-quota claims, thus establishing the concept of "rallonges." At the mid-1952 renewal of EPU, a uniform arrangement with major creditors for half-gold-half-credit settlements within beyond-quota rallonges replaced dependence on *ad hoc* arrangements. At the same time, special arrangements were made to reduce Belgium-Luxembourg's beyond-quota cumulative surplus, partly by payment in gold, partly by conversion into a bilateral claim on the United Kingdom, and partly by consolidation into a medium-term debt of the Union.

At the time of this settlement, the troublesome Belgian surplus seemed likely to keep on growing. Like Portugal and Italy, Belgium tried to stimulate imports of goods and services from and exports of capital to other member countries. Belgium and Portugal began temporary partial blocking of export proceeds to discourage exports and lessen the internal inflationary influence of their surpluses. Belgium even resorted to licensing to divert exports from the EPU to the dollar area. These measures, together with antideficit measures in other EPU countries and post-Korea changes in the world economy, kept the monthly Belgian EPU accounts close to balance after mid-1952. Portugal's cumulative surplus, though in excess of her small quota at one time, never was large enough in absolute terms to be really troublesome; and a series of monthly deficits began whittling it away early in 1952. Italy's cumulative surplus also began declining about the same time, turned into a cumulative deficit by the spring of 1953, and had become a beyond-quota cumulative deficit a year after that.

The problem of extreme creditors did not vanish, however. The cumulative surplus of the Netherlands reached the limit of the quota around mid-1953 (but did not grow substantially more); and Germany, by this time, had already been experiencing a year of beyond-quota surpluses that were ultimately to grow to mammoth and troublesome proportions.

Increased scope for private exchange markets

Stabler economic trends in the EPU financial year 1952–1953 permitted further liberalization of imports and financial transactions. A number of members began permitting *multilateral* currency arbitrage: the transferability of member currencies, instead of being carried out solely by central banks and the EPU, could now be carried out on the ordinary foreign-exchange markets also. The United Kingdom had paved the way for this step as early as December 1951 by permitting banks to deal on their own account and no longer as mere agents of the authorities. Forward-exchange rates were allowed to move freely, and the range of possible spot-rate fluctuation within the official buying and selling limits was widened from 0.125 cent to 2 cents on either side of sterling-dollar parity. The British authorities granted freedom for *bilateral* arbitrage transactions with banks in the U.S.- and Canadian-dollar areas and soon extended it to transactions with Switzerland and the French and Belgian monetary areas. In 1952 the Netherlands and Sweden widened their ranges of possible fluctuation in intra-European exchange rates. These changes lessened the need for daily central-bank intervention in the foreign-exchange market and introduced some limited risk into speculative positions. Finally, in May 1953, the authorities of eight EPU members agreed to standardize the spreads between the official buying and selling limits of their currencies at about 0.75 percent on either side of parity and to permit banks to deal with each other in any of the eight currencies. (Previously, this freedom had been limited to bilateral operations.) Much of the multilateral offsetting of balances previously done once a month by central banks through the EPU could now be done day by day by banks trading in the ordinary market. Much work remained for the EPU, however, in handling balances arising from direct transactions between central banks (for example, direct inter-

16. *Ibid.*, p. 182. Triffin himself had been the chief architect of EPU.

17. *Essays in Positive Economics*, Chicago: University of Chicago Press, 1953, p. 163.

18. International Monetary Fund, *Annual Report*, 1953, p. 13. For details on the crisis and policy responses, see pp. 447–448 below.

vention in support of currencies, intergovernmental payments, repayment of old bilateral debts, and third-currency transfers). Multilateral arbitrage was authorized only for spot transactions at first but was extended to forward transactions in October 1953 and (more fully) in May 1956. The volume of forward arbitrage transactions was still affected by controls over capital movements enforced by most participating countries.

The new arbitrage arrangements were a step toward leaving multilateral compensation to private dealings in ordinary markets, with central banks intervening only to keep spot exchange rates from fluctuating sharply or from going outside the fixed limits. These reforms illustrate the spirit that guided EPU itself. Its managers apparently favored a cautious, gradual return to "normal" conditions in which their own services would no longer be needed.[19]

EPU modifications of 1954 and 1955

During the 1953–1954 financial year, Germany's cumulative surplus and the cumulative deficits of France and Italy grew markedly (yet Italy had had a troublesome surplus as recently as 1952). Credit granted by surplus countries to deficit countries through the intermediary of the EPU was no longer serving, as originally intended, to meet temporary balance-of-payments fluctuations only; some credits had remained outstanding for three or four years. Persistent creditors faced internal financial problems related to their loans to the union, while debtors worried about their narrowed scope for meeting further deficits. By mid-1954, four of the seven creditor countries had long exceeded their quotas, and only $70 million out of an initial $1100 million remained available for settlements with the other three. Three of the eight debtor countries had far exceeded their quotas and were having to settle further deficits fully in gold, while only $200 million out of an initial $1350 million of quota credits remained available to the other five debtors.[20]

How could some of this outstanding credit be removed from the framework of the Union so as to reopen lines of credit for future EPU settlements? The renewal of the Union in mid-1954 brought a compromise. Some debts to and claims on the Union were converted into bilateral debts to and claims on particular creditor and debtor countries. Thirty-three separate agreements (and a few more in later years) had to be worked out. Most of them called for partial payment in gold or dollars at once and payment of the remainder in installments over several years. Each bilateral payment, when made, was to cancel an equal amount of the debtor's debt to the creditor's claim on the Union (until then, the amounts were to remain on the books of the Union, subject to its usual conditions and interest rates). The immediate payments plus the obligations for subsequent installments covered about three-fourths of the debts and claims outstanding at the time. Besides sponsoring the bilateral repayment system, the Union itself divided a special repayment of $130 million out of its dollar assets among the seven countries that were creditors in mid-1954. The immediate reduction in debts and claims outstanding within the Union correspondingly rebuilt the credit lines offered to or by the countries concerned.[21]

The arrangements of mid-1954 also extended the total borrowing privileges of deficit countries beyond the regular lines of credit within quotas. Creditor countries, in return for the partial repayment of their claims, agreed to new and higher limits to future credits to the Union in part settlement of surpluses.

When the EPU was again renewed in later years, some further bilateral agreements similar to those of 1954 were made, but for smaller amounts. All creditors' claims, with the notable exception of Germany's, were brought well below the limits of their lending commitments.

Other important changes at the mid-1954 renewal of EPU were the 20 percent increase in quotas and the already mentioned agreement to settle future imbalances half in gold and half in credit. The latter uniform rule removed any danger that larger payments than receipts of gold or dollars might some time embarrass the Union.

When the EPU agreement expired again at the end of June 1955, it was prolonged for one month and then renewed with important modifications from August 1. The shift from 50–50 to 75–25 settlements moved further toward ultimate full settlement of all balances in gold or convertible currency rather than credit and also cut incentives to keep on discriminating against expenditures in the dollar area. The new settlement percentages were accompanied, as already mentioned, by a doubling of the quotas as adjusted the year before.

The 1955 renewal of the EPU for the first time contained a special termination clause. It remained in subsequent renewal agreements until finally put into effect in December 1958. The EPU was to be disbanded at any time when members holding at least 50 percent of the total amount of quotas requested it and if the standby European Monetary Agreement was brought into force at the same time. If major EPU members were to adopt external convertibility, the Union would no longer be needed to make their currencies transferable; and most settlements would then probably take place through the ordinary foreign-exchange markets. Still, a centralized settlement system was to be kept available for occasional use if members so desired. Under the new system, with settlements made entirely in convertible currency, the automatic credit characteristic of the EPU would no longer apply. Hence the standby agreement provided for loans on a nonautomatic basis to countries in balance-of-payments trouble.

Meanwhile, European steps toward convertibility included a pair of arrangements that, though not actually a part of the EPU, affected its members and shared its general purpose. These were the "Hague Club" and the "Paris Club."[22] The first resulted from revision in 1955 of the bilateral trade and payments agreements between Brazil and several EPU members. Brazil would no longer have a purely bilateral position with each. Brazilians could now collect for their exports and pay for their imports in the currency of any of the participants. Taken together with the existing wide facilities for transferring sterling, marks, and Belgian francs, the new arrangement made Brazilian earnings of any "club" currency available for expenditure throughout most of the nondollar world (and, by way of unofficial markets in sterling and marks, for expenditure in the dollar area itself). The Brazilian authorities agreed not to discriminate among the European participants in controlling imports. A similar arrangement with Argentina, the "Paris Club," was developed in 1956 and 1957 and eventually expanded to include all but a few EPU members, as well as Finland. It enabled Argentina freely to transfer its earnings of one member currency to other members.

Strains and adjustments of 1955–1958

During the 1955–1956 financial year, four EPU members had conspicuous imbalances. After a respite the year before, France and the United Kingdom again faced growth in their large cumulative deficits. Among creditors, Belgium-Luxembourg ran a new surplus almost triple that of the year before, and Germany's yearly surplus roughly doubled. These Belgian and German surpluses accounted for over 90 percent of the total net surpluses and for all of the new credit granted to the union during 1955–1956. Debtor and creditor positions changed much more moderately than cumulative deficits or surpluses, however, because of the new rule for 75 percent gold settlements within quotas, settlement of certain net positions wholly in gold, and some repayments outside the regular monthly settlements.

EPU reports attributed the growth of imbalances during 1955–1956 to differences from country to country in demand pressures and price increases and in the effectiveness of governmental measures. Some exceptional influences also made themselves felt in 1956–1957 —the Suez crisis, which raised fuel and freight costs, deprived the United Kingdom in particular of some oil earnings, and touched off speculation against sterling (see Chapter 22); frost damage to crops in February 1956, particularly in France; France's Algerian expenditures,

---

19. See EPU, *Fifth Annual Report*, pp. 27–28, 67, *Sixth Annual Report*, p. 24; IMF, *Annual Report*, 1953, pp. 66–68, *Annual Report*, 1954, pp. 87–88; and Triffin, *op. cit.*, pp. 212–214.

20. EPU, *Fifth Annual Report*, pp. 67–68; Triffin, *op. cit.*, pp. 193–194.

21. EPU, *Fifth Annual Report*, pp. 34–36, 68; BIS, 25th *Annual Report*, 1954–1955, pp. 173ff.

22. Cf. IMF, *1956 Annual Report*, pp. 100–101, *1957 Annual Report*, p. 100, *1958 Annual Report*, p. 127; BIS, 26th *Annual Report*, 1955–1956, p. 140; EPU, *Sixth Annual Report*, pp. 24–25; Triffin, *op. cit.*, p. 217; Rolf Sannwald and Jacques Stohler, *Wirtschaftliche Integration*, Basel: Kyklos-Verlag, Tübingen: Mohr, 1958, pp. 156–157.

worsening an inflationary budget and credit situation; and the mobilization of French reservists, which handicapped mine production in particular. The French deficit and German surplus grew notably. The gold and dollar assets of the German central bank rose by about one-third between mid-1956 and mid-1957, almost entirely as a result of transactions with other EPU members. The EPU positions of most other members tended toward better balance over the 1956–1957 financial year as a whole.

In the summer of 1956 the OEEC set up a Ministerial Working Party to study the growing disequilibriums and related internal policies. Its report in November recommended that debtor countries intensify their anti-inflation policies and that creditors try to increase their imports and use their surpluses so as to avoid strain on other members. In June 1957 the deputies of the Working Party agreed that measures taken since the November recommendations had been insufficient and that France and Germany had special responsibilities for finding remedies. The deputies regretted that France had reacted to her balance-of-payments crisis that very month (June 1957) by completely suspending import liberalization under the OEEC code. They urged Germany to consider further unilateral tariff reduction, to limit capital imports through EPU channels, to facilitate capital export, and repay some government debt in advance.[23]

Intra-European disequilibrium became critical in the late summer of 1957. In France, the suspension of trade liberalization and restrictive budget and monetary policies were failing to stop foreign-exchange losses. A piecemeal *de facto* devaluation in August and October 1957 changed the rate from 350 to 420 francs per dollar. Speculation against the pound sterling had already been feeding on worries about British labor costs and about weakness of demand for primary products of the overseas Sterling Area. The Dutch guilder also felt some bear speculation. The corresponding bullishness centered on the mark, considered a candidate for upward revaluation. Intensified speculation drove the British government to drastic measures in September. The annual meeting of the International Monetary Fund that month heard firm declarations against exchange-rate alterations. France, Belgium, the Netherlands, Sweden, and the United Kingdom were taking steps to tighten credit. The Germans were easing their monetary policy and making ad-

vance transfers to the United Kingdom for debt repayments and arms purchases. The crisis thus blew over. Germany even ran monthly deficits in its EPU account in November and December 1957 and in February 1958.[24]

The measures taken to stem the 1957 intra-European crisis did not prevent renewed growth of Germany's cumulative surplus early the following year or the continued growth of the French deficit. France drew on $655 million of assistance provided in January 1958 by the OEEC, the International Monetary Fund, and the United States, tightened foreign-exchange regulations, and postponed reversing the suspension of trade liberalization. In mid-1957, when the EPU was again extended for what proved to be the last time, the overall degree of intra-European trade liberalization was about the same as it had been a year before. During the final six months of EPU, the German surplus continued growing. The next largest current surpluses were those of the Netherlands, Italy (which continued paying off old debt), and Belgium-Luxembourg. France again had the largest deficits, followed by the United Kingdom.

Western Europe as a whole escaped a repetition in the EPU's 1957–1958 financial year of the exceptional influences (Suez, poor harvests, and so forth) that had halted the growth of gold and dollar reserves the year before. Developments in capital movements and in the prices of several raw-material imports were favorable in 1958, while a temporary slackening of European economic growth occasioned cutbacks in inventories and imports. From mid-1957 to mid-1958 the total official gold and foreign-exchange reserves of all EPU member countries grew by some 14 percent. European reserve gains were especially rapid during the second half of 1958, and between mid-1957 and the end of 1958, they totaled 27 percent.[25] During 1958, Western Europe obtained by far the largest share of the record-breaking increase in total foreign gold and dollar reserves that corresponded to the swollen deficit in the balance of payments of the United States. The much publicized American gold loss of $2.3 billion was more than matched by the gains of West European central banks, which traditionally hold the bulk of their international reserves in gold.

These developments were but the last of a series that had paved the way for a return to European currency convertibility. In earlier years, international commodity markets had been reopened in London and other European centers and EPU currencies made acceptable in payment for reexport even of goods imported from other currency areas. Multilateral currency arbitrage had been restored among most EPU members. Sterling, marks, and some other EPU currencies had become widely transferable even for holders outside the EPU and dollar areas, and sterling had been made practically convertible into dollars by the start of official support operations in transferable sterling in February 1955. (See p. 449.) Increased transferability enabled any EPU member to alter its position with the Union almost at will by using another EPU currency in settlement of non-EPU transactions or by dealing in it against dollars in the unofficial market. Such operations violated the logic of an automatic credit arrangement supposedly designed to settle net imbalances within the EPU area alone.[26]

The end of EPU: a retrospect

At last, on December 27, 1958, Belgium-Luxembourg, France, Germany, Italy, the Netherlands, and the United Kingdom, holding more than the required one-half of all EPU quotas, announced that they wished to make their currencies externally convertible, terminate the EPU, and bring the European Monetary Agreement of 1955 into effect. All the other members except Greece (no longer an exception after May 1959), Iceland, and Turkey, together with Finland, followed suit in making their currencies convertible for nonresidents. (The Swiss franc had already been fully convertible for residents of Switzerland itself and of other hard-currency countries.) Foreigners currently earning any of the newly hardened currencies could now freely sell it for any other currency, including dollars, at exchange rates maintained within official support limits.

The Bank for International Settlements, as agent, proceeded to liquidate the EPU. Funds corresponding to the Union's capital were transferred to a new European Fund. The Union's small net interest earnings were distributed among member countries as increases in their claims on or reductions in their debts to the Union. The remaining convertible assets of the Union were distributed among its creditors. Finally, each creditor's remaining claim

on the Union and each debtor's debt to it were split up among all other member countries in proportion to their respective quotas, and each of the resulting pairs of bilateral positions was then netted. Germany, as the largest creditor (holding more than three-fourths of the total claims against the Union), acquired claims on all other member countries; and France, as the largest debtor (with 43 percent of the total liability, not counting the special credit of January 1958), incurred debts to all others. In all, 105 bilateral positions were thus established.[27] Repayments were scheduled over periods ranging from a few months to several years.

A description of the system that replaced EPU will follow some remarks in summary and appraisal. Table 21.2 classifies the ways that the cumulative total of the monthly bilateral positions of all members with one another were settled over the entire life of EPU. Explaining each item in the table will review the logic of the system. Item 1 is explained as follows: Each month each participating central bank may have used or granted overdrafts in dealings with each of the other participating central banks, running up a corresponding deficit or surplus (or a zero balance either if no bilateral credit had been used or granted or if any credit had been fully reversed during the same month). In the total, each bilateral position is counted twice, as one country's surplus and another's deficit, and all of the monthly totals are added together for the whole period of operation of the Union. The $46.4 billion figure refers to *net* bilateral transactions only, that is, the total of the balances left on each bilateral account after offsetting all debits and credits that had passed through it during the month; the value of the underlying commercial transactions was many times greater.

Item 2, "multilateral compensations," refers

23. EPU, *Seventh Annual Report*, pp. 24–30, 33.

24. EPU, *Eighth Annual Report*, pp. 15–17.

25. *International Financial Statistics*, May 1959, p. 16.

26. Cf. Triffin, *op. cit.*, pp. 214–219.

27. BIS, 29th *Annual Report*, pp. 215–220.

TABLE 21.1. *Cover for total bilateral positions in EPU over its entire existence*

	Billions of dollars	Percentages of total
1. Total bilateral positions (deficits plus surpluses)	46.4	100
2. Multilateral compensations	20.0	43 ⎱ 70
3. Compensations through time	12.6	27 ⎰
4. Effect of special settlements and adjustments	0.5	1
5. Balance (= 1 minus 2, 3, & 4)	13.4	29
Of which settled in —		
6. Gold	10.7	23
7. Credit	2.7	6

SOURCE: EPU, *Final Report*, p. 39.

to bilateral positions cleared through the EPU at the end of the month when they arose. It is the total of the amounts by which each country's surpluses with some members were offset against its deficits with other members. The difference between items 1 and 2 is the cumulative total over the whole period of each member's monthly deficits and surpluses with all other members as a group. The table shows that rather less than half of the bilateral imbalances were multilaterally compensated away; more than half represented members' net imbalances with the rest of the group.

Item 3, "compensations through time," is the amount by which these consolidated deficits or surpluses were later—perhaps very many months later—offset by corresponding surpluses or deficits. (If a cumulative deficit country developed a surplus in some later month or a cumulative surplus country developed a deficit, the current monthly position was settled by repayment of gold previously paid or extinction of credit previously granted.)

Item 4, "effect of special settlements and adjustments," refers to settlements by positions initially allocated as grants, by transfers from initial holdings of national currencies, by the net effect of interest due to or from the Union,

and by adjustments in connection with special gold credits.

Imbalances that had not been multilaterally offset, had not reversed themselves over time, and had not been specially settled or adjusted were necessarily met either by credit received or granted within the framework of the Union and not yet repaid or by transfers of "gold" not yet reversed. ("Gold" is not meant in the strict sense; it also includes dollars and other currencies acceptable to creditors.)

As Table 21.1 implies, the cumulative total of members' deficits and surpluses *not* multilaterally cleared each month (item 1 less item 2) was $26.4 billion. Of this total cumulative imbalance of individual members with the rest of the group, only $12.6 billion, or less than half, reversed itself over time. The major part of the imbalance had to be met either by payments and receipts of gold and foreign exchange drawn from or added to national reserves or earned or spent in opposite imbalances with non-EPU countries or else by credit received or granted within the framework of the Union and not repaid by December 1958. This nonreversal of half of the net intra-Union imbalance emphasizes, for one thing, how little reason there is to expect a country's external accounts to be in balance with any group of trading partners smaller than the entire rest of the world, even over a span of several years, so long as any multilateralism prevails in worldwide trade. Restriction of multilateralism to a limited area would interfere with the international division of labor, as was recognized in the merely temporary status of the EPU.[28]

A second lesson of EPU experience serves once more to discredit the hope that balance-of-payments disequilibriums will prove minor and self-reversing. There were some spectacular reversals of position within the Union, it is true: the deficit crisis of Germany in 1950–1951 gave way to the persistent problem of mounting cumulative surpluses; the Sterling Area's surplus in 1950–1951 switched abruptly into deficits that later became troublesome; the Italian surplus in 1951–1952 later reversed itself; and the early deficits of the Netherlands later yielded to comfortable surpluses. But rather than being mere minor alterations first one way and then the other from a balanced position over the long run, these reversals illustrate how empty the notion is of a long-run equilibrium rate of exchange. Balances of payments are often inconveniently sensitive even to comparatively minor changes in domestic or international conditions. Experience under the EPU also provides several striking examples—notably the German and French—of severe disequilibriums accumulating over several years *without* any major reversal.

Several related aspects of the EPU illustrate the lack of adjustment mechanism. The Union was called on to provide emergency credits in time of balance-of-payments crisis, as with Germany late in 1950 and France early in 1958. The concept of rallonges was introduced to palliate the problems of cumulative deficit and surplus positions beyond quotas. For Germany, an unlimited creditor rallonge was established in November 1956 and was renewed up to the termination of EPU. At the termination, though, Germany had the only postquota creditor position; 55 percent of the outstanding total credit granted to the Union was by way of rallonge.[29] The corresponding figure had been only 27 percent in mid-1954, when the persistence of large debtor and creditor positions had nevertheless been considered troublesome enough to call for special bilateral repayments to deal with the problem. Balance-of-payments troubles caused a good deal of temporary backsliding from trade liberalization, as by Austria in 1951, Iceland in 1952, Turkey in 1953, and most notably by Germany and the United Kingdom in 1951 and France in 1952 and 1957.

EPU combined a regional payments scheme with preferential relaxation of trade barriers among the members. One disadvantage is that imbalances may result from differences among member countries in rates of domestic inflation, in degrees of currency overvaluation, and in the stringency of restrictions on imports from outside the area. Businessmen have an incentive to import outside goods into the member countries with the relatively most liberal trading policies for transshipment into the countries whose restrictions against outside imports are among the tightest and whose currencies are among the most overvalued in relation to the degree of domestic inflation. Or, if direct transshipment is effectively controlled, the inducement remains to import outside goods into the relatively least restrictive countries and then sell to other members of the preferential area either locally made substitutes for the imported goods or locally made goods embodying the imports or substitutes for them as ingredients. The relatively liberal intermediary countries thus face a drain of hard cur-

rencies in exchange for an accumulation of relatively soft claims on fellow members of the preferential area. Belgium, for example, experienced some of these difficulties until about mid-1952. Transit trade was subjected to licensing and extra restrictions imposed on imports paid for in dollars. The National Bank of Belgium was worried about undue domestic credit expansion based on the financing of the surplus of exports to other EPU countries. The steps taken to meet this danger and promote better balance in intra-European trade included a temporary partial blocking of the intra-European earnings of Belgian exporters.[30]

The EPU felt called upon to concern itself with the relation between balance-of-payments troubles and domestic financial policies. Some remarkably frank passages appear in its Sixth *Annual Report* (pp. 21–22, 30–31):

With the increasing freedom of intra-European trade and payments, countries have become more vulnerable to the measures taken by their neighbours . . . a disequilibrium in intra-European trade and payments could not fail to become worse if the financial policies of the Member countries were not co-ordinated.

. . . this increasing and freer flow of trade and of capital between Member countries, together with the gradual extension of the multilateral links with nonmember countries, makes the economy of each country more sensitive to developments in the economy of each of its partner countries and requires to a much greater extent than before that their economies should develop on parallel lines and that all should maintain internal financial stability. . . .

This situation gives new emphasis to the role already played by the E.P.U. in providing a framework within which Member countries discuss their problems and the co-ordination of their financial and economic policies in the common interest.

28. On this and some of the following points, cf. L. W. Towle, *International Trade and Commercial Policy*, 2nd ed., New York: Harper & Row, 1956, pp. 393–397.

29. BIS, 29th *Annual Report*, pp. 202, 206.

30. BIS, 22nd *Annual Report*, 1951–1952, pp. 108, 198, 200, 24th *Annual Report*, 1953–1954, p. 109.

A final observation about balance-of-payments adjustment is that although the EPU countries did not tolerate fluctuating exchange rates, some of them did make deliberate rate changes. In October 1950 Austria simplified its multiple-exchange-rate system in a way that amounted to a devaluation of the schilling, and another simplification to a single-rate system in May 1953 amounted to a further devaluation. The French franc was devalued in 1957 and again when the EPU was dissolved in December 1958. The Greek drachma was devalued by 50 percent in 1953, after some earlier modifications of multiple-rate practices. Iceland made several changes in its multiple-rate structure during the life of the EPU. Modifications in the exchange value of the Turkish lira were even more numerous and complicated. EPU members also made numerous modifications in taxes and tariffs and other aspects of commercial policy serving as *ad hoc* measures for coping with balance-of-payments difficulties.

Despite lack of a continuous balancing mechanism, the lapse of 13 years since the end of World War II allowed time to overcome the war-created disorders so often loosely referred to as urgent import "needs" and damaged export "capacities." It allowed time for the financial policies and the price and income levels of the various European countries to become better aligned with one another at established exchange rates. What the EPU itself achieved was not so much a solution of each member country's actual or potential balance-of-payments problem as a simplification of it. Each member no longer had to concern itself with its position vis-à-vis each fellow member separately, but it still had to strive for overall balance.

Unlike the International Monetary Fund, the EPU was based on no ambitious blueprint for an ideal future state of affairs. It was designed as an immediate and temporary palliative for glaring defects in earlier arrangements. It loosened the rigidities of bilateralism and destroyed incentives for discrimination in controlling imports from fellow member countries. By encouraging gradual adjustments in national policies and by twice raising the percentage of gold payments in intra-European settlements, it helped prepare its members for increasingly liberal policies toward hard-currency countries as well.[31] One may wonder whether the gadgetry and gradualness really were necessary, but by the tests usually applied

to international economic institutions, EPU was an outstanding success.

The outlook for convertibility

How fully convertible did European currencies become? For many years, of course, the word "convertibility" has not had its traditional gold-standard meaning. It now means nothing more than unrestricted salability for other currencies. Even in this sense, most European currencies became freely convertible only for nonresidents of the country concerned; most Europeans still did not regain complete freedom to spend or lend or invest their money wherever they wished.

With all currency acquired by foreigners (in current if not capital transactions, anyway) becoming salable for dollars at officially supported rates, European governments lost any apparent financial reason for continued discrimination against imports from the dollar area. The level of a country's official gold and dollar reserves no longer depended on *where* in the outside world its residents made purchases. One country after another announced further liberalization of import quotas and licensing and an abatement of discriminations against the United States.[32]

Convertibility unified and broadened the markets in spot and forward exchange, made competition in them more keen, narrowed the spreads between buying and selling quotations, and apparently made forward premiums and discounts more responsive than before to international differences in short-term interest rates. The increased interest-sensitivity of short-term capital movements and the reemergence of an international money market was not entirely an unmixed blessing; as will be mentioned in some of the chapters to follow (particularly the one on the United States), heavy and volatile transfers of funds have occasionally embarrassed monetary authoritites. Convertibility also increased the attractiveness of the London gold market and contributed to a sharp increase in the volume of transactions in 1959.

Early experience suggested that European countries had moved toward convertibility at an opportune time. In February 1961 nine of them (Belgium, France, Germany, Ireland, Italy, Luxembourg, the Netherlands, Sweden, and the United Kingdom), as well as Peru, joined the United States, Canada, and the eight countries of northern Latin America that had already been operating under Article VIII rather than Article XIV of the International Monetary Fund Charter. By this step, which was more a symbol of liberalization already attained than an immediate step toward further liberalization, the ten additional countries at last waived the postwar-transition-period excuse for exchange restrictions and agreed to impose or maintain them thereafter only with the specific permission of the International Monetary Fund. Practically all currencies used to finance international trade and payments thus became "convertible" under IMF rules and eligible for use in repayment of drawings from the Fund.

It was still too early, however, for complacency. Piecemeal liberalization had stretched over the ominously long period of 13 years between the end of World War II and the important measures of December 1958. Many countries, particularly outside Europe and North America, still maintained controls over trade and payments that on the whole were restrictive not merely in comparison with the period before World War I but even in comparison with the late 1930s. Perhaps currency convertibility would eventually become complete for residents as well as nonresidents; perhaps controls for balance-of-payments purposes would become unnecessary. On the other hand, backsliding was destined to occur in the future, as it had in the past. There may have been an element of fortunate historical accident in Europe's early experiences with convertibility. The strength in European balances of payments corresponded to an apparent shift from "dollar shortage" to "dollar glut" in the balance of payments of the United States. Payments worries had not disappeared: their focus had simply shifted. This point and others will be developed in chapters on the experiences of several individual countries.

The European Monetary Agreement and successor arrangements

The shift from EPU to the European Monetary Agreement involved few administrative changes. The members of the Managing Board of EPU became the Board of Management of the new European Fund. The Bank for International Settlements continued as agent for financial operations. When the Organisation for European Economic Co-operation was reorganized in September 1961 as the Organisation for Economic Co-operation and Development (with Canada and the United States and later some other countries added as members), the enlarged organization carried on as sponsor of the European monetary arrangements.

Under the post-1958 system, member central banks made settlements entirely in gold or dollars. The European Fund—something of a European miniature of the International Monetary Fund—replaced the automatic credit facilities of EPU. Its capital consisted of the original U.S. contribution to EPU and of subscriptions by its members, part being paid in and the rest remaining subject to call if needed. The European Fund had the purpose, expressed in familiar language, of "providing all members with a potential source of short-term credit in order to aid them to withstand temporary overall balance of payments difficulties, in cases where these difficulties endanger the maintenance of the level of their intra-European liberalisation measures."[33] The OECD and the managers of the Fund had wide discretion in granting or withholding credits and could make aid conditional on adoption of their policy recommendations. Over its whole life, actually, the Fund made loans only to Greece, Iceland, Spain, and—mainly—Turkey. The total amount of drawings outstanding at the end of any year never exceeded 145 million units of account (at the end of 1968).[34] (The unit was equivalent to one pre-1971 U.S. dollar.)

The only remnant of automatic credit still available under the European Monetary Agreement was "interim finance": each member was required to make its own currency available

---

31. On the success of EPU, see Triffin, *op. cit.*, pp. 161–163, 199–200, 208–209, and *passim*.

32. See Federal Reserve Bank of Kansas City, *Monthly Review*, May 1960, pp. 14–15.

33. EPU, *Fifth Annual Report*, p. 50.

34. Facts such as these about the EMA, the European Fund, and their liquidation are conveniently assembled in BIS, *Annual Report*, 1972–1973, pp. 175–182.

between settlement dates to any other member so requesting. The arrangement was the same as under EPU, except that each member had a limit on the total amount it might draw from or advance to all other members.

The greatest change from EPU operations was that central banks were no longer expected to bring into the monthly settlements all balances acquired during the month. They had to bring only balances arising from credit under the very few bilateral payments agreements still in existence or from interim finance not repaid during the month when drawn. This Multilateral System of Settlements was basically a mere standby. Balances not required to be centrally cleared would usually not be, and any interim finance drawn would usually be repaid within the same month. The reason was that a central bank reporting a bilateral balance for centralized clearing would have to make payment (if a debtor) or accept payment (if a creditor) at the exchange rate at the limit of permissible fluctuation most unfavorable to itself; it would almost always do better to deal in the ordinary market at an exchange rate fluctuating *inside* the official support limits. These expectations were in fact borne out; and during the whole lifetime of the EMA, the cumulative total of multilateral settlements amounted to only US $94.5 million.

Being relatively unimportant in its actual operations, the EMA system was liquidated at the end of 1972. The United States was to get back the capital that it had contributed to the EPU and that the EPU had transferred to the European Fund. Part of the repayment took the form of transfer to the United States of the Fund's outstanding claim on Turkey.

When the EMA came to an end, the central banks of Australia and Finland joined the old participants in a new agreement. Echoing an exchange-guarantee provision of the EMA, the new agreement provided for maintaining the foreign-exchange value of working balances of one member's currency held by another member. On April 6, 1973, the member countries of the European Community set up a European Monetary Co-operation Fund. In the first stage of its activity, the new Fund was to carry out operations connected with narrowing the margins of fluctuation between EC member currencies and multilateralizing positions and settlements resulting from central-bank intervention in EC currencies. (What "multilateralization" means should be clear from the earlier discussion of EPU.) The Bank for International Settlements is Agent for carrying out the technical aspects of the new Fund's operations.[35]

Exchange rates within the European Community

Following the Smithsonian Agreement of December 1971,[36] the International Monetary Fund authorized each of its members to allow its currency to fluctuate as much as 2¼ percent (instead of the old limit of 1 percent) up or down from its par or central rate with the U.S. dollar. If, at a particular time, the Ruritanian crown is at its upper limit and the Graustark florin at its lower limit against the dollar, then the crown-florin rate is 4½ (= 2¼ + 2¼) percent away from the crown-florin cross-parity in the direction of a strong crown and weak florin. If, in time, this extreme position should reverse itself, the change would represent a 9 (= 4½ + 4½) percent depreciation of the crown against the florin or appreciation of the florin against the crown.[37]

The EC member governments decided to keep the range of possible fluctuation between their currencies only *half* that large (and eventually to narrow the range still further). They began operations for this purpose on April 24, 1972 (the currency crisis of May 1971 having shelved earlier plans of the same general kind).[38] Suppose the parities are 6 florins per Special Drawing Right and 3 crowns per Special Drawing Right. (We continue referring to mythical EC currencies and parities to keep the arithmetic simple, and we drop reference to the dollar to take account of the possibility that the EC currencies have no effective parities with it.) The cross-parity is then 2 florins per crown. The 2¼ percent upper and lower limits around this cross-parity—limits only half as wide as under the unsupplemented Smithsonian rule—are 2.045 and 1.955 florins per crown. An exchange-rate movement from the upper to the lower of these extremes would be a 4.4 percent depreciation of the crown against the florin; an opposite movement would be a 4.6 percent appreciation of the crown against the florin. The average of these two percentages—or, equivalently, the range between the extremes expressed as a percentage of parity—is 4.5 percent. We arrive at the same 4½ percent maximum range of fluctuation, of course, if we express the parity and the 2¼ percent limits around it as 0.5, 0.51125, and 0.48875 crowns per florin.

Central-bank intervention keeps the fluctuations between EC currencies within the prescribed limits. When a currency is at its upper or lower limit not merely against the currencies of other participating countries but also against the dollar, then the central bank concerned may intervene by buying or selling dollars. Dollar intervention may also be allowed by special dispensation, such as was temporarily granted to Italy in 1972. Otherwise, however, intervention must be carried out only in the currencies of the participating countries. The central banks of strong-currency countries either buy weak currencies directly or lend their own currencies to the weak-currency central banks for the latter's use in supporting their currencies. Liabilities arising from such support are ordinarily to be settled by the end of the following month by the transfer of reserve assets. The intervention mechanism was called into operation for the first time when sterling came under speculative attack in the middle of June 1972. All participants except Italy and Denmark supported sterling. This intervention tended to strengthen sterling and weaken the other currencies in relation to the dollar. When Britain allowed the pound to float, it temporarily quit the EC scheme.

Before March 1973 the EC arrangements were nicknamed "the snake in the tunnel," with reference to the narrow band of fluctuation of EC currencies against each other within the wider band of fluctuation of those (and other) currencies against the dollar. (The still closer pegging of the Benelux currencies was called "the worm in the snake.") In March 1973 the EC countries ceased, at least temporarily, to limit the fluctuations of their currencies against the dollar. With the "tunnel" thus abolished, "the snake in the tunnel" became "the snake in the lake." The latter arrangement is a "joint float" of the participating currencies against the dollar and other nonparticipating currencies: while the arrangements described hold the exchange rates between the participating currencies within narrow limits, no limits apply between each of them and the dollar or between their "snake" and the dollar. All EC countries originally participated in the joint float except the United Kingdom and Ireland and Italy, whose currencies were floating separately. Norway and Sweden, though not EC members, soon joined the joint float. France left it in January 1974.

The changing role of gold

After being closed or all but closed since 1939, the London gold market reopened in March 1954. The market was calm for 6½ years, and the price remained within a few cents of the U.S. Treasury's buying and selling prices of $34.9125 and $35.0875 per ounce. In the autumn of 1960, however, nervousness developed over the impending presidential election in the United States and the policies of a new Administration. The German ban of interest on foreign deposits and the Swiss *charge* of 1 percent a year on foreign deposits was presumably helping make gold more attractive relative to currencies. Speculators could hope for a rise and be confident of no cut in the official price of gold. (So that some two-way uncertainty might restrain speculation, some academic economists recommended, in vain, that the United States stand ready to make occasional small cuts in its official gold price.) Some central banks were doing their gold-buying in London so as not to embarrass the U.S. Treasury with requests for the redemption of dollars.[39] Under these influences, the price of

35. BIS, 1972–1973, pp. 194–195.

36. See p. 580 in particular.

37. This simple addition of percentages is only an approximation, of course, as will become clearer from the numerical example to follow.

38. Already, when a period of generally floating rates began in August 1971, the Belgian-Luxembourg and Dutch authorities had decided to intervene in each other's currency to keep the rate from moving more than 1½ percent away from the cross-parity of 13.81 Belgian-Luxembourg francs per Dutch guilder. This franc-guilder arrangement remained in effect within the new EC context.

Facts on the EC arrangements are given in BIS, 1971–1972, pp. 131–132, and BIS, 1972–1973, pp. 136–137.

39. Chapter 29 sketches the broader background of these events. Most but not all of the details in the following paragraphs come from the chapters on "Gold, Reserves and Foreign Exchange" in various *Annual Reports* of the Bank for International Settlements and from Fred Hirsch, *Money International*, London: Allen Lane, The Penguin Press, 1967, pp. 199–205.

gold rose to $35.20, high enough to attract attention. Speculative buying then sent the price to $35.35 on October 18, to $40 on October 20, and even to $41 in a few transactions. It became clear that the U.S. selling price plus cost of transatlantic shipment had been a merely psychological ceiling on the London price: only foreign monetary authorities, not private arbitrageurs, could redeem dollars in gold; and the United States would not have tolerated arbitrage by central banks even if they had felt tempted to carry it out.

This "gold rush" marked a watershed in the evolution of the Bretton Woods system. It called attention to an impending shortage of gold at the existing price and under existing policies and to how this threatened the dollar's redeemability. Although the gold market and gold price soon returned temporarily to normal, the former extreme confidence in the dollar never returned.

After first trying to talk down the gold price with mere words about the dollar's strength, the American authorities fed gold to the market through the intermediary of the Bank of England in the last weeks of 1960. The price sank and remained below $36 but continued for a while to fluctuate in a wider range than before the gold rush. Early next year President Kennedy, newly inaugurated, reaffirmed the $35 price.

In November 1961 the central banks of England and six continental countries joined the United States in supplying the gold needed to keep the market calm and the price near $35. The U.S. share in this Gold Pool was 50 percent. U.S. reserves felt half the impact of the Pool's operations immediately and might feel the other half ultimately, since the Europeans had not agreed permanently to hold the dollars received for sales of gold. By early 1962, market conditions had so changed that the Pool could buy back all the gold sold earlier. An oversupply of gold permitted it to take gold off the market, which helps explain why U.S. gold losses fell off, especially in 1963. Russian sales of gold to pay for North American grain were supplementing current gold production in the free world. On at least two occasions, in the autumn of 1963 and again two years later, the prospect of these sales came at a critical time, when gold speculaton might otherwise have gotten out of hand.[40]

The Pool remained a net buyer on balance until around the end of 1965. Then, however, the Soviet Union stopped selling gold (and apparently did not resume significant sales until 1970 or 1971). A decline in total monetary gold stocks of Western countries in 1966 was followed by further declines in the next two years.

Gold in the mid-1960s was changing from a commodity whose price was supported by official purchases to one whose price was being held down by official sales. (This is not to deny that even then, policies of continuing to hold gold for monetary purposes kept the price higher than it otherwise would have been.) The basic idea of the Gold Pool had been that private supply and demand at the official price would leave some gold over for addition to official reserves; the Pool would have to sell only to smooth over temporary disturbances. But in the mid-1960s, gold production in the Free World ceased growing, Russian sales stopped, and demands for gold in industry and as a medium of savings were increasing, not to mention speculative demands.

The Gold Pool and the $35 price grew more precarious late in 1967. As the flight from sterling grew in the fourth quarter, so did the demand for gold. After the pound's devaluation on November 18, the dollar also came under suspicion, and the demand for gold reached unprecedented levels. Speculation intensified when it became known that France, in June, had stopped taking part in the supply of gold to the market. At first the Pool's active members reaffirmed their intention to continue defending the $35 price. Their sales are reflected in a decline in noncommunist monetary gold stocks (including those of international institutions) by $1.4 billion during the last quarter of 1967. The U.S. balance-of-payments program announced at the beginning of 1968 briefly helped calm the market. A fresh buying wave began early in March and persisted despite another statement by the Gold Pool countries on March 10. The first quarter of 1968 saw a further $1.4 billion drop in Western official gold stocks. The London and Zurich markets were closed on Friday, March 15, while the Paris price rose above $44.

A meeting in Washington over the weekend resulted in an announcement on Sunday the 17th that the central banks would no longer supply gold to the market. In view of the prospective creation of Special Drawing Rights as a new reserve medium, furthermore, the central banks no longer felt it ncessary to buy gold from the market. The Gold Pool was at an end, and the market would now have two tiers:

the \$35 price remained in effect for official transactions, but the price on the open market would be left to supply and demand.

The London market remained closed until April 1. After it reopened, variations in the supply of gold coming onto the market were governed largely by the volume of sales from South Africa, which depended in turn on the state of that country's balance of payments and the policies of its authorities. At first gold traded at slightly under \$38. The price then rose to a peak of over \$42 in the second half of May 1968. Hopes of resumption of South African sales contributed to some easing in the

TABLE 21.2. *London gold price, dollars per fine troy ounce, at ends of quarter-years, 1967 through 1974*

1967	IV	\$ 35.20
1968	I	...
	II	40.90
	III	39.60
	IV	41.90
1969	I	42.90
	II	41.20
	III	40.68
	IV	35.20
1970	I	35.30
	II	35.40
	III	36.40
	IV	37.38
1971	I	38.88
	II	40.10
	III	42.60
	IV	43.62
1972	I	48.38
	II	64.65
	III	64.20
	IV	64.90
1973	I	90.00
	II	123.25
	III	100.00
	IV	112.25
1974	I	173.00
	II	144.25
	III	151.25
	IV	186.50

SOURCE: *International Financial Statistics,* various issues, U.K. pages.

early autumn, and the price hovered around \$39 through October.

From November 1968 the price began a fairly steady uptrend. The rise partly reflected the mark-franc-sterling crisis, but South African gold sales moderated it. In December and January, conjectures about the gold policy of the incoming Nixon Administration supported the uptrend. Amidst bearishness on the French franc, the price reached a new peak of nearly \$44 in March 1969. A foreign-exchange crisis in early May had little further effect; and from that month, South African sales of gold, connected with weakness in that country's balance of payments, contributed to a decline in the price. The decline was reinforced toward the end of July by agreement among the Group of Ten countries on activation of the SDR scheme. In the last quarter of 1969, several conditions still further depressed the gold price: the impending issue of SDRs, the return of confidence to the exchange markets following devaluation by France and revaluation by Germany, the strengthening of sterling, and the continuing high level of Eurodollar interest rates. The gold price touched down to \$35 in December and even dipped 25 cents below in mid-January 1970.

At the end of 1969 the International Monetary Fund and South Africa reached an agreement that effectively put a floor of \$34.9125 on the price received by that country. With South Africa not having to sell any cheaper, the market price must have been affected, though only indirectly.

The gold and foreign-exchange markets enjoyed a calm before the storm in 1970. The gold price remained near \$35 for most of the first quarter, briefly peaked at \$36.25 in the first week of May, and began rising again around the end of August. It reached almost \$39.25 in late October before relapsing again.

Demand for gold was strong in 1971 in view of increasing industrial use and worldwide inflation. The Russians seemed to be selling significant amounts for the first time since 1965. The price trended upward fairly steadily, gaining 16.7 percent over the course of the

40. Hirsch, *op. cit.,* pp. 203–204.

year. Two bulges above the trend were note-worth: to $41.25 in mid-May, in the wake of the mark-dollar crisis, and to nearly $44 on August 9, after a U.S. Congressional subcommittee had reported that the dollar was over-valued. Although the United States suspended redeemability of dollars in gold on August 15, denials that the official price would be raised helped bring the price down to about $41 at the end of August, when the uptrend resumed. The Smithsonian Agreement in December scheduled an increase in the official price to $38, about $5 below the market price at the time.

The first seven months of 1972 brought a steep rise. At $70 on August 2, the price was 60½ percent above its end-of-1971 level. An 8.1 percent rise occurred in January alone, not only reflecting renewed weakness of the de-valued dollar but also reflecting expectations, which apparently proved correct, that the Smithsonian devaluation of the rand would improve the South African balance of pay-ments and curtail sales of gold. As South Africa added to its own gold reserves and as Soviet sales appeared to have been temporarily suspended, speculation intensified the trend; and the price rose by 37.6 percent in less than two months, between April 11 and June 8. Contributing to the early-August peak were (incorrect) rumors of an increase in the price for official settlements within the Common Market. Then reports that Russia might have to sell gold to buy grain, together with recovery of the dollar after a bear attack on it in July, had their effect. The price dipped to about $60 in mid-November.

Spectacular increases in the market price in the first half of 1973 reflected new currency crises, including a second devaluation of the dollar and then its renewed weakness against many currencies temporarily set afloat, as well as the heating-up of U.S. and worldwide infla-tion. Japanese gold purchases began rising in March in advance of the April 1 easing of re-strictions on the import of bullion into Japan. By early June the market price passed $120 an ounce, nearly double the end-of-1972 price and nearly three times the new official price of $42.22.

A moderate relapse of the price of gold around mid-1973 was widely attributed to the course of international discussions on monetary reform. It appeared likely that the monetary role of gold would be downgraded, and the possibility was discussed that central banks might even sell gold on the market.

Temporarily, at least, gold had become pretty much immobilized as a medium of offi-cial settlements: central banks were reluctant to part with gold at an official price so far below the market price. Gold had also lost ground as a numéraire of currencies: a number of governments had taken to expressing their parities in terms of SDRs rather than gold.

A background for the experiences of individual countries

Chapters 22 through 27 survey postwar mone-tary events, classified by the country chiefly concerned with each. Each of these chapters emphasizes events and conditions about which the country concerned offers particularly in-structive experience. The chapters on the United States and the United Kingdom pre-sent the experience of key-currency countries. The U.K. chapter, as well as the chapter on Japan and Italy, shows the orientation of do-mestic financial policy around the balance of payments. The chapter on Germany highlights an on-and-off struggle with imported inflation.

The arrangement must be somewhat arbi-trary, since a monetary event hardly affects a single country alone. Each country's experi-ences can hardly be appreciated outside their international context. The concise chronology that follows is an attempt to sketch this context.

End of World War II to the late 1940s or early 1950s. In contrast with floating rates after World War I, exchange rates are held steady, but with the aid of strict controls. Bi-lateralism, disorderly cross rates, and multiple-currency practices are common. The "dollar shortage" leads foreign countries to maintain discriminatory controls on payments to the dollar area. (Worry about the dollar shortage persists until the late 1950s, years after it had ceased being a reality.) Three countries re-value their currencies upward as an anti-in-flationary measure: Canada and Sweden in July 1946 and New Zealand in August 1948.

1947. The International Monetary Fund opens for business. A British experiment with currency convertibility fails. Europe launches multilateral payments schemes, presaging the European Payments Union.

1948. The Marshall Plan begins. Germany reforms its money and returns to a market economy.

1949. A sterling crisis touches off a world-wide wave of devaluations.

1950. The Korean War touches off a boom in primary commodities, obscures the consequences of the currency devaluations, and contributes to a temporarily large U.S. payments deficit. The Canadian dollar begins floating. The EPU is organized; and in parallel with it, the Organisation for European Economic Co-operation pursues a program of trade liberalization. The German mark goes through a bear crisis in the winter of 1950–1951.

1951. The commodity boom collapses. Sterling suffers another crisis, extending into 1952.

1952. The International Monetary Fund makes its first standby arrangement.

1952–1953. International payments positions generally move toward equilibrium.

1954. Britain simplifies exchange controls and reopens the London gold market.

1955. Sterling becomes externally convertible, unofficially, as the Exchange Equalisation Account begins intervening to support transferable sterling.

1956. The Suez War and closing of the Suez Canal contribute to a sterling crisis. The International Monetary Fund aids in the rescue with its largest-scale activity up to that time.

1957. Intra-European disequilibrium becomes critical, France devalues the franc, and sterling undergoes a major crisis. The United States runs an exceptional balance-of-payments surplus because of repercussions of the closing of the Suez Canal. Prospective members of the European Common Market sign the Treaty of Rome.

1958. The United States runs a large deficit and loses gold heavily, marking the start of an epoch of dollar weakness. European countries gain gold and dollar reserves, make their currencies externally convertible, and dismantle the EPU. France devalues the franc again.

1959. The European Monetary Agreement and European Fund come into operation (but are destined to remain relatively unimportant).

1960. The London "gold rush" reflects bearishness on the dollar.

1961. The major European countries accept the obligations of convertibility under IMF rules. German and Dutch revaluations cause widespread anticipation of further exchange-rate changes. The Basel Agreement provides for central-bank cooperation to soften the impact of hot-money movements on countries' external reserves. A sterling crisis forces Britain into austerity measures. The Gold Pool takes definite shape. The United States begins intervention, on a small scale, in the foreign-exchange market.

1962. After a switch the year before from a substantially free to a flexibly manipulated rate, the Canadian dollar is devalued to a new fixed parity, which then requires defense from a bear attack. The United States begins building a network of inter-central-bank swap credits and issuing "Roosa bonds" to alleviate drains on its gold reserves.

1963. President Kennedy proposes the Interest Equalization Tax, to restrain outflows of capital from the United States; the tax, when finally enacted the following year, is made retroactive to the time of its proposal.

1964. Under a standby arrangement negotiated the year before, the United States makes its first drawing on the International Monetary Fund. The Italian lira is rescued in noteworthy fashion from a crisis that began the year before. Sterling suffers a severe crisis but is rescued; Britain imposes an import surcharge. The General Arrangements to Borrow, adopted in 1962, are activated for the first time.

1965. The United States imposes "voluntary" controls on capital outflows. The heating-up of U.S. inflation as a result of the Vietnam war begins setting the stage for the events of 1971–1973. Sterling experiences recurrent weakness but receives new international support.

1966. A sterling crisis brings severe domestic measures in Britain and an unequivocal end to three years of flirtation with a doctrine of "equilibrium through expansion"; still further international support is arranged.

1967. The Arab–Israeli War brings a new and longer-lasting closure of the Suez Canal. Germany undergoes recession. IMF members agree in principle on the plan to introduce

Special Drawing Rights. Devaluations of the pound sterling and several other currencies intensify worries about the dollar.

1968. U.S. controls on capital outflows become mandatory. Canada undergoes a brief crisis of bearish speculation. A run from sterling and the dollar into gold brings collapse of the Gold Pool and introduction of a two-tier gold market. Speculative crises of bearishness on the French franc and bullishness on the German mark heat up in May–June and November, but controls and other palliatives avoid parity changes. Renewed weakness of sterling leads Britain to introduce an import-deposit scheme. Britain negotiates agreements to avoid wholesale dumping of sterling reserves held by other countries. Brazil adopts a policy of frequent small devaluations. Japan experiences its first year of large chronic balance-of-payments surpluses.

1969. Major countries reinforce their mutual-aid arrangements by informal agreement to "recycle" funds back to central banks whose reserves are drained by speculative outflows. Europe gets through a franc-mark crisis in May without parity changes; but France devalues the franc in August, and Germany floats the mark in September and revalues it upward in October. Late in the year, Britain and France move decisively into payments surplus, marking a new phase in the long-drawn-out collapse of the gold-and-dollar system.

1970. Calm prevails before the storm. The IMF makes the first allocation of Special Drawing Rights. The Canadian dollar is set afloat again. Italy rides through a currency crisis. The U.S. official-settlements balance worsens sharply.

1971. Crises occur in the spring and midsummer, with flights from the dollar into the mark and later into the yen and other currencies, as well as gold. Speculative capital outflows join a merchandise trade deficit in creating an overall U.S. deficit of unprecedented size. The mark and Dutch guilder are set afloat in May. After the United States "closes the gold window" and imposes a temporary import surcharge in mid-August, intervention-plagued floating becomes general for four months. A new pattern of fixed parities (or "central rates") is negotiated, with the dollar devalued, and margins of permissible fluctuation are widened.

1972. The members and prospective members of the European Community introduce the "snake in the tunnel" to narrow the fluctuations among their currencies. Speculation puts the Smithsonian exchange-rate structure to several tests. A speculative attack cuts sterling adrift, then shifts to the dollar and Italian lira; their defense is temporarily successful. The price of gold rises 60 percent by early August. The European Monetary Agreement is terminated at the end of the year.

1973. Speculation involving the lira, Swiss franc, mark, yen, and other currencies brings a second devaluation of the dollar, which soon comes under renewed attack. The major countries allow their currencies to float, temporarily and "dirtily"; eight European countries operate a joint float. The dollar depreciates further, then recovers; the price of gold zooms. Worldwide inflation accelerates, partly as a consequence of the last-ditch defense of the Bretton Woods system. Reform discussions drag on under IMF auspices. Another Arab–Israeli war breaks out, the Arabs temporarily embargo oil shipments to the United States and the Netherlands, and the oil-exporting countries sharply increase their selling prices.

1974. Numerous exchange rates continue to float "dirtily" amidst extreme difficulties, including those associated with the sharp increase in petroleum prices and with persistent worldwide inflation. France drops out of the European joint float. The SDR is redefined in terms of a "basket" of currencies, and the International Monetary fund suggests guidelines for the management of floating rates, but ambitious international monetary reform is tacitly shelved for the time being. The price of gold continues to rise. The U.S. government legalizes private gold ownership at the end of the year.

Singapore, and other countries have also been accepting deposits denominated in United States dollars. Deposits in sterling, marks, and a few other currencies are also accepted by banks outside the home countries of those currencies. Although Fritz Machlup has suggested the broader and more accurate label "xenocurrency," the usual label for operations of this sort remains "Eurodollar" or "Eurocurrency." Even the term "deposits" may be slightly misleading, since banks with foreign-currency liabilities, far from having just passively accepted deposits, have actively borrowed foreign funds for relending.

A simplified (and not necessarily typical)

Appendix to Chapter 21: The Eurodollar Market

One institutional feature of world finance in the 1960s and 1970s deserves special notice. A market in foreign-currency deposits arose in London in the 1950s. It grew in size and geographic scope in the 1960s, after the chief European currencies had become convertible in 1958. The market has facilitated borrowing and lending across national boundaries, has contributed to financial integration, and has thereby presumably heightened the sensitivity to interest-rate differentials of international capital movements. Its development illustrates the dominance of the dollar in international finance and the rapid adaptability of financial institutions on the international scene as well as within countries.

How the market works

The term "Eurodollar" is hard to define because it often serves as a loose label for a range of operations rather than as the name for a specific thing. "It has been said that there does not exist, strictly speaking, a Market for the Eurodollar, but a 'Euromarket for the Dollar.'"[1] Narrowly defined, Eurodollars are deposits held with British or Continental banks but denominated in dollars instead of local currency. Actually, banks in Canada, Japan,

---

1. G.-P. Menais, *Les Relations Monétaires Internationales Financières et Économiques*, Paris: Editions J. Delmas, 1971, p. 87. Other literature consulted includes Paul Einzig, *The Euro-Dollar System*, 2nd ed., New York: St. Martin's Press, 1965; Einzig, *A Textbook on Foreign Exchange*, New York: St. Martin's Press, 1966, chap. 14; Ernest Bloch, *Eurodollars: An Emerging International Money Market*, New York University, *The Bulletin*, No. 39, April 1966; Federal Reserve Bank of Richmond, "The Euro-Dollar Market," *Monthly Review*, April 1967, pp. 8–10; Alexander K. Swoboda, *The Euro-Dollar Market: An Interpretation*, Princeton Essays in *International Finance*, No. 64, Princeton, N.J.: Princeton University, February 1968; Fred H. Klopstock, *The Euro-Dollar Market: Some Unresolved Issues*, Princeton Essays, No. 65, Princeton, N.J.: Princeton University, March 1968; Jane Sneddon Little, "The Euro-dollar Market: Its Nature and Impact," Federal Reserve Bank of Boston, *New England Economic Review*, May/June 1969, pp. 2–31; Milton Friedman, "The Euro-Dollar Market: Some First Principles," *Morgan Guaranty Survey*, October 1969, pp. 4–14; Federal Reserve Bank of Cleveland, *The Eurodollar Market*, June 1970, a reprint of articles from the Bank's *Economic Review* of March, April, and May 1970; Helmut W. Mayer, *Some Theoretical Problems Relating to the Euro-Dollar Market*, Princeton Essays, No. 79, Princeton, N.J.: Princeton University, February 1970; Mayer, "Multiplier Effects and Credit Creation in the Euro-dollar Market," Banca Nazionale del Lavoro *Quarterly Review*, No. 98, September 1971, pp. 233–262; Fritz Machlup, Edward M. Bernstein, and Carl H. Stem, discussions in *International Monetary Problems*, Washington: American Enterprise Institute, 1972, pp. 3–57; and papers presented at American Enterprise Institute, Washington, October 17 and 18, 1974, and to be published, notably Carl H. Stem, "The Eurocurrency System: Problems and Prospects." For citations to earlier literature, see the first edition of the present book, p. 467n.

example will help explain the system. A European has acquired a dollar deposit in or a check drawn on a New York bank. He wants to continue holding dollars for a while, neither spending them nor converting them into his home currency. Instead of having to hold the dollars on deposit in New York, he can hold them in the form of a deposit claim on a European bank, to which he transfers ownership of the deposit in New York. The European bank can in turn transfer this deposit to someone wanting to borrow immediately spendable dollars. The European bank will hold such positions with many customers at the same time, owing dollars to many depositors and holding dollar claims on many borrowers. The bank will not lend away the full amount of U.S. bank balances transferred to it. It will keep a small fraction of them in reserve to pay off depositors who may wish to cash their Eurodollar demand deposits or—much more typically—their maturing time deposits into dollars actually spendable in the United States. Suppose the Eurobank has dollar deposit liabilities of $1 million, reserve balances in New York of $100,000, and outstanding dollar loans of $900,000. Sellers of goods or services or securities to whom the borrowers have made payments actually have the $900,000 in the form of balances in U.S. banks. Yet the depositors of the Eurobank still have their $1 million, only now in the form of their claims on that bank. The bank has intermediated transfers of balances in the United States from its depositors to its borrowers while still leaving its depositors holding claims that they regard as dollars. One million dollars has become $1,900,000. In a sense, the Eurobank has taken part in creating $900,000. And $1 million of Eurodollars is backed by only $100,000 of New York funds. (Actually, the 10 percent reserve ratio, assumed to keep the arithmetic simple, is unrealistically large.)

For Eurobanks in the aggregate or as a system, the multiple creation of Eurodollars on the basis of additional reserves of United States dollars is more narrowly limited than the multiple creation of demand deposits by the American commercial banking system on the basis of additional domestic reserve funds. This is true even though Eurobanks operate with much smaller reserve ratios (and, for the most part, with self-chosen rather than required reserve ratios). The reason is that the Eurobanking system is more fully exposed than the American banking system to drainage of re-

serves out of its possession as borrowers spend the proceeds of their loans. Unlike demand deposits in U.S. banks and apart from minor exceptions, Eurodollars do not circulate as a medium of exchange. Within the United States, when bank customers obtain loans to buy goods, the sellers of the goods or the subsequent recipients of the money hold most of it in the form of bank deposits; and most of the reserve funds involved remain in the possession of the banking system. Recipients of dollars borrowed from Eurobanks, however, do not typically retain that money in the form of dollar deposits with Eurobanks, since Eurodollars do not serve as a medium of exchange. Whereas U.S. holders of demand deposits routinely receive and pay them in transactions with one another, holders of Eurodollar deposits hold them only if they relatively deliberately choose to hold funds in that particular form. The operations of Eurobanks in creating Eurodollars and serving as intermediaries in loans of U.S. dollars are analogous to the operations of nonbank financial intermediaries in the United States. Institutions of both kinds create liquid (but noncirculating) claims against themselves and serve as intermediaries in loans. Both alike take part in creating dollar-denominated near-moneys on the basis of fractional reserves held in the form of demand deposits with U.S. commercial banks. Both take part in transferring around ownership of existing media of exchange.

The close analogy between Eurobanks and Eurodollars on the one hand and American nonbank financial intermediaries and their near-money liabilities on the other hand has further instruction to offer us. Eurodollars are no more a special kind of dollar than are the dollars in which deposits in savings-and-loan associations and mutual savings banks and the commercial paper of sales finance companies are denominated. Similarly, whether an American businessman borrows dollars from an American friend or a Belgian businessman borrows dollars from a French friend, the dollars in which the debt is denominated are the same. The ordinary U.S. dollar serves as unit of account or standard of deferred payments in all such cases. Either on demand or after a specified lapse of time and either directly or at the end of a chain of transactions, as the particular contracts involved specify, the debt is collectible in paper money issued by the Federal Reserve Banks or coin issued by the U.S. Treasury. The various cases differ not in the unit of account used but rather in the national ity and other characteristics of the debtor and in the terms on which the debt is payable. Similarly, the most liquid dollar reserve funds of Eurobanks and of U.S. savings-and-loan associations are alike: demand-deposit balances with U.S. commercial banks.

Eurodollars and other near-money claims also resemble each other in being close substitutes for each other for some holders. Someone who acquires a Eurodollar deposit may not have regarded a demand deposit in an American bank as his next best alternative asset. Consider an oil sheik who holds a maturing certificate of deposit (CD) issued by a New York Bank. Perhaps he renews the CD; perhaps he lets it run off and places the funds on deposit with the London branch of the New York bank, which then relends the funds to its head office. In the first case, the bank acts as a direct intermediary between the sheik as ultimate lender, from whom it borrows money by issuing a new CD, and the ultimate borrower to whom it relends the funds. In the second case, the bank obtains funds from the sheik in a more indirect way, through the intermediary of its London branch. Since the London branch counts as part of the Eurodollar banking system, that system plays a part in intermediation between ultimate lender and ultimate borrower that might otherwise have taken place within the United States. Similarly, the holder of a Eurodollar deposit might have considered a U.S. Treasury bill his next best alternative. Thus, holders of Eurodollar deposits have not necessarily switched away from holding demand deposits in U.S. banks. If people were making such switches on a large scale because of a change in their asset preferences, they would indeed be promoting the multiple creation of Eurodollars, just as they would be promoting the multiple creation of savings-and-loan deposits if their preferences shifted in that direction and away from bank demand deposits. Furthermore, the very existence of the Eurodollar market must make the ratio of the total quantity of dollar-denominated near-moneys to the quantity of dollar demand deposits in U.S. banks higher than it otherwise would be because that market provides an additional alternative to holding demand deposits. Still, it would be wrong to suppose that the very existence of the Eurodollar market is continually promoting the multiplication of Eurodollars by continually promoting the shift of asset preferences away from demand de-

posits, just as it would be wrong to suppose that the very existence of savings-and-loan associations is continually promoting the multiplication of deposits in them by continually promoting the shift of asset preferences away from demand deposits. No such idea should be read into our earlier example of the European who exchanges a New York demand deposit for a Eurodollar deposit.

Why does the system exist? Why should anyone care to hold Eurodollars? The familiar advantages of financial intermediation provide part of the answer. Lenders of dollars—and these have often been American banks—can let better-placed and better-informed European banks bear the trouble and risk of lending to ultimate European borrowers. A European without regular American banking contacts can borrow dollars from his bank at home. By conducting their dollar banking transactions in their home countries, Europeans can avoid the problem of the transatlantic difference in business hours. The advantages of intermediation also help explain why several banks may stand in a long chain between the ultimate lender and the ultimate borrower, the banks inside the chain accepting dollar deposits from some banks and placing dollar deposits with others.[2] Intermediation also provides opportunities to tailor loans and deposits to the desires of borrowers and depositors, to share or reallocate risks, and to shape asset and liability portfolios to the desires of the banks involved. Because of the law of large numbers, for example, dollars received on short-term deposit may be relent at longer term. The spread between borrowing and lending rates in the interbank Eurodollar market is small, but the participating banks get other advantages besides an explicit profit mar-

2. "When a Japanese city lacks money at the end of the month to pay its subway-construction workers, it quickly borrows dollars from an English bank and exchanges them for yen. The English bank obtains the dollars in Zurich, and the Zurich bank perhaps in Paris. But the initial lender will turn out to be, for example, a German firm that has deposited in a large German bank the dollar receipts arising from its exports." Menais, *op. cit.*, p. 87, quoting in French translation from an unspecified German financial journal.

gin, such as the opportunity to pave the way for other types of business by cultivating contacts and keeping their names familiar in the international banking community.

The Eurodollar market offers a way around certain government controls. During the sterling crisis of 1957, the British government prohibited British banks from financing trade between third countries (non-British trade) in pounds. To retain a lucrative business, the banks offered the same kind of financing in dollars instead, attracting the dollars by offering interest on short-term deposits.[3] Under Regulation Q, the Federal Reserve forbids interest on demand deposits and limits interest on time deposits in the United States. On a Eurodollar deposit, however, the holder can receive a competitive rate of interest. The Eurobank's motive is that it can relend the dollars at a higher rate of interest than it pays. The source of the interest-rate advantage shared between the Eurobank and its borrowing customer is the opportunity to borrow dollars relatively cheaply from a depositor whose alternatives would have been to hold demand deposits or near-moneys paying zero or unattractively low rates of interest in the United States. Similar reasons partly explain transactions in Eurosterling and in deposits of Continental currencies outside their home countries. A foreign bank, not bound by the cartel agreements, reserve requirements, and other regulations and practices of the country where a currency circulates domestically, may be able to operate on smaller margins, paying higher rates of interest on deposits of it and charging lower rates on loans of it. The more competitive international money market also provides scope for letting interest rates in wholesale transactions reflect economies of scale.

Events of 1968 and 1969 illustrate the role of Eurodollar transactions in getting around the Regulation Q ceilings. At that time of tight credit in the United States, when market interest rates were rising above the ceiling rates on time deposits, including CDs, banks had trouble selling new CDs to replace ones coming due. They had to scratch around for other sources of time funds for relending. In particular, they borrowed dollars in the Euromarket, especially from their own overseas branches. These Eurobanks, in turn, obtained funds largely from short-term investors who, in the absence of Regulation Q, might have placed their funds directly with the head-office banks in the United States. (Recall the example of the oil sheik who shifts from a maturing CD into a Eurodollar deposit.) Through the intermediation of their Eurobank branches, the U.S. banks were able to accomplish pretty much what they would have been able to accomplish in a more direct and economical way in the absence of Regulation Q. Their operations brought a relatively complete and rapid leakage out of the Eurobank system of the dollars being temporarily detoured through it. The artificial necessity for this roundabout financial intermediation helps explain why U.S. banks established so many foreign branches in the late 1960s. At the end of 1965, 13 banks belonging to the Federal Reserve System had a total of 188 branches abroad. By the end of 1968 these figures had grown to 27 head-office banks and 340 foreign branches, and by mid-1972 to 106 and 558.[4] In 1970 and 1971, after the Federal Reserve had relaxed CD interest ceilings and after market interest rates had receded, repayments of Eurodollar borrowings by U.S. banks caused reverse distortions of balance-of-payments figures, just as the growth of those borrowings had distorted the figures in the first place. Meanwhile, the Federal Reserve introduced and altered marginal reserve requirements on the Euromarket borrowings of U.S. banks in efforts to manipulate borrowings and repayments.[5]

Dollars deposited by ultimate lenders by no means form the only basis for Eurodollar operations. Eurobanks can buy dollars on the foreign-exchange market with domestic currency or with holdings of third-country currencies. Furthermore, West European business firms and banks are by no means the only suppliers and borrowers of funds in the Euromarket. From about 1963 until the Johnson Administration imposed "voluntary restraint" on capital exports in 1965, much of the supply consisted of funds lent by corporations in the United States. Especially in the 1950s, in the early stages of the market's development, banks of communist countries reportedly acted on their supposition that dollars were safer from legal attachment or restriction when on deposit in a European rather than in an American bank. Central banks of many countries have fed the market at times by holding parts of their external reserves as Eurodollar deposits. They have either handed over dollar balances to commercial banks or to the Bank for International Settlements in return for a dollar deposit claim or have sold dollars to commercial banks for local currency under repurchase agreements. In some cases the central banks have wanted to influence international capital movements or the size or composition of their officially reported external reserves; in other cases they were seeking a higher yield on Eurodollars or Eurosterling than on U.S. or U.K. bank deposits or Treasury bills. More than $1 billion—an estimated 45 percent—of the total increase in foreign-exchange reserves of national monetary authorities in 1960 reportedly took an untraditional form, largely dollar and sterling deposits in banks outside the United States and the United Kingdom.[6] Total central-bank placements sagged after 1961 or 1962. Not until the late 1960s did the central banks of the main financial centers make sizable placements in the Euromarket.

Discrepancies between published figures on total foreign-exchange-reserve holdings of monetary authorities and the total of reserve-type liabilities of the United States and the United Kingdom eventually aroused suspicions that central bankers were helping multiply the dollars flowing in unwanted volume into their own reserves. Before 1966 this discrepancy was generally under $1 billion and could plausibly be explained by holdings of reserves of other countries' currencies. In 1966 the discrepancy reached $2.4 billion, in 1968 $4.4 billion, in 1969 $8.1 billion, and by the end of 1970 $13.2 billion.[7] It turned out that the typical European central bank had been depositing in the Eurodollar market, either directly or through the intermediary of the Bank for International Settlements, some of the dollars that it had been reluctantly acquiring in its exchange-rate pegging. This action tended to depress interest rates on the Eurodollar market and so increase the incentive for European businessmen to borrow dollars cheaply there and then sell them for their home currencies. Furthermore, dollars deposited by a central bank with a Eurobank were available for relending, including relending to borrowers who would convert them into their home currencies. Thus, dollars would come back into the possession of central banks, be again deposited in the Eurodollar market, and so on and on. The central banks were frustrating the leakage that ordinarily restrains the multiplication of Eurodollars. As a result, they were reluctantly buying up dollars in amounts several billion dollars larger than the increase in U.S. liabilities to them. In effect, the European authorities were unintentionally manufacturing

some of the dollars whose influx they had been so bitterly blaming on the United States. Meeting in Basel in May 1971, European central bankers and the Bank for International Settlements agreed that they would soon stop, if they had not already stopped, feeding the "Eurodollar carousel" in this way, and that they would gradually diminish their existing placements in the Eurodollar market. Central banks outside the main industrial countries, however, including the central banks of the Middle East oil countries, apparently persisted longer in placing reserve funds on the Euromarket. At the end of 1972, deposits owed to official monetary institutions amounted to an estimated $20 billion, about 22 or 15 percent of total external foreign-currency liabilities of commercial banks in eight European countries (the percentage depending on elimination or nonelimination of some double-counting from the total).[8] Central banks have not been moti-

---

3. Benjamin J. Cohen, *The Future of Sterling as an International Currency*, London: Macmillan; New York: St. Martin's Press, 1971, pp. 130–131n.; Paul Einzig, *The Destiny of the Dollar*, New York: St. Martin's Press, 1972, p. 43.

4. *Federal Reserve Bulletin*, October 1972, p. 855.

5. See pp. 575–576.

6. Reinhard Kamitz, "Ein neuer internationaler Geldmarkt," *Der Österreichische Volkswirt*, XLIX, 15 November 1963, pp. 1–2; International Monetary Fund, 1961, pp. 112–114.

7. Menais, *op. cit.*, p. 95. Different sources give somewhat different figures. My calculation from *International Financial Statistics*, May 1973, pp. 23, 360, 366, gives total foreign-exchange reserves exceeding U.S. and U.K. reserve-type liabilities by $15.1 billion at the end of 1970.

8. *Wall Street Journal*, 20 May 1971, p. 6, 27 May 1971, p. 8, 1 March 1973, p. 1; *Federal Reserve Bulletin*, October 1972, pp. 862–863; Mayer, Princeton Essays in International Finance, No. 79, February 1970, pp. 12–13; Federal Reserve Bank of Cleveland, *Economic Review*, March 1970, pp. 8–10, 15; Banca d'Italia, *Assemblea* 1970, pp. 12, 17, 350; IMF, 1971, p. 82n.; IMF, 1972, pp. 16, 29; Bank for International Settlements, 1971–1972, pp. 115–116; BIS, 1972–1973, pp. 155, 163; Bundesbank, 1971 *Bericht*, p. 37 (the Bundesbank says that it took no part in reserve placements on

vated solely by eagerness to earn interest. At times they and the Bank for International Settlements have intervened with the intention of smoothing and stabilizing Euromarket interest rates.[9]

The basic trend of Eurodollar interest rates seems to be largely determined by interest-rate developments in the United States, with seasonal factors, the strength or weakness of the dollar in foreign-exchange markets, and monetary developments outside the United States accounting for fluctuations around the trend. Interest rates for deposits and loans in other Eurocurrencies are subject to wider fluctuations than dollar interest rates because of narrower national money markets, the effects of controls over capital flows, and changing exchange-rate expectations as reflected in forward premiums or discounts of these other currencies against the dollar.[10]

Size of the market

How large is the Eurodollar market? It is hard to say with any confidence. The difficulties are conceptual as well as statistical. One of them is that the market has a heavily wholesale character, with much of the business taking place between banks rather than between the banks and the ultimate suppliers and borrowers of funds. The Bank for International Settlements estimated the net size of the market, excluding interbank deposits, at about $7 billion in 1963. About $5 billion of the deposits were in dollars and about $2 billion worth in European currencies. By the end of 1972, the gross foreign-currency liabilities of commercial banks in eight European countries had grown to an estimated $131.9 billion. Banks in the United Kingdom accounted for 45 percent of this total. About 73 percent of the deposits were denominated in dollars, about 15 percent in German marks, and about 6 percent in Swiss francs. With double-counting attributable to interbank deposits eliminated, the end-of-1972 total was about $91.0 billion, of which about 77 percent was in dollars. (By the end of March 1973, this estimated net total had grown to nearly $100 billion.)

It may help give an impression of how large or small these figures are to note that the total U.S. narrow money supply (demand deposits and currency) at the end of 1972 was $262.9 billion; the broad money supply (M_2 as reported in the *Federal Reserve Bulletin*) was $530.3 billion. The narrow money supplies of the eight European countries, translated at end-of-1972 exchange rates, totaled $251 billion; their broad money supplies (including quasi money, as reported in *International Financial Statistics*) totaled $502 billion. Thus, the gross foreign-currency deposits in the banks of the eight countries at the end of 1972 totaled an amount 50 and 25 percent as large as the narrow and broad U.S. money supplies, respectively, and 52 and 26 percent as large as the narrow and broad domestic money supplies of the European countries. Similar comparisons for Eurocurrency deposits with double counting eliminated work out to 35 and 17 percent of the narrow and broad U.S. money supplies and 36 and 18 percent of the narrow and broad European domestic money supplies.[11]

The foregoing figures refer to the banks' foreign-currency *external* liabilities and do not include liabilities to local residents. Neither do they include figures for Canada and Japan, whose banks had gross external foreign-currency liabilities amounting to $8.1 billion and $7.5 billion, respectively, at the end of 1972.

Eurobonds

The Eurodollar market paved the way for development of the Eurobond market. The latter is the market for bonds floated mainly in countries other than those in whose currencies the bonds are denominated. From the nineteenth century onward, many international bond issues were denominated in currencies other than those of the borrowers, but in practically every case the currency involved was that of the market on which the bonds were floated. Canadian and European borrowers had long floated U.S. dollar bonds in the New York market. Beginning in 1963 under the impetus of the impending Interest Equalization Tax and U.S. official discouragement, European borrowers began floating their dollar bond issues in Europe itself. The Eurobond issues are usually underwritten by a multinational syndicate and are floated in several countries at the same time. The most prevalent currency of denomination has been the dollar, with the German mark second. There has been some slight experimentation with bonds denominated in international units of account rather than in one particular currency only. U.S. capital-export controls encouraged U.S. corporations or their European subsidiaries to do their borrowing for purposes of investment in Europe on the European capital market rather than in the United States. Many of their bonds have been convertible into common stock.[12] Despite the shakiness of the dollar, the volume of new Eurobond issues expanded by 73 percent in 1972 over the 1971 figure. Bonds denominated in dollars made up $3.9 billion of the $6.5 billion total in 1972, with issues in marks, French francs, and Dutch guilders following in that order.[13] Activity in the Eurobond market declined in 1973 and 1974.

Appraisal

How is the Eurodollar market to be appraised? It "plays an important and constructive role in providing additional means for arbitrage," according to Paul Einzig, a leading authority on the subject; it "has greatly contributed towards increasing and redistributing the world's international liquid resources."[14] It has helped meet the growing demand for credit to finance international transactions. For good or ill, it is a long step toward a competitive international market.

In conformity with its interbank character, the Euro-dollar market operates first and foremost as a link between the various national credit systems, and therefore the bulk of the Euro-banks' external dollar liabilities and assets are vis-à-vis other banks, whereas taking the market over the whole of its life direct deposit-taking from or lending to nonresidents other than banks has been rather the exception. At the end of 1970 over 80 percent of both external dollar liabilities and assets of the banks of the eight European countries which furnish Euro-currency statistics were vis-à-vis other banks.[15]

As a wholesale market and as a set of arrangements that circumvent controls and cartel restrictions, that gather and transmit information, that reduce transactions costs, and that intensify competition, the Euromarket welds national credit markets more closely together. It can even help erode or bypass segmental barriers within national credit markets, as is illustrated by how resort to it in 1968–1969 enabled U.S. banks to perform their domestic financial-intermediation functions despite

the Euromarket). In its 41st *Annual Report*, published June 14, 1971, the Bank for International Settlements mentioned in several passages—though of course did not emphasize—the role of central banks, and its own role, in the multiplication of dollars. The report even acknowledged (e.g., pp. 164, 166) that central banks had made large deposits in the Eurodollar market to obtain attractive interest yields on their foreign-exchange reserves.

The danger had been recognized as early as March 17, 1967 by Dr. Edwin Stopper, President of the Swiss National Bank:

> Even the central banks can hamper one another in their fight against inflation if they lend the dollars they have received to banks of other countries in the Euro-market. Every time that the amount of dollars in question must be taken in by another central bank, the latter, by exchanging it for national currency, cannot avoid increasing the national money volume. As a rule, therefore, central banks ought to stay away from the Euro-market.

—Speech quoted in Ruth Logue, *Imported Inflation and the International Adjustment Process*, Washington: Board of Governors of the Federal Reserve System, 1969, p. 80.

Probably the leading analytical article on the topic is Fritz Machlup, "The Magicians and their Rabbits," *Morgan Guaranty Survey*, May 1971, pp. 3–13.

9. Donald R. Hodgman, "Euro-dollars and National Monetary Policy" (manuscript prepared for Irving Trust Company, September 1969), p. 6; Federal Reserve Bank of Cleveland, *Economic Review*, March 1970, p. 8; Menais, *op. cit.*, p. 90.

10. BIS, 1972–1973, p. 168.

11. BIS, 1963–1964, p. 130; BIS, 1972–1973, pp. 154–167, *Federal Reserve Bulletin, International Financial Statistics*, and calculations with figures from those sources. According to Carl H. Stem's paper of October 1974, cited in footnote 1, Eurocurrency deposits, including deposits in Eurocurrency centers outside Europe, such as the Bahamas, had grown by mid-1974 to about $185 billion.

12. IMF, 1966, pp. 73–75; Robert Solomon in Randall Hinshaw, ed., *The Economics of International Adjustment*, Baltimore: Johns Hopkins Press, 1971, p. 121; Federal Reserve of Cleveland, *Economic Review*, May 1971, pp. 3–17.

13. BIS, 1972–1973, p. 171.

14. *A Textbook on Foreign Exchange*, New York: St. Martin's Press, 1966, p. 162.

15. Helmut Mayer in Banca Nazionale del Lavoro *Quarterly Review*, September 1971, p. 244.

interest-rate ceilings that were too low in relation to market interest rates. The Euromarket foreshadows a unified worldwide credit market comprising itself and the national credit markets.

This is not to say that the Euromarket makes interest rates everywhere the same. Unless exchange rates are so rigidly and perpetually fixed that national currencies effectively blend into a single currency, exchange-rate uncertainties remain as an obstacle to complete equalization. A well-functioning forward-exchange market enables interest arbitrage to eliminate covered interest differentials, but not differentials pure and simple.[16]

Even so, the Euromarket has rendered national credit policies less independent of one another. As the German Bundesbank has complained, the market has facilitated money transfers by bringing together market partners in different countries and continents. In that way, and also because of the large funds at the disposal of multinational corporations, relatively slight interest differentials among countries suffice to set large amounts of money in motion. The market has also facilitated the financing of short-term foreign-exchange speculation. Finally, it has been active not only as a middleman and transmission belt but also as a creator of funds, especially through the dollar reserve placements of central banks.[17] As illustrated by the transatlantic flows of 1971, interest-sensitive capital movements may become awkwardly heavy and then turn destructively speculative. A country cannot ward off interest-motivated inflows merely by forbidding payment of interest on foreign-owned deposits in its banks if holders of such balances can collect interest after all by redepositing them on the Eurocurrency market.[18] Thanks to the Euromarket, business firms and banks have become more able to evade a domestic anti-inflationary tight-credit policy by borrowing abroad and forcing their country's central bank to create additional "high-powered" domestic bank reserves as it buys up the foreign money to keep the exchange rate pegged. With this in mind, some observers have called the system "an international Federal funds market." This evasion has led governments to resort to more and more controls over borrowing abroad.

Euromarket operations impair domestic monetary policies much less in the United States than abroad. As long as other countries rather than the United States attend to the pegging of their currencies to the dollar and as long as the Federal Reserve and Treasury do not create and destroy domestic high-powered money by any sizable purchases and sales of foreign currencies, the stock of domestic high-powered money, and thus the total money supply geared to it, remains under the control of the Federal Reserve, if only the Federal Reserve chooses to exercise that control. The heavy bank borrowing in the Euromarket in 1968–1969, for example, did not bring new high-powered money into existence. It was simply overcoming the impairment by Regulation Q of domestic financial intermediation and of the attendant redistribution of existing high-powered money among the banks. Only to the extent that the funds acquired by detouring through the Euromarket were effectively subject to lower reserve requirements than funds acquired directly at home did Euromarket operations tend to promote expansion of the U.S. money supply by permitting a somewhat higher degree of pyramiding of ordinary money on a given base of high-powered money. The base, however, remained under the control of the Federal Reserve.

Partly because "liquidity" is such a vague term, opinions differ on whether the Euromarket has had a beneficial or harmful effect on liquidity. Some European bankers have hailed the system as disproof of worries about an inadequate growth of international liquidity and as an example of how liquidity can adapt itself to the needs of trade through increased velocity of circulation. It has helped meet the growing demand for credit to finance international transactions. Expanded holdings of foreign exchange by banks and business firms increase the scope for the financing of international payments to take place outside of official reserves, leaving the reserves freer for absorbing fluctuations in balances of payments.[19] The extent to which international liquidity is created or stretched in these ways is haphazard, however, and difficult to assess.

Some observers worry that the Eurodollar market, interpreted broadly as the xenocurrency market, haphazardly expands the world money supply by creating bank balances whose quantities are under the systematic control neither of the national monetary authorities of the countries whose currencies are used or where the banks and their customers are located nor of any international authority.[20] This worry seems less compelling than the more familiar worry about how the xenocurrency market facilitates international flows of funds, sometimes causing imported inflation and the unwanted expansion of ordinary national money supplies. As for the xenocurrencies themselves, they are not media of exchange but near-moneys;[21] and their creation may well be largely a substitute for creation of other near-moneys instead. In 1968–1969, for example, the expansion of the Eurodollar deposits of the European branches of American banks largely corresponded to shrinkage of the CD liabilities of the banks' head offices.

Even so, Eurodollars and demand deposits in circulation at home may compete for holders, conceivably with awkward consequences. (In other words, Eurodollars may conceivably speed up the circulation of demand deposits in ways that are hard to cope with.) In countries whose ordinary money supplies incurred this competition of deposits created by foreign banks, the monetary authorities would face a trickier job than otherwise of regulating the money supply. Within the United States, this worry remains rather farfetched unless the volume of Eurodollars should become large in relation to the ordinary domestic money supply and unless assetholders should regard dollar deposits in foreign banks and demand deposits in American banks as close substitutes. As they affect U.S. monetary management at present, Eurodollars seem analogous to the liquid liabilities of a moderately important class of nonbank financial intermediaries. A still more conjectural worry is that the chance to escape from the interest prohibition and reserve requirements applicable to the demand deposits of U.S. banks might bring Eurodollars into routine use as a medium of exchange, being transferred by check in payments among Americans.

The problem of an excess supply of dollars appears (or appeared, in 1973) even more acute on the international scene than within the U.S. economy. After the devaluations of December 1971 and February 1973, one might have expected the dollar to be strong at its new low parity. Yet the market strength or weakness of a currency is not determined solely by the flows of supply and demand arising from current international commercial transactions; it also reflects the stock demand relative to the existing quantity. After inflationary money creation from 1965 had brought about large foreign holdings of liquid dollar claims and after two devaluations had fostered an idea of the dollar's inherent devaluation-proneness, the pool of dollar liquidity abroad appeared excessive in relation to the demand for it, at least in the short run and at official exchange rates.[22] This problem must be exacerbated by the expanded volume of Eurodollar deposits, which

16. Even with interest arbitrage completely free of impediments and frictions and completely successful in maintaining the interest-parity relation among spot and forward exchange rates and different countries' interest rates, *uncovered* interest differentials could persist if the following conditions held: (1) uncertainty about exchange rates; (2) absence of a sufficient amount of non-risk-averse speculation to eliminate discrepancies between each forward exchange rate and the average expectation of the corresponding future spot rate, and *either* (3) dominant expectations that the spot rate would move up or down, as distinguished from neutral or balanced expectations, *or* (4) virtual interest-rate differentials (conditions of supply and demand for loans in the national money markets such that their interest rates would be different in the absence of interest arbitrage).

17. Bundesbank, 1971 *Bericht*, p. 37.

18. Paul Einzig, *The Destiny of the Dollar*, p. 49. It is true that foreign acquisition of mark claims on banks outside Germany, for example, does not directly force the Bundesbank to acquire foreign-exchange reserves and supply marks. However, interest arbitrageurs or speculators may have acquired non-interest-bearing mark balances in order to redeposit them on the Euromark market; and the Eurobanks will hold some mark balances in Germany as reserves against their own mark deposit liabilities.

19. Special West European correspondent of the *Eastern Economist* (New Delhi), "Euro-Dollars Versus Triffin," **XXXVII**, 21 July 1961, pp. 111–112; IMF, 1963, p. 43.

20. Menais, *op. cit.*, p. 89; Fritz Machlup in AEI, *International Monetary Problems*, 1972, pp. 17–18.

21. There is admittedly room for debate about the significance of the distinction between near-moneys and money. Some writers, such as Machlup, would argue that xenocurrencies and other near-moneys are to all intents and purposes actual money. See, on the other hand, my "Essential Properties of the Medium of Exchange," *Kyklos*, **XXI**, No. 1, 1968, pp. 45–69.

22. The First National City Bank of New York makes this argument in its *Monthly Economic Letter*, March 1973, pp. 1–2.

in the minds of some holders compete closely with the liquid obligations of U.S. banks and other U.S. debtors.

Critics of the gold-exchange or dollar standard may view Eurodollars as a new basis for their fears. They form a new layer in the inverted pyramid of various kinds of money and near-money onto a narrow ultimate reserve base. (As already explained, however, the drainage of dollars spent by ultimate borrowers restrains the pyramiding.) Financial practice has now evolved beyond a mere pyramiding of deposit money in U.S. banks onto Federal Reserve funds, which in turn may be pyramided onto some more ultimate reserve. Dollar deposits in European banks are now pyramided onto a fractional reserve of ordinary deposits in American banks, which are pyramided onto a fractional reserve of deposits in the Federal Reserve banks, which in turn are pyramided onto the ultimate reserve. And this is not all. Insofar as some foreign authorities peg their currencies to fractional reserves of foreign exchange consisting partly of Eurodollars rather than entirely of ordinary dollars, foreign currencies are pyramided onto something that is in turn pyramided onto something that is further in turn pyramided fractionally onto Federal Reserve deposits, which are pyramided fractionally onto the ultimate reserve. The "ultimate reserve" was gold until March 1968 and even—or so one might argue—until as late as August 1971.[23] Since then the role of gold has been ambiguous; and it is not clear what, if anything, the ultimate reserve might be.

The higher the pyramid and the more tiers it has, the bigger the crash if it should come apart. Paul Einzig argues that Eurodollar multiplication means multiplication of the amounts that speculators can dump on the foreign-exchange market when they become bearish on the dollar.[24] Bearish forward speculation is encouraged, since people have larger dollar balances on which they can draw, if necessary, to make delivery on their maturing forward sales. Furthermore, the Eurodollar market facilitates lending dollars into the hands of people who want to sell them spot; it mobilizes the New York funds that change hands in the foreign-exchange market. The

sales are made either by spot speculators or by arbitrageurs responding to the profit opportunities created when forward speculation tends to disrupt the interest-parity relation. But similar complaints could be made about other types of institutions and near-moneys that enhance the mobility of funds.

In summary appraisal, it would be rash to conclude that the Euromarket is harmful on balance. It offers genuine advantages, including the familiar advantages of intermediation and the enhancement of financial competition. As for its disadvantages, it is well to remember that the market is partly a response to regulations of questionable wisdom, such as interest-rate regulation. Policy expedients and market innovations provoke each other in an unnecessary escalation of what might be called "institutional instability." Exchange-rate pegging probably enhances the interest-sensitivity of international flows of funds and surely promotes speculative flows. It plays a part in the rise of the Euromarket and is responsible for national monetary policies sometimes getting out of the control of the domestic authorities. The Eurodollar-multiplying activities of central banks, which finally received due attention in 1971, were associated with exchange-rate pegging and with the particular form in which central banks accumulated their growing dollar reserves. Considering the origin of the most questionable aspects of the Euromarket, it seems strange to look for a solution in still more regulation, carried onto the international plane and administered by people such as those who blundered into the central-bank Eurodollar carousel.

As the Eurodollar market continues changing rapidly in its details, observers will continue finding much material both for satisfaction and for alarm.

---

23. For the significance of these particular dates, see pp. 574–575, 580.

24. *The Destiny of the Dollar*, chap. 6. Einzig says that the Euromarket played an important role in the crises of 1971: dollars were borrowed in the Euromarket and sold for German marks (pp. 48–49).

CHAPTER TWENTY-TWO

Sterling
Since World War II

Britain's postwar experience is particularly worth reviewing not only because of sterling's role as a key currency but also for the sake of insights into the administration and gradual simplification of exchange controls and into the "stop-and-go" character of an economy in which policy interacts with recurrent external crises.[1]

The legacy of war finance

During World War II Britain's balance-of-payments deficit meant a welcome net inflow of goods for maintaining essential consumption and fighting the war. This import surplus was financed mainly by American Lend-Lease aid and by disinvestment and borrowing abroad. Foreign investments estimated at nearly one-third of the prewar total were sold. Most of the borrowing took the form of paying for overseas purchases with sterling deposits or other short-term sterling obligations. During the war, the British added roughly £3 billion of such debt to the £½ billion or more already outstanding. By the end of 1946, these externally held "sterling balances" had risen to about £3.7 billion. India, Egypt, and the colonies were the chief creditors. Sterling Area countries had

tended passively to accumulate sterling because of the linkage of their monetary systems with the British. Sterling earned by exporters in these countries, when sold for local currency at a fixed exchange rate, served as the legal reserve basis for local monetary expansion. The resulting inflations were part of the process of transferring real resources to Britain in exchange for paper or bookkeeping claims.

The end of the war cut off Lend-Lease aid. Britain now suddenly had to balance her external accounts or find new sources of finance. Devaluation of the pound was not seriously considered. Rightly or wrongly, people believed that an early postwar import surplus would be due not so much to wrong prices and exchange rates as to physical limitations on export capacity and to urgent and relatively incompressible import needs. The exchange rate was to remain pegged at $4.03; controls were to continue coping with balance-of-payments problems, and further foreign credits were to be sought.

The American loan agreement

A loan agreement signed in December 1945 and ratified by the United States Congress in July 1946 gave Britain a $3.75 billion line of credit, available at any time up to the end of 1951, carrying interest at 2 percent, and repayable in 50 annual installments beginning at the end of 1951 but subject to modification in years of severe British balance-of-payments

---

1. General references include Judd Polk, *Sterling: Its Meaning in World Finance*, New York: Harper & Row, 1956, chaps. 3 and 4; Philip Bell, *The Sterling Area in the Postwar World*, Oxford: Clarendon Press, 1956, chaps. 2 and 3; Brian Tew, *International Monetary Co-operation, 1945–1960*, 6th ed., London: Hutchinson's University Library, 1962, chaps. 10–15; Bank for International Settlements, various *Annual Reports* and also *The Sterling Area*, Basel: 1953; International Monetary Fund, various *Annual Reports*; R. G. Hawtrey, *Towards the Rescue of Sterling*, London: Longmans, Green, 1954, esp. chaps. 1–3; Peter B. Kenen, *British Monetary Policy and the Balance of Payments, 1951–1957*, Cambridge: Harvard University Press, 1960; M. FG. Scott, "The Balance of Payments Crises," chap. 7 in G. D. N. Worswick and P. H. Ady, eds., *The British Economy in the Nineteen-Fifties*, Oxford: Clarendon Press, 1962; and E. Victor Morgan, pp. 404–424 in his revision of Albert Feavearyear, *The Pound Sterling*, 2nd ed., Oxford: Clarendon Press, 1963.

difficulties. Canada lent another $1.25 billion. These loans were originally intended largely to cover the estimated (and, as it turned out, underestimated) British current-account deficit with the dollar world during the first three or four postwar years. The small size of the American loan had, in fact, disappointed the chief British negotiator, Lord Keynes. Besides granting the loan, however, the United States cancelled any British obligation on account of wartime Lend-Lease and provided a further long-term credit of $650 million to cover both civilian goods in the Lend-Lease pipeline at the end of the war and the purchase at bargain prices of American military installations and surplus goods located in British territory.

The loan agreement carried some noteworthy "strings" to prod the United Kingdom back into a multilateral international payments system. Britain promised not to restrict payments and transfers to the United States for current transactions and promised to avoid restrictions on the use of practically all American-owned sterling (but did not forswear nondiscriminatory trade restrictions, as distinct from exchange restrictions, on imports from the United States). Within one year after the agreement went into effect, furthermore, sterling currently earned by foreigners was to be freely convertible into dollars at the official exchange rate for purposes of current spending. Britain was to work out arrangements with Sterling Area countries so that their citizens also could freely convert currently received sterling for current use outside the Area; the agreement intended "that any discrimination arising from the so-called sterling area dollar pool will be entirely removed and that each member of the sterling area will have its current sterling and dollar receipts at its free disposition for current transactions anywhere."[2]

The convertibility provision did not cover sterling balances already in existence. The British and American negotiators hoped that the creditor countries would write off part of their claims in thanks for Britain's great share in the common war effort. Parts of the remaining balances might be blocked by mutual agreement at first and gradually made available in later years. These hopes were in vain. Australia and New Zealand did later write off a token of £46 million of their claims as a gift, but the major creditor countries, poor compared with Britain, were unwilling to scale down their claims. Around £3½ billion of the

balances thus remained. The threat of their expenditure was met only by loose short-term blocking arrangements and by the regular practice in some countries of holding sterling as external reserves. Egypt, incidentally, left the Sterling Area because of disagreement over which government was to do the blocking.

The failure of convertibility

July 15, 1947, was the date for convertibility to begin under the Anglo-American agreement. Early that year, in preparation, the British authorities began liberalizing their bilateral payments regime by establishing a system of transferable accounts. Residents of specified countries were authorized to transfer sterling among themselves and into the Sterling Area for current transactions, and in February, transfers to residents of the dollar area were also authorized. Between then and July, more and more countries were added to the transferable-account list. To gain this status under the British exchange controls, a country had to agree to report transfers to the Bank of England, to accept sterling from the Sterling Area or from other transferable-account countries without limit or restriction in payment for current transactions, and to prevent capital transfers to nonresident accounts.[3] Finally, on July 15, convertibility was generalized to residents of all but a few countries with which the necessary agreements had not yet been reached. Persons living outside the United Kingdom could now sell currently acquired sterling or officially released old balances at the $4.03 parity for dollars or other currencies needed for current transactions.

Actually, the time was not ripe for convertibility on these terms. A very severe winter had been followed in February by a fuel shortage that stalled much of industry and caused heavy if temporary unemployment. The loss of production, together with continuing inflation at home, swelled Britain's external current-account deficit. A hot dry summer now threatened a poor harvest. Quite possibly the pound was not really worth $4.03 in view of the terms on which and the amounts in which the British were prepared to supply exports. It is true that a comparison of British and American price indexes on a prewar base suggests, if anything, an *under*valuation of the pound;[4] but the British indexes remained more distorted by price and other controls than did the American. Lengthy delays in filling foreign orders for British goods further restricted the actual purchasing power of the pound. The countries of the outer Sterling Area were also running an increased dollar deficit. British surpluses in trade with some parts of the world were not convertible to meet the dollar deficit. On the contrary, the aftermath of war left much of the world still dependent on American supplies and anxious to snatch at any source of dollars. Knowing the date when convertibility would become effective, foreigners had an incentive to postpone their sterling receipts until then. A number of countries tightened currency or trade restrictions to increase their net earnings of newly convertible sterling. The segregation of currently earned sterling from old and supposedly inconvertible sterling proved far from airtight.

In short, foreigners leapt at the chance to convert. Britain lost about $1 billion worth of gold and dollars before abandoning convertibility, with American consent, on August 20. These losses contributed to the unexpectedly early exhaustion of the American loan in March 1948.[5]

The failure of 1947 colored British attitudes for several years afterward, seeming to demonstrate more than ever the necessity for controls. Actually, what had failed was an exchange-rate-stabilization loan, for this is what the American financing of the supposedly temporary British payments disequilibrium amounted to. American aid might well have proved more constructive if it had been granted without the conditions that bedeviled the 1946 loan.

After convertibility failed, British exchange-control regulations reverted to the earlier type. What a holder of sterling could do with it depended not only on whether he lived in or out of the United Kingdom or Sterling Area but also on *where* he lived in the outside world. *American-account countries* included the United States and its dependencies, Canada, the Philippines, and several countries in northern Latin America. Residents of this "dollar area" could transfer sterling elsewhere with little or no restriction and could sell it for dollars at the official rate. Without these privileges, they would probably have refused to accept sterling altogether. In dealing with other nonsterling countries, the British authorities aimed in general to avoid gold and dollar losses but to make sterling widely usable so it

would be an attractive currency to hold. With sterling no longer convertible for payments to dollar countries, a number of countries quit the *transferable-account* group. Its relatively few remaining members were countries that were willing to use and hold sterling as an international means of payment, whose transactions with one another and whose sterling receipts and payments could be expected to stay in reasonably near balance, and whose authorities were willing and able to administer the necessary controls. Their residents could use sterling for payments into the Sterling Area and could transfer it for current purposes to residents of other transferable-account countries. More countries now fell into the *bilateral* classification, however, than into any other. With some exceptions, residents of a bilateral country could use their sterling freely only for payments to their fellow countrymen or to Sterling Area residents; transfers elsewhere required special administrative permission. For a small group of *unclassified countries*, the British authorities dealt with each proposed transfer as the question arose.

Membership in the transferable and bilateral groups changed from time to time. The progressive simplification of Britain's postwar exchange controls is largely a story of reclassification of bilateral countries into the transferable group. As will be mentioned later, practically all bilateral accounts became transferable in March 1954; and in December 1958, the transferable and American-account classifications merged.

2. Quoted in Bell, *op. cit.*, p. 53.

3. W. M. Scammell, *International Monetary Policy*, 1st ed., London: Macmillan, 1957, p. 425; Raymond F. Mikesell, *Foreign Exchange in the Postwar World*, New York: Twentieth Century Fund, 1954, pp. 43–44.

4. Cf. Lloyd A. Metzler, "Exchange Rates and the International Monetary Fund," *International Monetary Policies*, Postwar Economic Studies, No. 7, Washington: Board of Governors of the Federal Reserve System, 1947, pp. 24–27, 38–41, 44–45.

5. The debt has not been forgiven; the British are still repaying it in the prescribed installments.

Crisis and devaluation in 1949

For several weeks early in 1948, after Britain had used up the American loan and until Marshall Plan dollars became available, Sterling Area reserves were without American support. The drain on them was cut during the year, however, by import restrictions and favorable export trends. The improved strength of sterling in world financial centers and the reduced discount on British banknotes in the Swiss and American markets seemed to justify optimism in early 1949. But the position weakened that spring. American exports to the Sterling Area, financed in part by the Marshall Plan, were holding up; but the value of American imports from the Area was being cut in half. A recession had begun in the United States late in 1948 and was still under way. American manufacturers were drawing down their raw-material inventories and currently buying less abroad. Prices of primary products exported by the overseas Sterling Area were softening. With domestic expenditures booming and their international current accounts in deficit, several overseas sterling countries were using their sterling balances to draw on the dollar pool in London. The main trouble did not lie in the United Kingdom itself, since its balance of payments was in approximate overall equilibrium in the year and a half before mid-1949. Surpluses earned in soft currencies or in old sterling balances were not usable, however, to cover a continuing dollar deficit.

As the year went on, sterling weakened further under speculative pressure.[6] Americans paid for larger and larger fractions of their imports from the Sterling Area with "cheap sterling," consisting of sterling bank accounts held by nonresidents of the Sterling Area and supposedly not convertible into dollars. Holders anxious enough for dollars to accept less than the official rate could sell their sterling through "commodity-shunting" or "switch" arrangements. Wool, rubber and other Sterling Area commodities ostensibly destined for nondollar countries could be paid for in non-American-account sterling, yet were in fact delivered to the United States. Sterling suffered in two ways. First, dollars that exports to the United States might otherwise have earned were sidetracked to countries holding supposedly inconvertible sterling. Second, the discounts on cheap sterling that made commodity-shunting attractive strengthened impressions that the

pound was definitely overvalued at $4.03.[7] Traders were aware that British exporters were having difficulty competing in price and especially in delivery dates and suspected that the official rate misrepresented relative production costs in Britain and the United States. Though this is not clear from price and wage indexes, speculation did seem to be feeding on something fundamental.

As rumors of devaluation spread, traders sought to shift their borrowing to London in order to owe sterling rather than dollars. Foreign buyers of goods from the Sterling Area delayed their purchases and payments, while importers in the Area hastened to buy and pay before dollars and dollar goods should cost more in sterling. U.S. merchandise imports from the entire Sterling Area fell from $364 million in the first quarter of 1949 to $283 million and $224 million in the second and third quarters, rebounding, after the devaluation, to $290 million in the fourth quarter. The ratio of U.S. imports to exports in commodity trade with the entire Area fell from 0.72 in the first quarter to 0.49 and 0.51 in the second and third before recovering to 0.74 in the fourth.[8]

Speculative influences on the timing even of ordinary trade thus show up in statistics despite at least two obscuring circumstances. First, devaluation and the resulting shift in expectations occurred while the third quarter still had almost two weeks to run. Second, a number of emergency measures were adopted in the summer of 1949, including tighter import controls designed to cut imports into the United Kingdom from the dollar area to three-fourths of their 1948 level. At a meeting in London in July, all of the Commonwealth finance ministers except the South African agreed to recommend similar measures to their own governments.

As late as September 6, Sir Stafford Cripps, the Chancellor of the Exchequer, made another one of his numerous denials that devaluation was impending, even though he must have had the step under very serious consideration by then and although American officials were confidentially urging it.[9] Cripps's denials failed to stop the speculative drain on London's gold and dollars. This drain, as well as the discounts quoted on banknote, transferable, and forward sterling, cumulatively intensified the distrust. By midyear the reserves were less than half as large as at the beginning of

1938, and less than one-fourth as large in real buying power, in view of the rise in American prices in the meanwhile. In the 11 weeks until September 18, the reserves fell nearly 20 percent further to $1340 million, or only about half the end-of-1946 level. The accelerating drain reached an annual rate of almost $1.4 billion. In the picturesque words of R. F. Harrod, "When some low-browed international financier, swirling the brandy around in his glass, uttered his profound thought, 'I don't believe the pound is worth four dollars', there was a run on the bank and all was over."[10]

On September 18, after consultations with the International Monetary Fund so scant as to be hardly more than mere notification, the British government announced a devaluation of the pound to $2.80. Its sharpness, 30.5 percent, came as a surprise. Twenty-three countries followed the British move within one week, and seven more followed later. In all, the wave of devaluations engulfed 31 countries (not counting colonies separately). The devaluing countries accounted for approximately two-thirds of all world trade and included the entire Sterling Area (except Pakistan, which staved off devaluation until August 1955), as well as Canada and most other countries of importance in world trade.[11] The chief currencies not devalued were the U.S. dollar and some Latin American currencies tied to it, the Swiss franc, the Curaçao guilder, and the currencies of Turkey, Brazil, Pakistan, Japan, and the Iron Curtain countries. In Western Europe, Ireland, the Netherlands, Greece, Iceland, Finland, and the Scandinavian countries, all devalued to about the same extent as Britain. (Finland's 30.5 percent devaluation came on the heels of a 15 percent devaluation in July, and Iceland's devaluation was followed in March 1950 by a further 43 percent devaluation.) Austria devalued by more than Britain (counting a further devaluation in 1950), and Belgium-Luxembourg, Germany, Italy, and France devalued by less.

These currency upheavals invite comparison with those of almost exactly 18 years before. (See pp. 342–344 and Bank for International Settlements, 20th *Annual Report*, pp. 148–149.) Both episodes fell within periods of postwar reconstruction. Both involved heavy bearish speculation. On both occasions, the depreciation of sterling touched off chain reactions of exchange-rate adjustment. But there were differences. The commodity price declines that preceded the 1931 episode were severe and general and had been going on for at least two years (and more for wheat and other grains); the price declines in 1949 were of short duration and chiefly affected primary products imported by the United States. The 1931 episode occurred while a worldwide depression was still growing worse. The mild American recession in 1949, on the other hand, was a mere interval in a still generally inflationary period, and an interval already coming to an end at the time.

6. Cf. Samuel I. Katz "Leads and Lags in Sterling Payments," *Review of Economics and Statistics*, XXXV, No. 1, February 1953, esp. pp. 79–80; BIS, 20th *Annual Report*, pp. 149–150.

7. Quotations on "cheap" sterling during the summer of 1949 varied from $2.80 to $3.20 according to the country of the holder. After April, British banknotes also weakened again on the Swiss and American markets, going to a discount of more than 30 percent by late summer. BIS, 20th *Annual Report*, p. 150 and graph on p. 149.

8. In 1950, by contrast, both U.S. imports from the Area and the import-export ratio rose from each quarter to the next. On both merchandise and goods-and-services accounts, U.S. transactions with the Sterling Area showed only a negligible surplus in the first quarter and moved into substantial deficit in the remainder of 1950. Exchange-rate expectations are of course not the sole explanation of these trade shifts; seasonal and business conditions (and Korea in 1950) also played a part. The figures are calculated from U.S. Department of Commerce, Office of Business Economics, *Balance of Payments Statistical Supplement*, rev. ed., Washington: Government Printing Office, 1963, pp. 94–95.

9. According to R. G. Hawtrey, *op. cit.*, p. 34, the decision to devalue was actually made at the end of August. Another British economist, speaking off the record nine years after the decision, dated it in July.

10. Roy F. Harrod, *The Pound Sterling*, Essays in International Finance, No. 13, Princeton, N.J.: Princeton University, International Finance Section, 1952, p. 28.

11. Federal Reserve Bank of New York, *Annual Report* for 1949, pp. 32, 36.

Finally, the chain reaction of devaluations ran its course more quickly on the later occasion.

Recovery after the devaluation

How effective were the 1949 devaluations? An answer would require knowing how things would have turned out otherwise. In a limited sense, though, the devaluations did work; they met a problem of speculation that would hardly have responded to any other treatment. The controls already in effect were proving inadequate, and additional controls would have had to be drastic and far-reaching indeed to cope with leads and lags and other ways of speculating through legitimate commercial transactions. It is only fair, however, to record the contrary judgment of the leading critic of the decisions of 1949. According to Sir Roy Harrod, the British devaluation was "a disaster of the first magnitude"; it would have been better to freeze every nonresident sterling balance and pay gold out of the reserve down to the last penny; it would have been better to adopt a firm policy of deflation while repudiating any thought of devaluation.[12]

In any case, the gold and dollar drain did stop promptly. Between September 18 and September 30, the British reserves rose from $1340 million to $1425 million; and by the end of the year, they were 26 percent above the September 18 level. They kept on growing throughout 1950 and in mid-1951 reached almost triple the predevaluation low. The total gold and dollar holdings of countries other than the United States rose from $14.7 billion at the end of September 1949 to $18.2 billion a year later. A net inflow of $341 million of gold into the United States during the first three quarters of 1949 gave way to a net outflow of $150 million in the fourth quarter and another net outflow of $1709 in 1950. Between the first half of 1949 and the first half of 1950, the annual rate of current-account surplus in the United States balance of payments fell from $3.7 billion to $1.9 billion with the OEEC countries and from $7.6 billion to $3 billion with the entire world. After the devaluations, the major European countries enjoyed a "spectacular improvement" in their position.[13] Britain's net trade position within Europe shifted from monthly deficits of over $150 million just before the devaluation to monthly surpluses of from $20 to $90 million in late 1949 and the first half of

1950. Britain agreed to stop receiving Marshall Plan aid at the end of 1950, two years ahead of schedule.

So far, this account of what happened is probably too favorable. In part, the improvements were due to reversal of speculative positions, including resumption of delayed American purchases from the Sterling Area. Imports into the Sterling Area remained subject to the controls that had been tightened in the months before the devaluation. Britain's anti-inflationary measures presumably accomplished some of the intended restraint on imports. Reconstruction in Europe continued boosting the output available for use at home and for export. A business revival had gotten under way in the United States toward the end of 1949. Even before the Korean War broke out in June 1950, but especially afterwards, world demand was strengthening; the dollar prices of most American raw-material imports rebounded to and eventually above their predevaluation levels. (Largely reflecting these price trends, the terms of trade of the United States worsened by about 26 percent between August 1949 and the middle of 1951, while the British terms of trade worsened by about 33 percent.)[14]

These are only some of the influences that almost hopelessly blur a view of how sensitively the flows of trade responded to the price adjustments accomplished by the devaluations. Between the first half of 1949 and the first half of 1950, the physical volume of European exports to the United States did apparently rise by just about enough to offset their reduced dollar prices; the aggregate dollar value of European exports to other markets in the Western Hemisphere actually rose about 10 percent. The European countries that devalued by 20 percent or more generally increased their shares of overseas markets, while countries devaluing little or not at all suffered relative losses in export markets. The Economic Commission for Europe ventured the conclusion that devaluation did indeed help improve the current-account balances of devaluing countries.[15]

The effect on imports is particularly hard to gauge because of the tariffs and controls already in effect and tightened in mid-1949. Even a highly price-sensitive shrinkage in the volume of *frustrated desires* to import would hardly show up in the statistics. On the export side, also, price was by no means the only determinant of trade volume. Britain was still apparently experiencing over-employment and latent or suppressed inflation; with some industries handicapped less by uncompetitive prices than by difficulties in obtaining factors of production and in making sufficiently rapid deliveries, a failure of devaluation to make exports boom would hardly be surprising.[16] But by the same token, it would hardly teach any general lesson about the effectiveness of devaluation. Furthermore, the worldwide prevalence of controls explicitly *designed* to hamper the response of trade to price and profit incentives was bound to obscure how price-sensitive trade might be in a more liberal world. Simultaneous devaluation by so many countries in 1949 also made estimating the price sensitivity of any particular country's trade especially difficult.

Although they could not give due weight to the various specific historical influences at work reinforcing and neutralizing one another and obscuring the effects of devaluation, at least two prominent British economists (Harrod and Hawtrey) did imply that the "perverse-elasticities" case characterized the British balance of payments in 1949, at least in the short run.[17] A "colossal and unnatural rise in the volume of exports" strained Britain's manufacturing capacity, but to no avail. The devaluation of their prices in foreign currency shrank the total import-buying capacity of British exports, especially on the assumption that the uptrend of export volume would have continued even without the devaluation.[18] It is true that the dollar value of British exports to the dollar area rose not only above the depressed level of 1949 but also above the level of 1948. On the other hand, the physical volume of total British exports, after rising in 1950, slumped slightly again in 1951–1953.

Actually, the perverse-elasticities interpretation seems a strained one in the absence of any balance-of-payments deterioration and in view of the striking improvement in Britain's gold and dollar reserves.

Another of Harrod's objections to the devaluation was that, through import prices, it unleashed an inflationary cost-push on the British economy whose effects stretched out over several years. This may be true, but the question remains whether an alternative policy of relying on still stricter exchange and import controls could have warded off inflation. The latent or suppressed inflation already existing (and evidenced, perhaps, by delays in filling orders) should not be forgotten.

The crisis of 1951–1952

The Korean War boom in the raw-material exports of Sterling Area countries benefited the postdevaluation position of sterling so much that rumors of its impending upward revaluation (as well as revaluation of the Danish and Swedish crowns) circulated in the winter and spring of 1950–1951. Merchants now tended speculatively to delay receipts and hasten payments due in sterling. Traders outside the Sterling Area tended to accumulate sterling in anticipation of commercial needs.[19]

The bullish rumors ceased as the pound rather suddenly came under renewed pressure. The speculative inflow of funds in the first half of 1951 gave way to an apparently even larger outflow in the second half. The London gold-

12. Harrod, *op. cit.*, pp. 28–29; *Policy against Inflation*, New York: St. Martin's Press, 1958, p. 151.

13. Robert Triffin, *Europe and the Money Muddle*, New Haven: Yale University Press, 1957, p. 160.

14. Mikesell, *op. cit.*, pp. 146–151.

15. *Ibid.*, pp. 147–148, citing J. J. Polak in IMF *Staff Papers*, September 1951, and *Economic Survey of Europe in 1950*.

16. For this view, see Hawtrey, *op. cit.*, pp. 30–32, 44; Harrod, *The Pound Sterling*, p. 26, and Harrod, *Policy against Inflation*, p. 132. Even in such a situation, however, a plausible if not conclusive case could be made for devaluation. Devaluation might increase the local-currency prices of export goods, thereby bidding some of them away from home consumers and also making it possible for the export trades to bid additional factors of production away from production for the home market. Devaluation might be part of a process of opening up a suppressed inflation and correcting the disequilibrium pattern of prices and apparent real incomes that had been accounting for "absorption" in excess of the national means. Compare Chapter 8 above.

17. Harrod, *The Pound Sterling*, pp. 30, 34; Harrod, *Policy against Inflation*, pp. 147–148; Hawtrey, *op. cit.*, p. 32.

18. Harrod, *The Pound Sterling*, p. 29.

19. BIS, 21st *Annual Report*, pp. 128, 168, and 22nd *Annual Report*, p. 24.

and-dollar pool fell by 40 percent between midyear and the end of 1951. The high prices and incomes previously received by Sterling Area exporters of primary products were having their full impact on imports only after some delay. Further time elapsed before goods ordered abroad were delivered and had to be paid for. Import payments thus peaked after the export boom had already begun to subside. The increased imports during 1951 apparently went mostly for additional private consumption, but increased investment in economic development was also important. To meet growing external deficits, country after country in the overseas Sterling Area drew on the London dollar pool. In the spring of 1952, several overseas sterling countries even developed a sterling shortage and for the first time since the war resorted to significant restrictions on imports priced in sterling.[20]

The United Kingdom was having troubles of its own. Its worsened payments position with the United States and EPU countries in 1951 was not fully offset by its shift from deficit in the first half of the year to surplus in the second in trade with the outer Sterling Area. For 1951 as a whole, import expenditure was 49 percent above the year before, while export value rose only 19 percent. The surge of imports went partly to replenish—and at increased prices—the business inventories run down during 1950, when the tightened import restrictions of 1949 were still in effect. Strategic stockpiling and an expanded rearmament program also absorbed imports. A steel shortage accompanying the defense program and a recession in world textile demand hampered exports. The invisible accounts suffered from the nationalization of British oil properties in Iran, a slump in the profits of companies engaged in the overseas production of commodities whose prices were now receding, an increase in overseas military expenditures, and the start of repayments on the American and Canadian loans. At home, shortages of steel, coal, and skilled manpower dramatized an inflationary atmosphere that affected business decisions. Speculative changes in the timing of import and export payments made matters worse.

Amidst the crisis, the Labor government lost the elections of October 1951. The next month the new Conservative government took several steps toward ending the cheap-money era that had lasted since 1932: it changed Bank rate for the first time since October 1939

by raising it from 2 to 2½ percent, discontinued pegging of the Treasury bill rate at about ½ percent, successfully converted about £1 billion of treasury bills into somewhat longer securities, tightened restrictions on installment buying, and maintained and intensified qualitative controls over new security issues and bank loans. The Chancellor of the Exchequer described a further increase of Bank rate to 4 percent in March 1952 as "an essential part of our campaign to fortify the currency" and demonstrate readiness to take "whatever firm measures may be necessary, however unwelcome they may be."[21]

At an emergency session in London late in 1951, the Commonwealth finance ministers had already agreed to tighten controls again on imports from the dollar area and to backslide from trade liberalization under the OEEC Code. A 25 percent cut in dollar imports was generally taken as a target. But until tight money and the tightened import controls took hold, the reserves continued falling, reaching a level in mid-1952 some 56 percent below that of just one year before.

The crisis blew over in 1952 for several reasons. The 4 percent Bank rate and an end to rumors of a convertible floating pound had a healthy effect on capital movements. Some elements of the crisis had been inherently temporary, such as the rebuilding of depleted inventories and the speculation through leads and lags. Basically, current-account transactions overshadowed short-term capital movements; the crisis had been largely a gigantic fluctuation in the current account of both the United Kingdom and the outer Sterling Area. A dollar deficit in the first half of 1952 gave way to a dollar surplus in the first half of 1953. The reserves rose in the last quarter of 1952 and throughout 1953 and the first half of 1954.

The simplification of controls

Even at the worst of the crisis, around the turn of the year 1951–1952, discussions with the U.S. Treasury and the IMF were exploring how sterling might eventually be made fully convertible. One step, effective in December 1951, was to allow banks to deal in foreign exchange as principals and to hold limited foreign balances for the purpose. (From 1939 until then, banks had dealt only as agents for the Bank of England.) Even now, the banks could buy foreign exchange only for permitted payments to the country concerned; and arbitrage remained forbidden until introduction of the multilateral scheme of May 1953.

Sterling's strength during 1953 permitted removing some domestic and import controls, as well as most of the restrictions imposed in March 1952 on loans to traders outside the Sterling Area. Sterling fared well even during the 1953–1954 business recession in the United States: easy money there created an interest-rate differential that apparently drew funds to London.

A more notable simplification in British controls came early in 1954. Until then, sterling payments had been largely bilateral (though decreasingly so as time went on; already the Bank of England was usually granting requests for transfers among important bilateral accounts). Officially, the transferable-account group included only the monetary areas of 18 countries agreeing to accept sterling payments for current sales to other transferable-account countries and the Sterling Area and agreeing to permit sterling transfers for current transactions only. Actually, enforcement languished. Transferable sterling changed hands readily and was even salable for dollars on active free markets in New York, Zurich, and other centers. By March 1954 it was quoted at a discount of only about 1 percent. The British authorities now added all bilateral-account countries, with three minor exceptions, to the transferable group. From now on someone living almost anywhere outside the Sterling Area could convert currently earned sterling at the official rate into almost any other currency except dollars. The new regulations even recognized the futility of trying to distinguish between current and capital transactions in transferable sterling. Facilities for holding it were extended to individuals and corporations as well as banks. Sterling's major classes were reduced to three: accounts belonging to Sterling Area residents, "American accounts" (belonging to residents of the dollar area, including Canadians), and the newly liberalized transferable accounts. (In addition there remained the minor category of "security sterling," consisting mostly of funds derived from legacies, sales of capital assets, and the like.) The only important simplification not yet undertaken was official convertibility of resident and transferable sterling into dollars.

A new minor category, "registered sterling," was created when the London gold market reopened in March 1954, after being closed or all but closed since 1939. Persons living outside the sterling and dollar areas could obtain registered sterling in exchange for gold or dollars and use it to buy gold or dollars or to make payment into almost any other type of sterling account. Sterling Area residents could buy gold only if they held special licenses as traders or industrial users. All gold transactions had to take place through a small number of authorized dealers (banks and specialist bullion firms).

In the second half of 1954 and at the beginning of 1955, a combination of fundamental and expectational factors weakened the sterling exchange rate and widened the discount on transferable sterling to 2 or 3 percent. In earlier years, such a discount would have been too small to make commodity shunting worthwhile; but since the simplifications of March 1954 had made the transferable-sterling market broader and more dependable, shunting developed again, especially in tin, and deprived the official reserves of some dollar proceeds of Sterling Area exports.

Partly to stop these transactions, the Exchange Equalization Account began, in February 1955, to support transferable sterling on its unofficial markets abroad.[22] It is not certain whether this support cost the official reserves fewer dollars than the discouragement of commodity shunting saved. Anyway, the discount was held to within about 1½ percent at most from then on except for a brief period during the Suez crisis of 1956. In fact, though unofficially, the British authorities were making nonresident sterling convertible into dollars at no more than a slight discount from the rate on American-account sterling. So important was this decision that Harrod dates the postwar

20. Cf. BIS, 22nd *Annual Report*, p. 24; Samuel I. Katz, "Sterling's Recurring Postwar Payments Crises," *Journal of Political Economy*, LXIII, No. 3, June 1955, esp. pp. 221–224; and figures in *International Financial Statistics*.

21. BIS, 22nd *Annual Report*, p. 28.

22. "Shunting could not in practice be prevented by controls; it could only be discouraged by making it unprofitable." Tew, *op. cit.*, p. 147.

restoration of *de facto* sterling convertibility in late February 1955.[23]

Problems of 1955 and 1956

Despite Bank-rate increases from 3 to 3½ percent on January 27 and to 4½ percent on February 24, as well as tighter controls on installment buying, sterling's recovery in early 1955 was short-lived. Unemployment was down and unfilled vacancies up in the United Kingdom, investment was booming, and prices were rising again after a pause. Some overseas sterling countries were also feeling inflationary strains. Rising imports were eating into the gold and dollar reserves. Wage increases during the early months of 1955, an income-tax cut in the April budget, retirement pension increases, uncertainty preceding the elections in May, dock and rail strikes in May and June, and discouraging trade figures for June and July— all helped sap confidence in sterling. Rumors circulated concerning the eventual end of the European Payments Union and possibilities that the pound would be allowed either to "float" or to depreciate within widened support limits. During the third quarter of the year, until the Chancellor of the Exchequer scotched these rumors at the Istanbul meeting of the International Monetary Fund in September, speculation joined with current-account deficits in causing heavy reserve losses. Pressure on the banks during the summer to cut their lending, government budget adjustments in October 1955 and February 1956, and a further rise of Bank rate to 5½ percent in February helped defend sterling. The strain never reached true crisis proportions.

Disinflationary domestic policies, reinforced in the April 1956 budget, helped shrink Britain's current-account deficit with nonsterling countries and expand her surplus with the outer Sterling Area. American-account sterling fluctuated above par during the winter and spring, the discount on transferable sterling remained within 1 percent, and the reserves grew. Increasingly high interest rates in Germany began attracting funds, however. These transfers grew as rumors of an upward revaluation of the mark fed on the German Economics Minister's proposal for "a discussion of the problem of exchange rate parities" at the July 1956 meeting of the OEEC.

Sterling's intra-European troubles developed into something more general after Egypt seized the Suez Canal on July 26. The resulting need for heavier dollar outlays on imports showed how all European countries were vulnerable together. The already weakening rate on American-account sterling now fell close to the $2.78 limit, requiring official support that depleted the reserves by $272 million during the last five months of the year. Without special receipts of $177 million in September from sale of the Trinidad Oil Company to American interests and of $561.5 million in December from the International Monetary Fund, the reserve loss would have amounted to $1010 million in these five months (as a matter of mere arithmetic, not of cause and effect). The net loss for the entire year 1956 would have been $725 million, or slightly more than one-third of the reserves held in January. The deterioration occurred although the United Kingdom continued to run an overall surplus on current account. A number of countries, notably India and Japan, were drawing on their sterling balances. The speculative outflow of funds by way of leads and lags was particularly heavy after fighting broke out at Suez in October, since the closing of the Canal and the resulting switch in sources of imported oil threatened payments problems.

The British finally restored confidence in December by statements of determination to maintain sterling's $2.80 parity and by recourse to international assistance. The International Monetary Fund provided not only the cash already mentioned but also a standby credit for a further $738.5 million. The United States added a $500 million line of credit from the Export-Import Bank and waived the December interest payment due on the loan of 1946. At the end of the year, American-account, transferable, forward, and banknote sterling all were recovering from several months of weak quotations; and the reserve drain stopped early in 1957, permitting a cut of Bank rate to 5 percent in February. No tightening of controls had proved necessary. The International Monetary Fund had successfully enabled a member to ride out a temporary and nonfundamental crisis; on this occasion, at least, it carried out the intentions of the Bretton Woods conferees.

The 1957 crisis and 1958 recovery

Even after the Suez crisis blew over, confidence in sterling suffered from strikes and strike threats in February and March and from worry that prices and wages had a stronger upward tendency in Britain than in competing countries. Long-term capital still escaped through gaps in Sterling Area controls. The British balance of payments continued running a current-account surplus, however, both globally and with the United States; and the overseas sterling countries more than met their current deficit with the United States by dollars received on capital account.

The next crisis was therefore not due to any obvious fundamental disequilibrium. On the contrary, it illustrates the especial vulnerability of a currency widely used in international transactions and widely held by private parties. Such a currency "is prone to speculation not only *against* its own parity, but also *in favour of* other currencies' parities."[24] The Rome Treaty for a European Common Market had been signed in March 1957, and negotiations were pending for a Free Trade Area of broader membership. The opinion grew that properly implementing these projects would call for adjusting exchange rates, in particular those of the reputedly overvalued French franc and undervalued German mark. Yet the Germans, whose overall trade surplus masked a heavy deficit with the dollar area, were reluctant to appreciate against the dollar. Any appreciation of the mark would probably have to be *relative* only, by way of a devaluation of sterling and a still sharper devaluation of the franc. A *de facto* devaluation of the franc in August and the persistence of Germany's trade surplus and foreign-exchange accumulations sharpened expectations. Discussions of exchange-rate policy were in prospect at the International Monetary Fund meeting in Washington in September and the OEEC meeting in Paris in October. Speculative transfers became heavy. The International Monetary Fund "estimated that outflows of this kind from official reserves in the third quarter of 1957 were of the order of $600–$700 million in the United Kingdom, and of about $175 million in the Netherlands; the inflow into Germany and into the United States may have amounted to $500 million in each case."[25] The German representative at the IMF meeting stated that more than half of the increase in Germany's reserves during the first eight months of 1957 had resulted from speculative operations. Much of the shift in short-term funds operated through the familiar commercial leads and lags.

Speculative opinion in the summer of 1957 was strikingly reflected in abnormally large spreads between spot and forward rates of exchange. Although German banks were forbidden to pay interest on foreigners' deposits (with a few exceptions not relevant here), the spread became so large at one time that by buying marks spot and selling them forward, an English bank, for example, could obtain a *de facto* interest rate of no less than 17 percent a year. A German firm borrowing at 8 percent in London could similarly earn 9 percent (17 minus 8) by thus going into debt. Another sign of the low confidence in sterling was the drop in the banknote quotation from almost $2.80 in July down almost to $2.56 in September.

At the worst point of the crisis, the official British gold and dollar reserves fell to about $1850 million, 22 percent below the level of just three months before. The loss attained a rate that would have spelled total exhaustion in a matter of months—and the prospect of exhaustion would doubtless have further accelerated withdrawals.[26]

As early as July the British authorities tightened exchange controls by forbidding residents of the United Kingdom to buy foreign securities even from residents of other Sterling Area countries without express permission. This departure from freedom of payments within the Area seemed necessary to check capital outflows operating through free markets in some parts of it, such as Kuwait, where dollar securities could be bought with resident

23. *The Pound Sterling, 1951–1958*, Essays in International Finance, No. 30, Princeton, N.J.: Princeton University, 1958, p. 27; *Policy against Inflation*, New York: St. Martin's Press, 1958, p. 174.

24. Benjamin J. Cohen, *The Future of Sterling as an International Currency*, New York: St. Martin's Press, 1971, pp. 158–159. Cohen goes on to explain how sterling in 1957 suffered from a "backlash" of bullish speculation on the mark.

25. IMF, 1958 *Annual Report*, p. 48.

26. Lionel Robbins, "Thoughts on the Crisis," *Lloyds Bank Review*, April 1958, n.s., No. 48, pp. 1–26, esp. p. 9.

sterling.[27] In August and September, to limit the availability of funds for speculation, the authorities put new restrictions on granting sterling credits to nonresidents. (British banks then resorted to the Eurodollar market—see page 434—and offered dollar credits in place of the prohibited sterling credits.)

The main response to the crisis came in domestic financial policy. Although the current account of the balance of payments posed no immediate danger, foreigners and residents alike were worrying that Britain "had lost control over the internal value of her money . . . in the summer there were times when even the British Government found increasing difficulty in marketing its longer-term securities."[28] The government announced a pause in the upward trend of investment by central and local authorities and nationalized industries and asked banks to hold loans to the level of the year before. On September 19 the Bank of England raised its discount rate by two points to the highest level since 1921, pushing up the entire structure of money rates along with it. Instead of being seen as "panic action," an interpretation the governor of the Bank later admitted fearing, the "rather sensational" 7 percent Bank rate symbolized a determined internal policy.[29]

Solemn British and German promises at the September IMF meeting, together with cancellation of the OEEC meeting scheduled for October, helped restore confidence in existing exchange parities. Britain drew $250 million in October under the line of credit granted by the Export-Import Bank the previous December and renewed her standby arrangement with the International Monetary Fund. Private short-term capital began returning to England. Gold and foreign-exchange reserves rose by September 1958 to 69 percent above the crisis level of one year before.

The external recovery was not without domestic cost. By the summer of 1958 unemployment and excess capacity, slight by prewar but heavy by postwar standards, were breeding some fear of an actual recession. Bank rate, already lowered in three steps down to the pre-crisis level of 5 percent by June, was further lowered to 4½ and then 4 percent before the end of the year. At the beginning of July the ceiling on bank advances imposed during the crisis was removed, as were installment-purchase restrictions soon afterwards. When the control of the Capital Issues Committee for almost all domestic borrowing was abolished, the banks became free, for the first time since before the war, to make whatever domestic loans they saw fit, subject only to the overall restriction of their cash and liquidity ratios.[30]

During 1958 the British current-account surplus grew with sterling and nonsterling countries alike. Although a continuing fall in primary commodity prices hit the overseas sterling countries, gold production and capital inflows more than covered their deficits with the outside world and so shielded the London reserve pool. Britain and other European countries benefited from improved terms of trade. In December Britain was able to join the other major European countries in establishing nonresident currency convertibility. From then on holders of sterling in any country, and not just members of the Sterling Area, had ready access to London's dollar reserves. One of the chief *raisons d'être* of the Area—members' discrimination in each other's favor in wielding balance-of-payments controls—thus disappeared.[31]

Early experience after convertibility

In 1959 British domestic economic activity continued recovering from the slowdown of the year before, and imports rose relative to exports. In contrast to their growth the year before, the gold and foreign-exchange reserves fell, though by less than the amount of debt repayment and additional gold subscription to the International Monetary Fund.

The sharply shrunken current-account surplus of 1959 gave way in 1960 to the largest deficit in nine years. Imports were responding to further trade liberalization of the year before, strong domestic economic activity, and further rebuilding of depleted inventories. Export growth remained disappointing. The trade balance worsened particularly in transactions with the United States. Net invisible earnings suffered from more competitive foreign shipping, greater foreign travel by Britons, larger interest payments on foreign funds in Britain, and rising government outlays abroad for aid and defense. The net outflow of private and official long-term capital, while smaller than the year before, continued above $500 million.

Paradoxically, and even despite accelerated repayment of debt to the IMF, the official gold and foreign-exchange reserves *rose* by 18 percent in 1960. Under the circumstances, this did not indicate an improvement in overall net external liquidity. Overseas sterling countries drew upon their sterling reserves to finance adverse balances of payments of their own, but

U.K. sterling liabilities to nonsterling countries rose by considerably more than did the gold and foreign-exchange reserves. An inflow of short-term capital from Continental Europe and North America, partly recorded and partly concealed in "errors and omissions," was masking the more basic payments deterioration. Suggested explanations include an excess of British over foreign money-market interest rates, speculative pressure against the dollar in the autumn, and German and Swiss resistance to inflows of funds (mainly from the United States).

The interest-rate differentials reflected British policy. Beginning early in 1960, prospects of excessive domestic demand, as well as the basic balance-of-payments situation, had prompted monetary restraint. Bank rate went up from 4 to 5 percent in January and to 6 percent in June. Installment-credit controls came back in April. Requirements for special deposits at the Bank of England (rather like reserve requirements) were imposed on the commercial banks in April and raised in June. Long- and short-term interest rates were allowed to rise. Whether or not as a result of these measures, growth of industrial production did pause after the first quarter of 1960. Bank rate cuts to 5½ percent in October and 5 percent in December, following interest-rate reductions in the United States, meant no reversal of generally tight policy; the British authorities had become concerned over a possibly excessive interest-motivated inflow of short-term funds.

Early in 1961, seeking other measures to affect demand besides interest-rate manipulation, the authorities relaxed consumer credit terms and encouraged easier bank credit for exports. The expansion of bank lending in the first half of the year occurred only at the expense of a further decline in the banks' general liquidity position. The budget of April scheduled a smaller overall government deficit than in recent years and authorized the Treasury to vary the main customs, excise, and purchase taxes within limits, as well as a surcharge on employers similar to a payroll tax.

Deficits on current plus long-term capital account persisted in the first half of 1961. Narrowing of the interest differential in favor of London and abatement of the speculative pressure experienced by the dollar late in 1960 contributed to reversing the earlier inflow of short-term funds. The British exchange rate was weakening even before revaluation of the German mark in March touched off bearish-

ness on sterling. (See Chapter 24.) During the first week or so after this event, support of sterling on the exchanges cost an amount widely estimated at nearly $300 million, or nearly 10 percent of the total British reserves. (The reported reserve drop of only $174 million for the entire month of March understates the extent of hot-money movements and support operations, since Continental central banks provided much of the support by acquiring and holding on to sterling.)[32] Announcement of

27. The "Kuwait gap" had been troublesome for years. To keep the oil-rich Persian Gulf sheikdom in the Sterling Area, Britain tolerated its virtual lack of payments restrictions; Kuwaitis could use their abundant foreign-exchange earnings as they wished. As residents of the Sterling Area, they could also sell securities they owned to residents of the United Kingdom. Arbitrageurs profited by the resale in London of sterling securities bought in New York at a discount roughly in line with the discount on security sterling. Kuwaiti arbitrageurs also bought dollar securities in New York and resold them in London at the prevailing premium. By liquidating blocked sterling balances in London and adding to private British holdings of dollar securities, these transactions diverted foreign exchange from the official reserves. Under the new restrictions of July 1957, the arbitrageurs could operate only in sterling securities.

28. Quoted from the *First Report* of the Cohen Council (1958), p. 34, in Samuel I. Katz, *Sterling Speculation and European Convertibility: 1955–1958*, Essays in International Finance, No. 37, Princeton, N.J.: Princeton University, 1961, p. 20.

29. Cf. Paul Einzig, *A Dynamic Theory of Forward Exchange*, New York: St. Martin's Press, 1961, p. 517. Despite appearances in retrospect, says Einzig, speculators were not mistaken at the time in being bearish on sterling, given the financial policy prevailing before their very attack forced action to slow down wage inflation. Scott, *op. cit.*, p. 223, expresses more skepticism about the deflationary measures.

30. Morgan in Feavearyear, *op. cit.*, p. 412.

31. "Twilight of the Sterling Area," Bank of Nova Scotia, *Monthly Review*, December 1972, p. 2. Cf. Cohen, *op. cit.*, pp. 84–86.

32. *Business Week*, 18 March 1961, p. 31; *Wall Street Journal*, 6 April 1961, p. 2; *The Economist*, London, 6 May 1961, p. 572.

cooperation among central banks, together with denial of any intention to devalue sterling and Swiss, French, and Italian denials of any intention to revalue their currencies, helped ease and later reverse the pressure. Still, the British external difficulties were due to more than a speculative episode. Growth of industrial production was reviving and bank loans expanding. By midyear the unemployment percentage had sunk to a four-year low. Some prosperous manufacturers had grown rather indifferent to export markets. A slump in the foreign demand for British automobiles continued, and net receipts from invisibles remained at a low level. In the six months February through July, nearly one-fourth of the external reserves went to support sterling; and the loss would have been worse except for special receipts in connection with American Ford's purchase of the minority interest in its British subsidiary, special debt repayment from Germany, and massive aid from Continental central banks. Spot sterling continued weakening, and in mid-July the three-months forward quotation sank as low as $2.75½. By early summer Continental speculators on a devaluation were reportedly making heavy sales of sterling.

Britain responded with an austerity program. On July 25 the Chancellor of the Exchequer announced a 10 percent surcharge on customs and excise duties and purchase taxes, a 7 percent Bank rate and further increases in the banks' special-deposit requirements to squeeze credit and restrain inventory and other investment, refusal or postponement of wage increases in government and the nationalized industries, and efforts to stiffen resistance against wage increases in private industry as well. (A widespread opinion blamed wage increases in excess of productivity gains for several years of worsening in Britain's international competitive position.) The government would try to economize at home, hold the line on foreign-aid expenditures for a while, and reduce military spending abroad. Britain drew $1.5 billion in nine currencies from the International Monetary Fund and used some of the proceeds to repay Continental central banks for their earlier support. The Fund made another $500 million available under a standby arrangement. The Treasury toughened its policy on British business investment outside the Sterling Area and tried to improve the rate of remittance of overseas earnings.

Even before its details were announced, the program to defend sterling reversed speculative sentiment. Before the end of July, apparently, speculators began covering their short positions. Leads and lags went into reverse. The spot sterling rate strengthened 3 cents between July and late September. By the end of the year, reserve gains had permitted full repayment to the Continental central banks and partial repayment to the IMF. An improvement in the current account of the balance of payments continued in the first half of 1962.

Apparently worrying about an inflow of undependable hot money from the Continent and the United States, the authorities cut Bank rate to 6½ percent in October 1961. But the unwelcome inflow persisted and apparently even grew in haste to take advantage of high interest rates in London not expected to remain available much longer. Bank rate came down again in November and March and reached 4½ percent in April 1962.

By this time some relaxation of financial restraint seemed wise to help production resume growing after the pause that followed the crisis measures. The April 1962 budget remained cautious, however, so that the government deficit turned out to be smaller than the year before. Not until June were the banks' special deposit requirements reduced. Consumer credit restrictions were eased. Then, with the home economy still sluggish, the banks were entirely freed from their special deposit requirements and from earlier urgings to be restrained and selective in granting credit. Market rates of interest were allowed to sag further. Late 1962 and early 1963 brought cuts in the purchase tax, some other expansionary fiscal measures, and a 4 percent Bank rate.

The balance of payments seemed strong enough by mid-1962 to justify paying off the remaining debt owed to the IMF. Improvements in both basic transactions and short-term capital movements allowed 1962 as a whole to register an overall surplus, following the deficit of 1961. The current account showed strength again in the first half of 1963. Official intervention successfully resisted brief speculative pressure against the pound after General de Gaulle vetoed Common Market membership for Britain in January. Early March saw a second and stronger movement against sterling, following discussion in the press and elsewhere of the merits of devaluation. A number of Continental central banks supplemented vigorous official support. Around midyear, Britain's surplus on goods and services practically vanished. Over 1963 as a whole, the external reserves sagged some 5 percent, continuing a generally downward drift since 1960.

The doctrine of equilibrium through expansion

At budget time in April 1963, however, the balance of payments still seemed strong enough to warrant experimentation with a doctrine of "equilibrium through expansion," supported in both major parties.[33] Breaking away from the stop-and-go of the past, the new policy would seek steady growth.[34] (The government had become committed to a target rate of nearly 4 percent.) Fixed investment would be stressed. Gains in productivity, together with a policy of wage restraint, would make British industry more competitive and strengthen the balance of payments. A deficit in the short run could be financed—as an investment in achieving fuller use of the country's economic potential—by drawing on the external reserves or on credit.[35] In accordance with this theory, the 1963 budget liberalized investment allowances, cut personal taxes, raised government spending, and avowedly planned a government deficit for the first time since 1947. Over 1963 as a whole, the money supply rose 6.8 percent.

By early 1964 wages were rising strongly and the balance of payments was weakening. Publication of January figures showing an all-time record monthly deficit in merchandise trade fed speculation against the pound. In framing the April 1964 budget, policy-makers intended "not to give up the experiment with sustained growth, but to confine the expansion to the longer-term real growth potential and, thereby, also to limit the external deficit."[36] The election due later that year may have been a reason,[37] but probably not a dominant one, for the decision to keep restraint mild. Even some senior Treasury civil servants believed in the experiment, wanted to persuade industrialists that stop-and-go had been abandoned at last, and were anxious to avoid shocking business confidence by a large tax increase.[38]

The crisis of 1964

During most of 1964, overseas Sterling Area countries were building up their balances in London, which helped obscure the fundamen-

tally precarious payments position.[39] By the time the narrowly victorious Labour Party took office on October 16, however, another crisis was brewing. Within a day or two, it is thought, Prime Minister Harold Wilson made an "irrevocable" decision not to devalue. He apparently feared that devaluation would be politically disastrous for his party, would alienate the Americans, and would not remedy what he thought were the basically physical and structural problems of the British economy. From then on, devaluation became "The Unmentionable" in government circles.[40]

33. The Bank for International Settlements (1964–1965 *Annual Report*, p. 10) quotes both Conservative Chancellor of the Exchequer Reginald Maudling, presenting the 1963 budget, and Labor leader Harold Wilson, speaking in 1964, to show that the "basic policy formula of 1963 and 1964 was in accordance with a bipartisan economic model."

34. Perhaps in response to criticism of stop-and-go, money growth had already accelerated in mid-1962. Michael Keran in Federal Reserve Bank of St. Louis, *Review*, November 1967, p. 15.

35. BIS, 1964–1965, pp. 10, 52, 164–165; Samuel Brittan, *Steering the Economy*, Harmondsworth: Penguin Books, 1971, pp. 270–279.

36. BIS, 1964–1965, pp. 10–11.

37. Keran, *op. cit.*, p. 16.

38. Brittan, *Steering the Economy*, p. 283.

39. Bank of Nova Scotia, *Monthly Review*, August 1966, p. 1.

40. Brittan, *Steering the Economy*, p. 292; Henry Brandon, *In the Red*, Boston: Houghton Mifflin, 1967, chap. 4.
Views similar to Wilson's prevailed widely. In the autumn of 1964, "Almost everyone . . . agreed that, though an overload of home demand had aggravated the situation, the chief cause of the deficit was uncompetitiveness in some sense or other: the result of the painfully slow increase in Britain's productivity. Everyone agreed that the ultimate solution must be sought through changing attitudes of mind—'a national reawakening'—toward restrictive labour practices, pricing agreements, innovation and research, mobility, money incomes etc." Francis Cassell, *Gold or Credit?*, New York: Praeger, 1965, p. 9.

On October 26 the government issued a White Paper announcing partial rebates of indirect taxation to spur exports. More important, it announced a 15 percent import surcharge, roughly doubling the average tariff level. It applied to manufactured and semi-manufactured products, which accounted for about one-third of all merchandise imports in 1964.[41] Although the White Paper estimated an £800 million balance-of-payments deficit for 1964, it doubted that any generally excessive demand pressure required correction. The import surcharge would strengthen the external position without a return to stop-and-go. The idea was still in effect of keeping output and employment high and encouraging investment in order to improve productivity and competitiveness.[42] The hasty preparation of the White Paper, however, as well as its substance, tended to weaken confidence.[43]

The budget of November 11, implementing the proposals of the White Paper, also foreshadowed proposals for corporation and capital-gains taxes, to be revealed in full the following April. Furthermore, it increased welfare benefits. Damage to confidence showed up on both the securities and foreign-exchange markets.[44]

In a speech on Monday the 16th, Prime Minister Wilson said he would not shrink from further steps to strengthen sterling. However, an increase in Bank rate, widely expected for Thursday of that week, did not occur then. Following emergency discussions over the weekend, Bank rate was belatedly raised from 5 to 7 percent on November 23. (In the United States, the Federal Reserve responded by raising its discount rate.) Some critics thought that a Bank rate increase coming on Monday, rather than on a Thursday as usual, struck the market as a sign of panic. Others worried that the government was representing the Bank-rate increase to overseas and financial opinion as a sign of readiness to take harsh defensive measures while representing it at home as a technical measure "not intended to deflate demand." On Tuesday and Wednesday, sales of sterling were "massive and growing."[45] Speculation[46] was carrying the external reserves to a seven-year low. Around this time, during the first weeks of the Wilson administration, Economics Minister George Brown pinned the label "gnomes of Zürich" on the foreign speculators supposedly to blame for the troubles of sterling.[47]

On Wednesday the 25th the Bank of England announced that 11 central banks, together with the Bank for International Settlements and the U.S. Export-Import Bank, had put together $3 billion of short-term credits to supplement an existing $1 billion standby credit with the International Monetary Fund. This international rescue operation, the largest in history at the time, blunted but did not immediately defeat the largest speculative attack ever mounted against a currency. Spot sales of sterling dropped off, but forward selling of sterling remained heavy throughout December.[48] By this time the Bank of England was supporting sterling in the forward market to keep a sizable discount from dramatizing the speculation. (Forward support was repeated from time to time over almost three years.) Evidently the authorities had dropped their opposition, expressed to the Radcliffe Committee in June 1958, to pegging forward rates during a crisis.[49]

On December 2 Britain drew $1 billion from the IMF and with it paid off the bulk of the central-bank credits actually used. On December 8 the government dropped its pretense of not deflating, though with a mild first move. It warned the banks to "expect no relief from their liquidity troubles in the period of seasonal pressure in March, as it was official policy to slow down the rate of growth of bank advances."[50]

As 1965 began, pressure on sterling was still requiring substantial official support in the spot and forward markets. In mid-January, borrowings by local authorities in the Eurodollar market brought some improvement. Publication of better trade figures for December also helped. In February, as already in December, the government seemed to be making progress in lining up agreement on a program of wage restraint. On the other hand, announcement of the American balance-of-payments program in February was adverse to sterling.

By April 1965, it seemed evident that domestic demand had strengthened beyond the degree envisaged in the theory of external balance through expansion. The new budget tightened restrictions on foreign travel and modified rules affecting investment in foreign securities in a way analogous in substance, though not in form, to the U.S. Interest Equalization Tax.[51] It tightened restrictions on direct investment outside the Sterling Area. Moreover, the budget adjusted taxes and government spending in ways viewed as deflationary. It discontinued the tax-deductibility of business entertainment expenditures—except, rather comically, expenditures to entertain foreign buyers. Measures to check bank-credit expansion followed in May, and consumer-credit down-payment requirements were raised in June. Still, the equilibrium-through-expansion doctrine had not been clearly abandoned. According to one observer, the 1965 budget turned out deflationary enough to undermine the credibility of the economic-growth-rate target of 3.8 percent "but not nearly deflationary enough to eliminate the payments deficit at the $2.80 exchange rate."[52]

In a speech to the Economic Club of New York on April 14, Prime Minister Wilson expressed "unalterable determination to maintain the value of the pound" in a way that seemed to impress his audience deeply.[53] These and other assurances that large resources would be used if necessary to defend the exchange rate helped soothe the market.[54]

Gradual abandonment of the growth experiment

In mid-June, publication of bad trade figures touched off another burst of sterling sales. Still another followed in the second half of July. In 1965, as in 1949 and 1957, an increase in the payments deficit of the overseas Sterling Area with the outside world was contributing to the decline in Britain's reserves.[55]

A "mini-budget" of July 27 contained what was intended to be the Labor government's severest package of restrictions. Some central and local government investment projects were postponed, large private construction projects subjected to licensing, the maximum repayment period of consumer credit shortened, all direct investment outside the Sterling Area excluded from the official exchange market, and the types of foreign-exchange proceeds eligible for sale on the investment currency market further restricted.[56]

It took time for this package to improve the foreign-exchange market. Aggravated by figures on reserve losses in July, selling pressure on sterling seemed not to exhaust itself until around the end of August. Around the same time, it became known that the government was talking to unions and employers about compulsory early notification of intended wage and price increases.[57] On September 10 the Bank of England announced a new package of

41. Richard Cooper in Richard E. Caves and associates, *Britain's Economic Prospects,* Washington: Brookings Institution, 1968, p. 166. The surcharge was reduced to 10 percent in April 1965 (as announced the preceding February) and was eliminated in November 1966 (as announced the preceding May).

42. BIS, 1964–1965, p. 50; Keran, *op. cit.,* p. 16.

43. Brittan, *Steering the Economy,* pp. 296–297.

44. *Ibid.,* pp. 300–302.

45. *Ibid.,* p. 303, quoting the latter phrase from a Bank of England report.

46. "Speculation" may not be quite the right word for what was going on. In late 1964, as typically, according to Sir Roy Harrod, outright speculation was not the major factor in the crisis. Instead, merchants were covering their commercial commitments, and foreign investors were hedging their assets valued in sterling. "A great many people, thousands and thousands of small traders, get told by their bankers, you must get those currencies that you will be needing *at once,* whether in the forward or the spot market." The run on sterling in 1964 consisted of "covering forward commitments, and also, even more important, it was hedging the sterling assets. People who have sterling assets may not want to sell them outright, but as soon as there is a risk of devaluation, they say, we must hedge on our position; and that was done on a big scale" in November 1964. Harrod in American Enterprise Institute, *International Payments Problems,* Washington: 1966, pp. 184–185, quotation from p. 185.

47. Brandon, *op. cit.,* pp. 51, 53.

48. Brittan, *Steering the Economy,* p. 304, quoting the Bank of England.

49. John H. Kareken in Caves, *op. cit.,* p. 95. Large forward support is also mentioned in BIS, 1964–1965, p. 13.

50. Brittan, *Steering the Economy,* p. 304.

51. Cooper in Caves, *op. cit.,* p. 178; BIS, 1965–1966, p. 133.

52. Brittan, *Steering the Economy,* p. 305.

53. *Ibid.,* p. 307; Brandon, *op. cit.* p. 67.

54. BIS, 1964–1965, p. 15.

55. Cooper in Caves, *op. cit.,* p. 186.

56. Brittan, *Steering the Economy,* p. 309; Bank of Nova Scotia, *Monthly Review,* August 1966, p. 2; BIS, 1965–1966, pp. 135–136.

central-bank standby credits to replace the earlier one and to supplement a $1 billion line still available from the United States. Market sentiment responded decisively. Foreign-exchange technicians at the Bank of England and the Federal Reserve Bank of New York collaborated to squeeze speculators against the pound. Bearishness and adverse leads and lags shifted into reverse. Already, the current-account position had improved, and net long-term capital outflows were smaller than the year before. By the end of September the spot pound was comfortably above par on the dollar for the first time since early 1963. The forward discount shrank, turning covered interest arbitrage margins in favor of London. Between September and February, the Bank of England repaid earlier drawings on short-term credits, reduced its forward-exchange commitments, and gained reserves. Apart from some seasonal weakness near the end of the year, sterling remained firm during the last quarter of 1965 and in early 1966.[58]

Sterling was enjoying what soon proved to be a "false dawn." The encouraging trade figures would turn out attributable to unsustainably rapid growth of world trade and to random fluctuations. The measures taken in 1965 had not been deflationary enough to raise unemployment, and Labor increased its majority in the election of March 31, 1966.[59] Already under intermittent pressure in February and March, sterling weakened further in April, in part because of dearer money in New York and renewed balance-of-payments worries.

The budget, postponed until May 3, responded with a compromise tendency toward deflation. It included a notable piece of gimmickry—a hastily drafted Selective Employment Tax, effective in September. All employers were to pay a wage tax; but those in transport, agriculture, and most of the public sector would receive full refunds, and manufacturing employers would receive refunds with a premium. Since the refunds would not begin until February 1967, the tax would take money out of the spending stream in the meanwhile. The net burden of the tax would fall on employment in services and construction. In effect, the tax extended to these sectors a counterpart of the excise taxes already borne by commodities. It would supposedly promote "redeployment" of labor from services to manufacturing; and since manufactures are exported to a larger extent than services, the tax would serve as a minor spur to exports and

substitute for devaluation.[60] May 1966 also brought a "voluntary program" limiting direct investment in developed countries even inside the Sterling Area.[61]

The budget's mild restraints on demand were not immediately convincing or effective.[62] To make matters worse, British seamen began a 6½ week strike on May 16. Announcement of a large reserve drop in May heightened the tension. Devaluation of the Indian rupee, effective June 6, 1966, stimulated thought on the general topic. An announcement from Basel on June 13 that earlier arrangements among central banks for support of the pound had been put on a continuing basis helped for only a few days. Funds attracted earlier by high interest rates in London were now moving out again as rates rose in New York, on the Continent, and in the Eurodollar market. Figures published at the end of June revealed a much increased payments deficit in the first quarter. This, followed by disclosure of further reserve losses in June, intensified the sales of sterling. Market confidence also suffered from a dispute within the Labour Party over a proposed tightening of incomes policy. On July 10 the *Observer* published an article on the case for devaluation. On July 12 Prime Minister Wilson tried to blame the crisis on the press. He also announced that banks would not be allowed to pierce their loan ceilings to accommodate businesses paying the Selective Employment Tax. On July 13 another set of bad trade figures appeared. On July 14 Bank rate was raised from 6 to 7 percent, and special bank reserve requirements were increased. Instead of announcing further measures at that time, as expected, the Prime Minister merely promised more in a couple of weeks. This delay intensified the speculation, and sterling had its worst day of the crisis on Friday the 15th. By about this time—that is, between November 1964 and July 1966—Britain had lost an estimated $4.5 billion of reserves (owned and borrowed). Wilson tried to limit the damage by making it clear over the weekend that he would introduce his remedial package earlier, on Wednesday the 20th, after returning from a trip to Moscow.[63]

The chief measures announced on July 20 were a 10 percent surcharge on consumer taxes, tightening of installment-purchase terms, cuts in government spending at home and abroad for 1967–1968, tightening of building controls, higher postal rates, and a six-month freeze (later extended to one year) of wages, salaries, and dividends, to be followed by six months of "severe restraint." Prices were frozen also, with exceptions for nonabsorbable increases in taxes or import costs. The package also included a few gestures, such as a cut in the foreign-travel allowance and a one-year surcharge on the income surtax, designed to show that well-to-do people were being hard hit.[64] Following the emergency measures of almost exactly one year earlier and the budget of May, this massive austerity program of July 1966 spelled final abandonment, as a failure, of Britain's experiment with "the novel theory that forced-draught expansion of the economy would itself eventually right the balance-of-payments deficit . . . "[65] Industrial production and private capital investment sagged in the succeeding months, while unemployment rose.[66]

The severity of Wilson's program impressed American officials, among other observers.[67] The outflow of hot money slackened, ceasing in September. Then, as one year earlier, market moods responded to a support operation for sterling (a bigger swap line with the Federal Reserve and new central-bank credits). In view also of Sterling Area credits negotiated in June, the pound seemed adequately protected against purely short-term movements. The fourth quarter of 1966 saw a dramatic return flow of funds, attracted by high sterling interest rates as well as by improved confidence. The basic balance of payments ran the largest surplus that quarter since 1959. Imports remained virtually level after July, and exports gained 11 percent between then and February 1967, thanks partly to postponement of imports pending the scheduled removal of the surcharge at the end of November and partly to exceptionally favorable overseas markets; so even commodity trade ran a large surplus.[68]

The 1967 devaluation

This strength of sterling was another "false dawn." By the end of March 1967 practically all earlier central-bank assistance, though not IMF assistance, had been repaid. In April it seemed safe to simplify exchange controls by unifying the security-sterling market and the official foreign-exchange market.[69] The new

57. Brittan, *Steering the Economy*, pp. 309–310; Brandon, *op. cit.*, chap. 10.

58. Brittan, *Steering the Economy*, p. 310; Brandon, *op. cit*, pp. 95–97; BIS, 1965–1966,

p. 133; Federal Reserve Bank of New York, *Monthly Review*, September 1966, p. 192; Bank of Nova Scotia, *Monthly Review*, August 1966, p. 2.

59. Brittan, *Steering the Economy*, pp. 320–324. Keran, *op. cit.*, pp. 15–16, notes that the introduction of a restrictive monetary policy, as measured by the money growth rate, cannot be observed until around the first quarter of 1966, about two years after the trade position had weakened.

60. On the Selective Employment Tax, see Brittan, *Steering the Economy*, pp. 325–327; BIS, 1965–1966, pp. 9–10; IMF, 1967, p. 61; and Richard and Peggy Musgrave in Caves, *op. cit.*, pp. 63–65. For a formal analysis and the judgment that the standard argument for the tax was "a piece of partial analysis of the worst kind," see I. F. Pearce, *International Trade*, New York: Norton, 1970, pp. 533ff.

61. BIS, 1965–1966, pp. 135–136; Cooper in Caves, *op. cit.*, p. 177.

62. BIS, 1966–1967, p. 174.

63. Brittan, *Steering the Economy*, pp. 330–333; Federal Reserve Bank of New York, *Monthly Review*, September 1966, p. 193; Bank of Nova Scotia, *Monthly Review*, August 1966, p. 3; Chase Manhattan Bank, *World Business*, May 1967, p. 15 (on the $4.5 billion).

64. Brittan, *Steering the Economy*, pp. 335–336; Brandon, *op. cit.*, p. 110; Federal Reserve Bank of New York, *Monthly Review*, September 1966, p. 194; Chase Manhattan Bank, *World Business*, May 1967, p. 13; *Wall Street Journal*, 16 June 1967, p. 1.

65. BIS, 1966–1967, p. 12.

66. Chase Manhattan Bank, *World Business*, May 1967, p. 14; *Wall Street Journal*, 16 June 1967, pp. 1, 10.

67. Brandon, *op. cit.*, p. 110.

68. Brittan, *Steering the Economy*, pp. 340–341; Chase Manhattan Bank, *World Business*, May 1967, pp. 13–14.

69. Proceeds of the sale of sterling securities owned by nonresidents, except residents of Rhodesia, became external sterling, freely convertible into foreign currencies at official exchange rates. Security sterling had for some years traded in markets abroad at rates close to official rates. Bank of England, *Report*, February 1968, p. 22.

budget, however, called for steadiness on the course of restraint in demand, wages, and prices. Monetary policy was already being relaxed slightly.[70] By midyear, however, economic activity had not recovered as well as hoped. Growing unemployment prompted steps to stimulate demand, including relaxation of installment-buying controls in June and again in August. Unfortunately for sterling, imports were still catching up, following removal of the surcharge in November; and exports were sluggish, presumably suffering from an economic pause in the United States in the first half of 1967 and a recession in Germany. Closure of the Suez Canal as a result of the Arab-Israeli war in June menaced the trade balance, while capital movements were responding to rising interest rates abroad. When Britain again applied for Common Market membership on May 11, the widespread belief became relevant that Britain could not accept the obligations of membership at the $2.80 sterling rate. "[F]rom the middle of May 1967 until well into 1969 the course of sterling and the reserves was almost one continuous slide."[71] Dock strikes occurred in London and Liverpool in the third quarter. Up to mid-July, anyway, the government could flirt with reflation of demand, alarmed at unemployment figures and forecasts and consoled by the thought that the drain on reserves had been smaller than in earlier crises and by the hope that the expanded network of central-bank swap lines would protect sterling. When the freeze on prices and incomes came to an end on August 1, however, wages resumed rising. Consumer expenditures grew, and the rise in unemployment stopped.

At the beginning of October the Common Market Commission released its report on the United Kingdom's application for membership. It took a dim view of the Sterling Area and by implication questioned the exchange rate of sterling. The French foreign minister underlined this message in a speech on October 25. A loan to Britain from a consortium of Swiss commercial banks, announced on October 10, seemed inadequate in size and humiliating in its terms. Trade figures published in mid-October were also disturbing. An increase in Bank rate on October 19 from 5½ to 6 percent, smaller than expected, brought a perverse reaction. So did a further increase to 6½ percent on November 9.[72]

From Saturday, November 11, the leading central bankers and finance officials of Western countries were due to be in almost continuous session at a series of routine meetings scheduled long before. Sterling suffered when dramatic announcements failed to emerge. Sales of sterling, both spot and forward, grew more massive late on Thursday the 16th, after the Chancellor of the Exchequer had been questioned in the House of Commons about rumors of new international assistance. His laconic and uninformative reply was taken as unwillingness to repeat once more his frequent promises not to devalue. That morning, apparently, the Cabinet had secretly decided otherwise. The decision became irrevocable on Friday evening, when the government informed President Johnson and the Managing Director of the International Monetary Fund.

The official announcement of devaluation from $2.80 to $2.40 came on Saturday evening the 18th. The same statement announced that the IMF and central banks were making approximately $3 billion of standby credits available to defend the devalued pound. For the first time, the devaluation of a reserve currency had been internationally agreed on in advance. Chancellor James Callaghan resigned, then moving to the Home Office. "Having had to give so many assurances about the parity to his overseas colleagues, he did not wish to stay on as Chancellor. . . ."[73] On Monday Bank rate was raised to 8 percent, the highest level since 1914. Other measures taken at the same time included reimposition of ceilings on bank credit to the private sector (except for exports) and the tightening of installment-credit terms.[74]

Before devaluation, the pound had not gone to a large forward discount. Aware of how important the forward rate was as an indicator of expectations and as an incentive to outward arbitrage, the Bank of England had been intervening since 1964. The discount on three-months-forward sterling remained smaller than 1 percent per annum from early 1967 until the end of October and reached only 1.73 percent on the eve of devaluation. This artificial cheapening of the cost of hedging investment in British assets against devaluation undoubtedly encouraged such hedging.[75] Devaluation, when it came, left the authorities with massive commitments to buy pounds at a rate well above the new spot price. These commitments cost the government a total of £356 million as they were gradually unwound in 1967 and 1968.[76] Disillusioned by this costly experience, the government seems to have refrained thereafter from significant forward support.[77] The "enormous support" given the forward market in the three years before November 1967, when devaluation was always quite possible, contrasts with "the subsequent complete departure from the forward market, when the parity was less unrealistic than it had been for a long time."[78] By the end of October 1968 the Exchange Equalisation Account's outstanding forward commitments to take sterling from the market had been reduced to about one-fifth of the peak reached before devaluation.[79]

Hindsight revealed an underlying deterioration in Britain's balance of payments since the late 1950s, with the deficit becoming severe in the 1960s. Even the rough overall balance of 1952–1959 was less satisfactory than it seemed. It had been aided by a downdrift in world commodity prices. The large current-account surplus was deceptive, for example, in 1958, a year when import prices dropped 8 percent while domestic output was hardly any higher than three years before. In the years before devaluation, while the reserves of Continental countries had been growing several-fold, Britain's had been fluctuating widely around a level of roughly $3 billion. While the United States, Germany, France, and Italy held reserves worth about half a year's imports, Britain's reserves covered not quite two months' imports. In the last three years before devaluation, moreover, Britain had kept her reserves even at that level only by "continual recourse to the international begging-bowl"—extensive borrowings from foreign central banks and the IMF. By the end of 1967 Britain's liabilities to official monetary institutions outside the Sterling Area had increased by well over £1,000 million net.[80] At that time, British official reserves were worth about £963 or £1123 million (depending on use of the old or the new exchange rate in the translation),[81] so unborrowed reserves had become approximately zero and probably negative. In 1967 an adverse shift of one week in the timing of payments for imports and exports could deplete Britain's reserves by £200 million; a shift in timing of only a few weeks would equal all of the reported official reserves.[82] Paul Einzig understandably designated leads and lags as "The Main Cause of Devaluation" in 1967.[83]

In 1949, most of the rest of the world had followed Britain in devaluing, depriving the move of much of its desired effect on Britain's price-competitiveness. In 1967, 14 other IMF members followed Britain within 10 days, but nothing like the earlier general adjustment of

70. Money-supply growth accelerated from the fourth quarter of 1966, and Bank rate was cut in three stages from 7 percent in January 1967 to 5½ percent in May. Keran, *op. cit.*, p. 16.

71. Brittan, *Steering the Economy*, p. 348.

72. Brittan, *Steering the Economy*, pp. 348–350, 355, 358; IMF, 1968, p. 51.

73. Brittan, *Steering the Economy*, pp. 360–364, quotation from p. 364; Paul Einzig, *The Destiny of the Dollar*, New York: St. Martin's Press, 1972, p. 57; Bank of England, *Report*, February 1968, p. 2.

74. IMF, 1968, p. 49.

75. Samuel I. Katz, *Exchange-Risk Under Fixed and Flexible Exchange Rates*, New York University, *The Bulletin*, Nos. 83–84, June 1972, pp. 57–58.

76. Offsetting this figure were profits of some £45 to £60 million that the government had made on its forward intervention in the three years before devaluation, estimated on plausible assumptions about the volume of forward intervention and the size of the forward discount on the pound. The *net* cost of forward intervention thus amounted to roughly £300 million. Cohen, *op. cit.*, pp.185–186.

77. *Ibid.*, p. 186. For an opinion that forward support in 1964–1967 had proved ill-advised, see Einzig, *The Destiny of the Dollar*, pp. 26, 31.

78. Brittan, *Steering the Economy*, p. 86.

79. Bank of England, *Report*, February 1969, p. 7.

80. Brittan, *Steering the Economy*, pp. 357, 422–424, 434–435. At the time of devaluation in 1967, the European portion of central-bank and BIS lines of credit for Britain was increased to an amount officially reported as "in excess of" $1.5 million. Meanwhile, the Federal Reserve swap line had been raised in several steps to $2 billion. By 1969, indications are that the short-term facilities at British disposal considerably exceeded the publicly revealed minimum of $3.5 billion. Cohen, *op. cit.*, p. 97 and footnote.

81. Dollar figure from *International Financial Statistics*, June 1973, p. 360.

82. Katz, *Exchange Risk*, p. 49.

83. This is the subtitle of his book *Leads and Lags*, London: Macmillan, 1968.

exchange rates occurred.[84] Even many of the major Sterling Area countries, including Australia, South Africa, India, and Pakistan, failed to follow sterling downward. Devaluing to the same extent as Britain, 14.29 percent, were 11 countries or territories in the Sterling Area, West Indian countries other than the Bahamas, and other British dependent territories. Iceland, Ceylon, New Zealand, Fiji, and Hong Kong[85] devalued by larger or smaller percentages. Outside the Sterling Area, not one country devalued specifically to maintain a fixed relation with sterling, although six did devalue for competitive reasons—Israel and Spain by Britain's 14.29 percent and Nepal, Brazil, Denmark, and Macao by other percentages. Thus the number of currencies pegged to sterling shrank.[86]

Early disappointment after the devaluation

Devaluation was slow in bringing the results sought. The postdevaluation return flow of short-term funds lasted only a few days, and by December funds were flowing out again. The merchandise trade balance worsened slightly in 1968. Imports rose even faster than in 1967; and exports, while rising strongly in volume, did not quite maintain their share of world markets as valued at the new exchange rate. The real worsening was greater than the bare figures show, since special circumstances had already affected the trade balance adversely in 1967. Imports had surged following removal of the import surcharge in November 1966; and the dock strikes of late 1967 delayed exports, their catch-up coming in early 1968. One of the factors promoting imports was a strong rise in consumer spending, which had begun around mid-1967, under the influence of earlier reflationary measures, and which intensified after the devaluation because of expectations that price increases would result and that the March 1968 budget would raise indirect taxes.

The pound's devaluation had come at a bad time for the dollar, with the Vietnam war raging, the U.S. economy overheated, and gold reserves falling toward the supposedly critical $10 billion level. Sterling suffered from the backlash of bearishness on the dollar and bullishness on gold. Rumors circulated in the winter of 1967–1968 that sterling, though already devalued, would at least match any devaluation of the dollar. Even in social circles where currency problems were not normally discussed, people asked when sterling's second devaluation would take place; "and it was often just those who had most vigorously contested the need for any devaluation at all who were most firmly convinced that a fresh one was imminent."[87] The short-term outcome, however, was tighter U.S. capital-outflow controls in January 1968 and replacement of the central-bank gold pool by a two-tier gold market in March.[88] In Britain, January brought additional steps to restrain government spending. An early budget in March raised various purchase and excise taxes and the rates of the Selective Employment Tax. Consumer spending dipped but regained buoyancy in the second half of 1968.[89]

Sterling suffered in 1968 not only from the gold crisis that climaxed in March but also from the speculation centering on Germany and France that climaxed in November.[90] Not only did spot sterling stand at a discount from par during most of 1968 and early 1969,[91] but forward quotations in the March and November crises reflected absence of official support. The forward discount reached 18.5 percent per annum on March 11 and 11.0 percent on November 18.[92]

During the November crisis the British authorities placed a surcharge of 10 percent on the purchase tax and on duties on tobacco, beer, wines, mineral oils, etc. The commercial banks, which had already been asked in November 1967 and May 1968 to limit their lending, were given more stringent instructions on November 22. An import-deposit scheme came into force on November 27, affecting roughly one-third of total U.K. imports, almost wholly manufactures. Importers were required to make a non-interest-bearing deposit with H.M. Customs of 50 percent of the value of the goods before withdrawing the goods from the port area. The deposits would be refunded six months later. Having to pay or forgo interest on the deposited money would presumably discourage imports. During the first six months, furthermore, before any refunds began, some of the funds available to importers would be drained off. Bank lending for import deposits was tightly restricted. The scheme was reinforced on December 18 by a ban on borrowing foreign currency or sterling owned by non-Sterling-Area residents to finance the deposits.[93]

The trade-balance deterioration of 1968 was more than offset by an increase in the surplus on invisibles and a cut in long-term capital outflow, so that the basic deficit shrank and actually turned into a small surplus in the second half of the year. On the other hand, short-term capital flows, including errors and omissions, continued heavily outward for most of the year, except in the third quarter. Thus the overall deficit, at around $3 billion, was more than twice that of 1967 and more than twice the 1964–1967 average overall deficit.[94]

The Basel arrangements of 1968

In connection with capital flows, one institutional development of 1968 deserves mention. The 1967 devaluation imposed windfall losses on the sterling reserves of overseas members of the Sterling Area. This experience intensified the diversification of sterling balances into other reserve assets. By the second quarter of 1968 this movement seemed to threaten a new and serious run on the pound. Britain responded by offering the negotiate some kind of guarantee against future losses. One outcome was the "Basel arrangements," announced in September. Concerned for the stability of the international monetary system as a whole, the central banks of 12 major industrial countries provided Britain with a $2 billion line of credit through the Bank for International Settlements "on which the United Kingdom could draw . . . to offset fluctuations below an agreed base level in the sterling balances of sterling area holders, both official and private . . ."[95]

The central bankers had reached agreement in principle in July; but before finally agreeing, they sought assurance that the Sterling Area countries would do their part by not drawing their sterling reserves down too far. Some of those countries, furthermore, should be asked to place part of their nonsterling reserves on deposit with the Bank for International Settlements to help meet Britain's drawings on the credit. Accordingly, the U.K. negotiated a series of agreements with individual members of the overseas Sterling Area. Coming into force on September 25, 1968, most of these agreements ran for three years initially but were renewable. Each overseas member agreed to hold an individually specified proportion of its total official external reserves in sterling. On this condition, the U.K. guaranteed the value

in U.S. dollars of the country's official holdings of sterling in excess of 10 percent of its total official external reserves. "Thus, taking account of their existing gold and non-sterling currency reserves, together with guaranteed sterling, 90% of each country's reserves would be safeguarded, in one way or another, against any loss that might be directly entailed by a future devaluation of sterling against the U.S. dollar."[96] The Basel credit line and the Sterling Area agreements, including the dollar guaran-

84. IMF, 1968, pp. 50–51.

85. Hong Kong initially devalued by 14.29 percent, then revalued by 10 percent a few days later, making a net devaluation against the dollar of 5.71 percent.

86. Cohen, *op. cit.*, p. 193 and footnote.

87. For the last two paragraphs, IMF, 1969, pp. 74, 76; Milton Gilbert in H. W. J. Bosman and F. A. M. Alting von Geusau, eds., *The Future of the International Monetary System*, Lexington, Mass.: Heath, 1970, pp. 54–55; Brittan, *Steering the Economy*, pp. 376–378 (source of the quotation).

88. See pp. 574–575.

89. IMF, 1969, pp. 74–75.

90. See pp. 482, 507.

91. IMF, 1969, pp. 123.

92. On the latter occasion, the French franc went to an 11.0 percent per annum forward discount and the German mark to a premium of 6.6 percent. These figures refer to transactions of the first National City Bank of New York, charted in E. A. Reichers and H. van B. Cleveland in George N. Halm, ed., *Approaches to Greater Flexibility of Exchange Rates*, Princeton, N.J.: Princeton University Press, 1970 (hereafter cited as Bürgenstock Papers), p. 329. According to Wednesday New York figures charted in IMF, 1969, p. 125, the greatest forward discounts on sterling amounted to about 11 percent in March and about 7 percent in December 1968.

93. Bank of England, *Report*, February 1969, p. 22; IMF, 1969, p. 75.

94. IMF, 1969, pp. 10–11, 59.

95. Bank of England, *Report*, February 1969, p. 13.

96. Bank of England, *Report*, February 1969, p. 13.

tee of sterling reserves, freed the British authorities to devalue sterling again without fear of recrimination from its official holders.[97]

Further details of the 1968 agreements came to light in November 1972, when the downward float of the British pound was about to bring the guarantee into effect. If the pound rate dropped below $2.3760 (i.e., 1 percent below the $2.40 parity in effect at the time of the agreement) and remained below for 30 consecutive days, then the United Kingdom would compensate holders with the sterling equivalent of the amount of guaranteed sterling reserves multiplied by the shortfall from $2.40 of the actual pound rate on the thirtieth day. With about £2920 million under guarantee (as of the end of June 1972) and with the pound quoted at $2.3506 on November 23, 1972, the compensation due at that time amounted to about £60 million.[98]

The generosity of the guarantee suggests how the British were negotiating with their backs to the wall in 1968. In a sense, overseas official holders received double protection against the risk of devaluation. They enjoyed a capital guarantee while still receiving a competitive interest rate on their sterling assets reflecting the risk premium demanded by non-guaranteed holders. Proposals were made for modifying this generous feature in renegotiations scheduled for 1973.

The Basel arrangements promptly stopped the flight of official holders from sterling; in fact, the long decline in official sterling balances gave way to a dramatic reversal. Those withdrawn before the 1967 devaluation returned to London long before the British balance of payments moved into surplus. By the end of March 1969, Sterling Area reserve balances were already larger than one year before. In later years, as the U.K.'s balance of payments improved, as the overseas sterling countries in general ran payments surpluses and complied with their agreements about specified proportions of their total reserves in sterling, and as the U.S. dollar grew more obviously shaky, official Sterling Area holders accumulated still larger sterling reserves. By mid-1972 they totaled about twice their amount at the time of the 1968 agreements.[99]

These developments were unforeseen. Instead of being a program for consolidating and strengthening the Sterling Area, the Basel arrangements were a response to the danger of its disorderly collapse. They downgraded sterling in making the U.S. dollar the measure of value for even the bulk of sterling reserves.

The delayed success of the devaluation

Let us return to the story as it unfolded in time. During the first months of 1969, the unwinding of leads and lags built up during the November 1968 crisis, together with the seasonally high earnings of Sterling Area countries, enabled the British authorities to buy foreign exchange in the market. A favorable turnaround in Britain's balance of payments was still not evident, however, as illustrated by a return of Bank rate to 8 percent on February 27 and by the provisions of the budget in April. To restrain domestic demand and speed up a shift of resources from the domestic to the foreign sector, the budget raised the corporation and selective employment taxes.[100] Sterling weakened toward the end of April 1969 as expectations revived of franc devaluation and mark revaluation. The spot rate dropped to the lower intervention point, and three-month-forward sterling widened to a discount of over 15 percent per annum against the dollar at the worst before recovering around mid-May.[101] On June 20, Britain arranged a $1 billion standby with the IMF; on June 27 Britain drew $500 million, raising her total outstanding drawings from the Fund to $2700 million.[102] By early August, the British authorities had recouped the foreign exchange lost during the crisis of April and May. Soon afterwards, though—to skip ahead to another similar situation—sterling came under renewed selling pressure after devaluation of the French franc on August 8. Sterling's spot rate against the dollar was allowed to fall slightly beyond the usual intervention point both in mid-August and again at the end of the month. By that time, the three-month-forward discount had widened to 8.5 percent per annum. At the end of September, as the newly floating mark began to appreciate and money flowed out of Germany, sterling was one of the main beneficiaries.[103] It is noteworthy that speculation should have produced sizable forward discounts in the spring and late summer even though sterling itself was the focus of neither crisis.

Basically, the favorable turnaround in Britain's position had already occurred by midyear. Three cheery news items appeared on June 12. First, invisible earnings had outweighed the trade deficit in the first quarter of 1969, producing a surplus on goods-and-services account. Second, the trade deficit had narrowed in May. Third, the fact came to light that a gradually increasing proportion of British exports had gone unrecorded since 1964; a statistical inaccuracy that had been undermining confidence in sterling was thus cleared up. Later, when confidence in sterling was shaken temporarily in the wake of the French devaluation, announcement of a surplus even in merchandise trade in August brought a change in market sentiment practically overnight.[104]

In 1969 as a whole, the British balance of payments was transformed. Current and long-term capital transactions yielded a basic surplus of nearly £400 million, compared with a deficit of the same order in 1968. The Bank of England attributed a "steep rise in exports" and moderation in the growth of imports to the competitive advantage achieved by devaluation.[105]

In 1970, although Britain's surplus on current account was the largest ever recorded,[106] and although the international monetary scene was relatively tranquil, the year was not entirely uneventful for sterling. Bank rate was reduced in March and again in April. Then the trend changed. In May and early June, sterling suffered from rising Eurodollar interest rates and falling domestic interest rates and the floating of the Canadian dollar. By the end of August, under the influence of adverse seasonal factors and the acceleration of wage and price increases, the pound had sunk almost to its lower support limit against the dollar. In early September, before the IMF annual meeting, sterling felt heavy but temporary pressure from talk of exchange-rate flexibility. At one point in the second week of September, the discount on three-month-forward sterling widened to nearly 3 percent per annum. The minicrisis proved short-lived. Sterling recovered in the last quarter of 1970, partly because of improved trade figures and partly because declining Eurodollar interest rates brought a renewed inflow of funds into London.[107]

After the turn of the year, sterling quotations began rising rapidly, almost reaching the upper support limit of $2.42 in mid-February 1971 and again in mid-April. Interest-rate movements and expectations in Britain and in the Eurodollar market were having an evident influence. Sterling remained firm during the mark-dollar crisis of early May 1971.[108] After President Nixon closed the "gold window" in August 1971, sterling joined many other currencies in a "dirty float" against the dollar until the Smithsonian Agreement of December

18, 1971. At that time it retained its gold parity, so that its "central rate" against the dollar rose from $2.40 to $2.60571.

In the late months of 1971, sterling gained in stature as a reserve currency in some respects and lost in others. A heavy inflow of funds enabled the British authorities to repay much of their outstanding debt to the International Monetary Fund and to increase their reserves to well above £2 billion.[109] In August through December, a number of Sterling Area countries, including South Africa, moved from a peg on sterling to a peg on the dollar. At the time of the Smithsonian Agreement, South Africa, India, Ghana, and other countries changed their rates against both the dollar and sterling, South Africa devaluing by 12.3 percent against gold and sterling and by 4.4 per-

97. Harry G. Johnson in Bürgenstock Papers, p. 110.

98. *IMF Survey*, 20 November 1972, p. 126, 11 December 1972, pp. 131–132.

99. On the Basel arrangements, see Cohen, *op. cit.*, pp. 77–79, 183, and chap. 11; Brittan, *Steering the Economy*, pp. 386ff.; Brittan, *The Price of Economic Freedom*, New York: St. Martin's Press, 1970, p. 69; Bank of England, *Report*, February 1969, pp. 13–14; IMF, 1969, pp. 64, 75; *IMF Surveys* just cited; Bank of Nova Scotia *Monthly Review*, December 1972, pp. 2–4.

100. IMF, 1969, p. 76.

101. BIS, 1969–1970, pp. 132–133. According to a chart of Wednesday noon quotations in New York, however, the widest three-month-forward discount of sterling against the dollar was about 11½ percent, during May. IMF, 1969, p. 125.

102. IMF, 1969, p. 76.

103. BIS, 1969–1970, p. 134.

104. Brittan, *Steering the Economy*, pp. 397–398, 400.

105. Bank of England, *Report*, February 1970, p. 5, with details on following pages.

106. Bank of England, *Report*, February 1971, p. 8.

107. BIS, 1970–1971, p. 145.

108. BIS, 1970–1971, p. 145 and chart on p. 146.

109. Einzig, *The Destiny of the Dollar*, p. 134.

cent against the dollar. A number of Sterling Area members that had switched to a dollar peg in the preceding months, including Ceylon, Jordan, Kenya, Pakistan, Uganda, Tanzania, and Zambia, decided after the Smithsonian Agreement to remain pegged to the dollar instead of sterling. At the same time, Australia and New Zealand went over to a dollar peg, while South Africa returned to pegging the rand against sterling.[110]

The British balance of payments was stronger in 1971 than ever before. The surplus on current account, already large in 1970, became "massive" at nearly £1 billion in 1971.[111] The net official overall payments surplus for the year as a whole derived about equally from the basic balance of payments and from inflows of funds. During the first half of 1971 the inflows reflected the payments surpluses and reserve gains of the overseas Sterling Area, while during the second half they were largely speculative.[112] The growth of Britain's reserve position, net of debts, amounted to $8.2 billion in 1971, more than twice as large as the growth in 1970 and second only to Japan's gain of about $10½ billion in reserves. During the year, the use of the gross inflow of funds shifted away from debt repayment to accumulation of assets. At the end of 1971 gross official reserves stood at $6.6 billion; and if the amounts placed with overseas monetary authorities by special swap transactions are added, the figure comes to $8.8 billion.[113]

The external gains of 1971 were not unrelated to less attractive developments on the home front. The authorities were still giving top priority to the balance of payments, second to combating inflation, and only third to reducing unemployment. Total output in 1971, the third year in succession of slight growth, rose only some 1 percent from the year before, the smallest increase in over 10 years. Unemployment increased substantially in 1971, while the capital utilization index fell.[114]

Sterling afloat

Sterling remained firm on the exchanges through much of the first half of 1972. End-of-month market quotations were above the new Smithsonian central rate of $2.6057 in February through May. Britain's gold and foreign-currency reserves reached an all-time high during the spring.

By June, however, the pound came under sudden selling pressure. The outflow of funds amounted to $2.8 billion in the third week of June alone.[115] Market participants were noting serious labor difficulties, the worsening wage-price situation, and the fall-off in monthly export receipts. The week before the crisis was one of almost unrelieved bad news. An official report predicted a drop in manufacturing investment in 1972, following the drop in 1971. A rail strike was averted by a 13 percent pay increase, and a dock strike was headed off only at the eleventh hour. The trade accounts had moved into deficit for the three months ending in May. Market participants could recall the March budget speech, in which Chancellor Anthony Barber had announced a 5 percent growth target and suggested that he would rather sacrifice the exchange rate than squeeze the economy.[116] When Bank rate was raised from 5 to 6 percent on Thursday, June 22, some currency traders thought that the increase might have a favorable psychological effect; others worried that it might appear as a panic move. Paul A. Volcker, U.S. Under Secretary of the Treasury for Monetary Affairs, testifying before a Congressional committee that same day, scoffed at the idea that the pound was ripe for devaluation, pointing out that Britain had been running a large balance-of-payments surplus.[117]

The next day, Friday the 23d, Britain set the pound free to float as "a temporary measure." Thereupon, "a brief but intense attack on the U.S. dollar sent at least $1-billion in hot dollars, and probably a good deal more, cascading across borders in just a few minutes."[118] Already, the flight from sterling had been forcing unwanted dollars onto Continental and Japanese central banks because of the dollar's role as intervention currency. European foreign-exchange markets closed abruptly on Friday, reopening Tuesday the 27th in London and on Wednesday on the Continent.[119] In London, the newly floating pound dipped as much as 5.2 percent below its Smithsonian parity on Tuesday the 27th but recovered to close only 3.9 percent below.[120]

Amidst the relatively extreme fluctuations of the first few days, the pound rate (and the dollar, too) was helped temporarily by announcements of intensified controls by capital-receiving countries such as Germany and Switzerland. Switzerland imposed an 8 percent a year charge on new foreign deposits.[121] A notable piece of specific news on July 5 was the resignation of German Finance and Economics Minister Karl Schiller, who was known to have opposed the exchange controls.[122] Germany slapped new restrictions on its own citizens, who might be tempted to borrow pounds or dollars and try to convert them into marks. The Swiss prohibited foreigners from buying Swiss securities and real estate for a period of up to two years.[123]

The British float was historic. Never before had a country abandoned support of its currency with such large reserves as Britain's. At the end of May, British central bank reserves of gold and foreign currencies stood at $7.15 billion, nearly double the $3.8 billion of a year earlier.[124] Britain's total international reserves dropped by about 2 percent in June, but this small figure is misleading. Most of the support of the pound before its float came from purchases of pounds by the central banks of Britain's prospective partners in the Common Market. Britain had to buy back $2.61 billion worth of these pounds in July, paying from its own reserves and with funds borrowed from foreign central banks and from the International Monetary Fund. Between the ends of May and July, in fact, Britain's gross reserves, as reported in *International Financial Statistics*, fell by nearly one-third.[125]

The sudden speculative attack that cut the pound adrift had not been touched off by such usual factors as clear balance-of-payments weakness or meager reserves. Instead, the basic cause seems to have been inflation, dramatized by large wage increases, and prospects of further inflation. Speculation simply hastened the weakness of the pound. Henry Wallich drew one lesson: "so long as countries will not curb their inflations, it will be difficult to attain even short-run stability of exchange rates."[126]

The British float hastened the crumbling of the Sterling Area. Ireland, India, South Africa, and about a dozen other countries initially kept their currencies pegged to sterling and allowed them to float with it. By the end of the year, however, South Africa, Malaysia, Singapore, Hong Kong, and several other countries shifted their currencies to a U.S. dollar basis. Jamaica joined them in January 1973, repegging its dollar from 0.5 pound sterling to US $1.10.[127]

---

110. BIS, 1971–1972, pp. 145–146.

111. Bank of England, *Report*, February, 1972, p. 7; some details on p. 8.

112. BIS, 1971–1972, pp. 118–119.

113. BIS, 1971–1972, p. 118.

114. Bank of England, *Report*, February 1972, pp. 5–7.

The fight against inflation does not appear to have gone very well, as indicated by the following percentages of increase in the money supply. (Each end-of-year figure is compared with the previous end-of-year figure for money as defined in *International Financial Statistics*): 1966, −0.0; 1967, 7.6; 1968, 4.1, 1969, 0.3; 1970, 9.3; 1971, 15.3; 1972, 14.0; 1973, 5.1.

115. BIS, 1972–1973, p. 127. According to Chancellor Anthony Barber's speech to the IMF 1972 annual meeting (p. 48), the outflow of funds had amounted to around $2.5 billion in six working days.

116. Bank of Nova Scotia, *Monthly Review*, December 1972, p. 1; *Business Week*, 1 July 1972, p. 13. Also, on the budget speech, *Washington Post*, 25 June 1972, p. A 11.

117. *Wall Street Journal*, 23 June 1972, p. 38.

118. *Business Week*, 1 July 1972, p. 12, probably exaggerating.

119. On market closings and reopenings, *Washington Post*, 28 June 1972, p. D 1; *Wall Street Journal*, 28 June 1972, p. 3; *Wall Street Journal*, 29 June 1972, p. 12.

120. Calculated from *Wall Street Journal*, 28 June 1972, p. 3.

121. *Wall Street Journal*, 5 July 1972, p. 3.

122. *Wall Street Journal*, 5 July 1972, p. 3; 6 July 1972, p. 4.

123. *U.S. News and World Report*, 10 July 1972, p. 20.

124. *Wall Street Journal*, 26 June 1972, p. 14.

125. *Wall Street Journal*, 3 August 1972, p. 9; Federal Reserve Bank of Chicago, *International Letter*, 4 August 1972; *International Financial Statistics*, November 1972, p. 359.

126. Wallich in *Newsweek*, 17 July 1972, p. 67. Chancellor Anthony Barber drew a further lesson: ". . . we cannot afford to have the stability of a rational and economically sensible structure of parities wrecked by ephemeral surges of short-term capital around the world. The degree of freedom for capital markets which is compatible with international monetary stability is clearly one of the more difficult and controversial matters in this whole subject. But we must find a solution." Speech at IMF meeting, September 1972, p. 48.

127. *International Financial Statistics*, November 1972, p. 3n., January 1973, pp. 2–3; IMF, 1972, p. 3; Bank of Nova Scotia, *Monthly Review*, December 1972, p. 3; *IMF Survey*, 12 February 1973, p. 46.

These shifts and Britain's modification of Sterling Area arrangements partially motivated each other. In June 1972, many of the U.K. exchange controls on capital transactions that had applied only to investment in nonsterling countries and securities were extended to the overseas Sterling Area. The reason officially given was that a speculative outflow of funds from Britain could otherwise have taken place through the Sterling Area countries no longer linking their currencies to the pound. Although the new rules did not remove the preferences in effect for payments for trade, travel, interest, and dividends between the United Kingdom and the overseas sterling countries, and· although they even preserved some preferential element in the capital controls, they could be regarded as delivering a nearly final blow to the Sterling Area. In the fullest sense of the term, the Area shrank from some 60 countries to basically just the British Isles (including the Republic of Ireland, the Channel Islands, and the Isle of Man).[128]

Let us see how the floating rate behaved. The pound ended June 1972 at 6.53 percent below its end-of-May market rate against the dollar, gained 0.25 percent during July and August, dropped 1.16 percent in September and 3.22 percent in October, and from then until late January 1973, before coming under the influence of the dollar crisis, fluctuated in the range of $2.34–$2.36. At first, the gradual covering of speculative short positions taken in June before the float tended to buoy the rate; but by late September this technical support dried up, and sterling became more exposed to downward pressures. By then, too, the British government was extensively negotiating for voluntary wage and price restraints. On several occasions in mid- and late October, the day-to-day drop of the pound rate amounted to about $\frac{2}{3}$ of 1 percent. Suggested reasons for the relatively sharp decline included news of substantial trade deficits in August and September; concern that the deficit might worsen when Britain joined the Common Market in January; concern about the balance-of-payments effect of Britain's contribution to the Common Market budget; publication of wage figures that heightened concern about British inflation, contrasting with milder inflation in the United States; reports of a possible slowdown by electrical workers; and signs that negotiations for voluntary restraints were failing. Most notably, speculative sentiment responded to discussions of the rate at which Britain would repeg the pound upon joining

the Common Market. Through the first half of October, when the market rate was hovering around $2.42, that rate, or perhaps the pre-Smithsonian parity of $2.40, seemed a plausible choice. When the rate was allowed to sink below $2.40 and then below the old support floor of $2.38, however, the piercing of these psychological resistance points inflamed conjectures about a lower parity. A German economic research institute issued a report saying that the pound was currently overvalued and might have to be repegged at $2.25. Even the figure of $2.20 appeared in press and market commentary. At one point on Friday, October 27, the rate sank as low as $2.32 before staging a moderate recovery. As the pound slumped, the Bank of England sold dollars but did not try to hold the rate at any particular level. Fear that a pound drifting too low could force other countries to devalue their currencies showed itself in market weakness of the Italian lira and French franc; the Smithsonian Agreement seemed in danger of coming apart.[129]

Early in November the British authorities revealed that they had spent $230 million of reserves supporting the pound in October. Though hardly indicating a major effort, that figure rather surprised money brokers, who thought that the Bank of England had been giving only token support.[130]

Signs that the British government would take a firmer hand against inflation affected the exchange rate in November. On Monday the 6th Prime Minister Heath introduced legislation calling for a compulsory freeze of prices, wages, rents, and dividends. The freeze was effective immediately, was to run for three to five months, and was then to yield to a longer-run policy negotiated in the meanwhile.[131] As the market assessed prospects for the policy's failure or success, hinging largely on the vigor of labor's opposition, the sterling rate ranged rather widely. A tightening of special deposit requirements, equivalent to bank reserve requirements, on November 9 (repeated on December 21) also affected the rate. November ended with the pound 0.46 percent higher than at the end of October. The Bank of England supported the pound on occasion but not on balance, and the external reserves rose by $36 million over November as a whole.[132]

By December, European authorities seemed to have quietly agreed that the pound probably should continue floating well after Britain's entry into the Common Market on January 1. A prolonged float seemed preferable to a parity that might have to be changed a half-year or so later in a disruptive wave of speculation. Delay in repegging found support in influential British circles and was advocated in a report of the private National Institute of Economic and Social Research.[133]

By late January 1973, traders in sterling had to weigh several conflicting considerations—the probable effectiveness of "Stage Two" of anti-inflation policy, the probable effects on British trade of sterling's accomplished depreciation of roughly 10 percent against other currencies, the probable consequences of temporarily tight liquidity conditions at home, the relations to be worked out between the pound and the other EC currencies, and the exchange-market turmoil following introduction of Italy's dual exchange market and the Swiss float. A sharp rise of the pound against the dollar reflected the crisis that led to the dollar's devaluation on February 12 rather than specifically British developments. "As the exchanges remained highly nervous in the wake of the dollar devaluation, sterling moved widely from day to day and even from hour to hour between $2.43 and $2.48. Then, as the turmoil built up to a peak on Thursday, March 1, the rate moved above $2.50. Early in the following week, with the markets officially closed, sterling settled back to trade around $2.46."[134]

The circumstances in which the pound was set afloat illustrated the weaknesses of the pegged-rate system. The relatively large—though certainly not wild—fluctuations of late October 1972 seem to have hinged largely on conjectures about the probable effectiveness of anti-inflation efforts[135] and about the rate at which the pound would be repegged. The fluctuations of January–March 1973 were influenced by bearishness on the dollar and bullishness on other pegged-rate currencies. Other countries responded with drastic exchange controls; Britain got off rather easily with a few cents' rise in the dollar-pound rate. The pound has not been *freely* floating. Its rate has been subject to intervention by the British authorities, to devaluations and revaluations of foreign currencies, and to expectations of and conjectures about such official actions.

Review and appraisal

After surveying the postwar British crises, recoveries, and policy responses, we may step back to draw some broad impressions. Sterling has been one of the two currencies most widely used in international payments and used as a reserve for overseas authorities and banks. Britain's gold and other liquid reserves have amounted to only a fraction of its liabilities of similar character. Normal as it is for a banker,

128. Bank of Nova Scotia, *Monthly Review*, December 1972, pp. 3–4.
For an earlier appraisal of the costs and benefits to Britain of a phase-out of sterling's international role, see Cohen, *op. cit.*, esp. chaps. 10 and 12.

129. Charles Coombs in Federal Reserve Bank of New York, *Monthly Review*, March 1973, pp. 55–56; *Wall Street Journal*, 25 October 1972, p. 18, 26 October 1972, p. 6, 27 October 1972, p. 12, 31 October 1972, p. 42, 3 November 1972, p. 14.
An institutional development of October 1972 deserves notice. Bank rate was abolished because its symbolic significance was no longer desired; it was replaced by a minimum lending rate ("last-resort rate") to be announced every Friday and set equal to half a percentage point above the Treasury bill rate, rounded up to the nearest quarter-point. According to Chancellor Anthony Barber, "What is needed is a rate which can respond more flexibly to the changing conditions of the money market and one whose week to week movements are not interpreted as signalling major shifts in monetary policy." *Wall Street Journal*, 10 October 1972, p. 7; Richmond *Times-Dispatch*, 10 October 1972, p. A15; BIS, 1972–1973, pp. 51–52. Briefly in late December this floating Bank rate reached 9 percent.

130. *Wall Street Journal*, 3 November 1972, p. 14.

131. "Stage 2" controls were unveiled on January 17, 1973. Pay increases would be limited over the next year to an average of 7 percent—about half the prefreeze rate—and prices, rents, and dividends would be restricted. A new element in the package was to be control of business profit margins. *Newsweek*, 29 January 1973, pp. 35–36; Federal Reserve Bank of Chicago, *International Letter*, 19 January 1973; Coombs, *op. cit.*, p. 57.

132. *Wall Street Journal*, 13 December 1972, p. 8; *Wall Street Journal*, 5 December 1972, p. 16; *International Financial Statistics*.

133. *Wall Street Journal*, 13 December 1972, p. 8.

134. Coombs, *op. cit.*, p. 57.

135. Britain's rate of price increase in 1972, 8.6 percent, was the highest of all major industrial countries. Federal Reserve Bank of Chicago, *International Letter*, 19 January 1973.

a fractional-reserve system can be awkward when many depositors wish to cash their claims.

A second characteristic of sterling's postwar position has been striking variability of the reserves, of exchange rates (the spot rate within official support limits and the forward rate), and of the tone of anticipations and discussion. Strength and weakness have alternated rapidly. For example, the weakness that brought devaluation in 1949 gave way to strength and rumors of upward revaluation in 1950–1951 and then in turn to the crisis of 1951–1952. Only weeks before the downward float of June 1972, the British balance of payments had seemed healthy; and the pound had been quoted well above its central rate against the dollar. Some observers may prefer to emphasize disturbances caused by definite historical events, such as the Korean War, the Arab-Israeli and Suez difficulties of 1956 and 1967, various hot-money episodes involving expectations of German revaluation, and the wage explosions and labor difficulties of 1972. But historical events are always occurring and are all too readily available as easy explanations for the jerky operation of economic institutions. Lionel Robbins made an apt comment early during Britain's postwar experience: "If a car fails to reach its destination, if it is continually running into the side, or if it is continually having to solicit hauls from passing lorries, we should not regard it as a sufficient explanation that the roads are not level and straight, that there are hills to ascend and corners to turn."[136]

The last point provides evidence for a third one: some of the crises, particularly before the agonies of the middle and late 1960s, were of a more speculative than fundamental nature. Short-term capital flows proved volatile. On some occasions, as in 1960 and most of 1964, short-term inflows masked underlying deficits and protected the reserves.[137] On other occasions, outflows precipitated a crisis. Controls proved nearly powerless to prevent speculation through speed-ups and delays of payments and even of actual purchases and sales. In Katz's words, "recurring speculative movements against the pound . . . could make any weakness in the balance of current payments into a serious crisis within a few weeks."[138]

A fourth characteristic, evident particularly in the early postwar years but also at the time of the import surcharge of 1964–1966 and of the import-deposit scheme of 1968, was the use of import restrictions to resist reserve drains.

Since the payments positions of the United Kingdom and the overseas sterling countries sometimes tended to strengthen or weaken together, speculation playing a part, Britain at times tried to persuade those countries to adopt import or exchange restrictions paralleling her own. At times, controls cut back imports and incidentally depleted inventories of imported materials;[139] at other times, imports spurted to make up for earlier cutbacks or to anticipate impending controls. One clear example is the run-down of inventories in 1950 and their subsequent replenishment as one aspect of the 1951–1952 crisis.

A fifth point is something of a catchall. It concerns conditions actually or allegedly responsible for Britain's relatively poor performance both in domestic economic growth and in exporting. A "danger of spurious profundity" plagues the whole lengthy discussion. A thousand different explanations of what was really wrong could be suggested—alleged shortcomings in management, design, salesmanship, delivery dates, and so on.[140] In 1966 the London *Times* published a long list of suggested reasons for the weakness of the pound, including: too many working hours spent on games and betting; prevalence, in all classes of society, of the idea that money is something one takes away from others or wins by gambling rather than earns by work; too much preference for old ways and too little dynamism and imagination; and too slow a transfer of power from privileged people to competent people.[141] Paul Einzig has written much of the "English disease," apparently meaning laziness, irresponsibility, and greed on the part of workers.[142] Sidney Rolfe has noted Britain's "structural" problems—a laggard business investment policy, anticompetitive practices of unions and business, and the inefficiency of management (connected, in turn, with snobbish attitudes about social class, vocational education, and materialistic ambitions).[143] An uncautious reader might suppose that such observations provide the key to Britain's balance-of-payments problem. Profundities like these may have their place, as in explaining Britain's relatively slow growth and waste of opportunity for higher real income, but they are unnecessary in explanations of balance-of-payments trouble and currency crises. British export-price and unit-labor-cost movements, compared to those of Britain's competitors at prevailing exchange rates, were bad enough "to explain by themselves what happened, on the principle of Occam's razor, without calling in aid the more profound explanations."[144]

For an analogy, consider a man who refuses any job paying less than $25,000 a year. One might blame his unemployment on his poor education, laziness, undependability, and rudeness and recommend training and psychotherapy to make him *worth* $25,000. Or one might emphasize his unrealistic salary expectations and recommend that he take a job at whatever salary he is worth to employers. That recommendation does not rule out measures to make the man worth more—his having a job would itself help—but it does focus attention on the consequences of a wrong or right price. Similarly, even a country much less prosperous and dynamic than Britain can, with appropriate monetary and exchange-rate policies, avoid balance-of-payments crises. Just as a man's insistence on too high a salary keeps him unemployed and in turn lessens his value to employers, so Britain's insistence on too high an exchange rate for sterling probably worsened the country's economic "fundamentals."

A sixth point blends with and helps explain the last one: a complex and partly psychological interaction between domestic financial policy and the foreign-exchange situation helped make policy *unsteady* and thereby probably hampered growth. The responsiveness of short-term capital movements to interest-rate differentials since adoption of convertibility in 1958 was sometimes a nuisance—even when inflows temporarily masked fundamental weakness in the balance of payments. The widely welcomed "discipline" of external crisis against lax inflationary drift sometimes worked perversely. "Successive British governments have been forced to throttle down the economy each time it began to build up steam, in order to restrain inflation, hold down imports, and erase any doubts as to maintenance of existing exchange rates."[145] The government would not squarely face the conflict among such diverse objectives as foreign aid and military activity, growth, high employment, external balance, and the fixed exchange rate. It tried to avoid hard choices by *ad hoc* expedients and by vacillating, in particular, between emphasis on employment and emphasis on the balance of payments. Since the unemployment rate tended to lag behind changes in economic activity, emphasis on it contributed to wrong timing as well as unsteadiness in application of the "brake and accelerator" of demand policy.

Interruptions and reversals of the growth of aggregate demand threw added risk into business decisions on fixed investment and innovation. Whether or not growth was more unstable in Britain than elsewhere, it remains true that a variation of, say, 2 percentage points is more serious in an economy growing slowly than in one growing rapidly. The recession phase of stop-and-go brought growth to a near

136. *The Balance of Payments*, Stamp Memorial Lecture, London: Athlone Press, 1951, p. 16.

137. Brittan, *Steering the Economy*, pp. 454–455. Deficits on current plus long-term-capital account were especially large in 1955, 1960, 1964, and 1965, years which are interestingly different from the years of the sterling crises, 1955, 1957, 1961, 1964, and 1966. On the other hand, sharp declines in reserves (including U.K. positions in the EPU and IMF) occurred in 1955, 1956, 1961, 1964, 1965, and 1966. Cooper in Caves, *op. cit.*, p. 152. The discrepancies suggest that short-term capital movements sometimes masked and sometimes aggravated underlying imbalance.

138. *Journal of Political Economy*, June 1955, p. 223.

139. *Ibid.*, p. 220; cf. pp. 217, 222.

140. Brittan, *Steering the Economy*, p. 440.

141. Reproduced in French translation in André Piettre, *Monnaie et Économie Internationale*, p. 522, from the *Times*, 10 March 1966.

142. *The Destiny of the Dollar*, pp. 41, 52, 107–108.

143. *Gold and World Power*, New York: Harper & Row, 1966, chap. V.

144. Brittan, *Steering the Economy*, p. 440.

145. Chase Manhattan Bank, *Report on Western Europe*, August–September 1961, pp. 2–3. Cf. "Britain: Slowdown Bolsters Sterling," *Business Week*, 4 November 1961, p. 116. For more recent and more detailed comments on the relation between unsteadiness and slow growth, see Brittan, *Steering the Economy*, pp. 449–450, 452, 457–458, and Cooper in Caves, *op. cit.*, p. 197. For a concise chronology of major monetary and fiscal policy reversals in the restrictive direction, see Richard and Peggy Musgrave in Caves, *op. cit.*, pp. 43–44.

standstill more often in Britain than in other countries.

British governments had an incentive to try to break out of the economic vicious circle, particularly when unemployment had drifted above a level thought acceptable. The temptation to expand demand strengthened as elections approached; in the meanwhile, the balance-of-payments deterioration might be financed by drawing on the country's external reserves or borrowing power. Policy would switch to deflation when necessary to defend the exchange rate, *"provided that there seemed a good chance of being able to bring unemployment down again early enough before the next election."*[146] As we saw, Chancellor Maudling did try, starting in 1963, to break out of the stop-go cycle by a policy of steady demand expansion, intended to promote investment and productivity and in turn the strength of sterling, with balance-of-payments deficits simply being tolerated in the short run until these longer-run benefits were achieved. As we also saw, this experiment had to be abandoned—piecemeal and unavowedly at first, but undeniably by no later than the relatively spectacular anti-inflationary measures of July 1966.

Unsteadiness in the growth of aggregate demand not only impaired growth but may well have been more inflationary than a policy of steadier demand pressure over time, since price and wage spurts during or following periods of strong demand do not fully reverse themselves in periods of restraint. Sharp expansionary bursts, according to an analogous argument, also make imports for final consumption higher than they would be if the same level of output were reached more gradually and domestic supplies given more time to adjust.[147] If so, ill-timed oscillations between brake and accelerator aggravated the underlying weakness of the balance of payments both indirectly and directly.

The rapid reversibility of British policy—to summarize—has been almost comical at times. Balance-of-payments troubles have brought a variety of *ad hoc* responses, including two devaluations and one abandonment of exchange-rate pegging, the Selective Employment Tax of 1966, the import surcharge of 1964, the import deposit scheme of 1968, the tightening and loosening of various exchange controls on current and capital transactions, and various attempts at wage and price control, as well as turnarounds in domestic financial policy. Reliance on such expedients creates dangers of improper timing, of anticipatory private actions, of overshooting the mark, and of intensified instability as a result. Financial policy can impair economic performance not only if it is consistently too tight or consistently too loose but also if it is inconsistently too jerky.

Samuel Brittan foresaw a great prize awaiting any British government that would banish self-created problems and the need to distort other policies for balance-of-payments reasons.[148] Time would tell whether Prime Minister Heath's government began to earn this prize in June 1972 by allowing the pound to float. The loss of the anti-inflationary "discipline" of the fixed exchange rate might eventually prove to have been regrettable, after all.

Actually, assessment of the British experiment has been confused by collapse of the entire Bretton Woods system amidst acceleration of worldwide as well as of British inflation in 1973, by the British coal strike and its severe repercussions in late 1973 and early 1974 (sterling dipped as low as $2.15 in mid-January), by the world petroleum crisis of 1973–1974, and by conditions related to the indecisive outcomes of two British general elections in 1974. From surpluses of about US$1.1 and $2.9 billion in 1970 and 1971, the British balance of payments on account of goods, services, transfers, and long-term capital shifted into deficits of $1.6 and $3.0 billion in 1972 and 1973. Short-term capital flows and official financing, however, caused exceptional discrepancies between these figures and the overall balance-of-payments position, which moved slightly back into surplus in 1973 after a $3.0 billion deficit in 1972.[149]

---

146. Brittan, *Steering the Economy*, p. 455; cf. Harry G. Johnson in Bürgenstock Papers, pp. 109–110. Brittan speaks of an "electoral policy cycle," Johnson of a "political cycle."

147. Brittan, *Steering the Economy*, pp. 453–454, citing F. Brechling and J. N. Wolfe in *Lloyds Bank Review*, January 1965.

148. Brittan, *The Price of Economic Freedom*, p. 91.

149. Calculations and figures from *International Financial Statistics*, November 1974, p. 368, and 1974 IMF 21.

Mention of what has happened since this chapter was written is necessarily brief. Final updating of material relevant to this and other country chapters appears in Chapter 28, which reviews "The Crises of 1973 and Generalized Floating."

CHAPTER TWENTY-THREE

The French Franc Since World War II

Multiple rates and broken cross rates

In December 1945, France devalued the franc from its wartime rate of 50 per dollar to 119.107 per dollar. This became the initial French parity registered with the International Monetary Fund in 1946. In January 1948 a complicated system of multiple exchange rates replaced it.[1] As the system evolved during the year, so-called free rates were quoted for the U.S. dollar, Portuguese escudo, and Swiss franc. Fully applicable mainly to tourist and financial transactions in the three "hard" currencies, these rates were "free" only in not being rigidly pegged. Occasional official intervention, together with manipulation of supply and demand by adjusting the stringency of exchange controls and import licensing and the classification of imports as "basic" and "nonbasic," kept the dollar rate in the range of about 305 to 312 francs for most of the year (with equivalent rates on the other two currencies). A new official rate of 214.39 francs per dollar applied to certain favored, or "basic," imports, including coal and wheat. The dollar, escudo, or Swiss-franc proceeds of exports could be sold half at the free and half at the official rate; and except at first, when the free rate alone applied, foreign exchange for authorized "nonbasic" imports from the three

currency areas was bought half at each rate. The effective rate for most trade with the three areas was thus an average of the official and free rates. This middle rate on the dollar hovered in roughly the 260–264 range.

For currencies other than the designated three, the rates for all transactions corresponded to the official dollar rate of 214.39. Since the parity of the pound sterling was still $4.03, the French rate for sterling was 214.39 × 4.03 = 864 francs per pound. The cross rate for sterling diverged from it: the official rate on sterling and the effective dollar rate of 260 francs implied only 864/260 = 3.32 dollars per pound. French merchants found it profitable to buy rubber in Malaya with cheap pounds, for instance, and then sell it in the United States for dollars. A Frenchman might buy £1 at the official rate of 864 francs, buy a pound's worth of commodities with it somewhere in the Sterling Area, sell the commodities for $4.03 in the United States, and realize 4.03 × 260 = 1048 francs on the transaction (less costs of transportation, administration, and the like). In this way, France could intercept some of the dollar earnings of the Sterling Area. Disorderly cross rates involving the lira made similar commodity-shunting operations profitable for Italians, also. In cheap-sterling deals such as this, Australian wool was resold to the United States through France and Italy, costing Australia some dollar earnings. Britain lost dollars because of furs bought in London on French account and then resold in the United States. American importers bought Indian tea through Italian merchants. Conversely, it was profitable for Britons to buy goods in hard-currency areas and reexport them to France or Italy, so far as controls permitted or could be circumvented. A British merchant might obtain $4.03 for £1, buy American goods and sell them for 4.03 × 260 = 1048 francs in France, and then sell the francs for pounds at the official 864 rate, yielding approximately £1⅕. This sort of operation would eat into the British dollar reserves for commodities going to France. Similarly,

---

1. Cf. Bank for International Settlements, 18th *Annual Report*, 1947–1948, pp. 91–93, 19th *Annual Report*, 1948–1949, pp. 119–122; International Monetary Fund, 1948 *Annual Report*, pp. 36–38, 76–78, 1949 *Annual Report*, pp. 23, 60–61; F. Bloch-Lainé *et al.*, *La Zone Franc*, Paris: Presses Universitaires de France, 1956, p. 325; Emil Küng, *Zahlungsbilanzpolitik*, Zürich: Polygraphischer Verlag, 1959, pp. 594–597; and various issues of *International Financial Statistics*.

French soda manufacturers had an incentive to sell their output to Swiss firms, compelling British users to buy in Switzerland. Britain's hard-currency reserves thus suffered to the benefit of the French. The countries harmed could not stamp out such operations entirely, since the difficulty might stem from combinations of individually legal transactions.

Because it had foreseen this sort of thing and, more generally, because discriminatory multiple exchange rates with broken cross rates ran counter to its basic principles, the International Monetary Fund refused to approve the French system. (It did not object to devaluation of the franc as such and had in fact urged devaluation to a realistic single rate.) The French government went ahead with its own proposal, anyway, whereupon "the Fund considered that France had made an unauthorized change in its par value and had therefore become ineligible to use the Fund's resources."[2]

As French prices rose during 1948, the trade deficit with the Sterling Area grew. For this and other reasons, the government decided to carry out an "alignment of the exchanges" in October 1948. Franc rates for all currencies were brought into line with the average of the free and par rates on the dollar, then about 264 francs. For all currencies except the three directly traded on the "free" market, official rates were fixed once a month at the mean dollar rate multiplied by the dollar parity of each currency in question. Cross rates were no longer disorderly. The free rate remained applicable only to financial and tourist transactions in the designated three currencies. The IMF "welcomed" the unification of French exchange rates for trade transactions but did not get around to restoring France's eligibility to draw on its resources until October 1954.

In the fall and winter of 1948–1949 the discount on French banknotes abroad and on the Paris "parallel" market widened, at one time reaching more than 60 percent from the authorized free rate. Tourists and others had incentives to use this market rather than convert their foreign currency into francs at legal rates. To improve the quotation of French banknotes on the unofficial markets by raising the demand for them, the authorities repeatedly raised the amount that travelers could legally bring into France. A recovery in the parallel rate for franc banknotes to a range of around 350–370 to the dollar in the spring of 1949 and a deterioration of the authorized free rate to about 329 narrowed the gap between these two markets to about 10 percent. Even after the "alignment" of October 1948, the official dollar parity had been kept at 214.39 francs. In mid-1949 the free rate was being kept stable by official operations at around 330 per dollar. The average rate, effective for most transactions and serving as the basis for the official rates on currencies other than the dollar, escudo, and Swiss franc, had worsened to about 273 in the months before the devaluations of 1949.

From 1949 through 1956

The events of September 1949 provided an opportunity to apply a single exchange rate to all transactions again. The new rate of 350 francs per dollar, with properly aligned rates on other currencies, represented a devaluation of about 22 percent from the old average dollar rate but only of about 6 percent from the "free" rate that had still applied to tourist expenditure and financial remittances. Relative to the more sharply devalued pound sterling, the franc appreciated by about 12 percent. At the same time, the unity of the franc area was reestablished by a decision to keep the parities of the overseas currencies and the metropolitan franc in line from then on; the former became mere multiples of the latter.[3]

During 1950, France was able to relax foreign-exchange restrictions. Travelers were permitted to take with them out of France twice as many francs in banknotes as before, and restrictions were dropped on bringing French banknotes back into the country from abroad. Forward-exchange regulations were also relaxed. In November 1950, in connection with the newly established European Payments Union, balances in French francs held by residents of other EPU countries were made freely transferable. French authorities noted that each new liberalization measure brought increasing amounts of foreign exchange into France through official channels.[4]

In the first quarter of 1951 France was still gaining gold and dollar reserves. After that, however, a drain set in. It became particularly heavy in the fourth quarter of the year and continued into the first quarter of 1952. A domestic inflationary spurt was being fed by increased spending on the Indo-China war and perpetuated by political obstacles to sufficiently prompt and firm countermeasures. Tightened import restrictions, new tax rebates and other encouragements to exports, and a respite from the inflation all then came to the aid of the situation. During the first half of 1953, however, the overall French balance of payments was again seriously passive. The premium on the one-month forward dollar widened from about 5 to about 11 percent, indicating fear of devaluation. French importers speculated by anticipating their future requirements in foreign currencies, while exporters, delayed selling their foreign-exchange receipts. By the early summer of 1953, the French Stabilization Fund's holdings of convertible currencies were badly depleted. France received special aid from the United States in order to meet its current obligations in the EPU and also obtained an advance of $100 million from the Export-Import Bank in anticipation of later receipts from off-shore contracts with the U.S. government. In the second half of the year the overall balance of payments shifted into surplus, forward quotations on the franc improved, and the French gold and foreign-exchange reserve recovered. The improvement continued into 1954. The French government was able to begin advance repayments on its loan from the Export-Import Bank. Exports grew (most were still subsidized in one way or another), and the franc area as a whole ran a surplus on current account (even excluding all receipts due to foreign aid) in the first half of 1954, in contrast to a deficit in the first half of 1953. During 1954, even after repayment of foreign debts totalling some $300 million, the IMF estimate of France's official gold and foreign exchange holdings rose by over 50 percent. Domestic price stability for more than two years was helping to increase the flow of available saving and was bringing some gold out of private hoards.

The improvement continued in 1955, with estimated reserves again rising more than 50 percent. France benefited from strong European demand for and increased domestic production of its foodstuffs, coal, and steel.

The following year was less favorable. In the winter of 1955–1956 war expenditures in Algeria and frost damage to crops threatened fresh inflationary pressures. Europe's total gain of external reserves was uneven in 1956, and France was an especially big loser. Taking not only gold and dollar holdings but also other items into account, especially France's deficit position within the EPU, French reserves fell by more than 45 percent during 1956 and the first quarter of 1957. They had been equivalent

to the value of five months' imports at the end of 1955; at the end of 1956 they were worth only 2½ months' imports. A boom at home was spurring imports of raw materials, fuel, and equipment, while an expanding government budget deficit was absorbing a bigger share of the savings of the economy and leaving other activities more dependent than before on bank credit. Speculation by way of commercial leads and lags, as well as increases in the exchange holdings of banks, also sapped the reserves. In mid-October—even before fighting broke out at Suez—France arranged with the International Monetary Fund to draw up to $262.5 million from the Fund within the following 12 months. Although France did not begin to use this credit until February 1957, $220 million had already been drawn by the middle of May.[5]

Crises and devaluations in 1957 and 1958

The heavy loss of foreign exchange in 1956 gave little room to relax foreign-exchange re-

2. IMF, 1948 *Annual Report*, p. 37.

3. Bloch-Lainé, *op. cit.*, pp. 346–347. This decision particularly affected French colonies in the Pacific, whose franc had not followed the various postwar devaluations; and its parity in metropolitan francs was rounded off to 5½. The Djibouti (French Somaliland) franc was something of a curiosity. Its parity was established in March 1949 at 214.392 per dollar (then still the official but scarcely applicable parity of the metropolitan franc). It was fully backed by dollar reserves and was made freely convertible into dollars. French Somaliland abolished exchange controls and became a hard-currency country, outside the franc area from the standpoint of French exchange regulations. The Djibouti franc remained aloof from the devaluations of 1949 and later years.

4. BIS, 21st *Annual Report*, 1950–1951, p. 137.

5. The preceding paragraphs draw in particular on BIS, 22nd *Annual Report* (1951–1952), p. 171, 24th *Annual Report* (1953–1954), pp. 128–129, 160, and 27th *Annual Report* (1956–1957), pp. 20–21, 180, 183, as well as the *Annual Reports* of the International Monetary Fund.

strictions; some (governing French purchases of foreign securities, for example) were even tightened a bit. In February 1957 the foreign-exchange allowance for Frenchmen traveling abroad was cut in half. March brought new measures to restrain imports. Import licenses became valid for only three instead of six months, importers had to make advance deposits at their banks of 25 percent of the value of their licensed imports, and an existing special compensatory import tax was extended to a wider range of goods and was standardized at the previous maximum rate of 15 percent. At the beginning of June, the import predeposit requirement was raised to 50 percent, and half of the predeposited amounts were to be transferred to a special account at the Bank of France. On June 18, 1957, the liberalization of imports from quantitative restrictions under the Code of the OEEC was suspended entirely. These measures came too late to keep France's external reserves from practically running out (except for the supposedly "untouchable" gold stock of the Bank of France). Even the credit arranged with the International Monetary Fund in October 1956 and all of the French entitlement to credit in the European Payments Union had been used. By early August, speculation was pressing heavily against the franc.

The government's response came on August 12. For all transactions except imports and exports of certain specified commodities, a 20 percent surcharge or premium was applied to purchases and sales of foreign exchange at the official rate of 350 francs per dollar. This absorbed the special 15 percent import tax previously in effect and also replaced export subsidies in the form of tax rebates. Various controls were liberalized. The maximum duration of import licenses was again extended to six months and the import predeposit requirement was dropped. As long as certain imports continued enjoying the old 350-per-dollar exchange rate instead of the generally effective new rate of 420, speculative buying mounted. On October 28, therefore, the devaluation was generalized to these commodities also. Meanwhile, the reserves had fallen so much that the French authorities felt they could not wait for the devaluation to take effect and replenish them. Toward the end of the year France sought new foreign credits. Early in 1958 arrangements were made for a total of $655 million from the European Payments Union,

the International Monetary Fund, and the United States government.

The year 1958 saw further profound changes in the international status of the franc.[6] Before General de Gaulle came to power early in June, the French economy had been experiencing productive strength but financial crisis. Real gross national product had been increasing at an average rate of more than 5 percent a year since 1953, with industrial production growing even more rapidly. Prices were on the rise again, and between the end of 1956 and the middle of 1958, the cost-of-living index had risen about 18 percent. A current-account deficit in the balance of payments was persisting if not growing. Sagging confidence had been worsening the drain on France's foreign-exchange reserves, especially from early 1956 on. Commercial leads and lags when the franc looked particularly weak are thought to have drained several hundred million dollars from the reserves in 1957.[7] At the end of 1955 the gold and foreign-exchange reserves had been around $2 billion; by the beginning of June 1958, the reserves (not counting the currency reserve of the Bank of France) had fallen as low as $169 million, with $104 million having been lost in the politically turbulent month of May alone.[8] A loss continuing at this rate would have exhausted the reserves by mid-July.

The formation of de Gaulle's government and the return to the Finance Ministry of Antoine Pinay, known for conservative views, had a healthy psychological effect. The previous massive outflow of funds gave way to a small-scale repatriation. Pinay imposed new taxes and, repeating an operation that had proved successful in 1952, issued a loan with repayment indexed to the franc price of gold and offering tax advantages. To encourage the repatriation of foreign assets, a 25 percent fine on reimported flight capital, in effect since 1948, was removed provided that the repatriation took the form of gold to be promptly offered for sale on the Paris market. The loan raised about 300 billion francs, including about 60 billion in foreign exchange or gold. A slight industrial slowdown under way since the spring of the year also presumably helped the balance of payments. But the problem was not fully solved: a worsening of the psychological climate could easily have touched off a new exchange crisis.

In September 1958 the government appointed a committee of financial experts headed by Jacques Rueff. The committee's report of early December stressed France's vicious circle of inflation. A shortage of genuine saving coming onto the loan market—itself largely due to fear of inflation—had left the government unable to borrow enough funds to cover its chronic budget deficit in a noninflationary way. Fiscal expedients that fed inflation had been intensifying this problem. Large private hoards of gold symbolized the attitude of the public. No one really knew their aggregate size, but it was often estimated at several thousands of tons, worth some billions of dollars.

The Rueff committee recommended cutting the French government budget deficit to a level that could be financed by borrowing the genuine savings of the public. Increased excise and income tax rates and withdrawal of certain exemptions were to expand budget revenue. On the expenditure side, the committee recommended cutting subsidies, including those paid on food, fuel, and public utilities in struggles to hold down the cost-of-living index. Reorganization of the social services and increased prices of postal and other services supplied by the government were to achieve further economies.

Unfortunately, some of these economy measures—especially the removal of subsidies—would directly tend to raise some prices and indirectly tend to raise wages and other payments linked to the cost-of-living index. Therefore, the committee recommended and the government decreed an end to all arrangements tying wages and agricultural prices to a price index. The only exception was the continued indexing of the minimum wage rate. The decree did not cut all connection between wages and prices, of course, but only the most mechanical one. Further to check price increases, the committee recommended opening French markets to intensified foreign competition. Most of the import quotas reimposed during the 1957 crisis were to be taken off, and France was to proceed with its obligations under the Code of Liberalization and the Common Market Treaty.

To make renewed import liberalization possible, something else had to be done to keep the balance of payments in order, and on December 27 the franc was devalued by 14.93 percent to 493.7 per dollar. At the same time, along with most other West European currencies, it became freely convertible for nonresidents. A so-called "new franc" was also announced and was finally introduced in January 1960. Two zeros were lopped off all prices, including the price of the dollar, and the exchange rate became 20¼ U.S. cents.

Initial success of the reforms

According to its author, Jacques Rueff, the financial reform had a breadth, coherence, and systematic character unprecedented in French history. The de Gaulle government had the advantage of operating under emergency powers. For the first time a devaluation was undertaken "in cold blood" and accompanied by associated measures needed for success.

The financial rehabilitation did indeed seem to stop endless inflation and recurrent external crisis. The annual indexes of wholesale and consumer prices rose by an average of only about 5½ percent between 1958 and 1959 and less than 3 percent between 1959 and 1960—not too bad a record in comparison with the 13 percent rise between 1957 and 1958 and considering price increases in the nationalized industries and the removal of subsidies that had been falsifying the cost-of-living index. In 1961 prices averaged 3⅕ percent higher than the year before, and the following year the rise averaged 3½ percent. The weakening of inflationary expectations encouraged saving by households and was reflected in a decline in

6. Cf. Jacques Rueff, "The Rehabilitation of the Franc," *Lloyds Bank Review,* No. 52, April 1959, pp. 1–18; "France Beats Back Inflation," *Business Week,* 16 May 1959, pp. 68ff.; BIS, 29th *Annual Report* (1958–1959), pp. 45–47, 77–81, 140–143, 175–176, 191–193; "The French Stabilization Program," Federal Reserve Bank of New York, *Monthly Review,* January 1960, pp. 11–15; and Michael A. Heilperin, "Accelerating France's Expansion," *The Banker,* April 1961, pp. 247–254.

7. *Wall Street Journal,* 1 May 1959, p. 8.

8. These are Rueff's franc figures converted into dollars at the 420 rate then in effect.

long- and short-term interest rates. The growth of production did slow down at first (hardly surprising when an ingrained inflation is brought under control), but forecasts of an actual recession were not borne out; and production soon surged ahead again. The balance of payments improved even though the removal of quotas on intra-European trade, which France had suspended in June 1957, was restored in December 1958 and made almost complete soon afterwards, even though liberalization of imports from the dollar area was reintroduced and extended, even though travel allowances and other aspects of exchange control were liberalized, and even though the 10 percent tariff cuts and the quota enlargements made in favor of the other five members of the European Economic Community at the beginning of 1959 were extended to other countries during the year. Both in dollar value and in physical volume, total imports actually fell between 1958 and 1959. French exports fell about 7 percent in yearly average dollar price (higher franc prices partly offsetting the cheapening through devaluation) and rose about 10 percent in total dollar value and 20 percent in physical volume. The balance of merchandise trade thus shifted from a deficit of nearly $300 million in 1958 to a surplus of about $435 million in 1959. The invisibles account improved also, especially because of a rise in tourist earnings. The capital account benefited from reversal of the previously adverse leads and lags, a return of French funds held abroad, and an inflow of foreign investment (apparently attracted in part by the relaxation of exchange restrictions). For France and the rest of the franc area together, the total balance on current and private capital accounts swung from a deficit in 1958 to a surplus of $1.3 billion in 1959. Despite heavy repayments on debts to the EPU, the IMF, and other creditors, the French official reserves and the foreign assets of the commercial banks combined were able to rise almost $1 billion during 1959.[9] Part of this early improvement stemmed from lucky coincidences or temporary responses, including recovery from the 1957–1958 recession in the United States and other customer countries, an immediate postdevaluation shift in leads and lags and an initial cutback of imports previously stockpiled to beat devaluation or tighten restrictions, and a heavy repatriation of private long-term capital. With these influences spent, the recorded surplus shrank in 1960; otherwise, the basic bal-

ance would have risen then and again in 1961. From $645 and $1050 million at the ends of 1957 and 1958, the gold and convertible-currency holdings of the monetary authorities rose to $1720 million at the end of 1959, continued growing every year, and reached $4457 million at the end of 1963. In 1961 France displaced Germany as the country with the world's biggest balance-of-payments surplus and biggest gain of official external reserves.

The first four years after the reforms of 1958 brought a growth of $4.7 billion in France's *net* external assets, counting the official reserves, the net IMF position, and the prepayment of debt. External surpluses over the four years totaled $1.4 billion on trade account, $1.7 billion on invisible account, and $1 billion on ordinary long-term capital account.[10] Imports rose moderately in relation to the uptrend of production, while exports grew strikingly. Autonomous factors were partly responsible, such as growing supplies of petroleum and petroleum products and natural gas from inside the franc area and the export success of the new Caravelle airplane. Reequipment and capacity expansion in capital-goods production and modernization of farm techniques promoted export growth in these sectors. Foreign capital flowed in, partly for investments previously postponed.

Nevertheless, the evidence permits supposing that the correction of the franc's overvaluation did work as standard theory envisages. The devaluation of 1958 may even have been excessive.

France began learning the German lesson: large and persistent external surpluses can cause trouble. The French authorities took advantage of their opportunity to relax controls further. They raised the foreign travel allowance for residents in June 1961 and February 1962. In April 1962 they authorized Frenchmen to make portfolio investments abroad via the official exchange market. At the end of 1962 they further relaxed rules concerning the surrender of export proceeds for francs. Early in 1963 they even adopted one measure against capital imports by forbidding interest payments on the franc accounts of nonresidents.

Renewed inflation in the early 1960s

These and other measures were designed not only to help the international payments situation but also to resist a tendency toward imported inflation.[11] They fell short of what was needed. Perhaps the continuing monetary expansion caused demand-pull inflation; perhaps it came as the mere passive support of wage-push inflation. Anyway, it occurred. Its relation to the balance of payments is suggested by the fact that the domestic monetary reserve base in the form of currency and bankers'-deposit liabilities of the Bank of France expanded by very roughly as much as the Bank's net foreign assets. (In earlier postwar years, in contrast, expansion of its *domestic* assets, including loans to the commercial banks, had matched expansion of its monetary liabilities.) From the end of 1958 to mid-1963, the net foreign assets of the Bank of France grew by 27 percent more than its liabilities serving as the domestic monetary reserve base. Over the shorter period from the end of 1959 to mid-1963, it is true, this "high-powered" money grew by 23 percent more than the Bank's net foreign liabilities.[12] Apparently a massive sterilization of foreign-asset acquisitions in 1959 was partially undone in the following years.

The ordinary money supply (demand deposits and currency, as distinguished from its reserve base) grew by *larger* percentages *after* the famous Rueff reform, and especially after 1959, than in the several preceding years. (The percentages of growth each year averaged 10.2 and were falling in 1954 through 1958 · but averaged 14.3 and were generally rising from then through mid-1963.) This monetary expansion was by no means fully matched, of course, by growth of the foreign assets of the central and commercial banking system as a whole. As usual, its main counterpart was loans to domestic business (while, for a change, bank loans to cover the government budget deficit were *not* an important factor).

So much creation of ordinary money would hardly have been possible, however, without an expanding reserve base of new high-powered francs. French official reports explicitly recognize that while expansion of bank credit to domestic borrowers was the chief immediate source of new money, the banks enjoyed the necessary liquidity because the Bank of France was buying up foreign exchange yielded by the balance-of-payments surplus.[13]

Another expansionary factor was the French public's growing willingness to hold demand deposits. Currency fell from 50 percent of the demand-deposit-and-currency total at the end

THE FRENCH FRANC SINCE WORLD WAR II

of 1953 to 47 percent at the end of 1958 and to 39 percent by mid-1963. Not only the total stock of high-powered francs was growing, but also the fraction of it held by the banks as reserves rather than held by the public.

The unfamiliar—to Frenchmen—basis of the monetary inflation perhaps helps explain why the process was not more generally understood and resisted. The moderate—for France —pace of price rises in the first few years after 1958 may have contributed to complacency. In

9. BIS, 30th *Annual Report*, 1959–1960, pp. 47–48, 122–124, 142–144, 157; and *International Financial Statistics*.

10. BIS, 33rd *Annual Report*, 1962–1963, p. 103.

11. Advance repayments of government external debt are sometimes listed among these measures. Actually, though, any anti-inflationary effect from them depends on the accompanying domestic financial policy. The effect would be strongest if the government bought foreign exchange for debt repayment with francs raised by taxation or noninflationary borrowing at home. So far as the authorities continue buying up the surplus foreign-exchange receipts of the private sector with newly created francs, the effect of these open-market operations (which is what they amount to) remains expansionary whether the authorities repay foreign debt with the foreign exchange bought or simply hold it.

12. These and the figures to follow are calculated from *International Financial Statistics*.

13. Cf. Conseil National du Crédit, *Dix-Septième Rapport Annuel, Année 1962*, Paris: Imprimerie Nationale, 1963, esp. pp. 35–36, 44–46, 62, 77; Banque de France, *Compte Rendu des Opérations*, 1962, Paris: Imprimeries Paul Dupont, 1963, esp. pp. 5–6, 25–26. For other comments on the inflationary impact of the French external surplus, see BIS, 32nd *Annual Report* (1961–1962), pp. 28, 30, 64, and 33rd *Annual Report* (1962–1963), pp. 11, 13; IMF, 1962 *Annual Report*, p. 96, and 1963 *Annual Report*, pp. 108–109; and *The Economist*, 6 April 1963, p. 77. According to Professor Fritz Machlup, inflation in France and some other European countries during this period was due "entirely" to purchases of foreign-exchange reserves at pegged exchange rates. *The United States Balance of Payments*, statements submitted to the Joint Economic Committee, November 1963; Washington: Government Printing Office, p. 308.

comparison with a 90 percent monetary expansion from the end of 1958 to October 1963, the home-and-import-goods price index rose only 18 percent and the cost-of-living index only 28 percent. The explanation (on the level of mere arithmetic) involves not only the continued growth of real output but also a decline in the velocity of money: the ratio of gross national product to money supply (average of beginning- and end-of-year money) fell from 3.30 in 1958 to 2.93 in 1962 and 2.79 in 1963. In the opinion of the French authorities,[14] the apparent success of monetary stabilization was encouraging the public to demand larger stocks of money and other liquid assets in relation to income. Furthermore, the authorities seemed timid about resisting a process that they could describe as spontaneous rather than as due to any unsound positive actions of their own. After all, growth of population and incomes and increased wages and costs and prices were supposedly creating a *need* for more money. "The development of the money supply is linked to these different movements by such diverse relationships that it seems to be their effect as well as their cause." "Brutal" measures of monetary restriction, unaccompanied by other anti-inflationary policies, would have risked jeopardizing the expansion of the economy.[15] Monetary policy, by itself, was inadequate to reconcile the goals of price stability, "expansion, full employment, a sufficient volume of investments, and the saving necessary to finance them."[16]

As the rise in prices became less gradual, concern about creeping inflation revived. The authorities continued wanting both easy medium-term and long-term credit for industry and commerce and some mild restraint on the growth of liquidity. In January 1961 they imposed on the banks a new required ratio of liquid assets (cash, Treasury bills, and certain specified paper) to demand and time deposit liabilities. The new ratio was first set at 30 percent, raised to 32 percent a year later, and raised again to 35 and 36 percent in March and May 1963. Meanwhile, attempts continued to manipulate the structure of interest rates so as to promote the development of the capital market and encourage medium- and long-term lending at the expense of short-term lending. When prices and liquidity continued rising into 1963, the banks were asked to hold the expansion of credit to the private sector down to 12 percent in the ensuing 12 months (about two-thirds of the rate of increase of

recent years), while discriminating in favor of export credit and medium-term investment credit. The different strands of policy were not fully consistent with each other.[17]

As early as April 1963 the authorities began controlling the prices or retail mark-ups of many manufactured consumer goods. In September the government announced further measures against inflation. These were to include requiring government approval for price increases on industrial products, controlling factory prices of nearly all manufactures, controlling some retail prices and limiting distributors' profit margins, cutting some gasoline and cigarette prices for symbolic effect, lowering import duties on many consumer goods, taking a tough line (without an actual freeze) on wages in the public industries and using a profit and credit squeeze to pressure private employers into tough wage bargaining, advancing the discharge dates of Army draftees and stepping up the recruitment of foreign workers to ease the labor market, further reducing the government budget deficit, tightening the limit on bank credit expansion, and floating a bond issue to drain off bank funds. Further tightening of credit restrictions and price and profit controls was scheduled for early 1964, as well as continued resistance to wage increases. As so often in recent French history, suppressing inflation seemed to get at least as much emphasis as stopping it.

Trends of the mid-1960s

By around that time, inflation seemed again, for a while, to be undermining French international competitiveness. The surplus on current account (including transfers) had peaked in 1961 and had since been shrinking. In transactions with countries outside the franc area in 1964, the current surplus dropped to below $0.1 billion, while the merchandise account registered a small deficit.

The deterioration of the merchandise and current accounts was interrupted in 1965; stabilization policies apparently worked in slowing down the growth of imports, while exports continued rising rapidly, in line with foreign demand.[18] It may be just coincidence, but the same year brought an intensification of the French campaign to undermine the gold-exchange standard, the special status of the dollar, and the dominance of the Anglo-Saxons in the Western alliance. In a press conference on February 4, General de Gaulle delivered a notable paean to the gold standard; and that spring, France converted nearly $1 billion of dollar reserves into gold. Ever since 1959, France had added more gold than foreign exchange to its reserves; and in 1965 and 1966 it reduced its foreign-exchange reserves while adding gold. When the French authorities needed dollars to support the franc in 1966, they did not pay out gold, as the gold standard they advocated would have called for; instead, some official agencies and nationalized industries borrowed dollars in the Eurodollar bond market.[19]

In the late summer of 1966 the series of large external surpluses that had followed the franc's devaluation and stabilization in 1958 came to an end. The spot rate of the franc against the dollar, which had long remained near its upper intervention point, eased rapidly.[20] For 1966 as a whole, the trade balance with nonfranc countries turned slightly negative, and the current-account surplus again practically vanished. The following year brought no marked recovery. Thanks in part, however, to continuing inflows of long-term capital, French international reserves continued through 1967 the growth that they had begun in 1958. The downtrend of French payments surpluses in the 1960s had been a move toward rather than away from equilibrium, and there was no question of actual balance-of-payments trouble at the beginning of 1968.[21]

The strikes of 1968 and their repercussions

After resolution of the international gold crisis in March 1968, the next crisis centered around the franc. The French balance of payments was already in deficit in the first quarter, though not seriously, and the official reserves fell. Then, in May and June, social and industrial unrest erupted in strikes of students and workers. "Almost overnight the franc lost its place among the stable currencies of the world. More important than concern about the stability of the French government, which proved to be unfounded, was the specter of inflation."[22] The strikes directly caused a loss of output estimated at 2 percent of gross national product, and the agreement that ended them raised hourly wage rates by some 12 percent. Mini-

mum wage rates and social security benefits were also increased. Consumer spending received an abrupt stimulus at a time when economic policy was already directed toward expansion to combat unemployment associated with rapidly increasing productivity.[23] The lapse of confidence not only caused a flight of short-term capital but also contributed to a deficit in the basic balance of payments: the previous net import of long-term capital turned into a substantial outflow, foreign workers hastened to transfer accumulated savings as well as current earnings abroad, and exchange-rate anticipations affected the timing of commodity transactions.[24] During 1968, French international reserves (including IMF position) dropped by $2.8 billion, or 40 percent, even though some recovery occurred in December.

The Paris foreign-exchange market was unable to function from May 20 to June 7. On foreign markets, the Federal Reserve Bank of New York and the Bank for International Settlements acted for the Bank of France in

14. BIS, 33rd *Annual Report* (1962–1963), p. 60.

15. Conseil National du Crédit, *op. cit.*, pp. 217, 218.

16. Banque de France, *op. cit.*, p. 27.

17. BIS, 32nd *Annual Report* (1961–1962), pp. 6, 67; 33rd *Annual Report* (1962–1963), pp. 13, 60–62; IMF, 1963 *Annual Report*, p. 109.

18. IMF, 1966, pp. 100–101.

19. Fred Hirsch, *Money International*, London: Allen Lane, Penguin Press, 1967, p. 277 (quoting de Gaulle's statement); Charles P. Kindleberger, *Power and Money*, New York: Basic Books, 1970, p. 214.

20. BIS, 1966–1967, p. 135.

21. Milton Gilbert in H. W. J. Bosman and F. A. M. Alting von Geusau, *The Future of the International Monetary System*, Lexington, Mass.: Heath, 1970, pp. 46–48.

22. Federal Reserve Bank of Cleveland, *Economic Commentary*, 22 September 1969, p. 3.

23. IMF, 1969, p. 78; Gilbert in Bosman and Alting von Geusau, *op. cit.*, pp. 49–50.

24. Gilbert, *op. cit.*, pp. 48–49.

supporting the franc at its lower limit. Exchange control was temporarily reintroduced on May 31. Outward payments were no longer freely allowed and were required to take place through authorized banks. Residents of France could no longer acquire assets abroad or hold means of foreign payment in France without official authorization. Export of means of payment or securities and imports and exports of gold also required permission.[25] The French government tried to offset the effect of price inflation on exports by cheap export credit and by subsidies (replaced early in 1969 by an adjustment of the value-added tax). Yet France's international price competitiveness worsened.[26]

The French authorities hoped to restrain the rise in costs following the generous wage settlements by promoting rapid recovery and expansion of output and fuller utilization of productive capacity. They cut business taxes to lessen incentives for price increases, reintroduced tax credits for new investments, and budgeted an increased government deficit. Monetary ease accompanied fiscal ease. Direct price control was extended. An expansionary monetary and fiscal policy may seem farfetched as part of an anti-inflationary program, yet that is what France adopted.[27] As might have been expected, it did not succeed in checking the rise in costs and did adversely affect the balance of payments. A shift toward restraint became necessary before the year was up. Industrial production, however, scored good gains.

At the end of August 1968, rumors of a possible revaluation of the German mark revived more strongly than before. Uneasiness over the Soviet occupation of Czechoslovakia was already contributing to weakness of the franc as well as of sterling. Around the beginning of September, French funds moved into Germany in increasingly heavy volume. On September 4, in an effort to help restore confidence, the exchange controls imposed in May were lifted. Open-market operations were carried out to reduce the liquidity of the banks, and their rediscount ceilings were lowered.[28] Although speculative outflows were not stopped, the crisis was papered over for a while.

It became virulent again in November. On Wednesday the 20th the principal European foreign-exchange markets were closed for the rest of the week while the finance ministers and central-bank governors of the Group of Ten met in emergency session in Bonn. The meeting was generally expected to result in

exchange-rate adjustments—devaluation of the franc, at least. On Sunday the 24th, though, de Gaulle surprised the world with a decision not to devalue. (Fear of an upward impact on prices in France, as well as considerations of prestige, reportedly influenced his decision.) Instead of devaluing, the French government sought severe fiscal and monetary restraint. Domestic price controls were tightened further. The value-added tax—payable on imports but reimbursable on exports—was raised. The recently lifted exchange controls were restored in more severe form. Official authorization was required for all payments to nonresidents, for import and export of gold, and for all acquisitions of foreign securities other than with the proceeds of selling securities previously held. Forward purchases of foreign exchange were restricted. All foreign transactions by residents had to take place through authorized intermediaries, and all foreign means of payment and securities held in France had to be deposited with authorized intermediaries. Residents were required to repatriate all foreign claims and earnings acquired or received during the preceding four months. Exchange restrictions were imposed on travel abroad. Restrictions were tightened, in December and again in January 1969, on foreign operations of French banks. France received aid in the form of a new $2 billion line of credit from the other members of the Group of Ten.[29]

When the European markets reopened on Monday, November 25, bearishness on the franc and bullishness on the mark had subsided. By February 1969, the heavy November losses of French official net foreign assets had been recovered. This was largely the result of the exchange controls, including the requirements for repatriation of funds held abroad. France remained in payments deficit, though, partly because of the inflationary sequels of the events of May and June.[30]

Successful devaluation

Balance-of-payments figures for 1969 as a whole are distorted both arithmetically and substantively by devaluation in August; but for what they are worth, they show French commodity trade with the rest of the world, including the franc area, moving from near-balance in 1968 to a deficit of $0.9 billion, the current-account deficit deepening from $1.1 to $1.8

billion, and the overall deficit settled by the monetary authorities shrinking from $3.7 to $1.1 billion. Transactions with nonfranc countries alone in 1969 resulted in a big trade-deficit, an increased current deficit, a slightly reduced basic deficit, and a reduced but still heavy overall deficit.[31]

After losing a referendum concerning regional government organization, President de Gaulle resigned on April 28. Existing speculation against the franc grew more intense. The three-month forward discount of the franc against the dollar had reached almost 17 percent per annum in mid-March and widened to almost 27 percent on April 30 and almost 32 percent on May 7. In the final days of April and the first days of May, the inflow of funds into Germany totaled over $4 billion. This was stopped by announcement on May 9 that there would be no change in the mark's parity.[32]

An 11.1 percent devaluation, to 5.5542 francs per dollar, came as a surprise when announced during a period of relative calm, on August 8.[33] The reversal of speculative flows after the upward revaluation of the German mark in October benefited the French payments position, as well as the British.[34]

As early as 1970 the balance of payments showed the intended results of devaluation. In French transactions with the rest of the world, including the franc area, merchandise trade returned from deficit to surplus, the current deficit (including transfers) shrank drastically, and the overall balance settled by the monetary authorities moved to a surplus of nearly $2.0 billion. In transactions with nonfranc countries, merchandise trade returned to surplus, the current account showed approximate balance, a small basic surplus appeared, and various concepts of overall balance showed a healthy surplus.

In 1971 the combination of well-sustained economic growth in France and relatively weak activity abroad might have-tended to affect the external current account adversely.[35] This tendency was outweighed by the continuing benefits of the parity changes of 1969. In transactions with the rest of the world, including the franc area, the trade surplus grew to $1.1 billion, and the overall balance settled by the monetary authorities grew to nearly $3½ billion. The French surplus was the largest, after Germany's, of any continental European country.

25. BIS, 1967–1968, p. 144.

26. Gilbert, *op. cit.*, p. 50.

27. See BIS, 1968–1969, pp. 15–16; IMF, 1969, pp. 12, 78.

28. Federal Reserve Bank of New York, *Annual Report 1968*, pp. 37–38; BIS, 1968–1969, pp. 18, 130–132; IMF, 1969, p. 79.

29. BIS, 1968–1969, pp. 18–19, 137–138; Federal Reserve Bank of N.Y., *Annual Report 1968*, p. 39. France's receipt of international support in May, June, and November 1968, and again in the spring of 1969, contrasts with its having occasionally held out, in a show of independence, against earlier such arrangements for rescuing other currencies. Kindleberger, *op. cit.*, pp. 214–215.

30. BIS, 1968–1969, pp. 11–12, 19; Federal Reserve Bank of New York, *Annual Report 1969*, p. 34.

31. The figures in *International Financial Statistics* and its supplements refer to the transactions of metropolitan France with countries outside the franc area through 1966 and with the rest of the world, including the franc area, from 1967 on. Figures on different bases are conveniently assembled in Organisation for Economic Co-operation and Development, *Economic Surveys—France*, Paris: OECD, February 1972, pp. 82–83.

32. IMF, 1969, pp. 125–126; BIS, 1969–1970, p. 4. For further details, see the chapter on Germany.

33. The forward discount on the franc had narrowed sharply after the May crisis and did not exceed around 4 percent in August (chart in 1970 IMF 119), suggesting, if not forward support, lack of strong expectations of early devaluation. According to Gordon L. Weil and Ian Davidson (*The Gold War*, New York: Holt, Rinehart and Winston, 1970, pp. 166–167), newly elected President Pompidou decided on devaluation on July 16 but for three weeks shared his secret with only seven other persons in Paris. The international consultation required by IMF and EEC rules did not take place. At the time of the surprise announcement, the new finance minister revealed that published figures had concealed the full amount of loss of external reserves during the preceding 12 months; to all intents and purposes it had been no less than $4.7 billion.

34. BIS, 1969–1970, pp. 5, 137.

35. BIS, 1971–1972, pp. 96–97.

The French side of the dollar crises

In this year of mark-yen-dollar crises, 1971, the balance-of-payments picture of France, as of many other countries, was distorted by short-term capital flows. Trying to limit the added monetary expansion caused by inflows, the Bank of France provided the bulk of its credit to the commercial banks at money-market rates calculated to avoid any incentive to borrow abroad. In April the banks' franc liabilities to correspondents abroad were made subject to reserve requirements, and from then to early August various reserve requirements were raised substantially. In September the government tightened regulations on prices and profit margins. Inflows of funds in July and early August added $2.1 billion to official net foreign assets, some of which amount was used to repay debt to the International Monetary Fund. When the foreign-exchange markets reopened on August 23 after being closed for a week during the dollar crisis, the franc, in contrast with other major currencies, was not set afloat. Instead, following the Belgian example of May, France split the foreign-exchange market, continuing to peg the franc for commercial transactions but allowing the rate to float in financial transactions. Strict regulations were introduced to combat arbitrage between the two submarkets.[36] At the time of the Smithsonian Agreement, the franc retained its gold parity and was thereby revalued 8.57 percent against the dollar.

In 1972 the French overall surplus settled by the monetary authorities in transactions with franc and nonfranc countries shrank to roughly half the 1971 figure. Among other changes, net long-term capital flows shifted from approximate balance into substantial deficit, and inflows of short-term funds shrank. Despite the dual exchange-market system, however, inflows of funds through the banking sector caused trouble in June and July, when the pound sterling and then the dollar came under bearish speculation. By the late summer, price inflation

had begun to accelerate, while the authorities were struggling to maintain control over domestic liquidity. Repercussions of the drop of the floating pound sterling after mid-October tended to weaken the franc rate. Later that year and early in 1973, the fluctuating prospects of leftist victory in the parliamentary elections scheduled for March had evident influence on fluctuations of the commercial franc within its support limits. When the European exchange markets reopened on March 19 after the second dollar crisis of 1973, the franc joined other Common Market currencies in their joint float.[37]

In 1973 the French surpluses in trade and goods and services shrank. Taking transfers and movements of nonbank capital into account also, the balance shifted into deficit. So did the overall balance settled by the monetary authorities, which moved from a surplus of about $1.8 billion in 1972 to a deficit of about $1.9 billion in 1973.[38] Along with other European currencies, the franc generally strengthened against the dollar in the first half of the year and weakened in the second half.

Effective January 21, 1974, France cut loose from the European "snake." Spain followed suit the next day with an independent float of the peseta. Though originally scheduled for six months only, the floating of the franc has continued. At first the franc dropped by about 5 percent, but through most of the remainder of 1974 it trended mildly upward against the dollar. On March 21 France abolished the dual foreign-exchange market, in which, since August 1971, commercial and financial transactions had supposedly been separated. Italy similarly unified its markets the following day.

---

36. BIS, 1971–1972, pp. 60–61, 122, 136–137.

37. BIS, 1972–1973, pp. 57–61, 101–102, 132; Charles Coombs in Federal Reserve Bank of New York, *Monthly Review*, March 1973, pp. 59–60.

38. For this and the preceding paragraph, see balance-of-payments figures in IMF, 1974, p. 21, and in *International Financial Statistics*.

The German Struggle Against Imported Inflation

The German balance of payments, 1951–1960

Germany's external disequilibrium after 1950 offers an instructive contrast to the experiences of other countries. Tracing it will give some fresh slants on how internal and external conditions can interact and on how well or how poorly various expedients can succeed in reconciling internal and external policy objectives. The story of primarily German events also helps describe the environment in which the experiences of other countries unfolded.

Earlier chapters have already mentioned German developments up to the time when emergency measures stemmed a balance-of-payments crisis early in 1951. The shift within a few months from a critical deficit to an eventually troublesome surplus illustrates how sensitively trade and capital movements can respond to changes in expectations and to even rather small changes in objective conditions when no "automatic" adjustment mechanism is at work.

Let us first broadly survey the German balance of payments from that time until the end of 1960 (after which its development was interrupted). As measured by the annual growth in official reserves of gold and foreign exchange,[1] the overall surplus rose between 1951 and 1953 to a level equaling over one-sixth of the value of merchandise exports. The continuing gain of gold and foreign exchange shrank in 1954 and 1955, rose again to peak levels in 1956 and 1957, and shrank in 1958. An actual decline in the reserves in 1959 was due to special circumstances and policy expedients and is misleading by itself, especially since the surplus from trade in goods and services remained not far below its peak levels. In 1960 the gain of reserves again set a new record.

The largest single contribution to the surplus on current account and to the growth of reserves was an excess of merchandise exports over imports. It even exceeded the growth of reserves in most of the years of the decade. This trade surplus grew without much interruption.

Between 1950 and 1960, German exports rose at average annual rates of 19 percent in money value and 16 percent in physical volume.[2] This rapid export growth would hardly have been possible without rising total industrial production and real gross national product (GNP in current marks deflated by the cost-of-living index); their growth rates averaged 9½ and not quite 9 percent a year respectively over the same period. Among the suggested explanations of such rapid economic advance[3] are an expanding labor force fed by refugees from the East (which, incidentally, helped keep wage demands moderate), the legendary German industriousness, and a sustained rise in productivity, based in part on restoration of an

---

1. The concept used here corresponds to line 10 in issues of *International Financial Statistics* of 1961 and earlier. The continuity of this series is broken by the exclusion, from the beginning of 1959, of net bilateral claims arising from liquidation of the European Payments Union. Where it makes any difference in discussion of changes in reserves during 1959, these net bilateral claims have been added back in to preserve continuity with the figures reported for the end of 1958. A conceptual change first adopted for line 10 in *International Financial Statistics*, August 1961, should also be noticed.

2. If $8.35x^{10} = 47.93$, $x = 1.19$, where the 8.35 and 47.93 are exports in 1950 and 1960 in billions of marks. Other growth rates mentioned in this first section are similarly calculated from figures in *International Financial Statistics*.

3. See Federal Reserve Bank of New York, *Monthly Review*, December 1960, p. 207.

efficient price system after June 1948 and in part on a higher ratio of saving and investment to national income than in most other countries. Fiscal measures encouraged accelerated depreciation and the plowing-back of profits. The smallness of the drain of national resources into defense contributed to the export supply capacity of the German economy as well as to investment; and a lag of defense spending even behind appropriations enabled the Federal government, until late in 1956, to run budget surpluses. This fiscal restraint, coupled with anti-inflationary monetary policy, contrasted with strong demand throughout most of the rest of the world and so helped promote German exports of machinery, automobiles, and other highly fabricated products. German industry promoted exports aggressively through trade fairs and otherwise and flexibly adapted its wares to foreign requirements. Tax incentives and government export credit insurance played a part. German capital goods especially appealed to businessmen in countries whose balance-of-payments controls still discriminated against imports from the United States.

Imports rose not quite as strongly as exports, though still at annual rates averaging 14 percent in money value and 15 percent in physical volume between 1950 and 1960. Decades of tariff protection and other policies to promote a large measure of self-sufficiency may have somewhat restrained a rise in the fraction of German income spent on imports. Also, the postwar emphasis on production of capital goods with a relatively low content of imported materials helped restrain the growth of total imports.[4] (These observations do not, of course, justify any notion that the German export surplus has been of "structural" origin. So-called structural conditions that apparently predispose a country to an export surplus at one set of domestic and foreign price relations would not do so at another.)

In comparison with merchandise trade, the net position from ordinary services (including travel, transportation, and investment income,

TABLE 24.1. *Relations between changes within calendar years in net foreign assets and other balance-sheet items of the consolidated German monetary system*

Change in net foreign assets expressed as percentage of change in:	1952	1953	1954	1955	1956	1957	1958	1959	1960	Entire period between ends of 1951 and 1960
Total net assets	35%	31%	22%	20%	43%	36%	30%	−2%	36%	26%
Money + quasi money	50	46	32	33	70	46	36	−3	57	38
Money	138	157	84	70	219	134	89	−9	207	107

NOTES: All figures refer to *changes* within the periods indicated and have been calculated from end-of-year figures published in *International Financial Statistics*, February and April 1961, which may be consulted for detailed definitions. The consolidated monetary system comprises the central bank (called the Bank deutscher Länder at first, later reorganized as the Deutsche Bundesbank), the Reconstruction Loan Corporation, the deposit money banks, and the Treasury coin circulation. Net foreign assets are the foreign assets minus foreign liabilities of the central bank and the deposit money banks. Other assets include loans to and investments in the private sector of the economy and net claims on government. Claims on all levels of government and some government agencies are recorded net of government deposits, counterpart funds (which originated in connection with receipts of U.S. aid in earlier years), and government loans made to certain types of banks for relending to the private economy. Other assets include the country's net position with the International Monetary Fund, as well as unclassified assets. Nonmonetary liabilities include bonded indebtedness of banks, which is much more common in Germany than in the United States, as well as unclassified liabilities and capital accounts. Money is coin, currency, and sight deposits held by the public; quasi money is time deposits.

among others) fluctuated more widely. This balance was negative except in 1957; and though apparently in an unsteady trend toward still larger deficits, it remained too small fully to offset the positive trade balance. Its component parts showed opposed trends during the 1950s, including a shift from surplus to deficit in foreign travel, a shift from deficit to surplus in transportation, rising net outpayments of foreign investment income, and a growing deficit in other nonmilitary services.

Sales of services to NATO forces stationed in Germany grew year to year without interruption. This military item ranked second only to the merchandise export surplus, and was gaining ground on it, as the biggest contributor to the net surplus on current account and so to the growth in external reserves. About four-fifths of these services were sold to United States forces and the remainder to British and other NATO forces.

Among net debit balances, the one ranking second only to nonmilitary services from 1955 on was official donations. Germany's earlier heavy net inflow of foreign aid had almost vanished by 1953, and after then Germany became a net donor on a growing scale. German unilateral transfers consisted mainly of indemnification payments to Israel and to victims of Naziism living in other countries, but aid to underdeveloped countries promised to become an increasing share of the total.

The long-term capital account usually but not always showed a negative balance, particularly because the government was repaying its external debt in installments and because private Germans were generally net buyers of foreign securities. Short-term capital movements, whether recorded or concealed in "errors and omissions" and whether undertaken by the government, the banks, or other firms and individuals, fluctuated widely.

The net imbalance from all the items just surveyed made the official reserves of gold and foreign exchange grow not only in every year from 1951 through 1960, with the sole exception of 1959, but even in every single month from early 1952 until October 1957. Even thereafter, monthly reserve losses occurred only in October 1957 through February 1958 and in January through April and June through September 1959. No further losses occurred until after the exchange-rate adjustment of March 1961. The increase in reserves from $274 million at the end of 1950 to $7199 mil-

lion at the end of 1960 amounts to an average annual growth rate of 39 percent.

Monetary expansion in Germany

A current-account surplus tends to withdraw goods and services from the home economy, expand money income through the foreign-trade multiplier, and expand the home money supply as reserves grow. One way to throw light on this last aspect of the problem is to compare increases in the net foreign assets and other assets and in the monetary and other liabilities of the consolidated monetary system. A paradox, however, bedevils the comparison. In a fractional-reserve banking system, the normal tendency (unless counteracted by deliberate policy) is for central-bank purchases of foreign exchange to expand the volume of bank reserves and the ability of the commercial banks to acquire additional domestic loans and investments through additional deposit creation. Growth of the consolidated system's foreign assets amounting to only a small percentage of money-supply growth might suggest, on the one hand, that external factors had been relatively insignificant. On the other hand, this very smallness might suggest that external factors had had a strong *multiple* impact in the way just mentioned. Table 24.1, superficially inspected, would understate the role of foreign-exchange acquisitions in monetary expansion. Even so, it is noteworthy that over the period considered, the change in net foreign assets accounted directly for more than one-fourth of the change in total net assets,[5] more than the full amount of the monetary expansion, and

---

4. *Ibid.*

5. How large the change in foreign assets looks in relation to the change in total assets depends very much, of course, on the degree of netting done. For example, the change in total assets is smaller, and therefore the change in foreign assets looms larger relatively, if claims on the government are taken net of liabilities to the government (as seems appropriate and as is done here) than if claims on the government are considered gross.

TABLE 24.2. *Growth of monetary liabilities of the central bank in relation to other annual changes*

	1951	1952	1953	1954	1955	1956	1957	1958	1959	1960	End of 1951 through end of 1960
Change billions of deutschemarks, in											
Gross foreign assets	1.0	2.8	3.4	3.0	1.8	5.0	5.7	2.7	−2.4	7.9	29.9
Net foreign assets		3.3	3.6	2.8	2.0	4.6	5.0	3.0	−2.1	8.2	30.4
Total assets (= total liabilities)	0.2	0.3	0.8	1.3	3.5	3.2	5.3	2.0	−0.1	6.4	22.7
Total assets net of selected liabilities		1.5	1.4	1.3	1.7	1.8	4.1	2.3	2.8	5.3	22.2
Total note and deposit liabilities	0.8	1.3	1.2	1.4	3.8	2.8	4.4	2.1	0.2	6.5	23.7
Note and deposit liabilities to banks and the private sector	1.2	1.6	1.3	1.5	1.7	1.7	3.8	2.4	2.5	5.1	21.6
Change in gross foreign assets expressed as percentage of change in											
Total assets	500%	933%	425%	231%	51%	156%	108%	135%	(2400%)	123%	132%
Total note and deposit liabilities	125	215	283	214	47	179	130	129	−1200	122	126
Note and deposit liabilities to banks and the private sector	83	175	262	200	106	294	150	113	−96	155	138
Change in net foreign assets expressed as percentage of change in											
Total assets net of selected liabilities		220%	257%	215%	118%	256%	122%	130%	−75%	155%	137%
Total note and deposit liabilities		254	300	200	118	164	114	143	−1050	126	128
Note and deposit liabilities to banks and the private sector		206	277	187	53	271	132	125	−84	161	141

NOTES: The figures are derived from *International Financial Statistics*, February and April 1961. Net foreign assets is gross foreign assets minus foreign liabilities. Total assets (= total liabilites) is the balance-sheet total as printed in IFS. Total assets net of selected liabilities is this last figure minus foreign liabilities, monetary liabilities to government, and counterpart funds. Total note and deposit liabilities include monetary liabilities to government.

nearly two-fifths of the expansion in money plus time deposits.

The likelihood of multiple expansion of monetary liabilities and domestic assets on the basis of additional reserves suggests examining separately, apart from the rest of the monetary system, the institution that issues the "high-powered" deposit liabilities and currency usable as bank reserves. Table 24.2 considers certain key assets and liabilities of the central bank with two different degrees of netting. Shown first are changes in gross foreign assets, total assets (equaling total liabilities), and total monetary liabilities, including central-bank notes and deposits held by the banks, the private sector of the economy, and government units. Also shown are changes in foreign assets net of foreign liabilities, total assets net not only of foreign liabilities but also of both monetary liabilities to government and counterpart funds, and currency and deposit liabilities to banks and the private sector only. In most years and over the entire period, the change in foreign assets, whether gross or net, was actually larger than the changes in the other items with which comparisons suggest themselves. Evidently the central bank sought, in its domestic operations, to counteract rather than reinforce the expansionary effect of its foreign-exchange acquisitions.

No one single comparison—no one single percentage—will unambiguously measure the domestic monetary importance of the balance-of-payments surplus and the growth in foreign-exchange reserves. Nevertheless, the unmistakable impression emerges that external influences have been large and significant. A survey of how often balance-of-payments considerations have dominated decisions about monetary policy will reinforce this impression.

The issue of imported inflation

Granted that acquisitions of gold and foreign exchange were large in relation to domestic monetary changes, one still might question whether this posed any problem. It might even have been a fortunate coincidence that balance-of-payments developments helped create the money needed by a rapidly growing economy. On the other hand, expansionary external influences narrow the scope for the monetary system to acquire domestic assets. Avoiding inflation may even call for actually shrinking domestic assets. (In Germany between 1951

and 1960, the consolidated monetary system reduced its net claims on the government, and the central bank reduced the aggregate of its domestic assets.) Furthermore, acquiring foreign-exchange reserves represents passively giving foreigners loans that might not have been attractive in their own right. Without such passive lending abroad, noninflationary extension of credit and therefore real capital formation at home could presumably have been all the greater.

In questioning whether the theory of imported inflation did actually apply to Germany, one might point out how mildly German prices rose. Between 1950 and 1960, the deutschemark lost purchasing power over consumer goods and services at a compound average rate of only 2.1 percent a year, compared with 3.9 percent for the pound sterling and 5.4 percent for the French franc. Money lost purchasing power at about the same rate in Germany as in the United States, and very few countries (Portugal, Switzerland, and Belgium, in Europe) recorded slower rates of depreciation.[6]

An answer to this skepticism about imported inflation has at least three strands. First, the money supply *did* expand rapidly in Germany between the end of 1950 and the end of 1960; compound annual growth rates averaged 10.8 percent for currency plus demand deposits and 15.5 percent for currency plus demand and time deposits. Had not Germany enjoyed conditions permitting real production to grow very rapidly, such rapid monetary expansion could hardly have failed to breed unmistakable price inflation. Second, an "identification problem" is involved: whether or not we expect to find inflation associated with a balance-of-payments surplus depends on the direction of cause and effect considered. The surplus, as a cause, tends to produce inflation as an effect. On the other hand, the surplus itself may be largely the effect of having less inflation than other countries, if any. Since the surplus merely *tends* to undermine the freedom from inflation that was one of its causes, the absence of conspicuously rising prices is no disproof of inflationary

6. First National City Bank of New York, *Monthly Letter*, May 1961, p. 59.

tendencies. (Had these tendencies been allowed full scope, they might have kept the balance-of-payments surplus from persisting, as the theory of the adjustment mechanism under international monetary linkage explains; and *imported* inflation would again have been difficult to demonstrate "empirically" because no balance-of-payments surplus would be persisting as its obvious source.) A third reason for recognizing the danger of imported inflation as a real problem is that the German authorities were continually preoccupied with it and were continually experimenting with various expedients to cope with it. The mildness of the uptrend in prices may mean not that the problem was nonexistent but rather that policy dealt with it more or less successfully—dealt with it, however, at the cost of imposing tighter domestic financial conditions than would otherwise have been necessary. Landing on one horn of a dilemma rather than the other does not disprove the dilemma.

Foreign criticism of the German choice between horns further suggests that the dilemma was genuine. Sir Oliver Franks, reporting to the stockholders of Lloyds Bank Limited at the end of 1957, criticized Germany's monetary and credit policies as inappropriate for a surplus country with big reserves; they threatened "to disrupt the whole system of European payments." The proper policy, observed Sir Oliver with excessive ingenuity, would be to fight inflation not by raising interest rates and restricting credit but by "expand[ing] incomes and allow[ing] the external account to swing back into balance again, thus obtaining additional real resources on which the larger money incomes can be spent." Moreover, lower interest rates would influence capital flows appropriately. If Germany could not avoid pressure on the exchange reserves of other countries by making long-term foreign loans, and if she remained unwilling to appreciate the mark, then "The only remaining recourse, if the surplus continued, would be to allow money incomes and the standard of living to rise, even if that meant abandoning the dogma of absolute stability in internal prices." No loyal member of an international system, said Sir Oliver, could reject *all* of these possible remedies.[7]

The danger recognized

Until sometime around 1955, the payments surplus and related monetary problems had

persisted for too short a period to arouse serious worry. From 1953 through 1955, in fact, the current-account surplus and the annual growth of external reserves had been shrinking under the influence of import liberalization, rising domestic demand, and increased capital outflows. The earlier absence of worry about the surplus shows up in maintenance until 1954–1955 and even later of exchange controls typical of a country with *deficit* troubles. These controls concerned the use of old blocked mark balances owned by foreigners, the transfer of earnings on foreign-owned capital in Germany, the export and reimport of German currency, limits on foreign travel expenditure by Germans, the obligation to surrender earnings of foreign exchange, and restrictions on German ownership of foreign bank accounts and investments.[8]

Other evidence besides tardiness in relaxing controls shows an early lack of worry about imported inflation. Increases in the liquidity of the German money market were allowed to lead to cuts in the official German discount rate in May and August 1952 and January and June 1953. A final cut to 3 percent came in May 1954. Market rates of interest also sagged. The money supply, defined as currency plus demand deposits, was allowed to grow somewhat more rapidly in 1952 and 1954 than at the average rate for the decade; defined as currency plus demand and time deposits, it grew at considerably above the average rate in each of the three years 1952, 1953, and 1954. In its annual report for 1954, the Bank deutscher Länder explained that its policy corresponded

not only to the internal monetary position but also to the rules of the traditional gold-standard mechanism, as determined by the balance of payments, when it had not only refrained from intervening by employing the instruments of credit policy to curb the expansionist tendencies connected with its purchases of foreign exchange but had rather admitted these tendencies by the reduction in its discount rate in May 1954.[9]

In 1955, concern about credit expansion, rising wages and prices, and a possibly excessive boom finally crystallized into a shift toward restriction. The Bank deutscher Länder rearranged the rediscount quotas of the commercial banks early in the year and undertook contractive open-market operations. In August it raised its discount rate from 3 to 3½ percent and raised bank reserve requirements. In

March and May 1956 the Bank raised its discount rates in full-point steps to 4½ and 5½ percent. Monetary expansion slowed down in 1955 and 1956. The tightening of money and credit drew criticism as a threat to continued economic growth, but the central bankers justified it as a timely action to safeguard the mark and preserve the basis for continued and orderly economic expansion. The Bank deutscher Länder felt that unfortunate repercussions on the desired revival of the capital market should not deter it from safeguarding the currency.[10]

A Federal government budget surplus supplemented monetary restraint. It had prevailed since 1952 and had been growing. Taxation was geared to defense appropriations in excess of actual expenditures. This "leakage" out of the domestic spending stream luckily tended to offset the "injection" from the active balance of payments. The bank deposits of all levels of government grew throughout the decade. The deposits corresponding to unspent defense appropriations and accompanying the growth of the country's gold and foreign-exchange reserves came to be known as a modern Julius-Tower, in allusion to the tower in Spandau where the Imperial Government had accumulated treasure for future war purposes. Surpluses continued accruing until late in 1956. When the budget position then shifted into deficit, the increased expenditures that were responsible went largely for increased purchases of or for prepayments for imported defense materials and to that extent were not additional direct injections into the domestic spending stream.

By this time various observers were pointing out how internal measures to counteract liquidity of external origin tended to be self-defeating. Effectively resisting internal inflation, explained Wilhelm Röpke, makes the balance-of-payments surplus and its expansionary effects all the more stubborn. If countries such as Germany, Switzerland, or Belgium were denied the possibility of protecting themselves against imported inflation, the fate of their currencies would become dependent in the last analysis on "the steel workers of America, the election tactics of the Republican Party, the trade unions of England and the confusion of parties of France."[11]

Writing in a similar vein, L. Albert Hahn likened internal measures against external inflation to

the activity of the Danaids with the opposite algebraic sign. As is well known, the Danaids sought to fill a bottomless barrel with water, which they didn't succeed in doing because of the outflow of water. The B.d.L. seeks to hinder the rise of the water level in a barrel into which water again flows from all sides as soon as the water level sinks a bit.[12]

Internal measures to mop up liquidity of external origin, far from preserving a neutral situation, involved tighter credit and higher interest rates than would otherwise be appropriate. On the one hand, Hahn argued, this tended to attract capital, perpetuating the inflationary acquisitions of foreign exchange. On the other hand, deflationary credit policy

---

7. Sir Oliver Franks, in *The Economist*, Vol. 186, January 25, 1958, pp. 352–353.

8. See Bank for International Settlements, 24th *Annual Report*, pp. 129–130; 26th *Annual Report*, p. 129.

9. Quoted in BIS, 25th *Annual Report*, p. 45n. The Bank for International Settlements found the German monetary expansion appropriate both to match the rapid growth in German production and to promote international equilibrium. Even in its following annual report (the 26th, pp. 52–53), the Bank continued to describe the German current-account surplus and reserve growth as an "entirely satisfactory" situation. The balance of payments did not give "any cause for concern"—almost as if only a deficit could be considered a "cause for concern."

10. Cf. Dr. Wilhelm Vocke, then president of the Bank deutscher Länder, writing in a supplement to Federal Reserve Bank of New York, *Monthly Review*, June 1959, and his Bank's annual report for 1955, paraphrased in BIS, 26th *Annual Report*, pp. 54–55.

11. "Das Dilemma der importierten Inflation," *Neue Zürcher Zeitung*, July 29, 1956, Handelsteil, sheet 11. Röpke sympathized with the German authorities for behaving in the reverse of the way that a balance-of-payments surplus would have called for under the international gold standard, since it was precisely the absence of that standard that permitted other countries to have the inflation whose contagion menaced Germany.

12. *Autonome Konjunktur-Politik und Wechselkurs-Stabilität*, Frankfurt/Main: Knapp, 1957, p. 12.

hampered the development of the German capital market and so tended to restrict the production of investment goods in favor of consumption goods and of excess sales to foreigners. By involuntarily lending to foreigners at zero or low rates of interest through passive accumulation of external reserves—something hardly compensated for by interest- and speculation-motivated transfers of short-term funds into Germany—the Germans were actually subsidizing foreign economic growth at the expense of their own.[13] (That this situation was not generally recognized and condemned is presumably due to the fact that *other* conditions were so favorable to German capital formation and economic growth.)

In its faithfulness to fixed exchange rates, the German central bank (like the International Monetary Fund) would not admit, said Hahn, "that a single country must either howl along with the others, so to speak, or break out of the international currency-zoo. It seeks to remain in the currency-zoo without howling along. It wants to remain in the water of currency stability without getting wet with the inflation of other countries."[14]

As the analyses just mentioned would suggest, the newly intensified policy of restraining domestic demand may have contributed to reversing the 1953–1955 shrinkage of the balance-of-payments surplus. In 1956, exports rose 20 percent while imports rose roughly 13 percent above the previous year's value. Exports benefited from the especial German restraint in the investment-goods sector, while foreign demand remained strong. The surpluses in merchandise and goods-and-services trade grew so much between 1955 and 1956 that the gain in external reserves rose by about 170 percent. The German reserve gain in 1956 was more than triple that of Western Europe as a whole.

Contributing to this overall surplus was the virtual disappearance of net capital exports. Expanded German long-term (mostly direct) investment abroad was outweighed by foreigners' greater long-term investment and short-term lending in Germany. The swollen "errors and omissions" item probably reflected such short-term capital inflows as prepayments for German export deliveries.[15] The tightened credit and increased level of interest rates in Germany, relative to rates abroad, was an important attraction to foreign capital, especially in the first half of the year. While short-term interest rates and the central-bank discount rate turned downward in the second half of 1956, bond yields continued to rise for a while. Speculation on possible exchange-rate adjustments also contributed to capital inflow through leads and lags. Funds were already flowing in from Britain in May, June, and July, and the Suez crisis made itself felt in the fourth quarter.

Policy in 1956–1958

The German authorities adopted several measures in 1956 to resist growth of the external surplus and also to help stabilize prices. In June they freed imports from the dollar area from quantitative restrictions to about the same extent as they had already done for intra-European trade. Various tariff cuts followed, both unilaterally and under the General Agreement on Tariffs and Trade. The duty on most manufactured imports was lowered to a maximum of 21 percent *ad valorem*, and duties on fuel oil and machine tools were suspended altogether in order to hold down prices in the investment sector. In the two years 1956–1957, the tariffs on most industrial products were lowered by nearly 50 percent. Partly as a result, imports of finished products rose in 1959 to 138 percent above their level of 1955, and their share in total imports rose from 19 to 31 percent, though these effects were obscured by the sluggishness of food and raw material imports and the continuing export boom. In August 1956 the official export-credit-guarantee agencies began narrowing their protection of German exporters. Official imports of defense materials and payments on foreign debt were accelerated somewhat, and measures were taken to discourage short-term capital inflow and further to relax restrictions on private capital exports.[16]

Begun earlier, an easing of domestic financial policy was symbolized in September by a half-a-point cut in the 5½ percent discount rate prevailing since May. The change continued toward the end of the year with tax reductions, increases in public spending, and a shift from surplus to deficit in the government budget. The continued growth in external reserves prompted the change in policy, and so did some signs of a slowdown in the investment boom and of an impending seasonal winter decline in economic activity. When the central bank cut its rate again to 4½ percent in January 1957, it explained that external conditions called for the change and internal conditions did not bar it.[17]

The shift toward easier credit continued into 1959. The initial discount-rate cuts in September 1956 and January 1957 were followed by further one-half-point cuts in September 1957 and January and June 1958 and a final cut to 2¾ percent in January 1959. These and other measures of monetary ease presumably contributed to the faster rate of money-supply growth recorded in 1957 through 1959 than in the relatively tight years 1955 and 1956 and than over the decade as a whole. (Currency plus demand deposits grew by 12.1, 13.1, and 11.8 percent in 1957, 1958, and 1959, while currency plus demand and time deposits grew by 18.0, 15.7, and 16.3 percent. The average annual rates for the two concepts of money over the entire decade were, to repeat, 10.8 and 15.5 percent respectively.)

Monetary ease during this period was by no means unambiguous. If the apparent inconsistency among various strands of policy does not indicate an imperfect understanding of how the interest-rate, bank-reserve, and money-supply aspects of monetary ease or tightness are interrelated, it at least provides further evidence of the conflict of objectives that perplexed policy-makers. Despite repeated discount-rate cuts, the central bank continued relatively heavy open-market sales of securities. On repeated occasions—five times during 1957 alone—it arranged with the government for conversion of some of the "equalization claims"[18] it held into government securities salable on the open market. So reequipped, the central bank could continue trying to mop up bank liquidity. Other exceptions to the general policy were the measures of May 1, 1957: bank reserve requirements were raised so as to sterilize over half a billion marks of the banks' resources; rediscount quotas were lowered; and the banks' borrowings abroad, except for the financing of imports, were deducted from these rediscount quotas. In May and September 1957 the reserve requirements applicable to the deutschemark deposits of nonresidents were raised to the highest level allowed by law. In December, as a feeble weapon against the boom in commodity exports, the Bundesbank excluded export bills from rediscounting privileges altogether.

The measures taken for the sake of the balance of payments did not operate strongly or promptly enough to keep the surplus on goods-and-services account from rising a further 36 percent between 1956 and 1957. The most notable shift was from deficit to surplus on transportation account. The larger surplus on goods and services was offset, however, by larger government advance payments for military imports and transfers for restitution and indemnification. The flow of private long-term investment capital was more heavily outward; and in 1957, for the first time since the war, the German banking system made loans to the governments of other European countries. Other short-term capital moved heavily inward during most of the year, however, especially as rumors circulated of impending depreciation of certain European currencies and appreciation of the mark. As measured by "errors and omissions," this movement amounted to about half a billion dollars in the third quarter of the year alone, and the Bundesbank estimated that about two-thirds of the exceptionally large $800-million net increase in its external reserves during that quarter could be attributed to the speculative capital inflow. Much of the

13. *Ibid.*, esp. pp. 13–15, 23–24.

14. *Ibid.*, p. 11.

15. International Monetary Fund, 1957 *Annual Report*, pp. 44–45.

16. BIS, 27th *Annual Report*, 1956–1957, pp. 143–144; IMF, 1957 *Annual Report*, p. 33; Federal Reserve Bank of New York, *Monthly Review*, December 1960, p. 208.

17. Samuel I. Katz, *Sterling Speculation and European Convertibility: 1955–1958*, Essays in International Finance, No. 37, Princeton, N.J.: Princeton University, 1961, p. 13; Federal Reserve Bank of New York, *Monthly Review*, February 1957, p. 17.

18. The reforms of 1948 cancelled government debts and scaled down claims on other debtors. Financial institutions holding large amounts of claims on the government would have been made insolvent if they had not been given amounts of equalization claims sufficient to equate assets and liabilities in their first post-reform balance sheets. The equalization claims were essentially government bonds subject to special restrictions.

funds apparently came from London.[19] This hot-money flow partially reversed itself toward the end of the year, after declarations at the International Monetary Fund meeting in September had helped calm down speculation. For 1957 as a whole, the overall effect on the external reserves was an increase little if any larger than the year before. Germany took the bulk of its reserve gain in gold and again, as in 1956, acquired more than the estimated world total increase in official gold holdings.[20]

Measures taken to resist the balance-of-payments surplus in 1957 included the increased government outpayments already mentioned; a notable example, helpful to the United Kingdom in its balance-of-payments difficulties, was German acquisition of £68 million in sterling to hold against future repayments of debt to the United Kingdom. Private capital exports were encouraged by removal of the last remaining restrictions on foreign investment by German residents, but high long-term rates in Germany remained a deterrent. Imports of manufactures were already running above the year before when duties on them were further reduced in September, and in the last quarter of the year their value was 40 percent above that of 1956. The proportional impact on total imports was much less because finished and semifinished goods still accounted for hardly more than one-fifth of the total value and because German agriculture continued to enjoy extreme protection against import competition.

In 1958, for the first time since World War II, estimated total industrial production in the free world fell below the level of the year before, and the dollar value of world trade declined for the first time since a slight dip in 1952–1953. Germany, by exception, recorded continued (though smaller) growth in both production and trade. Imports grew more than exports as a percentage of the previous year's physical volume but grew less in absolute money value, so that the merchandise export surplus actually rose.[21] A large increase in sales of services to foreign troops failed to outweigh a still larger shift from surplus to deficit in ordinary services, and the net change in the overall balance on goods and services was small, though still positive. The modest rise in this balance was far outweighed by an increase in net capital exports. It is true that official capital exports in the form of advance payments for military imports were temporarily stopped and reversed, but other official capital exports rose by way of subscription to the capi-tal of the European Investment Bank (one of the institutions of the European Economic Community) and German participation in international loans to France and Turkey. Recorded and unrecorded private capital shifted outward, partly in response to a continued decline of German relative to foreign interest rates and the liquidity of the German financial system. Trade financing by German exporters continued to revive; in fact, the decline in German interest rates promoted a lengthening of payments terms and in turn facilitated commodity exports. Other short-term foreign lending had resumed late in 1957, foreign direct investment by German industry continued to develop, and long-term lending to foreigners began on a small scale. Success in reviving the German capital market was symbolized in September 1958 when a South African corporation floated the first foreign industrial bond issue in Germany since before World War I. An Austrian power loan followed early in 1959. In addition to these capital exports, the "errors and omissions" item for 1958 included a large outward shift, partly reflecting a continuation into the early months of the year of the hot-money reversal that had taken place late in 1957 after abatement of the speculative crisis. The net effect of all transactions so far mentioned was that the external reserves still grew during 1958, but by only half as much as the year before. They had fallen, in fact, in the five months from October 1957 through February 1958 but began rising again in March and by early June had regained the peak level of the previous autumn.

Despite the smaller growth in external reserves, the increase in the German money supply was slightly larger in 1958 than in 1957 (13 as against 12 percent). Medium-term and long-term bank loans and investments in both the public and private sectors played a part in this monetary expansion. On the one hand, the authorities were continuing (though less vigorously than before) to offset the effects of reserve gains by open-market operations; on the other hand, they were continuing to reduce official discount rates and permit the continued expansion of bank liquidity. A cash deficit in the Federal budget continued at a reduced size and corresponded to official payments abroad; domestic cash transactions continued in substantial surplus.[22]

When the major European countries adopted external currency convertibility late in December 1958, Germany merged the limited-convertibility mark accounts with the freely convertible accounts that had already existed. Next month virtually full convertibility privileges were extended to residents and nonresidents alike. With minor and temporary exceptions, exchange control vanished. Actually, all of this did little more than formalize arrangements that had prevailed *de facto* for some time. As early as 1956, the obligation to surrender foreign-exchange receipts after a certain period had been abolished. In 1956 and 1957, the rationing of foreign exchange for travel abroad had been discontinued and restrictions on holding foreign portfolio and direct investments and bank accounts had been greatly relaxed. Various steps to liberalize gold transactions culminated in January 1959 with an end to the remaining German restrictions on domestic and international trade in coined and uncoined gold.[23]

The 1959 interlude

By early 1959, the policies for influencing capital movements were apparently succeeding so well, in comparison with previous (and subsequent) experience, that the official reserves fell by $879 million, or 14 percent, in the first four months alone. For the year as a whole, net exports of long-term private capital were much larger than in 1958, official capital movements for debt settlement and advance payment for military imports were again heavily outward, and Germany paid an additional gold subscription of 480 million deutschemarks to the International Monetary Fund. The surplus on goods-and-services account persisted in 1959 but was 9 percent smaller than before, mainly because of heavier German tourist spending abroad and larger earnings paid on foreign capital invested in Germany. Germany displaced the United Kingdom in 1959 as the world's second largest merchandise exporter. A sharp recovery of international reserves toward the end of 1959 was not enough to keep them from declining by 8¾ percent over the year as a whole.[24]

This first annual decline in reserves, instead of indicating a solution to the balance-of-payments problem, reflected some untypical influences. The burden of accumulating external assets had not been shed altogether but just temporarily shifted from official to private shoulders, which later proved inconvenient. During the first nine months of 1959, while

the official reserves were falling by almost $1 billion, the net foreign-exchange assets of the commercial banks grew by $540 million. Over the full year, the gold and dollar holdings of German banks and official institutions *combined* actually rose by about 1 billion marks' worth.[25] Especially during the early months of 1959, the private institutions had been responding largely to a changed pattern of international interest-rate differentials. The official

19. Federal Reserve Bank of New York, *Monthly Review*, January 1958, pp. 12–13; IMF, 1958 *Annual Report*, p. 97; Katz, *op. cit.*, p. 21.

20. IMF, 1958 *Annual Report*, pp. 56, 147.

21. Gerhard Fels sees world price movements from 1957 to 1960—a 13.2 percent decline in the average prices of German imports of raw materials, semifinished goods, and foodstuffs—as an important factor in the growth of Germany's trade surplus over that period. Goods of the kinds mentioned had accounted for four-fifths of Germany's commodity imports in 1955 and still accounted for two-thirds in 1960. Fels's interpretation depends on the plausible assumption that the import demand for such goods was inelastic in the medium run, so that the direct price effect of their cheapening did more to strengthen the German trade balance than the response of volume imported did to weaken the balance. In such circumstances, cheapened imports were restraining price inflation in Germany through their direct price effect rather than promoting inflation by increasing the growth of money supply through a larger balance-of-payments surplus. *Der internationale Preiszusammenhang, eine Studie über den Inflationsimport in der Bundesrepublik*, Köln: Heymanns, 1969, pp. 81–82.

22. IMF, 1959 *Annual Report*, pp. 67–68, 94.

23. See BIS, 27th *Annual Report*, p. 190, 29th *Annual Report*, p. 193; IMF, 1959 *Annual Report*, pp. 127, 129, 157, 1960 *Annual Report* p. 154; Federal Reserve Bank of New York, *Monthly Review*, February 1959, p. 27.

24. This figure, like those in the next paragraph and the first sentence of this one, refers to reserves defined as including net EPU claims. With reserves defined to exclude these claims, the decline is 4 percent.

25. The last two figures are from BIS, 30th *Annual Report*, 1959–1960, p. 145; IMF, 1960 *Annual Report*, p. 93.

discount rate went down to 2¾ percent in January, and in April the Bundesbank reduced the interest rates at which it sold money-market paper, bringing the German equivalent of the Treasury bill rate to its lowest level since the war.

As far as the German authorities could tell in the spring of 1959, without knowing what the future held in store, their policies were working well in influencing capital movements. In fact, the discriminatory features of bank reserve requirements and rediscount quotas that had been introduced in May 1957 to discourage speculation in favor of the mark no longer seemed necessary. From April 1, therefore, the Bundesbank lowered the reserve requirements for foreing-owned deposits to the same level as for domestic deposits. From May 1, for the first time since the war, German banks were permitted to pay interest on foreign-owned deposits. At the same time, sales of German money-market paper to nonresidents were permitted, and restrictions on loans from nonresidents to residents (such as that the loans had to be of at least five years' maturity) were removed.[26]

The removal of these special discouragements to capital inflows proved premature; the conflict between internal and external considerations of policy soon returned to prominence. Internally, low interest rates stimulated construction and helped promote the continued revival of economic growth in 1959 after the slowdown of 1958. (While briefer and less marked than in most other industrial countries, the slowdown had nevertheless been appreciable by recent German standards.) By early 1959 production was expanding again at a rising rate. Market rates of interest rose in the second half of the year. These domestic developments prodded the authorities into increasingly restrictive credit policies from September on. At first the Bundesbank raised its discount rate by one-fourth of a point, to 3 percent, and then, in October 1959 and June 1960, by full points to 4 and finally 5 percent. The rediscount quotas of the commercial banks were cut in October 1959 and cut again in March. An increase in bank reserve requirements was announced in October, became effective in November, and was followed by further increases in January, March, and June 1960. In late 1959 and early 1960 the Bundesbank repeatedly warned about upward pressures on wages and prices, threatened still stricter credit controls if demand should continue excessive,

and urged noninflationary budgets at all levels of government. Money-supply growth slowed down in 1960 to 6.8 percent for currency plus demand deposits and 11.2 percent for currency plus demand and time deposits, well below the annual growth rates for the preceding years and for the decade as a whole.[27]

Domestic considerations were overriding the desire to promote capital exports. The Bundesbank regretted but "deliberately accepted the possibility" that German funds might return from abroad and that the growth of foreign-exchange reserves might "again cause . . . headaches."[28] Events did bear out these fears. During the last quarter of 1959, the commercial banks reduced their foreign-exchange assets by well over $100 million and increased their deutschemark liabilities to foreigners by about twice the amount of their decline during the nine preceding months. The external assets of the Bundesbank (excluding EPU liquidation claims) grew by almost one-seventh during the last quarter of 1959 alone.

Swaps and other policies in 1960

These trends continued far into 1960. For the year as a whole, the trade and current-account surpluses increased only moderately over those of 1959, but the overall payments position (settled by official reserve transactions) shifted back from deficit into a surplus of nearly $2 billion.[29] The inflow of capital was growing, particularly after the excess of German over foreign interest rates began to rise sharply during the second quarter.[30] Though the repatriation of German capital seemed practically unavoidable, the authorities hoped at least to restrain the inflow of foreign capital. They reinstated discriminatory reserve requirements. Effective the first day of 1960, the Bundesbank raised to the legal maximum the reserve requirements against increases in foreign-owned bank deposits above their end-of-November levels. Effective July 1, German banks were again, as before May 1959, forbidden to pay interest on foreign-owned sight and time (but not savings) deposits and were also forbidden to sell money-market paper to nonresidents. The Bundesbank also withdrew an earlier exemption of foreign-owned deposits from reserve requirements to the extent that they were matched by foreign-currency assets.

These expedients apparently did work to some extent; the growth of foreign deposits in

German banks paused after May 1960. On the other hand, the "net errors and omissions" item in the balance of payments switched from negative in 1958 and 1959 to increasingly positive in the first three quarters of 1960. In large part this apparently reflected the repatriation of German capital and German borrowing of foreign capital through either unrecorded financial transactions or shifts in the timing of commercial payments. Widespread rumors of an exchange-rate adjustment intensified the demand for marks, especially in mid-June. Some transactions during a long holiday weekend were actually made at rates on the mark stronger than the official support limit of 4.17 per dollar,[31] and the premium on forward marks rose. A clear-cut denial by the Bundesbank and the government of any intention to revalue the mark helped shrink the inflow of funds at the end of June and in July. Another helpful factor was that the German banks were apparently at last nearing the end of their short-term foreign investments available for repatriation. But in the 13 months between the ends of August 1959 and September 1960, the banks did draw down their foreign short-term assets by $530 million, returning them to just about their level of late 1958, when the Bundesbank had begun to encourage the outflow of short-term funds. Over the same period, the German banks also increased their outstanding short-term foreign debt from $67 million to $257 million.[32]

The inflow of funds tended to replenish domestic liquidity, feeding the boom.[33] The Bundesbank responded, as already mentioned, not only by raising the discount rate to 5 percent in June 1960 and by discriminating further against foreign-owned deposits but also by again tightening domestic reserve requirements. In August the Bundesbank reached an agreement with the commercial banks under which the banks agreed to buy DM1 billion of nonnegotiable two-year 5½ percent government notes; this had the effect though not the form of a further increase in required reserves.[34]

Attempted restraints on capital inflow apparently had their main effect in merely changing its *form*. Foreign buying of German stocks and bonds spurted during the second half of 1960. Borrowing abroad by German banks and corporations continued despite a further deterrent adopted late in August.

At that time the Bundesbank attempted a more ambitious use of a policy instrument that it had already occasionally employed. It had sought to promote outward lending by providing forward cover for short-term money-market investments abroad. That is, it had repurchased dollars forward when selling them spot to guarantee German institutions against exchange risk. The Bundesbank now extended these "swaps" of spot for forward dollars to transactions connected with the financing of import and transit trade. The Bank would agree to forward maturities ranging from 15 days to six months. Furthermore, it would buy the forward dollars at a premium above the rate charged in the spot sale. This premium was set at 1 percent per annum in August 1960 and raised to 1.5 percent in September.[35] In effect the Bundesbank was now not only subsidizing short-term German investments abroad but was also subsidizing the lending to importers of dollars that commercial banks

26. BIS, 29th *Annual Report*, p. 193; IMF, 1959 *Annual Report*, p. 63; Federal Reserve Bank of New York, *Monthly Review*, June 1959, p. 84.

27. Both relatively high interest rates and relatively slow money-supply growth indicate the period from December 1959 to December 1960 as one of tight liquidity. Victor Argy and Zoran Hodjera, "Financial Integration and Interest Rate Linkages in the Industrial Countries," IMF *Staff Papers*, **XX**, March 1973, p. 69.

28. The President of the Bundesbank, quoted in Federal Reserve Bank of New York, *Monthly Review*, February 1960, p. 32.

29. Here and in the following pages, reference to the official-settlements balance means the balance-of-payments transactions of the monetary authorities as reported in *International Financial Statistics*.

30. Argy and Hodjera, *op. cit.*, pp. 69–70.

31. Federal Reserve Bank of New York, *Monthly Review*, July 1960, p. 134.

32. Federal Reserve Bank of New York, *Monthly Review*, December 1960, p. 208.

33. According to Fels, 1960 provides the best German example up to that time of inflation being imported through expansion of domestic liquidity. *Op. cit.*, pp. 82, 92.

34. Federal Reserve Bank of New York, *Monthly Review*, September 1960, p. 162.

35. Fels, *op. cit.*, p. 41.

would buy from its own swollen external reserves. In effect it was trying to encourage German importers to borrow foreign exchange from itself, through the intermediary of the commercial banks, rather than to borrow abroad, as they had recently been doing in large volume. International competition in import financing had become keen; Italian and Swiss banks in particular were offering funds to German importers on terms that German banks had been unable to match, especially in view of the domestic tight-credit policy. The Bundesbank's 1.5 percent swap premium was apparently too small to have strong effects of the kind desired, especially on short-term capital exports, since it still did not bring the yield on short-term funds transferred to the United States up to what could be earned in Germany.

The failure of the swap policy to be pressed more vigorously is hardly surprising in view of its inherent limitations. Ordinarily there exist open-market forward-exchange quotations as well as the special rates offered by the central bank to its partners in swap transactions. If the policy is to make any difference to the situation, the price in marks that the Bundesbank offers to pay the commercial banks for forward dollars must exceed the open-market price (or exceed what the open-market price had been before arbitrage does its work). This excess gives the banks an opportunity to profit by importing funds and reexporting them. Suppose the spot exchange rate is 4.00 marks per dollar, the open-market three-month forward rate 4.02 marks, and the Bundesbank's swap rate 4.04 marks. The banks borrow dollars abroad, sell them spot at 4.00 marks, and repurchase them forward at the open-market rate of 4.02. They use the mark proceeds of the spot sale of the borrowed dollars to buy spot dollars from the Bundesbank at 4.00 and at the same time, as part of the special swap transaction, sell the dollars forward at the Bundesbank's artificially favorable buying price of 4.04. From the standpoint of an arbitrageur bank, its borrowing and lending of dollars abroad cancel each other out, as do its spot sale and spot purchase of dollars. Its open-market forward purchase of dollars at 4.02 marks matches its forward sale to the Bundesbank at 4.04. The commercial bank cannot do so in a straightforward way, of course, because, by the very nature of what it is trying to accomplish, the Bundesbank links its own forward purchase of dollars with a spot sale. To describe what the commercial bank is doing in another way,

it is in effect engaging in the subsidized re-export of funds borrowed abroad, with much the same incentive as if it was receiving an interest-rate subsidy on the re-exported funds. Of course, the Bundesbank might try to prevent such arbitrage; but the greater the differential between the open-market and swap-contract forward rates, the greater the incentive arbitrageurs would have to circumvent the controls.

To the extent that arbitrage does transmit the artificial forward rate to the open market, the outcome resembles that of straightforward forward support of the dollar (and antisupport of the forward mark) by the Bundesbank on the open market. The Bundesbank would have found such an outcome undesirable for at least two reasons. To the extent that traders in German imports and exports respond to forward and not solely to spot exchange rates, the forward depreciation of the mark would normally affect the German current account in qualitatively the same way as a spot depreciation. In the situation considered, this strengthening of the German current account would hardly be desired. More important, a forward rate of the mark pressed below the mark's lower spot support limit would give speculators an intolerably advantageous opportunity. Suppose that the Bundesbank—or arbitrage of the kind described above—presses the forward mark to 22 cents, while the lower spot support limit is 23 cents. Speculators would buy marks forward on a massive scale, confident that when they took delivery at 22 cents upon maturity of their forward contracts, they could immediately resell the marks spot for at least 23 cents. They would hardly have to worry about devaluation of the mark below 23 cents; for in the kind of situation in which the Bundesbank was resorting to swap policy, the mark would be strong and much less likely to be devalued than to be revalued upward. Upward revaluation—or even a mark rate higher than the 23-cent floor—would give speculators even larger profits than their practically certain profit of 1 cent per mark. The situation described would provide especially favorable opportunities for one-way-option speculation. In effect, the Bundesbank would be playing a game with speculators that, from their point of view, amounted to a game not of "Heads we win, tails we break even" but of "Heads we win big, tails we still win something."

A truly vigorous forward-swap policy would be self-defeating in the ways described[36] unless supported by controls so elaborate and tight that they, rather than the swaps, would be the dominant aspect of policy. German experience does not discredit the theoretical conclusion that swap policy has strictly limited potentialities for manipulating capital flows.[37]

The measures adopted during 1960—the prohibition of interest on and the discriminatory reserve requirements for foreign deposits and the swap-premium system—dealt more with the symptomatic and aggravating element of short-term capital movements than with fundamentals. Exports of goods and services in 1960 still exceeded imports by a record $1.9 billion. By the autumn of 1960 mere palliatives were clearly failing to offset the double pull on short-term capital of the excess of German over foreign interest rates and of recurrent exchange-rate rumors. The first three quarters of 1960 contrasted sharply with the same period one year before: recorded capital movements and those concealed in "errors and omissions" turned heavily inward. Official reserves grew by $1805 million, or nearly 40 percent, from January through September 1960. The German government had to consider more basic correctives. Larger contributions to NATO would go some way toward reducing or offsetting Germany's large foreign-exchange receipts from NATO troop expenditures. The Reconstruction Loan Corporation, owned jointly by the Federal government and the states, might lend abroad for development purposes; and some part of the state government budget surpluses might also be used for foreign aid. The government might further hasten repaying foreign debts.[38] Domestic policy might shift emphasis from monetary to fiscal tightness.

"In the end, the authorities decided that the attempt to maintain a restrictive stance, superimposed on a strong payments position, was becoming self-defeating, since offsetting the domestic liquidity effects of reserve accruals only perpetuated the inducements to import capital." Although economic activity was at a high level and accelerating toward the end of 1960, the monetary authorities switched to expansion. "External considerations were allowed to dominate interest-rate policy."[39] The Bundesbank cut its discount rate on November 11 from 5 to 4 percent, "solely in the light of the external monetary situation," as its announcement said, and not because of any lessened domestic need for restraint. Discount-rate reductions abroad had made a similar step in lar step in Germany "unavoidable." Other

short-term interest rates followed the discount rate downward. Special reserve requirements that had been introduced in June were dropped on December 1. Money-supply growth was allowed to accelerate.

As German financial commentators noted, "Although it would be desirable for domestic reasons to continue a policy of tight money, experience has shown that it is impossible to achieve both aims, cheap and tight money, for any length of time."[40] Further cuts in January and May 1961 brought the discount rate down to 3 percent, where it remained until 1965. Additional credit-easing steps included reduced reserve requirements against domestic bank deposits, larger rediscount quotas for the banks, and reduced interest yields on money-market paper sold by the Bundesbank. During the first six months of 1961, German credit institutions were able to expand their loans and their deposit and other liabilities by roughly half again as much as in the same period the year before, yet they were able to turn their net short-term liability to foreigners into virtual balance.[41] After the banks' liquidity began coming under strain in August, the authorities pushed their earlier measures further and also removed the obligation imposed on banks the year before to

36. This description elaborates on Fels, *op. cit.*, pp. 39–42. Fels draws in turn on F. Meyer, "Wechselkurse," *Handwörterbuch der Sozialwissenschaften*, Vol. 11, pp. 119ff.

37. Fels says there is no historical example of swap policy working as desired. A successful policy would require absence of dominant expectations of parity alteration and an international interest-rate differential to be compensated for that was small in relation to the band between the upper and lower spot support limits. *Op. cit.*, p. 42.

38. But on the theory involved, see Chapter 23, footnote 11.

39. Argy and Hodjera, *op. cit.*, p. 70.

40. *Frankfurter Allgemeine Zeitung*, editorial of 3 December 1960, summarized in *International Financial News Survey*, 9 December 1960, pp. 597–598.

41. Calculated from BIS, 32nd *Annual Report*, p. 69. (The institutions' foreign liabilities grew, but their claims on foreigners grew more.)

hold 1 billion deutschemarks worth of special Treasury notes. By the beginning of 1962, the yield on three-month Treasury bills had reached its lowest level since the war.[42] The switch from monetary tightness to ease after November 1960, like the switches from ease to tightness in 1955, back to ease in 1956, and back again to tightness in 1959, was one more example of thrashing back and forth in efforts to reconcile internally and externally oriented strands of policy.

Revaluation and its immediate aftermath

The reorientation of financial policy got early support from something more dramatic. After repeatedly disavowing any such intention,[43] the government revalued the mark upward. Effective Monday, March 6, 1961, its parity went from 4.2 to 4 per dollar. This meant a 5 percent rise in the dollar price of the mark and a 4.76 percent cut in the mark price of the dollar. Commentators saw political and economic motives combined. The alternative proposed by Economics Minister Erhard, discontinuance of both the refund of turnover tax on exported goods and the "equalization" tax on imports, had drawn too much protest from industry. Germany's gold and foreign-exchange reserves, then second only to those of the United States and over twice the size of the British, had widely if not logically been seen as evidence of Germany's capacity to carry a still larger share of defense and development-aid burdens, especially in view of recent American balance-of-payments troubles. Yet the Adenauer government, facing an election in September, was wary of tax increases to pay for foreign aid; and Erhard was unenthusiastic.[44] By revaluing, the Germans would seem to be *doing something* about their embarrassing international imbalance and their bloated reserves. The step might lighten foreign pressures on them and leave them more nearly free to decide for themselves on the size of their defense and aid contributions. Inside Germany, furthermore, the new exchange rate would tend to cheapen imports for consumer-voters. More broadly, the revaluation might help resist the inflationary danger of the new policy of easier money.

One day after Germany acted, the Netherlands revalued the guilder by the same percent-age. As the Dutch finance minister explained to parliament, the country had been running substantial current-account surpluses in most years since 1951. Recent capital flows had been heavily inward. The gold and foreign-exchange holdings of the Netherlands Bank had climbed 23 percent in 1960 alone to a record level of $1.8 billion. Failure to follow the German lead would have intensified inflationary influences by spelling devaluation of the guilder against the currency of the country accounting for more than one-fifth of all Dutch foreign trade. The Dutch authorities hoped that a reduction in the payments surplus and cheaper imports would slow down price increases expected in 1961 and temper wage demands.[45]

At first the two revaluations boomeranged. Their very occurrence, especially without due international consultation in advance, reminded speculators not to trust official denials of impending exchange-rate adjustments. Their smallness suggested possible repetition, especially when a statement by the U.S. government welcomed the German revaluation as "a useful but modest step" only. As German officials complained, the word "modest" incited speculation on a further change. (American officials later interpreted the word as a call for bigger aid and defense contributions and emphasized that they were "entirely satisfied" with the extent of the revaluation.) Germany's merely "modest" adjustment also suggested that the dollar and sterling, still supposedly overvalued in terms of the mark, might contribute their share by devaluing. Hot money surged violently from London and New York into Germany. As one international banker put it, "The speculators have tasted blood, and no matter what you say, they won't believe that another revaluation isn't in the wind."[46] The Bundesbank absorbed $125 million worth of gold and foreign exchange during the week including two trading days after the revaluation, and $206 million more in the following week.[47] During the month of March as a whole, the German reserves rose by $362 million, or about 5 percent.

The initial burst of bullish speculation extended to other currencies, especially the Swiss franc and to a lesser extent the revalued Dutch guilder, the French franc, and the Italian lira. An official statement on March 6 ruled a Swiss revaluation "out of the question" because there was "no similarity" with the German situation; yet almost $300 million moved into Switzerland during the next nine or ten days, according to an estimate by the Swiss National Bank. For Switzerland as for Germany, the growth in reserves during the second week of March set a new record for so short a period.[48] The chief currency weakened by the corresponding outflows of funds was sterling (as detailed in Chapter 22).

At their regular monthly meeting for March at the Bank for International Settlements in Basel, the governors of eight leading European central banks issued a joint statement emphasizing that rumors of further currency adjustments had "no foundation." They emphasized their own close cooperation in the exchange markets to discourage speculation and cushion the impact of hot money on reserve positions. As President Blessing of the Bundesbank later argued when urging inclusion of the United States in a broadened scheme of cooperation, the speculator would have no chance against "an association of central banks operating in unison," and the sooner this was realized, the quicker speculative money movements would lose force. The European central bankers agreed, specifically, not only to make short-term loans of needed currencies but also to hold each other's currencies more extensively than before, instead of converting them at once into gold or dollars. In fact, they agreed to hold one another's currencies (including short-term securities) in unlimited amounts in order to meet hot-money movements. The British reserves would escape depletion by speculative attack, for example, to the extent that Continental central banks were willing to keep holding sterling acquired with their own currencies in pegging operations on the exchange market. The United States would benefit so far as the European banks were willing to absorb dollars without converting them into gold. These procedures were to be temporary, pending a more fundamental reform of methods for dealing with short-term capital movements and financial disequilibriums in general.[49]

Whether because of these pronouncements and actions or just of its own accord, speculation did die down by the end of March. Meanwhile, however, events had shown again how unsettling an official realignment of a major currency can be. Outright speculators had not made a real killing but had not been defeated, either. "As a British official put it, 'they've hurt us as much as we've hurt them.' "[50] The events of March had brought a change in market psychology. Before then, growing confidence in currency convertibility and the pattern of exchange rates had caused much international business to be conducted without forward-exchange protection. Afterwards the practice became more general of arranging forward cover for foreign-exchange positions.[51]

The shift to a short-lived external deficit

German trade took a while to respond clearly to the revaluation, partly because of a backlog of export orders. The commodity export surplus reached a record level for 1961 as a whole, though it shrank after the first quarter and was smaller in the fourth quarter than one year before. The surplus on services disappeared after the first quarter. Outward governmental and private transfers rose. The surpluses on goods and services and on goods, services, and transfers shrank from 1960 to 1961. The net

42. *Ibid.*, p. 71; IMF, 1962 *Annual Report*, p. 93.

43. Disavowals dated back six years or so, the most recent explicit one coming on 18 October 1960. *Wall Street Journal*, 6 March 1961, p. 3.

44. *Ibid.*; "Sterling after the Storm," *The Banker*, April 1961, pp. 235–237.

45. Federal Reserve Bank of New York, *Monthly Review*, April 1961, p. 63.

46. *Business Week*, 18 March 1961, p. 31.

47. Federal Reserve Bank of New York, *Monthly Review*, April 1961, p. 63.

48. *Ibid.*; BIS, 31st *Annual Report*, 1960–1961, p. 147. According to another estimate, the Swiss took in $350 million in a single week. *Business Week*, 22 April 1961, p. 48.

49. *International Finance News Survey*, 7 April 1961, p. 97; Federal Reserve Bank of New York, *Monthly Review*, April 1961, p. 64; *Business Week*, 8 April 1961, p. 76, and 22 April 1961, pp. 45–50; *U.S. News and World Report*, 3 April 1961, p. 113; *The Economist*, 6 May 1961, p. 572.

50. *Business Week*, 22 April 1961, p. 50.

51. IMF, 1961, pp. 6–7.

inflow of long-term private capital also shrank slightly and actually turned negative in the second half of 1961 under the influence of the Berlin crisis. The basic balance on account of all these ordinary transactions was still in surplus for the year, though slightly in deficit for the second half. Short-term capital movements and some special government transactions were large enough to make the Bundesbank's gold and foreign-exchange reserves decline slightly, though total reserves, including Germany's IMF position, did not quite fall back to their end-of-1960 level. The special transactions included advance debt repayments to the United States, United Kingdom, and France, military purchases abroad, and credits and contributions to the World Bank, International Monetary Fund, and the underdeveloped countries.

The move away from balance-of-payments surplus continued in 1962. Imports rose more strongly than exports, cutting the merchandise export surplus roughly in half. Further growth in German tourist spending abroad and in remittances by foreigners working in Germany pushed the balance on services (even including sale of German services to foreign troops) into deficit, after near-evenness in 1961 and surpluses in earlier years. The surplus on goods and services together was less than half as large as in 1961. Defined as also including private and government transfers, the current account registered a deficit in both halves of 1962 and Germany's first deficit for any calendar year since 1950. A slight net inflow of long-term capital was too small to prevent an overall "basic" deficit.

Mirroring these and all other items, including short-term capital movements, the Bundesbank's reserves of gold and foreign exchange fell by $87 million in 1962. This fall of only 1.3 percent, unlike the 2.9 percent fall of 1961, reflected a "genuine" overall deficit. In fact, the reserves would have fallen considerably in 1962 but for repayments collected on earlier loans made through the International Monetary Fund and sales of foreign assets by the banking system. (International liquidity, counting the IMF position along with gold and foreign exchange, fell by $208 million.) In 1961, by contrast, changes in the net IMF position and in the foreign position of the banking system (excluding year-end window-dressing) had more than offset the decline in gold and foreign exchange. A more important difference is that special compensatory government transactions such as advance debt repayment were unnecessary in 1962, whereas, without them, the reserves would have shown a big rise the year before.[52]

Was the revaluation really responsible for the shift in the balance of payments? A change in price-competitiveness was indeed one influence at work, among others. Import prices in marks fell to annual averages of 3 percent in 1961 and 4 or 6 percent (depending on the index used) in 1962 below their level of 1960, while German industrial and agricultural wholesale prices and the cost of living continued rising mildly and reached 1962 averages of 3, 4, and 7 percent, respectively, above their 1960 levels. German export prices in dollars averaged 6 percent higher in 1962 than in 1960, while over the same period the indexes rose only about 1 percent for Western Europe as a whole and 2 percent for the United States.[53] According to one authority, "the gradual evaporation of the large surpluses" was "clearly," if only "partly," a result of the revaluation, "which had cut into the competitive margin enjoyed by exporters . . . while also making imports cheaper." The Bundesbank noted some effects of revaluation—a prompt decline in export *orders* if not in shipments and some apparent restraint on imports, especially of finished goods.[54] Largely, though, the change in the current account after so small a revaluation resulted from the continuation of tendencies already at work.[55] One of these was the continued rise of incomes and of demand pressing on domestic resources. The slowdown in growth of German real national income from its unsustainable earlier pace to about the Continental European average of 5 percent between 1960 and 1961 was due not to financial tightness but rather to physical constraints such as labor scarcity, further accentuated in 1962 by a shortening of the average work week, longer paid vacations, and greater difficulty in recruiting foreign workers as skilled labor enjoyed full employment practically throughout Continental Europe. German expenditures abroad on "invisibles" were rising in a partially autonomous trend.

Perhaps the most notable influence on the balance of payments was the shift toward an easier domestic monetary policy that had already begun a few months before the revaluation. The move away from external surplus in 1961 did not neutralize this policy shift, since the official transactions making for a deficit—

debt prepayments and contributions and government expenditures abroad—were of a sort that allowed other parts of the balance of payments to continue actually adding liquidity to the domestic banking system.[56] As a combined result of the balance of payments and reinforcing domestic policy, then, the German money supply grew by 14.8 percent during 1961. (This relatively large increase contrasts with average and maximum annual increases of only 10.2 and 13.1 percent over the previous five years and 10.6 and 13.2 over the previous nine.) At the end of 1961, interest rates on the German money market were actually lower than in most other international financial centers.[57]

With the balance of payments no longer in either overall or basic surplus in 1962, the German authorities could pay more attention again to the problem of rising wages and prices. As the Bundesbank reported,

Continuance of the previous year's policy of relaxation aligned to the balance-of-payments situation was . . . not required. The Bundesbank was on the contrary able to cease applying the pressure, which it had exerted on the money market from the end of 1960 to the end of 1961 so as to reduce the inflow of foreign moneys or to inhibit its resumption and could thus in many respects give a different inflection to its monetary policy.[58]

A housing and construction boom, a return to a Federal government budget deficit, and wage-push were seen as the main inflationary pressures and, operating unevenly over the economy, were considered less effectively subject to money and credit restraints than to fiscal and direct restraints. The authorities took some direct measures to curb governmental and other construction. The Bundesbank left both its discount rate and bank reserve requirements for domestic liabilities unchanged in 1962. It did, however, at least passively allow the liquidity positions of the banks to tighten as the demand for bank credit continued strong, as the total of required reserves grew in step with deposits, as the public drained currency into circulation, and as the government budget absorbed loanable funds. The Bundesbank raised the interest yield on short-term securities it sold. Money-supply growth fell to 6.6 percent in 1962, a smaller rate than in any of the preceding 10 years. Gains in industrial production from the preceding year were relatively small in 1962 and 1963—only 4.3 and 3.0 percent.

The old worry once again

The monetary restraint and business slowdown presumably had something to do with another balance-of-payments reversal. Merchandise trade in 1963 recorded an export surplus larger than in any earlier year except 1961; and 1962's deficit on goods, services, and transfers gave way to the more familiar surplus. The decline of external reserves in 1962 gave way to a 10 percent gain (including IMF position) in 1963. The restored external surplus grew with particular vigor in the fourth quarter. Early 1964 brought further heavy reserve gains. An inflow of hot money into Germany was both feeding and feeding on rumors of another upward revaluation of the mark.[59]

What explains this return to earlier conditions? For one thing, prices were again rising more moderately in Germany than in neighboring countries. The rise in German wages slowed down noticeably in 1963. German dollar export price indexes had held steady or had even declined slightly since being raised by the 1961 revaluation, and export prices in marks had been steady for several years, while competitors' prices had risen. Germany's surplus contrasted with the growing external trade deficit of all six Common Market countries considered together.

Late in 1963 or early in 1964, for the first time since the revaluation, "imported inflation" again became a theme of public discus-

52. BIS, 33rd *Annual Report*, p. 130.

53. Calculated from *International Financial Statistics*.

54. Federal Reserve Bank of New York, 1962 *Annual Report*, p. 35; Bundesbank, *Geschäftsbericht für das Jahr 1961*, Frankfurt: 1962, p. 430.

55. *Ibid.*, p. 421.

56. *Ibid.*, pp. 29, 31, 34–35.

57. Bundesbank, *Report for the Year 1962*, Frankfurt: 1963, p. 14.

58. *Ibid.*

59. *Wall Street Journal*, 27 February 1964, p. 14, and 9 April 1964, p. 12.

sion.[60] Two apparent sources were France and Italy, where price inflation had come to arouse actual anxiety. The 1 July 1964 issue of *Der Spiegel*, the German counterpart of *Time* magazine, carried a picture on its cover of Economics Minister Schmücker surrounded by French and Italian banknotes. Besides an interview with the Minister, the magazine contained a popularized exposition of the mechanics of imported inflation and casually referred to the European Economic Community as the "European Inflation Community." Spectacular export gains were threatening to transmit inflation into Germany both by reducing the supply of goods on the home market and increasing the supply of money (whose growth rate recovered to 7.2 percent in 1963 and 8.9 percent in 1964).

Probably more important, in fact, was translation into marks at the fixed exchange rate of the rising foreign prices of internationally traded goods. From about 1962 until 1968, according to Fels, this effect overshadowed the liquidity or income-multiplier effects of payments surpluses. Over 1963–1966, Germany's basic balance was slightly in deficit;[61] and Table 24.3 does tend to document the absence of any clear-cut externally imposed expansion of domestic reserve money until that phenomenon returned in 1968, and returned on a massive scale in 1970. (The middle column of the table is calculated from changes in the *dollar* values of the Bundesbank's holdings of gold and foreign exchange in an effort to avoid distortions due to changes in the exchange rate, changes in IMF position, and SDR allocations.)

Worry about an inflationary payments surplus thus proved overdone or premature in 1964. Resistance was less difficult than on some earlier and later occasions. In March 1964 the Bundesbank revived its swap policy, granting the commercial banks forward-exchange protection on favorable terms to encourage them to invest funds in U.S. Treasury bills.[62] Soon afterwards, the authorities again forbade payment of interest on foreign-owned bank deposits and doubled the reserves required against them. The government also introduced a 25 percent withholding tax on income from foreign-owned German fixed-interest securities, which not only checked the inflow of long-term capital but also caused foreigners to liquidate some of the German securities they held.[63]

The trade surplus shrank as the year went

TABLE 24.3. *Changes in gold and foreign-exchange holdings and in domestic reserve-money liabilities of the German Bundesbank, 1961–1973*

Year or quarter	Gold and foreign exchange (billions of DM)	Reserve money
1961	−0.823, −0.784	1.2
1962	−0.352	1.9
1963	2.636	2.8
1964	−0.520	4.8
1965	−2.460	3.1
1966	1.672	3.1
1967	1.316	−1.1
1968	5.328	4.6
1969	−6.424, −5.878	1.8
1970	20.525	12.0
1971	16.682, 14.688	10.2
1972	14.624	20.5
1969 I	−6.328	−4.5
II	7.748	4.8
III	7.704, 7.639	2.7
IV	−15.416, −14.226	−1.2
1970 I	0.055	−0.7
II	4.952	3.3
III	7.953	5.8
IV	7.565	3.6
1971 I	7.078	−0.3
II	3.203, 3.060	7.7
III	0.720, 0.684	1.4
IV	5.120, 4.972	1.4
1972 I	3.732	−3.5
II	9.838	8.9
III	3.848	7.6
IV	−2.794	7.5
1973 I	26.876, 23.669	8.6
Total change in 12 quarters from 1970 II through 1973 I	78.091, 74.557	52.0

NOTES: Calculated from *International Financial Statistics*, various issues and 1972 Supplement. The changes in gold and foreign exchange are dollar figures converted into marks. Where two figures appear for a year or quarter, the first is the conversion into marks at the parity or exchange rate of the beginning of the period (end of preceding period), and the second is the conversion at the end-of-period parity or rate. The totals for 1970 II through 1973 I are the sums of quarterly changes converted at beginning-of-quarter and end-of-quarter parities or rates.

on. Domestic investment was replacing export demand as a leading stimulus to the German economy, and imports were rising in step with the increasing pressure of demand on resources. For 1964 as a whole the current account (including transfers) and the balance on official settlements were barely in surplus; external reserves (including the IMF position) rose only 3 percent, and gold and foreign exchange fell 2 percent. Giersch and Kasper draw the inference that the German economy was close to external balance around mid-1964 and that German price increases, as well as the 1961 revaluation, had left the mark undervalued only slightly if at all. They consider what would have happened if Germany had then widened the exchange-rate band to 5 percent on either side of parity and had allowed the parity to glide by as much as 2 percent a year. Inflationary disturbances from outside could have been neutralized and price stability nearly achieved. From mid-1964 to mid-1969 the mark would have risen by about 10 percent on the exchanges and would have lost only 5 percent in internal purchasing power instead of the actual 13 percent. With the task of domestic policy simplified, the recession of 1966–1967 might well have been avoided. The exchange rate would never have come so close to one edge or the other of the gliding band as to touch off one-way-option speculation.[64]

Recession and its background

In actuality, the boom and monetary ease of 1963–1964, followed by the balance-of-payments turnaround, brought a response in the form of a return to tight money. The episode dates from December 1964 to December 1966 by the interest-rate criterion, from June 1965 to December 1966 by the money-growth criterion.[65] Two circumstances facilitated a restrictive stance. As the German authorities pushed interest rates up, rates abroad happened to be rising also, restricting the rise in the differential in Germany's favor. Second, insofar as the interest differential attracted short-term capital—and inflows did seem to synchronize well with quarter-years when the differential in Germany's favor was largest— these inflows tended to stabilize Germany's international reserves (rather than destabilize them, as on earlier occasions), since a current-account deficit had developed late in 1964 and persisted until late in 1966.[66] For the calendar year 1965 the merchandise trade surplus was smaller and the current-account deficit larger than for many years before or after; and with the overall official-settlements balance also in deficit, the external reserves fell 5.7 percent.

The continuation of the restrictive policy until late in 1966, with the money-supply growth rate down to 7.5 percent in 1965 and 1.8 percent in 1966, apparently contributed to the 1966–1967 recession, Germany's most serious since World War II.[67] In comparison with the preceding year, yearly average industrial production gained only 1.5 percent in 1966 and fell 2.7 percent in 1967. Industrial employment averaged 7 percent lower in 1967 than in 1965.[68] Why did the authorities per-

60. Fels, *op. cit.*, p. 98.

61. *Ibid.*, pp. 59, 62, 67, 100. Fels's historical interpretation may be colored, however, by his emphasis throughout the book on the direct price connection.

62. Again, however, the swap policy failed to undergo and pass a real test; for from early 1964 to mid-1965 short-term interest rates were higher in the United States than in Germany anyway. Fels, *op. cit.*, p. 40.

63. Also, an existing tax on bond issues by foreigners in Germany was abolished. Herbert Giersch and Wolfgang Kasper in George N. Halm, ed., *Approaches to Greater Flexibility of Exchange Rates*, Princeton, N.J.: Princeton University Press, 1970 (hereafter cited as Bürgenstock Papers), p. 346.

64. *Ibid.*, pp. 345–355, as well as the editor's summary on p. 332.

65. Argy and Hodjera, *op. cit.*, pp. 69–70. The tight-money policy could become fully effective only in the late 1965 and early 1966, after the balance of payments had dipped into sizable deficit and the discount rate could be raised to 5 percent. Giersch and Kasper in Bürgenstock Papers, p. 346.

66. Argy and Hodjera, *op. cit.*, p. 70.

67. Although 1965 as a whole was still a boom year (IMF, 1969, p. 10), the peak, as judged by the index of capacity utilization in manufacturing, came in the first quarter of 1965; and the trough came in the second quarter of 1967. Argy and Hodjera, *op. cit.*, p. 70.

68. Calculated from *International Financial Statistics, Supplement*.

sist so long with tight money? Perhaps they underestimated the extent of the business downturn. Perhaps they were preoccupied with price inflation, which remained rapid until mid-1966. Perhaps they were concerned with the deficit that had emerged in the basic balance of payments (including long-term capital movements) and, despite a high level of international reserves, were willing to accept a domestic slowdown to correct the deficit.[69] For a short time, Germany was experiencing a conflict between the requirements of internal and external balance in the opposite direction from the conflict characterizing most of its postwar experience.

The 1966–1967 recession halted the inflationary spiral; wholesale prices actually declined from the preceding year in both 1967 and 1968.[70] It also helped turn the German balance of payments back from its short-lived deficit to its longer-run chronic surplus. The trade surplus amounted to $1.9 billion in 1966, and the official-settlements balance was back in surplus. Merchandise imports actually declined in value from 1966 to 1967, and the trade surplus grew to $4.2 billion. The current-account surplus (including transfers) rose from negligible in 1966 to $2.4 billion in 1967. With Germany returning to monetary ease and Eurodollar interest rates rising sharply above German rates, however, short-term capital movements responded, so that despite a surplus in the basic balance of payments, Germany's official-settlements balance recorded a slight deficit in 1967.[71]

Liquidity from abroad in 1968

The strengthening of the German trade balance in 1966 and 1967 and again in 1968 contrasted with its earlier fluctuation around a rather flat trend. Various measures relating to propensity to import, export performance, and price and cost movements attest to Germany's increased international competitiveness. While the home economy returned nearly to full employment in 1968, Germany's share in export markets rose; and the growth of imports relative to industrial production remained, as it had fallen in 1966–1967, well below the average measure for other industrial countries.[72] The recession had widened international price-level differentials too far for Germany's business revival to cancel them.[73] For the first time since 1960, according to Fels, a flood of

liquidity coming in through the balance of payments and feeding domestic demand was the key element in the imported-inflation process. The danger was widely recognized that an adjustment would require German prices to catch up with the inflation abroad.[74]

Despite growth of the trade and current-account surpluses, the basic balance of payments was approximately in balance for 1968 as a whole, and actually in deficit in the second and third quarters. The explanation hinges on Germany's suddenly, in 1968 (and 1969), becoming the world's largest exporter of long-term capital. Germans bought foreign securities heavily, and German enterprises and banks extended long-term loans abroad. Apparent causes were restrictions newly imposed by the traditional capital-exporting countries, the historically high levels of interest rates in those countries, and lower interest rates in Germany. (The German authorities had worked for low interest rates to promote business recovery and now welcomed their effect on capital movements.) Another odd feature of 1968 was an official-settlements surplus of $1.7 billion, the largest since 1960s despite the near-balance in basic payments. Short-term capital, unlike long-term capital, moved inward during episodes of speculation on revaluation of the mark, particularly in May, August, and November. The size and persistence of the trade surplus and the fact that the large net exports of long-term capital were dependent on an easy-money policy apparently made speculators realize that Germany's basic balance could easily swing back into surplus. Besides, several foreign currencies came under bearish pressure.[75]

Some events affecting speculation in 1968 concern other countries more directly than Germany and are discussed in other chapters—continuing weakness of sterling after its devaluation in November 1967, the announcement on January 1 of mandatory controls on capital exports from the United States, the Canadian crisis of the first quarter of the year, the bearishness on the dollar and bullishness on gold leading to adoption of the two-tier gold market in March, and the French crisis of May and June.

In August and September, sterling and the French franc weakened in the wake of the Soviet occupation of Czechoslovakia. Their weakness intertwined with renewed rumors that the mark would be revalued. Around the beginning of September, by coincidence at just about the time that the French exchange controls temporarily imposed in May were lifted, French funds began moving heavily into Germany. Firm denials of any intention to revalue the mark restored calm by the second week of September. To hold down the gain of official reserves, the Bundesbank again resorted to its "swap" expedient: it offered spot dollars to the commercial banks under forward repurchase agreements making it advantageous for them to place these funds in the Eurodollar market. The increase in Germany's reserves in September, which would otherwise have approached $2 billion, was limited to only $300 million.[76]

Again, however, resort to the swap expedient to promote reexport of funds through the commercial banks did not score a lasting success. Early in November, the inflow of funds grew massive with unprecedented speed. The Bundesbank gained $2.4 billion in reserves in the first three weeks of November, including almost $1.8 billion in three days around the middle of the month.[77]

On Wednesday, November 20, 1968, the principal European foreign-exchange markets closed for the rest of the week while the finance ministers and central-bank governors of the Group of Ten met in emergency session in Bonn. Exchange-rate adjustments were expected to result. That Sunday, though, General de Gaulle surprised the world by his decision not to devalue the franc. Instead of revaluing the mark, Germany reduced by 4 percentage points its value-added tax on imports and its tax rebate on exports. These adjustments were estimated as equivalent to a 3 or 4 percent revaluation of the mark for purposes of commodity trade. To discourage inflows of hot money, the Bundesbank imposed a 100 percent reserve requirement on increases in foreign deposits in German banks; and, with certain exceptions, the banks were temporarily required to have prior approval before accepting deposits or otherwise borrowing from nonresidents.[78]

On one view, the German government's resort to such mere palliatives was an attempt to avoid fundamental balance-of-payments adjustment by disarming speculative and political pressures calling for it. On another view, the decision not to revalue was more respectable. The authorities did not yet possess hindsight on the situation. The basic balance was not actually in surplus at the time. The current account had been substantially in deficit as recently as 1965, and the subsequent improvement of the balance of payments had been associated first with a tight-money policy and then with a business recession. Failure of the current surplus to shrink as the business recovery gained monetum in 1968 could plausibly be attributed to temporary factors. Made chiefly under the pressure of short-term capital inflows, such a hard-to-reverse move as revaluation would be inappropriate. Understandably, the Germans could feel that much of the responsibility for correcting international imbalances lay with France, the United Kingdom, and the United States.[79]

When the main European markets reopened on Monday, November 25, with exchange-rate changes ruled out, speculation had subsided.

69. Argy and Hodjera, op. cit., pp. 70–71; Michael Keran in Federal Reserve Bank of St. Louis, Review, November 1967, p. 14.

70. This and some of the following statements are based on figures in International Financial Statistics.

71. IMF, 1968, p. 7; Argy and Hodjera, op. cit., p. 72.

72. IMF, 1969, pp. 10, 53.

73. William Pollard Wadbrook, West German Balance-of-Payments Policy, New York: Praeger, 1972, p. 218.

74. Fels, op. cit., pp. 92, 99. The money-supply increase during 1968 amounted to 8.5 percent.

75. Milton Gilbert, in H. W. J. Bosman and F. A. M. Alting von Geusau, eds., The Future of the International Monetary System, Lexington, Mass.: Heath, 1970, pp. 32–34; IMF, 1969, pp. 10, 59, 77; Wadbrook, op. cit., p. 174.

76. BIS, 1968–1969, pp. 18, 130–132; Federal Reserve Bank of New York, Annual Report 1968, pp. 37–38; Gilbert in Bosman and Alting, op. cit., p. 34.

77. Gilbert in Bosman and Alting, op. cit., p. 34; Federal Reserve Bank of New York, Annual Report 1968, p. 38.

78. BIS, 1968–1969, pp. 11–12; IMF, 1969, p. 77; Federal Reserve Bank of New York, Annual Report 1968, p. 39; Wadbrook, op. cit., p. 151; Gilbert in Bosman and Alting, op. cit., p. 34.

79. The first view is that of Wadbrook, op. cit., p. 127; the second that of Gilbert in Bosman and Alting, op. cit., pp. 34–35.

(The first impact of the German border-tax changes, however, was to speed up the delivery of exports in December, before the changes came into effect.) Funds began to pour out of Germany; and by the end of January 1969, the inflows during the November crisis had been reversed. Official reserves fell back to their pre-November level.[80]

Crises, float, and revaluation in 1969

For 1969 as a whole, Germany's trade surplus declined by 13 percent, to $3.9 billion, and her current-account surplus (including transfers) declined 41 percent, to $1.6 billion. Strangely, her overall balance on official settlements shifted into a deficit of $3.0 billion; and her international reserves declined by $2.8 billion, or 28 percent. An outflow of long-term capital, estimated at nearly $6 billion, was covered only in part by short-term inflows as German banks repatriated funds exported earlier and as speculators acquired mark claims.[81] Figures for 1969 as a whole are misleading, however; for the year was an eventful one, seeing two major crises of bullish speculation and the revaluation of the mark. (That change, by the way, hampers straightforward interconversion of dollar and mark figures and impairs the continuity of time series of balance-of-payments figures.)

One change during 1969 occurred in the official attitude toward long-term capital outflows, formerly desired as a check to reserve gains. By early in the year the Bundesbank was warning that excessive outflows were endangering domestic investment and growth. Foreigners were borrowing heavily in response to Germany's relatively low interest rates. By early April the authorities acted to relieve congestion in the capital market by spacing out foreign issues.[82]

Although Germany was in basic payments deficit, a gradual return toward restraint in monetary policy[83] aroused concern that funds might flow back to Germany and cause renewed buying pressure on the mark. The demand for marks rose as April 27 approached, the date of a French referendum on which de Gaulle was staking his prestige. De Gaulle's defeat and resignation spurred a rush of funds out of France and into Germany. Rumors that Germany might be willing to consider revaluation as part of a multilateral realignment of parities fed on remarks by a German cabinet minister. Hedging, leads and lags, and outright speculation shifted heavily in favor of the mark. The Bundesbank bought over $850 million between Wednesday, April 30, and Friday, May 2. Pressures intensified during the following week. On May 8 the three-month forward premium of the mark against the dollar touched 9 percent per annum, and on May 9 the spot quotation actually pierced the support ceiling. In the first seven business days of May the international financial markets experienced their heaviest flow of funds in history until then. The countries hardest hit by the rush into marks were France, the United Kingdom, Italy, and smaller European countries such as Belgium and Denmark; the outflow from the United States was large also. In the first seven business days of May the reserves of the Bundesbank grew by over $4 billion, including $2.5 billion on May 8 and 9 alone.[84]

German elections were due in the autumn, and opinion polls showed the public's distaste for revaluation. Industrial interests did not want to lose the export subsidy and protection against imports provided by an undervalued currency. The reactions of exporters to even the small revaluation of 1961 had allegedly made its repetition "a practically unavailable alternative." Finance Minister Strauss emphasized that revaluation would entail writing down the mark value of foreign-exchange assets. It might also give the politically dangerous impression that Germany was being unfairly compelled to make up for the lax financial policies of its trading partners. Having rejected advice to revalue, the Christian Democrats had trapped themselves into acting accordingly.[85] On Friday, May 9, the government publicly rejected revaluation. Instead, it announced indefinite extension of the November 1968 border-tax changes, as well as more vigorous controls to discourage inflows of funds. The decision was also backed up by a declaration from central bankers meeting at Basel about agreement to recycle speculative flows.[86]

Speculation subsided immediately upon the decision to hold existing parities. Nevertheless, much of the previous inflow of funds remained in Germany. Traders were apparently awaiting the outcomes of the French presidential election in June and of the German election in late September. The foreign-exchange markets reacted calmly at first to the French devaluation of August 8. As the German election approached, however, it seemed significant that

Professor Karl Schiller, who would probably continue in office as Economics Minister if the Social Democrats should win, was in favor of revaluation. While government spokesmen refused to discuss revaluation prospects, both major parties declared their intention not to revalue.[87]

As the inflow of funds regained momentum in September, the German money supply again rose too fast. So said the Bundesbank. Attempts to neutralize this effect strengthened the speculation, or at least did not reduce it. "The restrictive measures, without alteration of the exchange rate, thus largely canceled each other out. The inflation into line with other countries, clearly apparent in the wage movement from the beginning of September onwards, ran faster and faster; a great potential inflation had been built up within the country. Germany's central monetary reserves again greatly rose, and strains on the international monetary system, of the kind already experienced in the currency crisis of May 1969 and November 1968, were repeated."[88]

The German government's announcement of May 9 had declared the existing parity of the mark "valid for eternity".[89] "Eternity" lasted until Wednesday, September 24 of the same year. After the close of that day's business, the German authorities announced that the official foreign-exchange market would remain closed through Sunday's election. This move forestalled a further influx of funds that might have approached the massive proportions of the previous November and May. With official intervention absent and with conflicting rumors in circulation, the mark moved above its former ceiling on foreign markets.[90]

The election results pointed to a change of government, subject to negotiation between the prospective coalition parties. The Bundesbank reentered the foreign-exchange market on Monday, September 29, and was flooded with $245 million in the first hour and a half of trading. The outgoing government thereupon accepted the Bundesbank's recommendation that the mark be permitted to float temporarily. It immediately jumped to a premium of more than 5 percent above its old parity. The premium rose to 7¼ percent by mid-October and then crept upward more gradually to almost 8 percent. The Bundesbank stood ready to buy marks at rates slightly below those prevailing in the market, thereby putting a floor just below each successive rise of the mark and

so nudging the mark upward. As some reversal of earlier speculative inflows got under way, the Bundesbank sold about 1 billion dollars from its reserves.[91]

The mark was not floating *freely* during this four-week episode. Traders found it less relevant to assess fundamentals than to guess what the German authorities might do; and the authorities, besides actually intervening, provided hints concerning how high they thought the new mark rate should be. Pressure was

80. Gilbert in Bosman and Alting, *op. cit.*, pp. 31, 35; BIS, 1968–1969, pp. 11–12; *Federal Reserve Bulletin*, March 1970, p. 228.

81. Most of the figures here come from *International Financial Statistics*; Wadbrook, *op. cit.*, p. 174, puts the long-term capital outflow at 23 billion marks.

82. Wadbrook, *op. cit.*, p. 174; *Federal Reserve Bulletin*, March 1970, pp. 228–229.

83. Argy and Hodjera date the restraint as beginning some time between December 1968 and June 1969 and ending in September 1970 by the interest-rate criterion, from March 1969 to possibly June 1970 by the money-growth criterion. *Op. cit.*, pp. 69, 71.

84. *Federal Reserve Bulletin*, March 1970, pp. 228–229; BIS, 1968–1969, pp. 19, 132; BIS, 1969–1970, p. 134; *Federal Reserve Bank of New York, Annual Report 1969*, pp. 37–38; Bundesbank, *Report for the Year 1969*, Frankfurt: 1970, p. 13; Robert Roosa in Bürgenstock Papers, p. 53.

85. Wadbrook, *op. cit.*, p. 129.

86. BIS, 1968–1969, pp. 12–13; *Federal Reserve Bulletin*, March 1970, pp. 228–229.

87. Federal Reserve Bank of New York, *Annual Report 1969*, pp. 38–39; *Federal Reserve Bulletin*, March 1970, p. 235; Wadbrook, *op. cit.*, p. 130.

88. Bundesbank, *Report* for 1969, p. 13.

89. Mordechai E. Kreinin, *International Economics*, New York: Harcourt Brace Jovanovich, 1971, p. 146. On the "immer und ewig" commitment, cf. Robert Roosa in Bürgenstock Papers, p. 53.

90. *Federal Reserve Bulletin*, March 1970, p. 230.

91. *Federal Reserve Bulletin*, March 1970 pp. 230–231; Federal Reserve Bank of New York, *Annual Report 1969*, pp. 39–40; BIS, 1969–1970, p. 135; Wadbrook, *op. cit.*, p. 130.

brought to bear on the Germans to end their experiment before it could yield useful evidence about a floating exchange rate for an advanced industrial country. This is not to say that the inadequate evidence was unfavorable; on the contrary, the chaos that many had predicted did not occur.[92]

On Friday, October 24, the newly formed government of Chancellor Brandt announced a revaluation of the mark by 9.29 percent, from 4.00 to 3.66 per dollar. The new 27.3224-cent parity was slightly higher than the level that the floating mark had reached. At the same time the government eliminated the November 1968 border-tax adjustments, which had already been suspended on October 11. Thus, the actual revaluation was accompanied by reversal of an earlier quasi revaluation. Being larger than generally expected, the revaluation removed the mark from the realm of bullish speculation. It traded at or near its new support floor most of the time through the end of the year while positions built up in September and earlier were being unwound. With interest rates still lower in Germany than abroad, moreover, foreign firms drew on credit lines previously established with German banks. Hence the Bundesbank sold dollars; and by year-end its sales totaled more than $6½ billion, including the $1 billion sold during the float. Maturing forward contracts offset these sales by about $1½ billion. The net outflow of $5 billion created internal and external problems. At home, it tended to make the (desired) monetary restraint too severe or abrupt, prompting reserve-requirement relaxations in November and December and, in mid-December, elimination of the ban on interest payments on foreign-owned bank deposits. Externally, covering the outflow of funds used up most of the Bundesbank's liquid dollar holdings by mid-November, though total official reserves remained very large. The Germans cashed some U.S. "Roosa bonds," made drawings from the IMF and through the General Arrangements to Borrow, and sold some gold to the U.S. Treasury. Germany's reserve losses were especially heavy in December as U.S. and European corporations met balance-of-payments targets or year-end needs by repatriating funds transferred to Germany earlier in the year. With the end of such year-end repositioning and with a sharp decline in Eurodollar interest rates, the outflows from Germany halted. Quotations of the mark firmed early in 1970, especially as further steps to tighten

German monetary conditions were taken in March.[93]

Although the 1969 revaluation quickly caused an awkwardly abrupt tightening of domestic monetary conditions, it could not, over the longer run, slow down internal cost and price increases to a degree worth mentioning. Such, at least, was the judgment of the Bundesbank. It came too late and was too small (especially as it was accompanied by reversal of the quasi revaluation of 11 months before). In particular, a strengthening of worldwide inflation overrode the tendency of the revaluation to dampen price increases in Germany.[94]

Even after the reversal of earlier German reserve gains in the last quarter of 1969, Germany and Japan ended the year together holding some 28 percent of the total international reserves of industrial countries other than the United States. In the ensuing two years those two countries acquired well over half of the extraordinary growth in that total.[95] Let us now turn to Germany's experience in those two years.

Capital flows in 1970

In 1970 Germany's trade surplus grew slightly in dollar amount, to $4.0 billion, but remained practically unchanged in revalued marks. An increased deficit on services and transfers cut the current-account surplus to less than half that of 1969. Yet the overall balance settled by official reserve transactions shifted from a deficit of $3.0 billion to a surplus of $6.2 billion, larger than ever before (and not to be exceeded until 1973). Net capital movements shifted from heavily outward to substantially inward. This reversal was partly attributable to policy, which remained motivated for a while by a desire to reduce the heavy private long-term capital ouflows characteristic of 1968 and 1969. The Bundesbank explained its high-interest-rate policy of 1970 as needed to reduce these outflows, as well as to help damp the inflationary boom then raging. After the 1969 revaluation, the authorities had eliminated income-tax withholding from interest payments on foreign-owned German securities, and the capital-market committee of the German banks had acted to cut back foreign security issues on the German market. Even so, long-term net capital flows were still outward, and the German *basic* payments position was roughly in balance through 1970 and early 1971. The overall net inflow was attributable to *short-term* capital. The quarterly average call-money rate in Germany rose from a low of 3.04 percent in the second quarter of 1969 to a high of 9.18 percent in the second quarter of 1970, sagging thereafter. Interest rates were falling, by contrast, in the United States and the Eurodollar market during most of 1970. The resulting differential, which persisted into the first half of 1971, attracted funds into Germany. Speculation accentuated these inflows when the Canadian dollar was set afloat and the Italian lira came under bear attack around midyear.[96]

The reversal of capital flows, counting short-term as well as long-term funds, thus went much further than desired. The German authorities responded, at various times, by manipulating the banks' rediscount quotas, by complicating the system of reserve requirements against foreign and domestic liabilities, and by manipulating the terms offered to the banks in forward swap transactions. To whatever extent these expedients did succeed in keeping the banks from borrowing funds abroad for relending at home, they unintentionally spurred *non*bank firms to borrow abroad directly. Finally, the Bundesbank felt obliged to try to shrink the international interest-rate differential by lowering its discount rate from 7.5 to 7 percent in July and by lowering it further in November and December (and again, to 5 percent, in April 1971). The Bundesbank made these cuts for balance-of-payments reasons and was anxious that they not be viewed as an easing of monetary policy for domestic purposes.[97] The discount-rate cut of November 1970 was accompanied by a further rearrangement of reserve requirements, which the banks apparently feared would prove restrictive. Accordingly, they brought home funds from abroad, while German corporations stepped up their borrowings in the Eurodollar market. This set off a groundswell of demand for marks. In just over one week of November, the Bundesbank had to absorb more than $1 billion.[98]

Eventful 1971

The conditions of 1970, growing more intense in early 1971, suggested a bigger-scale replay of 1960 and early 1961: strong reserves, a large excess of German over foreign interest rates,

heavy borrowing abroad by German nonbank corporations, and speculation intensifying the capital inflows. On both occasions, furthermore, the mark was allowed to move up against other currencies. Again a classic dilemma case illustrated the difficulty of restricting both domestic and foreign sources of funds in a non-reserve-currency country with exchange rates fixed and currencies convertible.[99]

The balance-of-payments results for 1971 as a whole were obscured by the exchange-rate changes of that eventful year. Germany's trade surplus grew to $4.6 billion, but the current-account surplus (including transfers) shriveled. Private capital movements, including errors and omissions, were heavily inward for the year as a whole, though outward in the second half. The officially settled overall balance ran a record surplus of $2.3 billion in the first quarter alone, much smaller surpluses in the remaining quarters, and a surplus of $4.5 billion for the year as a whole, down 28 percent from that of 1970. The IMF attributed this reduction in

92. Samuel Brittan, *The Price of Economic Freedom*, New York: St. Martin's Press, 1970, pp. 54–55.

93. *Federal Reserve Bulletin*, March 1970, pp. 231–233.

94. Bundesbank, *Geschäftsbericht für das Jahr 1971*, pp. 11–12.

95. IMF, 1972, p. 14.

96. Wadbrook, *op. cit.*, pp. 174–175, 285; Argy and Hodjera, *op. cit.*, p. 71; figures from *International Financial Statistics*.

As for the boom, the peak of manufacturing-capacity utilization was probably passed after the first quarter of 1970, but activity remained high throughout the year and into the first half of 1971. Monetary policy remained tight into middle or late 1970. From about the third quarter, interest-rate policy was dominated by inflows of funds, despite signs that the home economy was still overheated. Argy and Hodjera, *op. cit.*, p. 71.

97. Wadbrook, *op. cit.*, *passim*.

98. Federal Reserve Bank of New York, *Monthly Review*, March 1971, p. 51.

99. Argy and Hodjera, *op. cit.*, pp. 71–72; Wadbrook, *op. cit.*, p. 285.

the overall surplus to the floating of the mark in May and other measures taken to restrain the inflow of foreign funds.[100]

Scarcely ever before, according to the Bundesbank, were monetary developments in Germany as strongly influenced by the balance of payments, and by net capital imports in particular, as in 1971. Short-term foreign borrowing of German nonbank enterprises dominated the capital inflow, although long-term capital imports were significant also.[101] These German borrowings on the Eurodollar market and elsewhere were motivated primarily by interest-rate differentials, in the view of the Bundesbank, although speculation played an increasing role. Between the end of 1969 and May 1971, the foreign financial-loan debt of German enterprises grew by some DM15.4 billion, equivalent to $4.2 billion at the parity then in effect, not counting borrowings concealed in errors and omissions. In the first half of 1971 foreign borrowings accounted for as much as 40 percent of total net borrowings of German firms. The late Bundesbank President, Karl Blessing, came to regard lack of control over direct foreign credits to German industry as the chief inadequacy in the central bank's monetary weapons.[102]

The chain of causation began, according to the Bundesbank, with the cheap-money policy adopted in the United States during the recession there. Under what was practically an international dollar standard, that policy could have effects that were perhaps stronger in other countries than in the United States itself. Interest-rate incentives to move funds were increasingly accompanied by loss of confidence in the dollar.[103] The flows took place not so much bilaterally as through the revolving door [Drehscheibe] of the Eurodollar market. The reserves of the Group of Ten countries, not counting the United States but adding Switzerland, rose by almost $31 billion in 1971. The acquisition of dollars by monetary authorities entailed creation of domestic central-bank money and provided the basis for multiple expansion of ordinary domestic money. German experience illustrated—still according to the Bundesbank—the difficulty of successful offsetting by restrictive domestic measures. In 1971, the total money volume of the ten countries mentioned grew some 18 percent above its end-of-1970 level, giving excessive scope for price and wage increases.[104]

The weakness of the dollar relative to the mark in early 1971 was ironic in some ways. The anti-inflation efforts that led to recession in the United States should have fundamentally tended to strengthen the dollar, yet the recession had the opposite effect through its influence on monetary policy and interest-rate differentials. German price inflation was temporarily outpacing the American. The German current account, including transfers, was moving into deficit and did in fact record a deficit in the second and third quarters of 1971.

Quasi-official talk intensified the flow of funds into Germany. The Joint Working Group of German Economic Research Institutes released its annual report on Monday, May 3. Among other things, the report said that the German authorities had to choose between fighting inflation and maintaining a fixed exchange rate; it recommended revaluation or a float. Economics Minister Schiller called the report "worthy of further consideration" and a "usable contribution." Numerous saver- and consumer-oriented groups quickly joined in publicly appealing for revaluation.[105]

Speculators began furiously selling dollars for marks on Monday, May 3. In three days the Bundesbank absorbed some $2.1 or $2.2 billion, including about $1 billion in the first 40 minutes of trading on Wednesday alone. Trading was then immediately suspended on the Frankfurt foreign-exchange market; the market was to remain closed for the rest of the week. Within hours, Belgium, the Netherlands, Austria, Switzerland, Portugal, and Finland followed suit. Other central banks from Spain to Israel imposed currency controls of various kinds.[106]

When the markets reopened on Monday the 10th, the Austrian schilling had been revalued upward by 5.05 percent and the Swiss franc by 7.07 percent, the Dutch guilder and German mark were floating, and the Belgian franc was floating on a financial market while still pegged for commercial transactions. By floating the mark in May, Germany, according to the Bundesbank, largely escaped further disturbance from capital movements for the rest of the year.[107] Other countries were not to be so fortunate.

Were the events of May 1971 a mark crisis, specifically, or a more general crisis centered on the dollar? Milton Friedman argued the former, noting that there was no great rush into French, British, Canadian, or Japanese currency, even though the yen, like the mark, was widely regarded as undervalued. He might also have noted the absence of any great increase in gold speculation. Later, even in the light of the August crisis, Milton Gilbert agreed that May had seen essentially a mark crisis. He blamed it chiefly on the Germans' extreme use of monetary tightness for domestic purposes, without due regard for external considerations and without measures to keep German firms from borrowing abroad.[108] At the convention of the American Bankers Association in Munich later in May, and on other occasions, American and other foreign officials complained to each other about the "madness" of the exceptionally high German interest-rate structure and about the German talk that had fanned speculation.[109] Some even suspected German domestic politics at work. A straight revaluation of the mark would have incurred the bitter opposition of German export interests. Allowing a crisis to force an upward float of the mark would be a subtle way of blaming Germany's troubles, including inflation, on the inflow of unwanted dollars—that is, on foreigners.[110]

Within two weeks after the float began, the mark rose to 4½ percent above its old (1969) dollar parity, then sank to a 2½ percent premium at the very beginning of June, partly in connection with a rise in Eurodollar interest rates. The Bundesbank had remained aloof from the foreign-exchange market for the first few weeks but returned on June 2 by offering to sell dollars at a price equivalent to a premium on the mark of 2.59 percent above the old parity. The Bundesbank had apparently been concerned that the mark was relapsing too fast in relation to the dollar. On June 3 it offered dollars at successively lower rates, so that the mark stood 3.67 percent above parity at the end of the day's trading. Earlier, the German government had said that the old parity would ultimately be restored, but now the Bundesbank's readiness to sell dollars at flexible rates was widely taken as a sign that the authorities had given up on that move and that they might revalue the mark upward instead. The premium reached nearly 4¾ percent in late June, 5¾ percent at the end of July, and over 8 percent by mid-August.[111]

The mark crisis, if such it had been, turned into a dollar crisis during the summer of 1971; the events are detailed in other chapters.[112] When the world's official foreign-exchange markets reopened on August 23 after being closed for a week, other major currencies, soon joined by the Japanese yen, were floating in addition to the mark. At first the mark's premium

100. IMF, 1972, p. 14; *International Financial Statistics.*

101. Bundesbank, *Geschäftsbericht*, 1971, p. 22.

102. Samuel I. Katz, *Exchange-Risk Under Fixed and Flexible Exchange Rates*, New York University, *The Bulletin*, June 1972, pp. 54–55. Wadbrook, *op. cit.*, p. 288, says that net short-term inflows between the beginning of 1970 and May 3, 1971, *including* unrecorded transactions, amounted to almost DM46 billion and that over two-thirds of this total constituted foreign borrowing by nonbank enterprises.

103. For more details on American aspects of the situation, including repayment by U.S. banks of their earlier mammoth borrowing in the Eurodollar market, see Chapter 27.

104. Bundesbank, *Geschäftsbericht*, 1971, pp. 22–23. This same report, pp. 59–60, argues, though perhaps not convincingly, that the central bank can hardly control the primary money expansion that occurs when nonbanks sell foreign-exchange acquisitions to their commercial banks and that even the control of the secondary monetary expansion that the banks carry out on the basis of their increased liquidity is extremely difficult in the face of interest- or speculation-motivated inflows of funds. Earlier, Otmar Emminger, a member of the Bundesbank Board, had complained of Germany's "pretty desperate situation," with its monetary policy in effect being dictated in Washington. *Wall Street Journal*, 6 May 1971, p. 20.

105. Wadbrook, *op. cit.*, p. 289; *Business Week*, 8 May 1971, p. 17; *Newsweek*, 17 May 1971, p. 76.

106. Bundesbank, *Geschäftsbericht*, 1971, p. 33; *Newsweek*, 17 May 1971, p. 75.

107. Bundesbank, *Geschäftsbericht* for 1971, p. 34.

108. Milton Friedman and Clem Morgello in *Newsweek*, issues of 24 May 1971, p. 72, and 10 May 1971, p. 80, respectively; Gilbert in *Morgan Guaranty Survey*, December 1971, pp. 6–7.

109. Hobart Rowen in *Washington Post*, 30 May 1971, p. G-1; Wadbrook, *op. cit.*, p. 292.

110. *U.S. News and World Report*, 31 May 1971, pp. 17–18.

111. *Wall Street Journal*, 3 June 1971, p. 8, 4 June 1971, p. 4; *New York Times*, 5 June 1971, p. 42; BIS, 1971–1972, p. 133; Wadbrook, *op. cit.*, p. 292.

112. See pp. 578–580 in particular.

sank to 6¾ percent, but towards the end of September it reached 10½ percent. After sagging below 10 percent in October, when monetary policy was eased, the premium reached 12¼ percent just before the Smithsonian Agreement in December. That Agreement raised the mark a bit further, revaluing it from the 1969 parity of 3.66 per dollar to a central rate of 3.2225 per newly devalued dollar, spelling a 4.61 percent increase in the value of the mark in gold and SDRs and a 13.58 percent increase in its dollar value. As with other currencies, the float remained "dirty" until the Smithsonian Agreement ended it; from time to time the German authorities countered what they considered too strong an appreciation of the mark by buying dollars both forward and spot.[113]

After early May, Germany's involuntary reserve gains were slight in comparison with those of other countries, especially in the third quarter; the stampede of funds into Germany had come earlier and had been checked by Germany's early float. Even so, the process of imported inflation illustrated itself again in parts of 1971, especially in the first few months. At least, this is the judgment of the Bundesbank. Placement of inflowing funds in the German banks directly expanded bank deposits, and the attendant growth of the banks' domestic reserves then promoted a secondary expansion of bank deposits. The rate of monetary expansion was especially rapid in January to May, before the float, slackened in June through September, as funds flowed outward on balance, and picked up again in October and after the repegging of exchange rates as funds again flowed in from abroad. The Bundesbank's offsetting measures were not nearly adequate to keep foreign-exchange inflows from increasing the liquidity of the banks.[114] Table 24.3, as already mentioned, provides some indication of this process.

Speculation and controls in 1972

In 1972 Germany's trade surplus, measured in devalued dollars and at increased prices, rose to $6.1 billion. The strength of exports, particularly in the fourth quarter, suggested that the realignment of parities had not canceled Germany's competitive advantage in world markets. The overall surplus settled by monetary authorities rose to $5.0 billion. Long- and short-term capital movements and errors and omissions—quite changeable during the year—netted to an inflow equivalent to $4.5 billion at the Smithsonian parity.[115]

Early in 1972, doubts about the Smithsonian exchange-rate structure were motivating flows of funds into Germany, which again boosted monetary expansion. The Bundesbank acted late in February to curb these inflows and absorb the bank liquidity resulting from them. It cut its discount rate from 4 to 3 percent, cut the banks' rediscount quotas, and raised reserve requirements on growth of their foreign liabilities. A so-called Bardepot (cash-deposit) requirement went into effect on March 1: German firms were required to keep the equivalent of 40 percent of their borrowing abroad in excess of DM2 million on non-interest-bearing deposit with the Bundesbank. An announcement at the end of May scheduled a further cut in the banks' rediscount quotas and an increase in their reserve requirements for July 1.[116]

In June and July the mark was the target of new speculative rushes, first out of sterling and then, after the pound's float,[117] out of the dollar. To meet this demand for marks while holding the rate within its Smithsonian ceiling, the Bundesbank had to take in $4.5 billion worth of foreign currencies. Pressures remained strong until beyond mid-July, when the Finance Ministers of the European Community reaffirmed their determination to hold the Smithsonian rates and when the Federal Reserve Bank of New York began supporting the dollar by selling marks (on a small scale).[118] Meanwhile, the German authorities raised the Bardepot on borrowing abroad from 40 to 50 percent and cut the exempted amount from 2 to 0.5 million marks, raised bank reserve requirements on foreign-owned deposits, and raised the special reserve requirement on increases in banks' liabilities to foreigners. They made prior approval necessary for sales of domestic fixed-income securities to nonresidents, who had increasingly taken this route to get into mark-denominated assets. Anticipations of some such measures, or even sterner ones, had intensified the rush into marks on the last day of June, requiring the Bundesbank to absorb nearly $0.9 billion in less than two hours.[119] Switzerland tightened its controls about the same time as Germany, imposing an 8 percent annual tax on new foreign deposits in Swiss banks, banning foreign investment in

Swiss securities and real estate, and barring Swiss residents or companies from borrowing abroad without government approval.[120]

The German measures to ward off foreign funds were widely interpreted as spelling abandonment of the country's traditional opposition to capital controls. In apparent disappointment over the change, Economics and Finance Minister Karl Schiller resigned. Events of the first two or three weeks of July tended to bear out Schiller's skepticism about the effectiveness of controls. On July 13 and 14 alone some $2.5 billion in hot dollars poured into central banks, most of that amount into the Bundesbank. Yet almost every frontier in Europe was guarded by the tightest controls in many years. The mark was under massive upward pressure; yet after two floats followed by revaluations in three years and with an election due in December, the German government found the idea of still another revaluation against the dollar intolerable.[121]

Not until August, after the speculation against the dollar had been stopped, did the Bundesbank gain a measure of autonomy in its monetary policy. But by that time—more precisely, during the first seven months of 1972 —the German money supply, whether narrowly or broadly defined, was averaging more than 13 percent above what it had been 12 months earlier. The Bundesbank raised its rediscount rate and rate on secured loans four times between October and January and cut the banks' rediscount quotas twice in early 1973. Yet money-supply growth continued exceptionally rapid. At the end of 1972, narrowly defined money was 13.9 percent and money plus quasi money 15.4 percent above the levels of one year before. Consumer prices were 5.5 percent higher, and the rise was accelerating.[122]

The German side of the dollar's troubles, 1973

Reflecting temporary recovery of the dollar, the mark declined from its upper support range almost to its Smithsonian central rate in October 1972 and again in January 1973. Then, over the weekend of Saturday, January 20, the Italians introduced a two-tier market for the lira. The Swiss responded on the 23rd by letting their franc float. The mark followed the jump in the Swiss franc and, after a few days,

came under great buying pressure, the counterpart of bearishness on the dollar.[123] Market operators were well aware the mark was now the major European currency neither floating nor, like the Italian, French, and Belgian currencies, trading on a financial market separated from the commercial market. People wondered how firmly resolved the Germans were to maintain the Smithsonian ceiling. On February 1 and 2 the Bundesbank took in more than $1 billion, and a further $4.9 billion over the week of Monday, February 5, while the Federal Reserve intervened on a smaller scale in New York. After the devaluation of the dollar on February 12, the mark at first declined to its new lower limit. The Bundesbank could sell nearly $1 billion, while the Federal Reserve bought marks to repay swap drawings. In a second phase of the dollar crisis, the mark rose

113. BIS, 1971–1972, pp. 133–135; Bundesbank, *Geschäftbericht*, 1971, p. 41.

114. Bundesbank, *Geschäftbericht*, 1971, pp. 19–20.

115. *International Financial Statistics*; Charles Coombs in Federal Reserve Bank of New York, *Monthly Review*, March 1973, p. 51; BIS, 1972–1973, pp. 30, 99.

116. BIS, 1972–1973, p. 54.

117. See p. 466.

118. Charles Coombs in Federal Reserve Bank of New York, *Monthly Review*, March 1973, pp. 50–51.

119. *Washington Post*, 2 July 1972, p. G-2; Federal Reserve Bank of Chicago, *International Letter*, 7 July 1972; First National City Bank of New York, *Monthly Economic Letter*, March 1973, p. 10.

120. BIS, 1972–1973, p. 68; *Newsweek*, 17 July 1972, p. 60.

121. Federal Reserve Bank of Chicago, *International Letter*, 7 July 1972; *Business Week*, 22 July 1972, p. 16, 29 July 1972, pp. 38–39.

122. First National City Bank of New York, *Monthly Economic Letter*, March 1973, p. 10; Coombs, *op. cit.*, p. 51; BIS, 1972–1973, p. 56; *International Financial Statistics*.

123. For details, see pp. 595–596.

to its new upper limit on March 1. On that day alone the Bundesbank took in a record amount of more than $2.6 billion. Its total net purchases from February 1 now totaled nearly $8 billion. Next day the mark rose to more than 4½ percent above its new central rate, just before the authorities closed the market.[124]

Before the European markets reopened on March 19, Germany revalued the mark upward by 3.00 percent in terms of Special Drawing Rights. (Austria followed with a 2¼ percent revaluation of the schilling.) The revaluation had no particular significance for the mark-dollar rate, which would now be floating, but it did affect the support limits to be maintained between the mark and the other European currencies taking part in a joint float against the dollar. After the heavy inflows of funds into Germany in February and at the beginning of March, it was not surprising that the mark was the weakest of the jointly floating currencies for some time. New bear speculation against the dollar, among other things, changed that situation. In the 12 days before June 29 the Bundesbank had to buy 4 billion marks' worth of other European currencies to hold rates within the support limits of the joint float; DM2.2 billion of the buying came on Thursday the 28th alone. On Friday Germany revalued the mark by a further 5.5 percent in terms of Special Drawing Rights. The move was seen as an attempt to maintain anti-inflationary policies without having to quit the joint float. (Austria again followed, revaluing by 4.8 percent on July 3.)[125] On Friday, July 6, 1973 the mark was quoted at 44.1 cents in New York, up 76 percent from the 25-cent parity in effect until September 1969.

During and even before the dollar crises of 1973, the German authorities again tightened their capital controls and antiinflation efforts. Effective January 1, the amount of borrowing abroad exempt from the Bardepot requirement was cut further to 50,000 marks. From February 2 foreign purchases of German stock were made subject to prior official approval, as bond purchases had been since July 1972. (These new controls were soon eased to permit shifting back and forth between bonds and stock so long as foreigners made no net increase in their holdings.) Also from February 2, foreign corporations would need official approval to increase their direct investment in subsidiaries or plants in Germany by more than DM500,000, and Germans would need permission to draw more than DM50,000 of credit abroad or arrange payment terms with nonresident creditors. The government also decided to ask parliament to raise the Bardepot requirement on borrowing abroad from 50 to 100 percent. Having again tightened banks' reserve requirements and rediscount quotas, the Bundesbank was seeking new policy tools. In February the government launched a tax-and-loan package intended to sop up liquidity and purchasing power.[126]

Over 1973 as a whole, Germany recorded a $10.1 billion surplus on goods-and-services account. The International Monetary Fund attributed this phenomenal performance partly to booming conditions in German export markets, moderation in the expansion of demand at home, and, in the face of the mark's appreciation, relatively low price elasticities of foreign demand for German exports of durable goods. (Furthermore, the dollar, as unit of measurement, had shrunken in both foreign-exchange value and purchasing power.) Germany's overall official-settlements surplus reached $9.2 billion, of which more than 70 percent appeared in the first quarter alone. (The last quarter of 1973 even brought an overall deficit, attributable to transfers and capital movements.) With the Bundesbank no longer committed to supporting the dollar at a fixed rate, growth of Germany's international reserves, domestic reserve money, and ordinary money supply was pretty well checked after early 1973. German consumer prices rose 6.9 percent in 1973 and in August 1974 stood 7.4 percent higher than one year before; these rates of inflation, though disturbing, were much more moderate than those being recorded in most other countries at the same time. The German mark, still pegged to other currencies in the European joint float, remained the focus of bullish rumors from time to time.[127]

Disputed lessons

What lessons emerge from Germany's experience? Manfred Willms has argued that it was —or would have been—feasible to offset imported inflation in Germany; even in an open economy with fixed exchange rates, the authorities can control the money stock.[128] If they shrink the stock of domestic high-powered or base money and interest rates rise as a result, the amount of external reserves attracted will be smaller than the domestic base-money contraction. International flows of funds are not perfectly interest-sensitive; they react not to the international interest-rate differential but rather to the differential adjusted for the divergence between spot and forward exchange rates. In his statistical study for the period 1958–1970, Willms distinguished between the directly controlled components of the monetary base and the noncontrolled or only indirectly controlled components. The latter are the part of the money base determined by commercial-bank borrowing at the Bundesbank and by international capital movements; the former are the part controlled at the initiative of the Bundesbank. In fact, "the German monetary authorities have been relatively successful in neutralizing the impact of the noncontrolled or indirectly controlled components of the money supply process by changing the directly controlled components. The most important instruments for offsetting the impact of changes in the noncontrolled components of the money supply process have been the required reserve policy and a change in Government deposits or special anticyclical deposits at the Bundesbank." Statistically estimated interest-rate elasticities of the endogenous variables of the money-supply process were low enough to indicate "that control of the money supply can be maintained in the short-run." International flows, in particular, would counteract domestic policy actions *less than fully*.

Several comments are in order. First, Willms himself makes frank qualifications to his own analysis. His reassuring conclusions apply, he says, on the average or in the short run over the period considered (a period including two upward revaluations of the mark), but not necessarily on all occasions. "In the long-run the use of monetary and fiscal policies to offset domestic inflationary pressure arising from an inflow of foreign reserves means that Germany trades investment and consumption goods for foreign currency. Hence, in real terms a policy of controlling inflation in a fixed exchange rate system results in welfare losses for the German economy." If Willms's study is a fair example of what sort of reassurance is available against the usual worries about imported inflation, the very weakness of that reassurance points up those worries.

Second, the period that Willms considers ends before the crises of 1971–1973, which dramatized the problem more than ever. Third, by referring to forward exchange rates and covered interest-rate differentials, rather than to interest-rate differentials pure and

simple, Willms is tacitly (and even explicitly, on his p.12) assuming that some exchange-rate risk exists. This variability or potential variability of exchange rates is what keeps capital movements from being so interest-sensitive that resistance to imported inflation would be impossible. Willms does not really contradict, therefore, the theory that a country cannot enjoy monetary and price-level independence under firmly fixed and trusted exchange rates.

Fourth, as Michael Porter argues, Willms's statistical work bears an interpretation roughly the opposite of his own. As the dependent variable in his econometrically fitted equation, Willms used the quarterly change in that portion of base money supposedly controlled by the authorities (total change in base money minus change due to foreign-asset accumulation). His independent variable was change in base money corresponding to change in foreign assets. His calculations indicated to him that the authorities successfully varied the controlled component so as to offset about 86 percent of changes in base money due to changes in foreign assets. Perhaps, however, changes in reserve requirements *induced* capital inflows.[129] Willms's use of quarterly data makes it impossible to sort out which came first.

124. Coombs, *op. cit.*, pp. 52–53; BIS, 1972–1973, p. 140; First National City Bank of New York, *Monthly Economic Letter*, March 1973, p. 9.

125. BIS, 1972–1973, pp. 140–141, 145; Federal Reserve Bank of Chicago, *International Letter*, 29 June 1973; *IMF Survey*, 9 July 1973, p. 208.

126. *Wall Street Journal*, 7 December 1972, p. 26; Foreign Exchange Letter (of the *Journal of Investment Finance*), 15 February 1973, p. 3; *IMF Survey*, 12 March 1973, p. 69; First National City Bank of New York, *Monthly Economic Letter*, March 1973, pp. 10–11.

127. *International Financial Statistics*; IMF, 1974, pp. 20–21.

128. "Controlling Money in an Open Economy: The German Case," Federal Reserve Bank of St. Louis, *Review*, April 1971, pp. 10–27.

129. Michael G. Porter, "Capital Flows as an Offset to Monetary Policy: The German Experience," IMF *Staff Papers*, **XIX**, July 1972, pp. 395–424.

Porter got around this difficulty by using monthly data for January 1963 to January 1971 and by noting that changes in reserve requirements, which affect the base money effectively available to banks, take effect at the *beginnings* of months. Porter's regressions indicated that a rise in the required reserve ratio sufficient to cause a DM1 billion increase in required reserves was *followed* by capital inflows, mostly through errors and omissions, of approximately DM820 million in the same month. His interpretation is that corporations turned rapidly to foreign sources of loans when they anticipated being denied loans at home. This behavior was particularly noticeable in 1970, when inflows offset substantial increases in reserve requirements. The Bundesbank seemed to have reached much the same conclusion. In its June 1971 *Monthly Report* it said that the floating of the mark had released it "from the compulsion of having to create central bank money by the purchase of foreign exchange. . . . The Bundesbank thus no longer has to fear that its restrictive course in credit policy is more or less automatically undercut by money inflows from foreign countries."[130] For an analogy concerning the frustration of monetary policy under a fixed exchange rate, Porter considered discriminatory imposition of a reserve-requirement increase on a group of banks in upstate New York. The banks' disappointed customers would borrow outside the area, without local interest rates necessarily increasing. If German banks were prevented from borrowing abroad, then disappointed corporate and individual borrowers might obtain funds from foreign banks or affiliates. Capital would flow in without any change in German interest rates being necessary. Thus, changes in reserve requirements, the major weapon of German monetary policy, were substantially and rapidly offset in their effect on bank liquidity by capital inflows mainly concealed among errors and omissions. In trying to neutralize the domestic monetary impact of capital flows, Germany obtained a small degree of monetary independence at the cost of much fluctuation in its external reserves. Striving for internal balance seems to have worsened the external imbalance.

Victor Argy and Zoran Hodjera, two other economists on the staff of the International Monetary Fund, drew similar lessons from German experience between 1958 and 1971, when money markets were closely integrated with markets abroad and when the German currency was strong in the foreign-exchange markets. Monetary restraint, appropriately applied for conditions of boom at home, would provoke capital inflows, swelling the external reserves. The growth of reserves would in time feed expectations of exchange-rate changes, which would in turn induce further capital inflows.[131]

Gerhard Fels is another student of German experience who found the reality of imported inflation well documented there.[132] He puts less than the usual emphasis, though, on the importation of inflation through a surplus in the balance of payments. He describes two aspects or theories of that supposed mechanism. The first is the liquidity theory: the central bank's purchases of foreign exchange inflate the reserves of the banking system and, in turn, the ordinary money supply. The second is the income theory, focusing on the multiplier and accelerator effects of a surplus on current account.[133] These theories may well apply to 1960 and 1968; but neither, in Fels's judgment, accounts for what he views as Germany's continuing import of inflation even during most of the mid-1960s, when the balance of payments was roughly in equilibrium on the average. Instead, he focuses on what he calls the international price-connection—the direct linkage of foreign and German prices through the fixed exchange rate. In accordance with the Law of One Price for an integrated market, inflation abroad directly raises the prices of German imports and of the goods competing with German exports on foreign markets.[134] In Germany, price increases radiate from the sector of internationally traded goods by way of direct and indirect links (as through costs) to goods and services in general. This international contagion of inflation has been a trend phenomenon, working with complicated and changeable lags, not a series of isolated shocks whose impact could be discerned in neat time sequences. The transmission process works partly through wage rates, whose adjustments are far from closely synchronized with price movements or balance-of-payments developments. Understandably, and contrary to oversimplified theories of the transmission mechanism, periods of largest price and wage increases do not necessarily coincide with, or follow with a stable lag, periods of largest balance-of-payments surplus. Diagnoses of inflation based on a simple balance-of-payments theory are likely to go wrong because the balance of payments reacts to German deviations from the international inflationary trend, not to the trend itself.

At full employment, everything *looks* like "homemade" inflation: the balance of payments tends less than otherwise to be in surplus, wages rise more strongly than would be compatible with stable costs, and price increases become virulent. Import of inflation seems almost ruled out by definition. Yet what may really be going on is that domestic boom weakens resistances to adjustment of domestic to foreign prices and costs, an adjustment for which pressures had been building up over the longer run.

Homemade inflation is of course readily conceivable. But how does one pinpoint where and when the causes arose of an inflation spread out in time and over space? How would businessmen, unions, the government, and the central bank have behaved if price stability had reigned abroad or if appreciation of the mark had impeded the transmission of foreign inflation? Homemade inflation tendencies no stronger than the international trend only speed up the process of adaptation. What part of a price inflation is really attributable to domestic causes if, without them, the inflation would have occurred anyway, only somewhat later? Under fixed exchange rates, one could justifiably conclude that an inflation was homemade only if the price trend was steeper at home than abroad and if external payments tended to be in deficit. Even then, such a process might represent a mere exaggeration or overshooting of adaptation to foreign inflationary influences that began earlier.

Fels makes a good case for the direct price connection as an element in the transmission of inflation to Germany. In my opinion, though, he exaggerates the rivalry between that theory and the liquidity and income or multiplier-accelerator strands of the balance-of-payments theory. They all fit together in an eclectic theory. (What is so wrong with eclecticism if it corresponds to how the world really works?) No particular strand of an eclectic theory is discredited merely because the effects that it stresses fail to occur simultaneously with or in a dependable lead or lag relation with the effects stressed by other strands. Furthermore, a direct linkage of import and export prices to rising prices abroad and its spread to the whole domestic price and wage level could hardly persist indefinitely without being "ratified" by monetary expansion. If homemade expansion does not occur, the tardiness of adjustment of

domestic to foreign prices will promote a balance-of-payments surplus after all, with monetary expansion as a result. Like monetary tightness to resist strong domestic wage pushes, resistance to the push of rising import and export prices by a policy tight enough to mop up monetary expansion resulting from the balance of payments would tend to bring on a recession, also tending toward payments surplus. Direct price linkage cannot be the *whole* story. Sooner or later the process must be ratified by monetary expansion provided either by a balance-of-payments surplus or by domestic actions merely hastening what would have happened anyway.

Wadbrook has reached a compatible conclusion. German measures of credit policy proved to be self-defeating palliatives. As rises in German prices and money incomes lagged behind rises in the outside world and as German interest rates rose relatively, the balance of payments brought funds in on current and capital account. Yet German prices and interest rates could not be effectively sealed off from those of the outside world. "Credit policy [had to] vacillate between fostering 'homemade' and provoking imported inflation. The resulting stop-and-go short-term-oriented credit policy [was] injurious to the long-term planning of firms, and constitute[d] an obstacle to consistent economic policy." Monetary tightness could not set aside direct linkages among prices and

130. Quoted by Porter *op. cit.*, p. 416.

131. *Staff Papers*, March 1973, p. 68.

132. *Op. cit.* Fels published his book in 1969, before the particularly striking episodes of the following years. My attempt to compress the main argument of a whole book necessarily involves some degree of interpretation, as distinguished from straightforward paraphrase.

133. See pp. 78–80 above.

134. If above-average productivity gains would otherwise have pressed German import-competing and export enterprises to cut their prices in the context of a stable general price level, price increases abroad soften that competitive pressure. Under fixed exchange rates, in the long run, price cuts would only have brought bigger export surpluses and their inflationary consequences.

wages. The timing of shifts in credit policy was further confused by a tendency of specific rounds of wage increases to lag behind price rises. Often the Bundesbank and others responded to each wage rise as if it were a new inflationary threat, when it was merely the lagged consequence of an inflationary movement already under way. Such problems of timing and flexibility led the German Council of Economic Experts, in a 1968 report, to characterize a balance-of-payments policy based on credit restriction as dangerous to both price stability and growth.[135]

The German authorities avoided a clear-cut choice between either relaxing and enjoying the worldwide inflation or adopting adequate measures of insulation, including either a floating exchange rate or sufficiently prompt and sizable revaluations. They shrank from forthright balance-of-payments adjustment in one way or another. Wadbrook suggests reasons of domestic and international politics for their vacillation. Fully adjusting the balance would have meant loss of some export markets, possible loss of financial prestige and power, and—if the exchange rate were to be kept fixed—abandonment of the goal and slogan of price stability in an inflationary world. Nonadjustment appeared to entail loss of financial and political harmony in the Atlantic community,

the domestic difficulties and distortions of combating the automatic adjustment tendencies created by disequilibrium, and the constant embarrassment of ultimately incurable imported inflation. German officials even engaged in some wishful thinking about solving their dilemma by somehow exporting Germany's monetary stability to the outside world.[136]

Both economic and political reasons make it understandable, then, why the Germans vacillated in handling their problems of payments disequilibrium and inflation. At some times and to some extent, the authorities allowed and even passively promoted internal inflation. If they did choose occasionally—or even if they had chosen consistently—to undergo homemade rather than imported inflation, that fact would be no evidence against the necessity, at fixed exchange rates, of making that unpleasant choice. The choice of one horn of a dilemma over the other does not disprove the existence of the dilemma. The dilemma is really what the problem of imported inflation is all about.

---

135. Wadbrook, *op. cit.*, pp. 218–219. In the quotation, I have changed the verbs to the past tense.

136. *Ibid.*, especially pp. 220, 251–257.

CHAPTER TWENTY-FIVE

Domestic Responses to External Imbalance: Japan and Italy

JAPAN

At least three reasons warrant discussing Japan. (A concluding section on Italy notes some instructive parallels in the experiences of the two countries.) Most obviously, Japan's balance of payments and currency have played a key role in the international monetary disorders of recent years. Japan has achieved the second largest gross national product in the Free World. Japan ranks third in value of exports and fourth in value of imports (as of 1973). A second reason is the notable orientation of its monetary and fiscal policies around its balance of payments. While apparently exerting a healthy anti-inflationary "discipline," external deficits responded sensitively to curative measures, without painful deflation. Until around the beginning of the 1970s, Japan's experience was often cited as evidence that the system of fixed exchange rates can work well.[1] A third reason is the puzzle that Japan seemed to have become increasingly competitive on world markets despite rapid growth and inflation. The explanation provides further insights into the purchasing-power-parity doctrine.

Prices and the exchange rate

Japan's balance of payments was generally strengthening, though with noteworthy inter-ruptions, over the period 1949–1971, when the exchange parity was held at 360 yen per dollar, and even after the upward float and upward revaluation of the yen in 1971. Yet Japan experienced a great degree of money-supply and consumer-price inflation than other major industrial countries. Between the end of 1953 and the end of 1971, the money supply and consumer price index rose by 1330 and 113.7 percent respectively, as against corresponding figures of 80.1 and 51.5 percent for the United States. Purchasing-power-parity calculations have notorious shortcomings as indicators of equilibrium exchange rates (as noted in Chapter 11), and these shortcomings might be extreme in view of the tight controls wielded by the Japanese government over both domestic business and international transactions. For what they are worth, however, purchasing-power parities calculated with consumer price indexes suggest that the yen was becoming increasingly *over*valued at the 360 rate; the number of yen per dollar should have been increasing. Calculated on a 1949 base—and the yen was almost surely overvalued already in 1949[2]—the purchasing-power parity for July 1972 is an incredible 567.2 yen per dollar. On a 1953 base, the parity for July 1972 is 514.5 yen per dollar; on a 1963 base, 428.10.[3] Actually, though, the yen strengthened against the dollar in 1971 and again in 1973; the yen-per-dollar rate moved down first to 308 and later, briefly, to below 265.

The apparent paradox rests on exclusive attention to the money supply and *consumer* prices. Japan's rapid monetary expansion was largely absorbed by a growing demand for money connected with rapid real economic

---

1. Tadashi Iino in George N. Halm, ed., *Approaches to Greater Flexibility of Exchange Rates*, Princeton, N.J.: Princeton University Press, 1970 (hereafter cited as *Bürgenstock Papers*), pp. 357, 362–363; E. M. Bernstein in Randall Hinshaw, ed., *The Economics of International Adjustment*, Baltimore: Johns Hopkins Press, 1971, pp. 70–71.

2. That is, pegged at too few yen per dollar. See page 528 below.

3. The figures necessary for the calculations are available in the monthly issues of *International Financial Statistics* and its 1971 *Supplement*. Various calculations are presented in William R. Henry, "The Application of the Purchasing Power Parity Theory to the Rate of Exchange between the Japanese Yen and the American Dollar," unpublished M.A. thesis, University of Virginia, 1972, particularly in the table on p. 119.

growth and also, presumably, with an increasing market orientation of the economy and a finer division of labor as resources shifted from agriculture to industry.[4] Japan's wholesale, import, and export price indexes not only fail to parallel the consumer index but even exhibit periods of mild downtrend. While the consumer index rises with little interruption from 1950 on, the wholesale index, after jumping sharply from 1949 to 1951, shows hardly any uptrend thereafter until the mid-1960s. From a peak in 1951, the export and import price indexes trend downward together to the early 1960s, move almost level in the mid-sixties, and trend mildly upward toward the end of the decade. The wholesale and export (as well as import) price indexes rise less rapidly than the corresponding U.S. indexes, so that purchasing-power parities calculated with Japanese and U.S. *wholesale* parities calculated on a 1953 base range, over the period 1951–1970, between a high of 365.822 yen per dollar for 1953 to a low of 329.247 for 1970; and by July 1972, the monthly figure was down to 298.279.[5]

Such calculations gain some qualitative plausibility from parallelism between the downtrends of wholesale purchasing-power parities and of black-market exchange rates. These rates reflected the demand for and supply of dollars in transactions forbidden or restricted by the Japanese government. Since the volume of illegal transactions was small in relation to total Japanese trade, and for other obvious reasons, the black-market rates hardly coincide with the rates that would have equilibrated the balance of payments in a fully free market. Movements in them serve as a clue, however, to how free-market equilibrium rates would have moved. The black-market rates trended generally but unsteadily downward from a peak of 475 yen per dollar at the end of January 1954 to 313 yen per dollar at the end of December 1971. They were always higher than 1953-base purchasing-power parities (as well as higher than the official rates); but the percentage discrepancy between the two series remained practically trendless over the 20 years from 1952 through October 1971, ranging between 10.51 and 17.32 percent around an average of 13.18 percent.[6]

Japan became increasingly competitive on the world market. In 1970, Japan's index of export unit values in dollars had risen 3.7 percent above its 1956–1960 average, while the corresponding rise for industrial countries as a group was 17.2 percent.[7] Taking 1960 as a base, the ratio of Japan's export price index to the average index of ten other countries trended downward through 1966; and though it rose thereafter, it was still below the 1960 ratio through the end of the decade. A similar ratio of wholesale price indexes trended downward through 1965 and ended the decade still below the 1960 figure.[8] Comparisons of unit labor costs in manufacturing and of unit values of manufactured exports, expressed in dollars, give a similar impression: Japan gained an advantage over competitors in the early and middle 1960s and held that advantage, even though it stopped widening, through the end of the decade.[9] From 1960 to 1970, the wholesale prices of manufactured goods (comprising over 80 percent of Japan's total exports) rose less on the average than those of any other country. Their average annual rise was 1 percent in Japan, 2⅔ percent in the United States. From 1965 to 1971, Japan's average yearly rise in the export price index was less than half as large as the U.S. figure—1.6 percent as against 3.5 percent.[10] A plotting of export unit values relative to those of competitor countries against the change in export market shares between 1961 and 1969 for 10 industrial countries shows the expected negative relation, with Japan having the biggest decline in relative export prices and the biggest gain in market share.[11]

In purchasing-power-parity calculations, use of a consumer price index more closely approximates use of a *general* price index,[12] than does use of a wholesale or a traded-goods index. In view of this and of a bias tending to make a general-price-index calculation underestimate the equilibrium foreign-exchange value of the currency of a wealthy, high-productivity country, the results of *consumer*-price purchasing-power-parity calculations for Japan are not so paradoxical after all. Japan has been coming closer to the position of a wealthy country for which such calculations have the bias mentioned.[13] To an increasing degree over time, a general- or consumer-price-index calculation yields an exchange rate of more yen per dollar than what would be the equilibrium rate.

A "structural" change in the Japanese economy has been altering relative prices. This fact and its consequences hardly discredit the purchasing-power-parity doctrine as presented in Chapter 11. The Japanese case does indeed highlight the inadequacy of the rate-calculation aspect of the doctrine—and the difficulty of *any* nonmarket determination of an equilibrium exchange rate. Comparative-version calculations are emphatically a makeshift, unavoidably distorted by dragging irrelevant historical developments into the picture, including changes over time in economic structures and in controls. The stabilizing-pressures aspect of the doctrine, by contrast, concerns *current* determination of exchange rates in a free market. It explains why random fluctuations would tend to be self-limiting and self-correcting. The fact that an economy has been experiencing real changes, including differential rates of productivity growth among industrial sectors, in no way destroys these stabilizing pressures.

It is not surprising that Japan's balance of payments should have strengthened at the 360 exchange rate if the extreme divergence between the movements of her consumer and other price indexes can be explained. This divergence was not exclusive to Japan during the 1960s. In the EEC countries, also, domestic price increases were accompanied by small or negligible increases in export unit values. In the United States and United Kingdom, by contrast, domestic and export prices moved nearly in parallel.[14] The relation between domestic and export price developments varied widely from country to country.

One factor contributing to a spread over time between different price movements, and to differences among countries in the degree of this spread, is that the product composition of a country's exports generally contrasts with the composition of its total output. Internationally traded products generally tend to be less susceptible to price increases than many of the goods and services figuring in GNP deflators. Export sales often meet more intense competition than prevails on home markets. Export industries are typically achieving larger gains in productivity than the gains achieved in more

4. Henry, *op. cit.*, p. 91.

5. *Ibid.*, table on p. 119. Henry argues (pp. 48–49, 53, 56, 108–109) that the 1953-base wholesale parities are rather good approximations to equilibrium exchange rates and that their movements show responsiveness to such influences as the increasing price-competitiveness of Japanese exports.

6. *Ibid.*, pp. 65–72, 108, 117–118, including charts and table. Henry obtained the black-market rates from various issues of *Pick's Currency Yearbook*.

DOMESTIC RESPONSES TO EXTERNAL IMBALANCE: JAPAN AND ITALY

7. Calculated from tables in International Monetary Fund, 1970, p. 54 and IMF, 1971, pp. 63–64. The percentages refer to increases over the entire period, not to annual-average increases. From 1955 to 1970 the ratio of Japan's export price index of *manufactures* to a weighted average index of competitors' prices trended generally downward; this ratio was roughly 22 percent lower in 1970 than in 1955. Organisation for Economic Co-operation and Development, *OECD Economic Surveys—Japan*, Paris: June 1972 (hereafter cited as *OECD Japan*, with the date), chart on p. 37.

8. Japan, Economic Planning Agency, *Economic Survey of Japan (1969–1970)*, Tokyo: Japan Times, 1970, charts on p. 9 (the charts end with 1969). (Hereafter, this annual publication is cited as *Economic Survey*, with the dates.)

9. See charts in IMF, 1970, p. 56 and IMF, 1971, p. 66. The comparisons are of trends rather than of absolute levels. Conceivably, therefore, they could mean that Japan was narrowing a cost-and-price disadvantage rather than widening an advantage.

10. Henry, *op. cit.*, pp. 57–58, citing *OECD Japan*, 1971, p. 23.

11. IMF, 1970, p. 53. (There, the Belgium-Luxembourg Economic Union is counted as a single country.)

12. The GNP deflator, like the consumer price index, has usually risen faster in Japan than in other industrial countries. Over the period 1958–1967, the annual average rate of increase of the deflator was 4.6 percent in Japan and 2.5 percent in industrial countries as a group. The rise was again greater in Japan than for the group in 1970 but smaller in 1969 and 1971, with the comparison for 1968 unclear. Tables in IMF, 1970, p. 54, IMF, 1971, p. 63–64, and IMF, 1972, p. 7.

13. The bias is explained on pp. 216–217. Its dynamic aspects involve the fact that service prices and the cost of living tend to increase more rapidly in relation to commodity prices in rapidly growing than in slowly growing countries. Samuel Brittan explicitly relates such considerations to Japan, noting that they "cannot determine the exact equilibrium exchange rate of a currency, but they do help to explain what would otherwise seem puzzling discrepancies." *The Price of Economic Freedom*, New York: St. Martin's Press, 1970, p. 37.

14. IMF, 1970, p. 54.

sheltered or purely domestic sectors (especially the service industries). Moreover, some discrepancies between domestic and international price movements probably resulted in several countries from tax increases that affected domestic price levels while exports received rebates.[15]

A sharpening contrast between the compositions of exports and of total output has been notably characteristic of Japan. Japan's exports have been growing nearly twice as fast as world imports,[16] and their composition has been shifting rapidly toward commodities for which world demand has been growing particularly fast. By 1971, manufactures made up some 95 percent of Japan's exports.[17] The share of the products of the heavy and chemical industries in Japan's exports rose from 44 percent in 1960 to 69 percent in 1969. Exports of machinery in several categories, of primary metals, and of chemicals soared by more than 20 percent a year during the 1960s. In the commodities with strong export markets, moreover, and particularly in transportation machinery and electric machinery, Japan has achieved higher rates of productivity growth, by and large, than other countries. Japan's relative gain in productivity is also noteworthy in radios and television, motorcycles, ships, textiles, iron and steel, and optical instruments. Japan has not strengthened its comparative superiority in all goods, of course, but it has succeeded in putting export emphasis on one comparatively superior good after another.[18] Corresponding changes have occurred, of course, in domestic resource allocation. Shifts from agriculture into manufacturing and other "secondary" sectors have been even more pronounced in Japan than in other countries, such as Italy and Spain, that experienced qualitatively similar "structural" changes.[19]

Another factor in the spread between wholesale and export price trends on the one hand and the consumer price index on the other lay in the latter's composition. Japan's rapid money-supply inflation was bound to show up in some prices, and consumer prices were the likeliest candidate. As Japanese resources shifted from agriculture to industry, services tended increasingly to be bought on the market rather than performed within the household. Services tended to rise in price rapidly as high-productivity industries competed for labor. Food prices, carrying more than two-fifths of the weight in the consumer index, tended to rise differentially as farmers moved into higher-

paying industrial jobs and because some government price supports checked the price-reducing effects of gains in agricultural productivity.[20]

Not only was productivity growth relatively slight in its restraining influence on prices of services and food, but the average incomes of their producers rose relatively rapidly (in the first half of the 1960s, anyway) as gaps narrowed between income levels in different sectors of the economy. In the manufacturing industries, prices rose more conspicuously for consumer goods produced by smaller firms than for capital goods, mostly produced by large enterprises and carrying heavy weights in the wholesale price index. One reason, besides differential gains in productivity, was that wages increased at a greater rate in small than in large firms against a general background of labor scarcity.[21]

Seen from the other point of view, several factors worked to help maintain the near-stability of wholesale and export prices. The high propensity to save of the Japanese people[22] facilitated investment in plant and equipment. This and technological innovation, including the adoption of foreign technology, as well as relatively little resistance by labor to innovation and modernization and relatively little insistence on craft lines (advantages apparently related to a high degree of job security and employer paternalism), resulted in gains in the productivity of labor that kept pace with wage increases particularly well in sectors producing goods entering heavily into the wholesale and export price indexes. Relative steadiness and sometimes even declines in the world prices of imported raw materials have affected the Japanese wholesale price index not only directly but also by helping hold down the costs of manufactures made from those materials.[23]

Raw material imports also affected the Japanese balance of payments (and what would be the equilibrium exchange rate) by declining relative to total imports, in which their share has been high and the share of manufactured goods low in comparison with the import compositions of other advanced countries, and relative to gross national product. The obvious reason is that the structure of total Japanese output has been shifting toward services and toward sophisticated processing and assembling and away from the simple processing of raw materials. Protectionism has also been a factor. In contrast, therefore, with the uptrend of imports relative to gross national product in the United States and the chief European countries (except Italy), that trend has been downward in Japan.[24]

Demand policy and the balance of payments

Another notable feature of Japan's postwar experience is that her macroeconomic policy, like her microeconomic policy of tariffs and controls,[25] was oriented to the balance of payments. Until the late 1960s, Japan repeatedly experienced a policy cycle of "import expansion—worsening of balance of payments —tight money policy—slowdown of economic growth." As long as the balance of payments seemed healthy, the authorities pursued an expansionary policy to stimulate economic growth. An "overheating" of the economy— this seems to be a favorite term in Japanese publications in English—would show up in a balance-of-payments deficit, which would itself exert a moderating influence on business activity and expectations and would also cue the monetary authorities to take a tighter stance. The resulting business slowdown would restrain the growth of imports, intensify incentives to seek sales abroad, and so turn the balance of payments around before a currency crisis developed. Then monetary policy could be relaxed and rapid economic growth resumed until another weakening of the balance of payments started the whole cycle again.[26] Not until around 1968–1969 did Japan happen to experience a major "dilemma" case, when balance-of-payments and domestic considerations called for opposite demand policies.

Monetary policy was the main tool used for responding to payments disequilibria. Japan's Economic Planning Agency noted a close cor-

15. IMF, 1970, pp. 54–55.

16. The compounded annual rates of growth from 1960 to 1970 were 9.5 and 16.9 percent for world imports and Japanese exports in dollar value, 8.4 and 16.4 percent in physical volume. In 1971, the corresponding world and Japanese increases amounted to 11.5 and 24.3 percent in dollar value, 5.8 and 17.0 per cent in physical volume. IMF, 1972, p. 9.

17. In imports, food and raw materials made up over 70 percent. The United Kingdom is the only other major country whose foreign trade structure is at all similar to Japan's, but the emphasis on manufactures in exports and nonmanufactures in imports is less extreme for the U.K. *OECD*, 1972, p. 39.

18. *Economic Survey*, 1969–1970, pp. 77–83.

19. *OECD Japan*, 1972, pp. 53–57.

20. Henry, *op. cit.*, pp. 92–94, citing a 1967 UN publication on the 42.4 percent weight of foods in the consumer price index. *Economic Survey*, 1969–1970, pp. 115–118, emphasizes the rapid rise in land prices. Although the *Survey* does not explicitly say so, it seems plausible to suppose that this rise must have affected housing and food costs.

21. *Economic Survey*, 1969–1970, pp. 40–41, 113, apparently referring to the first half of the 1960s in particular.

22. The ratio of personal savings to disposable income trended upward from 9½ percent in 1954 to 21 percent in 1971. Chart for 1954–1971 in *OECD Japan*, 1972, p. 13.

23. Iino in Bürgenstock Papers, pp. 361–362; Henry, *op. cit.*, pp. 96–102; *U.S. News and World Report*, 16 January 1967 (on the labor situation). In 1970, for example, tendencies toward recession "had little apparent effect in retarding the consumer price advance, which reflected the tendency for the distributive and service industries to raise their charges to consumers as wage increases outstripped productivity gains by a wide margin. In the innovating and high-investment manufacturing sector, increased wage costs were absorbed to a much greater extent by continuing advances in productivity. . . ." IMF, 1971, pp. 92–93.

24. *Economic Survey*, 1969–1970, pp. 83–92; *OECD Japan*, 1972, p. 63.

25. ". . . Japan as a late participant in the family of advanced nations has sought to gear its industrial and trade structures to the principles of promoting exports and curbing imports, in an effort to overcome handicaps in the sphere of balance of payments." The high self-supply ratio of the Japanese economy has been due partly to the growth-and-technology pattern and partly to cautiousness in import liberalization to protect the country's balance of payments. *Economic Survey*, 1969–1970, p. 83 and around p. 87. On protectionism, see also p. 534 below.

26. For general descriptions of this policy cycle, see Iino in Bürgenstock Papers, p. 360; *Economic Survey*, 1968–1969, p. 2; *Economic Survey*, 1969–1970, foreword, and pp. 3–4, 33, 52–54, 78 (source of the quotation). The chronology reviewed later in this chapter tends to bear out the generalization stated above.

relation "between fluctuations in aggregate demand and those in the money supply. Results of measurement show that there exists a close relationship between fluctuations in the money supply in the three quarters preceding the given quarter and fluctuations in aggregate demand in the given quarter (particularly close is the relationship with fluctuations a quarter ago)."[27]

From figures for the second quarter of 1950 through the fourth quarter of 1966, Michael Michaely also concluded that the Japanese authorities did indeed use monetary policies to adjust the balance of payments.[28] Fiscal policy seems not to have been so used; the government budget was generally near balance. The main policy weapon was the discount rate of the Bank of Japan (supplemented at times by moral suasion and by ceilings on central-bank credit to the commercial banks); other weapons of monetary policy were comparatively unimportant. The Bank of Japan cut its discount rate when the country was gaining external reserves and raised its rate when the reserves were falling.[29] The discount rate does not—not before the late 1960s, anyway—appear to have responded to changes in the unemployment rate, the rate of price inflation, or the growth rate of industrial production.

Not only the discount rate but also the money supply seemed "to react to imbalances of payments in an adjusting direction at least from the beginning of 1954. From that period on, the rate of increase in money supply most of the time was less during periods of downward imbalances of payments, and greater during periods of upward imbalances." Although the pattern was rather weak, the rate of increase of the money supply appeared generally higher when the external reserves were growing than when they were falling.[30]

This relation was largely automatic. Gains or losses of external reserves promoted or restrained growth of bank liquidity and in turn of the money supply. When gaining liquidity through the balance of payments, the commercial banks would respond by borrowing less from the Bank of Japan, even though the Bank cut its discount rate at such times; when the balance of payments was not contributing to their liquidity, the banks would borrow more from the Bank of Japan, even though the discount rate was raised.

For this reason, what a cut or increase in the discount rate did was not so much actually to expand or contract the commercial banks' borrowing from the central bank as to make the quasi-automatic contraction or expansion smaller than it otherwise would have been. Changes in external reserves were allowed to affect bank liquidity and the money supply in the automatic way that tended to promote balance-of-payments adjustment, and the discount rate was used to resist offsetting changes in bank borrowing from the Bank of Japan. But this complication does not contradict the proposition that the discount rate was consistently oriented toward balance-of-payments adjustment.[31]

Why was monetary policy as effective as it seems to have been in regulating domestic demand and, in turn, the external balance?[32] For one thing, policy was not inhibited by worries about the interest cost of carrying the public debt, for the wartime and early postwar inflation had practically wiped out the debt in real terms. The government budget was generally balanced, with some element of countercyclical built-in stability. Businesses, by and large, had weak liquidity positions, had relatively little capacity to finance expansion internally, and were dependent on external finance, especially bank credit. The commercial banks, in turn, had substantially no excess reserves and were dependent on the Bank of Japan. Bank reserves tended to tighten automatically in boom periods as consumers, who still used mainly currency rather than checking accounts, drained currency into hand-to-hand circulation. Exchange controls limited resort to borrowing abroad at times of domestic tight money. The banks' willingness to respect the controls was promoted by their dependence on the Bank of Japan for credit—access to the central bank was considered a privilege, not a right—and perhaps also by Japanese traditions of discipline and respect for authority. (These points are also relevant to compliance with moral suasion, or informal "guidance" of bank operations in general.)

For these reasons, a money and credit squeeze could succeed in restraining spending. Restraint did not have to be disruptive, given the famed resilience, flexibility, and responsiveness of the Japanese economy. Japan supposedly had the advantage over other industrial countries of favorable labor-management relations, including absence of industry-wide collective bargaining and a bonus element in workers' incomes depending on their employers' profits. Such conditions facilitated prompt labor-cost reductions in recessions and rapid return of the economy to full employment.[33]

Another favorable circumstance was the context of rapid growth, related in turn to a shift of resource into industries of the most advanced types, to high rates of investment and technological advance, and to the resulting gains in productivity. The ample long-run monetary expansion accommodating this real growth did not cause significant inflation of unit labor costs in manufacturing or of export prices. The share of income saved and invested was so high, anyway, that the authorities did not have to fear serious lasting damage from occasional restraint on investment. Successful restraint did not require actually reducing wage rates and sticky commodity prices, but merely moderating uptrends. Relative shifts of resources among sectors could be accomplished less painfully in a context of growth than in a context of stagnation, in which resources would actually have to be forced out of some sectors to move them to others. Briefly if ever in Japan did restraint require an actual decline in production and incomes; a mere slowdown in growth would suffice. Growth in imports would slacken while exports would be, if anything, stimulated.

Japan and the United Kingdom were alike in using monetary and fiscal policy for balance-of-payments purposes.[34] The pains of British "stop-and-go" illustrate, by contrast, the advantages that rapid growth offered to Japan. Japan's success with economic management at a fixed exchange rate rested on rather special circumstances and warrants no sweeping generalizations. Around the end of the 1960s, as we shall see, Japan wound up in a dilemma reminiscent of Germany's nearly chronic one.

Experience through the mid-sixties

Let us turn to a chronology of Japan's experience. In the first years after World War II, the country's foreign trade took place through the Japanese and occupation authorities. Beginning in 1946, private trade was gradually reopened. In October 1948 a system of commodity-by-commodity multiple exchange rates was introduced. In April 1949 the occupation authorities imposed a unified rate of 360 yen per dollar. Although the reasons for its choice were not revealed, that rate was close to a purchasing-power parity calculated with U.S. and Japanese wholesale price indexes on a 1935

27. *Economic Survey*, 1969–1970, pp. 136–137. The close relation mentioned is evident in a chart (p. 138) of the percentage changes from the previous quarter of seasonally adjusted three-month moving averages of currency plus demand deposits and actual and calculated nominal GNP from 1957 through 1969.

28. *The Responsiveness of Demand Policies to Balance of Payments: Postwar Patterns*, New York: National Bureau of Economic Research, 1971, chap. 8.

29. Michaely says that the discount rate, "moved consistently—indeed with no exception—in an adjusting direction" (*ibid.*, p. 161), but the accompanying chart casts some doubt on such an unequivocal statement.

30. *Ibid.*, pp. 164 (for the quotation), 168–169.

31. For a one-paragraph summary of Michaely's findings, see *ibid.*, pp. 174–175.
Another study, focusing on the period 1960–1970 in particular, reached similar conclusions. The monetary-restraint episodes of July 1961 to October 1962, end of 1963 to end of 1964, and September 1967 to August 1968 came in response to balance-of-payments deterioration and were successful in cooling the domestic economy and turning the balance of payments around. The restraint from September 1969 to October 1970, however, during a longer period when the balance of payments was generally strengthening, came in response to faster than usual domestic price increases. Organisation for Economic Co-operation and Development, *Monetary Policy in Japan*, Paris: December 1972.

32. Some answers are suggested by Iino in *Bürgenstock Papers*, p. 361; and OECD, *Monetary Policy in Japan*, esp. pp. 67–68.

33. Gottfried Haberler, "Some Observations on Japanese-American Economic Relations," Banca Nazionale del Lavoro *Quarterly Review*, September 1972, separately reprinted by American Enterprise Institute, February 1973, p. 7.

34. Surveying the experiences of nine countries, Michael Michaely notes that

In two countries—the United Kingdom and Japan—monetary policy appears to have been played consistently according to the classical "rules of the game"; that is, to have been guided by the fluctuations in the country's external position. (*Op. cit.*, p. 62)

base. It must have overvalued the yen, since controls and subsidies kept the Japanese index from accurately expressing how far the yen's purchasing power had really fallen. To make matters worse, 1949 brought business recession in the United States and the devaluation of sterling and other currencies. Japan's goods-and-services deficit in 1949 was large (but was more than covered by U.S. aid). Still, Japan kept the 360 rate and embarked on austerity and deflation to make it tenable. Bankruptcies and unemployment followed. The outbreak of the Korean War in June 1950 brought an increase in exports, including sales of war materials to the U.N. forces, and rapid improvement in the balance of payments. In 1951, however, the United States suspended its purchases of strategic goods and its aid to Japan. Anti-inflationary fiscal and monetary policies then contributed to an economic slump, reflected in a slowdown of growth of industrial production between 1951 and 1952. Thus began the Japanese policy, later repeated, of tightening financial policy when the balance of payments worsened and relaxing it when the balance improved.[35]

Japan gained international reserves until 1953, when they dropped by 19 percent. Exports, already below 1951's peak, remained practically unchanged, while imports rose 19 percent in value over the level of 1952. Money-supply expansion was held to 3.9 percent in 1954. This, as well as rise in industrial production over the year before (8.9 percent) was slight by Japanese standards; and 1954 counts as a recession year.[36] The growth of international reserves resumed.

Its next interruption came in 1957, when the reserves dropped 35 percent as exports fell 33 percent short of imports in value. This was the first of three episodes during the period from mid-1956 to mid-1967 when the trade balance deteriorated sharply, monetary policy tightened, and the growth of production slowed down.[37] On each occasion, imports rose sharply in the late boom phase of the business cycle; monetary policy, as measured by the quarter-to-quarter growth rate of the money supply, was then tightened; and production and imports finally decelerated. On the first occasion, to judge by quarterly data, the trade balance was at its weakest in mid-1957, money growth at its slowest also in mid-1957, and the rate of growth of industrial production smallest (negative, actually) late in the year.

(Industrial production averaged slightly lower, in fact, in 1958 than in 1957.)

The second episode of monetary restraint in response to balance-of-payments deterioration was preceded by three years of rapid economic expansion. In early 1961 the economy began to show signs of overheating, with wholesale prices rising almost 2 percent above the previous year. The trade balance went into deficit in the first quarter and was at its weakest late in the year. The current balance, already in deficit because of invisibles, worsened as the year went on.[38] Money growth became slowest around the turn of the year 1961–1962, and industrial-production growth was slowest late in 1962 (when it became negative, after declining since mid-1961). On the third occasion, the trade balance was weakest around the turn of the year 1963–1964, money growth relatively slow throughout 1964 and even slower in mid-1965, and industrial-production growth practically at its trough during most of 1965.[39]

Let us consider in more detail how the third episode developed from the second. In 1962, with the trade balance improving as domestic business languished, the monetary authorities switched to ease to encourage domestic recovery.[40] In late 1962 and early 1963, the money stock was growing about twice as fast as in previous periods of early cyclical upswing. Strong economic expansion resumed early in 1963, and imports accelerated more rapidly than in previous such episodes. Wholesale prices ceased to decline late in 1962 and then rose. In December 1963, with the trade balance still weakening and money-supply growth already decelerating, the authorities modestly raised reserve requirements against demand deposits. In January 1964 they asked the banks to observe specified limits on increases in their lending. Such measures slowed the growth of money and credit quickly. Business activity responded with a lag. Imports stopped rising around the beginning of 1964, and exports began a strong recovery. By the end of the year, the turnaround in the external accounts had been large enough to rebuild the reserves to within 2 percent of their level of one year before. A year or so of monetary restraint had succeeded in restoring external balance.[41]

As 1965 began, the favorable trend of exports was continuing, while symptoms of recession were spreading at home. During the year "Japan experienced once again one of the rather dramatic adjustments of its current account position which have become characteristic of its postwar balance of payments. . . ." Even though hampered by a shipping strike in the closing months of the year, exports in 1965 as a whole rose 24 percent in dollar value above the level of 1964, while imports rose only 1.6 percent. The current account swung from a deficit of about $0.4 billion in 1964 to a surplus of about $1.0 billion in 1965. The current-account improvement was mostly offset by an opposite change in capital movements, partly undertaken by the banks with official encouragement.[42]

At the same time, Japan was suffering its first acute postwar recession. The authorities responded as early as the turn of the year 1964–1965. They reduced bank reserve requirements and relaxed credit guidelines in December and lowered the Bank of Japan's discount rate in January. Further discount-rate cuts followed in April and June 1965 and another cut in reserve requirements in July. Limits on credit expansion were suspended by mid-year. The Bank of Japan also used open-market operations for monetary ease.[43]

Even so, the shift toward ease was more cautious and moderate than it had been in the past, although the ease was to prove longer-lasting.[44] Thanks, perhaps, to increased cautiousness with policy switches, the volatility of Japan's balance of payments was reduced thereafter; and the average deficits of 1961–1964 gave way to an annual average overall surplus of about $700 million in the period 1965–1969. Especially from 1968 until 1970, strong economic expansion and a large payments surplus continued to coexist.[45] This is not to say, however, that the earlier cycle was entirely abolished.

Because the shift toward monetary ease was only moderate, so was the response of business activity. Slackness of demand was reflected in

---

35. Iino in Bürgenstock Papers, 359–360; for industrial production, *International Financial Statistics, Supplement.*

36. Figures from *International Financial Statistics, Supplement.*
Subsequent recessions have been dated as follows (Roman numerals indicating quarters of the year): 1957 II to 1958 II, 1961 IV to 1962 IV, 1964 IV to 1965 IV, and 1970 III to some time in 1972. None of the recessions except the latest one lasted much more than a year; and during all of them real gross national product continued growing, though at a much reduced rate. *OECD Japan,* 1972, pp. 6–7.

DOMESTIC RESPONSES TO EXTERNAL IMBALANCE: JAPAN AND ITALY

37. Michael Keran has studied this period in detail; and the following description draws on his "Monetary Policy, Balance of Payments, and Business Cycles—The Foreign Experience"; Federal Reserve Bank of St. Louis, *Review,* November 1967, pp. 11–12. I have added references to annual figures of money supply, balance-of-payments items, industrial production, and nominal GNP.

38. OECD, *Monetary Policy in Japan,* p. 87, as well as Keran, *op. cit.*

39. Keran considers it significant that only one such cycle began in the four years from the third quarter of 1956 to the third quarter of 1960, whereas two occurred in the subsequent period from the third quarter of 1960 to the third quarter of 1964. During the second four years, Prime Minister Hayato Ikeda favored an aggressively easy monetary policy in pursuit of a goal of doubling national income in 10 years; and the money supply grew by 120 percent, as contrasted with 60 percent during the first four years. Price and imports also rose faster under Ikeda, while international reserves sagged; yet the total growth of industrial production, at 70 percent, was the same over both four-periods. Comparing not only the two Japanese periods but also Japan with Germany, Keran emphasizes a contrast between a monetary policy of making delayed but large adjustments in response to balance-of-payments deterioration and a policy of making small, prompt, and frequent adjustments to keep price inflation from heating up.

40. The ease is rather obscured in end-of-year money-supply figures. However, discount-rate cuts occurred in October and November 1962 and March and April 1963. OECD, *Monetary Policy in Japan,* pp. 87–88, dates the period of ease from October 1962 to the end of 1963 and the subsequent period of restraint from the end of 1963 to the end of 1964.

41. Keran, *op. cit.,* pp. 11–12; Bank for International Settlements, 1964–1965, pp. 74–75; OECD, *Monetary Policy in Japan,* pp. 88–89.

42. IMF, 1966, pp. 103–104 (source of the quotation); BIS, 1964–1965, p. 75.

43. BIS, 1964–1965, p. 75; BIS, 1966–1967, p. 77.

44. Money-supply growth amounted to 18.2 percent in 1965 as against 34.6 percent in 1963. OECD, *Monetary Policy in Japan,* pp. 88–89, dates the period of ease from the end of 1964 to September 1967.

45. *Economic Survey,* 1969–1970, p. 67.

business failures, involuntary accumulation of finished-goods inventories, and lower investment in plant and equipment than a year earlier. During the summer of 1965 the government began fiscal actions to stimulate the economy. The rapid rise of exports was also providing stimulation. The start of a boom may be dated late in 1965.[46]

Two years of full-fledged boom followed. Around the turn of the year 1966–1967, however, exports began to weaken as economic growth slackened in Japan's major trading partners, including Germany. For 1967 as a whole, Japan's surplus on goods and services disappeared. The policy problem had changed from promoting business recovery to keeping unexpectedly strong expansion, with price increases, under control. Moderate moves away from fiscal and monetary ease began early in 1967. Restraint was intensified in September and again after the devaluation of sterling in November and after the announcement of U.S. balance-of-payments measures in January 1968. The Bank of Japan increased its discount rate in September and January; and on the average in 1966, 1967, and 1968, money-supply growth was held below 14 percent a year, which is moderate by Japanese standards.[47]

The late sixties: A new combination of problems for policy

Import growth in 1968 slowed to 13 percent in physical volume, as compared to 23 percent the year before. The capital account strengthened on increased borrowing abroad by Japanese corporations and on increased foreign purchases of Japanese securities, whose prices had fallen. An economic upswing in other industrial countries, particularly the United States, favored Japanese exports; and the export market was strong in Southeast Asia also. From an overall deficit in 1967, Japan's balance of payments switched into record current-account and overall surpluses in 1968; and the external reserves rose 43 percent. At the same time, real gross national product grew about 14½ percent. This dual achievement of external surplus and strong domestic expansion stood in noteworthy contrast with earlier experience. As the external balance continued to strengthen and as the restrictive policies seemed to have achieved their purpose, the authorities moved

to a relatively neutral financial policy. The discount rate was cut in August 1968, and credit limits eased in October.[48]

Domestic expansion remained vigorous in 1969, sustained in part by continuing strong growth of exports. Accelerating inflation in the United States and Europe presumably aided Japan's export performance. In Japan, too, price increases were accelerating: by the autumn, the year-to-year increase in wholesale prices amounted to 3.1 percent, compared to only 0.8 percent in the preceding 12 months. Anyway, the overall balance-of-payments surplus (surplus on nonmonetary transactions) hit a new record, rising to $2.4 billion from $1.1 billion the year before. Since there had been an overall deficit as recently as 1967, the turnaround over the course of two years amounted to roughly $3 billion at an annual rate, the bulk of the turnaround occurring in merchandise trade. Only one-third of 1969's overall surplus showed up as a rise in the official reserves; the other two-thirds of the settlement consisted of a shift from negative to positive in the net-foreign-asset position of the Japanese commercial banks. This shift was in part the natural consequence of a widening excess of Eurodollar over Japanese interest rates, but the authorities gave it additional encouragement to restrain the growth of the official reserves.[49]

The first major tightening of policy for domestic rather than balance-of-payments reasons began around the late summer of 1969. Wholesale prices had been almost trendless since the early 1950s, and export prices had shown, if anything, a downtrend.[50] Even in the early years of the post-1965 boom, price levels had been reasonably stable despite wage increases of over 10 percent a year. Cost-of-living increases, one could argue, had not been excessive for a country experiencing such rapid socioeconomic change. By mid-1969, however, intensified upward price pressures were evident. Over the whole year, the rise in wages exceeded 16 percent, as against less than 12 percent in 1968. As the rise in wholesale prices steepened, the earlier so-called "divergence between consumer and wholesale price trends" diminished.[51] Increases in export and import prices and in the wholesale index were not due to domestic supply-and-demand conditions alone; overseas inflation also apparently contributed an upward push. Taking account of their weights in the wholesale price index, the Japanese Economic Planning Agency estimated that export and import prices contributed—as a matter of arithmetic—either 16 or 22 percent (not percentage points) to the rise in the index in the first half of the fiscal year beginning on April 1, 1969, and either 18 or 30 percent in the second half of that year. (The higher of the alternative percentages results from attributing to overseas inflation not only the price rises of exports and imports but also of Japanese import-competing goods.)[52]

In view of these price trends and of a mounting labor shortage, a marked increase in lending by financial institutions, and other signs of overheating, the Bank of Japan made an increase in the discount rate and demand-deposit reserve requirements effective in early September 1969. In addition, the so-called "reserve position guidance" given to city banks was made stricter in the last quarter of the year.[53]

The early seventies

The boom continued headlong for about six months after these moves toward restraint. Effects became noticeable from the spring of 1970. The rate of output growth dropped markedly after midyear, and seasonally adjusted industrial production actually dipped in the fourth quarter. Growth of real gross national product dropped to an annual rate of 8.3 percent in the fourth quarter—a recession by Japanese standards—and gain for 1970 as a whole was only some 10 to 11 percent, as against growth rates of 12 to 14 percent in the preceding three years. The uptrend of wholesale prices leveled off.[54]

The year brought little lasting success, however, in checking the price and wage increases that had accelerated the year before. After merely pausing in the second and third quarters of 1970, the rise in consumer prices brought the fourth-quarter average to 3.7 percent above that of the third quarter and to 7.8 percent above that of one year before. Increases in wage costs were absorbed instead of being transmitted to prices to a lesser extent in the distributive and service industries than in the innovating and high-investment manufacturing sector.[55]

Although unit labor costs in Japanese manufacturing increased in 1970, they did not close the advantageous gap that had opened up from 1966 to 1969 between Japan's and competitor-countries' costs and prices. Despite business

stagnation in the United States and the United Kingdom and a cooling off in Western Europe after midyear, as well as a slowdown of expansion in the developing countries, overseas inflation continued to favor Japanese exports. The trade surplus rose to a record of $4.0 billion. Because of changes in service and long-term-capital transactions, however, the overall surplus (on the concept whereby change in the net foreign position of the commercial banks counts "below the line") shrank by nearly $1 billion from the 1969 level. Even so, and even though the Bank of Japan made some special

46. BIS, 1965–1966, p. 83; BIS, 1966–1967, pp. 77–78; IMF, 1969, pp. 74. *Economic Survey*, 1968–1969, p. x, dates the start of the boom in November 1965.

47. Keran, *op. cit.*, p. 12; BIS, 1966–1967, pp. 77–78; IMF, 1969, p. 74; calculations from *International Financial Statistics*. OECD, *Monetary Policy in Japan*, p. 89, dates moderate restraint from September 1967 to August 1968.

48. IMF, 1969, pp. 10, 74; BIS, 1969–1970, p. 25; Milton Gilbert in H. W. J. Bosman and F. A. M. Alting von Geusau, *The Future of the International Monetary System*, Lexington, Mass.: Heath, 1970, pp. 42–44; Bank of Japan, *Annual Report 1968*, pp. 1–5; *Economic Survey*, 1968–1969, p. 2. OECD, *Monetary Policy in Japan*, pp. 89–90, classifies policy as "neutral" from August 1968 to September 1969.

49. OECD *Japan*, 1972, p. 78; OECD, *Monetary Policy in Japan*, p. 90; BIS, 1969–1970, pp. 25–26, 130; Bank of Japan, *Annual Report 1969*, pp. 1–5.

50. Henry, *op. cit.*, chart on p. 52.

51. BIS, 1969–1970, p. 25; *Economic Survey*, 1969–1970, pp. 111–112.

52. *Economic Survey*, 1969–1970, p. 42.

53. Bank of Japan, *Annual Report 1969*, pp. 1–5; BIS, 1969–1970, pp. 25–26. Restraint does not show up clearly, however, in the year-to-year or quarter-to-quarter figures for the narrowly defined money supply.

54. BIS, 1970–1971, p. 30; IMF, 1971, p. 92; Bank of Japan, *Annual Report 1970*, pp. 1–3; OECD *Japan*, 1972, p. 6.

55. BIS, 1970–1971, p. 31; IMF, 1971, p. 92; and *International Financial Statistics*.

foreign loans of its own, as well as encouraging the commercial banks to repay foreign debt, the official reserves went up by a record annual amount of $1.0 billion in 1970, not counting the first allocation of Special Drawing Rights.[56]

The domestic cooling-down begun in 1970 continued in 1971. At about 6 percent, the year's gain in real GNP was less than half the long-run average rate. Business fixed investment also rose at about half the usual rate. Mining-and-manufacturing production registered the smallest annual percentage gain since 1965, and seasonally adjusted manufacturing employment actually declined throughout 1971 and the first half of 1972. The recession showed some signs of bottoming out around July 1971; but, according to the Bank of Japan, the "Nixon shock" of August and the floating of the yen worsened business uncertainties and contributed to a relapse. Although annual-average consumer prices were 6.1 percent higher in 1971 than in 1970, the rise slowed down from the early autumn. At 4.4 percent, the rise in the GNP deflator was close to its long-run average; and for the first time since 1962 the annual-average wholesale price index decreased in 1971, though only fractionally.[57]

The recession at home (with a deceleration of inventory-building), together with continuing price inflation overseas and a general expansion of world trade, helped produce a massive merchandise trade surplus of some $7.8 or $7.9 billion. It is true that the yen was allowed to float upward in August and was revalued in the Smithsonian Agreement of December 1971. A habit of fixing export contracts in dollars, however, meant that the external price effects of the yen's appreciation against the dollar were partly absorbed. A reduction in the yen unit values of exports after August kept their rise for 1971 as a whole down to about 2½ percent. Before the appreciation of the yen, furthermore, its very prospect had apparently spurred exports.[58]

Short-term capital movements, including errors and omissions and the commercial banks' borrowing or repayment of debt abroad, joined with current transactions to produce an overall (official-settlements) surplus of about $10.7 billion for 1971. (Net *long*-term capital flows, though smaller than in 1970, were still sizably outward.) The inflow of short-term funds amounted to some $3¾ billion in the third quarter, mainly through receipt of advance payments for exports and through bank borrowing abroad. Inflows had occurred but

had been smaller during the mark-dollar crisis of the spring, thanks to various controls and to general belief in the determination of the Japanese authorities not to revalue the yen upward. The increase in Japan's overall surplus in 1971 was more striking than that of any other country, and the official reserves tripled.[59]

In June 1971 the Japanese cabinet decided to work for better external and internal balance by a program including tariff reductions, acceleration of import liberalization, gradual abolition of tax concessions to exporters, removal of the limit on outward direct investments, promotion of development aid, and the flexible operation of fiscal and monetary policies so as to remove the effects of slack domestic demand on the trade surplus. June brought some import liberalization, greater freedom for residents to invest abroad, and curtailment of tax incentives for exporters. July brought still greater freedom for capital export. After August 15, banks were instructed not to increase their Eurodollar borrowings. After the floating of the yen at the end of August, the receipt of advance payments for exports was virtually banned, nonresidents' free yen accounts were strictly controlled, and banks' dollar positions were subjected to day-to-day control. At the same time the amount of yen banknotes that Japanese tourists could take abroad was raised. From October 1 some further import quotas were removed. Some of these capital controls were lifted in January 1972; but the ban on receipt of advance payments for exports was reintroduced in February in the face of renewed inflows of funds. In view of the balance-of-payments situation, the Bank of Japan extended yen loans to the IBRD in January, March, June, and September 1971. In June, it took further measures to promote the switch of import financing from foreign to domestic banks. In August, it reduced the preferential treatment accorded export financing.[60]

In view of recession at home and declining interest rates overseas, the Bank of Japan had already begun steps toward monetary ease in 1970. It eased its "position guidance" toward city banks and lowered its discount rate in October. Further cuts in that rate followed in January, May, July, and December 1971, bringing it to its lowest level since 1948. With expansionary fiscal measures accompanying it, money-supply growth over 1971 as a whole amounted to 29.7 percent. The balance-of-payments surplus brought about a huge increase in bank liquidity; and the banks not only ended their long history of indebtedness to the central bank virtually at one stroke (despite the discount-rate cuts) but also were able to expand their lending by one-fourth during 1971. The increase in the foreign assets of the monetary authorities in 1971 was more than three times as large as the increase in the stock of reserve or "high-powered" money; changes in the authorities' claims on government and on the commercial banks were in the direction of resisting the growth of reserve money. The Bank of Japan sold securities to mop up liquidity, ran short of securities to sell, and introduced a new instrument, bills drawn on itself, to meet the deficiency. Although the authorities did desire monetary ease in 1971, the figures suggest that they did not desire as much as was occurring spontaneously through the balance of payments; they were attempting partially to offset the imported monetary inflation.[61]

In December 1971 an advisory committee to the Minister of Finance recommended changes, subsequently adopted, in the system of deposit reserve requirements. The changes extended coverage to certain financial institutions formerly outside the system, raised the maximum ratios, and introduced the possibility of reserves depending on the growth rather than level of deposits and of a special ratio applicable to nonresident yen accounts. "This latter step was another example of the necessary adaptation of monetary policy to take account of potentially undesirable external influences, such as had been experienced for the first time in 1971."[62]

Something further should be said about the Japanese exchange rate during 1971. From early February the yen clung to its upper limit against the dollar in the exchange market. On August 28, extreme and involuntary gains in reserves in the two weeks following the "Nixon shock" led the authorities to set the yen afloat. The yen rate immediately jumped 5½ percent above the old dollar parity. Despite additional heavy official purchases of dollars—the float was "dirty"—the yen continued rising, reaching a premium of 9½ percent by mid-October. Little further movement occurred from then until early December, when a rise began that carried the premium to 12½ percent just before the Smithsonian Agreement. That agreement revalued the yen upward by 7.66 percent in terms of gold and Special Drawing Rights. A new central rate of 308 yen per dollar meant a

16.88 percent increase in the dollar value of the yen and a 14.44 percent cut in the yen value of the dollar. With the margins of fluctuation widened to 2¼ percent on either side of the central rate, the yen closed 1971 at 314.8 per dollar, near its new floor; but during the first half of 1972 it rose to its ceiling of 301.1. From then through the events of early 1973, the market apparently kept considering the yen still undervalued, since the Bank of Japan kept having to acquire dollars to keep the rate from piercing the ceiling.

Recovery from Japan's lengthy recession came in 1972, and real GNP averaged 9.2 percent higher than in 1971. In November 1972, for the first time in 31 months, Japan's Economic Planning Agency detected signs of overheating. After pausing during the recession, the rise of wholesale prices had resumed. The authorities also worried about soaring land and stock prices and near-record increases in banknotes in circulation. Yet desires to continue promoting economic recovery and to reduce the external surplus, and perhaps also concern for the election scheduled for December 10,

56. IMF, 1971, pp. 65, 93; BIS, 1970–1971, p. 31: Bank of Japan, *Annual Report 1970*, pp. 1–3; *OECD Japan*, 1972, p. 78.

57. Bank of Japan, *Annual Report 1971*, pp. 1–5; BIS, 1971–1972, pp. 51, 63; and *International Financial Statistics*. On the international monetary events of August–December 1971, see pp. 579–580.

58. *OECD Japan*, 1972, p. 78; BIS, 1971–1972, pp. 51, 91; IMF, 1972, pp. 14–15; Bank of Japan, *Annual Report 1972*, pp. 1–5; and *International Financial Statistics*.

59. IMF, 1972, p. 14; BIS, 1970–1971, p. 32; BIS, 1971–1972, pp. 91–92, 128, 143; *OECD Japan*, 1972, pp. 31, 33, 78; *U.S. News and World Report*, 7 June 1971, pp. 79–80; and *International Financial Statistics*.

60. IMF, 1971, p. 93; BIS, 1971–1972, p. 144; Bank of Japan, *Annual Report 1971*, pp. 1–5.

61. Bank of Japan, *Annual Report 1970*, pp. 1–3, *Annual Report 1971*, pp. 1–5; BIS, 1971–1972, pp. 52–53; and calculations from *International Financial Statistics*.

62. BIS, 1971–1972, p. 53.

inhibited a decisive switch to tighter policy.[63]

Externally, the merchandise trade surplus swelled to practically $9 billion in 1972 from $7.8 billion in 1971. The current-account surplus, at $5.8 billion, was by far the largest of any country and amounted to about 2½ percent of Japan's gross national product. As the Bank for International Settlements reported, "the biggest non-event of 1972 was the failure of Japan's trade surplus to show any signs of contracting in the face of both the large effective revaluation and the strong pick-up of the domestic economy." Japan's net gain of reserves was indeed much smaller than the year before, but this resulted entirely from changes on capital account and from official efforts to avoid or disguise the gain in reserves.[64]

During 1972 Japan's new Prime Minister, Kakuei Tanaka, embarked on a "third yen defense program" to deflect pressure for a new upward revaluation of the yen by restraining exports and encouraging imports. Elements of the program included tariff cuts on industrial and processed agricultural products; increases in import quotas; agreement to make emergency purchases of $1.1 billion of U.S. goods by July 1973; a 1 percent interest-rate increase on export loans and decrease on import loans; and end to the "buy-Japan" rule for government purchases and foreign aid; relaxation of rules to permit U.S. firms to warehouse, wholesale, package, and retail their products in Japan; quantitative curbs on exports in several product categories, including automobiles and motorcycles; and measures to impede capital inflows, liberalize capital outflows, and promote Japanese investment abroad. With his election victory on December 10, 1972, Tanaka seemed to be in a better position to extend his policy of opening Japan economically to the world and work for his commitment to cut Japan's payment surplus to 1 percent of GNP. A lessened concentration on exports and import-substitution would go along with a program of higher real incomes and of measures to remedy crowding, pollution, shabby housing, inadequate sewage systems, and the lamentable state of public transportation, telecommunications, roads, schools, hospitals, bridges, and harbor facilities. In general, Tanaka was interpreted as wanting to divert resources from net exports into public investment, social services, and social security.[65]

As for the government's intention to reduce protectionism, skeptics could point out that a mercantilistic outlook was deeply ingrained in Japan. The Japanese had a reputation for "thinking poor," for worrying about their trade and payments position even as fantastic surpluses belied their worries, and, partly because of these worries, for being willing to work hard and long, save a high proportion of their incomes, and neglect the natural environment. To make trade liberalization—or yen revaluation—work as intended, the skeptics said, there would have to be changes in the industry-government partnership nicknamed "Japan, Inc." As things traditionally stood, "administrative guidance" required foreign and domestic companies alike to obtain approvals from various government bureaus before making virtually any major move. The system could interpose all kinds of red tape and hurdles. Complaints of unfair treatment could trigger reprisals, such as tax audits. Because of a notoriously complex and costly product-distribution system, with many stages of middlemen operating at low volume and charging large markups, imported products could cost several times as much at retail as at the pier, making purchases rather insensitive to trade liberalization or exchange-rate adjustments. On the export side, a change to lesser emphasis there would be long and painful. Japanese exporters, many of them traditionally paternalistic small businessmen, had geared their expansion plans to past policy and could hardly meet a lag in sales by laying off workers. The mentality of the past could not be shed overnight.[66]

As the U.S. dollar came under renewed suspicion in February 1973, the yen, along with the German mark, became a target of bullish speculation.[67] In the eight trading days through February 9, total intervention by the Bank of Japan amounted to $1.1 billion. The authorities then closed the exchange market.[68] After the dollar's devaluation on the 12th, the yen was set afloat. Before mid-1973 it had strengthened to roughly 265 per dollar. By then some signs of a turnaround in Japan's merchandise trade balance had at last appeared.

For 1973 as a whole, the surplus on goods and services nearly vanished; the balance on goods, services, transfers, and movements of nonbank capital shifted to a deficit of $7.4 billion; and the overall balance settled by the monetary authorities shifted to a deficit of $6.0 billion. The appreciation of the yen against the dollar seems to have worked as standard theory would suggest. Late in 1973 and early in 1974 the informal pegging of the supposedly floating exchange rate retreated temporarily from around 265 to around 300 yen per dollar, amounting to an effective devaluation of roughly 12 percent.

ITALY

Italy's balance-of-payments experience offers some instructive similarities and contrasts with Japan's. The events of 1964, in particular, have been widely cited as an example of relatively easy adjustment of the balance of payments by domestic demand policy, and even of the workability of a fixed exchange rate. On the other hand, Italy has at times provided an example of speculative capital flight even when the balance of payments seemed fundamentally sound. Italy's troubles were a factor in precipitating the dollar-mark-yen crisis of February 1973.

The background to noteworthy events

Italy, like Germany and Japan, was often identified as the scene of a postwar "economic miracle." Between 1952 and 1971, real gross national product grew at an average annual rate of some 5⅓ to 5½ percent. Growth was particularly steady up to 1964. Over the 12 years to then, nonagricultural output rose by 6 percent a year on the average; yet price increases were moderate, the GNP deflator rising by an average of no more than 2½ percent.[69] In the 12 years from 1953 to 1965, real domestic product more than doubled and exports more than tripled. Unemployment fell from an average of 1.9 million persons in 1953–1957 to 0.5 million in 1963 (rising to 0.7 million in 1965).[70] By 1961, to judge from end-of-year figures in *International Financial Statistics*, Italy gained third rank, behind only the United States and Germany, as a holder of external reserves.

According to Michael Michaely, referring to the period from the second quarter of 1950 to the second quarter of 1966 in particular, monetary policy was left more to automatic mechanisms in Italy than in other major countries. Changes in the discount rate of the Bank of Italy occurred rarely (until 1969) and were of little significance.[71] Changes in commercial-bank reserve requirements were similarly unimportant. Other variables of monetary policy seem not to have been overridingly oriented either to the balance of payments or to domestic targets. Budgetary or fiscal measures also appear not to have been used with any consistency for adjustment of the balance of payments. The rate of money-supply expansion was allowed, by and large, to fluctuate automatically in the same direction as the country's foreign-exchange reserves. As in Japan, the external influence on bank liquidity and the money supply tended to be neutralized, but only in a partial and not very consistent way, by the tendency of the commercial banks to borrow from the central bank when the exter-

63. BIS, 1972–1973, p. 46; *Wall Street Journal*, 6 December 1972, p. 33.

64. BIS, 1972–1973, p. 29. On the masking of reserve gains, see, for example, *Wall Street Journal*, 1 November 1972, p. 7, 1 December 1972, p. 12, 1 March 1973, p. 8.

65. *Wall Street Journal*, 1 November 1972, p. 7; Walter W. Heller in *Wall Street Journal*, 12 December 1972, p. 24; *Newsweek*, 11 December 1972, pp. 88–90.

66. *Newsweek*, 11 December 1972, pp. 88–90; *Wall Street Journal*, 10 October 1972 pp. 1, 37.

67. According to some observers, Japan had contributed to the turmoil by tightening stock-market credit in mid-January, which tended to strengthen the demand for yen at the expense of dollars. Compare *Wall Street Journal*, 2 March 1973, editorial on p. 8, with Federal Reserve Bank of Chicago, *International Letter*, 19 January 1973.

68. Charles Coombs in Federal Reserve Bank of New York, *Monthly Review*, March 1973, p. 63.

69. Organisation for Economic Co-operation and Development, *Economic Surveys—Italy*, Paris: November 1972 (hereafter cited as OECD, *Italy*, 1972), p. 27 and table on p. 28.

70. André Piettre, *Monnaie et Économie Internationale*, Paris: Cujas, 1967, p. 505.

71. Quantitative limits on the Bank of Italy's rediscounting for the commercial banks render its interest rate "of secondary importance." *International Financial Statistics*, February 1973, p. 205.
The contrasting roles of the discount rate in Japan and Italy illustrate a general point: analysis with statistics alone is treacherous; one must understand the relevant institutions, which can vary greatly from country to country and over time.

nal reserves fell and to repay debt when the external reserves rose. Another partially offsetting factor, at times, was the tendency of the commercial banks to borrow abroad when the other parts of the balance of payments were failing to expand their liquidity. Since the offsetting was only partial, the money supply did tend to change in the direction, if not to the full extent, consistent with the automatic mechanism of adjustment of the balance of payments under fixed exchange rates. The money growth rate tended to rise or fall with surplus or deficit in the country's balance of payments.[72]

A detailed chronology of Italy's balance-of-payments vicissitudes would be tediously repetitive of what we have seen happening in other countries. It will be helpful, however, to sketch in the background of the events that do command attention. Italy's wartime and postwar inflation was brought under control by orthodox measures of monetary restraint, applied under the leadership of Luigi Einaudi, economist and Governor of the Bank of Italy and later the first President of the Republic. The exchange rate, which had been 19 lire per dollar before the war, was stabilized at 575 in January 1948.[73] During the devaluation wave of 1949, the lira was pegged at 625 per dollar. That parity held—precariously at times—until 1971.

During each of the years from 1949 through 1962, except only in 1952, Italy was gaining international reserves.[74] From mid-1953 to the end of 1959, the balance of payments was consistently in surplus, often substantial. The resulting automatic expansion of the money supply was evidently not sufficient to lead to full adjustment. Had balance-of-payments adjustment been desired, domestic reinforcement of monetary expansion would have been called for; yet the Bank of Italy's lending to the commercial banks was small and falling slightly. The absence of domestic reinforcement suggests that the accumulation of external reserves was welcome.[75]

One element in the background of the 1963–1964 crisis appears to be the continuing momentum of a monetary expansion previously fed in part by payments surpluses. The annual rate of monetary expansion had increased to an average of 14⅔ percent over the five years 1958–1962 and of 15⅔ percent over the last four years of that period. In a report written early in 1960, the Bank for International Settlements noted that "it was the balance-of-payments surplus which created additional liquidity in the banking system and made possible the expansion of bank credit both to the government and to the private sector."[76] During 1959 the external reserves had grown by $842 million, or 37 percent. By the end of that year, the economy was booming, with exports giving the impetus. The authorities let the boom roll on, undamped, in 1960. They had the external surplus in view. Furthermore, prices were still stable, gains in productivity were still keeping pace with wage increases, unemployment was still heavy in southern Italy, and production had been showing substantial capacity to expand. The authorities counted on expansion of output and of liberalized imports to meet growing demand without serious inflation. A widening of the merchandise trade deficit and narrowing of the current-account surplus, as well as the commercial banks' foreign investment, reduced the growth of the external reserves in 1960; but their growth increased again in 1961. In its report for 1961, the Bank of Italy commented on how a strong development of exports and a balance-of-payments surplus was tending to transfer foreign pressures of excess demand into Italy. Still, the authorities continued in 1961, as the Bank for International Settlements reported, "to encourage domestic expansion while further liberalising the foreign payments regime. As in previous years, the growth in the volume of money and credit was allowed to reflect the increase in the country's reserves." Instead of desiring to accumulate more international reserves, they wished "to employ the country's external savings to stimulate economic growth and the absorption of remaining unemployed resources at home." In 1962 as a whole, external transactions continued contributing to monetary expansion, though to a lesser degree than before, since the balance of payments was in the process of shifting into deficit. As the expansionary foreign impulses slackened off, but before a menacing deficit appeared, the monetary authorities acted to maintain domestic credit expansion. Apparently they feared a check to economic growth if the monetary expansion, fed so long from external sources, should be interrupted. A further clue to this attitude is the fact that in the last quarter of the year, when an actual payments deficit had at last appeared, the commercial banks not only obtained loans from the Bank of Italy but were again permitted to incur net debt to foreigners.

Passages in its report for 1962 suggest that the Bank of Italy felt some sort of need for partially ratifying cost inflation. Understandably, the authorities did not squarely choose price stability over production and employment. Reassured by the fact that the balance of payments was still in surplus for the year 1962 as a whole, they "introduced enough liquidity to impede checks in this or that sector of productive activity, resulting . . . in an increase in internal demand in excess with respect to the expansion of internal supply and thus in the partial reabsorption of the surplus of the current accounts of the balance of payments."

One element in the rise of costs was the crumbling of a wage pause enforced in earlier years; wages began catching up. They rose at a 15 percent annual rate from mid-1962 to mid-1964. Civil servants and employees of semigovernmental agencies gained large salary increases, and pensions were also raised. For several years, moreover, Italian agriculture had been plagued by poor harvests, loss of its best workers to industry, and other troubles. In this atmosphere, and reinforced by continuing bank-credit expansion, demand surged for investment and consumer goods, including automobiles. The annual-average consumer price index, which had risen 4.6 percent from 1961 to 1962, rose 7.5 percent from 1962 to 1963. Yet the authorities hesitated to apply restraint, fearing to stop the "miracle" of growth.[77]

The 1963–1964 crisis and recovery

Italy's current account (including transfers) shifted from a surplus of $281 million for 1962 as a whole to a deficit of $715 million in 1963 as imports jumped 19.5 percent in physical volume and 25.0 percent in lira value. Approximate overall balance turned into a deficit of $1.2 billion, and from October 1963 to March 1964 the overall deficit was running at an annual rate of $1.8 billion.[78]

Capital movements played a noteworthy role in the reversal. Around 1962, the introduction of new short-term government securities contributed to the development of an active money market in Italy and to the international mobility of capital. With the external convertibility of European currencies restored, Italian banks began administering their balances of lire and foreign exchange almost as if they formed a single holding of liquid funds. Several

government agencies were preparing to issue debentures to finance the nationalization of electricity and other expenditures. Electric-company shares were widely held by middle-class savers; and the expected nationalization, on unknown terms, was one reason why the Italian stock market dropped in mid-1962. Another reason was the expected introduction of a tax on dividends, which would make tax evasion more difficult. Part of the funds withdrawn from the stock market went to inflate the real-estate market; another part began being illegally transferred abroad. Italian entrepreneurs began to hedge against risks on their lire-denominated investments by transferring

72. Michael Michaely, *The Responsiveness of Demand Policies to Balance of Payments: Postwar Patterns*, New York: National Bureau of Economic Research, 1971, chap. 7, particularly pp. 151, 153–154.

73. Figure and date from Piettre, *op. cit.*, p. 504.

74. *International Financial Statistics*, 1972 Supplement, pp. 30–31. The current account, consisting of goods-and-services transactions and private and governmental transfers, was slightly in deficit in 1956 (the first year for which IFS gives the figures) but in surplus in each of the years thereafter (through 1972), except only for 1963.

75. Michaely, *op. cit.*, chap. 7, esp. pp. 149, 153–154.

76. This and the following paragraphs draw on my "Discipline, Inflation, and the Balance of Payments," in N. A. Beadles and L. A. Drewry, eds., *Money, the Market, and the State*, Athens: University of Georgia Press, 1968, especially pp. 15–18, to which, except as otherwise indicated, the reader is referred for detailed citations.

77. Marcello de Cecco, "The Italian Payments Crisis of 1963–1964," in Robert Mundell and Alexander Swoboda, eds., *Monetary Problems of the International Economy*, Chicago: University of Chicago Press, 1969, pp. 383–384; Milton Gilbert in Bosman and Alting, *op. cit.*, p. 40; Piettre, *op. cit.*, pp. 505–506; and calculations from *International Financial Statistics*, Supplement.

78. Calculations from *International Financial Statistics*, Supplement; Gilbert in Bosman and Alting, *op. cit.*, p. 40.

funds abroad and substituting bank credit as operating capital for their firms. Capital export also occurred through underinvoicing of commodity exports and overinvoicing of imports and through purchases of emigrants' remittances and tourist receipts before they reached Italy. The physical export of Italian banknotes, as estimated by their deposit in Italian banks by "nonresidents," nearly doubled between 1962 and 1963, reaching $1.5 billion. Another clue to the export and reimportation of banknotes is the fact that the errors-and-omissions debit item in the balance of payments more than doubled, to $1.5 billion, almost half again as large as the deficit on goods and services.[79]

At first the authorities decided to shelter the official reserves by allowing commercial banks to borrow short-term funds abroad, mainly on the Eurodollar market. Then, in the summer of 1963, a cabinet crisis developed, dashing hopes of prompt budgetary measures to deal with the balance of payments. The Bank of Italy resorted to a credit squeeze, beginning in September. To implement it, the authorities asked the commercial banks not to increase their foreign borrowings beyond the level reached in August 1963, and if possible to reduce them. This stoppage of capital import by the banks left the official reserves to bear the brunt of the payments deficit, and they fell $458 million between September 1963 and March 1964. This unmasking of the deficit came as a shock to international financial opinion and inflamed speculation. The forward lira went a widening discount against the dollar, until the authorities finally intervened.[80]

The credit squeeze, including tighter restrictions on consumer credit, was in other respects effective. The growth rate of money plus time deposits was cut from 4 or 5 percent *per quarter* in 1962 and the first half of 1963 to 1.2 percent in the first quarter of 1964. The expansion of narrow money was cut from 18.6 percent in the full year 1962 and 13.7 percent in 1963 to 7.7 percent in 1964. In February 1964 a new government that had taken office a few months before was finally able to take such energetic measures as a 30 percent increase in taxes on companies, an 8 percent tax on purchases of new cars, an increase in the gasoline tax, an obligatory 30 percent down payment on credit purchases, and draconian sanctions against capital export. Merchandise imports, which had been rising at an average 5.7 percent per quarter in 1963, decreased by 2.1 percent in the first quarter of 1964, while the

growth of exports accelerated. Between the full years 1963 and 1964, imports fell by 5.1 percent in physical volume and by 4.5 percent in lira value, while exports rose by 16.3 percent in volume and 17.9 percent in value. The dramatic reversal hinged partly on strong export demand, particularly from Germany (whose boom had apparently been feeding partly on contagion of inflation from Italy itself). Tourist receipts also rose.[81]

At the beginning of 1964, devaluation of the lira had seemed almost inevitable; the London *Economist* saw no other solution. But international assistance, including credits of $1 billion from the United States and $225 million from the IMF in March 1964, joined the stern Italian measures in reversing speculative sentiment. Within 12 or 13 months, a trade deficit running at an annual rate of well over $1 billion had been transformed into a surplus of around $2 billion. Italy shifted from having the largest balance-of-payments deficit of any country at the beginning of 1964 to having the largest surplus by the third quarter of the same year. In 1965, Italy's current-account surplus, at $2.2 billion, was more than twice as large as in any earlier year.[82]

The quick cure of the payments crisis imposed internal costs in the form of bankruptcies, unemployment, and retarded growth. Between October 1963 and August 1964, the indexes of production of investment and consumption goods dropped by 19.4 and 11.9 percent respectively. The index of the volume of total investment in machinery and equipment declined in both 1964 and 1965, falling by more than 30 percent from the level of 1963. During 1964–1967, the average annual growth rate of real GNP was 4½ percent, as against 6½ percent during 1960–1963.[83] Unemployment rose, and not until 1968 did manufacturing employment regain its 1963 average level.

If Italy furnishes an exception to the unwillingness of countries actually to deflate for balance-of-payments reasons, the mildness of the exception tells in favor of the general rule. Deflation was not pushed to the extent of reversing the uptrend of prices. Annual figures of money supply, prices, wages, gross national product in both current and constant prices, and total industrial production all continued rising, though more slowly than before. Furthermore, Italy did not choose actual deflation at home solely for the sake of external balance. The country was experiencing a "nondilemma case": inflation at home happened to join with the external deficit in calling for a tighter financial policy.

The second half of the 1960s

Restrictive measures gave way to antirecession measures in 1965, and economic expansion regained momentum in 1966–1968.[84] Even so, and whether or not it is coincidence, the policy-induced recession of 1964 does seem to mark a break in the trend of Italy's real economic growth. Real gross national product had grown at average rates of 5.3 percent in 1952–1958 and 5.9 percent in 1959–1964; but in 1965–1971, even with a start from a depressed base, the growth rate was only 4.9 percent. Slack in the economy was evidenced by generally unsatisfactory levels of unemployment and by emergence of net exports of goods and services averaging 2.8 percent of gross national product in the period 1965–1971, in contrast with small net imports before.[85] In 1965–1971, the current account, including inward net transfers, ran a surplus averaging $1.9 billion, with a peak of $2.6 billion in 1968 and a trough of $0.8 billion in 1970.[86]

Capital outflows kept gains in external reserves much smaller. In 1968, despite the strong current account, the reserves actually registered a small drop. The Italian authorities were deliberately promoting capital exports to offset the current surplus; to keep interest rates below rates prevailing abroad, they employed open-market operations and direct central-bank financing of part of the government budget deficit.[87] Since 1964, as much as 10 to 15 percent of domestic saving was being exported, mostly to countries with higher incomes and capital stock per head than Italy. Suggested explanations, besides occasional official action, include deficiencies of the Italian capital market, deficiencies of the fiscal system and tax evasion, growing government transfers to households, and attitudes and recurrent crises of confidence that apparently made some wealth-owners prefer placements abroad almost regardless of opportunities at home.[88]

Capital outflows also apparently responded to steps that a newly formed government took late in 1968 and during 1969 to stimulate economic activity and reduce unemployment. Increases in government spending and tax incentives for investment and consumption were reinforced by a relatively easy monetary policy.[89] By early 1969, "massive capital outflows" were

79. De Cecco in Mundell and Swoboda, *op. cit.*, pp. 384–386, and calculations from IFS Supplement.

The reimportation of banknotes fulfills rather than cancels the significance of their having been smuggled out in the first place. The Italian capital-exporters acquire and presumably retain bank accounts or other assets abroad, while the foreign purchasers of the smuggled notes use them for payments in Italy that they would otherwise have covered in some other way.

80. De Cecco in Mundell and Swoboda, *op. cit.*, pp. 387–388; cf. Michaely, *op. cit.*, p. 149, on changes in the banks' net foreign-exchange position.

81. De Cecco in Mundell and Swoboda, *op. cit.*, p. 387; Piettre, *op. cit.*, p. 506 and footnote; calculations from IFS Supplement; and other sources as referred to in footnote 76 above.

82. Piettre, *op. cit.*, p. 506; E. M. Bernstein in Randall Hinshaw, ed., *The Economics of International Adjustment*, Baltimore: Johns Hopkins Press, 1971, p. 70; IMF, 1965, p. 89; IMF, 1966, pp. 102–103.

83. Calculations from table in De Cecco in Mundell and Swoboda, *op. cit.*, p. 388, and chart in *OECD Italy*, 1972, p. 8; Gilbert in Bosman and Alting, *op. cit.*, pp. 40–41.

84. Piettre, *op. cit.*, p. 506; Gilbert in Bosman and Alting, *op. cit.*, p. 41.

85. *OECD Italy*, 1972, pp. 27–29.

86. The main factor in the persistently large current-account surplus, according to Milton Gilbert (in Bosman and Alting, *op. cit.*, p. 40), was the reduced growth rate of domestic demand. The IMF (IMF, 1969, p. 10) points to growth rates below the economy's high potential and to increased competitiveness in international markets. Italy's index of average dollar unit values of manufactured exports generally fell relative to the average index of her competitors from 1964 to 1969, both indexes rising roughly in parallel thereafter. (Chart in *OECD Italy*, 1972, p. 46.) The exceptional surplus of 1968 was related in part to a slowdown of economic expansion in the first half of the year, when imports remained stationary while exports rose at a 17 percent annual rate. (IMF, 1969, p. 79).

87. IMF, 1969, p. 80.

88. *OECD Italy*, 1972, pp. 28–29.

89. IMF, 1970, pp. 87–88. Rates of narrow-money-supply expansion were 12 percent in 1968, 16 percent in 1969, and 27 percent in 1970.

already causing concern.[90] The first half of the year saw exceptionally large outflows of nonbank capital. Reasons, in addition to persistent features of the Italian scene, included a growing interest-rate differential as rates staged an unprecedented upsurge on the Eurodollar market and in foreign countries. In 1969 the Italian authorities faced an example of the difficulty of effectively applying monetary stimulus for domestic purposes while credit demands were strong and monetary policies restrictive abroad. As the outflow of nonbank capital, outweighing the surplus categories of the balance of payments, drained the official reserves, the authorities responded by raising the cost of forward cover for the foreign-currency assets of the commercial banks, requesting the banks to liquidate their net foreign asset positions, and raising domestic short-term interest rates, including (in August) the discount rate. Toward the end of the year, weakness developed on current as well as capital account. The last four months were marked by strikes, attendant losses of output, and large wage settlements, which reinforced an upturn in prices that had already begun in the spring.[91]

The eventful early seventies

In 1970 the current surplus was only one-third as large as in 1969 and merchandise trade was in deficit, yet the reserves rose. The balance-of-payments situation fluctuated sharply over the year. As the year began, costs were accelerating in the wake of the strike settlements, price increases were exceeding the 6 percent annual rate regarded as a danger signal, demand was buoyant, imports were rising, and the lira was under pressure from capital outflows. A tightening of credit seemed appropriate for internal as well as external reasons. The authorities raised interest rates (including the discount rate, which went from 4.0 to 5.5 percent in March), encouraged government-controlled enterprises to borrow abroad, and tightened capital controls.[92] In mid-February the Bank of Italy centralized with itself the crediting to bank accounts of Italian banknotes returned from abroad. This measure made the export and reimportation of banknotes more costly by lengthening the time necessary to have reimported notes credited to bank accounts and by increasing the discount on Italian notes abroad. Its immediate effect is shown by reductions in the second half of February in comparison with the first half of 54 and 79 percent, respectively, in amounts of banknotes

arriving from abroad and amounts credited. For this initial period, the difference between arrivals and creditings is an indicator of the above-mentioned cost. By the second half of 1970, banknote remittances had been cut to a monthly average of about $50 million worth, in comparison with a monthly average of about $200 million worth in 1969. The cutback in capital outflow thus reflected was due not only to the control measures but also to a rise in Italian interest rates while rates were falling abroad.[93]

Signs of business recession became evident in 1970; and although real output gained significantly in the last quarter of 1971, the recovery lost momentum in the first half of 1972. Rates of increase over the previous year in gross national product at constant prices had amounted to 6.4 percent in 1968 and 5.7 percent in 1969 but were down to 4.9 percent in 1970, 1.4 percent in 1971, and between 3 and 3½ percent in 1972.[94] Factors mentioned as contributing to this longest postwar Italian recession include the wage explosion that preceded it, the deterrence to business investment decisions of uncertainties created by further wage negotiations, uncertainties arising from repeated delays in introduction of the value-added tax and their effect on inventory investment in particular, the deterrent effect on consumer spending of "the unstable social climate and the weakening of the labour market," impairment of business and household confidence alike by political uncertainties, and a prolonged housing slump.[95] As shown in footnote 89 and on page 542, money-supply expansion was rapid but unstable. The phenomenon deserves closer study than it can receive here.

Domestic recession did not improve the balance of payments quickly and powerfully enough to prevent a minor currency crisis. From the beginning of 1970 until mid-August, the spot exchange rate of the lira moved practically at its floor against the dollar. Its weakness was attributed partly to the current-account weakness but more importantly, and especially from May onwards, to capital outflows induced by domestic labor unrest and political uncertainties, including resignation of the government. By early July, rumors of imminent devaluation were circulating. Later in the month, with the Bank of Italy refraining from forward intervention, the three-month forward discount on the lira widened to 17 percent per annum. The Bank's spot support of the lira totaled about $450 million for July and the first half of August. A new government was formed early in August. Announcement of tax increases and other fiscal measures, together with favorable seasonal factors, brought the spot lira above par by the end of August for the first time since February 1969. By early November, aided by falling Eurodollar interest rates, the spot lira rose to 0.5 percent above par, while the three-month forward discount narrowed to only 1 percent per annum. The sudden turnaround in the lira's prospects reportedly imposed heavy losses on bear speculators.[96] The official reserves recouped their earlier losses and ended 1970 higher than at the beginning of the year.

Even though the speculative attack on the lira was successfully resisted, it seems odd—superficially—that it should have occurred at all during a year when the capital account and the overall balance of payments were moving into surplus from the deficits of the year before. The explanation hinges on the sharp reversals of conditions and market sentiment during the year, the contrasting movements of the current and capital accounts between 1969 and 1970, and the special nature of the capital-account improvement. That improvement was attributable to declines of interest rates abroad and a rise in Italy, to contraction in the repatriation of banknotes from abroad, and to borrowing abroad by Italian enterprises and medium-term credit institutions. The authorities were encouraging heavy foreign indebtedness with the double intention of equilibrating the overall balance of payments and regulating the inflow of investment finance. Without the recourse to external financial markets, according to the Bank of Italy, the balance of payments would have registered an overall deficit of more than $1½ billion.[97]

The balance-of-payments improvement permitted increased attention to the recession at home. Fiscal measures to stimulate investment, even at the expense of consumption, were adopted in August and December 1970; but their results apparently came slowly. Monetary policy also eased in the second half of the year. With the recession worsening, with the rise in prices, though worrisome, becoming more moderate than the rise in most foreign countries, and with the balance-of-payments constraint temporarily gone, the authorities persisted in 1971 in their expansionary efforts. A discount-rate cut in April was intended to aid domestic recovery and keep Italian interest rates in step with the decline abroad.[98]

With domestic activity still depressed and

DOMESTIC RESPONSES TO EXTERNAL IMBALANCE: JAPAN AND ITALY

with buoyant demand—even inflation—prevailing in world markets, Italy's merchandise account moved back into a small surplus in 1971; and her goods-and-services surplus rose to $1.7 billion. Net capital outflows increased, but not enough to keep the overall balance-of-payments surplus, settled by official and banking transactions, from rising to $0.9 billion. Italy's biggest reserve gains came in the first and third quarters of 1971, although the lira was not an especial object of bullish speculation during the international currency crises of May and was involved only relatively slightly in the August crisis.[99]

In the Smithsonian Agreement of December, Italy devalued the lira by 1.0 percent against gold and SDRs, thereby appreciating it by only 7.48 percent against the dollar and making the new central rate 581.5 per dollar.

Through most of 1972 the domestic situation was characterized by strong wage and price inflation, sporadic strikes, a profit squeeze, disappointingly poor business recovery, and persistently high unemployment. The monetary authorities continued aiming at easy credit conditions.[100]

90. IMF, 1969, p. 80.

91. IMF, 1970, pp. 87–88.

92. IMF, 1970, pp. 10–11, 88; IMF, 1971, p. 99; Banca d'Italia, *Assemblea Generale Ordinaria dei Partecipanti, Anno 1970*, Rome: Banca d'Italia, 1971 (hereafter cited as *Assemblea 1970*), p. 93; BIS, 1970–1971, pp. 148; *International Financial Statistics*.

93. *Assemblea 1970*, pp. 172–173.

94. *OECD Italy*, 1972, pp. 6, 85; *IMF Survey*, 12 March 1973, p. 72.

95. *OECD Italy*, 1972, pp. 5–10 (quotation from p. 10).

96. IMF, 1971, p. 135 and chart on p. 137; BIS, 1970–1971, pp. 148–149; *Assemblea 1970*, pp. 181–182, 368.

97. *Assemblea 1970*, pp. 153–154, 164–165.

98. IMF, 1971, p. 99; *OECD Italy*, pp. 16, 19.

99. *OECD Italy*, 1972, pp. 11, 14, 99; BIS, 1970–1971, p. 149; BIS, 1971–1972, p. 138.

100. Charles Coombs in Federal Reserve Bank of New York, *Monthly Review*, March 1973, p. 57; BIS, 1972–1973, pp. 61, 63.

Italy's external current account registered a surplus second in size only to Japan's in the first half of the year, and even for 1972 as a whole.[101] This would seem to be a curious background to a speculative run on the lira; but the capital accounts were so heavily in deficit, even despite net compensatory borrowing abroad by public and semipublic agencies, that the reserves declined almost every month. (During the first five months, however, the decline was essentially attributable to advance repayment of foreign borrowing done by public agencies the year before.) Adverse leads and lags and other forms of speculation grew more intense after the float of the British pound late in June as rumors kept circulating of devaluation or float of the lira. Political and economic uncertainties and a widening differential between Italian and foreign interest rates also affected capital movements. Heavy intervention was necessary in July to keep the lira within the band prescribed by rules of the European Community,[102] and the lira rate persisted at or near the bottom of the band throughout the early fall. Heavy intervention was necessary again when increasing talk of devaluation, float, or complete withdrawal from EC currency arrangements produced a speculative squall at the end of November. Over the 8½ months from the beginning of June 1972 until the floating of the lira on February 13, 1973, total official support of the lira amounted to $5.2 billion, equaling nearly four-fifths of Italy's reserves at the beginning of that period. (The decline in the net reserves was much smaller, however, thanks to compensatory borrowing abroad by public agencies and to special banking transactions.) From the time of the British float until the end of 1972, incidentally, Italy was granted an exemption from EC rules to permit support of the lira with dollars rather than with EC currencies (since debts incurred in those currencies would supposedly have to be repaid in gold).[103]

Italy again tightened exchange controls right after the float of sterling in June 1972: the Bank of Italy would no longer convert lira banknotes mailed in from abroad or allow them to be deposited with Italian banks for conversion into foreign exchange. In effect, this decision instituted a floating market for banknotes; and early in January 1973 the discount on lira notes abroad reached 9 percent.[104]

The regular lira itself was especially weak in January 1973, and expectations grew that the authorities would soon have to take some exchange-rate action. On Saturday the 20th they announced a split-off of a floating financial rate from the still-supported commercial rate. They also reduced the period of settlement of export and import payments in an effort to stop and even reverse the buildup of leads and lags against the lira. As we shall see in Chapter 28, the splitting of the lira market was an important link in a chain of events that led to the dollar's devaluation on February 12. Instead of setting a new central rate on the dollar, the Italian authorities allowed the commercial as well as the financial rate to float.[105]

Since then the lira has been floating independently of EC arrangements. It was almost as weak as the dollar at first and even weaker later on. By the beginning of December 1974 it was quoted at 666 per dollar, representing a depreciation of 6 percent from its pre-Smithsonian parity of 625; yet the dollar itself had deteriorated badly both in foreign-exchange value and purchasing power. Although balance-of-payments figures change their meaning under fluctuating exchange rates, it may be relevant to mention that the balance on goods and services had shifted into a deficit of $1.9 billion in 1973. Italy was hit particularly hard by the rise in oil prices in 1973–1974. Furthermore, it was having troubles enough at home. Inflation was raging. Increases in the narrow money supply amounted to 27.4 percent in 1970, 19.0 percent in 1971, 24.1 percent in 1972, 17.4 percent in 1973, and 19.3 percent between mid-1973 and mid-1974. The consumer price index averaged 10.8 percent higher in 1973 than in 1972, and in December 1974 it stood 24.5 percent above its level of one year before. The question of the exchange-rate system ranked relatively low on the list of Italy's problems.

---

101. OECD 1972, p. 5; BIS, 1972–1973, chap. III. The lira figures, translated at the Smithsonian central rate, are equivalent to $1.6 billion for the first half and $1.5 billion for 1972 as a whole. *International Financial Statistics* shows a surplus on goods and services and private and government transfers of $1.5 billion for 1972.

102. On this "snake in the tunnel," see pp. 424–425 above.

103. Coombs, *op. cit.*, pp. 57–58; BIS, 1972–1973, pp. 102–104, 135, 142–143.

104. Federal Reserve Bank of Chicago, *International Letter*, 7 July 1972; OECD *Italy*, 1972, p. 19n; BIS, 1972–1973, p. 143.

105. Coombs, *op. cit.*, p. 58.

CHAPTER TWENTY-SIX

Canada's Fluctuating Exchange Rate

The pegged-rate background

Canada adopted a fluctuating exchange rate in 1950 after several years of trouble with pegging. During 1945 and the first half of 1946, a growing opinion that the Canadian dollar was undervalued at its wartime rate of 90.9 U.S. cents led Americans to buy Canadian securities heavily, while Canadians cut their holdings of American securities. The resulting rise in official Canadian holdings of U.S. dollars, together with hopes of checking the contagion of American price inflation, led the Canadian government to revalue its dollar to parity with the U.S. dollar on July 6, 1946.

Revaluation soon proved a mistake. Canada's current-account deficit with the United States had traditionally been met by a surplus with the United Kingdom and Western Europe, but in the early postwar years these impoverished customers were unable to pay fully in gold or convertible currencies. Canada was in effect making foreign loans and grants out of her reserves of U.S. dollars. While her overall balance on current account remained positive (though shrunken), her pent-up demand for imports led to unprecedentedly large current deficits with the United States in 1946 and 1947. Another difficulty was that the inflow of capital from the United States fell off

after the revaluation of 1946 and reversed itself in 1947. Official Canadian holdings of gold and U.S. dollars fell from US $1667 million in May 1946 to only US $480 million in November 1947. A loss continuing at the same average monthly rate would have wiped out the remaining reserve by the early summer of 1948.

Instead of devaluing to meet the crisis, in November 1947 the government imposed severe restrictions on imports from and travel in the United States and other countries. The controls were discriminatory in fact though not in form. Canada also cut its foreign lending and borrowed from the U.S. Export-Import Bank. This program stemmed the crisis. Still, inconvertible pounds earned in trade with Great Britain did not satisfactorily meet the continuing (though much shrunken) deficit with the United States. In the summer of 1949 (a year of American recession), Canada's Acting Prime Minister warned that tighter austerity measures might again be necessary. And when the worldwide devaluations of September 1949 threatened Canadian exports with intensified competition, Canada returned to the rate of 90.9 U.S. cents.

People soon felt that the Canadian dollar was now undervalued. Expectations of revaluation crystallized under the influences of a boom in exploration and development of Canadian natural resources and of external inflationary pressures resembling those that had led to the revaluation of 1946. Rumors gained support from the Commerce Minister's statement in Parliament on June 5, 1950—*before* the Korean outbreak and the resulting boom in raw materials—that the discount on the Canadian dollar might not last much longer. Of the roughly C$1 billion of net capital inflow in 1950, only about one-fourth was for direct long-term investment; most of the remainder represented speculation.[1] Foreigners acquired Canadian banknotes, bank deposits, and government and corporation securities, either for cash or on margin. The item "other capital movements" in the Canadian balance of payments swelled tremendously: many U.S. companies with Canadian affiliates delayed taking their profits out of Canada and delayed paying for things bought in the United States for use in Canada; foreigners due to receive payments in Canadian dollars were glad to

---

1. Samuel I. Katz, "The Canadian Dollar: A Fluctuating Currency," *Review of Economics and Statistics*, **XXXV**, August 1953, pp. 236–237.

wait, while Canadians due to make payments in foreign currencies were anxious to stall.

The fixed exchange rate forced the Foreign Exchange Control Board to meet this speculative capital inflow by buying all U.S. dollars offered—still at a 10 percent premium in terms of Canadian dollars. Official Canadian holdings of gold and U.S. dollars rose from $1117 million at the end of December 1949 to $1255 million at the end of June 1950 and, by a further 43 percent in the third quarter of 1950 alone, to $1790 million at the end of September. The monthly increases amounted to $73 million in June, $65 million in July, $184 million in August, and $285 million in September. The sharp peak for September dramatizes the snowballing speculation.

Finding the Canadian dollars to buy the foreign exchange offered to the Control Board became a serious problem. The government had to supplement funds from its budget surplus by borrowing from the chartered (commercial) banks and by turning to the Bank of Canada for help in absorbing foreign exchange. Like a giant open-market operation, these purchases of foreign exchange provided the chartered banks with reserves and the public with Canadian money. The Bank of Canada tried to offset these inflationary effects by selling government securities on the open market. As the Governor of the Bank later told a parliamentary committee, these sales, relative to the size of the Canadian economy, constituted the largest open-market operation in the history of central banks. Still, they did not suffice to keep the reserves of the chartered banks from rising during 1950.

Toward the end of September 1950, official holdings of gold and U.S. dollars had climbed to nearly $1.8 billion. Announcement of this figure, due early in October, was sure to spur speculation still more as long as the Canadian dollar stayed pegged at 90.9 U.S. cents. The Finance Minister felt there was "no telling how much further this movement might have gone so long as the fixed rate of a 10% premium on U.S. dollars was maintained and people believed in the possibility or probability of an official change to another fixed rate such as parity." The Minister went on to say that "an influx of funds on this tremendous scale would, if continued, be likely to exercise an inflationary influence in Canada at a time when government policy in all fields is directed to combatting inflationary developments."[2]

Something had to be done. But what? Raising the Canadian dollar to parity with the American dollar would probably have reversed the capital movement as speculators took their profits at the expense of the Canadian authorities. The Finance Minister emphasized that adoption of parity or any other fixed rate "would not necessarily be justified by fundamental conditions and might be found to require reversal or further adjustment within the not too distant future."[3] Emerging weakness in trade and service items in the balance of payments made the problem still more delicate. With all alternatives open to serious objection, Finance Minister Douglas Abbott persuaded the cabinet to try a fluctuating rate. The government tried to make the free rate palatable to the International Monetary Fund by giving lip-service to the idea that it was tentative and experimental and that fixity might be reimposed in more appropriate circumstances.

On Friday evening, September 29, the government instructed Canadian banks to suspend foreign-exchange dealings and invited the chiefs of their foreign-exchange departments to a briefing in Ottawa the next morning. There the authorities announced their surprise decision.[4] Over the weekend the banks reshuffled their personnel, established departments for free-market exchange trading, and installed extra telephones. The free market opened on Monday morning, October 2.

The immediate results were gratifying. Though American investment funds kept moving into Canada, the heavy speculative inflow ceased without giving way to a speculative outflow. For a while Canada cautiously kept its general structure of control over international transactions (though not over the exchange rate itself). Finally, after 14 months of progressive relaxation, exchange controls were completely abolished on December 14, 1951. Canada then notified the International Monetary Fund and so became the first member country that had imposed exchange controls during and after World War II to give up the "transition-period" excuse for them. These results contrast with the unsatisfactory conditions that had led to upward revaluation of the Canadian dollar in July 1946, to a tightening of trade and exchange controls in the fall of 1947, to the devaluation of September 1949, and finally to abandonment of rate-pegging at the end of September 1950.

Fluctuations

The free Canadian dollar was first quoted at about 93½ U.S. cents. It reached parity with the American dollar on January 22, 1952 and, apart from dipping briefly back to parity late in 1955, remained at a premium until the end of the free-rate period. The end came in June 1961, though with hindsight one might perhaps date the first steps away from the free rate as early as December 1960 (the relevant events will be described below). The first and last full calendar years, full quarters, and full months of the free-rate period are therefore 1951 and 1960, the fourth quarter of 1950 and the first of 1961, and October 1950 and May 1961.

Over the whole period, the Canadian dollar fluctuated in a range of fractionally more than 13 U.S. cents, reaching a low of 93 cents in the very first month of free rates and a high of nearly 106.2 cents on August 20, 1957.[5] Much of this fluctuation can readily be explained by "objective" economic conditions. As was to be expected, however, the state of the balance of payments on current account bore no clear relation to the level of the rate; each was partly a cause and partly an effect of the other, creating an "identification problem" akin to that found in statistically deriving demand or supply curves for individual commodities. The rate was positively correlated with purchasing-power parity (calculated with wholesale price indexes) and with the excesses of Canadian over American long-term and short-term interest rates.[6]

If the theory of perversely low price elasticities of demand had been applicable to Canada, or if seriously destabilizing speculation had taken place, the exchange rate would presumably have fluctuated sharply. Yet the fluctuations were mild and orderly. Rarely were they as large as a full U.S. cent during a single day. Samuel I. Katz found that during 1955 the daily high and low quotations in New York diverged by one-fourth of a cent or less on 223 days and by more on only 26 days; the average daily high-low spread was only 0.07 of a cent.[7] Over the whole flexible-rate period, day-to-day changes averaged 0.08 percent (ignoring sign). Only 4.7 percent of the changes exceeded one-quarter of 1 percent in absolute value, and only 0.55 percent of them exceeded one-half of 1 percent.[8] Even within months and years the range between highest and lowest quotations

was small. In only six of the 128 months of free rates—October 1950, December 1951, November 1952, February 1955, and May and December 1960—did the high Canadian quo-

2. Bank of Nova Scotia, *Monthly Review*, September, 1950, p. 4.

3. Raymond F. Mikesell, *Foreign Exchange in The Postwar World*, New York: Twentieth Century Fund, 1954, p. 162.

4. The *Financial Post*, in its last issue before the announcement (September 30, p. 2) had characterized "reports of imminent revaluation" as "completely unfounded."

5. The great bulk of this range of fluctuation is attributable to the period from the unpegging to September 1952, when the Canadian dollar reached 104.2 cents. Paul Wonnacott, *The Floating Canadian Dollar*, Washington: American Enterprise Institute, 1972, p. 27.

Regarding this early period as one of *transition* to a free exchange rate—because, for one reason, exchange control was not abolished until December 1951—several students begin their statistical studies of the free rate with 1952 or 1953.

6. For the period up to mid-1957, details, figures and calculations concerning these relations and others to be mentioned below appear in "Some Facts About the Canadian Exchange Rate," *Current Economic Comment*, **XX**, November 1958, pp. 39–54. Constraints of time and space made presenting updated versions of all these computations here seem hardly worth while, especially since students of the Canadian experience hardly disagree any longer about the broad facts themselves (as distinguished from the general lessons they may or may not teach). On speculation, in particular, see the studies cited on later pages.

7. *Two Approaches to the Exchange-Rate Problem: The United Kingdom and Canada*, Essays in International Finance, No. 26, Princeton, N.J.: Princeton University, 1956, p. 6.

8. William Poole, "The Stability of the Canadian Flexible Exchange Rate, 1950–1962," *Canadian Journal of Economic and Political Science*, Vol. 33, May 1967, p. 205. It should be noted that Poole's figures cover the entire flexible-rate period, including the period of official manipulation in 1961–1962.

tation on the U.S. dollar exceed the low by more than 2 cents; and in no month was the range larger than $2^{11}\!/_{16}$ Canadian cents. The range stayed below 1 percent of the monthly average rate in more than two-thirds of the months and averaged only 0.87 percent over the entire period. The largest high-low range within a full calendar year was 5.82 percent of the annual average rate (in 1951); the smallest, 2.47 percent (in 1954); the average of the 10 yearly ranges was 4.17 percent.[9]

Official intervention in the free market

How much credit for this orderliness belongs to the Exchange Fund Account, managed by the Bank of Canada? Would the record have been worse or better without the Fund? The Canadian authorities repeatedly stated that they allowed the rate to respond to the normal play of economic forces; the Fund made no attempt to resist persistent trends and dealt in the market only to dampen whatever excessive short-run wobbles might otherwise have occurred.[10] According to no less an authority than the International Monetary Fund, "From October 1950 to June 1961, the Canadian exchange rate was permitted to fluctuate freely, being determined by market forces and with a minimum of official intervention. . . ."[11] Details of the Exchange Fund's operations were not made public, for obvious reasons, but published figures on official Canadian holdings of gold and U.S. dollars at the end of each month offer some clues suggesting that the Fund's influence was indeed peripheral. In the 123 months of free rates through the end of 1960 (thus not counting the five following months of possible transition to a new system), net monthly changes in official reserves did not exceed $20 million in over five-eighths of the months and remained under $40 million in 87 percent of the months. The net change was (slightly) over $100 million in only two months (August 1951 and May 1960). The average monthly change was US $21.0 million, or well under 5 percent of the size of monthly total balance-of-payments credits or debits on current account.

This restrained Fund activity contrasts sharply with average monthly reserve changes of $54.5 million in 1946 through the third quarter of 1950, even though the volume of Canada's international transactions had expanded greatly since then and even though direct controls over trade and payments and two deliberate adjustments in the pegged exchange rate had supplemented use of reserves in that earlier period. In the possibly transitional first five months of 1961, the average change in reserves amounted to $24.0 million. In the 12 following months, during all or part of which the authorities were avowedly manipulating a flexible exchange rate, the monthly change amounted to $75.1 million on the average and to over $175 million in two months (October 1961 and February 1962).

A further clue to policy during the free-rate period is the fact that the Exchange Fund was usually acquiring gold and U.S. dollars (that is, tending to restrain or depress the Canadian dollar) during months when the Canadian dollar was generally rising and drawing down its reserves (that is, tending to support the Canadian dollar) during months when the Canadian dollar was generally falling. Such passive resistance occurred in 100 out of the 123 months from October 1950 through December 1960; in only 23 months did Exchange Fund operations appear to be reinforcing or determining the trend. (For the period through May 1961, the corresponding breakdown is 104 months and 24 months.) Another way of considering intervention was to correlate the monthly changes in official reserves from October 1950 through December 1960 with the average daily change in the Canadian dollar rate as computed by fitting a least-squares straight-line trend to the daily New York quotations within each month.[12] (Up-trends in the rate and intervention tending to support the rate—i.e., reserve losses—counted as positive, the opposites as negative.) The resulting correlation coefficient of -0.66 (derived from 123 monthly "observations" and significant at better than the .01 level if the usual test is applicable) also suggests that the Fund's practice was indecisively to resist rather than to intensify or determine rate movements. A further experiment was to correlate the two sets of figures just mentioned without regard to algebraic sign. If large Fund operations went with small exchange-rate trends, yielding a negative correlation, this would suggest that the rate was stable or unstable according to whether the Fund was especially active or inactive and would favor giving the Fund considerable credit for the observed exchange-rate stability. If, on the other hand, large operations went with large rate trends and small operations with small trends, this would suggest that relatively large Fund activity occurred primarily in response to but was not dominant enough to suppress rapid change in the market and that steadiness when it occurred was due primarily to private supply and demand rather than to heavy intervention. The latter interpretation receives some support from a correlation coefficient of +0.41 (also significant at the .01 level).

Daily reserve figures as well as daily exchange rates point to a similar conclusion: up to 1961, official intervention generally tended to resist rate movements, but its influence was slight relative to that of private capital movements.[13]

Evidence of mild resistance to short-run trends in the exchange rate does not cast doubt on the Fund's announced policy of refraining from intervention except to counter excessive short-run wobbles. For the Fund could not know at once whether a given change was only a brief wobble. It apparently tried to steady the rate but stopped trying when a continuing market tendency showed the change to have been more than random. If the general tendency of the exchange rate during a particular month turned out to have been mainly in one direction, the Fund's continual "testing" of the market produced an unintentional net gain or loss of reserves and appeared, misleadingly, to indicate deliberate resistance to the trend.[14] In summary, the managers of the Exchange Fund

---

9. Calculated from various issues of Bank of Canada, *Statistical Summary*, and annual *Supplement*. For additional calculations concerning the extent of fluctuations, see three articles by Donald B. Marsh: "Kanadas Erfahrungen mit Beweglichen Wechselkursen," *Ordo*, **XIX**, 1968, pp. 389–401; "Canada's Experience with a Floating Exchange Rate: A Vindication of Free Markets in Exchange," in Robert Z. Aliber, ed., *The International Market for Foreign Exchange*, New York: Praeger, 1969, pp. 138–157; and "Canada's Experience with a Floating Exchange Rate, 1950–1962," in George N. Halm, ed., *Approaches to Greater Flexibility of Exchange Rates*, Princeton N.J.: Princeton University Press, 1970, pp. 337–344.

10. See, for example, statements by Finance Minister Abbott on February 19, 1953, and Finance Minister Harris on April 5, 1955, printed in House

of Commons, *Parliamentary Debates* for these dates, pp. 2120 and 2729, respectively.

11. 1962 *Annual Report*, p. 56.

12. Details on procedure appear in my article in *Current Economic Comment*, November 1958.

13. G. Hartley Mellish, "Official Intervention and the Flexible Canadian Dollar, 1950–1962," in Mellish and Robert G. Hawkins, *The Stability of Flexible Exchange Rates*, New York University, *The Bulletin*, Nos. 50–51, July 1968, pp. 5–27.

14. Cf. Samuel I. Katz, "Le dollar canadien et le cours de change fluctuant," *Bulletin d'Information et de Documentation de la Banque Nationale de Belgique*, 30th year, Vol. I, May 1955, pp. 7–8. Several later writers have reached similar conclusions. In *The Canadian Dollar, 1948–1958*, University of Toronto Press, 1960, p. 123, Paul Wonnacott notes that the Fund's stabilizing activity usually seemed greater shortly after the rate movement had changed direction than some time later. In *Bank of Canada Operations and Policy*, University of Toronto Press, 1958, p. 208, E. P. Neufeld notes the Fund's policy of "backing away" from the market when the rate movement persisted in one direction. In "Canada's Foreign Exchange Market: A Quarterly Model," IMF *Staff Papers*, **VII**, April 1960, p. 447, Rudolf R. Rhomberg notes the relative smallness of official intervention and its apparently much smaller influence than stabilizing speculation exerted in limiting rate fluctuations. In "The Canadian Exchange Rate, 1950–57," *Southern Economic Journal*, **XXVI**, January 1960, p. 207 and footnote, James C. Ingram mentions the apparent smallness of Exchange Fund transactions and finds it reasonable "to treat the Canadian dollar as if it were a freely fluctuating currency." R. E. Artus found little evidence that the Fund intervened any more actively between 1952 and December 1960 than to smooth day-to-day fluctuations, "and the movement of the rate seems to have been determined wholly by the play of demand and supply in the market." "Canada Pegs its Dollar," *The Banker*, **CXII**, June 1962, p. 362. "The operations of the stabilization fund were relatively modest in scope, . . . so that it did not determine the stability of the market, but instead augmented other larger forces stabilizing the rate." Robert M. Dunn, Jr., *Canada's Experience with Fixed and Flexible Exchange Rates in a North American Capital Market*, Washington & Montreal: National Planning Association & Private Planning Association of Canada, May 1971, p. 64.

Account showed remarkable restraint.[15] Until the government set a new policy in 1961, they apparently avoided determining the rate and limited themselves to trying to moderate minor short-run wobbles. The managers avoided the market disorder likely to result from giving speculators "one-way options" under a system of actively managed rates. It is an open question whether exchange-rate instability would have been greater or still slighter than what was actually observed if there had been no Fund and no official practice of first countering rate movements and then abandoning resistance to them when they proved more than random.

Speculation

We may infer something about speculation not only by observing whether the exchange market behaved in an orderly manner but also by studying capital movements as classified into two categories: (1) investment capital movements—direct investment and new issues and retirements of securities, and (2) short-term capital movements—transactions in outstanding securities and changes in Canadian-dollar holdings of foreigners, as well as the "other capital movements" listed in the Canadian balance of payments. These "other" movements include changes in international commercial indebtedness associated with hastening or delaying payments for Canadian imports and exports, changes in balances owing between corporate affiliates, loans between unaffiliated parties, changes in the foreign-exchange holdings of banks, various capital movements not directly recorded, and other errors and omissions. No one supposes that the capital movements in the first category are entirely nonspeculative and those in the second category entirely or even overwhelmingly speculative; the distinction between nonspeculative and speculative actions is unavoidably loose. Still, it does seem that the second category is more likely than the first to contain a significant speculative element. The rather obvious reasons for this belief are supported by the heavy short-term capital inflows in the summer of 1950, when upward revaluation of the pegged Canadian dollar was generally expected, and by the rather opposite events of the second quarter of 1962, when the flexible rate was again pegged. During the free-exchange-rate period, also, the two types of capital movement behaved in characteristically different ways.[16]

It would be interesting to know how, if at all, movements of short-term capital and the exchange rate were related. By the same method as already described for trends within months, a daily average rate change was computed to measure how sharply the Canadian dollar was rising $(+)$ or falling $(-)$ on the average over each quarter-year. Short-term capital movements were taken from quarterly balances of payments, a plus sign indicating an inflow and a minus sign an outflow. Simple correlation of the two sets of figures yielded coefficients of -0.17 for the 42 quarters from the fourth of 1950 through the first of 1961 and of -0.21 for the 41-quarter period through the fourth of 1960. These coefficients are too small to be statistically significant, but they do have the same sign as some others to be mentioned. The same short-term capital movements correlated to the extent of -0.55 with indicators of the strength of the Canadian dollar in relation to the recent past, that is, with quarterly average exchange rates expressed as percentages of each preceding quarterly average, for the 41 quarters from the first of 1951 through the first of 1961. (The fourth quarter of 1950 was not included because the ratio of its exchange rate to the preceding rate would have involved a quarter when the Canadian dollar was not yet unpegged.) The corresponding coefficient for the 40 quarters through only the fourth of 1960 was -0.53. Small as they seem, these last two coefficients are statistically significant at better than the 1 percent level for the 41 or 40 "observations" involved if the usual criterion is applicable. Apparently, short-term capital movements generally tended to resist exchange-rate movements. Familiar qualms about correlation of time-series data apply here with less than the usual force because none of the series is dominated by obvious trends; the short-term capital movements and the indicators of exchange-rate behavior often changed sharply from one quarter to the next.

Whether quarterly movements of short-term capital and of the exchange rate generally went in the same or in opposite directions is hardly a complete test of whether speculation was destabilizing or stabilizing. Even if capital movements did sometimes tend to reinforce or even cause rate movements, they might still have tended to iron out deviations from a longer-run average rate, provided that the current rate at those times was still below average though rising or still above average though falling. The third quarter of 1957 provides an example. For the quarter as a whole, the trend of the Canadian dollar was definitely downward; a continuing mild rise that carried the rate to an all-time peak of over $1.06 on August 20 was followed and outweighed by a sharp depreciation that continued throughout the rest of the quarter (and year). Yet short-term capital moved out of Canada to the extent of 72 million for the quarter as a whole. An English financial columnist, writing in mid-September, commented on "a wave of bear speculation" and detected signs of profit-taking by former bulls and of bearish delays in making payment by buyers of Canadian goods. (Interestingly enough, the columnist attributed the bear speculation to growing expectations of "a basic change in Canadian exchange rate policy" designed to force down the premium on the currency.[17] Although no such policy change in fact occurred until 3¾ years later, expectations were able to feed on the common knowledge that an Exchange Fund existed and was in the market to at least some extent.) Although the Canadian dollar was falling at this time, its quarterly average quotation was still higher than ever before and higher than in any succeeding quarter until the fourth of 1959. It is thus by no means clear that the capital outflows must be called destabilizing; after all, they were tending to *lessen* the deviation of the exchange rate from its longer-run average.

This episode suggested another approach to the statistics. To measure the strength of the Canadian dollar in each quarter in relation to both the recent past and near future, I expressed each quarter's rate as a percentage of the average of itself with the rates of the two preceding and two following quarters. These percentages were correlated with short-term capital movements in the 38 quarters from the second of 1951 through the third of 1960. (Use of this shorter period avoided having any of the five-quarter moving averages involve quarters before or after the free-rate period.) The coefficient turned out to be −.43, significant at the 1 percent level for the 38 "observa-

tions" by the usual criterion. Yet this coefficient seems surprisingly low when one sees a time-series chart of the underlying figures. Ordinary correlation is perhaps too exacting a test. Perfect inverse correlation would require not merely that capital movements were inversely related to exchange-rate deviations from a longer-run average but that they were related in size by a definite linear formula. Any departure from a rigid linear relation would hold down the computed coefficient, even if capital movements were always in the "stabilizing" direction. Exchange-rate changes and speculative capital movements were each undoubtedly subject to many influences besides the other. While the statistics hardly indicate any close rigid connection between the two series, they do at least definitely fail to support the standard theoretical worries about destabilizing speculation.

Besides the relation between short-term capital movements and exchange-rate changes, other evidence also suggests that speculation tended to buoy up the Canadian dollar when it was falling or relatively low and to restrain it when it was rising or relatively high. Despite a substantial seasonal pattern in Canadian trade, the exchange rate showed no economically meaningful seasonal fluctuation (though with only 11 years of data to work with, one cannot be sure of this conclusion). Day-to-day rate changes, moreover, were not serially correlated in the way one would expect if speculators had been riding and reinforcing trends.[18]

In one way or another, several scholars have

---

15. Extended periods of almost automatic market stability in the 1950s "sometimes left the authorities with nothing to do; and they sometimes expressed puzzlement (but no regrets!) at this state of affairs." Marsh in Aliber, *op. cit.*, p. 148.

16. For details and statistics and other variants of the approach to assessing speculation used here, see the article cited in footnote 6.

17. Lombard, "About Turn for Canadian $," *Financial Times*, London, 17 September 1957, p. 3.

18. Poole, *op. cit.*

reached pretty much this same conclusion.[19] At least one observer, though, dissents from the usual interpretation of the equilibrating capital movements.[20] The so-called "other capital movements" form a usually dominant, though highly variable, part of total short-term capital movements. These "other" movements are thought largely to reflect changing balances of commercial indebtedness. In an almost mechanical way, then, these movements were likely to be inward into Canada when the Canadian dollar was weak or falling and outward when the Canadian dollar was strong or rising. Weakness of the Canadian dollar, Harry Eastman suggests, seemed typically due to a sluggishness of Canadian exports (and other independently motivated credit or plus transactions) relative to imports (and other independently motivated debit or minus transactions). This then meant, incidentally, that the volume of short-term credit extended to foreign buyers of Canadian exports dropped relative to credit extended to Canadian importers by their foreign suppliers. Strength of the Canadian dollar, on the other hand, was likely to result from strength of export demand relative to import demand, and the difference between commercial credit granted by and received by Canadians then shifted in the direction of a capital outflow. This interpretation raises doubts whether the capital movements had been motivated by exchange-rate expectations. Few businessmen had enough faith in their rate-forecasting ability. Firms with large foreign transactions, despite their presumed access to expert opinion, generally found it best to deal in exchange as their ordinary business required, without hastening or delaying transactions in hope of profiting from moves in the rate. More active forms of speculation were also unimportant, partly because of the disapproval of the banks. Professionals most familiar with the market reportedly believed that deliberate speculation, at least after the first two or three years of the fluctuating rate, had been sporadic, on a small scale, and without significant influence.

This line of interpretation invites four comments, not necessarily dissenting. First, it is not clear that the trade balance was closely related to the exchange rate (the "identification problem" looms again). Second, it is doubtful whether the "other capital movements" always reflected nothing more than normal commercial credit; the massive surge of "other" capital into Canada in the summer of 1950, when people expected an upward revaluation of the pegged Canadian dollar, is striking evidence of this. The actual speculative character of commercial leads and lags has also often been clear in the postwar experience of other countries. Third, regardless of the motivation behind the equilibrating capital movements, the fact remains that they apparently did occur. If they were largely automatic, rather than dependent on speculators' forecasts and moods, their implications are in some respects still reassuring. Fourth, even if conscious speculation actually was negligible, this fact itself fails to bear out the usual theoretical worries.

All this forms just one reason why we cannot unequivocally cite the Canadian experience as an example of speculation that was unquestionably equilibrating in the sense of being based on a correct diagnosis of objective market conditions and prospects. Another reason hinges on a theoretical point. Speculation might be considered equilibrating, even when intensifying rate movements, if it hastened reaching the rate appropriate for emerging price-level and interest-rate relations and for other "fundamental" supply and demand conditions in international trade. On the other hand, it might be considered disequilibrating if, by delaying rate movements in accordance with "fundamental" conditions, it made adjustments all the sharper when they finally occurred. Speculation could conceivably stabilize an exchange rate "too much" and so hamper adjustment to changed conditions. The Canadian experience is significant only in a modest sense: it fails to bear out standard worries about speculative intensification of functionless fluctuations. Furthermore, the Canadian free rate did what it was originally intended to do: it solved the earlier problem of exchange crises and hot-money movements.[21]

Trade and investment

Did the risk of exchange-rate fluctuations impede Canada's international trade and capital movements? Their greater size after the unpegging of the rate than before in large part simply reflects general economic growth. A more meaningful comparison is of the *rates* of year-to-year growth in the postwar period before and after the unpegging. Because the war continued through most of 1945 and because the exchange rate remained fixed only during the first three quarters of 1950, some doubt exists about just which "before and after" periods to consider. Table 26.1 shows the various possibilities for the physical volume of exports plus imports, both of goods and services and of commodities alone.

TABLE 26.1. *Growth of Canadian exports plus imports before and after 1950*

AVERAGE YEARLY PERCENTAGE INCREASE

Period	Quantum of commodity trade	Value of trade in goods and services at constant prices
1945–1949	−1.74%	−2.60%
1945–1950	−1.00	−1.47
1946–1949	+1.06	−0.30
1946–1950	+0.99	+0.39
1950–1960	+4.26	+4.16
1951–1960	+3.73	+3.77

NOTES AND SOURCES: A quantum index of commodity exports *plus* imports was obtained by averaging separate export and import quantum indexes (given in various issues of *International Financial Statistics*), using base-year money values as weights. Goods-and-service trade in "constant (1949) dollars" is given in Bank of Canada, *Statistical Summary*, 1960 *Supplement*, pp. 124–125. The yearly average percentages of increase (or decrease) were obtained by fitting exponential trends to the trade figures for the years indicated (i.e., by fitting linear trends to their logarithms).

19. See, for example, R. Craig McIvor, *Canadian Monetary, Banking and Fiscal Development*, Toronto: Macmillan, 1958, p. 218; L. Albert Hahn, *Autonome Konjunktur-Politik und Wechselkurs-Stabilität*, Frankfurt: Knapp, 1957, p. 34; Ingram, *op. cit.*, esp. pp. 213, 215; Rhomberg, *op. cit.*, esp. p. 447; and Rhomberg, "A Model of the Canadian Economy under Fixed and Fluctuating Exchange Rates," *Journal of Political Economy*, **LXXII**, February 1964, esp. p. 12. Rhomberg's econometric model for the period 1952–1959 implies that a 1-U.S.-cent depreciation of the Canadian dollar would tend to attract approximately the same *inflow* of short-term capital into Canada as a 1-percentage-point excess of Canadian over U.S. short-term interest rates. Additional statistical studies include T. L. Powrie, "Short-Term Capital Movements and the Flexible Canadian Exchange Rate, 1953–1961," *Canadian Journal of Economics and Political*

Science, Vol. 30, February 1964, pp. 76–94; Richard E. Caves and Grant L. Reuber, *Capital Transfers and Economic Policy: Canada, 1951–1962*, Cambridge, Mass.: Harvard University Press, 1971, especially chap. 2; Caves and Reuber, "International Capital Markets and Canadian Economic Policy Under Flexible and Fixed Exchange Rates, 1951–1970," in Federal Reserve Bank of Boston, *Canadian-United States Financial Relationships*, 1972, esp. pp. 11, 21, 25; and R. G. Hawkins, "Stabilizing Forces and Canadian Exchange-Rate Fluctuations," in Mellish and Hawkins, *op. cit.*, pp. 28–65. Marsh in Aliber, *op. cit.*, p. 148, attributes a stabilizing effect to the skillful timing by Canadian commercial banks of conversion into Canadian dollars of the proceeds of their customers' bond flotations in New York. Artus, *op. cit.*, p. 363, commented on the "very effective equilibrating mechanism associated with short-term capital flows" and concluded that "As regards stability . . . , the floating rate performed eminently satisfactorily." Dunn, *op. cit.*, esp. pp. 9, 63–64, also commented on the strongly stabilizing influence of speculation. Wonnacott, *The Canadian Dollar* (1960), pp. 128–130, 139, found evidence on short-term capital movements less persuasive than these other students; yet he too judged that on balance they were more stabilizing than destabilizing.

Even the 1953 *Annual Report* (p. 70) of the International Monetary Fund, surveying the earlier period when the exchange rate had behaved less stably on the average than it proved to do over the remainder of the free-rate period, observed that "capital movements, on the whole, have been equilibrating rather than disturbing. Canadian trade and normal capital movements have accordingly not lost the important benefits that are commonly associated with rate stability."

20. Harry C. Eastman, "Aspects of Speculation in the Canadian Market for Foreign Exchange," *Canadian Journal of Economics and Political Science*, **XXIV**, August 1958, esp. pp. 361–365, 368–372.

21. After emphasizing this "overwhelming advantage" of the free-rate policy, the President of the Royal Bank of Canada took note of the argument that hot money was no longer a problem and that changed conditions required new policies. "But hot money is no longer a problem for Canada precisely because we *have* the free exchange rate." He went on to draw a contrast with the way that inflows and outflows of hot money had plagued European countries and even the United States. W. Earle McLaughlin, address at the annual meeting of his bank's shareholders, Montreal, January 12, 1961, p. 3.

Another clue may lie in the total of Canadian imports and exports expressed as a percentage of total world imports and exports. This figure averaged 5.56 percent in 1947 through 1949, 5.53 percent in 1947 through 1950, and 5.63 percent in the 10 years 1951 through 1960.[22] Although Canada and the United States together supplied a share of world exports in the early postwar years that was considered abnormally large and was expected to decline[23] and although the growth in Canadian trade did slacken in the late 1950s, comparison of the entire "before and after" periods is not unfavorable to the fluctuating rate. Another impression emerges from seeing whether the growth of imports and exports of goods and services kept pace with general economic growth, as judged from their total expressed as a percentage of Canadian gross national product. This figure averaged 49.7 percent from 1946 through the third quarter of 1950 and 44.7 percent from the fourth quarter of 1950 through the first quarter of 1961. In the light of the other before-and-after comparisons, it is uncertain whether this difference shows interference from exchange-rate fluctuations; to suppose so would be to rule out, among other things, any possible connection between growth of gross national product (especially during the early part of the free-rate period) and the freedom from exchange and other controls permitted by a free exchange rate. It seems probable, however, that other particular historical circumstances had much more to do with the growth both of trade and of the Canadian economy in general than did exchange-rate policy.

How badly did exchange-rate fluctuations impede international investment? As already explained, capital movements by way of foreign direct investment in Canada, Canadian direct investment abroad, and new issues and retirements of securities are less likely to reflect mere speculation than are short-term capital movements. These investment capital movements were heavier after than before the exchange rate was freed in 1950, whether one considers their net inflow into Canada or—as seems more appropriate for detecting the possible influence of exchange risk—one considers the items reported in the balance of payments totaled without regard to algebraic sign. The same is true of a before-and-after comparison of growth—if growth rates are meaningful for such widely fluctuating magnitudes.[24]

For movements of investment capital as also for trade, it is probably true that their size and growth depended less on exchange-rate policy than on other influences, including particular historical circumstances (for example, continued exchange-rate pegging and the slow removal of controls in other countries, close economic ties with the United States, the Korean and cold wars, and Canada's own boom in natural-resource development). No one knows, of course, "what would have happened" to Canada's international trade and capital movements if the exchange rate had been kept fixed in the 1950s. What can be said is that any damage in accordance with the standard theoretical worries was slight enough to be covered up by other influences.[25]

Abandonment of the free rate

"On the whole, the Canadian experience with a flexible exchange rate has been a happy one"—to use the words of a Canadian economist who appears to have reached this conclusion without enthusiasm and who would regret seeing his country's example widely followed. Canada in the 1950s enjoyed "one of the most remarkable periods of rapid and relatively stable growth" in its history. The flexible exchange rate did not *cause* Canadian prosperity, of course, but neither did it appear to dampen it significantly[26]—not, at least, until toward the end of the decade. Yet Canada abandoned its free rate in 1961. Had it proved unsatisfactory after all?

Before judging, we must look at the background of economic developments and policy proposals. Unemployment, in particular, had become a conspicuous problem. As a percentage of the labor force, it had reached 10 percent early in 1958, had averaged 6.7 percent over 1958–1960, and had averaged above 11 percent in the first three months of 1961. It still stood at 7 percent in May. In part the trouble supposedly stemmed from a continuing rapid rise in the labor force as the wartime crops of babies grew up, as people left the farms, and as refugees from Hungary migrated into Canada after the events of 1956. A shortage of vocational training schools and the influence of a heavy demand for unskilled labor some years before, when the primary industries had been growing so rapidly, left an excess of unskilled labor.[27] In addition, the problem seemed partly cyclical and partly related to an apparent slowdown in economic growth. Over the 10 years from 1950 to 1960 as a whole, Canadian gross national product in constant prices had increased 45 percent (compared with 39 percent for the United States), but the growth had been less rapid in the last four years of the decade than in the first six. Table 26.2 summarizes some contrasts.

The total of construction and other investment had been declining since 1957. Production was lagging in such labor-intensive industries as transportation equipment, machines, electrical goods, clothing, rubber, and leather goods. Total exports set new records in 1959 and 1960, but longer-term prospects seemed doubtful. Canada's postwar boom had largely concentrated on export-oriented basic industries, such as wood and pulp products, oil, and uranium and other metals. Overestimation of future demand and prices at the time of the Korean War had prompted construction of what later proved to be excess capacity. Exports of wheat, forest products, and some metals and other minerals were already reflecting a weak world demand or the intensified competition of rival suppliers. Good trade with Britain and Western Europe was helping to offset the relative stagnation of exports to the United States, but the European Common Market threatened discrimination against Canadian goods; and if Britain joined, most Canadian exports would probably lose their duty-free

on the success of the Canadian experiment, but few dissenters. Perhaps the most skeptical is Jacob Viner, who sees "no important lesson to be drawn from it, given the relevant circumstances of the period, except that in some circumstances the adoption of a floating currency does not lead to disaster—or does not lead to it quickly." "Some International Aspects of Economic Stabilization," in Leonard D. White, ed., *The State of the Social Sciences*, Chicago: University of Chicago Press, 1956, p. 296.

The most prevalent reason for seeing little general significance in the Canadian experiment is the idea that Canadian circumstances were so untypically favorable. The fact that the Canadian and American currencies are both "dollars" may have bred a stabilizing "parity psychology." (Egon Sohmen persuasively questions this widespread notion, however, in *International Monetary Problems and the Foreign Exchanges*, Princeton, N.J.: Princeton University, 1963, pp. 27–28.) Canada had relatively sound monetary and fiscal policies and a relatively slight bias toward inflation, a fine record of economic growth, abundant natural resources to be developed, and good prospects for the future. Her international current-account balance adjusted relatively easily to changes in long-term capital movements because of the tendency to import a sizable fraction of the capital goods used. Canadian corporations and governments had easy access to the American capital market. (Wonnacott, *The Canadian Dollar* (1960), pp. 130, 140, makes these points.) In other respects, too, Canada had very close economic ties with the United States (though it is uncertain whether this dependence was more an advantage or a disadvantage).

For all these reasons, it is interesting to compare the operation of a free exchange rate under quite different circumstances. Austria-Hungary in the late nineteenth century, for example, lacked most of Canada's special advantages, yet her exchange rate was if anything *less* unstable than the Canadian. See my "Fluctuating Exchange Rates in the Nineteenth Century: The Experiences of Austria and Russia," in Robert A. Mundell and Alexander K. Swoboda, eds., *Monetary Problems of the International Economy*, Chicago: University of Chicago Press, 1969, esp. pp. 65–67.

22. The underlying figures are from *Intenational Financial Statistics*, December 1961, pp. 38–39, and earlier issues. Comparable figures for 1946 are not available. In 1938, the Canadian share of world imports plus exports was 3.85 percent.

23. Cf. Ivar Rooth in International Monetary Fund, *Summary Proceedings of the Tenth Annual Meeting of the Board of Governors*, September 1955, p. 11.

24. See the reference in footnote 6.

25. Marsh in Aliber, *op. cit.*, p. 150, concludes that the floating rate did not discourage long-term investment. "Investment followed interest-rate and rate-of-return differentials, not the ups and downs of the exchange market." Dunn, *op. cit.*, p. 9, also notes that the flexible exchange rate does not appear to have significantly discouraged foreign trade or international investment, both of which grew rapidly in the 1950s.

26. Wonnacott, *The Canadian Dollar* (1960), p. 130. Numerous scholars could be cited who agree

27. Some facts here and later come from Alfred Zänker, "Centralbankkonflikt och expansionssträvanden i Kanada," *Ekonomisk Revy*, **XVIII**, September 1961, pp. 483–492; and "Canada's New Economic Measures," Federal Reserve Bank of New York, *Monthly Review*, February 1961, pp. 22–24.

TABLE 26.2. *Canadian and U.S. economic growth, 1950–1956 and 1956–1960*

	Real gross national product		Total industrial production		Physical volume of total exports	
	Canada	U.S.	Canada	U.S.	Canada	U.S.
Total percentage increase						
1950–1956	36.3%	26.7%	44.9%	33.3%	37.2%	48.9%
1956–1960	6.6	9.9	8.1	8.8	9.3	8.8
Arithmetic mean of year-to-year percentage increases						
1950–1956	5.4	4.1	6.4	5.1	5.6	7.4
1956–1960	1.6	2.4	2.0	2.4	2.3	2.9

NOTES AND SOURCES: Bank of Canada, Statistical Summary, 1960 *Supplement*, pp. 124–125, 128, 152; *Economic Indicators*, November 1961, pp. 1, 14; and various issues of *International Financial Statistics*. Canadian GNP is given in 1949 prices, U.S. GPN in 1960 prices. U.S. exports exclude military aid goods.

entry into the British market.[28] Even in the home market, Canadian producers of finished goods faced competition not only from the United States but also from Germany, Japan, and other countries.

One more factor impairing Canadian competitiveness was the high exchange rate. The premium on the Canadian dollar had oscillated around an average of 2.7 U.S. cents over the years 1952–1960 inclusive. The combination of these various real and monetary factors gave rise to a current-account balance-of-payments deficit averaging about C$385 million a year in 1951–1955 and C$1343 million in 1956–1960 (that is, about 7 percent of total current-account credit items in the first half of the decade and 20 percent in the second half). A persistent deficit in transactions with the United States far overshadowed a usual positive balance in overseas trade. Numerous categories of goods and services, together with net outpayments of interest and dividends, contributed to the overall current deficit. Ordinarily one might have expected depreciation of the free exchange rate to cure or prevent this deficit, but a heavy inflow of investment capital kept sustaining the rate. Funds flowed in, mostly from the United States, to establish or expand Canadian operations of American firms, to buy corporation stocks and other outstanding securities, and to buy new bond issues that corporations and provincial and local governments floated in the American market in response to the interest-rate differential. This was nothing new; foreign funds had traditionally fed every major expansion in Canada's history.

Despite some intimations in the financial press, the state of the balance of payments did not demonstrate a failure of the exchange-rate mechanism. The rate did maintain equilibrium between *total* supplies of and *total* demands for foreign exchange. The current account deficit and the capital-account surplus were the real and the financial sides of interwoven developments. Worry could not logically center on the current-account alone.

The capital account did receive critical attention. In the 15 years since the end of World War II, the gross total of foreign capital invested in Canada had more than tripled; net of Canadian capital invested abroad, the figure had more than quadrupled. Net outpayments of interest and dividends on these investments had reached a level of nearly $½ billion a year and were still growing. Besides this, American corporations might some day decide to bring home the earnings that they had been leaving in Canada. Pessimists foresaw an awkward day of reckoning when the capital inflow on which Canada had come to depend should dwindle; the country's natural-resource industries were already losing some of their attractions as fields of investment. Some saw too much reliance on foreign capital as the root of the country's economic difficulties: foreign capital had pushed efforts to do much too fast, had contributed to unbalanced expansion, and, by discouraging exports and promoting imports through the exchange premium, had aggravated unemployment.[29] From this point of view, the strengthening of the Canadian dollar in 1958 and 1959 seemed particularly untimely.

Some critics even blamed the heavy capital inflows on the exchange-rate system. Yet one can hardly have one's criticism of the free rate both ways: if it fostered too heavy a capital movement, then the risk of fluctuations in it was not too great an interference.[30] Before passing judgment, one should also consider the two alternative exchange policies. If the Canadian dollar had been kept pegged *below* the free-market level for the sake of the current account and employment, the inflow of private capital might have been even heavier (entailing awkward official accumulations of foreign exchange); the reasons had already been well illustrated in the summer of 1950. Pegging *above* the free-market level would probably have restrained the capital inflow, but at the cost of a current-account response opposite to the one desired for the sake of employment and at the risk of a balance-of-payments crisis. Two ways of restraining capital imports are vastly different: artificial exchange appreciation and either direct obstacles or domestic cheap money to get free-market depreciation as a desired by-product.

A more optimistic view saw the productive contribution of venturesome foreign capital as well worth the interest and dividends paid on it. Relative to export earnings, the burden of debt service had not greatly increased since the war. Over half the foreign investment in the country consisted of direct investment that would probably never have to be repaid. If Canada ever should become a mature debtor country, with interest, dividend, and amortization payments exceeding new receipts of capital, the free exchange rate, still equating *total* supplies of and demands for foreign exchange, would automatically solve the supposed problem of providing enough foreign exchange for the foreign remittances. Besides, asked the optimists, if an eventual cessation or reversal of the capital inflow is something to fear, why do anything to hasten the evil day, especially as long as foreign capital is still finding constructive employment?

Further reasons for worrying about the inflow of foreign capital—thus indirectly promoting the eventual shift in exchange-rate policy— were as much political and emotional as economic. Critics played on fear of foreign domination. They cited such facts as that U.S. investments in Canada amounted to over $17 billion and were growing by about $1 billion a year. Foreigners owned or controlled more than one-half of Canadian manufacturing, nearly two-thirds of all mining and smelting, and more than three-fourths of the petroleum and natural-gas industry. American corporations and their subsidiaries were accused of discriminating against Canadians in various ways. Though the best customer for U.S. manufactures, Canada was exporting much of its own produce in a raw or semifinished state for processing abroad. American investment was allegedly stifling industrial development, keeping Canada a mere "hewer of wood and drawer of water."

The Diefenbaker government felt heavy pressure to embrace economic nationalism and ward off further foreign capital, thereby presumably causing exchange depreciation as an easy answer to unemployment and other problems. The revised budget of December 1960 made mild—but only mild—concessions to this pressure. It withdrew the existing preferred tax treatment for earnings on foreign loans and investments in Canada and adopted tax incentives for private domestic investment. The Dominion government had already been exhorting provincial and municipal governments to reduce their bond issues in New York, and from early 1960 until late 1962, this type of borrowing virtually dried up.[31] Hindsight

28. More than 95 percent of Canada's exports entered Britain duty-free; under Common-Market tariff policy, only about 25 percent would. *Business Week*, 9 December 1961, p. 36.

29. Federal Reserve Bank of New York, *Monthly Review*, February 1961, pp. 23–24, summarizes some of the opposing views. A good example of the pessimistic view is Wm. Stix Wasserman's pamphlet, "A Study of the Canadian Dollar," New York: Wm. Stix Wasserman & Co., Inc., February 1961. Mr. W. Earle McLaughlin's speech already cited, pp. 9–14, is a good example of the optimistic view considered below.

30. It is hard to see, furthermore, why the system should have especially promoted capital movements in one direction only. Sohmen, *op. cit.*, p. 26.

31. Bank of Nova Scotia, *Monthly Review*, March 1963, p. 3.

makes one suspect a more direct though quiet alteration in exchange-rate policy, also, around the end of 1960: a $120 million rise in the official reserves during the first five months of 1961—a change exceeded (slightly) in only one of the full calendar years of the free-rate period—points to official intervention as what was keeping the premium on the Canadian dollar from rising more than fractionally above 1 U.S. cent.[32]

The most prominent advocate of more vigorous action against foreign investment was James E. Coyne, Governor of the Bank of Canada. Among other things, he proposed an increase in withholding taxes on foreign earnings. Measures to promote domestic saving and investment, including heavier taxes on luxury consumption and establishment of a National Development Corporation, would partially displace American capital, and higher tariffs would protect Canadian manufacturing. As for unemployment, Coyne felt that it was "structural." Monetary expansion and cheaper credit would not solve the problem but would promote inflation.[33] Any remedial increases in spending would have to be selective. The Bank of Canada had accordingly allowed the money supply to sag after the summer of 1958 and to recover by two years later to only just about the earlier level.[34] "With Mr. Coyne it appeared to be an article of faith that Canada's unemployment problem was not amenable to correction through an expansion of the money supply."[35] Many Canadian economists took a dimmer view of tight money, and a number of them sent a rather vaguely worded petition to the Finance Minister in December 1960 calling for Coyne's resignation. By the end of May 1961, Finance Minister Fleming apparently had concluded that Governor Coyne's many politically tinged public speeches advocating tight money and economic nationalism had invaded the government's prerogatives, and he called for Coyne's resignation. Coyne delayed resigning until July, after the Canadian Senate had given him what he considered a clean bill of health for his personal integrity in conducting the Bank's affairs.

Meanwhile, on June 20, the Finance Minister introduced his delayed budget for the fiscal year ending March 31, 1962. It eliminated the excise tax on automobiles, boosted depreciation allowances on new plant and equipment, and gave tax incentives for scientific research. Altogether, the budget cut taxes by some $101 million annually and increased government spending. Canada was to run an administrative deficit of $650 million in fiscal 1961–1962, almost double that of the year before, and the cash deficit was to be about $1 billion, or more than triple the preceding year's. Further to stimulate business activity (as well as to discourage capital inflow), interest rates were to be brought down. Fleming saw no danger of inflation as long as heavy unemployment persisted, along with excess capacity in several industries. Further adjustments were made in taxes on foreign investment earnings, but the budget included no provisions for direct restrictions on foreign capital or for general tariff increases. It rejected outright economic nationalism.

In his budget speech, the Finance Minister also announced the government's intention to push the Canadian dollar to an unspecified but "significant" discount. Not only interest-rate cuts but also direct intervention by the Exchange Fund Account would be the method. Instead of just embarking on expansionary monetary and fiscal policy and letting the free exchange rate adapt, the government hoped to stimulate employment and production by artificially pressing the currency down. A new example was apparently at hand of the "competitive exchange depreciation" commonly but mistakenly said to have been a widespread practice in the 1930s.

Developments on the manipulated market

Even before Finance Minister Fleming confirmed the new policy, growing awareness of his controversy with Governor Coyne had affected the exchange market. The Canadian dollar had already been weakening fractionally during the first week and a half of June 1961. On Tuesday the 13th, when the controversy broke into the open, the market closed with the premium at ¾ of 1 U.S. cent, down from 1.2 cents the day before. By the end of the week the Canadian dollar was practically down to par for the first time since December 1955; in fact, it dipped briefly below par in the Montreal market on Friday the 16th. Prospects of Coyne's departure and the drop already begun in interest rates apparently prompted a rush to sell Canadian dollars, as well as pressure from leads and lags.[36]

A more dramatic change occurred the moming after Fleming's budget speech of Tuesday the 20th. The Canadian dollar dropped slightly more than 3 cents overnight. Its discount ranged from 3½ to 2¼ cents during the morning alone. Quotations rose on stocks of companies selling in export markets, particularly pulp and paper and gold companies.

Speculation continued to aid the new policy for a while; but the authorities did not rely on announcement effects alone, and over the entire month of June (two-thirds gone at the time of the change) official holdings of gold and U.S. dollars rose by $36 million. From July until late September, however, these reserves actually fell (mostly reflecting Canada's contribution to a British drawing on the International Monetary Fund), suggesting that no further official intervention was necessary to maintain the discount. Difficulties began late in September. Investors and merchants who had been waiting to see where the discount would settle apparently felt that the time had come to move funds into Canada. Official intervention kept the rate practically rigid at 97⅛ U.S. cents during almost all of October, and the external reserves rose $186 million during the month. On October 27, a mistaken impression that the rate would be allowed to float back upward forced the Exchange Fund Account to buy an estimated $50 million of U.S. dollars to maintain the discount.[37]

This decisive intervention, together with a reminder from the Finance Minister that the rate might be pushed still lower, turned the tide.[38] From then on, in fact, the Canadian dollar sagged from an average of 97.1 U.S. cents in October 1961 to an average of 95¼ cents the following April. Preventing any larger depreciation cost $516 million, or practically one-fourth of the official reserves, between the end of October and the end of April. Around the turn of the year, when the Canadian dollar stood at a discount of slightly more than 4 cents, the Canadian government would apparently have liked to see the rate stabilize on its own. The government's silence about how low a rate it wanted contributed, however, to reduced demand for and increased supply of Canadian dollars. Experienced bankers saw signs of bearish leads and lags.[39]

Early in April 1962, at the time of the annual budget message, the government reaffirmed its intention not to set a fixed rate through "any hasty action which might prove premature or impossible to sustain."[40] The speculative outflow of funds continued. What

had begun early in 1961 as an operation to depress the Canadian dollar had changed, one year later, into an uncomfortable support operation. "The decisive and most devastating blow" came from short selling by Canadians rather than Americans. When Canadians' confidence in their own currency weakened, a "marked reduction in the exchange rate be-

32. Artus, *op. cit.*, p. 362, also infers that "the Canadian authorities . . . moved away from a true floating rate" after the latter part of 1960. Other authors finding reasons for dating the end of the period of a genuinely free rate at around December 1960 include H. H. Binhammer, "Canada's Foreign Exchange Problems: A Review," *Kyklos*, **XVII**, 1964, pp. 645–646; and Alex N. McLeod, A *Critique of the Fluctuating-Exchange-Rate Policy in Canada*, New York University, *The Bulletin*, Nos. 34–35, April–June 1965, pp. 40–41. (McLeod believes that a 1960 mimeographed draft of his monograph had some influence on the decision to move away from a free rate.)

33. Facts on Coyne's views and his controversy with the government have been taken from Bank of Canada, *Annual Report* for 1960 (Ottawa: 1961) and from the already cited articles by Zänker and in the Federal Reserve Bank of New York's *Monthly Review* of February 1961, as well as from press items.

34. Plus or minus 1 or 2 percent. The ambiguity lies in the definition of the Canadian money supply held by the general public: holders of personal savings deposits are in practice allowed to write some checks against them. Money defined as including these deposits rose somewhat more than money defined as excluding them.

35. Artus, *op. cit.*, p. 367.

36. *New York Times*, 17 June 1961, pp. 25, 32.

37. A speech by the Finance Minister the day before had evidently been misinterpreted. See Marsh in Aliber, *op. cit.*, p. 143, and Alex N. McLeod in American Enterprise Institute for Public Policy Research, *International Payments Problems*, Washington: AEI, 1966, p. 103.

38. In addition to the usual statistical sources, see *Wall Street Journal*, 7 November 1961, p. 13, and *Business Week*, 11 November 1961, p. 138.

39. *Wall Street Journal*, 16 April 1962, pp. 1, 6.

40. *Ibid.*, p. 1.

came inevitable."[41] On May 2, the Canadian government devalued its currency by 2.9 percent from the prevailing market rate to a new fixed parity of 92.5 U.S. cents. Finance Minister Fleming noted that the move had been precipitated by speculative pressures and by the International Monetary Fund's urging that Canada peg its dollar.[42]

Significance of fixing the rate

That action brought rejoicing in the IMF, the Organisation for Economic Co-operation and Development, and the U.S. Treasury. "Joy shall be in heaven over one sinner that repenteth, more than over ninety and nine just persons, which need no repentance."[43] Respectability had triumphed. *Business Week's* issue of May 12 (p. 44) saw abandonment of the fluctuating rate as a confession that "Canada's experiment had proved a failure." So, years later, did the Swiss banker Max Iklé; for if it "had proved successful, it would surely have been continued. Canada's example, therefore, does not speak in favor of flexible exchange rates."[44]

What is the supposed proof of failure? The much-deplored persistent current-account deficit during the free-rate period was actually the real counterpart of the inflow of foreign capital that had been contributing to Canadian development. The free rate had not been balancing the current account alone—nor does theory suggest that it should have—but it had been equilibrating *total* supplies and demands on the exchange market. Worry about the current account in particular is more relevant when the exchange rate is fixed and its tenability uncertain; it is hardly logical to appraise a free-rate system by criteria appropriate only to a different system. The worry about a future crisis when capital inflow might dwindle in the face of continuing interest and dividend outpayments was an *a priori* worry about the future, not a defect of the system already "proved" by experience. Political and emotional worries about excessive dependence on foreign capital certainly received much attention in Canada but were hardly relevant in appraising the performance of the exchange market.

As for problems related to unemployment and slow economic growth, expecting any particular exchange-rate system to solve them by itself was almost as naïve as expecting it to prevent alcoholism or juvenile delinquency.

The main thing a free exchange rate can be expected to do is to avoid balance-of-payments crises, without controls, and so clear the way for whatever policies seem best on domestic economic grounds. But doing that is doing a lot. Failure to make good use of this opportunity is essentially what the economist critics of Governor Coyne were complaining about.

Monetary restraint continued from 1957 to 1961 "in spite of growing unemployment. High interest rates attracted foreign capital and caused an appreciation of the Canadian dollar, which discouraged exports and encouraged imports when the state of the economy would have required opposite policies."[45] "The economic system worked much as theory suggests it should have[;] . . . the restrictive effects of tight monetary policies were increased."[46] Because the monetary policy thus being intensified happened to be an inappropriate one, "the whole floating-exchange-rate experiment fell into unwarranted discredit in the eyes of the Canadian authorities. . . ."[47]

A troublesome and unusually large spread of Canadian over U.S. interest rates toward the end of the free-rate period, though not actually intended, was partly a result of deliberate policy. A major refunding operation to lengthen the average life of the outstanding government debt had been attempted at an unfortunate time, in mid-1958. The bond market became demoralized; Coyne and the Bank of Canada, fearful of inflation, ceased cushioning bond prices in the open market; and for a year or so afterwards, the market appeared unresponsive to any official attempts to reduce interest rates significantly.[48] The resulting impact on capital flows and the exchange rate made it seem superficially plausible to blame "inadequate demand for domestic output . . . on foreign investment or foreign competition." The uneven incidence of weakness in demand, including the quite normal incidence of general unemployment on the least skilled workers in particular, lent plausibility to emphasis on structural maladjustments and inadequate training of labor. In the words of one observer, "errors in Canadian monetary policy [were] the sole (and insufficient) justification for the abandonment of the floating rate of exchange. . . ."[49]

Easier money and credit would have expanded the demand for Canadian goods and services and labor not only in the usual direct way but also through the effect of exchange depreciation on the current account. Instead of spelling manipulation, this depreciation would simply have meant a free-market balancing of exchange supply and demand in the light of the total economic situation, with domestic policy one of its facets. Recognizing this is not to hail easy money under free exchange rates as a cure-all. The Canadian trouble with unemployment and slackened growth may indeed have been partly "structural," possibly involving the pattern of the labor supply and the country's vulnerability to shifts in foreign demand because of its close gearing into the world economy and particularly the U.S. economy. The important freedom to manage the overall level of demand cannot,·after all, make shifts in the *composition* of demand harmless, nor can it dispel any domestic dilemma of having to choose between unemployment and inflation.[50]

As for the performance of the exchange market itself, narrowly considered, the evidence already shown for the period up to early 1961 is reassuring. The speculation and crises and alternation of heavy gains and losses of external reserves that then followed in the 11 months before adoption of the new fixed parity occurred under a regime of officially manipulated flexible rates, *not* of free rates. This distinction is crucial, yet often missed.[51] Once again, as in France in 1936–1938, experience showed the absurdity of classifying the two flexible-rate regimes together and comparing this blurry hybrid concept with fixed rates. In important respects, on the contrary, a rate manipulated to the extent of actually being fixed and a flexibly manipulated rate have more in common with each other than either has with a free rate. It is important to be clear about *what* system had "failed" by May 1962.

Like the troubles before October 1950, troubles experienced in the foreign-exchange market after official manipulation began in

41. George H. Chittenden, speech reprinted in *Morgan Guaranty Survey*, April 1963, p. 8. Cf. Bank for International Settlements, 32nd *Annual Report*, p. 150.

42. *Wall Street Journal*, May 4, 1962, p. 20.

43. *Wall Street Journal*, 4 May 1962, p. 20; A. F. Wynne Plumptre, *Exchange-Rate Policy: Experience with Canada's Floating Rate*, Princeton Essays in International Finance, No. 81, Princeton, N.J.: Princeton University, June 1970, p. 8 (where a variant appears of the passage from Luke 15).

44. Iklé in Halm, ed., *op. cit.*, p. 194.

45. Editor's summary, p. 332, of Marsh's argument in Halm, *op. cit.*

46. Wonnacott, *The Floating Canadian Dollar* (1972), p. 30. On the theory of how a floating exchange rate intensifies the domestic impact of monetary policy, recall pp. 114, 198.

47. Ronald I. McKinnon and Wallace E. Oates, *The Implications of International Economic Integration for Monetary, Fiscal, and Exchange-Rate Policy*, Princeton Studies, No. 16, Princeton, N.J.: Princeton University, 1966, p. 28. Dunn, *op. cit.*, pp. 60–61, explains his own very similar diagnosis: the Canadian authorities acted with a general lack of understanding of the relations between a flexible exchange rate, monetary policy, and the business cycle. "Virtually all of the students of Canada's history with a flexible rate conclude that the difficulties of 1958–62 [sic] were not the fault of the system, but instead grew out of a series of unfortunate or perhaps disastrous policy decisions in Ottawa." P. 60n.

48. Artus, *op. cit.*, pp. 364–365, 367.

49. Harry C. Eastman, Review of Harry G. Johnson, *Canada in a Changing World Economy*, Toronto: University of Toronto Press, 1962, in *American Economic Review*, LII, December 1962, p. 1172. As Harry Johnson put it, "the Canadian return to a fixed exchange rate . . . involved a failure of governmental competence, not of the floating rate system. . . ." "The International Competitive Position of the United States and the Balance of Payments Prospect for 1968," *Review of Economics and Statistics*, XLVI, February 1964, p. 28.

50. McIvor, *op. cit.*, p. 249, mentions some of the special limitations on Canadian monetary autonomy.

51. Belief in stabilizing speculation could find little support, wrote Hal B. Lary, in Canada's experience before May 1962. "Its difficulties, first in depressing the Canadian dollar from a level deemed too high and then in preventing the fall, once it had started, from becoming excessive, show how drastically private evaluations and behavior can shift." *Problems of the United States as World Banker and Trader*, Princeton, N.J.: Princeton University Press for the National Bureau of Economic Research, 1963, p. 112. "[I]n the popular view, and even in the official view," even the exchange crisis that followed the repegging "is usually considered to be the inevitable result of weaknesses inherent in a floating exchange-rate system!" Marsh in Aliber, *op. cit.*, p. 144.

1961 and after the repegging in 1962 made the performance of the free exchange rate look good by contrast. For some time, the new policy did not even bring greater exchange-rate stability. In the 12 months after May 1961, the Canadian rate fell 9½ percent. The spread between calendar-year highest and lowest Canadian quotations on the U.S. dollar reached 6 percent of the year's average in 1961 (larger than the spread in *any* of the full years of free rates) and 4.4 percent in 1962 (larger than the average of the spreads in the 10 full years of free rates).

The crisis of 1962

Canada was not yet out of the woods. The exchange rate was permitted to fluctuate in a narrow range around the new 92.5-cent par. By the middle of May 1962 it stood below 92 cents. Only support from the official reserves, which shrank $102 million in May alone, kept the rate from sinking below 91¾¢. During just three weeks of June the government had to spend over a third of its remaining unborrowed reserves to buy Canadian dollars unloaded by speculators.[52] Another ironic example was at hand of official action to depress the Canadian dollar overshooting the mark through its effect on expectations; the authorities were having to struggle to keep the rate from falling further than they had desired. Even the International Monetary Fund, hardly likely to exaggerate the difficulties of a return to its fold, described "the speculative flow of funds out of Canada" as the "most serious instance of a disequilibrating movement of short-term funds" occurring during the period covered by its 1963 *Annual Report* (p. 5).

The June 1962 elections kept the Conservatives in office precariously, without an absolute majority in Parliament. Immediately afterwards the government took emergency action. It cut the duty-free exemption on purchases brought home by returning Canadian tourists from $300 to $75 a year and imposed surcharges ranging from 5 to 15 percent on about half of Canada's imports.[53] Fiscal and monetary policy tightened. Cuts in government spending amounting to $250 million in the fiscal year were scheduled. The Bank of Canada strove for higher interest rates to attract a big enough capital inflow to cover the current-account deficit and help rebuild reserves. Its discount rate, which since November 1956 had been set every week at ¼ of 1 percentage point above the market-determined fluctuating tender rate on Treasury bills, was raised on June 24 to a fixed 6 percent. This and other measures caused a conspicuous upward bulge for several months in the time-series chart of yields on government securities of various maturities. To keep yields from coming down again too far and too quickly when their high levels began stimulating non-bank security purchases, the authorities let the tightening of liquidity force banks to run down their own security holdings.[54] Another indicator of relatively tight money in 1962 was the mere 3½ percent growth in the money supply (more or less, depending on whether or not personal savings deposits are included); this compares with growth rates of either 8.7 or 12.4 percent in 1961 and either 6.8 or 7.2 percent in 1963 (depending on the same matter of definition).

In September, amidst signs that the emergency program was affecting the balance of payments as desired, monetary policy shifted toward ease. The authorities began replenishing bank liquidity. A series of cuts carried the Bank of Canada's discount rate down to 4 percent in November 1962 and 3½ percent in May 1963. (It went back to 4 percent in August 1963 in response to developments in the United States—a rise in the Federal Reserve discount rate and threats of other measures to discourage capital outflow.) Meanwhile, Canada had seen the ironic adoption of *contractionary* monetary and fiscal policies to cope with an emergency stemming from official action to depreciate the Canadian dollar, in turn undertaken in hopes of *expanding* employment and production.

Besides resorting to special tariffs and financial tightness, Canada obtained $1050 million in foreign credits at the time of the crisis in June—$300 million worth of European currencies from the International Monetary Fund, a $400 million line of credit from the Export-Import Bank, and credits of $250 million and $100 million under reciprocal currency arrangements with the Federal Reserve System and the Bank of England.

The package of measures brought confidence in the devalued Canadian dollar. The flows of both long-term and short-term capital turned heavily inward, far exceeding the deficit on current account and causing Canada's external reserves to increase by more during the second half of 1962 than they had fallen in the first half. (This contrast holds true whether or not changes reflecting the foreign credits are counted.) The bilateral credit arrangements (as distinguished from the IMF drawing) made in June were all terminated or converted to stand-bys by the end of 1962.

Further experience with the repegged rate

The emergency of the first half of 1962 had been largely psychological, involving speculation first on official manipulation of the flexible exchange rate and then, in May and June, on possible collapse of the new parity. Fundamentally, the 92½-cent parity more probably undervalued than overvalued the Canadian dollar. Most of the time until official support limits were again abolished in 1970, the Canadian dollar fluctuated against the U.S. dollar in the upper half of its band. The balance of payments was in official-settlements surplus (with capital inflow outweighing a current-account deficit), and the official international reserves were growing in each year but one. In 1966 the reserves sank by 11 percent. Instead of a crisis, that reserve loss reflected official purchases of securities, including Canadian securities held abroad, as well as outflows of bank funds, largely in response to an unusual rise of U.S. short-term interest rates above the Canadian level.[55] The uptrend of reserves in the 1960s contrasts with their near-steadiness at around US$2 billion in the free-rate period.

After the 1962 crisis blew over, notable bearish pressures on the fixed rate occurred only during brief periods when U.S. balance-of-payments programs[56] were thought to apply to Canada. In July 1963, when President Kennedy proposed an Interest Equalization Tax on American purchases of foreign securities, a wave of apprehension swept through Canadian financial markets; and the Exchange Fund Account suffered substantial losses. After urgent consultations, the U.S. Administration agreed to exempt new Canadian issues. In return, Canada declared that it neither desired nor intended to increase its foreign-exchange reserves through borrowing in the United States. In 1965, after the United States government imposed "voluntary" guidelines for capital

movements, Canada again received an exemption in return for a further commitment to limit the growth of its international reserves.[57]

Only the events of early 1968 deserve the label "crisis." Although sterling's devaluation in November 1967 posed no immediate threat, it contributed to general exchange-rate uncertainty that eventually spread to Canada. After President Johnson announced mandatory controls over capital movements on January 1, commentators exaggerated the program's probable impact on Canada. Already there had been considerable talk in Canada about an ultimate need for devaluation if inflation were not kept under control, and newspaper headlines did not always distinguish between what might "ultimately" happen and what might "immediately" happen. In February Canada's minority government suffered temporary defeat on a tax-increase bill. A worldwide rush into gold was gathering momentum. Concern arose about substantial transfers of funds out of Canada by U.S. corporations. American banks were making forward-exchange contracts with customers desiring to hedge their Canadian assets; and to protect themselves, the banks sold Canadian dollars spot. Reactions by Canadian importers contributed to the pressure. Speculators against the Canadian dollar saw a one-way option. Canada lost reserves heavily and drew on the IMF and on the Federal Reserve under its swap line. Canadian bank rate was raised to record levels of 7 percent on January 22 and 7.5 percent on March 15. On March 7 Canada was exempted from

52. *Wall Street Journal*, 7 December 1962, p. 1, puts the drain during these three weeks at $US400 million.

53. These surcharges were temporary and were finally removed in April 1963, after being gradually relaxed.

54. BIS, 33rd *Annual Report*, 1962–1963, pp. 70–71.

55. IMF, 1967, p. 84; BIS, 1966–1967, p. 130.

56. Described in Chapter 27.

57. Wonnacott, *The Floating Canadian Dollar* (1972), pp. 40–43.

substantially all U.S. controls on capital out-flows, agreeing in return to avoid being used as a conduit for funds moving from the United States to other foreign countries and also agreeing to invest all its U.S. dollar reserves, beyond working balances, in nonliquid U.S. government securities. On March 17 the international gold crisis ended in agreement on a two-tier market. These announcements, as well as the international assistance, restored confidence in the Canadian dollar.[58]

The crisis was an excellent example of speculation, unwarranted by fundamentals, directed against a pegged exchange rate. "The Canadian dollar was basically strong even during this period: speculation was based on a complete, and, in the event, costly misreading of Canada's real economic position."[59]

Before the end of 1968, the problem reversed itself into one of gains considered excessive in Canada's official external reserves. Until then, Canada's commitment to limit her gains (given in return for exemptions from U.S. capital-export restrictions), together with the fixed exchange rate, had tended to inhibit tight monetary policies in Canada. The substitute had been a series of expedients "which kept the Canadian exchange rate pegged, and thus prevented an appreciation which would have partially offset the domestic inflationary effects of domestic policies." In 1968 Canada's borrowings outside the United States soared to $540 million because of tight money in North America and relatively greater supplies of funds in Europe. In this changed situation, Canada's steps to discourage capital inflow could work against the U.S. objective "of reducing European holdings of U.S. dollars. Also, incidentally, they could cause a statistical deterioration in the U.S. liquidity balance, since Canada had undertaken to put her reserves in excess of working balances into nonliquid U.S. government securities." Toward the end of the year, continuing reserve increases and the existence of the upper reserve target were threatening severe limitations on Canadian monetary policy. The U.S. Treasury then took note of the shift of Canadian borrowing to Europe, of Canada's need for flexible reserve levels to permit a domestically appropriate monetary policy, and of the altered U.S. stake in the matter. In effect, the United States no longer expected Canada to keep its reserves within a target limit.[60]

The Canadian balance of payments had been strengthening since the mid-1960s. The current account went from deficits of about US$1 billion in 1965 and 1966 to a surplus of roughly the same size in 1970. Canada continued to import growing amounts of long-term capital through 1969 (after which date government policy succeeded in restraining the inflow), but growing outflows of short-term capital maintained approximate equilibrium in the overall balance of payments from 1965 to 1969 and probably masked an increasing overvaluation of the Canadian dollar. Canada's reserves rose only slightly in 1967 and 1969 and rose substantially only in 1968. In 1970, however, the emerging Canadian surplus, with its implication of an undervalued Canadian dollar, became far more evident.[61]

Here, before we describe the events of 1970, is a good place for some generalizations about the repegged exchange rate. Only on brief occasions during the period did strong expectations prevail that the parity might soon be changed. In response to fluctuations of the spot exchange rate within its official band, as earlier in response to free fluctuations, capital movements were generally stabilizing. On the other hand, reported gains and losses of official reserves (especially as adjusted for government purchases of World Bank bonds made to conceal reserve gains) appeared to provoke short-term capital inflows and outflows respectively; that is, reserve gains were seen as bullish and losses as bearish signs for the Canadian dollar. "Although short-term capital flows tended to reinforce the stability of the exchange rate during the fixed-rate period," econometric work by Caves and Reuber provides "some evidence of their potentially destabilizing tendencies in their response to recently reported changes in Canada's official reserves."[62]

Caves and Reuber doubt whether the repegging of the Canadian dollar improved the integration of the U.S. and Canadian capital markets. On the contrary, flows of portfolio capital apparently became *less* sensitive to changes in U.S. and Canadian interest rates, suggesting that "the fixed rate increased uncertainty about the expected yields of international transactions," since the effective yields involve not only interest rates but also the exchange rate "and various rationing constraints." The reduced "sensitivity and reliability of the response of capital flows to the price of loanable funds . . . seems hardly consistent with the virtues of financial integration which have been alleged to flow from fixed exchange rates." Although the increased uncertainty may have stemmed partly from occasional flurries of exchange-rate speculation, most of it seems to have resulted from policies adopted by the United States and Canada to defend their fixed parities. For example, when President Kennedy proposed the Interest Equalization Tax, uncertainty prevailed for a while about whether or not Canadian security issues would be exempt. After its enactment in 1964, with the Canadian exemption, some catch-up in Canadian borrowing occurred. After U.S. capital controls were tightened early in 1968, the exemption in Canada's favor was made contingent on Canada's taking steps to avoid serving as an intermediary for transmission of U.S. short-term funds to Europe and on investment of official reserve gains in long-term U.S. and World Bank bonds. Beyond adopting these and less significant measures, both governments, throughout the period, subjected borrowers and lenders to moral suasion and jawboning.[63]

Floating again

Events pointing to the Canadian dollar's undervaluation at 92½ cents came to a head in 1970. They were a replay of what had happened 20 years before. Then, however, the upward pressures had resulted essentially from large capital inflows, whereas the pressures of 1970 were broadly based. Historically, Canada had run a deficit on current account, the most recent surplus coming in 1952. From a deficit of about US$0.9 billion in 1969, 1970 brought a sharp swing to a surplus of US$1 billion (more or less, depending on the concept employed). The swing was especially striking in merchandise trade, which registered a surplus of nearly US$3.0 billion for 1970 as a whole. Most types of goods contributed to a strong export expansion, thanks partly to continuing effects of the U.S.–Canada automotive agreement of 1965 and to more buoyant demand in overseas markets than in Canada. Although the inflow of long-term capital was smaller in 1970 as a whole than in 1969, it was strong, at US$595 million, in the first quarter. In the second quarter the capital inflow took on a short-term, speculative character. The Canadian dollar rose close to its upper intervention

point, and the authorities had to buy large amounts of foreign exchange. The increase in net official foreign assets in the first five months of the year came to $0.9 billion, and a further $0.4 billion was bought for future delivery. The reserve growth threatened a faster and more extreme domestic monetary expansion than the Canadian authorities considered appropriate. The very announcement of May's particularly heavy reserve gains would probably flag on the speculators.[64]

Accordingly, effective Monday, June 1, Canada returned to a fluctuating exchange

58. IMF, 1968, pp. 49–50; IMF, 1969, p. 73; Wonnacott, *The Floating Canadian Dollar*, pp. 43–44; and esp. W. Earle McLaughlin, "The State of the Canadian Union," address delivered to The Canada Club, London, November 13, 1968, duplicated by the Royal Bank of Canada.

59. Marsh in Halm, *op. cit.*, p. 341n.

60. Wonnacott, *The Floating Canadian Dollar*, pp. 39, 44–46. Although the source is not explicit, the figure quoted is apparently in U.S. dollars.

61. Andrew F. Brimmer in *Canadian-United States Financial Relationships*, Boston: Federal Reserve Bank of Boston, 1972, pp. 59–61.

Conceptual or other differences cause discrepancies among Brimmer's balance-of-payments figures and those appearing in *International Financial Statistics*, July 1972 and July 1973, and Organisation for Economic Co-operation and Development, *OECD Economic Surveys—Canada*, Paris: OECD, 1973 (hereafter cited as *OECD*), pp. 38, 90. The general picture of the trend, however, is unaffected.

62. Richard E. Caves and Grant L. Reuber, "International Capital Markets and Canadian Economic Policy Under Flexible and Fixed Exchange Rates, 1951–1970," in *Canadian-United States Financial Relationships*, esp. p. 32.

63. *Ibid.*, especially pp. 27–28, 32–35. See also the concurring comments by Ronald Jones, pp. 42–43, and Robert Mundell, p. 54, in the same volume.

64. BIS, 1970–1971, pp. 32, 64, 96–98, 140, 144; Wonnacott, *The Floating Canadian Dollar*, pp. 61–63; Dunn, *op. cit.*, pp. 67–69. According to Dunn, the Bank of Canada had to buy "over $1 billion in foreign exchange in the spot market and an undetermined amount forward during the first five months of 1970."

rate.[65] Especially in view of the fact that the government had forced the Canadian dollar *down* in 1961–1962 as part of a package of policies for dealing with heavy unemployment, it might seem odd that the government allowed the rate to float *up* at a time when unemployment was again a problem. The government, however, faced a dilemma. Unemployment and inflation had coexisted as major problems since 1967. Far from being part of an overall restrictive policy, the upward float of 1970 was part of a change in the policy mix. The tight fiscal and monetary policies that had been pursued were relaxed. The degree and pace of relaxation were to suit domestic conditions, however, and not be forced by further gains of external reserves. In addition, it was hoped, the direct linkage of foreign and Canadian prices at a higher value of the Canadian dollar would put some direct restraint on increases, much as a price-and-incomes policy might have done. It may be more than coincidence that the rise of the Canadian consumer price index did slow down for several months after June 1970.[66]

Immediately after being unpegged, the Canadian dollar jumped to between 97 and 98 U.S. cents and then fluctuated rather markedly before settling down in late June to a little above 96½ cents. It began rising again in July, peaked at above 99 cents in mid-September, then sagged and moved narrowly at around 98 cents before rising to close the year 1970 above 99 cents. It reached equality with the U.S. dollar in February 1971. Subsequent reductions in Canadian interest rates, together with increases in U.S. and Eurodollar rates, brought the Canadian dollar below 99 U.S. cents late in May and to a low of around 97½ cents in mid-June. The Canadian–U.S. exchange rate showed only slight response to the monetary shocks of 1971; but official holdings of U.S. dollars did rise 34.4 percent over the course of the year, mostly in the second half. The rate rose from almost 99 cents just before to practically 99½ cents just after the U.S. actions of mid-August, easing to 98½ cents later in the month on fears about how the U.S. import surcharge would affect Canadian trade. The two dollars reached equality again late in October; and immediately before the Smithsonian Agreement, the Canadian dollar stood at a half-cent premium. Unlike most other major currencies, it was not then fixed at a new parity. After sinking slightly below US$1.00

early in 1972, it strengthened again in March and in midyear was standing at a premium of 1½ cents. Through the summer and early fall the rate moved narrowly between 101½ and 101¾ cents. Although the Canadian current account had returned to deficit[67] and although Canadian money-market interest rates had become generally lower than those elsewhere, long-term capital inflows continued to support the Canadian dollar. The outcome of the October 30 election, in which no party won a clear majority, and expectations that the minority government would pursue more expansionary policies in response to the voters' evident concerns, as well as moderate cuts by Canadian banks in the interest rates they paid on certificates of deposit, contributed to weakening the Canadian dollar. The rate sank to 99¾ cents on December 7 before partially recovering. By early 1973 the rate had settled at around $1.00. Partly because of expectations of expansionary domestic policies, the Canadian dollar was largely ignored amidst bullish speculation on European currencies and the yen. After the U.S. devaluation in February, official intervention absorbed a spurt of demand for Canadian dollars. After reaching 101¼ cents, the rate bottomed out just below 100¾ cents, closing February at that level.[68] Despite the vicissitudes of the U.S. dollar in the ensuing months, the rate between the two dollars remained very close to one-for-one. Beginning late in 1973, a renewed rise brought the Canadian dollar to a peak monthly average of 104.1 U.S. cents in April 1974.

The Canadian authorities were continuing an intervention policy announced at the very beginning of the float in 1970: they would resist what they considered undue oscillations of the Canadian dollar, particularly in the upward direction. To judge from end-of-year and end-of-quarter exchange rates and reserve figures, intervention tended more often to resist than to reinforce rate movements, and the Canadian dollar was more often tending upward than downward against the U.S. dollar (a mild downdrift from late 1972 to late 1973 providing the main exception). From mid-1970 (one month after the unpegging) through September 1974, the Canadian dollar appreciated by 4.93 percent, this rise being restrained by a 34.1 percent rise in the country's international reserves and a 41.1 percent rise in official holdings of U.S. dollars specifically. Besides intervening directly, the Canadian au-

thorities repeatedly exhorted provincial governments and other Canadian borrowers to use
the Canadian capital market rather than New
York. In addition, the Bank of Canada pursued an interest-rate policy intended to discourage recourse to the U.S. capital market. In
effect, the Canadian dollar followed the U.S.
dollar in its devaluations of 1971 and 1973
against the currencies of both countries' major
overseas trading partners. The Canadian dollar
of the early 1970s, unlike the dollar of the
1950s, was *not* an essentially free-floating currency.[69]

---

65. In taking that anti-inflationary step, said
Mundell, Canada did what other major countries
were forced to do the following year and what she
herself should have done earlier. An upward-floating
rate would have spared Canada the world inflation
of 1965–1970. By holding the rate, Canada "accepted the world inflation until 1970. By that time
prospects for stopping inflation internationally did
not appear any better than in the preceding years;
the fight against inflation had been lost and new
inflationary expectations had set in." Robert Mundell in *Canadian-United States Financial Relationships*, p. 45.

66. This is Paul Wonnacott's interpretation of
the policy; *The Floating Canadian Dollar*, pp. 63–
72, 79, 95.

67. This shift reflected a merchandise trade surplus only half as large in 1972 as in 1970 and was
no doubt fostered by the appreciation of the Canadian dollar above its old 92.5-cent parity, though
a business upswing in Canada and strikes that
harmed exports were also at work. BIS, 1972–1973,
p. 92; *OECD*, p. 37.

68. BIS, 1970–1971, p. 151; BIS, 1971–1972,
pp. 138–139; Charles Coombs in Federal Reserve
Bank of New York, *Monthly Review*, March 1973,
pp. 63–64; and *International Financial Statistics*.

69. The figures used appear in *International
Financial Statistics*. Statements on intervention
policy are quoted and episodes of intervention are
mentioned in Wonnacott, *The Floating Canadian
Dollar*, pp. 72–85. *OECD*, pp. 45, 49, 53, also
mentions the use of domestic interest-rate policy to
resist unwanted appreciation of the Canadian dollar.

CHAPTER TWENTY-SEVEN

The United States Balance of Payments

The large gains of gold and dollars that helped Western Europe back to external currency convertibility at the end of 1958 mirrored a deterioration in the balance of payments of the United States. After several years of worry about a supposed "dollar shortage" (canvassed in the appendix to this chapter), its opposite began causing alarm. A review of these developments and of policies for dealing with them will lead into questions of diagnosis of the U.S. deficit and of lessons that might emerge.

From the War to the mid-1960s

Tables 27-1 and 27.2 serve as reference. Over the first four postwar years, merchandise exports totaled more than twice as much as imports. The export/import ratio fluctuated comfortably over 100 percent from 1950 through 1964. Beginning with 1965 it fell steadily, except for mild recovery in 1970, and fell under 100 percent in 1971. The current-account balance covers trade in commodities and services, including military transactions and earnings on international investments, as well as pensions, nonmilitary foreign aid, and other private and governmental transfers. Whether in surplus or deficit, the current balance always amounted to less than 1 percent

of gross national product after the 1940s, and often to much less. After the 1940s, the merchandise and current accounts both appeared exceptionally strong in 1956–1957 and 1960–1964 and exceptionally weak in 1950, 1953, and 1959. After the mid-1960s their weakness became the rule rather than the exception. The basic balance is the current-account balance less the excess of outflow over inflow of private and government long-term capital. This net long-term capital flow always was outward; yet in only a few years—1950, 1953, 1958–1959, 1971–1972—did a basic deficit exceed one-half of 1 percent of GNP. By and large, the basic balance shows relatively great strength or weakness in the same years as the merchandise and current accounts.

Short-term capital flows, including those concealed under errors and omissions, are reflected in the overall balance. As measures of it, the tables use the balance on official reserve transactions, also called "official settlements," and the gross or net liquidity balance, all as defined in Chapter 3.[1] From 1960 to 1969, the ORT balance oscillated widely on a generally improving trend, followed by massive deterioration. (Official ORT figures are not published for each year before 1960.) The gross liquidity balance, after recovering in 1951 from an exceptional $3.5 billion deficit in 1950, deteriorated to 1953, improved to 1957, and deteriorated to 1960. After oscillating but generally improving in 1961 through 1968, it deteriorated sharply in 1969 and again in 1971. The net liquidity balance, for which figures begin in 1960, oscillated with some trend toward improvement around an average of $2.8 billion from then through 1968, then deteriorated sharply.[2]

Over the four years 1946–1949, the U.S. surplus on goods-and-services transactions totaled over $32 billion. Even granting aid and loans amounting to over $26 billion, the United States added almost $6 billion to its external reserves.[3]

The devaluation of most foreign currencies late in 1949 was eventually to prove a crucial turning point for the dollar. The United States was usually in external deficit thereafter, losing gold and building up liabilities to foreign official institutions. The devaluations were not the only reason, however, why the overall, basic, and current-account balances shifted sharply into deficit in 1950 and why falling exports and rising imports brought a $4.2 billion drop in the merchandise trade surplus. The trade shift owed much to the Korean War and to the continuation of postwar readjustments.

Deficits averaging about $1.2 billion a year on the official-settlements basis ($1.5 billion on the gross liquidity basis) over the period 1950–1956 showed no clear trend up or down and caused no alarm. They were attributed to the exchange-rate changes, to direct and indirect effects of the Korean War, and to U.S. government loans and grants, which exceeded them in size. Most countries were aiming at some growth of their dollar reserves in step with their external transactions. Redistribution of gold away from the United States was considered a healthy development. The dollar hardly seemed overvalued up to and beyond the middle 1950s. On the contrary, theories of chronic dollar shortage—of a chronic tendency toward *surplus* in the U.S. balance of payments—were still being implemented overseas in widespread discriminations against imports from the dollar area and still remained fashionable in academic circles. Well into the 1950s the world's early postwar thirst for U.S. goods persisted with relative disregard for price; and U.S. exports responded to the supply of dollars furnished by U.S. imports and foreign aid.

Trade, current-account, and overall surpluses in 1957 were large and freakish. The closing of the Suez Canal the year before boosted oil and agricultural exports. The European reconstruction boom was reaching its climax, furthermore, while the American economy was turning into recession.

The years 1958–1968 contrasted dramatically with 1950–1957. The yearly average overall (ORT) deficit nearly doubled, from $0.9 billion in the earlier to $1.7 billion in the later period. A change in merchandise trade dominated the sharp worsening of 1958. The balance worsened further in 1959 as exports remained flat while imports rose. The deterioration in 1958–1959 from 1956–1957 seemed due basically but not solely to Europe's being in recession while the United States was recovering from recession. The reopening of the Suez Canal and the U.S. steel strike of 1959 were other influences. In addition, the jump in imports, particularly of cars, suggested that foreign countries had gained competitive strength during the 1950s. U.S. price trends from 1950 to 1957 had compared favorably with those of other industrial countries; but the others' wages, costs, and prices had been much lower to start with. Reconstructing rapidly, Europe and Japan gained the export capacity to derive a trade advantage from their lower price levels. At the exchange rates fixed in 1949, the United States could not afford the price increases of the Korean War years and of the 1955–1957 boom. In iron and steel, transport equipment, and machinery, for example, the rise of U.S. prices apparently contributed to declines in the U.S. shares of world exports.

The cyclical situation changed in 1960, when the United States again suffered recession while business expanded rapidly in Europe. U.S. exports spurted by 19.4 percent in value, aided by special factors affecting cotton, airplanes, and steel. Despite the strong recovery in trade, the overall (gross liquidity) balance registered a larger deficit in 1960 than ever before. A new element in the picture was a heavy outflow of short-term capital, mostly lending abroad by banks. The errors-and-omissions item, thought to consist mainly of unrecorded short-term capital flows, turned negative for the first time since 1950 (and, with two small exceptions, remained negative thereafter through 1973). The "gold rush" of October 1960 suggests that a significant body of

---

1. Since the growth of dollar balances held by private foreigners for transactions and liquidity purposes appears "below the line" in the calculation of the liquidity balance, the balance on official reserve transactions usually, before 1970, gave a better impression of the overall trend. Even so, the situation may often be obscured by shifts of funds between central banks and the private banking systems. Bank for International Settlements, 1967–1968, p. 29.

2. Words like "improve," "deteriorate," "strengthen," "weaken," "better," "worse," "favorable," and "unfavorable," used in connection with international trade and payments, admittedly may seem to convey questionable value judgments. Such judgments—for example, whether shrinkage of a trade deficit is good or bad—are not intended. Particularly in some of the remaining passages of this chapter, however, avoidance of the questionable words is not worth the awkward style that would result.

3. BIS, 1971–1972, p. 3. Chapter I of this *Annual Report*, entitled "The Crisis of the Dollar and the Monetary System," conveniently assembles many of the historical facts mentioned in the following pages.

TABLE 27.1. *United States balance of payments, 1950–1973*

Items (net *credit or debit*, except that exports and imports of merchandise are shown separately)	YEARS OR ANNUAL AVERAGES						
	1950–59	1960–64	1965–69	1970	1971	1972	1973
	(*billions of dollars*)						
Merchandise trade							
Exports	14.8	21.7	31.3	42.0	42.8	48.8	70.3
Imports	−11.8	−16.2	−28.5	−39.8	−45.5	−55.8	−69.8
Military transactions	−2.3	−2.4	−2.9	−3.4	−2.9	−3.6	−2.2
Travel and transportation	−0.3	−1.1	−1.6	−2.1	−2.3	−3.1	−2.7
Investment income, fees, and royalties	2.1	3.9	5.7	6.3	8.0	7.9	8.5
Other services and transfers	−0.5	−0.6	−0.7	−0.8	−1.9	−1.8	−1.7
U.S. government nonmilitary grants	−2.0	−1.9	−1.7	−1.7	−2.0	−2.2	−1.9
Balance on current account	−0.1	3.3	1.4	0.4	−3.8	−9.8	0.5
Long-term capital flows							
Official	−0.4	−1.0	−1.9	−2.0	−2.4	−1.3	−1.5
Private	−1.3	−2.9	−1.8	−1.4	−4.4	−0.1	0.1
Basic balance	−1.9	−0.7	−2.3	−3.1	−10.6	−11.2	−0.9
Short-term private capital flows	0.3	−0.5	3.1	−6.5	−10.1	2.0	−1.8
Errors and omissions	0.3	−1.0	−0.9	−1.2	−9.8	−1.8	−2.6
Allocations of SDRs	—	—	—	0.9	0.7	0.7	—
Official-reserve-transactions balance	−1.3	−2.2	−0.0	−9.8	−29.8	−10.4	−5.3

NOTE: Addition may not be exact because of rounding. "Other services and transfers" is calculated as a residual for 1971–1973.

SOURCES: Bank for International Settlements, *Forty-Second Annual Report*, Basel: 1972, p. 4; *Economic Report of the President together with the Annual Report of the Council of Economic Advisers*, Washington: Government Printing Office, 1973, pp. 293–294, 1974, pp. 350, 351; *Survey of Current Business*, March 1973, pp. 23, 31, September 1974, pp. 35ff., S-3.

opinion considered the deficits of 1958–1960 (averaging almost $3 billion on the official-settlements basis and $3.6 billion on the gross-liquidity basis) to be more than cyclical and chance aberrations and considered the dollar overvalued and its devaluation more than a theoretical possibility.

Private long-term capital outflows had already become substantial in the late 1950s. After averaging $0.7 billion a year in 1950 through 1955, the excess of long-term outflows over inflows jumped to averages of $2.3 billion in 1956–1959 and $3.1 billion in 1960–1967, before imposition of mandatory controls.[4] The development of overseas raw-materials sources, reconstruction and active prosperity in Europe and elsewhere, the formation of the Common Market, and greater confidence in political stability created investment opportunities or incentives for American business at a time when most of the world outside the United States was still short of capital. The return to convertibility of the chief European currencies at the end of 1958 also improved the climate and scope for international capital movements. Capital flows became more sensitive to interest-rate differentials, which partly explains the recurrence of sizable short-term movements. These economic and political developments during the middle and late 1950s were to show their full impact on capital movements only in the 1960s.[5]

The trade surplus recovered from the depressed $1.1 billion of 1959 to an average of

$5.4 billion in 1960–1964. Europe was in sustained boom for most of this period, while U.S. recovery from the 1960–1961 recession was sluggish. Exports also benefited from growing "tied" aid grants and loans, from milder price inflation in the United States than abroad, and from occasional bad harvests abroad. Rising foreign-investment earnings also helped improve the current account. Most but not all of this improvement was offset by larger outflows of short- and long-term capital. After averaging $2.7 billion in 1958–1959 and reaching $3.4 billion in 1960, the deficit on official reserve transactions fell to an average of $1.9 billion in 1961–1964. Some of this apparent improvement traces to advance repayments of long-term debt to the United States undertaken to narrow the overall deficit.[6]

Table 27.3 compares the relatively satisfactory first half of the 1960s with the years that preceded and followed. The basic balance, which includes long-term capital movements, was worse than the current account by 0.43 percent of GNP in 1951–1959, by 0.70 percent in 1960–1964, and by 0.48 percent in 1965–1969. Thus, the greater strength of the basic balance in 1960–1964 than before and after was more than entirely due to the current account.

Though smaller in 1961–1965 than in 1958–1960 in particular, the overall deficit remained substantial. The dollar remained under pressure in the foreign-exchange markets, and foreign central banks absorbed sizable amounts. Nevertheless, the decline in U.S. gold reserves was much smaller on the average in 1961–1965 than in 1958–1960. Other countries, with the notable exception of France, hesitated to rock the boat by converting dollars into gold. On balance, the United States even gained gold from the operations of the gold pool, which had been formed in the wake of the 1960 gold rush.[7] Several notable steps were taken in the early 1960s to hold down gold losses, including formation of the inter-central-bank swap network, the start of Treasury and Federal Reserve intervention in the exchange markets, the issue of marketable securities denominated in foreign currencies (Roosa bonds), advance repayment of long-term debts to the United States by several European countries, removal of the interest-rate ceiling on time deposits held in the United States by foreign official institutions, and occasional drawings on the U.S. gold tranche in the International Monetary Fund.[8] In 1961 (or

late 1960), furthermore, "Operation Twist" began—an experiment in holding long-term interest rates down to benefit domestic investment while holding short-term interest rates up to safeguard the balance-of-payments against short-term capital flows. The experiment met with only limited success. Domestic lenders and borrowers moved freely enough between long-term and short-term securities to bar any substantial twist of the rate structure; and long-term capital, though less so than short-term capital, was growing more internationally mobile.[9] In 1963–64 an Interest Equalization Tax (see p. 429) began penalizing capital outflows.

The year 1964 was unusual, a burst of sunshine before the storm. Thanks partly to inflationary demand and a poor agricultural season in Europe,[10] the United States ran the largest surpluses on merchandise and current accounts (measured in current dollars) since 1947, and larger than ever subsequently. The net outward total of private long- and short-term capital movements (including errors and omissions) increased, however, from $4.0 billion in 1963 to $6.0 billion in 1964. Although the basic deficit practically vanished, the official-settlements balance was still in deficit by $1.5 billion.

Capital moved outward in particularly heavy volume in the last quarter of 1964 and in the

---

4. Averaged from the St. Louis publication cited in Table 27.2.

5. BIS, 1967–1968, p. 32, mentions some of these influences.

6. BIS, 1967–1968, pp. 29–36, BIS, 1971–1972, p. 5.

7. For a review of the rise and fall of the gold pool, see BIS, 1971–1972, pp. 17–19, as well as pp. 425–427 above.

8. BIS, 1967–1968, pp. 29–36, BIS, 1971–1972, pp. 19–21.

9. Richard Caves and Ronald W. Jones, *World Trade and Payments*, Boston: Little, Brown, 1973, p. 405.

10. Milton Gilbert in H. W. J. Bosman and F. A. M. Alting von Geusau, eds., *The Future of the International Monetary System*, Lexington, Mass.: Heath, 1970, p. 62.

TABLE 27.2. United States balance of payments, selected accounts, 1946–1973

Year	MERCHANDISE TRADE Exports as percentage of imports	Exports minus imports $ billions	% of GNP	Current account balance $ billions	% of GNP	Basic balance $ billions	% of GNP	ORT balance $ billions	% of GNP	Liquidity balance (1946–1959 gross, 1960–73 net) $ billions
1946	232.2	6.7	3.21	4.9	2.34	1.4	0.67			1.0
1947	269.5	10.1	4.38	9.0	3.89	3.9	1.69			4.2
1948	175.5	5.7	2.22	2.0	0.77	0.0	0.00			0.8
1949	177.7	5.3	2.08	0.6	0.23	−0.7	−0.27			0.1
1950	112.4	1.1	0.39	−2.1	−0.75	−3.3	−1.16			−3.5
1951	127.4	3.1	0.93	0.3	0.09	−0.6	−0.18			0.0
1952	124.1	2.6	0.76	−0.18	−0.05	−1.5	−0.43	} −1.2 average		−1.2
1953	113.1	1.4	0.39	−1.9	−0.53	−2.5	−0.69			−2.2
1954	124.9	2.6	0.71	−0.32	−0.09	−0.9	−0.25			−1.5
1955	125.1	2.9	0.72	−0.35	−0.09	−1.3	−0.33			−1.2
1956	137.1	4.8	1.13	1.7	0.41	−0.9	−0.21			−1.0
1957	147.2	6.3	1.42	3.6	0.81	−0.3	−0.07	1.1		0.6
1958	126.7	3.5	0.77	−0.01	−0.00	−3.5	−0.78	} −2.7 average		−3.4
1959	107.5	1.1	0.24	−2.14	−0.44	−4.1	−0.85			−3.6

1960	133.3	4.9	0.97	1.82	0.36	−1.2	−0.23	−3.40	−0.68	−3.7
1961	138.5	5.6	1.07	3.09	0.59	0.004	0.00	−1.35	−0.26	−2.3
1962	128.1	4.6	0.81	2.50	0.45	−1.00	−0.18	−2.65	−0.47	−2.9
1963	130.8	5.2	0.89	3.22	0.54	−1.29	−0.22	−1.93	−0.33	−2.7
1964	136.6	6.8	1.08	5.81	0.92	−0.004	−0.00	−1.53	−0.24	−2.7
1965	123.0	4.9	0.72	4.26	0.62	−1.85	−0.27	−1.29	−0.19	−2.5
1966	115.0	3.8	0.51	2.28	0.30	−1.74	−0.23	0.22	0.03	−2.2
1967	114.2	3.8	0.48	2.06	0.26	−3.28	−0.41	−3.42	−0.43	−4.7
1968	101.9	0.6	0.07	−0.48	−0.06	−1.44	−0.17	1.64	0.19	−1.6
1969	101.7	0.6	0.07	−1.04	−0.11	−3.01	−0.32	2.70	0.29	−6.1
1970	105.4	2.2	0.22	0.36	0.04	−3.06	−0.31	−9.84	−1.01	−3.9
1971	94.0	−2.7	−0.26	−3.82	−0.36	−10.56	−1.00	−29.75	−2.82	−22.0
1972	87.5	−7.0	−0.60	−9.81	−0.85	−11.24	−0.97	−10.35	−0.89	−13.9
1973	100.7	0.5	0.04	0.52	0.04	−0.90	−0.07	−5.30	−0.41	−7.8

NOTES: Exports exclude those supplied under military grants. The current account covers trade in goods and services, investment income, and transfers (including government nonmilitary grants). The basic balance covers the current and long-term-capital accounts. The balance on official reserve transactions and gross and net liquidity balances are as defined in Chapter 3.

SOURCES: Same as in Table 27.1, and Federal Reserve Bank of St Louis, U.S. Balance of Payments Trends, April 1973, pp. 2–3.

TABLE 27.3. *U.S. merchandise, current, and basic balances, annual averages, 1951–1969*

	Trade balance		Current account		Basic balance	
	$ billions	*% of GNP*	*$ billions*	*% of GNP*	*$ billions*	*% of GNP*
1951–59	3.1	0.79	0.1	0.01	−1.7	−0.42
1960–64	5.4	0.96	3.3	0.57	−0.7	−0.13
1965–69	2.8	0.37	1.4	0.20	−2.3	−0.28

SOURCE: Derived from Table 27.2.

first two months of 1965, evidently because repercussions of the British crisis and the French policy of exchanging dollars for gold were arousing anxieties about the dollar and because certain remarks by U.S. officials were breeding anticipations of capital controls.[11]

A technicality of IMF rules led the United States to make its first drawing on the Fund in 1964. In February the Fund's holdings of dollars came to exceed 75 percent of the U.S. quota, barring the Fund from accepting dollars in repayments (technically, repurchases) by other members who had previously borrowed from it (bought foreign currencies with their own). From time to time, therefore, the United States borrowed (bought) other currencies from the Fund and sold them for dollars to members needing to repurchase their own currencies from the Fund. The United States made its first *nontechnical* drawing (one not related to other members' repurchases) in July 1965, when it drew $300 million worth of five currencies.[12]

The middle and late 1960s

After 1964 the trade surplus shrank and the basic balance worsened. A regression line of U.S. imports on GNP is steeper for 1965–1970 than it had been for 1950–1964, and the ratio of growth rate of imports to growth rate of GNP was twice as high for 1965–1971 as it had been for 1950–1964. The rise in imports relative to domestic demand was particularly pronounced for capital goods, cars, and consumer goods.[13] Costs and prices rose faster in the second half of the 1960s than in the first half. Increases were at least as large on balance in the United States as in a number of European countries from 1965 to 1967 and were larger thereafter (until 1970 brought a spurt of inflation in Europe). Unit labor costs in manufacturing rose at an average annual rate of 4 percent in the United States from 1965 to 1968 while rising only slightly in such Euro-

pean countries as Germany and Italy and declining in Japan. Unit values in dollars of manufactured exports rose substantially in the United States while increasing little or even declining in these latter countries and in Great Britain (because of the 1967 devaluation). A related influence on current-account positions was a shift to fuller utilization of resources and to excess demand in the United States, while Continental Europe went through an economic slowdown in the late 1960s. Although a loss of competitiveness from inflation, tracing in turn to the Vietnam escalation beginning in 1965, goes part way toward explaining the deterioration of the U.S. trade balance, growth of the trade surplus had already been sluggish for more than a decade. Other countries had been building up their productive capacity and technological strength. Industrialization proceeded apace abroad, facilitated by shifts of labor out of agriculture and by ready assimilation of new technologies. Expansion of the scale and efficiency of industry abroad were gradually eroding the dominance of U.S. products.[14]

The figures for 1965 are not particularly bad in themselves, but they mark the beginning of an ominous trend. Several important shifts hid behind overall figures. The trade surplus, though still larger than in most of the postwar years, began a deterioration not significantly interrupted until 1970. Influenced by buoyant demand at home and an economic slowdown in Western Europe and Japan, imports rose by 15.3 percent in value (the highest growth rate since 1959), while exports rose only 3.8 percent. This development interrupted an uptrend of several years' standing in the current-account surplus, which had been largely attributable to rising investment income from abroad. This deterioration was restrained by an improvement of a few hundred million dollars in invisibles as a further rise in investment income more than offset higher payments for travel and other services. Despite the current-account deterioration, the overall deficit (on gross and net liquidity and official-settlements concepts) shrank slightly, thanks to complex shifts in private capital movements (including errors and omissions) that on balance reduced the net outflow. U.S. direct investment abroad rose sharply during the first half and particularly during the first quarter of 1965 as corporations acted in anticipation of subsequent restrictions; but in the second half, the program of voluntary restraint announced in February appeared to be taking effect. The government's directives to banks and other financial institutions curtailed their foreign lending. An unfavorable shift in movements of long-term foreign capital largely reflected the sale of about $500 million of U.S. corporate securities by the British Exchange Equalization Account,[15] only partly offset by U.S. corporate borrowing in European markets. The inflow of liquid funds held by foreign commercial banks nearly vanished; this $1.3 billion change appeared, in part, to be a side effect of the program to restrain capital outflows.[16]

The introduction of so-called voluntary controls over capital exports was a notable event of 1965. Not only the long-run economic effectiveness of the program was open to question, but also its wisdom on grounds of political philosophy.[17] The Executive Branch of government obtained the effect of momentous legislation without Congressional enactment. In many of their decisions, businessmen were supposed to set aside the profit motive in favor of the Administration's notions of what the national interest required. The program's spurious voluntary character and its inherent vagueness (particularly as far as foreign direct investment was concerned) ran counter to cherished legal principles. Voluntariness, vagueness, and appeals to patriotism put a premium on compliance with the spirit as well as with the letter of the program, creating an atmosphere unfavorable to vigorous dissent and democratic debate.

Although the current-account deterioration sharpened in 1966, the basic and overall deficits shrank, the official-settlements balance even showing small surplus. The explanation lies, of course, in the capital accounts. The voluntary restraint program had some effect. Tight credit conditions in the United States contributed to an inflow of foreign capital through U.S. corporate security issues in Europe and increases in long-term foreign debt of U.S. banks and of liquid liabilities to foreign

banks. Foreign official purchases of U.S. government agency securities were substantial. The reduction in the net capital outflow put severe pressure on financial markets throughout the world.

Over half of the current-account deterioration came in merchandise trade. As Vietnam repercussions and a domestic investment boom were intensifying the strain on domestic resources and as the import growth of several other industrial countries was slowing down, U.S. imports rose 18.5% in value in 1966. Imports of automobiles almost doubled, coming mainly from Canada (thanks to a special trade agreement) and Germany. Imports of capital equipment and industrial materials also rose notably. Besides commodity trade, the other chief element of deterioration in the balance of payments was a rise in the deficit on military transactions from $2.1 billion in 1965 to $2.9 billion in 1966.[18]

---

11. Gottfried Haberler in American Enterprise Institute, *International Payments Problems*, Washington: 1966, pp. 16–17.

12. International Monetary Fund, 1966, pp. 7, 35.

13. BIS, 1971–1972, pp. 6–7.

14. BIS, 1967–1968, pp. 29–36; BIS, 1971–1972, pp. 8–9, with table; IMF, 1969, p. 6, with chart on p. 5.

15. This liquidation of the Account's secondary reserves creates a problem in measuring the deficit in 1965. In the U.S. statistics, it appears "above the line" as adding to the deficit, while the corresponding increase in liquid liabilities appears "below the line" as part of the financing of the deficit. IMF, 1966, p. 93.

16. BIS, 1965–1966, pp. 90–92; IMF, 1966, pp. 93–95.

17. See my "Balance-of-Payments Cure Worse Than the Disease," *Commercial and Financial Chronicle*, 2 September 1965, pp. 3, 29.

18. Some of the figures here and elsewhere in this chapter are calculated from appendix tables in annual issues of *Economic Report of the President*. On 1966 generally, IMF, 1967, pp. 76, 81–82, 84, 87; BIS, 1966–1967, pp. 87, 89–90; BIS, 1967–1968, pp. 25, 36.

In 1967 the official-settlements balance shifted back to deficit, and the net-liquidity deficit more than doubled. This overall deterioration was attributable not to any spectacular change in one or two categories of transactions but rather to relatively small changes in most of the main categories of the current account and especially of the capital account. Net outflows on government loans increased, while inflows connected with liquid liabilities to private foreigners fell. Exports again appeared sensitive to the level of economic activity in Western Europe, where the growth of industrial production slackened in late 1966 and early 1967. The difficulty that had started late in 1965 was continuing: Vietnam expenditures were worsening the balance of payments not so much by their direct foreign-exchange costs as by promoting domestic inflation. Worsening of the trade balance was especially noticeable in the fourth quarter of 1967. At the same time, the capital-account deficit grew, partly because the British Treasury was selling investments in the United States to bolster official reserves. The devaluation of sterling in November had further repercussions by spurring a speculative wave of gold-buying that brought U.S. gold losses, small until then, to $1170 million for the year.[19] These events led to mandatory capital controls on 1 January 1968. An earlier policy change, effective in January 1967, was an extension of the Interest Equalization Tax, with its rate increased from the equivalent of 1 percent to 1½ percent.

The overall figures for 1968 conceal an odd and unfavorable pattern of shifts. A $5.1 billion turnaround brought a surplus on official reserve transactions. The net liquidity deficit fell almost by two-thirds. The basic deficit was less than half that of 1967. Yet the trade surplus nearly vanished, more than fully accounting for a $2.5 billion shift of the current account into actual deficit. The aggregate of all capital accounts (other than official settlements, but including errors and omissions), improved by a massive $7.6 billion. U.S. government net long-term capital outflows declined slightly from 1967 to 1968. Special transactions shifted $2.4 billion of U.S. liabilities from the liquid to the nonliquid category. Private net long-term capital flows turned from $2.9 billion outward to $1.2 billion inward. Direct investment abroad declined only slightly, but U.S. corporations financed an increased proportion of it by issuing new securities abroad. Foreigners more than doubled their purchases of existing corporation securities on U.S. markets. A rise of $3.8 billion in U.S. liquid liabilities to nonofficial foreigners counted as an above-the-line capital inflow on the official-settlement basis. This figure included short-term borrowing abroad by U.S. banks and corporations, even for domestic financial needs. (This inherently volatile and reversible capital-account item was also significant the following year.) The overall capital turnaround traced partly to U.S. controls, partly to tight conditions in the U.S. capital market, partly to a boom on Wall Street, and partly to political uncertainties arising from events in France and Czechoslovakia that encouraged European investors to place funds in the United States.[20]

The trade deterioration of 1968 represented a sharpening of a trend already under way since 1965. While exports grew rather satisfactorily, imports rose by an unprecedented 22.8 percent. Strikes and strike expectations had some effect, but the main influence was pressure of excess domestic demand, with unemployment falling and wages and prices rising faster than the year before.[21]

New controls, as already mentioned, were announced at the beginning of 1968. The President claimed authority under the Trading with the Enemy Act of 1917. Limits on direct investment outflows were made mandatory and made more severe than the previous guidelines. The Federal Reserve was given standby authority to impose mandatory controls on foreign lending by banks and other financial institutions, and it tightened the restrictions previously announced for 1968. In August 1968 the rates of the Interest Equalization Tax on new foreign portfolio investments by Americans were again raised. The impact of these measures cannot easily be sorted out from that of other factors tending to improve the capital account, but the direct-investment controls do seem to have promoted offshore financing, as well as heavy repatriations of investment funds in the last weeks of 1968 by corporations seeking to bring their net direct investment outflows for the year within the ceilings. Besides the capital controls, the January announcements urged Americans to postpone nonessential travel outside the Western Hemisphere for two years and mentioned steps to cut the government's foreign expenditures and steps to promote U.S. exports, including increased scope for financing by the Export-Import Bank.[22]

The inter-central-bank gold pool collapsed in March 1968 and was replaced by a two-price system. This event is a landmark in the piece-meal discontinuance of the gold convertibility of the dollar, a movement that climaxed in August 1971. Under the gold pool, the United States had made the major contribution to the members' sales of gold on the London market whenever necessary to keep the price down in the vicinity of the official price. In effect, then, though not avowedly, the dollar had been convertible into gold bullion at the official price not only for foreign official agencies but also for private residents of countries where owning gold was legal. This *de facto* private convertibility of the dollar came to an end in March 1968. In a less clear-cut way, convertibility seems to have ended for foreign official agencies also. After the separation of the official and free-market values of gold, "the convertibility of the dollar was little more than formal. . . ." After March 1968, "it was a matter of common knowledge that, although in theory the dollar was supposed to be convertible into gold for foreign governments and Central Banks, in practice the United States would refuse to comply with this obligation if some Central Bank should demand an embarrassingly large amount. Its conversion into gold for official holders ceased in 1968 to be a matter of routine. It became a matter of negotiation."[23] Figures on the U.S. gold stock are consistent with these statements: major declines no longer occurred. With convertibility at an end, the world was on a *de facto* dollar standard rather than on a genuine gold-exchange standard.[24] To some extent, this development began even before 1968. In 1967, for example, Germany, the major surplus country at the time, had publicly agreed not to buy gold from the United States. Some other countries followed a similar policy in practice, and there was "a widespread perception that the United States, if confronted with demands for large gold conversions, would suspend the gold convertibility of the dollar rather than suffer further large losses of reserves."[25]

Like 1968, 1969 brought further current-account deterioration but an official-settlements surplus; and that surplus even increased. Reflecting strange cross-currents in capital flows, however, the balance on the old gross-liquidity concept shifted from slight surplus to a $7.1 billion deficit, while the net liquidity deficit widened by $4.5 billion from the year before. (As for the gross-liquidity balance, the previous practice was discontinued of window-dressing it by encouraging foreign official holders of dollars to transfer their claims from

liquid to nonliquid form.) Sizable "circular flows" of U.S. funds occurred—into the Euro-dollar market and then back again through the U.S. banking system in response to exceptionally tight domestic credit conditions and interest-rate ceilings. In a spectacular steepening of a trend already noticeable for several years, Eurodollar-market borrowings of U.S. banks from their foreign branches rose by almost $8 billion in the first half of 1969 alone, more than doubling the amount outstanding at the beginning of the year.[26] Owing to the current-

19. BIS, 1967–1968, pp. 25–27.

20. IMF, 1969, pp. 10, 57, 60, 72; BIS, 1971–1972, p. 11; BIS, 1968–1969, pp. 31–32; and additional figures from *Economic Report of the President*.

21. Gilbert in Bosman and Alting, *op. cit.*, pp. 57–62.

22. BIS, 1967–1968, pp. 27–28 (compare IMF, 1968, pp. 58–59); IMF, 1969, p. 72; Gilbert in Bosman & Alting, *op. cit.*, pp. 60–61.

23. Quotations from BIS, 1971–1972, p. 32, and Paul Einzig, *The Destiny of the Dollar*, New York: St. Martin's Press, 1972, p. 128, respectively. Compare Einzig, pp. 65, 85; Samuel Brittan, *Steering the Economy*, Harmondsworth: Penguin Books, 1971, p. 385; Samuel Brittan, *The Price of Economic Freedom*, New York: St. Martin's Press, 1970, p. 3.

24. Émile James, "L'avvenire del 'gold exchange standard,'" *Mercurio* (Milan), **XV**, October 1972, pp. 1–5, esp. p. 3.

25. C. Fred Bergsten in George N. Halm, ed., *Approaches to Greater Flexibility of Exchange Rates*, Princeton: Princeton University Press, 1970, p. 73.

26. To arrest further developments of this type, the Federal Reserve imposed a 10 percent marginal reserve requirement on the Euromarket debt of U.S. banks, and its growth soon ceased (IMF, 1970, p. 78). This debt amounted to something over $7 billion at the start of 1969, peaked at over $14½ billion late in the year, dropped with little interruption to under $8 billion at the end of 1970, hit a low of about $1½ billion in the summer of 1971, jumped briefly back to $3 billion late that year, fluctuated between roughly $1 and $1½ billion during 1972, and touched down to $1 billion early in 1973.

account deterioration and a shift of private long-term capital flows back to their normal net outward direction, the basic deficit rose from $1.4 billion in 1968 to $3.0 billion in 1969. The current-account deterioration, incidentally, occurred only in invisibles. Because of sharp increases in U.S. interest rates and in U.S. bank borrowing in the Eurodollar market, outward interest payments increased enough to cause a slight but unusual decrease in the net surplus on investment income account. Net military and travel expenditures rose somewhat.[27] Despite the largest price and unit-labor-cost increases in almost two decades, with the GNP deflator up nearly 5 percent,[28] the shrunken merchandise trade surplus shrank no further; presumably these changes would work with lags.

1970 and 1971: background of crisis

By 1970, a highly unusual pattern of changes had itself become usual. The net liquidity deficit shrank by $2.3 billion while the official-reserve-transactions balance shifted fom a surplus of $2.7 billion into the largest deficit until then recorded, $9.8 billion.[29] An only fractionally increased basic deficit masked an improvement of $1.4 billion in current transactions and a $1.4 billion deterioration on account of private and government long-term capital. Recovery of the merchandise trade surplus explained siightly more than the entire net current-account improvement. This improvement largely reflected the combination of recession in the United States and a high level of demand in Western Europe and Japan. The rapid influence of a favorable change in unit costs is not very plausible. Still, if the figures are to be taken seriously, U.S. manufacturers regained in late 1969 and in 1970 the ground that they had lost relative to foreign competitors between the end of 1965 and mid-1969. Their comparative cost position even seemed to have become more favorable than in 1963 and 1964, years of healthy trade surplus. In export prices however, only a small part of the divergence between U.S. and foreign trends was reversed.[30] Actually, in view of the exceptionally favorable pattern of world business cycles, the trade-balance recovery—by $1.5 billion, in contrast with a $3.8 billion recovery in the earlier recession year 1960, when U.S. trade was less than half as large—was ominously small. Furthermore, the bulk of the improve-

ment came in the first half of the year, partly reflecting the settlement of the 1969 dock strike. U.S. export growth tapered off sharply in the second half of 1970 as demand pressures abroad began to ease.[31]

The U.S. recession of 1970 reversed the tight credit conditions that had induced abnormal capital inflows in 1968 and 1969, camouflaging the underlying weakness of the balance of payments. Interest rates fell sharply in the United States while boom and supposedly anti-inflationary monetary policies still prevailed in Japan and most of Western Europe, notably Germany. Changes in flows of U.S. and foreign long-term capital very nearly matched the improvement on current account. Dramatic reversals of short-term flows dominated changes in the overall liquidity and official-settlements balances. In particular, U.S. banks set about repaying their earlier heavy borrowing in the Eurodollar market. The suspension of certain interest-rate ceilings on certificates of deposit in June 1970 enabled the banks to raise more time-deposit funds at home, without resort to the Euromarket carousel; and repayments to the Euromarket gained momentum. From the end of November onward, the Federal Reserve tried to retard this reflow of funds by raising the reserve requirement applied against the banks' borrowings from their overseas branches in excess of a reserve-free base; repayments would shrink this base and make the raised requirement applicable to any subsequent increase in borrowing. (In short, the Federal Reserve acted to raise the potential reserve-requirement cost to banks of reductions in their Euromarket debt.) This policy move had no clear effect, however; and over 1970 as a whole, the banks paid back some $6 to $6½ billion.[32]

As late as 1970, according to Federal Reserve Governor Andrew Brimmer, some hope remained that the United States could sufficiently improve its international competitiveness by reducing excess demand at home. The results for 1970 and early 1971 ended this hope. The merely modest recovery and then the further deterioration of the trade balance, together with capital outflows, brought unprecedented overall deficits. It became clear that the United States "could not expect to recover through demand management the losses in competitiveness that had accumulated in the 1960s. Our absolute levels of costs and prices were too far above those of our competitors."[33]

At the turn of the year 1970–1971 the U.S. basic balance was very weak, with hardly any trade surplus left, and was bound to weaken further as the economy recovered from recession. Monetary policy to promote recovery, especially in contrast with opposite policies abroad, was bound to cause further capital outflows. The climate of discussion was unfavorable: U.S. reserves had sunk to near their supposed minimum tolerable level, members of the Group of Ten were talking about the need for greater exchange-rate flexibility, and the French franc had been devalued, the German mark floated and revalued, and the Canadian dollar floated between August 1969 and June 1970. An explosion was near.[34]

Before noting the events of 1971, let us glance at the bare figures. A $4.9 billion deterioration in the merchandise trade balance brought the first deficit since 1935.[35] The current account shifted to a deficit of $3.8 billion, and the basic deficit more than trebled to $10.6 billion. Reflecting, in addition, massive outflows of short-term funds (including errors and omissions), the overall deficit reached unprecedented levels of $22.0 billion on the net liquidity basis and $29.8 billion on the official-reserve-transactions basis, larger than the total of all ORT deficits from 1960 on, even including the exceptionally large one of 1970.

From 1970 to 1971, merchandise exports rose only 2 percent in value and declined slightly in volume. Imports rose some 14½ percent, more than one-third of this rise reflecting increased prices. More than four-fifths of the trade-balance deterioration came in trade with Western Europe and Japan. Various estimates attribute about half of the deterioration to slower growth than usual in overseas markets at a time when the United States was recovering from recession. Other apparent influences were a weakening trend in U.S. price competitiveness over the previous six years, strikes in the United States, and responses to the exchange-rate uncertainties prevailing both before and after the announcements of August 15.[36] Leads and lags—speculative or precautionary adjustments in timing—affected not only payments for commercial transactions but also such transactions themselves: foreign buyers delayed their purchases in the United States and American importers hastened their purchases abroad in anticipation that the dollar would depreciate against foreign currencies.[37]

The current account worsened less in 1971

than the merchandise account, thanks to a rise in investment income, lower outpayments because of a decline in U.S. interest rates, and reduction in net military outlays, chiefly through increased sales of military equipment. A deficit of $6.8 billion on long-term capital account, compared with $3.4 billion in 1970, contributed to swelling the basic deficit.[38] "On balance, foreigners reduced their new long-term investments in the United States and increased their outstanding dollar obligations in an effort to reduce or eliminate any positions taken in dollars. At the same time, United States firms transferred large amounts of funds to their overseas affiliates and subsidiaries; early in the year these transfers were motivated mainly by interest rate differentials but later reflected expectations of exchange rate changes. These various responses were reflected in a sharp reduction of net new foreign invest-

27. BIS, 1969–1970, p. 83; IMF, 1970, p. 78.

28. IMF, 1970, pp. 76–77.

29. This calculation counts an SDR allocation of $867 million "above the line." With this amount left out, the $10.7 billion ORT deficit in 1970 almost equals the cumulative deficit of $11.0 billion for all of the 1960s.

30. IMF, 1971, p. 65 and chart on p. 66.

31. BIS, 1970–1971, pp. 93–94; BIS, 1971–1972, p. 16; Federal Reserve Bank of New York, Annual Report, 1970, pp. 43–44.

32. IMF, 1971, p. 90; IMF, 1972, pp. 14–15; BIS, 1970–1971, pp. 93–94; BIS, 1971–1972, pp. 23–24; Federal Reserve Bank of New York, Annual Report, 1970, pp. 40–45; the same, 1971, p. 34; Bank of England, Report, February 1971, p. 11.

33. Brimmer in Federal Reserve Bank of Boston, Canadian-United States Financial Relationships, 1972, p. 58.

34. Paraphrased from BIS, 1971–1972, pp. 24–25.

35. BIS, 1971–1972, p. 87.

36. BIS, 1971–1972, pp. 87–89.

37. Federal Reserve Bank of New York, Annual Report, 1971, p. 45.

38. BIS, 1971–1972, p. 89, with revised figures from Economic Report of the President.

ment in the United States and a sustained increase in United States long-term investment overseas."[39]

Short-term capital movements, however, accounted for the bulk of the overall deficit. The net outflow, including errors and omissions and movements of liquid and nonliquid short-term private capital, amounted to around $21 billion. Americans and foreigners alike were flying from the dollar.

With hindsight, one can name several specific factors that brought a trend of several years to a climax in 1971. The increasing integration of the world economy, epitomized by the growth of multinational corporations, had contributed to exposing the international monetary system to strains of capital movements in the late 1960s. The size of the potential movement of short-term funds became more fully apparent in 1970, when American and European monetary policies moved in opposite directions for the first time in several years. During 1969, most European countries had moved toward tighter monetary restriction, first as a defense against increasing capital outflows and then to resist inflation. The need for countercyclical monetary restraint lasted longer in Europe than in the United States. By 1970, stagnation of real output and rising unemployment brought a shift to monetary ease in the United States. Throughout the year, the excess of European over U.S. and Eurodollar interest rates widened. Funds moved heavily out of dollars into other currencies.[40] In 1970 and early 1971, American banks more than fully reversed their Euromarket borrowings of 1968–1969. These inflows and outflows may not have disturbed American monetary policy excessively, thanks to the great size of the U.S. monetary system. According to the German Bundesbank, however, the rest of the world could scarcely cope with such changing baths of liquidity [Liquiditäts-Wechselbäder], especially because inflows of dollars led to expansion of central-bank money. It would hardly have been possible for Germany or other affected European countries to lower domestic interest rates quickly and decisively enough to impede these American repayments to the Eurodollar market.[41] The role of interest differentials appears in the contrast between heavy movements of funds into marks and smaller movements into Japanese yen: "although it was much more undervalued than the Deutsche Mark, the yen was not subjected to significant speculative pressure until after 15th August" 1971.[42]

It is ironic that a decline in American interest rates should have promoted a flight from the dollar, for the decline was due chiefly to the recession the United States had suffered in efforts to stop inflation. These efforts should have tended, fundamentally, to strengthen the dollar. When the recession became unmistakable, Federal Reserve policy reinforced the decline of interest rates to promote business recovery.

The interest-motivated flow of funds continued in early 1971. In the first quarter alone, the seasonally adjusted official-settlements deficit in the U.S. balance of payments reached $5.6 billion.[43] Between January and early April the Export-Import Bank and the U.S. Treasury tried to keep repayments to the Euromarket from swelling other countries' reserves by selling a total of $3 billion of special three-month notes to the foreign branches of U.S. banks. The parent banks were allowed to count their branches' subscriptions to these notes toward maintenance of their own reserve-free Eurodollar bases.[44]

Dramatic changes in 1971–1974

By this time, exchange-rate expectations were gaining ground over interest-rate differentials as the chief motor of the transatlantic flow of funds. Analysts increasingly realized that the improvement in the U.S. current account in 1970 had been the temporary result of a favorable business-cycle pattern; the tapering off of the European boom, together with the start of economic recovery in the United States, was again exposing fundamental weakness.[45] Publication in February 1971 of the discouraging balance-of-payments figures for 1970 worsened the general mood.

Further developments leading to the crisis of May 1971 have been described in Chapter 24. The immediate outcome was the upward floating of the German mark and Dutch guilder, upward revaluations of the Swiss franc and Austrian schilling, and a fuller separation of the commercial and financial foreign-exchange markets in Belgium. Even at this late date, one could plausibly argue that the essence of the crisis had been bullishness on the mark rather than bearishness on the dollar.[46]

The piecemeal exchange-rate adjustments in

May soon proved to have been mere palliatives. In fact, they aroused fears that other countries might revalue or float their currencies. As an actual U.S. merchandise trade deficit registered in April persisted in subsequent months, confidence in the dollar was increasingly shaken. After a brief reflux of funds into dollars in June, one foreign currency after another became the target of funds running out of dollars.[47] As European countries, notably Switzerland and France, adopted controls to ward off unwanted funds, the apparent breakdown in international monetary cooperation further undermined confidence.

Despite swap drawings and the sale of new foreign-currency-denominated obligations to foreign official institutions to absorb dollars that their holders might otherwise have converted into gold or other reserve assets, the United States paid out almost $2 billion of reserve assets over the first seven months of 1971. It lost a further $1.1 billion in the first two weeks of August alone. By then, liquid dollar liabilities to foreign official institutions were more than three times as large as U.S. reserves, and even larger losses were threatening.[48]

By early August, newspapers and news magazines were full of stories about the weakness of the dollar, possibilities of its devaluation, and complaints that the government was applying only Band-Aids to a hemorrhage. Reporters for the *Wall Street Journal* interviewed executives and economists of some three dozen corporations based in the United States, many of them having extensive foreign operations. By and large, these companies were trying to shift cash balances from dollars into foreign currencies and to incur debt expressed in dollars. Executives were taking such precautions not so much to engage in outright speculation as to protect the assets of their corporate employers.[49] On Friday the 13th, efforts to switch from dollars into strong currencies were so intense that over-the-weekend Eurodollar interest rates hit as high as 22 percent per annum.[50]

Practically the last straw had been the release of a report by a subcommittee of the Joint Economic Committee over the weekend of Saturday, August 7. The subcommittee declared that the dollar was overvalued and recommended that exchange rates be changed somehow or other. Significantly, the chairman of the subcommittee, Representative Henry

Reuss, had until comparatively recently been one of the firmest defenders of the old parity of the dollar. His switch suggested that Congress would no longer bar action by the Administration.[51] Although the U.S. Treasury replied that the Reuss report reflected only a narrow and untypical slice of Congressional sentiment, it had to admit that the United States did face balance-of-payments problems, that France was going to convert $191 million into gold on Monday, and that the United States was going to make its biggest borrowing ever from the International Monetary Fund (in connection with French and British repur-

39. Federal Reserve Bank of New York, *Annual Report*, 1971, p. 45.

40. *Ibid.*, pp. 33–35.

41. *Geschäftsbericht*, 1971, pp. 33–34.

42. BIS, 1971–1972, pp. 189–190.

43. *Economic Report of the President*, 1974, table on p. 351.

44. Federal Reserve Bank of New York, *Annual Report*, 1971, p. 35; BIS, 1971–1972, p. 25; Bank of England, *Report*, February 1972, p. 11.

45. IMF, 1972, p. 16.

46. Recall footnote 108 and the accompanying text in Chapter 24.

47. Federal Reserve Bank of New York, *Annual Report*, 1971, p. 40; BIS, 1971–1972, p. 190.

48. Federal Reserve Bank of New York, *Annual Report*, 1971, p. 41; German Bundesbank, *Geschäftsbericht*, 1971, p. 40.

49. *Wall Street Journal*, 13 August 1971, p. 1. Significantly, this article appeared before President Nixon's speech of the 15th.

50. *Wall Street Journal*, 16 August 1971, p. 3. On August 17, the settlement date for currencies purchased on the 13th, overnight Eurodollar rates rose above 40 percent. *Federal Reserve Bulletin*, March 1972, p. 254. Earlier, on some days in April and early May, overnight Eurodollar rates had reached 45 percent or more. On the last day of August, the overnight rate soared to 200 percent. Federal Reserve Bank of St. Louis, *Review*, April 1972, p. 9.

51. Einzig, *The Destiny of the Dollar*, pp. 59, 61.

chases). Even so, the Treasury cited speeches by Secretary Connally to the effect that the dollar would be neither devalued nor made inconvertible into gold. Predevaluation disclaimers were, of course, almost standard practice.

On Sunday the 15th President Nixon imposed a domestic price-and-income freeze. Hoping "to generate momentum toward the negotiation of new international monetary arrangements,"[52] he formally suspended the convertibility of the dollar into gold or other reserve assets and imposed a 10 percent import surcharge.

The major wholesale (interbank) foreign-exchange markets remained closed for the entire week of August 16 through 20. The first few days were difficult for U.S. tourists abroad. No one could know what market-clearing exchange rates would be, and a bewildering variety of fast-changing retail rates developed. Foreign banks, hotels, and shops either refused to accept dollars at all or took them only at deep discounts. On Monday the 16th, thousands of travelers had to wait an hour or more outside the American Express Company in London to exchange their travelers' cheques.[53]

When the wholesale markets reopened, all major currencies were left to float, except that French controls separated a pegged "commercial" rate from a floating "financial" rate for the franc and that Japan kept pegging the yen until August 28. After absorbing $4.4 billion in August alone, the Japanese authorities finally gave up.[54]

The resulting pattern of floating exchange rates was heavily influenced by official interventions, proliferating controls, and rumors and conflicting reports about government negotiations concerning levels at which rates would be repegged. The temporary U.S. import surcharge tended to reduce normal commercial demands for foreign currencies. "Under these circumstances, the exchange markets provided very limited guidance as to the currency relationships that would restore a more balanced pattern of international payments."[55]

The United States, with Treasury Secretary Connally as its chief spokesman, at first resisted devaluing the dollar against gold; other countries could revalue their currencies upward against the dollar if they wished. Furthermore, exchange rates and monetary reform, the import surcharge, foreign import barriers against U.S. goods, and a fairer sharing of defense burdens should form the subject of negotiations in a single package. Other countries insisted on piecemeal negotiations. A meeting of the Group of Ten in November saw a softening of the U.S. position against dollar devaluation, a shift formalized at a meeting between President Nixon and French President Pompidou early in December. In negotiations with the other Group of Ten countries at the Smithsonian Institution in Washington on December 17 and 18, the United States agreed to raise to $38 the official price at which it was in fact neither buying nor selling gold. This spelled a 7.89 percent devaluation of the dollar.[56] The United States also removed the import surcharge. The Smithsonian Agreement also widened the band of permissible fluctuation of exchange rates to 2¼ percent above and below the new parities or "central rates."

Over the next few days the major industrial countries announced effective upward revaluations of their own currencies against the dollar, ranging downward from 16.88 percent for the Japanese yen. Any currency with an unchanged gold parity, such as the British pound or French franc, was automatically revalued by 8.57 percent. The effective trade-weighted average devaluation of the dollar against the currencies of the 14 countries with which the United States did about two-thirds of its trade amounted to 10.35 percent. Against all currencies revaluing relative to the dollar, whose countries accounted for about 80 percent of U.S. trade, the average dollar devaluation was about 9.7 percent. Against all currencies of the world, including those remaining pegged to the dollar, such as most Latin American currencies, the average devaluation was about 7.5 percent.[57] A long-drawn-out agony had thus resulted in an effective devaluation of the dollar by somewhat less than 10 percent.

The Smithsonian Agreement left other currencies pegged to an inconvertible dollar. It—or, rather, the crises that had preceded it—also "left an enormous residue of inconvertible dollar balances with foreign official institutions. . . ."[58] As recently as the end of 1969, U.S. liabilities to foreign central banks and governments of types counted as reserves by those institutions had totaled $16.00 billion (a figure not including liabilities to private foreigners). Between the end of 1970 and the end of 1971, those reserve-type liabilities grew from $23.78 billion to $50.65 billion. Their increase in 1971 alone thus exceeded the amount to which they had grown in all previous history. Their continued increase even from August to December is evidence that the floating exchange rates of that period were "dirtied" by official intervention. The officially held "dollar overhang," as it became known, was destined to grow further in 1972 and early 1973, reaching $71.33 billion at the end of the first quarter. It came to be considered a serious problem in discussions of international monetary reform.[59]

In 1972 the official-reserve-transactions deficit shrank by nearly two-thirds to $10.4 billion, still the second largest in history. Most of this deficit was recorded during the early months of the year and during the summer weeks immediately after the floating of sterling, when the Smithsonian exchange-rate structure seemed particularly shaky. As a matter of arithmetic, the great bulk of the $19.4 billion shrinkage in the ORT deficit can be accounted for by an $8.0 billion shrinkage in outflows under errors and omissions and a $11.4 billion switch from reduction to increase in liquid dollar holdings of private foreigners. The latter figure includes a sharp rise in the liabilities of U.S. branches and agencies of foreign banks to their head offices. The chief factor reducing short-term outflows was probably the temporary abatement of concern about exchange rates during most of the year. However, no large return flow took place.[60]

The basic deficit, at $11.2 billion, remained almost the same in 1972 as in 1971. Its composition, however, changed drastically: the deficit on long-term capital account shrank and the deficit on current account grew, each by about $5 billion. Long-term *private* capital movements shifted to an actual net inflow of $0.1 billion. U.S. direct investment outflows receded from their 1971 record level as U.S. firms reduced the rate of growth of their overseas spending on plant and equipment. Net foreign direct investment in the United States recovered from the speculatively induced outflows of 1971. Partly because of vigorous U.S. economic expansion and renewed confidence in the U.S. stock market, foreign investors showed increased interest in U.S. corporate stocks and in offshore bond issues, largely convertible into stock.[61] In the current account, part of the deterioration came in invisibles. As in 1969, the excess of U.S. receipts over payments of interest, dividends, and fees on international loans and investments registered an

unusual drop, though very slightly. In particular, outward interest payments rose sharply on the "dollar overhang" of Treasury bills and other U.S. securities accumulated by foreign official agencies during years of U.S. deficits and currency crises.[62] The bulk of the deterio-

52. Federal Reserve Bank of New York, *Annual Report*, 1971, p. 41.

53. *Wall Street Journal*, 17 August 1971, p. 6.

54. BIS, 1971–1972, p. 190; Federal Reserve Bank of New York, *Annual Report*, 1971, p. 42.

55. Federal Reserve Bank of New York, *Annual Report*, 1971, p. 43.

56. The change took effect at once, although the necessary act of Congress was not passed and signed until March 31, 1972. Formal notification to the International Monetary Fund came on May 8, 1972.

57. Federal Reserve Bank of St. Louis, *Review*, April 1972, p. 12.

58. Federal Reserve Bank of New York, *Annual Report*, 1971, p. 44.

59. The figures are taken from line 4a of the U.S. pages of *International Financial Statistics*.

Dollars held privately—and presumably voluntarily—pose no comparable problems in the absence of sudden massive change in the reasons or incentives for holding them. There seems to be no profound distinction between foreign-held and domestically held cash balances, near-money balances, and securities. The peculiarity with officially held dollar balances is that they have been acquired more or less involuntarily in connection with exchange-rate pegging or intervention. Dumping of official balances, though unlikely, could bring disruptive sudden changes in exchange rates and balances of payments.

By 1974, amidst the changes wrought by the world oil situation, worry about the "dollar overhang" had pretty much gone out of fashion.

60. Federal Reserve Bank of New York, *Annual Report*, 1972, pp. 37–38; Federal Reserve Bank of St. Louis, *U.S. Balance of Payments Trends*, 24 April 1973, p. 1. I have made use, however, of slightly revised balance-of-payments figures.

61. Federal Reserve Bank of New York, *Annual Report*, 1972, p. 38; figures revised from more recent government publications.

62. *Business Week*, 12 May 1973, p. 26.

ration, however, was a $4.3 billion increase in—a 2½-fold multiplication of—the merchandise trade deficit. The trade deficit grew during the first four months of the year and shrank slowly, on balance, during the last eight months.[63] For 1972 as a whole, exports rose 14 percent in dollar value. Imports, however, rose 23 percent, and from a 1971 figure already in excess of exports. Rapid business expansion in the United States pulled in additional imports. The initial impact of the dollar devaluation of December 1971 was to raise the dollar prices of imports with relatively little short-run response of volume to the price changes. In fact, imports were probably swollen during the early months of 1972 by deliveries on orders speculatively placed ahead of that devaluation. Toward the end of 1972 "imports from Japan may have been increased by expectations that the yen would again be revalued. Finally, a growing shortage of domestic supplies led to a rise of close to $1 billion in our fuel imports."[64]

Though less so than 1971, 1972 was an eventful year. The foreign-exchange markets initially greeted the Smithsonian Agreement with relief, and some reversal began of earlier speculative outflows of funds. This small return flow ended, however, early in January. Downward pressure on the dollar at times in January and February led foreign central banks to support it with additional purchases. The dollar strengthened on improved market sentiment in the spring. In June a sudden crisis set sterling afloat. Amid rumors of a joint EC float, over $6 billion shifted from dollars into European currencies and the yen. The market began calming down on July 17 after the EC Finance Ministers reaffirmed support of the Smithsonian parities. On July 19 the Federal Reserve began supporting the dollar by selling foreign currencies. Actual sales of only $31.5 million worth between then and September 1 were enough to improve the mood in the market, since they signaled that central banks on both sides of the Atlantic were now actively defending the Smithsonian exchange rates. The dollar again strengthened as a return flow of speculative funds brought the United States roughly into official-settlements balance in the late summer, although a large current-account deficit persisted. The foreign-exchange markets remained generally calm as the year ended.[65]

The crisis of early February 1973 therefore represented a sudden reversal of the situation. The outcome was a 10 percent devaluation of the dollar against most other major currencies.

The Japanese yen, however, was allowed to float upward. Within about two weeks, a second crisis erupted, destroying the new parities and inaugurating a period of widespread currency floating. The next chapter presents the details.

In the first quarter of 1973 alone, the seasonally adjusted ORT and net-liquidity deficits reached $10.2 billion and $6.6 billion respectively, nearly equaling the figures for all of 1972. These deficits largely reflected capital outflows during the two periods of market turmoil that occurred in close succession. For 1973 as a whole, the balances on merchandise trade, on goods and services, and on current account registered surpluses of $0.5 billion, $4.3 billion, and $0.5 billion respectively. Trade was apparently responding to the devaluation of the dollar as theory leads us to expect. Already by the spring of 1973, some evidence was discernible that the Smithsonian devaluation was working. In April the United States posted its first merchandise trade surplus in 19 months.[66] In 1974, however, largely under the influence of the international petroleum situation, deficits returned in merchandise trade and on current account. With exchange rates floating and with immense petroleum-related international flows of funds taking place, the very meaning of the various balance-of-payments measures, and especially of the official-settlements and liquidity balances, was thrown into doubt.[67]

After exchange rates were set afloat in March 1973, the dollar generally depreciated to mid-year, recovered to January 1974, depreciated again through April, recovered partially until August, and then resumed a depreciation that persisted into 1975. Details appear in the following chapter.

Diagnosis and appraisal

Standing back from details about exports of cotton and airplanes, imports of oil and cars, international patterns of business cycles and interest rates, and palliatives tried and remedies proposed, let us see what generalizations our chronological survey of the balance-of-payments problem invites. Measures of the overall deficit by the gross-liquidity, net-liquidity, and official-reserve-transactions concepts have often diverged widely from each other and from the basic deficit. These divergences underline the inherent vagueness of the distinction between "above-the-line" and "below-the-line" items and thus the vagueness of the very concept of deficit or surplus, especially for a reserve-currency country such as the United States.[68] Overall deficits and the major deficit categories have been small in relation to gross national product; yet those relatively small amounts have caused much worry at home and abroad. Furthermore, the size and makeup of the deficit have varied sharply. While some components have improved from one year to the next, others have worsened—sometimes trade in goods and services, sometimes long-term capital movements, sometimes short-term capital movements.

These facts are trite but important; they emphasize how changeable conditions are. Balances of payments can react sensitively to slight differences among countries in rates of interest or price rise or economic growth, to changes in so-called "structural" conditions, and to special historical circumstances, including expectations and moods.[69] A trade surplus or deficit is a difference between sums of differences, since imports and exports of particular goods are themselves differences between domestic production and domestic use. A search for stable functional relations between balance-of-payments positions and their innumerable determinants is practically hopeless; forecasts can be little better than short-run extrapolations. A sensible policy would not have to depend on them.

For many years, actual policy consisted of poorly coordinated *ad hoc* expedients, including piecemeal suspension of the dollar's convertibility into gold and controls that added up to its piecemeal devaluation. Its actual devaluations in 1971 and 1973 came amid agonizing crises, and the full normal effectiveness of the devaluations was delayed by so-called "structural" distortions that had been accumulating for years.

Now let us look for generalizations about the shape and even about the causes of the chronic U.S. deficit. It may be described, arithmetically, as consisting of net military expenditures and government and private loans, investments, grants, and other transfers abroad in excess of an export surplus of goods and services. (This description holds until mid-1971, when even the goods-and-services account shifted into deficit.) In Fritz Machlup's terminology, "financial transfers" exceeded "real transfers."[70] Among the financial transfers, thus defined, government grants held top rank only in the early years of deficit (1950–1952)

and were overtaken first by military expenditures and beginning in 1956 by private capital exports. The net deficit on government account, chiefly in military transactions and foreign aid, averaged $4.0 billion a year from 1960 through 1970 and reached $6.2 billion in

63. Federal Reserve Bank of New York, *Annual Report*, 1972, p. 37; Christopher Bach in Federal Reserve Bank of St. Louis, *Review*, April 1973, p. 18.

64. Federal Reserve Bank of New York, *Annual Report*, 1972, p. 37; also Bach, *op. cit.*, pp. 17–18, 20; and *Business Week*, 12 May 1973, p. 72.

65. Federal Reserve Bank of New York, *Annual Report*, 1972, pp. 28–29, 32.

66. *Business Week*, 12 May 1973, pp. 72, 74; other news items; and figures from *Economic Report of the President*, 1975, pp. 350–351.

67. See *Survey of Current Business*, September 1974, esp. p. 36.

68. Not only the variety and changeability of concepts but also frequent large revisions of the published official numbers plague anyone trying to put together a consistent historical survey.

69. Consider the attempt by Walter Salant *et al.* to look ahead at *The United States Balance of Payments in 1968*, Washington: Brookings Institution, 1963. The authors worked with two different sets of assumptions about U.S. and European prices and real gross national products in 1968. Those of the figures that differed at all between the two sets of assumptions differed by only a few percent at most. Yet the discrepancy between the two resulting projections of the "basic" U.S. payments position was practically as large as the average actual "basic" deficit over the years 1958–1962.

70. "The Transfer Gap of the United States," Banca Nazionale del Lavoro *Quarterly Review*, September 1968, Reprints in International Finance, No. 11, Princeton, N.J.: Princeton University, International Finance Section. Machlup makes the classification he does (including, for example, military expenditures with the financial transfers) because he wants the "real" balance "to consist chiefly of such items as are sold and bought out of incomes and at market prices, or at least under conditions that allow income elasticities of supply and demand to come into play" (p. 203).

1971.[71] Private long-term capital outflows in excess of inflows averaged $2.3 billion a year from 1960 through 1970 and reached $4.4 billion in 1971. (More than matching these capital outflows was private net investment income, including royalties, averaging $4.9 billion a year from 1960 through 1970 and reaching $9.0 billion in 1971.)[72] For an impression of how large or small these figures are, we may note that the government-account deficit amounted to 0.6 percent and the private long-term capital deficit to 0.4 percent of gross national product in 1971. These subdeficits were about two-thirds and less than half, respectively, the size of the "basic" payments deficit for 1971.

The foregoing statements are matters of arithmetic and do not demonstrate cause and effect. Even if the causes of the overall deficit could be pinpointed, they would not necessarily coincide with conditions that "ought" to be eliminated. If the cost of urgently needed surgery threatens a deficit in an individual's personal balance of payments, it hardly follows that he "ought" to cancel his plans for the operation.[73] Similarly, curbing the government's overseas expenditures might hamper American foreign policy, as well as reduce exports that had been tied to American aid.[74] Curbing new foreign investments would impair interest and dividend returns in future years. One might reasonably argue (as Machlup did) for somehow expanding the real export surplus enough to cover the "financial transfers."

The United States balance-of-payments deficit has not been due to any single factor and certainly not to clear-cut motives of the country as a single decision-making unit. On the contrary, the deficit stems from the decisions made—or evaded—for a variety of reasons by innumerable American and foreign officials, firms, and individuals. The United States has, to be sure, received some gains (as well as some disadvantage) from the deficit. The country could acquire goods and services and investment assets from the rest of the world and could make donations abroad without currently paying for them in full. In concrete terms, the government could bear its overseas military burdens and grant foreign aid, corporations could acquire plants and offices abroad, investors could buy foreign stocks and bonds, and consumers could enjoy wines, small cars, tape recorders, and European trips, all more cheaply than they could have done if foreign monetary authorities had not been supporting

the dollar on the foreign exchanges and had instead allowed exchange rates to keep balances of payments is equilibrium. The United States could finance its deficit largely by running up dollar liabilities to foreign central banks at relatively low interest rates. The foreigners, from their own point of view, were making automatic loans to the United States of indefinite duration and of increasingly involuntary character. This situation was comfortable for the United States, on the whole, as long as it could last without degenerating into crisis. Many foreigners, notably including the French economist Jacques Rueff, complained of America's special privilege of being able to run "deficits without tears."

The existence of such benefits is no proof, however, that they were consciously sought. It hardly seems plausible that the United States kept the dollar overvalued to hold down the cost of seeking military, political, and economic domination of foreign countries. The U.S. deficit can be linked more plausibly with several conditions that evolved without being consciously intended. These include: (1) the Bretton Woods system of pegged exchange rates, with its lack of any "automatic" mechanism for correcting the imbalances always tending to arise from divergent cost and price trends or from changes in tastes, technology, and national economic structures; (2) the special roles of the United States and of the dollar within that system; (3) the special position and responsibilities of the United States in addition to those directly connected with the international monetary system; and (4) specific historical developments.[75]

The first point is fundamental but too familiar to need further emphasis here. The second point has several aspects. For private transactors, the dollar has been by far the most important currency used in international transactions and held as working balances. As world trade and payments grew in the 1950s and 1960s, private transactors were glad to acquire additional dollar balances. For monetary authorities, the dollar has been the most important currency used in exchange-market intervention and held in external reserves. Central bankers were glad, until recent years, to acquire additional dollar reserves, particularly as the growth of gold reserves came nowhere near meeting the requirements of the Bretton Woods system.

These last observations deserve elaboration. Because the dollar spelled liquidity for private and official foreigners alike, foreigners willingly accumulated short-term claims on the United States by incurring long-term liabilities or selling investment properties. These financial exchanges were promoted by the large size, elaborate organization, efficiency, and competitiveness of the U.S. money and capital market and its extension in the Eurodollar and Eurobond market. Failure to understand this process promoted what some economists considered the error of counting American long-term lending and investing in Europe toward a United States deficit while counting European lending and investing in short-term claims on the United States not toward avoiding a deficit but toward precariously financing one.[76] In the American balance-of-payments position, correctly understood, these flows of American long-term capital and European short-term capital largely offset each other. They represented constructive exchanges motivated by a generally stronger desire of Europeans than of Americans to place their savings at short term and to do their borrowing at long term. On this view, the money and capital markets of the United States served as a gigantic financial intermediary for the world; they adapted the characteristics of claims and debts to the different preferences of lenders and borrowers. Part of the reported outflows of capital from the United States, therefore, did not represent any intended net transfer of capital in the form of goods and services. Instead, these outflows arose from the intermediary role of the United States in enabling foreigners to acquire short-term assets by incurring long-term debt or by transferring ownership claims to American investors. Just as financial intermediation within a country aids capital formation and growth even though the banks and other financial institutions may not themselves be ultimate providers of real resources, so flows of capital into and out of the United States were aiding capital formation and growth abroad, even apart from any real transfer of capital in the form of goods and services. Banking, broadly conceived, happened to be a service in which the United States had a comparative advantage and which it was selling to the rest of the world. To some extent, even central banks counted among the foreigners actively acquiring short-term dollar assets. So far as a genuine foreign demand for liquid dollar holdings offset the outflow of long-term capital from the United States, the dollar came under no pressure on the foreign-exchange market.

71. Calculated from International Economic Policy Association, *The United States Balance of Payments*, Washington: IEPA, 1972, p. 13.

72. Calculated from *Economic Report of the President*, 1974, pp. 350–351.

73. Wilson E. Schmidt, *The Rescue of the Dollar*, Washington: American *Enterprise Institute*, 1963, esp. p. 28.

74. Machlup, *op. cit.*, noted by fitting a regression equation for 1950 through 1966 that changes in net financial transfers were reflected to the extent of 92 percent on the average in changes in net real transfers. Why, he wondered, should an adjustment mechanism work so well in forcing the flows of goods and services to adjust to changes in transfers while not correcting the gap that averaged around $2.3 billion? His hunch was that political considerations caused U.S. monetary and fiscal policies to tighten or ease whenever the external deficit moved up or down from its accustomed size.

75. I owe the inspiration for the last two paragraphs to a conversation with Mr. Gernot Volger, who would probably not, however, agree with their content.

76. For the view summarized here, see Charles P. Kindleberger, *Balance-of-Payments Deficits and the International Market for Liquidity*, Princeton Essays in International Finance, No. 46; Princeton, N.J.: Princeton University, International Finance Section, 1965; Emile Despres, Charles P. Kindleberger, and Walter S. Salant, "The Dollar and World Liquidity—A Minority View," *The Economist*, 5 February 1966, pp. 526–529, reprinted with some additions in Lawrence H. Officer and Thomas D. Willett, eds., *The International Monetary System*, Englewood Cliffs, N.J.: Prentice-Hall, 1969, pp. 41–52; and Walter S. Salant, "Financial Intermediation as an Explanation of Enduring 'Deficits' in the Balance of Payments," in Fritz Machlup *et al.*, eds., *International Mobility and Movement of Capital*, New York: National Bureau of Economic Research, 1972, pp. 607–659. Robert Mossé expresses agreement—noteworthy, coming from a Frenchman—with the Despres-Kindleberger—Salant thesis and disagreement with the thesis of his fellow countryman Jacques Rueff and many other Europeans that the United States was enjoying undue privileges in international monetary affairs. See "I falsi privilegi del dollaro," *Mercurio* (Milan), September 1972, pp. 1–11.

Until around 1970, anyway, a number of eminent economists were inclined largely to explain away the U.S. deficit with this consoling line of argument. It was a mistake to see a deficit in America's serving the world as a giant bank. The deficit was a mere statistical construct—a spurious problem rather than a true disequilibrium needing to be worried about and corrected. While so complacent a view is not fully justified, one can properly recognize international financial intermediation as one element in the U.S. deficit as conventionally measured. Unfortunately, worry can sometimes be self-justifying; it can *make* a problem out of what would otherwise not have been a problem. Worry about balance-of-payments weakness can bring bearish speculation against the country's currency at its fixed exchange rate, as well as unwise policy responses. Through leads and lags, bearishness can even weaken the merchandise trade balance.

Until 1971, at least, the dollar's role as numéraire of the international monetary system—the currency in terms of which other countries set and altered the par values of their currencies[77]—also contributed to the deficit. The dollar was subject to a quadruple bias. Other countries felt keener pressures to devalue when in deficit than to revalue upward when in surplus. Devaluations tended to be too large. Revaluations tended to be too small. Any single devaluation tempted other countries to follow suit, both for competitive reasons and because such a response to the action of another country was relatively easy to justify politically.[78] The dollar itself, however, as numéraire, could not readily be devalued. This fact was illustrated by the delay of its devaluation until 1971, after crises had occurred and after shock treatment had initiated a process of devaluation that stretched from August to December, amid intergovernmental bickering. The very belief that the dollar could hardly be devalued reinforced that delay. As a result, the actions of other countries exposed the dollar to passive and piecemeal upward revaluation. Its amount has been estimated at 4.7 percent on the average against other currencies from 1959 to the beginning of 1970 (even after the German revaluation of 1969).[79] The amount may not be large, but the direction was wrong.

As foreign willingness to accumulate dollars became ever more sorely tried, the special role of the dollar contributed to the U.S. deficit in another way, through capital movements. Pre-

cisely because the dollar was the dominant transactions, intervention, and reserve currency, attention focused on it; it was particularly susceptible to coming under distrust. Large foreign (and American) holdings of dollars meant that plenty were available to be dumped out of private into official hands whenever doing so seemed prudent or profitable. Once the devaluation of the dollar had ceased being unthinkable, the dollar came under the sort of speculative pressures that the pound sterling, as a lesser reserve currency, had repeatedly suffered on a smaller scale. By February and March 1973, many hedgers and speculators had apparently come to consider the dollar as inherently devaluation-prone, just as they considered the mark and yen as revaluation-prone. Such notions are characteristic of a system of fixed-but-adjustable rates.

The third point listed on page 584 is something of a catchall. As citadel of the capitalist system, center of technological innovation, generator of current saving from the world's largest national income, and home of a highly developed capital market, the United States was a natural source of large-scale direct and portfolio investment for the rest of the world. U.S. earnings on past foreign loans and investments have indeed exceeded current outflows of new loans and investments. Still, these current outflows are significant, arithmetically, in the U.S. deficit. And, in the sense indicated, they are natural. In the face of foreign expectations and exhortations, furthermore, America's size and wealth have contributed to transfers of foreign aid which, though small in relation to gross national product, have been sizable in relation to payments deficits. Its size and wealth also saddled the United States with exceptional responsibilities for the defense of the Free World, including the thankless burden of Vietnam. Finally, America's size and wealth and corresponding position in world trade and finance made its currency the natural focus of the Bretton Woods system, with all the special consequences already mentioned.

Fourth comes the role of special historical developments in the U.S. deficit. Japan and Western Europe, particularly Germany, experienced remarkable recovery and growth after World War II, thanks in part to U.S. aid and transfers of technology. Their export industries became increasingly competitive on the world market. The formation of the European Community and the discriminations it posed against American goods, especially agricultural goods, presumably held down the growth of American exports. At times, the United States ran a faster rate of inflation than other major industrial countries. This discrepancy was not persistent, but it appeared during part of the Vietnam period. Over longer periods, several competitor countries held their export price trends in check relative to their general price trends better than the United States did. Because of the smallness of foreign relative to domestic trade in the U.S. economy and for historical reasons, American businessmen tend not to be such hustlers on the world market as Europeans and Japanese—or so a common observation goes. Special historical developments include such things as business-cycle phasings, the vogue for small cars, oil import needs, increasing interest in tourism abroad, and so on. Changes of that general character are always occurring within and among advanced countries. Not they, but the absence of any automatic balancing mechanism, is what deserves emphasis.

Indecisive policies

Until 1971, the policies pursued by the United States government consisted of palliative "bits and pieces," some of them rather ridiculous.[80] The specific measures implementing this approach to the payments problem were objectionable for the same general reasons why tariffs, import quotas, and exchange controls are objectionable. The indecisiveness itself, however, is understandable. Coming much earlier than it came in fact, decisive U.S. action against the deficit would probably have met strong foreign resistance. Other countries were enjoying the luxury of moralizing at the United States for its deficit while hesitating to accept the turnaround in their own balances of payments that an end to the U.S. deficit would have entailed. Why should the United States have quarreled with those countries over trade barriers or monetary policies or exchange rates, especially when there were grounds for hope that the deficit might somehow cure itself, in accordance with the "breath-holding" philosophy of the Bretton Woods system?[81] Perhaps foreign inflation would speed up relative to U.S. inflation; perhaps some unforeseeable technological or structural change would benefit the U.S. position. Respectable economists, after all, were viewing the deficit with complacency. Mere fiddling with "bits and pieces" is also understandable on the part of elected and

appointed officials, whose responsibility in a particular office is likely to be brief. Besides, many influential advisers are likely to be technicians whose financial and diplomatic skills have their greatest value within a bits-and-pieces approach of applying cosmetics to balance-of-payments figures, inventing swap arrangements and Roosa bonds, devising and administering controls, negotiating offset agreements, and flying around the world endlessly conferring on global monetary reform.

77. Legally, the numéraire was the quantity of gold contained in the dollar at the time when the charter of the International Monetary Fund was negotiated; in effect, it was the dollar pure and simple.

78. Bergsten in Halm, *op. cit.*, p. 68. On the devaluation bias of a system of fixed-but-adjustable exchange rates, also see pp. 112–113 above.

79. Peter G. Peterson, *The United States in the Changing World Economy, Volume II: Background Material*, Washington: Government Printing Office, 1971, pp. 29, 31.

To recognize the dollar's piecemeal revaluation in the exchange-rate sense is not to deny that U.S. imposition of capital and other controls was amounting to piecemeal *de*valuation in a broader sense.

80. As early as 1963, Professor Milton Friedman incisively deplored the adoption of

one expedient after another, borrowing here, making swap arrangements there, changing the form of loans to make the figures look good. Entirely aside from the ineffectiveness of most of these measures, they are politically degrading and demeaning. We are a great and wealthy Nation. We should be directing our own course, setting an example to the world, living up to our destiny. Instead, we send our officials hat in hand to make the rounds of foreign governments and central banks; we put foreign central banks in a position to determine whether or not we can meet our obligations and thus enable them to exert great influence on our policies; we are driven to niggling negotiations with Hong Kong and with Japan and for all I know, Monaco, to get them to limit voluntarily their exports. Is this posture suitable for the leader of the free world?

The United States Balance of Payments, Hearings before the Joint Economic Committee, Part 3, November 1963, pp. 458–459.

81. On breath-holding, see p. 403.

Academic recommendations of a passive balance-of-payments policy[82] presumably carried some weight in favor of fiddling with bits and pieces as a compromise between passivity and decisive action. Although the United States had not sought the gains reaped through a payments deficit, those gains (mentioned on page 584) did exist; and curing the deficit would have meant losing them. True, those benefits could not have gone on forever; but policy-makers could understandably think, "Après nous le déluge." Meanwhile, the palliatives might gradually accumulate into a mass of mercantilistic negations of a market or price system. A further disadvantage was that the United States would sooner or later, and perhaps suddenly, face the necessity of major action and the disruption that would be involved, as in currency crises, large exchange-rate adjustments, and loss of accustomed benefits. A chronic deficit poses these dangers for any country. The United States did not have to face them as long as foreigners would automatically finance its deficit, but that advantage would not continue forever.

The case for full-fledged passivity, expressed more bluntly than usual, was somewhat as follows. A continuing deficit was not hurting the United States. We Americans needed only to express sympathy with countries that had been absorbing unwanted dollars into their central banks, risking imported inflation. We could merely suggest that they stop doing so. Each country could ward off unwanted dollars in whatever way seemed best for its own particular circumstances—by accepting faster inflation, by reducing tariffs and dismantling other controls over imports, or by upvaluing or floating its currency against the dollar. We did not have to press other countries to act; their unwanted accumulations of dollars exerted pressure enough. Exhaustion of the U.S. gold stock would not seriously harm us and would only sharpen the question addressed to foreign countries of whether they wanted to keep their currencies pegged to the dollar and, if so, at what exchange rate. Unfortunately, each individual foreign country might have to worry that an upward revaluation of its own currency would put it at a competitive disadvantage if its trading partners did not go along. That problem is characteristic of fixed-but-adjustable rates. The United States could not entirely

spare other countries that or a similar problem by devaluing the dollar against gold or SDRs. As in fact happened in 1971 and 1973, such action would force other countries to decide—and with awkward haste—whether to go along with the dollar or with gold and SDRs or take some intermediate course. The best the United States could do would be to set a good example by adopting the policy that it hoped most countries would eventually follow: "hands off" international trade and payments and "hands off" foreign-exchange markets and rates. If other countries failed to follow our advice and our example, then their resulting accumulations of dollars would be their worry, not ours. Actually, the United States government did not adopt so forthright a position.

Recommendations of passivity did not spell indifference to problems of trade and money. On the contrary, they concerned *how* the United States might best contribute to solutions. In particular, they did not mean indifference to erosion of the purchasing power of the dollar. Avoidance of inflation was quite in the spirit of those recommendations. Passive policy got a bad reputation and aroused resentment abroad by being stuck with a smart-alecky label of unfortunate connotations—"benign neglect."

By devaluing in 1971 and 1973, the United States went a long way toward abandoning its haphazard compromise with passive policy. As long as the dollar retains any substantial part of its former special role in the international monetary system, the United States, more than any other country, will find its balance-of-payments and monetary issues tied up with issues of reform of that system. To this topic we turn in Chapters 29 through 32.

---

82. See, for example, Gottfried Haberler and Thomas D. Willett, U.S. *Balance of Payments Policies and International Monetary Reform*, Washington: American Enterprise Institute, 1968; Lawrence B. Krause, "A Passive Balance of Payments Strategy for the U.S.," *Brookings Papers on Economic Activity*, 1970, No. 3; and my "Unilateral Action on International Monetary Policy," prepared for a Congressional subcommittee in 1966 and excerpted in Lawrence H. Officer and Thomas D. Willett, eds., *The International Monetary System: Problems and Proposals*, Englewood Cliffs, N.J.: Prentice-Hall, 1969, pp. 212–215.

Appendix to Chapter 27: The Dollar Shortage

An assortment of ideas

The balance-of-payments troubles of many countries for several years after World War II suggested the diagnosis of a "dollar shortage" that, with hindsight, could be traced back several decades. Most of the world outside North America supposedly suffered from a persistent or recurrent tendency to spend more than it earned (or borrowed at long term) in dealing with North America. Its reserves of gold and dollars seemed in continual danger of running out unless protected by direct controls over international trade and payments and by resort to loans or grants from the United States or from American-financed international agencies.

Writings on the dollar shortage kept piling up even in the late 1950s, years after the gold and dollar reserves of foreign countries as a whole had begun a sustained rise, years after the external position of the United States had actually shifted from surplus to slight deficit, and right up to the time when the fashion shifted toward worry about an American *deficit* and a dollar *glut*.[1] If the whole discussion now seems hopelessly dated, this very fact suggests a lesson worth emphasizing. Fashionable and ex-

cessively ingenious theories that read deep-seated significance into temporary conditions do not deserve quiet oblivion as soon as brute facts crush them; they should be remembered to permit recognizing their counterparts in the future. Continuity is of value in scientific disputes.

No amount of chronicling the balance-of-payments troubles of particular countries could illuminate the dollar shortage unless these troubles could be shown to share common characteristics and causes. Rather than a thing or a series of historical events, the dollar shortage was a theoretical concept. It was the idea of a long-term imbalance in international payments stemming not from remediable errors of policy but from deep-seated objective circumstances. Kindleberger, for example, spoke of tendencies rooted in "climate, geography, causes of war, the growth of productivity and consumption, the distribution of income, etc."[2]

More nearly specific explanations were legion: a secular tendency for a greater degree of economic stagnation or lesser degree of inflation in the United States than elsewhere (Kindleberger, Bollier, de Vries); low elasticities of demand and supply in international trade (Balogh, Harrod); a great shrinkage of international liquidity relative to international trade because of the failure of the price of gold to rise in step with the prices of other things (Harrod); America's great size and strength, leading to greater dependence of the rest of the world on the United States than conversely (Williams, the London *Economist*, Crowther); various kinds of "deep-seated structural changes in the world economy" (Zupnick, who, with particular reference to British problems, mentions among other things American dominance in the world petroleum industry, increasing industrialization in the overseas Sterling Area, and Britain's failure to adapt to basic changes in the world's economic structure); an international demonstration effect prodding

1. For surveys of the literature in the late 1950s, see Charles P. Kindleberger, "The Dollar Shortage Re-Revisited," *American Economic Review*, XLVIII, June 1958, pp. 388–395; and Raymond F. Mikesell's refreshingly iconoclastic note on "Dollar Shortage: A Modern Myth," *Journal of Political Economy*, XLVII, June 1959, pp. 307–309.

2. Charles P. Kindleberger, *The Dollar Shortage*, New York: The Technology Press of MIT and John Wiley & Sons, Inc., 1950, pp. 170–171.

foreigners to live beyond their means in an attempt to imitate the American standard of living (Kindleberger); a more rapid pace of innovation and productivity growth in the United States than elsewhere or in some sectors of the American economy than in others (Hicks, Balogh, de Vries, Croome, Williams, Crowther); or asymmetry in trade adjustments because the United States specializes in research-intensive commodities and the rest of the world in traditional commodities (Hoffmeyer).[3]

Wary of sweeping insights, at least one writer scrutinized the American balance of payments item by item and projected the probable future size of each item under various assumptions. His method is epitomized by his observation, in discussing U.S. raw-material imports, that the successful efforts were being made to reduce the use of tin in tin cans.[4] He concluded that structural developments were likely to keep the foreign demand for American goods growing more strongly than the American demand for foreign goods; only under improbably optimistic assumptions would a long-term dollar problem fail to persist. This approach is reminiscent of W. Stanley Jevons's fears, in the last century, of impending shortages of coal and paper.[5] Once one has become convinced that a shortage of something or other is or is not likely, diligent study and thought can produce numerous "considerations" in support of that opinion.

Some of the arguments contradicted each other. The argument about America's superior dynamism in innovation and productivity ran counter to the one about America's greater tendency towards economic stagnation. Emphasis on the ability of efficient American producers to undersell foreigners almost all across the board ran counter to the supposition of low price elasticities of demand in international trade. The apparent contradictions might have been reconciled somehow, but this was not really necessary. The notion of dollar shortage actually thrived on the many kinds of supporting considerations, even mutually contradictory ones, that kept coming forth. "Dollar shortage" was a label that lumped together a vaguely defined *range* of conditions or developments that might lessen countries' gains from international trade, or that might impose awkward internal economic readjustments, or that might tend to create balance-of-payments deficits, or that might hamper adjustment

mechanisms. The rise of a dollar-shortage fad —a fashionable topic for books, articles, and doctoral dissertations—gave economists a positive incentive to devise new products marketable under that label and to devise new "explanations" for the range of problems it so vaguely suggested. The billowing academic smoke strengthened belief in a real-world fire.

Growth of productivity

A particularly influential line of argument emphasized differential rates of growth in productivity. Even within this line, contradictions abounded. Harrod worried about especially rapid productivity growth in the export sectors of the more progressive economy, Hicks about productivity growth concentrated in import-competing sectors, Balogh about random increases in productivity, and Williams even about uniform productivity growth in the more progressive economy.[6] Whether or not wage levels rose in step with productivity also entered the discussion. If productivity kept growing in the United States faster than abroad and faster than American wage levels, then the American price level would fall, tending to stimulate exports relative to imports. Foreigners would have import surpluses unless they endured deflation or unless the dollar were allowed to appreciate on the exchanges. The foreigners would probably share in America's increased productivity by way of improved terms of trade. This outcome could occur without major changes in exchange rates or foreign price levels if American wage levels did rise along with productivity in such a way that the price level held roughly steady.

J. R. Hicks took a dimmer view. His "Inaugural Lecture"[7] had a remarkable influence in keeping the whole discussion respectable and topical. He saw American productivity growing more rapidly in import-competing industries than in export industries. To hold their American markets, foreigners would have to accept ever lower prices while enjoying only slightly cheapened American exports. If foreigners resisted the necessary decline in their terms of trade and their real incomes, as by delaying devaluation relative to the dollar, balance-of-payments disequilibrium would develop.

A stronger argument, perhaps, pointed to constant American dynamism not only in cutting the real-input production cost of existing products but also in developing improved products or entirely new products not soon available from other sources. In both ways the pattern of comparative advantage kept changing. Foreign countries might have a comparative advantage in certain industries one year, a comparative disadvantage the next. The smaller and poorer countries, with their industries continually becoming obsolete, kept on having to retreat into specialization in less and less advantageous lines of production. American dynamism set a killing pace of adjustment. Painful adjustments would be undertaken only under the pressure of actual balance-of-payments deficits; and even so, the foreign economies might not succeed in adjusting fast enough. Adaptations were likely to be obsolete even before they could be completed.[8]

The differential-productivity-growth arguments were open to questions of fact[9] and also of analysis. The various hypothesized patterns of productivity growth would not necessarily, without further assumptions, intensify foreign eagerness to trade relative to American eagerness. And even if this result did occur and did, rather implausibly, tend to shrink foreigners' gain from trade with the United States, this still would not be the same thing as turning their gain into actual loss. As for continual American development of new and improved products not available elsewhere, one wonders why the job only the American machine could do had to be done. If foreigners would buy American goods at whatever cost, something was peculiar and in need of explanation about their overall propensity to spend, and not merely about their propensity to import.[10] If

University Press, 1957, esp. pp. 183, 226; J. R. Hicks, "An Inaugural Lecture," *Oxford Economic Papers*, n.s. **V**, June 1953, pp. 117–135; Honor Croome, "The Dollar Siege," *Lloyds Bank Review*, July 1950, pp. 30, 37, quoted in Zupnick, *op. cit.*, pp. 206–207; Erik Hoffmeyer, *Dollar Shortage and the Structure of U.S. Foreign Trade*, Copenhagen: Ejnar Munksgaard; Amsterdam: North-Holland Publishing Co., 1958.

R. F. Harrod's participation in the discussion is interesting because of his earlier much-quoted remarks that "dollar famine" is "one of the most absurd phrases ever coined" and that the "allegation of a 'world dollar shortage' is surely one of the most brazen pieces of collective effrontery that has ever been uttered." *Are These Hardships Necessary?*, 2nd ed., London: Rupert Hart-Davis, 1947, pp. 42–43. Hoffmeyer, *op. cit.*, pp. 27, 38–39, refers to Harrod's "conversion" to belief in the dollar shortage.

4. Donald MacDougall, *The World Dollar Problem*, London: Macmillan, 1957, p. 193 and footnote. Similarly, Hoffmeyer, to bolster his thesis about the special research intensity of American production, provided historical-statistical surveys of various categories of U.S. foreign trade—wool, sugar, shipping, newsprint, copper, oil, and business machines. He also reviewed developments in trade policy. This sort of thing gave an unwarranted air of specificity and empiricism to the idea of dollar shortage.

5. Cf. John Maynard Keynes, *Essays and Sketches in Biography*, New York: Meridian Books, 1956, pp. 128–133.

6. See Zupnick, *op. cit.*, p. 208.

7. *Oxford Economic Papers*, June 1953. Cf. the discussion in de Vries, *op. cit.*, pp. 11–14.

8. This paragraph combines points raised in Balogh, *op. cit.*, pp. 8–9; Croome, *loc. cit.*; Dennis H. Robertson, *Britain in the World Economy*, London: Allen & Unwin, 1954; and de Vries, *op. cit.*, esp. pp. 15–16, 23–24, 28–30, 32.

9. Cf. J. Kymmell, "Het dollar probleem; duurzame realiteit of tijdelijk fenomeen?," *Economisch-Statistische Berichten*, **XLI**, March 14, 1956, esp. pp. 216–217; and J. M. Letiche, "Differential Rates of Productivity Growth and International Imbalance," *Quarterly Journal of Economics*, **LXIX**, August 1955, pp. 371–401.

10. Kindleberger, *American Economic Review*, June 1958, p. 393.

---

3. The references are to Kindleberger, *Dollar Shortage*, esp. pp. 170, 181; René D. Bollier, *Die These einer chronischen Dollarknappheit*, Zurich: Polygraphischer Verlag, 1956; T. de Vries, "De theorie van het comparatieve voordeel en het dollartekort," *De Economist*, Vol. 104, January 1956, pp. 1–39; T. Balogh, *The Dollar Crisis*, Oxford: Basil Blackwell, 1949, esp. pp. 8–9, 229; Roy F. Harrod, "Imbalance of International Payments," IMF *Staff Papers*, **III**, April 1953, pp. 1–46; John H. Williams, *Economic Stability in the Modern World*, Stamp Memorial Lecture, London: Athlone Press, 1952; *The Economist*, Vol. 145, 4 December 1943, pp. 750–751; Geoffrey Crowther, *Balances and Imbalances of Payments*, Boston: Harvard University, Graduate School of Business Administration, 1957, esp. p. 48; Elliot Zupnick, *Britain's Postwar Dollar Problem*, New York: Columbia

the pessimistic theories were correct, incidentally, why were the less dynamic regions of the United States not suffering from a conspicuous dollar shortage in their trade with the more dynamic regions?

These questions fail, however, to press the main objection. Much ingenuity went to waste demonstrating possibilities no one ever doubted: *of course* changes in wants, resources, and technology can shift the pattern of comparative advantage and reciprocal demand to the benefit of some countries and the harm of others. (Most obviously, one country could suffer from new and cheaper competing supplies of the things it exports and from new and intensified competing demands for the things it imports.) What remained to be shown was that such changes had decisively characterized the decades of dollar shortage and were fated to keep on doing so in the future. It especially remained to be shown—depending on just what the dollar-shortage thesis was, anyway—either that these changes unavoidably caused intractable external deficits or else that their harmful effects could largely be avoided by controls to replace market adjustment mechanisms.

Adjustment mechanisms: the crucial question

Here was another fundamental ambiguity in the dollar-shortage thesis. Did it contend that no "automatic" market processes *could* work to equilibrate balances of payments? Or that reliance on controls was preferable? Or that political realities made acceptance of market processes unlikely? Apart from terminology, there would have been nothing basically new or particularly disturbing in either of the two latter contentions. What was disturbing was the denial, on the first interpretation, of the theory of self-regulation of the balance of payments by way of changes in incomes, prices, and exchange rates. What, exactly, was wrong with standard economics?

Ridicule was one way of dismissing this question. Kindleberger found wrong exchange rates responsible for disequilibrium only in the sense that "there is never a shortage of anything, but merely wrong pricing." Eisenhower's troops in World War II never ran short of

ammunition; "the price was merely too low."[11] Vagueness supplemented quips. Standard analysis was called static, while reality is dynamic.[12]

A matter of sheer public relations handicapped the traditional analysis. Any simple explanation of dollar shortage seemed *too* simple. See how many laws and regulations had been promulgated to deal with it, how many crises experienced, how many international conferences held, and how many loans arranged. See how many books and articles had appeared with complex and impressive theorizing, massive statistical tabulations, learned historical surveys, and detailed technological investigations (penetrating even to the fabrication of tin cans). Criticism emphasizing adjustment mechanisms was damned for its simplicity—for its very merit of abstracting the relevant main truths from the incidental details. It was orthodox or classical, furthermore, and thus behind the times practically by definition.[13] Finally, disparagement of orthodox analysis had the same sort of strength as the positive case for dollar shortage: it had so many strands to it, even vague and mutually contradictory strands, that it could hardly be pinned down.

If what the dollar-shortage theorists had in mind was the *disadvantages* of automatic adjustment mechanisms, their saying so openly would have helped bring their opinions into relation with the existing literature on the issue.[14]

Some of the dollar-shortage literature did explicitly acknowledge the central question of whether "automatic" equilibrating tendencies could work. The answer often implied was "no." One writer saw the problem as primarily the result not of "wilful policies" but rather of "basic forces which have transformed the nature of the world economy . . . and precluded adequate adjustment. . . ."[15] On another page, however, he defined a dollar shortage as existing when more dollars were demanded than supplied "at an acceptable level of employment, real income, and import restrictions. . . ." The key word was "acceptable," whose imprecision was frankly recognized by the remark that an acceptable level of real income is one below which "tensions" would "threaten the stability of the social and political equilibria." This minimum acceptable level of income might be ascertained in a general way of knowing "a country's history,

customs, traditions, and institutions. . . ."
The problem of dollar shortage was "one of
restoring equilibrium without inducing an intolerable decline in the levels of real income
and employment."[16]—Such statements slide
from a denial of market adjustment mechanisms to a judgment that their operation would
be intolerable.

Policy arguments

Other writers frankly accepted the latter interpretation. Thomas Balogh, for instance,
emphatically recognized that equilibrium in
international payments could easily be achieved
without controls. He predicted the consequences: worsened terms of trade, diminished
real income, worsened maldistribution of
income in the poorer countries, worsened prospects for a decrease in international inequality,
a need for periodic further readjustments by
the poorer countries, and probably even "mass
unemployment and starvation."[17] Unfortunately, the fact that a country's trading opportunities have changed adversely does not necessarily mean that controls and tariffs could do
much about it. What if the country lacks any
great monopoly-monopsony power on the
world market? If anything, the thesis about the
overpowering economic strength of the United
States and about how one-sidedly the rest of
the world depended on trade with it suggested
little opportunity for the rest of the world to
twist the terms of trade in its favor. The two
strands of argument do not mesh well.

By now the implication is out in the open
that the dollar-shortage thesis sometimes served
as a vehicle for policy arguments. Balogh developed a sizable list of arguments against free
or freer trade. Crowther predicted, and quite
apparently recommended, that in the future
trade between the dollar world and the sterling-
EPU world would be balanced only "by the
brute force of control and restriction." Williams found the world more than ever "in need
of close cooperation looking toward the conscious development of an integrated pattern of
trade. . . ." Hoffmeyer pleaded for a more
liberal U.S. import policy. Zupnick listed
numerous recommendations, including measures to modify the structure of the British
economy, the screening of British capital exports to the overseas Sterling Area as well as to

the outside world, a rise in the dollar price of
gold, cuts in American tariffs, continued temporary toleration by the United States of currency inconvertibility and of discrimination

11. Kindleberger, *Dollar Shortage*, pp. 175–176.

12. E.g., Balogh, *op. cit.*, p. 229; Balogh, "The
Dollar Shortage Once More; a Reply," *Scottish
Journal of Political Economy*, II, June 1955, p. 151;
Williams, *op. cit.*, pp. 13–14.
As Machlup and Samuelson have noted, the term
"static" often is little more than an epithet to
disparage other people's theories while describing
one's own, and the world they supposely refer to,
as "dynamic."

13. De Vries, *op. cit.*, pp. 1–2, implies that
refusal to take the dollar shortage seriously is
reminiscent of the classical economists' insistence
on Say's Law and refusal to worry about depressions
and unemployment.

14. De Vries, whose dollar-shortage argument
is one of the most nearly plausible known to me,
recognized that fluctuating exchange rates might
perhaps be a solution. He dismissed this possibility,
however, as too complex a topic for the scope of
his paper. *Op. cit.*, pp. 30, 39.

15. Zupnick, *op. cit.*, p. 226. Similar passages
occur in Williams, *op. cit.*, p. 7, and Crowther,
op. cit., p. 52. Crowther thinks (p. 50) that exchange-rate adjustments, no matter how large,
might not provide equilibrium; even a 50 percent
devaluation of the pound would not balance Britain's international payments. Similarly, but in a
more general context, Seymour E. Harris, *International and Interregional Economics*, New York:
McGraw-Hill, 1957, p. 440, insists on the possibility
"that at *no* value of a currency will there be equilibrium. . . ."
Perhaps the denial of equilibrating processes
stems from a vague idea that equilibrium is a Good
Thing by definition, coupled with the judgment
that reliance on market processes would be a Bad
Thing in the modern world. Cf. F. Machlup,
"Equilibrium and Disequilibrium: Misplaced Concreteness and Disguised Politics," *Economic Journal*, LXVIII, March 1958, esp. pp. 13–14.

16. Zupnick, *op. cit.*, pp. 3–6.

17. Balogh, *Scottish Journal of Political Econ-
omy*, June 1955, p. 154; *Dollar Crisis*, p. 136; "The
Dollar Crisis Revisited," *Oxford Economic Papers*,
VI, September 1954, pp. 276–277.

against itself, and continuance of U.S. foreign aid. On this last point, the dollar-shortage thesis did often seem to convey tacit approval of international imbalance so far as it meant that the rest of the world was obtaining more goods and services from the United States than it sent in return. This would be a sophisticated variant of the view that balance-of-payments difficulties are in themselves an argument for American aid. As the main conclusions of his *Dollar Crisis*, Balogh frankly called for "the international development of the poorer, financed out of *free* contributions of the richer, countries. . . ." De Vries argued that convertibility of European currencies would probably have to be supported for a few years by American military grants and special dollar expenditures in Europe.[18]

One could reject the dollar-shortage thesis, of course, and still agree with some recommendations made in its name. The most forthright and ultimately most persuasive way of stating the case for aid, for example, would seem to be to show that the recipients are poor and deserving.

Confusion of value judgments and positive analysis

Despite occasional openness about policy preferences, the entire texture of the dollar-shortage discussion made these preferences appear to have been imposed by inexorable developments that had destroyed or seriously impaired the traditional adjustment mechanisms. Normative judgments and policy proposals thus took on the prestige of positive propositions of fact and logic.

If a writer purporting to analyze dollar shortage really meant that many foreign countries were so desperately poor as to have an understandable and forgivable tendency to try to live beyond their means; or if he was comparing the relative merits of rival balance-of-payments adjustment mechanisms; or if he thought he had found some crucial flaw in the traditional analysis of those mechanisms; or if he had in mind some political or other reason why no otherwise-workable mechanism would be tolerated; or if he was calling for tariffs and other trade controls to improve terms of trade, safeguard home employment, affect income distribution, foster infant industries, or promote economic diversification and so reduce vulnerability to changes in world markets; or if he was discussing some other familiar matter, he should have said so openly. Unnecessary new terminology appearing to deal with a new and distinct topic only interferes with bringing to bear on a topic any analyses and arguments that are already familiar. If these precautions had been taken in the first place, the dollar shortage would never have seemed to be a distinct reality requiring explanation by distinct and novel theories.

18. See the following works already cited: Balogh, *Scottish Journal of Political Economy*, June 1955, pp. 153–154; Crowther, p. 35; Williams, p. 33 (and cf. p. 26 for musings about a fundamental reshaping of British production and trade); Hoffmeyer, p. 206; Zupnick, pp. 227–232; Balogh, *Dollar Crisis*, pp. xxxiv–xxxv and chap. 6; de Vries, p. 39.

CHAPTER TWENTY-EIGHT

The Crises of 1973 and Generalized Floating

Background of the February crisis

With hindsight, the monetary crisis of February 1973 traces back several weeks. The Vietnam agreement that had seemed "at hand" in October 1972 was delayed until late January. Meanwhile, the American bombing of Hanoi resumed in December. Although price inflation was still running at a lower pace in the United States than in other major countries, uneasiness apparently fed on the Vietnam disappointments and on the announcement of January 11 that the price and wage controls of Phase II would give way to looser enforcement under Phase III.[1] Worriers could see a connection between a Federal budget deficit running in the neighborhood of $20 billion a year and money-supply expansion. Money had grown by 8.3 percent in 1972, as compared with 6.6 percent in 1971, 6.0 percent in 1970, 3.6 percent in 1969, and 7.8 percent in 1968.[2] Big jumps in wholesale prices late in 1972 seemed likely to carry over into consumer prices early in the new year. The stock market slumped, apparently on fears of faster inflation and of interest rates reflecting it; and the slump reacted on the mood in the foreign-exchange market. The Federal Reserve seemed to be persisting in its traditional preoccupation with interest rates, even at the expense of money-supply control.[3] Strong business recovery in the United States in the face of slackened economic growth abroad had been swelling the U.S. trade deficit; discouraging figures—revealed only later, on revision, to have exaggerated the imbalance—became available late in January. Japan's balance of payments was heavily in surplus, still showing no sign that the imbalance in Japanese-American trade was diminishing. In mid-January, moreover, Japan tightened stock-market credit in a way that seemed likely to promote capital imports.[4]

Against this background, several specific events brought matters to a head. Italy had been chronically plagued by capital flight, partly through export of banknotes; and the lira was the weakest of the Common Market currencies. Yet a large Italian trade surplus argued against a straightforward devaluation. By a decision announced on Saturday, January 20, the authorities allowed the lira to float downward in financial transactions while continuing to support it for current-account transactions. They also sought to curb capital exports accomplished through leads and lags in commercial payments. In the first day or two of the two-tier market, the "financial lira" slumped some 6 to 7½ percent below the lira's current "commercial" rate and its Smithsonian central rate. Italian banks tried to adjust to the new system partly by buying Swiss francs to cover outstanding indebtedness. Their intensi-

---

1. Treasury Secretary Shultz, although maintaining that the move to Phase III "shouldn't have been a factor" in triggering the crisis, later acknowledged its psychological effect. *Wall Street Journal*, 16 February 1973, p. 4.

2. M₁, revised; *Federal Reserve Bulletin*, February 1973, p. 63.

3. As the international financial community shifted its keenest worries about inflation back onto the United States, the markets became concerned that interest rates in the United States, even though rising sharply for short maturities, might not be allowed to rise enough to protect the dollar in the face of rising interest rates in Europe. This, anyway, is the interpretation of Charles A. Coombs, Federal Reserve Bank of New York, *Monthly Review*, March 1973, pp. 47–48.

4. Federal Reserve Bank of Chicago, *International Letter*, 19 January 1973; and *Wall Street Journal*, 2 March 1973, p. 8.

fied demand for Swiss francs joined a strong demand from Swiss banks, which had been selling Eurodollar holdings to meet domestic credit demands in the face of a restrictive monetary policy. The dollar was also involved as a vehicle currency. To keep it from sinking below its Smithsonian floor, the Swiss National Bank had to absorb dollars on a scale that, although not massive by historical standards, was large enough to grate on Swiss worries about imported inflation. The National Bank imposed new restrictions on banks' use of Swiss funds obtained for dollars. More important, it announced on Tuesday, January 23, that it was suspending its support of the dollar. This floating of the Swiss franc, though supposedly only temporary, underlined the shakiness of the Smithsonian structure. Perhaps, thought market participants, the Swiss authorities knew something not generally known. Anyway, the franc's rise above its Smithsonian ceiling put upward pressure on the currencies of Switzerland's major trading partners. Perhaps Germany (and Japan) would also have to float or revalue. Still, the first week of the Swiss float passed with no general crisis.

The attention already focusing on the mark grew more intense after release of strong German trade figures on Monday, January 29. On Tuesday, despite central-bank support (on a moderate scale), the dollar weakened in Frankfurt, Paris, London, Tokyo, and Zurich and in the Italian financial market. Wednesday the 31st was a relatively tranquil day, thanks in part—or so some foreign-exchange dealers said—to the official support of the dollar on Tuesday. Foreign-exchange trading swelled on Thursday, February 1. Multinational corporations prudently switching out of dollars were reportedly joined by speculators testing the determination of central banks to keep on supporting the dollar.[5] On Friday the 2nd, by some accounts, central banks in Europe and Japan absorbed about $1 billion of dollars in addition to about $1 billion earlier in the week. Over the weekend the German authorities tightened their controls over foreign direct and portfolio investment in Germany and over borrowing abroad by German corporations.

The second devaluation of the dollar

Monday the 5th was the last day before the assault on the dollar turned massive. During the week, such prominent members of Congress as Representatives Henry Reuss and Wilbur Mills and Senator Jacob Javits contributed to talk that the outlook for the U.S. trade balance was bleak, that the dollar was (in Reuss's words) "patently overvalued again" in relation to the mark and yen, that the latter currencies should be revalued or floated upward or the dollar devalued again, that exchange rates should be renegotiated in an international conference and made more readily adjustable, that Germany was considering a two-tier foreign-exchange market, and that the German government would impose a virtual ban on all corporate borrowing abroad. By the close of the market on Friday, the Bundesbank's gain of reserves in the first seven business days of February had mounted to $6 or $7 billion, at least half on Thursday and Friday alone. The Bundesbank's intake of dollars was the highest ever recorded for a period of that length; it contrasts with the $2.2 billion taken in from April 29 to May 5, 1971. (Meanwhile, the Federal Reserve Bank of New York sold $339 million worth of marks and guilders.)[6] Financial experts watched with surprise and skepticism as the Bundesbank traded on such a scale, paying marks likely to rise in value for dollars likely to fall.

Until then, the Tokyo foreign-exchange market had been open for business on Saturdays. The crisis would have focused there on the 10th if the Japanese government had not closed the market. The leading European countries ordered their markets to remain closed on Monday the 12th, while New York banks remained closed anyway for Lincoln's Birthday.

Late that night, Treasury Secretary Shultz announced a 10 percent devaluation of the dollar against SDRs.[7] By advance agreement, Japan allowed the yen to float. Italy allowed the lira to float in its commercial as well as its financial market, thus emulating Canada, Britain and Ireland, Switzerland, and Japan. Apart from these floaters, most major industrial countries retained their parities against gold or SDRs, thereby passively revaluing by 11.1 percent against the dollar. Many smaller and less developed countries kept their existing pegs to the dollar. Taking account of New York quotations for 14 currencies on February 20 and the importance of their countries in U.S. trade, the Morgan Guaranty Trust Company calculated the weighted average devaluation of the dollar as 5.3 percent from the Smithsonian rates and 15.8 percent from the rates prevailing just before Canada's upward float in 1970.[8] (The Canadian dollar appreciated only slightly further against the U.S. dollar when the latter was devalued.)

It is not clear that the February crisis and devaluation reflected a fundamental disequilibrium. Since the time of the Smithsonian Agreement, when econometric models had been employed in an effort to set equilibrium rates, the dollar had lost purchasing power more slowly than other major currencies. The purchasing-power-parity doctrine, as explained in Chapter 11, is useful chiefly for purposes *other* than estimating equilibrium exchange rates; but for what they may be worth, comparative-version calculations using plausible base years in the 1950s and 1960s fail to show the dollar overvalued at the end of 1972. Only weeks before the crisis, the U.S. trade position and the dollar were widely assessed as growing sounder. The contrary evidence of the widening of the trade deficit in 1972 might be explained away in terms of the country's strong business recovery and of normal lags in the working of any exchange-rate adjustment. The dollar overhang of $60 to $70 billion in foreign official hands, another element of weakness in the situation, was a result of earlier conditions and no measure of any current overvaluation. None of this is to say that the dollar's Smithsonian parity was still correct in February 1973; but no one knows how large an adjustment, if any, was required. The herd instincts of hedgers and speculators and even the sheer *habit* of regarding the yen and mark as undervalued currencies and the dollar as an overvalued currency had contributed to an atmosphere of crisis. To pick a number—10 percent—out of such an atmosphere is a questionable method of revising exchange rates.

Involuntary floating
after fixed rates crumble again

For about ten days the dollar was strong in relation to its new reduced parity. Early in the week of Monday the 19th, the dollar reached its ceiling against the mark. The unwinding of speculative positions in marks was encouraged by Germany's imposition of a 10 percent a year negative interest rate on nonresident deposits.[9]

The Bundesbank was able to sell nearly $1 billion of its recently acquired dollars. Nevertheless, the dollar's second devaluation had evidently come as a profound shock, sensitizing holders of dollars around the world to the possibility of further changes. Treasury Secretary Shultz somehow passed up the opportunity to answer with a firm "no" a television reporter's question about the possibility of further devaluations, and remarks in a press conference by German Finance Minister Helmut Schmidt inflamed talk already circulating about the possibility of a joint float of European currencies.[10] By Friday the 23rd, the pressure had become intense, with the Swiss franc floating buoyantly and the dollar at its new floor against the mark, the guilder, and the French and Belgian francs. The Federal Reserve raised its discount rate from 5.0 to 5.5 percent.

5. Arab holders are said to have played a major role in the flight from the dollar, converting $1 to $3 billion of Eurodollars into German marks in February alone. *Farmand*, 20 October 1973, p. 66.

6. *IMF Survey*, 26 February 1973, citing the *Monthly Report* of the Bundesbank; *Washington Post*, 11 February 1973, p. A-28, 12 February 1973, p. A-12; *Wall Street Journal*, 14 February 1973, p. 3.

7. Legalistically, the Administration would ask Congress to cut the par value of the dollar from SDR0.92106 to SDR0.82895 and raise the official price of gold from $38 to $42.22 per ounce. This devaluation became effective legally on October 18, 1973, but effective actually at once.

8. *Wall Street Journal*, 21 February 1973, p. 2. Alternative calculations from daily figures currently appearing in the *Wall Street Journal* show the dollar on February 15, 1973 averaging 6 percent below its Smithsonian level and 16 percent below its level of May 1970.

9. Federal Reserve Bank of Chicago, *International Letter*, 23 February 1973. Effective March 1, Switzerland tightened its negative-interest-rate penalty on nonresident accounts. *IMF Survey*, 12 March 1973, p. 69.

10. These incitements to uncertainty are mentioned in, respectively, *Newsweek*, 12 March 1973, p. 71, and *Wall Street Journal*, 26 February 1973, p. 4.

The weekend, together with announcement of improved trade figures for January, brought only a brief respite. By Wednesday the 28th the dollar was sinking again. The following day, March 1, brought an unprecedented rush into Continental currencies. It seems no mere coincidence that this rush occurred on the very day when Prime Minister Heath and Chancellor Brandt were meeting in Bonn to discuss "monetary cooperation." The Bundesbank bought $2 billion of dollars by noon and a total of $2.5 billion during the day, recording its most massive intervention ever in a single day. Other European central banks also supported the dollar with purchases totaling around $1 billion. That night the major foreign-exchange markets were ordered officially closed until further notice;[11] and on Sunday the EC finance ministers decided to continue this suspension of official exchange transactions.

On March 11, Germany, France, Belgium-Luxembourg, the Netherlands, and Denmark agreed to float their currencies jointly. At the same time, Germany revalued the mark upward by 3 percent against SDRs. Norway and Sweden, though not members of the European Community, soon joined the joint float. When the markets reopened officially on Monday, March 19, with the float abolishing the Smithsonian tunnel, the "snake in the tunnel"[12] became the "snake in the lake." Japan, Canada, Switzerland, Italy, and Britain and Ireland continued floating independently.

The dollar generally strengthened against Continental currencies in March and April 1973 and even to mid-May. Then those currencies, notably the mark, began a sharp rise that would continue with little interruption through early July. Several developments were apparently at work. A policy of tight money in Germany was expected to intensify. A further upward revaluation of the mark was rumored. The price of gold was jumping, rising $10 in just three days and reaching $120 on June 1. Prices were escalating and the stock market sinking in the United States. The Watergate affair was widely regarded as a major factor: perhaps President Nixon would be too weakened in his dealings with Congress to take strong economic measures. Hopes for decisive action against inflation were disappointed on June 13 when President Nixon announced a 60-day price freeze, widely viewed as a superficial and inappropriate gesture. On Tuesday, June 26, after disappointing U.S. trade figures had appeared and after the Germans had announced further liquidity-tightening measures, heavy demand for marks drove the spot rate up almost 2½ percent in four hours. The mark gained another 3 percent against the dollar on June 28. Central banks participating in the joint float had to sell marks heavily to support the other currencies, bringing the 12-day intervention total to $1.5 billion worth. The following day, June 29, Germany announced a 5½ percent further revaluation.

Between then and Friday, July 6, amid (false) rumors of still another revaluation, the mark gained more than 9½ percent against the dollar.[13] At 45.25 cents, the mark had risen 31.2 percent above its central rate implied by the February devaluation of the dollar. It stood 45.8 percent above its Smithsonian central rate, 65.6 percent above its parity of before May 1971, and 81.0 percent above its parity of before September 1969.

Other quotations on July 6 also reflected the dollar's weakness. At 37.74 cents, the Swiss franc stood 30.4 percent above its rather fictitious February parity with the devalued dollar and 44.9 percent above its Smithsonian central rate. At 40.00 and 26.26 cents, respectively, the Dutch guilder and French franc stood at 16.8 and 20.9 percent above their new February central rates.

By ordinary standards, conditions were chaotic on July 6. In New York, spreads between bid and offer rates widened to almost 1 percent for the mark and to over one-half of 1 percent for the guilder. Several banks temporarily discontinued trading in those currencies. In Switzerland, the Director-General of the National Bank characterized the foreign-exchange market as "completely out of control."[14]

Meeting over the weekend at the Bank for International Settlements in Basel, central bankers completed negotiations for increases in the lines of "swap" credit they made available to each other. On Tuesday, July 10, the Federal Reserve announced an increase from $11.7 billion to nearly $18.0 billion in its swap network. The day before, the Federal Open Market Committee had authorized resumption of intervention in the foreign-exchange market, to be financed by swap drawings if necessary.

The markets were already expecting such measures. On Tuesday the 10th the dollar rose against European currencies to some 7 percent above its all-time low of Friday. Market operators were presumably hedging against the possibility of sudden massive intervention by the Federal Reserve. Later, when intervention proved limited to a modest scale, the dollar began slipping back, though not to its earlier lows.

Another influence was the Bundesbank's persistence in "a ruthless two-month credit squeeze that bore hard on West German borrowers and created turmoil for the dollar, the pound, and five Continental currencies linked to the mark."[15] On July 26, the interest rate on overnight loans among German banks hit 38 percent. Then, as the Bundesbank loosened its credit squeeze, as the New York money market tightened, and as figures for June showed improvement in U.S. trade, the dollar recovered strongly through the first two weeks of August.

By mid-August, as the dollar gained, the Federal Reserve repaid the swap drawings it had used in July. From late August through October, the markets were more orderly than before, with narrower fluctuations. Signs appeared that the U.S. balance of payments was moving decisively into surplus, and the impression fleetingly prevailed that inflation was under better control in the United States than in Europe and Japan. The Arab oil situation[16] exerted a strong influence. The market took the view that the United States was less dependent on imported oil than Europe and Japan and that a major share of oil producers' revenues would move into dollar investments. From November until mid-January 1974 the dollar's recovery gained momentum. The unwinding of speculative positions in foreign currencies intensified the trend. Although various foreign central banks sold dollars to cushion the declines of their currencies, the dollar rates on the German mark and Swiss franc, for example, fell by mid-January to roughly 23 percent below their peaks of early July.

Indeed, this movement entirely reversed the average depreciation that the dollar had suffered while floating and even erased the bulk of its February 1973 devaluation. By noon on Monday, January 21, 1974, the first day of trading with the French franc floating independently of the European snake, the dollar's trade-weighted average value in New York in terms of 14 currencies stood only 0.54 percent below its Smithsonian average value.[17] The dollar showed more than its Smithsonian value

in relation to the British pound, French franc, Italian lira, and Swedish crown and nearly that value in relation to the Japanese yen. It remained weaker even than it had been right after the February 1973 develuation, however, in relation to the German mark, Dutch guilder, and Australian dollar, and was also below its theoretical February parity with the then already floating Swiss franc.

The dollar's renewed average strength in part merely reflected the especial weakness of particular foreign currencies, notably the Italian lira and British pound. Floating since June 1972, the pound had become fairly steady against the dollar from early November 1972 to late January 1973 in a trough about 10 percent below its Smithsonian central rate of $2.6057. It jumped when the dollar was devalued. Negotiations for an end to sterling's float against other EC currencies reached an impasse in March 1973. A moderate uptrend against the dollar accelerated in May. At its peak around the middle of 1973, the pound stood only about 1 percent below its Smithsonian rate. Sterling had been rising less sharply

11. The Paris market did open on Friday but closed after 90 minutes.

The technicality of "closing" the European markets meant that central banks would not buy or sell, but trading among commercial banks and between banks and their customers was not forbidden. In limited trading on Monday the 5th the dollar actually gained somewhat against most major currencies as some speculators were evidently closing out their positions. *Wall Street Journal*, 6 March 1973, p. 5.

12. Recall pp. 424–425.

13. Most of the exchange-rate figures that follow come from Charles A. Coombs, Federal Reserve Bank of New York *Monthly Review*, September 1973, pp. 215–231.

14. *Ibid.*, pp. 221, 223, 227.

15. *Business Week*, 4 August 1973, p. 17.

16. See the section on "The Oil Situation" later in this chapter.

17. *Wall Street Journal*, 22 January 1974, p. 2, citing calculations of the Morgan Guaranty Trust Company.

against the dollar than Continental currencies, however, and so was depreciating substantially against them. One apparent influence was a decline in London interest rates as rates rose elsewhere.

In early July, sterling declined more than the dollar against Continental currencies and then lagged behind when the dollar began to rally. It went below $2.50 on July 26 and kept sinking. During that summer, the British authorities were encouraging public agencies to borrow in the Eurocurrency markets, partly to bolster Britain's external reserves. Early in September, the pound suffered a selloff on bad economic news and on rumors (later falsified) that Britain would soon let its guarantees of the sterling balances lapse. Speculation then contributed to a drop of about 3 percent in the pound rate in just three days. In mid-November the coal miners banned overtime and weekend work; the implications for electricity and for the whole economy intensified bearishness on the pound. December brought a three-day work week in Britain and a doubling of international oil prices. Talk of an early election grew. In January 1974 the pound dipped briefly almost down to $2.15.

These were the circumstances of the dollar's apparent strength. In late January the dollar began relapsing again. In February, March, and April 1974, it fell as much as 17 percent from its January highs against the German mark and other major European currencies. Observers linked this weakness to elimination in January of the Interest Equalization Tax and other U.S. controls on capital outflows, while European countries eased their curbs on inflows, to disappointing U.S. trade figures and unexpectedly strong German figures, to accelerating inflation and a decline in output in the United States, and to moves in prospect to impeach the President. Furthermore, the market turned bearishly away from its initially favorable assessment of how the oil situation would affect the United States. Arab deposits of oil profits in U.S. banks proved smaller than expected, while the banks were lending heavily to European countries scrambling to pay for more expensive imports of oil.

As the dollar weakened, the Federal Reserve sought to support it, selling $428 million worth of marks and French and Belgian francs in the three months of February through April 1974. It obtained the marks sold mostly by drawings on its swap line with the Bundesbank. Support of the dollar was particularly heavy in March,

"amidst intense rumors of an increase in the mark's value" and of collapse of the European joint float.[18] The dollar continued relapsing against other major currencies until mid-May, when it stood 21 percent below its January high in relation to the mark. During the late spring and summer of 1974, the dollar recovered again, apparently in connection with improvement in the U.S. trade position and with tightened credit and increased interest rates in New York.[19] Then the decline resumed. Comparing monthly average rates of January 1975 and September 1974 shows the dollar down 15.9 percent against the Swiss franc, 11.2 percent against the German mark, and 5.7 percent against the nondollar currencies included in the SDR basket; and the decline was continuing.

The oil situation

Floating exchange rates functioned in an environment in which fixed rates had broken down and could not have been soon restored. The world oil situation brought what has been called the "biggest international financial crisis since the 1930s" and "the largest structural shift in international payments since the German reparations problem after World War I."[20] After the outbreak of another Arab-Israeli war in October 1973, the Arabs temporarily embargoed shipments of oil to the United States and the Netherlands. The Organization of Petroleum Exporting Countries approximately quadrupled the price of oil in late 1973 and early 1974. There were signs that this move by a classic cartel was attracting imitators among producers of other commodities.

Divergent early estimates appeared of how big an impact the higher oil prices were having. Projections of the new value of international oil trade ranged as high as $100 billion a year. (For comparison, *total* exports of free-world countries had amounted to about $510 billion in 1973.) In September 1974, the U.S. Treasury estimated—and later figures suggest that its estimate was on the low side—that OPEC oil revenues would reach $80 billion for the whole year, up from about $25 billion in 1973 and $15 billion in 1972. About $5 billion worth of other exports would bring the OPEC countries' total export revenues to $85 billion in 1974. Their expected imports of only about $30 billion worth of goods and services would leave a current-account surplus of about \$55 billion. The International Monetary Fund, assuming that the oil prices of the first half of 1974 would persist throughout the year, estimated that the combined current-account surplus of the major oil-exporting countries would jump from about \$5 billion in 1973 to roughly \$65 billion in 1974. The current account of all other countries combined would deteriorate by a similar amount, of which the industrial countries would incur about two-thirds and the non-oil primary-producing countries about one third. Various projections of the increase in external financial assets of OPEC member countries ranged as high as \$60 billion or even \$75 billion for 1975.

There were two main reasons why the higher oil prices were expected to have so large an impact on international payments. First, it would take time for higher prices to promote substantial economies in oil consumption and development of new energy sources. Second, the major oil-exporting countries could not, in the short run, advantageously spend the bulk of their additional export earnings on additional imports. Roughly half of government revenue from oil exports accrued to countries mostly having small populations, high ratios of external reserves to imports, and a history of some capital exports. These characteristics cast doubt on whether additional resources could be quickly and productively invested at home. Most of the other (non-Arab) oil-exporting countries, however, had large populations, had borrowed abroad in the past to finance domestic investment, and seemed to have a good potential for economic development. In time —but not quickly—these countries with relatively high absorptive capacities would spend the bulk of their sharply expanded foreign-exchange earnings. Meanwhile, they too would be accumulating financial assets.

One cannot, of course, predict imbalances in payments simply by evaluating a given physical pattern of oil trade at the higher prices. Trade would adjust as energy consumption and production responded to changed prices and as people in the oil-exporting and oil-importing countries responded to their respectively improved and worsened real circumstances. Still, the actions of the oil cartel had balance-of-payments impacts that were massive in relation to payments surpluses and deficits of earlier historical experience. The yearly transfer from the oil-importing to the oil-exporting countries—

THE CRISES OF 1973 AND GENERALIZED FLOATING

the tax, so to speak, levied by the latter on the former—probably amounted to only 2 or 3 percent of gross world product. The burden of this transfer, however, fell very unevenly; India and Italy, among other countries, were particularly hard-hit.

It was crucial to the world economy how the oil countries would split their earnings between domestic consumption and real investment and external financial investment and, further, what directions and forms their external investment would take. (Like most investors in an inflationary world, they had no easy and obvious way of safeguarding the real purchasing power of their financial claims.) The oil-importing countries as a group would not necessarily experience major changes in their *overall* balance-of-payments positions. They might receive large enough capital inflows from the oil countries to match their oil-related trade deficits. It was unlikely, though, that the oil exporters would place their surplus funds just where they had earned them, country by country. Individual countries receiving relatively small capital inflows would face deterioration of their balances of payments and external reserves or of their exchange rates or both. The question arose of how flows of "petrodollars" could be "recycled" from the oil countries to their customers and from countries receiving

18. *Wall Street Journal*, 6 June 1974, p. 8, citing a report of the Federal Reserve Bank of New York.

19. Charles A. Coombs in Federal Reserve Bank of New York, *Monthly Review*, September 1974, p. 207.

20. *Business Week*, 28 September 1974, p. 32, and Wilson E. Schmidt, briefing for the "Shadow Open Market Committee," 6 September 1974, mimeographed, p. 1, respectively. Sources for this section include IMF, *Annual Report*, 1974, esp. Chapter 1; First National City Bank of New York, *Monthly Economic Letter*, March and July 1974; Joseph G. Kvasnicka in Federal Reserve Bank of Chicago, *Business Conditions*, June 1974; Federal Reserve Bank of New York, *Monthly Review*, September 1974; and various issues of *IMF Survey*, Federal Reserve Bank of Chicago, *International Letter*, *Business Week*, *Newsweek*, *U.S. News & World Report*, *Forbes*, and *Wall Street Journal*.

disproportionately large amounts of those funds to countries initially left short.

Several channels of recycling seemed possible. Short-term placements of oil revenues would most likely take the form of deposits with banks in the United States and Europe, including the Eurocurrency banks. Eurobonds were a related outlet. Direct investments in business operations and real estate in individual countries were another possibility, as well as portfolio investments through their stock and bond markets. Various special channels (to be mentioned presently) might be arranged.

Early data on the use of petrodollars were sketchy and fragmentary. In the eight months of January through August 1974, according to U.S. Treasury estimates, the OPEC countries ran a combined export surplus of some $25 to $28 billion. An estimated $7 billion of this amount was invested in the United States (about $4 billion in short-term government securities and the remaining $3 billion mostly in short-term bank deposits; Arab investment in U.S. corporate securities and real estate had thus far amounted to only a few hundred million dollars). Another $2 billion or so was invested in Europe in private securities, real estate, and loans to local government institutions. Perhaps $3 billion was invested in British government securities or deposited in British banks. Long-term loans to developing countries or international development agencies accounted for some $3 billion. The remaining $10 to $13 billion was thought to have been placed largely with· London banks as Eurodollar deposits.

During 1974 OPEC countries placed a large share of their temporarily surplus funds in the Eurocurrency market, mainly on very short-term deposit. Official and semiofficial agencies of oil-importing countries borrowed there, as well as from U.S. banks, trying to extend the maturities of their debts as far as possible. Following news of foreign-exchange losses by several banks, notably the Herstatt Bank in Germany and Franklin National in the United States, bank managements reacted by tightening their credit limits for all but the most creditworthy borrowers. As a result, many smaller banks and even large banks in some countries had to pay premiums over rates at which prime banks could obtain funds. Yet despite this segmentation, the Eurocurrency market continued expanding at an impressive rate during the first half of 1974.

Early experience with recycling suggested certain worries about the adequacy of the private financial markets. Initially, it seemed, the oil countries were placing most of their deposits in a few dozen of the largest European and U.S. banks, while several hundred smaller banks faced a possible loss of deposits as their customers made payments for oil. By way of reassurance, it was suggested that if the major banks found their deposits or loans or both becoming too concentrated, they could refuse additional oil-country deposits or widen the spread between their interest rates on deposits and loans, thereby deflecting depositors and borrowers to the smaller banks.[21] A second worry was that the oil-country deposits had been mostly subject to withdrawal on very short notice, while the consuming countries were seeking long-term loans. Banks could be squeezed and foreign-exchange markets disrupted if OPEC countries should suddenly withdraw their deposits or shift them around from bank to bank and from currency to currency. Amidst such possibilities, long-term lending was especially risky. On the other hand, the oil-country money managers were unlikely to behave irresponsibly; they understood the expense and risk of shifting funds around erratically. Short maturities made little difference as long as the managers renewed their deposits at maturity, which they would do for lack of good alternatives; in fact, they would need growing outlets for petrodollars as time went on. If individual banks felt that the maturities of their deposits and loans were getting uncomfortably out of line, they could adjust their deposit and loan interest rates to promote the appropriate shift in maturities. As a last resort, should it ever become necessary, banks in the Eurocurrency market could seek loans from their head offices and ultimately from the central banks of their home-office countries. Furthermore, national and Eurocurrency banking systems would by no means have to handle all petrodollar recycling; other channels were available.

Another worry concerned whether the oil-importing countries could generate enough exports to cover interest payments on their accumulated borrowings. A rather complacent suggestion (made by the First National City Bank of New York in its July 1974 *Letter*) was that countries could borrow to cover their interest payments as well as their oil bills. Would such borrowing really be warranted, especially if undertaken not by private businesses assessing the productivity of capital but by governments concerned with the short-run apparent strength of their external reserves and the market quotations of their currencies? What about the long run?

Official arrangements for recycling were being made and proposed. A special "oil facility" of the International Monetary Fund began operations in September 1974. It obtained lending commitments from the major oil exporters and Canada and offered medium-term loans, supplementary to assistance obtained under other IMF policies, to countries suffering oil-related balance-of-payments strains. (Not to be confused with the oil facility was another new facility to aid IMF "members in certain special circumstances of balance-of-payments difficulty." It would provide drawing privileges for up to three years, in contrast to traditional stand-by arrangements, which ran no longer than 12 months.) The World Bank (IBRD) was trying to float bonds in oil countries to obtain funds for relending to developing countries. European delegates at the IMF-IBRD meetings of September 1974 favored expansion of the capacity of these two institutions to borrow and relend oil funds, partly through a new facility that would accept medium-term deposits. British Chancellor of the Exchequer Denis Healey was proposing a fund of $30 billion, operated through the IMF, to borrow oil funds for relending to importing countries. The Shah of Iran recommended a new international institution to channel loan funds mainly from oil producers to developing countries. Bilateral loans between governments were also being negotiated. Britain and France borrowed from Iran. In the late summer of 1974, Germany and Italy negotiated a swap arrangement whereby the Bundesbank would make $2 billion in dollars available to the Bank of Italy against collateral of about 500 tons of gold valued at about 80 percent of the recent market price, or about $118 per ounce. (This arrangement contributed to blurring the distinction between the still-official $42.22 price of gold and the market price, making it seem likely that further gold transactions between central banks would also be based on a market-related price.)

These and other actual and proposed schemes might, unfortunately, prove mere short-run devices to postpone facing up to the real adjustments required by massive transfers to the OPEC countries. Perhaps Federal Reserve Chairman Arthur Burns was right: "What recycling really means is piling debt

upon debt. . . . All the talk about recycling is an escape from reality." The financial problems caused by high oil prices could not be managed, Burns continued, by finding ways to pay those prices through international borrowing and lending. The only solution was to force those prices down by concerted action of the consuming countries to conserve energy and develop new sources.[22] "Somehow the consumer nations must show the producers—especially the Arabs—that they are destroying the very markets they are trying to exploit."[23]

Even the International Monetary Fund expressed worry that official financing might "bulk too large compared with adjustment, referring here to both exchange rate changes and demand policy adaptations." Unduly heavy official borrowing would let countries keep the foreign-exchange values of their currencies and their levels of domestic expenditure and of imports higher than otherwise, possibly placing inflationary pressure on the resources of other countries.[24]

International loan programs would presumably tend to compete with and reduce some of the recycling through equity investment that might otherwise take place and that would have certain advantages, relatively. In the absence of massive official recycling and with commercial banks reluctant to keep on expanding their financial intermediation in established ways, market incentives might promote invention of new ways of coping.

The oil situation raised thorny analytical

21. Some of these worries and reassurances are described in First National City Bank of New York, *Monthly Economic Letter*, July 1974, pp. 13–15; *Newsweek*, 14 October 1974, pp. 91–92, 97; *Wall Street Journal*, 10 October 1974, p. 16; and IMF, 1974, p. 26.

22. Quoted and paraphrased in *Wall Street Journal*, 11 October 1974, p. 3.

23. Editorial in *Business Week*, 28 September 1974, p. 116.

24. IMF, 1974, p. 28. The report also noted an opposite danger: some countries, reacting to the prospect of mounting debt, might seek to adjust their current-account balances too rapidly, harming trading partners already in similar difficulties.

points. On a neo-Keynesian view, the much greater increase in the value of imports than in the value of exports of oil-importing countries would have a deflationary foreign-trade-multiplier effect. To the extent that larger oil-import payments were financed by diversion of spending out of other channels, the "tax" or "reparations" aspect of increased oil prices might also be deflationary. To be persuasive, however, such interpretations would have to be rationalized in terms of downward effects on the velocities of countries' money supplies.

An inflationary impact seems more plausible. Most obviously, the oil-price increase means a large increase in the prices of energy, of petroleum-derived and of competing chemicals and materials, and thus of a wide range of costs throughout the world. Higher oil prices spell worsened terms of trade for the importing countries, formally quite similar to a decline in the productivity of their factors of production and thus of the real sizes of their economies. With demands for real cash balances correspondingly reduced, higher price levels are necessary to equate demands for nominal cash balances with given nominal money supplies. Higher oil prices might even lead, in various ways, to nominal money expansion. Countries might pursue expansionary policies to resist the unemployment tending to result from the tax-like diversion of spending away from some sectors of their economies. If sectoral unemployment caused by real disturbances is always to be fought by macroeconomic policies, inflation is practically bound to result. On the international scene, swap arrangements among central banks and other schemes for oil finance might lead in effect to the creation of additional international liquidity. So could certain forms of investment of the growing official reserves of the oil countries, such as their placement in the Eurodollar market. Greater liquidity provides greater scope for the import of inflation into countries running balance-of-payments surpluses from time to time. One might reply that this cannot happen under floating exchange rates. True, except that exchange rates have not been floating freely from 1973 on. Central-bank intervention continues, though no longer committed to the defense of specific rates, even outside the European "snake" and other programs of continued actual pegging. The purpose of recycling, after all, is to delay or avoid the supposed pains of sudden adjustment effected by allowing exchange rates to move to whatever levels would keep balances of

payments in equilibrium even in the short run. Some elements of the international creation and transmission of inflation were still possible, though weaker (one hopes) than they had been in 1970–1973.

Given the downward inflexibilities of many types of cost and price nowadays, the orientation of government policies toward full employment at almost whatever cost, and the persistence of remnants of exchange-rate pegging, all sorts of disturbance—and the oil situation is one—have a bias toward raising rather than reducing price levels and money supplies. The oil situation has made the pursuit of monetary stability more difficult. It has massively disturbed balances of payments and the pattern of exchange rates that would equilibrate international transactions. It is in the face of such major handicaps, and also of the official interventions and controls described later in this chapter, that the system of floating exchange rates has been functioning.

Appraisals of the float

How well did floating exchange rates work in 1973–1974? For what little they may be worth, let us note some opinions. Commenting on the first few months, the senior vice president of the Federal Reserve Bank of New York said, in effect, that floating rates had failed their test. "The market was overwhelmed by irrational and emotional forces. The dollar was driven down in recurrent bursts of heavy selling to levels unjustified and undesirable on any reasonable assessment of the U.S. payments position. . . ." In early July 1973, several New York banks refused to deal in some foreign currencies, and "trading was grinding to a standstill. . . ." Then, in an effort to restore orderly market conditions, the Federal Reserve and other central banks intervened.[25]

In August 1973, Robert Roosa, former Under Secretary of the Treasury and designer of the system of "swaps" among central banks, took a similarly dim view. "Instead of insulating the U.S. from external inflationary pressures, floating has aggravated inflation here and abroad." "The ups and downs of business requirements and of other money transfers have resulted in fluctuations of as much as 2% or 3% in spot quotations for the dollar within a single day, and fluctuations have been even wider through the cross rates among other currencies." "During most of June and until July

9, the cumulative effect of the defensive actions of individual banks and firms, operating on their own in the international markets, was to create the wide gyrations in exchange rates against the dollar just described." Then, fortunately, came official intervention.[26]

According to Joseph Slevin, "Floating rates did curb speculation but . . . they greatly aggravated inflationary pressures in a desperately inflationary world.

"The inflation flaw took the free world's top financial officials by surprise. Most never shared [Treasury Secretary] Shultz's enthusiasm for floating rates but they thought they would be more useful than proved the case."[27]

At a convention in April 1974, George H. Chittenden, senior vice president of Morgan Guaranty Trust Company, and some other bankers alleged that "combines" or "syndicates" of some European banks had been engaging in concerted manipulations of the foreign-exchange market. Other bankers at the convention were skeptical. No one alleged that the abuses mentioned were widespread.[28]

The foregoing comments—and particularly the charges that floating exchange rates promoted inflation—are further examples of something drearily familiar in monetary history: floating exchange rates, left on the scene after fixed rates have broken down, are routinely blamed for the economic disorders that had caused the breakdown and to which the fixed rates had themselves contributed. Actually, both the Bretton Woods system and its collapse had inflationary consequences. This is not to say that the shift to floating exchange rates was itself inflationary. The trouble came from the *way* that the system collapsed, that is, from its last-ditch defense that stretched out over several years. During this period, from 1969 or perhaps even from 1967 until March 1973, speculators against pegged exchange rates enjoyed one-way options on a mammoth scale. During the single year 1971, foreign monetary authorities added more dollars to their official reserves than in all of human history up to that time. Speculative funds surged across boundaries and oceans, inflating the countries of destination without deflating the countries of origin. Once the damage had been done, no early cure was possible. Rapid inflation develops a momentum of its own. Even if excessive money-supply expansion were to be stopped, it would take time for price trends to respond. Months and even years are required for lagging prices and costs to catch

up with those that rise earliest and most sensitively in an inflationary process. Expectations and wage demands play a part. A policy of trying to bring inflation to a rapid halt threatens more unemployment than authorities are likely to find politically tolerable. Heaven knows that powerful domestic factors pose inflationary biases in the modern world. But when the acceleration of *worldwide* inflation around 1973 is the topic under discussion, the role of the last-ditch defense of the Bretton Woods system should be recognized. Belated abandonment of that system amounted to locking the barn door after the horse had been stolen.[29]

Not all observers, of course, have blamed floating rates for the flaws of the preceding system. "For the moment," according to *Business Week*,[30] "the world seems to be getting on nicely without a formal monetary system. Exchange rates have been floating for a year, and the exchange markets have coped with them very well." Milton Friedman, as one might expect, compared price controls discredited at home with floating exchange rates working on the international scene. "In sharp contrast, . . . the free market abroad has worked like a charm, confounding all those 'realistic' bankers who predicted unstable markets and recurrent chaos, and behaving just the way that

25. *Wall Street Journal*, 7 September 1973, reporting on a briefing given and a report written by Charles A. Coombs.

26. Roosa in *Business Week*, 11 August 1973, pp. 18, 23.

27. "Inflation Pressures Mount Under Floating Currencies," *Washington Post*, 14 April 1974, p. H 1.

28. *Wall Street Journal*, 11 April 1974, p. 4.

29. On imported inflation and on the inflation bias of a system of adjustably pegged exchange rates, recall parts of Chapters 6, 19, and 24, in particular. For evidence on the assertions of the foregoing paragraph, see David I. Meiselman, "Worldwide Inflation: A Monetarist View," in *The Phenomenon of Worldwide Inflation*, Washington: American Enterprise Institute, 1975, pp. 69–112.

30. 23 March 1974, p. 58.

starry-eyed academic theorists had said it would." Friedman emphasized "the crisis that did not happen" but that would have happened under the Bretton Woods system when the Arab-Israeli war and the oil crisis developed in the fall of 1973. As hot money poured across boundaries, central banks would have lost and gained billions overnight. "Foreign-exchange markets would have been closed while central bankers hastened to some pleasant locale for a crisis meeting to 'solve' the problem. None of this occurred. Instead, the price of the dollar in terms of other currencies rose some 5 to 10 per cent, subsequently declined again, and the world continued about its business." The United States was even able to end its exchange controls.[31]

The Joint Economic Committee of Congress reached a similar judgment. Floating rates "have not demonstrably impeded the expansion of trade and investment," and the "exchange markets have demonstrated the resilience and ability to maintain appropriate rates." This performance occurred even under adverse conditions. During the period of floating,

the United States has suffered repeated bouts of economic uncertainty. Exports of soybeans and substitute high protein feed were embargoed, the pace of domestic inflation has soared, dropped back, and then accelerated again, and prices of petroleum imports have tripled. Massive shifts in international economic prospects have occurred almost overnight. The ability of exchange markets operating under a fluctuating rate regime to adjust to these changes has been impressive. If the same events had occurred during a period when officials had been attempting to maintain fixed parities, exchange markets probably would have been closed periodically while the authorities met to calculate and negotiate a new structure of rates.

As international traders, investors, and exchange dealers acquire more experience with a fluctuating rate regime, the amplitude of fluctuations will tend to diminish.[32]

In addition to its other troubles, the world seemed, in 1974 and early 1975, to be suffering the worst business recession since World War II. Even Japan was suffering an actual decline in production, not a mere slowdown in growth. The oil situation was one causal factor. So, probably, was the failure of national money supplies to keep growing at the inflationary pace that had been intensified by earlier last-ditch attempts to defend the crumbling system of fixed exchange rates.

Fluctuations, interventions, and controls

A sound appraisal of *any* economic arrangements must take account of their environment. It must also be clear about precisely *what* arrangements are being appraised. The rates floating since March 1973 have been plagued by interventions, controls, and other remnants of the Bretton Woods system. This situation will, at best, eventually prove to have been a *transitional stage* in a movement toward freely fluctuating exchange rates.

By the standard of historical experience with essentially free rates, fluctuations under this transitional system have been wide. The German mark, for example, peaked early in July 1973 at 31.2 percent above its central rate implied by the February devaluation of the dollar. Not all of that rise occurred through floating, however; for revaluations in March and June had raised the mark by 8.66 percent against SDRs. It should be emphasized that the near-chaos on the markets in mid-1973 occurred in the context of speculation in anticipation of and then in response to the German revaluation of June 29. All of this is more characteristic of the Bretton Woods system than of freely fluctuating rates. After that revaluation, the mark rose more than 9½ percent further against the dollar by Friday, July 6. By that date, the French franc and other EC currencies had risen to some 18–21 percent above the rates established in February. Then, apparently under the partial influence of official intervention, the trend reversed itself. By late August, the Swiss franc dropped 13½ percent against the dollar. By the middle of January 1974, the Swiss franc and German mark had fallen by roughly 23 percent against the dollar from their peaks of early July. Then, from mid-January to the late spring of 1974, the dollar fell 17 percent or more against the mark and other European currencies. Fluctuations on the average against a weighted basket of foreign currencies were smaller, understandably, than fluctuations against some individual currencies. In the calendar year 1974 the effective value of the dollar ranged from approximately the Smithsonian level to an 8 percent depreciation, while the swing in the dollar-mark rate amounted to 18 percent of the central rate.

Short-term fluctuations were also notable. Toward the end of May and the first week of

June 1973, with bad trade figures published and a government crisis coming to a head, the Italian (commercial) lira fell about 7 percent in seven business days. In just one week of late June and early July, the Belgian franc rose some 6 percent against the dollar. On Monday and Tuesday, July 9 and 10, the dollar recovered more than 7 percent against the mark and French franc. In just three days in early September, sterling dropped 3 percent against the dollar. After the doubling of oil prices in late December and especially in the aftermath of the French float of January 19, 1974, sterling dropped by January 21 to some 7 percent below its end-of-December rate. From the end of 1973 to a low in early January, the Swiss franc fell more than 7 percent against the dollar, then recovered 5 percent by the end of the month.

Examples could be multiplied to document the following generalization: a number of leading exchange rates changed by 20 percent or more within a few months and by 7 or 8 percent in a few weeks—in early July 1973, even in a few days. Changes of 1 or 2 percent or more in a day were not uncommon.

All this, to repeat, occurred under a system quite different from *freely* floating rates. The European joint float has involved the pegging together of the participating currencies. Within this "snake," episodes of one-way-option speculation and of currency crisis have continued to occur. Besides the two revaluations of the mark, the Netherlands (to help ward off inflation) revalued in September and Norway in November 1973. Other parity changes were repeatedly rumored. "The snake," as *Business Week* noted in 1973,[33] "is an important part of any explanation of the curious behavior of the dollar this summer. . . . In a real sense, money flows this summer have been a run into the mark, and the pressure has not been confined to the dollar. The Bundesbank has been forced to buy over 4-billion DM worth of the currencies of other members of the joint float. And the mark has moved from the bottom of the snake to the top, pulling the rest of the float with it." By the beginning of August 1973, "Rumors were rife in exchange markets . . . that Germany's rebellious allies were insisting either that the mark be revalued again, to make the joint float tolerable, or else that margins of permissible fluctuation in exchange rates permitted by the rules of the joint float be loosened, so the mark would be left to rise more on its own."

The Dutch revaluation in September fostered speculation on revaluations of the mark and the Belgian franc, leading the Belgian authorities to impose a negative interest rate on new deposits by nonresidents. Support of the weak French franc required massive central-bank intervention, while the dollar and the pound suffered daily drops of more than 1 percent in Frankfurt. Repercussions of the Dutch revaluation, including speculation on a French devaluation, were still being felt more than a month afterwards.[34] The French decision of January 19, 1974 to float independently came, of course, in response to pressures that had built up within the snake. Spain's floating was one prompt repercussion.

Outside the snake, Japan provides perhaps the most notable examples of officially administered changes in exchange rates. Nominally, the yen had been floating since February 1973. Actually, though, the Bank of Japan pegged the rate for weeks and months at a stretch, occasionally changing the level of the

31. Friedman in *Newsweek*, 1 April 1974, p. 65.
Treasury Secretary Shultz, similarly, reminded reporters: "The one crisis you weren't writing about last October was the monetary crisis." "Floating rates have worked quite well," according to *Newsweek*, "helping avoid havoc when oil prices soared." *Newsweek*, 25 March 1974, p. 77.

32. Joint Economic Committee, *Report on the February 1974 Economic Report of the President*, Washington: U.S. Government Printing Office, 25 March 1974, p. 6.
The Managing Director of the International Monetary Fund also testified to the extremely adverse conditions under which floating rates were functioning—a "combination of circumstances [that] will place strains on the monetary system far in excess of any that have been experienced" since World War II. He recognized that floating rates would have to continue indefinitely. "Worst Monetary Strains Since World War II Are Expected by IMF Due to Oil Crisis," *Wall Street Journal*, 15 January 1974, p. 2, reporting on a speech in London by H. J. Witteveen.

33. 28 July, p. 60; 4 August, p. 18.

34. *Wall Street Journal*, 18 September 1973, p. 16, 21 September, p. 3, 23 October, p. 19, 24 October, p. 26.

peg. From March through October the peg remained in the neighborhood of 265 yen per dollar. Then came the impact of the international oil situation. In November the defense of the yen apparently retreated first to a peg of 270 and then to 275 and 280. Expectations of further devaluation became rampant late in December. January 1974 brought a retreat to 300. After the French float and a two-day closing of the Tokyo market, defense of that spot rate required massive intervention, while the six-month forward rate on the dollar briefly rose to 324 yen.[35] Intervention is reflected in a loss of $7.6 billion, or 40 percent, in Japan's official reserves in the 11 months of March 1973 through January 1974. In December alone the loss amounted to nearly $1 billion. Intervention was probably on an even larger scale, financed in part by the drawing down of earlier reserve gains that had been hidden outside of the official figures. The yen soon rebounded from its trough of January 1974 as the dollar in turn weakened on such developments as U.S. removal of capital controls and market reassessment of the oil situation.

In the rest of the world, numerous official changes in parities occurred. Early in June 1973, South Africa revalued the rand 5 percent against the dollar, while Finland also reduced its support price for the dollar. Thailand and Saudi Arabia revalued upward in terms of SDRs, by 4.00 percent in July and by 5.08 percent in August, respectively. Measures taken in July and September 1973 amounted to an effective revaluation of New Zealand's currency. Australia revalued upward by 5.00 percent against SDRs in September. One year later, however, in September 1974, New Zealand effectively devalued its currency by about 6 percent against the weighted basket of trading-partner currencies that it had been employing as a basis of valuation, while Australia severed its peg with the U.S. dollar and effectively devalued by about 12 percent. Greece temporarily abandoned its dollar parity in October 1973, in effect reversing the drachma's February devaluation against SDRs in parallel with the dollar. In March 1975 Greece more definitively abandoned its dollar peg, and the Bank of Greece began a daily fixing of the average rate of the drachma with the currencies of the country's main trading partners. In February and March 1975 Iran, Saudi Arabia, Kuwait, and Qatar switched their currencies from a dollar peg to an SDR peg, effecting small upward revaluations against the dollar.

This survey covers just the major changes. It does not include several devaluations by underdeveloped countries, which are familiar occurrences. (A noteworthy example is Chile's 91 percent devaluation in October 1973, from 25 to 280 escudos per dollar. By December 1974 the figure had reached 1680.) Nor does it mention all abandonments of parities. Yet such action occurs within—at the end of—a regime of pegging, and the shock of abandoning is much like the shock of changing a peg.

Intervention to support the British, French, Italian, and Japanese currencies, as estimated by growth of foreign debt and sales from official reserves, amounted to $15 billion in 1973 and $25 billion in 1974. The figures do not include a further $6 billion worth of deposits in sterling by oil-producing countries in 1974.[36]

Not only have exchange rates not been free of interventions and pegging and repegging; they have also not been free of controls. All sorts of capital controls, including restrictions and charges on foreign acquisition of local bank deposits, carried over from the Bretton Woods system. Some countries, like Belgium after the Dutch revaluation, introduced new controls. Italy did not permit its banks to deal in forward lire against the dollar unless invoices documented the commercial purpose of each transaction. Forward cover in Japanese yen, always difficult to obtain, became even more so when the government tightened restrictions on domestic and foreign banks operating in Japan, or so many U.S. corporations complained.[37] During the first few months of floating, against the background of a worldwide scramble for raw materials, the United States limited "the export of more than 40 commodities ranging from steel scrap to soybeans."[38]

Gold policies were subject to change. Tuesday, November 13, 1973 brought the announcement that the major central banks had terminated their two-tier agreement of 1968, thus freeing themselves to sell gold on the private market. The London gold price responded with the largest drop ever in a single day, by $6.90, or 7.1 percent.[39] Whether the central banks would in fact sell gold remained uncertain. Another brooding uncertainty concerned whether central banks would reactivate gold as a means of settlement among themselves by raising its official price from $42.22 to a figure more nearly in line with the much higher free-market price. France did revalue its gold reserves in January 1975. With gold a widely sought haven for funds fleeing out of inflationary paper currencies, the policy-linked volatility in its actual and expected prices must have affected exchange rates. Gold ownership became legal for private Americans at the end of 1974, and the U.S. Treasury auctioned off a small amount of its gold early in the new year.

The revision or even the removal of controls is a potentially disruptive event occurring within—albeit at the end of—the regime of controls. On January 9, 1974, for example, the dollar fell 2.26 percent in Frankfurt from the preceding day's close. Dealers attributed the selling pressure partly to Germany's decision gradually to lift its remaining controls over capital inflows.[40] That same month the Japanese government reversed its earlier policy of encouraging capital outflows, a policy introduced when its reserves of foreign exchange were embarrassingly large. Overseas travel expenditures were also newly discouraged.[41] Also in January 1974, one month after relaxing its restraints on capital outflows, the U.S. government abolished those restraints. President Nixon lowered to zero the rate of the Interest Equalization Tax, already due to expire on June 30, 1974. The Commerce Department terminated its controls over direct investments abroad by U.S. corporations, and the Federal Reserve terminated its restraints on foreign lending and investing by U.S. financial institutions. Canada emulated the United States by withdrawing its guidelines for capital exports. Germany removed curbs on foreign purchases of German securities and made it easier for German firms to borrow abroad. Belgium also lifted some of its restraints on capital inflows; France had already eased such restraints. (Switzerland, however, tightened restraints— on capital outflows, for the sake of domestic credit availability.) When the U.S. liberalization moves became effective on January 30, and again the next day, the dollar suffered daily drops of roughly 1 percent in the French and German markets.[42] On March 20 the French government announced abolition of the two-tier market, which had been an anachronism since the franc was cut adrift from the EC snake two months before. The Finance Ministry expected an end to "wasteful paper work." Then Italy abolished, as ineffective, its two-tier foreign-exchange market. It also cut to approximately $32 worth the amount of Italian banknotes that travelers might legally take out of the country. The availability abroad at a discount of lira notes exported for purposes of

capital flight had been diverting from official channels much of Italy's foreign-exchange earnings from tourism.[43]

Expectations about official intervention exhibited their influence on May 14, 1974, when the news tickers carried reports that Swiss, German, and American officials meeting in Basel had agreed on the desirability of concerted operations to counter overspeculation against the dollar. A scramble ensued to cover short dollar positions. By the following day, the German mark and Swiss franc had fallen 4½ percent against the dollar.[44] November 1974 brought further examples of expectations interacting with intervention (or surprising nonintervention) and with changes in controls. On Thursday the 14th the dollar dropped 2.5 percent in Zurich and 1.6 percent in Frankfurt after Chancellor Helmut Schmidt had said that he would not mind seeing the mark appreciate to help trim Germany's payments surplus. The dollar dropped further on Friday and on Monday the 18th, by 0.9 percent and then 2.9 percent against the Swiss franc, 0.8

35. *Wall Street Journal*, 5 November 1973, p. 15, 26 December, p. 2, 2 January 1974, p. 3, 8 January, p. 3, 24 January, p. 10.

36. *IMF Survey*, 3 February 1975, p. 43, citing the General Manager of the Bank for International Settlements.

37. *Wall Street Journal*, 3 July, pp. 1, 21.

38. Robert Roosa in *Business Week*, 11 August 1973, p. 23.

39. *Wall Street Journal*, 15 November 1973, p. 4.

40. *Wall Street Journal*, 10 January 1974, p. 6.

41. *Wall Street Journal*, 17 January 1974, p. 13, 22 February, p. 28.

42. *Wall Street Journal*, 30 January 1974, p. 3, 31 January, p. 13, 1 February, p. 20. Rumors of official intervention to push the dollar back to its February 1973 parity were also reportedly at work.

43. *Wall Street Journal*, 21 March 1974, p. 8; *Business Week*, 30 March 1974, p. 39.

44. Charles A. Coombs in Federal Reserve Bank of New York, *Monthly Review*, September 1974, p. 207.

and then 2.2 percent against the mark. Speculators were reportedly dumping dollars in surprise that central banks were not intervening more vigorously to support the dollar. Rumors of support did steady the Zurich market at one point on Monday, but the selling resumed after the Swiss National Bank issued a denial. The dollar's weakness was also attributed, in part, to a downtrend in U.S. interest rates, which made the dollar less attractive as a haven for speculative funds. On Friday the 22nd the dollar dropped from Thursday's level by 2.3 percent in Zurich and 1.9 percent in Frankfurt on news that five prominent German economists had advised their government to let the mark float freely upward to reflect Germany's relative success in moderating inflation. Meanwhile, in just a few hours on Wednesday of that week, the dollar had gained more than 5 percent in Zurich after the Swiss cabinet imposed a 12 percent a year charge on nonresidents' holdings of Swiss-franc deposits. A further rise on Thursday the 21st brought the dollar's temporary surge in Zurich to more than 8 percent in less than a week. In Frankfurt the dollar rose 1.9 percent over Tuesday's level (a holiday intervening). Signs that various governments were acting to push up the dollar seemed to be influencing the trading.

Also, the Swiss authorities were lowering bank reserve requirements and imposing a limit on sales of francs for future delivery. On Thursday the 28th, after the intervening fluctuations already mentioned, the dollar wobbled 0.7 percent in Zurich on news of still another action to discourage demand for francs—a rule requiring a Swiss bank lending francs to a foreigner to sell an offsetting amount of francs for foreign currency.[45]

Getting history straight

In summary, exchange rates have been floating under conditions quite different from those of an established and enduring free market. Many experts in official circles disparage, as politically just not in the cards, the policy recommendation that they suspect to be implicit in this diagnosis. Still, scholars should try to get history straight. The system of freely floating exchange rates should not receive a bad name through *mis*interpretation of experience with something rather different.

---

45. *Wall Street Journal*, 18 November 1974, p. 25, 19th, p. 14, 21st, p. 7, 22nd, p. 13, 25th, p. 19, 29th, p. 24.

CHAPTER TWENTY-NINE

Diagnoses of the Need for Monetary Reform

Topics of discussion

The concluding chapters of this book review shortcomings of the international monetary system and remedies proposed. This emphasis by no means implies that everything is wrong with the system. By its very nature, a discussion of reforms emphasizes conditions that could stand improvement.

First, what *is* the international monetary system? It consists of the arrangements that make the various national currencies exchangeable for one another: the foreign-exchange market, the banks and other institutions operating in the market, and the practices they employ. "The IMF, swaps, upper and lower bands, reserves, and all of the other agreements and arrangements which journalists and officials refer to as the 'international monetary system' actually are only mechanisms for governments' intervention, directly and via controls, in the private foreign exchange market. . . . It is these mechanisms which are in 'chaotic disarray' today, not the private market to which they are appended."[1] As the quotation suggests, discussions about reform of the system usually concern the machinery and practices of official intervention.

By the time these chapters appear in print, amendments to the IMF Charter may have adopted some particular set of reforms. Still, grounds for dissatisfaction and proposals for further reform will keep arising. Discarded proposals will be resurrected, or their features picked over and combined in new ways. The strengths and weaknesses of the proposals recently under discussion will remain relevant for years.

International monetary problems have traditionally been classified under the headings of "adjustment," "confidence," and "liquidity." These problems are most likely to prevail when exchange rates are pegged but subject to change. The first one concerns the lack—or destruction—of any dependable process of preventing or correcting imbalances of payments. Governments wait and hope that imbalances will either go away of their own accord or will yield to mild influences on wage and price trends. Occasionally, currency crises will prod governments to adopt controls over trade and capital movements or even to alter domestic financial policies or exchange rates. The second problem, narrowly conceived, is that confidence sometimes lapses in the continuing foreign-exchange value or gold value of key or reserve currencies. More broadly, confidence may lapse in the pegged exchange rate of any currency and not just of a reserve currency. Speculation can then cause massive capital movements. The third problem is that the "liquidity" held in reserve by monetary authorities may be too scarce or too abundant in total amount, that the nature or sources of some reserve assets may be unsatisfactory, that the relative quantities of different reserve assets may be unsuitable, or that the distribution of reserves among holders may be unsatisfactory in some sense.

These three problems intertwine closely. Stubborn imbalances of payments raise doubts about the durability of exchange rates, the adequacy of reserves of deficit countries, and the willingness of surplus countries to go on accumulating reserves. Shaky confidence makes more total liquidity necessary than otherwise would be. A full solution to the adjustment

---

1. John H. Watts III, Deputy Manager, Brown Bros. Harriman & Co., in American Enterprise Institute, *International Monetary Problems*, Washington: AEI, 1972, pp. 98–99.

problem would largely dispel the liquidity and confidence problems.

International settlements and liquidity

Despite its secondary or derivative character, the liquidity problem has received the most attention. Until a few years ago, worry about a shortage of international liquidity was more prominent than worry about a possible excess. Newspapers and magazines kept repeating the idea that as world income and world trade continued to grow, countries would need more liquidity for financing trade and for making payments to each other.

Such language personifies "countries" in a misleading way unless the user makes it clear just what his metaphors mean about the actions of definite business and government units. Quite a few journalists apparently do not realize that there is anything to be explained when they write of countries' trading with one another, having to pay each other, sometimes running deficits and surpluses, and needing liquidity with which to make settlements. Even academic economists, who presumably do understand their own shorthand language, all too often fail to tell their readers just what they mean when they write of "settling deficits" or "settling debts" that have arisen between "countries" and of proposed rules for the use in these "settlements" of the new "international liquidity" to be created under plans for reform.

Actually, exporters and importers quote prices and receive and make payments in the national currency of the exporting or the importing country or of some third country. Bank loans and other credits to finance international transactions are likewise expressed and repayable in ordinary national currencies. Even widely used "vehicle currencies," such as the dollar and pound, remain the ordinary money (bank deposits) of particular countries. None of the ordinary private participants in international trade and finance deals in any special kind of international liquidity.

Deficiency of a country's domestic money supply has a fairly clear meaning: if severe, it would show itself in deflation of employment, production, and prices. Nowadays, governments and central banks generally have the ability and the will to prevent any such defi-ciency. (Their errors tend to run in the opposite direction.) But what could a deficiency of international liquidity mean? Actually, it refers to the need felt by central banks and governments for additional holdings of reserves with which to intervene on the foreign-exchange markets to keep exchange rates fixed (or to constrain their floating) despite the pressure of imbalances in other transactions. With exchange rates pegged, these imbalances will presumably continue growing along with world production and trade, and all the more so as prices continue in an inflationary trend. Some considerations (not necessarily conclusive) even suggest that imbalances will grow more than in proportion to the total money value of trade. Technology and productivity are advancing, and demands keep changing; yet the appropriate responses within both deficit and surplus countries require time-consuming transfers of capital and labor among industries. As trade becomes freer, if it does, and as industrial countries draw closer together in technology, productivity, per capita incomes, and consumer tastes, changes in relative costs are likely to exert their influence over a broadened range of actual and potential trade. Trade balances are likely to become more sensitive to international price differences. As wealth increases, as privately held liquid balances grow, and as financial markets become more closely linked, interest-motivated and speculative capital movements may well magnify the volatility of overall balances of payments.[2]

No dependable relation holds between objective magnitudes such as volume of trade or deficits experienced in the past and a "needed" volume of reserves. The analogy between "needed" sizes of world reserves of gold and foreign exchange and a country's domestic money supply is faulty. While domestic money serves as the everyday medium of exchange, reserves serve only to fill in gaps between ordinary supply and demand on the foreign-exchange market at pegged rates. How large these gaps are depends on many circumstances, especially on how effective a mechanism for balancing international transactions is in operation.

Unless a country's reserves are either large enough or growing fast enough to forestall anxiety over them, its government is likely to slide into controlling trade and capital movements. The anxieties of government officials and central bankers are perhaps not quite as foolish as they appear in Fritz Machlup's comparison of their attitudes with Mrs. Machlup's passion for a huge or rapidly growing wardrobe.[3] Reserves must be more than ample to meet any likely nonspeculative drain if confidence is to endure, for losses of confidence and of reserves intensify each other. Even otherwise huge reserves could prove inadequate to defend a currency in the face of fundamental disequilibrium interacting with loss of confidence. But if the currency's exchange rate is approximately correct, huge reserves discourage bearish speculation (and may even encourage bullish speculation) and so make themselves all the more huge in relation to actual drawings on them. Either skimpiness or hugeness exaggerates itself through the behavior of speculators, which is one more reason why there can be no simple and dependable relation between the size and the adequacy of a country's reserves.

Vagueness about how much international liquidity is "enough" for a single country provides just one reason for doubting that the present or recent system provides a world total that is right in any definite sense.

"Official settlements" and "liquidity," to repeat, are connected with exchange-rate pegging. Under the traditional gold standard, governments and central banks refrained from regular intervention on the foreign-exchange markets. They usually stabilized exchange rates indirectly by maintaining two-way convertibility between their own currencies and gold at a fixed price. Until 1968–1971, when it suspended gold convertibility even for dollars held by foreign monetary authorities, the United States maintained the exchange stability of the dollar in this indirect way. (Some actual foreign-exchange dealings since 1961 provided only a sporadic and small-scale exception.) Nowadays, however, most countries maintain exchange stability, when they do, by dealing directly on the market in their own and foreign currencies. They do not intervene with gold itself because gold is not traded on the foreign-exchange market. Since about 1971, as explained a few pages later on, the active official use of gold has been even further attenuated.

Gold

What, then, could the familiar statement have meant that "Gold remains the ultimate means of settling balances among the principal trading nations"?[4] Under the bilateral payments agreements prevailing widely in the early years

after World War II, and even under the European Payments Union of 1950–1958, such statements could bear a fairly literal interpretation. Central banks routinely made short-run advances to each other to supply the currencies demanded on the market at fixed exchange rates. Periodically, central banks that had run up net debts to their partners would make full or partial settlement, as agreed, by transferring gold (or dollars). Such procedures were to some extent coming back into use under the monetary arrangements of the European Community. In general, though, central banks no longer routinely develop such debts to and claims on each other; and the terminology of "official settlements" seldom literally applies. Ordinarily, each country's authorities just keep its currency from appreciating or depreciating against the dollar (or, for some countries, sterling). A deficit country's central bank no longer typically makes payments to or obtains an advance from a surplus country's central bank; instead, the one simply runs down and

2. Walter S. Salant, "Does the International Monetary System Need Reform?," in J. Carter Murphy, ed., *Money in the International Order*, Dallas: Southern Methodist University Press, 1964, pp. 3–33; Walter S. Salant *et al.*, *The United States Balance of Payments in 1968*, Washington: Brookings Institution, 1963, pp. 236–238 of the Joint Economic Committee print; and J. M. Culbertson, "U.S. Policy and the International Financial System," in *Recent Changes in Monetary Policy and Balance-of-Payments Problems*, Hearings before the House Banking and Currency Committee, July 1963, Washington: Government Printing Office, 1963, p. 346. These authors, writing some seven or eight years before the final crack-up of the Bretton Woods system began in 1971, have turned out to be pretty good prophets.

3. Fritz Machlup, "The Need for Monetary Reserves," Banca Nazionale del Lavoro *Quarterly Review*, September 1966, reprinted by Princeton University, International Finance Section, October 1966.

4. Here quoted in the words of Miroslaz Kriz, article of December 1960 reprinted in Finn B. Jensen and Ingo Walter, eds., *Readings in International Economic Relations*, New York: Ronald Press, 1966, p. 87.

the other builds up its own reserves. Each deals not with the other specifically but with transactors in general on the interbank foreign-exchange market.

The foregoing paragraph describes practice before 1968, and even as late as 1971. The roles of gold and the dollar then became unclear, and they remain changeable at the time of writing. Since this chapter is concerned with the need for reform, it makes sense to continue describing the system *away from which* an evolution is under way.

Under that system, loose references to the use of gold in international "settlements" meant the sale of gold for the dollars a central bank needed to intervene with on the foreign-exchange market in support of its own currency. The central bank might sell the gold to the United States Treasury, to the International Monetary Fund, to some other central bank that happened to have a surplus of dollars for which it wanted gold, or to any buyers on the London gold market.[5]

Because of its ready salability for the dollars actually used in market intervention, central banks found gold an attractive asset in which to hold their "international liquidity." Until flooded with dollars in 1970–1971, the major central banks of Western Europe, like the United States itself, did in fact hold the bulk of their reserves in gold. But none held gold alone. The central banks wanted some dollars as working balances. Furthermore, they could invest their dollar reserves at short term and earn interest, while gold itself was sterile (apart from the possibility of its being marked up in price). Still another reason was that the United States pressured foreign authorities to limit their conversions of dollars into gold.

Why didn't the central banks go to the other extreme and hold practically all of their external reserves in interest-bearing dollar (or sterling) assets? The old gold-standard tradition of holding actual gold was part of the answer. Furthermore, taking a loss on gold seemed practically impossible, apart from storage costs and the loss of interest, while holding gold might conceivable bring a profit (or avoid a loss on dollars). Especially in view of American balance-of-payments deficits, no central banker worried that the dollar price of gold might be officially cut. There was no limit to how far the United States could go in keeping the dollar price of gold *up*; it could simply create dollars in any necessary amounts—a standard procedure—to buy all the gold offered to it at the official price. There was an objec-

tive limit, however, to how long the United States could persist in holding the price of gold *down*: if its reserves were to run out, it could no longer continue selling gold at the old price.

The limited capacity of the United States to hold the price of gold down but its unlimited capacity to hold the price up, together with prevailing policies and attitudes, put gold in the position that a corporation's stock would have if it were guaranteed against going down in price but might possibly rise. For investors, that feature might well outweigh the disadvantage of the stock's not paying dividends.

Because its price was adjustable only upward, gold was what J. M. Culbertson called "first-class international money." It was the reserve medium that central bankers preferred; dollars and sterling were mere "second-class" substitutes.[6] When the gold value of a reserve currency came under serious suspicion, central bankers were inclined to dump that substitute and scramble for the safety of gold itself, except as they restrained each other by formal agreements or informal pressures. Private hoarders felt less restraint. Something analogous to Gresham's Law was at work: the first-class money was hoarded, while second-class money remained in active use. After 1965, gold production (as distinguished from mark-ups in the price of gold) made no net addition to the reserves of monetary authorities; instead, slightly more gold than was produced went into industrial uses and private hoards.

Other circumstances contributed to the special monetary status of gold. Members of the International Monetary Fund were required to pay part of their subscriptions in gold and to declare the par values of their currencies in terms of gold itself, of the dollar as its gold "content" stood in 1944, or of Special Drawing Rights, the SDR itself being defined (until mid-1974) as equivalent to 0.888671 gram of gold. Especially as the official and free-market prices of gold diverged widely from 1971 on, gold's role as "a common denominator of currencies" became an incidental aspect of exchange-rate pegging.

Gold has traditionally enjoyed legal status as a domestic monetary reserve. The United States was among the last countries to abandon this tradition. The requirement for a 25 percent gold reserve was repealed for the deposit liabilities of the Federal Reserve Banks in March 1965 and for Federal Reserve notes in March 1968. The required percentage had already been cut in 1945. Not since 1933 had U.S. money been domestically redeemable in gold. Although purchases and sales of gold by the U.S. Treasury tended to expand and contract the supply of "high-powered" domestic bank reserves, the Federal Reserve ordinarily did not allow these spontaneous tendencies to prevail. It offset them by open-market operations, managing bank reserves chiefly by criteria other than the country's gold stock. The Federal Reserve was better able to do so than the central banks of countries whose foreign trade, balances and imbalances of payments, and losses and gains of gold and foreign exchange did bulk large among the influences on the supply of domestic high-powered money.

In some respects, the first-class status of gold was paradoxical. Not gold but the dollar was (and remains) the chief "vehicle currency" used in private and official transactions. Gold was serviceable as a reserve medium not because its official holders could use it to support their own currencies on the foreign-exchange market—they could not do so, directly—but because they could exchange it for the dollars (or other currencies) actually used in such support. Since 1971, with the free-market price of gold soaring far above the twice-increased official price, even this use of gold has become doubtful. Central bankers have become reluctant to sell or transfer gold to each other at the relatively low official price. As Gresham's Law explains, they would much prefer to exchange away dollars from their vastly swollen holdings. As a result, gold remains where it is, at least temporarily out of active use as a reserve medium.[7]

The gold-exchange standard

Like gold's first-class status, the dollar's second-class status was largely artificial. The dollar, not gold, is the home currency of the world's chief banking center and capital market. The Eurodollar and Eurobond markets illustrate the dominance of the dollar in international finance. Although the United States had experienced price-level inflation, especially since the start of Vietnam escalation, the dollar still had retained more of its purchasing power since World War II than almost any other currency. In the closing years of the gold-exchange standard, though perhaps only temporarily, other major countries were experiencing worse price inflation than the United States. The upward bias of expectations about the dollar price of gold resulted from United States gold policy. It contributed to the payments deficit that bred

uneasiness about the adequacy of the country's gold reserves. A vicious circle was operating: the weakness of the dollar, partly artificial though it was, contributed to the deficit, while the deficit contributed to the weakness. From the late 1950s, outflows of capital were a major element in the deficit, provoking the controls mentioned in Chapter 27. Short-term outflows were heavy at times, notably in the fall of 1960 (when the price of gold spurted dramatically on the London market), in the last quarter of 1964 (shortly before and apparently in anticipation of the imposition of "voluntary restraint"), after the British devaluation of 1967, and on even more memorable occasions since then. Speculative considerations may even have encouraged the outflow of long-term investment capital: the possibility of dollar devaluation or tighter controls gave potential American buyers of foreign securities or business properties an extra reason for not procrastinating. At least, that is how Professors Triffin and Machlup persuasively interpreted experience during the 1960s.[8] If they are right, the

5. In times of crisis, of course, central banks might still lend to each other, especially by activating bilateral "swap" agreements of the kind mentioned on pp. 569, 579, 587, 616. A debt between central banks could also arise and be settled as in the following example: the Federal Reserve Bank of New York, as agent for the Bank of England, supports sterling by buying it with dollars. The Bank of England later takes over the sterling bought on its behalf, paying with gold. But these transactions amount to the same thing as if the Bank of England had first sold the gold for dollars and then itself used the dollars in support of sterling.

6. Culbertson, op. cit., esp. pp. 337–338.

7. Norman S. Fieleke, "International Economic Reform," New England Economic Review, January/February 1973, pp. 23–24.

8. Robert Triffin, The Balance of Payments and the Foreign Investment Position of the United States, Princeton Essays in International Finance, No. 55, Princeton, N.J.: Princeton University, 1966; Fritz Machlup, "World Monetary Debate—Bases for Agreement," reprinted from The Banker, September 1966, by International Finance Section, Princeton University, 1966.

capital outflows figuring heavily in the U.S. deficit embodied an element of one-way-option speculation against the dollar, related in turn to the one-way-only changeability of the official price of gold. This interpretation rather obviously does apply to the big deficits of 1970, 1971, and early 1973 also.

Under the gold-exchange standard prevailing before the events of 1968–1971, gold still constituted the bulk of official reserves; but the foreign-exchange component was gaining ground. Between the ends of 1948 and 1966, 57 percent of the *increase* in total gold and foreign-exchange reserves of noncommunist countries (not counting drawing rights at the International Monetary Fund) consisted of foreign exchange. For noncommunist countries other than the United States, 72 percent of the increase in their reserves over the same period either consisted of foreign exchange or corresponded to U.S. gold losses. New gold production in noncommunist countries, together with Russian gold sales in the West, accounted for only a small fraction of the growth in reserves. New gold supplies were inadequate by themselves—especially with much of the new gold going into private hoards—to satisfy the growing reserve demands of monetary authorities.

Triffin's diagnosis

By the late 1950s, Professor Robert Triffin was already warning about these trends and about the "absurdity"[9] of the way the gold-exchange standard was working. Despite the impression created by some of his early writings, his worry was not that the world already faced a shortage of international liquidity. Mainly he worried about how haphazardly the growth of reserves was determined and about how undependable and plagued with contradictions its existing sources were. As one of his fellow thinkers phrased the problem, "Key currency reserves increase or decrease in supply, depending on whether the key currency countries happen to be running balance-of-payments deficits or surpluses and quite independently of the growth in need or demand for international liquidity."[10] Over the long run, the key-currency countries would have to keep running deficits to expand the reserves of other countries. The U.S. gold reserve would shrink not merely as a percentage of the growing foreign liquid claims pyramided against it but even in absolute

amount as foreign authorities converted into gold some of the dollars they acquired in pegging exchange rates. Curing the U.S. deficit would improve confidence in the chief element of growth in international liquidity, foreign-held dollars, but would restrict the supply. Continuing U.S. deficits were both necessary yet alarming. The system would become more and more precarious as time went on.

One particular type of international liquidity, namely, the "overhang" of dollars held by foreign official agencies, grew so excessively in 1970–1973[11] as to become considered a serious problem in itself. We should remember, in future years, that this problem—if in fact it persists as a problem—is a consequence of the crumbling Bretton Woods system and not of whatever new system may replace it.

A conservative diagnosis

Several conservative observers who were presumably shocked at the particular reform that Triffin proposed nevertheless offered an analysis remarkably similar to his. Probably the most prominent member of this school was Jacques Rueff, General de Gaulle's architect of French economic and monetary stabilization. Rueff saw the world repeating the gold-economizing practices adopted during the 1920s, partly under the inspiration of the Genoa Conference of 1922. Countries gaining sterling or dollars did not demand their full redemption in gold, as they would have done under a genuine gold standard. They left the funds on deposit in the countries of origin; the international monetary system became a "childish game" in which the winners returned their marbles to the losers; the key-currency countries learned "the marvelous secret of the deficit without tears." (One might add that by acquiring liquid claims on a relatively rich key-currency country, relatively poor countries were granting cheap loans to that country, moving capital in the perverse direction.) Balance-of-payments adjustment ceased being quasi-automatic and came to depend on deliberate measures of credit or trade-control policy. Growing claims of surplus countries on deficit countries could serve as a basis for credit expansion in the former without imposing contraction on the latter. Imbalances in trade or even capital movements (including repatriations of capital that had previously taken flight) could therefore promote inflation in some countries without promoting deflation in others. But this duplication of the credit pyramid on a relatively narrow gold base could not go on indefinitely. The house of cards was getting shakier and shakier and would eventually collapse, as in 1929–1931. The danger had developed not because the United States had lost so much gold since 1950 but because it had lost so *little*, delaying correction. Rueff viewed the system as "the product of a prodigious collective error"; it would "go down in history as cause for stupefaction and scandal." It would end in crisis and panic unless deliberately and carefully dismantled.[12]

Proliferating forms of liquidity

The introduction of Special Drawing Rights by the International Monetary Fund represents a partial response to the problem as Triffin diagnosed it and a partial step in the general direction of the reform he recommended. As matters now stand, however, the SDR has not displaced other types of international liquidity. On the contrary, it so far represents just one more of the ways in which older reserve media have been stretched or supplemented. These ways include ordinary IMF drawing rights, the General Arrangements to Borrow, the network of bilateral swap arrangements among central banks, the mutual currency-support arrangements of the European Community, some aspects of the Eurodollar market, official forward-market intervention intended to ward off drains on spot reserves, and occasional special rescue efforts for beleaguered currencies.[13] The multiplicity of these various ways of financing exchange-rate pegging warrants no complacency. On the contrary, it underlines the jerry-built character of the present system of international liquidity.

Capital movements

The liquidity problem, as we have seen, intertwines with the confidence and adjustment problems. The adjustment problem is too fundamental and too familiar to require much further comment here. Let us just note its relation to capital movements. Under pegged exchange rates, a short-term capital inflow not offset by other above-the-line items in the balance of payments means that private transactors are running down their short-term claims on foreigners or building up their short-term debt to foreigners, while the country's central bank is gaining external reserves. An expansion of domestic money and credit on the basis of this reserve gain would be precarious because the presumably temporary capital inflow might soon reverse itself. If the central bank wants to ward off imported inflation, it especially wants to ward off imported inflation followed by deflation. The central bank has reason to "neutralize" the monetary effects of an inflow of funds if it conveniently can. It has similar reason to neutralize an outflow: it would be perverse to impose deflation on the home economy to adjust to an outflow likely to prove only temporary. The more abundant

9. Triffin, *Gold and the Dollar Crisis*, New Haven: Yale University Press, 1960, p. 67. Triffin offered his diagnosis and proposal in this book and in numerous articles and statements for Congressional hearings, some of them reprinted in his *The World Money Maze*, New Haven: Yale University Press, 1966.

10. Tibor Scitovsky in *International Payments Imbalances and Need for Strengthening International Financial Arrangements*, Hearings of May and June 1961 and papers contributed to the Subcommittee on International Exchange and Payments of the Joint Economic Committee, Washington: Government Printing Office, 1961 (hereafter cited as "1961 Hearings"), p. 176.

11. See pp. 580–581.

12. "The West Is Risking a Credit Collapse," *Fortune*, LXIV, July 1961, pp. 126–127, 262, 267–268. A very similar article by Rueff, "Gold Exchange Standard a Danger to the West," is reprinted in Herbert G. Grubel, ed., *World Monetary Reform*, Stanford: Stanford University Press, 1963, pp. 320–328. Professor Michael A. Heilperin of the Graduate Institute of International Studies in Geneva gave a similar conservative analysis in "Monetary Reform in an Atlantic Setting," in 1961 Hearings, pp. 331–340, and in "The Case for Going Back to Gold," reprinted in the Grubel volume, pp. 329–342.

13. On some of the liquidity devices mentioned, recall pp. 279–282, 393, 396–399, 424–425, 435, 438.

liquid funds are and the more sensitively they move in response to changing interest rates and changing degrees of confidence in currencies, the more damaging it would be to allow zigzags of domestic inflation and deflation for the sake of balance-of-payments adjustment. The Bretton Woods system tacitly presupposed a low degree of capital mobility, whether because of inertia, high transactions costs, controls, or other inhibitions. In the present-day world, however, interest-arbitrageurs, hedgers, and speculators (including multinational corporations) are well financed and alert. Especially in these circumstances, neutralization of capital flows seems desirable for domestic reasons. Neutralization does, however, reinforce the lack of any automatic payments adjustment mechanism under pegged exchange rates. It leaves unimpaired the incentives for mobile funds to slosh across boundaries. For this reason, and also because it is difficult anyway to achieve complete domestic neutralization (particularly of the inflationary effects of inflows), national authorities have increasingly been resorting to controls over capital movements.[14]

For completeness, let us simply list some further actual or alleged problems: the dominance of the dollar in world finance; the special privileges of the United States in being able, until recently, to run Rueff's "deficit without tears"; discrimination in favor of advanced countries and against underdeveloped countries in provision of international liquidity; an apparent inflation bias; and the interdependence between monetary arrangements and tariff and trade policies. Some of these problems have a political aspect, even involving sheer national prestige.[15]

Most broadly, the troubles calling for reform stem from the philosophy underlying the Bretton Woods system.[16] Events have discredited it in key respects.

---

14. Recall examples from the chapters on individual countries.

15. On the French concern with politics and prestige in international monetary negotiations, see Edward Kolodziej's forthcoming book on French foreign policy.

16. Recall Chapter 20.

CHAPTER THIRTY

Reforms of International Liquidity

Questions about liquidity

The three types of problem reviewed in the last chapter intertwine so closely that it is arbitrary to classify most reform proposals as aimed at one problem in particular. Still, this classification will serve as an organizing device. The present chapter covers reforms concerned primarily with liquidity; the following two chapters cover reforms to deal with the adjustment and confidence problems.

How should the total stock of world liquidity be regulated? How should new liquidity be distributed among countries? Should first-class and second-class liquidity continue to coexist? How should different types of liquidity be tied together? Should key currencies be retained? Should their convertibility be restored into gold or SDRs, and if into gold, at what price of gold?

Raising the price of gold

One of the least fundamental reforms discussed in the 1950s and 1960s would have increased supplies of international liquidity and

given key currencies more adequate backing while leaving the gold-exchange standard unchanged in its essentials. The proposal was to double or triple the official price of gold at least. Unchanged since 1934 despite the worldwide inflation that had occurred in the meanwhile, the $35 price was said to be unrealistic. At a realistic price, gold could more fully perform its role as the ultimate monetary asset, an objective asset that could not be simply printed or written into existence and that was not the debt of any issuer. In contrast with other liquidity reforms, an increase in the price of gold would be delightfully uncomplicated.

Much, however, could be said against the proposal. The benefits would accrue haphazardly. The price increase would be least beneficial to those countries that had been particularly short of gold reserves. The chief gainers would be private gold hoarders, gold-mine owners, Russians, South Africans, and "any countries which had previously been 'rocking the boat' by switching out of dollars and pounds into gold."[1] The old joke about wasting resources to dig up gold in one place and rebury it in another would become more apt. An impending increase in the price of gold could not be kept completely secret and would be preceded by one-way-option speculation. The conditions calling for the initial price increase would probably develop again in later decades and require further increases. Variability in the price of gold would undermine even the *pretense* of linking currencies to gold. It would heighten the danger of flights from national currencies into gold and might discredit their use as international reserves. Unless the official price of gold were to increase gradually, either at a specified monthly rate or according to some formula, the price changes would come in discrete jumps. This way of keeping the effective supply of liquidity in step with the growing demand for it over the long run would mean that liquidity was inadequate before every price increase and temporarily excessive afterwards, causing inflationary tendencies that

1. Brian Tew in *International Payments Imbalances and Need for Strengthening International Financial Arrangements*, Hearings of May and June 1961 and papers contributed to the Subcommittee on International Exchange and Payments of the Joint Economic Committee, Washington: Government Printing Office (hereafter cited as "1961 Hearings"), p. 289.

would not be completely reversed later on. As a way of creating international liquidity, raising the price of gold is subject not only to its own special disadvantages but also the general disadvantages, described in later sections of this chapter, that bedevil any creation of international liquidity.

The Triffin plan

Professor Triffin's plan is worth describing even though it dates back to before 1960 and has in some respects been bypassed by developments. It spawned a number of other plans in reaction to it, and it influenced the official thinking that resulted in Special Drawing Rights. Triffin's ideas continue influencing proposals for further evolution of SDRs.

Under the Triffin Plan, a new international money would be created for use among central banks. It might be called "bancor," the name suggested by Keynes in his plan of 1943 for an international clearing union. Bancor might take the form of deposits with an expanded International Monetary Fund. As time went on, countries would hold more and more of their international liquidity in this new form. Ultimately, key currencies would be displaced, and gold would be restricted to a small percentage of each country's reserves. A central bank needing another country's currency for exchange-rate stabilization could buy it from the other central bank and pay by transferring ownership of some of its bancor deposit on the books of the IMF. The IMF could create bancor by giving it to the participating countries in exchange for transfers to itself of their conventional reserve assets, by lending to members with balance-of-payments deficits, by buying national securities or the bonds of development banks, or by giving it to participating countries outright according to some formula. The IMF could pay its members interest on their deposits because it would be earning interest on the foreign-exchange assets transferred to it and on the other loans and investments that it would buy. The total supply of bancor could supposedly be regulated to grow at some suitable moderate pace. No longer would international liquidity grow erratically according to the vagaries of gold production, industrial gold consumption, private hoarding, gold sales by the Soviet Union, the balance-of-payments positions of key-currency

countries, and the willingness of central banks to hold key currencies rather than redeem them in gold.

Gold would play a peculiar role. It, bancor, and national currencies would all be pegged together. The long-run growth of international liquidity would make gold become an ever smaller fraction of bancor deposits. Two things would avoid the otherwise obvious danger: a so-called gold or exchange guarantee to prevent loss of confidence in bancor, and narrow limits on the convertibility of bancor into gold. Restrictions on gold ownership by monetary authorities would almost certainly be accompanied by a ban on private gold ownership in all member countries. The fixed gold content of national money units and the bancor unit would retain little operational meaning: the gold guarantee of bancor would become empty. Under the Triffin Plan, bancor would displace gold as the ultimate international money. Gold would be a mere appendage, apparently serving only as a costly public-relations device to gain support for the plan.

Early counterproposals

Governmental officials and central bankers initially greeted the Triffin Plan with suspicion. It looked too radical. Various supposedly more acceptable substitutes were invented to remedy the absurdities Triffin had noted in the key-currency-reserve system. One early counterproposal would have had the key-currency countries cure their balance-of-payments deficits, yet continue supplying their own currencies as international liquidity, by buying foreign currencies to hold, along with gold, in their own external reserves. The dollar, while still a reserve medium for foreign countries, would itself be backed partly by foreign currencies. *Business Week* once called that scheme "monetary incest." Another idea was to multiply the sources of liquidity by having central banks hold their reserves in *several* currencies in at least roughly specified proportions. This idea of a "composite reserve unit" could be formalized by having each country deposit its own currency in an international pool, receiving in return international units matched in specified proportions by the currencies deposited. Alternatively, or in addition, countries could multiply the means of defending currencies under speculative attack by perfecting the patchwork system of bilateral and multi-lateral standby loan agreements, including the inter-central-bank "swaps," that has in fact been extensively developed since 1961 and 1962. The patchwork of gold or foreign-exchange guarantees of debtor-country currencies could be formalized and extended. (Under such an arrangement, a country's authorities guarantee that in the event of devaluation, they will credit designated foreign official holders of the home currency with enough additional amounts of it to keep the gold or foreign-exchange value of each guaranteed holding as large as before. The British example was described in Chapter 22.) Members' quotas in the International Monetary Fund could be increased again, as in the past. By itself, that approach would load up the Fund still further with "cruzeiros, bolivianos, rupees, rupiahs, bahts, kyats," and other such currencies, all to obtain more of the few major currencies that really are in demand.[2] Paying 25 percent of any additional subscription to the IMF in gold, as normally required, could be awkward for countries already worried about gold losses. The Fund's statutes could be modified to make as much as desired of each country's ordinary drawing rights—and not just the gold tranche—available without questions asked. Furthermore, these rights could change from being regarded as borrowing rights to being regarded as deposits in the Fund that their owners could draw down without obligation to reconstitute them. Additional amounts of such deposits could even be periodically credited to members' accounts, in exchange for nothing, as the world's "need" for liquidity grew. This new money would simply circulate in a closed circuit among central banks; each would agree to accept it in payment for its own money or for dollars supplied to fellow members for use in their foreign-exchange-market interventions. The new money would play much the same role as gold before 1968–1971.

Further development of Special Drawing Rights

In describing these possibilities, we have arrived at what would be a convergence between the Triffin Plan and the SDR scheme already in effect. How do SDRs and Triffin's bancor compare? Both are (or would be) a so-called paper gold, denominated in gold and guaranteed in gold value but not normally redeemable in gold. Both bear interest. Both circulate among central banks in exchange for the currencies used in market interventions, but a participant's obligation to accept SDRs is more limited than its obligation to accept bancor would be. SDRs are given outright, while bancor would be issued largely in exchange for reserve or loan or investment assets. Each new issue of SDRs requires approval of members holding at least 85 percent of the voting power, while the issue of bancor would be more at the discretion of the IMF. Bancor would be unambiguously an asset for its owners, while SDRs are partially an asset and partially a borrowing right, as the provision for partial reconstitution of drawings and as the name itself suggest.[3] Triffin envisaged a more nearly exclusive role for bancor in the scheme of international liquidity than is yet in prospect for SDRs.

The Triffin Plan in its ultimate form, with

2. Robert Triffin in the 1961 Hearings, p. 304.

For further comment on guarantees and other palliative reforms mentioned in this paragraph, see the first edition of this book, pp. 472–475. A guarantee scheme, as explained there, could have some merit but would do little toward solving problems of payments adjustment and international liquidity. The prospect of large and incalculable foreign-exchange costs would in some ways awkwardly tie the hands of the authorities giving a guarantee. Problems would arise concerning what types of home-currency asset and what types of foreign holder should be covered. It might be difficult to keep the coverage of a guarantee from effectively extending beyond the designated official holders to private parties abroad and at home; a credible guarantee would have to be limited in amount.

3. On the happy ambiguities that brought agreement among national delegations whose opinions on reform of the IMF diverged rather sharply, see Fritz Machlup, *Remaking the International Monetary System: The Rio Agreement and Beyond*, Baltimore: Johns Hopkins Press, 1968.

bancor displacing all other reserve assets except working balances of intervention currencies, would solve the confidence problem on the official level. No longer would the danger exist of a flight from one reserve asset into another or from second-class into first-class international money. Some reform plans[4] do call for a movement in this direction, exalting SDRs and downgrading gold and the dollar as reserve media. SDRs would also displace gold and the dollar as the numéraire in terms of which countries fix the parities of their own currencies. (For example, when the United States devalued in February 1973, it set the dollar's new parity as 0.82895 SDR.) A more radical move would turn SDRs into an intervention currency. For SDRs to become an object of trading on the foreign-exchange markets, they would have to become eligible for ownership by commercial banks, at least, and probably by the banks' customers as well. The international issue of a currency widely owned and used by private parties would probably lodge an unacceptable potentiality for inflation in the hands of an international body. So fundamental a change is unlikely in the foreseeable future.

Enhancing the role of SDRs could conceivably deal with the problem of dollar overhang.[5] Foreign authorities holding more dollars than they desire could turn them over to the IMF for a special issue of SDRs, on which the Fund would pay interest covered by the interest earned on the dollar assets turned over to it. The idea behind this proposal[6] is presumably that the IMF would behave as a more stable holder of dollar claims than their reluctant previous owners. Another way of achieving similar stability would be for the United States to fund its dollar-overhang obligations into long-term debt. Such debt would presumably have to bear interest rates high enough to compensate the creditors for the reduced liquidity of their claims. Skepticism is in order. Such proposals, if implemented, would lock the United States into obligations that might better be handled more flexibly as conditions evolve. In time, foreign official holders may be able to sell their unwanted dollars to private parties—perhaps to local importers as their countries move into trade deficits and the United States into surplus, perhaps to investors in U.S. corporate securities. It may be fortunate that worry about the overhang had, by 1974, largely gone out of style.

A dollar standard

Introducing Triffin's bancor or developing SDRs into essentially the same thing is not the only way to solve the problem of multiple forms of international liquidity. The U.S. dollar itself could displace gold and other reserve media. Demonetizing gold and forthrightly accepting the dollar as the basis of the international monetary system would carry to its logical conclusion a trend that had long been under way in private and official use of the dollar. Just as many countries forsook gold and clung to sterling when Britain left the gold standard in 1931, many countries might keep their currencies pegged to a nongold dollar. The crucial flaw that Triffin diagnosed in the gold-exchange standard was not the use of key-currency reserves as such, but the use as reserves of key currencies precariously pegged to gold on a fractional-reserve basis. With the dollar no longer backed by a gold reserve whose shrinkage could sap confidence, with the problem dispelled of having both first-class and second-class international moneys, and with no possibility remaining of one-way-option speculation on a devaluation of the dollar against gold, the precariousness of the old system would be gone. (If other key currencies served along with the dollar as international liquidity, however, and if they were pegged together at fixed rates, the possibility would remain of flights from relatively distrusted to relatively trusted key currencies. The system works best when there is only a single key currency.)

Since 1971, permanent acceptance of a world dollar standard seems unlikely. Repeated devaluations, depreciations, and speed-ups of inflation have shaken confidence in the dollar; and continuing U.S. deficits, the dollar overhang, and manifestations of supposed "dollar imperialism" have aroused resentment abroad. Still, a dollar standard remains instructive to contemplate. Under that system, any run from the dollar would have to be a run into American goods and services. (If some foreigners unloaded their dollars onto other foreigners, this would not be a run from the American point of view.) Unlike a run from a gold-standard dollar, this could cause no crisis for the United States; the capital outflow would finance itself by and coincide with surplus exports of goods and services. Even this development would be limited, to the extent that the dollars were held by foreign monetary authorities and banks rather than by business firms; for it is unlikely that central and commercial banks would fly on any large scale from dollars into commodities. To persuade residents of their own countries to take dollars off their hands and use them for purchases in the United States, the foreign authorities might relax import and exchange restrictions previously in effect or sell the dollars at a reduced price (that is, revalue their own currencies upward against the dollar). The only devaluation of the dollar against foreign currencies to worry about would have to come at the initiative of foreign authorities, since the United States would not have been pegging the dollar to anything in the first place.

Continuing American inflation might motivate a flight from foreign-held dollars into American goods and services. This would differ little from a flight out of domestically held dollars. Foreign and domestic flight would develop gradually together as a continuing inflationary drift in American policy undermined confidence in the purchasing power of the dollar. As in any other country, the monetary authorities might either succeed or fail in avoiding such a disastrous policy drift. But with the dollar no longer pegged to anything by U.S. action, the goal of stability in its purchasing power would no longer have to share attention with balance-of-payments considerations. With its objectives made fewer and simpler, monetary management would have a better chance of success. The interest of foreign countries as well as Americans in a stable dollar might even be given some sort of formal, institutional recognition.[7] Inflationary drift in government policy is too deep-rooted, however, to be curable by any easy institutional device.

Though less precarious than the gold-exchange standard, the nongold dollar standard would by no means solve all problems. Individual foreign countries would still occasionally face deficits, reserve losses, and one-way-option speculation on devaluation, or surpluses and unwanted large accumulations of dollar reserves. These are difficulties of exchange-rate pegging as such rather than of the choice of a particular reserve medium. For the United States, balance-of-payments problems would be less serious, though a conceivable run out of dollars into goods and services, meaning an export surplus, would presumably be more nearly troublesome than a deficit. Even such a surplus would be nothing worse than repayment of real resources previously lent cheaply by foreigners.

Over the long run, a deficit would be more likely as foreigners willingly accumulated dollar reserves. Far from being troublesome for the United States, the deficit would mean overabsorption of goods and services painlessly financed by cheap loans of indefinite duration. From the foreign point of view, this "coals-to-Newcastle" capital flow is a defect of the nongold dollar standard, but no worse than tying up capital through the accumulation of gold reserves.

The "link"

A nongold dollar standard would give to the United States the "seigniorage" available when new international liquidity is created by the strokes of bankers' pens rather than dug laboriously out of the ground.[8] This may seem

4. For example, the proposal of the U.S. government, reprinted in *Economic Report of the President together with the Annual Report of the Council of Economic Advisers*, January 1973, pp. 160–174.

5. Recall pp. 580–581, 616.

6. This and other proposals concerning the dollar overhang (as well as other problems) are listed in International Economic Policy Association, *The United States Balance of Payments*, Washington: 1972, pp. 102–107.

7. Charles Kindleberger has actually proposed replacement of the Federal Open Market Committee by an Atlantic Open Market Committee, which would seek to determine interest rates in the international capital market. *The Politics of International Money and World Language*, Princeton Essays in International Finance, No. 61, Princeton, N.J.: Princeton University, August 1967, p. 7.

8. On the concept of "seigniorage," see Robert Mundell and Alexander Swoboda, eds., *Monetary Problems of the International Economy*, Chicago: University of Chicago Press, 1969; Part 5 contains discussions of seigniorage by Herbert G. Grubel, W. M. Corden, Wilson E. Schmidt, Larry A. Sjaastad, and Harry G. Johnson.

unfair. Similarly, current arrangements for creating additions or supplements to international liquidity are widely regarded as unfair. The underdeveloped countries, in particular, are said to be short-changed. Not they but the industrialized countries get the benefit of the General Arrangements to Borrow, the inter-central-bank swap credits, and most of the special currency-rescue operations. Special Drawing Rights are allocated in proportion to countries' quotas in the International Monetary Fund; and in the assignment of quotas, national incomes, trade volumes, and reserve holdings—indicators of relative prosperity—carried great weight. "He that hath, to him shall be given. . . ."

The widely popular proposal for some sort of "link" between development aid and the issue of SDRs may conveniently be discussed against the background of a plan proposed by Sir Maxwell Stamp.[9] Stamp proposed that the IMF periodically issue certificates denominated in gold but not convertible into gold. Aid-coordinating agencies would distribute the certificates to underdeveloped countries, which would be pretty sure to spend most of them to cover balance-of-payments deficits. The certificates would thus come into circulation among central banks and would supposedly be considered practically equivalent to gold and reserve currencies. The plan would kill two birds with one stone—expand international liquidity and help poor countries. Stamp subsequently modified his plan to try to make it more acceptable: the issue of certificates and the amount of them any country would be expected to absorb would be more tightly limited than in his original plan.

Stamp's basic idea of the "link" could be grafted onto the SDR scheme. Under some new formula for allocating issues of SDRs, underdeveloped countries could receive shares larger than proportionate to their IMF quotas, while advanced countries would receive proportionately smaller shares. Unfortunately, the real resources thus transferred to the underdeveloped countries would not come out of some fourth dimension. They would come from countries running export surpluses and taking settlement, directly or indirectly, in SDRs that had been given to poor countries.

It is no objection to the "link" that it would tranfer resources to poor countries, for that is its purpose. The chief objection is that it would obscure where the resources transferred came from. No one could accurately foresee what amounts would come from whom. Countries would wind up providing aid in real terms without their legislatures having voted appropriations for it in the normal way. "Such aid would therefore be provided even though the electorate might prefer to devote the resources in question to other uses."[10] The chief merit or chief defect of the "link," then, depending on one's point of view, is that it would exploit ignorance to accomplish international transfers to which the donors might not otherwise agree. Rather than each being made on its own merits, decisions about liquidity and about aid would be muddled together.

Liquidity on two levels

Creating international liquidity in a suitable form and distributing it initially in an equitable way would not solve the problem of creating just the right amount. The quantity of international liquidity—let us say SDRs—in existence at any given time and the quantities and purchasing powers of national currencies must be connected. One reason is that the volume of SDRs "needed" to finance imbalances of payments at pegged exchange rates depends largely on the price levels of internationally traded goods. National inflations can thus increase the quantity of SDRs needed and presumably provided in response. Causation runs the other way, too: by allowing some countries to run larger or more persistent deficits than their reserves would otherwise have covered, creation of SDRs will strengthen demand and raise prices in the world markets for their imports and exports.

This is not to say that receipt of an SDR allocation automatically causes a country to expand its domestic money supply. But increased reserves *permit* expansion by relaxing the "discipline" of threatening balance-of-payments deficits. It is a weak reply to say that increased reserves need not be inflationary because central banks need not use them. "If central banks were not responsive to reserve holdings, most of the arguments for and against liquidity would fall to the ground. What has the whole liquidity issue been about if it has not assumed some connection between actual reserves and the incentives to use those reserves?"[11] Now, to the extent that some countries can run larger or longer-lasting deficits, other countries are exposed to stronger inflationary pressures of payments surpluses and of monetary expansion as their central banks gain reserves in pegging exchange rates. This transmission of inflation does not even presuppose that allocations of new reserves will directly relax monetary discipline in the deficit countries. Those countries may simply avoid, postpone, weaken, or reduce the controls or devaluations that the depletion of their reserves would otherwise have made necessary. In either case, the more ample financing of international imbalances has much the same impact on surplus countries.

International liquidity management cannot follow some simple criterion of stabilization, for the purchasing power of the SDR consists of the purchasing powers of the national currencies tied to it; and domestic policies affect national price levels. The difficulty inheres in money-supply management on two levels—the international and the national. This problem of two levels would be absent only if countries gave up their monetary independence and oriented domestic monetary conditions above all toward keeping their international transactions balanced. A country's money supply, price level, and state of business activity would then be geared to its holdings of international liquidity. A world liquidity shortage would be unambiguously deflationary. But when countries orient their policies toward maintaining full employment or toward financing government budget deficits and refuse to accept deflation to keep in step internationally, liquidity need not always be deficient or excessive on the national and international levels both at the same time. In particular, a shortage of international liquidity need not mean a deflationary shortage of domestic money. An international liquidity shortage may breed restrictions on international trade, but ordinarily not deflation. As the early years after World War II amply illustrate, domestic monetary inflation can coexist with impediments to international trade that might plausibly be blamed on a shortage of international liquidity available for riding out deficits (although the deficits themselves stemmed partly from divergent degrees of inflation within countries).

In such situations, remedying an international liquidity shortage would mean creating more SDRs even when they were not needed to avoid any deflation. The point is not that liquidity is inherently "bad" or "inflationary," but simply the creating more of it even when there would otherwise be no deflationary deficiency does tend toward inflation. Of course,

some conservative percentage limit might be set to the annual increase in the supply of SDRs. But then, as just shown, the supply might sometimes fall short of what was needed for covering balance-of-payments disequilibria.

Is the opposite conflict also possible—too much liquidity to lubricate international trade but not enough to prevent deflation within countries? This is unlikely. An excess of international liquidity hardly has any meaning, apart from its ultimate effect in raising price levels; and as for deflation, domestic policies can avoid it. The conflict is asymmetrical: the supposed needs of international trade may sometimes promote but never restrict the creation of SDRs when an opposite policy is advisable on domestic grounds. The inconsistencies of trying to manage liquidity on two levels at the same time shake the hope that SDRs would never be created in inflationary excess, but always created only to stave off a deflationary deficiency.

Let us consider this inflationary bias further. New SDRs would seldom be created to prevent deflation of prices and business activity; domestic policies would be taking care of that, anyway. Controls or devaluation, not severe deflation, are the ultimate response to balance-of-payments crisis. The supply of SDRs does not significantly restrict domestic money supplies, yet this in no way means that creating additional SDRs will not expand them. The very purpose of creating new SDRs is to let deficit countries avoid or postpone or mitigate the controls or devaluations otherwise necessary, financing larger or longer-lasting deficits. The hope that payments surpluses will alternate with deficits provides little reassurance, for the alternation will take place at generally higher levels of spending. A later balance-of-payments

9. See the 1961 Hearings and Stamp's paper reprinted in Herbert G. Grubel, ed., *World Monetary Reform*, Stanford: Stanford University Press, 1963, pp. 80–89.

10. N. Fieleke, "International Economic Reform," *New England Economic Review*, January/February 1973, p. 23.

11. Robert Mundell, *Monetary Theory*, Pacific Palisades, Cal.: Goodyear, 1971, pp. 124–125.

reversal does not undo the inflation that a country imports with a surplus; well-known "ratchet effects" are at work.

Any scheme for the more ample financing of international imbalances could partially defeat itself through its inflationary bias. Increased prices would make more international liquidity necessary to peg exchange rates at any given real flow of trade. Creating more SDRs to meet this need would enable the process to proceed for another round. Just as expanding the supply of a country's domestic money increases the total of cash balances demanded by raising prices—just as the supply of money creates its own demand—so an expanded supply of international liquidity creates its own demand by raising prices and the nominal sizes of imbalances to be financed. The chief difference is that the latter process is more roundabout and more subject to delays. If the SDR-issuing authority were determined to avoid feeding price inflation and guided itself by liquidity requirements on the national level, only coincidence could assure adequate liquidity on the international level as well. A further complication is that liquidity requirements even on the national level would diverge among countries.

M. June Flanders has noted a different but related aspect of this two-levels dilemma in arguing that "International Liquidity Is Always Inadequate."[12] If countries differ in the supposed trade-offs they face between unemployment and inflation, in their willingness to accept inflation to avoid unemployment, or in their propensity to engage in inflationary government finance, the more inflation-prone countries will run external deficits at fixed exchange rates. The countries running surpluses and accumulating reserves, though not actually compelled to adopt expansionary policies, will have trouble warding off imported inflation. Still, they will not be particularly unhappy about large reserves, as such, provided the reserves seem likely to retain their value. The deficit countries will avoid painful adjustment through deflation and unemployment as long as they can continue financing their deficits; and no amount of international reserves, short of infinity, can ever be enough to guarantee their continuing ability to do so. With countries unwilling to adopt the domestic financial policies necessary for payments equilibrium at fixed exchange rates and with small or shrinking reserves causing more worry than large or growing reserves,[13] the world will always appear short of reserves, whatever their actual total may be.

For several reasons, in short, it would be beyond the power of an international authority to provide adequate but not excessive liquidity for all countries at the same time.

No official reserves

This discouraging conclusion suggests a look at the idea of abolishing the international-liquidity problem by having national and international authorities stop concerning themselves with reserves and foreign-exchange operations. The following chapter considers the floating-exchange-rate aspect of this proposed solution; here, we are concerned with the liquidity aspect. Foreign balances would be held only by individuals, commercial banks, and other business firms and private organizations (as well as by government agencies solely to conduct their regular international transactions rather than to influence exchange rates). Holders would manage their foreign bank balances according to the same sorts of motives that govern their domestic bank balances and their inventories of ordinary commodities. (For private business, foreign exchange is indeed a kind of intermediate good, like fertilizer, office supplies, pig iron, or cloth; it is an "ingredient" in "producing" imported goods and services that is itself "produced" by domestic labor and resources in the export industries.)

Even with the SDR scheme elaborated along the lines of the Triffin Plan, private holdings of foreign exchange would remain substantial. With only *official* reserve-holding of other countries' currencies forbidden, private holdings of foreign exchange could still become the object of one-way-option speculation from time to time. A private flight from dollars into marks, for example, could force the German Bundesbank to buy dollars in pegging the exchange rate. Since the Bundesbank would be forbidden to continue holding these dollars, it would call on the United States to redeem them in SDRs. The drain on the SDR reserves of the United States could be quite as bothersome as a gold drain used to be. The United States might borrow from the IMF, but this would not so much prevent as palliate the dangers of one-way speculation.

By contrast, avoiding official intervention and allowing only private parties to hold foreign exchange would enlist the Law of Large

Numbers on behalf of a resilient monetary structure. Under the gold-exchange standard, the Law of Large Numbers was inapplicable in two ways: one or two currencies made up the great bulk of foreign-exchange reserves, and a small number of national authorities held the bulk of the total. When one key currency came under suspicion, a large fraction of all international reserves was thus under suspicion; and its fate might hinge on the decisions of a relatively few holders. But if all foreign-exchange holdings were private, there would be no dominant holders of particular currencies. No holder would hold more than a small percentage of the total amount of any currency. Each merchant would probably hold bank accounts in the currencies in which he ordinarily made and received payments. Each bank, similarly, would hold foreign balances in many currencies. Speculative opinion would be diffused over a large number of currencies and among many holders, none of whom would be of dominant size. In contrast with the gold-exchange standard, only a widespread realignment of opinion could seriously strain international monetary relations.

This distinction needs some qualification. As bank runs illustrate, distrust may spread and destroy the independence of decisions that the Law of Large Numbers presupposes. A similar linkage of opinion might affect private holdings of foreign exchange, though presumably less than when attention had been concentrated all along on one or two key currencies largely held by a few dominant holders. With exchange rates not pegged, incipient distrust of a currency could express itself in a slight weakening of its quotation, producing a new alignment of speculative opinion. Expectations would not be lopsided; there would be no one-way option.

With the pricing of currencies as free from official intervention as the pricing of ordinary commodities, the profit motive would usually keep inventories of foreign exchange, as of any ordinary commodity, tending toward a level appropriate to the needs of their holders and to the cost of tying up resources in that form. Foreign exchange even contrasts favorably with flour, paint, salt, and other ordinary commodities in that large amounts of it could, at a price, be "produced" quickly if necessary. Banks could borrow abroad; balances in one money could turn instantly into foreign exchange by mere change of ownership. Severe inflations or deflations might conceivably distort holdings of foreign exchange away from a socially optimum level, defined in any plausible way. But these distortions, stemming from price-level instability and the resulting expectations, would be similar for inventories of foreign exchange and ordinary commodities alike. This consideration strengthens the case for aiming at domestic monetary stabilization.

Under the system outlined here, there could be no such thing as a shortage of international liquidity apart from deflationary shortages of domestic currencies within countries. Anyone desiring more than he already held of some particular foreign currency could always obtain it at some price. Of course, adding an intensified foreign demand onto the domestic demand for cash balances of a particular currency would exert deflationary tendency on its home country. (The deflation can be understood in terms either of the demand for and supply of cash balances or of currency appreciation, the resulting import balance of goods and services, and contractionary operation of the foreign-trade multiplier.) Far from being burdensome, the opportunity to create additional domestic money to meet a growing foreign demand for it would allow the country to acquire real goods and services on indefinite loan from abroad at zero or low interest. In any country, stable economic growth requires satisfaction, somehow, of the accompanying growth of demand for real cash balances; and the fact that foreigners account for part of this growth of demand need not be a major problem for national monetary management. The exclusively private holding of foreign exchange at least avoids the troublesome conflict between domestic and international considerations caused by the existence and management of a separate international money in addition to the various national currencies. Monetary stabilization has a better chance of success when sought by national criteria and for national objectives than when the task is complicated by liquidity management for international objectives as well.

12. *Kyklos*, vol. 22, No. 3, 1969, pp. 519–529.

13. In accordance with the Mrs.-Machlup's-wardrobe principle; see pp. 612–613.

628

Exchange rates and liquidity

The more nearly rigid the exchange rates between distinct currencies are, the greater the so-called need for international liquidity. ". . . with completely rigid exchange rates, demand can become insatiable; and the fundamental weakness of the miscellaneous plans [for shoring up world liquidity] is that, for the most part, they concentrate only on providing liquidity, on filling this bottomless pit, instead of providing a mechanism of adjustment to achieve the international balance that would

make additional liquidity unnecessary."[14] By providing such a mechanism, flexible exchange rates would abolish any distinct problem of international liquidity: if money supplies were not excessive or inadequate from national points of view, they could not be wrong from the international point of view either. The next chapter compares that exchange-rate system with its alternatives.

---

14. Donald B. Marsh in Robert Z. Aliber, ed., *The International Market for Foreign Exchange,* New York: Praeger, 1969, p. 153.

CHAPTER THIRTY-ONE

Proposals for Thoroughgoing Reform

All but the last of the proposals so far reviewed aim at shoring up the system of fixed exchange rates by contriving a sounder basis and less haphazard growth of international liquidity. This and the final chapter compare alternative exchange-rate systems. No one is to be rejected merely because it has disadvantages; all do. A sensible choice cannot hinge on how long the lists of arguments are; some supposed advantages and disadvantages are spurious or unimportant, and any debater can increase or decrease the number of arguments by dividing or consolidating. A sound choice requires trying to understand and compare how the whole economic system would work under each of the alternative systems.[1]

The gold standard

Either an international gold standard or freely floating exchange rates would be a really radical reform. In some respects these two systems stand at opposite poles, but in one respect they stand together: both would let market forces equilibrate balances of payments in relatively automatic ways. Both stand opposed to efforts to escape adjustment or make adjustment depend on *ad hoc* policies or controls.

A genuine gold standard would tie national currencies together by having each one redeemable in and obtainable for gold at a permanently fixed price. Gold ownership and gold shipments would be unrestricted. Maintaining the fixed relation with gold would be the overriding aim of each country's monetary and fiscal policy; national money supplies and price and income levels would conform to the requirements of balance-of-payments equilibrium at fixed exchange rates. The more fully currencies coincided with gold alone instead of being based on merely fractional reserves, the more nearly would the quantity of money be determined by objective conditions and be immune from the influences of politics and self-seeking economic interests. Money supplies, price levels, and business conditions would be more stable than they have been under non-gold currencies as typically mismanaged in actual experience. Or so the argument goes. This argument blends with an argument about the anti-inflationary "discipline" of fixed-exchange-rate systems in general, an argument reviewed in more detail later on.

A genuine gold standard would end the present awkward hybrid character of international liquidity. Countries would hold their official reserves entirely in gold and no longer in key foreign currencies. The official price of gold in terms of all currencies would be raised at the time of return to the gold standard, supposedly for that one last time. Thereafter, a gradual and continuing process could theoretically sidestep the problem of the adequacy of liquidity. Adjustments in price levels would

1. Although I do try to give a fair account of the major points made by economists of different persuasions, I have reached a judgment of my own—one subject to revision, but rather definite at the time of writing. For the sake of balance, the reader should pay particular attention to contrary views, not only as summarized here but especially as presented by economists who hold them. See, for example, the works cited in this and the next chapter by Harrod, Ingram, Katz, Triffin, Einzig, Bernstein, and Roosa, as well as Ragnar Nurkse, *International Currency Experience*, League of Nations, 1944; Division of International Finance, Board of Governors of the Federal Reserve System, "A System of Fluctuating Exchange Rates: Pro and Con," reprinted in *Recent Changes in Monetary Policy and Balance-of-Payments Problems*, Hearings before the Banking and Currency Committee, U.S. House of Representatives, July 1963, pp. 57–70; and Margaret G. de Vries, J. K. Horsefield, et al., *The International Monetary Fund, 1945–1965*, Washington: IMF, 1969, esp. chaps. 3 and 7 of Vol. II.

keep real (purchasing-power) quantities of gold and gold-based currencies adequate to meet the demands for international liquidity and for domestic cash balances. Under the historical gold standard, as Sir Roy Harrod charitably described it, "The linkage of gold to the domestic circulation . . . meant that, if the increase in gold stocks was not keeping pace with the growth of world production and trade, the domestic circulations would not keep pace either, and there was a tendency for prices to fall." If the number of ounces of gold held by central banks "did not keep pace with the growth of world trade, the value of world reserves might none the less keep pace, because the value of each ounce tended to rise."[2] The firm link and substantial overlap between national and international moneys and the automatic adjustment of balances of payments would avoid any inconsistency between the amounts of money needed within countries and needed internationally.

The gold standard gains some of its appeal from an idealized view of its historical association with economic and personal freedom in the late nineteenth century. Progress in science and technology, in economic well-being, in individual freedom, and in political democracy then seemed fated to continue indefinitely. People could cross boundaries with few restrictions or formalities. Trade in goods and services was practically free from quantitative restrictions and from all but moderate tariffs. International investment took place with little interference and was conspicuously beneficial to the host countries. Use of coins with different names and sizes in different countries was a mere detail and did not keep gold from being the international money. Nationalistic governmental manipulation was kept away from money as from other human affairs. Monetary internationalism seemed to be the condition and corollary of internationalism in all policies affecting the movement of goods, services, capital, persons, and ideas.

Actually, this happy association may have been more a coincidence than a matter of cause and effect. (On the contrary, something besides coincidence may explain why the worldwide trend toward freer trade began to run down and give way toward renewed protectionism at just about the time the gold standard was becoming truly international in the 1870s.) But whether historically and logically warranted or not, the idea does have widespread appeal that monetary and other kinds of internationalism naturally go together, as do their opposites. Some people even call monetary nationalism the worst kind of nationalism and the root of all other kinds.

Some advocates of the gold standard build their case at least as much on political philosophy as on economics. Government is an actual or potential enemy. It is a necessary evil—necessary if anarchy would be intolerable, evil because it tends to push its coercive powers beyond their proper sphere. Government, on this view, is no mere committee appointed by ordinary citizens to administer their common concerns, no mere instrument for passively recording and implementing the desires of the voters. On the contrary, it is a group of officials pursuing their own interests. Throughout the ages, the state has used monetary inflation to wrest resources from its subjects and build up its own power at their expense. The gold standard can help resist this statism. Through its financial discipline, the citizens hold the purse strings and control their government more directly and effectively than they could do at the ballot box alone. Furthermore, gold coins are durable form of wealth, readily exchangeable, high in value in relation to bulk, easily hidden against confiscation, and easily transported by refugees from tyranny. With some such ideas in mind, presumably, no less modern an economist than Sir Roy Harrod has called gold "a sheet anchor of liberty," "a bulwark of human freedom."[3]

Ironically, the attempt to preserve a key role for gold in modern monetary systems, or the pretense of doing so, has deprived gold of whatever such serviceability it ever did have. Violating the traditionally prized automaticity of the gold standard, governments have sought to loosen the link between the quantities of gold and money. They have devised or tolerated methods of "economizing" on gold. Money has increasingly been pyramided onto a narrow gold base by such measures as the withdrawal of gold coins from circulation in favor of a gold bullion standard, by the spread during the 1920s of the practice of basing domestic money on a fractional reserve of foreign money, in turn only fractionally based on gold, by neutralizing the impacts of gold flows on domestic money supplies, and by prohibiting private gold ownership since the 1930s. Inconsistently, nations have tried both to preserve and to escape the linkage of money to gold. They have tried to preserve an appearance while destroying the substance.[4] So doing, they have undermined, among other things, the role of gold as "a bulwark of human freedom." In the United States (before 1975), possession of gold bullion not only failed to enhance a person's freedom but made him liable to criminal prosecution.

Reasons like these explain the emphasis, in earlier paragraphs, on a *genuine* gold standard. With good reason, Milton Friedman has insisted on the distinction between "Real and Pseudo Gold Standards."[5] Nevertheless, some advocates of the gold standard "resent" that distinction; more important, they say, is the distinction between being or not being on a gold standard at all. The vagueness of such a position gives the proposal for "the gold standard" much of its appeal. It serves as a slogan or rallying point for opposition to the twentieth-century record of inflationary government mismanagement of money. The gold standard enjoys the advantage of being a negative position; its features and operating properties are not carefully examined and its own defects do not come to the fore.

Perhaps it is not quite fair, after all, to complain that the gold-standard proposal is vague. A minority of supporters do say rather clearly what they want, how they propose to achieve it, and how it will work.[6] But because it does mean different things to different people, the gold standard retains the tactical advantage of being an ambiguous rallying cry for opposition to "things as they are."

A small minority wants a 100 percent gold standard. Gold would be the only money.[7] Government issue of any other kind would be forbidden, and even private banknotes, demand deposits, or other liabilities usable as media of exchange would be banned unless fully backed by gold. Supporters deny that enforcing these prohibitions would bring totalitarian government intervention into economic

2. *Reforming the World's Money*, New York: St. Martin's Press, 1965, p. 6.

3. *Op. cit.*, pp. 80, 172. Views of the kind mentioned on government in relation to money are expressed, for example, by Murray N. Rothbard in "The Case for a 100 Per Cent Gold Dollar," in Leland B. Yeager, ed., *In Search of a Monetary Constitution*, Cambridge, Mass.: Harvard University Press, 1962, pp. 94–136.

4. ". . . I consider the gold standard as dead as a dodo; I think it has been dead since the guns of

August 1914, since which it has only twitched." Howard S. Ellis in Randall Hinshaw, ed., *The Economics of International Adjustment*, Baltimore: Johns Hopkins Press, 1971, pp. 105–106.

5. *Journal of Law and Economics*, IV, October 1961, pp. 66–79, reprinted in Friedman's *Dollars and Deficits*, Englewood Cliffs, N.J.: Prentice-Hall, 1968, pp. 247–265.

6. A brief survey cannot report proposals and arguments of various advocates of the gold standard in the detail and with the nuances that they themselves would want. To avoid unfairness, it seems best not to attribute particular views to particular persons. For a sampling of diverse writings, see the articles by Rueff and Heilperin cited in Chapter 29, footnote 12; the lectures by Murray Rothbard and Arthur Kemp in *In Search of a Monetary Constitution*, Cambridge: Harvard University Press, 1962; the remarks of W. J. Busschau, Donald H. McLaughlin, Philip Cortney, O. Glenn Saxon, James Washington Bell, Philip M. McKenna, and Henry Hazlitt in the National Industrial Conference Board Economic Forum, *Shall We Return to a Gold Standard—Now?*, New York: NICB, 1954; W. J. Busschau, *Gold and International Liquidity*, Johannesburg: South African Institute of International Affairs, 1961; Walter E. Spahr, "The Gold Standard and Its Significance," *Modern Age*, Summer 1960, pp. 297–301; E. C. Harwood, *Cause and Control of the Business Cycle*, 5th ed., Great Barrington, Mass.: American Institute for Economic Research, 1957, esp. Chap. IX and Appendix D; Ludwig von Mises, *The Theory of Money and Credit*, new ed.; New Haven: Yale University Press, 1953, part four; Charles Rist, *The Triumph of Gold*, trans. with an introduction by Philip Cortney, New York: Wisdom Library, a division of Philosophical Library, 1961; Wilhelm Röpke, *Internationale Ordnung—heute*, Erlenbach-Zürich: Rentsch, 1954, pp. 30–31, 110–112, 219–220, 278, 334–335, 314–350; the monthly *Monetary Notes* and occasional other publications of the Economists' National Committee on Monetary Policy; Ian Shannon, *International Liquidity, A Study in the Economic Functions of Gold*, Chicago: Regnery, 1966; Francis Cassell, *Gold or Credit?*, New York: Praeger, 1965, esp. chap. 7; and several of the contributions to G. C. Wiegand, ed., *Toward a New World Monetary System*, New York: Engineering and Mining Journal, 1973.

7. Some of the properties of such a system are described in Chapter 4.

life; government would simply be doing its traditional duty of preventing force and fraud (for the issue of demand obligations that could not all be honored at once is fraudulent, on this view).

Less rigorous proposals would forbid governmental fiduciary money but tolerate the private creation of fractional-reserve money. Some proposals would impose reserve requirements on banks; others would subject them to no regulations beyond those governing all business, including the obligation to honor contracts. The gold reserve ratios that banks would voluntarily adopt to be safe and to guard their reputations for soundness would, it is hoped, gear the total supply of money in a stable enough manner to the unmanipulated total stock of gold. Still other proposals would tolerate fiduciary issues not only by commercial banks but also by governments or central banks. Gold reserve ratios might be constitutionally or legislatively set or might be left to the discretion of the monetary authorities. One well-known American committee of economists, now no longer active, believed that the gold standard could function with a ratio of gold to the total money supply as low as the ratio had fallen in the United States in the 1960s. As long as people knew they could redeem fiduciary money in gold coins whenever they wanted them, they would not want them; they would prefer the convenience of paper money and bank accounts. The smallness of fractional gold reserves would be an actual advantage, on this view: if the authorities should show signs of deviating from sound policies, even a small rise in demands for redemption of fiduciary money would promptly compel the authorities to mend their ways.

Opinions differ widely on how high, how rigid, and how automatic the gearing should be between the total quantity of money and the quantity of gold. At one extreme, advocates of a 100 percent standard want a completely automatic and rigid one-to-one linkage. Many more persons, toward the opposite extreme, envisage a rather high and flexible gearing under central-bank management. The view that would be satisfied with redeemability in gold bullion is more completely at the extreme of belief in high and flexible gearing than the view that insists on redeemability in and actual circulation of gold coins.

To make gold stocks and current gold production adequate in value for operation of a gold standard, the official price of gold in national currencies would have to be increased. The closer the system adopted came to a 100 percent standard, with its low gearing of money to gold, the larger the price increase would have to be. It is easy but not quite fair to make fun of gold-standard supporters for allegedly ignoring the essence of that standard— a supposedly fixed and permanent gold content of each money unit. In effect they are saying: give us just this one last opportunity to tamper with the gold contents of money units and we promise never to do it again. Actually, their position is defensible. Precisely because we have *not* been on a genuine gold standard for several decades, price levels have *already* gotten too far out of line with the price of gold to permit avoiding an initial adjustment. In making an adjustment that would indeed be subversive of an already existing gold standard, we would only be realistically facing up to the consequences of our not having been on one all along. Why start out hopelessly burdening a restored gold standard with those consequences?

The gold link versus other rules

Gold-standard advocates should recognize their dilemma. The tighter and more unchangeable the link is between a country's gold stock and money supply, the more fully sheer accident determines whether or not the money supply grows over time in step with the aggregate demand for real cash balances. Faster or slower growth burdens the economy with price inflation or with deflation. This consideration speaks in favor of only a loose and adjustable link between the gold stock and the money supply. But the looser this link, the more the money supply loses the objective fact-of-nature quality that was supposed to be the key advantage of a gold standard.

Perhaps we do want discretionary management, though within limits. If so, can't we enact some better rule for limiting discretion than keeping money redeemable at a fixed rate in a particular metal? Is that what we really want? Or, instead, do we want money of stable value that does not generate economic disturbances? It would seem more sensible to aim at what we really want than to hope for what we want as a by-product of an indirect approach. The rules that make the best economic sense should have the best chance of eventually commanding public respect and of becoming a new "monetary religion."

As this remark suggests, rules of economic policy are not self-enforcing. How durable a rule is depends ultimately on whether or not it operates satisfactorily. If the gold standard is a poor rule for regulating money supplies and avoiding balance-of-payments troubles, then its results impair its durability. In historical fact, the gold standard has not proved durable. Governments can and do go off it. No mythical or religious aura will do much to prevent departures from the rules of a restored gold standard.

An optional gold standard

Dollar devaluations and other events since 1971, including gyrations of the price of gold on free markets, have presumably lessened any possibility of restoring faith in a firm link between moneys and gold or in a stable purchasing power of gold over goods and services. A broader range of experience, together with theories of bureaucracy and democratic politics now being developed, weakens the hope that governments will in fact follow any of the sensible rules for nongold money that economists suggest. The difficulty is not mainly one of getting enough votes in favor of such a rule. Rather, it is one of making the rule stick. Government bureaus and democratic legislatures and electorates exert pressures toward ever greater government spending and for covering part of that spending in inflationary ways. Central banks tend to be compliant. Perhaps economists should divert some of their energy from devising ideal monetary rules to devising ways for people to have alternatives to the governmental monetary botch. Perhaps competitive monetary systems should be allowed. People would be allowed to quote prices, borrow and lend, make contracts, and make and receive payments in gold or any other commodity or composite of commodities. A plausible monetary unit would be 1 gram of gold. Banks would be allowed to issue notes and deposits denominated in commodity money, even without the government's setting any reserve requirements. Free competition would favor those banks that earned and guarded reputations for keeping their money issues sound and instantly redeemable. It

would be easier for governments to permit such a system, by the negative action of repealing many restrictions now in effect, than to take and keep taking the positive actions of observing sound rules for the management of governmental money. The option of using private commodity moneys might be inferior to having a government monetary system operated in accordance with the best economic advice; but in view of the way governments operate, the latter may not be a realistic possibility. The competition of private commodity-based moneys might eventually have a healthy disciplining effect on the operation of governmental monetary systems.

Establishing a private, voluntary gold money faces serious obstacles. One is that history has made gold a highly political commodity. What role governments and central banks accord to gold in their national and international monetary systems, what official price they set on it, and what they do with their present huge holdings of it are bound to affect the value of gold in terms of other goods and services. The very uncertainty about future official actions impairs the suitability of gold as a private unit of account and standard of value. Even if governments sincerely resolved to get rid of their dominant influence over its value, how to do so would remain a thorny question. There seems to be no quick, smooth way of depoliticizing gold and thus making it suitable as a private money.

Commodity reserve money

Setting aside cynicism about governments, we should remember that a gold standard is not the only kind of commodity-based monetary system that has been proposed for governmental operation. Instead of gold alone defining the money unit and being freely interchangeable with it at a fixed price, a definite physical assortment of commodities would perform those functions. For example, $100 might be defined as the value of and made interchangeable with 50 kilograms of pig iron *plus* 100 kilograms of wheat *plus* 10 kilograms of copper *plus* specified amounts of a number of other commodities. Commodities included in the standard bundle should be economically important, competitively traded, storable, and amenable to accurate specification of grade or quality. If countries defined their moneys in bundles of commodities in the same physical proportions, commodity-bundle arbitrage analogous to the gold arbitrage of the gold standard would hold exchange rates within commodity-bundle points analogous to the gold points, (though wider apart, because of the greater cost of shipping commodity bundles than gold of equal value). Conceivably, a world agency could issue money in the form of warehouse certificates for commodity bundles, with individual countries basing their own moneys on the international certificates rather than on commodity bundles directly.

The advantages claimed for some such scheme include those claimed for the gold standard—money whose quantity and value would be determined relatively objectively and automatically rather than by the vagaries of politics, reasonable stability of exchange rates, and the rest. One theoretical advantage of the gold standard could operate more effectively under the composite-commodity standard: a deflationary tendency would increase the profitability of producing the monetary commodities, assembling standard bundles, and exchanging the bundles for newly issued money at the fixed price; the deflation would be nipped in the bud. An inflationary tendency would check itself, conversely, as people removed money from circulation by redeeming it in commodity bundles. The general purchasing power of money would supposedly be more stable when money was based on a composite of widely used raw materials than when it was based on a single relatively unimportant metal. Furthermore, the scheme would presumably have some advantage in stabilizing the prices on the average of the primary commodities involved and in stabilizing the incomes of their producers.

Some of the objections to the scheme coincide with objections to the gold standard: its inferiority to sensibly managed fiat money (if only governments could somehow be forced to stick to the rules of sensible monetary management) and its sacrifice of the advantages, such as they are, of national monetary independence and free exchange rates. Further objections concern the complexities and costs of the scheme—warehousing and all that—and the scope for wrangling among producer and consumer interests and among countries over the composition of the standard commodity bundle and over the revisions in the bundle that technological and other changes would call for from time to time. Finally, when one actually tries to specify the standard commodity bundle and weeds out the commodities that are unsuitable for inclusion for one reason or another, one might well be left with little beyond a few metals, a composite of which would be unlikely to have a stable value in terms of goods and services in general.[8]

Financial integration

Thoroughgoing international financial integration could conceivably be achieved on the basis of the gold standard, the composite-commodity standard, national currencies tied to reserves of internationally issued "paper gold" (such as SDRs), currencies tied to a particular national currency such as the dollar, or currencies tied to one another without any one of them dominating. According to James Ingram,[9] financial integration would largely solve or sidestep all problems of balance-of-payments adjustment and liquidity among the countries taking part. Within the integrated area, trade in securities and other financial claims and transfers of capital and interest and dividends would be freed of all legal restrictions. Exchange rates would be fixed permanently and rigidly, with no band of fluctuation whatever. To make this permanent rigidity credible, "member governments might formally declare every currency legal tender in every country. They might also require commercial banks to pay all checks at par in any Community currency requested by the payee, and allow them to accept deposits denominated in any currency. Commercial banks would be allowed to count as reserves the cash balances they hold in the currencies of other member countries."[10] Local and foreign securities would become thoroughly intermingled in the portfolio of the typical bank, insurance company, or other financial institution. A sizable part of the entire stock of financial claims held by a country's residents could potentially enter into international payments adjustment, and the adequacy of a country's official external reserves in the traditional strict sense would become a relatively unimportant question. The pressure of an external imbalance would be widely diffused through the financial markets. Exchange rates would require little or no central-bank support: a kind of securities arbitrage would supplement or replace it. Suppose one member country developed an external deficit. As the customers of its banks drew down their deposits to pay for their overspending, the banks would individually feel the pressure of adverse clearing balances and would act to replenish their cash reserves by selling securities, by borrowing, and by curtailing their lending. Such actions would marginally raise interest yields in the deficit country, attracting foreign funds. International movements of capital and securities would be extremely sensitive to interest-rate differentials. For a member country of a financially integrated area, the traditional concept of balance-of-payments deficit or surplus would itself become blurred as the distinction between independently motivated and settlement transactions faded away.

Financial integration would thus prevent speculative currency crises in the absence of fundamental disequilibrium. But what would prevent fundamental disequilibrium? Skeptics sometimes pose the question of a disproportionate rise in money wages and costs in one country.[11] Under financial integration, however, a member country's money supply would not be independent and could not support a differential rise in wages and costs in the first place. As for a nonmonetary wage-and-cost push, unemployment would restrain it. But if the people of a country really were determined to keep *trying* to push up their real incomes substantially faster than productivity was rising, financial integration would come apart. Under those circumstances, no system, not even an independent currency with a flexible exchange rate, would provide both internal and external balance.

Ingram lists several requirements for extreme financial integration: (1) completely and permanently rigid exchange rates, necessary for the extreme interest-sensitivity of capital movements; (2) removal of restrictions on international payments; (3) removal even of *de facto* impediments to capital movements (such as tax provisions and other legal discriminations in favor of local securities in the portfolios of financial institutions); and (4) development of an efficient and unified market in securities and claims.

A single country could no longer pursue a separate national monetary policy in the sense of making its level or structure of interest rates diverge appreciably from those of its partners.

PROPOSALS FOR THOROUGHGOING REFORM

Yet, according to Ingram, the required *additional* sacrifice of monetary independence would be small. Independence is largely illusory anyway when exchange rates are fixed, when currency convertibility and commodity trade are mostly unrestricted, and when governments have to adjust their financial policies in response to balance-of-payments pressures. Furthermore, some room would remain for independent fiscal policy: a government could still engage in deficit spending to carry out or encourage productive investment if it borrowed at market rates of interest. (The scope for

8. For an introduction to a large literature, see Benjamin Graham, "The Commodity-Reserve Currency Proposal Reconsidered," in Yeager, *op. cit.*, pp. 184–218. The final objection mentioned in the text above, which Graham finds unconvincing, is developed in Milton Friedman, "Commodity-Reserve Currency," *Journal of Political Economy*, Vol. 59, June 1951, pp. 203–232, reprinted in Friedman's *Essays in Positive Economics*, Chicago: University of Chicago Press, 1953, pp. 204–250.

9. "A proposal for Financial Integration in the Atlantic Community," in *Factors Affecting the United States Balance of Payments*, studies compiled for the Subcommittee on International Exchange and Payments of the Joint Economic Committee, Washington: Government Printing Office, 1962, pp. 177–207; *Regional Payments Mechanisms: The Case of Puerto Rico*, Chapel Hill: University of North Carolina Press, 1962; *The Case for European Monetary Integration*, Princeton Essays in International Finance, No. 98, Princeton, N.J.: Princeton University, April 1973. Compare the section on interregional adjustment in Chapter 5 above.

10. Ingram, Princeton Essay No. 98, p. 11.
Egon Sohmen argues that to make irrevocably fixed rates credible, governments would have to stand ready to make forward contracts, with maturities as long as anyone might desire, to buy and sell currencies at rates identical to the established parities. Sohmen in R. Mundell and A. Swoboda, eds., *Monetary Problems of the International Economy*, Chicago: University of Chicago Press, 1969, p. 194.

11. See W. M. Corden, *Monetary Integration*, Princeton Essays in International Finance, No. 93, Princeton, N.J.: Princeton University, April 1972, esp. pp. 33–34.

independently stimulating aggregate demand to combat unemployment would be narrow indeed, though, if the essence of effective policy is what it does to the money supply.)

Ingram doubts the need for a common currency and supranational monetary and fiscal authorities, but the required coordination of national policies would amount to much the same thing. Proposals such as his are a valuable contribution to the discussion because they shun weak eclecticism. Starting from analysis of the inconsistencies of existing hybrid arrangements, they logically follow through to a consistent policy conclusion.

Is monetary unification—a common currency or firmly fixed exchange rates—necessary for or conducive to economic integration in the sense of fully reaping the advantages of geographic specialization in producing goods and services? Is it even necessary for financial integration in the sense of geographic specialization in saving, investment, and financial intermediation? It would be a shame to let a mere verbal or legalistic association of ideas prejudge these questions.[12] Questions of economic performance and optimum currency areas call for economic analysis.[13] A price system is, among other things, a network of communications linking together the different sectors of a national economy and of the international economy. Flexible prices serve as signals in this process of communication and linkage. It is far from clear that freezing some of these signals, namely exchange rates, necessarily does more to help than hinder this process.

Freely fluctuating exchange rates

If national authorities stopped pegging their currencies to the dollar, gold, SDRs, or anything else and agreed to refrain from intervention on the foreign-exchange markets, exchange rates would be freely flexible. Mere inaction by governments, rather than positive action, would accomplish this reform. It would abolish problems of balance-of-payments crises and of international liquidity. Governments could turn their attention from these manufactured problems to other problems that objectively exist.

Exchange-rate freedom permits aiming domestic financial policy squarely at internal balance, even in the face of depression or inflation abroad. A few economists have even argued that free exchange rates would make monetary

policy more effective.[14] Expanding the money supply and reducing interest rates to fight a recession, or even just letting interest rates fall spontaneously, as they typically do in a recession, tends to promote capital outflow. The balance of payments would move into deficit— except that the home currency depreciates on the exchanges enough to match an export surplus of goods and services to the capital outflow. This export surplus makes a timely addition to the total demand for domestic output and domestic labor and other factors of production. An anti-inflationary monetary policy, conversely, influences capital movements so as to make the home currency appreciate, bringing a net inflow of goods and services into the country and restraining any uptrend in prices.

This additional channel of operation of monetary policy may not be useful and important. Free exchange rates do not, of course, *guarantee* sensible and mutually consistent policies affecting domestic aggregate demand and international trade and capital movements. Nothing can. But free rates at least *permit* such policies.

They do so by banishing balance-of-payments complications. Just as there is only one main argument—efficiency—for free trade, so there is only one main argument for free exchange rates: the exchange rate is the simplest balance-of-payments equilibrator, while the alternatives require unpleasant changes in price levels or employment or breed restrictions on trade and capital movements. To work smoothly, the exchange-rate mechanism requires less flexibility of local-currency prices and wage rates than does the price-and-income mechanism of fixed exchange rates. The necessary changes occur largely through translation of prices and wages from one currency into another at exchange rates that are inherently flexible (but not necessarily unstable) because they are determined continuously by supply and demand in a competitive market. The changes occur mainly where they are most relevant to external balance—in the prices of internationally traded goods. Free rates both facilitate necessary adjustments and avoid unnecessary ones.[15]

Neither this nor any other reform would be a panacea. No policy for the real world is free of disadvantages. It will be convenient to organize a further discussion of free exchange rates around a list of their actual or supposed disadvantages. Some widely urged disadvantages will appear to stem from misreading of experience with a different system, that of the adjustable peg.[16] Unavoidably, our review of policy arguments will overlap with the theory and history of earlier chapters.

1. Free exchange rates, it is said, are subject to rapid, erratic changes. The assumption is questionable, however, that rate changes occur exogenously and without economic reason; it "reflects the mentality of the fixed-rate system," in which governments hold rates fixed despite accumulating pressures for change, creating severe uncertainty about the timing and size of eventual changes. Actually, changes in circumstances sharp and unexpected enough to make free rates move rapidly and erratically would probably cause even more disruption under fixed exchange rates, involving speculation, currency crises, devaluation, deflation, or new controls.[17] It is the pegged-rate system that exhibits the discontinuities of devaluation, "stop-and-go," or controls.

2. Free rates are subject to disruption by speculation. *Evidence* of disruptive speculation comes overwhelmingly, however, from experience with pegged or manipulated rates. The observations in earlier chapters need no repetition here.

3. Free rates burden international trade and investment with risks for which forward-exchange facilities are an inadequate answer. No system, however, banishes the risk that wants, resources, and technology will change and will require adjustments in trade and production. The question is how the necessary adjustments are to be made—how fast and in response to what signals and incentives.[18] (When countries' money-supply-growth and price-level trends diverge, the question is how to *avoid* false signals and incentives and inappropriate adjustments.) The risk of big, sudden responses to pent-up pressures is characteristic of pegged exchange rates.

An inquiry conducted by the head organization of German Chambers of Commerce suggests that most businessmen have become wary of "sporadic and drastic parity changes." Now they "would rather rely on a more flexible adjustment of parities in small steps and, not infrequently, even on flexible rates." Many recognize "that such a change would reduce the risk involved in sales calculations and decisions on production and investment and would improve the chances for a business strategy guided by genuine market data."[19]

What explains the inadequacy of forward markets? Wide divergences between forward and spot rates due to speculation and to inter-ferences with interest arbitrage are characteristic of pegged, not free, spot rates. It is misleading, incidentally, to interpret a forward premium or discount as if it were a net cost to business or to society: an apparent burden to a country's import or export trade is equally a benefit to its trade in the opposite direction; a forward discount on one of two currencies is a forward premium on the other.

Some critics note that flexible exchange rates would increase the demand for forward cover and worry that the supply of forward facilities might not increase enough to meet it.[20] The supposed difficulty, as Fritz Machlup has pointed out,[21] hinges on differences between the language of dealers and the language of economists. In the dealer's language, his customers seek (demand) forward cover; and he, whether buying or selling forward exchange, is supplying forward cover. In economists' language, flexible exchange rates would increase both the demand for and the supply of forward exchange; demand for forward cover from one point of view *is* supply of forward cover from the other point of view.

---

12. Recall the warning of Wolfgang Kasper quoted in footnote 4 of Appendix 2 to Chapter 6.

13. Recall Appendix 2 to Chapter 6.

14. Egon Sohmen, *Flexible Exchange Rates*, rev. ed., Chicago: University of Chicago Press, 1969, pp. 112–115, 119–123, 212–216.

15. Cf. pp. 104, 113–114.

16. Cf. Harry G. Johnson in Bürgenstock Papers, pp. 103–106.

17. *Ibid.*, p. 103.

18. Friedrich A. Lutz, article of 1954 reprinted in his *Geld und Währung*, Tubingen: Mohr (Siebeck), 1962, p. 178.

19. German Council of Economic Experts, *Toward a New Basis for International Monetary Policy*, Princeton Study No. 31, Princeton, N.J.: Princeton University, October 1972, p. 28.

20. See Paul Einzig, *The Case Against Floating Exchanges*, New York: St. Martin's Press, 1970, pp. 110–137, as well as my review in *Journal of International Economics*, I, August, 1971, pp. 362–365.

21. In Bürgenstock Papers, pp. 298–300, 303.

None of this is to say, however, that forward facilities can abolish all exchange-rate-related risk. (Recall Chapter 13.)

4. The fluctuations of a free exchange rate would allegedly cause costly and unnecessary shifts of resources back and forth between a country's export and import-competing industries on the one hand and its domestic industries on the other hand. This argument must logically be based—though that basis is seldom made explicit—on the idea that changes in a floating rate are random or erratic, are caused by ill-informed or emotional speculation, or are otherwise out of correspondence with economic fundamentals. In this respect, the argument overlaps arguments 1 and 2 above. It ignores the role that rate fluctuations, even temporary ones, can play in lessening rather than causing wasteful back-and-forth resource shifts.[22]

This buffer role is especially important when money and price-level inflation is proceeding at different rates at home and abroad. Suppose, for contrast, that the exchange rate is pegged in the face of more rapid inflation at home. At its pegged rate, the home currency becomes increasingly overvalued; the export and import-competing industries suffer. Subsidies and protectionist measures are mere palliatives. Finally devaluation must come. If the exchange rate is to be approximately correct on the average over time and if the authorities are to rebuild their depleted external reserves, the devaluation must be excessive at first. While the currency remains undervalued at its new parity, the export and import-competing industries are exceptionally profitable. Continuing inflation eventually makes the currency overvalued once again, until a new devaluation again temporarily reverses the disequilibrium. The export and import-competing industries alternate between feast or famine. The adjustable peg entails, and a floating rate would avoid, delayed lumpy devaluations and back-and-forth shifts of resources. To the extent, furthermore, that the prospective stability of profits affects investment decisions, a floating rate is more favorable than the adjustable peg to the export and import-competing industries, as well as to foreign trade itself. By lessening the effort that businessmen must spend coping with profit fluctuations, the floating rate would even permit firms to be more efficient.[23]

The same general conclusions emerge from the opposite example of better resistance to inflation at home than abroad. Export and import-competing industries flourish until a delayed upward revaluation reverses the shift of resources. An upward-floating rate would avoid the trouble due to the delay, suddenness, unpredictability, and clumsiness of discrete revaluations. The home-currency prices of imports and exports would remain more nearly stable.[24]

The foregoing comparisons of pegged and floating rates illustrate the general point that trying to enforce a price different from the market price manufactures problems. Agricultural price supports and urban rent controls are other familiar examples. An exchange rate intertwines with all of a country's foreign trade and so, directly or indirectly, with the prices of nearly all goods. When delayed adjustment of a wrong rate calls for a shift of resources, transitional unemployment is likely; for store clerks cannot be transformed overnight into factory workers, or vice versa. These pains of delayed correction of a misallocation of resources form part of the so-called burden of balance-of-payments adjustment. The prospect of them serves as an argument for interests opposed to exchange-rate adjustment. In a surplus country, export industries are likely to exert political pressure against a corrective upward currency revaluation.[25] An aggregate demand policy aimed at lessening the transitional unemployment associated with interindustry resource shifts could make even upward revaluation inflationary.[26]

5. Another objection to free exchange rates is that the price mechanism may work sluggishly because of low price elasticities, particularly of demand. The preceding paragraph is relevant to this worry. It is doubtful whether econometric elasticity estimates based on experience with stepwise parity changes really indicate how well flexible exchange rates would maintain international balance. One reason is that "conventional parity changes aim at correcting sizeable disequilibria, which would not arise with more flexibility. . . ."[27] If trade were to respond with evidently great price elasticity to a delayed large parity change, correspondingly large and seemingly "structural" shifts of resources would have to occur between the foreign-trade-goods and domestic-goods industries. Small and prompt exchange-rate movements, by contrast, entail only small and marginal resource shifts. As portrayed in the conventional convex-outward shape of the familiar transformation curve, the bigger the shift to be accomplished is, the more does

expansion of one line of production cost in other production sacrificed, and conversely for small changes. For analogous reasons, it is easier to achieve responses of resource-allocation and trade that are large *in relation to* an exchange-rate change when that change is small than when it is large.

These considerations help reconcile the sluggish response of trade often observed after big delayed parity changes with the moderateness of fluctuation in freely floating rates in the absence of sharp changes in purchasing-power parities. Moderateness of fluctuation implies high price elasticities in international trade—or if it does not imply high elasticities even in the short run, then it implies high long-run elasticities coupled with stabilizing speculation.

Discipline

The sixth and perhaps the strongest argument against free exchange rates deserves a section of its own. It centers on the issue of financial discipline. Though the monetary independence that free rates afford is an advantage from one point of view, it has disadvantages from the viewpoint of the discipline argument. What if the government finances spurts of expenditure by creating money? What if wage pushes and upward pushes on import prices (due to random exchange-rate depreciation) generalize and support themselves through monetary expansion? What if the money supply accommodates every little inflationary shock? What if the authorities react calmly to a rise of a few percent in the money supply or the price index? With no balance-of-payments crisis to force prompt action, inflation remains a problem to tackle *mañana*. Given this attitude, a persistent inflationary bias makes the requirements of internal and external balance both generally point in the same direction. If a country is somehow unable to follow the discipline of a price-level rule or of a rule limiting the growth of the money supply, the discipline of reserve losses at a fixed exchange rate is a welcome substitute. Under fixed but not under free rates, a government can cite the danger of balance-of-payments crisis when calling on labor-union leaders and businessmen patriotically to join in fighting inflation. A free exchange rate provides no rallying point, as a fixed rate might, in support of guidelines and moral suasion designed to restrain excessively

greedy wage demands and pricing policies and so shrink the wage-push element in inflation and improve the trade-off between unemployment and inflation.[28]

22. On seasonal fluctuations, recall pp. 239, 261.

23. Harold R. Williams, "Resource Allocation under Alternative Exchange Rate Systems," *Southern Economic Journal*, Vol. 38, April 1972, pp. 566–568. Geoffrey E. Woods makes the point about efficiency in a comment, same journal, April 1973, p. 650. Williams and Woods actually compare the adjustable peg with the crawling peg, but their points are equally valid in a comparison with a floating rate.

For supporting evidence from Brazil's experience since August 1968 with a policy of frequent minidevaluations (similar, in the respects here under discussion, to a floating exchange rate), see William G. Tyler, "Exchange Rate Flexibility Under Conditions of Endemic Inflation: A Case Study of the Recent Brazilian Experience," in C. Fred Bergsten and William G. Tyler, eds., *Leading Issues in International Economic Policy; Essays in Honor of George N. Halm*, Lexington, Mass.: Lexington Books, 1973, pp. 19–49; and Juergen B. Donges, *Brazil's Trotting Peg: A New Approach to Greater Exchange Flexibility in Less Developed Countries*, Washington: American Enterprise Institute, 1971.

24. Wolfgang Kasper in Bürgenstock Papers, p. 386; Ronald Jones, commentary in Federal Reserve Bank of Boston, *Canadian-United States Financial Relationships*, 1972, p. 43.

25. Samuel Brittan, *The Price of Economic Freedom*, New York: St. Martin's Press, 1970, pp. 10–11, 18–19.

26. See p. 642.

27. Herbert Giersch and Wolfgang Kasper in Bürgenstock Papers, p. 351n.

28. Lionel Robbins's emphasis on this argument has already been mentioned in an earlier chapter. Jacob Viner also values a commitment to exchange-rate fixity because in many countries, he believes, this "seems to be the only factor of any strength which puts a brake on inflation." "Some International Aspects of Economic Stabilization," in Leonard D. White, ed., *The State of the Social Sciences*, Chicago: University of Chicago Press, 1956, p. 294; cf. p. 296. The discipline argument is a leading theme in recent writings by Paul Einzig, including *The Case against Floating Exchanges*.

Professor Robert Triffin has stressed a related advantage of fixed rates that free rates lack.[29] Suppose that an inflationary innocent mistake occurs in a previously stable country. Under fixed exchange rates, the inflationary impulses spill out into spending on additional imports and on goods that would otherwise have been exported. The availability and price competition of imports restrain price increases at home, while the sale of foreign exchange from official reserves mops up some of the home money supply. The gearing of the home economy into a not-yet-inflated world environment and the balance-of-payments deficit thus provide anti-inflationary assistance.[30] The drain on the external reserves "disciplines" the monetary authorities to correct their inflationary mistake before it becomes irreversibly consolidated into prices and wages. A free exchange rate, by contrast, works almost too well in depreciating as severely as necessary to keep foreign transactions in balance. It bottles up inflationary pressures within the country and lets them raise the local-currency prices of foreign exchange, imports, exportable goods, and goods and factors of production in general. It gives inflationary mishaps or mistakes full scope to push costs and prices irreversibly upward. Correction of the mistake would come too late to prevent or reverse the damage; prices, and especially wages, would exhibit their characteristic downward inflexibility. To make matters worse, a speculative outflow of funds might intensify the exchange depreciation of the inflation-plagued currency, causing an export surplus of goods and services and so making domestic demand all the more excessive in relation to the goods and services available for domestic absorption. The depreciation would raise the local-currency prices of import and export goods more than the pull of demand would account for, and wage increases would follow.

The last-mentioned worry[31] is less persuasive than it seems at first sight. The idea that the currency would depreciate immediately in correspondence with its expected *future* loss of purchasing power overlooks how such expectations, if they really were definite, would raise interest rates at home and how covered interest arbitrage would hold the current foreign-exchange value of the currency above its forward and expected future spot rate. Triffin worried that a spurt of spending or other disturbance to the balance of payments, though temporary under fixed exchange rates, would cause irreversible price and cost inflation through depreciation of a free exchange rate. This worry appears to overlook the role of stabilizing speculation. If the disturbance really were temporary, speculators should understand that fact and cover the temporary payments deficit by supporting the exchange rate. These answers are admittedly conjectural, just as are the worries to which they apply.

Let us return to the "discipline" claim, strictly speaking: the loss of external reserves under a fixed rate would quickly compel the authorities to correct their inflationary error. Although this happy result is conceivable, so is its opposite. If a country has the reserves or the borrowing capacity to finance a persistent deficit, then, as one user of the discipline argument himself recognizes, the deficit's effect in holding down domestic prices and costs may actually encourage delay in taking corrective action.[32] That effect makes inflation of local origin inconspicuous by diluting it onto other countries in small bits. Instead of using this opportunity to correct their mistake, the local authorities may even reconcile for a while the inflationary attempts of different economic groups to divide among themselves more than the total national output, meeting these excessive claims from the external reserves. The country is less immediately and fully exposed to the wanted or unwanted consequences of its own policies than it would be under the monetary insulation offered by a floating exchange rate.

British experience hardly shows healthy discipline at work. On the contrary, according to Samuel Brittan, the British fixation with the balance of payments under a fixed exchange rate drew attention away from the sound domestic reasons for avoiding inflation. Because of inflation in the rest of the world or because of the long time lag between inflationary policies and resulting payments difficulties, governments allowed inflation to gather momentum. "Tough measures" came too late to prevent overvaluation of the home currency; and its unavoidable eventual devaluation gave "the inflationary screw a further turn, as well as providing the authorities with a few more years of freedom from currency worries."[33]

The notion that exchange depreciation is a distinct inflationary factor derives unwarranted support from confusion between floating and pegged rates. It is the latter system that brings abrupt and steep devaluations, resulting in elements of imported inflation. Devaluation raises import prices and may breed expectations of further price increases and of wage increases, as well as of higher excise taxes, credit restraints, and other measures to reinforce devaluation. Spending, including spending on imports, is thus likely to spurt.[34] Under a floating rate, by contrast, no such dramatic event as a devaluation upsets expectations and causes lumpy revision of wage and price decisions.

Far from imposing discipline consistently, the pegged-rate system has sometimes imposed an induced *lack* of discipline. The international cooperation that it fosters and depends on has turned out, to a considerable extent, to be cooperation in tolerating inflation. Or so argues the German Council of Economic Experts. Countries that were lax in resisting inflation, by helping each other out in financing payments deficits, could impose their error on the world as a whole. When a country did take corrective action, it seldom went beyond reducing its rate of inflation a little in the face of continuing inflation elsewhere. The pressure for discipline that ought to have come from countries aiming at greater stability was relaxed by increased supplies of international liquidity. At a fixed exchange rate, a country bent on stability could succeed only in favorable circumstances, and even then only temporarily and at high cost.[35] Although the discipline argument rests on the assumption of *limited* reserves, some advocates of fixed rates, such as Sir Roy Harrod, call for very ample international liquidity so that monetary and fiscal restraint need not be harsh. But ample liquidity or credit takes the teeth out of discipline, and incomes policies (wage controls and the like) provide no adequate substitute. Devaluation becomes unavoidable in the long run. The discipline argument is most nearly plausible when exchange rates are meant to remain *permanently* fixed.[36]

The phrase "induced lack of discipline" alludes to the processes of imported inflation.[37] If a country succeeds in pursuing domestic stability in a world of inflation, its currency becomes increasingly undervalued at a fixed exchange rate, and its balance-of-payments surplus grows. Success requires that the country forgo absorption of an increasing fraction of its current output of goods and services and that

1966, pp. 83, 140. Cf. E. M. Bernstein in Randall Hinshaw, *op. cit.*, pp. 161–162. Samuel Brittan effectively restates the argument, without finding it conclusive, in *op. cit.*, p. 66.

30. Converse benefits would occur, according to the argument, at a time of recession at home: an increase of exports of goods and services relative to imports would moderate the decline of production and employment. Whether domestic policy errs on the side of boom or of recession, a fixed exchange rate causes the world economy to absorb part of the excess or deficiency of domestic demand. This dilution of domestic instability onto a more stable outside world is the most favorable conceivable case, in contrast with cases in which the home economy suffers the contagion of instability in the outside world.

31. Stated by Bernstein in particular in Hinshaw, *op. cit.*, pp. 166–167.

32. Bernstein in Hinshaw, *op. cit.*, pp. 163–164.

33. *Steering the Economy*, Harmondsworth: Penguin, 1971, p. 483.
Earl Dwight Phaup, in a 1973 University of Virginia Ph.D. dissertation, surveyed the experience of major countries since World War II but was able to find extremely few instances of "discipline" apparently at work as the argument envisages.

34. Samuel Brittan, *The Price of Economic Freedom*, p. 19. Compare what happened after the British devaluation of 1967, as described in IMF, 1969, p. 74. The German experts believe that more flexible adjustment of parities "would also help to avoid structural distortions and the risk of wage explosions in the wake of imported inflation." Princeton Studies in International Finance, No. 31, p. 28. On the confusion in question between floating rates and pegging, compare Harry G. Johnson in Bürgenstock Papers, pp. 105–106.

35. Princeton Study No. 31, pp. 4–5.

36. George Halm in Bürgenstock Papers, p. 7.

37. The phrase is due to Donald B. Marsh in Robert Z. Aliber, ed., *The International Market for Foreign Exchange*, New York, Praeger, 1969, p. 155.
On imported inflation, see pp. 110, 379–382, 518–519, as well as my "Discipline, Inflation, and the Balance of Payments," in N. A. Beadles and L. A. Drewry, *Money, the Market, and the State*, Athens: University of Georgia Press, 1968, pp. 1–34; and Ruth Logue, *Imported Inflation and the International Adjustment Process*, Washington: Board of Governors of the Federal Reserve System, 1969.

29. Comments in National Industrial Conference Board Convocation (October 1965), *Gold and World Monetary Problems*, New York: Macmillan,

it neutralize the domestic monetary effects of its payments surpluses.[38] Successful monetary neutralization would not itself neutralize the direct price effect of inflation abroad—the translation at the fixed exchange rate of the rising foreign-currency prices of internationally traded goods.[39]

Successful resistance to imported inflation, even if technically possible, has real costs. External reserves accumulated by the central bank are hardly attractive investments in their own right, as indicated by the fact that private parties leave them to the central bank instead of undertaking them all themselves. Tightening monetary or fiscal policy to offset the inflationary impact of the central bank's purchases of foreign exchange means squeezing domestic borrowers or taxpayers for the sake of the cheap loans to foreigners that the foreign-exchange acquisitions represent. Another cost is the additional complexity imposed on framing and implementing domestic policy when the authorities must try to predict and allow for balance-of-payments developments and offset their domestic impacts.

Occasional upward revaluations by an inflation-resisting country provide no full remedy for the inflation bias of the adjustable-peg system.[40] Most obviously, each such revaluation confronts the stable country's trading partners with a partial devaluation of their own currencies.[41] For them, the resulting shocks of price increases and of having to cut back on overabsorption of goods and services may be more inflationary than a smooth upward float of the stable country's currency would have been.

Even for that country, discrete upward revaluations are not wholly anti-inflationary. When each revaluation becomes strongly anticipated, speculative funds flow into the country and tend to expand its money supply; and outflows after revaluation are unlikely to undo the damage fully. As the stable country's currency becomes more and more undervalued in advance of each revaluation, furthermore, its export and import-competing producers develop larger stakes in their markets than they could hold at an equilibrium exchange rate. They are likely to exert political pressure against revaluation, causing the revaluation, when it comes, to be later and larger than a free-market currency appreciation would have been. Then the unsustainable allocation of resources into the export and import-competing industries shifts into re-

verse.[42] This shuttling-around of resources is itself an element of inflationary waste.

All this suggests a way in which, contrary to intuition, an upward revaluation may actually be inflationary. A discrete exchange-rate change, in either direction, alters the distribution of aggregate demand between the export and import-competing industries on the one hand and the domestic-goods industries on the other hand. The pattern of resource allocation cannot promptly and fully match this shift of demand because of various frictions, including physical complementarities of resources, long-term contracts, and downward inflexibilities of prices and wages. Transitional unemployment threatens, and a macroeconomic policy to avoid it means expansion of aggregate demand. In accordance with a ratchet effect,[43] prices and wages rise more readily in the sectors to which demand has shifted than they fall in the sectors from which demand has shifted. Delay in currency revaluation and the necessity for seemingly "structural" shifts to reverse an accomplished misallocation of resources worsen the unemployment-or-inflation tradeoff. More inflation than otherwise must be accepted to hold unemployment down to a desired level. A prompt and gradual upward float of the currency would avoid these difficulties.[44]

On several grounds, then, the "discipline" argument for fixed exchange rates is open to question. Some advocates of floating rates even see a better element of discipline in that system: the warning against an inflationary lapse comes more promptly and conspicuously in the form of exchange depreciation. The money supply is also a better indicator of policy, whereas under fixed rates, much of an excessive domestic creation of money may "leak abroad."[45] Furthermore, free exchange rates make controls unnecessary for balance-of-payments purposes. By thus permitting (though of course not guaranteeing) free trade and free international competition, that system would help maintain the discipline of competition over economic groups whose excessive wage and price demands might otherwise pose the unemployment-or-inflation dilemma. Finally, freedom from balance-of-payments complications would facilitate (though, again, would not guarantee) greater steadiness in domestic monetary-fiscal policies. There could be less of the zig-zagging between expansionary and contractionary policies that contributes, in several ways, to a long-run inflationary bias.

Still, we must give the lack-of-discipline worry its due. A floating exchange rate is no panacea. Monetary independence and insulation mean freedom for prudence and recklessness alike. Freedom from unhealthy external constraints means freedom from healthy ones also. If these constraints are *needed*, then, by assumption, so are fixed exchange rates. The free-exchange-rate mechanism of payments adjustment would not work, anyway, if the home money supply were out of control and rose in proportion to the price of foreign exchange whenever the home currency weakened on the market. If a country cannot or will not maintain internal balance for itself, and if it needs the anti-inflationary discipline of potential balance-of-payments crises at fixed exchange rates, then, by assumption, exchange-rate flexibility is inflationary in a permissive sense. Such a country might be well advised to try tying its own currency to some relatively stable foreign currency.

The "discipline" argument for fixed exchange rates, and especially for the gold standard, appeals to people who mistrust their own governments. People who advocate free exchange rates despite the loss of external discipline do so partly because they mistrust foreign governments even more than they mistrust their own; they fear monetary linkage with governments whose inflationary propensities may be even worse.[46] The discipline argument seems most relevant for countries that have an intermediate propensity to inflate. The most inflationary governments are hardly restrained by fixed exchange rates; they cannot keep their rates fixed for long. Their currencies are pegged at disequilibrium rates most of the time: they are undervalued for a while after each devaluation but become overvalued again as inflation proceeds and makes another devaluation necessary. Wrongly pegged rates simply disrupt business without exerting effective discipline. At the other extreme stand the most prudent countries. Their resistance to inflation suffers rather than gains from monetary linkage to foreigners. In between stand the countries whose inflations are not fast enough to require

frequent devaluations. Their pegged exchange rates do not become quickly and seriously wrong again after each (infrequent) adjustment. Yet they can benefit from external restraint on inflation. Applied to such countries, the discipline argument is probably the strongest of the arguments for fixed and against free exchange rates. The peoples of the world badly need some sort of effective discipline over their governments.

38. Cf. Hinshaw, *op. cit.*, p. 5.

39. The role of the direct price effect in imported inflation is a leading theme of Gerhard Fels, *Der internationale Preiszusammenhang*, Köln: Heymanns, 1969.

40. On this bias, see pp. 110–112, 624–626.

41. For bordering countries doing a large proportion of their international trade with Germany, the upward revaluation of the mark in 1969 had a definite upward impact on prices. BIS, 1969–1970, p. 9.

42. Cf. Hinshaw, *op. cit.*, p. 6.

43. See p. 111.

44. Roger Shields and Thomas D. Willett, "Revaluation Can Be Inflationary: An Analysis of Demand Shifts with Downward Price Rigidity," lithoprinted discussion paper, Harvard University, November 1970, esp. pp. 1, 2, 11–13.

45. "Under a 'fixed' rate, there is a series of lags between the initial pumping of excessive purchasing power into the economy, the resultant domestic overheating and wage inflation, the payments deficit, and the eventual foreign exchange crises. The process is longer and more difficult for the public to grasp than the fall in a free-market exchange rate. The latter is an immediate index of failure, which affects the retail price index and which all can follow." Brittan, *The Price of Economic Freedom*, p. 61.

46. Harry G. Johnson, *The World Economy at the Crossroads*, New York: Oxford University Press, 1965, p. 28.

CHAPTER THIRTY-TWO

Compromise Reforms or Forthright Choice?

Controls

Several types of compromise between the extremes of permanently fixed and completely free exchange rates have been adopted or proposed. Resort to special import duties or various trade and capital controls at times of balance-of-payments trouble is one indication of reluctance to choose between the adjustment mechanisms appropriate to fixed and to free exchanges. The main claim for controls is that they can deal with payments disequilibrium relatively quickly and surely, even when other methods of adjustment might be slow and feeble. On the other hand, controls are open to the same sort of objections on efficiency grounds as are developed in the traditional analysis of protective tariffs versus free trade (and whatever qualifications apply to that analysis apply here also). Since resort to controls does not constitute a distinct system of international monetary relations, we need say no more here than to refer back to Chapter 7.

The adjustable peg

The adjustable peg envisaged in the Charter of the International Monetary Fund is itself a compromise system. The chief advantages

claimed for it, and its chief apparent disadvantages, including an inflation bias, have already been described. An additional problem is that adjustment of pegs had fallen almost into desuetude—until 1971, anyway, when the system itself began falling apart. National authorities understandably tended to postpone exchange-rate adjustments, hoping that payments disequilibriums would prove nonfundamental and would go away either of their own accord or in response to mild policy expedients.

Much recent discussion concerns how to make the adjustable peg work after all. At best, prompt and correspondingly small exchange-rate adjustments would both provide a payments adjustment mechanism and avoid the expectations of large changes that give rise to one-way-option speculation.[1] Governments might agree on "objective indicators" of the need for parity changes.[2] A country's loss of more than 10 percent of its international reserves within three months, for example, might call for devaluation of its currency. Other possible indicators are price indexes, current-account or basic balances of payments, or exchange-rate behavior (such as a rate's clinging to the upper or lower edge of its band around parity). Specified behavior of the agreed indicators might make parity adjustment mandatory or automatic; but it is more likely that governments would agree on a *presumption* in favor of adjustment, a presumption that special circumstances could override. Even more in vogue has been the proposal that agreed indicators trigger mere international *consultation* about adjustment.

Reforms employing objective indicators might introduce pressures for adjustment impinging as keenly on surplus countries as on deficit countries. A payments surplus, reserve gains, relative avoidance of price inflation, or an exchange rate persistently pushing against its support ceiling would carry a presumption in favor of currency revaluation. Furthermore, internationally agreed charges might be levied on the reserve gains of surplus countries, just as charges might be levied to promote devaluation by deficit countries. (Such a reform would implement a key idea of the Keynes plan of 1943.)

Hopes pinned on the readily adjusted adjustable peg seem overoptimistic. Under the old Bretton Woods system, the one-way-option problem was no worse than it was because adjustments were regarded as a measure of last resort. Denials that exchange-rate changes are coming will be credible only if the finance ministers believe them themselves and are fighting to make them hold true. "Once such denials were completely dismissed as routine noise, torrents of funds would flow across the exchange [sic] at the slightest suggestion that a parity might be out of line."[3] Under the old system of earnestly defended parities, speculators had to reckon with the prospect that the defense might succeed. Accepting parity adjustments as the normal response to payments disequilibrium would create a different speculative atmosphere. As for "objective indicators," speculators and hedgers would be as alert to them as monetary officials. The main hope for avoiding such problems is that parity adjustments would be so prompt and small as to make speculation on them hardly worthwhile.

Conceivably, each parity change might be so small that the bands of fluctuation around the old and new parities overlapped and that the overlap included the level at which the rate had been fluctuating at the time of the change. The change would cause little disturbance to the market when it occurred; yet a series of such changes could, when necessary, accomplish substantial adjustment over time.

The "band" proposal

These suggestions bring to mind the proposal for widened bands. According to the IMF Charter, a spot exchange rate was to be allowed to fluctuate no more than 1 percent up or down from the currency's declared parity; the Smithsonian Agreement of December 1971 increased this figure to 2¼ percent. The "band" proposal envisages widening this range to perhaps 5 percent or more on either side of parity.[4] One claim is that a widened band would lessen the problem of speculation. With fluctuations narrowly confined, speculators can count on winning if an expected change in parity does take place and on breaking almost even if it does not. With a wide band, speculators would realize that the rate could rebound substantially from whichever edge of the band it was pressing against. Speculation could prove costly if wrong.

Speculation might even be stabilizing. Given firm confidence that the band would hold, an exchange rate approaching one edge would seem more likely to rebound than to break through. Spectators would help cause the ex-

pected rebound—or keep the rate away from the edge of the band in the first place. Stabilizing speculation would reduce the need for official intervention and official reserves. So would nonspeculative exchange-rate variations within the band, since they should help adjust balances of payments and resource allocation to changed conditions.

On the other hand, situations could develop in which a standoff between bullishness and bearishness on a currency depended on confidence in successful defense of the lower edge of its band. Confidence might weaken, upsetting the standoff, because that defense was draining official reserves. With the exchange rate clinging to the lower edge, the very width of the band might emphasize the wrongness of the mid-band parity. The disadvantages of rigid pegging, including the danger of speculation on what had become almost a one-way option, would then appear. (But if free-market supply and demand were to keep the rate comfortably within the limits of the band, then those limits

1. Substantial parity changes, as for the currency of a country suffering rapid inflation, might be accomplished by changes of as little as 1 or 2 percent made as often as every few weeks. Making such small and frequent adjustments would amount to a discretionary crawling peg (see pp. 646–647). The experience of Brazil since August 1968 is said to illustrate the benefits of such a system; see the citations in Chapter 31, footnote 23.

2. A proposal made by the U.S. government in 1972 embodies this idea. See *Economic Report of the President together with the Annual Report of the Council of Economic Advisers*, January 1973, pp. 160–174.

3. Samuel Brittan, *The Price of Economic Freedom*, p. 18. Cf. Gottfried Haberler in George N. Halm, ed., *Approaches to Greater Flexibility of Exchange Rates*, Princeton, N.J.: Princeton University Press, 1970 (hereafter cited as Bürgenstock Papers), p. 117.

4. George N. Halm, *The "Band" Proposal: The Limits of Permissible Exchange Rate Variations*, Special Paper No. 6, Princeton, N.J.: Princeton University, International Finance Section, 1965; Leland B. Yeager, "A Skeptical View of the 'Band' Proposal," *National Banking Review*, **IV**, March 1967, pp. 291–297.

would be unnecessary.) Expectations concerning policy and market conditions have more material to feed on and to change sharply about under the band system, as under other compromise systems, than under a "hands-off" policy.

Another argument for the band scheme envisages greater scope for official forward-exchange-rate policy. Official support of the forward value of the home currency could prevent or reverse an outflow of funds by way of interest arbitrage that would otherwise exert downward pressure on the spot exchange rate and on the official reserves when home interest rates were lower than foreign rates or when bearish speculation against the home currency was active in the forward-exchange market. But as explained above,[5] a forward rate cannot go outside the support limits of the spot rate if those limits command confidence, as they would if the policies pursued were successful. A widened range of spot fluctuation would permit a substantial forward premium on the home currency when it was desired to retain or attract arbitrage funds.

This particular argument does not stand up well upon examination of the relevant technicalities; a widened band is unlikely to enhance forward support policy in an important way.[6] But some other arguments join with it in partially recognizing the case for exchange-rate flexibility. The band system would supposedly hold down the size of the reserve gains and losses that sometimes advertise disequilibrium under narrowly pegged rates, and exchange-rate movements within a broadened band would indicate the growing strength or weakness of a currency and thus serve as one useful guideline for domestic financial policy. This last point joins with the familiar claim that the need to hold the exchange rate within some limits exerts some anti-inflationary discipline.

The band scheme pure and simple could be combined with official smoothing operations: instead of leaving the rate free within the band and intervening only at its edges, the authorities might intervene continuously to counter short-run wobbles. Either with or without continuous intervention, the band scheme could be combined with a revitalized adjustable peg. As already mentioned, the parity of a currency, together with the band about it, could be made subject to prompt and small adjustments. With wide enough bands, each new parity could lie within the band around the old one.

The crawling peg

In that way the "band" and "crawling-peg" reforms could combine into a "crawling band." With the band kept narrow, however, the reform would be the crawling peg alone—more elegantly called the "gliding parity." A currency's parity and the two limits narrowly flanking it could be changed, either at the discretion of the authorities or by formula, perhaps every few months when necessary, perhaps as often as every day. Under an automatic version of the scheme, each day's parity might be a moving average of the actual daily exchange rates over a specified number of immediately preceding months. If changed conditions had left a currency definitely overvalued, its consequent bumping along the lower edge of its narrow band would pull down both the moving average and the band itself; in this way the rate could gradually approach a new equilibrium level. Details of the scheme would presumably be such as to hold the maximum change of an exchange rate under pressure to within a few percent a year. Exchange-rate variation could contribute to equilibrating the balance of payments in an orderly way, without speculation being incited by susceptibility of the rate to sudden sharp adjustments.[7]

Still, with parity adjustments frequent either by discretion or by formula, expectations would cause trouble. At least, so the skeptics worry. When people realize that correction of a disequilibrium exchange rate is being split up into small steps and strung out over time, they will expect the future value of the currency concerned to be lower or higher, as the case may be, than its current artificial value. A freely fluctuating rate, by contrast, can hardly be generally regarded as artificially high or artificially low; for if it were so regarded, market responses would promptly adjust it to a level no longer viewed with one-way skepticism.[8] Expectations of continuing—because restrained and strung-out—depreciation or appreciation of the spot rate affect forward rates and, through interest arbitrage, domestic interest rates.[9] A closely related source of pressure on domestic interest rates would be the fact that if interest rates did not adjust, people would be reluctant or eager to hold claims (and not just forward contracts) in a currency on which they were bearish or bullish. Incentives would be at work akin to those of deductions from or additions to interest rates in countries whose currencies were weakening or strengthening. If bothersome capital movements were not to result, actual interest rates would have to be kept higher in a weak-currency country and lower in a strong-currency country than they otherwise would be. Thus, the stringing-out of parity adjustments over time would affect not only the forward-exchange market but also the money and capital markets. It would pose an additional complication for domestic monetary-fiscal policy, even though the authorities have a hard enough job straddling among full employment, growth, price-level stability, desired credit conditions, and other domestic goals.

Some of these objections to stringing out rate adjustments by intervention apply also to controls recognized as keeping an exchange rate higher or lower than it would be in a free market. In general, guesses about possible changes in interventions and controls—guesses about what the authorities may be up to—add an additional element of potential instability to exchange-rate determination.

The suspendible par

Another modification of the adjustable peg would have each country keep the par-value system in effect most of the time. Most international transactions, being completed in the short run, would benefit from exchange-rate stability. In nondilemma cases, in which the aggregate-demand policies required for external and internal balance run in the same direction, such policy could take care of balance-of-payments adjustment. Occasionally, in dilemma cases, exchange rates would be made temporarily flexible. This suspendible par, as it might be called, is said to be especially suitable to the real world of uncertainty and imperfect information and imperfect stabilization policies.[10] Yet the monetary authorities would themselves have to exercise their continuing option to maintain or suspend the par-value system amid "uncertainty and imperfect information." Their having that option would introduce uncertainty of its own—uncertainty about what institutional arrangements were in effect. People cannot really rely on par values continually subject to suspension; nor can they count on free-market equilibrating processes when flexible exchange rates are affected by disequilibria accumulated during earlier periods

of fixed rates and are continually subject to being frozen, perhaps at levels other than their current levels. Private market institutions and practices are unlikely to develop the same way in intermittent episodes of floating rates as they would if floating rates were regarded as a permanent system. Coupled with demand policy forthrightly and steadily oriented toward domestic requirements, permanently floating rates would take care of both dilemma and nondilemma cases.[11]

5. Page 30. On forward support policy, see pp. 119–123.

6. Henry N. Goldstein, "A Further Comment on an Aspect of the 'Band' Proposal," *National Banking Review*, **IV**, June 1967, pp. 511–513.

7. John H. Williamson, *The Crawling Peg*, Princeton Essays in International Finance, No. 50, Princeton, N.J.: Princeton University, International Finance Section, 1965; J. Carter Murphy, "Moderated Exchange Rate Variability," *National Banking Review*, **III**, December 1965, pp. 151–161.

8. This is not to overlook the possibility of expectations of continuing inflation, which would be reflected in expected future spot rates below the current spot rate of the currency concerned, in a forward discount on that currency, and in increased domestic interest rates. The interest-parity relation between spot and forward rates could still hold; and the actual spot rate, though continually depreciating, could still be regarded by average market opinion as correct at each instant. The case discussed in the text is different: because official intervention is slowing down the adjustment of a disequilibrium rate, people realize that in the absence of intervention, the rate would already be different from what it actually is.

9. Cf. Robert Mundell in Randall Hinshaw, ed., *The Economics of International Adjustment*, Baltimore: Johns Hopkins Press, 1971, pp. 97–98.

10. Samuel I. Katz, *The Case for the Par-Value System*, Princeton Essay No. 92, Princeton, N.J.: Princeton University, March 1972, esp. p. 15.

11. Some of these answers are suggested by Gottfried Haberler, writing before the appearance of Samuel Katz's proposal, in Bürgenstock Papers, pp. 118–121.

648

Optimal flexibility

A similar answer, emphasizing that policy choices lie basically among alternative institutional arrangements, applies to the idea of optimal exchange-rate flexibility.[12] The notion of an optimal degree of flexibility—one in between perpetual rigidity and minute-to-minute unrestrained fluctuation—accords well with economists' general inclination to envisage an optimum between extremes. (The tariff rate best implementing the terms-of-trade argument is somewhere between zero and prohibitive; the best macroeconomic policy compromises between pursuing full employment at whatever cost and pursuing price-level stability at whatever cost; and the most profitable course for a businessman lies somewhere between pursuing extremely high per-unit profit margins and extremely high sales volume.) Furthermore, the notion of optimum flexibility over time bears an analogy—though only a loose one—with the concept of optimum flexibility over space, as worked out in the theory of optimum currency areas.

The optimality argument goes somewhat as follows. First, price-induced shifts of resources among industries and regions have costs; and the faster the shifts, the greater the costs. Second, balance-of-payments disturbances tend to be reversed or offset—the more so, the longer the time allowed. Third, owners of productive factors would gladly take somewhat lower incomes to have the instability of their incomes reduced. By financing payments disequilibria out of international reserves, countries can avoid some real adjustments simply by waiting for offsetting disturbances, can hold down the costs of other adjustments by making them more slowly, and can reduce the expected instability of incomes. The greater the total quantity of international liquidity, the greater the extent to which countries can reap these advantages. If Special Drawing Rights bore a higher rate of interest than they now do, more nearly equal to the rate of return on real capital goods, and if the supply of SDRs were adjusted to the quantity demanded at that higher rate, then the stock of international liquidity would be more nearly optimal; and so would the associated degree of exchange-rate variation. Optimal flexibility is thus defined only indirectly, as the degree resulting from stabilizing interventions conducted by authorities armed with the aggregate quantity of international reserves demanded at an interest rate on reserves equaling the rate of return on real capital.[13]

One reply to this line of argument is that it takes too seriously the concept of a definite demand function for reserves on the part of monetary authorities. Furthermore, is it generally true that keeping exchange rates from fluctuating freely reduces the shift of resources among industries? In plausible cases, as we have seen, rate fluctuations, even temporary ones, may reduce pressures for inappropriate shifts. And is it true that payments disturbances tend to offset each other over time? On the contrary, they may accumulate. The chief oversight of the optimum-flexibility doctrine, however, is failure fully to realize that what policy-makers face is a choice among alternative sets of rules and constraints, not the choice of the best size of a particular parameter along a continuous scale. Fixing exchange rates rigidly is one institutional arrangement, pegging them within a specified band is another, allowing them to float without intervention is still another. It is arguable whether intervention supposedly confined to smoothing the rate without influence on its long-run level or trend should be classified as an institution operationally distinct from that of intervention at the discretion of the authorities. It is not clear just what form of managed flexibility the optimum-flexibility doctrine recommends—readily adjustable pegs, gliding pegs or bands, unpegged rates guided by official intervention, or something else. As policy advice it is nearly empty, like advising legislators to arrange matters so that the marginal social costs of some activity equal its marginal social benefits.

Managed floats

Optimal flexibility might conceivably be achieved by official intervention operating on unpegged rates. That idea, already surveyed in Chapter 14, deserves some notice as a reform scheme. Ideally, a stabilization fund would trade routinely in the market to iron out excessive short-run wobbles; yet it would not resist fundamental trends and would allow the exchange rate to keep the country's payments in equilibrium over the long run. But how can the fund's managers know, before they have hindsight on the episode, whether an observed exchange-rate movement accords with or departs from the long-run trend? Even speculative rate movements may accord with the main trend, since speculators may be taking account of basic conditions affecting international trade and of reasonably expected changes in them. Even if the fund's managers could know that particular rate movements would prove purely temporary, it is far from clear that these movements would be functionless and should be blocked. If exchange-rate fluctuations would clearly be temporary or seasonal, private speculation would probably iron them out; but even if it did not, this failure would not necessarily be regrettable.

When official funds or central banks are at work in the market, rate determination becomes at least potentially a political matter. Different governments may operate at cross purposes. Though exchange funds *may* serve as instruments of international cooperation, the very fact of official trading designed to influence rates gives scope for suspicions, at least, of nationalistic manipulation. An internationally operated stabilization fund, occasionally proposed as an alternative to national funds, would presumably avoid these abuses; but even if diplomatic and administrative difficulties could be overcome, an international fund would still face most of the problems of national funds.

A policy supposedly confined to smoothing out unwarranted fluctuations can drift into one of pegging rates at levels that ultimately prove wrong; history provides examples. If a fund holds a currency steady for months at a stretch, changing to a new level occasionally, speculators are likely to enjoy one-way options—and more often than under the old adjustable-peg system. If a fund manages to avoid actual pegging, it still must keep some of its activities and intentions secret to avoid giving speculators tips on a sure thing. But then speculators will guess. The idea of a "normal" exchange rate, with its stabilizing influence, is less likely to prevail when speculators must guess at the whims of an official agency not limited to profit-seeking than when they need to consider only fundamental market factors. In important respects, a rate manipulated to the extent of actually being fixed and a rate manipulated flexibly have more in common with each other than either has with a free rate. Destabilizing speculation feeds on mysteries, gossip, and rumors. It is an open question whether a fund operating with enough self-restraint to avoid

these dangers would really be missed if abolished.

The worry about "competitive exchange depreciation," properly understood, is an argument against managed flexibility, not against truly free rates. So is the curious worry[14] that under a generalized system of fluctuating exchange rates, there would be no currency in which central banks could safely hold working balances for carrying out their market interventions. A final worry due to glossing over the distinction between managed and free flexibility suggests that the problem of international liquidity might be worse under flexible exchange rates than under the adjustable peg. As Sir Roy Harrod has suggested, national authorities might actually need larger external reserves to cope with temporary disequilibria promoted by the uncertainties of the new system itself.[15]

The criticisms just reviewed raise the question whether managed flexibility might not combine the worst rather than the best features of permanently fixed and fully free rates. It surely would lack the automaticity and impersonality of the otherwise quite different adjustment mechanisms of those two polar systems.

---

12. See Herbert G. Grubel in *International Monetary Problems*, Washington: American Enterprise Institute, 1972, pp. 96–98, with comments by John H. Makin, pp. 102–104.

13. Grubel in *ibid.*, acknowledging inspiration from Milton Friedman's concept of the optimum quantity of (domestic) money. My understanding or misunderstanding of Grubel's argument derives in part from a lecture whose substance he has since incorporated into "The Case for Optimum Exchange Rate Stability," *Weltwirtschaftliches Archiv*, Vol. 109, No. 3, 1973, pp. 351–381.

14. Expressed, for example, by Otmar Emminger, a member of the Board of Governors of the German Bundesbank, in National Industrial Conference Board Convocation, *Gold and World Monetary Problems*, New York: Macmillan, 1966, pp. 127–128.

15. *Reforming the World's Money*, New York: St. Martin's Press, 1965, chap. 2, esp. p. 51.

The distaste for automaticity

All the compromise proposals considered reject automaticity. The only exception is the crawling peg operated by formula rather than by discretion, and that proposal has found little favor with the expert practitioners of exchange-rate policy, central bankers and government and international officials. Rarely seeing print in a clear-cut version and lurking only as an undertone even in conversation, there seems to be a pervasive vague distaste for automaticity in balance-of-payments adjustment. This distaste may stem from uneasiness about the wide and unfathomable repercussions of market adjustments.[16] Somehow, the consequences of a country's balance-of-payments position should not spread themselves out inconspicuously in time and scope. They should remain concentrated and visible as a signal of need for policy changes, as a pivot for consultations, and perhaps even as an argument for international cooperation and aid from abroad.

The proposition that the par-value system has served the world well and only requires improvements in accord with its basic character is one of those propositions widely accepted as axiomatic. "[O]nce a case is treated as axiomatic empirical evidence becomes irrelevant. Whatever the actual course of events, it can always be adduced in support of a policy which is axiomatically deemed desirable; progress as evidence of its success and lack of progress as evidence of the need for its reinforcement."[17] The IMF's 1969 *Annual Report* provides an example of dealing in axioms. The report notes an enormous expansion in the volume of short-term funds ready to surge from country to country when exchange-rate changes are thought likely, a situation not envisaged at Bretton Woods. During the preceding year, the Fund's Executive Directors had been discussing ways of putting more flexibility into exchange rates. "They have not, at this stage, reached conclusions. . . . They intend to continue their study of this subject. They want to emphasize, however, that any changes that might be made should preserve the essential characteristics of the par value system, which remain as beneficial for the world as they were when written into the Fund's Articles of Agreement 25 years ago. . . ."[18]

Doesn't the nearly unanimous opposition to freely floating rates among monetary officials count as evidence against that system? May not academic economists be wrong in rejecting the par-value axiom? As Antony Flew writes in another context, "when one rejects any widely or respectably held view one needs to ask why so many or such considerable people have been misled into what is, apparently, error; and until and unless satisfactory answers are forthcoming one is not entitled to feel entirely sure that it is an error at all, or, if an error, that it is just a straightforward error and nothing more."[19]

A similar question is in order when appeal is made to the sheer *authority* of the practicing experts. Inquiry into people's occupational biases and probable motives is no substitute, of course, for inquiry into their analysis. But when their analysis is skimpy or unconvincing, doubters are entitled and forced to inquire how much respect their authority deserves.

If someone contends that the persistence of efforts to maintain par values or controls or a two-tier foreign-exchange market is evidence that such arrangements serve their intended purposes adequately, one is entitled to ask just what their intended purposes are. Serving the public interest, pure and simple, is not a clear answer, nor the whole one. The persons who devise and operate policy measures are, after all, human beings; and like all human beings, they have personal motives of their own.[20] They like to think that their work is useful and important. They are interested in the prestige and expansion of the offices or bureaus they work for.

It is understandable if central bankers savor their image as "cultivated gentlemen benevolently rescuing faltering currencies over truffles and wine at Basel."[21] The people engaged in international meetings and "frantic scurrying" and "midnight phone calls" to line up emergency support for beleaguered currencies "are important people and they are all persuaded that they are engaged in important activities. It cannot be, they say to themselves, that these important activities arise simply from pegging exchange rates." Their attitude, Milton Friedman suggests, is "one of the major sources of the opposition to floating exchange rates."[22]

An economist with one foot in the world of practitioners and another in the academic world has an additional reason to like the crises, excitement, and opportunities to engage in expertise that exchange-rate pegging causes. Preparing lectures becomes almost painless. He can walk into class and talk practically off the top of his head about "frantic scurrying" and "midnight phone calls" and reform negotiations and others of his activities as a practitioner. His students may well prefer these glimpses of the supposed real world to dry economic analysis. If he likes to write articles, he finds plenty of material in the problems he deals with, and plenty of scope for inventing and marketing his own new variants of reform proposals.

In fact, an academic economist need not have a foot in the world of practitioners to value, perhaps subconsciously, the material for lectures and articles that exchange-rate pegging provides. It would be a shame to have the problems that he specializes in solved at one stroke.

The need for choice

Were it not for considerations like these, it would seem odd that economists have not yet reached near-unanimity on the need, in framing international monetary policy, to sacrifice one or more individually desirable things. The necessity for choice is, after all, the most fundamental principle of economics.

In the area of policies for internal and external balance, many writers have perceived this necessity in a conflict between three things, each desirable in its own right: (1) freedom for each country to pursue an independent monetary and fiscal policy for full employment without inflation (or for the best domestically attainable compromise), (2) freedom of international trade and investment from controls wielded to *force* equilibrium in balances of payments, and (3) fixed exchange rates. Any two of these are possible together, but not all three. With controls ruled out, a country can maintain a fixed exchange rate only by sacrificing its monetary independence and allowing its domestic business conditions and price level to keep in step with foreign developments. Unless the outside world remains perpetually stable, a country must choose between domestic stability and exchange-rate stability.

Sometimes this so-called Doctrine of Alter-

and, to tell the truth, I have not seemed to generate any real argument. It has been a sort of tropismatic response, even below the level of instinct. . . . I have been unable to get any lucid discussion on this subject from any representative of the Federal Reserve Board. . . . [A]s this question has been put time and time again . . . there has only been a bland parry." *The United States Balance of Payments*, Part 3, "The International Monetary System: Functioning and Possible Reform," Washington: Government Printing Office, 1963, pp. 576, 581.

17. P. T. Bauer, *Dissent on Development*, Cambridge, Mass.: Harvard University Press, 1972, p. 73. Bauer introduces his concept of axiomatic propositions while considering the case for government-to-government aid and the case for development planning.

18. International Monetary Fund, 1969 *Annual Report*, pp. 31–32, quotation from p. 32.

Compare Katz, *op. cit.*, p. 22: "Countries have been anxious to retain the structure of the Bretton Woods arrangements because they have benefited so widely from the unprecedented postwar expansion in international trade and investment achieved under the par-value system. The modifications in exchange-rate practices thus far considered have been regarded merely as adaptations of, and not the supplanting of, the adjustable-peg variant of fixed rates."

19. *God and Philosophy*, New York: Dell (Delta Book), 1966, p. 80.

20. Cf. the work on the theory of bureaucracy of such economists as Anthony Downs, William Niskanen, and Gordon Tullock.

21. For examples of the enjoyment and pleasurable excitement involved in defending fixed parities, see John Brooks, "In Defense of Sterling," *The New Yorker*, Vol. 44, 23 March 1968, pp. 44ff., and 30 March 1968, pp. 43ff.

Richard H. Timberlake, Jr., citing Robert Roosa and other monetary officials, also conjectures that such men have a taste for the fixed-rate system because of their own "essential" roles in it; see his "The Fixation with Fixed Exchange Rates," *Southern Economic Journal*, Vol. 36, October 1969, especially p. 139.

22. Milton Friedman and Robert V. Roosa, *The Balance of Payments: Free versus Fixed Exchange Rates*, Washington: American Enterprise Institute, 1967, pp. 15–16.

16. On November 15, 1963, Senator Paul Douglas told the Joint Economic Committee: "For years I have urged the Federal Reserve, the Treasury, and our representatives on the IMF, to consider the flexible exchange rates, and I have been deeply disappointed by their refusal even to consider or study the matter. It has been an automatic reaction

native Stability is questioned.[23] A country with abundant external reserves and enough size to sway world economic conditions has some leeway for a full-employment policy, for example, even in the face of world depression. Use of this leeway counts as temporarily dropping the goal or external balance (or, alternatively, as adding the weapon of variability in reserves), so that policy goals and policy weapons remain equal in number. But this qualification to the doctrine is a clearly limited one. For a country that would benefit from diluting instability originating at home onto the outside world and whose domestic finances are so lax that internal instability and exchange-rate instability would intensify each other, the Doctrine of Alternative Stability is not wrong but irrelevant. Nobody supposes that exchange fluctuations themselves generate domestic stability.[24] The doctrine states not that each of the two kinds of instability rules out the other but that each of the two kinds of stability rules out the other (unless the world economy is stable). The doctrine is relevant for countries that have reasonable hope of doing better in monetary and fiscal policy than the general range of other countries.

If countries do not openly choose which one to sacrifice among monetary independence, external balance without controls, and fixed exchanges, the choice gets made unintentionally. Under the international gold standard before 1914, monetary independence was sacrificed to fixed gold parities. In the early years after World War II—the "transition period" of the IMF Charter—freedom from controls was sacrificed to national pursuit of full employment. Since then, the choice has become fuzzier as countries seek a compromise in the merely partial sacrifice of each of the three objectives. The progressive dismantling of controls has become an important goal, and indeed an accomplishment. But the accomplishment is not really secure. The historical chapters of this book include many examples of backsliding into controls and other mere palliatives of balance-of-payments troubles. While not sacrificed, national financial independence has been modified: witness Great Britain's "stop and go" and Germany's vacillation between resistance to and defeatist acquiescence in imported inflation. Without adopting flexible rates except temporarily, a number of countries have adjusted their pegs often enough to jeopardize whatever advantages fixed rates may offer. His-

torical evidence illustrates, in short, the logically inexorable need to sacrifice one of the three objectives forthrightly or two or three of them in part.

The only choice that has not been tried by numerous countries except as an unwelcome and avowedly temporary expedient is to maintain national monetary independence and freedom from controls and frankly sacrifice exchange-rate fixity. Saying this is by no means to recommend free exchange rates for all countries under all circumstances. The theory of optimum currency areas and the "discipline" argument may be relevent for some countries. If two or more countries want to integrate their monetary policies tightly enough so that fixed rates of exchange among their currencies never become disequilibrium rates and so that the processes of balance-of-payments adjustment among themselves become the same as the processes at work among the different states of the United States, then the principal arguments against fixed exchange rates do not apply. Those objections apply only to pegging exchange rates among currencies that remain effectively distinct.

Misinterpreted compromises

It would probably prove tactically unwise to advocate some sort of compromise reform as a way of trying out exchange-rate flexibility little by little and of approaching genuinely free floats gradually as businessmen and central bankers become accustomed to the idea. That approach may boomerang because any unsatisfactory experience with limited or managed flexibility is apt to be blamed on flexibility as such. This misinterpretation has occurred all too often: "the lessons of history" are commonly said to have discredited free exchange rates, although it was managed flexibility that prevailed instead in the episodes typically cited.

We should be wary of misinterpretation of the episodes of floating rates experienced since mid-1971. Floating rates "dirtied" by interventions and controls, avowed to be temporary, and subject to early repegging at who knows what levels do not add up to a system of freely floating rates. The German Council of Economic Experts regretted that many people viewed the four-month episode of 1971 as a test of flexible exchange rates. Speculative expectations unrelated to market fundamentals seemed to dominate exchange rates and thus countries' degrees of price-competitiveness. Actually, such results stemmed from expectations still conditioned by exchange-rate fixing. Exchange rates were bound to respond to expectations concerning new parities that might be imposed. Their movements "were determined by the expected outcome of an economic power struggle between the United States and its trading partners."[25]

The question of acceptability

A relatively last-ditch argument employed by defenders of exchange-rate pegging is that freely floating rates are simply not in the cards: rightly or wrongly, central bankers and government officials consider an exchange rate too important a price to leave to itself, and they will intervene. Fear of adverse intervention by other countries, furthermore, will keep each country from refraining from intervention in the first place. Some sort of full-fledged or modified par-value system is necessary to avoid disruptive intervention at cross-purposes.

The issue here is not of workability but of acceptability. For at least two reasons, "political impossibility" should not rule a proposal out of consideration. First, discussing how a proposed change is likely to work can be a way of conveying and testing understanding of economic principles and the facts and logic they rest on. Second, "political impossibility" is not an inherent operating property of an economic arrangement. If a particular reform really does have a more attractive set of operating properties than its rivals, experts and policy-makers may come to understand that fact. If the policy-makers are recalcitrant, the voters may eventually replace them. If an economist, concerned with his own reputation for practicality and reasonableness, makes amateur assessments of political feasibility and accordingly recommends policies other than those he truly considers best, he is shirking the responsibilities of the expert he claims to be.

Economy in value judgments

With some people, opposition to free exchange rates stems from nearly ultimate value judgments. This sort of opposition is found, for example, among some supporters of the gold

standard. They intimate that fixity in gold is the only really sound, decent, and honest monetary basis.

Another approach shuns moralizing in a choice among policies. Of course, it does not dispense with value judgments entirely; no policy whatever can rest on scientific grounds alone. Most of us presumably prefer social institutions allowing individuals to follow their own ideals and pursue their own goals with as little clash as possible among their respective pursuits. We value opportunities for effective cooperation in pursuing goals requiring common action, yet freedom from unnecessary private or governmental coercion. All this implies a preference for an economy coordinated by free markets and, in turn, for whatever monetary arrangements promise, *on purely technical grounds*,[26] to be most workable. No detailed ethical premises are appropriate in appraising, say, fiat money against a gold standard or fluctuating against pegged exchange rates. Ideology properly relates to general pictures of the good society, but what monetary arrangements

23. Wilhelm Röpke, *Crises and Cycles* (adapted from the German by Vera C. Smith), London: Hodge, 1936, pp. 164–173; Röpke, *Internationale Ordnung*, Erlenbach-Zürich, Rentsch, 1945, pp. 246–253.

24. John T. Walter, *Foreign Exchange Equilibrium*, Pittsburgh: University of Pittsburgh Press, 1951, esp. pp. 38–39, however, makes quite a point of refuting this unavowed supposition.

25. Princeton Studies in International Finance, No. 31, Princeton, N.J.: Princeton University, 1972, p. 15. Compare Wolfgang Kasper in American Enterprise Institute, *International Monetary Problems*, 1972, p. 94: "Many new developments hint in the direction of flexibility *and* controls. It should be made quite clear that many of the benefits from free exchange rates . . . will not be derived from the present 'polluted float.' And I fear that present developments may lead to serious distortions, which will in later years be attributed (as happened after the 1920s) to flexibility and not to the controls."

26. The relevant grounds are not limited to those illuminated by economics; sociology, political science (e.g., theories of bureaucracy), psychology, and other disciplines are also relevant.

are most conducive to the operation of a market economy in a free society is a technical matter. People who share common ultimate values should be able to discuss monetary issues among themselves on this technical plane, without bandying about suspicions of ethical deficiency. An Occam's Razor can be applied to value judgments as well as to analytical concepts: value judgments are not to be multiplied beyond necessity.

Index of Names

Index of Subjects

United Kingdom (*continued*)
    and devaluation, 429, 446–448, 453, 458–466
    and the EPU, 412, 414
    and the Exchange Equalisation Account, 282–
        284, 291, 344–346, 365, 371–372, 450
    and exchange controls, 141n, 343, 373–374, 443
    and free sterling, 344–346
    and the gold standard, 253–254, 295, 305,
        310–311, 321–324, 330
    and inflation, 86, 379, 384
    and the IMF, 391, 394–396, 445, 449–451, 454,
        572
    and the managed sterling standard, 305
    and reserves, 299–300, 371, 441–442
    and speculation, 265, 345–346, 372, 418, 445–
        446, 447–448, 452, 455–457
    and the Suez Crisis, 393–394, 417, 449–450
    and tariffs, 346, 470
    and terms of trade, 446
    and war, 310–312, 316–324, 377–379
United Nations, 400
United Nations Relief and Rehabilitation
    Administration, 384
United States
    aid, 378, 384–387, 442, 583
    and bimetallism, 295–296
    and capital movements, 566, 568, 573–574,
        576–578, 584–586, 601–602
    and depression, 335–338, 346–355, 373
    and devaluation, 54, 291, 353, 357, 373, 426–
        430, 580
    and the fluctuating dollar, 353–354, 515, 581–
        582, 598–600, 604–606
    and gold reserves, 50, 233, 335–336, 353,
        374–375, 569, 575
    and the gold standard, 296, 342, 349–350,
        352–353, 355, 566–576
    and the golden avalanche, 353, 375
    and the IMF, 43, 391
    and inflation, 605, 623
    and the oil situation, 600–604
    and prices, 572
    and productivity, 590–592
    and purchasing-power parity of the dollar,
        219–220
    and recession, 576, 595
    and the role of the dollar, 586, 590–593,
        622–623
    and silver policy, 334–356
    and tariffs, 257, 338
    and terms of trade, 446
    and war, 316, 378, 385–388, 567, 595
Uruguay, 331

Velocity, 70, 81, 88, 108, 177, 224–225
Venezuela, 331, 338, 379
Versailles Treaty (1919), 315, 332

Young Plan, 315–316
Yugoslavia, 330–331, 388